Bailey's
Illustrated and Useful Inventions

A Bailey turret clock in a private collection.

Bailey's Illustrated and Useful Inventions

Seventeenth Edition

(Circa 1880)

Edited by

Chris McKay

2017

Copyright © Chris McKay 2017
The right of Chris McKay to be identified as author of this work
has been asserted by him in accordance with the
Copyright, Designs and Patents Act 1988.

Designed and typeset by Chris McKay
Hinton Martell
WIMBORNE MINSTER

email chris.mckay@tesco.net

Self-Published by the Author
Printed by CreateSpace an Amazon.com Company
North Charleston SC United States

ISBN-13:978-1537180298
ISBN-10:1537180290

The Catalogue

W. H. Bailey & Co.
The company started as John Bailey & Co around 1832. In 1865 William Bailey took over the company on his father's retirement. The company changed name in 1876 to W. H. Bailey & Co. The company name changed again in 1889 to W. H. Bailey & Co Ltd. A knighthood was bestowed on William H. Bailey in 1894. William died in 1913 when the company name changed yet again, this time it was Sir W. H. Bailey & Co Ltd. The company became a subsidiary of Yorkshire Metals in 1966 and subsequently went through further name and ownership changes, eventually passing to Pentair who today run the Bailey Valve product line .

Bailey's Products
Bailey produced an amazing range of products. If it could be made in cast iron or was associated with boilers, steam production, control, regulation and safety valves then it was in the catalogue. Clocks appear regularly, mostly in the form of recording devices. A whole section on turret clocks lists their range. Surprisingly Bailey turret clocks in England are not numerous, possibly because the company was not solely a maker of clocks.

Source
My interest is principally in the field of turret clocks, so I was very pleased to be able to acquire this catalogue. It had been in a library and bore a hand-stamp to say "Duplicate Copy" and a date of 1919, presumably when the catalogue had been withdrawn from stock and disposed of. Although not a major maker of turret clocks, Bailey did produce movements that are found in Australia, India and other former British colonies. It is probably down to Bailey catalogues like this one that such clocks were chosen, rather than ordered from the many other turret clock makers in England in that period.

Date
W. H. Bailey published many editions of their catalogue and they can be found widely advertised in technical journals and books of the time. This version has got to be before 1889 when the company name changed to W. H. Bailey & Co. Ltd. Page 198 has an extract for the *Engineer* magazine June 1875. This gives a window between 1875 and 1889. In round numbers, the catalogue is likely to be ca. 1880.

Reproduction
This document is my Copyright. If you want to reproduce a page or more then email me with details of your requirements and the end use.

BAILEY'S
Illustrated Inventions

(SEVENTEENTH EDITION)

Published by W. H. Bailey and Co.,

LATE JOHN BAILEY AND CO.,

Brassfounders and Manufacturers of Engineers' and Contractors' Sundries,

AND EVERY DESCRIPTION OF

ENGINE AND BOILER FITTINGS

ELECTRIC TELEGRAPH ENGINEERS, & TURRET CLOCK MAKERS

DEPARTMENTS:

	PAGES
STEAM GAUGE, RECORDER, INJECTOR AND ENGINEERS' BRASS FOUNDRY AND STEAM FITTING DEPARTMENT	from 5 to 50
ENGINEERS', CONTRACTORS' TOOLS, TESTERS AND SUNDRIES' DEPARTMENT	„ 78 „ 162
PUMPS, FIRE ENGINES, ESCAPES AND PUBLICANS' DEPARTMENT	„ 162 „ 195
TURRET CLOCK, BELL AND TELEGRAPH, LIGHTNING CONDUCTOR DEPARTMENT	„ 196 „ 240
TOO LATE FOR CLASSIFICATION	See pages in Advertisements at end of Book.

ALBION WORKS, SALFORD, LANCASHIRE.

TERMS TO ADVERTISERS—SEE END OF BOOK.

POST FREE 3/6 IN THE UNITED KINGDOM, OR 4/0 IN THE BRITISH COLONIES.

Persons abroad may order this Book through the Chief London Publishers, or it will be sent Free, either at home or abroad, to those who order our Goods to the extent of £10 or more.

Free to Educational Institutions, Working Men's Clubs, Mechanics' Institutions, or Improvement Societies.

PRINTED BY
PIM BROTHERS AND CO.,
STEAM PRINTERS,
WILLIAM STREET, DUBLIN.

INDEX.

Steam Gauge, Recorder, Injector, and Engineers' Brass Foundry Department.

	Page
AIR VALVE for Blast Furnaces	58
Air Escape Valve for Water Main	58
Air Escape Valve	58
Alpha B.R. Boiler Fitting	36
Ashcroft's Low Water Detector and Alarm	44 to 47
Ashcroft's Patent Compound Safety Valve and Low Water Detector, and Ashcroft's Patent Spring Balance Safety Valve and Low Water Alarm	238
Ashcroft's Tallow Cup	69
Alpha Low Water Whistle	43
Anemometer	24
BLAST PRESSURE GAUGE	9
Blast Furnace Air Valve	58
" Pyrometer	28
Boiler Flue Conical Tubes	27
Boiler Mounting, B.R.	37
Ball Clack Valve	50
Boiler Alarm	43
Blow-off Cocks, Iron and Gun Metal	55
Bridgewater Tallow Cups	71
Bow Key Stop Cock	52
Bib Cocks (Gland)	55
Bow Key Bib Cocks	52
Balloon Escape Valves	72
Brewers' Thermometers	11
Boiler Mounting	36 to 42
Bayley and Bailey's Steam Valve	33
CONICAL TUBES for Boiler Flues	27
Clock, Watchman's Peg	21
" for Engine House, with Gauges	19, 20
Counter and Recorder, Watchman's	21
Compound Boiler Fitting, B.R.	39
Coils	39
" Copper	63
Combined Pressure and Vacuum Gauge	8
" Safety Valve and Gauge	39
" " Gauge & Water Gauge	39
Curtin's Patent Tell-tale Gauge	8
Compound Water Gauge Cocks	34, 35
Check Valves	55
" Feed	50
Clepsydra Low Water Alarms	43
Clement's Engine Lubricator	74
Cotton Mill Speed Clock	16
Cocks, Steam	55
" Gland	53
" Test	73
" Cast Iron	51
" Brass Plugs	55
" Test	73
" Steam Gauge	73
" Indicator	73
" Cylinder	73
" Safety Valve Test	73
" Gas, Cast Iron	51
Chandler's Water Gauge	33
Cock, Threeway	57
Crystal Tallow Cup	76
DANGER BAR PRESSURE GAUGE	6
Double B.R. Safety Valve	37
Detector, Ashcroft's, and Alarm	44 to 47

	Page
Detector and Tell-tale, Curtin's Patent Gauge	8
Double Safety Valve and Low Water Float	48
Double Bracket Safety Valve	53
Double Gland Mud Cocks	52
Dome Escape Valve	58
EQUILIBRIUM VALVE	58
Expansion Steam Trap	61
Ditto, Joints	63
Ejectors or Steam Jet Pumps	20
Engine Indicator, Richard's	25
" Hopkinson's	25
Engine House Recorder and Indicator	14
Estimate for Fittings for Small Boilers	56
Engine Cylinder Tallow Cup	68
Engine House Clock and Gauge	19, 20
Escape Valve	69
" Pump	52
" Dome	52
" Balloon	72
FEED REGULATING VALVE	42
Frictionless Throttle Valve	61
Fusible Plugs	29 to 32
Feed Pump Regulating Suction Valve	67
Feed Water Regulator	51
Fittings for Small Boilers	56
Farron's Taps	56
Floating Cistern Steam Traps	67
GAUGES, Danger Bar	6
" Steam	5, 6
" Gas	11
" Water	10
" Vacuum	5, 11
" Blast	9
" Hydraulic	10
" Vacuum and Steam combined	8
" Mercurial	9, 11
" Curtin's Tell-tale	8
" Pyrometrical	7
" Heat Thermometers and Pyrometers	28
" and Clock for Engine House	19
Gas Valves, Sluice	58
Governor Valves	62
Greenhalgh's Reducing Valve	62
Gravity Oil and Tallow Cup	77
Glass Tubes for Water Gauges	48
Governor for Steam Engines	75
Gainsborough's Fittings for Boilers	40
Gauge Cocks, various	33
Government Pattern Safety Valve	49
Gland Steam Cocks	53
" Bib	55
Gas Meter Indexes	17
HOT WATER THERMOMETERS	11
Hallam's Patent Injectors	25, 41
High Pressure Steam and Water Tap	56
Hydraulic Gauge	10
Hydrostatic Level	48
INDEXES	17
Ixion Steam Cock	61
Iron Coils	63
Injector, Hallam's Patent	25, 41

	Page
Iron Valves with G.M. Spindle & Seats	55
Iron Mud Cocks, G.M. Plugs	55
Indicator, Speed	15, 18
" Hopkinson's	25
" Richard's	25
" Low Water	43
" Cocks	73
" Spindle	22
" Printers'	15
" Ashton and Storey's	236
JUNCTION AND SAFETY VALVE COMBINED	55
KETTLE, STEAM	65
Kitchen Boiler Safety Valve	51
LOCOMOTIVE WHISTLES	71
" Spring Balances	12
" Safety Valves	42
" Marine & Portable Boiler Safety Valves	42
Low Water Float and Safety Valve	48
" Alarm	43
" Float Whistles	43
MEASURING INDICATOR	18
Measuring Instrument	239
Mud Cock Scavenger	56
Machine for Testing Metals, Thurston's Patent	19 and 239
Mud Cocks, Double Gland	52
Mercurial Gauges	9, 11
Mounting for Boiler	36 to 44
Mud Cocks	55
Nickel Pop Safety Valve	49
OXYGEN REGULATOR	27
Oil and Tallow Cup, Gravity	77
" " Ordinary	71
" " Bridgewater's	71
" " Ashcroft's	69
" " Bailey's	68
" " Crystal	76
" " Vertical Plug	69
Oil Syphons	71
PRESSURE GAUGES	5
" Danger Bar	6
" Curtin's	8
" Blast	9
" Hydraulic	10
" Water	10
" Gas	11
" Pyrometrical	7
Pedometer	18
Peg Clock, Watchman's	21
Peet's Patent Valves and Taps	59, 60
Pillar Water Gauge Cocks	35
Plugs, Fusible	29
Porter's Governor	75
Pet Cocks	73
Pressure Recorders	13
Pop Safety Valve	49
Pump Escape Valve	52
Printers' Indicator	15
Pyrometers	28 and 228
Pumps, Plunger	57
QUADRUPLE ENGINE HOUSE RECORDER	14

	Page
REGULATOR, OXYGEN	27
Regulating Feed Valve	42
" Suction Valve	67
Regulator, Feed Water	51
" Smoke	66
Recorder, Pressure	13
" Speed	13, 10, 17
" Watchman's	21
" Water	13
" Reservoir	23
Ramsbottom Safety Valves	42
Reducing Valve	62
Roscoe's Engine Lubricator	73
Roarers	70
STARTING VALVE	41
Suet Cup	71
Stillwell Heater and Lime Catcher	64
Sluice Valves, Steam	58
" Air	58
" Water	58
" Gas	58
Speed Indicator	15, 18
" and Recorder	13
Speed Recorder Clock	16
Steam Gauges	5
" Driers and Expansion Joints	63
" Kettle	65
" Thermometers	11
" Stop Valves	55
" Trap	42
" Royle's Patent	226
" Bailey's Patent	227
" Jet Pumps	26
" Engine Indicator, Hopkinson's	25
" " Richard's	25
" Gauge, Pyrometrical	7
" Registered Syphon for Testing	8
" Cocks	55
" Valves	55
" Taps	55
" Gauge Cocks	73
" or Water Universal Swivel	92
" Roarers	70
" Cock, Patent Improved	52
" Continuous Indicator, Ashton and Storey's	236
Self-Registering Turnstile	18
Syringe for Oil and Tallow	61
Smoke Preventor and Regulator	66
Spring Balances	12
Scumming Apparatus	236
Safety Valves	50, 55
" Double B.R.	36
" Ramsbottom's	37
" Spring Balance	38
" Kitchen Boiler	51
" Lock-up	50
" Gun Metal	50
" Iron	50
" Water Gauge and Gauge	38
" and Gauge	39
" and Spring Balance	38
" Registered	38
" Side Flange	39
" and Junction combined	55
" Ashcroft's Patent	49
" Government Pattern	49
" Double Bracket	53
" Test Cocks	73

	Page		Page		Page		Page
Spindle Indicator	{22, 24}	Tallow Cup, Vertical Plug	69	Valves, Water	58	Valves, Dome	50
Scavenger Water Gauge Cocks	34	Time and Speed Indicator	15	,, Air	58	,, Balloon	72
Stop-cock with Bow Key	52	Thurston's Patent Testing Machine	79	,, Gas	58	,, Bayley and Bailey's	53
Syphons, Oil	71	Tell-tale, Curtin's Steam Gauge	8	,, Throttle	58	WATER VALVES	58
TUBES, CONICAL, for Boilers	27	,, Ashcroft's Low Water	{44, 47}	,, Equilibrium	58	,, Heater, Stillwell's	64
Thermometers	11	,, Watchman's Electrical	{21, 23}	,, Starting	42	,, Wood's	66
,, Hot Water	11	,, ,, Watch	22	,, Iron and Gun Metal	55	,, Main Air	58
,, Brewers'	11	,, ,, Peg Clock	21	,, Governor	61	,, Escape Valve	
Turnstile, Self-Registering	18	,, Clepsydra Low Water Alarms	43	,, Safety Spring Balance	{37, 50}	,, Pressure Gauge	10
Throttle Valves	58	Three-way Cocks	57	,, Feed Regulating	42	,, Lifters	26
Test Cocks	73	UNION JOINTS	53	,, Reducing	{62, 189}	Water Gauge Glass Tubes	48
Time and Speed Indicator	15	Universal Swivel, for Steam or Water	69	,, Safety Lever and Spring	40	,, ,, Cocks, Scavenger	34
Tallow Cup, Ashcroft's	69	VACUUM GAUGES	5	,, Ball Clack		,, ,, Cocks, various	33
,, Bailey's Engine Cylinder	68	Vertical Plug Tallow Cup	69	,, Escape	50	Watchman's Watch	22
,, Bridgewater's	71	,, ,, Hot Water Cock	51	,, Peet's Patent	{59, 60}	,, Peg Clock	21
,, Crystal	76	Valves, Sluice	58	,, Steam	55	,, Recorder and Counter	21
,, Gravity	77			,, Pump Escape	52	Workman's Steam Kettle	65
,, Ordinary	71						

Engineers, Contractors' Tools, Testers and Sundries Department.

	Page		Page		Page		Page
AMATEUR'S LATHE	166	Casting Brushes	161	Hydraulic Motor	145	Moncreiff's Governor	78
American Rules	120	Cast Iron Pipes	235	,, Iron Tester	86	Milwaukee Lantern	161
,, Calipers	120			,, Jacks	99		
,, Squares	120	DRILLING MACHINES	{98, 105}	Hop Press	137	NUTS AND BOLTS	126
BUCKETS	152	Duppa's Bench Dogs	118	Hay Presses	230	Needle Lubricators	149
Blacksmith's Iron Fire Trough	95	Drilling Jib	108	Holdfast Cement	158	Nail Pullers	{103, 234}
,, Tools, &c.	113	Disintegrator	130	Hoffman's Hand Shears	102	Non-conducting Felt	157
Bone Crusher	134	Drills and Braces	107	Hot Water Meter	144		
Boot and Shoe Cleaning Machine	106	Drug Mills	132	,, ,, Goods	235	OIL TESTER	87
Bench Vices	98			Hoists	91	,, Cans	150
Bolts	125	ENGINES	155	Hoisting Crab	91	,, Feeders	151
Brewing Pans	152	Engineers' Hammers	113	Hydraulic Tire Fitter	138	,, Cup	151
Bench Dogs	118	,, Rules	120	Hore Lubricators	149	,, Cans, Buckingham's	{150, 151}
Belt Glue	154	,, Squares	120			,, ,, White's	151
Bellows	{127, 128}	Embossing Presses	135	IRON CUTTER, "Little Giant"	106	,, ,, Radcliffe's	151
Blowing Machine	129			,, Cisterns	152	,, Piston	151
Bear Punching	103	FIRE BUCKETS	152	,, Casks	152	Oiling Machines for Wagons, Halliday's Patent	229
Bar Iron Cropper	102	Fans, Schiele's	130	,, Testing Machines	83		
Bolt Cropper	{98, 112}	,, Exhaust	130	,, Cropper	102	PIPE WRENCHES, McComber's	100
		Files and Rasps	148	,, Shears	99	Planing Machine, Hand	97
Bread Makers	97	Forges and Bellows	{127, 128}	,, Barrows	113	Pillars, Wrought Iron Riband and Spiral	{232, 233}
Boiler Test Pumps	135	Flock Dressing Machines	161	India Rubber	156		
Bench Test Pumps for Cocks, &c.	79	Ferrule Extractor	112	,, ,, Hose	156	Pipe Tester	80
Breast Drill	79	Foundry Brushes	161	,, ,, Cord	156	Paper Tester	10
Bar Iron Shears	97	Felt	146			Piston Rings, Ramsbottom's	124
Bottle Washing Machine	99	,, for Steam Pipes	157	JEWELLERS' VICE	95	,, ,, Rubber	156
Braces	106	Foot Lathes	115	Jacks, Ratchet	96	Plumbers' Stove	161
Barrows	107	Flange Pipes	121	,, Screw	96	Punching Bear	103
Bread Kneader	113			,, Bottle	96	,, Simplex	103
	136	GRINDSTONES	95	,, Traversing	96	Punching and Shearing Machines	234
COAL AND COKE WEIGHING MACHINES	134	Grindstone and Trough	105	,, Hydraulic	99	Pipe Vices	103
Colliery Signal Bells	89	Gas Tubes	{140, 141}	KEGS	152	Pipe Felt	157
,, Winding Indicators	89	,, Cocks	139	LATHES	117	Packing Stand	{183, 159}
,, Wagon Oiling Machine	229	,, Fittings	139	,, Amateur	106	Parallel Vices	97
Cisterns, Iron	152	,, Regulator	139	,, Chucks	115		{115, 132}
Carr's Paint Mills	132	,, Tongs	107	Leather Driving Straps	155	Paint Mills	{132, 137}
Cement Tester, Michele's	86	,, Dogs	103	Lifting Jacks	96	Punches for Straps	155
Conical Grinding Mill	130	,, Wrench	107	,, ,, Railway	112	Punching Presses	99
Crickmer's Packing	123	,, Meters	144	Lubricators	149	Paint Mills	132
Cotton Waste	123	,, Pliers	107	,, Atmospheric	231	,, Mather's	132
Cotton Presses	230	,, Fitters' Tools	141	,, Needle	149	,, Carr's	132
Contractors' Barrows	113	,, Stocks and Dies	{109, 234}	,, Havre	149	,, Cans	153
Chucks	116			,, Marine	149	,, Oxide	231
,, Horton's	116	Governor, Moncreiff's	78	,, Skylight	151	Portable Drilling Machine	{112, 119}
,, Westcott's	116	Grinding Mill	130	Lanterns	161		
Calipers	120	Gas Machine	142	MIXING MACHINE	136	Pulley Blocks	91
Coach Wrenches	107	,, Alpha	233	Mallet Shafts	124	,, Eade's	95
Copying Presses	135	,, Pipe Screwing Machine	228	Metals, Prices	147	,, Weston's	90
Coal Tester	80			Metallic Kegs	{152, 153}	,, Pickering's	93
Crab for Hoists	91	HAMMERS	{105, 113}	Mitre Machines	118	,, Robinson's	94
Carpenters' Cramps	97	Hammer Shafts	124	Mortar Mills	132	Rain Water Goods	235
Chisels	105	Hydro Extractor	230	Mortar Temperers	132		
Cramps	107	Hand Trucks		Miners' Oil Lamps	161	ROTARY VICES	95
Cotter Pins	123	Howarth's Ventilators	160	Mechanics' Hammers	113	Road Scrapers	134
Cement	158			Malleable Iron Screw Keys	112		

	Page		Page		Page		Page		Page
Revolving Screen	134	Screw Keys, Baxter's	103	Tube Cutters	108	UMBRELLA STAND	116		
Railway Tools	101	" " McComber's	100	Trucks, Hand	122				
" Jacks	96	Shears	102	Tobacco Cutting Machines	133	VICES	{96, 105}		
Ratchet Braces	105	Steam Engines	155	" Crushing Machines	133	" Parker's	95		
" " Wilson's	103	Stocks, Taps and Dies	{109, 234}	" Spinning "	133	" Stephens's	115		
" " Weston's	108	Screw Stock, The Universal	234	" Cutters	161	" Jewellers'	95		
" " Anti-friction	108	Schiele's Fan	130	Tire Bending	137	" Bench	98		
Ratchet Drill, Moore's	100	Steam Joint Cement	{158, 231}	Testing Machine	{82, 83, 86}	" Pipe	103		
" Wrench, Moore's	100	" Packing	159	Testing Machine, Thurston's, Iron, Brass and Wood	{81, 239}	" Parallel	{97, 115}		
Ripley's Pipe Wrench	121	Steel yard	161			" Picken's	97		
Rules	120	Split Pins and Cotters	123	Tinman's Stove	161	Ventilators, Howarth's	160		
Ramsbottom's Piston Rings	124	Spiral Springs	123	Tools	103	Ventilator and Smoke Conductor, Hawksey's	146		
Roofing, Corrugated, &c.	233	Spiral Pillars	{232, 233}	" Gas Fitters'	107				
Roofing Felt	146	Sponge Cloths	123	" Railway	101	WINDING INDICATORS	89		
Rolls for Bending and Straightening Plates	146	Stud End Cutter	98	" Engineers'	107	Water Meter, Open	144		
Rasps and Files	148	Swivel Attachment	115	" Mechanics'	107	" " Clemesha's	145		
		Sack Hoist	93	Testing Apparatus	79	Washers	99		
STRAPS	155	Saw Spindle and Frame	107	Tester	79	Wilkinson's Hydraulic Pressure Reliever	144		
Strap Fasteners, Harris's	154	Spanners	108	" for Boilers	79	Wrenches	107		
" " Green's	95	Screw Cutting Lathes	117	" Pipes and Cocks	{79, 80}	" Moore's	100		
" Punches	155	Squares	120	" Paper	80	Wire Straining Machine	121		
Swivel Vice	95	Seaming Machines	122	" Coal	80	" Straightening Machine	121		
Swage Block and Stand	95	Scumming Apparatus	236	" Yarn	80	" Knotting Machine	121		
Stone Crushers	134			" Cotton	80	Wheel Hooping Slacking Pan	136		
Sack Barrow	122	TUBING, Gas and Steam	141	" Twine	80				
Signal Bells	89	Tube Scraper, Smith's	114	" Cement	86	YARN TESTER	80		
Safety Lamps	89	" " Mack's	124	" Oil	87				
Scroll Saws	106	Tube Brushes	114	" Wood	83				
Screw Jacks	96	" Wrenches	100	" Brass	83				
" Keys, Skarkop's	103	" " McComber's	100	" Steel	83				
" " Wilson's	103	" " Bewley's	108	Trough and Tuyere	95				

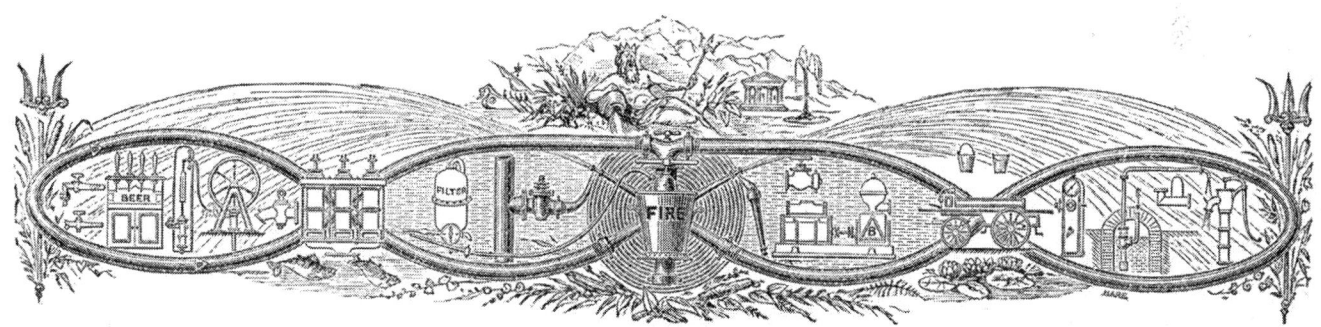

Pumps, Fire Engines and Escapes, Gas Machines and Publicans' Goods.

	Page		Page		Page		Page
AIR COMPRESSORS for Pumps	190	Fire Pump "Tozer's"	165	MEASURING TAP, Gooding's	194	REDUCING VALVES	189
Air Pumps for Gas Testing Machine	190	" Steam	181	" Instrument	239	Rams, Hydraulic	179
		" "Paddington"	166	Manchester Fire Pump	{165, 166}	Rotary Power Pumps	186
BOTTLING COCKS	194	" Engines	163	Manure Cart	174		
" Machine	192	" Steam	182	" Pumps	174	SPIRIT COCKS	194
Beer Machines	193	" Escape	163			" Racking	194
" Cocks	194	" Hill's	237	PUMPS	174	" Fountain	194
" Pumps	193	" Extinguishers, Steam	171	" Lift and Force	{173, 177}	Steam Pump, Excelsior	184
Bottle Washing Machines	192	" Brigade Cabinet	168	" Treble	178	" " Williamson & Walker's	181
Barrel Pumps, Brass Castings	186	Frictionless Pump	173	" Double	178	" " Fire Engine	182
Ball Hydrants	170	Frame Pump	178	" Horse or Bullock	176	" Jet Pumps	172
Bailey and Bayley's Valves	189	Filters, Self-Cleansing	191	" "Paddington"	166	" Fire Extinguishers	171
		Flax Hose	170	" "Manchester"	165	Self-acting Bottling Machine	192
COCKS, BOTTLING	194	Force Pump	183	" Beer	193	Syruping Pump	192
" Tapping	194			" Centrifugal	187	Swing Water Barrows	167
" Beer	194	GOODING'S MEASURING TAP	194	" Hand	187	Spreading Nozzle	164
" Leakless	194	Gas-Fitters' Test Pump	190	" Feed	181	Self-cleansing Filters	191
" Spirit	194			" Hand	187	Swivel Union	169
" Sundries	170	HYDRANTS	{170, 185}	" Brass	178	Stand Pipes	170
Corking Machines	192	Hand Pipes, Fire	185	" Frictionless	173		
Cork Drawing Machines	192	Hose	{170, 169}	" Frame	178	TAPPING COCKS	194
Compressors, Air	190	" Flax	169	" "Excelsior"	184	Tozer's Patent Fire Pumps	165
Centrifugal Pumps	187	" Leather	169	" Cameron's	183	" Swivel Unions	169
Cameron's Steam Pumps	183	Hose Carts	162			Testing Machines	190
Cistern Pumps	186	" Reel	162	" Force	{177, 181, 183}		
DONKEY PUMPS	185	" Union	167	" Barrel	186	UNIONS	185
Double Barrel Pump, Fire Engine	166	Horse Pumps	176	" Rotary	186	" Joints	185
Deep Well Lift Pumps	{176, 178}	Hydraulic Machine	186	" Cistern	186	VALVES, for Landings	170
		" Pump	186	" Pillar	175	" Bailey and Bayley's	189
"EXCELSIOR" STEAM PUMP		" Rams	179	" Double Action Lift & Force	175	" Greenhalgh's Reducing	189
Gas Machine	{184}	Hand Fire Engine, Single Barrel	166	" Steam Fire	182		
Engine Force Pump	183	Hall Fire Escapes, &c.	171	" Manure	175	WILSON'S DONKEY PUMP	185
"Express" Fire Engine	167			" Steam Jet	172	Water Valve	185
Edward's Frictionless Pump	173	JET PUMPS, Steam	172	" Power	180	" Cart	174
Ejectors	172	LANDING VALVES AND COCKS	170	" Williamson and Walker's Plug Hydrant	185	" Pillar	164
FIRE COCK	185	Leather Fire Buckets	169			Water Barrows	167
" Hand Pipes	185	Liquor Blenders	192	" Cock with Cap	170	Williamson and Walker's Pump	181
" Escape Pipes	172	Lift and Force Pumps	173				

BANK CLOCK IN BRONZE, BUENOS AYRES.

Turret Clock, Bell and Telegraph, Lightning Conductor Department.

	Page		Page		Page		Page
AUTOMATIC FOG BELL	212	Clocks, Double Dial	199	FOG BELL, Automatic	212	Speed Recorder	221
Alphabetical Telegraph Instrument	{219, 221}	,, Works	201	Fire Alarm, Electrical	219	,, Indicators	221
		,, Registered Design	202	,, Bells	219	,, ,, Reciprocating	221
BOXES, MUSICAL	212	,, Watchman's	204	Fittings, Telegraph	218	,, ,, Clocks	221
Burglar Detectors	219	,, Spring and Weight	204			,, ,, Counters	221
Bedroom Contacts	219	,, Regulator	206	"GALILEO" Billiard Marker	210	Spring Timepieces	204
Barometers	214	Cable Pattern Barometers	214	Gothic Timepieces	205	Semaphore Indicators	218
Bunsen's Battery Carbons	215	Colliery and Surface Barometers	214			Speaking Tubes	217
Billiard Marking Board, "Galileo"	210	Compound Magnets	215	LIGHTNING CONDUCTORS	{207, 208}		
Barometer, Polytechnic	213	Carbons for Bunsen's Battery	215	Leclanche Battery	222	TURRET CLOCKS	{195, 196, 197}
,, Cable Pattern	214	Chiming Machines	203				
,, Colliery	214	Card Table	211	MUSICAL BOXES	212	Telegraph Instrument, Alphabetical	{219, 221}
Bracket Time Piece	200			Morse Printing Key	219	,, Materials	218
Bell-Tolling Machine	203	DOUBLE AND SINGLE DIAL TIMEPIECE	199	Mean Time Regulator	206	,, Department, Prices	216
Bells	203	Dust and Damp Proof Electric Bells	222	Magnets	215	Tell-tale Clock, Watchman's	204
,, Electric	217			Magnetizing Machine	223	Time Regulator	201
,, Buttons	222	ELECTRIC BELLS	217			Terminals	217
,, Alarm Machine	203	,, Educational	223	PROJECTING DIALS, Timepiece	200		
Battery, Leclanche	222	,, and Indicators	218	Polytechnic Barometer	213	WATCHMAN'S Tell-tale Clock	204
		,, Speed Indicator	221	Pushes, Electrical	222	Works, Offices, &c., Time Regulator	201
CONDUCTORS, LIGHTNING	{207, 208}	,, Fire Alarm, adjustable	219				
Clocks	196	,, Bell Fittings	220	REGULATOR Clock, 12 months	212	Weight Timepieces	{204, 224, 225}
,, Turret	{195, 196, 197}	,, ,, Buttons	222	Railway Station Timepiece	199		
,, Bracket	200	,, ,, Pushes	222	SPEED INDICATOR, Electrical	221	,, Clocks	206
		,, Signal Bells, Dust and Damp Proof	222	Switch, Electrical	219	Whist Marking Table	211

Supplementary Matter Inserted too late for Classification.

See Advertisement Pages at the end of Book.

	Page		Page		Page		Page
Egg Boiler, for Bailey's Patent Steam Kettle	26	Tallow Cup, the Gravity	28	Fuel Economiser and Mechanical Stoker, 'Hallidays'	23	Stench Trap, Lowe's Patent	24
Low Water Alarm, "Syren"	26	Weighing Machinery	27	Tallow Cups, Bailey's Hollow Plug	23	Lathes, Manchester Pattern, (Amateurs')	24
Rotary Blower and Gas Exhauster, forced blast, Baker's Patent	10	Fusible Plug, Bailey's Patent	26	Ironfounders' Gauge, Bailey's Patent, for Indicating Low Blast Pressure	23	Domestic Machinery	25
		Grindstones for Tools	23				

NOTE.—There are a few pages of Sundries at the end of the Book, immediately before the Advertisements commence, which are not classed at all.

TERMS.

All Goods are delivered at our Works, carriage not paid. Cases charged cost price.

Strangers must send cash with first order in all cases, and trade references, if credit is wished for.

Foreign orders to be accompanied with bill on London banker at 3 months date, if nett amount deduct $2\frac{1}{2}$ for cash if bill at sight be sent. Our Bankers are the Liverpool and Manchester District Banking Co., Liverpool and Manchester. Bankers' London Agents, Messrs. Smith, Payne and Smith.

CASH DISCOUNT.—$2\frac{1}{2}$ per cent. allowed on all accounts, either cash with order, or if paid within one month after delivery. No discount allowed *if accounts go beyond that date.*

Merchants, Factors, Wholesale Ironmongers, and others, who can sell our goods abroad, or in this country, will receive our best attention ; and all will find that, in consequence of their popularity, they will meet with easy and profitable sale.—Full particulars on receipt of trade card.

To prevent *unnecessary correspondence*, W. H. B. & Co. state to *foreign purchasers*, that in no case will they depart from their terms *for goods sent abroad*, *i.e.*, cash, or bill on an accepted London house.

In as many cases as possible, *our friends are particularly asked to make orders out on a sheet separate from a letter.* State page of Catalogue, and by what route to be delivered.

CONDITIONS.

Toutes Marchandises sont expidiès des ateliers de W. H. B. & Co., frais de transport non payes, caisse et emballage sont facturés au prix coûtant.

Les étrangers doivent joindre le montant de leur premiere commission, et envoyer référence de commerce dan le cas de crédit.

Les demandes pour l'étranger doivent être accompagnées d'une remise sur une maison de banque de Londres.

Les Banquiers de W. H. B. & Co., sont Liverpool and Manchester District Banking Co., Liverpool and Manchester ; agents de Messrs. Smith, Payne and Smith, de Londres.

$2\frac{1}{2}$ o/o d'escompte sont alloués sur tout paiement, soit remise avec la commande, ou dans le casque le susdit paiement soit effectuè dans le mois qui suit la livraison ; apres cette époque, l'acheteur n'a plus de droit a l'escompte.

Marchands, facteurs, quincailliers en gros, et autres maisons qui se chargeraient de la vent des produits a l'étranger ou dans ce pays de W. H. B. & Co., peuvent etre assures que tous le soins seront apportés a la bonne exécution de leurs commandes ; la popularité des articles, leur sera une garantie pour en faciliter une vente courante et avantageuse ; plus amples informations seront fournies, sur la reception d'une carte d'affaires.

Pour éviter une correspondence inutile, W. H. B. & Co., ont l'honneur de prévenir les acheteurs étrangers que dans aucun cas, ils ne changeront rien a leur conditions pour les envois a l'étranger.

W. H. B. & Co., prient les maisons qui voudront les honorer de leur commande de la faire sur une feuille á part de la lettre, en avant soin de mentienner la page du Catalogue et le mode de transport.

The Goods advertised at the end of this Book may, in most cases be had direct from us at the same prices as supplied by the manufacturer, and can be packed at the same time.

Friends abroad who wish us to purchase goods for them may rely on having their interests forwarded in the best possible manner. Our knowledge of the manufacturing districts of the United Kingdom is, of a necessity, very great, and it is freely placed at the disposal of foreign purchasers. We have on our books alone as customers from five to ten thousand firms who are either Boiler Makers, Engineers, or in the Metal Trades, besides many thousands in other trades.

NOTICE CONCERNING REMITTANCES OF SMALL SUMS.

Post Office Orders may be made payable to W. H. BAILEY & CO. AT THE REGENT ROAD POST OFFICE, MANCHESTER.

Friends in the British Colonies can send their remittances of small amounts in this manner, and may deduct the cost of the order from the amount. Five per cent. should be sent in addition for cost of packing.

North Germany, Denmark, and other countries are now in connexion with the English Post Office, and Money Orders may be sent to us direct from those places.

Large Buyers, for Wholesale Purposes, may have full details of our terms on application.

PAMPHLETS BY W. H. BAILEY.

POST FREE, THREEPENCE,

"THE PATENT LAWS DEFENDED,"

A REPLY TO

R. MACFIE, Esq., M.P.,

A Paper read before the Manchester Association of Foremen, Masters and Draughtsmen of the Mechanical Trades. JAMES GRESHAM, Esq., *in the Chair*.

POST FREE, THREEPENCE,

"SOUND TELEGRAPHS,"

(ILLUSTRATED),

Being an Account of Telegraphs, Ancient and Modern, with a description of a Process of Telegraphing at Sea by means of Steam Whistles.

A Paper read before the Manchester Scientific and Mechanical Society. EVAN LEIGH, Esq., C.E., *in the Chair*.

POST FREE, FOURPENCE,

ON THE "PREVENTION OF EXPLOSIONS IN KITCHEN OR CIRCULATING BOILERS, AND THE PREVENTION OF ICE IN WATER SUPPLY PIPES,"

(ILLUSTRATED.)

A Paper read at the Manchester Town Hall, before the Society of Municipal and Sanitary Engineers. J. C. LYNDE, Esq., City Surveyor, *in the Chair*.

This Paper will shortly be published in a more extended form for the use of Architects, Plumbers, &c., by Messrs. LOCKWOOD & CO., Publishers, London.

"THE PYROMETER AND ITS USES,"

AND OTHER LISTS,

POST FREE, ON APPLICATION.

The Catalogue

Physical Details

The original catalogue is quarto size, section bound with rigid card covers that are finished with coloured prints. Overall the condition is poor: the binding has dropped apart, the pages are the colour of a pale coffee and are very brittle. It was decided that since the content was so interesting the document should be scanned and published for posterity. This involved completely dis-binding the book. Fortunately the pages were in the main complete, but edges were ragged and corners often missing. Two leaves, pages 1 to 4, were missing; it was decided to insert these pages, but with added suitable material.

Many catalogues of this era contained pictures of the factory and its interior. Often these were rather imaginative and exaggerated to create a good impression. Most likely pages 1 to 4 contained such images of the Bailey works since there are no items in the index for these pages. Perhaps the leaves were removed by a trophy hunter.

At the bottom of each page is the text 'When ordering, please quote No, (if any) and Page'. In order to keep the pages full size these footers were removed. The requirements of the print process demand certain margins and this legend was right on the edge of the page. Section signatures were also lost in this cropping. Minimal digital restoration of the internal pages has been undertaken.

In the adverts section some pages had a footer to state that these items could be supplied by Bailey.

The cover was in a very bad state with a large corner lost on the front plus tears and a similar size corner missing from the back. It was decided that the cover had a naive charm that reflected the era and this should be reproduced. Missing parts were reconstructed from what was left and the tears covered over. There was no attempt to to make it it look as new, only as close to the original as was reasonably possible.

Index to New Matter added since last Edition.

	Page		Page		Page		Page
BLACKSMITHS' DRILLING MACHINES	248	Fire Engine	262 & 263	Oil Pump, on Cast-iron Frame, Bailey's	275	Steam Pan Paste-pots, &c.	295
Belt Shipper, Patent Safety	252	Fire Apparatus	264	Organ Blower, Hydraulic	277	" Kettles, Double	296
Boiler Composition, &c.	255	Filter, Mud, Dirt, &c., Extractor	273	Oil Testers, Ingram and Stapper's	285	" Horses, &c.	296
Boiler Composition Injector	256	Fitter's Friend Shaper, Bailey's	276	" Thurston's	286	TAPS AND DIES	253
Blow Pipe, Chisels, Drill, &c.	256	Furnace Bars	279 to 282			Thermometer, Bailey's Steam, Hot Air and Liquor	264
Blow-off Cock, Bailey's Patent	264	Foot Warmers, Boiler, and Apparatus Complete for Railway Companies, &c.	294	PUMP, HYDRAULIC	245	Traps, Steam	269
Ball Valve, Equilibrium, Extra Size	268			Presses—Lard, Tallow, Cloth, Baling	250	Tally or Counter	288
Barrel Cocks, Improved Patent, &c.	270	GLUE POTS	294	Pulley Blocks, Henderson's Patent	251	Telegraph Wire Insulators, &c., &c.	289
Ball Joint and Union, Extra Strong Swivel	271	Gas, Water, and Steam Union Joints	273	Packing, Gun-Metal	257	UNION BALL JOINT, &c.	271
Biscuit Machine, American Patent	285	Grindstone Turner, Young's Diamond	278	Pumps, &c.	258 to 263	Union Joints, Gas and Water	273
		Gauges, Scavenger, &c., with Lamps	287	Paste Pots, Steam	295		
CLEAR WATER SEPARATOR, Plum's Patent	275			RUBBER WASHER CUTTER	247	VALVES	245
Crane, Improved Friction	252	HOLDFAST CEMENT	289	Ratchet Brace	248	Valves, Spindle	245
Composition Boiler	254	Hearth, Bailey's Patent Hot	297	Reservoir Regulator, J. G. Lynde, Esq., C.E.	268	Valves, Safety	245
Composition Injector	256			SAW BENCH	246	Valves, Water Waster Preventer, Howard's Patent	251
Counter, Engine	268	INJECTORS	272	Sawing Machine, Hand Power, Combined Circular, &c.	246	Valves, Starting, Anti-priming Pipe	256
Cock, Draw-off	275	Indicator Bell Signal	288	Steel Tool Holders, Smith and Coventry	247	Vertical Steam Boiler	259
Counter or Tally	288	" Float	297	Screwing Machines, Grindrod's	249	Valve, Reducing	264
Cement, Holdfast	289	" and Patent Well, &c.	278	Steel Bars	252	Valves, Lip and Double Lip, and Dead-weight Pattern	265 to 267
Clocks, Railway, &c.	296			Spirit Levels	254	Valve, Patent Cylinder-Relief, Bailey and Ashcroft	273
" Eight-Days, &c.	290	LEVELS, SPIRIT, &c., &c.	254	Steam Pumps	258	Vacuum Guage, Absolute, Baldwin and Bailey's	274
Clock, Baronial	291	MITRE CUTTER, PATENT	249	Secretaire, Wooton Patent	248	Valve, Safety, Ashcroft's Patent Alarm	287
" Drop Attachment and Alarum	292	Mill Boards	252	Steam Boilers	259		
" Tassell	292	Motors, Hydraulic	276	Steam Engines, Haag's Patent	278	WASHER RUEBER CUTTER	247
ENGINE AND BOILER, with B. R. Fittings	261	Motors, Haag's	277, 278	Suet Lubricators	271	Water Closet	251
Engine Counter	268			Signal Bell Indicator, Parkin's	288	Wire Netting	283
Engine, Steam, Haag's Patent	278	ORGAN BELLOWS AND INDICATOR	277	Screws	284	Wire Insulators, &c., Telegraph	289
FLOAT INDICATOR	297	Oil Cistern, Tell-Tale Pattern	275	Steam Kettles			
				" Glue Pots, Size, Paste,	294		
				" Stoves, Foot Warmers, &c.			

Insert facing page vi

For Further Particulars of Injectors, Water Motors, Hydraulic Organ Blowers, Water Heaters, Steam Jet Pumps, Safety Valves, &c., as well as other

BOILER FITTINGS,

See

"BAILEY'S SUPPLEMENT OF BOILER FITTINGS,"

Post Free.

Insert Facing page 41

CHEAP SECOND-HAND LATHES.

We have a few Lathes on Sale in good condition, Second-hand, as illustration page 117, with 7-in. centre, on Cast-iron Legs complete, as described the new Price being £17 10s. 0d. These are on sale at £12 10s. 0d. each, for cash. They are in good condition, our reason for parting with them being that we are placing down a number of heavier ones.

Insert Facing page 117

NOTICE

On page 247 of the present edition of our Catalogue, a Trade Mark, consisting of an Eagle holding a bow in one claw and and Arrow in the other, has, by an error of our printers, has been placed over a Patent Toolholder. This Trade Mark is the property of Messers. JOHN FLETCHER & SONS, Eagle Foundry, Booth Street, Salford, and is shewn in illustration of their Advertisement, on page 50 of the supplementary part of our book.

Insert Facing page 247.
Transcribed from the original that was printed on dark blue paper and thus difficult to scan.

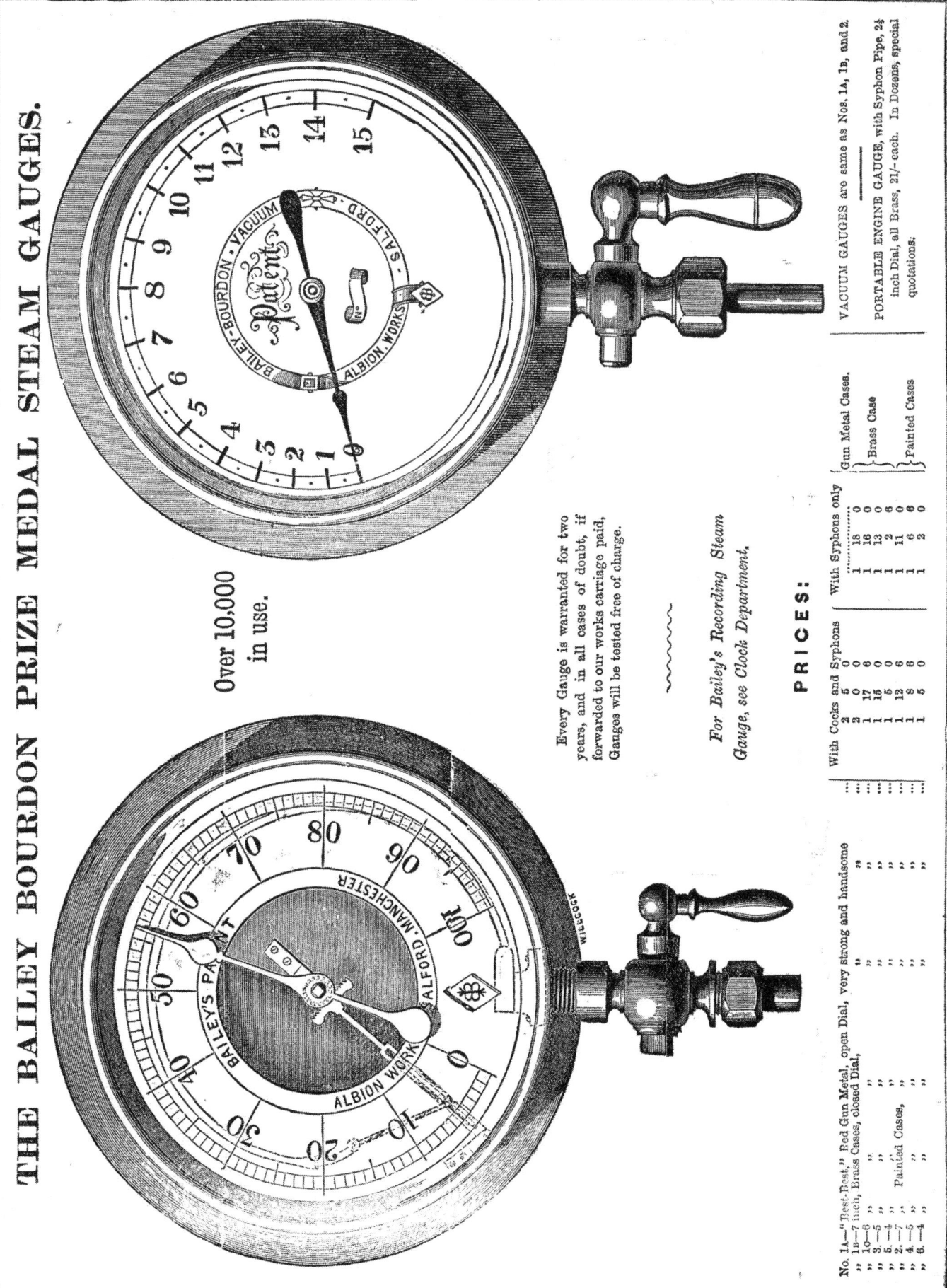

THE "DANGER" BAR GAUGE.
BAILEY'S PATENT, A.D. 1875.

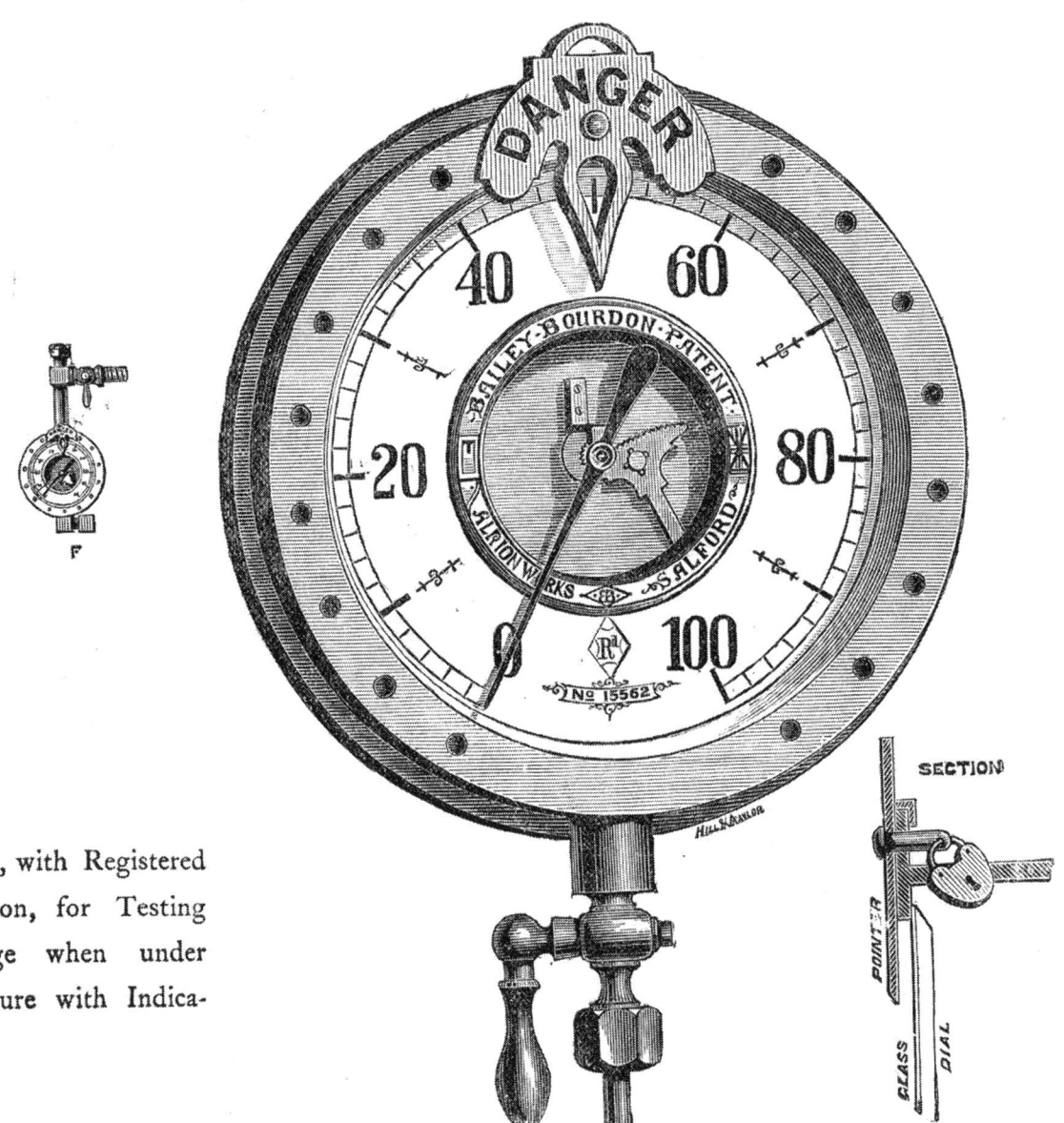

No. 11, with Registered Syphon, for Testing Gauge when under pressure with Indicator.

The improvement in Steam Gauges here illustrated consists of a Sliding "Danger" Bar, which can be adjusted and locked (see section) at the pressure which must not be exceeded by the attendants. In the event of accident or neglect of duty, the hearsay evidence of the stoker, or the mere word of mouth (verbal) instructions are not relied upon, as the manager's instructions are "plain on the face of it," and not to be contradicted.

These Bars are only fitted to the High-class 7in. Solid Gun Metal Gauges, and for best boilers are not only useful but really magnificently finished and handsome guards.

No. 9.—	7-inch, with Cock and Tail Pipe for Engine-houses,	…	£2 16 0
,, 10.—	,, with ordinary Syphon and Cock, … …	…	3 0 0
,, 11.—	,, with Registered Syphon—(See Cut F.) …	…	3 0 0

For BAILEY'S Patent Steam Gauges, Gauge Cocks, Stop Valves, &c., see other Lists.

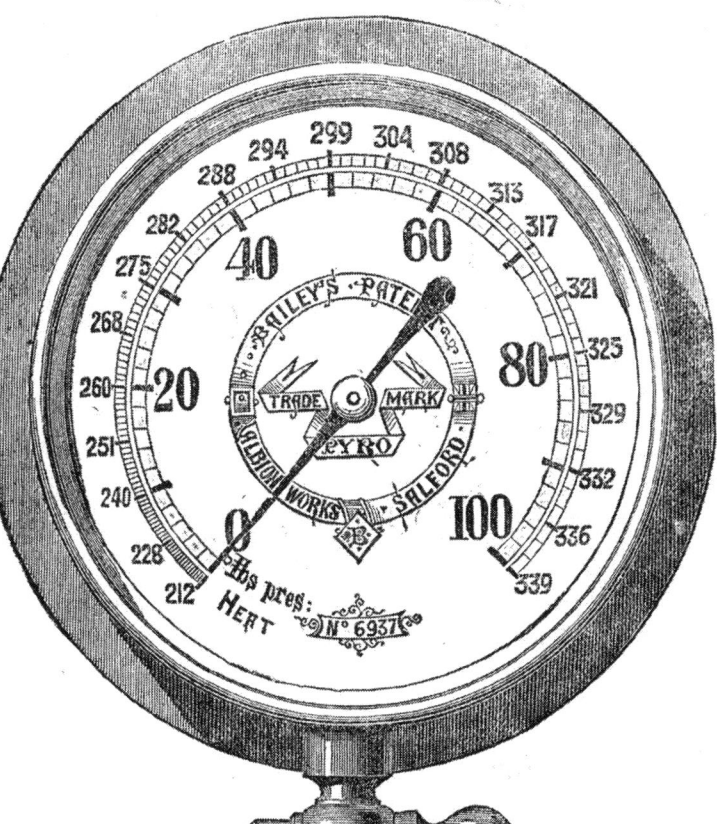

BAILEY'S NEW PATENT STEAM GAUGE	THE EDUCATIONAL GAUGE
Heat as a Means of Motion	TRADE MARK: "PYRO"
PRACTICALLY ILLUSTRATED.	
BAILEY'S PYROMETRICAL OR, EDUCATIONAL STEAM GAUGE	Protected by Letters Patent in England, America, &c., &c.
	INVENTORS AND MAKERS: J. BAILEY & CO., SALFORD.

The economical questions to be considered in relation to the "Pyro Educational Steam Gauge."
Coal is used by Manufacturers and others to produce heat, which Produces Steam, and, although it is known that High Pressure Steam is more economical than Low Pressure, it has not been presented to the minds of Engineers in a manner as vivid as the Pyro Gauge indicates it.

The Pyro Gauge not only indicates the Steam Pressure, but also its Temperature, in a most striking manner; causes a thinking man to consider the great question—How much does every pound pressure of Steam cost?

He will see that if 5 lbs. pressure from 0 to 5 costs 16 degrees of heat to produce it, and that quantity of heat costs one shilling's worth of heat or 16 degrees, 16 degrees will produce four times the amount of Steam at 80 lbs. pressure to 100. He sees on the dial that 50 lbs. pressure is only about 300 degrees of heat, while he is really producing 2,000 degrees of heat under the boiler, and often 1,000 in the chimney, presenting to his mind the enormous waste that is going on, and that he obtains, in many cases, only one-third of that which he buys; the other is lost by radiation, uncovered steam pipes, bad chimney arrangement, disproportionate fire-bars, and other causes known to practical men.

As an incentive to Economy.
As a continual reminder, ever presenting the exact amount of heat obtained as well as the pressure, the Pyro Gauge is useful, because it is a perpetual incentive to economy, and a dumb reproach against extravagance and the neglect of those means which men of science continually point out as the most rational in producing steam power.

Reason for Title.
Therefore, the "Patent Gauge" may be called the "Educational Gauge."

As a Heat Indicator for Heating and Stoving purposes
Apart from the considerations which are made in the preceding remarks, the Gauge is exceedingly beneficial to all who use Steam Power for Brewing, Heating, Baking, Drying, Stoving, Calendering, Boiling, Distilling, and many other purposes for which it is used for its heat and not for its pressure alone. In many cases a certain amount of heat is required, all superfluous heat being dangerous, or at least waste, and as a correct Indicator for such purposes, *dispensing with the Thermometer*, which is often being continually broken, and is a source of annoyance and trouble, this Gauge will be found very valuable.

Price, Workmanship, &c., &c.
Apart from all considerations of Heat, it is a first-class Gauge for indicating *Steam pressure only*, and its price being no higher than that of the ordinary Steam Gauges, the workmanship being essentially of first-class character, and every Gauge being warranted for two years, it is offered with confidence to the thinking portion of the mechanical community.

PRICES:

No. 1—In Gun Metal case, open Dial, 7 inch diameter, with cock and syphon	...	£2 10 0
2—In painted case, closed Dial, ditto ditto	...	2 2 0

The above are indicated to 60, 80, or 100 lbs. pressure.

3—Large Dial Gauge, 12 in. diameter, in Brass, most superior for large Engine House	...	5 10 0
For higher pressures, special Gauges are made 300, 400, 500, or 1,000 lbs., in Brass cases		6 10 0

CAUTION.—*Infringers of this Gauge will be prosecuted. Protected by Letters Patent in this Country and Abroad.*

THE BAILEY BOURDON
COMBINED PRESSURE & VACUUM GAUGE.

Much used by Steam-Boat Companies, and in large and handsomely-furnished Engine-houses.

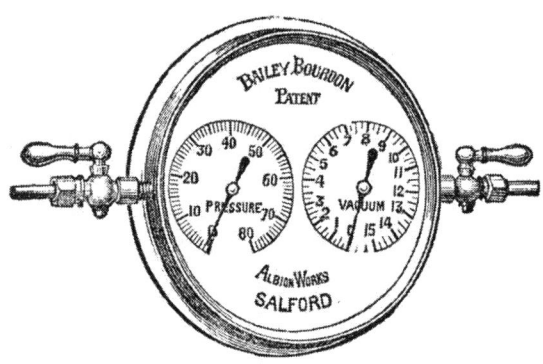

In strong Gun Metal Case. 12 inch dial.

Price complete, as shown, … …	£5	10 0
BAILEY'S LARGE STEAM GAUGE, with		
12 in. dial, in Gun Metal Case, … …	£5	5 0
10 in. ditto, … … … …	£4	10 0

THE BAILEY BOURDON
STEAM PRESSURE GAUGE.

Extra strong, most superior finish, and with Registered Test Syphon Pipe and Cock.

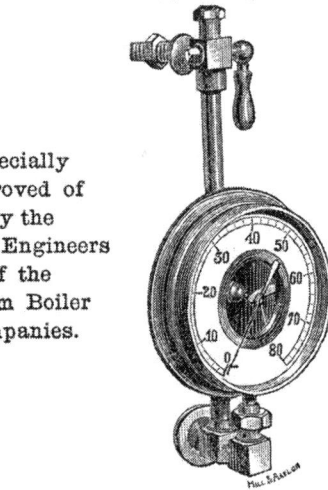

Specially approved of by the Chief Engineers of the Steam Boiler Companies.

7 inch dial.
No. 1a.

The above is highly recommended to all Engineers, as well worthy of their attention. The case is of solid gun metal—the syphon of registered pattern—has a strong two-way cock, to which, by unscrewing the top plug, a Test Gauge (see index) may be attached, and the accuracy of the Gauge at any time determined. M'Naught's, Richard's, or Hopkinson's Indicators may also be attached to the same syphon.

Price, complete … … … £2 18s. Guaranteed for two years.
With ordinary syphon & cock 2 15s.

☞ *Bailey's New Registered VACUUM AND PRESSURE GAUGE THERMOMETER AND LAMP will shortly be ready.*

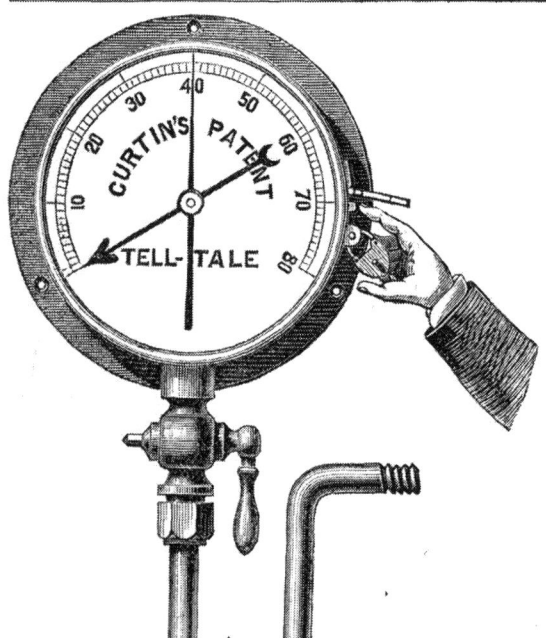

The Sketch shows the manner of bringing the Tell-Tale Hand to Zero, by simply pushing the button, which is protected from being tampered with by the padlock.

PRICE—In. 7 inch Brass Cases, £3 3s. each,
WITH SYPHON AND COCK.

CURTIN'S PATENT HIGH-STEAM
TELL-TALE & DETECTOR,

A Best Steam Pressure Gauge, with arrangement showing highest point the Steam has been in the absence of Manager or Employer.

It cannot be altered or tampered with.

TESTIMONIALS.

BRISTOL, *May* 22nd, 1871.
Your Patent Pressure Gauges are answering well.
    For the Great Western Cotton Co.
    [Signed] THOMAS LANG.

CANYNGE BUILDINGS, BRISTOL, *June* 23rd, 1871.
We have had two in use for some time. Our engineer says they answer admirably, and we have every reason to speak in the same manner of them.
    [Signed] CHARLES T. JEFFERIES & SONS.

ALBION FOUNDRY, TIPTON, *August* 11th, 1871.
I have used your Patent Check Gauges for some time past, and find them very reliable, and a very great improvement on the ordinary Gauges. Please forward on two more.
    J. DAVIES, Jun., C.E.

BOWER ASHTON, BRISTOL, *October* 18th, 1871.
I have had two of your Gauges at work for some time, and they are giving me every satisfaction. I consider them to be well made, very accurate, and a great improvement on the old Gauges.
    JOSEPH TINN, C.E.

CHEDDAR PAPER MILLS, WESTON-SUPER-MARE, *Dec.* 9th, 1871.
We have one of your Gauges at work, and it is giving every satisfaction. Should we require more, we should certainly come to you for them.
    [Signed] TANNER & BUDGETT.

BAILEY'S PATENT BLAST PRESSURE GAUGES,

As used by the chief Iron Manufacturers at home and abroad.

BAILEY'S REGISTERED OPEN COLUMN MERCURIAL PRESSURE, VACUUM, AND BLAST GAUGES.

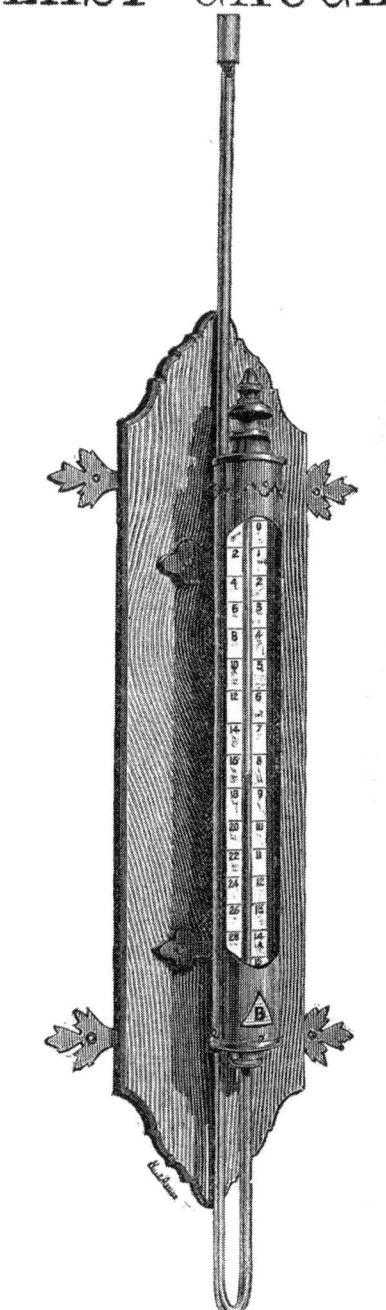

No. 1.—With 7 inch open Dials, Gun Metal Case, very handsome,	... £2	0	0
„ 2.—7 inch closed Dial, Painted Case,	... 1	16	6
„ 3.—12 inch Dial, Gun Metal Case,	... 5	5	0

In handsome Brass Case, on French Polished Oak Board. Complete with Mercury.

A Vacuum,	... £2	10	0
B Pressure,	... 3	10	0
C For Blast, 8 lbs., complete	2	10	0

10

Bailey's Patent Hydraulic Pressure-Gauges.

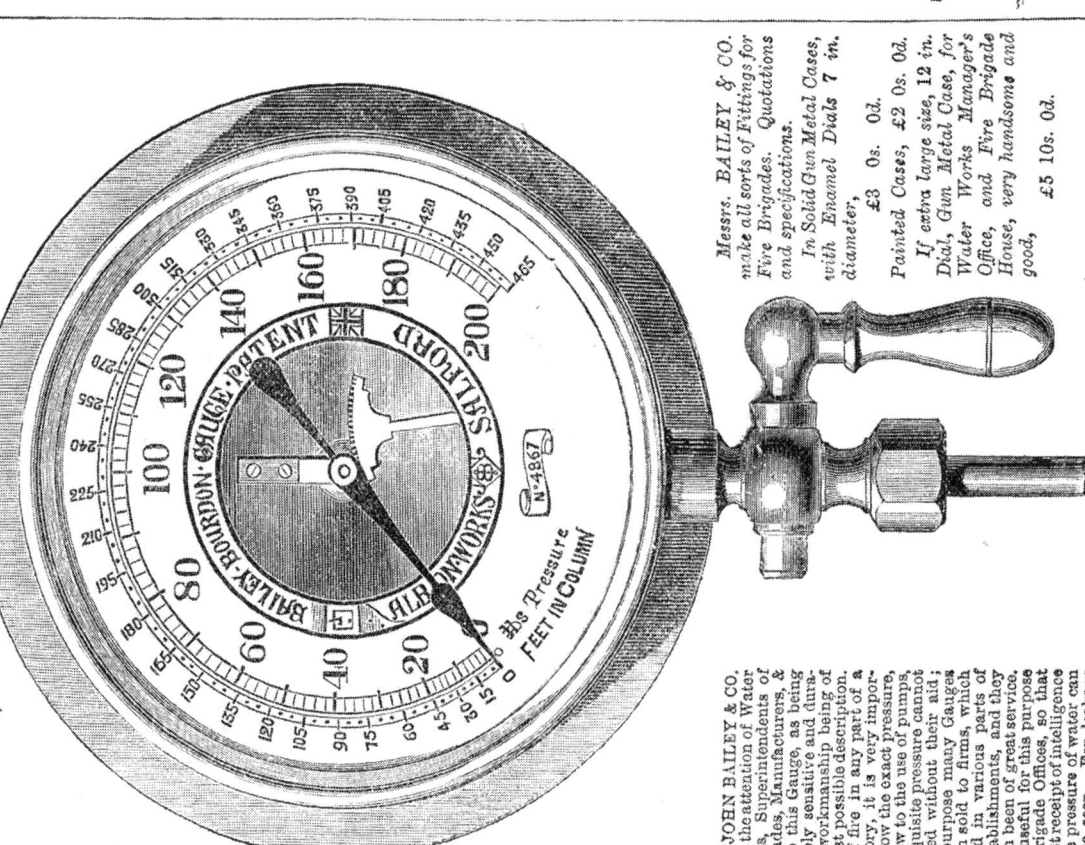

These Gauges are very Strong, Durable and Sensitive, and give universal satisfaction.

PRICES:—

		Gun Metal Cases	Painted Cases
With 7 in. Dials—to 4 tons	A	£4 0 0	D £3 10 0
,, ,, to 1,000 lbs.	B	£3 10 0	E £2 15 0
,, ,, to 500 lbs.	B	£3 5 0	F £2 10 0
,, ,, to 300 lbs.	C	£2 15 0	G £2 0 0

Bailey's New Water Pressure Gauge.

Indicated in lbs. and feet in column of water.

Messrs. JOHN BAILEY & CO. beg to call the attention of Water Companies, Superintendents of Fire Brigades, Manufacturers, & others, to this Gauge, as being remarkably sensitive and durable; the workmanship being of the highest possible description. In case of fire, in any part of a Manufactory, it is very important to know the exact pressure, with a view to the use of pumps, when a requisite pressure cannot be obtained without their aid; for this purpose many Gauges have been sold to firms, which are placed in various parts of large Establishments, and they have often been of great service. They are useful for this purpose in Fire Brigade Offices, so that on the first receipt of intelligence of fire, the pressure of water can at once be seen. For leakage of the Towns' Mains these are useful, as by placing them in various parts of a large town the constant usual pressure can be seen, and any extraordinary diminution of pressure at a given point at once leads to investigation, and leakages are thereby discovered.

Messrs. BAILEY & CO. make all sorts of Fittings for Fire Brigades. Quotations and specifications.

In Solid Gun Metal Cases, with Enamel Dials 7 in. diameter, £3 0s. 0d.

Painted Cases, £2 0s. 0d.

If extra large size, 12 in. Dial, Gun Metal Case, for Water Works Manager's Office, and Fire Brigade House, very handsome and good, £5 10s. 0d.

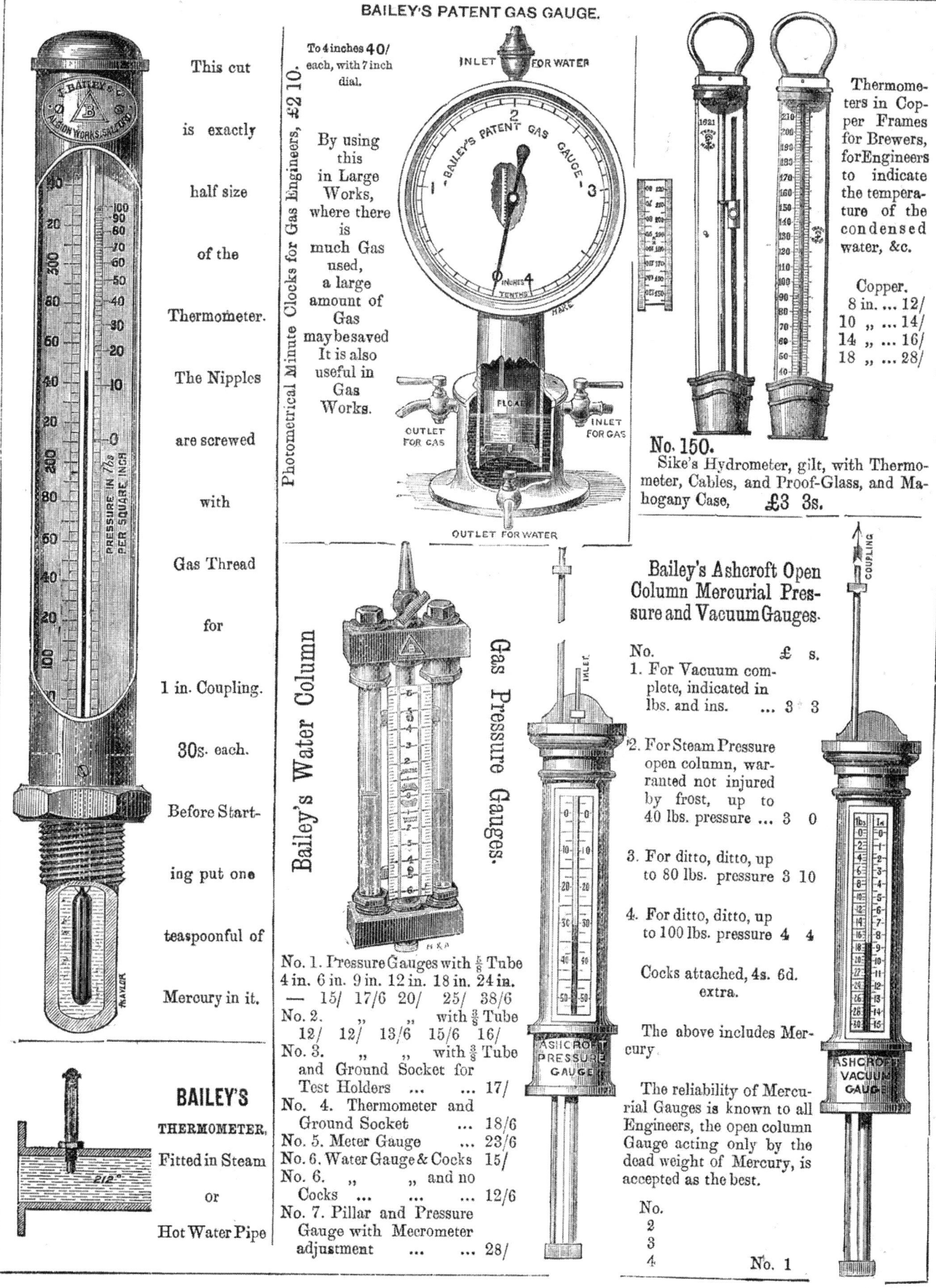

ROUND LOCOMOTIVE BALANCES,

WITH SCREW AND NUT.

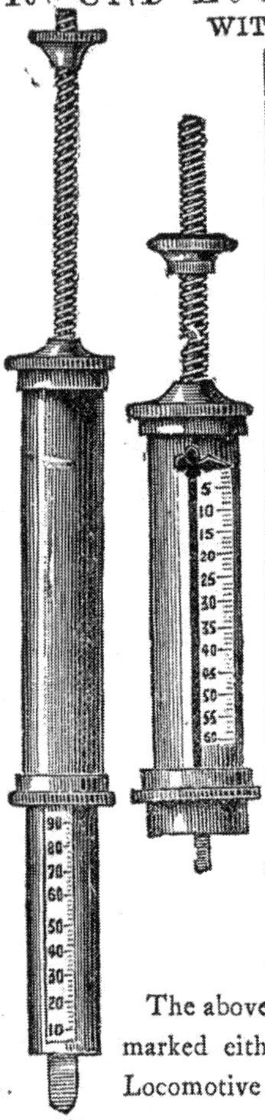

lbs.	5in.	6in.	7in.	8in.	9in.	10in.	11in.	12in. Range.
50	14/-	15/6						each.
60	14/6	16/-	17/6					„
70	15/-	16/6	18/-	19/6				„
60	15/6	17/-	18/6	20/-	21/6			„
90	16/-	17/6	19/-	20/6	22/-	23/6		„
100	16/6	18/-	19/6	21/-	22/6	24/-	25/6	27/- „
110		18/6	20/-	21/6	23/-	24/6	26/-	27/6 „
120		19/6	21/-	22/6	24/-	25/6	27/-	28/6 „
130		20/6	22/-	23/6	25/-	26/6	28/-	29/6 „
140		21/6	23/-	24/6	26/-	27/6	29/-	30/6 „
150		22/6	24/-	25/6	27/-	28/6	30/-	31/6 „
160		23/6	25/-	26/6	28/-	29/6	31/-	32/6 „
170		24/6	26/-	27/6	29/-	30/6	32/-	33/6 „
180		25/6	27/-	28/6	30/-	31/6	33/-	34/6 „
190		26/6	28/-	29/6	31/-	32/6	34/-	35/6 „
200		27/6	29/-	33/6	32/-	33/6	35/-	36/6 „

The above Prices include Patent Locomotive Balance, marked either on Outer or Inner Tube, and Round Locomotive Balances marked on Flat Side.

ROUND LOCOMOTIVE BALANCES,

WITH SCREW AND NUT,

MARKED ON FLAT SIDE,

For Portable Engines.

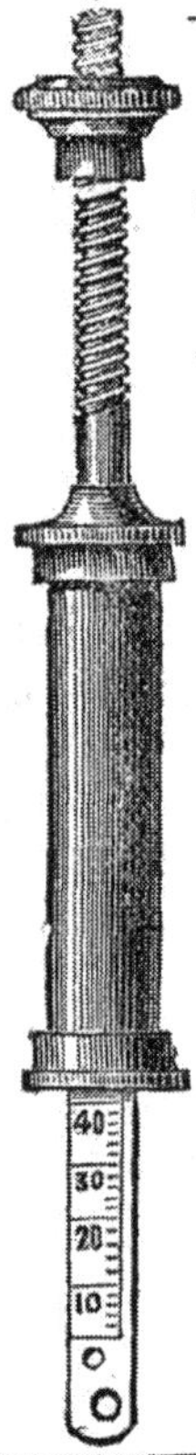

	2in.	2½in.	3in.	3½in. Range
20 to 45 lbs.	5/6	6/-	6/6	7/- each.
„ 50 „	5/9	6/3	6/9	7/3 „
„ 60 „	6/-	6/6	7/-	7/6 „
„ 80 „	...	7/-	7/6	8/- „
„ 100 „	...	7/6	8/-	8/6 „

FLAT LOCOMOTIVE BALANCES,

WITH SCREW AND NUT.

Indicated to	30lbs.,	...	4 inch Range	...	7/6	each
„	40lbs.,	...	4½ „	...	9/6	„
„	50lbs.,	...	4 „	...	10/6	„
„	60lbs.,	...	4 „	...	11/6	„
„	60lbs.,	...	4⅞ „	...	12/6	„
„	70lbs.,	...	4⅞ „	...	13/9	„
„	70lbs.,	...	5⅝ „	...	15/-	„
„	80lbs.,	...	5⅝ „	...	15/6	„
„	90lbs.,	...	6¼ „	...	16/-	„
„	100lbs.,	...	6¼ „	...	17/-	„
„	120lbs.,	...	5⅝ „	...	19/-	„

ROUND LOCOMOTIVE BALANCES,

MARKED ON ROUND IRON SPINDLE,

WITH SCREW AND NUT.

Indicated to			
160lbs.,	3½ inch Range,	11 in. × 2⅛ in. Barrel,	17/- each
200lbs.,	3½ „	13 in. × 2⅛ in. „	19/- „
160lbs.,	4½ „	14 in. × 2⅛ in. „	21/- „
200lbs.,	4½ „	15 in. × 2⅛ in. „	23/6 „

ROUND LOCOMOTIVE BALANCES,

WITH SCREW AND NUT,

MADE FOR SMALL PORTABLE ENGINES.

Indicated		2½ in.		3 in.		3½ in.		4 in. Range
20 to 45lbs.	...	7/-	...	7/6	...	8/-	...	8/6
50lbs.	...	7/6	...	8/-	...	8/6	...	9/-
60lbs.	...	8/-	...	8/6	...	9/-	...	9/6
70lbs.	...	8/6	...	9/-	...	9/6	...	10/-
80lbs.	...	9/-	...	9/6	...	10/-	...	10/6
100lbs.	...	10/-	...	10/6	...	11/-	...	11/6

The above prices include Balances, marked on inner or outer tube.

J. B. & Co. manufacture Valves complete with Spring Balances, all in one fitting, and having many designs for Steam Yachts, Portable Boilers, &c., they will be glad to quote, upon receiving particulars of Boiler, &c. Engineers, who send drawings of boilers, with request for a tender for a full set of fittings, will find our experience of value to them.

Bailey and Norton's Patent Pressure Recorders.

Now used by the Chief Engineers in Europe.

PRICE LIST.
(PATENTED IN ENGLAND, FRANCE, AMERICA, &c.)

NEW DESIGN, WITH RECENT IMPROVEMENTS, A.D. 1870.

For full Description, see "THE ENGINEER," April 29th, 1871.

REVISED PRICES.

	No.		£ s. d.
FOR STATIONARY BOILERS.	1.—For Steam Pressure, indicated to 100 lbs.		10 10 0
	2.—Indicated to 60 lbs. pressure,		10 10 0
	3.—Indicated to 30 lbs.,		10 10 0
WATER WORKS, &c.	4.—For Water Works, Fire Brigades, &c., to indicate Towns' pressure in lbs. and feet in column to 100 lbs.,		12 10 0
	5.—Ditto, ditto to 200 lbs.,		12 10 0
HYDRAULIC PRESSURE RECORDERS.	6.—For Hydraulic Pressure Pumps and Presses, indicated to 1,000 or 500 lbs.,		15 10 0
	7.—Hydraulic Recorder, indicated to 4 Tons on the square in.		15 10 0
FOR MARINE PURPOSES, STEAMBOATS, &c.	8.—Recorder, with Patent Lever Escapement; our best make, to go Eight Days, with Gauge to 30 lbs., or more,		15 10 0

FOR TIDAL OR RESERVOIR PURPOSES, ... £15 to £100.

These Recorders, for Indicating the Height of the Tide, or the Fluctuation of Water in Reservoirs, are made to order only.

COPY OF DIAGRAM (one-fourth full size.)

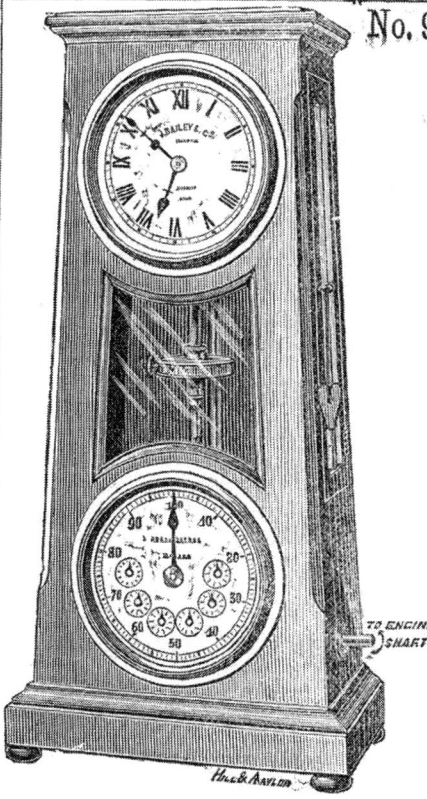

AWARDED
First-class James Watt Medal
By the Royal Cornwall Polytechnic Society, 1870.

No. 9

BAILEY'S
PATENT
SPEED INDICATOR AND RECORDER.

Copy of diagram (one-fourth full size.)

The Speed Recorder and Counter indicates the number of the revolutions of any Engine or Machine, and on a twenty-four hour diagram a puncture is made at the end of every 500 revolutions, thus indicating at what hour in the day the Engine went too fast or too slow.

PRICE, £10 10s. EACH.

☞ The above two instruments combined, see BAILEY's Quadruple Recorder, £20.

Bailey's Patent
QUADRUPLE ENGINE-HOUSE RECORDER AND INDICATOR,
EXHIBITING AT ONE VIEW, TIME, PRESSURE, SPEED, TEMPERATURE.

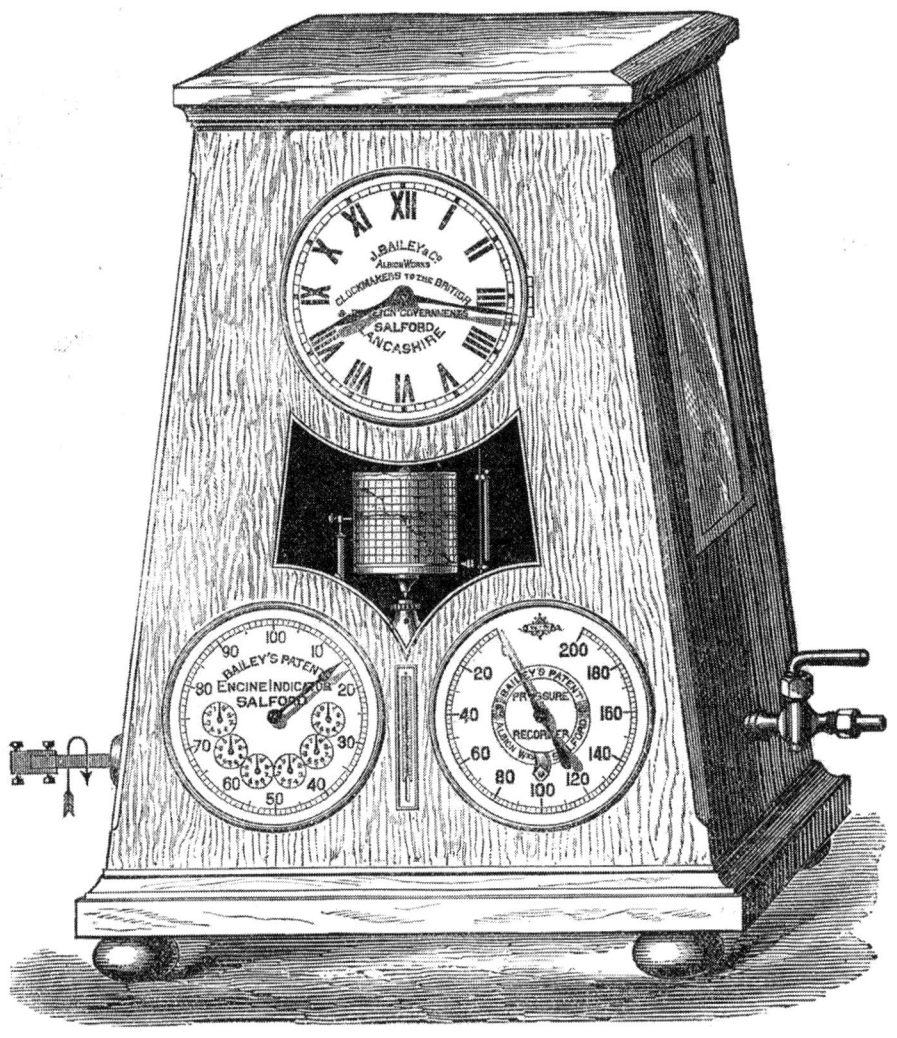

The above includes EIGHT DAYS' TIMEPIECE, 10-in. dial, with SPEED and PRESSURE DIALS 7-in., and DIAGRAM of DAILY PRESSURE and SPEED, recorded by a dot on Diagram at every 500 revolutions, also THERMOMETER, to indicate temperature of Engine-house. The whole in French-polished Case.

The Pressure Gauges are indicated to 80, 100, and 200lbs., for Blast Purposes to 8lbs. for Iron Works, and for Bessemer Steel Works to 30lbs. When required for Water Works' Engines, sometimes the pressure of the water in feet and lbs. is indicated.

This Instrument is in use in some of the most extensive Establishments in Europe, India, &c.

No. 248A.—High Pressure Engines, 100 to 200 lbs. £20 0 0
No. 248B.— Ditto, with Drum arranged for Striker for Watchman, thus indicating Speed, Pressure, and Watchman's punctuality, ... £25 0 0

☞ *When ordering, please say pressure.*

BAILEY'S SPECIALITY IN WORKS CLOCKS, FOR YARDS, STABLES, WORKS, &c.

Complete, with one two-feet Cast Iron Dial, painted blue, with O G mould, gilded hands and figures, to be fastened on wall, with strong eight-day movement, to be fixed on shelf behind wall; can be fixed by any mechanic in two days. Price, all complete, ready for fixing, £15.

BAILEY'S PATENT SPEED INDICATORS,
For Indicating the Speed of Engines, Pumps, Machines, Shafting, Printing Presses, Brick Machines, &c.

RECENT IMPROVEMENTS IN BAILEY'S PATENT SPEED INDICATORS.

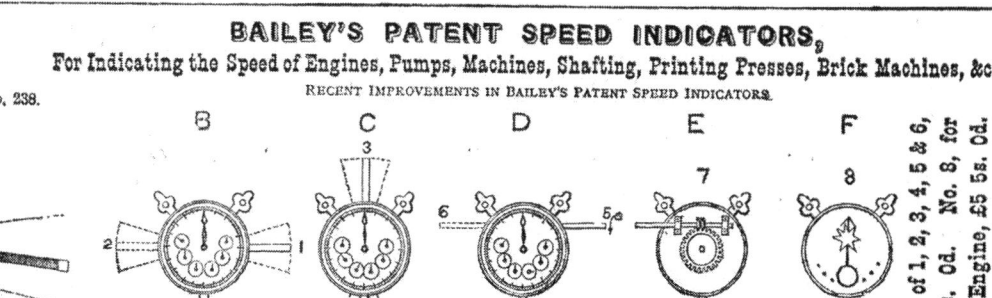

No. 238.

Price of 1, 2, 3, 4, 5 & 6, £4 4s. 0d. No. 8, for Beam Engine, £5 5s. 0d.

This well-known Speed Indicator has been well strengthened in parts where experience has dictated. The improvements consist in the facility with which any movement can be imparted for reciprocating motion: 1, 2, 3 and 4 show all the sorts, and for rotary 5 and 6 will do; 7 shows back view of the latter, and 8 shows the one for fixing on the axle of a Beam Engine, in such a manner that every time the engine beam swings the pendulum will move—a most desirable plan to prevent tampering with it. The parts are strong and substantial, the dials porcelain on copper, and the instrument looks well. All have dials 7in. in diameter, and indicate to 100 millions.

No. 240—SPEED INDICATOR AND CLOCK, Dial 14 in., Polished Oak Cases, Complete, with Eight-day Time-piece ... £8 10 0

Bailey's ENGINE HOUSE and Manager's Clocks,
And Combined Gauges and Indicators.

241—Oak case, French polished, with Eight-day Timepiece, 7 in. dial, and Bailey's Patent Speed Indicator, 7 in. dial, for rotary motion, with a small shaft through the side, ... £7/10/0

242—Ditto, ditto, with 7in. dial Steam Gauge; the three dials showing time, speed and pressure, ... £10/0/0

The Gauge can be connected with ¼in. high pressure lead pipe, with Boiler.

243—Ditto, ditto, with time, speed, pressure and vacuum, 4 dials £13/10/0

244—Ditto, ditto, with Blast instead, for vacuum, for Blast Furnace Engine-houses, ... £13/10/0

Any of the above with Gun Metal Bands, Gothic, like 245, £1 extra.

No. 245.

Bailey's Time and Speed Indicator,
Specially designed for Bombay Water Works.

Our cut represents an Indicator for the pumping engines of the Bombay Waterworks, of which two have been made by Messrs. J. Bailey and Co., of the Albion Works, Salford. The upper dial is an eight-day timepiece: the two lower dials are for the speed indications, which are connected to the shaft of the engine by the small shaft at the side of the case. The total number of revolutions made per day, per week, or per month, may be noted on the right-hand dial, and on the other "engine time" is seen. For instance, if an engine commences at fifty revolutions per minute at six o'clock in the morning, the engine time-dial should be set accordingly to that time, and then after working until say six o'clock in the evening, it will show six o'clock instead of 36,000, and the total number will be seen on the revolution dial. If 500 revolutions too few have been made, the engine time-dial would, of course, indicate 5.50 or ten minutes slow. It will be understood that by this means, if the chief engineer or person in charge wishes to see at a glance what sort of duty the engine has been making, he can do so by noting the engine time-dial, and if he has time to note the revolution dial, it can be then seen to a single revolution what duty has been done. Messrs. Bailey and Co. are introducing another description of speed indicator with only the revolution dial and the clock time-dial, which actuates a drum on which a paper is fixed making one revolution in twenty-four hours, and instead of taking a diagram of speed, which is difficult to understand, a simple pricker is actuated, which makes a mark on the paper for every thousand revolutions made. The same firm have in hand some recorders for the Greenock Water Trust, for indicating the time of the fluctuation of water in the reservoirs. We need scarcely point out the advantage to engineers of being able to arrive at the value of alterations, and to preserve uniform system, in order to obtain statistics upon which to base calculations of duty done in various engineering operations.—*Engineer*, Feb. 11, 1870.

245—As described, ... £16/10/0
246—Ditto, with Steam Gauge, in all 4 dials, ... £20/0/0

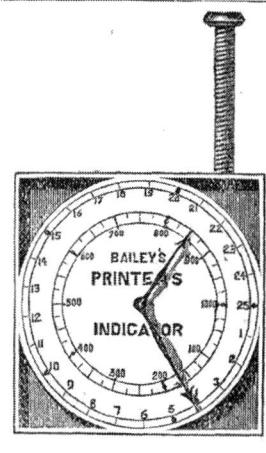

PRINTER'S INDICATOR,

For Jobbing Work, with dial 4 inches, or in box. The pressure screw, adjustable. Price 35/ each to 1,000; 6 at once, 30/ each; a dozen or more, 28/ each.

It is found on practice that indicators to 1,000 are quite sufficient, as they are parcelled as done.

BAILEY'S PATENT
SPEED RECORDER CLOCK,

No. 10.

FOR COTTON AND WOOLLEN OR OTHER MILLS,

WORKING 9, 9½, 10, OR 10½ HOURS PER DAY.

For indicating regularity of Starting, Stopping and performance generally of Engine.

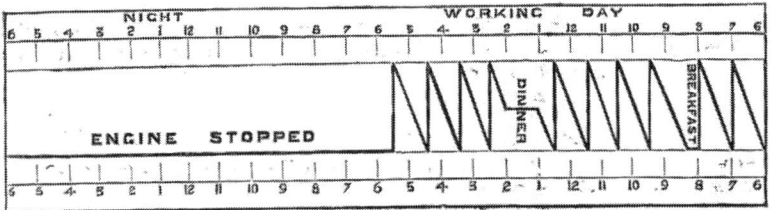

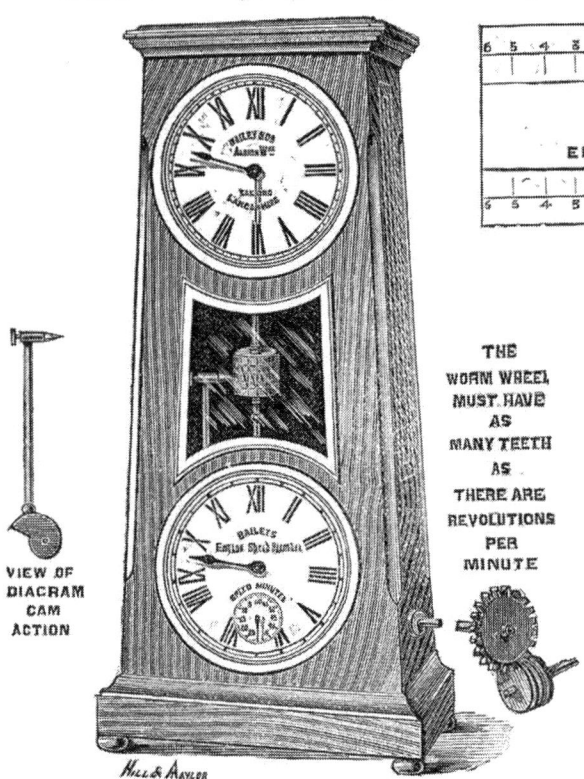

THE WORM WHEEL MUST HAVE AS MANY TEETH AS THERE ARE REVOLUTIONS PER MINUTE

VIEW OF DIAGRAM CAM ACTION

This diagram gives an indication every hour. After starting at six, this diagram shows good driving until stoppage for breakfast at eight o'clock, when there was a pause of half an hour; the next occurs at one o'clock when it shows the dinner hour and the start again at two o'clock; the engine stops at half-past five, and this completes the diagram. In order to take a fresh diagram it should be placed on the drum when the engine stops ready for the following morning; the engine may have stopped at five or half-past five; in that case, if starting time will be six in the morning, the engine dial must be set at six by means of the milled-headed screw inside the case.

If it is not considered desirable to take a diagram every day, the dial, if observed every evening at stopping, will show if the engine has been driven too fast or slow.

PRICE, £10 EACH.

Worm and wheel extra; the wheel should have as many teeth as the shaft makes revolutions in a minute; if there are eighty revolutions in one minute, there ought to be eighty teeth in the wheel.

BAILEY'S
Cotton Mill Speed Clock.
No. 236.

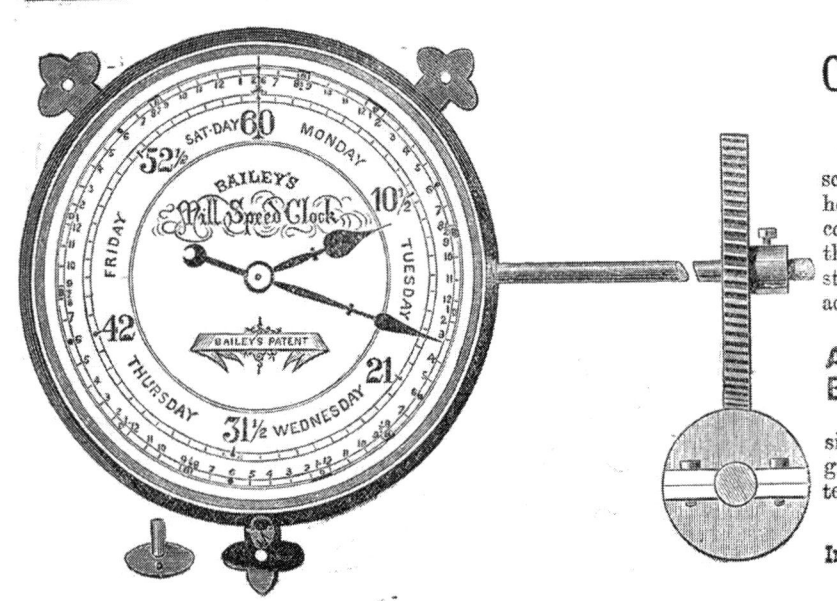

This is an enlarged view of the clock described on opposite page; if required for 57 hours, 54 or 50 per week, they are made accordingly. In all cases when an order is given the hours worked each day and the time of starting and stoppage should be given accurately.

Worm and Wheel, extra,

A   Price,   7-in. diam. of dial,   £4 4s.
B   ,,   with 12-in. dial,   -   £5 5s.

These are in use at the chief cotton, woollen, silk and hose mills in this country, and are great promoters of regular driving and detection of carelessness.

In ordering, be particular in giving proper times for meals, starting, and stopping.

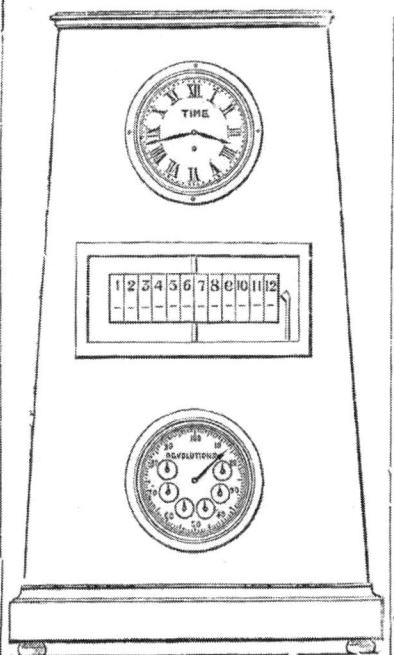

No. 237b.

BAILEY'S PATENT SPEED RECORDER,

For marking one dot on a diagram for every 1000 revolutions. Complete, with Eight-day Clock, in Oak Case, Price, £9 10s.

Recording Clocks for Turn-Stiles, Weighing Machines, &c., made to Drawing.

Clock-work for Engineers' Dials, Wheels for Models cast and cut, and instruments of every description for promoting statistics, will have attention, and the benefit of J. BAILEY and Co.'s great experience in this class of work.

No. 238a.

BAILEY'S small 4 in. Dial Brass Case INDEX or COUNTER, for Machines, with Shaft for revolutions to one hundred thousand.

Price, ... £2 10 0 each.
If ordered in Dozens,   ... 2 0 0 ,,

This Instrument, for Flax Machinery, and for other purposes, in quantities, in iron cases, made according to quantity, at from £15 per dozen.

GAS METER INDEXES AND INDICATORS, FOR TURN-STILES.

Price for the above, with 6 dials each, 8s. 6d., full size. Special quotations per dozen or gross.

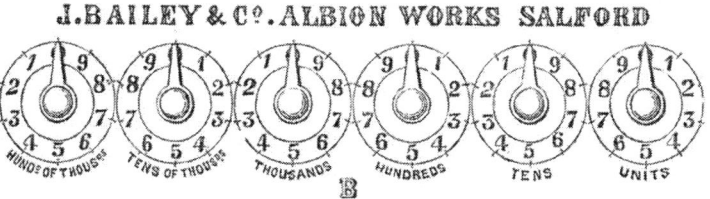

Indicators for Paper Makers, Paper Hanging Makers, Manufacturers, etc.

NORTON & LANDLESS' PATENT COTTON MILL SPEED RECORDER.

237a.

Fig. 1 represents the Speed Recorder, and it may be described simply an oak case in which is placed a first-class eight-day timepiece. By a proper arrangement of wheels in connection with the timepiece a drum is made to revolve once in every working day, say from six o'clock in the morning to six in the evening. The time of day is shown on the time dial, and the drum is made to rotate above the large dial, as shown in the illustration. The speed-indicating portion of the apparatus consists of a train of wheel-work, which is actuated by the main shaft of the engine, whose speed is required to be recorded by means of a small shaft with a wheel upon it, the number of teeth of which corresponds with the revolutions of the shaft per minute. This shaft is driven by a worm placed on the main shaft, and which is made in two parts for the facility of fixing. When the shaft performs its proper number of revolutions in a minute, the speed minute dial keeps the same time as the minute hand of a watch, and hence the day speed dial should always show the right time, and the large centre hand should indicate the exact number of hours the engine has worked in the week. To illustrate this let us suppose that a manager goes into the place where the clock is kept, on Thursday morning, at half-past ten, and he knows that that day and hour ought to be indicated on the dials. If he finds it to be otherwise he finds that the speed has been either faster or slower as the case may be, and he sees also the precise amount of the error. This may do for casual purposes, and in cases where strict exactitude is not necessary, and it is a good guide for an attentive engine-tenter; but the great feature of the invention is the simple manner in which the daily speed is recorded. The drum described above has fixed upon it a diagram of metallic paper, similar to that used with the Richards' indicator; as the drum rotates a metallic point pricks on the paper the speed: and, as this is done every half-hour, the increase or decrease of speed at any time may be detected. Complete, £10 10s.

BAILEY'S PATENT SPEED CLOCK,

No. 236.
For Reducing Revolutions to Hours.

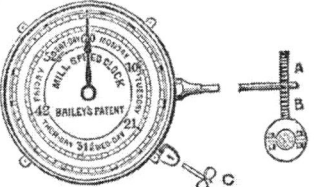

Since this block was cut, the Indicators are all fitted with centre seconds hands.

This Indicator, which is constantly in use in some of the principal Manufactories in the Kingdom, is specially designed to indicate *at once, and without calculation, if the engine has been keeping correct speed.* Those Indicators which indicate the speed or number of revolutions only, require a memorandum to be kept, and a calculation to be made, every time the speed is required to be known. This Indicator reduces the revolutions to hours,—suppose the speed of a shaft to be 2,000 per hour: instead of indicating 2,000, this indicates one hour, and if there be 60 hours in a week, 60 hours are indicated. The Indications are not all shown on the engraving, owing to its being so small.

If a manager or a proprietor goes into a works on Thursday morning at 11 o'clock, and he looks at an Indicator, it should (if the speed has been correct) indicate 11 THURSDAY, so that instantaneous indication of correct or irregular speed is given. If the Indicator shows too fast or too slow, it is a sign of irregularity.

The Indicators are strong and durable, and are the result of some years' experience, and they are highly approved of by all who have tried them.

DESCRIPTION.

A is a worm wheel, which is actuated by the worm B, which is fastened on the driving shaft, and is in two halves for ready application; the key C is to move the hand by, the key-hole being closed with a lock.

PARTICULARS REQUIRED FOR FIXING.

The diameter of the shaft to be indicated, and the number of revolutions it makes per minute, are required, in order that the worm and the wheel may be of the proper dimensions.

When required for different hours than those suitable for mills working under the "Ten Hours' Act," these dials show 10½ hours for every day except Saturday, and on that day 7½ hours only, i.e., from 6 a.m. to 6 p.m. every day except Saturday, and on that day from 6 to 2; meal times are allowed for on the dial, half an hour for breakfast and one hour for dinner. When required for night and day, or for 57½ hours, special ones are made at no extra cost.

Where irregular speed has been kept, a small premium might be added to the engineer's wage when a correct performance is obtained.

Price £4 4s. in brass cases, with 7 inch dials.

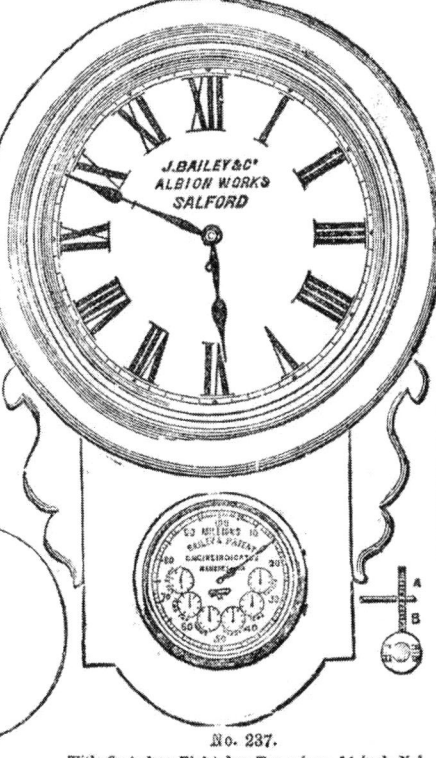

No. 237.
With first-class Eight-day Timepiece, 14 inch dial, in French Polished Oak Case, £8 10s.; if in case like No. 237B., £7 10s.

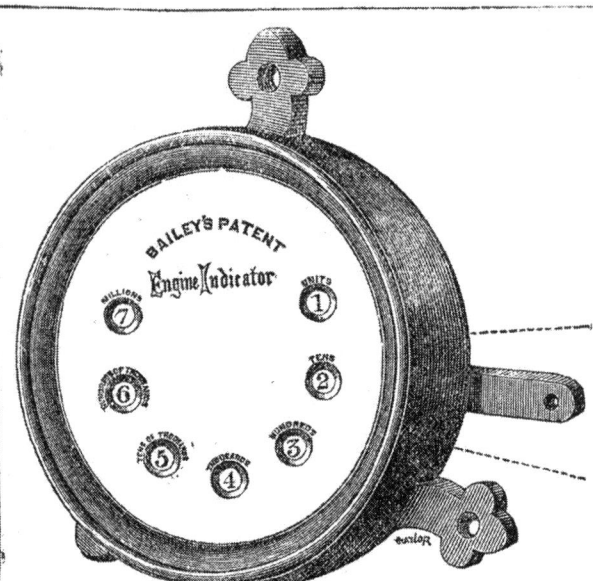

No. 240 A.

BAILEY'S
PATENT
SPEED INDICATOR,

With Reciprocating Motion,

7-IN. DIAL TO TEN MILLIONS.

PRICE, £4 4 0.

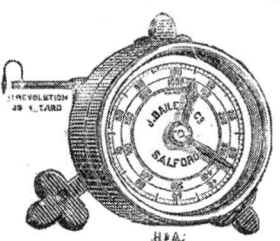

MEASURING INDICATOR.

4in. dial to 1,000 yards. No glass. The hands can be moved. The spindle makes one revolution for one yard.

PRICE, £2 2 0 Each.

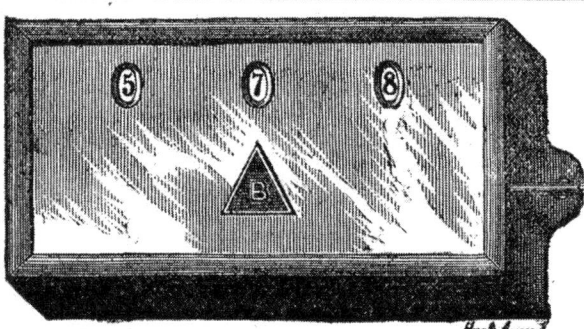

No. 241 A.

Small Speed Indicator.

5in. long by 3in. wide, to indicate to 999, with rotary shaft.

£2 0 0 Each.

Bailey's Pedometer, to measure distance walked by Wearer.
SILVER CASE. PRICE, £2 10s.
Free by post to any part of Great Britain, East Indies, Colonies, or Possessions.

DIRECTIONS FOR USE.—Suspend the Pedometer from the neck by a chain or ribbon, or wear it in the waistcoat pocket, suspended by the hook.

Move the hand on the dial plate with the finger, either backwards or forwards, and place it exactly on the XII. When the wearer has walked a mile the hand will point to I., when he has walked two miles it will point to II., and so on. Each dot indicates a quarter of a mile.

To REGULATE the Pedometer, walk a measured mile at your ordinary rate. If the hand has not then reached the I., unscrew the adjusting screw. If it has gone past the I., tighten the adjusting screw. A few trials will regulate it exactly to the wearer's ordinary rate.

No. 250 A.

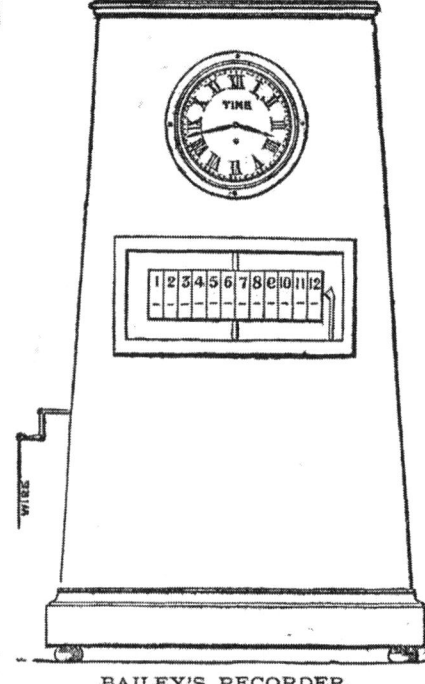

BAILEY'S RECORDER.

For indicating at what time any mechanical movement took place, such as the opening of a door, the movement of a wagon over a weighing machine, the pull by a watchman, the elevation of a crane or any similar movement; goes eight days, drum revolves 24 hours, can be connected by ordinary bell wire, or an electro-magnet can be used, and a copper wire, if the distance be far. PRICE, ... £6 10s.

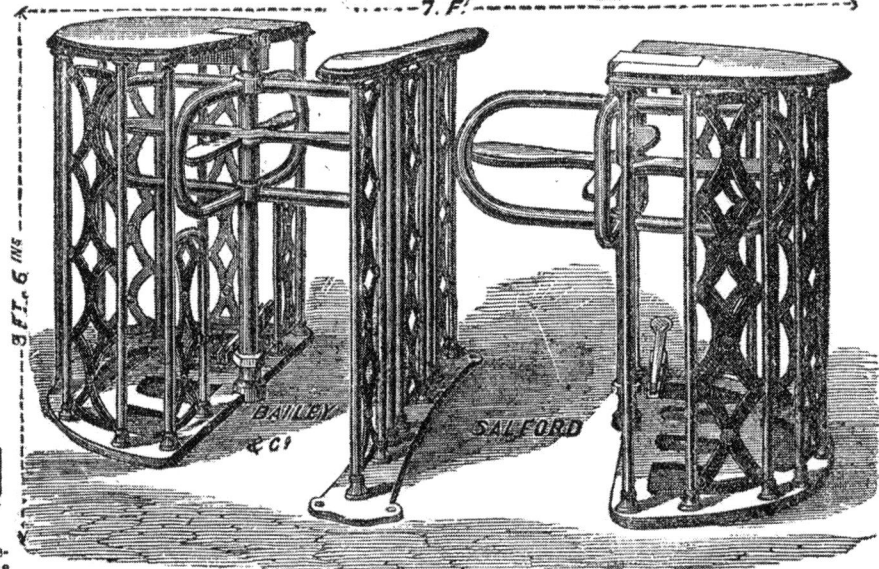

Bailey's Improved Self-Registering Turnstiles,
FOR BRIDGES, PIERS, TOLLS, PUBLIC EXHIBITIONS, &c.

These Turnstiles are offered as the most accurate and the best designed in the market, and are finished in a most superior manner. PRICE, £20; Middle Rail extra, £2; Non-Registering Turnstile, £15.

19

No. 247.

Engine House Clock and Gauges.

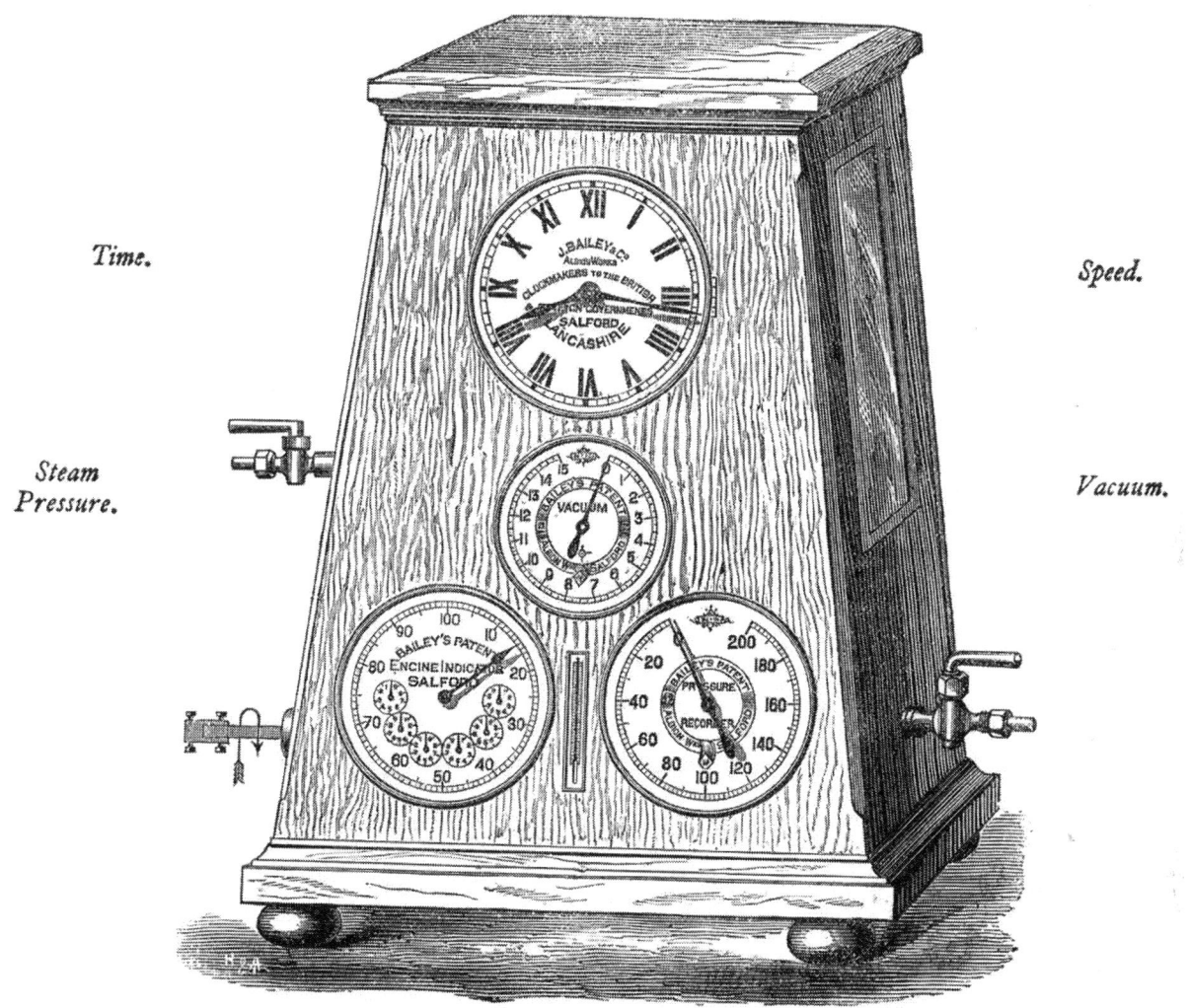

Time. *Speed.*

Steam Pressure. *Vacuum.*

The Time Dial, 10 inches diameter; Speed Indicator and Pressure Gauge, 7 inches diameter; Vacuum Gauge, 5 inches diameter, in French polished case; handsome brass well-lacquered rims.

Price £15, ready for fixing.

Professor Thurston's Patent Testing Machine,

FOR TESTING IRON, STEEL, WOOD,
AND OTHER MATERIALS OF CONSTRUCTION.

This machine is worthy of the attention of all those who are interested in obtaining the best results from the materials used. The information is too bulky for this volume, but it is expected that it will be published soon after. Enquire of us for *particulars*.

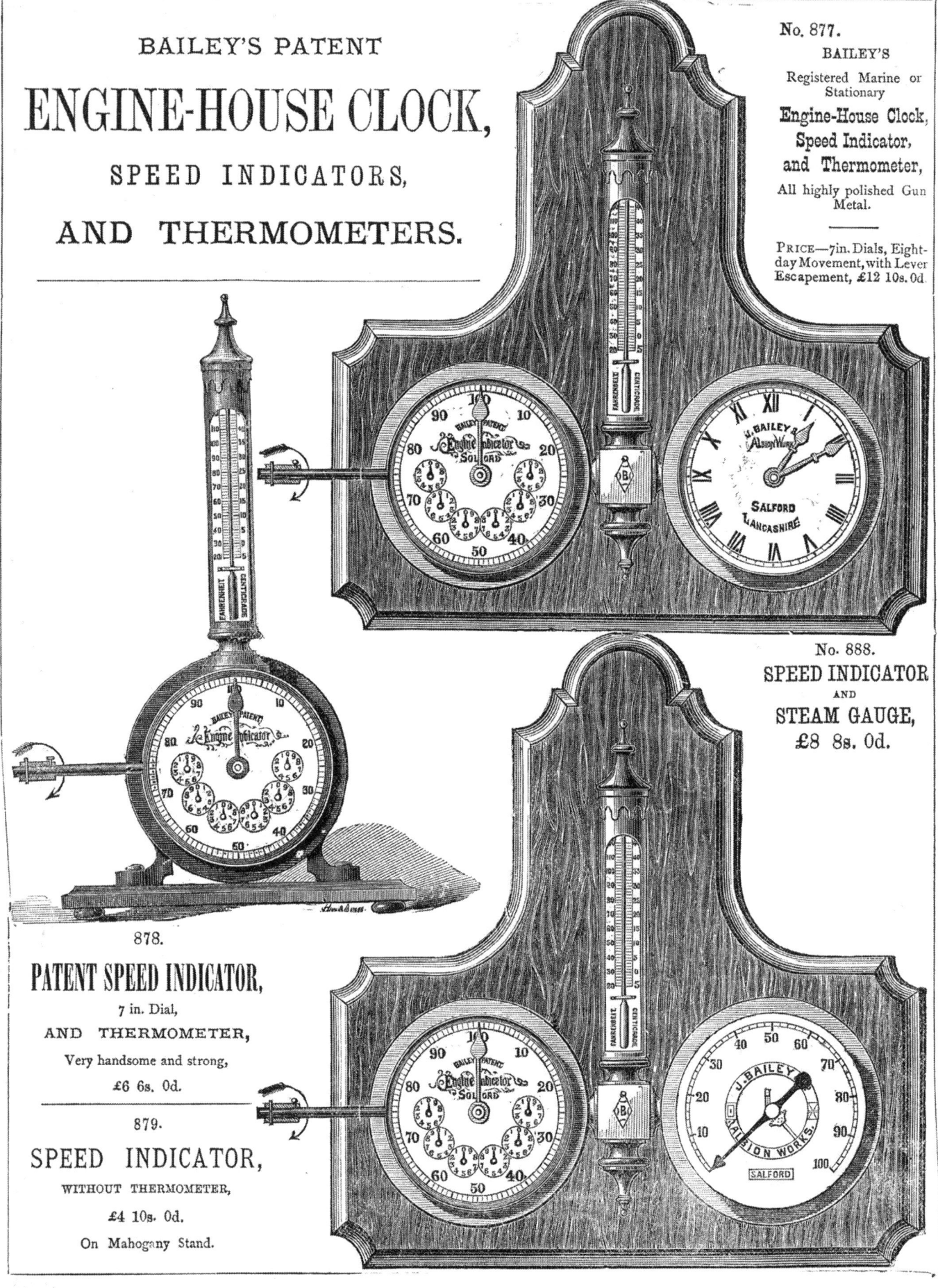

BAILEY'S
Office Watchman's Peg Clock.

With 14 inch dial, good English Eight-day movement, making a good Office Time-piece, as well as efficient Detector of Irregularity or Neglect.

Price, ready for hanging up, £5 5s.

No. 251.

Automatic in its action, the Pegs being pushed down every half-hour, with ten minutes' grace to the watchman. They remain down for twelve hours, and appear automatically for next night, giving time to take a record for office purposes.

As used by the Chief Government Departments and Manufacturing Concerns at home and abroad.

BAILEY'S
Office Clock, Watchman's Recorder, & Counter

For giving a Diagram, and also Counting Numbers or Attendances, and for other purposes.

Diagram.

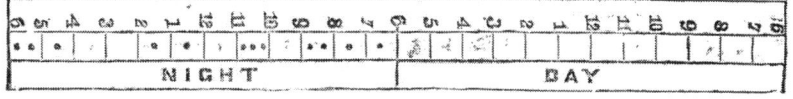

The paper is punctured at every pull.

Price, with Eight-day Clock, 7 in. dials, £7 7s.

No. 151.

This Instrument may be made use of either to give a Diagram on Paper every night, as well as the Number of Attendances, which are indicated on the dial below; or if it is not thought fit to use a Diagram every night, the Counter can be used only, but in this latter case only the number of Pulls will be recorded, and as the Clock will not be seen by the Watchman, it being generally in an office, the mere number may suit most purposes, with an occasional Diagram about once a month, as a test of time.

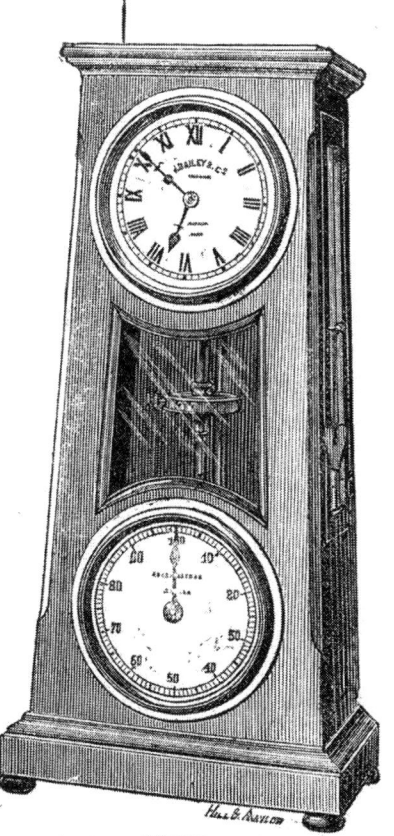

In the various stations of the watchman's beat, keys, twelve of which belong generally to each detector, are securely fastened **within or outside** the buildings on those places which have to be visited by the watchman. Those keys have different bits corresponding each with another number of the steel die situated beneath the stationary hand, so that each key being introduced through the key-hole on the cover of the case, and passing between the stationary hand and the pasteboard dial, imprints the corresponding number or numbers of the steel die on the pasteboard dial. So for each station to be controlled only a key is wanted, and with one watch and one watchman, twelve—if necessary even more—stations can be controlled; they may be inside or outside the buildings, depots, warehouses, workshops, stable, etc. The watch is set by turning the brass disc

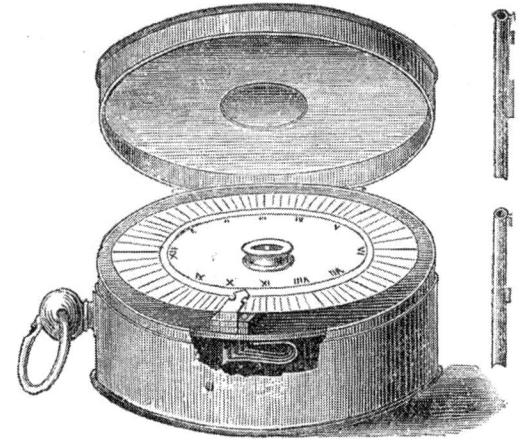

is set and locked, and protected by a leather pouch, carried by a strap round the body.

The watchman makes his rounds, and visits the different stations, according to instructions received from his employer. In making his rounds and arriving at a station, the watchman will insert the key which is fastened there through the keyhole on the cover of the case, and give it one turn. While doing this, the figure die corresponding to the key will be imprinted on the pasteboard dial of the detector at exactly the minute shown by the hand of the watch, or if the watch has been set right, at exactly the time the watchman has been at the station. Supposing the watchman was at station 6 at 3 o'clock, on the pasteboard dial will be imprinted the No. 6 exactly at 3 o'clock.

on the centre of the dial, and through it the movable pasteboard dial, in such a way that the right time corresponds with the stationary hand. If it is 7 o'clock, the figure 7 on the pasteboard dial must be just beneath the stationary hand. As the dial on those watches is moving and the hand is stationary, at 8 o'clock the figure 8 of the pasteboard dial will have arrived just beneath the stationary hand, and so forth. The figure dies being also just beneath the stationary hand, the different marks must be imprinted on the pasteboard dial always at the exact time and minute at which the watchman has been at the corresponding station, supposing the detector has been previously set right.

The watchman receives in the evening the watch, which has to be wound up every second day, and which is to be provided every day with a fresh pasteboard dial, and

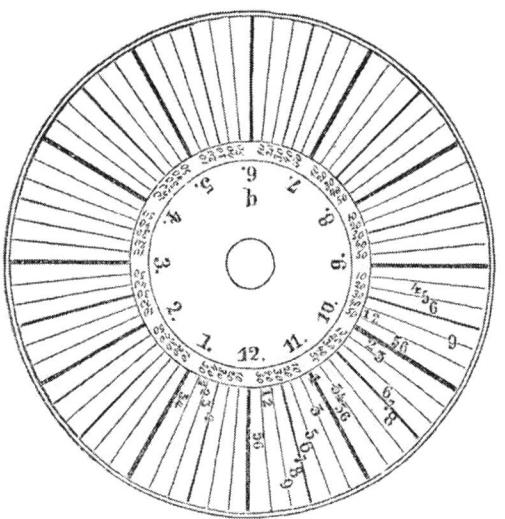

Keys No. 1—6 mark the corresponding numbers, Keys No. 7—12 mark the corresponding or 2 combined numbers on the dial.
Generally Keys No. 1—9 mark the corresponding numbers 1 to 9 on the dial | Generally Key No. 11 marks No. 3 and 4 together on the dial
" Key " 10 marks No. 1 and 2 together | " " " 12 " " 5 and 6 " "

On delivering the watch in the morning to the person in charge, the latter on opening the same can see at a glance how often and when the rounds have been made during the night, whether every station has been visited or any neglected at each round, and what space of time elapsed between the different visits; in short, it tells the history of the night's doings, of the vigilance or carelessness of the watchman. It shows also whether the watchman takes the trouble in making his rounds, and visits regularly the isolated stations, etc.

The dial A shows that the watchman has done his duty. It is supposed that he has to begin his round at 9 o'clock, and has to visit every hour 12 different places, where are fastened the keys 1 to 12. He began his round at 9 o'clock, and visited every 5 minutes another station—up to 5 minutes to 1 o'clock. He was at station No. 6 at 9.25, at 10.25, at 11.25, and at 12.25. At station No. 1 at 9, 10, 11 and 12 o'clock, and so forth.

The price of one Detector and six keys for six stations, one box dials, and one leather pouch is ... £6 10 0	Do. do. with twelve keys 8 8 0
Do. do. with nine keys 7 10 0	Do. do. with twenty keys 10 0 0

☞ *This invention is far simpler than any other for being understood, as the number of the rooms are legibly stamped on the dials.*

BAILEY'S SPINDLE INDICATOR.

This Indicator is much used in Cotton, Woollen, and Silk Mills, for indicating the speed of Spindles of high speed. The dial is 2½in. diameter. The spindle can be put in and out of gear by the thumb in a most simple manner, so that by means of a watch the speed for half a minute or a minute may be accurately taken.

COMPLETE IN CASE, 30/- EACH.

PRATT'S PATENT ELECTRICAL
TELL-TALE CLOCK and OFFICE TIME-KEEPER for WATCHMEN, etc.

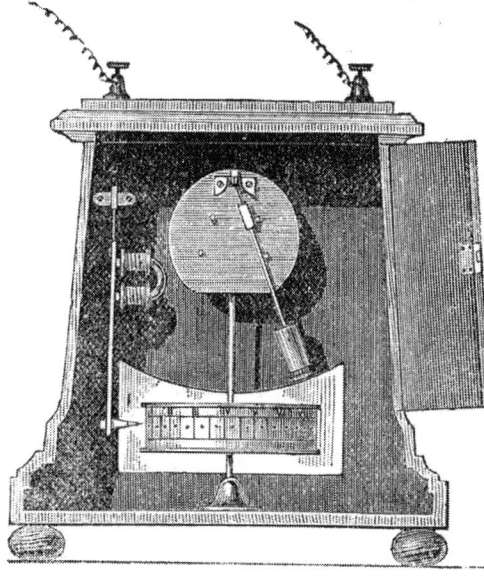
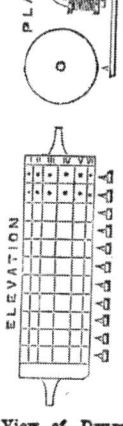

View of Drum for eleven separate Indications.

In large factories and extensive works the watchman is assumed to be an important institution, although the proper performance of his duties is a matter which has more or less to be taken for granted. For who watches the watchman? Who knows whether he goes to sleep or does his duty?

The apparatus we illustrate is the invention of Mr. F. M. Pratt, and a rear-elevation of it is seen in the annexed engraving, which shows to the left the electro-magnetic marking arrangement. It consists of an ordinary clock, to which is attached a cylinder, revolving upon a vertical axis, and driven by the mechanism of the clock. The cylinder is covered with a sheet of paper, attached to it by spring clips, so that it can be removed when used, and a clean sheet substituted for it. Each sheet of paper is divided longitudinally into hours, and, if necessary, parts of hours, and crosswise into as many divisions as there are places to be visited by the watchman. Each cross division has a corresponding marker, which indicates, by the impression it makes upon the paper, the time the watchman visits the place connected with that marker.

The markers are actuated by electro-magnetic apparatus, and in each room to be visited is an actuating knob. Upon the watchman pressing this knob, the electromagnet is brought into action, the current being completed. The armature is thus attracted, and gives a vibrating motion to the marker, which causes a dot to be imprinted in one of the squares. In our engraving a short cylinder only is shown, but it can be increased to any depth, and a number of armatures placed on either side of it, according to the number of rooms in the establishment. This is the case at Messrs. NOBLE and HOARE's Works, Cornwall Road, Stamford Street, London, where we recently examined this apparatus, and where there are thirty different apartments requiring the watchman's attendance during the night. Here, therefore, there are thirty divisions counted vertically for the rooms, and twelve counted horizontally for the hours. The watchman visits each room once an hour, and touches the actuating knob by which the time of his attendance in that particular apartment becomes registered. If, from any cause, he is detained in one room such a length of time that the cylinder has travelled the distance of one division, or will have done so before he reaches the next room to be visited, his instructions are to occasionally touch the knob in the room in which he is detained, whereby progressive dots will be formed on the paper, to "prate of his whereabouts," accounting for the absence of dots in the square belonging to the next room.

Of course the clock and cylinder are beyond the reach of the watchman? they may be locked away in a closet or case, or may even be placed in the bed-room of the manager of the works, who can thus, if he chooses, from time to time assure himself of the watchman's vigilance. If kept in the office the record is examined in the morning, and replaced by a clean sheet of paper.

It will thus be seen that we have here a very useful and reliable apparatus, as has been proved by over twelve months' use at Messrs. NOBLE & HOARE's works where the expenses of maintenance are found to be practically nil. Its application for other counting and registering purposes is obvious; such, for instance, as the registering of the number of times that a hoist is lifted, or loads of pig-iron are delivered, &c. Messrs. BAILEY & Co., who are sole manufacturers of this watchman's watcher, will doubtless find orders flow in fast as soon as the apparatus becomes known.—*Mechanics' Magazine*, Feb. 10, 1872.

Price	No. 1, with one Magnet					£5	15	0
,,	,, 2, ,, two Magnets	...	...	...	...	8	12	6
,,	,, 3, ,, three ,,	...	...	...	...	9	15	6
,,	,, 4, ,, four ,,	...	...	...	...	10	18	6
,,	,, 5, ,, five ,,	...	...	...	...	12	0	0
,,	,, 6, ,, six ,,	...	...	...	...	13	15	0

More than six 20/- extra per Magnet.

The battery power required for any of these will be 20s. extra in case, Ordinary black and gold porcelain. "Pushes" 2s. 6d. each extra, and wire 2d. per yard, well covered with rubber and felt. In most cases a No. 2 is used with a push fixed at the two extremities of a building, which compels the watchman to walk the whole distance, say every half-hour, in order to actuate the two.

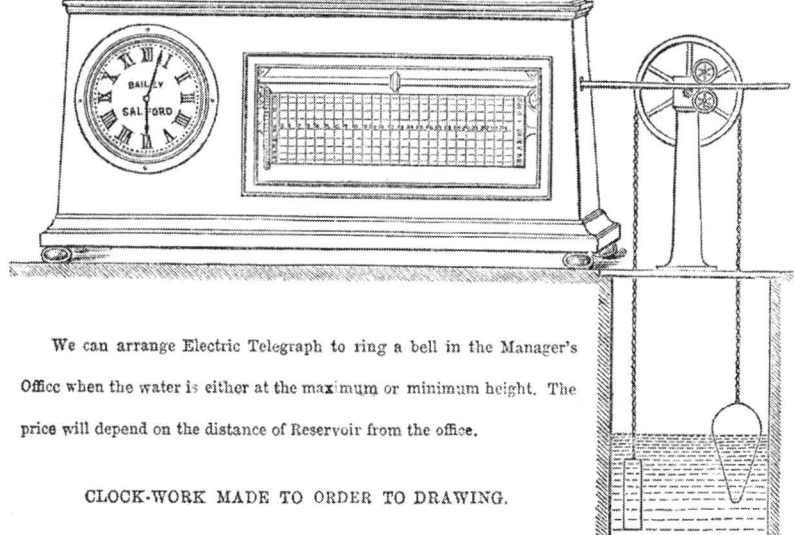

BAILEY'S RESERVOIR RECORDER,
For Indicating the Fluctuation of Water in Reservoirs, &c., &c.

We can arrange Electric Telegraph to ring a bell in the Manager's Office when the water is either at the maximum or minimum height. The price will depend on the distance of Reservoir from the office.

CLOCK-WORK MADE TO ORDER TO DRAWING.

J. BAILEY & Co. have designed and constructed many Recorders for Registering the Fluctuations of Water, &c., for Southport Water Works, for Birmingham Sewage Works, &c., &c.

Estimates on receipt of details.

BIRAM'S PATENT ANEMOMETER,

For Ascertaining the Current of Air in Mines, etc.

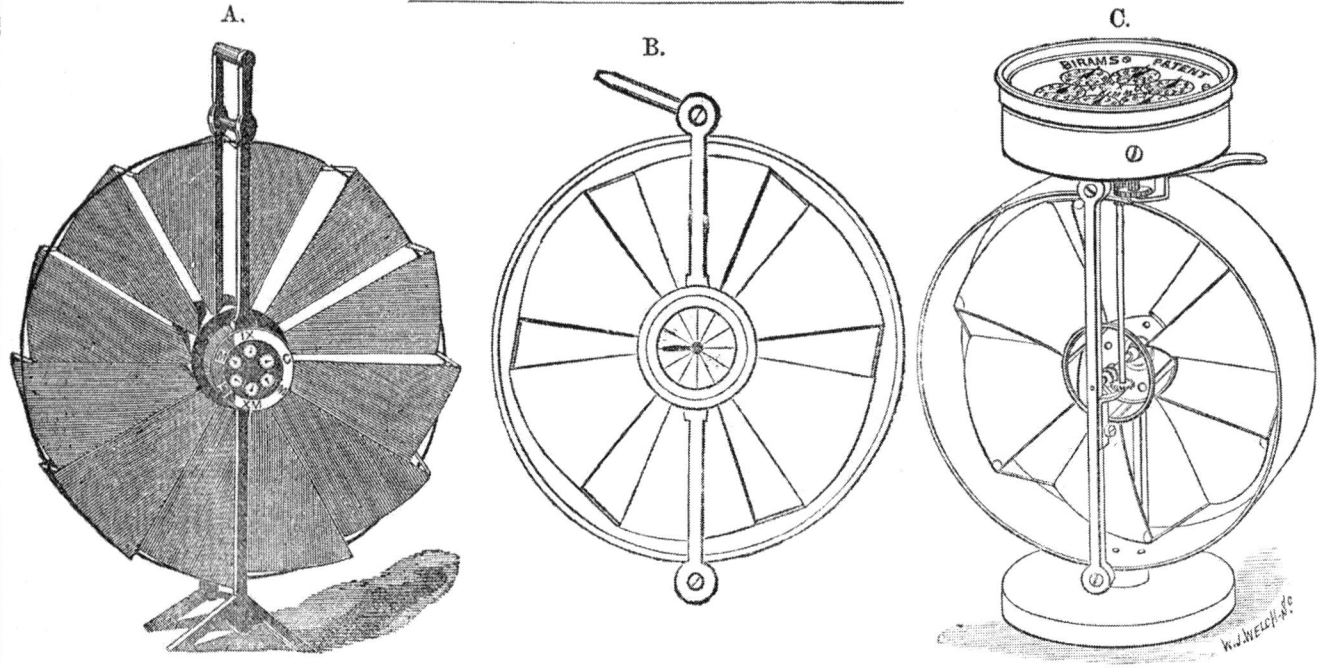

A. 12 in. Size.
B. 4 in. Size.
C. 4 in. new Anemometer.

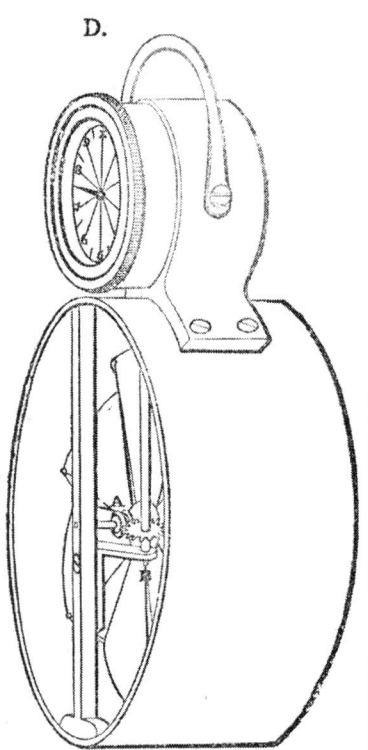

D. 3 in. Size.

		£	s.	d.
No. A.—12 in. diameter, reading up to 10,000,000 feet	...	4	4	0
6 in. ditto ditto 1,000 feet	...	3	3	0
6 in. ditto, with disconnecting motion, reading up to 1,000 feet	...	3	13	6
No. B.— 4 in. ditto, reading up to 100 feet	...	2	10	0
„ C.— 4 in. ditto, new, reading up to 10,000,000 feet	...	4	4	0
„ D.— 2 in. ditto, reading up to 100 feet	...	2	5	0
„ E.— 2 in. ditto, new Anemometer, reading up to 10,000,000 feet	...	3	15	0
2 in. ditto, reading up to 1,000 feet	...	3	3	0

TAYLOR'S PATENT SPEED INDICATOR.
DIRECTIONS FOR USING.

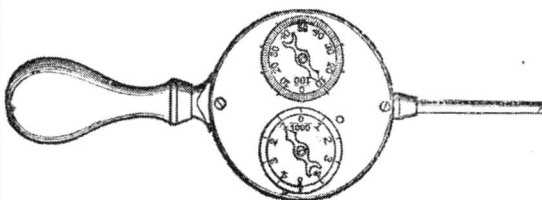

To ascertain the number of revolutions made by a shaft in any given time:—Take the Indicator by the handle in the right hand, hold your watch in the left, press the point of the spindle gently against the end and centre of the shaft. To every hundred revolutions of the shaft the Hundred Pointer will make one revolution, while the Thousand Pointer will indicate one number, the dial being marked into ten parts. It may be applied to a shaft revolving either to the right or to the left. Price, 30/- each.

POCKET SPEED INDICATOR.

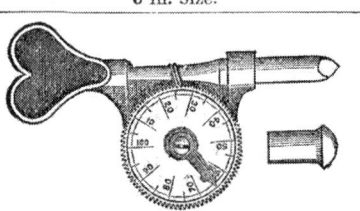

The dial revolves while the pointer remains stationary, though the latter may be turned to the starting point. It is made of the best composition and steel, nickel plated, and has a thimble to cover the point, so that it can be carried in the pocket. The above cut represents half size. To ascertain the number of revolutions of any shaft in a given time, place the point of the Indicator in the centre of the shaft, and for every hundred revolutions the dial will revolve once; less than one hundred will be indicated by the Pointer, which is to be placed at 100 before starting. Price, 8/- each.

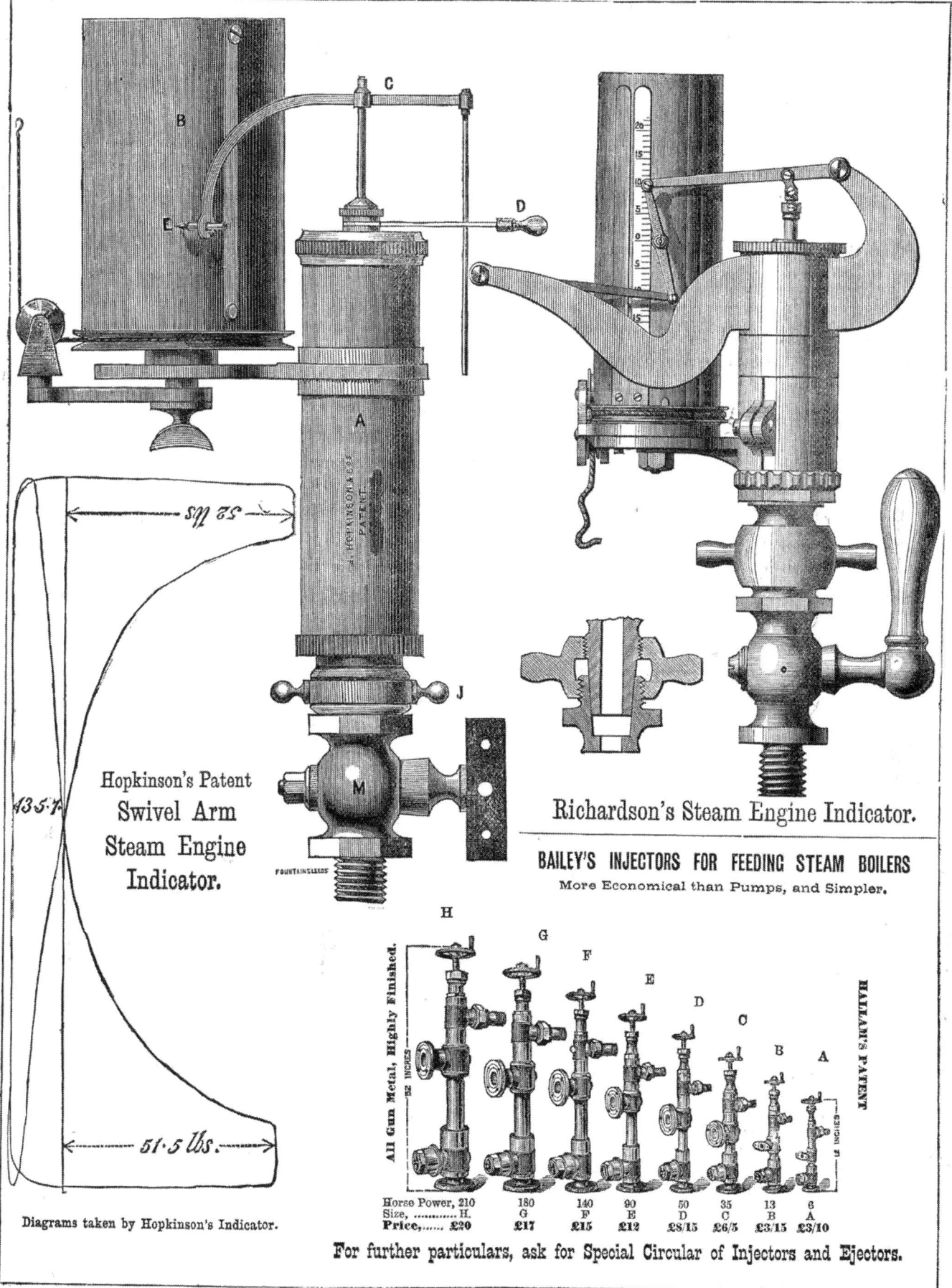

HOPKINSON'S PATENT DIRECT ACTING SWIVEL-ARM STEAM ENGINE INDICATOR.

The use and advantages of the Steam Engine Indicator are as follows:—

1st—Prevention of break-downs and unnecessary strain.
2nd—Economical Working.
3rd—Regularity of Speed.
4th—Proper adjustment of the Valves for the power required.
5th—The horse-power exerted, and the pressure indicated at the beginning or any part of the stroke.
6th—The exact opening or closing of the Ports, so as to get the full effect from the steam.
7th—The Indicator delineates the true working state of a Steam Engine, enabling the attainment of the greatest amount of power with the least expenditure of fuel.

This IMPROVED STEAM ENGINE INDICATOR is submitted as being the best Instrument ever produced for the purpose of ascertaining the working of a Steam Engine and recording accurate and faithful diagrams. It is constructed on the first principles of applied mechanics, viz.:—*Direct action*, and is free from all joints, slides, frictional parts and complicated multiplying motions. The piston is very much *enlarged* in area, with suitably arranged *springs*, and the light pencil arm is made to *swivel* on the top of the piston rod, by an ingenious arrangement of drop guiding bar, and swivel guiding arm: thus the pencil can be readily applied or removed from the paper on the revolving barrel, and diagrams taken with the greatest facility. Its durability is also unquestionable.

That a Direct Acting Indicator without joints is superior to any Indicator having a number of joints cannot be refuted; the simplicity of the construction, with the combined improvement of the Swivel-arm Indicator, makes it the best instrument for indicating Engines of any construction—speed and pressure. As many words, however, would not of themselves prove its value, an instrument will be sent to any intending purchaser subject to approval.

Each Instrument is supplied with four springs of 20lbs., 30lbs., 40lbs. and 60lbs., with measuring and dividing scale, complete, in Lock-up Mahogany Case.

Springs for Higher pressure made to order.

Prices, complete, with 3 Springs, 20lbs., 40lbs., and 60lbs., £7 10s.

RICHARD'S STEAM ENGINE INDICATOR.

Richard's Indicator has this distinguishing feature, that the throw of the piston is only one-fourth that of the pencil, while the latter still moves in a vertical line. By this means the defects common to all the forms of this Instrument hitherto devised, and which arise from the necessity of using a long, weak and tremulous spring, and of employing heavy reciprocating parts, which must have a considerable motion, are completely avoided.

This Indicator was introduced at the Great Exhibition of 1862, by Mr. Porter, the Patentee, by whom several thousand diagrams were taken with it from the "Allen Engine" at the speed of 150 revolutions per minute; and it was selected by Dr. Clark, the superintendent of the Machinery Department, to take diagrams from all the Engines remaining in the Exhibition.

Since the Exhibition the sale of the Indicators has steadily increased, and the great demand now existing shows that their excellence is well established.

They have been used with complete success on Locomotive Engines, running at a speed as high as 260 revolutions per minute, and indeed, it is found that there is not any practicable speed at which they will not give perfect indications, while their application to Engines making the fewest number of revolutions per minute reveals inaccuracies in the diagrams given by all other instruments.

The Springs are made to ten scales, as follows:—

No.				
1	$\frac{1}{8}$ inch on the Scale represents 11 lbs. pressure on the sq. inch. Indicates from		15 to x 10
2	$\frac{1}{12}$	"	"	15 " x 22
3	$\frac{1}{16}$	"	"	15 " x 35
4	$\frac{1}{20}$	"	"	15 " x 47
5	$\frac{1}{24}$	"	"	15 " x 60
6	$\frac{1}{30}$	"	"	15 " x 80
7	$\frac{1}{32}$	"	"	Atmosphere x 100
8	$\frac{1}{40}$	$\frac{1}{8}$ inch on the Scale represents 11 lbs. pressure on the sq. inch. Indicates from	Atmosphere	x 125
9	$\frac{1}{48}$	"	"	" x 150
10	$\frac{1}{65}$	"	"	" x 175

Spring No. 1 has been specially adapted to indicate the vacuum on a large scale, in engines or pumps which work at high pressure—the springs showing pressures. The springs showing pressures above 80lbs. are made to indicate the vacuum also, when so ordered, and springs are made also to any other scale desired.

All the springs will fit every instrument, and they can be readily changed by any one. Attention is especially invited to this novel and important feature. The size of the diagram is 3⅝ x 5 inches. It is drawn on Metallic paper by a pointed brass wire. The piston has an area equal to one-half of a square inch. This is double the size employed in the ordinary cheaper instruments; but it is believed to be the smallest that will ensure accuracy in the diagram. Instruments of any size, or peculiar in any respect, will be made on special order. A special attachment, enabling them to b applied to oscillating cylinders, is furnished when ordered.

The Indicator is neatly and securely packed in mahogany case, and is furnished with an admirable contrivance for laying off the diagram, when not otherwise ordered; the cock has Whitworth's ¾ inch thread.

The treatise on the use of the Indicator by Mr. Porter may also be had from J. B. & CO. Price Five Shillings. New edition.

Price £8 10s., with One Spring.

In sending orders, it is necessary to specify particularly the number of springs required, and the pressure they will have to indicate. If the Indicator is to be adapted for oscillating engines, 10/- extra.

Additional Springs with Boxwood Scales, 10/- each; extra Paper Cylinder Springs, 1/6 each. Metallic Paper, ready cut, 4/- per Quire, making 360 diagram sheets.

To obtain true diagrams, the communications with the engine must be short, large, and direct. This indicator should not be attached to the small bore cocks fixed for other Indicators.

BAILEY'S HALLAM'S PATENT STEAM JET PUMPS

Are exclusively used for Emptying Bilge Water, &c., &c.

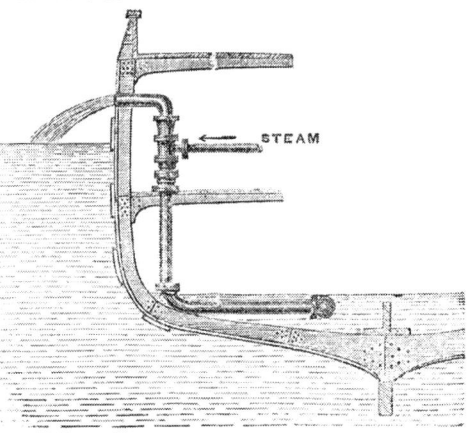

For prices and other particulars see "Bailey's Supplementary List of Boiler Fittings," Post Free.

BAILEY'S PATENT OXYGEN REGULATOR,

For Preventing Smoke and Economizing Fuel in Steam Boiler Furnaces.

Scarcely any description is required of this simple means of regulating the supply of air at the bridge of furnaces in boilers. It has been demonstrated by C. Wye Williams and other eminent authorities that the only effectual way of curing smokey chimneys and consuming coal in a rational manner, is by admission of air in this manner, and all attempts to do this hitherto have been so clumsy as to very often disgust all in connexion with them; the ultimate result being that they have been consigned to the limbo of the scrap heap.

The arrangement can be fixed by any Engineer of ordinary ability, and the facility of adjustment by means of the Dial soon educates him to the degree he must fix it at (1) after firing up and (2) when a good fire is burning.

The great length of time the fire bars last is one consideration in valuing this invention, as the cooling effect of the air passing to the bridge prevents much of the usual burning.

PRICE—Bridge, *Brass Dial, highly polished*, Chain, and Pulley, complete for fixing,	Diameter in feet	Single Flues	Double Flues
	2ft. 0in.	8 8 0	15 0 0
	2ft. 6in.	10 10 0	18 10 0
	3ft. 0in.	12 0 0	20 0 0
	3ft. 6in.	12 10 0	22 0 0

These Prices do not include Fore Tiles.
In Ordering, please give the exact diameter of Flue.

"GALLOWAY" PATENT CONE TUBES
For Steam Boilers.

DELIVERED FREE AT ANY RAILWAY STATION.

Patent Cone Tubes not exceeding 2ft. long	...	35/- each.
Do. above 2ft. and not exceeding 2ft. 6in.	...	40/- ,,
Do. above 2ft. 6in. ,, 3ft.	...	45/- ,,
Do. above 3ft. ,, 3ft. 6in.	...	50/- ,,
Do. above 3ft. 6in. ,, 4ft.	...	55/- ,,
Do. above these Sizes	...	special rates.

If the rivet holes are punched, 1/- per Tube extra.

These Tubes are almost universally used in the construction of either single or double-flued Boilers. They **Economise Fuel, Strengthen the Flues, and promote a thorough Circulation of Water.**

NOTE.—In ordering these Tubes, be careful to give EXACT dimensions of the boiler flue, *i.e., the internal diameter and thickness of plates.* When necessary, the Tubes can be forwarded immediately.

BAILEY'S PATENT PYROMETERS.

LIST OF PRICES.

A.—For Bakers, Tube 3ft. long (including length of Iron Pipe to build in wall) .. To 700° Enamelled Dial, 4in. dia. £2 15 0
B.—For Biscuit Bakers, tube 4ft. long .. To 1500° Enamelled Dial, 4in. dia. 3 10 0
C.—For Cooks, for Private Ovens, Gas Stoves, &c., tube 1ft. long .. To 800° Enamelled Dial, 2½in. dia. 2 10 0

Bailey's Vertical Dial Pyrometers.

Price List of Bailey's Patent Adjustable and Compensating Vertical Dial Pyrometers. No. 8

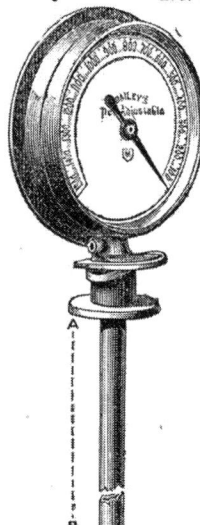

Prices of Vertical Dial Pyrometers, all with dials of white enamel, and very well made, & with Compensating Screw (Bailey's Patent):—

Catalogue	Dial diam.	A to B Length. Ft.	Indicated Fahrenheit degrees.	Price £ s. d.	Catalogue	Dial diam.	A to B Length. Ft.	Indicated Fahrenheit degrees.	Price £ s. d.
No. 8.—For Flues, Hot-air Chambers, Stoves, Galvanizers, &c.	7 inch	4	1500	4 4 0	No. 9A.—For Oil Stills, Varnish Makers, &c.	7 inch	4	700	4 4 0
No. 8A—Do. for Super-heated Steam, &c.	7 ,,	4	700	4 4 0	No. 10.—For Brewers, Soap Makers, &c.	7 ,,	4	300	3 10 0
No. 9.—For Oil Stills, Varnish Makers, &c.	7 ,,	3	700	3 10 0	No. 10A.—Ditto		3	300	3 10 0
					No. 10B.—Ditto	18 ,,	4	300	2 10 0

No. 7. Fig. 1.

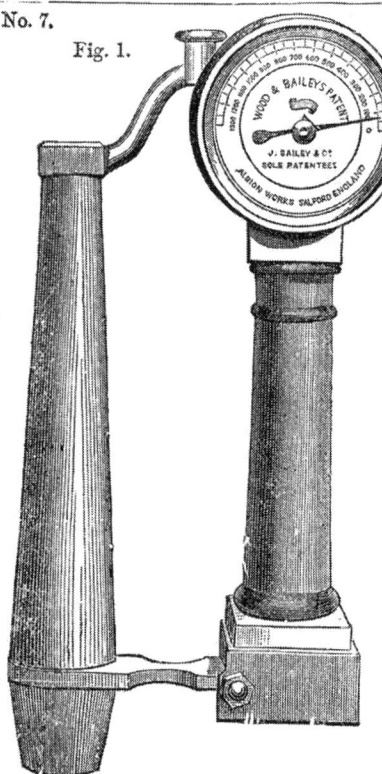

WOOD AND BAILEY'S PATENT PORTABLE PYROMETERS, For Hot Blast Furnaces.

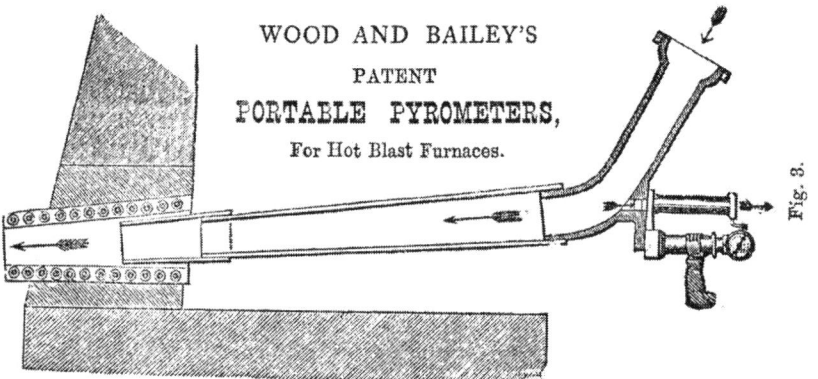

Fig. 3.

This Pyrometer consists of a porcelain pillar, fastened to a taper tube of a metal composed of a peculiar bronze mixture. It will be seen from the illustration—Fig. 3—that the plug being taken out of the tuyre, and the taper tube inserted, the hot blast rushes through, actuating the quadrant, and thus indicating the temperature. If after continued use, the hand should not go back to the temperature of the atmosphere, the hand can be adjusted by means of a screw. It is desirable to screw up the bolt at the bottom of the pillar occasionally, to keep the instrument in working order. Fig. 3 is section of Blast Furnace Tuyre, with Pyrometer being used.

PRICES.

No. 7.—To 1,500 degrees £5 5 0
,, 7A—With maximum and minimum pointers 6 6 0

For full details of Pyrometers, ask for "BAILEY'S SUPPLEMENTARY LISTS OF FITTINGS," which contains full particulars of Pyrometers for Bakers, Engineers, &c. Any of our friends requiring one extra to give to a Baker in their neighbourhood, will oblige us by asking for two or three.

BAILEY'S PATENT FUSIBLE PLUGS

☞ NOTE.

That it is impossible to burn a Boiler Flue if it be fitted with BAILEY'S PATENT FUSIBLE PLUG.

Let sceptics (if there be any) try one.

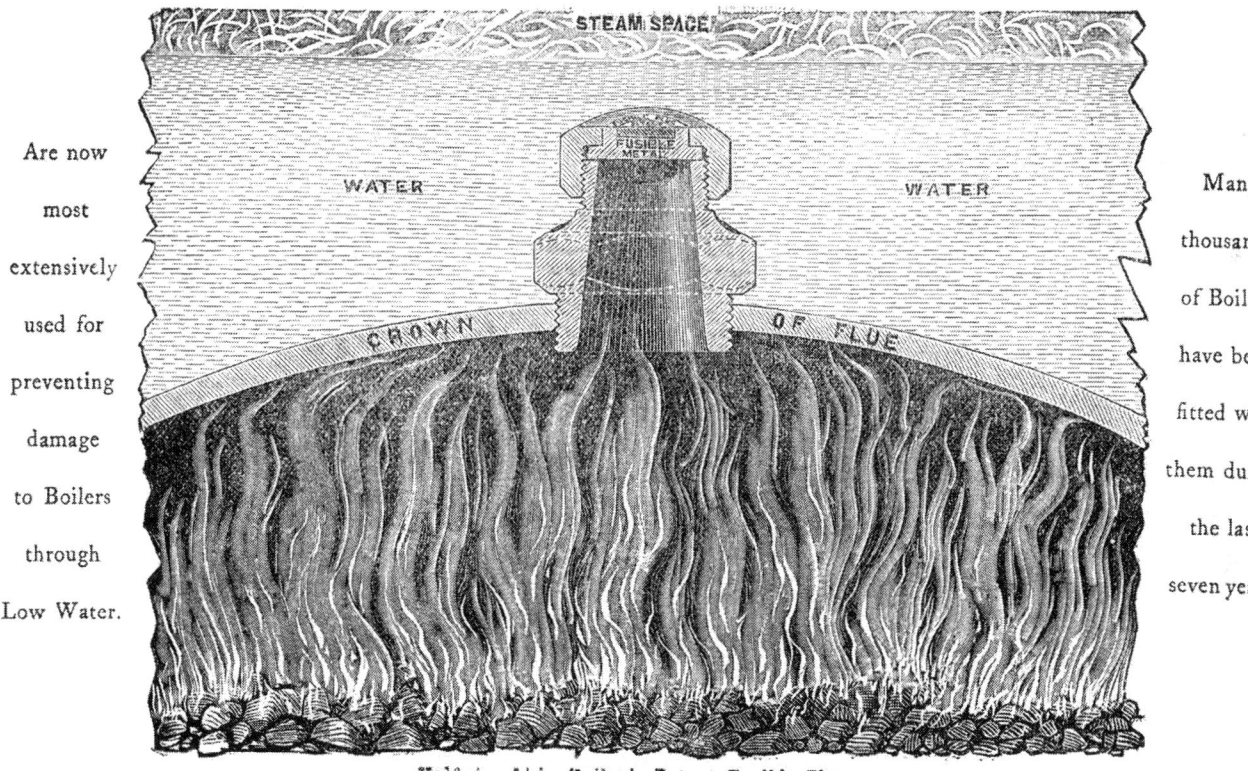

Are now most extensively used for preventing damage to Boilers through Low Water.

Many thousands of Boilers have been fitted with them during the last seven years.

Half size 1½ in. Bailey's Patent Fusible Plugs.

A Fusible Metal Disc, in the centre of which is a Disc of Copper. When the water becomes dangerously low, the fire causes the Copper Disc to be blown through the fusible metal, and the fire is extinguished, thus

Rendering Damage to the Boiler Impossible, at a Cost of One Shilling and Threepence,

That being the amount charged for the Fusible Discs.

The fatal accident at Menia Bridge, which killed two men and a boy, in June, 1875, would not have taken place if the Boiler had been fitted with a Plug.

EXTRACT FROM THE EVIDENCE OF THOS. WOOD, ESQ., C.E., OF MANCHESTER AND ST. PETERSBURGH.

"I have no hesitation in saying that the accident would not have happened had the boiler been fitted with a Patent Fusible Plug. These had been in use for some time with success.

This was supported by Mr. OWENS, the well-known local Engineer of the Menia Foundry. The Jury found a verdict of accidental death, coupled with the suggestion that *Fusible Plugs should be used by Proprietors of Steam Power.*

No. 1—Screwed to 1½ in. Gas Thread, the above sketch being half size ... 10/- each.   Fusible Discs, 15/- per doz.
No. 1A—   „   2 „   „   „   „   „   „   ... 15/- „   „   30/- „

No. 1 are used for Boilers of 10 to 30 horse power ; No. 1A for Boilers from 20 to 60 horse power.
They are placed on the hottest place in the flue, immediately above the fire.

IMPORTANT IMPROVEMENTS IN FUSIBLE PLUGS.

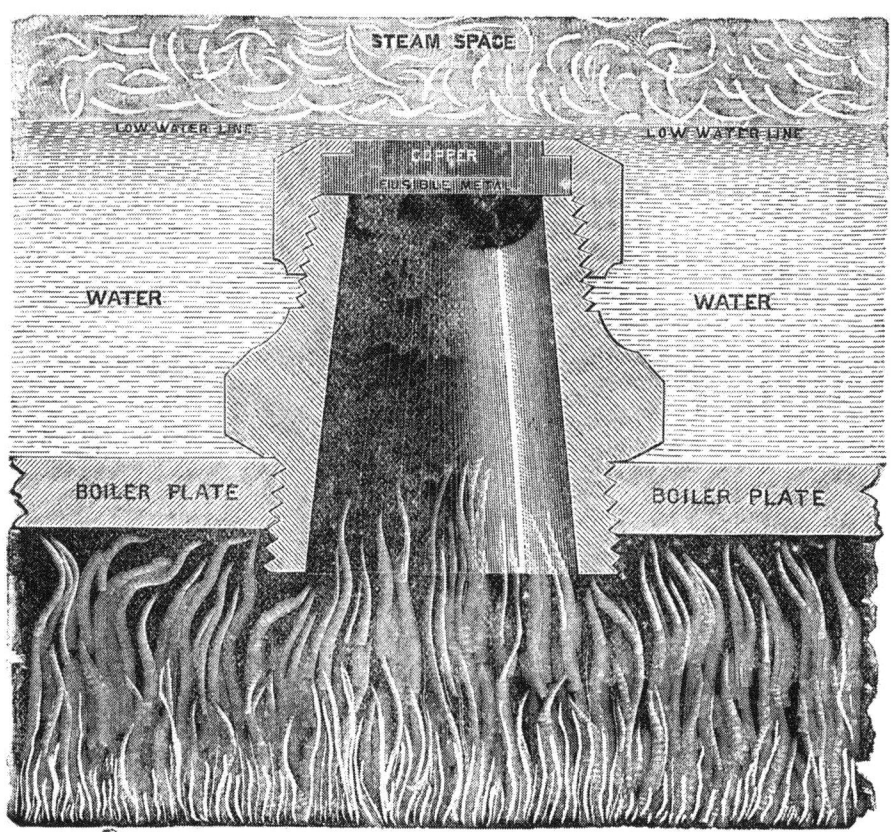

Full-size 1½ in. Bailey's Patent Fusible Plugs.

A.D. 1876—The last improvement in Bailey's Patent Fusible Plugs will be understood when the following remarks are read:—

Those who have been supplied with Bailey's Fusible Plugs may have noticed that occasionally a complaint has been made of the centre Copper having become loose;—this looseness may have been caused by a slight error in workmanship, or through the unequal expansion and contraction of it and the surrounding Fusible Metal;—the result was, that water, percolating through, caused a sediment to be deposited, especially so if the water contained much Carbonate or Sulphate of Lime; this blocked up the passage subject to the action of the fire, and materially interfered with the perfect action of the Plug. In some cases of very high pressure the Copper has been blown out, although sufficient water existed over the flue, that is if we are to believe the assertions of those who have had charge of the Boilers.

In order to prevent this imperfection we have made extensive experiments, which have resulted in our being able to introduce the improvement illustrated above, which is a full-size drawing of the Plug. It will be seen that we face the fusible metal with a Copper Disc, which gives all the advantage of a Copper Centre (of which see next page) without the disadvantages to which we have alluded

Taking into consideration the price at which immunity from danger through low water in boilers may be purchased, this invention should have the careful examination of all proprietors of Steam Boilers.

Bailey's Patent Fusible Plug Preventing an Accident.

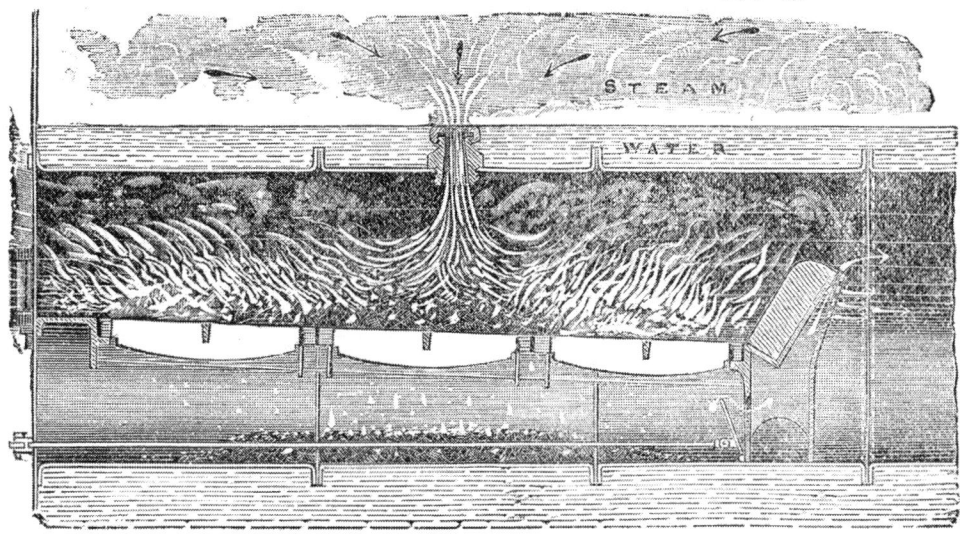

AN ESSAY ON FUSIBLE PLUGS IN GENERAL,
AND
Bailey's Patent Fusible Plug in Particular,
BY THE
PATENTEE OF BAILEY'S PATENT FUSIBLE PLUGS.

Their object, Firstly

Fusible Plugs, when they fulfil their object, and are fixed in a proper manner, melt when the water in a steam boiler becomes dangerously low, thus allowing the steam to put the fire out, and prevent danger to the flue plates, which would otherwise become, if not red hot, sufficiently so as to cause a collapse of a very serious nature.

Their object, Secondly

Although most cases of injured flues are caused by low water, another important cause is the great deposit of scale which is formed on them by the deposit of sulphate or carbonate of lime, and other earthy matters, which prevent the water from keeping the plate at a relatively low temperature; therefore, it being assumed that if any heat that will damage a boiler plate will fuse a proper plug *if it also* be covered, as is likely, with sediments, it will be seen that a Fusible Plug prevents damage through low water, or if caused by great deposit of scale on the plates.

Old Fusible Plugs not preventives of danger

The writer had the benefit some years ago of the friendship of the late Richard Roberts, the inventor of the self-acting Mule, the Planing Machine, and many other well-known apparatus in the manufacturing districts, which will for ever cause his name to be associated with the history of mechanical engineering. This gentleman was called to inspect a boiler that had its flue collapsed at Bury, in Lancashire; he found it had been caused by a deficiency of water, and although a fusible plug existed in it of the old sort *i.e.,* a piece of lead driven into the crown, this had not prevented the accident. Mr. Roberts made a sketch similar to the figure A.

From it only one conclusion is to be drawn, and that is, the fire having melted the metal of the plug, causing a hole of a conical shape, with only a diameter of 3-16th of an inch for the steam to rush through.

This small hole just allowed steam enough to pass to *blacken the fire* only immediately below it, and the fire having ceased, of course, to act upon it, to melt it further, the remaining portion of the furnace sufficiently softened the flue, as to cause a collapse attended with serious loss of life and property.

Bailey's Patent Improvement on the old system

Mr. Roberts pointed out to the writer that the only way to prevent this effete action would be to block up the middle of the fusible plug to prevent it melting, until the impediment could be blown out, thus creating a large hole in the fusible metal quite sufficient to allow the escape steam to put the fire out, and at once prevent further danger. He suggested this to the writer, and made him a present of the idea, and told him to whip it into shape. The result is, Bailey's Patent Fusible Plug, which, having a piece of copper in the centre in all cases, has been found an effectual remedy against collapse, although several of the first plugs made on this system were failures, owing to circumstances which cannot here be detailed. After going through many shapes and alterations, having been dictated by that most powerful educater, experience, the present Bailey's Patent Fusible Plugs are probably as perfect as fusible plugs ever will be. The facility by which the loose caps can be removed and examined, the easy way in which they can be fixed, the actual experience of benefit received by those who have used them, coupled with the low price at which they are supplied, have made them familiar to users of steam boilers in nearly all parts of the world.

Experiencia Docit
Beware of servile Imitations

Over seven years' experience has proved, beyond all doubt, that the suggestion of blocking up the centre made by the venerable inventor was correct. Other plugs have since been brought out, and in one special case a piratical and colourable imitation. Our friends are therefore requested to see that when they order Bailey's Patent Fusible Plugs, that they obtain them, and not infringements introduced by brass-founders having well developed parisitical instincts, combined with a minimum of originality and a very low morality.

IMPORTANT NOTICE.—£50 Reward will be paid to anyone giving information of any infringement of this Patent.

120,000 have been Sold, and the demand is ever on the increase.

BAILEY'S PATENT FUSIBLE PLUGS,

For Preventing Accident to Steam Boilers through Low Water.

This invention has received the approbation of several of the learned Societies and of eminent Engineers in this country and abroad. The letters of approbation and illustrations of various Prize Medals would fill a huge volume. Messrs. BAILEY & Co. beg to call attention to the fact, that the enormous quantity of ten thousand were sold in the first year of the Patent.

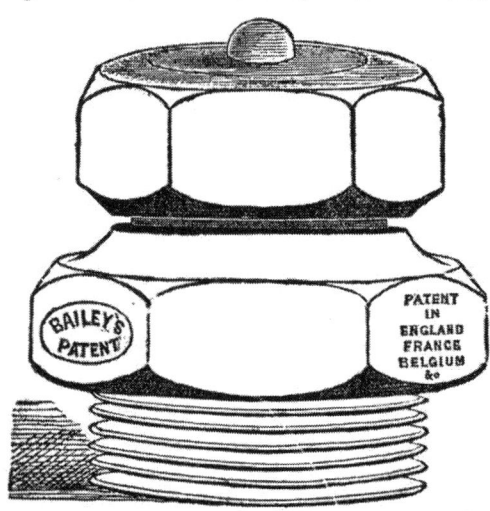

Screwed to	Suitable for Boilers of*	Price each	1 dozen loose Caps in boxes always ready
No 1 1½in. gas thread	10 horse power and less	10/-	15/-
1A. 2in. ,,	30 ,, ,,	15/-	30/-

* The dimensions here given of the Plugs suitable for Boilers of certain H.P. are merely nominal. Some will put two No. 1 in a flue of a large boiler in preference to No. 1A.

A sample Plug will be sent to any address on receipt of Stamps or Post Office order for the amount. Sample one will be sent for trial, and no charge made if returned un approved.

INSTRUCTIONS FOR FIXING.

The Plug must be fixed on the flue, in the place where the fire is most fierce. When the body of the Plug is once fixed, it does not require removing. If at any time the fusible alloy should melt, a new cap can be inserted by unscrewing the lock-nut. Every time the boiler is cleaned, the cap should be removed, and taken to the chief engineer or manager for his inspection: when cleaned it may be replaced.

Instructions are also sent with each case of loose Caps.

WHY RUN ANY RISK WHEN THE EXPENDITURE OF A FEW SHILLINGS WILL PREVENT IT.

FOR LOCOMOTIVE, PORTABLE, AND MARINE ENGINE BOILERS.

No. 2 (full size.)

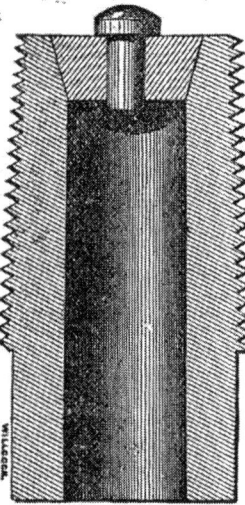

**8/- each.
Loose Caps, 1/3**

If any Railway Company will send an old Plug with their order, the Plugs shall be made to the dimensions and pitch of the old one.

Special quotations for large quantities.

No. 3.

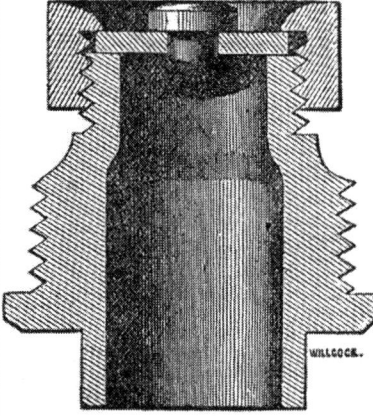

10/- each. Loose Caps, 1/3.

Locomotive Plugs, full size, screwed 1⅜ in. gas thread; they are also used for Marine and Upright Boilers, as being easier to fix for such than the No. 1 Plug.

If any purchaser has a doubt as to which sort of Plug would be best adapted, a Pen sketch of the boiler being sent, we will at once say which we would recommend.

No. 4.

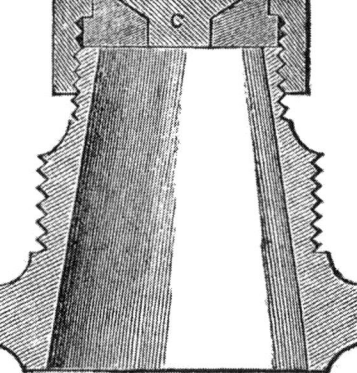

8/- each. Loose Caps, 1/3.

Screwed 1¼ in. gas thread.

In consequence of the number of accidents which have occurred of late to Portable Engine Boilers, Messrs. Bailey & Co. have been requested to design a Plug specially applicable to them, and the result has been of a satisfactory nature to both makers and users of that class of Boilers.

Section showing Plug in use.

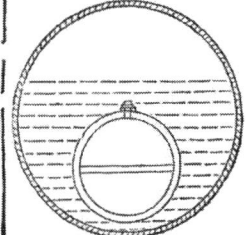

In Stationary Boilers.
No. 1, 1A, 1B.

Showing Plug.
Nos. 2, 3 and 4 in use.

The best way to test the efficiency of these Plugs is to let the water low and see it act. £50 will be given to any person who will give information of this Patent being infringed, and which will lead to a conviction. Several have been stopped infringing.

Bailey's Stuffing Box Gauge Cock.

London Pattern, finished all bright

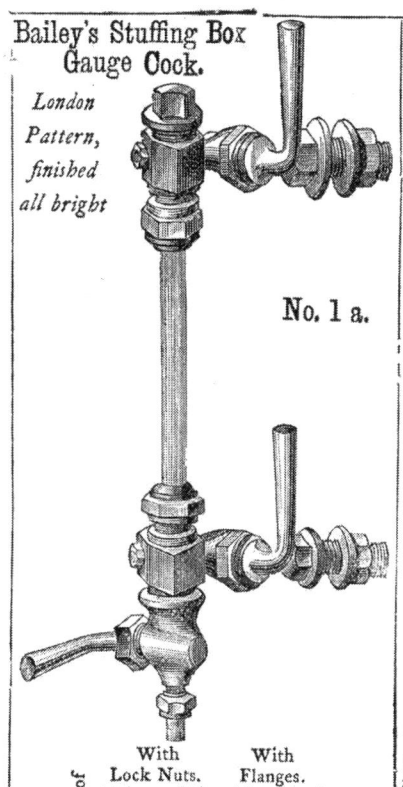

Diam. of Glass	With Lock Nuts		With Flanges	
	⅝-in.	32/-	⅝-in.	37/6
	¾ ,,	42/-	¾ ,,	50/-
	⅞ ,,	50/-	⅞ ,,	58/-

If black finished, 15 o/o less.

No. 2—Howat's Patent.

No. 1 a.

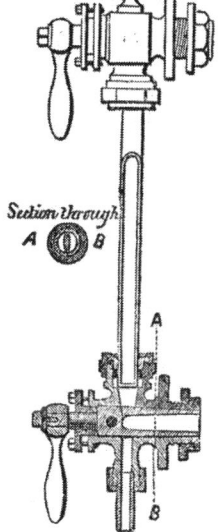

Section through A B

Diam. of Glass	With Lock Nuts		With Flanges	
	½-in.	30/-	½-in.	32/-
	⅝ ,,	38/-	⅝ ,,	40/-
	¾ ,,	42/-	¾ ,,	44/-
	⅞ ,,	44/-	⅞ ,,	46/-

No. 3—Bailey's Ordinary.

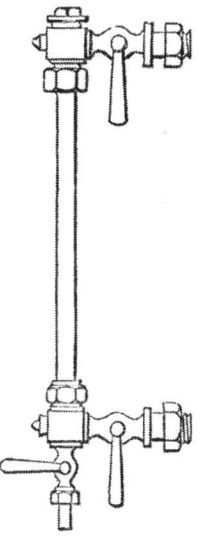

Diam. of Glass	With Lock Nuts		With Flanges	
	½-in.	16/-	½-in.	22/-
	⅝ ,,	18/-	⅝ ,,	27/-
	¾ ,,	24/-	¾ ,,	33/-
	⅞ ,,	28/-	⅞ ,,	38/-
	1 ,,	34/-		

No. 4 Extra—With Glands, Nuts and Stuffing Boxes.

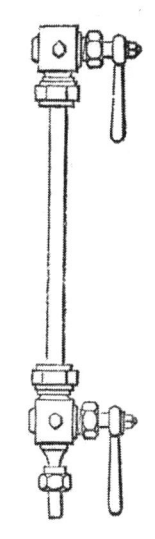

Diam. of Glass	With Lock Nuts		With Flanges	
	½-in.	26/-	½-in.	28/-
	⅝ ,,	30/-	⅝ ,,	32/-
	¾ ,,	32/-	¾ ,,	36/-
	⅞ ,,	36/-	⅞ ,,	40/-
	1 ,,	40/-		

No. 4.—Bailey's Gauge

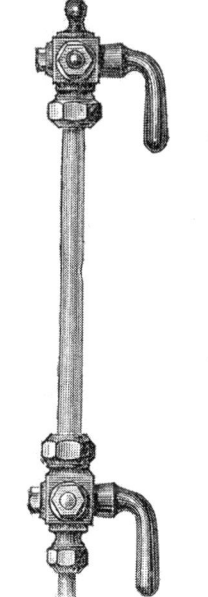

With Lock Nuts		With Flanges	
½-in.	15/-	½-in.	21/-
⅝ ,,	17/-	⅝ ,,	26/-
¾ ,,	23/-	¾ ,,	30/-
⅞ ,,	26/-	⅞ ,,	36/-
1 ,,	32/-		

These are similar to No. 4 extra, being lighter, and with screwed Plugs.

Bailey's "Consett" Pattern Water Gauge Cocks.

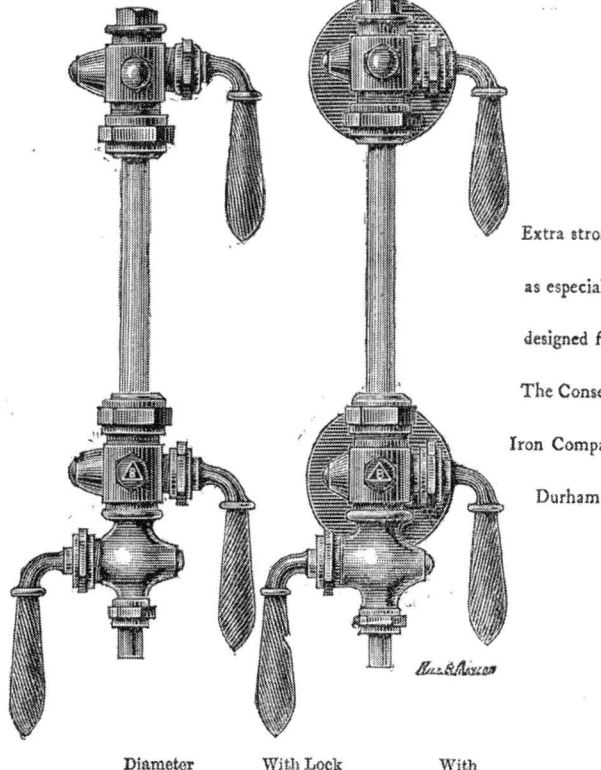

Extra strong, as especially designed for The Consett Iron Company, Durham.

Diameter of Glass	With Lock Nuts	With Flanges
⅝	35/-	40/-
¾	46/-	55/-
⅞	55/-	60/-

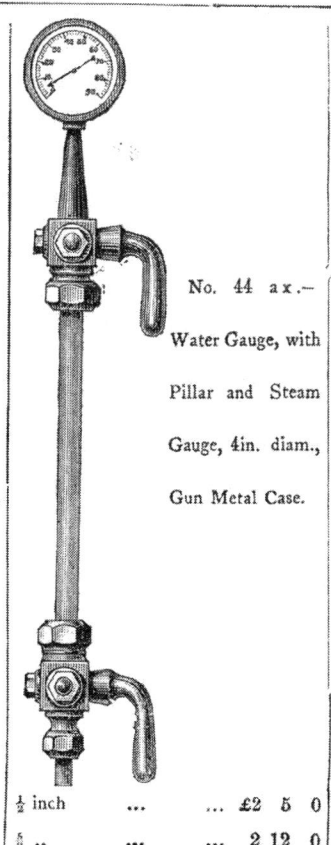

No. 44 ax.—Water Gauge, with Pillar and Steam Gauge, 4in. diam., Gun Metal Case.

½ inch	...	£2 5 0
⅝ ,,	...	2 12 0
¾ ,,	...	2 15 0

A very handsome and useful fitting.

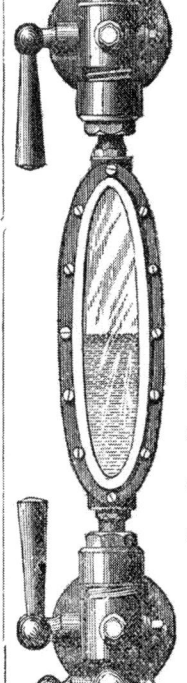

CHANDLER'S Patent Flat Water Gauge Glasses,

Supplied to any of the above description of Water Gauge Cocks, Patent Case.

Prices of Patent Cases only.

4½	6	7½	9 inch.
18/-	24/-	30/-	36/- each.

These are more costly than tubes, but experience teaches they are cheaper in the long run.

Bailey's Patent Fullway SCAVENGER WATER GAUGE COCKS.

Self-Acting, Strong, Safe, and not liable to derangement.
Many Thousands in use.

NOTICE OF NEW PATENT AND TRADE MARK.—J. BAILEY AND CO. having recently taken out Letters Patent for improvements in Water Gauge Cocks—the chief feature in which consists of a revolving scraper, which is actuated every time the bottom cock is opened and closed, thereby removing the sediment, and preventing a false indication of the state of the water—they beg to inform the engineering public that all such bear the Trade Mark as illustrated, and the title BAILEY'S PATENT "SCAVENGER" WATER GAUGE COCKS. They may be obtained through all Engineers and Boiler Makers in this country, and through the chief Machine Factors, or direct from the works, on application.

Prices for Set with Lock Nuts for Glass Tube.

Outside Diam.	Price
½-inch	£1 6 0
⅝ "	1 10 0
¾ "	1 16 0
⅞ "	2 0 0

Prices, with Flanges instead of Lock Nuts.

Outside Diam.	Price
½-inch	£1 8 0
⅝ "	1 12 0
¾ "	2 0 0
⅞ "	2 5 0

Extra Large for Steam-Boat Boilers.
For Inch Glass, with Flanges £2 15s

Bailey's Patent Self-Cleansing Scavenger Water Gauge Cocks

Are in constant use by such extensive firms as the Barrow Hæmatite Steel and Iron Co.; the Butterly Iron Co.; the Bridgewater Collieries, &c., &c. Over 5,000 sets have been sold, and the results are most satisfactory.

TWIN WATER GAUGE

The Top Cock may also be used to Screw on Steam Gauge or indicator.

SCAVENGER COCK.

Price complete for ¾-inch Glasses
£3 5s. 0d.

BAILEY'S BARROW PATTERN FURNACE Boiler Cocks,

Where Long Glasses are required,
£2 15s. per Set,
For ¾-inch Glass.

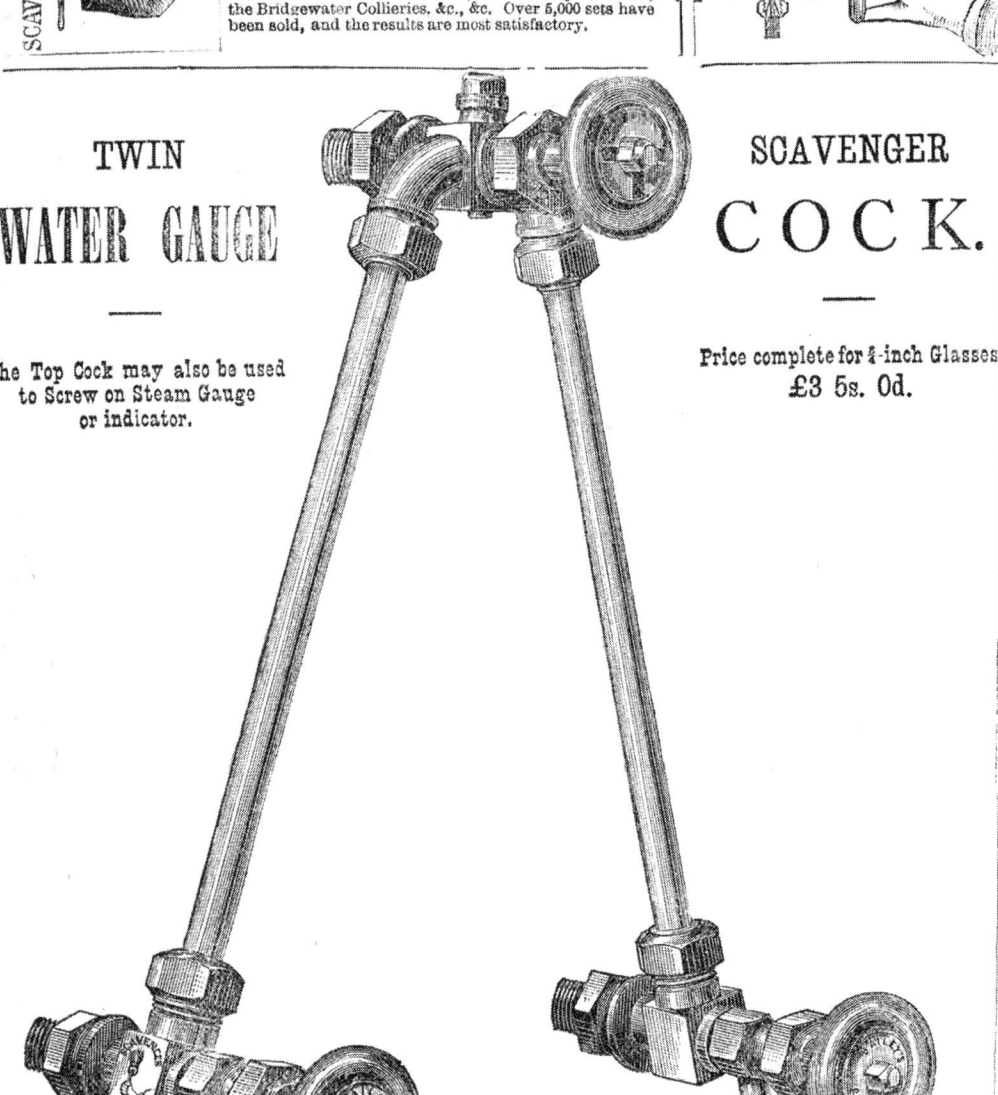
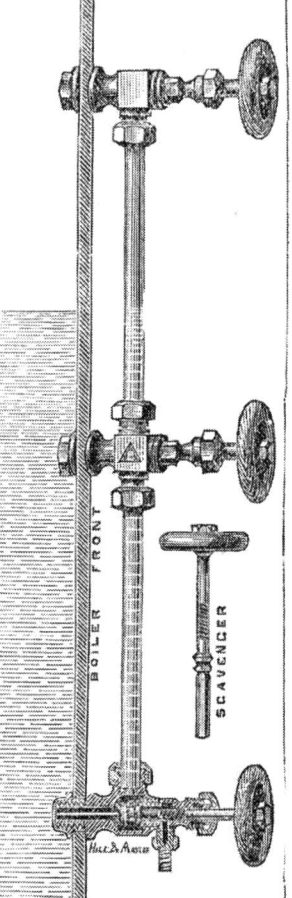

BAILEY'S PATENT PILLAR WATER GAUGES.

BAILEY & CO.'S PATENT BOILER FITTING.

DESCRIPTION.

From the "Engineer," September, 1867.

"* * * we illustrate a neat arrangement of a boiler fitting just brought out by Messrs. BAILEY & CO., of the Albion Works, Salford. The importance of having two sets of Water level testing apparatus is always acknowledged, and here we have them combined. The steam gauge on the top is Bourdon's Patent, improved by Messrs. BAILEY, and fitted with a 7in. dial. The entire apparatus is neat and simple: but two holes require to be made in the boiler, and the design is so pleasing to the eye that it must become a favourite with those who like handsome boiler fittings."

No. 1AX,
WITH FLANGES.

With best 7in. Dial Gauge and ¾in. Gauge Cocks.

PRICE,
With figures cast on the Pillar,

£8 15s. 0d.

Do., with Brass Engraved Plate, 15s. extra.

These are exclusively used for High Class Boilers of 50 and 60 H. P. in the Indian, Russian, and other Foreign Mills, as well as the Boilers of the large Iron Works at home.

No. 1AX., with Flanges, No. 1A., 1B., 1C.—All are fixed on Boiler front by Lock Nuts and Tubes, which are supplied complete.

No. 1C.

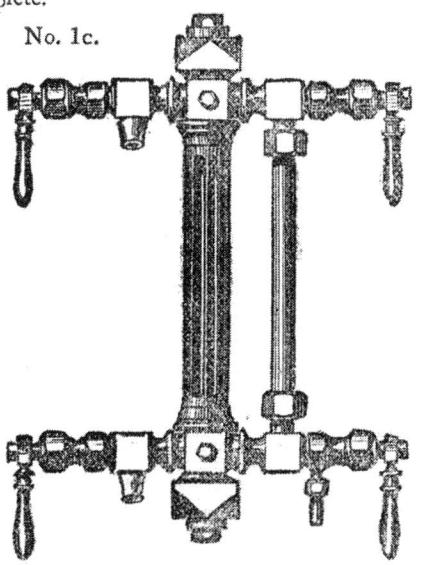

SCAVENGER GAUGE AND TEST COCKS,
WITH PILLAR.

Size.	Price.
Inch.	£ s. d.
½	2 17 6
⅝	3 5 0
¾	3 17 6

The above are with Pipes and Lock Nuts.

No. 1A.

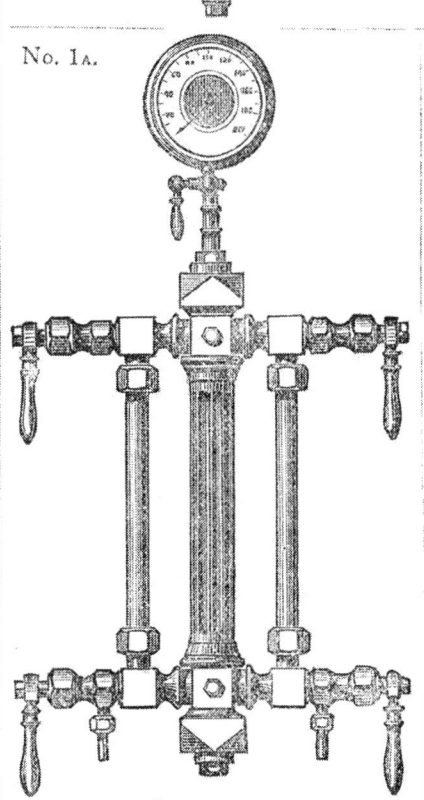

PRICES.

No. 1.—With ½in. Gauge Cocks, and 4in. Dial Gauge, £5 8s.
No. 2.—With ⅝in. Gauge Cocks, and 5in. Dial Gauge, £6 14s.
No. 3.—With ¾in. Gauge Cocks, and 7in. Dial Gauge, £8.
All with Scavenger Gauge Cocks.

No. 1B.

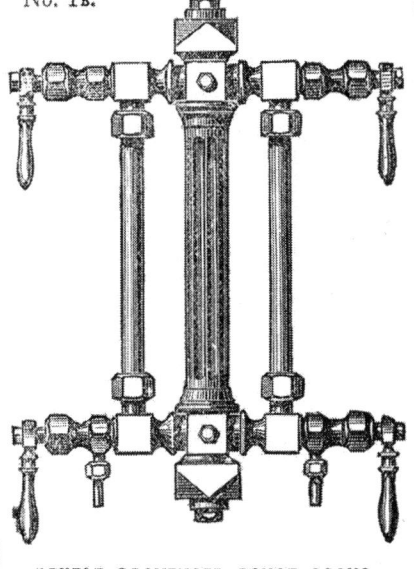

DOUBLE SCAVENGER GAUGE COCKS,
WITH PILLAR.

Size.	Price.
Inch.	£ s. d.
½	3 12 0
⅝	4 0 0
¾	4 15 0

☞ **SPECIAL NOTE**—The above only require Two Holes in Boiler Front for fixing.

THE ALPHA "B R" PATTERN.

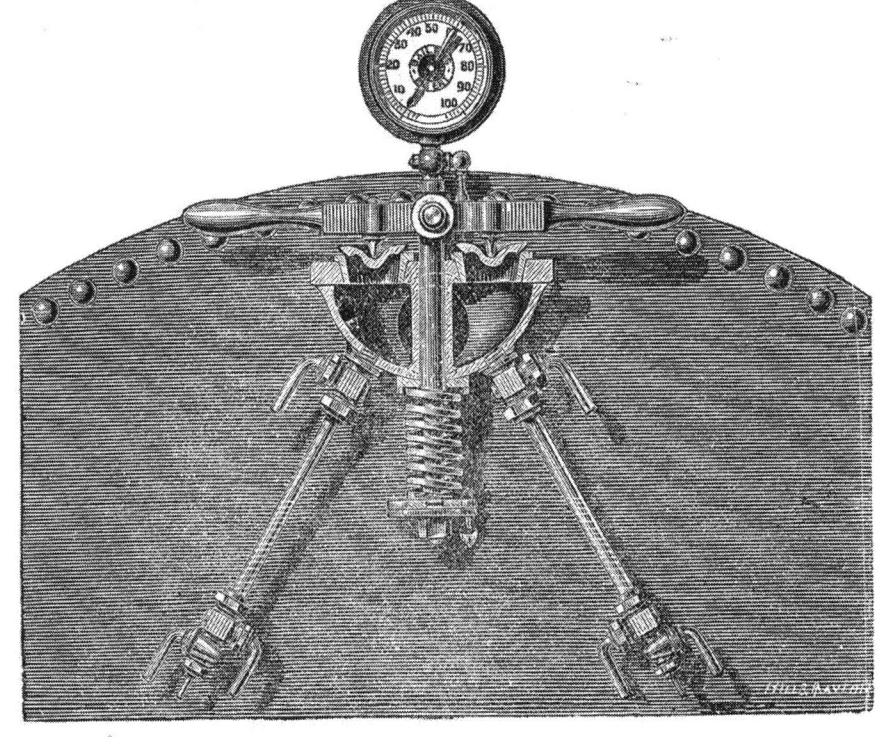

These Valves, for Stationary Boilers, are recommended as Lock-up Auxiliaries, and not to dispense with the ordinary Weight Valves on Boilers.

BAILEY'S "B R" PATENT BOILER FITTING.

BAILEY'S PATENT IMPROVED "RAMSBOTTOM VALVE."

The above woodcut represents a pattern used where the A pattern cannot be fixed. The Prices are the same as the A pattern, the latter being, however, more compact and preferable, sometimes in single Flue Boilers, as the above.

The Double Valve, long associated with the name of Mr. Ramsbottom, the invention of that gentleman when the Locomotive Superintendent of the London and North Western Railway Company, and Engineering Manager of their extensive Works at Crewe, is familiar to most engineers, found its extensive use on English and Foreign Locomotives. Its principle is, that if one Valve sticks the Spring immediately has upon it double the pressure in consequence of the inactive valve being used as a fulcrum, by which the live Valve raises it. J. BAILEY & CO. have patented improvements in this Valve, in order that it may be placed with facility on the front of large boilers as an AUXILIARY VALVE to the weight or lever Valve, always locked up, and under the eye of the Man in charge.

It will be seen by the illustration with what success their efforts have been met, as a more compact, durable and handsome Fitting has never yet been introduced. The Springs are bare and exposed to view, and, to prevent oxidation, are plated with nickel Silver.

The Valves are made in many forms, either with Gauge Cocks and Steam Gauge combined, or without.

Only two holes having to be cut in the Boiler, its advantages are obvious to those who understand these matters.

For Steam-Boats, as well as for land Boilers, this Fitting has many advantages to recommend it.

Contracts made with Boiler Makers, Yacht Builders, and Engineers, for special adaptations.

The use of the Adjustable Danger Bar on the Gauge is fully explained in our Steam Gauge List.

For very small Boilers and Portable Engine, as well as Steam Launch Boilers, we are preparing Illustrations of Safety Valves on the patent principle, all Brass, from $\frac{1}{2}$in. to 2in. diameter, at reasonable prices.

THE B R PATENT STEAM BOILER FITTINGS.

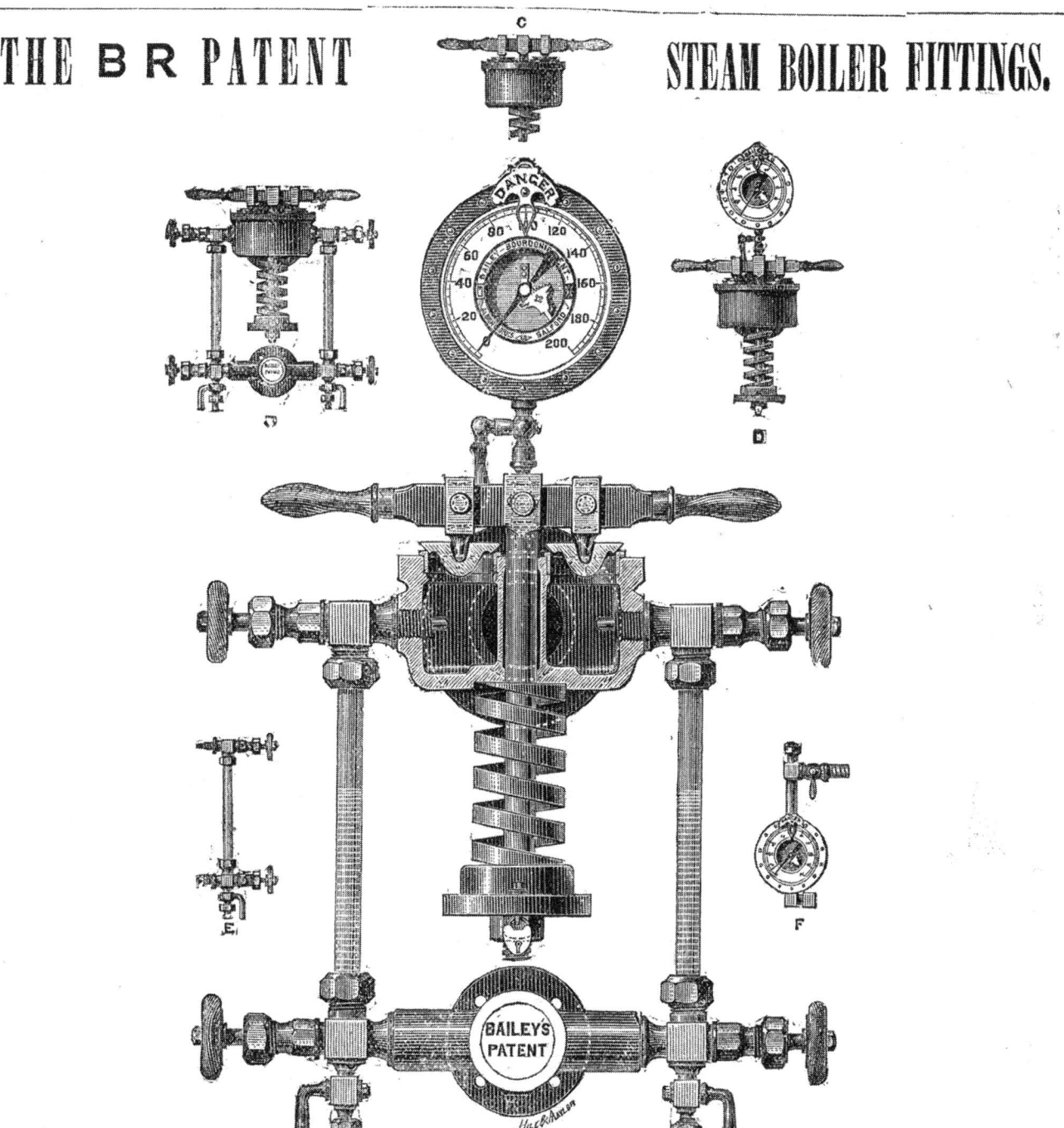

☞ When our friends order New Boilers, please insert on order that the Fitting must be supplied. It is not higher in price than the separate articles of old pattern.

A Pattern						B Pattern	C Pattern	D Pattern	E Pattern		F Pattern
Danger Bars Steam Gauge, Water Gauge Cocks, Safety Valves, complete	Suitable for Boilers of	Diameter of Safety Valves	Diameter of Gauge Cock Glasses	Diameter of Steam Gauge Dials	PRICE	Safety Valves and Gauge Cocks	Safety Valves only	Safety Valves and Steam Gauge	Bailey's Patent Scavenger Water Gauge Cocks		Bailey's Patent Danger Bar Steam Gauge, with registered Syphon
The B R Fitting. In ordering, please quote this and the diameter of the valve.	H.P. 0 to 10	In. 1	In. ½	In. 4	£ s. d. 6 6 0	£ s. d. 4 15 0	£ s. d. 2 10 0	£ s. d. 4 0 0	In. —	£ s. d. —	7in. dial of best quality Red Gun Metal Case and open Dial, Each £3.
	6 to 12	1½	⅝	5	8 10 0	6 8 0	3 5 0	5 10 0	½	1 6 0	
	12 to 30	2	¾	7	12 10 0	8 12 0	5 0 0	7 15 0	⅝	1 10 0	
	30 to 80	2½	⅞	7	15 5 0	11 10 0	7 7 0	10 10 0	¾	1 16 0	
	50 to 100	3	1	10	17 10 0	12 5 0	8 10 0	14 0 0	⅞	—	

Please quote the diameter of the valve and the initial when ordering.
The Springs of the above are all plated with Nickel or with Silver to prevent oxidation, the general finish is of the highest quality.

BAILEY'S PATENT BAILEY-RAMSBOTTOM SAFETY VALVE,
For Locomotive, Marine, and Portable, or other Boilers.

No. 603

This modification, patented by J. Bailey and Co., of the Ramsbottom Valve, is highly recommended for Locomotives, Marine, and other Boilers. Special modifications to drawing for Engine Makers.

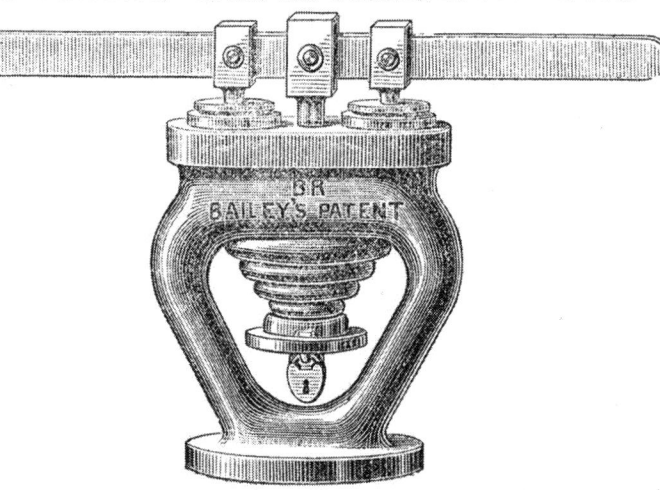

"THE MOST COMPACT VALVE EVER DESIGNED."

PRICES,
with Bright Lever Gun Metal Valves and Spindle Padlock and Key Valves:—

2 in.	... ...	£5 0 0
2½ ,,	... ...	7 7 0
3 ,,	... ...	8 10 0
3½ ,,	... ...	10 10 0
4 ,,	... ...	13 0 0

No. 602

BAILEY'S PATENT
Portable Boiler Double B. R. Safety Valve.
All Gun Metal.

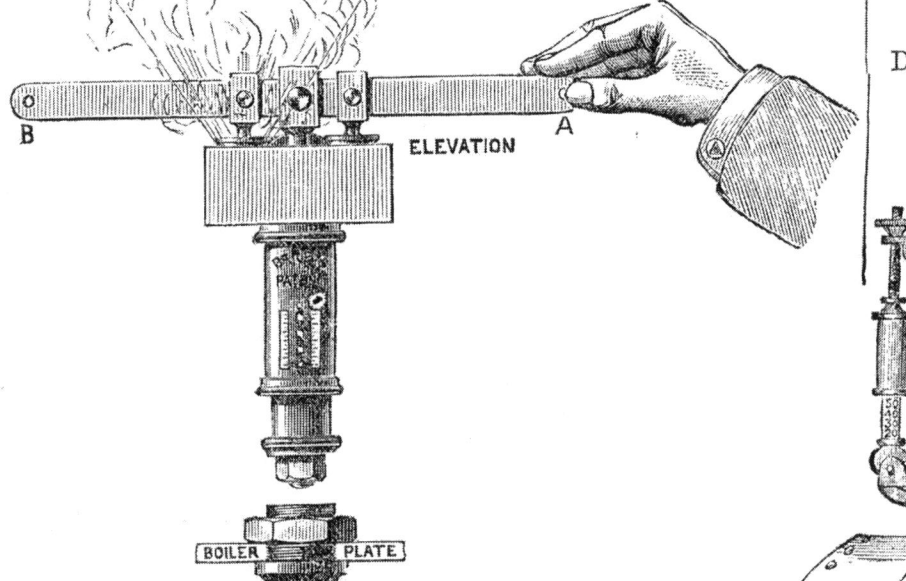

Bore of Valves for Boiler	£	s.	d.
6 h. p.—1 screwed nut	2	2	0
10 h. p.—1½ flanges	3	10	0
12 to 20 h. p. 2 flanges	6	10	0

This Double Valve is a compact and reliable instrument, suitable for Portable Land or Marine Boilers.

No. 601

SPRING BALANCE SAFETY VALVE,
IN IRON CASE.

Diameter of Valve, 2 inches.	Price complete, £4 10s. 0d.

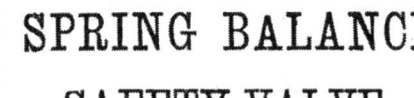

Injectors for feeding Boilers, Water Heaters, Steam-Jet Water Lifters, Steam Traps, Pyrometers, with an Essay on their use in relation to the generation of Heat and Steam fully described and illustrated. Ask for "Bailey's Supplementary Lists," *free.*

39

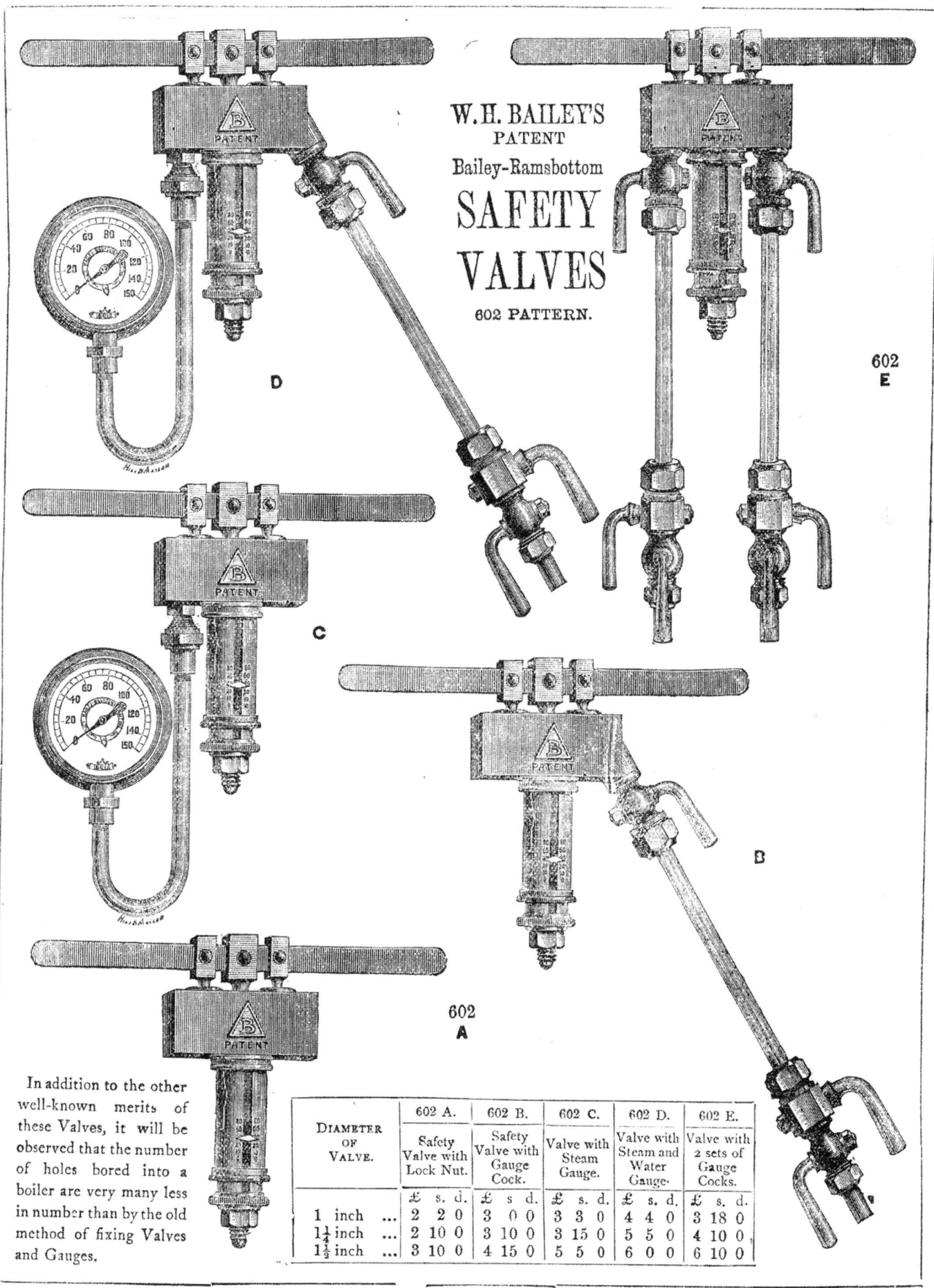

W. H. BAILEY'S PATENT Bailey-Ramsbottom SAFETY VALVES 602 PATTERN.

In addition to the other well-known merits of these Valves, it will be observed that the number of holes bored into a boiler are very many less in number than by the old method of fixing Valves and Gauges.

DIAMETER OF VALVE.	602 A. Safety Valve with Lock Nut.	602 B. Safety Valve with Gauge Cock.	602 C. Valve with Steam Gauge.	602 D. Valve with Steam and Water Gauge.	602 E. Valve with 2 sets of Gauge Cocks.
	£ s. d.	£ s. d.	£ s. d.	£ s. d.	£ s. d.
1 inch	2 2 0	3 0 0	3 3 0	4 4 0	3 18 0
1¼ inch	2 10 0	3 10 0	3 15 0	5 5 0	4 10 0
1½ inch	3 10 0	4 15 0	5 5 0	6 0 0	6 10 0

BAILEY'S PATENT "GAINSBOROUGH" FITTINGS
FOR BOILERS.

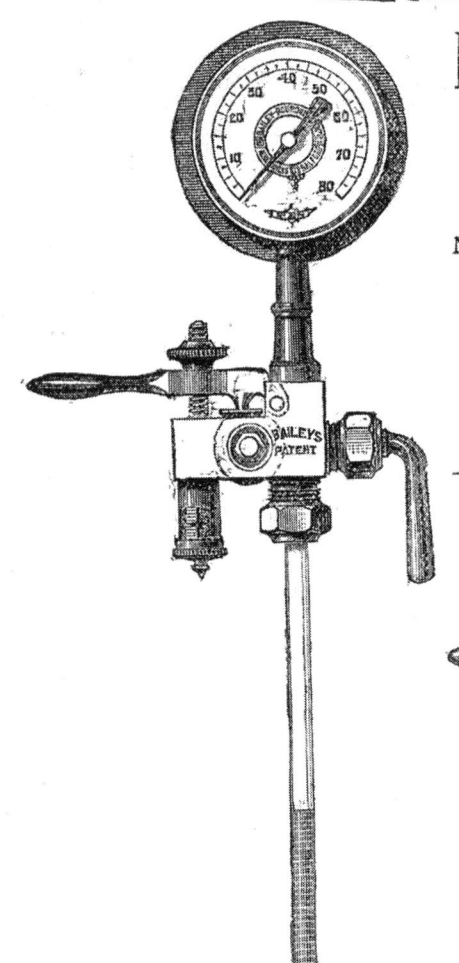

No. 510, with Steam Gauge 2½ inches diameter :—

A	Safety Valve ½ inch, Spring Balance and Water Gauge for ⅜ in. Glass		£2 2 0
B	Do. Gauge 4 inches, Valve ¾ inch, Gauge ½ inch	...	2 10 0
C	Do. Gauge 5 inches, Valve ¾ inch, Glass Gauge ⅝ inch	...	2 17 6
D	Do. Gauge 6 inches, Valve ¾ inch, Glass Gauge ¾ inch	...	3 5 0

BAILEY'S PATENT SAFETY VALVE AND SPRING BALANCE.

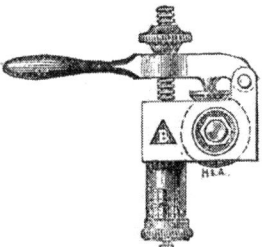

No. 512.

A	½ inch Valve	...	...	...	£0 12 6
B	¾ inch Valve	...	...	...	0 16 0
C	1 inch Valve	...	...	...	1 0 0
	1¼ inch Valve	...	...	...	1 6 0
	1½ inch Valve	...	...	...	1 15 0
	With Flange, 2 inch Bore	...	...	...	2 5 0

Brass Castings, Glass Tubes, Rubber Rings, &c., see lists.
For ordinary and other Safety Valves, see lists.

These elegant designs, for the Fronts of Steam Boilers, supply, at a less cost than the separate articles, good sound fittings; the cost of fixing is much reduced, and fewer holes required.

No. 511

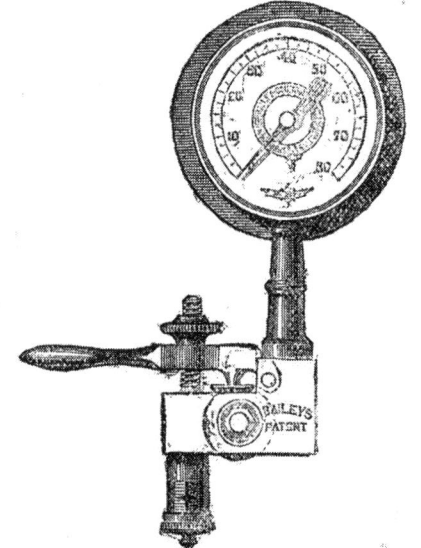

BAILEY'S
Patent Steam Gauge
AND
SAFETY VALVE AND SPRING BALANCE
For Front of Boiler, with Lock Nut.

A	2½ inch Steam Gauge and Safety Valve ½ inch	...	...	...	£1 10 0
B	4 inch Gauge, Valve ¾ inch	...	...	...	1 18 0
C	5 inch Gauge, Valve ¾ inch	...	...	...	2 3 0
D	6 inch Gauge, Valve ¾ inch	...	...	...	2 10 0

Bailey's (Hallam's Patent) Injector.

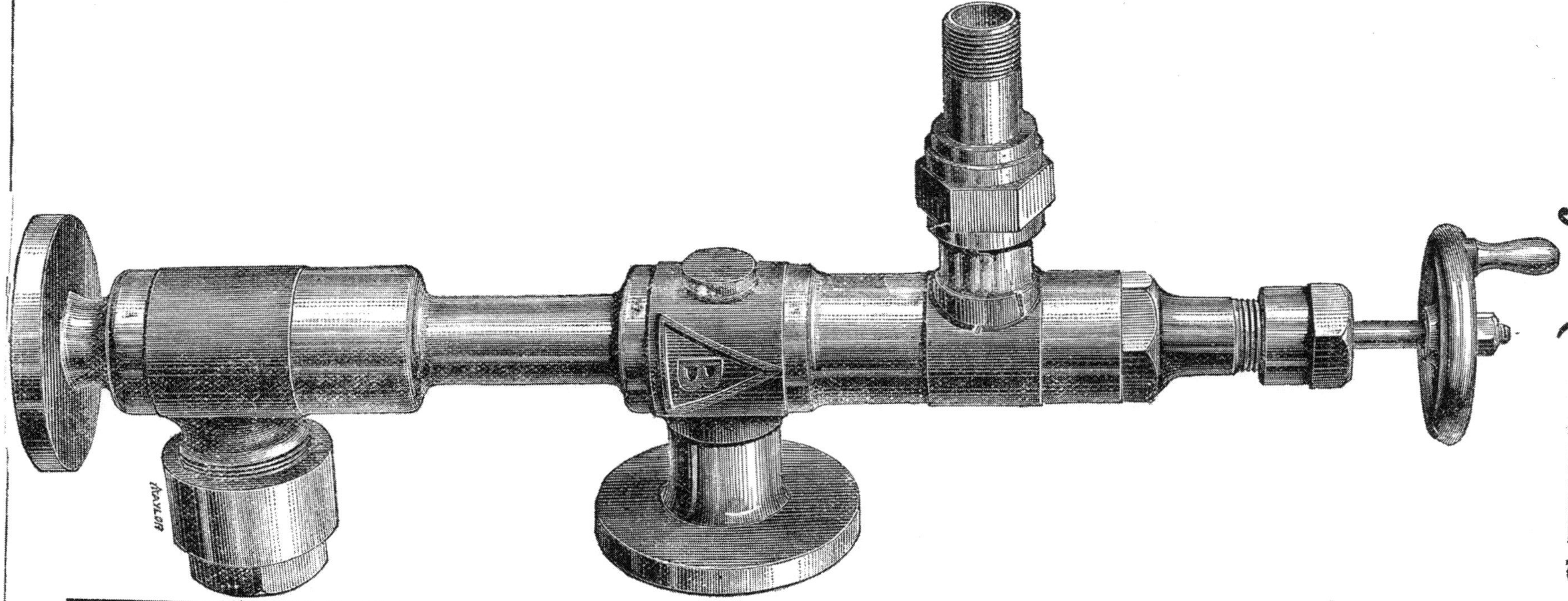

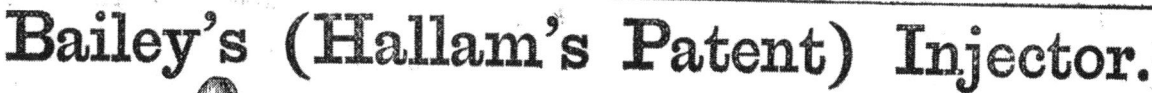

No.		A £ s. d. 3 10 0	B £ s. d. 3 15 0	BX £ s. d. 5 0 0	C £ s. d. 6 5 0	D £ s. d. 8 15 0	E £ s. d. 12 0 0	F £ s. d. 15 0 0	G £ s. d. 17 0 0	H £ s. d. 20 0 0	I £ s. d. 24 0 0	K £ s. d. 29 0 0	L £ s. d. 35 0 0	M £ s. d. 43 0 0	N £ s. d. 50 0 0	O	P	Q
1	All Gun Metal	3 10 0	3 15 0	5 0 0	6 5 0	8 15 0	12 0 0	15 0 0	17 0 0	20 0 0	24 0 0	29 0 0	35 0 0	43 0 0	50 0 0	Special Quotations		
2	Iron Bodies	...	...	...	...	6 5 0	8 10 0	11 0 0	13 0 0	14 0 0	18 0 0	21 10 0	25 0 0	31 10 0	38 10 0			
	Horse Power at 50 lb. pressure	6	12	20	35	50	90	140	180	210	250	300	490	595	665	730	795	860
	Delivery in gals. per hour at 50lb. pressure	63	135	210	375	540	958	1498	1813	2155	2935	3383¾	4912	5992	6620	7252	7936	8620
	Internal diam. of Pipes	½ in.	½ in.	¾ in.	1 in.	1 in.	1¼ in.	1½ in.	2 in.	2 in.	2½ in.	2½ in.	3 in.	3 in.	3 in.	3½ in.	3½ in.	4 in.

The small numbers are only made in gun metal, as our experience of them in iron cases does not justify their being retained in the list. When used for pressure above 80 lbs., the steam nozzle may be screwed down a little, as it is adjustable.

☞ When ordering this class of Injectors, if it cannot be stated the horse power or the number of gallons, please state the length and diameter of boiler, and the working pressure.

A Special Circular is published of Injectors, Jet Pumps, Water-Heaters, etc.—Ask for Bailey's "Supplementary Lists of Boiler Fittings," post free.

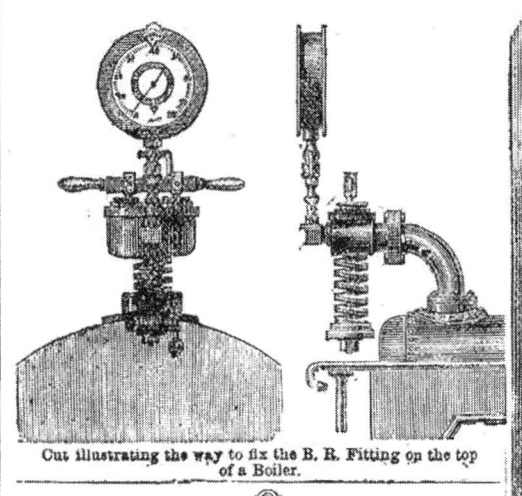

Cut illustrating the way to fix the B. R. Fitting on the top of a Boiler.

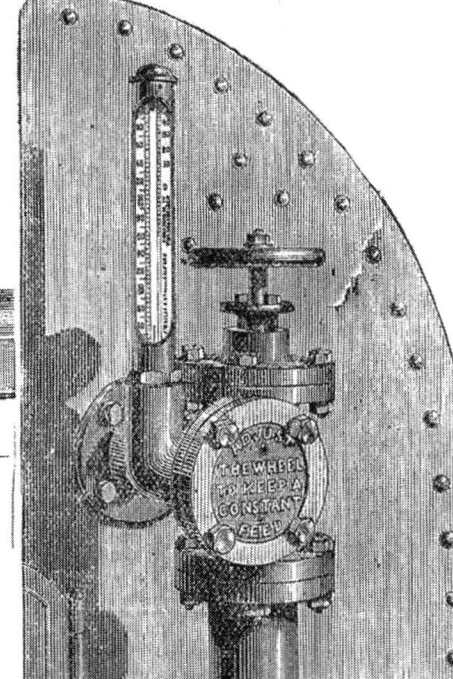

No. 876.
BAILEY'S IMPROVED

Feed Regulating Valve
AND
Feed Water Tell Tales for Boilers,

As recommended by the Steam Boiler Insurance Companies.

PRICES.
All first-class finish.

Bore.	Without Thermometer.
	£ s. d.
1½ in.	2 0 0
2 in.	2 10 0
2½ in.	3 10 0
3 in.	4 10 0

Thermometers 30/- each extra.

For instructions about Thermometers, see Thermometers.

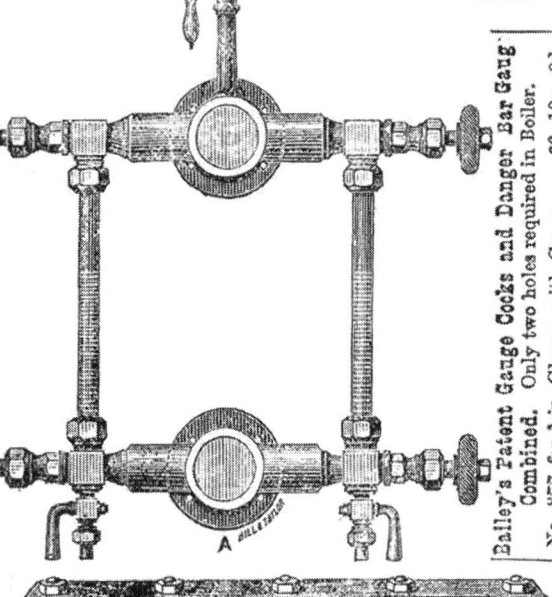

Bailey's Patent Gauge Cocks and Danger Bar Gauge Combined. Only two holes required in Boiler. No. 877 for ¾ in. Glasses with Gauge, ... £6 10s. 0d.

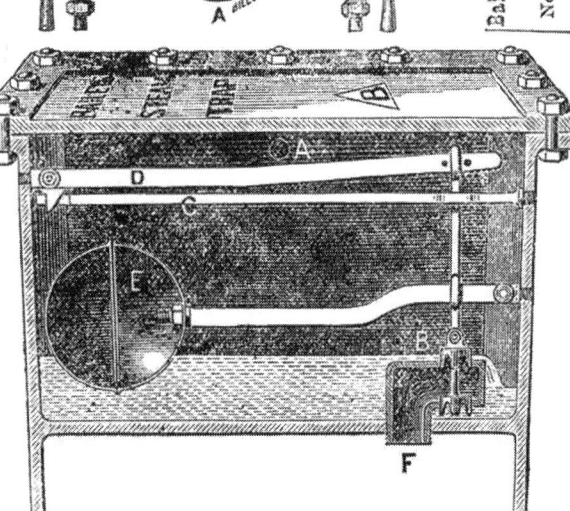

LEVER STARTING VALVE,
Sluice Pattern,
FOR WATER OR STEAM.

	£ s. d.
2 in. bore	2 15 0
3 ,,	3 10 0
4 ,,	5 5 0

Other sizes quoted for.

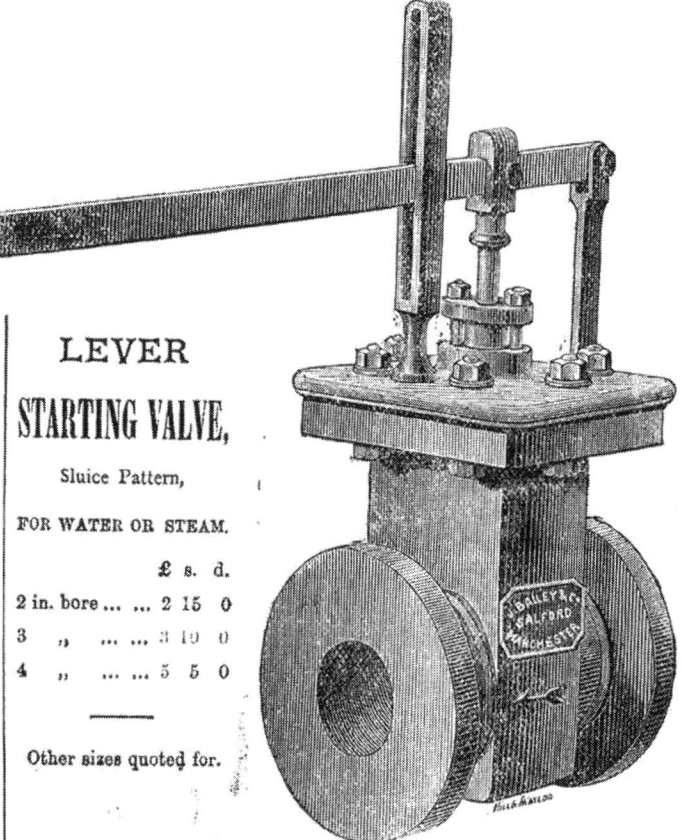

JONES' PATENT COLD AIR WATER AND STEAM TRAP.
2,000 IN USE.

PRICES.—Inlet, ¾ in. £2 12s. 6d.; 1 in. £3 3s.; 1¼ in. £4 10s.; 1½ in. £6 5s.
The Ball allows the pressure to come inside and outside, and cannot collapse. The hot steam forces any condensed water out of the ball when it gets hot by the expansion at E.

For further particulars of this Steam Trap, Water Heaters, Injectors, &c., see "Bailey's Supplementary Lists of Boiler Fittings," post free on application. All Engineers should have this.

LOW WATER ALARM.
No. 31.

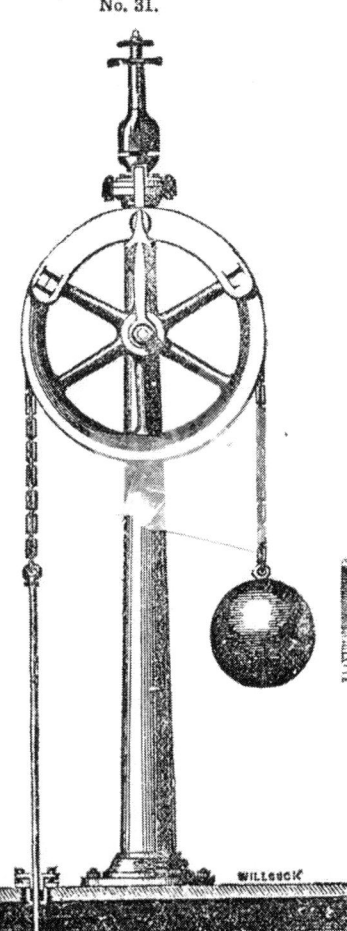

BAILEY'S CLEPSYDRA ALARM.

This alarm, as will be seen from the illustration, is to be fixed on the top of the boiler, and the float actuates the wheel; behind the wheel on the top is a cam, which raises a valve when the boiler has high water at H, and low water at L; when the valve is raised the whistle (which is 2¼ inches in diameter) makes a loud noise.

The Arrangement for an Alarm at High Pressure.

The small valve mentioned above as being raised when the water is high or low, will also be raised at any given pressure of steam. The best way to make it whistle at high pressure, say 50lbs., is to cause the steam to be raised to that pressure, and gradually to unscrew the lock-nut on the top of the whistle until the steam raises the valves and causes the alarm.

All the working parts are outside, and it can readily be tested as to its working order by the engineer turning the wheel to H or L.

In addition to being good for all stationary boilers, these are particularly useful for upright boilers, in IRON WORK, for instance, where steam is generated from the hottest furnace heat, and where, in consequence of the height, the ordinary water gauges are difficult to see.

PRICE complete, with float, stuffing-box, chain and weight-balance, £3 3s.

No. 31B.

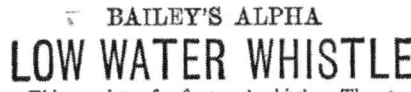

BAILEY'S ALPHA LOW WATER WHISTLE.

This consists of a float and whistle. The steam connection is by means of a small hole which is in the tube. When the hole is below the stuffing-box, the steam enters and blows the whistle, thus indicating low water in a most simple manner.

PRICE COMPLETE, £2 10s.

LOW WATER INDICATOR.
No. 21.

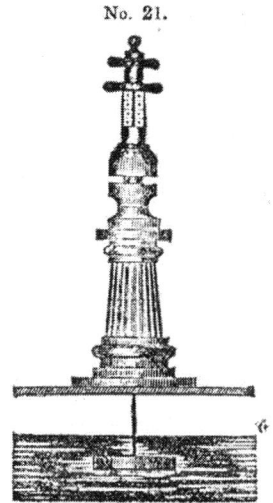

Bailey's Low Water Alarm.

This Low Water Alarm, on account of its simplicity, is a general favourite among engineers. The stone float is much better than the hollow metal balls, which often cause other alarms to be inoperative when they leak. The action in this is caused by the different specific gravity of stone and water. It will easily be understood that when the water leaves the stone, it (the stone) becomes heavier, in consequence of not being buoyed up by the water: this causes a valve to be opened and a loud alarm to be sounded on the whistle, which continues whilst the water is below level.

PRICE £2 5s

No. 32.

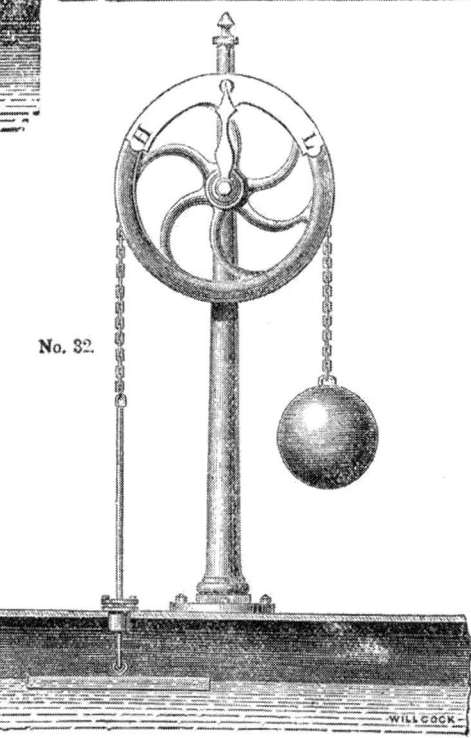

LOW WATER FLOAT.
30/- EACH COMPLETE.

No. 201.

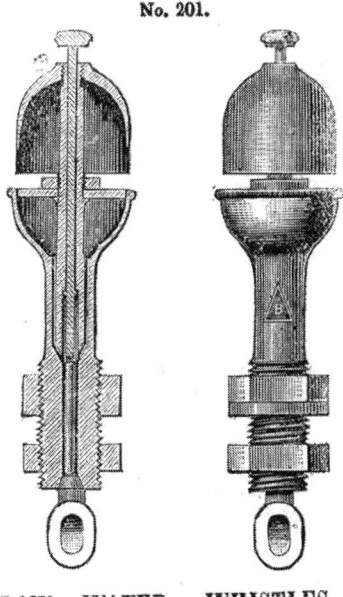

LOW WATER WHISTLES.

For attachment to Floats, or the end of Levers for special arrangements of Engineers and Safety Valve Makers.

Diameter of Whistle

PRICE EACH, £

AWARDED AT THE   **THE ASHCROFT PATENT**   1870 MEETING

LOW-WATER DETECTOR
AND ALARM,
For Steam Boilers,
PATENTED IN ENGLAND, AMERICA, &c.

The only Alarm without Valves, Springs, Cranks, Floats, or Moving Machinery.

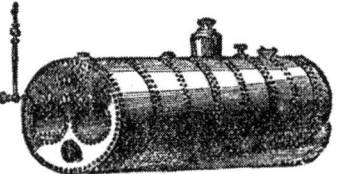

It is eminently fitted to guard against those accidents caused by low water. It needs not the care or attention of the engineer or fireman to keep it in order. Operating by the force of natural laws, it takes care of itself, and is only called into action by the fall of the water below any fixed level, and then it gives the alarm to all within the sound of the whistle of a deficient supply of water.

It stands as a watchful monitor over the magazine of power on which it is placed, and not only guards it, but notifies the attendant, if he is forgetful or negligent of his duty.

The following are a few of the eminent Firms who have the Ashcroft Low-Water Alarms in use, and speak highly of them:—

The Bridgewater Trustees Collieries	Manchester
The Trustees of Marquis of Bute	Cardiff
Sir R. Burnett and Co., Vinegar Works	London
Sir Sidney Waterlow and Sons, London Wall	London
Sir John Power and Sons, Distillers	Dublin
Truman, Hanbury, Buxton and Co., Brewers	London
R. and A. Chambers, Bleachers	near Manchester
West Cumberland Hæmatite Iron Co.	Workington
Joseph Ashwood and Son, Ainsworth Mill	Bolton
James Hardcastle, Bradshaw Bleach Works	Bolton
Thomas Hardcastle and Son, Firwood Bleach Works	Bolton
Barrow Hæmatite Steel and Iron Co.	Barrow
Stanier and Co., Silverdale Colliery	Newcastle-under-Lyne
W. H. and G. Dawes, Milton Iron Works	near Barnsley
Farmer and Co., Vitriol Works	London
Jackson and Ashworth, Smedley Bridge Works	Manchester
William Higginbottom, Alexandra Mills	Derby
Overton and Gibbons, Brewers	Croydon
Phœnix Gas Co., Vauxhall	London
Carter and Walker, Engineers	London
Wentworth and Sons	Wandsworth
John Bailey and Co., Engineers and Brass Founders	Salford
Hennetts and Co., Engineers	Bridgewater
Thomas Stephens and Green, Paper Manufacturers	Woodburn
Adventurers of Wheal Basset	Redruth
J. T. Jackson, Engineer	Brighton
B. Davies, Engineer	Brighton
Kirk, Bros. and Co., Iron Works	Workington
Wm. Griffiths and Co., Tin-Plate Works	Workington
T. Briggs, Springfield Works	Manchester
John Holmes and Sons, Engineers	Norwich
J. Marsden and Sons, Cotton Spinners	Bolton
Riches and Watts, Iron Works	Norwich
John Knowles, Cotton Spinner	Bolton
May and Baker, Garden Wharf	London
W. H. Horsefall, Waterside Mills	Hebden Bridge
Ransome, Suns and Head	Ipswich
Hick, Hargreaves and Co.	Bolton
D. Adamson and Co.	Hyde
Cater and Walker	London
Marshall, Sons and Co.	Gainsboro'
Fletcher and Co.	Litchurch, Derby
Galloway and Sons	Manchester
J. and F. Howard	Bedford
Clifton and Kersley Coal Co.	near Manchester
Close, Ayre and Nicholson, Iron Works	York
Riddell and Co.	Donegall Place, Belfast
Topp and Hindley, Cotton Spinners	Farnworth
E. Blundell, Builders, etc.	Nottingham
W. Benson, Engineer	Nottingham
V. and J. Robbins, Foundry	Dover
Alum and Ammonia Co.	Bond Common, London
W. Gibson	Nottingham
The York Railway Plant Co.	York
Hopkins, Gilkes and Co., Iron Works	Middlesborough
The Crossfield Iron Ore Co.	Crossfield
Jonathan Edge and Co., Engineers	Bolton
Solway Hæmatite Iron Co.	Maryport
John Hill and Co.	Ilkeston
Jackson, Gill and Co., Iron Works	Middlesborough
W. N. Nicholson, Engineer	Newark
Rossendale Printing Co.	Rawtenstall
E. and B. Tremnier, Brewers	Gloucester
Victoria Dock Engine Works	London
Kirk and Valentine, Iron Works	Workington
S. Fox and Co.	Deepcar, near Sheffield
Ince Hall Coal Co.	near Wigan
Strangeways Hall Coal Co.	near Wigan
John S. Deed and Sons	London
John Reid, Tannery	Edinburgh
Lewis and Grundy, Engineers	Nottingham
Pearson and Spurr, Iron Founders	Birstall
Stock and Co., Silver and Lead Mines	Swansea
J. and F. Howard, Britannia Iron Works	Bedford
Sir Titus Salt, Bart. Sons, and Co.	Saltaire
Ransomes, Sims and Head, Engineers	Ipswich
Cotton and Slater, Boiler Makers	Blackburn
H. J. Coulthurst, Robert Street Foundry	Darwen
Hendry Bros., Engineers	Glasgow
The Rhymuey Iron Co., Limited	Rhymuey
J. Crossley and Sons, Limited	Halifax
Southport Baths and Assembly Rooms Co.	Southport
Llwydrath Tin-Plate Co.	Maesteg, near Bridgend
Manlove, Alliott and Co., Broomsgrove Works	Nottingham
S. Bottomley and Brothers, Buttershaw Mills	Bradford
Broughton Moor Colliery Co.	Maryport
G. W. Risien, Engineer, The Leonora, West Coast	Demerara
North Staffordshire Coal and Iron Co.	Talk-o'-th'-Hill, Staffordshire

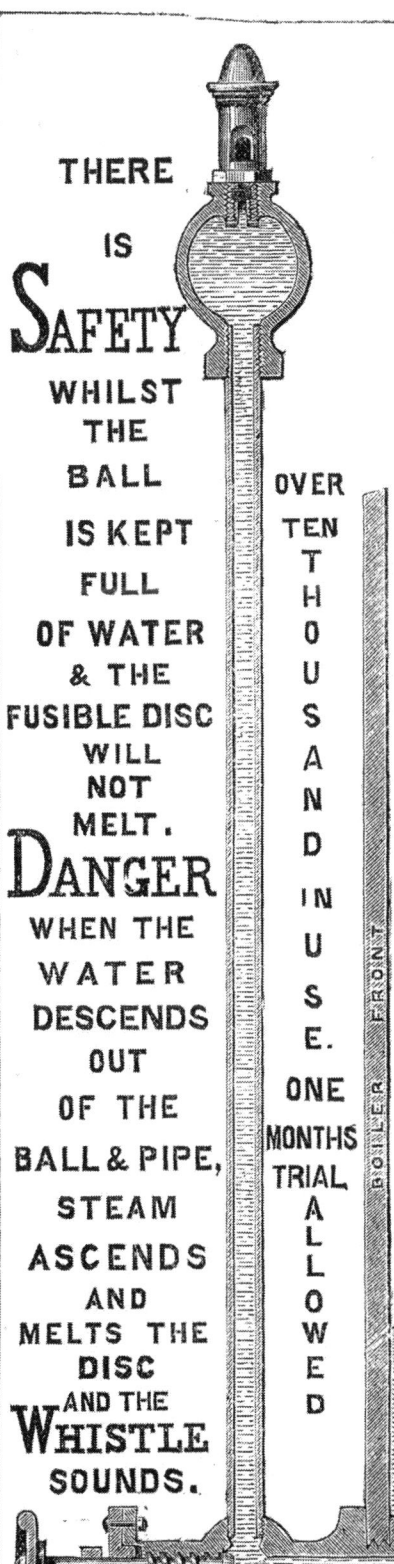

SAFETY.

THERE IS **SAFETY** WHILST THE BALL IS KEPT FULL OF WATER & THE FUSIBLE DISC WILL NOT MELT. **DANGER** WHEN THE WATER DESCENDS OUT OF THE BALL & PIPE, STEAM ASCENDS AND MELTS THE DISC AND THE **WHISTLE** SOUNDS.

OVER TEN THOUSAND IN USE. ONE MONTHS TRIAL ALLOWED

BURNT BOILERS

AND

Boiler Explosions

PREVENTED BY

THE ASHCROFT

PATENT

LOW WATER DETECTOR,

WHICH,

On account of its extreme simplicity, recommends itself to all USERS OF STEAM POWER.

The VERY FAIR and perfectly equitable principle upon which we have successfully introduced this invention to new districts, indicates our desire to give anyone the OPPORTUNITY OF SUBMITTING IT TO THE MOST SEVERE CRITICISM, One Month's Trial being allowed before purchase.

Nearly all accidents to Boilers are caused by deficiency of water.

To be had direct, or through any Boiler Maker, Engineer, or Ironmonger.

THERE IS **SAFETY** WHILST THE BALL IS KEPT FULL OF WATER & THE FUSIBLE DISC WILL NOT MELT. **DANGER** WHEN THE WATER DESCENDS OUT OF THE BALL & PIPE, STEAM ASCENDS AND MELTS THE DISC AND THE **WHISTLE** SOUNDS.

OVER TEN THOUSAND IN USE. ONE MONTHS TRIAL ALLOWED

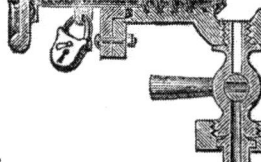

DANGER.

ENGLISH TESTIMONY.

From BOOTHROYD, SON, and RIMMER, *Southport.*
Aug. 29th, 1870.

Dear Sirs,—The Alarm answers first-rate. Boiler has been blown out twice (for slight alteration to feed-pipe), and both times as soon as water was below the level of the Alarm, the whistle commenced making noise enough to drive a nervous person crazy. We have no doubt this Alarm will have, as it deserves, a very extensive sale, being so vastly superior to the old system of floats with so-called "stuffing-boxes," or really sticking-boxes.

Report of trial of the Ashcroft Patent Low-Water Detector or Alarm, before the Committee of the Royal Cornwall Polytechnic Society, Mr. John St. Aubyn, M.P., presiding, given in the "Western Morning News," Sept. 13th, 1870.

"Ashcroft's Patent Low-Water Detector and Alarm was tried, and found to be an unqualified success."

Falmouth September 13th, 1870.

Dear Sirs,—We have exhibited your two Alarms at the Polytechnic Meeting, and the judgment of the Committee was suspended until practical trials were had on a boiler. We are happy to say that the trials took place yesterday, and the Alarms answered admirably. All with whom we talk express themselves much in favor of them. Mr. John St. Aubyn, in his opening address at the Meeting, spoke of it in the highest terms, and said how great was the need in Cornwall of such an apparatus.— Very truly yours, COX, FARLEY, & CO.
Falmouth Docks Iron Works.

From THE WEST CUMBERLAND HÆMATITE IRON WORKS,
Workington, September 23rd, 1870.

The Alarm has now been in use some time, and we have much pleasure in saying that it is the right thing in the right place, and we have no doubt of its being universally adopted in course of a short time.—Yours truly,
The second order was for Twelve.

From Messrs. THOMAS, STEPHENS and GREEN,
Soho Mills, Woburn, near Beaconsfield,
Buckinghamshire, Sept. 26th, 1870.

We have this morning tested the Low-Water Alarm, and are so well satisfied with its efficiency, that we shall order three more, and apply them to all our boilers. We worked the water down, particularly noticing when the tube in which the plug is began to get warmer, and found, in less than two minutes from the time was concluded the water had left the tube, and the plug was out. We therefore consider the Detector, when fitted in its proper place, will be a great safeguard.

Memorandum from WHITLEY PARTNERS *to Messrs.* THE ASHCROFT PATENT ALARM CO. *Essex Street, Salford.*

We are glad to hear of the progress you are making in the sale of your Patent Detectors. We have pleasure in bearing testimony to their efficacy and usefulness.

New Yard Ironworks, Workington, Oct. 5th, 1870.

We have had the Ashcroft Alarm in use about a month, during which time it has gone off twice, and the last time we believe it prevented a new boiler from being injured by a deficiency of water. Had we adopted them a few months sooner, we should have been saved the annoyance and great loss caused by the collapse of a boiler flue. We believe the Detector a sure preventive of boiler explosions through shortness of water, and we will thank you to supply us with two more of them for new boilers we are now putting in.—Yours faithfully,
KIRK BROTHERS & CO.

Memorandum from JOHN BAILEY & CO., *Albion Works Salford,*
Nov. 3rd, 1870.

The Detector fixed on our boiler is a perfect success.

Phœnix Iron Works, Nov. 22nd, 1870.
THE ASHCROFT PATENT DETECTOR CO.

Gentlemen,—Be so good as to forward us another "Low-Water Detector," the same as last sent. We have tested the one we have, and have much pleasure in testifying to its efficiency and usefulness. Please send us monied invoice for both.—Yours truly,
CLOSE, AYRE, & NICHOLSON,
Per J. Close, Junr.

Victoria Docks, London, December 8th, 1870.
ASHCROFT DETECTOR AND ALARM CO.

I had the Alarm fixed to my satisfaction, and have made trial to-day, when its action is all we could desire. We will shortly have all our boilers supplied.—Yours truly,
T. FARMER & CO.
Per Henry Glover.

Teeside Iron Works, Middlesborough, Dec. 27th, 1870.
Messrs. THE ASHCROFT ALARM CO.

Gentlemen,—Please send goods as under; Six Alarms, No. 2, same as last, and oblige. Pro. HOPKINS, GILKES, & CO., Limited.
R. WEATHERILL.

Derwent Tinplate Works, Workington, Dec. 22nd, 1870.

Gentlemen,—Within please find cheque for £3 15s. Receipt will oblige. So far as we have yet been able to judge of the Alarms, we are satisfied with them.—Yours faithfully,
W. GRIFFITH & CO.

Powburn, Edinburgh, March 13th, 1871.

Gentlemen.—I have pleasure in testifying that it completely answers the purpose for which it is intended. It was carefully tested on being fitted to the boiler, and one night, about a month afterwards, gave the alarm, when the boiler had been accidentally allowed to get too low in water.—I am, Gentlemen, yours respectfully,
JOHN REID.

Memorandum from THOMAS FARMER & CO., *Chemical Manure Works, Victoria Docks, London, April 18th,* 1871.

Please supply us with two more of your Patent Low-Water Indicators and Alarms No. 2. quality, same as you last supplied us with.

A BOILER SAVED FROM DESTRUCTION.—

"We fixed your Alarm on Saturday last on our Boiler, and on Monday night, about Twelve o'clock, were aroused by a terrific screaming coming from it. It seems our mudhole lid had not been properly fastened after cleaning out on Saturday, thereby causing a leakage. Our Water, consequently, went down in the boiler, and, if it had not been for the Detector, we have no hesitation in saying that we should have had a very serious accident. We would advise all persons using Boilers, who study their own safety, to have one.".

This is an Extract from a letter received from Messrs. H. J. & A. COULTHURST, Engineers, Darwen.

☞ We allow trial before purchase, under the most adverse circumstances, if any can be imagined, and are therefore prepared to receive orders on condition that if returned within one month, no money to be paid.

There are several thousand of these Low-Water Detectors in use in different parts of this country and the United States, and we might print many testimonials of their efficiency, but the evident simplicity of the instrument renders any additional testimony unnecessary. Every instrument warranted. These Alarms are used by Messrs. Hick, Hargreaves & Co., the celebrated Engineers, of Bolton; also used by Messrs. Howard, of Bedford, for the Howard boilers.

UNSOLICITED TESTIMONY.

Under the head of "WATER GAUGES OUT OF ORDER," *the Chief Engineer of the Yorkshire Boiler Insurance and Steam Users' Co., Limited,* JOHN WAUGH, ESQ., *Associate Inst. C.E., says, in the* 1874 *Report :—*

"Ashcroft's Alarm Whistle is an appendage no Boiler ought to be without; when sounded through shortness of water, the fires ought to be withdrawn without a moment's delay."

Extract from "MECHANICS' MAGAZINE," February 10th, 1872.

THE ASHCROFT
LOW-WATER DETECTOR AND ALARM.
10,000 IN USE.

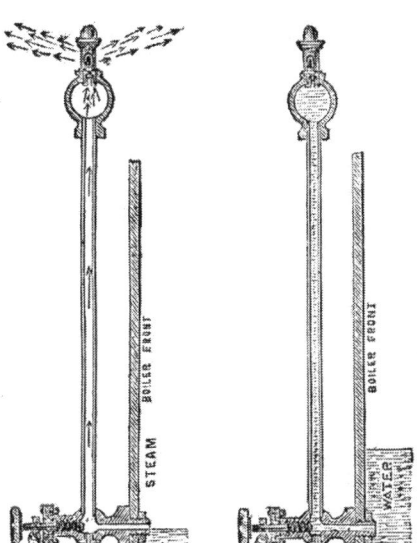

A STEAM-BOILER—like a fortress—is no stronger than its weakest part; and, contemplating the fearful results that continually ensue on neglect resulting in weakness, every device that promotes security must be regarded as of essential interest and importance. As a matter of course, it is a *sine-quâ-non* that, in point of original construction, the plates and joints of a steam generator should be capable of resisting a higher strain than they are intended to be exposed to; and as a corollary, the prevention of any excess over that pressure by means of safety-valves becomes equally necessary.

But it is of at least as great, if not greater importance, that the proper level of water in the boiler should be continuously maintained, and especially that any lowering thereof, by neglect or accident, should not only be indicated, but remedied at once, so as to prevent the burning of the plates, with all the unknown and illimitable risks attendant thereon. This is an office that is fulfilled, automatically, by the Detector and Alarm, which is illustrated in the accompanying engravings; and which in its operation is independent of mechanism, of valves, springs, floats, cranks, or other moving parts, but efficient and reliable solely through the natural effects of heat and gravitation. Its action depends entirely on a fusible plug, made of a metal or alloy, that melts at the boiling point of water, or the ordinary temperature of steam, under the pressure of one atmosphere, i.e. at 212 deg. F. This fusible disc is so placed, that under the usual conditions it is accessible only to water having a temperature below its melting point; and whenever the water in the boiler falls below the proper level, immediate access is given to the steam, which at once melts the plug and escapes, blowing the whistle, and sounding an alarm. The other parts of this useful appliance are a metal tube, connected to the boiler by a stop-valve (which is locked when open), and carrying an air-chamber with a half-inch fusible disc, secured to its seat by an union with a whistle on its stem, and capable of bearing a pressure of 250 lbs.

The fusible plug has been applied in other ways, but with the disadvantage of complete emptying of the boiler, when requiring renewal—a manifest drawback to general use; an objection to which the arrangement here shown is not liable, as by closing the connecting cock—accessible only with the key—and unscrewing the whistle and union-joint, a fresh disc can be put in the seating, without emptying the boiler; and until this be done the whistle will continue to be sounded by the escaping steam. Thus not only is accident or injury prevented, but neglect infallibly detected by the principal or his representative keeping the key.

PRICES—Complete and ready for fixing, with One Dozen extra Fusible Discs. Discs 12s. per Dozen.	No. 1. All Brass, highly polished, very handsome and good. £5 0s. 0d.	No. 2. With Iron Pipe and Ball. £3 15s. 0d.

Where this shape cannot be fixed to the front, the Marine Pattern may be used

Extra Highly-Finished Pattern, called the "Saltaire" Pattern, so called because first used for the boilers of Sir Titus Salt & Sons, of Bradford; the pipe is 1¼ inch diameter, and the ball is massive, a costly and august appearance, with very heavy valve, all bright, £6 10s. 0d.

MARINE PATTERN.

This is the only invention that will give an alarm when the water is dangerous in Steamboat Boilers.

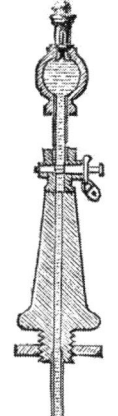 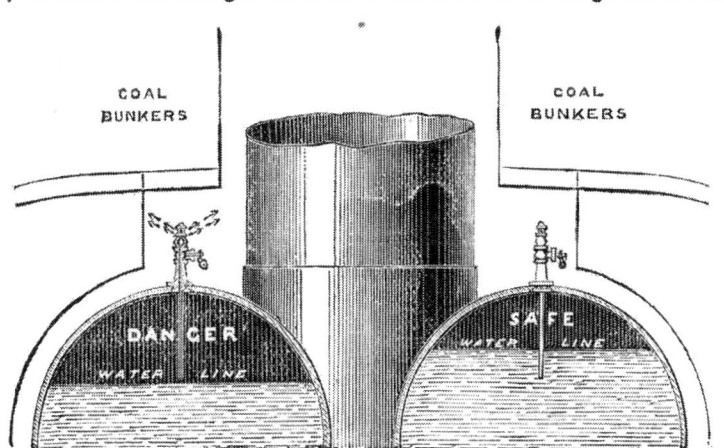 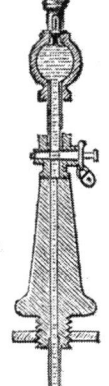

BOILERS OF THE STEAMSHIP, "GORDON CASTLE," OF GLASGOW,
SHOWING THE
ASHCROFT PATENT DETECTOR, AS FIXED FOR MARINE BOILERS.
As in use in the American Navy, and the Chief Steamship Companies.
One Month's Trial allowed. (See Testimonials.)

PRICES.

No. 1.—Brass Ball, and superior finished, with one dozen discs, ... £5	No. 2.—With Iron Ball, quite as good, but not so handsome or durable, with one dozen discs, ... £3 15s.

BAILEY'S GAUGE GLASSES FOR STEAM BOILERS.

BEST GREEN TINTED GLASS TUBES

One Half-penny per Inch.

½ inch, ⅝ inch, or ¾ inch diameter

ALL ARE GROUND ON THE ENDS

AND THE QUALITY UNEQUALLED.

Double 4 in. Safety Valve & Low Water Float
No. 33.

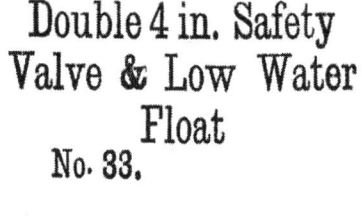

BAILEY'S HYDROSTATIC LEVEL,
FOR CIVIL & MECHANICAL ENGINEERS, SURVEYORS, BUILDERS, &c.,
FOR MEASURING LARGE DISTANCES.

This instrument will be found valuable by Railway Engineers, Manufacturers, &c.

PRICE, complete, with 6 feet of Tube, 35/-

This new and exceedingly useful instrument is constructed as follows:—Two Glass Tubes fitted in heavy Gun Metal Pedestals, with Cocks connected with a pipe as long as the distance to be levelled. One of the Tubes is filled with water till it will be seen in the other tube—the difference in the tubes gives the result of the level or plane.

Two 4 in. Valves, gun metal seats, with weights and levers, with one low water float, with brass plate and raised figures, with chain and flag float, as extensively used at the large iron works in Staffordshire, the Cleveland districts, &c.

Price, complete, ...	£8 10 0
With 3 in. Valves, ...	£6 10 0
With 2½ in. ,, ...	5 10 0

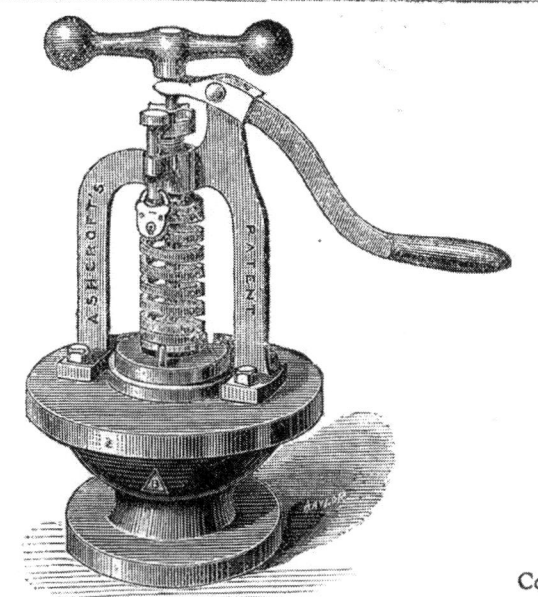

BAILEY AND ASHCROFT'S
PATENT NICKEL SEAT
"POP" SAFETY VALVE.

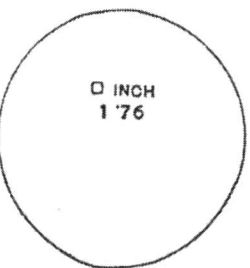

Area of Common Valve.

Area of Nickel "Pop" Valve.

Comparative Diagram, showing the Areas of the Common Valve when open, and the Nickel "Pop." Size of Valve, 3 inches.

DISTINGUISHING FEATURES.

1.—The seat of the Valve being of nickel bronze as hard as steel and as non-oxydisable as gold, corrosion is prevented.
2.—It lifts higher from its seat than any other Valve, and discharges as much as five Valves of the ordinary construction; when it discharges, the great rise of the Valve causes a great noise to be made, hence its name, the "Pop" Valve.
3.—The Valve may be moved whilst under pressure to test its condition.
4.—It can be locked up, and therefore cannot be tampered with.
5.—There are no levers, pins, or joints to interfere with its free action.
6.—It is excellently well made, so that full justice is done to the invention.

PRICES.

Diameter Inches.		£	s.	d.
2	FOR STEAM YACHTS AND PORTABLE ENGINES, 10 H.P.	4	4	0
3	STATIONARY BOILERS, SMALL LOCOMOTIVES, &c., 20 H.P.	5	10	0
4	DITTO, AND FOR LOCOMOTIVE MARINE BOILERS, &c., 60 H.P.	8	0	0

BAILEY'S
GOVERNMENT PATTERN
SAFETY VALVES.

(Bailey and Ashcroft's Patent.)

These consist of one Lever Safety Valve, and one Spring Safety Valve, locked up with Test Lever and Rotary Spindle for trying.

Price, complete, both 3-inch diameter,

£8 10 0.

Spring, Electro-plated with Nickel Silver, 4-inch Valves,

£12 0 0.

SAFETY VALVES

No. 40

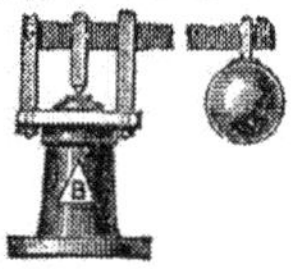

CAST-IRON SAFETY VALVES.

With Flange to bolt on the Boiler; with Wrought-Iron Lever, Gun Metal Valve and Seatings

1in. diameter	18/0
$1\frac{1}{2}$ „	26/0
2 „	35/0
3 „	52/0
4 „	75/0
5 „	95/0
6 „	103/6

Safety Valves, with Junction Flanges, same price as above

No. 40B.

DOUBLE SAFETY VALVES.

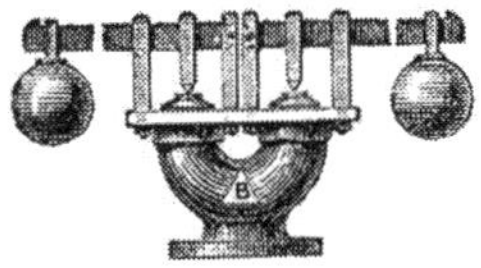

2in diameter	70/0
3 „	97/9
4 „	132/6
5 „	170/0
6 „	210/0

No. 46

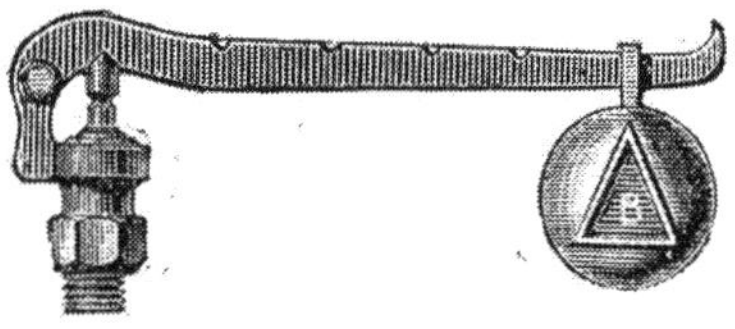

SMALL GUN METAL SAFETY VALVES,

With Lever and Weight to screw on the Boiler.

$\frac{1}{2}$in. diameter... ...	13/0
$1\frac{3}{4}$ „	20/0
2 „	30/0

AIR VALVES

FOR

Steam Chests, Drying Cylinders, &c.

$\frac{1}{2}$ in. diameter... ...	1/3
$\frac{3}{4}$ „	1/6
1 „	1/9
$1\frac{1}{2}$ „	2/0
2 „	

Every description of Valves and Clacks made to order, and prices quoted to drawing.

EXTRA STRONG

BEST GUN METAL UNION JOINTS,

FOR STEAM.

	s.	d.		s.	d.
$\frac{1}{4}$ inch ...	1	7	1 inch ...	4	0
$\frac{3}{8}$ inch ...	1	10	$1\frac{1}{4}$ inch ...	6	8
$\frac{1}{2}$ inch ...	2	6	$1\frac{1}{2}$ inch ...	9	0
$\frac{3}{4}$ inch ...	3	3	2 inch ...	16	0

A very useful Valve for many purposes,

Especially to prevent accident to Engine Cylinders from condensed water.

GREENHALGH'S

PATENT GUN METAL

ESCAPE VALVE,

For Engine Cylinders, Pipes, &c.,

WITH GRADUATED INDEX.

No. 45a.

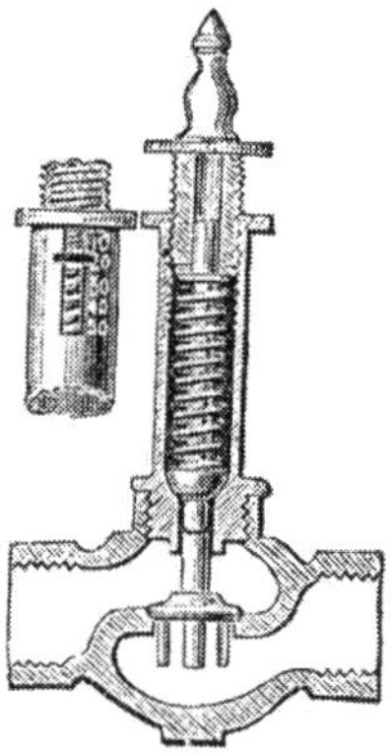

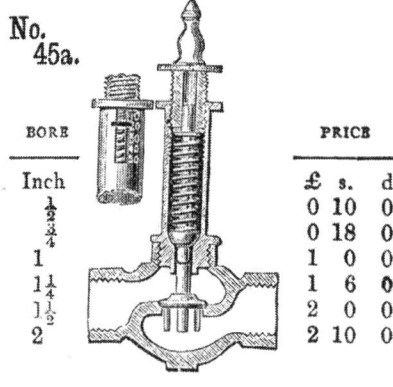

BORE	PRICE		
Inch	£	s.	d.
$\frac{1}{2}$	0	10	0
$\frac{3}{4}$	0	18	0
1	1	0	0
$1\frac{1}{4}$	1	6	0
$1\frac{1}{2}$	2	0	0
2	2	10	0

No. 145

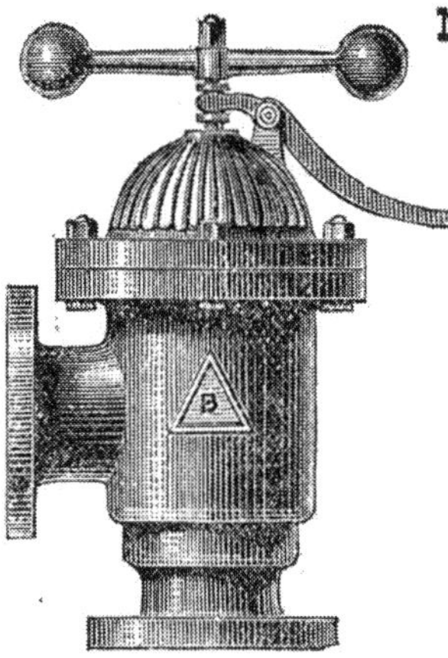

LOCK-UP SAFETY VALVE,

With Junction Flange on Iron, Cast and Gun Metal Fittings, with Nickel-Plated Spring and Adjustment inside Dome.

Diameter of Valve	2 inches ...	50/0
	3 inches ...	75/0
	4 inches ...	120/0
	5 inches ...	146/0
	6 inches ...	165/0

The above are also used for Escape Valves for Pumps, to prevent overpressure breaking the Pipes.

Important to Makers & Proprietors of Portable Boilers.

SAFETY VALVE AND SPRING BALANCE

Combined.

Price for 2in. Valve, all bright, highly polished, complete, £3 3s.

Very Liberal Discount to Wholesale Buyers.

No. 146

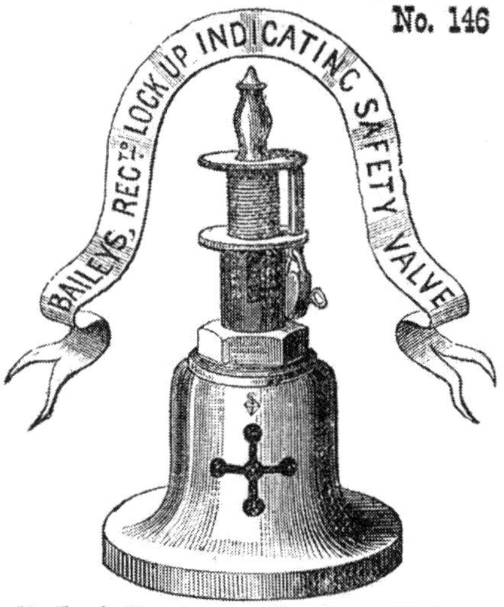

Bailey's Registered Lock-up Valves.

[From *The English Mechanic*, June 1868.]

This Valve is made all of gun metal, and is designed for portable engine, marine, and other Boilers. It will be seen that it combines the indications of the spring balance with the valve, so that it may be screwed down to blow off at any pressure. In addition to being useful and good, being made entirely of gun metal, highly polished, it is an ornamental addition to any boiler. The Valve is being rapidly introduced by the makers, Messrs. J. Bailey and Co., of the Albion Brass and Steam Gauge Works, Salford, Lancashire.

No. 147.

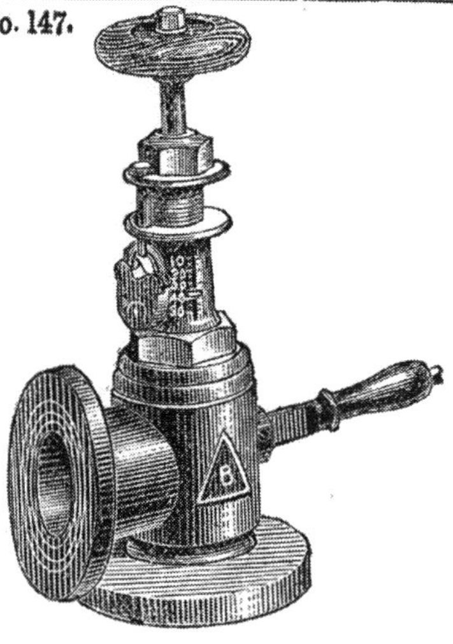

SAFETY VALVE AND SPRING BALANCE

Combined, with side Flange for carrying away waste Steam.

	£	s.	d.
Valve all Gun Metal, 2 inch diameter complete,	3	12	0
Iron Body and Gun Metal Fittings	2	10	0

Both Inlet and Outlet Flanges $7\frac{1}{2}$-inch diameter.

No. 148

BALL CLACK VALVES.

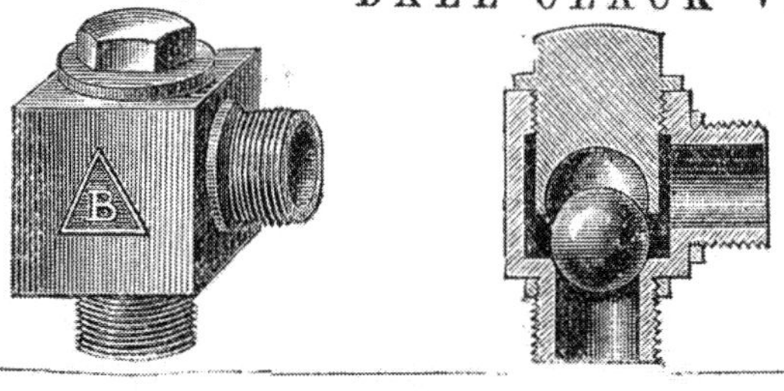

$\frac{1}{2}$ inch	5/6
$\frac{3}{4}$ inch	7/6
1 inch	8/6
$1\frac{1}{4}$ inch	13/0
$1\frac{1}{2}$ inch	15/6
2 inch	23/6

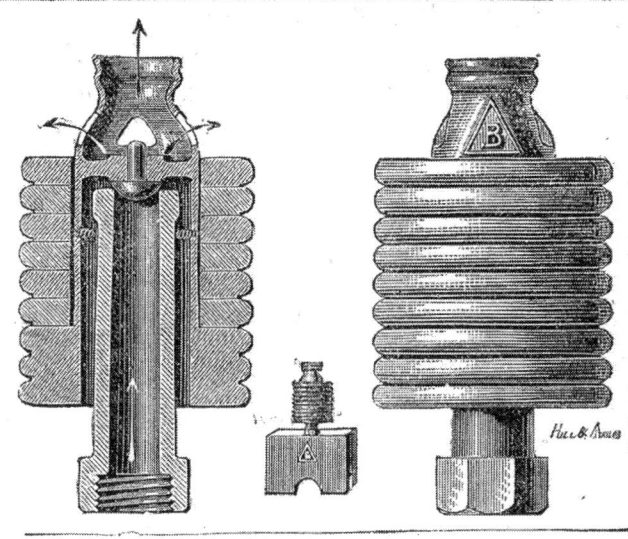

Bailey's Kitchen Boiler Safety Valve.

The great number of kitchen boiler explosions which occur every winter through the frost, very often ending in a fatal manner, has caused a demand for this Dead-weight Valve, which is recommended strongly by Mr. Fletcher, the Chief of the Manchester Steam Users' Association. Stoppage of the pipes from many other causes than ice, have caused many fatal explosions; and in all cases where boilers are used for circulating hot water, if a safety valve is not fixed on it, having in view the many deaths which occur every winter, it seems very much like what is called criminal negligence. Several deaths from this cause have occurred in our own neighbourhood of Manchester during the past few years, many of which we have investigated, and we affirm in the strongest possible manner, that every death would have been prevented if safety valves had been adopted.

10s 6d each.

Bailey's Feed Water Regulator,

For Boilers having a head of water of greater pressure than the Steam; for low pressure boilers.

Price £2 2s. each.

SUITABLE FOR ½ in. PIPE—NOT INCLUDING PIPE.

RULE.—For every lb. pressure carried, the head of water should be over 2 feet 3 inches in height; for instance, if 20 lbs. pressure is carried, the height of the water cistern should be 50 feet or more above the boiler.

French Pattern Vertical Plug Hot Water Cock.

No. 69.   Bore,

CAST IRON COCKS.

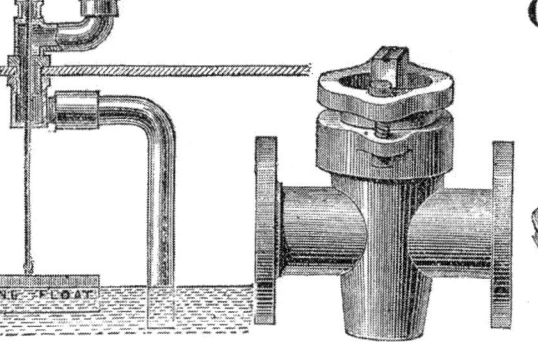

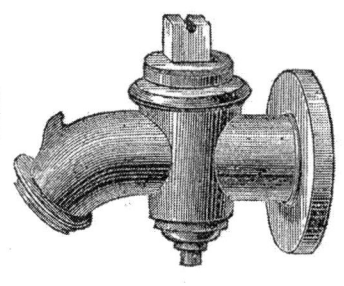

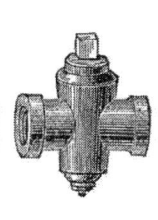

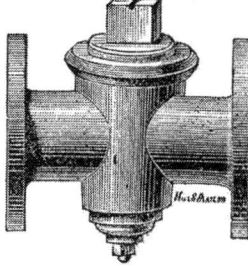

	Inches,	⅜	½	¾	1	1¼	1½	2	2¼	3	3½	4
503—Iron Gas Main Cocks,	... ...	2/-	2/6	3/-	4/-	7/-	9/-	14/6				
503B—Iron Gas Main Cocks, with brass plugs		3/7	4/5	5/5	7/10	13/3	17/3	27/3				
502B—Iron Bib Cocks, for Water		...	...	...	...	...	7/6	12/-	18/9	21/-		36/9
504—Iron Flange Cocks, for Water		...	...	...	...	...	6/9	11/3	18/-	22/6	30/-	39/-
501—Cast Iron Gland Cocks, for Steam		...	...	...	...	...	15/-	26/3	37/6	42/-		56/3
502A—Iron Bib Cocks, with Brass Plugs		...	...	...	...	...	18/-	21/9	30/-	42/-		63/-
504A—Iron Flange Cocks, with Brass Plugs		...	...	...	...	...	16/6	20/3	28/6	40/6		60/-

For Gland and other Cocks, see Steam Cock List.

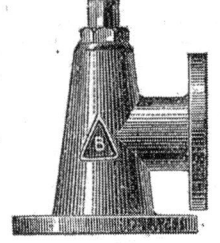

No. 801.
Inverted Plug Blow-off Tap.

Bore In.	All Iron £ s. d.	Brass Plug £ s. d.	All Brass £ s. d.
1	...	...	0 18 0
1½	...	...	1 10 0
2	1 7 0	2 5 0	3 4 0
2½	1 12 0	2 15 0	4 0 0
3	1 18 0	3 7 0	4 19 6
3½	2 4 0	4 4 0	6 2 6
4	2 12 0	4 18 0	7 9 0
5	3 6 0	6 10 0	10 12 6
6	4 0 0	8 10 0	14 12 0

No. 802—Stop Cock for Bow Key, Screw Bottom.

½	¾	1	1¼	1½	2 inch.
3/6	5/-	8/6	12/6	13/6	30/-

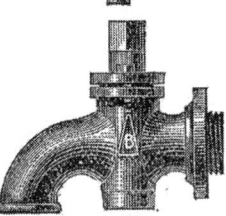

No. 803—Gland Bib Cock, with Flange and Screwed Male End.

½	¾	1	1¼	1½	2 inch.
4/-	5/6	9/-	13/-	20/-	32/-

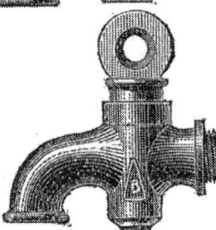

No. 804—Bib Stop Cock for Bow Key, Screw Bottom.

½	¾	1	1¼	1½	2 inch.
3/6	5/-	8/6	12/6	18/6	30/-

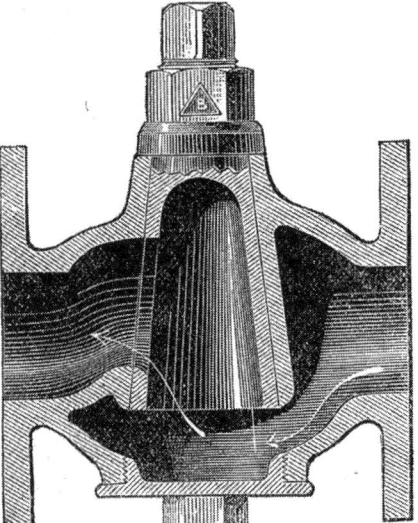

No. 805.
Patent Improved Steam Cock.

¼	⅜	½	¾ inch.
3/3	3/9	5/6	7/9

1	1¼	1½	2 inch.
11/6	17/-	25/6	40/-

With Flanges

1½	2	2½	3 inch.
35/-	50/-	67/6	90/-

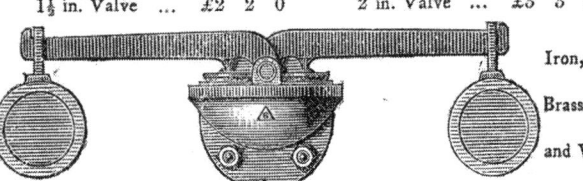

No. 807—Bailey's Double Bracket Safety Valve.

1½ in. Valve ... £2 2 0   2 in. Valve ... £3 3 0

Iron, with Brass Seats and Valve.

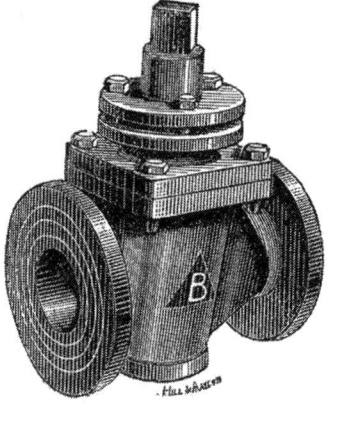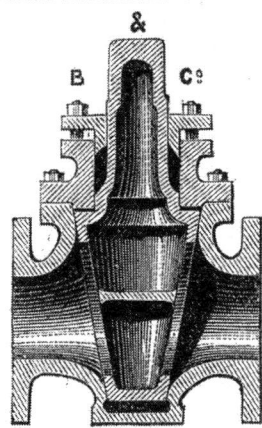

No. 806—Bailey's Double Gland Mud Cocks,
As recommended by the Steam Boiler Associations.

Bore	£ s. d.	Bore	£ s. d.	Iron Bodies Gun Metal Plug Bore	£ s. d.
1	1 15 0	2½	5 15 0	2	2 16 0
1½	2 5 0	3	8 0 0	2½	3 10 0
2	4 10 0	4	13 10 0	3	4 6 0
				4	10 16 0

The above are same price, Angle Flange Pattern

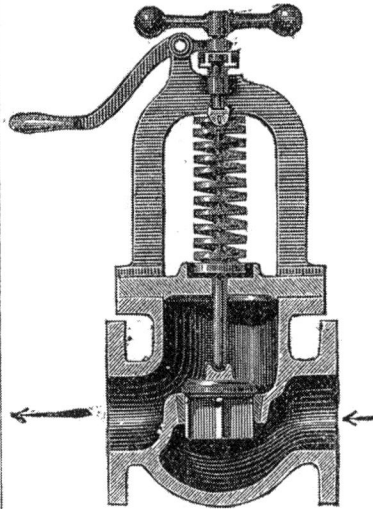

No. 808.
Patent Pump Escape Valve,

For Surplus Water from Feed Pump, for fixing on Overflows, with Nickel-plated Spring.

2 in.	50/-	5 in	130/-
2½ „	60/-	6 „	160/-
3 „	75/-	8 „	220/-
4 „	110/-	10 „	300/-
		12 in.	400/-

These are lower in price if supplied with Lever and Weight.

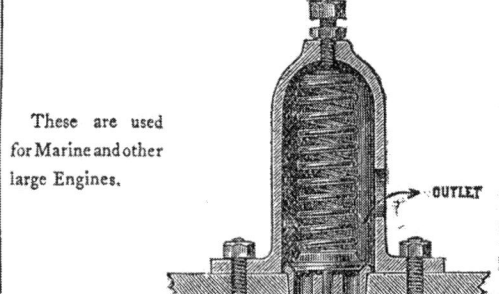

These are used for Marine and other large Engines.

No. 809.
Dome Escape Valves,

With Seating to drive into Cylinder Lids.

Dome Cast Iron, turned bright, Gun Metal Screw and Lock Nut, Nickel-plated Steel Springs. Valves, 3 inch diameter, £4 each.

Special Cocks in best Gun Metal, made to Engineers' own patterns, at low quotations. Our facilities and Special Tools enable us to do this very often much better than Engineers can who make their own Brass Work at a loss to themselves.

Bayley & Bailey's Patent Steam Valves.

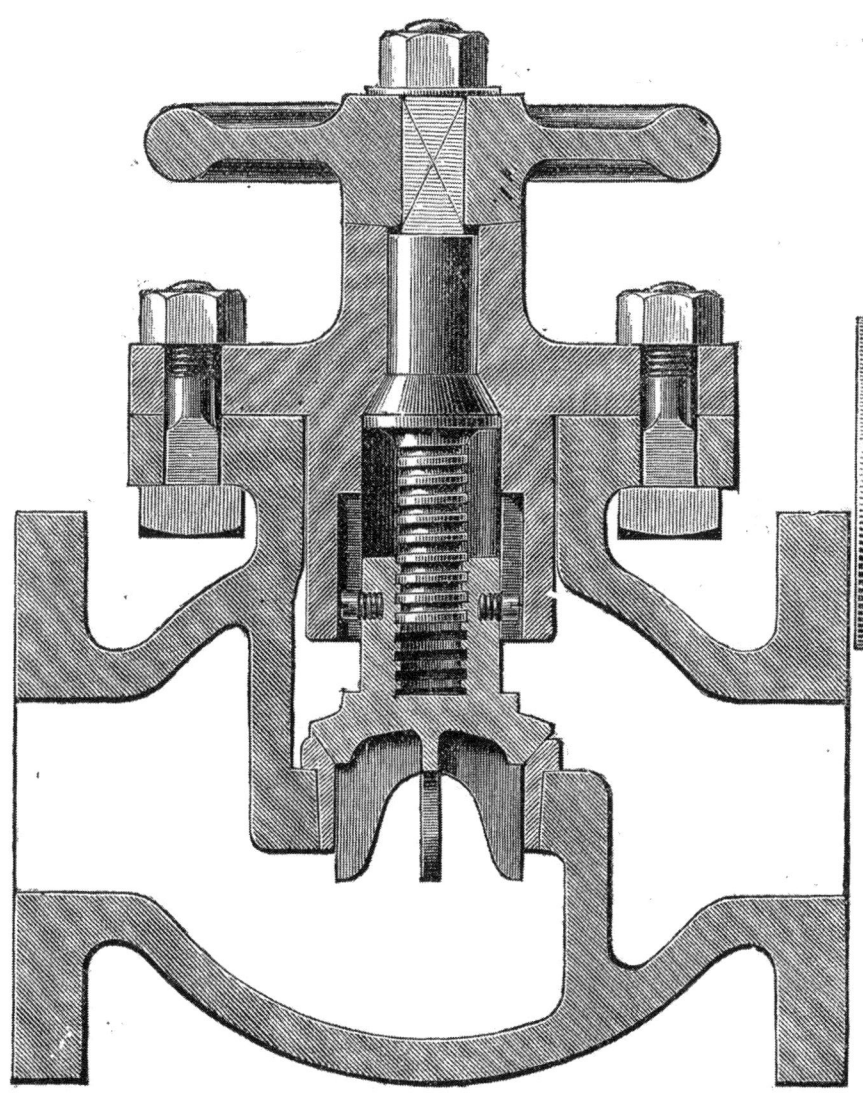

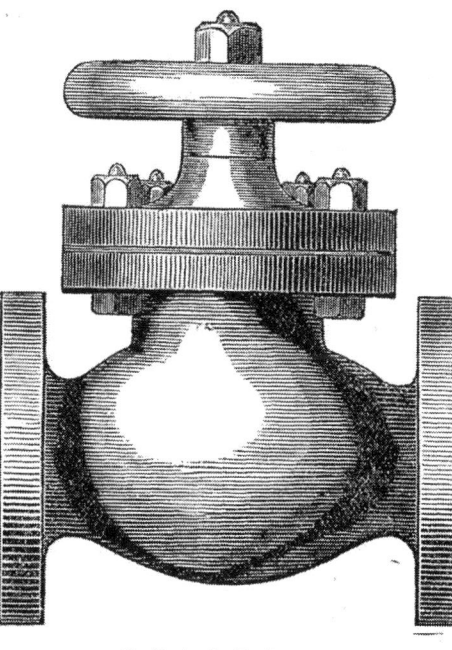

PRICES:

Iron Bodies; Gun Metal Spindle and Seatings,

Bore			£	s.	d.
2 in.	...	...	1	7	6
2½ ,,	...	...	1	18	6
3 ,,	...	...	2	7	6
4 ,,	...	...	3	10	0
5 ,,	...	...	4	15	0
6 ,,	...	...	6	5	0
8 ,,	...	...	9	5	0
10 ,,	...	...	13	10	0
12 ,,	...	...	17	15	0

No. 30 C Screwed Cap Gland Cock.   No. 30 B Extra Strong Gland Cock.

GLAND STEAM COCKS.

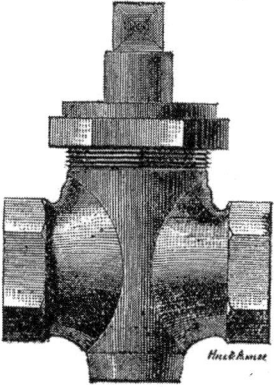
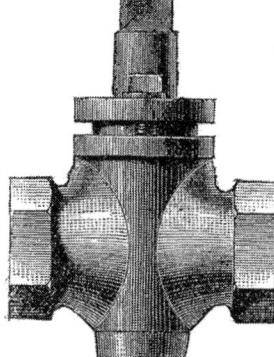

Screwed to Bore	¼	⅜	½	¾	1	1¼	1½	2
No. 30 B	3/4	4/2	5/-	7/6	12/-	17/6	26/6	40/-
Screwed to Bore	¼	⅜	½	¾	1	1¼	1½	2
No. 30 C	2/8	3/4	4/-	6/-	9/6	13/6	21/-	32/-

Heavy Cocks made to order from our patterns at 1/4 per lb. subject to the fluctuations of the market.

BAYLEY AND BAILEY'S
PATENT STEAM STOP VALVES.

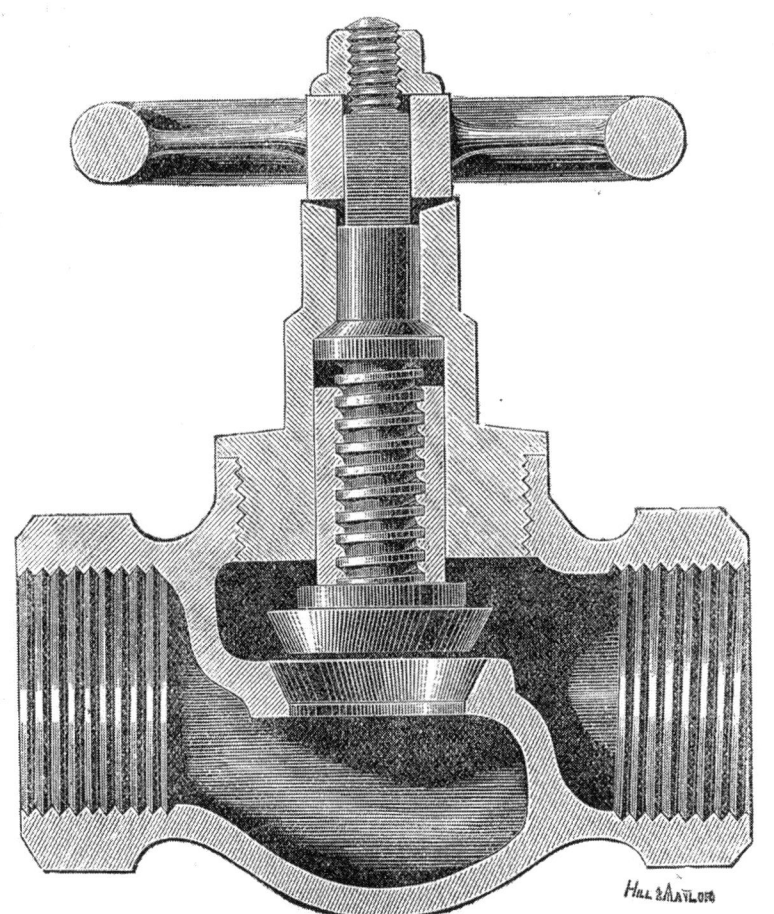

The ordinary Stuffing Box entirely dispensed with.

More durable, less wear and tear, no "drip," or trouble in packing.

This simple invention, already in extensive use, meets a great want. No explanation is requisite besides the cut, the non-liability to leak, the broad seat, the general design, and the first-class metal and workmanship, have made it an extensive favourite. Although double the wear, prices vary little from the ordinary valves. All screwed gas-pipe pitch.

Screwed In.	$\frac{1}{4}$	$\frac{3}{8}$	$\frac{1}{2}$	$\frac{3}{4}$	1	$1\frac{1}{4}$	$1\frac{1}{2}$	$1\frac{3}{4}$	2	$2\frac{1}{4}$	$2\frac{1}{2}$	3
Price each,	3/6	4/3	5/	7/6	10/	12/6	17/	25/	30/	35/	40/	60/
,, per doz.	41/	50/	59/	89/	119/	149/	202/	298/	358/	418/	478/	718/

It will be observed that when these Valves are ordered by the Dozen there is an advantage to the Buyer.

Valves made on this principle for Water in various shapes. See Special List.

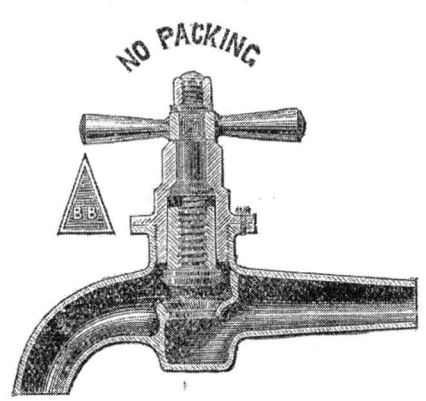

Bailey's First-Class Valves,

WITH GUN METAL SEATS & SPINDLES.

No 1

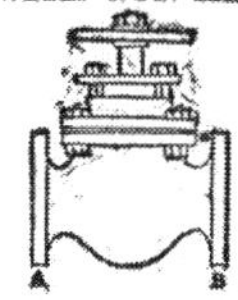

No 2

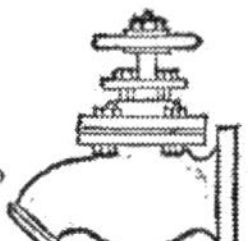

Bore	Diam of flange.	Length from A to B	Prices
IN.			£ s. d.
2	6½	9	1 5 0
2½	7	9½	1 15 0
3	7½	10	2 3 0
3½	8	12	2 12 0
4	9	14	3 3 0
5	10	16	4 6 0
6	12	18	5 12 0
7	13	18	6 18 0
8	14	20	8 7 0
9	15½	22	10 0 0
10	17	23	12 2 0
12	19	26	16 2 0

No 3

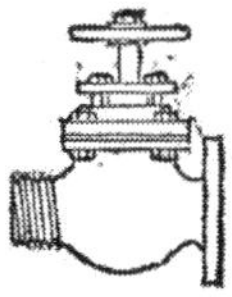

VALVE FOR HOSE PIPES.

For list of Hose Pipe and the Manchester Fire Pumps see index.

Bore	2	2½	3
Price	30/0	36/6	46/0

No 4

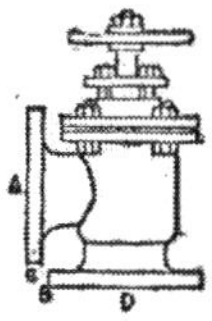

After cleansing a boiler and making the joints, use Bailey's Test Pumps. See index.

No. 4 same price as Nos. 1 and 2.

No 5

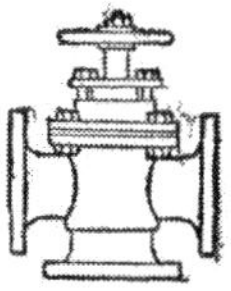

Bore	2	2½	3	4	5	6
Price	34/6	46/	57/6	82/	110/	140/

Bore	7	8	9	10	12
Price	172/6	207/	247/	293/6	400/

No 6

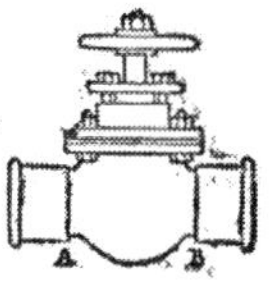

Same price as Nos. 1 and 2.

No 7

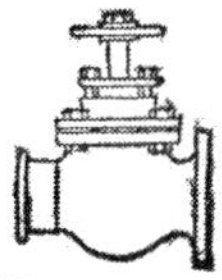

Same price as Nos. 1 and 2.

BAILEY'S FIRST-CLASS

ALBION BLOW-OFF COCKS,

All Gun Metal and First-Class.

No 52

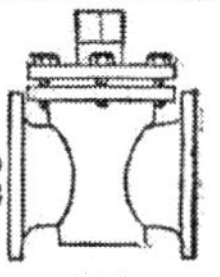

Bore	1	1¼	1½	2	2½	3	4
Price	18/	23/	32/6	50/	98/	140/	
Iron Bodies & Gun Metal Plugs							
Price	14/	17/6	21/6	40/6	46/	57/6	74/9

No 53

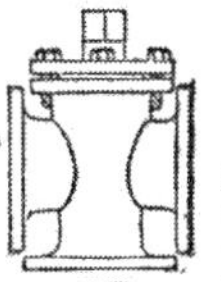

Gun Metal.

Bore	1	1¼	1½	2	2½	3
Price	20/9	26/6	37/6	57/6	112/	160/
Iron Bodies & Gun Metal Plugs.						
Price	16/3	20/3	24/	32/9	46/	66/

No 54

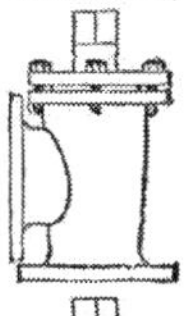

Gun Metal.

Bore	1	1¼	1½	2	2½	3
Price	18/	23/	32/6	50/	98/	140/
Iron Bodies & Gun Metal Plugs.						
Price	14/	17/6	21/6	28/9	40/6	57/6

No 55

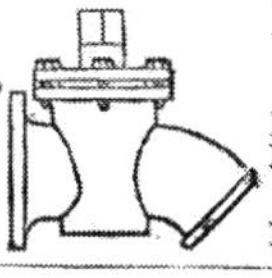

Gun Metal.

Bore	1	1¼	1½	2	2½	3
Price	17/3	22/	31/	47/6	93/	133/
Iron Bodies & Gun Metal Plugs.						
Price	13/3	16/6	20/6	28/3	38/6	55/

BAILEY'S STEAM VALVES,

STRONG GUN METAL.

21.

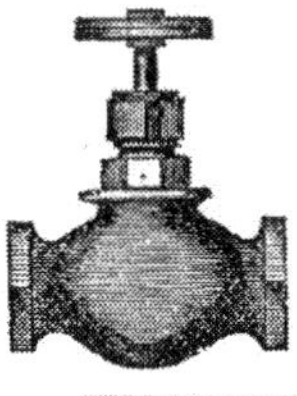

22.

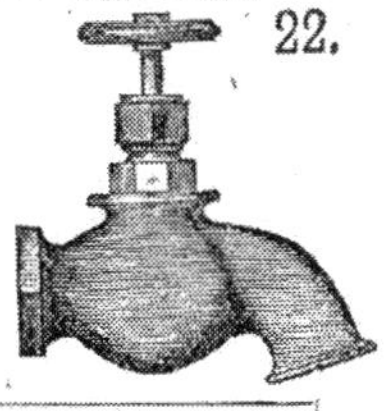

Bore	Price	Bore	Price
INCH	£ s. d.	INCH	£ s. d.
⅜	0 4 0	1¼	0 11 0
½	0 4 6	1½	0 14 0
¾	0 6 0	1¾	0 18 0
1	0 8 6	2	1 5 0

No. 21 are made according to Bailey's Patent Fast Valve arrangement.

½ inch......4/0
¾ inch......5/0
1 inch......7/0

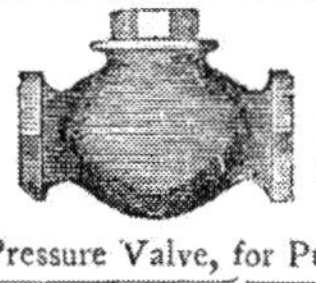

1¼ inch...... 9/0
1½ inch......11/6
2 inch......18/6

Back Pressure Valve, for Pumps, &c.

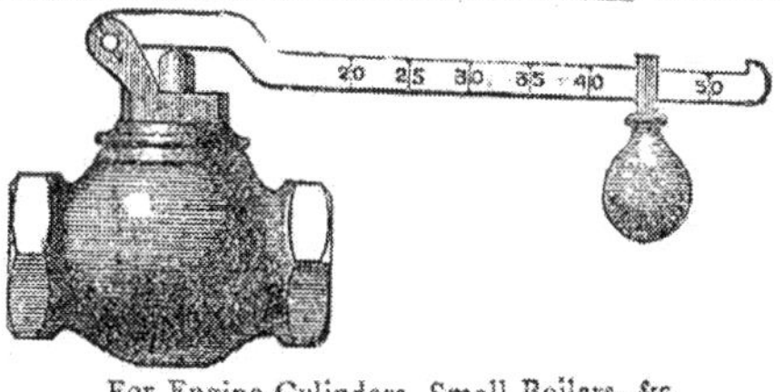

For Engine Cylinders, Small Boilers, &c.

45. Gun Metal Escape Valve.

½ inch...... 9/0	1 inch......16/0	1½ inch......27/0
¾ inch......12/0	1¼ inch......22/0	2 inch......42/0

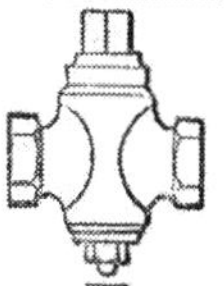

Gun Metal Main Steam Tap, Extra Strong

No. 29

Bore	¼	⅜	½	¾	1	1¼	1½	2in.
Price	2/10	3/6	4/	5/9	10/	15/	21/	32/6

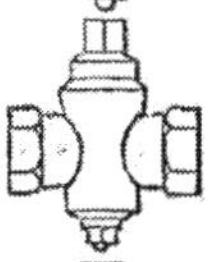

No. 29a

Gun Metal Main Steam Tap.

Bore	¼	⅜	½	¾	1	1¼	1½	2in.
Price	2/3	2/9	3/3	4/6	8/6	12/	17/6	26/

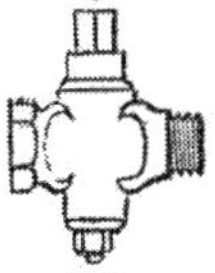

No. 29b

Gun Metal, London Pattern, Steam Tap.

Bore	¼	⅜	½	¾	1	1¼	1½	2in.
ROUGH								
Price	2/9	3/3	4/	6/6	10/	15/	20/	38/
POLISHED								
Price	3/3	3/9	4/6	7/6	12/	18/	23/6	44/9

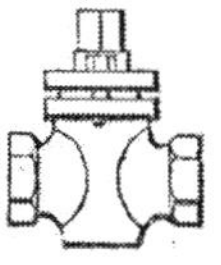

No. 30

Gun Metal Gland Steam Tap, Extra Strong

Bore	¼	⅜	½	¾	1	1¼	1½	2in.
Price	3/4	4/2	5/	7/6	12/	17/6	26/6	40/

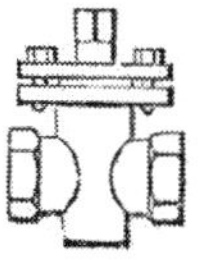

No. 30b

Gun Metal Gland Steam Tap.

Bore	¼	⅜	½	¾	1	1¼	1½	2in.
Price	2/8	3/4	4/	6/	9/6	13/6	21/	32/

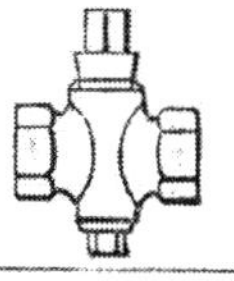

No. 29c

Gun Metal, London Pattern, Steam Tap.

Bore	½	⅜	½	¾	1	1¼	1½	2in.
ROUGH								
Price	2/9	3/3	4/	6/6	10/	15/	20/	38/
POLISHED								
Price	3/3	3/9	4/6	7/6	12/6	18/	23/6	44/9

Bailey's New Junction Valve & Safety Valve combined.

No. 44.

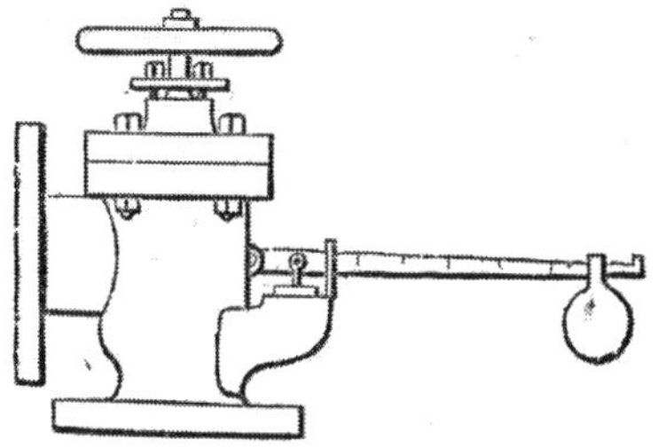

Bore of Valve.	Bore of Safety Valve.	Diam. of Flange	Price
	INCH		£ s. d.
2	1½	6½	2 17 6
3	2½	7½	4 12 0
4	3	9	6 4 3
5	4	10	8 1 0
6	5	12	10 1 3

This useful design of Safety Valve is rapidly being introduced; and it does not require anything at all to prove to Boiler Makers and users of Boilers the advantage of having as few holes and as few joints as possible in a boiler; these, of course, only requiring one hole where under ordinary circumstances two would be required.

Bailey's Patent Gun Metal Steam Valve

No. 21.

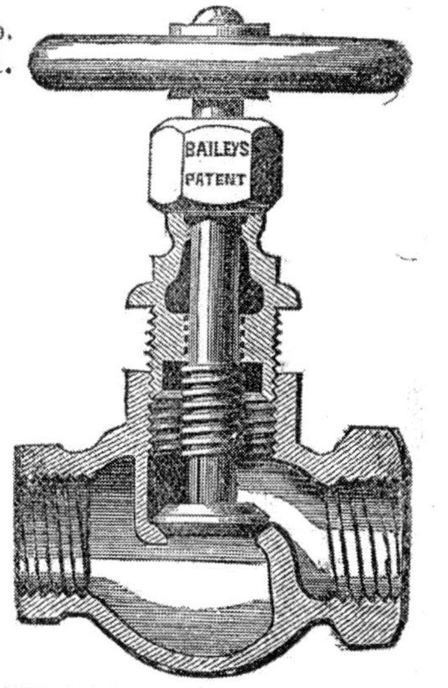

BORE	PRICE	BORE	PRICE
INCH	£ s d	INCH	£ s d
⅜	0 4 0	1¼	0 11 6
½	0 4 6	1½	0 14 0
¾	0 6 0	1¾	0 18 0
1	0 8 6	2	1 2 6

The principle of this Valve is that which is so well known in connection with Bailey's Patent Water Gauge Cocks—(*See page* 10.)

1—In consequence of the Valve being fast on the spindle, and the metal being of the best quality, and very hard, any sediment that may become deposited on the face of the Valve-seat becomes ground to powder by the action of the Valve, which, when closed, has a circular vertical motion: such is not the case when the Valve is loose on the spindle.

2—When the Valve requires grinding, the gland-nut is simply to be raised out of the body-casting, and thus disengaging the screw, (as shown in the illustration), it can be ground without removing it from its place. This is so important and so apparent that mechanical men appreciate the improvement at once.

3—In consequence of the Valve being double-faced, steam cannot get to the packing, and new packing can be inserted whilst in action.

4—The Valves are of the best Gun Metal, and the prices are the same as for the ordinary Valves.

Valves of any other shape to drawing made on this principle.

FARRON'S PATENT SELF-ADJUSTING
HIGH-PRESSURE STEAM & WATER TAP.

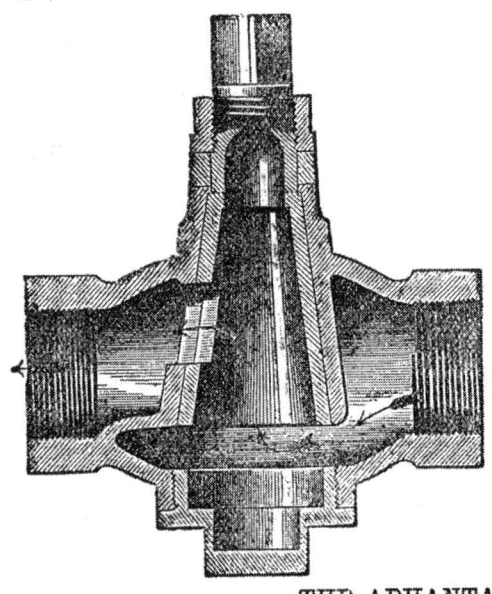
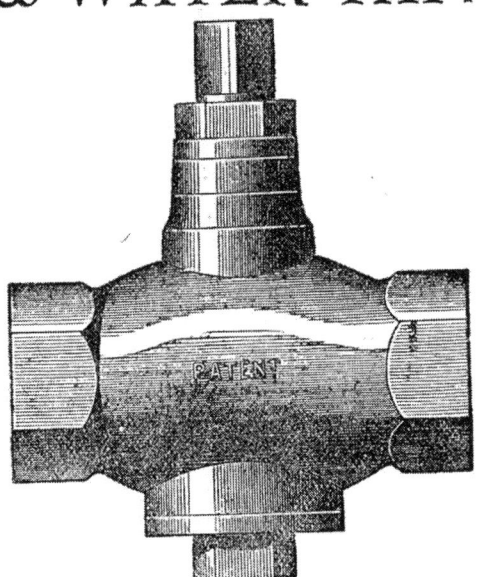

LIST OF PRICES:

	s.	d.
¼ inch	3	0
⅜ ,,	3	6
½ ,,	5	0
¾ ,,	7	6
1 ,,	12	6
1¼ ,,	18	6
1½ ,,	27	6
2 ,,	41	6

To thoroughly open and shut, the Tap must be turned half round.

THE ADVANTAGES OF THIS TAP ARE AS FOLLOWS—

1st.—It is not so liable to get fast, as the Plug and Barrel are of one equal temperature, which is maintained by the steam passing in a cavity between the body of the Tap and the Barrel, which is a shield to the Barrel from the atmosphere.

2nd.—There is no action of the steam on the ground face of the Plug, as the pressure is at all times inside the Plug, which presses the Plug inside the Barrel and keeps the bearing good without any other appliance. No packing is required, which renders the Tap not liable to derangement.

3rd.—The construction of the Tap necessarily makes it very strong, so as to resist any strain that might be caused with the pipes contracting or being out of square.

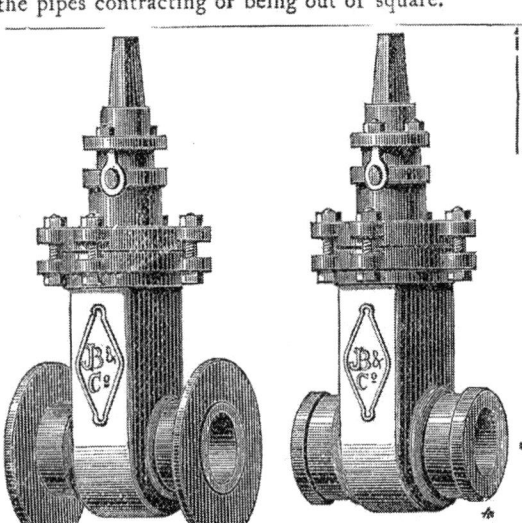
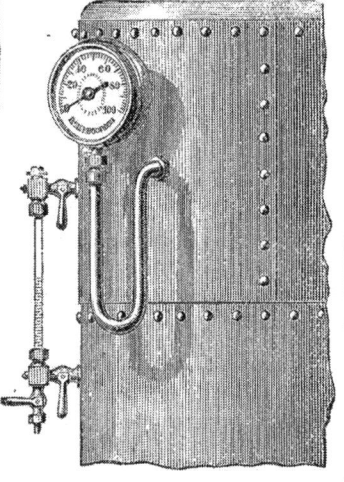
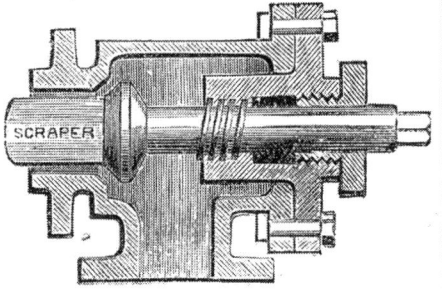

Bailey's Iron Main Sluice Valves,
With Gun Metal Valve Faces and Seats.

PRICES.

2	2½	3	4	5	6
36/-	44/6	53/3	71/-	91/6	110/-
7	8	9	10	11	12
133/-	162/-	194/-	215/6	251/-	285/-

Special contracts for very large quantities.

Estimate for Fittings for Small Boilers.

	£	s.	d.
1 No. 6 Gauge, page 5,	1	5	0
1 Set Water Gauge Cocks, No. 4,		15	0
1 Safety Valve, 1in., No. 46, page 13,		13	0
	£2	13	0
Cash discount 2½ o/o		1	6
	£2	11	6

Prices quoted for Brass Fittings to Drawing.

Bailey's Patent Scavenger Mud Cock

The principle of this consists in the valve face being very broad, and being fast on the spindle, every time it is closed, if there be any sediment deposited on the seat, it is ground to powder.

The Scraper, which is fast to the spindle of the valve, effectually, and in the most simple manner, prevents the valve becoming inoperative through sediment.

The satisfaction these Mud Cocks give to all who use them is such, that they recommend them in the highest terms.

PRICES.
With Cast Iron body, Gun Metal spindle and seating.

1½-inch	30/0	3 inch	50/0
2 ,,	35/0	3½ ,,	65/0
2½ ,,	42/0	4 ,,	75/0

BAILEY'S Floating Cistern Steam Traps,
No. 901.

It will be observed that when the floating cistern becomes full of water it sinks, thus opening the bottom end of the pipe through which the water is forced by the pressure of the steam. There is one peculiar advantage in this trap, and that is the facility in which it can be placed at a low level, and the water forced up a few feet after it has left the trap. The large ones will force the water several feet above it, thus giving a constant supply of hot water, which in small quantities may be found useful. The air-valve allows cold air to escape.

No. 1, cover 16 inches in diameter,
and   inches deep   ... £2 12 0

No. 2, cover 12 inches in diameter,
and   inches deep   ...   2 2 0

HORIZONTAL THREE-WAY COCKS,
With Gland Packing Iron Body and Gun Metal Plug.

2 in.	£2	15 0
2½ ,, ...	3	15 0
3 ,, ...	4	7 6
4 ,, ...	5	10 0

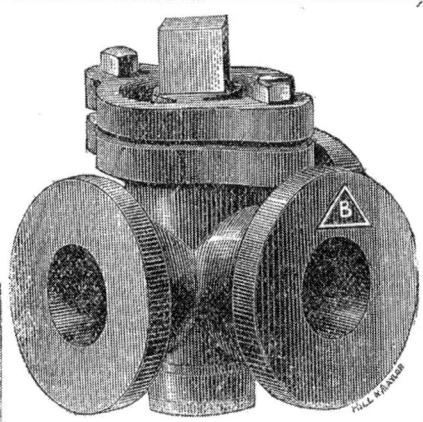

HEAVY COCKS,
All Gun Metal,

At   per lb., according to price of copper.

No. 158.
PLUNGER PUMPS.
For heavy pressure,
Cast Iron, with gun metal Plunger and Fittings

3 in. ...	£7 10 0	4½ in. ...	£17 10 0
3½ ,, ...	9 10 0	5 ,, ...	22 0 0
4 ,, ...	15 0 0		

No. 159.
Stoneware Pumps for Acids.

1½ in. ...	£3 12 6	4 in.	£7 10 0
2 ,, ...	4 7 6	6 ,, ...	8 15 0
3 ,, ...	5 18 9		

These Pumps are suitable for heavy lifts, feeding boilers, &c.

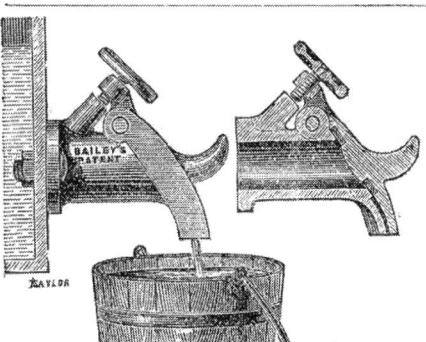

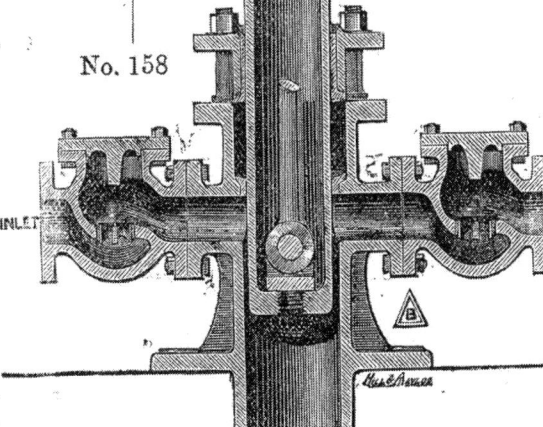

No. 158

BAILEY'S PATENT
"LID VALVE" STOP COCK.
2 inches bore, 12s. 6d. each, complete, with RUBBER VALVE.

It will be seen that this Valve is exceedingly cheap, simple, and effective; and whenever the valve leaks, a new ring can be inserted, and the valve made equal to new.

BAILEY'S SLUICE VALVES, &c.

Air Valve for Blast Furnaces, 9 in. diam., £9 9 0. No. 1,116.

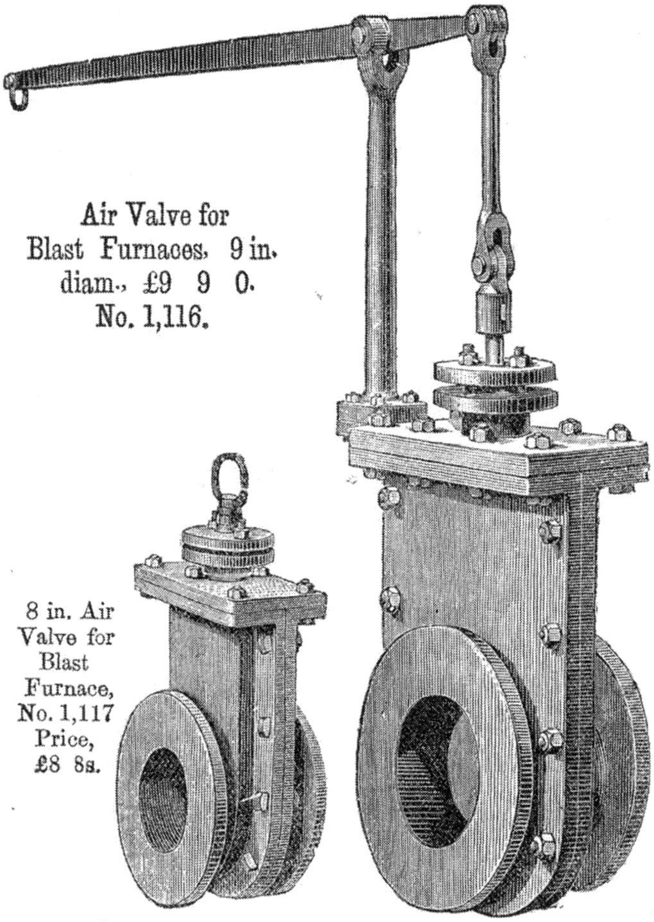

8 in. Air Valve for Blast Furnace, No. 1,117 Price, £8 8s.

Water Valves.

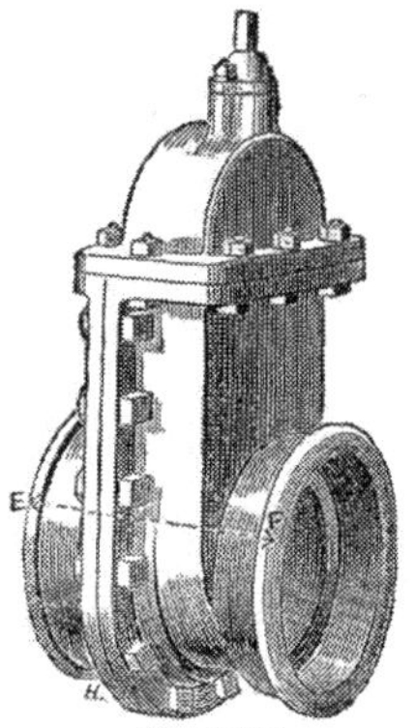

No. 1,111

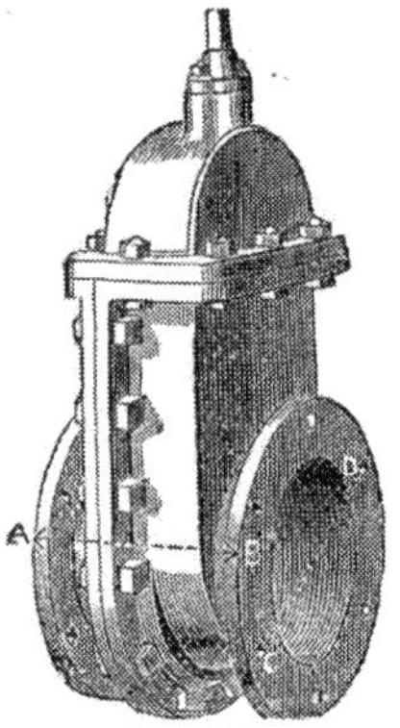

No. 1,112

Size of Bore of Valve	Length from Face to Face of Flanges over all from A to B	Diameter of Flanges	Diameter of circle through centre of bolt holes from C to D.	Number of holes in Flanges	Size of holes in Flanges	Length over ends of Sockets from E to F	Depth of Sockets	£	s.	d.
Inches	Inches	Inches	Inches		Inches	Inches	Inches			
2	7½	6½	4¾	4	5-8	9	2½			
2½	8	7	5¼	4	5-8	10	2½			
3	8	8½	6½	4	11-16	12	3			
4	10	10	8	4	11-16	13	3¾			
5	10	10½	8½	4	3-4	13	4			
6	11	12	9½	6	13-16	13	4			
7	11	14½	12	6	13-16	14	4			
8	12	15½	13	6	⅞	15	4½			
9	13	17	14	6	1	16	4½			
10	13	18	15	6	1	17	4½			
12	14	20	17	6	1⅛	18	5			

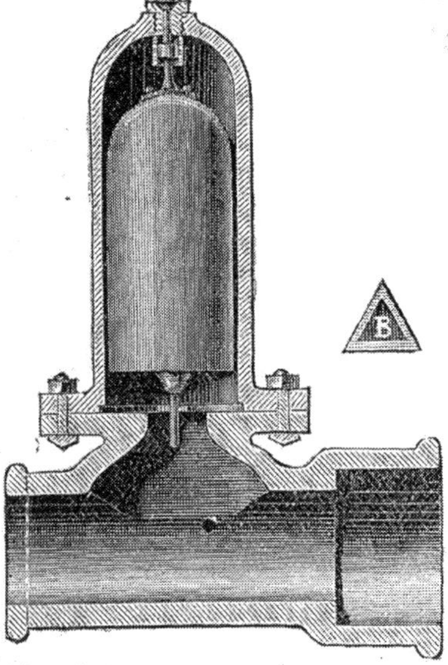

No. 1,116.

BAILEY'S

Water Main Air Escape Valve,

With Cast Brass Float, and Trap, and Valve, in Cast Iron Case, with Sockets or Flanges made to order only, complete

4-in.	... ...	£5 10 0
5 ,,	.. ...	6 17 6
6 ,,	... ...	8 8 0

Specialities for Managers of Water Works made to order.

Gas Sluice Valves.

No. 1,113

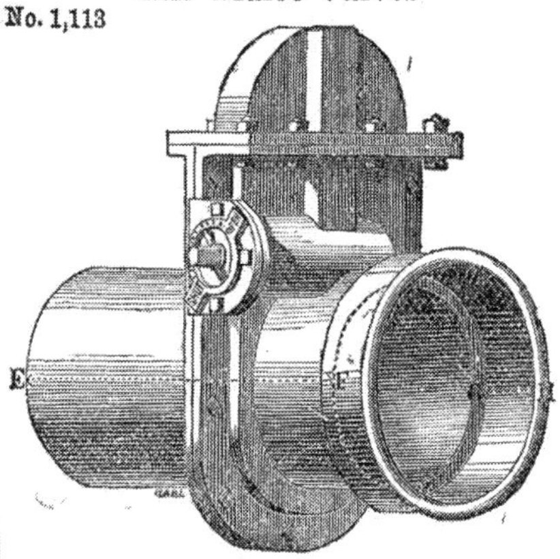

Spigot & Fawcet.

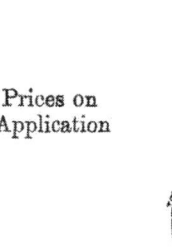

Prices on Application

Gas Valves.

No. 1,114 With Flanges.

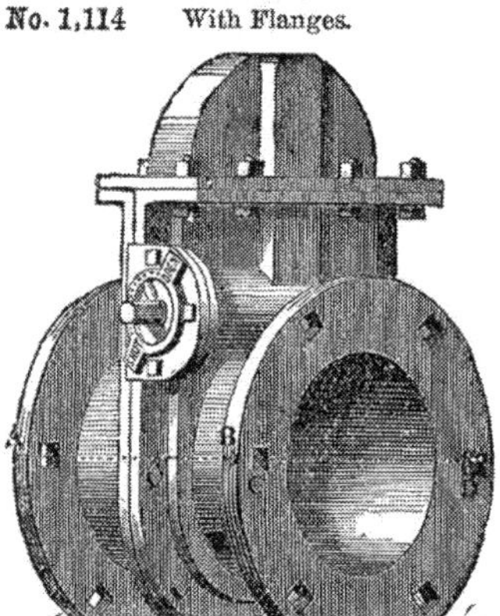

BAILEY'S Equilibrium Throttle Valves for Steam Engines.

No. 1,115 2 in.	£4	0	0
2½	5	0	0
3	6	0	0
3½	7	0	0
4	8	0	0
5	10	0	0
6	12	0	0
8	16	0	0
10	20	0	0
12	24	0	0

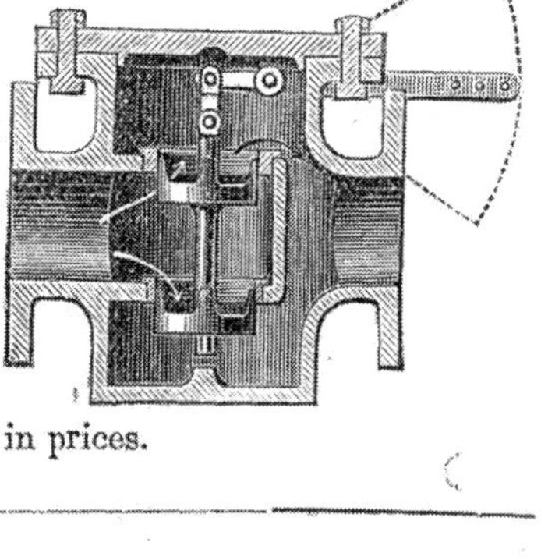

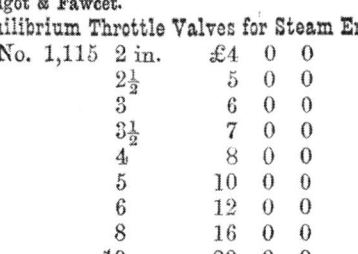

These are prepared for levers, but levers are not included in prices.

No. 1

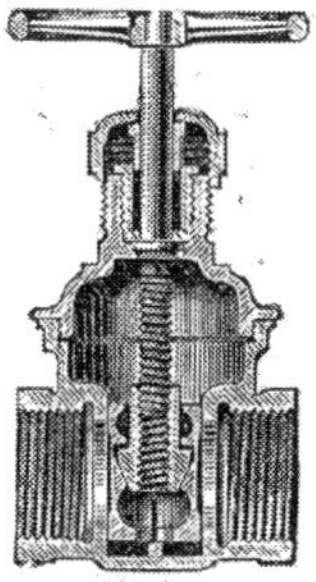

PEET'S PATENT VALVE TAPS.

Gun Metal Peet Valves.

No. 2

No. 3

No. 4

No. 5

No. 6

No. 7

No. 8

No. 8A

No. 9

No. 10

No. 11

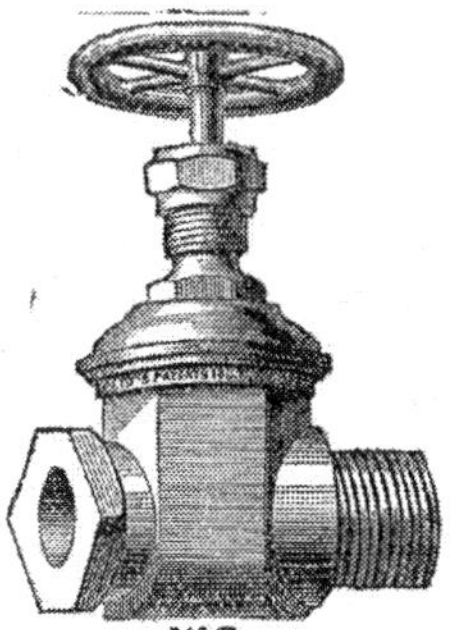

Cast Iron Peet Valves (with Gun Metal Wearing Parts and Faced Flanges.)

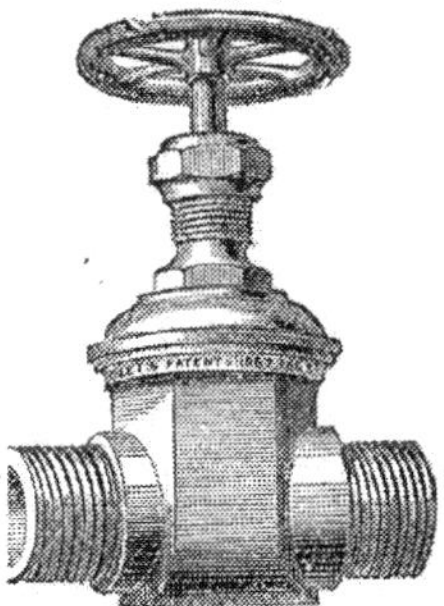

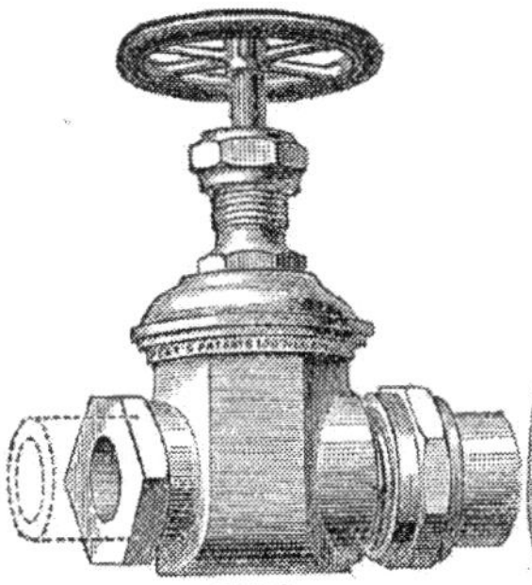

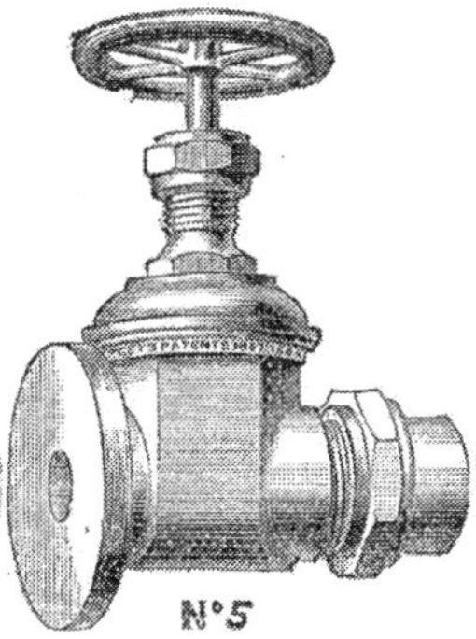

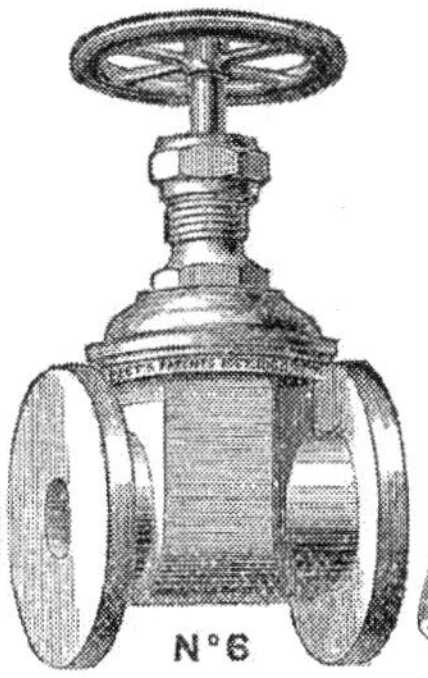

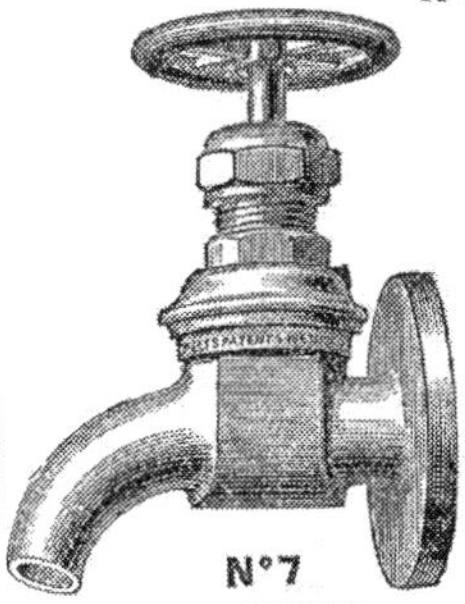

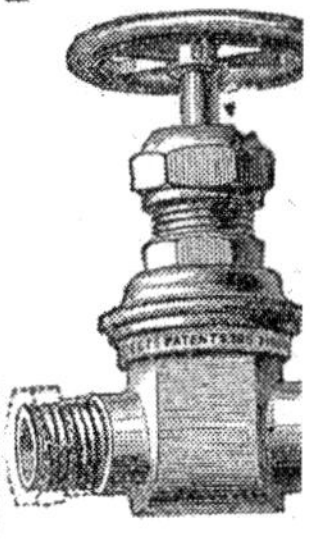

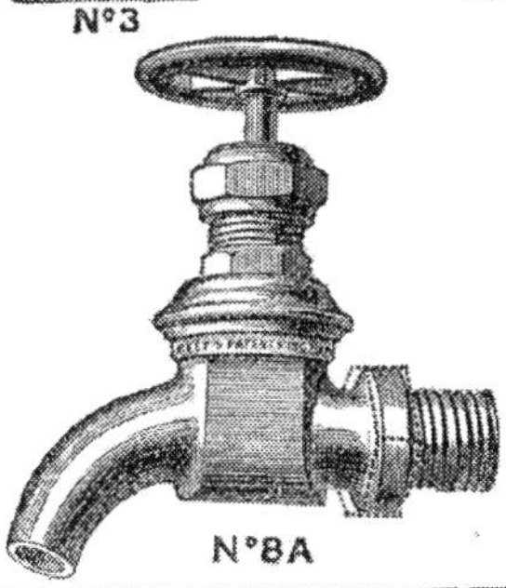

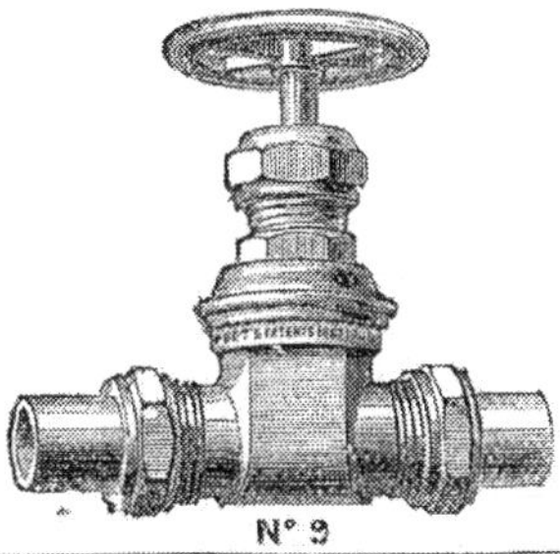

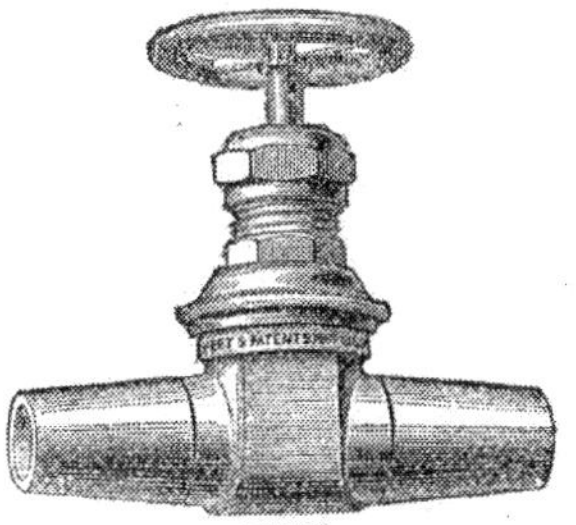

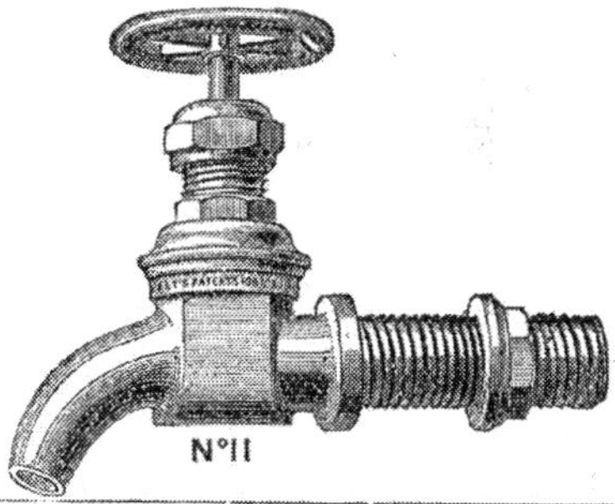

Nos. 12, 13 and 14 are supplied with wheel or top of spindle; Nos. 15, 16, 17 and 18 are supplied with square-headed spindle, unless ordered to have wheel, same

No. 12

No. 13

No. 14

No. 15

No. 16

ast Iron Peet Valves

(All Iron) with W.I. Spindle and Faced Flanges.

In ordering, please state if No. 19, is requir with wheel or square-headed spindle.

No. 19A is supplied with wheel.

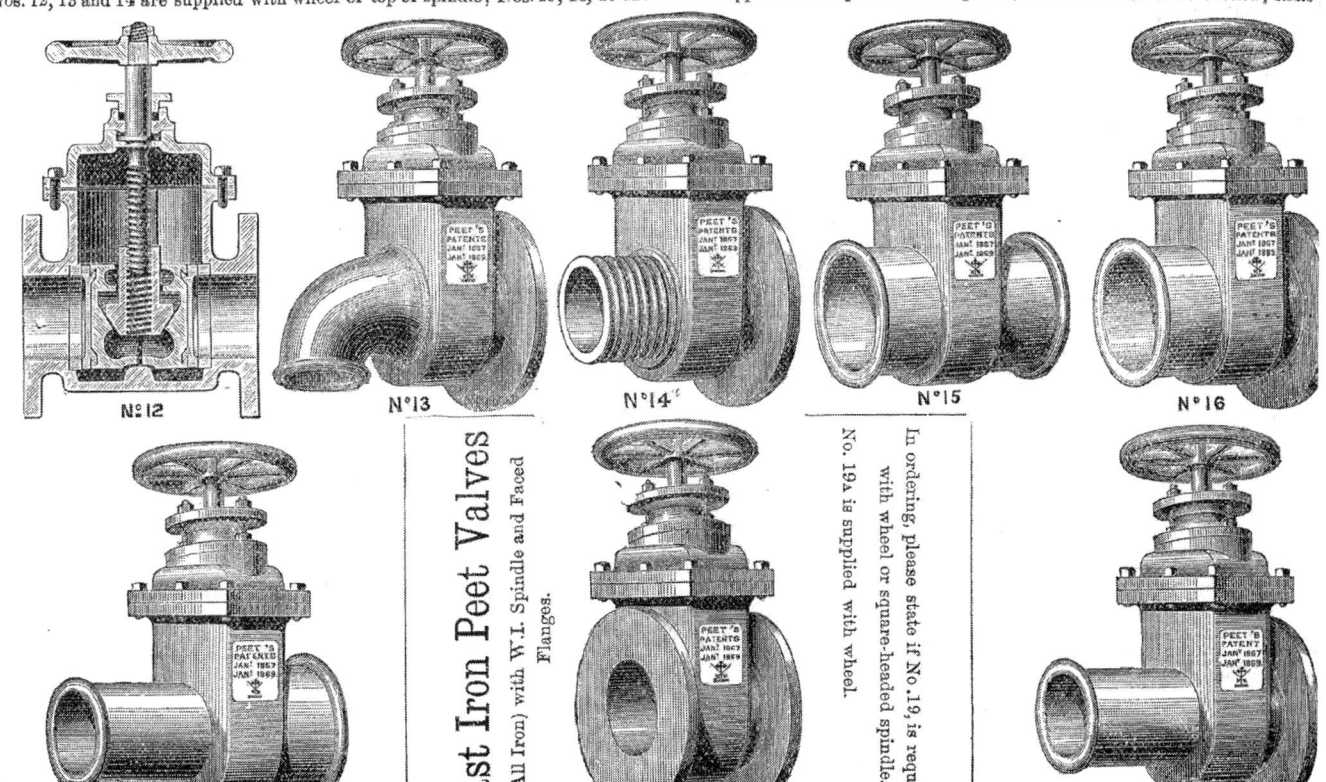

PEET'S PATENT VALVE TAPS,
FOR STEAM, WATER, AND GAS.

PATENTED IN ALL EUROPEAN COUNTRIES. THOUSANDS IN CONSTANT USE IN EUROPE AND AMERICA.

QUOTATIONS GIVEN FOR LARGER SIZES.

Gun Metal Valves, Nos. 1, 2 and 3, viz. :—No. 1, with two female ends ; No. 2, male and female ends ; No. 3, two male ends ; all screwed for W. I. Pipe.

Bore	$\frac{1}{2}$	$\frac{3}{4}$	1	$1\frac{1}{4}$	$1\frac{1}{2}$	$1\frac{3}{4}$	2	$2\frac{1}{2}$	3	$3\frac{1}{2}$	4	5	6 inch.
Price	5/-	7/-	10/-	13/-	16/6	22/6	26/-	50/-	[	Prices on application			] each.

No. 4 Gun Metal Valve, with one male or female end screwed for Iron Pipe, and one end with Union Joint attached.

Bore	$\frac{1}{2}$	$\frac{3}{4}$	1	$1\frac{1}{4}$	$1\frac{1}{2}$	$1\frac{3}{4}$	2	$2\frac{1}{2}$	3	$3\frac{1}{2}$	4	5	6 inch.
Price	8/-	10/-	14/-	20/-	26/-	34/-	40/-	[	Prices on application				] each.

No. 5 Gun Metal Valve, with round or oval Flange on one end and Union Joint on the other (all flanges will be sent round unless ordered oval).

Bore	$\frac{1}{2}$	$\frac{3}{4}$	1	$1\frac{1}{4}$	$1\frac{1}{2}$	$1\frac{3}{4}$	2	$2\frac{1}{2}$	3	$3\frac{1}{2}$	4	5	6 inch.
Price	9/-	10/6	17/6	22/6	30/-	37/6	50/-	[	Prices on application				] each.

No. 6 Gun Metal Valve, with two round or oval Flanges (all flanges will be sent round unless ordered oval).
" 7 Gun Metal Valve, with round or oval Flange and Bib ("   "   "   ").

Bore	$\frac{1}{2}$	$\frac{3}{4}$	1	$1\frac{1}{4}$	$1\frac{1}{2}$	$1\frac{3}{4}$	2	$2\frac{1}{2}$	3	$3\frac{1}{2}$	4	5	6 inch.
Price	7/-	11/-	15/-	20/-	27/6	38/-	46/-	85/-	£5/5	£6	£7/10	£15	£20 each.

No. 8 Gun Metal Valve, with one male or female end, screwed for iron pipe, and one end with round or oval Flange (all flanges will be sent round unless ordered oval).
" 8A with one male or female end screwed for iron pipe and one end with Bib.

Bore	$\frac{1}{2}$	$\frac{3}{4}$	1	$1\frac{1}{4}$	$1\frac{1}{2}$	$1\frac{3}{4}$	2	$2\frac{1}{2}$	3	$3\frac{1}{2}$	4	5	6 inch.
Price	6/6	9/-	11/-	16/-	20/-	27/6	34/-	68/-	80/-	[	Prices on application		] each.

No. 9 Gun Metal Valve, with a Union Joint attached to each end.

Bore	$\frac{1}{2}$	$\frac{3}{4}$	1	$1\frac{1}{4}$	$1\frac{1}{2}$	$1\frac{3}{4}$	2	$2\frac{1}{2}$	3	$3\frac{1}{2}$	4	5	6 inch.
Price	9/6	12/-	15/-	22/6	30/-	38/-	44/-	[	Prices on application				] each.

No. 12 Cast Iron Valve, with Gun Metal wearing parts and faced Flanges ; No. 13, ditto, ditto, with Flange and Bib ; No. 14 ditto, ditto, with Flange and screwed end for union, **or grooved to receive Hose Pipe (state which in ordering)** No. 15, ditto, ditto, with two Faucet ends ; No. 16, ditto, ditto, with Flange and Faucet ; No. 17, ditto, ditto, with Spigot and Faucet ; No. 18, ditto, ditto, with Spigot and Flange.

Bore	1	$1\frac{1}{2}$	2	$2\frac{1}{2}$	3	$3\frac{1}{2}$	4	5	6	7	8	9	10	11	12	14	16	18	20	24	30	36 inch.
Price	18/-	28/-	35/-	40/-	50/-	60/-	70/-	85/-	£6	£7	£8/10	£10	£12	£16	£20	[	Prices on application					] each.

With respect to all Peet Valves, 10 in. bore and above, *when required for Steam*, we have found it advisable to fix a "relief valve" with branches of W. I. tube to each disc, to equalise the pressure, and thus facilitate the raising of the discs by the spindle. The "relief valve" is a $\frac{3}{4}$ in. one, for which we charge £1/7/6, subject to same discount as the valves. Please state, therefore, when ordering valves of 10 in. bore, or above, if for steam or water. This "relief valve" is not necessary when Peet's Valves are used for *water*.

DIMENSIONS OF No. 12 PEET VALVES.

Bore of Valve	1	$1\frac{1}{2}$	2	$2\frac{1}{2}$	3	$3\frac{1}{2}$	4	5	6	7	8	9	10	11	12	14	15	16	17	18 inch
Diameter of Flanges	$3\frac{3}{4}$	6	$6\frac{1}{2}$	7	$7\frac{1}{2}$	8	9	10	12	13	14	15	17	18	19	22	23	24	25	26 inch
Approximate distance from face to face of Flanges	$5\frac{1}{2}$	$7\frac{3}{4}$	8	$8\frac{1}{2}$	9	10	$10\frac{1}{2}$	11	12	$12\frac{1}{2}$	$13\frac{1}{2}$	$14\frac{1}{2}$	15	$15\frac{1}{2}$	16	18	18	20	20	20 inch

No. 19 Cast Iron Gas Valve, similar in shape to No. 12, but all iron (with Wrought Iron Spindle).

Bore	$1\frac{1}{2}$	2	$2\frac{1}{2}$	3	$3\frac{1}{2}$	4	5	6	7	8	9	10	11	12	14	16	18 inch.
Price	20/-	22/6	27/6	34/-	40/-	52/-	65/-	90/-	£5/5	£6	£7/10	£9/10	£11	£12/10	[	Prices on application	] each.

No. 19A Cast Iron Valve with two female ends screwed for Iron Pipe, with Wrought Iron Spindle, all other parts Cast Iron.

Bore	$1\frac{1}{2}$	2	$2\frac{1}{2}$	3	4	5	6 inch.
Price	27/6	30/-	35/-	40/-	[	Prices on application	] each.

☞ All Flanges will be sent round unless ordered otherwise.
Any other modifications of Peet's Valve Taps (not named on this List) made to order, will be charged extra.

All Peet's Valves, with Threads, are screwed to Whitworth's Standard Gas Threads, and only this kind kept in stock ; if required with other pitches of Threads, they will have to be made special and charged extra.

BAILEY'S GUN-METAL FRICTIONLESS EQUILIBRIUM THROTTLE VALVES

No. 1,115 A.

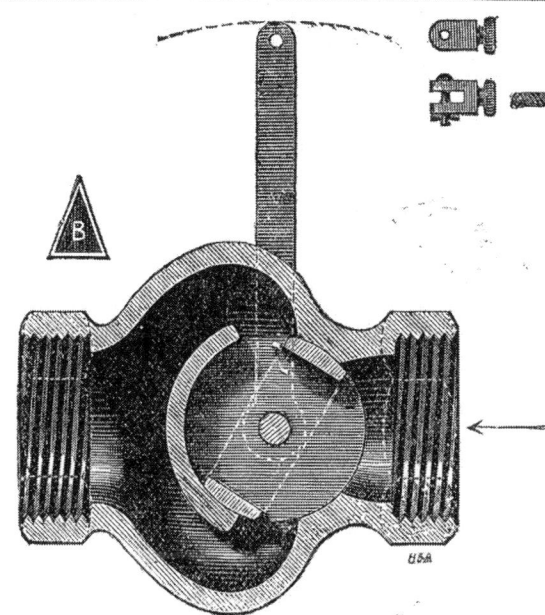

An excellent substitute for the ancient fly and double-beat Valves, which never give proper satisfaction.

Bore of Pipe,	½	¾	1	1¼	1½	2 in.
Screwed Gas Thread each,	10/-	15/-	20/-	25/-	30/-	40/-

Squared for, but not including, Lever.

When ordered in dozens by Engine makers, prices are, of course, reduced.

With a Pulley on the Spindle, and a Stone Float and Chain, these Valves make excellent Cistern and Reservoir Regulators.

BAILEY'S LONG-BARREL "IXION" STEAM COCK

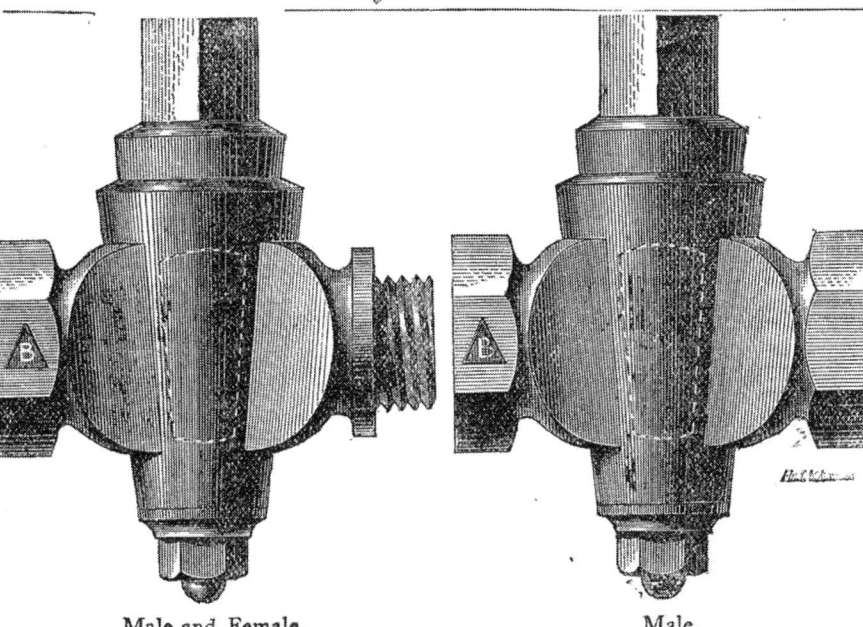

Male and Female.　　　Male.

No. 705.　GUN METAL.

Specially designed for wear and tear, for use in the Iron Works and the Colonies, where constant renewals are considered unprofitable and foolish. All tested to 200lbs. pressure.

Inch.	Black.	All Bright.
½	4/-	5/-
¾	6/6	7/6
1	10/-	12/6
1¼	15/-	18/-
1½	20/-	23/6
2	38/-	44/9

When Ordering the IXION Cocks, say if female, or male and female ends.

OIL AND TALLOW SYRINGE, ALL BRASS.

PRICES ACCORDING TO LENGTH.

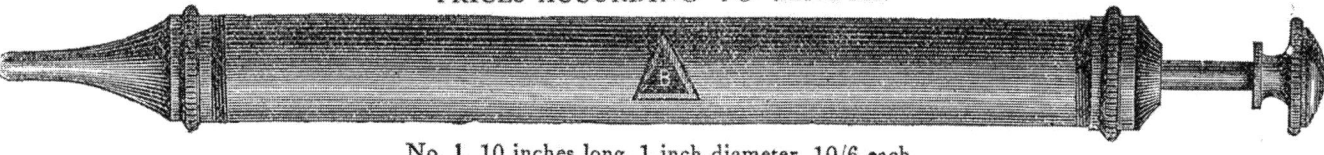

No. 1, 10 inches long, 1 inch diameter, 10/6 each.

No. 902. BAILEY'S EXPANSION STEAM TRAP,

For the delivery of Cold Water from Steam Pipes.

PRICE, EACH.

⅜ in.	...	4/0	1 in.	...	8/6
½ in.	...	4/6	1¼ in.	...	12/0
¾ in.	...	6/0	1½ in.	...	15/0

This efficient and simple Trap is used to let the cold water out of Steam Pipes; it is fastened to the end of Iron Pipe, about 8 or 10 feet long, the Spindle is made fast to the wall or a board; when the pipe becomes cold it contracts, and thus the Valve is opened and the water blown out, the hot steam causes the pipe to expand and the Valve then closes.

Important to Bleachers, Brewers, Calico Printers, Hat Manufacturers, Engineers, Manufacturers of Drying Cylinders, &c.

GREENHALGH'S PATENT REDUCING VALVE.

ALL BEST RED GUN METAL, STRONG AND DURABLE.

No. 1.—1 inch ... ... £2 10 0   No. 3.—2 inch £5 0 0
" 2.—1½ " ... ... 3 15 0   " 4.—3 " with flanges all gun metal 7 10 0

All those under 2 inch diameter are made to suit iron pipe, are screwed gas-thread, and are made of the best gun metal throughout. All above 2 inch bore are made of cast-iron, with flanges.

In ordering, please state the ordinary working pressure, and the amount required to be reduced to.

In consequence of the great superiority of this valve, since making terms with the patentee, we have ceased to make Bailey's Patent Reducing Valve.

Without one word of comment, *we simply guarantee the efficacy of these valves.* Whenever the pressure at which steam is required is exceeded, in the most simple manner the two pistons raise and close the aperture. As they have been working successfully for over four years, time has proved them to be good. We may add the inventor is a working millwright and engineer, who invented this valve in consequence of the difficulty experienced by his employers in obtaining a really good "Reducer."

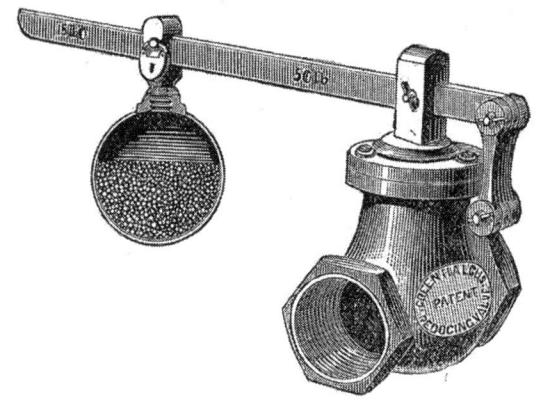

TESTIMONIALS.

Hat Manufactory, Denton, near Manchester,
Messrs. Bailey & Co.,—Gentlemen.—We have used the valve of Greenhalgh's for three years, and find it very useful as well as economical.—Yours truly,
T. WALKER, Sen.

Bent Grange Iron Works, Oldham,
Messrs. Bailey & Co.,—Gentlemen.—In answer to your favour, we have used several of Greenhalgh's Patent Reducing Valves, and have found in every case entire satisfaction.—Yours respectfully,
JOHN MILLS.

No. 1,116 B.

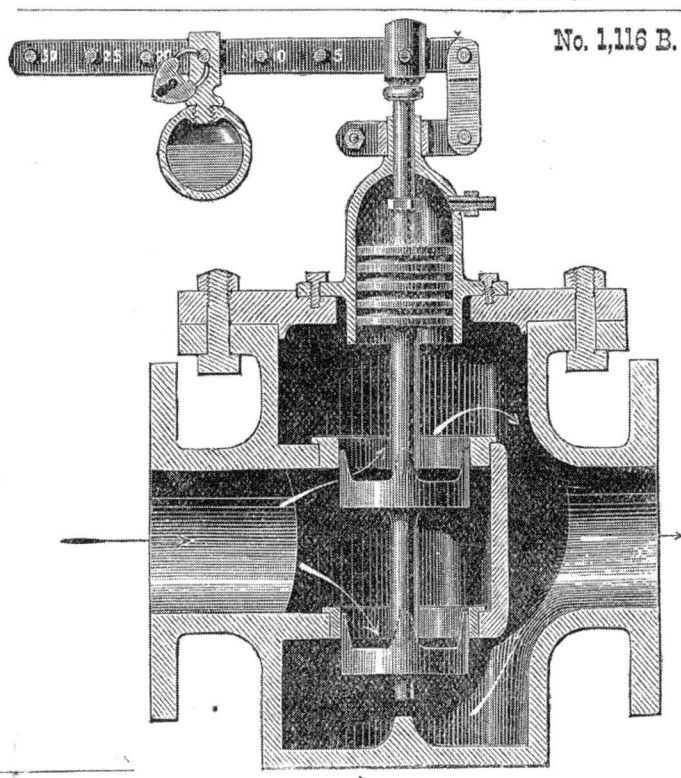

BORE	DIAMETER OF FLANGE	PRICES £ s d
2 inch	6½ inch	5 0 0
2½ "	7 "	6 5 0
3 "	7½ "	7 10 0
4 "	9 "	10 0 0
5 "	10 "	12 10 0
6 "	12 "	15 0 0
8 "	14 "	20 0 0
10 "	17 "	30 0 0

These Valves are excellently well made, the Cases are of iron, and the Cylinders and internal piston and fittings are of brass, the joints are of best brass, and the greatest care is taken in testing and indication. It is advisable to fix a small pipe to the union and nut, to take away the slight amount of steam which might pass the piston. No oil must be used to lubricate these pistons.

BAILEY'S
FRICTIONLESS EQUILIBRIUM GOVERNOR VALVES
From Half-inch to 12 inches.

Specially designed for the Moncrieff Governor, of which Circulars may be had on application.

No. 1,115 A.

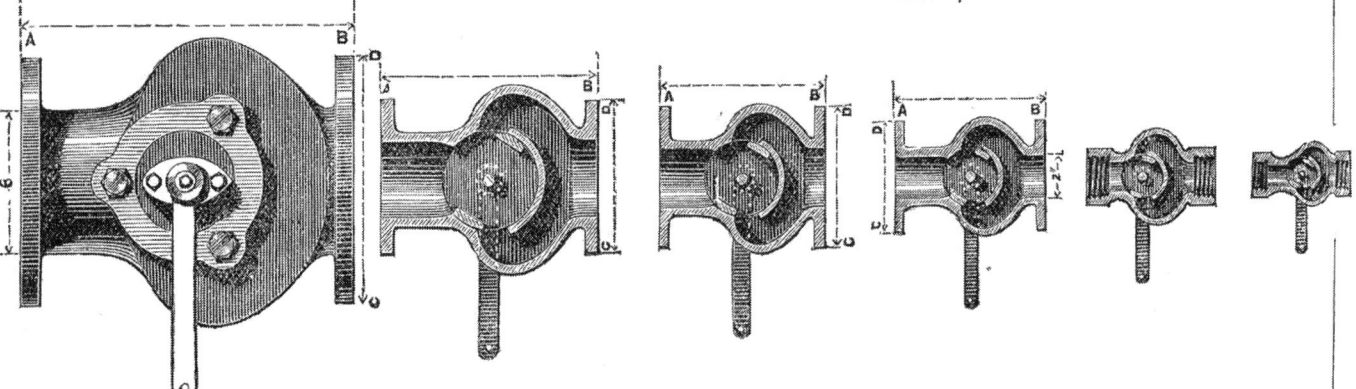

These Valves are also useful as Baffler Valves for Winding Engines, and as Stop Valves for semi-fluids, &c., &c. With Flanges, price 30/- per inch bore. The dimensions outside are the same as Bailey's No. 1 Stop Valves. 2 in. bore and larger are of iron, with brass glands; below 2 in. are screwed, and all brass.

BAILEY'S PATENT
Steam Dryers and Expansion Joints,
FOR STEAM PIPES OF STATIONARY AND MARINE ENGINES, STEAM HAMMERS, DRYING STOVES, &c.

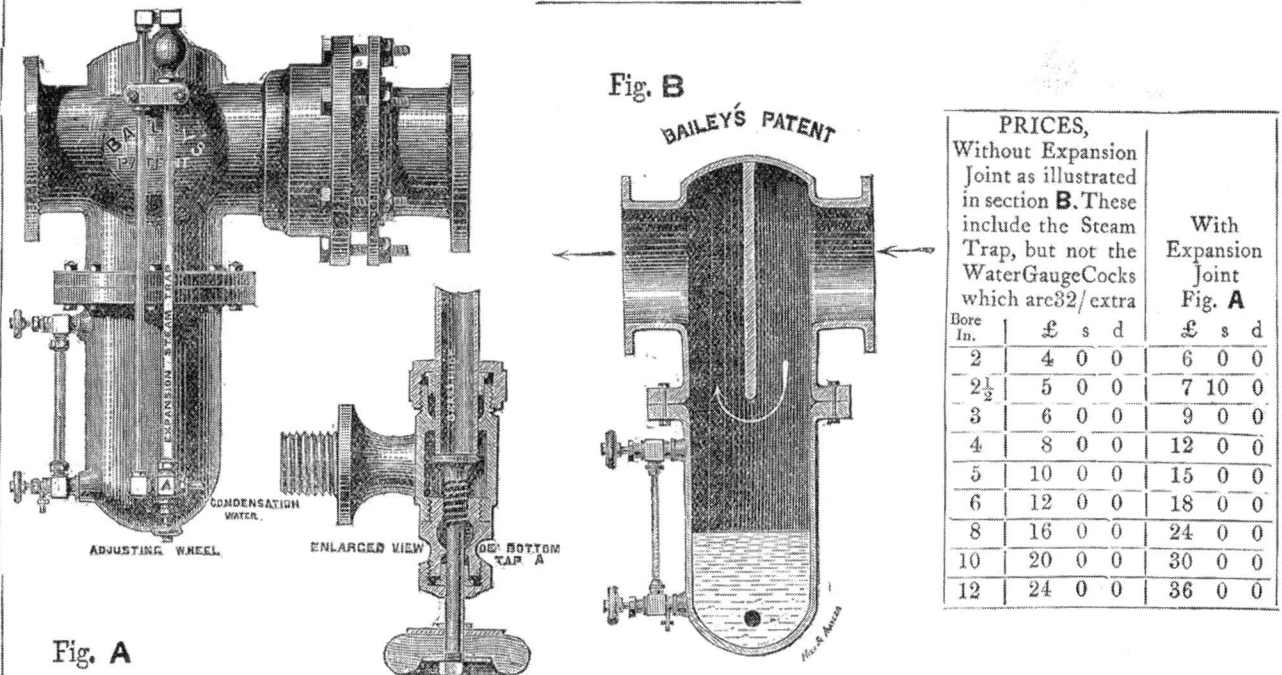

Fig. B — BAILEY'S PATENT

Fig. A — CONDENSATION WATER. ADJUSTING WHEEL. ENLARGED VIEW OF BOTTOM TAP A.

Bore In.	PRICES, Without Expansion Joint as illustrated in section **B**. These include the Steam Trap, but not the Water Gauge Cocks which are 32/ extra			With Expansion Joint Fig. **A**		
	£	s	d	£	s	d
2	4	0	0	6	0	0
2½	5	0	0	7	10	0
3	6	0	0	9	0	0
4	8	0	0	12	0	0
5	10	0	0	15	0	0
6	12	0	0	18	0	0
8	16	0	0	24	0	0
10	20	0	0	30	0	0
12	24	0	0	36	0	0

The sectional view of this invention will cause the instrument to be understood. Much injury is often done to engines in consequence of the introduction of condensed water into the cylinders, often causing serious "break-downs." The reduction in the temperature of the steam by its coming in contact with water, is a well-known source of loss. When engines prime, or the pipes are a distance from the boiler, this invention is found useful.

This operation will be readily understood. When the water collects in the catcher, the pressure of the steam blows it up a tube of iron, and it descends down one of brass, which has a valve at its end. The tube expands and closes the valve when steam alone is blown out, and this operation may be adjusted to the exact requirements. When it is cold it is wide open, when the engine starts, and then all accumulation will be readily allowed to escape.

Bailey's Expansion Joints for Steam Pipes.

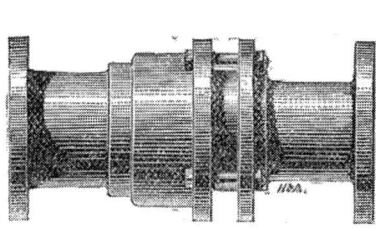

EXPANSION JOINT.

In.	£	s	d
2	2	0	0
2½	2	10	0
3½	3	10	0
3	3	10	0
4	4	0	0
5	5	0	0
6	6	0	0
8	8	0	0
10	10	0	0
12	12	0	0

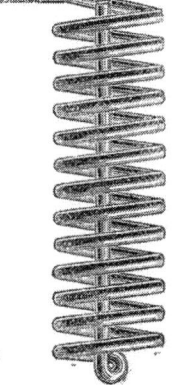

Copper or Iron Coils for Fuel Economisers. Water Boilers made to order. Estimates given for Special Designs.

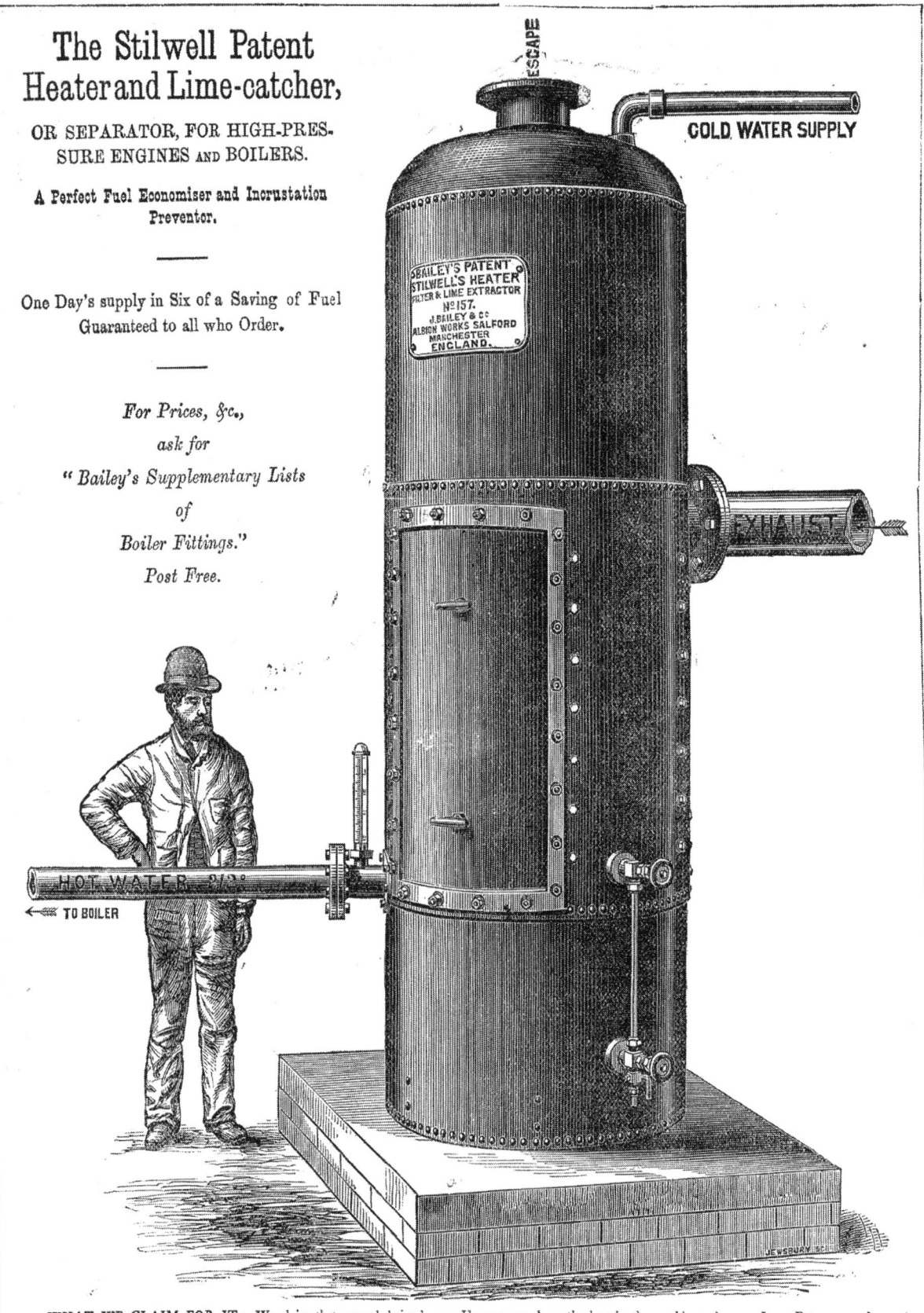

The Stilwell Patent Heater and Lime-catcher,

OR SEPARATOR, FOR HIGH-PRESSURE ENGINES AND BOILERS.

A Perfect Fuel Economiser and Incrustation Preventor.

One Day's supply in Six of a Saving of Fuel Guaranteed to all who Order.

For Prices, &c., ask for "Bailey's Supplementary Lists of Boiler Fittings." Post Free.

WHAT WE CLAIM FOR IT.—We claim that, regarded simply as a HEATER, we have the best in the world; and, as a LIME EXTRACTOR, it stands alone, unrivalled in its perfect action. We claim that the use of our Heater will effect a saving of at least *ten per cent.* of fuel where *soft water is used*, and when "hard" and impure water is used, it will effect a saving of from *fifteen to fifty per cent. of fuel*, not to mention the saving to the boilers, in time, and in obviating the necessity, occasioned by "scale," of frequently "blowing-off" and cleaning boilers, a job so dreaded by engineers, and so expensive to employers.

BAILEY'S PATENT STEAM KETTLE,

For supplying Clean Hot Water, direct from the Main, for Cooking purposes, for Workpeople for Meal times, for Pork Butchers, Cooking and Washing Establishments, for Prisons, Hospitals, Asylums, Workhouses, Bleachers, Dyers, &c., &c.

When used for Hotel Washhouses, &c., where the water is required in upper rooms, it is obvious that the water will ascend, the Kettle being placed in lower room.

To be seen at work at

Mr. SUMMERS,

Iron Works, Stalybridge.

Messrs. DERBYSHIRE & Co.,

Glass Works, Salford;

At our own Works, and other places.

No. 1 is considered large enough for works employing 100 men, and if greater capacity is required, in most cases, it is advisable to have two or three, instead of one larger, although for special purposes we make to order, where informed of the requirements.

Price each, No. 1, complete, £8 10 0.	Height 4 feet.	Diameter, 8 inches.	Steam-pipe inlet, ½-inch.	Double Hot Water Cocks and Outlets, ½-inch each.

The action of this will be understood from the following description:—The inlet at the top allows steam to enter, and this surrounding the copper pipe, boils the water which it contains; the water which is connected with the town's main passes through the hot pipe at its full pressure, and going down the pipe and up to the top outlet is made to any temperature, which can be regulated by the valves.

Clean hot drinking water can thus be readily obtained in this manner, as the water touches nothing but the clean copper pipe through which it passes. The steam condenses in the cistern, and to allow it to escape, the pressure of the steam forcing on the top of it causes the water to ascend, and as it passes moderately cold down the outside expansion pipe, it is caused to contract, and thus automatically opens a valve which allows the water to escape; it is obvious that when the steam blows through, the pipe expands and closes the valves, the amount it opens and closes is regulated by the screw as indicated in the cut.

WOOD'S PATENT WATER HEATER, CONDENSER & REFRIGERATOR.

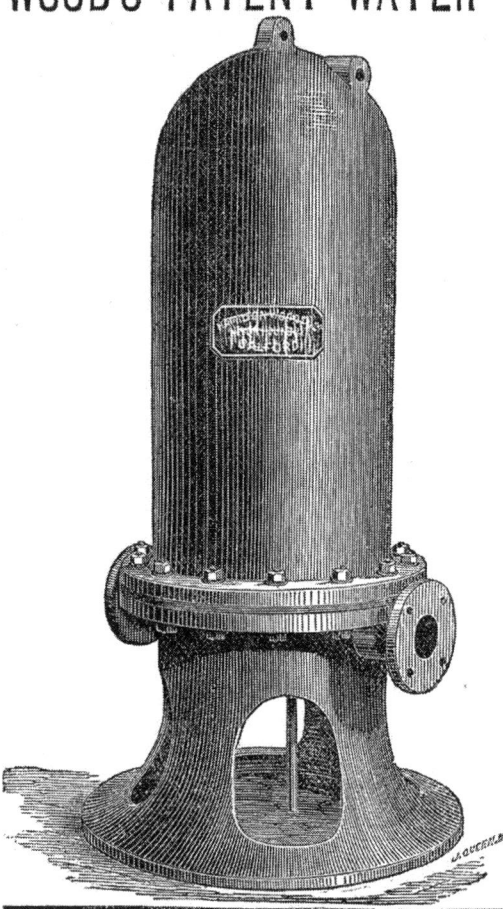

Every Heater tested to 150lbs. per square inch before leaving the Works.

Prices of Water Heaters
8-Horse Power.
12 do.
16 do.
20 do.

When used as Water Heater to economise Exhaust Steam, the Feed Water delivered into the Boiler at Boiling Point.

No Back Pressure in the Cylinder.

Water can be supplied from a constant Head or Pump.

The advantages over other similar Heaters will be seen by any Engineer in consequence of the shape of the pipes, the expansion and contraction of the tubes will not break the joints, a constant source of weakness where pipes are used fixed in the ordinary manner.

On receipt of particulars, estimates will be forwarded for any size on application.

NEW SMOKE PREVENTOR.

BAILEY'S BROADBENT'S PATENT REGULATOR OR METER FOR BOILER FURNACE DOORS.

J. BAILEY & CO., LICENSEES.

PRICE, without Louvre, £3 10s.

If Boiler Doors are not already fitted with Louvres, they are supplied at from £1 to £2 each according to size, and can be fitted to any door. Send the size of the door in ordering.

That the combustion of Coal in Boiler Furnaces can be effected without producing dark-coloured smoke is now proved beyond all doubt by numerous and well-tried experiments, and that it can be accomplished by an economy of fuel is equally certain. This result, however, can only be attained by a compliance with certain conditions, which are absolutely necessary to success, and the neglect of which has led to so many previous failures.

DESCRIPTION OF BROADBENT'S PATENT SMOKE PREVENTOR.

The figure is a front view of a Boiler, fitted with the "Patent Smoke Preventor." It may easily be understood from the following description:—The box contains the self-acting motion (which is exceedingly simple and strong, and is guaranteed in all cases not to get out of order); from it projects a lever, which is attached by means of a light chain to the balance weight, and patent louvres fixed in the ordinary fire doors.   The action of the Apparatus is as follows:—

Upon opening the door for the purpose of charging or distributing the fire, the chain becomes slack, and the weight, descending by its own gravity, raises the lever. The louvres open on the shutting of the door, but are gradually closed by the falling of the weight, the speed at which this is accomplished being regulated at will, so as to be adapted to any quality of coal by simply altering the position of the slide on the lever. By this means the louvres can be gradually closed in any fixed time, varying from two to twelve minutes. One of the peculiarities in these louvres is in the arrangement of the laths, which are so mounted upon their pivots that upon being drawn back to their full extent, which takes place upon the closing of the doors, they only admit about one-half the quantity of air of which they are capable, but upon the gradual falling of the weight C the louvres open to their full extent. A continuation of the same motion, however, eventually closes them, in which position they remain until the door is again opened. It is entirely self-acting, requiring no winding up, and not being dependent upon either water or mercury. It thoroughly diffuses the air in its admission to the furnace, secures the proper mixtures of the gases, and the quantity can be regulated to the greatest nicety without any action on the part of the fireman, its working being in perfect harmony with the requirements of the Furnace. Its durability is guaranteed for five years, and is constructed to work efficiently for upwards of twenty. It has already been supplied to upwards of Fourteen Hundred Furnaces, with the most satisfactory results.

Bailey's Patent Feed Pump Regulating Suction Valves,

For regulating the action of Pumps for feeding Steam Boilers, in order that one constant feed may be maintained, and the level of the water kept at a regular height.

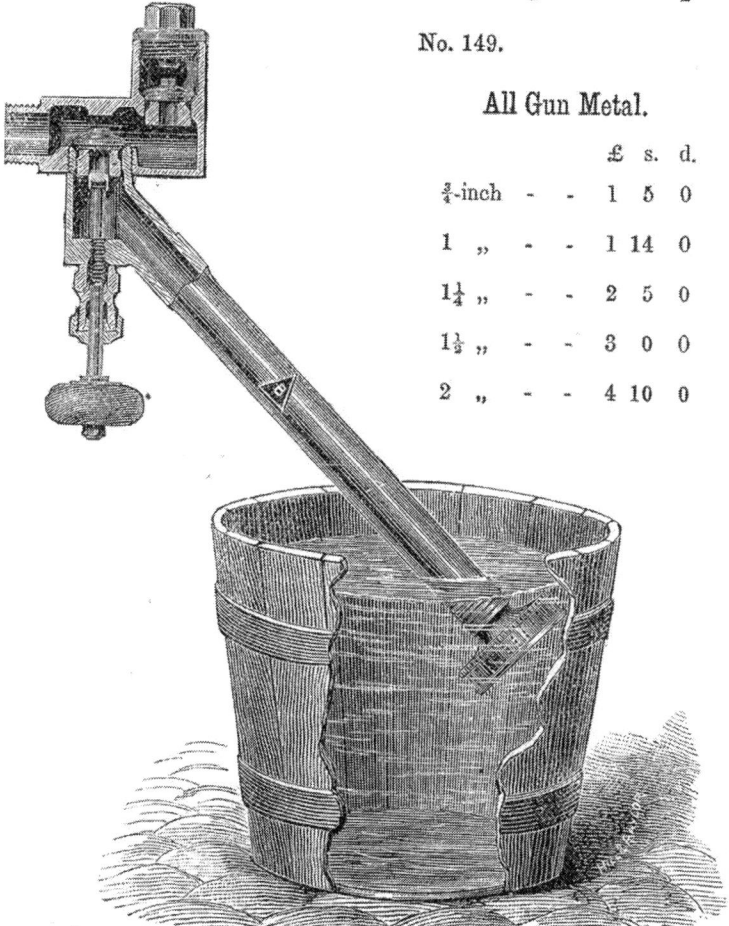

No. 149.
All Gun Metal.

	£	s.	d.
¾-inch	1	5	0
1 ,,	1	14	0
1¼ ,,	2	5	0
1½ ,,	3	0	0
2 ,,	4	10	0

As applied to Portable and Launch Boilers.

This important little invention, when applied to Agricultural, Portable, or Steam Launch Boilers, as sketch, enables the Pump to continually work, and by the adjustment of the Section Valve to either stop, the pump lifting any water, or to permit it only to force in sufficient for the requirements, the surplus being forced, by leakage, back, thus entirely doing away with escape valves or with "knocking off" gearing to stop the pump when water sufficient is in the boiler. This will be appreciated by all makers of Portable Engines. The illustration shows the invention as adapted for Pumps working in an horizontal position. Special adaptations for special purposes.

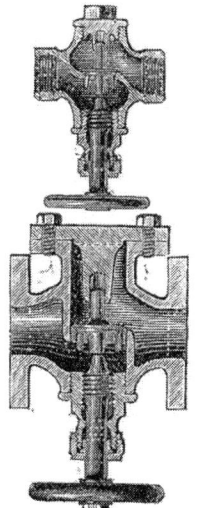

No. 151.
All Gun Metal.

	s.	d.
½-inch	6	0
¾ ,,	7	6
1 ,,	10	6
1¼ ,,	13	6
1½ ,,	17	6
2 ,,	26	6

No. 152.
Cast-Iron Case, with Gun Seatings.

Bore.	£	s.	d.
2-inch		1	7	6
2½ ,,		1	17	6
3 ,,		2	10	0
3½ ,,		2	16	3
4 ,,		3	8	9
5 ,,		4	13	9
6 ,,		6	5	0
8 ,,		9	0	0
10 ,,		13	2	6
12 ,,		17	10	0

For Large Stationary Boilers.

The Steam Users' Association, as well as all other authorities on the use of Steam, recommend as a most important object the use of apparatus to maintain a constant feed; the full duty of "Economizers" can only be obtained by the slowest possible passage of water through them, and in order that the invention may be readily and cheaply adapted and adopted to existing large Boilers in Cotton Mills, Iron Works, and extensive establishments, we have designed the annexed Feed Suction Valves in all Brass and Iron Cases and Gun metal Fittings. Of course, it is obvious that where these Valves are applied the pump must be able to do a little in excess of the requirements, in order that an adjustment may be obtained by leakage.

Reduce your Friction; Economise your Steam Power, and save your Tallow. Make your Coal Account less, and keep your Engine Cylinders good, by using

BAILEY'S PATENT ENGINE CYLINDER TALLOW CUP, OR LUBRICATOR,

With recent Improvements and an entire new set of patterns of improved design and greater strength—the result of experience.

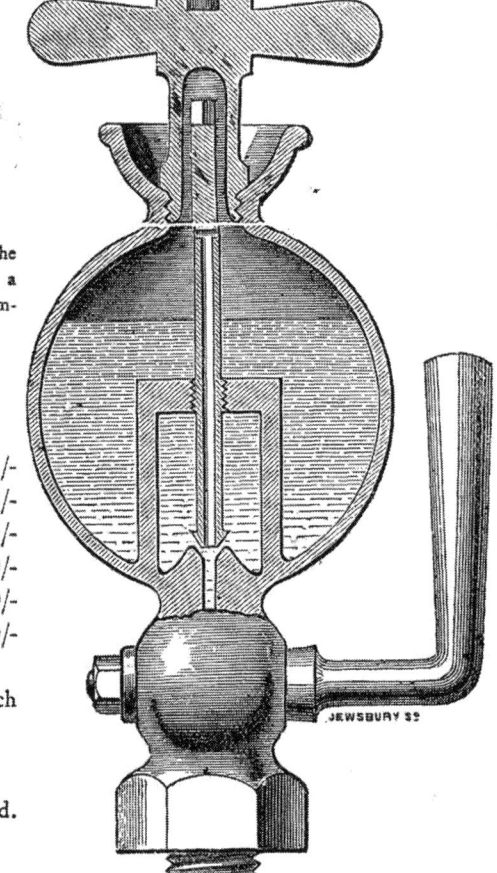

2,500 in use.

Although the improvements have increased the weight, the prices have not been increased, a greater demand being depended upon to compensate for smaller profits.

PRICE:

Diameter, 1¾ inch,	... ...	15/-
,, 2 inches,	... ...	23/-
,, 2¼ ,,	... ...	25/-
,, 3¼ ,,	... ...	30/-
,, 4 ,,	... ...	40/-
,, 5 ,,	... ...	50/-

An extra large one, very strong, 7 inch diameter, 80/-

Sample orders from Engineers solicited.

North Bridge Mill, Burnley, *July 12th*, 1867.

GENTLEMEN,—I have much pleasure in stating that I have tried your Patent Cylinder Lubricator, and have found it to answer for us very well, both with regard to economy and efficiency.

They cause a great saving in Tallow.

Yours truly,

For J. HARTLEY & SONS,

J. HOWARTH, Engineer.

Grimsby, *May 9th*, 1867.

We hereby certify that we are using one of BAILEY's Tallow Lubricators to our Engine. WE USE ABOUT HALF THE TALLOW we did when we had the old cup.

W. MARSHALL & SONS.

The simplicity of this Cup has made it a general favourite with users of Steam Power. By means of the Valve, the Tallow is easily regulated according to the requirements; and, in consequence of the Steam being able to get at the top of the Tallow through the hollow spindle of the Valve, Tallow can be introduced at any pressure whilst the Engine is at work. They can be fixed on the steam pipe, or on the cylinder lid.

The Cups are very well made, of the Best Gun Metal, and will bear rough usage. There are no stronger Cups made, and are as cheap as ordinary Tallow Cups of the same weight.

TESTIMONIALS.

(From Messrs. T. W. & J. HEATON, Egyptian Mill, Bolton).

We are satisfied, so far as we have been able to judge, with the working results of the Patent Cylinder Lubricators you lately applied to our two Steam Engines. THERE IS A CONSIDERABLE SAVING IN THE AMOUNT OF TALLOW CONSUMED, though we are not prepared to say to what precise extent. We have not had any trouble with the Lubricators since completed, and the Cylinders keep in good condition, with smooth and even surfaces.

(From Mr. T. G. HORRIDGE, Raikes' Bleach Works, near Bolton).

I have tried five of Bailey's Patent Lubricators on my Engines, and find them VERY EFFECTIVE.

(From Messrs. G. CLAYTON & BROS., Victoria Mills, Upworth, near Bury).

We have tried Bailey's Patent Lubricators, and approve of them very much, as they cause a very GREAT SAVING IN TALLOW AND COAL.

(From Messrs. M. & M. SCOTT, Tranmere Foundry, Cheshire).

We have much pleasure in stating that the Patent Cylinder Lubricators MORE THAN EQUAL OUR HIGHEST EXPECTATIONS; OUR ENGINE WORKS IN A MUCH BETTER MANNER THAN HITHERTO.

(From Messrs. T. H. SIDEBOTHAM & BROS., Bridge Mill, Waterside, near Hadfield).

We beg to say that we are perfectly satisfied with your Patent Cylinder Lubricator: IT SAVES TALLOW.

(From R. SIDEBOTHAM, Esq., Mill Brook, near Hadfield).

I have three of your Patent Cylinder Lubricators at work, and am satisfied as to their EFFICIENCY AND ECONOMY IN SAVING TALLOW.

(From Messrs. W. HOLLAND & CO., Adelphi Mills, Salford, Manchester).

Respecting the Patent Cylinder Lubricators you applied to our Engines, we have great pleasure in stating we highly approve of them. THE SAVING OF TALLOW IS VERY CONSIDERABLE; our Cylinders are kept in better order: they also effect a SAVING IN FUEL, and the SPEED OF THE ENGINES IS MORE REGULAR.

(From Messrs. P. NIGHTINGALE & CO., Mesne Lea Colliery, Worsley).

We have much pleasure in stating that we have had one of your Lubricators at work, and have never had any trouble with it. We greatly approve of them; THEY CAUSE A GREAT SAVING IN TALLOW.

(From Messrs. J. KENWORTHY & CO., Heys Colliery, Ashton-under-Lyne).

We have had applied two of your Patent Lubricators for regulating the supply of tallow to the Cylinders of our Steam Engines, and find them EFFECT A VERY GREAT SAVING, and to answer the purpose exceedingly well, quite to our satisfaction.

(From THE HOPEFIELD DYEING & PRINTING CO., Broughton).

The Lubricators we had from you are giving every satisfaction, by FREEING THE PISTONS AND SAVING TALLOW. We are perfectly satisfied with them.

(From Messrs. J. & F. JACKSON, Macclesfield).

We have one of your Patent Cylinder Lubricators at work, and feel satisfied with its efficiency and ECONOMY IN SAVING TALLOW.

(From T. L. OPENSHAW, Esq., Brooksmouth Mill, Bury).

I have used your Patent Lubricators four months on my high and low pressure Cylinders. The pistons are now in very good condition, AND SAVING OF TALLOW IS MORE THAN ONE-HALF.

(From the "Warrington Guardian."—NEW INVENTION).

Within the last few days we have had brought under our notice a new Patented Invention for Improving Steam Engines, and manufactured extensively by Messrs. BAILEY & CO., of Albion Works, Salford, Manchester. The design of this apparatus is to furnish a supply of lubricating matter to the Cylinders of Steam Engines, Steam Chests, &c., in a more regular manner than is generally done by the attendant thereof, and none will be more disposed than Engineers themselves to estimate the importance of constant supplies of lubricating matter for this useful purpose.

The Ashcroft Patent Regulating Tallow Cup, for Engine Cylinders.

Entirely without Bottom Cock. The most Durable and Economical Cup ever introduced.

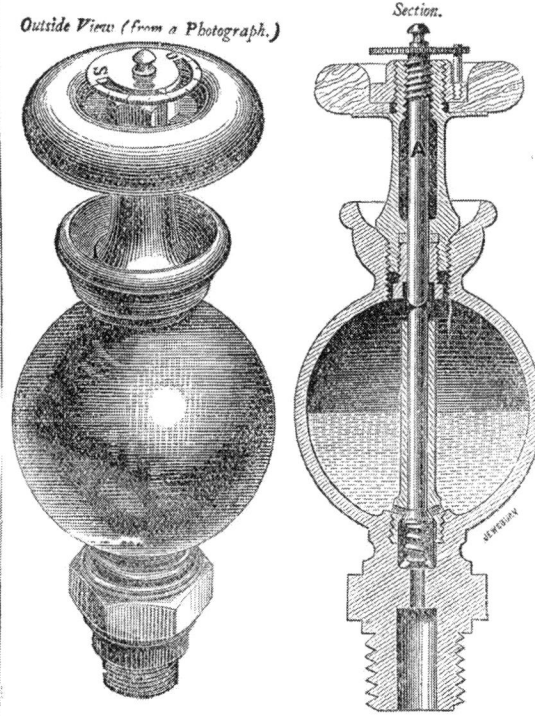

Outside View (from a Photograph.) Section.

PRICES.

1.—Outside Diameter,	2in.	16s. 0d. each.		4.—Outside Diameter,	3½in.	38s. 0d. each.
2. "	"	2½in.	25s. 0d. "	5. "	"	4in.	43s. 0d. "
3. "	"	3in.	32s. 6d. "	6. "	"	5in.	58s. 0d. "

The Prices are not any higher than common Tallow Cups. No. 1 has not any regulating dials.

They may be fixed on the engine Cylinder, or on the Steam Chest, or Inlet Steam Pipe.

DESCRIPTION OF ITS ADVANTAGES.

The bottom cock in ordinary Tallow Cups, on High-pressure Cylinders, is an intolerable nuisance, in consequence of its leakage, and Engineers will recognise that a very desirable improvement has been made.

Most Tallow Cups and Lubricators allow all the tallow to go into the Cylinder at once; this invention places the power of regulation in the hands of the Engineer, economising tallow and reducing friction, saving steam power and coal.

The inverted valve is kept to its seat by the pressure of the steam, and by a spiral spring when the top handle valve is unscrewed, to enable the cup to be filled, the bottom valve closes, and allows the cup to be filled even when the engine is at work. When filled with lubricating matter the aperture is closed, and the projecting spindle A comes in contact with the spindle of the bottom valve and depresses it, allowing the tallow to descend from the cup: this may be adjusted in a very sensitive manner by the dial on the top. The moment the handle is unscrewed to refill, the valve closes. We invite the criticism of mechanical men on the construction of this cup; and if they will compare it with others they know of, the result will be their patronage. The cups being all in one piece, are very strong and good; and in consequence of this alone, even supposing it only to be as good as the ordinary cup, it is worthy of attention.

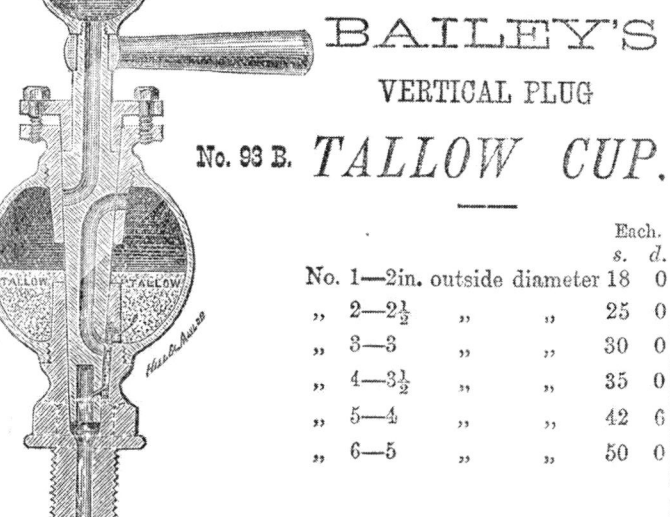

BAILEY'S VERTICAL PLUG TALLOW CUP.
No. 93 B.

			Each.
			s. d.
No. 1—2in.	outside diameter		18 0
" 2—2½	"	"	25 0
" 3—3	"	"	30 0
" 4—3½	"	"	35 0
" 5—4	"	"	42 6
" 6—5	"	"	50 0

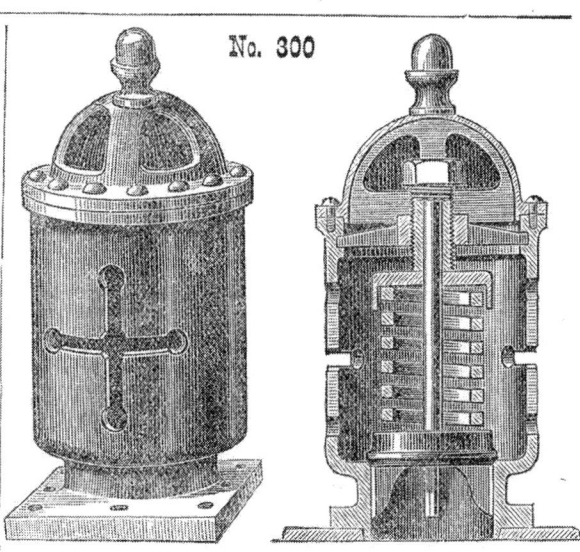

No. 300

BAILEY'S GUN METAL Escape Valves

For Large Engine Cylinders.
All Gun Metal, highly polished.
Registered Design.
The Flanges are Square.

Diameter of Valve.				Price.
2½ inch.	...	...	...	£4 4 0
3 "	...	...	...	5 5 0
3½ "	...	...	...	6 6 0

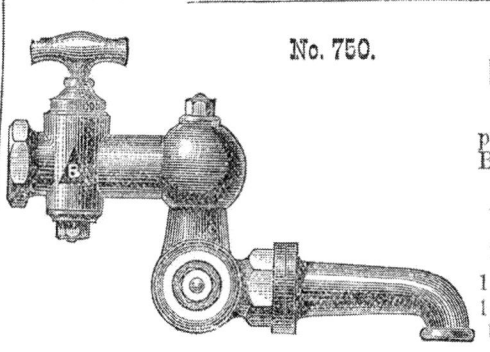

No. 750.

STEAM OR WATER UNIVERSAL SWIVEL.

Extra Strong, used for many purposes, in Dye Works, Bleach Works, etc.

	Each.
½ in. bore	15/-
¾ " " {screwed for Gas Thread}	20/-
1 " "	28/-
1¼ " "	35/-

Universal Swivels of other descriptions to Drawing.

W. H. BAILEY'S STEAM-ROARERS.

(W. H. BAILEY'S PATENT.)

Cast Iron Plates, with the Code in raised characters, **BAILEY'S PATENT STEAM TELEGRAPH MORSE CODE** 5/- Each.

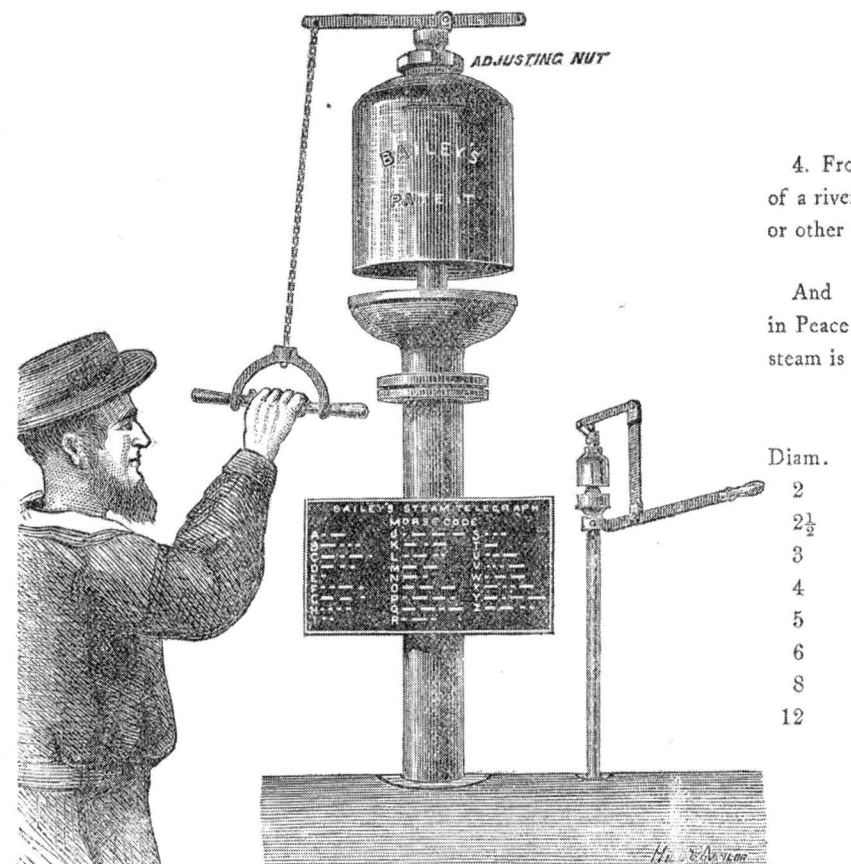

The only Telegraph which can be used by ships in a fog. All Harbour Authorities, Commanders, Admiralty and Lighthouse Controllers, should investigate this.

1. For use on Steam Boats as the ordinary whistle, or for speaking with other boats.

2. For War Ships for the word of command.

3. For Tramways in the Mining districts, instead of electric telegraphs, where there are steam boilers at each end.

4. From opposite sides of a river for steam ferry or other purposes.

And many purposes in Peace or War where steam is available.

Diam.	£	s.	d.
2	1	0	0
2½	1	10	0
3	2	0	0
4	2	10	0
5	3	10	0
6	4	10	0
8	6	0	0
12	15	0	0

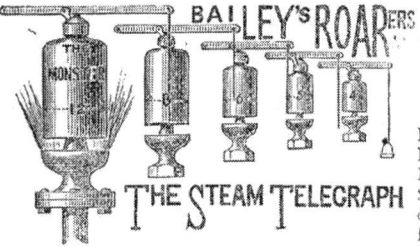

BAILEY'S PATENT FULL-BORE STEAM-ROARER OR TELEGRAPH,
As used on the Mail Packets, River Boats, &c.

Used instead of BELL for WORKS, and a PERCUSSION TELEGRAPH for Colliery Tramways. Recommended by Capt. Brent, of H.M. Navy, at a United Service Institute Meeting, for use in the British Navy as a Fog Signal and Steam Telegraph. Extensively used by the Chief Marine Engineers, Messrs. Maudslay, Field and Co., Stothert and Co., Bristol, Forrester and Co., Liverpool, Oswald and Co., Sunderland, Southampton Dock Co., Wilson Line of Packets, &c., &c., &c. All best gun metal. 6in. diameter, for Steamboats, Works, &c.; 5in. diameter for ditto, 4in. diameter for yachts,; extra large for line packets, harbours, &c., 8in. diameter. "The Monster," 12in. diameter, weight about 112 lb., for 3in. steam pipe, with flange (for lighthouses, large boats, and harbours).

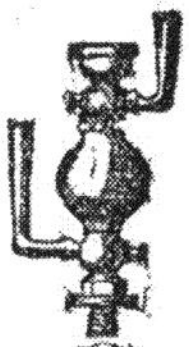

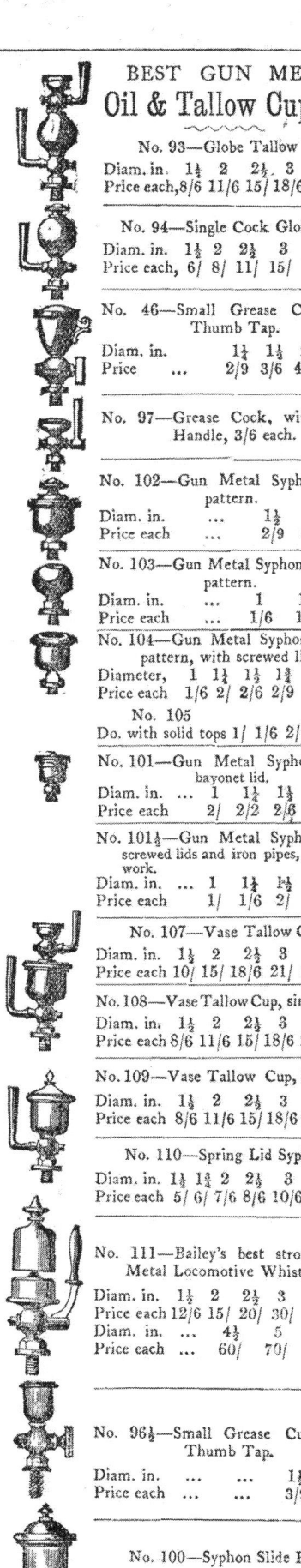

BEST GUN METAL

Oil & Tallow Cup List

No. 93—Globe Tallow Cup.

Diam. in.	1¼	2	2½	3	3½	4
Price each,	8/6	11/6	15/	18/6	25/	32/6

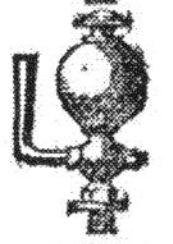

No. 94—Single Cock Globe Cup.

Diam. in.	1½	2	2½	3	3½	4
Price each,	6/	8/	11/	15/	18/6	25/

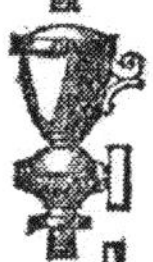

No. 46—Small Grease Cup, with Thumb Tap.

Diam. in.	1¼	1½	2	2½
Price ...	2/9	3/6	4/6	5/6

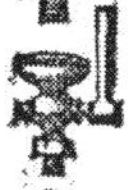

No. 97—Grease Cock, with Lever Handle, 3/6 each.

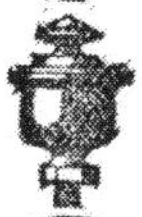

No. 102—Gun Metal Syphon, vase pattern.

Diam. in. ...	1½	2	2½
Price each ...	2/9	3/6	4/6

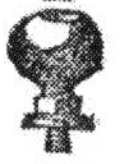

No. 103—Gun Metal Syphon, balloon pattern.

Diam. in. ...	1	1½	2
Price each ...	1/6	1/9	2/8

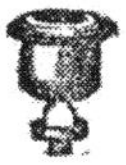

No. 104—Gun Metal Syphon, inkpot pattern, with screwed lids.

Diameter,	1	1¼	1½	1¾	2	2½	3
Price each	1/6	2/	2/6	2/9	3/	4/	6/

No. 105

Do. with solid tops 1/ 1/6 2/ 2/3 2/6

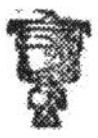

No. 101—Gun Metal Syphon, with bayonet lid.

Diam. in. ...	1	1¼	1½	1¾	2
Price each	2/	2/2	2/6	3/	3/6

No. 101½—Gun Metal Syphon, with screwed lids and iron pipes, for cheap work.

Diam. in. ...	1	1¼	1½	1¾	2
Price each	1/	1/6	2/	2/3	2/6

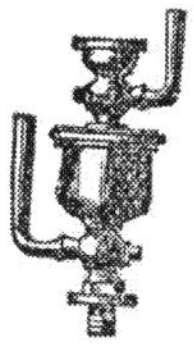

No. 107—Vase Tallow Cup.

Diam. in.	1½	2	2½	3	3½	4
Price each	10/	15/	18/6	21/	29/	35/6

No. 108—Vase Tallow Cup, single cock

Diam. in.	1½	2	2½	3	3½	4
Price each	8/6	11/6	15/	18/6	25/	32/0

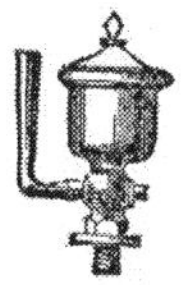

No. 109—Vase Tallow Cup, loose lid.

Diam. in.	1½	2	2½	3	3½	4
Price each	8/6	11/6	15/	18/6	25/	32/6

No. 110—Spring Lid Syphon.

Diam. in.	1½	1¾	2	2½	3	3½	4
Price each	5/	6/	7/6	8/6	10/6	14/	18/

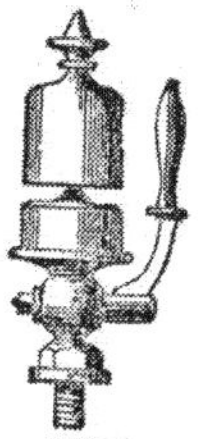

No. 111—Bailey's best strong Gun Metal Locomotive Whistles.

Diam. in.	1½	2	2½	3	3½	4
Price each	12/6	15/	20/	30/	35/	50/
Diam. in. ...	4½	5	6			
Price each ...	60/	70/	90/			

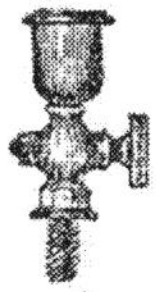

No. 96½—Small Grease Cup, with Thumb Tap.

Diam. in.	1½	2
Price each	3/9	3/3

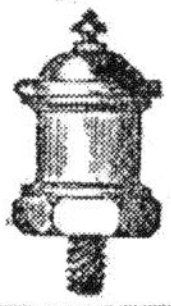

No. 100—Syphon Slide Bars

Diam. inch ...	1	1½	2	2½
Price each ...	2/0	3/	3/9	4/6

BAILEY'S

BRIDGEWATER

TALLOW CUP.

93 A.

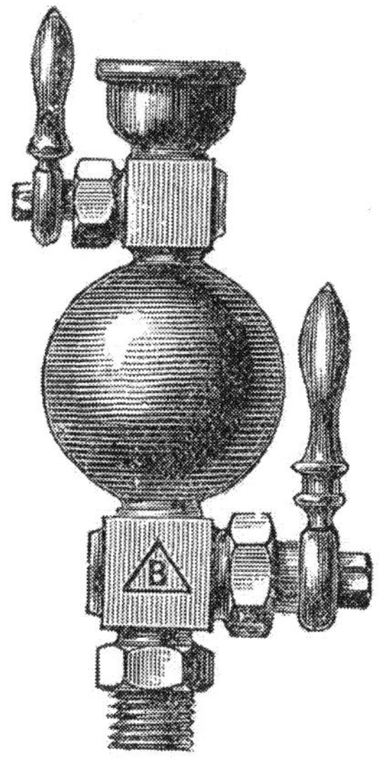

"A good thing is always cheapest in the end," and Mr. Timmins, the long resident Chief Engineer of the Bridgewater Trustees' Collieries, near Manchester, some time since ordered special Cups of the above pattern, as the ordinary pattern, although good value for the price, would not stand the rough night and day work of Colliery Engine use. For the metal and workmanship the prices are reasonable.

2 in. diam.	...	22/-
2½ "	...	25/-
3 "	...	30/-
3½ "	...	35/-
4 "	...	40/-
5 "	...	50/-
7 "	...	80/-

BAILEY'S

PATENT

SUET CUP.

No. 598.

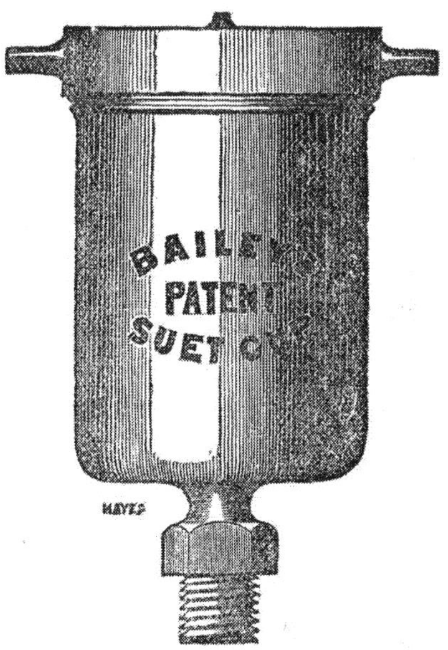

This Cup is especially designed for the use of those who prefer mutton suet in the leaf for lubricating, and having no plug taps to leak and get out of order, it is a general favourite.

ALL ARE OF THE BEST

RED GUN METAL.

The suet is placed in the cup in the leaf, and when the cover is screwed on, a small inverted valve is thrust open, which allows the steam to enter and melt the suet, which gradually enters the cylinder or steam pipe on which the cup is placed.

Inches diam.	2	2½	2¾	3	3½	4
Prices each...	15/-	20/-	30/-	35/-	40/-	50/-

THE BALLOON ESCAPE VALVE,
FOR ENGINE CYLINDERS AND STEAM HAMMERS.

(Chatwood's Patent in England, France, America, &c.)

TRADE MARK

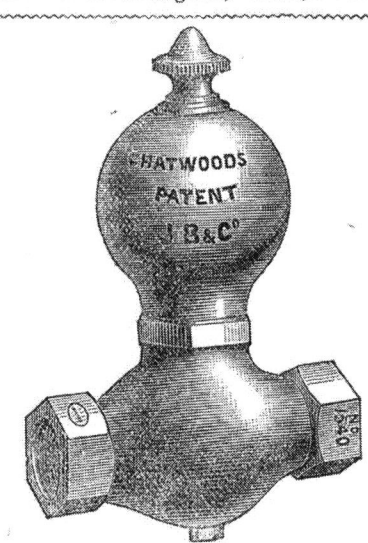

"A most admirable invention for allowing the condensed water to escape from Cylinders."

Vide the opinions of all mechanical men who have tried them.

It does not require any attention, is perfectly self-acting, can be fixed with little trouble, and is a general favourite.

Many Inventions have been introduced for allowing the cold water to escape from Steam Engine Cylinders, but none are entirely self-acting. The danger and damage caused by an engineer who starts his engine without blowing off the cold water are well known. Often joints about a steam engine are continually leaking and out of order, causing disorder, irregularity, and waste of steam, WITHOUT THE CAUSE BEING KNOWN. We often, in attempting to cure an evil, imagine that we know the cause, and many in this case will say, "it is the bad packing"—"it is the bad cement; those bolts have come unscrewed;" or, "that valve face wants grinding," when it is not so at all; but the true cause of the damage is rendered obscure because of its being only the result of a few drops of condensed water, which have not been allowed to escape at the proper time, before the engine has started.

Mr. S. CHATWOOD, C.E., well known by his celebrated Safes and the Safe Contest at Paris, during the last International Exhibition there, and who is also interested in Steam Hammers, found great difficulty in working them without such an invention. The result has been this essentially SAFE contrivance.

DESCRIPTION.

The sketch above shows a section of the Balloon Escape Valve. The pressure of the steam on entering the inlet closes the valve seat by raising the ball. The moment the engine stops the valve becomes wide open, in consequence of the descent of the ball, there being no pressure to keep it up, and thus allows all the condensed water to run out whilst the engine is at rest. The moment the engine is started the steam enters the ball, and the valve is closed. Should any water by any chance, such as priming or any other cause, be in the cylinder whilst the steam pressure is on, it will suddenly be dashed against the plate inside the ball, and, diverted to the sides, will cause the valve to open and let it out.

If at any time the engineer wishes to blow off a little steam, or see that the Balloon Valve is in good order, a slight pressure on the knob will cause it to open.

Being perfectly self-acting, it is far superior to anything yet in the market; and so great is our confidence in it, that any firm may have one to try, if they doubt the facts herein stated.

EACH CYLINDER SHOULD HAVE TWO.

PRICES.

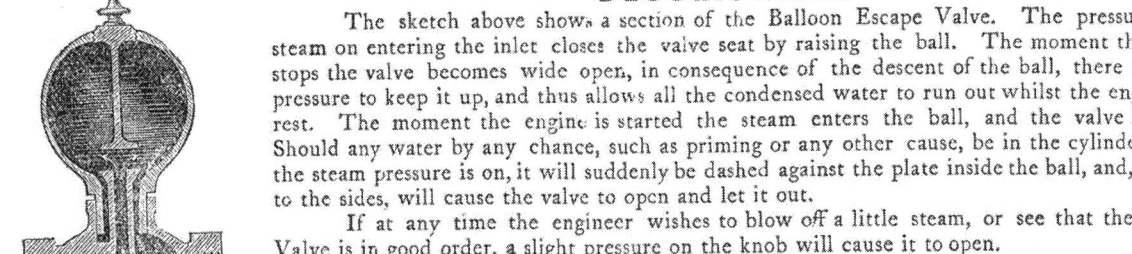

Screwed for ¼in. Gas Thread	... 6s. 0d. each.		Screwed for ¾in. Gas Thread	... 20s. each.	ALL BRIGHT
,, ⅜in. ,,	... 7s. 6d. ,,		,, 1in. ,,	... 25s. ,,	AND
,, ½in. ,,	... 15s. 0d. ,,		,, 1½ & 2in. ,,	35s. & 40s. ,,	WELL FINISHED.

Special Contracts with Engineers and Steam Hammer Manufacturers. Since these Engravings were made the patterns have been slightly altered; the Inlet is screwed male and the Outlet female.

SOLE LICENSEES AND MANUFACTURERS,—

JOHN BAILEY & CO.,
BRASSFOUNDERS AND ENGINEERS' SUNDRYMEN,
ALBION WORKS, SALFORD, LANCASHIRE.

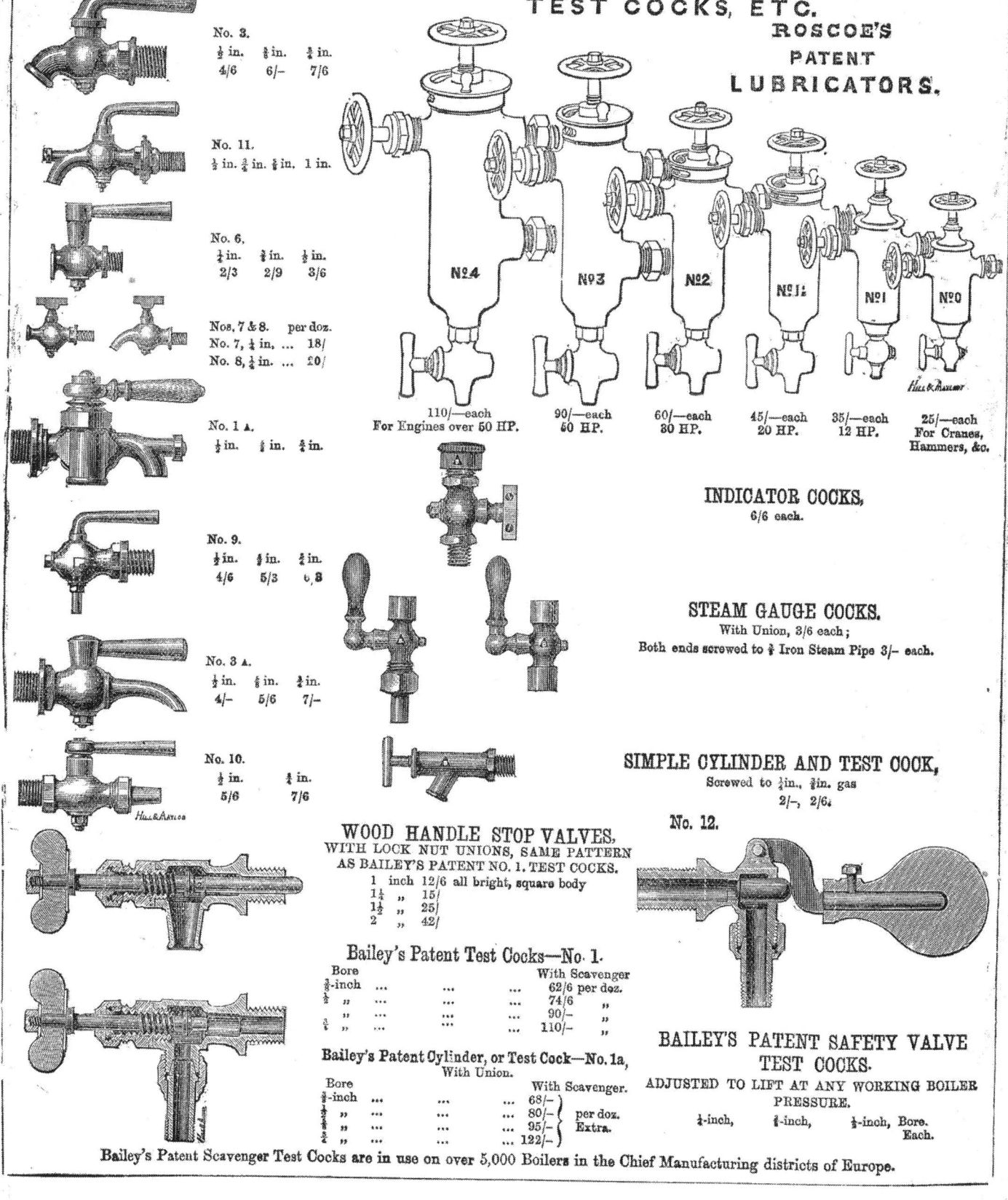

CLEMENTS' PATENT ECONOMIC LUBRICATOR,
FOR
MARINE, STATIONARY, AND LOCOMOTIVE ENGINES.

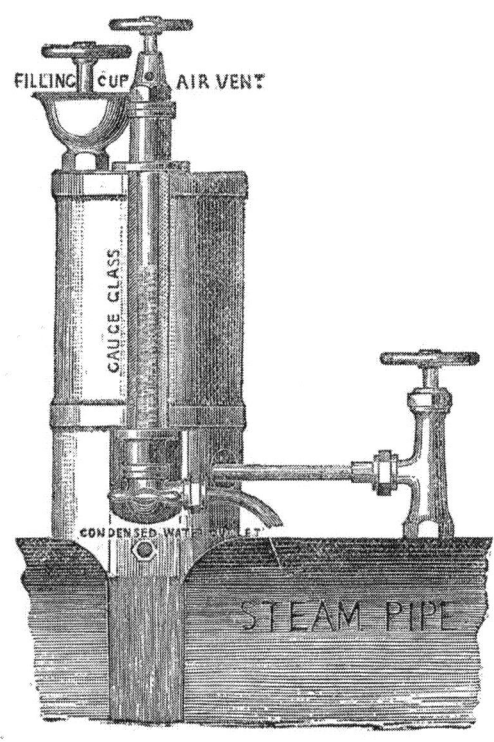

No. 130

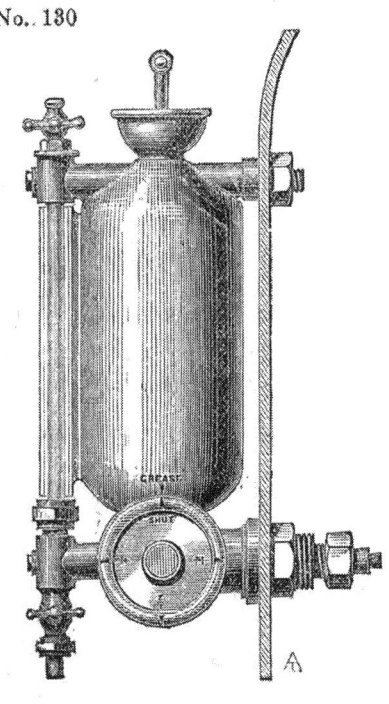

This Lubricator offers a perfect and cleanly method of lubricating all the internal parts of the Steam Engine by the diffusion of the lubricant in the steam; saving, at least, half of the oil or tallow generally used, and lessening the wear and tear consequent upon imperfect lubrication.

The largely extended use of these Lubricators amongst many of the most eminent Engineers testifies as to their value; and the Makers have had the perfect condition of the Cylinder and Slide Valves, resulting from their use, frequently brought under their notice.

They are made in bright gun-metal, in sizes varying from 1 pint to 6 pints.

A Form of this Patent Tallow Cup is suitable for screwing into Steam Pipe or Valve Chest, applicable for all purposes where the common Double Grease Cup is used.

PRICES

Of the **A** and **C** Forms.

To contain in Pints	1	2	3	4
Cast Iron Body	55/	60/	70/	80/
All Gun Metal	65/	75/	85/	100/

Of the **B** and **D** Forms.

To contain in Pints	1	2	3	4
Cast Iron Body	65/	70/	77/6	87/6
All Gun Metal	75/	85/	95/	110/

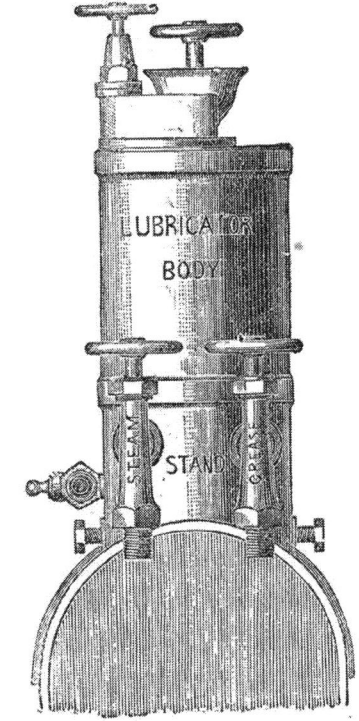

No. 130 A

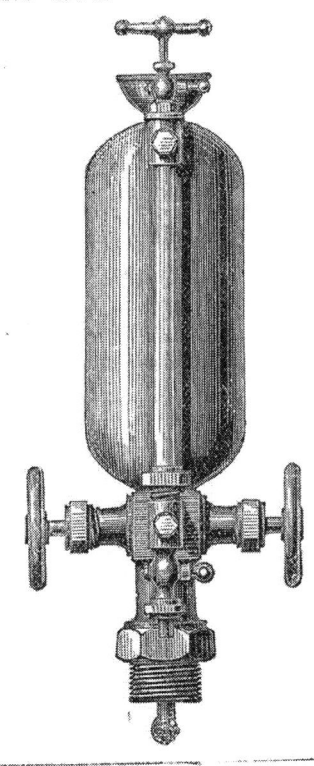

CLEMENT'S PATENT LUBRICATOR.

REMARKS AS TO THE FIXING.

This Lubricator is made in various forms, to suit round or flat surfaces in a vertical or horizontal position. It can be fixed upon Copper Pipes by brass bands (see the A and B forms), or where the substance is sufficient, can be screwed into iron pipes, the valve-chest, &c. (see the C and D form). The A form can be made with flat back, and the B with flat base, so that it may be bolted against the valve-chest, or upon it,—or, by using longer pipes, against the "bulk-head" or wall of Engine-room. In short, it can be placed in any position most convenient for observation, provided it be hot and free from draughts

The Connection should be made with the stem-pipe, so that the grease may fall into the current of steam near the valve-chest, and the perforated stem on the grease cock should project into the steam way, to prevent the grease trickling down the inside of pipe. The object of the invention being to impermeate the steam with grease, the grease should be so applied that it can be readily taken up in minute particles.

With a little attention to the following instructions, and especially when dry or super-heated steam is used, it will be found to give very satisfactory results, and require little attention.

INSTRUCTIONS FOR USING.

The Lubricator should be occasionally "blown out" by opening all the valves, and so keep clean. If it becomes foul with the passage choked, it will not act well.

To charge it, open the Charging Valve and Air Vent and observe the Gauge Glass.

The Lubricator being properly charged with tallow, freed from any foreign matter, by filtration if necessary, and all the valves closed,—Open the steam valve fully and blow off through the condense outlet the condense water, which may accumulate until the Lubricator is heated.

The Grease Valve can then be opened and regulated to the requirement of the Engine, which will be indicated by the appearance of the piston-rod, the valve-faces, &c. This must be a matter of experience, and upon the care bestowed in properly regulating the supply, will depend the saving of grease, and consequently much of the value of the invention. The grease should not be let in at intervals, but allowed to constantly dribble into the steam, so that it may be properly diffused; and occasional attention is necessary, in order that any condense water may be let off, as this will otherwise impede the flow of grease.

If the steam is very wet or the situation cold, so that condensation goes on rapidly, and it be thus preferable to work by condensation, keep the Grease Valve closed altogether, and the condense water accumulating at the bottom of the Lubricator will raise the grease, and cause it to overflow and trickle down the inside of the same tube which forms the steam inlet. This Lubricator will then have only the one way for both steam and grease, and will thus resemble in use and possess all the advantages of those Lubricators now extensively introduced to work by condensation alone.

The first plan is, however, considered the best, if the conditions are in its favour, it being independent of condensation, which is uncertain and uncontrollable, and having distinct ways for the steam and grease.

The Makers think they cannot do better than here annex a copy of a letter which was kindly sent them from the Chief Engineer of H.M.S. Himalaya.

Portsmouth, January 16th, 1866.

SIR,—With reference to your Patent Tallow Lubricator, fitted in June last, to the Engines of H.M.S. Himalaya, 700 horse power (Penn & Co. direct acting Trunk principle), and working at an average of fifty revolutions per minute, and since which time a distance of 17,000 miles has been run, giving us ample opportunity of testing its efficiency as well as its economy, every portion of the working parts in steam, viz.:—Pistons, Slides, Trunks, &c., were thoroughly and constantly lubricated, causing the packings, &c., to last much longer, as well as to materially reduce friction. As for its economy, we effected a saving of 60 per cent. in Tallow, and can highly recommend its adoption in Steam Engines of either high or low pressure.

I am, Sir, yours respectfully,

R. S. CONWAY, Chief Engineer H.M.S. Himalaya.

DIRECTIONS FOR WORKING TALLOW LUBRICATOR.

Steam in pipes and ready for starting, cocks F G H closed; unscrew cocks C and D, and pour in melted tallow until the Glass is full. Close cocks C and D, and open cock G for steam, wide, viz., two or three turns, also open cock F for tallow, but only a quarter turn, or even less will be sufficient, especially for engines working at a high velocity, because the current of steam passing the Lubricator Pipe has a tendency to draw in more tallow than necessary on increasing speed—Cock H may be opened one or two turns occasionally about every half hour, to blow out any water that condenses in the Lubricator, which would otherwise have a tendency to lead one to suppose, on examining the various working parts, that the Lubricator was not efficient, owing to the water instead of tallow being the lubricating material. It will perhaps be better to open the cock H seven or eight times once in three or four days, while the steam cock G is open, to clear the bottom of the Lubricator of any sediment. I would also recommend that the tallow should be strained through muslin or bunting while melted, before using.

These suggestions I would beg to offer from experience I gained in working the one on board the Himalaya.

Yours truly,

R. S. CONWAY, Esq.,
Chief Engineer.

RICHARD BIDDLE,
Senior Engineer, late Himalaya

It is respectfully requested that this should be HUNG UP in the Engine Room.

PORTER'S Governor for Stationary Steam Engines.

Size	Size of Engine for which each Governor is suitable	PRICES IN MANCHESTER	Distance of centre of Fulcrum-pin of Lever from centre line of the Governor.	Height to centre of Fulcrum-pin of Lever.	Motion of Slide	Weight of Counterpoise	Diameter of the largest circle described by the balls, over all	Length of Arms between centres	Number of revolutions of the Pulley per minute	Distance from centre line of Governor, to centre of Pulley, where not otherwise ordered.	Face of Pulley	Diameter of Pulley	Height of Centre of Pulley	Extreme Height	Size of Base
A	Not ex. 4-h.p. nom.	£10/10/0	in. 5	in. 13¾	in. 2	lbs. 40	in. 15	in. 8¼	210	in. 6¼	in. 1½	in. 3	in. 2¼	in. 31⅜	3⅜ × 6
B	,, ,, 10 ,,	13/13/0	5½	16¼	2¼	50	16½	9¼	220	6¾	2	3⅝	3¼	35⅜	3⅞ × 6¼
C	,, ,, 20 ,,	17/10/0	6	19	2½	60	17½	10½	230	7⅜	2	4	3½	41	4 × 8¼
D	,, ,, 40 ,,	21/0/0	7	25	2¾	80	19½	11	230	8⅛	2¼	5	4¼	50	4¾ × 9
E	,, ,, 60 ,,	24/5/0	8	31⅜	3	100	21	13	120	11¼	2½	6	5½	59	5⅞ × 11¼
F	,, ,, 90 ,,	27/17/6	9¼	35	3¼	120	23	14¼	124	13	2¾	7	6¼	66	6¾ × 13
G	,, ,, 120 ,,	31/10/0	10¼	36	3¾	150	25	15	124	13½	3	8	6⅜	68	6¾ × 13
H	above 120	35/15/0	12	37	5	180	27	16⅝	124	15	3¼	9	6¾	71	7¼ × 15

BAILEY'S
PATENT REGULATING CRYSTAL TALLOW CUP
FOR ENGINE CYLINDERS.

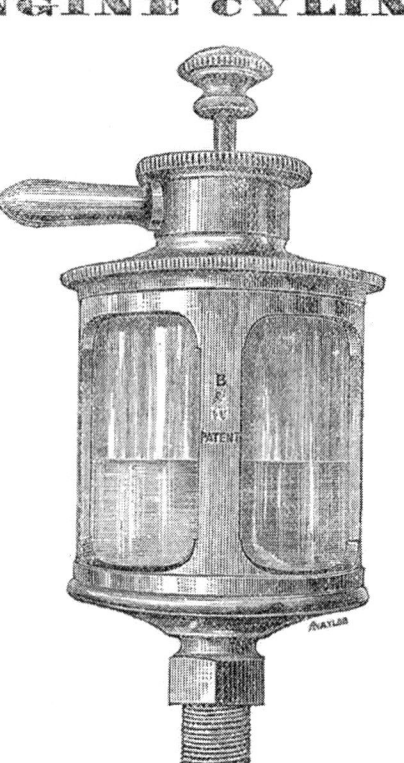

Simple in construction; strong, and economical in use.

It can be adjusted to the exact requirements of the Engine.

Scarcely a word is required to demonstrate the value of an Engineer being able to see "at a glance" if his cup is full of tallow. Simplicity is the great feature of this invention. The tallow may be regulated to enter into the cylinder or steam pipe at any speed, according to the requirements, and by simply closing the bottom valve with the milled headed nut at the top, the handle may be turned and the cup filled.

PRICES.

Diameter in Inches.	£	s.	d.
5	4	4	0
4	3	3	0
3	2	2	0
2½	1	7	6
2	0	18	6
1¾	0	12	6

A great number are in use, giving great satisfaction.

Purchasers of new Engines should by all means instruct the makers to fit these Tallow Cups.

SOLE MAKERS:

J. BAILEY AND CO.,
ALBION WORKS, SALFORD, LANCASHIRE.

LOWTHER AND BAILEY'S

PATENT GRAVITY

OIL AND TALLOW CUPS,

For Engine Cylinders, for Oil or Tallow.

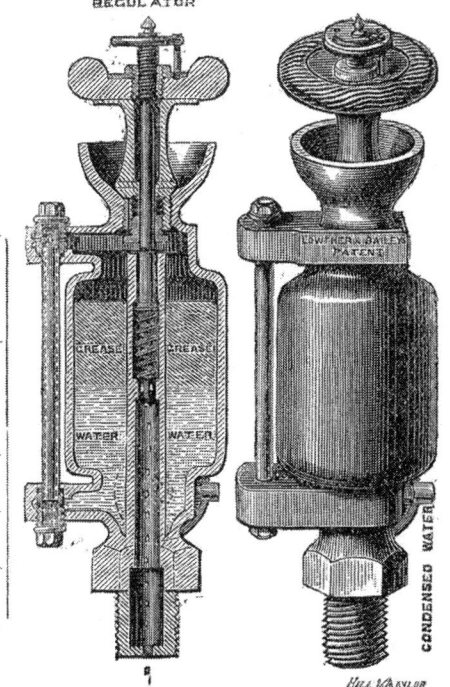

PRICES,
With Glass to see height of Lubricator.

Diameter of Cup.	Price.		
2½	£1	12	6
2¾	£1	16	0
3	£2	0	0
3½	£2	7	6
4	£2	17	6
5	£3	7	6

These Cups are especially adapted for use with Crane's Patent Oil, instead of Tallow. They are used also with Tallow. The Regulator enables the internal valve to be opened or depressed according to the requirements.

    These Cups are extensively used for lubricating the Slide Valves and Cylinders of large and small Land or Marine Engines. The principle upon which their action is based is upon the known condensation of steam, which, as it enters the Cup at the top, through the upright piece in the centre, it condenses and becomes water. This water displaces a certain amount of oil, which goes into the engine cylinder as it is required. It will be observed that only one valve at the top has to be moved, for, when the valve is taken away, the inverted valve closes and allows oil to be poured in without stopping the engine. A large quantity of tallow may be Injected for starting purposes, by filling the Cup full, and when the stopper is closed down, all will be injected into the cylinder until level with the top of the glass. The use of the condensed steam for heating the feed water, or even the use of the condensed water as a means of economy in feeding a boiler is often very injurious, and has to be prohibited where a great amount of carbonate or sulphate of lime exists in the water, as this coming in contact with ordinary greasy water which has passed through the cylinder and become impregnated, so causes a most extraordinary hard scale, in consequence of its soapy combination with the salts mentioned. The use of Crane's Patent Oil in these Cups, by its non-affinity for the minerals held in solution, is not attended with these difficulties, but really does a deal to prevent the incrustion which is detrimental to Steam Boilers. (For other properties of this Oil, see opposite page.)

    These facts having come under our observation, we note them for the benefit of our friends, and ourselves at the same time, as the more the Oil is used the greater will be the quantity of the Cups required.

THE MONCRIEFF PATENT
GYROMETRIC GOVERNORS
FOR LAND AND MARINE ENGINES,
THE MOST SIMPLE AND RELIABLE EVER INVENTED—HIGHLY APPROVED OF BY ALL WHO HAVE USED THEM.

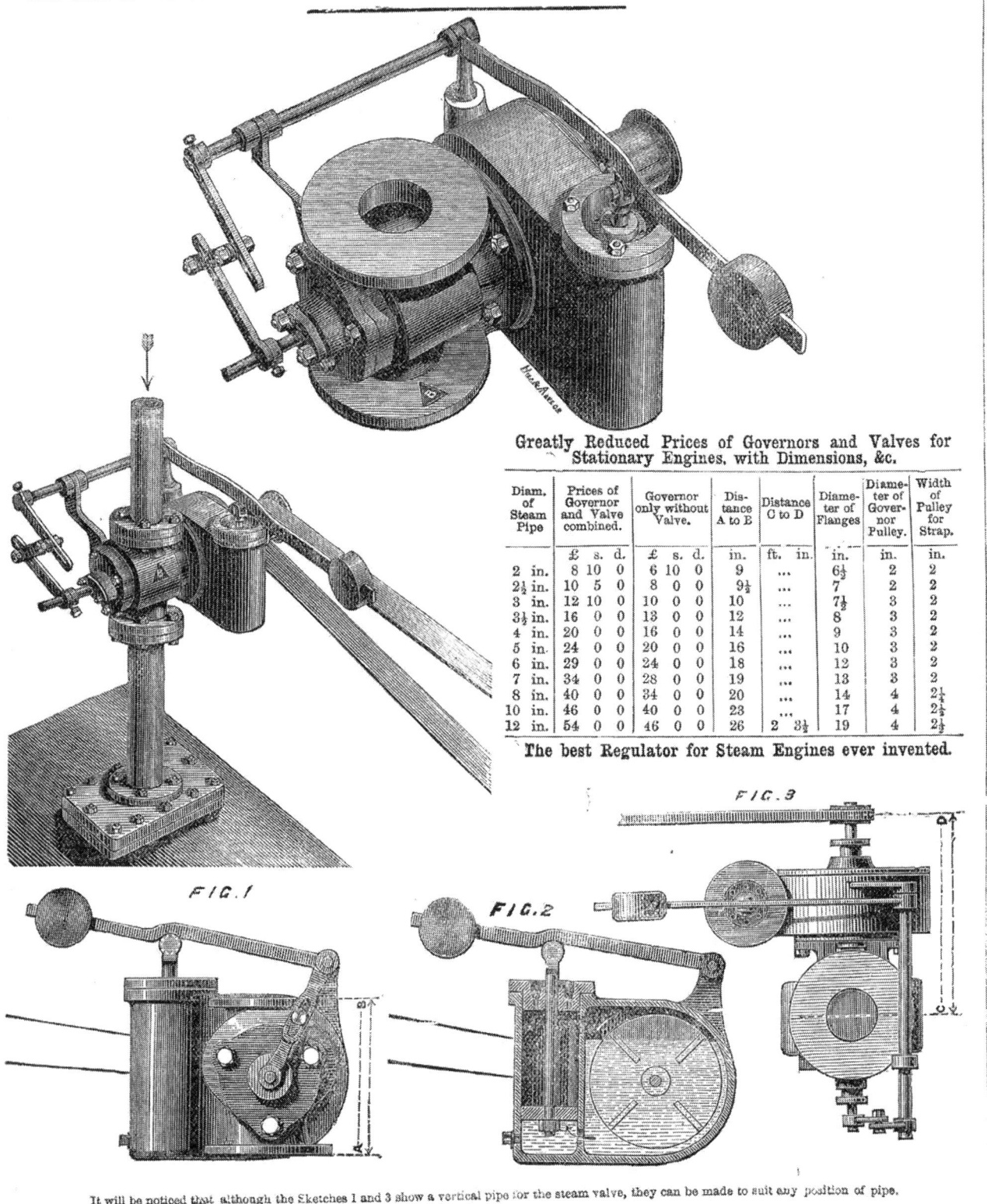

Greatly Reduced Prices of Governors and Valves for Stationary Engines, with Dimensions, &c.

Diam. of Steam Pipe	Prices of Governor and Valve combined.			Governor only without Valve.			Distance A to B	Distance C to D		Diameter of Flanges	Diameter of Governor Pulley.	Width of Pulley for Strap.
	£	s.	d.	£	s.	d.	in.	ft.	in.	in.	in.	in.
2 in.	8	10	0	6	10	0	9	...		6½	2	2
2½ in.	10	5	0	8	0	0	9½	...		7	2	2
3 in.	12	10	0	10	0	0	10	...		7½	3	2
3½ in.	16	0	0	13	0	0	12	...		8	3	2
4 in.	20	0	0	16	0	0	14	...		9	3	2
5 in.	24	0	0	20	0	0	16	...		10	3	2
6 in.	29	0	0	24	0	0	18	...		12	3	2
7 in.	34	0	0	28	0	0	19	...		13	3	2
8 in.	40	0	0	34	0	0	20	...		14	4	2¼
10 in.	46	0	0	40	0	0	23	...		17	4	2¼
12 in.	54	0	0	46	0	0	26	2	3½	19	4	2¼

The best Regulator for Steam Engines ever invented.

It will be noticed that although the Sketches 1 and 3 show a vertical pipe for the steam valve, they can be made to suit any position of pipe.

BAILEY'S
NEW HYDRAULIC TESTING APPARATUS.

This pump is used by the chief employers of Steam power at home and abroad.

Total weight, 100 lbs.

Complete ... ... £10 0s. 0d.

Other prices see opposite side.

Model Pump for Bench use for testing Steam Cocks, Steam Gauges, &c., complete, with Gauge to 200 lbs, £5 10s.

Since this Engraving was made the Pumps are made much stronger.

To Boiler Makers in Testing New Work these Pumps are recommended, and in consequence of their portability and general adaptability, we can give the names of several boiler makers who have cast on one side the old cumbersome apparatus in order to use ours.

To India-rubber and Woven Hose Pipe and Tube Makers these Pumps are useful for testing purposes, and we beg to refer, among others, to the Manchester Rubber Co.; Messrs. Foster and Williams, London; &c., who have them in daily use.

To Managers of Gas and Water Works Companies—For testing Iron and Brass Pipes and Tubes, Cisterns, Valves, Cocks, &c., this invention is useful. Special unions for special purposes are made.

To Makers of Hot Water Apparatus this invention is useful. Much damage and expense is created by defective pipes being laid, the fault often being only discovered when a job has been completed, and which might have been prevented by the timely use of the hydraulic test to each pipe.

It is an additional source of profit to Engineers, Boiler Makers, and others. Many of our friends, who have purchased Pumps, test boilers, and make a charge for so doing of £1 1s., or lend the Pump for one day for 10s. 6d.

In testing Boilers, Messrs. J. Bailey & Co. recommend them not to be tested to a pressure any higher than one-third more than ordinary working pressure.

"Messrs. J. Bailey & Co., eminent Pressure Gauge Makers, have recently produced a neat, compact, portable apparatus for testing Boilers."—*English Mechanic.*

"A suitable Pump fitted in a tank, and connected with a good pressure gauge."—*Engineer.*

"The most complete thing for the purpose."—*All who have tried them.*

All Boilers should be tested after being cleansed before being again used.

Those Boilers in which are many tubes and flues, such as those for agricultural, marine, and locomotive purposes, can only be efficiently tested by hydraulic pressure, in consequence of the impossibility of examining or testing internal deficiencies by any other means.

This unsolicited Testimonial is one of a great many of a similar nature, which are constantly being received:—

From Messrs. GEORGE THOMPSON & Co., the eminent Contractors, Greenhill, near Sheffield.

March 23rd, 1867.

GENTLEMEN,—The Hydraulic Test Pump, which we purchased from you six months ago, gives general satisfaction, and answers our purposes very well. We can highly recommend it as being reasonable in price and very efficient.—We are, gentlemen, yours very truly,

GEORGE THOMPSON & Co.

A Complete gun metal working parts, flexible tube, union joint, and nipple, and gauge to 250 lbs. ... £10 0 0
B Small Pumps for testing Steam and Gas Cocks ¼ in. to 2 in., with nipples, complete, with gauge to 100 lbs. ... 9 0 0
C Pump Hose Pipe, ¼ in. to 3 in., with clips and nipples ... 16 13 0
D For Locomotives, with gauge to 500 lbs. pressure, is extra strong in all its parts, all gun metal and first-class Hydra-Pump, with Ram 1-in. diameter, all gun metal, with cross head and extra strong (without gauge), with Valve and Weight, for Oil Presses, Packing, &c. 20 0 0

Pumps for Special Testing purposes made to Drawing.

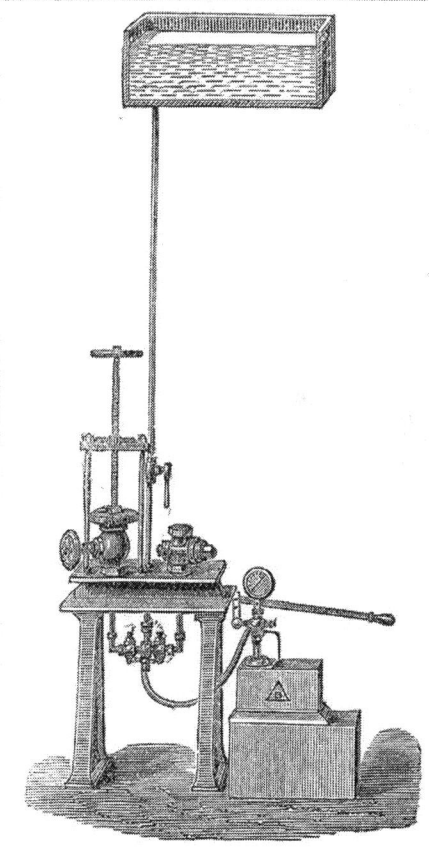

TESTING BENCH & PUMP

Complete for Chief Engineer's office, for Testing Tubes, Cocks, Valves, Fittings, &c.; also much use by Plumbers, Brass-Founders, *et hoc genus hominum*.
Price, complete, without cistern, ... £15 10 0
Model Bench Pump, separate from Bench, ... £5 10 0

Estimates for Hydraulic Work on application.

BAILEY'S TESTING MACHINES,

FOR PIPES, PAPER, IRON, STEEL, COKE AND COAL, COTTON AND LINEN YARN, &c.

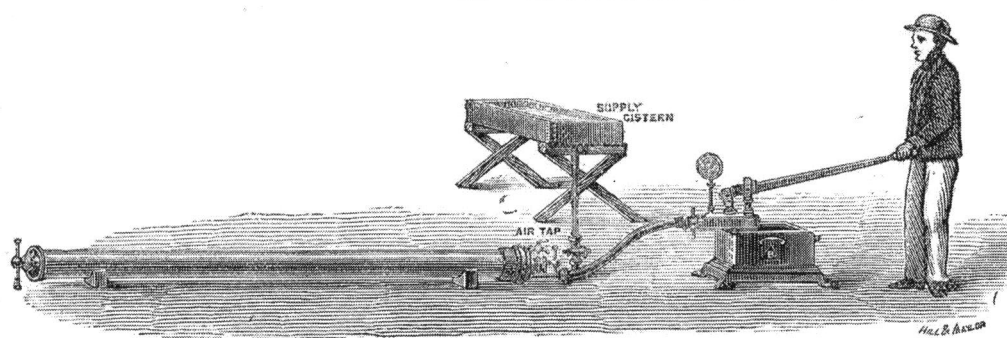

BAILEY'S HYDRAULIC PUMP, FOR TESTING PIPES.

BAILEY'S PIPE TESTING MACHINE for testing pipes from 2in. to 3 feet in diameter, for the use of Gas and Water Works Managers, Pipe Makers, &c. The pipes are blocked by Stuart & Walker's Patent Bevel Stops, which, by the aid of rubber washers, enables a good joint to be made.

Price, complete, with Test Pump to 250 lbs. pressure, with Stoppers for 2, 2½, 3, 3½, 4, 6 and 8 inches for Flange Pipes, £40. Special quotations for special pipes. Pump, without Stoppers, £10. Circulars are in course of preparation of the Testing Machine for Iron, Brass, Cement, &c., invented by Professor Thurston, of which J. BAILEY & CO. are Sole Makers.

This Machine has been awarded the Gold Medal of Progress of the American Institute; this is their highest award for 1874, only two others having been given. This Machine tests and records Strength, Elasticity, Limits of Elasticity, Ductility, Homogeneousness, Resistance.

Patent Paper Tester for Paper Buyers, Paper Makers, &c.

For testing the strength of Paper,   Complete, £2 10s.

As used by *Daily Telegraph*, *Standard*, &c., &c.

WILKINSON & BAILEY'S COAL TESTING APPARATUS.

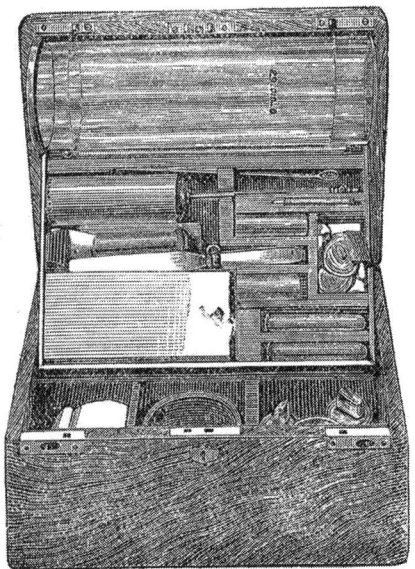

Apparatus for ascertaining the Heating Power of Coal, Coke, and other Fuel.

Instructions are furnished with the Apparatus, which render the manipulation easy, and in the hands of any moderately careful person, will give MORE CORRECT results than can be obtained by any of the expensive, laborious, and intricate processes previously in use.

	£	s.	d.
Apparatus complete in plain Wood Case	4	15	0
Ditto, ditto, polished Mahogany Case, lined with Cloth, with additional Tests for Lignite, and Sulphuretted Hydrogen Gas, Test Tubes, Box-end Beam, and Glass Scales	5	10	0

The want of a simple and certain method of ascertaining the calorific or steam generating power of the various samples of Coal, Coke, &c., now in use, has been long felt. The Apparatus now offered to supply this need, is constructed on principles that will bear the test of the closest scrutiny by the scientific, is easily understood by practical men, and may be used without the necessity of making intricate calculations.

BAILEY'S YARN TESTERS

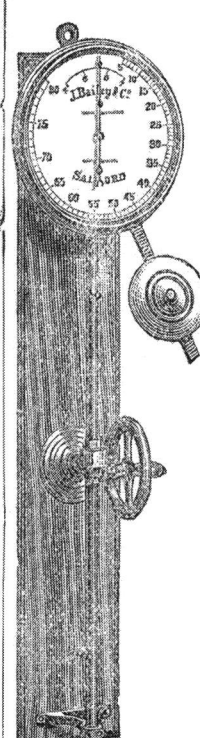

Dead Weight	Price
	£ s. d.
No. 1, for Yarn up to 100 lbs.	6 10 0
No. 2, for Yarn up to 100 lbs., and also for single threads in ounces to 5 lbs.	7 10 0
No. 3, for Paper Makers, to 100 lbs., with elliptical jaws	6 10 0
No. 4, for Flax, Cotton Cords and special purposes, to 200 lbs.	8 8 0
No. 5, for Twine, Thin Wire, &c., to 500 lbs. on cast iron back plate	20 0 0

Important to Iron and Steel Manufacturers, Civil Engineers, Bolt Makers, Brassfounders, &c.

PROFESSOR THURSTON'S TESTING MACHINE,
WITH
AUTOGRAPHIC REGISTRY.

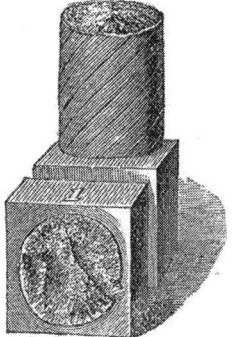
Swedish Iron.

Softened Cast Iron, specially prepared.

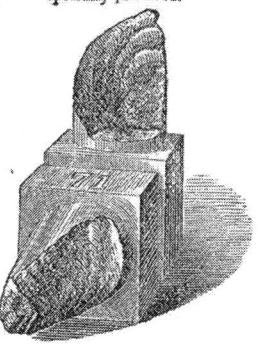
American Tool Steel, of fine quality.

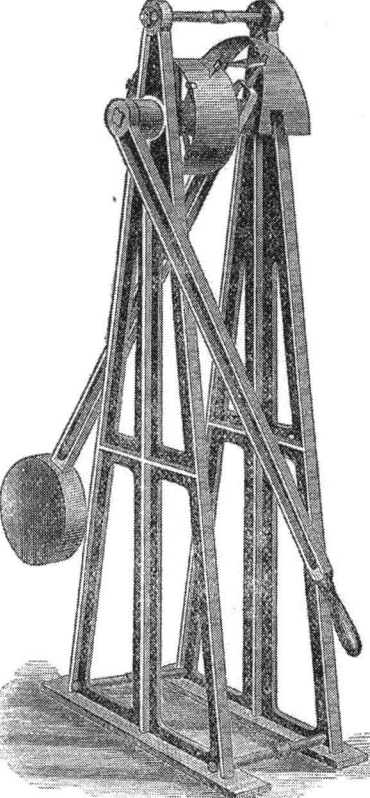

Strength,

Elasticity,

Limit of Elasticity,

Ductility,

Homogeneousness,

Resilience.

Good Ordinary Iron.

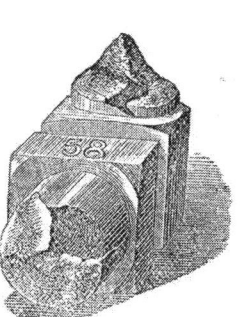
German Crucible Steel.

White Iron, Cast.

The illustrations here shown are from the proceedings of the American Institute of Engineers, Professor THURSTON having kindly lent them to illustrate our book.—[See *Journal of Franklin Institute*, April, 1874.]

No. 22 is Metal Wrought Iron of the highest possible character. It will be observed that the other illustrations do not present so great an appearance of ability to resist torsional strains.

We have a few copies of the paper read by Professor THURSTON, and shall be glad to send one to any one interested in these experiments.

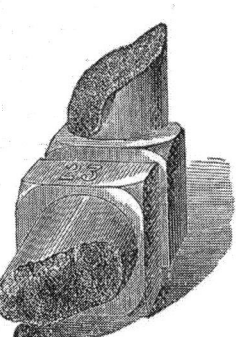
Pennsylvania Foundry Iron.

Low Steel, Tough.

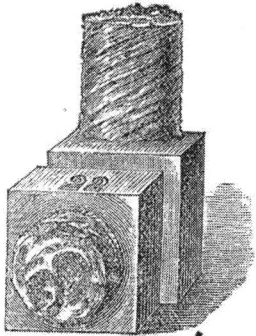
Best Iron, Very Superior.

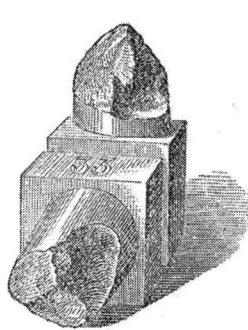
Cast Iron.

AMERICAN SOCIETY OF CIVIL ENGINEERS.

A NOTE ON THE RESISTANCE OF MATERIALS OF CONSTRUCTION.

By Prof. ROBERT H. THURSTON, Member of the Society.

READ AT THE REGULAR MEETING, NOVEMBER 19TH, 1873.

On the 13th ultimo, an *apparatus for determining the torsional resistance of materials*, which I had designed for use, in illustration of my course of instruction, and to which I had fitted an automatic recording attachment, was exhibited to the National Academy of Science, at the late session held at this place, for the purpose of showing the peculiar adaptability of the machine for the determination and analysis of the action of physical and molecular forces in resisting stress, and to illustrate the bearing of experiments already made upon scientific investigations of molecular relations.

At the close of the meeting a test piece of wrought-iron was left in the machine, exposed to a strain which had passed the limit of elasticity, and with a distortion of 45 degrees, the intention being to determine whether, as has been suspected by some writers and by many engineers, "viscosity" is a property of solids, whether a "flow of solids"* could occur under long-continued strain just equilibrating, when first applied, the resisting power of the material, or whether the "polarity" of Professor Henry is an absolutely unrelaxing force.

The metal was left under strain twenty-four hours, and had not then yielded in the slightest degree. This result, and the results of other similar experiments since made confirming it, indicates, that metal strained far beyond the limit of elasticity, as above described, does not lose its power of resisting unintermitted static stress.

The important bearing of this fact upon the availability of iron, and of steel, which also behaves similarly, for use in constructions exposed to severe strains, is readily seen.

After noting the result obtained as stated, it was attempted to still further distort the test piece, when the unexpected discovery was made that its resisting power was greater than when left the previous day, an increase of resistance being recorded amounting to about 25 per cent. of the maximum registered the preceding day, and approximating closely to the ultimate resistance of the material. Repeated experiments, continued up to the date of writing, confirm the following previously undemonstrated principle: that iron and steel, if strained beyond the limit of elasticity, and left under the action of the distorting force which has been found just capable of equilibrating their power of resistance, gain resisting power to a degree which has a limit in amount, approximating closely, if not coinciding with the ultimate resistance of the material, and which had a limit, as to time, in experiments hitherto made, of three or four days.

Releasing the piece entirely, and again submitting it to the same force immediately, does not produce this strengthening action.

There is some evidence, that is confirmed by theoretical dynamic principles, that the increase of strength noted is not accompanied by a change of resilience, but that the gain of resisting power is at the expense of a proportional amount of ductility.

The diagrams obtained during this research will be presented at a future time, when the investigation shall have been completed.

The interest and importance attaching to the discovery of the principles above enunciated, to our profession as well as to science, will, I hope, justify the presentation of this note.

OFFICIAL REPORT

OF UNITED STATES GOVERNMENT OFFICIALS

On Prof. THURSTON'S TESTING MACHINE.

Navy Yard, New York,
May 2nd, 1874.

SIR,—In obedience to your order of the 25th ult., that we should proceed to the Stevens' Institute of Technology, in Hoboken, New Jersey, and witness the operation of the Machine designed by Professor R. H. Thurston, of that Institute, for Testing the strength of materials, &c., to examine those in course of construction, to inspect the work already done, and the designs of machines proposed for special purposes, and to report in duplicate the results of our examination, and our recommendations in view thereof,

We have the honour to report that we have visited the Stevens' Institute, and witnessed the operations of a machine, which has for its purpose to subject specimens of different materials to strains of torsion, continuously, from the initial strain through all the succeeding stages to final rupture; the machine being furnished with an automatic registry, by which means the relation between the moment of torsion and the angle of torsion is graphically represented throughout the entire process of any experimental inquiry of the kind.

We have also examined several machines in course of construction, with improved features in the details of their operation, besides examining drawings of other and larger machines.

We are satisfied that this form of Testing Machine admits of being used with great facility in the practical study of the properties of woods, the metals, and their alloys, especially with reference to their elasticity, ductility, and ultimate resistance; that it is capable of revealing characteristic physical properties of great value in forming a practical judgment of their relative usefulness under different circumstances of their production or manufacture.

We find the machine an extremely simple one, and of small cost (estimated $350 each), and while we do not think it can judiciously replace the machines for direct tension, we are of opinion that this machine would be found quite useful in the different departments of the Navy Yards requiring the kind of information furnished by it.

We are, Sir, very respectfully,

Your obedient Servants,

(Signed),

ROBERT DANBY, Chief Engineer, U.S.N.
W. L. HANSCOM, Naval Constr., U.S.N.
RICHARD W. MEADE, Commander, U.S.N.
H. C. WHITE, Lieut.-Commander, U.S.N.
B. F. GREEN, Prof. of Math., U.S.N.

Vice-Admiral,
S. C. ROWAN, Commandant,
Navy Yard, N.Y.

Vice-Admiral's Office,
Navy Yard, N.Y., Approved May 5th, 1874.

(Signed),

S. C. ROWAN, Vice-Admiral Commanding.

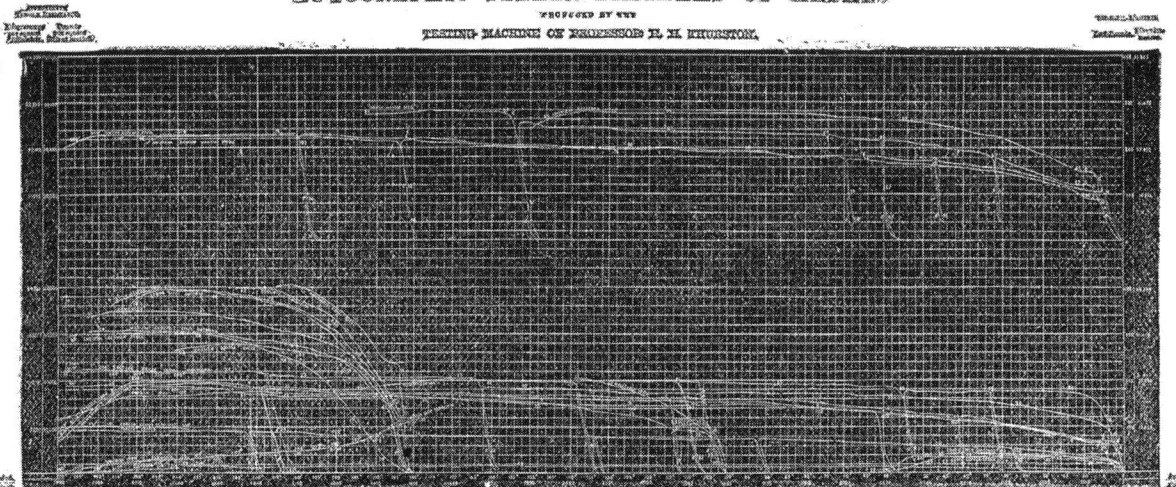

AUTOGRAPHIC STRAIN-DIAGRAMS OF METALS PRODUCED BY THE TESTING MACHINE OF PROFESSOR R. H. THURSTON.

THURSTON'S PATENT TESTING MACHINE.

SOLE MAKERS,
J. BAILEY & CO., MANCHESTER.

Awarded the Gold Medal of Progress by the American Institute, 1874.

Bolt Makers, Brass Founders, &c., may test Specimens of Metal in five minutes with this Machine.

No. 1 Machine for Iron, Brass, Wood, &c., £45 each. Height 6 feet.

INSTRUCTIONS.

Prepare test specimens of standard size and form as shown in the accompanying sketch,

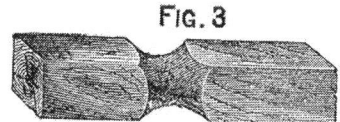

making them 3½ inches long, and turning the middle down to a neck one inch long, ⅜ inch diameter, and with fillet turned out at each end to a radius of one-sixteenth inch. Centre them in the machine, block them carefully, adjust the paper under the pencil, and then twist the sample off very slowly and steadily, taking off all strain again once or twice, before ultimate fracture, to form the "elasticity line."

Remove the strain diagram and measure. The scale of the diagram of the "Standard" machine is 300 foot pounds in torsion, equivalent to 30,000 pounds per square inch tensile resistance. Interpret the diagram as directed in the following instructions:

1. *To determine the homogeneousness of the material.*

Examine the form of the initial portion of the diagram between the starting point and the first sudden change of direction which indicates the elastic limit. Notice also its inclination from the vertical, and compare with it the inclination of the "elasticity line."

A perfectly straight line between the elastic limit, perfectly parallel with the "elasticity line," shows the material to be *homogeneous as to strain*, i.e., to be free from internal strains, such as are produced by irregular and rapid cooling, or by working too cold. Any variation from this line indicates the existence and measures the amount of strain. A line considerably curved exhibits the existence of such strain.

Next examine the form of the curve immediately after passing the elastic limit.

A line rising from the elastic limit, regularly and smoothly, approximately parabolic in form, and concave toward the base line, indicates *homogeneousness in structure*, and the absence of such imperfections as are produced in wrought iron by cinder, or in cast metals which have been worked from ingots, by porosity of the ingot.

A line turning the corner sharply, when passing the elastic limit, and then running nearly or quite horizontal, as in irons usually and in low steel, or actually becoming convex toward the base line, as with some of the woods, and then, after a time, resuming upward movement by taking its proper parabolic path, indicates a decided want of this kind of homogeneity. The relative length of the depressed portion of the line, and the amount of depression measures the relative defectiveness of materials compared in this respect.

Finally, compare the diagrams produced by several specimens of the same kind of material or from the same mass.

Homogeneousness in general character and *homogeneousness in composition* are proven by the precise similarity of these diagrams, while a greater or less variation of the curves compared indicates a greater or less difference in the specimens of which they are autographs.

Materials should usually exhibit great homogeneousness in all these three ways, to be perfectly reliable. Perfect homogeneousness is not to be expected in either respect.

(2.) *To determine the elastic resistance of the specimen.*

Measure the height of the curve at the elastic limit, using the scale of torsion, or for tension, which is given for each machine and for each standard size of test piece.

(3.) *To determine the resistance offered to any given amount of extension or that producing a given set.*

Measure the height of the curve at the point whose distance from the origin measures the assumed degree of set.

(4.) *To determine the ultimate resistance of the material.*

Measure in a similar manner the maximum height of the curve.

(5.) *To determine the resilience of the piece within the elastic limit*, i.e., the work required to produce an evident and permanent set, approximately proportional in amount to the degree of change of form of the specimen. (*This quantity measures the power of the material to resist blows*, and its determination is evidently quite as important as that of resistance to simple stress, which latter forms one of the factors of the former.)

Measure the area comprised between the ordinate of the curve at the elastic limit and the initial part of the curve. This quantity is proportional to the required value.

Or, multiply the elastic resistance of the material by the extension within the elastic limit. Two-thirds this product is the quantity required in inch pounds or foot pounds, according as measures of extension are taken in inches or feet as an approximate result.

(6 *To determine the resilience of the material within any assumed limit of extension*, i.e., the magnitude of blow required to produce a given set.

Measure the area of the curve up to the assumed limit.

Two-thirds the product of the resistance measured by the altitude, and the extension box gives as before an approximate value for ordinary purposes.

(7.) *To determine the total resilience* or shock-resisting power of the material.

Measure the total area of the diagram.

For ductile materials an approximate value is obtained by taking two-thirds the product of the maximum tenacity by the maximum extension. For hard and very brittle materials one half the same product gives very accurately its values. For intermediate qualities the true value is more nearly two-thirds this product, also Swedish wrought iron, white cast iron and hardened steel illustrate the first and the second classes; ordinary tool steels are examples of the third class.

(8.) *To determine the effect of a load given in pounds per square inch of stress.*

Find a point in the curve having an altitude which measures the given stress. This altitude of that point measures the extension under that load.

In other words, a point being found in the curve, the height of which above the base line is equal to the load per square inch, its distance from the origin measures the extension of the material as produced by that stress.

9. *To determine the effect of a blow or a shock, whose measure is given in inch pounds of energy, i.e., of which the work which it is capable of doing is known.*

Find a point on the curve whose ordinate cuts off an area between itself and the origin, representing the given amount of work.

Or, find such a point that two-thirds the product of the stress measured by its ordinate, and the extension corresponding to its abscissa is equal to the number of inch pounds given. The position of this point shows the maximum strain and the maximum extension of the material under the assumed conditions. Drawing a line through this point parallel to the nearest "elasticity line," the distance of the point at which it intersects the base line from the origin indicates the resulting set.

10. *To determine the effect of a blow upon the material when already strained by a dead load.*

Determine first the extension produced by the application of the static stress as in (8), and then find that point on the curve between the ordinate of which and the ordinate of the point indicating the strain just found as due the dead load, an area is intercepted which measures the work done by, or the energy of, the shock which has been assumed or calculated.

15. Examples.

(1.) Given, a load of 30,000 pounds per square inch. Determine its effect upon good qualities of cast and wrought iron, low steels, tool steel and the weaker metals.

Referring to examples we find that neither cast copper, lead, tin, nor zinc would sustain such strain. All would be broken.

Good iron would be strained beyond its limit of elasticity, and would take a set after an extension of about 1 or $1\frac{1}{4}$ per cent. Exceptional iron would be strained to a point which is so nearly its elastic limit that it would remain practically uninjured.

The low steels would bear the stress with a similar degree of safety, very nearly.

If the strain were torsional, the weaker metals would be twisted off by a force corresponding to that here assumed, the good irons would take a set of about 25°, the best iron and the stronger steels would take no appreciable set, and the softest of the latter would set at about 10°. In these cases the specimens are supposed of standard size. For other sizes the forces producing similar effects would vary as the cubes of the diameters.

(2.) Given, the magnitude of a shock or blow, e.g. as equal to that due a weight of one ton, 2,000 pounds, falling one foot, the rod taking the strain being of one square inch area of section and one foot long. Determine the effect for each of the above-named materials.

The effect of this blow is equivalent to an expenditure of energy amounting to $2,000 \times 12 = 24,000$ inch pounds.

The weaker materials, not possessing an ultimate resilience of this amount, would be broken.

Forged copper would be strained and would take a set after very nearly 12.5 per cent. of extension, since, for a tested specimen,

$$0.125 \times 12 \times \frac{24,000 \times 2}{3} = 24,000$$

the work done by the blow being equilibrated by the product of two thirds the resistance,

$$\frac{24,000 \times 2}{3},$$

into the extension $0.12\frac{1}{2} \times 12$ inches. Perfect accuracy of figures may be insured by perfectly accurate measurements.

A specimen of iron would be given an extension and set of nearly 0.068, since the resistance, under this amount of stretch, would be approximately 45,000 pounds per square inch, and the work during extension would be

$$0.068 \times 12 \times \frac{45,000 \times 2}{3} = 24,000 \text{ inch pounds.}$$

Iron of special grade would be elongated

$0.058 = 0.69$ inch, as $0.069 \times 12 \times \dfrac{52,000 \times 2}{3} = 24,000$, nearly.

The same blow would produce on the rod, if made of such steel as one specimen tried, an extension of $0.0384 \times 12 = 0.461$ inches, estimated thus, $x = 24,000 \div \frac{2}{3}.78,000 = 0.461$, it being found by "trial and error," that the extension 0.0384 developes a maximum resistance of 78,500 pounds per square inch.

It is evident that where extreme accuracy is required, the curves should be transferred to a new scale in which the abscissas should be a scale of elongation instead of angular distortion, and the area should be carefully measured. For the latter work an Amsler "Planimeter" is useful.

(3.) Given, a bolt of dimensions as last assumed, strained with the effect of a load of 30,000 pounds, as in example (1), determine the effect of a blow of 24,000 inch pounds energy, occurring while the bar is sustaining the static load.

The effect of the dead load, as already calculated, is to produce a strain upon the low steels, and upon iron of very high grade, which would keep them extended only a very minute fraction of their original length, this extension being, even with the latter material, but 0.05 of one per cent. The effect of the blow would be, practically, the same as has just been estimated for the unloaded bar.

Two other irons would be, as already shown, extended one and one and a-half per cent. respectively, by the simple load. The added effect of the blow would be to produce an additional extension and set of 0.0533 and 0.0555 respectively, since the main resistance, during this extension, is found to be

$$\frac{45,000 + 35,000}{2} \text{ and } \frac{42,000 + 30,000}{2}$$

respectively, and the extension must be,

$$24,000 \div \frac{45,000 + 30,000}{2} \div 12 = 0.0533 \text{ and}$$

$$24,000 \div \frac{42,000 + 30,000}{2} \div 12 = 0.0555$$

The bar is stretched in the first case, 0.64 inch; in the second, 0.666 inch, by the blow, if made of such iron as that supposed.

It should be remarked here, that although the diagrams obtained from the various materials tested give data from which to estimate their relative value in resisting shock, the absolute results of calculation, with no modification for varying rapidity of action, will be but approximate.

This is a consequence of the facts that the inertia of the body struck will affect the result, and the actual resistance varies with the velocity of rupture. A rod which will sustain safely the blow of a heavy body, would yield readily under a blow of similar energy struck by a light weight moving with proportionally increased velocity. A rod of uniform section and homogeneous in structure, will be uniformly extended by a force slowly applied. A blow received at one end will extend it most at the portion nearest that end, and the more rapid the blow the more is its effect concentrated. It is possible to produce actual fracture at one end by a very rapid blow, and for rupture to become complete before the shock is felt at the opposite end. This action is seen daily in every workshop where pieces are broken from heavy masses by the blow of a hammer.

The effect of a blow depends, therefore, not only on the magnitude of that product of mass into height due its velocity which we call *vis viva* but also upon the magnitude of the factors.

In general a rod should be somewhat larger at the end receiving the shock, and this enlargement should be greater as the blow is more rapid. Conversely, blows of equal energy are the most injurious when given by bodies of light weight moving at high speed.

16. Peculiar problems sometimes present themselves in practice which can be readily solved by the use of this machine, but not by any other means.

Of these the following is an example:

To determine the effect of a succession of stresses, whether static or dynamic, each of which strains the material beyond the original or the acquired limit of elasticity.

(An illustration of this action is given by the repeated bending, stretching or other form of distortion by external force, of any material producing at each application a new set. The same case is illustrated by the gradual elongation of rod by repeated blows, the energy of each of which exceeds the elastic resilience of the material.)

Determine the elastic resilience of the material existing previous to the application of each stress, by taking the area comprised between two lines drawn through that point on the curve of the material chosen, whose abscissa represents the existing extension, one of which lines is an ordinate and the other of which is parallel to the nearest "elasticity line." This represents the elastic resilience of the piece; *i. e.*, a blow having an equivalent energy would leave the piece uninjured and without set. Deducting this amount from the energy of the given blow, the remainder of the work done by that blow is expended in producing set or extension, and may be determined as already described.

The effect of a simple force may be determined by deducting from the total distortion producted by each application of that force the elastic range of the material.

It is thus readily ascertained, in either case, how much each application will add to the set, and how many applications will be required to produce rupture.

The effect of repeated bending or other form of strain can thus be inferred from an examination of the strain diagram of the material, obtaining from a single experiment a determination hitherto only obtained by a long and tedious process of repeated distortion. Such investigations of the "fatigue" of metals are often of great importance.

STRAIN DIAGRAMS AND THEIR REVELATIONS.

BY PROFESSOR R. H. THURSTON.

In the figure here given are rough copies of several complete Strain Diagrams produced by the Autographic Torsion Machine, by which this novel internal examination of materials, and its revelations can be more completely exhibited. The original Strain Diagrams of iron occupy a space nearly a yard long and but two and a half inches high. Those of steel are five or six inches high. The column of figures at the right of the engraving represents the maximum stress per square inch of section exerted upon the fibres of the metal by tension, when the product of the weight on the end of the lever by its leverage is equal to the figure at the opposite end of the plate.

Referring to the figure: the curve, A, is that of zinc. Its form at the commencement, concave toward the base, shows its inelastic nature. Its gradual rise shows that it may take a set under the action of the smallest forces. Its maximum height is small in comparison with its companion curves, and this shows its weakness; it actually has proportional to its distortion, is at a very low strain, less than 10,000 lbs., and it yields very considerably before it offers its maximum resistance. Its ductility is its most remarkable quality. Cast copper contrasts strikingly with the forged metal. Its limit of elasticity occurred at about 5,000 lbs. per square inch, its ultimate strength was between 12,000 and 13,000 lbs. per square inch, and its elongation was but two and a-half per cent. This piece was from carefully selected ingot copper, cast in dry sand. It, like the majority of the specimens here described, is therefore an unusually good example of cast copper; and were it of an impure scrap, or had it been cast in green sand, its inferiority to forged copper would have been still more marked. Green sand seriously injures the metal by the production of porous castings, rendered spongy by vapours from the damp mould.

Good wrought iron gives the line D. The beginning of the diagram, a line nearly straight but slightly curved in a direction the reverse of the preceding, and inclined toward the left, shows plainly that this is a somewhat elastic material, having a little internal strain. The short stretch of nearly horizontal lines, which appears far more distinctly in the original diagram, indicated that it is a fibrous iron, well worked and rather hard. It takes a set at nearly 20,000 lbs. per square inch, and its maximum resistance is nearly 60,000 lbs. It finally breaks at some point beyond 240o; its maximum elongation is about one-half, on some lines of fiber.

On this strain diagram will be noticed two of the lines exhibiting elasticity. They are apparently perfectly parallel, a fact which proves, what had already been suspected and almost proved by more than one distinguished philosopher, that elasticity remains unimpaired until fracture actually commences. Comparing the inclination of these lines, e e, with that of the initial part of the diagram, we find all very nearly of the same inclination; and the deduction, already made from the slight curvature of the beginning of the diagram, that this iron is very slightly weakened by internal strain, is thus confirmed. The line, E E, shows the form of the terminal portion of the diagram when the metal is very tough and ductile, like Swedish iron, for example. With ordinary irons and with steel, the curve ends abruptly, as shown in all those here given. The diagram, F F, is that of the excellent iron, referred to in the previous article as having given a curve of such beautiful regularity. The line exhibits perfection in quality by its great symmetry and smoothness. Were it shown in extenso, it would be seen that the specimen only broke after a complete revolution, and that the metal is as remarkable for its strength and ductility as for its homogeneousness and purity.

The effect of the presence of carbon upon the properties of iron is shown by the succeeding diagrams. A low steel, containing 0·4 per cent. carbon, and produced by the Bessemer process, tells its story at G. The line H, is that of a Siemens-Martin steel, containing one-half per cent. or a trifle more of carbon, while I and J are tool steels; K and L are medium and spring steels, and M is the strain diagram of double shear steel. It is seen, at a glance, that the introduction of carbon lessens the ductility of the metal, while increasing its strength and raising the elastic limit. The least ductile are the tool steels containing one per cent. and upward of carbon. The most ductile is pure iron, containing no measurable quantity of that element. Intermediate degrees of ductility are produced by intermediate proportions of carbon. Their strengths vary in the opposite direction, increasing with the dose of carbon, in a pretty regular proportion, which is expressed quite accurately, for unhardened steel, by a formula, constructed by the writer: $T = 60,000 + 70,000\,C$, in which T represents the tenacity in pounds per square inch, and C, the percentage of carbon present in the given steel. In the low steels, the lack of homogeneousness, due to porosity in the ingot, is seen to be much more noticeable than in the tool steels, which are rendered more quiet in the mould by their higher proportion of carbon and of manganese.

In these high steels, the limit of elasticity, for the unhardened, is seen to rise to 60,000 lbs., and the ultimate strength to over 120,000 lbs. per square inch. The elongation is reduced by the maximum dose of carbon to about one and a-half per cent.

N and P are the strain diagrams of white and of gray cast iron. The one is stiff, hard, strong and brittle, its line rising steadily upward without a sign of curvature or ductility until it suddenly snaps, after sustaining a very heavy stress. The other offers barely a half as much resistance; the curve bends sharply and runs a little way to the left, and breaks after the piece has twisted less than 20o, indicating a strength of but a half of one per cent. It has, however, five times the ductility of the white iron.

Malleableizing the white iron, a material of which the line O, represents the characteristics. It is very homogeneous, has lost no strength, and has gained immensely in ductility. For many purposes it is better than average wrought iron; and the readiness with which irregular forms may be made of it, if of small size, makes malleableized cast iron a very useful material. "Steel" castings are usually made of an exceptionally good quality of this metal.

Glancing over the collection of strain diagrams, it is easy to select the proper kind of iron for any specified purpose. If mere strength is required, it is evident that the tool steels are the best materials. If ductility is desired, something resembling Swedish iron is the proper metal. Comparing the qualities of several metals experimented upon with the price lists, we may readily determine which is cheapest for the specified work. When shocks are to be resisted, or blows sustained, strength alone is not sufficient. Tool steel is too brittle a material to be used in such situations, and even moderately hard steels were long ago found to be less valuable than moderately good iron for such purposes. That metal which is at once strong and ductile is the proper one to choose. The power of a substance to sustain live loads—its resilience—is measured by the product of its main resistance into the distance through which it stretches before breaking. A close approximation may be obtained by multiplying two-thirds the ultimate strength by the distance through which elongation takes place. The metal giving the highest product is the safest against rupture by blows. Of two metals giving equal products, choose that which is strongest.

An area of the strain diagram measures precisely the value of a material to meet shocks. It is exactly proportional to the product just referred to, and its construction affords the only means yet discovered of determining resilience with precision. Examining the diagram, it is seen that, except the very purest and most expensive wrought iron, the low steels excel all other materials in this respect, while they are stronger than any iron; and we perceive a very excellent reason for the wonderfully rapid introduction of Bessemer and Siemens steels, in rail and machinery making, which has recently taken place. A steel containing less than one-half per cent. carbon is not affected injuriously by changes of temperature, cannot be hardened, has at once great strength and considerable ductility, and is the best known metal, all things considered, to be placed wherever a structure is liable to severe blows and heavy strains, and therefore must be both light and strong.—*From the "Scientific American."*

Circulars and further information are being prepared of the THURSTON TESTING MACHINE, which is interesting to Civil Engineers, Architects, Engineering Iron Masters, Bolt Makers, Carriage Builders, Railway Companies, &c.

SOLE MAKERS IN EUROPE,

J. BAILEY & CO.,
ALBION WORKS, SALFORD, MANCHESTER.

TENSILE TESTING MACHINE,
For Testing Bar Iron, &c.,

Is adapted for Iron Works, Shipbuilding Establishments, and other places where the quality of Iron has to be tested. It is capable of testing to a strain of 40 tons. **A** the piece of Iron being tested, having first been reduced to an area of one square inch. **B** a strong lever acted upon by the worm-wheel and spindle. **D** the weights applied to end of the scale-beam levers. **E** balance weight for the scale-beam levers **G, H,** and **I.**

MODE OF USING.

Put 4 oz. at **D**, then tighten the test-bar attachments with the hand-wheel, until the beam just begins to lift. Keep on adding weights and adjusting the levers by means of the hand-wheel until fracture ensues.

No. 1.—Length, 5ft. 8in.; width, 2ft.; height, 6ft.; weight, about 2 tons, ... Price

No. 2.—A modification of this, on a smaller scale, for testing Cast-iron Bars up to 4ft. long × 1in. square, ... Price

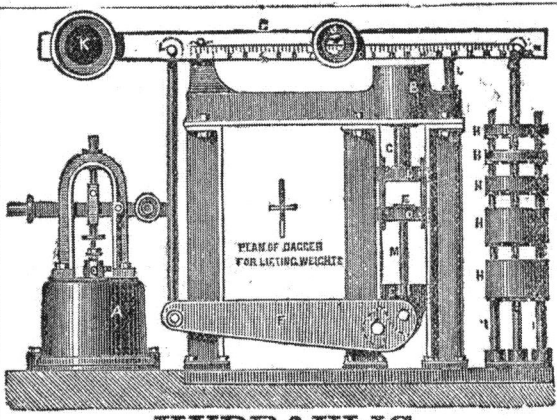

HYDRAULIC DEAD-WEIGHT TESTING MACHINE.

This Machine is adapted for applying tensile strains up to 30 tons. Referring to our Engraving, it will be seen that the Machine consists of a simple cast-iron frame supporting a short hydraulic cylinder B; the piston rod C, of this cylinder passing through the bottom and being attached to a crosshead D D. This crosshead slides between suitable guides formed in the adjoining frame pillars, and its lower crossbar is furnished with steel wedges, or gripping pieces E, for holding the specimen M, to be tested. The lower end of the specimen is held by similar wedge-pieces fitted to a second crosshead, which is traversed by a pin connecting the two parts of the double lever F.

The lever F has arms bearing the proportion of 8 to 1, and it is connected by a link, as shown, to a second lever G. The shorter arm of the lever G is prolonged and fitted with the counterbalance K, which is proportioned so as to place all the parts in equilibrium. The strain applied by the hydraulic press is resisted by weights hung from the end of the longer arm of the lever G; and the total leverage being $8 \times 14 = 112$ to 1, each pound of weight thus lifted represents 1 cwt. of strain thrown upon the specimen under test. The manner in which the weights are attached to the end of the lever G is very convenient. It will be seen that a series of five weights, representing 2, 3, 4, 10, and 20 tons respectively, are mounted on a kind of stand which allows each weight to be lifted freely; while down through the centre of the whole set of weights there passes a rod hung from the end of the lever G. This rod is pierced with a hole just below each weight, and by inserting in these holes "daggers" of the form shown in the detached figure, any number of the weights can be lifted at pleasure. A sliding weight J, fitted to the lever G, serves to apply strains varying from 0 to 1 ton, the lever being graduated, as shown. The water is forced into the hydraulic cylinder by an ordinary hydraulic press pump, as shown.

PRICE—30 Tons,   50 Tons,

Important to Civil Engineers, Contractors, Builders, &c.

MICHELE'S PATENT CEMENT TESTING MACHINE.

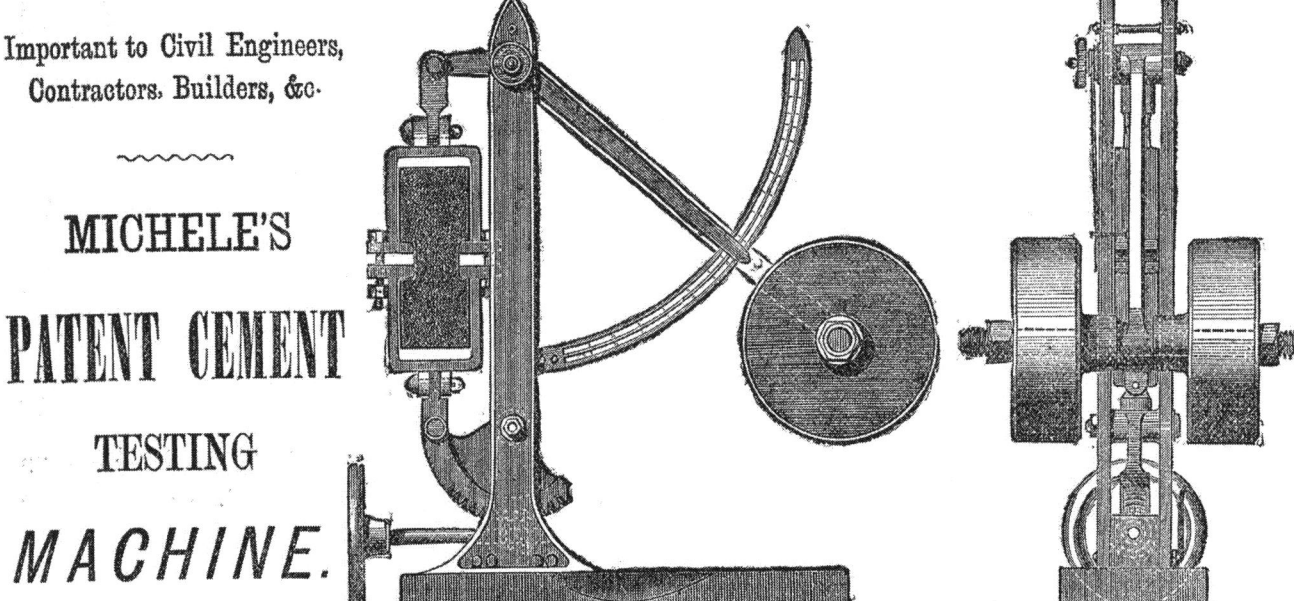

The block of Cement to be tested is placed in the jaws prepared to receive it; the hand-wheel is then turned, which raises the weighted lever by exerting a pull on its short end through the medium of the Cement block. When the leverage is so increased as to exert a force too great for the cement to sustain, it breaks, and the lever falls, leaving the index pointer at the spot to which it had been raised. The arc along which the pointer moves is graduated to show the number of pounds of tensile strain applied. A suitable arrangement, when the Cement block breaks, prevents the lever from falling more than half an inch.

As the force is thus gradually applied to the block of Cement, it is impossible that its breaking point can be influenced by any jerk or uneven strain.

Price of a Machine to exert a tensile strain not exceeding 1,000 lbs.,

BAILEY'S OIL TESTER

For indicating the Lubricating Properties of Oil.

UNDER THE EXACT CONDITIONS IN WHICH IT IS USED.

Under the distinguished patronage of the British Government, Royal Arsenal, Woolwich; The Russian Arsenal, Cronstadt; The Belgian Government, The South Australian Government, The Right Hon. Earl Fitzwilliam, The Right Hon. Earl Dudley, The Great Eastern, The Great Western, The Carlisle and Maryport, The Belgian and other Railway Companies; J. Watson and Sons, Price's Patent Candle Co., and other eminent Oil Refiners; Sir W. Armstrong, W. Robey and Co., and other Engineers at home and abroad, &c.

PRICE £8 8 0

Extra Large Size for Railway Companies £20.

Packed for Export £9 0 0

All Foreign Orders should be accompanied with Draft on London.

REPORT
OF THE IMPLEMENT JUDGES
Of the Royal Agricultural Society, Leicester Show, Stand No. 3,587—1868.

"The Oil Tester seems really to test the lubricating properties of Oil most satisfactorily."

Extract from the Journal of the Society, Vol. 4, No. 8, page 148.

ADDITIONAL

Testimony in favor of

BAILEY'S OIL TESTER,

which has been awarded *Three Silver Medals* this year.

"Your Oil Tester is the best I have seen, and is most accurate in its results."

LOUIS CROSSLEY,

Director of J. Crossley & Sons, Limited, Halifax, Nov. 3rd, 1868.

Important Testimonials, selected from many received.

FARNWORTH OIL DISTILLERY,
Lancashire, May 6th, 1868.
Messrs. BAILEY & Co., Salford.

Gentlemen,—I have carefully tested a considerable number of both Virgin and Compound Oils, on your Oil Tester, and my unqualified opinion is, that yours is the only Tester which enables the exact cash value of oil to be ascertained, because by it their durability is clearly indicated.

It must be useful to all Oil Refiners and Consumers, and you deserve to be pre-eminently successful in its introduction.

Yours truly,

J. STIRRIT.

SPINDLE AND MINERAL OIL MANUFACTORY,
Wigan, June 9th, 1868.
Messrs. J. BAILEY & Co.

Gentlemen,—We have much pleasure in testifying to the excellence and usefulness of the Oil Tester. It is "a ready reckoner" in the hands of oil consumers, and will undoubtedly be the means of putting Lubricating Oils on a proper level, especially mixed oils; and will give the *real* oil distiller and refiner his proper place in the market.

We are, Gentlemen,

Yours truly,

WILLIAMS AND LAMB.

OIL WORKS,
Mold, Flintshire, June 13th, 1868.

Gentlemen,—We have carefully tested many Mixed and Virgin Oils on Ingram and Stapfer's Patent Oil Tester. It is the most perfect machine of the kind we have seen, and when carefully worked will show to a nicety the true value of any oils used as lubricants.

We are, Gentlemen,

Yours truly,

LAVENDER & CO.

Messrs. J. Bailey & Co., Salford.

Opinions of the Press.

"The instrument we illustrate is being rapidly introduced. Scarcely any description is requisite, as the illustration, which is from a photograph, shows the instrument very clearly. A bed-plate, two pedestals, fast and loose pulleys and strap, fork, two brass steps, with weighted levers to reduce friction, an indicator to show the revolutions, and a thermometer to indicate the temperature produced, make the thing complete.

"The exact money value of oil may be arrived at as follows:—Suppose a certain quantity of No. 1 oil on the machine shows 200 deg. by being driven 10,000 revolutions, No. 2 oil shows 200 deg. and 7,500 revolutions, or 25 per cent. less value; in addition to this practical way of obtaining a result, the machine may be driven to a higher temperature, to see which oil produces the worst residue.

"Of course, it will be seen how valuable such an instrument is to consumers of oil, and to oil merchants and refiners, to enable cheap oils to be tested, and various mixtures experimented upon, by the machine, at various speeds for quick machinery and for heavy bearings."—*Engineer*, February 25th, 1868.

See also *Brewers' Journal, Engineer, Glasgow Advertiser, Glasgow Daily Herald, Morgan's British Trade Journal, Builders' Weekly Reporter, Oil Trade Review, Mechanics' Magazine, Manchester Courier, Blackburn Times, English Mechanic,* and *Colliery Guardian.*

Directions for Fixing and Using
BAILEY'S INGRAM & STAPFER'S PATENT OIL TESTER

Quantity of Oil to be used in Testing

The oil must be measured in a small glass tube (an homœopathic bottle will do, or the hole in a small key, if it is smooth inside); in emptying its contents the measure should be gently warmed over a flame, to enable the oil to pass freely from it. The measure must be well cleaned out each time. Two drops only have often been used; and a glass pencil dipped into the oil, and then held until the drops accumulate, will be found useful; but a definite weight or measure is the best.

Temperature at the commencement and expiration of each experiment

The Thermometer should always indicate the same temperature at starting. It is found that 200 degrees is the best to try all oils to, if their lubricating power is to be consumed, and the machine should be always driven until that temperature is indicated, and then immediately stopped. The machine should be fixed in a place not liable to sudden changes of temperature.

General Instructions

The top and bottom steps should be well cleaned before each experiment, and kept free from dust; the bearings of the spindle should be well oiled, to prevent friction in the wrong place. *It should run half a day well oiled before a test takes place when first fixed.*

The speed of the Tester

When a temperature of 200 degrees has been obtained (the speed index showing zero at the start), it should then be seen the number of revolutions taken to produce the temperature (see table below). The speed should be about 1,500. A uniform speed should be maintained in all tests.

To indicate the friction of bad Oil after being used

After obtaining figures from an oil, stop the machine, and let the oil remain on the machine, and in twelve hours after see how soon 200 degrees can be obtained. The second experiment will indicate which oil is the inferior on machinery when stopped.

Bad residue in Oils

If Oils have once been tested, special tests may be made, or the tests continued, to see which oil produces the most offensive residue. This may be done by driving until 200 degrees are obtained.

The Cash Value of Oils.

That oil which allows the greatest heat to accumulate with the fewest revolutions must be a bad oil. The cost of the extra power required when a bad lubricant is used is very great; the heat produced on the bearing costs as much as the coal costs that will produce the same heat in the same amount of metal in a smith's fire: in other words, heat must not be allowed to reproduce itself, for, undoubtedly, if 20 deg. of heat above the temperature of the atmosphere are produced in a bearing, 20 deg. of heat are lost under the boiler, *and the money lost for ever is the cash paid for the coal to produce that heat*, and the cost of the extra wear and tear of the machinery.

Each oil should be tested three times, and the total result of them put down. If there is any error, it will easily be seen by too great a discrepancy between each.

The following table may serve as a guide to those using the Tester.

Quality of the Oils	Temperature produced	Total indicated speed of 3 Tests	Market Price per gallon as bought		Real value of the Oils, taking No. 1 as a standard	
			s.	d.	s.	d.
No. 1	200	120,000	6	0	6	0
No. 2	200	180,000	4	0	9	0
No. 3	200	60,000	2	6	3	0

It will be seen that No. 2 oil will allow 50 per cent. more revolutions to be performed than No. 1, and must, therefore, be worth 50 per cent. more money.

THE FOLLOWING LETTER GIVES INSTRUCTIONS
How to Test the Value of Lubricating Oil.

Highfields Foundry and Iron Works,
Bilston, March 11th, 1872.

GENTLEMEN,

We have found your "Tester" of the greatest service in detecting bad Oils; *it has, no doubt, saved us some hundreds of pounds.*

We always test the sample we buy from, and again test some out of the bulk when received, and can easily discover any deficiency in the latter. The first test shows its lubricating power; the second test is always made after the machine has rested twenty-four hours, and is started without adding fresh oil, so that it exactly shows the amount of *viscidity* or *gumminess* which it has acquired in the interval.

We find some oils give a high lubricating power the first trial, but a low result the second: as a rule we prefer those that do not lose more than from ten to fifteen per cent., even if the first trial should not be as high as some other sorts. By taking the average of two results you may compare the relative commercial values of any two oils.

We send you a few slips from our trial register.

Yours faithfully,

THOMAS PERRY & SONS,
Per F. R. WHEELDON.

NOTE.—One or two drops from the end of a glass rod are quite sufficient to test.

	Name of Oil.	Price	No. of Revolutions.	Degrees of Temperature		No of Degrees raised	No. of Revolutions to 1 degree	REMARKS
				From	To			
1st day	No. 1 Ox.	5/6	13005	80°	200°	120°	108 $\frac{45}{120}$	1st trial new Oil
2nd day	Do.	5/6	11787	78°	200°	122°	96 $\frac{75}{122}$	No fresh Oil was added to the second trial.
1st day	Sperm Oil	9/0	16044	65°	200°	135°	118 $\frac{114}{135}$	1st trial new Oil.
2nd day	Do.	9/0	13104	62°	200°	138°	94 $\frac{132}{138}$	No fresh Oil was added for the second trial.
1st day	Minrl. Oil	3/6	11831	65°	200°	135°	87 $\frac{86}{135}$	1st trial.
2nd day	Do.		0	0	0	0	0	2nd trial, after standing 24 hours, the saddles were found to be so glued to the drum that the machine could not be started, though the belts were tightened, showing that the oil was of so gummy a nature as to be useless after once using.

NOTE by J. B. & Co.—The Tester may be briefly described as a piece of 3-inch shaft and two brass steps upon which frictional pressure is obtained by the weighted levers. The Speed Indicator shows the number of revolutions required to make the Thermometer indicate 200 degrees.

BAILEY'S WINDING INDICATORS, FOR COAL MINES, WELLS, &c., &c.

Bailey's WINDING INDICATORS FOR MINES.

The Winding Indicator is the best instrument yet in use for indicating the exact height of the cage; the bell is struck before the cage arrives at either the top or the bottom.

When ordering the diameter of the drum shaft is required for the worm, and also the number of revolutions it makes in sending the cage to the bottom of the pit.

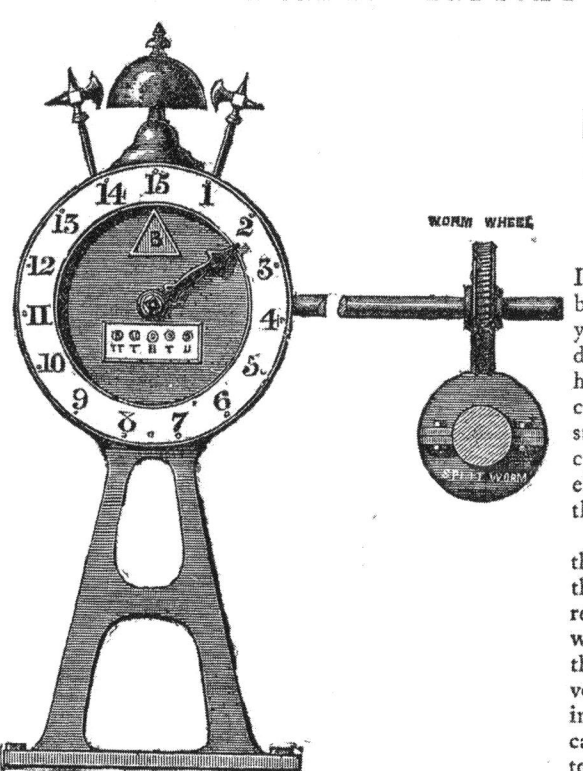

Bailey's Bridgewater Pattern Winding Indicator.
24 Inches to Centre of Dial.
Diameter of Dial, 16 Inches.

Price, complete, without worm and wheel, £5 10 0
If with counter on to indicate the number of loads per month or year to tens of thousands, ... 10 0 0

Bailey's Pendleton Pattern,
(As used at Messrs. A. Knowles & Son's Collieries, Shortleys.)
Distance to Dial Centre, 18 Inches.
Diameter of Dial, 16 Inches.

Price, ... £4 10 0
If with counter to tens of thousands, ... 9 0 0

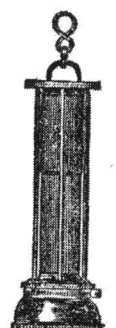

The Bridgewater Safety Lamp.

J. BAILEY & Co. are makers of all sorts of Lamps, but specially recommend this; it locks through the bottom, and is a first-class lamp. They are in use at some of the largest Collieries in the kingdom.

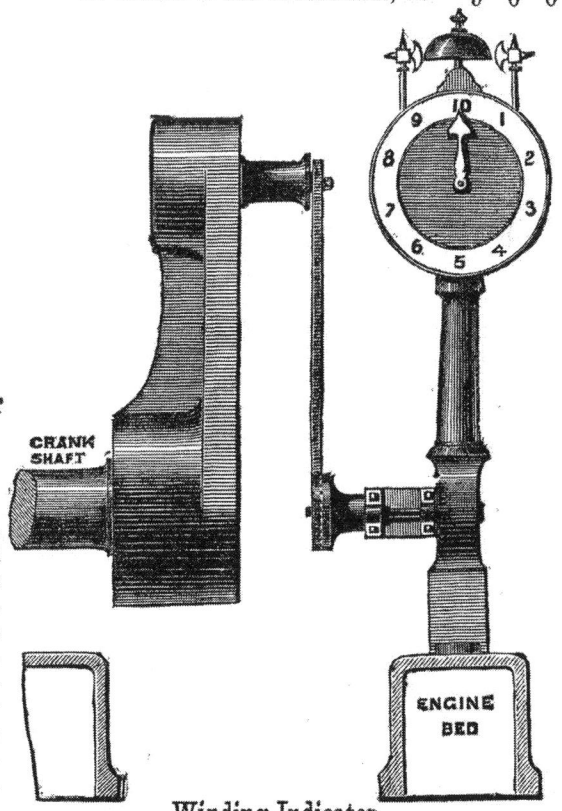

Winding Indicator,
For actuation by cranks, to be fixed on engine bed. When ordering this design, the distance from engine bed to the centre of crank shaft and also the length of crank should be given. PRICE, each, £7 10 0

Bailey's Extra Strong Signal Bells,
For Collieries, Steam-Boats, Locomotives, &c.
11 inches in diameter, with strong spring, to keep the wire tight, ... £4 10 0
7 inches, ... 1 15 0

For Coal Pit Barometers, see another portion of the Book.

WESTON'S PATENT
DIFFERENTIAL PULLEY BLOCKS.

The peculiar merit attached to these Pulleys is, that while they are more powerful than ordinary Pulley Blocks, they also possess the novel and invaluable quality of not "running down" under any circumstances, whilst the load is suspended to them. Wherever weights have to be lifted, this hoisting tackle WILL BE FOUND INVALUABLE.

In ordering either kind, please specify height of lift, or state what chain is required. When worked from above with Rachet or Spocket, it takes about three times the length of lift. When worked from below, by pulling the chain, about four times the length of lift is required.

UPWARDS OF 70,000 SETS HAVE BEEN SOLD.
ADOPTED IN ALL THE PRINCIPAL WORKSHOPS IN THE WORLD.

PULLEY WITH SPOCKET WHEEL.

Tested to	Price of Blocks per set	Bright Chain per foot
2 tons	75/-	11d.
3 ,,	110/-	1/1
4 ,,	135/-	1/3

SUPERIOR ROPE, MADE SPECIALLY FOR THESE PULLEY BLOCKS, EXTRA.

THIS IS WORKED BY PULLING AT THE CHAINS.

Tested to	Price of Blocks per set	Bright Chain per Foot
5 cwt.	12/6	6d.
10 ,,	20/-	6d.
12 ,,	20/-	7d.
20 ,,	30/-	9d.
30 ,,	40/-	10d.
40 ,,	50/-	11d.
60 ,,	100/-	1/1
80 ,,	120/-	1/3

PULLEY WITH RACHET,
BY WHICH ONE MAN CAN LIFT THE WEIGHT SPECIFIED.

Tested to	Price of Blocks per set	Bright Chain per Foot
1 ton	50/-	9d.
1½ ,,	60/-	10d.
2 ,,	70/-	11d.
3 ,,	100/-	1/1

PULLEY WITH TANGYE'S PATENT GEAR.

Tested to	Price of Blocks per Set	Bright Chain per Foot
4 tons	135/-	1/3
5 ,,	200/-	1/6
6 ,,	240/-	2/4
8 ,,	320/-	3/-
10 ,,	400/-	3/6

SUPERIOR ROPE, MADE SPECIALLY FOR THESE PULLEY BLOCKS, EXTRA.

NOTE—In sending Blocks for Repairs, or in ordering parts to repair same, it is necessary to give the number stamped on the side strap of top frame.

BAILEY'S BEST LONDON-PATTERN PULLEY BLOCKS,
WITH TURNED SHEAVES AND PINS.

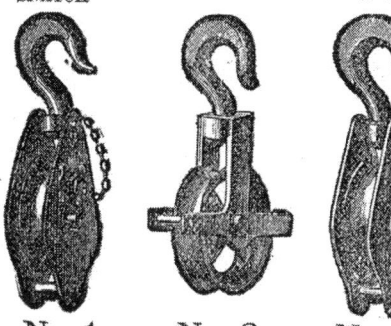
SNATCH No. 1   No. 2   No. 3

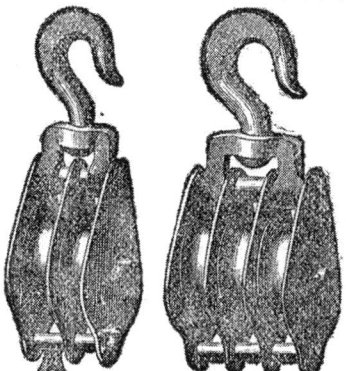
No. 4   No. 5

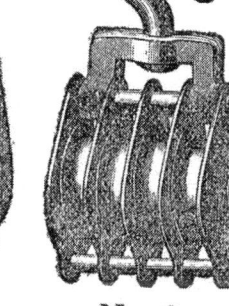
No. 6

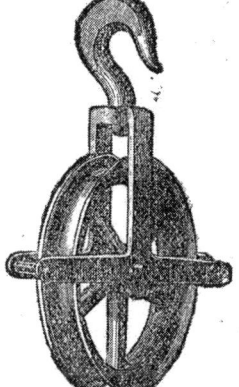
GIN BLOCK

CALOW'S PATENT SAFETY HOIST.

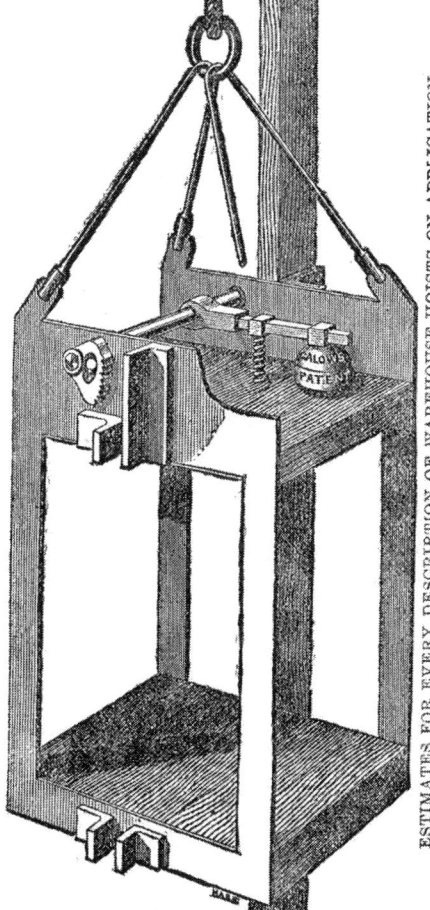

For Prices, see Page 92.

ESTIMATES FOR EVERY DESCRIPTION OF WAREHOUSE HOISTS ON APPLICATION.

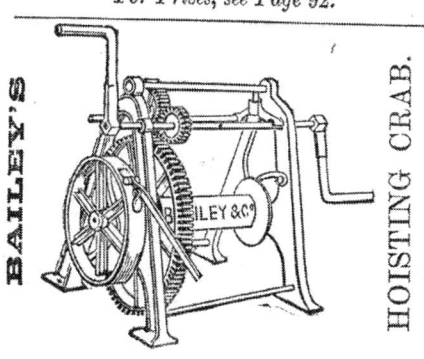

BAILEY'S HOISTING CRAB.

THE PATENT HOIST GOVERNOR,
For Preventing Accidents in Hoists of Mills, Warehouses, &c.

The following are a few of the many firms that have been supplied in Manchester:—
Messrs. S. & J. WATTS
Messrs. SCHUNK & Co.
Messrs. D. LEE & Co.
Messrs. J. P. & E. WESTHEAD and Co.
Messrs. LOMNITZ & Co.
Messrs. GRAFTON & Co.
Messrs. BROWN, SON & Co.
Messrs. ROBERTS & Co.
And most of the chief Packers and Merchants in Manchester.

Extracts from Testimonials and Opinions of the Press.

Valuable lives and property saved by this apparatus, at the Warehouse of Messrs. S. and J. WATTS, the eminent Merchants, Manchester.

"I have much pleasure in saying that the Patent Apparatus was the means of preventing a very serious accident. A few days ago there were three men and a quantity of goods descending in our hoist, and when they were about seventy feet from the bottom, the down strap broke, and immediately the governors acted upon the apparatus, and fixed the cage that the men were in perfectly fast to the sides of the shaft, and, of course, prevented it from coming down, which it would have done with fearful velocity, had we not had the Patent Governor Apparatus attached to it.

"We are so well satisfied with its performance, that we immediately gave an order to fix the Patent Apparatus to our other hoist.

DESCRIPTION.

On the top of the hoist is placed a pair of governor balls, receiving motion through a pulley and bevel wheels, from a friction pulley, which is held against the guide by a spring; on each side are two shafts, on the end of which are fixed four serrated cams. When the hoist is in motion, it will work freely without hindrance from the break cams; but the instant that the hoist exceeds the limit at which it is intended to work, the governor balls fly apart, release the latch, and set free the cams, which are thrown out against the guide by means of the weighted levers, and instantly stop the further descent of the hoist.

There is also a further contrivance for ensuring safety in case of the winding rope breaking, consisting of a weighted lever suspended by a cord to the winding rope. When the rope breaks the lever falls, releasing the latch, and setting free the serrated cams as before, thus making it impossible for an accident to occur either from overspeeding, rope breaking, keys coming out of top gearing, &c.

Reduced Price, complete, £15.

ESTIMATES for Hoist Gearing for Mills and Warehouses, sent on application.

WROUGHT IRON PULLEY BLOCKS. LONDON PATTERN.

In this arrangement of Block, each plate forms a support for the Centre Shaft, besides protecting the Pulley from damage. The Eye as shown in No. 4 is supplied with the smallest Block of each pair ordered. The MEASUREMENTS are given as at A in No. 1, but the diameter of the Pulley at the bottom of the groove is one diameter of rope less than at A. The actual width of the grooves is from $\frac{1}{16}$ to $\frac{1}{8}$ more than list, so that the $16 \times 3\frac{1}{4}$ is really $16 \times 3\frac{3}{8}$, and so on, to allow for new rope being larger.

		ins.	ins.	ins.	ins.	ins.	ins.	ins.	ins.	ins.	ins.	ins.	ins.	ins.	ins.	ins.	
	Diameter of Pulley	$2\frac{1}{2}$	$3\frac{1}{2}$	4	$4\frac{3}{4}$	5	6	7	8	9	10	11	$12\frac{1}{2}$	14	15	16	
		×	×	×	×	×	×	×	×	×	×	×	×	×	×	×	
	Width of Groove	$\frac{3}{8}$	$\frac{1}{2}$	$\frac{5}{8}$	$\frac{3}{4}$	$\frac{7}{8}$	1	$1\frac{1}{4}$	$1\frac{1}{2}$	$1\frac{3}{4}$	2	$2\frac{1}{4}$	$2\frac{1}{2}$	$2\frac{3}{4}$	3	$3\frac{1}{4}$	
Snatch	Price	6/3	6/3	7/-	10/-	11/6	13/6	16/6	21/6	32/-	46/-	61/6	84/6	107/6	130/-	160/-	All parts of these Pulley Blocks being interchangeable, duplicate parts can be had by ordering.
	Weight ... lbs.	$1\frac{1}{2}$	$3\frac{3}{4}$	5	$9\frac{1}{2}$	15	16	23	35	48	65						
1 Sheave	Price	5/6	5/9	6/2	8/6	10/-	11/6	14/-	19/-	28/-	38/6	52/6	70/-	85/-	100/-	125/-	
	Weight ... lbs.	$1\frac{1}{4}$	$3\frac{3}{8}$	$4\frac{1}{2}$	$8\frac{1}{4}$	14	15	21	32	44	60						
2 Sheave	Price	7/-	8/6	10/-	12/6	15/6	17/-	24/6	35/6	46/-	70/-	88/6	100/-	130/-	155/-	185/-	
	Weight ... lbs.	2	$5\frac{1}{2}$	$7\frac{1}{4}$	$14\frac{1}{2}$	21	28	38	57	79	114						
3 Sheave	Price	8/6	10/-	11/6	15/6	19/6	21/6	30/6	48/6	65/6	92/6	108/-	130/-	170/-	200/-	245/-	
	Weight ... lbs.	3	$7\frac{1}{4}$	9	18	27	36	49	75	107	146						
4 Sheave	Price	12/-	14/-	15/6	20/-	25/6	28/6	46/-	63/-	87/6	115/6	135/-	155/-	215/-	270/-	307/-	
	Weight ... lbs.	4	$7\frac{1}{2}$	12	24	36	48	65	100	140	192						
	Brass Sheave Blocks per Sheave extra	9d.	1/6	2/-	3/-	4/6	6/3	7/9	11/6	15/3	21/6						

CALOW'S PATENT SAFETY HOIST.

PRICES:—For a Cage, with a working load of not more than 10 cwt. £10 0 0
    Do.   do.   do.   20 ,, ... 12 10 0
    For all above 20 cwt. 15 0 0

GIN BLOCKS OR RUBBISH PULLEYS.

$3\frac{1}{4}$	$4\frac{3}{4}$	6	7	8	9	10	11	12	14	16	18	20	22 inch.
3s. 9d.	6s. 3d.	7s.	7s. 9d.	8s. 6d.	9s. 3d.	10s.	11s.	12s.	13s.	16s. 6d.	21s.	24s.	27s. 6d.

BAILEY'S HOISTING CRABS.

SINGLE PURCHASE.

To lift with 1 & 2 Sheave		Without	With	To lift with 1 & 2 Sheave		Without	With
No.	Pulley Blocks	Break	Break	No.	Pulley Blocks	Break	Break
1	1 Ton	£3 0 0	£4 2 6	4	3 Tons	£5 0 0	£6 10 0
2	1½ ,,	3 7 6	4 12 6	5	4 ,,	6 5 0	7 15 0
3	2 ,,	4 5 0	5 10 0	6	6 ,,	7 5 0	8 15 0

If Brass Bushed, 25/- extra.

DOUBLE PURCHASE

To lift with 1 & 2 Sheave		Without	With	To lift with 1 & 2 Sheave		Without	With
No.	Pulley Blocks	Break	Break	No.	Pulley Blocks	Break	Break
10	2 Tons	£5 0 0	£6 10 0	14	8 Tons	£10 0 0	£12 0 0
11	3 ,,	6 0 0	7 10 0	15	10 ,,	13 12 0	15 15 0
12	4 ,,	7 7 6	8 17 6	16	12 ,,	17 5 0	19 10 0
13	6 ,,	8 5 0	9 17 6	17	16 ,,	20 0 0	23 10 0

If Brass Bushed, No. 10 to 12, 27/6 extra.
  ,,   ,,   ,, 13 ,, 14, 35/- ,,
  ,,   ,,   ,, 15 ,, 17, 40/- ,,

WESTON'S PATENT DOUBLE LIFT SAFETY "E" HOIST.

One man—with ordinary exertion—can lift the weight, and by hooking up the end of the chain, and using a single sheave block in the loop thus formed, double the weight may be lifted:—

	2½ Cwt.	5 Cwt.
Price of Hoist	£3 0 0	£7 10 0
Best Tested Chain, per foot ...	0 0 7	0 0 10
Rope, per foot	0 0 4	0 0 4
One Sheave Pulley Block	0 5 0	0 7 6

The chief advantage of this Hoist is that it is self-sustaining. If the hand rope be let go the load will not run down, but remain suspended. The lowering is effected by pulling the rope on the other side of the wheel. The chain has two hooks, the one descending while the other ascends, so that when one hook has arrived at the top of the lift, the other will be at the bottom, ready for a fresh load; thus no time is lost in running up and down the empty hook.

EADES' PATENT EPICYCLODIAL PULLEY BLOCKS.

Patented in England, America, France, Prussia, Italy, Austria, Holland and Belgium.

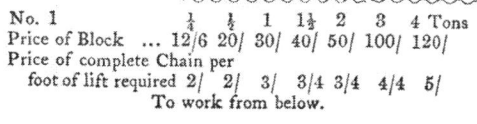

No. 1	¼	½	1	1½	2	3	4 Tons
Price of Block	12/6	20/	30/	40/	50/	100/	120/
Price of complete Chain per foot of lift required	2/	2/	3/	3/4	3/4	4/4	5/

To work from below.

No. 3			2	3	4 Tons
Price of Block			85/	115/	140/
Price of Chain per foot of lift			3/8	4/4	5/5

These work with sprocket wheel, by which two men can lift weight specified, and they have another speed for lift weights.

No. 2		1	1½	2	3 Tons
Price of Block		63/	70/	77/	107/
Price of complete Chain per foot of lift required		2/3	2/6	2/9	3/3

These work from above, with Ratchet Lever.

No. 4.	5	6	8	10 Tons
Price of Block	200/	240/	320/	400/
Chain per foot of lift	6/	9/4	12/	14/

Worked with sprocket wheel and compound gear. One man can lift 4 tons—two men 8 tons.

The great superiority of these Blocks consist of the following advantages:—

1. Speed and Power.
2. Being Self-sustaining.
3. Double Lift, the empty Hook descending while the Load rises, thus they never require winding down for a fresh Load.
4. All the Wearing Parts are hardened, and the Lifting Chain working only at the same speed which the rod rises, make them very durable, and not likely to get out of order.
5. The endless hand Chain being one loop, may be used on drum, as in a Crane, for which it is suitable.
6. Any Block may be converted into one of double strength and power by simply hooking one end of the Lifting Chain to the place on which the Block hangs, and placing a Snatch Block in the loop thus formed.
7. The Chains do not require any attention after the Block has been removed, as, hanging loose, they cannot twist.
8. Light weights may be raised or lowered quickly, as with an ordinary Pulley Block, by forming a noose in the hand Chain, or attaching a hook to it.

PICKERING'S PATENT PULLEY BLOCKS.

THE ADVANTAGES OF THESE BLOCKS ARE—

Simple, strong, and powerful. Sustain the load, and cannot slip.

Very easy to work, and not liable to get out of order.

The Lifting Chain being supplied with a hook at each end, no lowering is required for a fresh load.

Longer or shorter Chains can be changed by simply unscrewing the bolts.

The working parts run on STEEL, and being internal, are not liable to accident, and are free from dust or dirt.

Having two Chains independent of each other, they work with much less friction, and with more speed than has been attained by any other Pulley Blocks, enabling one man to lift from 15 to 20 cwt.

Can be worked at an angle, thereby enabling the workman to stand from under the load. Made to lift from 5 cwt. upwards.

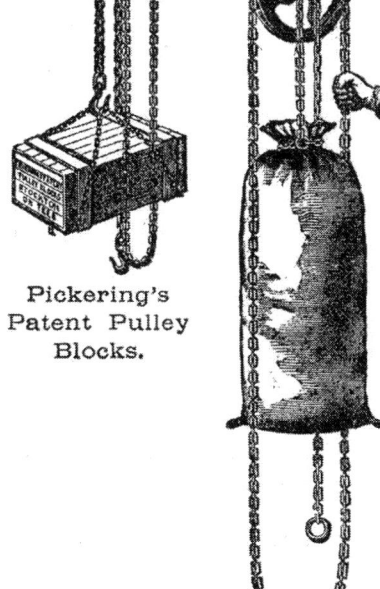

Pickering's Patent Pulley Blocks.

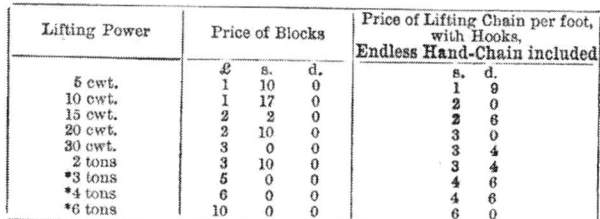

Pickering's Patent Sack Hoist.

Lifting Power	Price of Blocks			Price of Lifting Chain per foot, with Hooks, Endless Hand-Chain included	
	£	s.	d.	s.	d.
5 cwt.	1	10	0	1	9
10 cwt.	1	17	0	2	0
15 cwt.	2	2	0	2	6
20 cwt.	2	10	0	3	0
30 cwt.	3	0	0	3	4
2 tons	3	10	0	3	4
*3 tons	5	0	0	4	6
*4 tons	6	0	0	4	6
*6 tons	10	0	0	6	0

Example—A set of Chains for a ½-ton Block to lift 10 ft., at 2s. per foot, £1.

* Blocks and Hoists marked (*) have double lifting chains.

PICKERING'S PATENT SACK HOISTS.

These Hoists are so arranged that a man may lift or lower a sack of grain or any other load at a quick motion. They are manufactured in two forms, with or without Ratchet for sustaining the load, and by the comparative ease with which the load is held in the hand, the workmen are enabled to raise, lower, or stop at any moment, in the most rapid succession. They will be most useful for Builders, Warehouses, Granaries, and all purposes where light loads are required to be lifted or lowered quickly.

PRICE OF HOIST for Lifting 5 cwt. 35s.; Chain, including Hooks or Rings, 7d. per foot. With Ratchet to sustain the load, 10s. extra.

PRICE OF HOIST for Lifting 10 cwt. 45s.; do. do. for Lifting 20 cwt. 65s.; Chains, including Hooks or Rings, 8d. per foot. With Ratchet to sustain the load, 10s. extra.

PRICE OF HOIST for Lifting 20 cwt. with Shaft and Frame, from 65s. upwards. Break, 20s. extra.

In ordering Chains the height of Lift MUST be given. In many cases it will not be necessary to order the endless hand-chain the same length as the lifting chain, as the Hoist can be worked on the top floor when the Lift Chain can be loaded at the bottom, or *vice versa*; but if not specified otherwise, the full length will be sent.

Bailey & Robinson's Patent Pulley Blocks

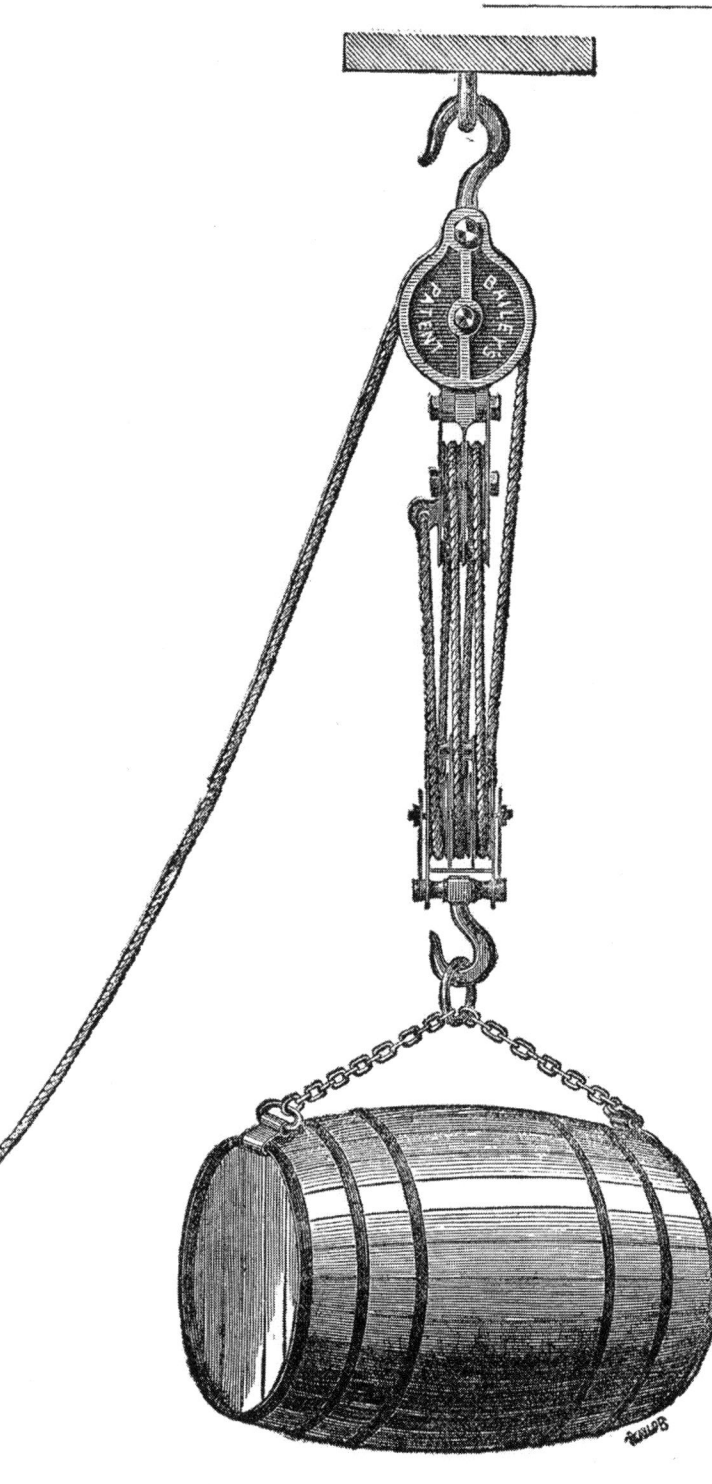

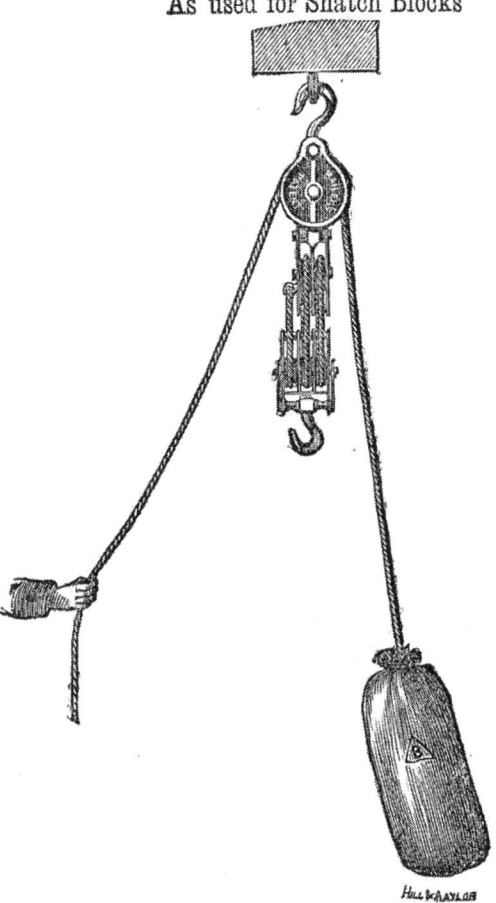

As used for Snatch Blocks

These, as will be seen from the Engravings, consist of the ordinary Rope Blocks, so made that the leading Sheave or Pulley is larger in diameter, and above the others, enabling a direct pull, less friction, and, as a consequence, greater power, with less expenditure of force. Those who have used them are loud in their praise, and many have called our attention to the great saving in wear and tear of ropes over the old system of Blocks, with which a great portion of the force expended in hauling or lifting is spent in destroying the Ropes, by the friction created by the rubbing against the sides of the frames.

One important feature in these Blocks, which should not be overlooked by those who require Blocks for general Yard work and sundry Jobbing purposes, is the great ease with which the end of the rope may be put through the leading Sheave, and at once it is made into a Snatch Block for light lifts.

The prices are not higher than those of first-class Blocks of the old pattern.

Diameter of Sheave,				$3\frac{1}{2}$in.	4in.	$4\frac{1}{2}$in.	5in.	6in.	7in.
Width of Groove,				$\frac{1}{2}$in.	$\frac{5}{8}$in.	$\frac{3}{4}$in.	$\frac{7}{8}$in.	1in.	$1\frac{1}{4}$in.
Price of a Pair of 3-and-3 Sheave Blocks,				32/6	37/6	45/0	55/0	75/0	85/0
Rope per Hundred feet,									

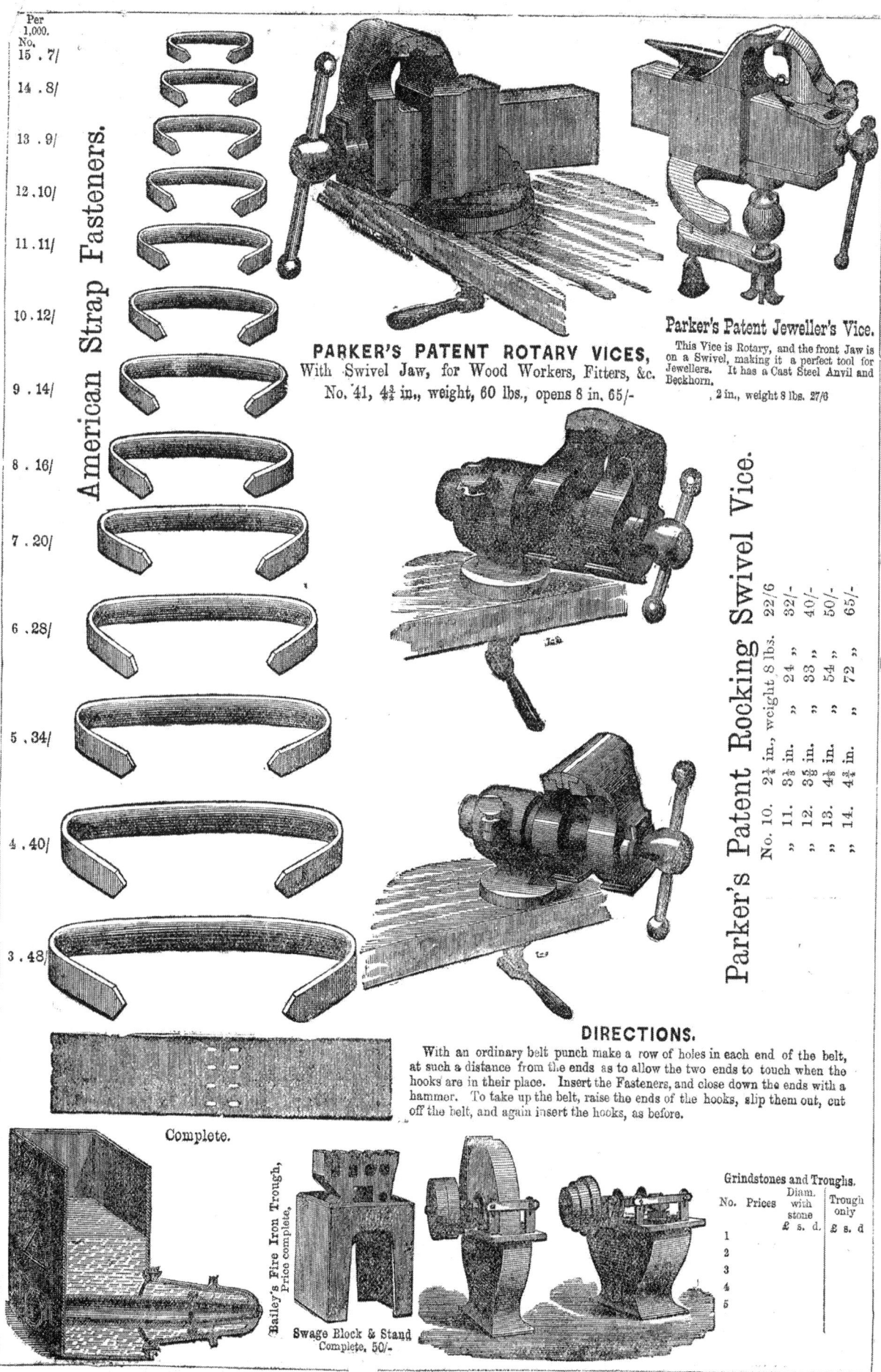

Per 1,000. No.	
15	7/
14	8/
13	9/
12	10/
11	11/
10	12/
9	14/
8	16/
7	20/
6	28/
5	34/
4	40/
3	48/

American Strap Fasteners.

PARKER'S PATENT ROTARY VICES,
With Swivel Jaw, for Wood Workers, Fitters, &c.
No. 41, 4¾ in., weight, 60 lbs., opens 8 in. 65/-

Parker's Patent Jeweller's Vice.
This Vice is Rotary, and the front Jaw is on a Swivel, making it a perfect tool for Jewellers. It has a Cast Steel Anvil and Beckhorn.
2 in., weight 8 lbs. 27/6

Parker's Patent Rocking Swivel Vice.
No.	Size	Weight	Price
10	2¼ in.	8 lbs.	22/6
11	3¼ in.	24 "	32/-
12	3⅝ in.	33 "	40/-
13	4⅛ in.	54 "	50/-
14	4¾ in.	72 "	65/-

DIRECTIONS.
With an ordinary belt punch make a row of holes in each end of the belt, at such a distance from the ends as to allow the two ends to touch when the hooks are in their place. Insert the Fasteners, and close down the ends with a hammer. To take up the belt, raise the ends of the hooks, slip them out, cut off the belt, and again insert the hooks, as before.

Complete.

Bailey's Fire Iron Trough, Price complete,

Swage Block & Stand Complete, 50/-

Grindstones and Troughs.
No.	Prices	Diam. with stone	Trough only
		£ s. d	£ s. d
1			
2			
3			
4			
5			

BAILEY'S IMPROVED PORTABLE AND BENCH VICES, LIFTING JACKS, &c.

No. 3

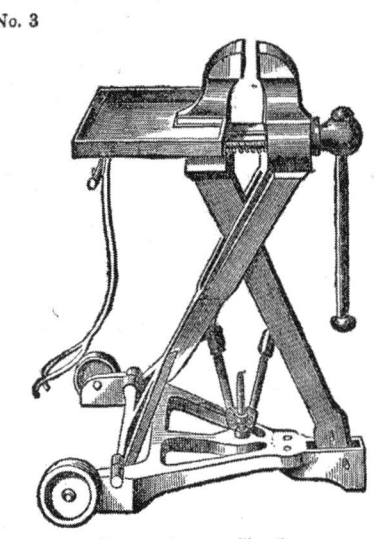

5	6	7in. Jaws.
138/-	150/-	162/6

No. 4

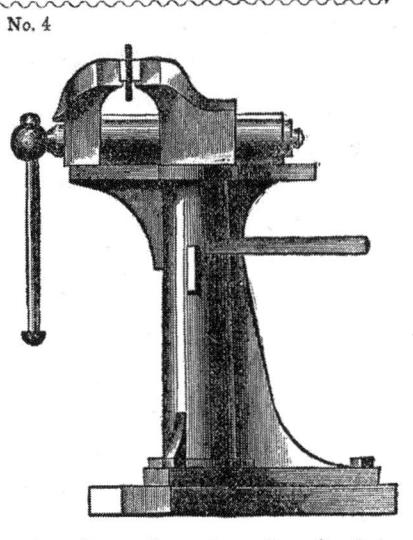

4	4½	5	6	7	8in. Jaws.
115/-	121/-	135/-	155/-	180/-	207/-

No. 2

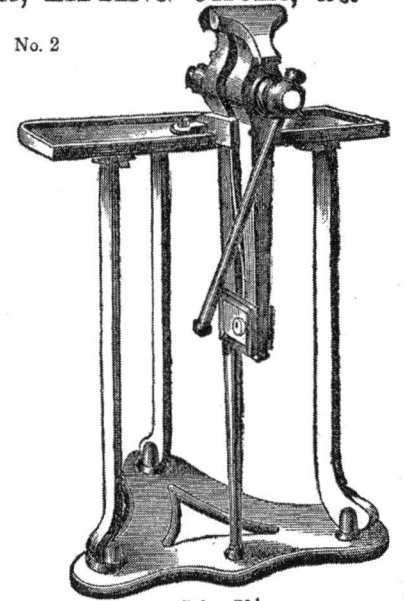

Price 70/-

No. 1

Price ... 55/- ... With Drawer ...65/-

Patent Lifting Jacks.

No. 5

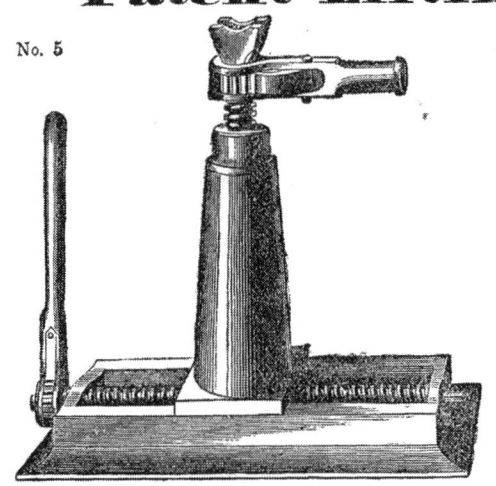

England's Patent Traversing Jack.

6 Tons	£6 10 0	12 Tons	£7 15 6
8 „	7 0 0	20 „	12 5 0

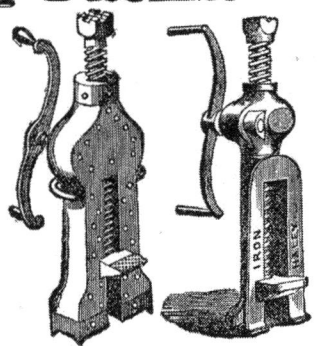

Haley's Lifting Jacks.

Height when down.	Will Lift.	Price.
No. 1—29 inch	2 Tons	£4 10 0
„ 2—31 „	4 „	5 0 0
„ 3—32 „	6 „	5 15 0
„ 4—34 „	8 „	7 0 0
„ 5—37 „	12 „	9 0 0
„ 6—40 „	16 „	15 0 0
„ 7—44 „	20 „	18 10 0

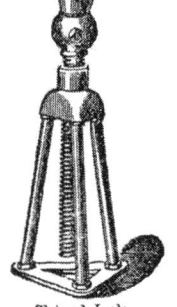

Tripod Jack.   Bottle Jack.

Tripod and Bottle Jacks.
(OR COTTON SCREWS.)

No.	Height when down.	Will lift.	Prices.
1	9 inches	1½ Tons	£1 4 0
2	12 „	2 „	1 7 6
3	15 „	3 „	1 12 0
4	18 „	4 „	1 18 6
5	21 „	5 „	2 5 0
6	24 „	6 „	3 0 0
7	27 „	8 „	3 13 0
8	30 „	10 „	4 10 0
9	33 „	12 „	5 10 0
10	36 „	14 „	6 7 6
11	42 „	16 „	6 17 6
12	48 „	18 „	7 15 0

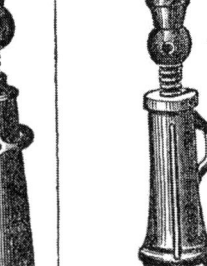

Bottle Jack,
(With Cast-Iron Frame).

No.	Height when down.	Will lift.	Prices.
1	12 „	1½ Tons	£0 17 6
2	15 „	2 „	1 0 0
3	18 „	4 „	1 2 6
4	21 „	5 „	1 6 0
5	24 „	6 „	1 10 0
6	24 „	8 „	2 0 0
7	24 „	10 „	2 10 0

Ratchet Screw Jack.

No.	Height when down.	Will lift.	Prices.
1	21 „	6 Tons	£3 17 0
2	24 „	8 „	4 10 0
3	27 „	10 „	5 7 6
4	30 „	12 „	6 10 0

Tripod Windlass Screw Jack.

No.	Height when down.	Will lift.	Prices.
1	32 „	4 Tons	£5 12 6
2	33 „	6 „	6 10 0
3	33 „	8 „	7 7 6

Windlass Screw Jack.

SINGLE PURCHASE.

No.	Height when down.	Will lift.	Prices.
1	29 „	2 Tons	£5 0 0
2	30 „	4 „	5 17 6
3	31 „	6 „	6 10 0
4	32 „	8 „	8 0 0

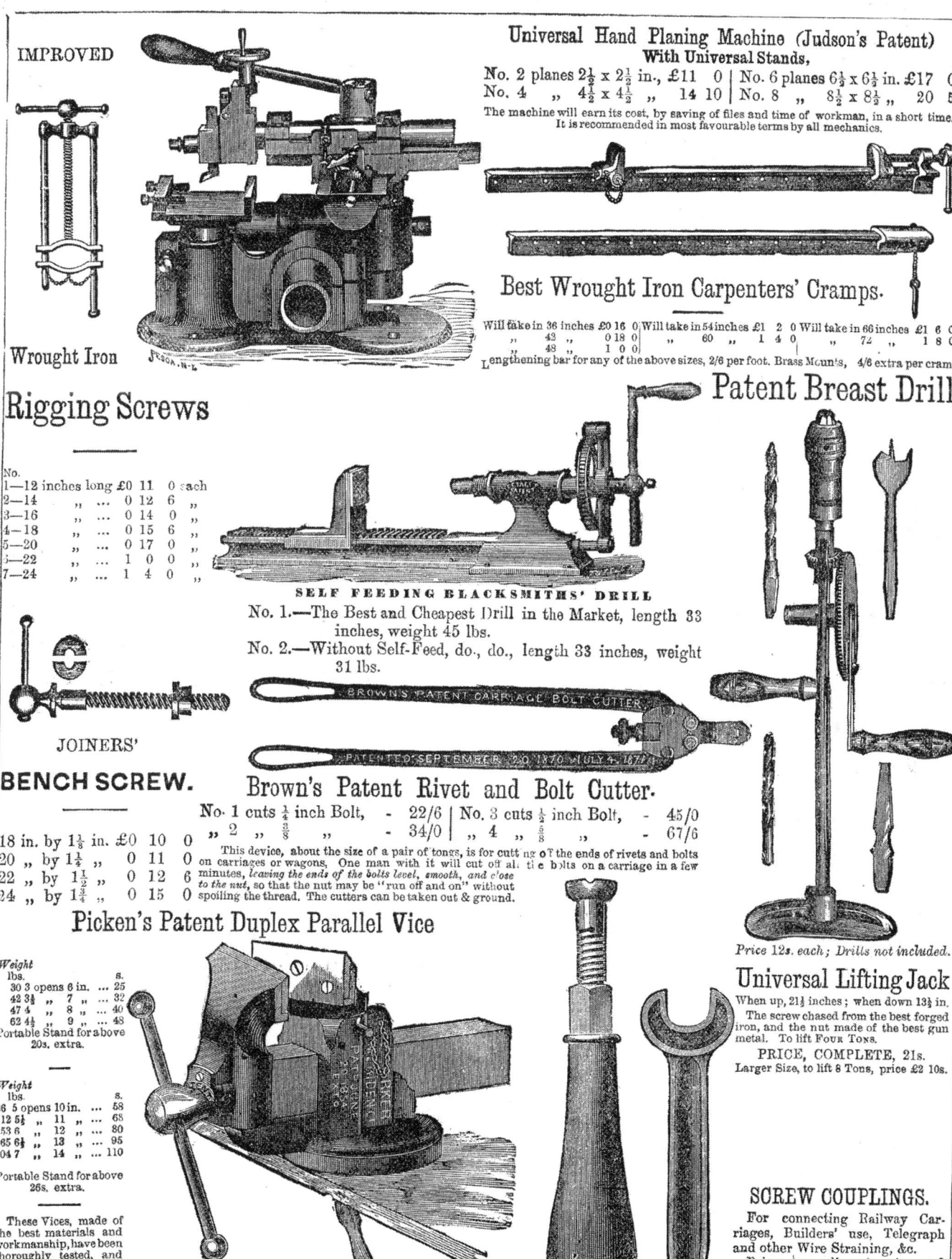

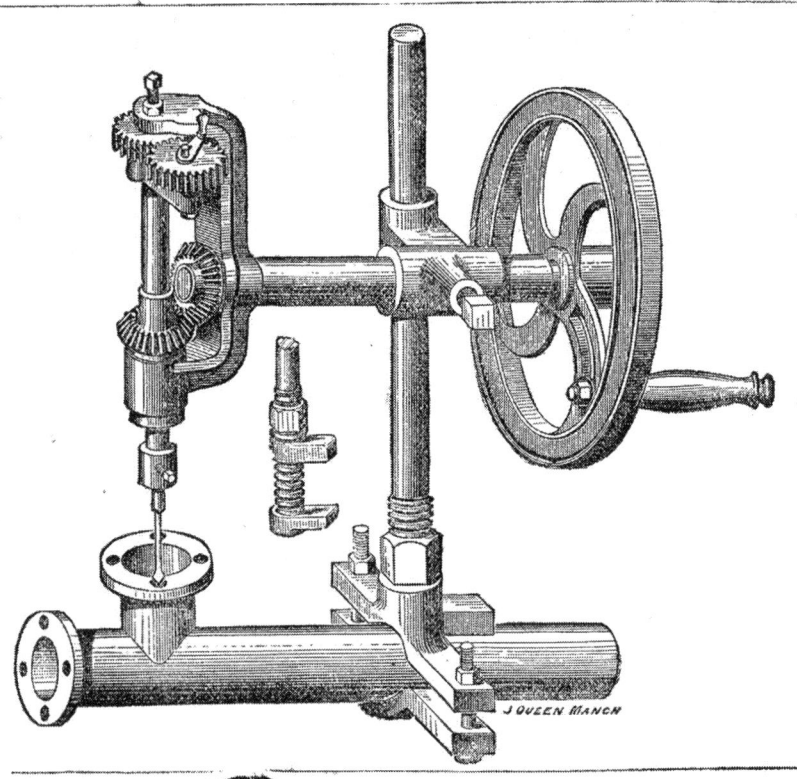

SELF-FEEDING DRILLING MACHINE.

A.—Machine to drill up to 1 in. diam. £5 0 0
B. do. do. 1½ do. 6 0 0
C. do. do. 2 do. 7 0 0

This Machine entirely supersedes the Ratchet or Swing Brace in point of time and efficiency, as well as being adapted to Drill at almost any angle.

For huge and ponderous work, not easily removed to the Drilling Machine, it will be found a desideratum long wanted.

Screw the Drill-stock or Bracket firmly to the work-bench or the article to be drilled. This being done, lock the upper tooth wheel, by turning the eccentric gearing against it to the left hand. Then run down the spindle, by turning the handle until it reaches the article being drilled. Put on the feed motion, by turning the eccentric to the right hand. After the hole is drilled, the spindle is immediately drawn back, by locking the upper wheel, as before, and reversing the handle.

The above Drills are capable of drilling holes at almost any angle, or in almost any position, and will be found a most invaluable tool in Mills and Workshops of any kind.

No. 41,270.

BAILEY'S PATENT PARALLEL ALL WROUGHT-IRON BENCH VICE.

	3,	3½,	4,	4½,	5,	5½,	6,	7,	8in.
Best Black Vice, Planed Sides, Solid Boxes,	40/-	46/-	52/-	60/-	75/-	82/-	100/-	120/-	148/-

As a First-class Vice this has never been equalled. It is well adapted for Engineers and all classes of Mechanics, and the cost is no more than an ordinary Bench Vice of the same strength.

No. 41,280.

BAILEY'S ALL WROUGHT-IRON PARALLEL BENCH VICE.

5 in.	6 in.	7 in.	8 in.
65/-	80/-	100/-	120/-

The Vices open the width of Jaws.

Nelson's Patent Stud End Cutter.

This Machine is for rounding off the ends of bolts and studs and cutting them down to the required length. It can be used after the studs are in their places, or for bolts in the vice.

The Advantages of using it are—

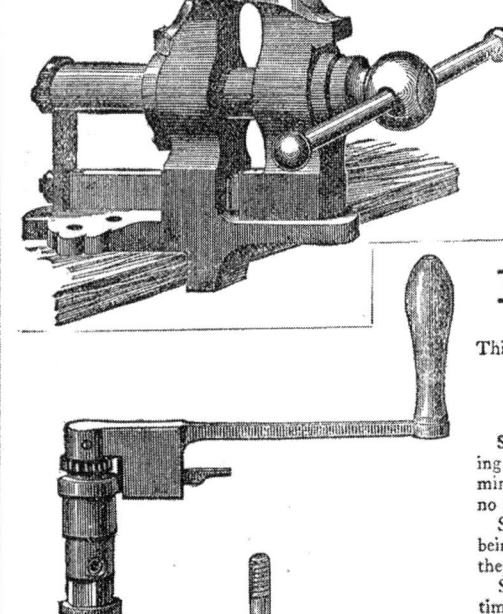

SAVING IN LABOUR.—It is fixed firm and true, ready for work in an instant, by simply screwing it on the stud end on which it is going to operate; the handle is then turned round, and in one minute a stud or bolt can be finished to the exact height, bright and regular as if it had been turned; no centre is left in.

SUPERIORITY OF WORKMANSHIP.—Studs are not liable to get damaged or loosened, and being finished after they are in their places they are more accurate than if they were turned before they were put in. The finish is equal, if not superior, to the best lathe work.

SAVING IN TIME.—Stud or bolt ends are rounded and finished off in half or one quarter the time they could be turned, and in a fiftieth part of the time hand labour would require.

All parts are made to exact gauges, and polished bright, forming a useful little appliance for every engineer and machinist.

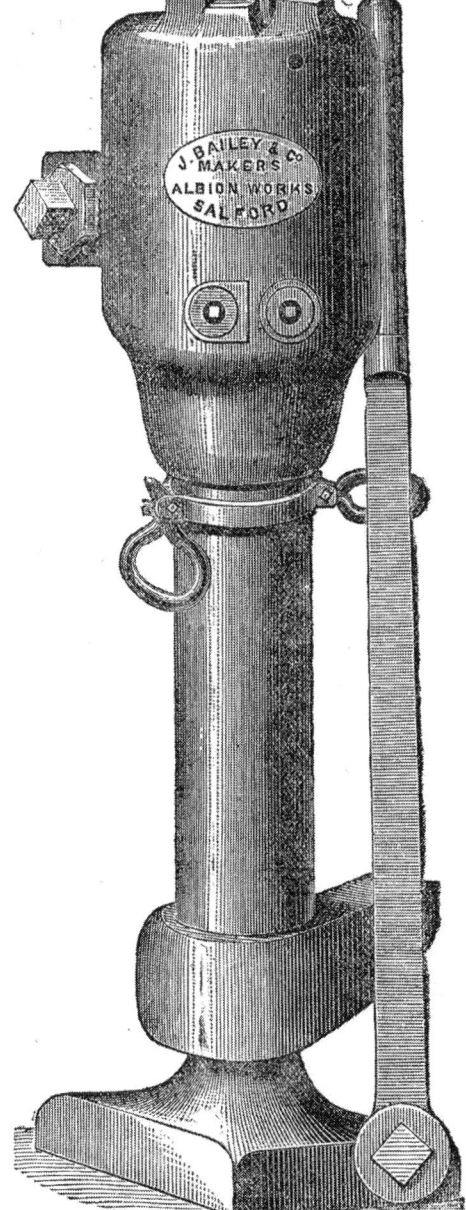

Bailey's Hydraulic Jacks.

PRICES:

	£	s.
To lift 5 tons 6 in. high, without Ground Lift	7	0
,, 10 ,, 12 ,, with Ground Lift	10	0
,, 15 ,, 12 ,, with ditto	13	10

DIRECTIONS:

To fill the Jack remove the slotted Screw in the head. The best fluid for this purpose is made of half soapy water, and in cold climates half whiskey.

If air be in the cylinder, it will be readily discovered by the springing motion of the lever and its unsteady stroke, in which case *screw down* the square Socket in the boss, so as to partly open the valve, and give a few sharp strokes, until the pump works with a steady and solid motion; then withdraw Socket again to its highest point.

 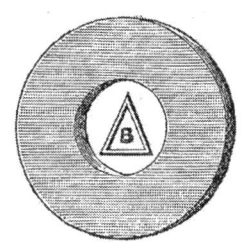 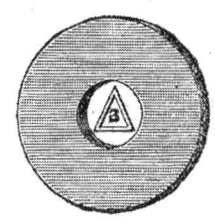

Patent Machine-made Iron Washers.

Cut from New Iron (not Scrap) warranted uniform in thickness and size, with the hole always in the centre.

Size No.	Outside Diameter	Diameter of Hole	14 Per Gross s. d.	12 Per Gross s. d.	10 Per Gross s. d.	8 Per Gross s. d.	6 Per Gross s. d.
00	3/8	—	0 6	—	—	—	—
0	1/2	—	0 6	0 7	—	—	—
1	5/8	1/4	0 6	0 7	0 8	—	—
2	3/4	5/16	0 7	0 8	0 10	1 0	—
3	7/8	7/16	0 9	0 11	1 1	1 3	1 6
4	1	1/2	0 11	1 1	1 3	1 6	1 10
5	1 1/8	9/16	1 1	1 3	1 6	1 10	2 2
6	1 1/4	5/8	1 4	1 7	1 10	2 3	2 8
7	1 3/8	11/16	1 8	2 0	2 4	2 10	3 4
8	1 1/2	3/4	2 0	2 5	2 10	3 4	4 0
9	1 5/8	13/16	2 5	2 11	3 4	4 1	4 10
10	1 3/4	7/8	2 10	3 5	4 1	5 0	5 10
11	1 7/8	15/16	3 6	4 1	4 9	5 8	6 10
13	2	1	4 0	4 9	5 7	6 8	8 0
13	2 1/8	1 1/16	4 7	5 5	6 5	7 7	9 2
14	2 1/4	1 1/8	5 2	6 2	7 2	8 7	10 4
15	2 3/8	1 3/16	5 9	6 10	8 0	9 7	11 6
16	2 1/2	1 1/4	6 4	7 7	8 10	10 6	12 8
17	2 5/8	1 5/16	6 11	8 3	9 8	11 6	13 10
18	2 3/4	1 3/8	7 6	9 0	10 6	12 6	15 0
19	2 7/8	1 7/16	8 1	9 8	11 4	13 6	16 0
20	3	1 1/2	8 8	10 5	12 2	14 6	17 4
21	3 1/8	1 9/16	9 4	11 2	13 1	15 6	18 8
22	3 1/4	1 5/8	10 0	12 0	14 0	16 6	20 0

PATENT COMBINED Hand Punch and Shears, and Wire Cropper.

No. 0 will cut 3-16 wire and smaller, and will punch and cut hoop iron.
Price, £3 10 0

This size will be found useful and convenient for light bench work.

No. 2 will cut 1/2 round iron, and 1 1/4 x 1/2 bar iron, will punch 1/2 inch hole in 1/2 iron, 3 3/4 inches from edge to centre of hole; it will be found a most convenient machine for general use.
Price, £14 15 0

SHEARS FOR CUTTING FLAT BAR IRON.

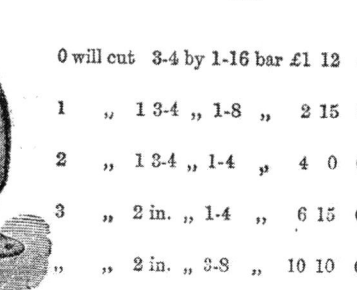

			£	s.	d.
0 will cut	3-4 by 1-16 bar		1	12	0
1 ,,	1 3-4 ,, 1-8 ,,		2	15	0
2 ,,	1 3-4 ,, 1-4 ,,		4	0	0
3 ,,	2 in. ,, 1-4 ,,		6	15	0
,,	2 in. ,, 3-8 ,,		10	10	0

Punching Presses.

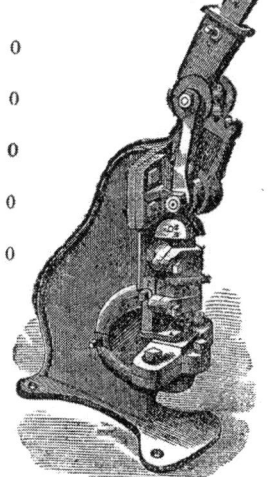

SHEARS FOR CUTTING ROUND IRON.

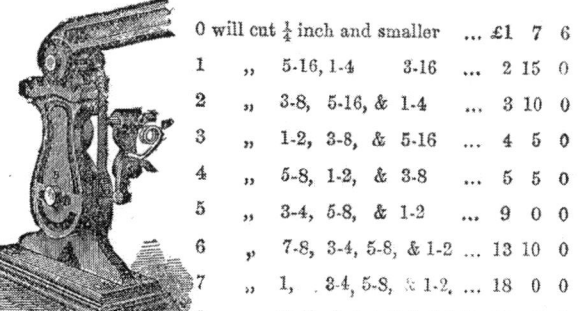

			£	s.	d.
0 will cut	1/4 inch and smaller	...	1	7	6
1 ,,	5-16, 1-4 3-16	...	2	15	0
2 ,,	3-8, 5-16, & 1-4	...	3	10	0
3 ,,	1-2, 3-8, & 5-16	...	4	5	0
4 ,,	5-8, 1-2, & 3-8	...	5	5	0
5 ,,	3-4, 5-8, & 1-2	...	9	0	0
6 ,,	7-8, 3-4, 5-8, & 1-2	...	13	10	0
7 ,,	1, 3-4, 5-8, & 1-2	...	18	0	0
8 ,,	1 1/8, 1, 7/8, 3-4, 5-8, & 1-2	...	22	0	0

Diam. of Punch	Thickness of Iron.	Hole from Edge.	Price.
0	1/4	1/8	2 1/2 in. £5 15 0
1	3-16	3-16	3 1/2 ,, 8 0 0
2	1/4	1/4	3 1/2 ,, 11 10 0
3	5-16	5-16	4 ,, 15 15 0
3 1/2	3/8	5-16	4 ,, 21 10 0
4	3/8	3/8	4 ,, 29 5 0
5	1/2	1/2	7 1/2 ,, 45 0 0

MOORE'S PATENT TRIPLE-ACTING RACHET DRILL.

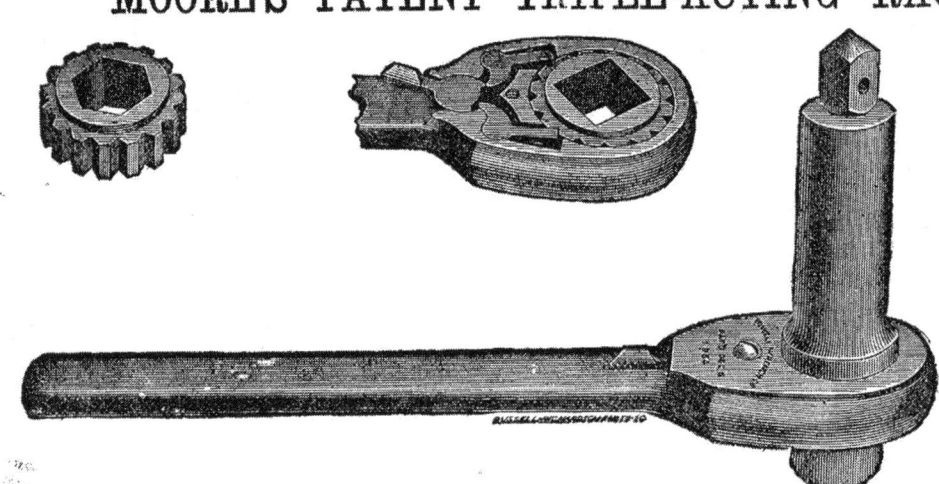

PRICE LIST OF DRILLS.

No. 1.	8 inch Lever	...	20/-
,, 2.	10 ,,	,,	26/-
,, 3.	15 ,,	,,	32/-
,, 4.	18 ,,	,,	40/-

This DRILL commends itself to all practical men whose business requires a Ratchet. Its superiority consists mainly, like the Wrench, in its triple movements, ACTING IN OPPOSITE DIRECTIONS AND CENTRALLY WITHOUT REMOVING, and its ready adaptation to both DRILLING and WRENCHING. It may be converted into a WRENCH by removing the cap and changing the Drill Socket for a Wrench Gear of corresponding number.

Both Drill and Wrench require but little space; are strong, and will not get out of order.

MOORE'S PATENT TRIPLE-ACTING RACHET WRENCH,

Adapted to turning the Nut on or off WITHOUT DISPLACING the Wrench, thus SAVING ONE-HALF THE TIME.

We desire to call attention to this WRENCH, acknowledged to be superior as a Rachet to any other. The smaller sizes are especially adapted to the wants of GAS FITTERS, PLUMBERS, and all who are engaged in putting in STEAM, GAS, or WATER PIPE, for Ratcheting side and corner boring, &c., &c. The larger sizes are almost indispensable to ENGINEERS, MANUFACTURERS, RAILWAY and STEAMBOAT COMPANIES. A nut or bolt is turned either way WITHOUT TAKING OFF THE WRENCH.

We beg to call the attention of railroad men to this adaptation of our PATENT RATCHET WRENCH to their use in turning the nut on FISH JOINT BOLTS. The workman always using the wrench in the position giving the greatest mechanical advantages, we claim *increase of efficiency* as well as *great saving in time* from not displacing the wrench.

The cut shows the wrench in position for operation. By a slight motion the action is changed from turning on to turning off. This wrench is made in a very substantial manner, the workmanship and working parts being the same as those which have stood the test of use for six years in our well known DRILLS and WRENCHES.

It will work when there is a clearness of only *three sixteenths* of an inch between the nut and the flange of the rail.

PRICE LIST OF WRENCHES.

No. 1.	8 inch Lever. Any size Gear on the List	...	12/-
,, 2.	10 ,, ,, ,, ,, ,, ,, ...	...	16/-
,, 3.	15 ,, ,, ,, ,, ,, ,, ...	...	20/-
,, 4.	18 ,, ,, ,, ,, ,, ,, ...	...	28/-
,, 5.	23 ,, ,, (Double handle) ...	...	40/-

PRICE LIST OF WRENCH GEARS.

	Inch Square Nut				Inch Hexagon			
No. 1.	$\tfrac{3}{8}$	$\tfrac{1}{2}$	$\tfrac{5}{8}$	...	$\tfrac{5}{8}$	$\tfrac{3}{4}$	...	2/- each.
,, 2.	$\tfrac{5}{8}$	$\tfrac{3}{4}$	$\tfrac{7}{8}$	...	$\tfrac{3}{4}$	$\tfrac{7}{8}$	1 ... 2/6 ,,
,, 3.	$\tfrac{3}{4}$	$\tfrac{7}{8}$	1	$1\tfrac{1}{8}$... 1	$1\tfrac{1}{8}$	$1\tfrac{1}{4}$	... 3/- ,,
,, 4.	$1\tfrac{1}{8}$	$1\tfrac{1}{4}$	$1\tfrac{3}{8}$	$1\tfrac{1}{2}$... $1\tfrac{1}{4}$	$1\tfrac{3}{8}$	$1\tfrac{1}{2}$	... 4/- ,,

PRICE LIST.

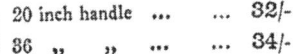

20 inch handle	...	...	32/-
36 ,, ,,	...	...	34/-

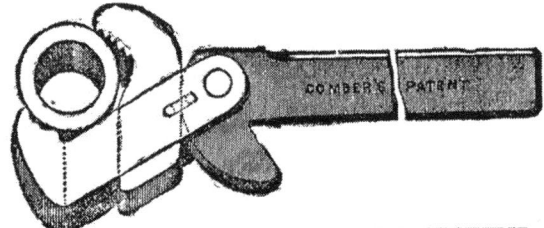

THE "COMBER" SELF-ADJUSTING PIPE WRENCH & SPANNER.

	PIPE WRENCHES.				SPANNERS.		
No.	B 1	B 2	B 3	No.	A 1	A 2	A 3
Length	10in.	17in.	24in.	Length	10in.	15in.	20in.
Taking PIPES	To $\tfrac{3}{4}$in.	1 to 2in.	2 to 3in.	Taking NUTS	To $\tfrac{5}{8}$in.	$\tfrac{5}{8}$ to 1in.	1 to $1\tfrac{1}{2}$in.
Span	To 1in.	$1\tfrac{3}{16}$ to $2\tfrac{1}{2}$in	$2\tfrac{1}{4}$ to $3\tfrac{3}{4}$in	Span	To $1\tfrac{3}{16}$in	1 to $1\tfrac{3}{4}$in.	$1\tfrac{1}{2}$ to $2\tfrac{5}{8}$in
Price	8/-	12/6	18/-	Price	7/-	10/6	15/-

BAILEY'S RAILWAY TOOLS.

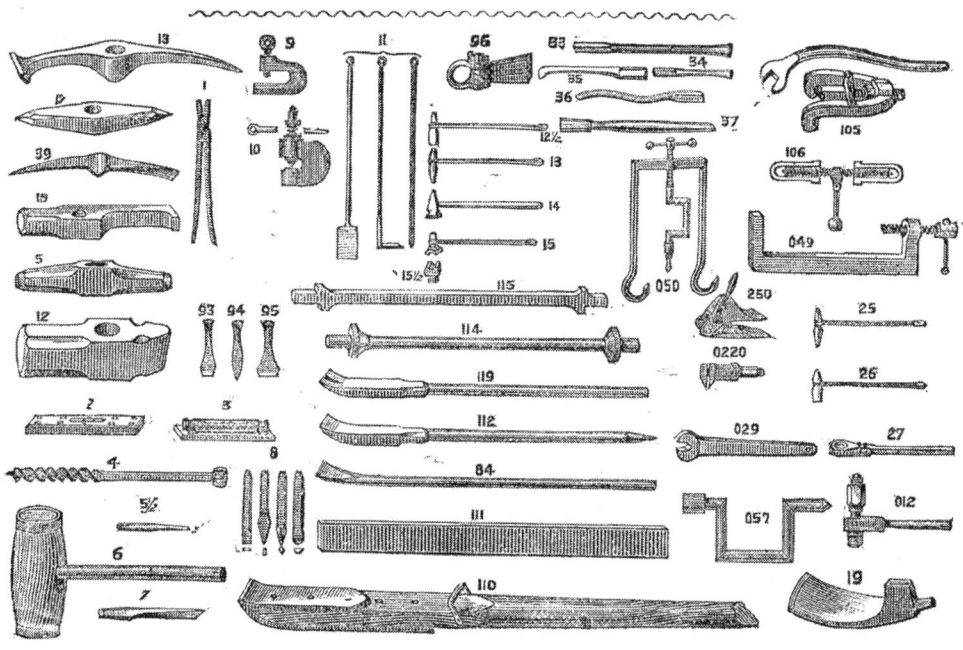

No. 18—Platelayers Benting Pick, -/9 per lb
" 17—Stone Pick, 1/6 per lb
" 39—Pickaxe
" 16—Keying Hammer, -/10 per lb
" 5—Spiking Hammer, 1/6 per lb
" 12—Sledge, Iron and Steel, -/8 ; Cast Steel, 1/3 per lb
" 6—Wood Mall, iron hooped, 16/6 each
" 7—Pin Cutter, -/8 per lb
" 2—Plated Spirit Level, -/10 per inch
" 3—Metallic Spirit Level, 1/4 per inch
" 4—Platelayer's Solid Eye Screw Augur

$\tfrac{3}{8}$ $\tfrac{1}{2}$ $\tfrac{5}{8}$ $\tfrac{3}{4}$ $\tfrac{7}{8}$ 1 $1\tfrac{1}{16}$ $1\tfrac{1}{8}$ $1\tfrac{3}{16}$ $1\tfrac{1}{4}$ $1\tfrac{5}{16}$ $1\tfrac{3}{8}$ $1\tfrac{7}{16}$ 2in.
22/- 23/- 26/- 29/6 33/- 36/- 39/6 48/- 50/- 55/- 66/- 67/- 78/- 80/-

" 5½—Cast Steel Drift Pin, 1/2 per lb
" 1—Smiths' Tongs, -/9 per lb
Nos. 93, 94, 95—Stone Chisels
No. 8—Chipping Chisels, 1/- per lb
" 9—Boiler Cramp, Light 12/-, extra Heavy -/10 per lb.
" 10—Boiler Bear, fitted with one Bed and Punch, Plain Lever, ½in. 66/-, ⅝in. 90/-, ¾in. 110/-
Extra Beds and Punches, 12/- per pair
With Ratchet Lever extra, 45/-
100—Hand Punch, 1/2 per lb.
" 11—Smiths' Hearth Tools, 12/- per set
" 96—Stone Lifting Lewish
" 12½—Cast Steel Sates, 1/2 per lb
" 13—Cast Steel Punch, 1/2 per lb
" 14—Set Hammer, 1/2 per lb

No. 15—Top and Bottom Swages, assorted, $\tfrac{3}{8}$ in. to 3 in., 1/2 per lb.
" 115—Plain Rail Gauge, 12/- each
" 114—Travelling Rail Gauge, with Turned Ends, -/10 per lb
" 119—Crowbar, with Steeled Claw, -/7 per lb.
" 112—Pointed Crowbar, both ends steeled, -/7 per lb
" 84—Birmingham Pattern Crowbar, 40/- per cwt
" 111—Wood Straight Edge or Level, 10/6 each
" 110—Strong Wood Lever, with Iron Shoe,
9 ft. 30/-, 10 ft. 36/-, 12 ft. 42/-
" 33—Sledge Hammer Handle, 34, 36, 38 inches long
" 34—Hand Hammer Handle
" 35—Axe Handle
" 36—Adze Handle
" 37—Pickaxe Handle
" 050—Brace and Cramp for Pipe Boring, 38/-
" 250—Rail Jack, 164/- each
" 0220—Best Railway Wrench, 10in. 13/3, 12in. 14/9
14in. 17/-, 16in. 21/6, 18in. 24/-
" 029—Fish Joint Spanner, -/8 per lb
" 057—Strong Crank Brace, 12/- each ; Drills, 14/- per doz
" 105—Permanent Way Cramp, -/8 per lb
" 106—Screw Coupling, -/8 to -/10 per lb
" 049—Drill Cramp, 22/6 each
Nos. 25 and 26 as Nos 12½ and 13
No. 27—Ratchet Spanner, Fish Bolt Size, 44/- each
" 012—Ratchet Brace, 14in. 21/-, 16in. 24/-, 18in. 26/6,
20in. 30/6, 24in. 36/-
" 19—Platelayer's Adze, Solid Eye, 12/- each

These Prices are subject to fluctuations of the Metal Market.

SHAW'S PATENT BAR AND ROD-IRON CROPPER,

For Cutting Round or Square Rods Square at the end.

Sole Makers, J. BAILEY & CO., Albion Works, Salford, Lancashire.

No. 3.

The most useful Tool ever invented for either ENGINEER, BLACKSMITH, MACHINIST, TOOL-MAKER, or any other user of Iron

REDUCED PRICES.

No 1—To Cut up to ¾in. £5 10 0
  „ 2   „   „   ½in. 3 3 0

BENCH CROPPER.

To Cut up to ¼in. Price 32/- Complete, with Sliding Gauge for Length.

HOFFMAN'S PATENT HAND SHEARS.

No. 3—To Cut not more than ¼in. Plate £5 10 0
Extreme length, 3ft. 9in.; extreme width, 8in.

No. 2.
To Cut not more than 3-16in. plate, £3 3 0
Extreme length, 3ft.
  „   width, 6in.

These compact and efficient Shears are decidedly amongst the most useful Tools ever offered for the purpose of Cutting Iron Plate. They can be either bolted or cramped to a bench, and can be easily moved about.

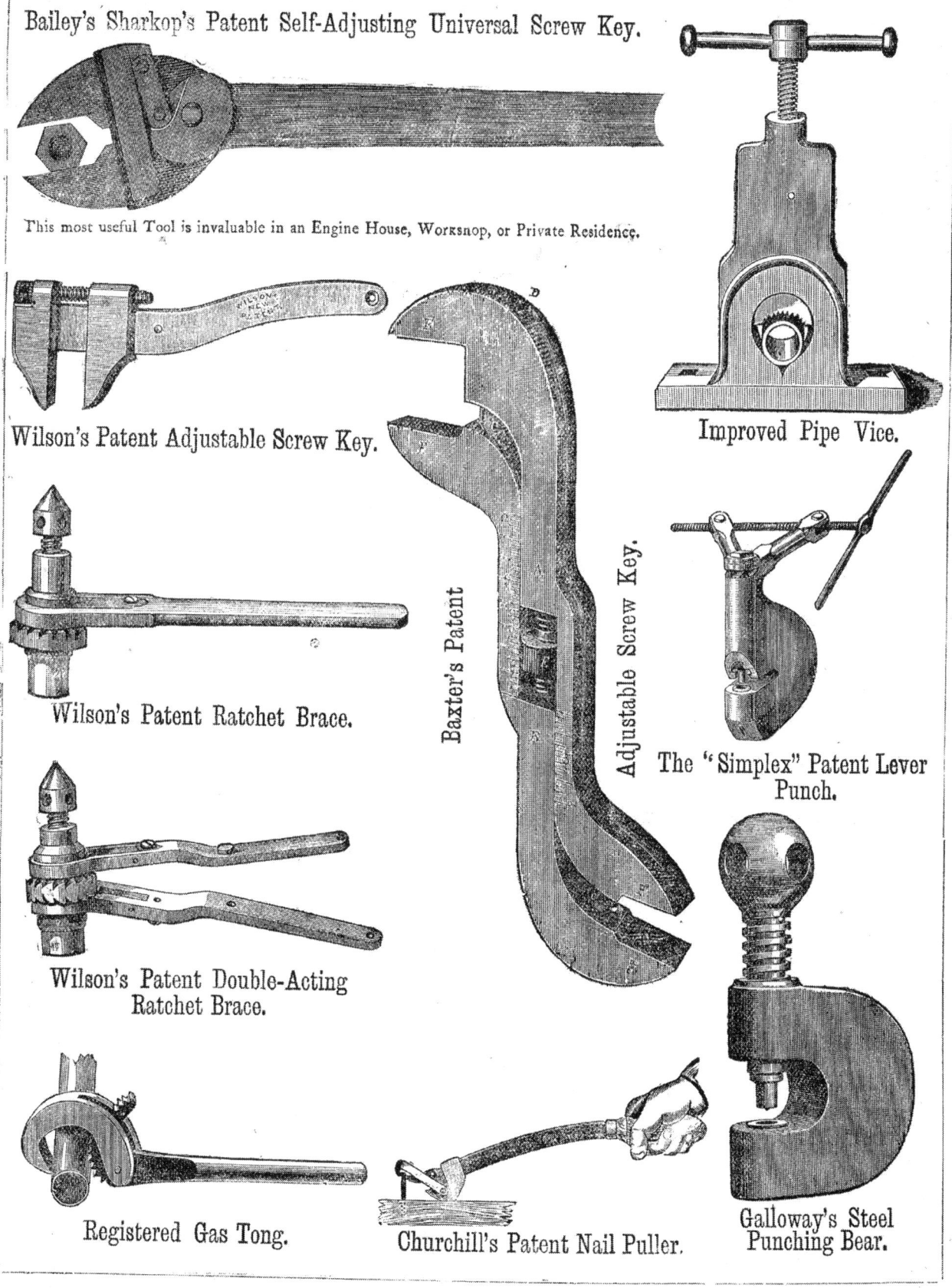

BAILEY'S SHARKOP'S PATENT SELF-ADJUSTING UNIVERSAL SCREW KEY.

REDUCED PRICES.

No. 1 will take any Nut from $\frac{7}{16}$ to $1\frac{1}{8}$ inch, ... 15/- each.
" 2 " " " $\frac{11}{16}$ to $1\frac{11}{16}$ " ... 18/- "
" 3 " " " $1\frac{1}{4}$ to $2\frac{5}{8}$ " ... 30/- "

WILSON'S PATENT ADJUSTABLE SCREW KEY.

This Screw Key is pronounced the strongest, handiest, and most complete tool of its class hitherto produced; it is cheap, well made, and of good material; its moving Screw is of Steel, which from its construction and arrangement, is easily and rapidly adjusted to its work.

Size -	7	8	10	12	14	16	18	inches.
Span -	1	$1\frac{1}{4}$	$1\frac{1}{2}$	$1\frac{3}{4}$	2	$2\frac{1}{4}$	$2\frac{1}{2}$	inches.
Price-	3/6	4/-	5/-	6/-	7/-	8/6	10/-	each.

BAXTER'S PATENT ADJUSTABLE SCREW KEY.

This is a very good and cheap tool, and is so constructed that no pressure is thrown on the adjusting Screw when in use, consequently it is very durable.

Size -	4	6	8	10	12	inch.
Price -	32/-	48/-	65/-	96/-	120/-	per doz.
" -		3/-	4/6	6/-	8/6	10/6	each.

WILSON'S PATENT RATCHET BRACE.

The advantages of this Ratchet Brace consist in the improved construction and arrangement of its driving pawl and ratchet wheel, by which greater compactness, strength, and durability are obtained; the pawl being situated in the lever, is held firmly to its work, and at the same time completely protected from external injury, while the ratchet teeth being formed on the side instead of the circumference of the wheel, are equally removed from danger, as well as stronger and more durable than those of the ordinary construction. The brace is strong, handy, well-made, and of good material, and the cheapest tool of the kind in the market.

Size -	12	14	16	18	inch.
Price -	11/-	12/-	14/-	16/-	each.

WILSON'S PATENT DOUBLE-ACTING RATCHET BRACE.

This Rathet Brace possesses, in addition to the improvements above described, the great advantage of being double-acting It is constructed with double ratchet, teeth, pawls, and levers, which on being moved from and towards each other simultaneously, impart to the ratchet wheel continuous motion, thereby enabling it to effect its work in half the time of a single-acting brace. By connecting the handles and using them as one, the brace is rendered single-acting, and may be thus used when desired. This brace is also well adapted for the working of lifting jacks and other purposes where continuous motion is a desideratum. The above advantages, combined with its simplicity, cheapness, and general handiness for mechanical use, must insure for it a wide market.

Size -	12	14	16	18	inch.
Price -	18/-	21/-	24/-	27/-	each.

REGISTERED ECCENTRIC GAS TONG.

A NEAT AND DURABLE TOOL.

No. 1 ... ... $\frac{1}{4}$ to $\frac{3}{4}$ inch 7/-
" 2 ... ... $\frac{1}{2}$ to $1\frac{1}{4}$ " 9/-
" 3 ... ... 1 to 2 " 11/-

CHURCHILL'S PATENT NAIL PULLER.

This tool is intended to supply a want long felt by everyone having to open Cases, Casks, &c.

By its use the Covers and Cases will both be saved from breakage, all the nails being drawn out in less time than they can be removed in the old way with mallet and chisel.

The Nails are also preserved straight for further use.

INSTRUCTION.

Standing beside or over the nail to be drawn, force the point of the lever or handle into the wood just behind the nail head; then holding it firmly in place, bear down the lever, causing the claw to grip the nail and draw it out. By first making a small hole in the wood with the point of the lever, on the opposite side of the nail head, will aid the claw in taking a firm hold of the nail, and insure rapid working.

Price 72/- per Dozen.

IMPROVED PIPE VICE,

STRONG AND DURABLE.

$1\frac{1}{4}$ to 2 inch 26/6

SIMPLEX PATENT LEVER PUNCH.

This Punch is the best Hand Punch ever invented, combining simplicity with durability and strength. It is far more easily worked than any Punching Machine yet made. Its peculiar construction renders it almost an impossibility for it to get out of repair. The prices, as compared with other Hand Punches, will be found much lower, and the weight of each machine considerably less.

PRICES.

No. 2 ... ... to Punch $\frac{3}{4} \times \frac{3}{8}$ £9 10 0
" 3 ... ... " $\frac{3}{4} \times \frac{5}{8}$ 12 10 0

GALLOWAY'S STEEL PUNCHING BEAR.

These Punching Bears are made of the best quality of steel, and from their *Lightness, Strength, and Durability*, are much superior to those hitherto in use.

They can be used by a common labourer without fear of breakage, and are so *light and portable* that they may be carried about with ease.

We can confidently recommend them to all Boiler Makers as being the best for general work.

PRICES, &c.

Approximate Weight. / Prices Nett, including Punch and Die.

No. 1 Size, 20lbs. to punch $\frac{3}{4}$-in. hole in $\frac{5}{16}$-in. plate ... £4 0 0
" 2 " 38lbs. " $\frac{3}{4}$-in. " $\frac{1}{2}$-in. " ... 4 12 0
" 3 " 56lbs. " $\frac{3}{4}$-in. " $\frac{3}{4}$-in. " ... 5 3 6

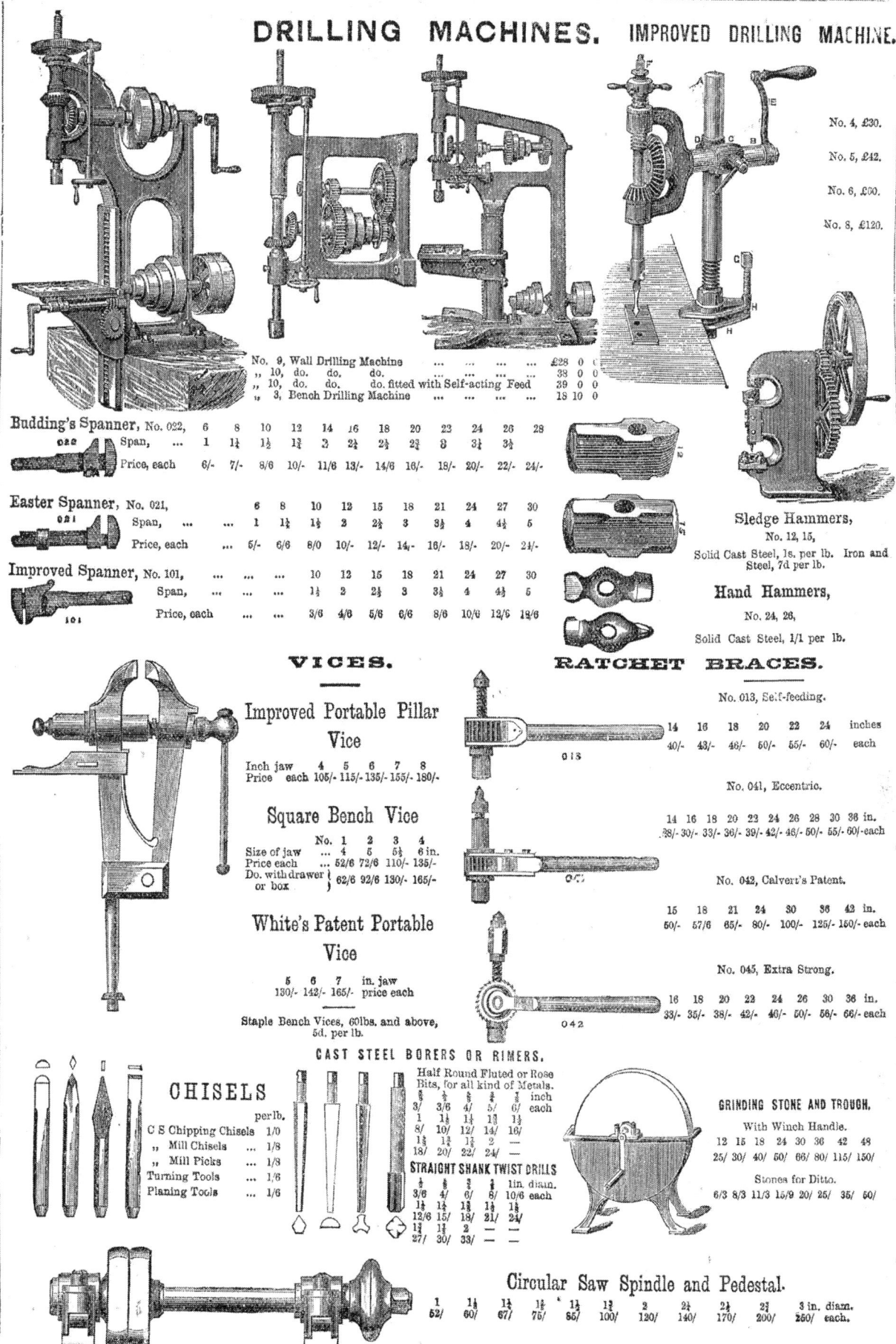

LITTLE GIANT IRON CUTTER.

	Weight.	Cuts.	£	s.	d.
No. 1.	16 lbs.	¼ in. x 1 in.	4	4	0
No. 2.	175 lbs.	½ in. x 3 in.	8	8	0
No. 3.	315 lbs.	¾ in. x 4 in.	12	12	0

One man, with this Machine, can easily and rapidly cut all sizes of round or square iron up to 1¼ inches, or flat iron ¾ x 4 inches. Both blades of the Shears move alike, so that no jar or recoil is felt when the iron is cut off. No one will believe the truth in regard to it until they see it work, as such results were never obtained before. They will cut double the size of any other Machine that costs the same price.

AMATEUR LATHE.

Weight 75 lbs., Foot Lathe, Price £6.

The above Cut shows a Foot Power Lathe. It is 5 inch centres, and 30 inches between centres. A speed of 2,000 revolutions may be made per minute. This Machine will be found suitable for Wood Turning, &c.

Fig. 1.

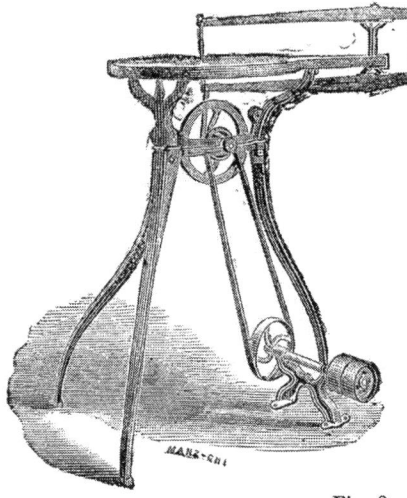

Fig. 2.

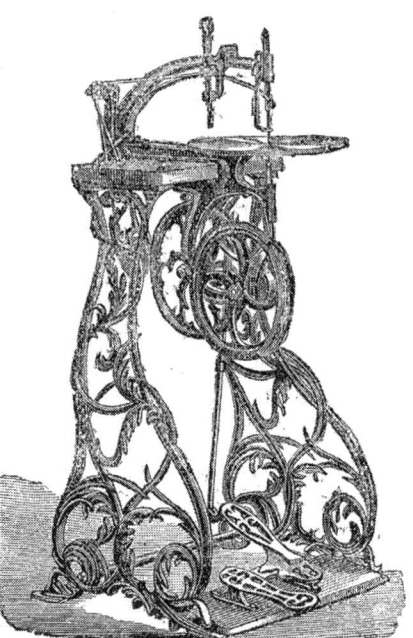

BARNES' PATENT FOOT-POWER SCROLL SAW.

Cabinet Maker's Machine, weight 56 lbs. £5 0 0 | Amateur Machine, weight 25 lbs. £4 0 0
Extra Saws, per doz. ... ... 0 4 0 | Extra Saws per doz. 0 1 0

The Amateur Machine is complete in itself. Is made suitable height for Adults to work sitting, or for boys to work standing. Will cut from 2 in. down to the thinnest wood. Take the ordinary fret saw.

See Fig. 2.—For Steam Power only. Price £6 10s. We now supply the Barnes' Saw, Cabinet Makers' size, to be worked by power as shown in the above cut. The table of this machine is 38 inches high. It will swing 24 inches under the arm.

Fig. 1.—This Saw is adapted to the entire range of scroll or fret sawing from the cornice bracket *three* inches thick to the finest wall bracket *one-eighth* of an inch thick. It takes up no more room than a sewing machine, and runs but little harder. The machine, all complete, weighs about 56 lbs. Being so light, and taking so little room, it can be used beside the workman's bench, and for most straight sawing, he will turn to the machine and do it quicker and better than he can fasten it to his vice or lay it on his horse and do it.

Fleetwood Saw mounted on Table
with Boring Machine attachment £6 0 0
Without attachment 4 15 0
Table only 1 5 0
Weight complete, 58 lbs.

IMPROVED BOOT AND SHOE CLEANING MACHINE.

The great saving in time and labour effected by the use of this machine would scarcely be believed by those who have not given it a trial. In large establishments, gentlemen's houses, schools, hotels, public institutions, &c., the time spent in cleaning Boots and Shoes is very considerable, and the work often very imperfectly done. By the use of this machine the Shoes are cleaned in one-fourth the time, besides being done in a very superior manner, unattainable by the usual hand method. Those who have the machines speak highly of the work done by them, and of the great economy in time effected by their use. £3 10s.

IMPROVED BOTTLE WASHING MACHINE, £3 10.

For soda water manufacturers, wine merchants, &c., this machine is the most convenient, compact, and efficient yet introduced to the public. The man sits comfortably at his work, two bottles are cleaned at the same time, and no exertion is required, the mere weight of the foot being sufficient to turn it.

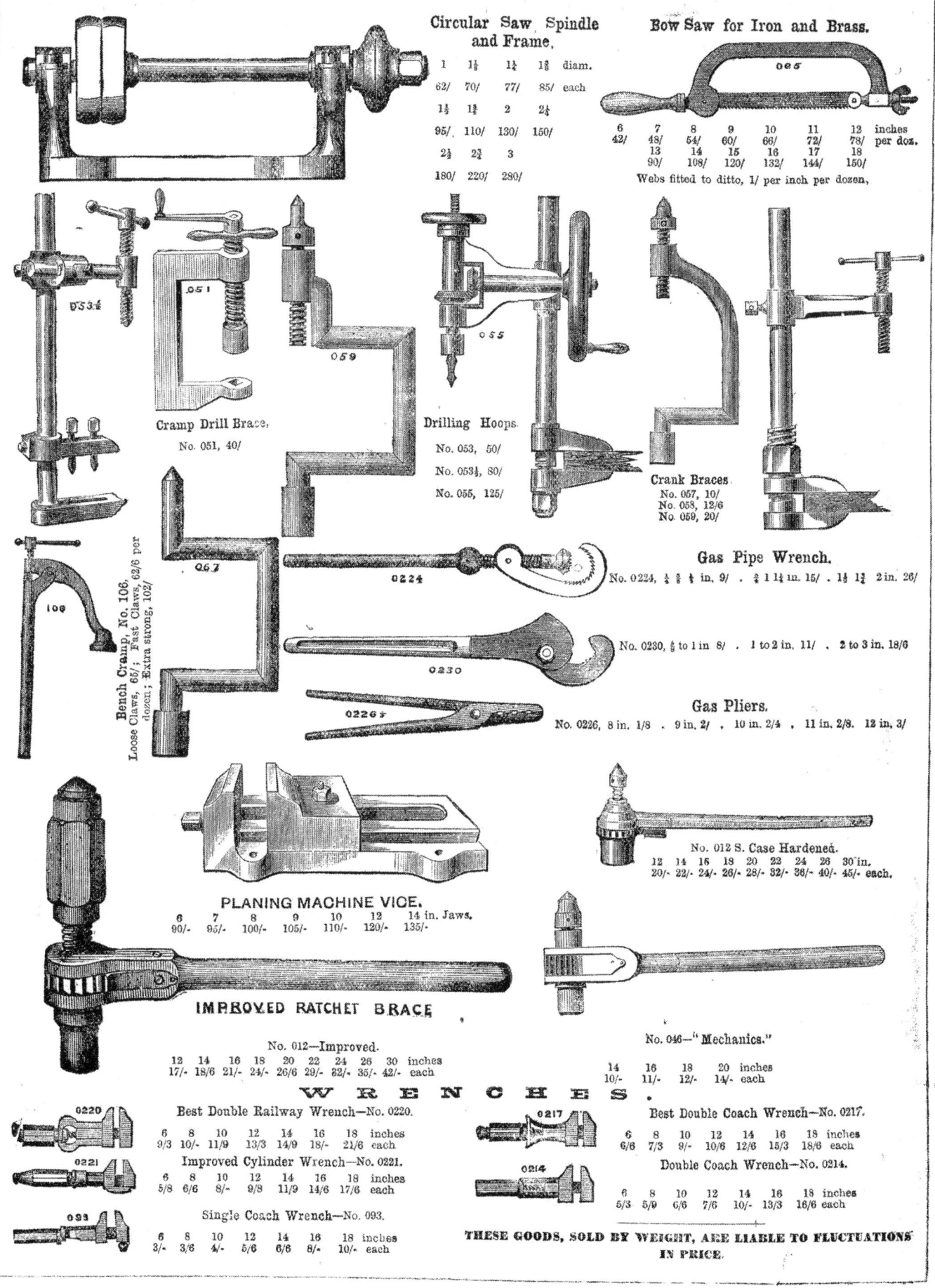

Patent Rotary Tube Cutter, with 3 Knives

No. 17—¼ to 1 inch, 23/6 per set.
" 18—1 to 2 inch, 30/- "

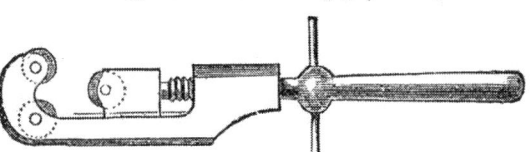

Nos. 17 and 18 have only to be turned one-third to and fro, when the tube will be cut through.

Patent Tube Cutters

No. 1—¼ to 1 inch, 15/6 per set.
" 2—1 to 2 inch, 22/6 "
" 3—2 to 4 inch, 40/- "

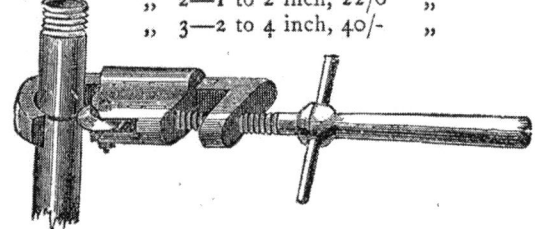

Bailey's Patent Spanner

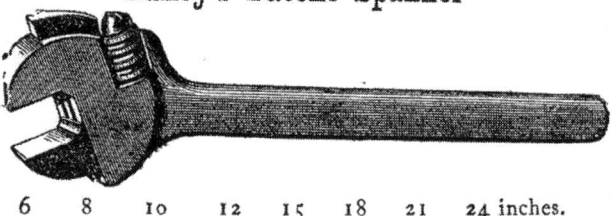

6	8	10	12	15	18	21	24 inches.
⅝	¾	1	1¼	1½	1¾	2	2¼ in. opening
4/-	4/9	5/6	6/9	8/6	11/-	12/6	14/6 each.

Bewley's Patent Tube Wrench

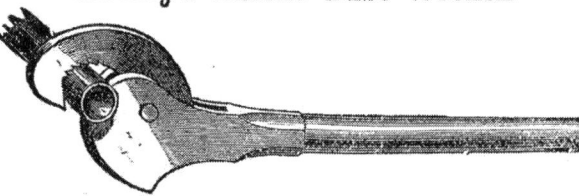

Very simple and strong. It instantly adjusts itself to the various-sized tubes, and it is not liable to get out of order. The claw is steel-faced.

A man can work one of the small sizes for small tubes with one hand, and can hold the other length of tube fast by a second wrench in his other hand.

A—For ⅛ to ½ in. Tube ... Price £0 7 6
B— " ⅝ to 1 in. " ... " 0 10 6
C— " 1 to 2 in. " ... " 0 17 6

Weston's Patent Ratchet Brace

Strong, simple, well-made, and at a very reasonable price. The two ratchets and wheels working alternately, give the greatest possible results for the labour expended.

Prices, fitted in "Lancashire Black."

12	14	16	18	20	22 inch.
11/6	12/6	13/6	15/-	16/-	18/6 each.

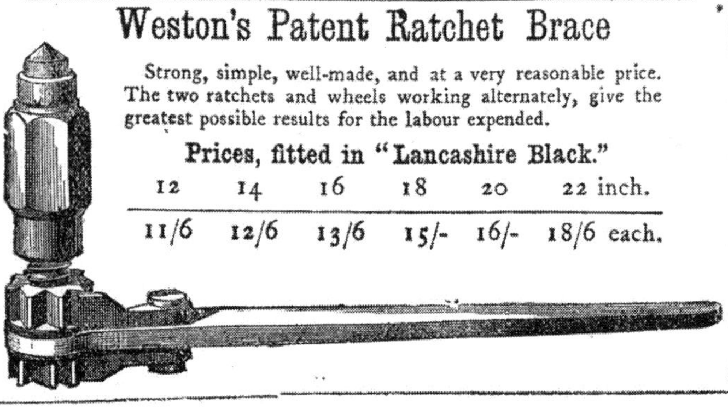

Patent Main Cutter

No. 4—To cut 2 to 4in. Cast-Iron Pipe, inside measure, 51/- per set.
" 5—To cut 5 to 8in. inside measure, Cast-Iron Pipe, 60/- per set.

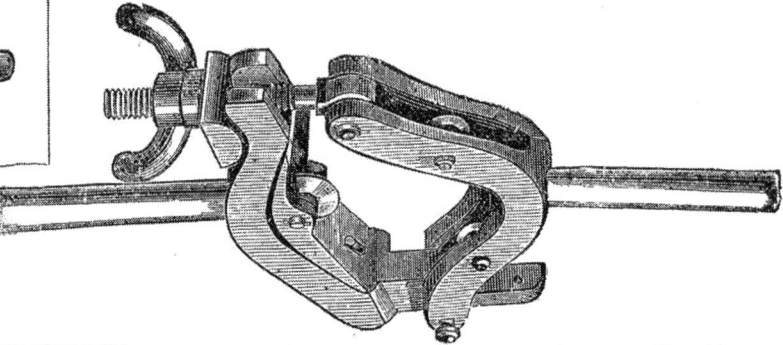

N.B.—After fixing and setting straight the Main Cutters, work to and fro till the circle is formed, then turn at pleasure, applying the thumb bit at each turn round. The size of each hole in the heel is numbered.

Extra Circular Knives or Tube Cutters

Nos. 1, 17, 19, and 21, 16/- per dozen.
" 2, 11, and 22, 20/- "
" 3, 4, 5, and 6, 24/- "

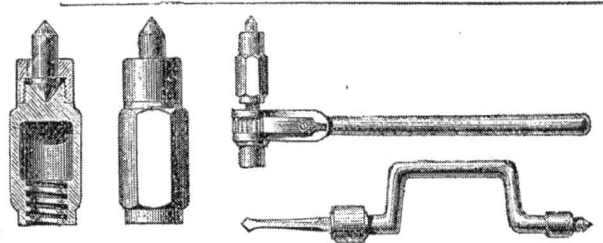

PATENT ANTIFRICTION LOOSE CENTRE.

AS APPLIED TO RATCHET AND CRANK BRACES.

This Ratchet is designed to obviate the friction and wearing away of the Working Centre. The she centre, acting as an oil cup, keeps the working centre constantly lubricated, and reduces the friction to a minimum. This brace will last longer, and requires less power to work it than any brace yet made.

PRICES.

12	14	16	18	20	22	24 inches
19/-	20/-	21/-	22/-	23/-	27/-	31/- each

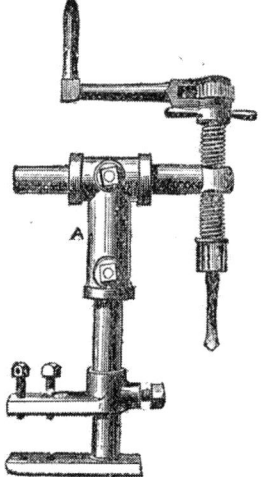

IMPROVED UNIVERSAL DRILLING JIB,

A very useful Tool,

Will Drill at any angle, up to 1½ inch.

Price—£4/5/-

J. BAILEY & CO.'S
BEST SCREW STOCKS, DIES, AND TAPS, FOR ENGINEERS, &c.

With Dies, Taper and Plug Taps, Tap Wrenches, Lever, &c.

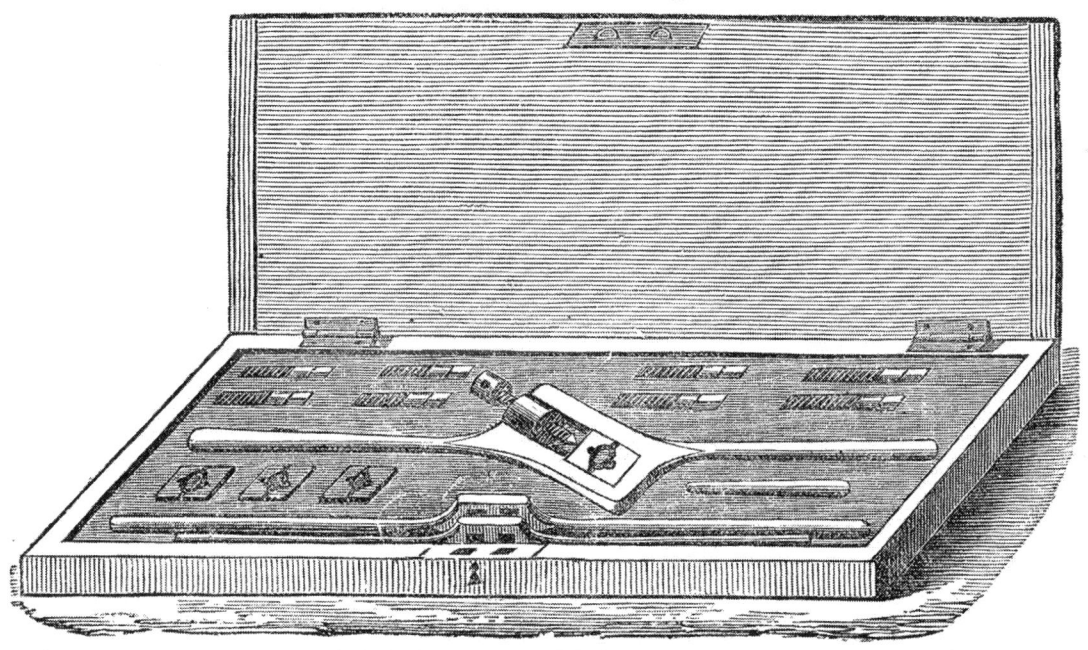

FIVE SERIES OF SCREW STOCKS AND DIES, FITTED IN PAINTED WOOD CASES.

The Cases in each Series are Priced separately, so that any selection may be made; and two sets of STOCKS, &c., may be fitted into one case.

Case containing set of Stocks and Dies, viz., 1 set $\frac{1}{4}$, $\frac{5}{16}$, $\frac{3}{8}$, $\frac{7}{16}$, $\frac{1}{2}$, & 1 set $\frac{5}{8}$, $\frac{3}{4}$, $\frac{7}{8}$, 1 inch, with Taper and Plug Taps to each size, and Tap wrenches	£9 3s. 0d.
Case containing 1 set of Stocks and Dies, $\frac{1}{4}$, $\frac{5}{16}$, $\frac{3}{8}$, $\frac{7}{16}$, $\frac{1}{2}$, $\frac{5}{8}$, $\frac{3}{4}$, and 1 set $\frac{7}{8}$, 1, $1\frac{1}{8}$, $1\frac{1}{4}$, with Taps, &c., complete	£13 2s. 0d.
Case containing 1 set of Stocks and Dies, $\frac{1}{4}$, $\frac{3}{8}$, $\frac{1}{2}$, $\frac{5}{8}$, $\frac{3}{4}$, and 1 set $\frac{7}{8}$, 1, $1\frac{1}{8}$, $1\frac{1}{4}$, with Taps and Tap Wrenches complete	£12 0s. 0d.
Case containing 1 set $\frac{1}{4}$, $\frac{3}{8}$, $\frac{1}{2}$, ... 1 ,, $\frac{5}{8}$, $\frac{3}{4}$, $\frac{7}{8}$, 1, ... Complete as above. 1 ,, $1\frac{1}{8}$, $1\frac{1}{4}$, $1\frac{3}{8}$, $1\frac{1}{2}$, ...	£18 10s. 0d.
Case containing 1 set $\frac{1}{4}$, $\frac{3}{8}$, $\frac{1}{2}$, ... { This set can be } 1 ,, $\frac{5}{8}$, $\frac{3}{4}$, $\frac{7}{8}$, 1, ... { had either in one } 1 ,, $1\frac{1}{8}$, $1\frac{1}{4}$, $1\frac{3}{8}$, $1\frac{1}{2}$, ... { or two cases at } 1 ,, $1\frac{5}{8}$, $1\frac{3}{4}$, $1\frac{7}{8}$, 2, ... { the same price. } { Complete as above. }	£35 0s. 0d.

	$\frac{3}{16}$	$\frac{1}{4}$	$\frac{5}{16}$	$\frac{3}{8}$	$\frac{7}{16}$	$\frac{1}{2}$	$\frac{5}{8}$	$\frac{3}{4}$	$\frac{7}{8}$	1	$1\frac{1}{8}$	$1\frac{1}{4}$	$1\frac{3}{8}$	$1\frac{1}{2}$	$1\frac{5}{8}$	$1\frac{3}{4}$	$1\frac{7}{8}$	2	$2\frac{1}{8}$	$2\frac{1}{4}$	$2\frac{3}{8}$	$2\frac{1}{2}$	$2\frac{5}{8}$	$2\frac{3}{4}$	$2\frac{7}{8}$	3 in.
Extra Working Taps, each	2/-	2/6	2/6	3/-	3/6	4/-	5/-	6/-	7/-	8/-	9/6	11/-	12/6	15/-	17/-	19/-	22/-	26/-	30/-	34/-	38/-	43/-	50/-	55/-	62/-	70/-
,, Master ,, ,,																										
Machine Taps, each	2/6	3/-	3/-	3/6	4/3	5/-	6/-	7/-	8/-	10/-	12/-	14/-	16/-	19/-	22/-	24/-	27/-	32/-	36/-	40/-	45/-	50/-	60/-	65/-	72/-	82/-
Screw Tools, per pair	5/6			6/-			6/6			8/-					9/6				11/-				12/-			

BAILEY'S BEST QUALITY SCREW STOCKS,

DIES AND TAPS,

For Bolts and Nuts, Machinery, &c.

All the Taps of Whitworth's Thread, Gauge, and Pattern.

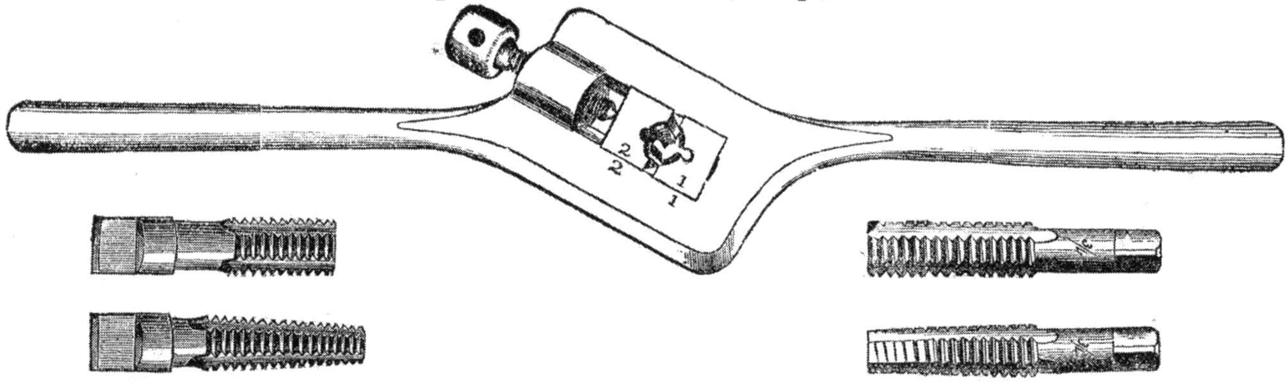

SERIES OR RANGE OF SIZES—To Screw						With 2 Taps to each size, Taper Plug	With 3 Taps to each size, Taper, Second, and Plug	Case Hardened Wrenches to suit Taps	Wood Case Painted
Inch	Inch	Inch	Inch	Inch	Inch	£ s. d.	£ s. d.	£ s. d.	£ s. d.
3-16	1/4	3/8	...	...	...	1 8 0	1 17 0	0 5 0	0 7 6
3-16	1/4	5-16	3/8	...	...	1 15 0	2 5 0	0 5 0	0 7 6
1/8	3-16	1/4	5-16	3/8	...	2 0 0	2 11 0	0 5 0	0 7 6
1/4	3/8	7-16	...	...	...	1 9 0	2 0 0	0 7 0	0 8 0
1/4	5-16	3/8	7-16	...	...	1 14 0	2 8 0	0 7 0	0 8 0
3-16	1/8	5-16	3/8	7-16	...	1 19 0	2 14 0	0 10 0	0 8 0
1/4	3/8	1/2	...	...	...	1 11 0	2 2 0	0 7 6	0 10 0
1/4	5-16	2/3	1/2	...	...	1 18 0	2 10 6	0 7 6	0 10 0
1/4	5-16	3/8	7-16	1/2	...	2 4 0	2 17 0	0 10 3	0 10 0
3/8	1/2	5/8	...	...	...	1 18 0	2 10 0	0 9 3	0 12 0
1/4	3/8	1/2	5/8	...	...	2 5 0	3 1 0	0 9 3	0 12 0
1/4	3/8	7-16	1/2	5/8	...	2 11 0	3 10 0	0 11 0	0 12 0
1/2	5/8	3/4	...	...	...	2 2 0	2 17 0	0 11 0	0 17 6
3/8	1/2	5/8	3/4	...	...	2 15 0	3 10 6	0 11 0	0 17 6
3/8	7-16	1/2	5/8	3/4	...	3 5 0	4 10 0	0 14 0	0 17 6
5/8	3/4	7/8	...	...	...	2 12 0	3 8 0	0 13 6	1 2 0
1/4	7-16	1/2	5/8	3/4	...	3 5 0	4 7 6	0 16 6	1 2 0
7-16	1/2	5/8	3/4	7/8	...	3 17 0	5 2 6	0 16 6	1 2 0
3/4	7/8	1	...	...	...	3 0 0	4 0 0	0 17 9	1 6 0
5/8	3/4	7/8	1	...	...	3 15 0	5 0 0	0 17 9	1 6 0
1/2	5/8	3/4	7/8	1	...	4 7 0	5 16 0	1 1 0	1 6 0
7/8	1	1 1/8	...	...	...	3 6 0	4 12 0	1 0 0	1 8 0
3/4	7/8	1	1 1/8	...	...	4 4 0	5 15 6	1 3 0	1 8 0
5/8	3/4	7/8	1	1 1/8	...	5 0 0	6 14 6	1 3 0	1 8 0
1	1 1/8	1 1/4	...	...	...	3 12 0	5 0 0	1 1 6	1 10 0
7/8	1	1 1/8	1 1/4	...	...	4 14 0	6 7 6	1 6 0	1 10 0
3/4	7/8	1	1 1/8	1 1/4	...	5 12 0	7 11 0	1 6 0	1 10 0
1 1/8	1 1/4	1 3/8	...	...	...	4 5 0	5 18 0	1 10 0	1 15 0
1	1 1/8	1 1/4	1 3/4	...	...	5 5 0	7 6 0	1 10 0	1 15 0
7/8	1	1 1/8	1 1/4	1 3/8	...	6 10 0	8 8 0	1 14 0	1 15 0
1	1 1/4	1 1/2	...	...	...	4 18 0	6 12 0	1 14 0	2 5 0
1 1/4	1 3/8	1 1/2	...	...	...	5 4 0	7 2 0	1 14 6	2 5 0
1 1/8	1 1/4	1 3/8	1 1/2	...	...	6 2 0	8 10 6	1 14 6	2 5 0
1	1 1/8	1 1/4	1 3/8	1 1/2	...	7 2 0	9 18 0	2 0 0	2 5 0
1 1/4	1 1/2	1 3/4	...	...	...	7 0 0	9 15 0	1 18 0	2 10 0
1 1/4	1 1/2	1 5/8	1 3/4	...	...	8 10 0	11 12 0	1 18 0	2 10 0
1 1/4	1 3/8	1 1/2	1 5/8	1 3/4	...	9 17 0	13 10 0	2 8 0	2 10 0
1 1/8	1 1/4	1 3/8	1 1/2	1 5/8	1 3/4	11 4 0	15 6 0	2 8 0	2 10 0
1 1/2	1 3/4	2	...	...	...	8 12 0	11 10 0	2 10 0	3 15 0
1 1/4	1 1/2	1 3/4	2	...	...	10 12 0	13 4 0	2 10 0	3 15 0
1 3/8	1 3/4	1 7/8	2	...	...	11 0 0	14 3 0	2 10 0	3 15 0
1 1/2	1 5/8	1 3/4	1 7/8	2	...	12 18 0	17 17 0	2 10 0	3 15 0
1 3/4	2	2 1/4	...	...	...	10 5 0	14 4 0	2 17 0	4 10 0
1 3/4	1 7/8	2	2 1/4	...	...	12 5 0	17 5 0	3 5 0	4 10 0
2	2 1/4	2 1/2	...	...	...	12 0 0	17 3 0	3 15 0	5 0 0
1 3/4	2	2 1/4	2 1/2	...	...	14 10 0	21 12 0	3 15 0	5 0 0
2	2 1/8	2 1/4	2 3/8	2 1/2	...	17 10 0	26 10 0	3 15 0	5 0 0

BAILEY'S BEST SCREW STOCKS & DIES

For Screwing Iron Gas Tube, with Taper and Plug Taps, to each size.

	in.	in.	in.	in.	in.		£	s.	d.
To Screw				1/8	1/4	Gas Tube	1	0	0
,,				1/4	3/8	do.	1	2	0
,,			1/8	1/4	3/8	do.	1	7	0
,,				3/8	1/2	do.	1	11	0
,,			1/4	3/8	1/2	do.	1	18	0
,,		1/8	1/4	3/8	1/2	do.	2	7	0
,,			3/8	1/2	5/8	do.	2	10	0
,,					3/4	do.	1	15	0
,,			1/2	5/8	3/4	do.	2	16	0
,,			3/8	1/2	3/4	do.	2	16	0
,,		1/4	3/8	1/2	3/4	do.	3	2	0
,,		3/8	1/2	5/8	3/4	do.	3	4	0
,,					1	do.	1	18	0
,,				3/4	1	do.	2	12	0
,,			1/2	3/4	1	do.	3	3	0
,,		3/8	1/2	3/4	1	do.	3	15	0
,,		1/2	5/8	3/4	1	do.	3	15	0
,,			3/4	7/8	1	do.	3	12	0
,,	1/4	3/8	1/2	3/4	1	do.	4	5	0
,,	1/2	5/8	3/4	7/8	1	do.	4	10	0
,,					1 1/4	do.	2	13	0
,,				1	1 1/4	do.	3	8	0
,,			3/4	1	1 1/4	do.	4	4	0
,,			7/8	1	1 1/4	do.	4	10	0
,,		1/2	3/4	1	1 1/4	do.	4	18	0

	in.	in.	in.	in.	in.		£	s.	d.
To Screw					1 1/2	Gas Tube	4	1	0
,,				1 1/4	1 1/2	do.	5	15	0
,,			1	1 1/4	1 1/2	do.	6	10	0
,,		3/4	1	1 1/4	1 1/2	do.	7	8	0
,,	1/2	3/4	1	1 1/4	1 1/2	do.	8	0	0
,,				1 1/2	1 3/4	do.	6	8	0
,,			1 1/4	1 1/2	1 3/4	do.	7	0	0
,,		1	1 1/4	1 1/2	1 3/8	do.	8	10	0
,,					2	do.	5	0	0
,,				1 3/4	2	do.	7	0	0
,,				1 1/2	2	do.	6	12	0
,,			1 1/2	1 3/4	2	do.	8	10	0
,,			1 1/4	1 1/2	2	do.	8	0	0
,,		1	1 1/4	1 1/2	2	do.	9	5	0
,,		1 1/4	1 1/2	1 3/4	2	do.	9	15	0
,,					2 1/4	do.	6	0	0
,,				2	2 1/4	do.	8	14	0
,,			1 1/2	2	2 1/4	do.	10	5	0
,,					2 1/2	do.	7	0	0
,,				2 1/4	2 1/2	do.	11	0	0
,,			2	2 1/4	2 1/2	do.	13	10	0
,,					3	do.	12	0	0
,,				2 1/2	3	do.	16	0	0
,,			2 1/4	2 1/2	3	do.	20	0	0
,,			2 1/2	2 3/4	3	do.	22	0	0

GASFITTERS' SCREW STOCKS AND DIES,

With Three Taper and Three Plug Taps for Screwing Brass Tube.

	1/4	3/4	1/2 inch	...	24/
	3/8	1/2	5/8 ,,	...	26/
1/4	3/8	1/2	5/8 ,,	...	28/
3/8	1/2	5/8	3/4 ,,	...	35/

5/8	3/4	7/8 inch	...	40/
3/4	7/8	1 ,,	...	52/
1	1 1/8	1 1/4 ,,	...	60/

Best Quality.

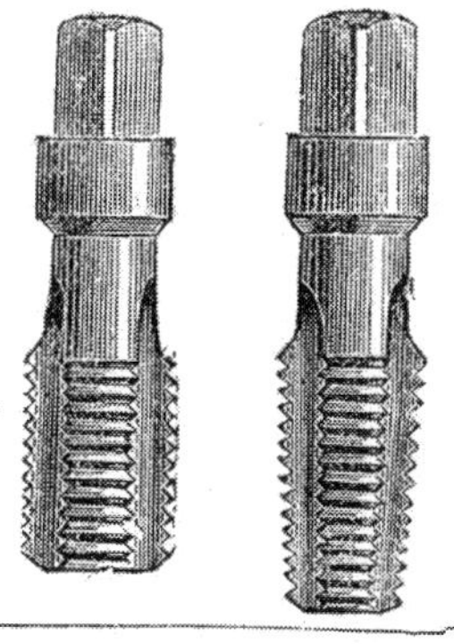

SEPARATE PRICE OF GAS TAPS.

[BEST.]

1/8	1/4	3/8	1/2	5/8	3/4	7/8 inch.
2/3	2/8	3/2	4/-	4/6	5/6	6/4 each.

1	1 1/4	1 1/2	1 3/4	2	2 1/4	2 1/2	3 inch.
7/2	10/10	12/8	18/-	21/8	32/6	43/-	57/8 each.

2nd Quality.

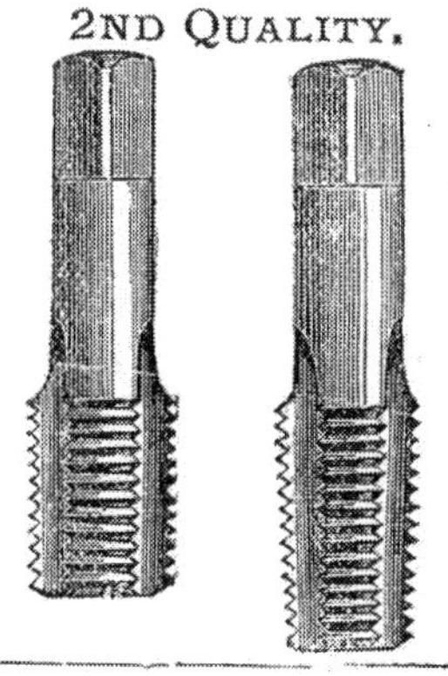

BEST SCREW STOCKS AND DIES—2nd Quality.

For SMITHS, &c. All Whitworth's Thread, WARRANTED.

With 3 Pairs of Dies and 6 Fluted Taps. | 4 Pairs of Dies and 8 Fluted Taps | 5 Pairs of Dies and 10 Fluted Taps.

		3 Sizes.		4 Sizes.		5 Sizes.
To Screw 1/2 inch down	...	27/-	...	34/-	...	40/-
,, 5/8 ,,	...	32/-	...	40/-	...	47/-
,, 7/8 ,,	...	38/-	...	48/-	...	55/-
,, 3/4 ,,	...	47/-	...	57/-	...	66/-
,, 1 ,,	...	56/-	...	66/-	...	76/-
,, 1 1/8 ,,	...	60/-	...	72/-	...	82/-

		3 Sizes.		4 Sizes.		5 Sizes.
To Screw 1 1/4 inch down	...	63/-	...	80/-	...	92/-
,, 1 1/2 ,,	...	84/-	...	105/-	...	120/-
,, 1 3/4 ,,	...	130/	...	155/-	...	160/-
,, 2 ,,	...	160/-	...	185/-	...	210/-
,, 2 1/4 ,,	...	190/-	...	226/-	...	260/-
,, 2 1/2 ,,	...	220/-	...	268/-	...	310/-

PRICE OF SEPARATE TAPS FOR SMITHS' USE, &c.—(See the above.)

1/4	3/8	7-16	1/2	5/8	3/4	7/8	1	1 1/8	1 1/4	1 3/8	1 1/2	1 5/8	1 3/4	1 7/8	2 inch.
3/8	4/-	4/6	6/4	8/2	10/-	12/8	14/4	15/4	16/2	18/10	22/6	24/4	28/-	31/6	36/- per pair.

BAILEY'S PORTABLE "ENGLISH" DRILLING MACHINE.

TOTAL WEIGHT, 28 lbs.

PRICE, ... £6 each.

Grooved Pulley for Steam Power, 7/6 each.

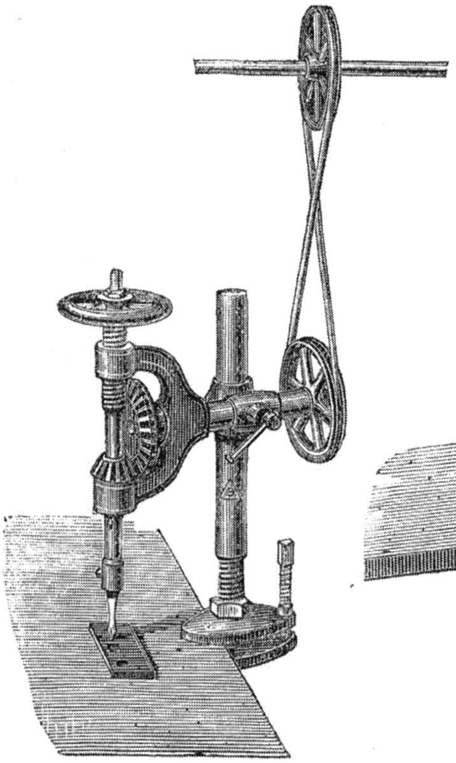

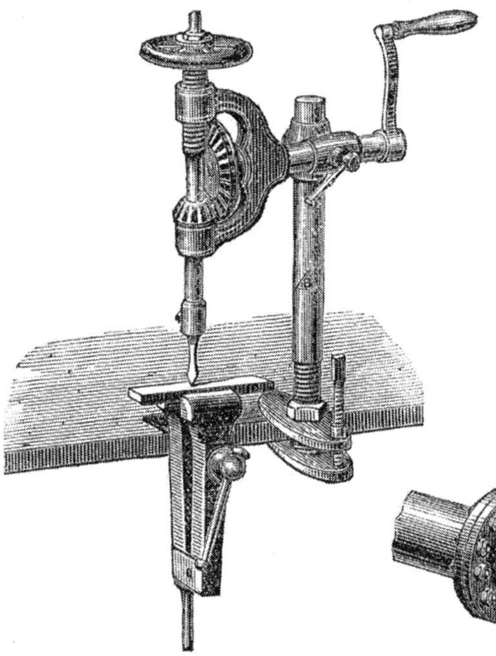

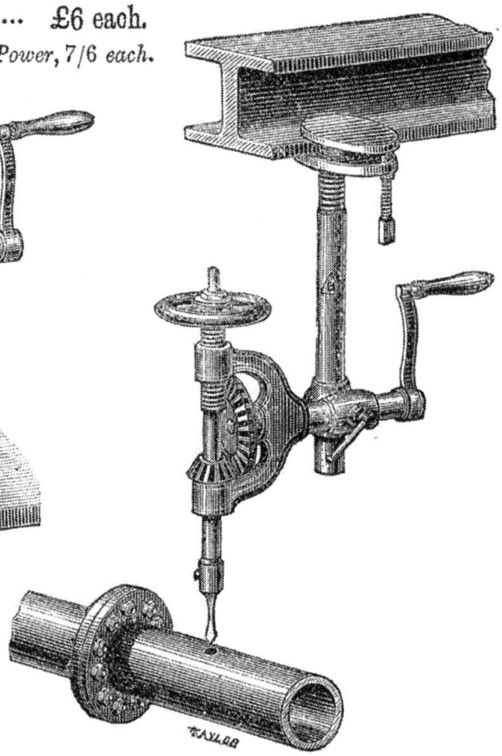

Specially manufactured to compete with the "American" Drilling Machine, being 10/- lower in price, and workmanship and quality much superior; useful, compact, light, cheap and strong. The demand for this Tool is a very satisfactory proof of its popularity. £6 0 0 each. In Half Dozens, £5 10 0 each.

Bailey's Tube Cutter

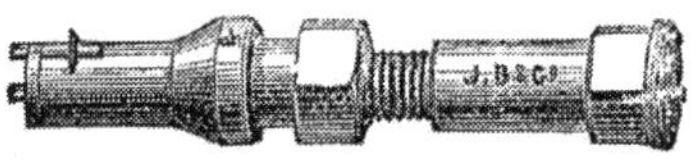

For cutting Boiler Tubes internally, for removal when worn out, or any other purpose. Much used for Locomotive and Portable Engines, and highly recommended:—
Price, complete, to cut to $1\frac{1}{2}$ inch, £4 10
Extra for arrangement to cut to $1\frac{3}{4}$ inch, 15/-

Bailey's Bolt Cropper

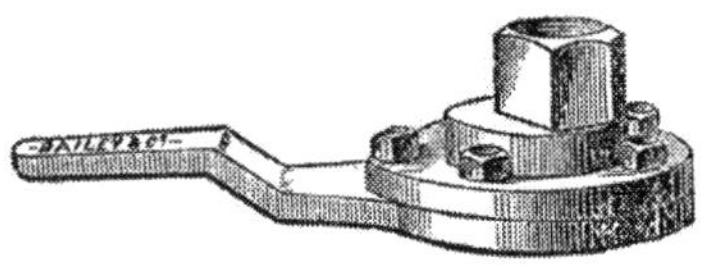

For cutting off the long ends of Firebox Stay Bolts of Locomotive and Tubular Boilers, leaving the Bolts just long enough for riveting. Will cut from $\frac{1}{2}$ inch to $1\frac{1}{8}$ inch. Very strong and good, price £4 10s.

Bailey's Tube Ferule Extractor

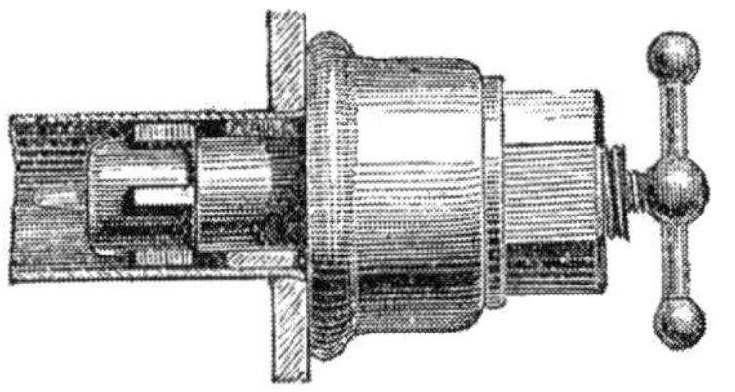

For removing old Boiler Tubes. Specially designed for the South Australian Government Railways, and approved of by W. Dempsey, Esq., Civil Engineer to the Government, of Great George Street, Westminster.

PRICES:

No.	inter. diam.	£	s.	No.	inter. diam.	£	s.
1	—For 1 in.	3	0	10	—For $2\frac{3}{4}$ in.	5	15
2	„ $1\frac{1}{8}$ „	3	5	11	„ 3 „	6	0
3	„ $1\frac{1}{4}$ „	3	10	12	„ $3\frac{1}{2}$ „	6	10
4	„ $1\frac{3}{8}$ „	3	15	13	„ 4 „	6	15
5	„ $1\frac{1}{2}$ „	4	0	14	„ $4\frac{1}{2}$ „	7	0
6	„ 2 „	4	10	15	„ 5 „	7	5
7	„ $2\frac{1}{8}$ „	4	15	16	„ 6 „	8	0
8	„ $2\frac{1}{4}$ „	5	0	17	„ 7 „	9	0
9	„ $2\frac{1}{2}$ „	5	10	18	„ 8 „	10	0

Bailey's Railroad Jack for Lifting Rails

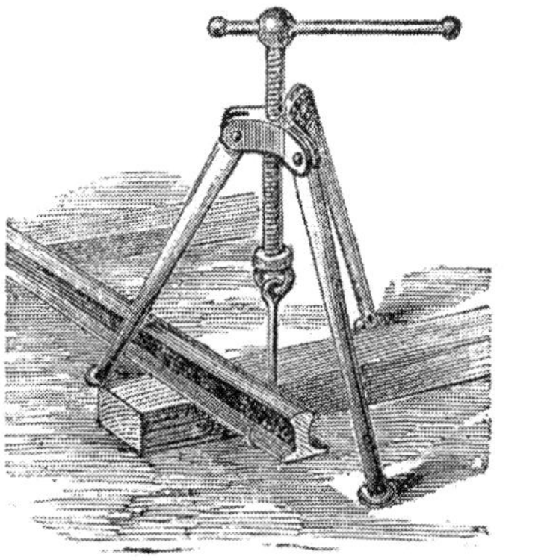

This useful Tool consists of a hooked link, attached by a swivel, to a screw working a nut to which the legs are pivoted, as shown. The legs, working independently, render it easy to adjust the nut directly over the rail, and a few turns of the screw will then raise the rail from the sleeper.
Price £2 2s each, or £18 per doz.

Double-Ended Malleable Cast Screw Keys—$\frac{1}{4}\times\frac{5}{16}\times\frac{3}{8}$; $\frac{7}{16}\times\frac{1}{2}\times\frac{9}{16}$; $\frac{5}{8}$; $\frac{3}{4}$; $\frac{7}{8}\times1$ inch; $1\frac{1}{8}\times1\frac{1}{4}$; $1\frac{3}{8}\times1\frac{1}{2}$.

Single-Ended do. do. $\frac{3}{16}$; $\frac{1}{4}$; $\frac{5}{16}$; $\frac{3}{8}$; $\frac{7}{16}$; $\frac{1}{2}$; $\frac{9}{16}$; $\frac{5}{8}$; $\frac{3}{4}$; $\frac{7}{8}$; 1 inch; $1\frac{1}{8}$; $1\frac{1}{4}$; $1\frac{3}{8}$; $1\frac{1}{2}$; $1\frac{5}{8}$; $1\frac{3}{4}$; $1\frac{7}{8}$; 2 inches.

All kinds of Malleable Cast Iron Bushes for Casks.

ENGINEERS' AND MECHANICS' HAMMERS.

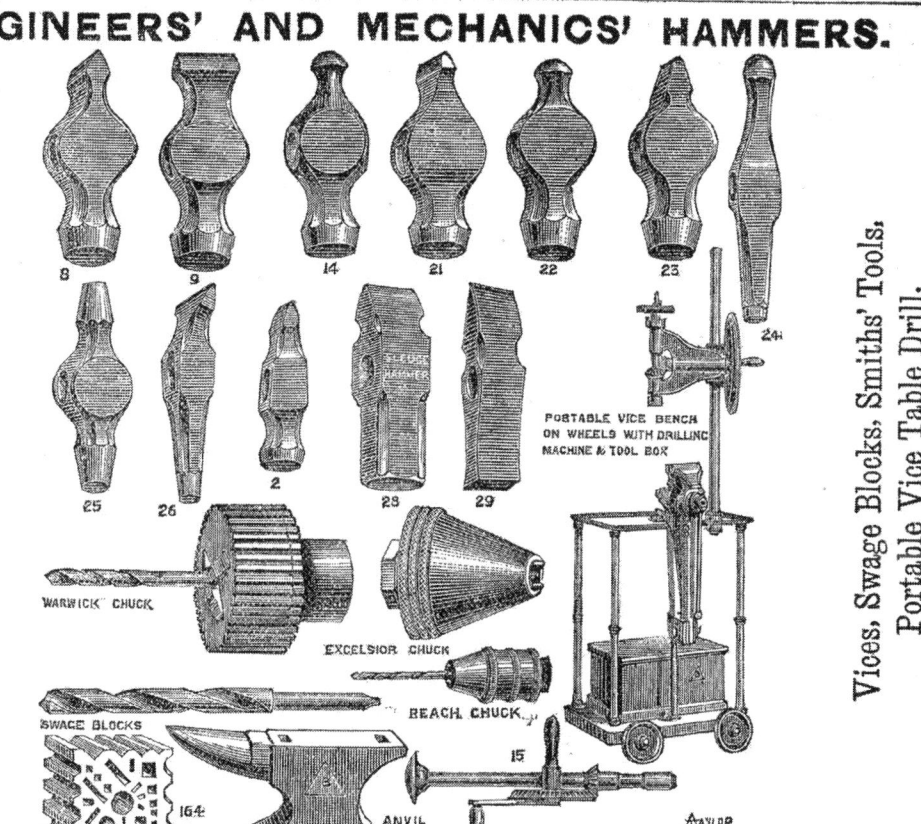

Prices vary with Metal Market. Anvils according to Metal Market.

Vices, Swage Blocks, Smiths' Tools, Portable Vice Table Drill.

Portable Vice Bench with Drilling Machine and Tool Box, on Wheels, 4 Jaws, of Vice. Price, £16 2 6
Small Breast Drill Machine, No. 15. Price, with 6 Cast Steel Drills.

	BLACK.		BRIGHT.
No. 1.	... ...	£0 10 0	£0 15 0
,, 2.	... ...	0 15 0	0 17 6
,, 3.	... ...	0 17 6	1 2 6

CONTRACTORS' WHEEL BARROWS, OF IRON,
with special adaptations for Export.

No. 1.

This article is light, yet firm, and is much superior to the wooden barrow. Size for general purposes.

Price ... 30/0 ... Galvanized 10/6 extra.

No. 2.

Similar to the preceding, but with larger body, for Stable use.

Price ... 32/0 .. Galvanized 12/0 extra.

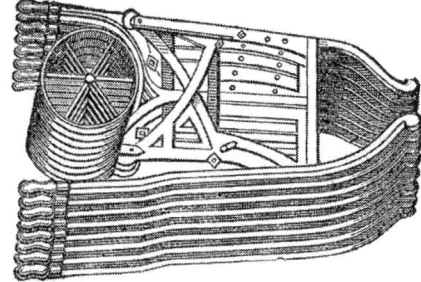

The above shows Frames as packed for Exportation.

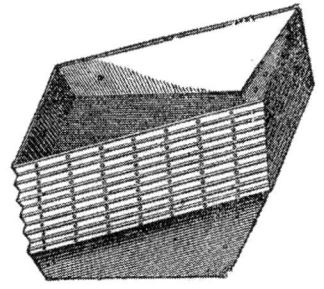

Bodies as packed for Exportation.

PATENT BRUSHES FOR TUBULAR BOILERS.

SMITH'S PATENT SELF-EXPANDING BRUSHES & SCRAPERS.

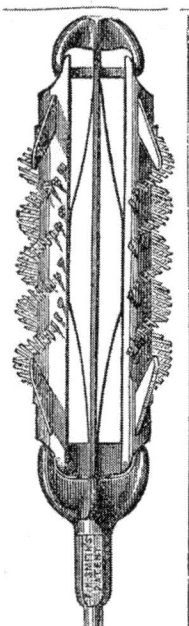

Fig. 1—BRUSH.

Diameter.	Brushes, per pair.		Stems, each.		Complete.		Diameter.	Brushes, per pair.		Stems, each.		Complete.	
Inches.	s.	d.	s.	d.	s.	d.	Inches.	s.	d.	s.	d.	s.	d.
1½	3	6	1	9	5	3	3	6	0	2	1	8	1
1¾	3	10	1	9	5	7	3¼	6	6	2	1	8	7
2	4	2	2	1	6	3	3½	7	0	2	6	9	6
2¼	4	6	2	1	6	7	3¾	7	9	2	6	10	3
2½	5	0	2	1	7	1	4	8	3	2	6	10	9
2¾	5	6	2	1	7	7							

This invention consists of a Brush, or Scraper, made in two or more parts, attached by springs to a handle. These springs act outwards, and force parts of the Brush, &c., against the interior surface of the tube with more power, and, therefore, with far greater efficiency than can be obtained by the ordinary cleansers.

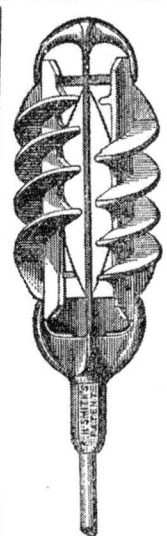

Fig. 2—SCRAPER.

PRICES:
2¼ in. to 3 in. 10/-
3¼ ,, ,, 4 ,, 11/-

SPIRAL WIRE BRUSHES.

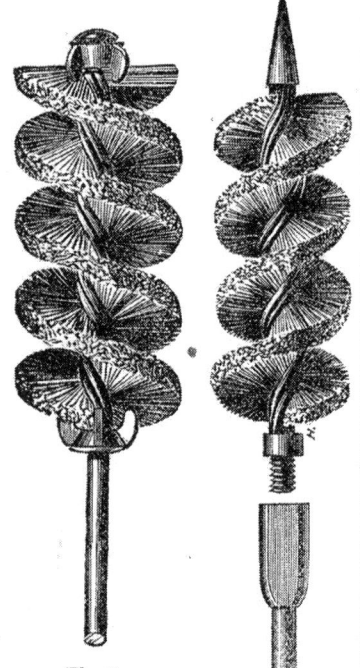

Fig. 3. WITH GUARDS.

Fig. 4. WITH COLLAR, AND SCREWED

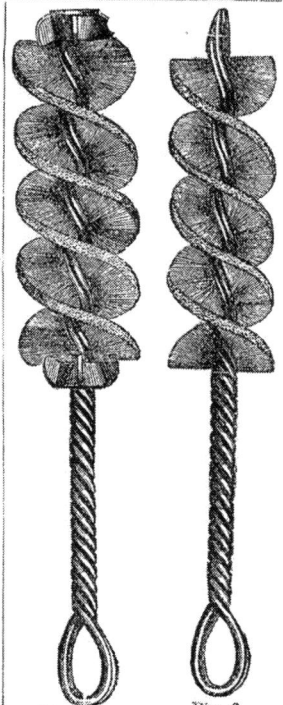

Fig. 5. With Guards.

Fig. 6. Without Guards.

Diameter.	FIBRE.				WHALEBONE, BRISTLE, OR WIRE.				Brass Wire.	
	Without Guards.		With Guards, or with Collar and Screwed.		Without Guards.		With Guards, or with Collar and Screwed.			
Inches.	s.	d.	s.	d.	s.	d.	s.	d.	s.	d.
2	1	9	2	3	2	1	2	7	3	2
2¼	1	11	2	5	2	3	2	9	3	4
2½	2	1	2	7	2	5	3	0	3	7
2¾	2	3	2	9	2	7	3	2	3	9
3	2	5	2	11	2	9	3	4	4	0
3¼	2	7	3	2	3	0	3	6	4	2
3½	2	9	3	4	3	2	3	8	4	6
3¾	3	0	3	6	3	4	3	10	4	8
4	3	2	3	8	3	6	4	0	5	0

Nut and Piece Handle, 8d.

SOLID BRUSHES.

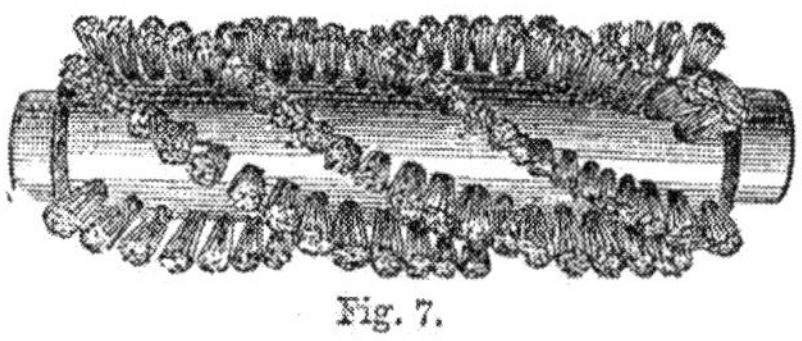

Fig. 7.

Diameter, inches.	Fibre.		Bristle.		Diameter. inches.	Fibre.		Bristle.	
	s.	d.	s.	d.		s.	d.	s.	d.
2	1	3	2	0	3¼	2	1	3	0
2¼	1	5	2	3	3½	2	3	3	2
2½	1	7	3	6	3¾	2	6	3	4
2¾	1	9	2	8	4	2	9	3	6
3	2	0	3	0					

Steel Wire Brushes for cleaning Castings, Iron or Brass, when hot. *(See page 161).*
No. 1, 36/-; No. 2, 30/-; No. 3, 32/6; No. 4, 45/- per doz.

Stephen's Patent Parallel Vice.

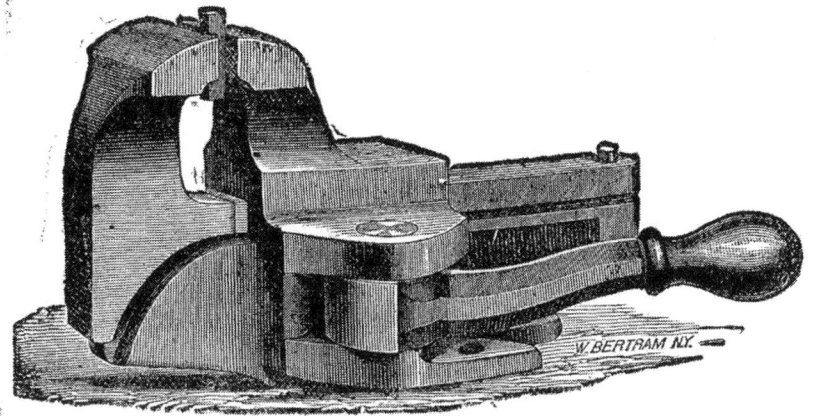

By pressing the handle hard back the movable Jaw can be slipt in and out to its extreme limits with perfect ease, and an article be held with great power, simply by placing between the Jaws of the Vice, then pressing the movable Jaw against it, and pulling the handle out.

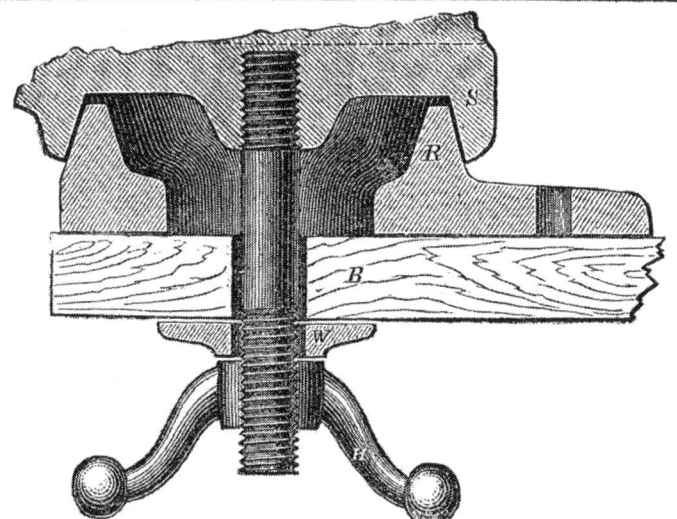

Stephen's Patent Swivel Attachment.

Width of Jaw.	Opens.	Weight.	Plain.	With Swivel.
2 inches	2 inches	2 lbs.	24/	24/
2¾ ,,	2¾ ,,	12 ,,	27/6	32/
3½ ,,	5 ,,	35 ,,	45/	52/
4½ ,,	6½ ,,	65 ,,	62/6	72/
5½ ,,	8½ ,,	115 ,,	115/	130/
6½ ,,	11 ,,	165 ,,	165/	195/

FOOT LATHES.

Class A.—Amateur Foot Lathe, Heads 4 inches to centres, with Wood-driving Pulley, Pair Centres, Driver, Rest Socket and Top Rest, 3 feet Planed Iron Bed, Iron Standards, Driving Wheel, Crank and Treadle Motion, Wood Shelf at back.   Price. £

Amateur Foot Lathe as above, but with grooved-stepped Iron Pulley and turned grooved-stepped Driving Wheel to correspond, round Catgut Band with Hook and Eye.   Price, £

Class B.—Pair Lathe Heads, with Wood-driving Pulley, Pair Centres, Rest Socket and Top Rest.

Height to Centres	4½	5½	6½	7 inches.
Price	£	£	£	£

Heads, &c., as above, with Planed Iron Bed, Iron Standard, Plain turned Driving Wheel, Double Crank and Chain, Treadle Motion, Wood Shelf at back.

Height to Centres,	4½	5½	6½	7 inches.
Length of Bed	4	4	5	5 feet.
Price	£	£	£	£

Turned-stepped Iron Cone, or Fast and Loose Iron Pullies instead of Wood Pulley, added to any of the above, 17s. 6d.
Turned three-stepped Driving Wheel, to suit Cone instead of Plain Turned Wheel, adds 25s.
Lathe Carriers, with Steel Screws.

Span	⅜	½	¾	1	1¼	1½	1¾	2	2¼	2½	2¾	3 inch.
Price	1/9	2/-	2/8	3/4	4/-	4/8	5/8	7/-	8/-	9/-	10/6	12/-each.

Improved Lathe Chuck.

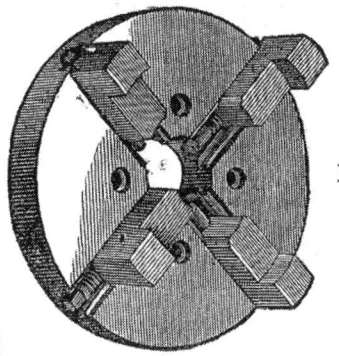

No. 1.

The above represents a Chuck, with set screws in the horn of the Jaw for holding extra tight, or for chucking an eccentric, and is made extra heavy.

PRICES:
9 inch	£5 8 0
12 ,,	6 15 0
15 ,,	8 2 6
18 ,,	10 2 6
21 ,,	13 10 0

No. 2.

Same as No. 1, but without set Screws, and made a little lighter.
PRICE:
6 inch ... £4 2 6
Larger sizes as above.

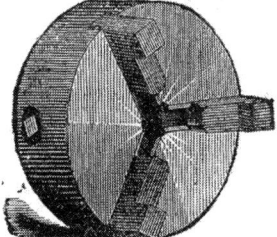

No. 3.

Made very strong. It is operated with a key, is very handy, and will hold very firm.

PRICES:
4 inch	£3 7 6
5 ,,	3 12 6
6 ,,	4 10 0

No. 4.

For Amateur Mechanics, Jewellers, &c. Is made with the Nut on the back as large as the diameter of the Chuck, so that it can be fitted to an ordinary-sized Lathe, and screw to a face-plate.

PRICES:
3 inch diam.	£2 5 0
4 ,,	2 15 0

These Chucks are in constant use in our own works, and are very economical.—J. BAILEY & CO.

THE HORTON CAR WHEEL CHUCK.

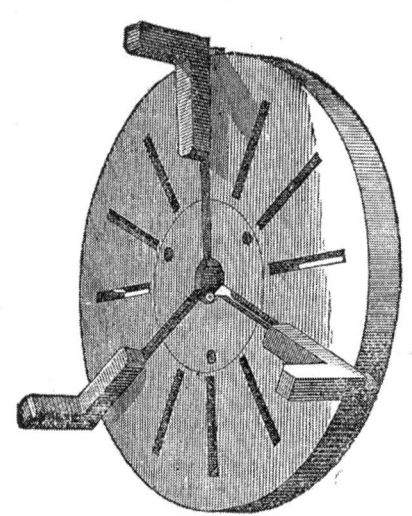

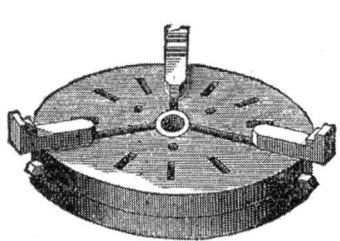

This cut gives a view of all Horton Chucks over 12 inch.

These two cuts show the Horton Chuck as adapted for holding Railway Carriage Wheels for boring, the jaws are made long, so as to fit the tread of the Wheel.

The Chuck may be attached to a boring machine table, as well as to a lathe. It will hold a wheel 37 inches diameter or less.

It is equally suitable for ordinary work.

HORTON'S PATENT LATHE CHUCK.

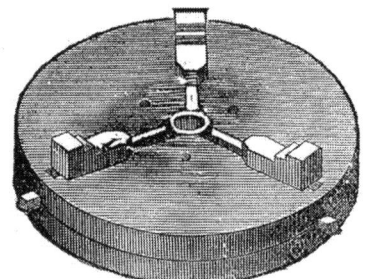
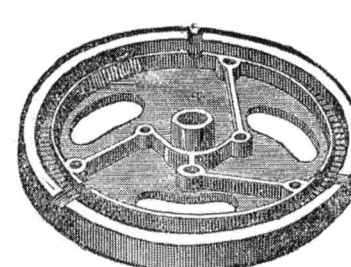

Chucks with Three Jaws.

6 inch diameter	£5 5 0
9 ,, ,,	7 0 0
12 ,, ,,	9 0 0
15 ,, ,,	10 10 0
18 ,, ,,	12 10 0
21 ,, ,,	16 0 0
24 ,, ,,	20 0 0
30 ,, ,,	34 0 0
36 ,, ,,	46 0 0
For Railway Carriage Wheels	50 0 0

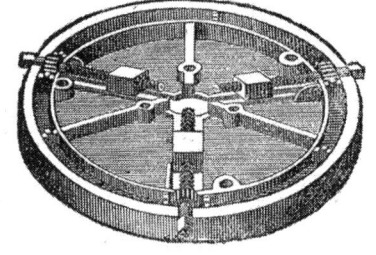

Chucks with Four Jaws.

6 inch diameter	£6 10 0
9 ,, ,,	8 10 0
12 ,, ,,	11 10 0
15 ,, ,,	13 0 0
18 ,, ,,	15 0 0
24 ,, ,,	24 0 0

WESTCOTT PATENT LATHE CHUCK.

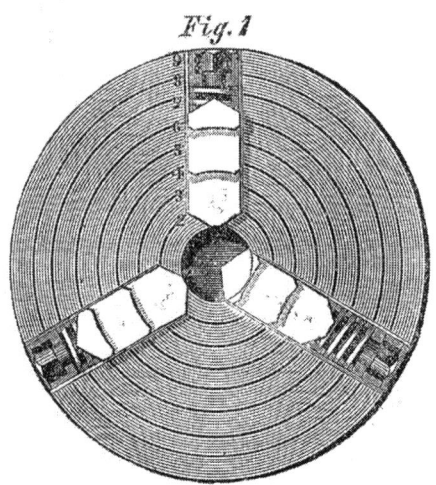
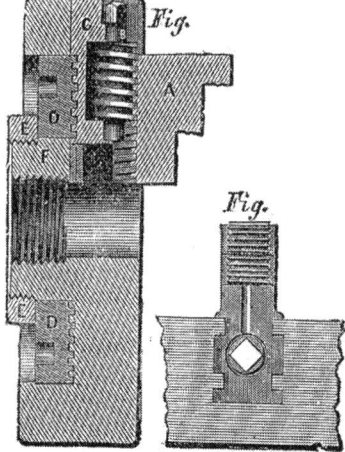

THREE JAWS.

6 inch diameter	£5 17 6
9 ,, ,,	7 15 0
12 ,, ,,	10 0 0
15 ,, ,,	11 15 0
18 ,, ,,	14 0 0
21 ,, ,,	18 0 0
24 ,, ,,	22 10 0
30 ,, ,,	38 10 0
36 ,, ,,	52 0 0
For Railway Carriage Wheels	56 0 0

FOUR JAWS.

6 inch diameter	£7 5 0
9 ,, ,,	9 10 0
12 ,, ,,	12 15 0
15 ,, ,,	14 10 0
18 ,, ,,	17 0 0
24 ,, ,,	27 0 0
30 ,, ,,	45 0 0

BAILEY'S 7-INCH HAND LATHES,

DESIGNED FOR OUR OWN USE.

These Lathes are useful for Jobbing purposes, for the Mechanic Shops of Manufactories, Steamship Companies, Builders, Ironmongers, &c., &c. We have a great number in constant use by our own brassfinishers and iron turners

No. 1.
PRICE COMPLETE, £17 10s. 0d. } With   feet Lathe-bed, Planed Legs, Back Board and Loose-fast Headstocks, Hangers, Top-driving Apparatus, Countershaft, 1 Hard-rest for turning or boring, 1 Face Plate, 2 Centres.

PRICE of Headstocks and Top-driving Apparatus and all as above, except Lathe-bed and Legs, £10.

Self-Acting, Sliding and Screw-Cutting Lathe, Complete.

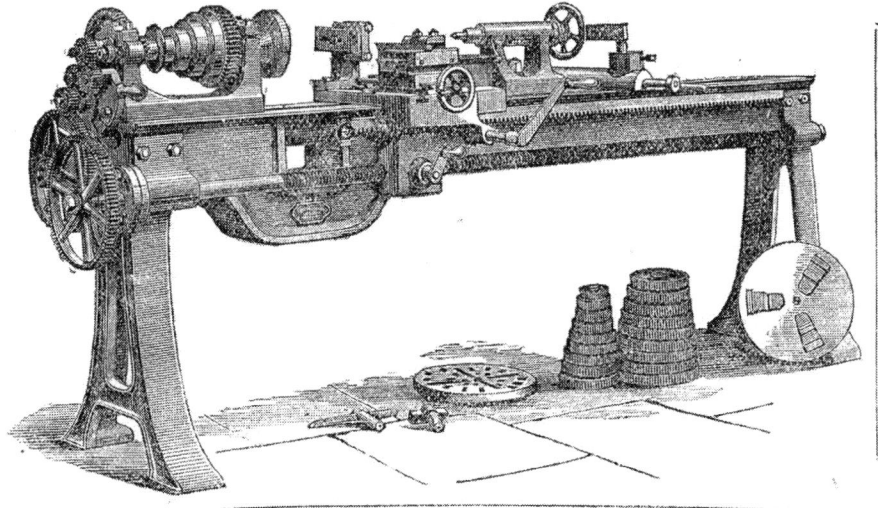

Centres.	Length of Bed.	Prices.	Extra if with Gap.			Additional Length per Foot of Bed.		
		£	£	s.	d.	£	s.	d.
6	6 feet	48	2	0	0	1	15	0
7	8 feet	58	2	5	0	2	0	0
8	10 feet	68	2	10	0	2	5	0
9	12 feet	78	2	15	0	2	7	6
10	16 feet	95	3	0	0	2	12	6
12	16 feet	115	3	10	0	3	0	0

BAILEY'S CIRCULAR SAW TABLES—CLASS A—(FOR GENERAL PURPOSES.)

These tables are entirely of iron, with planed tops, parallel guide-plates of improved construction, and are fitted with steel spindles, &c., complete, with driving pulley.

Class A, No. 1 Saw Table, with 24in. Saw, ... £
" " 2 do. 30in. " (will admit a 36in. Saw)
" " 3 do. 36in. " " " 42in. "

An adjustable Boring Bench, with a set of Augers, may be attached to any of the above tables, at an extra cost of £4 10s. 0d.

The sizes Nos. 2 and 3 are also furnished, when required, with a set of rails 50 feet long, and two timber carriages, at an extra cost of ... ... £

Hand Winch for drawing up the timber ... ...

No. 4 Self-acting Saw Table, with 42in. Saw, fitted with Self-winding Gear adjustable to varying speeds, for drawing up the timber; rails 50 feet long, and two timber carriages; also Boring Tables and Augers, complete, ...

CIRCULAR SAW TABLES—CLASS B.—FOR CROSS-CUTTING.

These Tables are designed especially for use in Bobbin Mills, but are suitable for all purposes of cross-cutting large or small timber.

The Tables are constructed of iron, with planed tops and parallel guides. The sizes Nos. 1 and 2, for cutting small wood, have fixed tops; the remaining sizes have movable tops.

CLASS B.
No. 1 Saw Table, with fixed top. Saw 18in. diameter, £
" 2 do. do. 24 in "

No. 3 Saw Table, with movable top, Saw 30in. diameter, £
" 4 do. do. 36in. "
" 5 do. do. 42in. "

RACK CIRCULAR SAW BENCH.

The Saw is fitted upon a strong Cast-Iron Table, with adjustable fence, &c. The travelling bed upon which the timber is laid is of wrought-iron; it runs upon rollers, and is worked by a rack, with self-acting gear both for the forward and return motion. All the iron work is complete, but the bed is to be placed upon timber beams, which are not included in the price. Price, including 42in. Saw and travelling top 40 feet long, £

CIRCULAR SAWS, WITH SPINDLE, &c., FOR FITTING ON TIMBER BENCHES.

The Saws are of the best Cast Steel, and are fitted upon Spindles, with Collars, &c., complete. The prices include the Saw, Spindle, Pedestals with gun-metal Steps, and one Pulley.

Diameter of Saw,.....................18in.   24in.   30in.   36in.   42in.
Price of Saw, Spindle, &c.,.........£   £   £   £   £

CIRCULAR SAWS.

Circular Saws adapted for use on any of the Tables described. Warranted of the best Cast Steel.

Diameter, ...12in.   16in.   18in.   24in.   30in.   36in.   42in.   48in.
Price, ...

TIMBER FRAME, WITH VERTICAL SAWS.

For cutting up logs into planks or boards. It may be used with any number of Saws down to one to the inch. It is fitted with timber carriages and rails 80 feet long. It will take in a log of 30in. diameter ... £
Saws, with buckles and cottars, each ... ...

SWEEP SAW.

For cutting out Felloes for Wheels and other Curved Work. Will cut up to 8 inches in depth. Price £

Duppa's Patent Bench Dog.

This Tool for Joiners' Benches, first made and introduced by J. BAILEY & Co., about three years ago; and since that time thousands have been sold in this country and abroad.
Price 3/- each, or 30/- per dozen.
J. BAILEY & CO., SOLE LICENSEES.

The Mitre Machine,

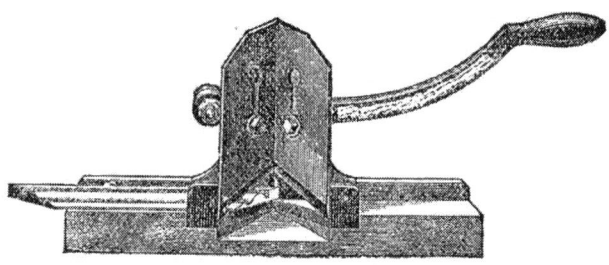

For Cutting and Fitting Panel Mouldings, Joinery, Cabinet Work, &c.
Price,....................£2 10s. 0d.

IMPORTANT
To Millwrights, Contractors, Engineers, Gas Managers, etc.

Patent Portable Drilling Machine.

This Tool is especially adapted for drilling or boring holes in any piece of work too heavy to be moved to an ordinary Machine. Also for outwork, repairs of boilers, &c., and is in every respect more efficient than the ordinary Ratchet Brace wherever it can be applied, and works at about four times the speed.

"Upon an upright pillar, with a cranked base, which, for greater strength, is made of cast malleable iron, a cast-iron bearing is made to slide from end to end. The flange of this bearing is cut in the mould, and when the two parts are drawn together by the bolts shown, the bearing is caused to grip the pillar. At the opposite side of the bearing there is a circular face or flange upon which another bearing with a similar face or flange bears and turns, one of the faces being recessed, and the other having a corresponding projection turned upon it. The first bearing has circular or quadrant-shaped slots cut in it, through which set pins are screwed into the face of the bearing. The first can thus be turned to any angle on the face of the second bearing, and fixed in position by tightening the set pins.

"This movable bearing is cast in a similar way to that upon the pillar, and grips a hollow cast-iron crossbar with a forked end. This crossbar is free to move from end to end in the bearing, and also turn round within it, and when placed in any position can be firmly fixed there by tightening the screws in the flange.

"In the hollow crossbar a shaft or spindle is placed, with a small fly-wheel (having a handle) keyed on at one end. At the other end a bevel pinion is fixed, working into a bevel wheel, with a long boss that fills the space in the forked end.

"The second bevel wheel drives a spindle similar to an ordinary drilling machine, which slides within it, but by means of a long keyway and fixed key in the wheel, is made to revolve with it. The feed-motion is imparted by a screw working through the forked end of the crossbar, and receiving the end of the drilling spindle. The drills are fixed in the spindle in the usual manner.

"It will be seen that the first bearing, being free to move from end to end of the pillar, the other bearing being arranged to turn upon it, the crossbar free to move endway in the first bearing, and also to turn round within it, the drill can be fixed so as to drill a hole anywhere within range of the machine."—*Engineer*, April 3rd, 1868.

This useful tool is of great utility in the Colonies, as it can be used as an ordinary Bench Drilling Machine, and for Steamships it is of incalculable service for jobbing purposes. The workmanship is of the most excellent quality.

This Drill is made to drill holes up to One inch, with a Feed-motion of Two inches deep ... ... Price £10 0 0
With Three-inch Feed ... ... „ 10 10 0

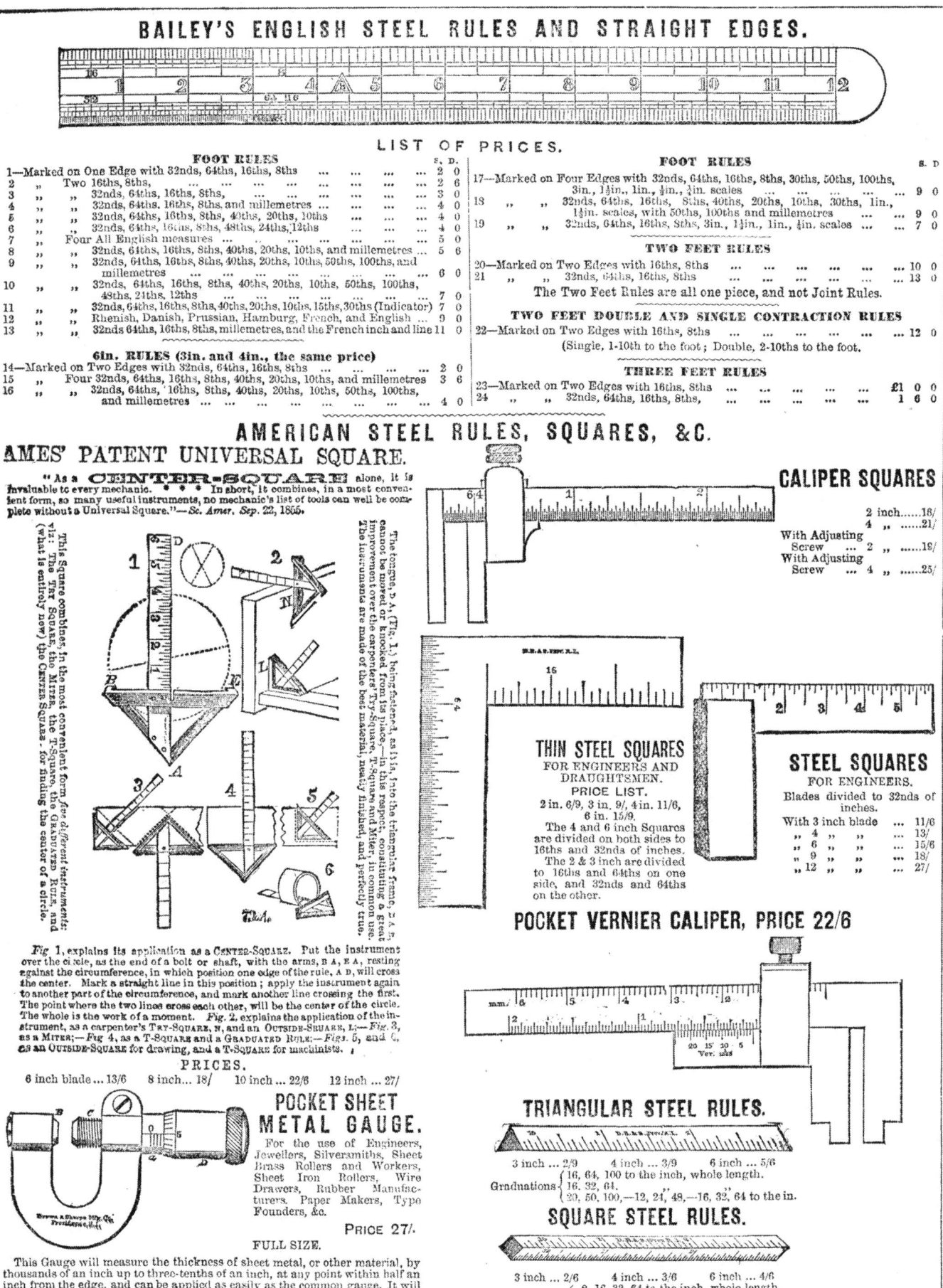

The Patent Pipe Wrench and Universal Spanner

Consists of an ordinary Spanner, with the jaws spread open to form the mouth, into which the pipe to be turned is inserted. One of the jaws is plain and the other is formed with ratchet teeth, as shown. Pipes such as are used for Gas, Water, &c., Round Rods, Studs, &c., can be screwed or unscrewed by means of this Wrench, in an easy simple manner, any article which will pass between the jaws being seized and held fast by the teeth. IT IS MADE OF THE BEST CAST STEEL, carefully tempered. If the teeth become dull after long wear, they should be sharpened with a file in the same manner as a saw. It ENTIRELY SUPERSEDES GAS TONGS, and will be found invaluable to **ENGINEERS, FITTERS, BLACKSMITHS**, and jobbers of all kinds, as it will grip and hold fast any Nut or Bolt which will go between the jaws, whether Round, Square, Octagon, Hexagon, OR ANY OTHER SHAPE. It is SIMPLE, EFFECTIVE, LIGHT, and PORTABLE—a set being HALF THE WEIGHT of a Set of GAS TONGS OF EQUAL CALIBRE.

PRICES:

No. 1, to take from ¼ to ½ inch Pipe	...	2/6 each
,, 2, ,, ,, ½ to 1 ,,	...	5/- ,,
,, 3, ,, ,, 1 to 1½ ,,	...	7/6 ,,
,, 4, ,, ,, 1½ to 2 ,,	...	10/- ,,
,, 5, ,, ,, 2 to 3 ,,	...	12/6 ,,

Or Set of five complete, 35s. Larger sizes made to order.

TESTIMONIAL.

Sheffield, October, 1870.

We have tried Ripley and Wormald's PIPE and STUD WRENCH, and are so far satisfied with it, that it is our intention not to renew any of our present stock of Tongs and Wrenches, but to replace them by this Wrench, as from time to time may be necessary.

SHEFFIELD UNITED GAS-LIGHT CO.,
Per THOMAS ROBERTS, Manager.

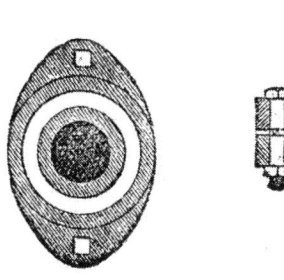 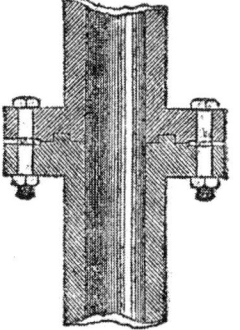 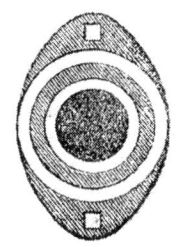

W. O. JOHNSTON'S PATENT CHILLED FLANGE PIPES.

Hitherto pipes with flanges have been cast in sand or loam, and afterwards faced in a lathe or other suitable machine. Under this invention the flanges are formed by the fluid metal being caused to flow into spaces between accurately turned and polished plates or chills, inserted in the mould at the flange end of the pipe, thereby producing pipes with flanges accurately faced. By this process the metal of the flanges, instead of having its skin broken by tools, is actually *chilled*, and thus resists the action of corrosion; they cannot be otherwise than true and smooth.

These pipes are especially adapted for Colliery purposes, being easily removed from one working to another. They are largely in use for Syphons, Steam, Compressed Air, and Pumping Arrangements and are laid 50 per cent. cheaper than ordinary socket pipes.

Improved Apparatus for Erecting Wire Fence.

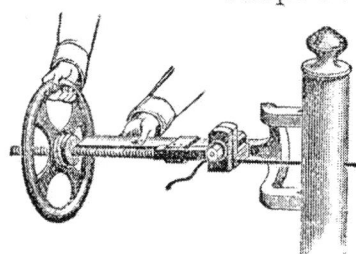

IMPROVED WIRE STRAINING MACHINE.

This tool is now most extensively used by gentlemen who erect their own fencing. It is most convenient to hold, easily applied to any description of straining post, and there is no danger of breaking or bending the machine.

Price complete, with Wrench, £1 2s. 6d.

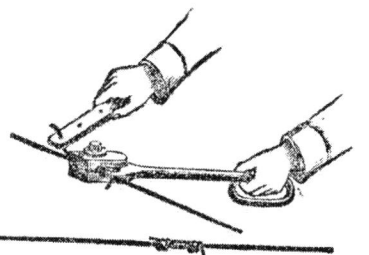

IMPROVED KNOTTING TOOL, WITH WRENCH.

This tool forms a knot, as shown in the annexed wood cut; the Wrench serves as a folder to turn over the ends of the wire.

Price, with Wrench, 7s. 6d.

THE COLLAR VICE

Is used to take hold of the strained wire, and keep it tight whilst the end is secured to the straining post, or an additional length of wire knotted on.

Price 3s. 6d.

WIRE STRAIGHTENING MACHINE,

For taking all coil and bends out of the wire before passing it through the posts, saving both time and trouble in erecting. Price 15s.

J. BAILEY AND CO. supply best Fencing Wire of the finest quality, plain or galvanized, of the usual sizes, and will quote prices for any quantity.

Wilmott's Patent

Self-Locking Hand Truck.

| No. 3. | ... | ... | £1 4 0 | No. 5. | ... | ... | £1 14 0 |
| No. 4. | ... | ... | 1 8 0 | No. 7. | ... | ... | 2 10 0 |

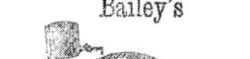

Bailey's Wrought-Iron Sack Barrow.
PRICES—31. 15/6   32. 17/6

Bailey's Portable Grindstone.
PRICES,
On Wheels £2 5 0
Without Wheels ... 2 0 0

Seaming Machines for Bleachers, Dyers, and Printers.

FOR WET GOODS.

Any of our Machines will sew wet goods as well as dry, and are being used by most of the Manufacturers for this purpose.

IN THE DYEWORKS,

We recommend the above Machine, made in composition, as a matter of durability, by prevention against rust.

Our ordinary Machine will do the work equally as well, and, if properly taken care of, will last a long time.

We refer to Dunnell Manufacturing Company, Pawtucket, Rhode Island; Greenwich Printworks, Greenwich, Rhode Island; and Cocheco Printworks, Dover, New Hampshire, who are using the Brass Seamer in the Dyeworks.

Price in either length:—
No. 1 Machine £28 10 0
Ditto Brass 36 10 0

No. —SEAMER AND STRETCHER. (Portable.)

We are now making, for the convenience of Manufacturers short of room, our PORTABLE HAND SEAMERS, in three different lengths, viz.—for 30, 36, and 42-inch goods.

Our 30-inch Machines will sew goods 30 inches in width, or less, and can be used conveniently behind the Printing Machine for joining the rolls, one Seamer doing the Sewing for two Printing Machines.

The large loss by damaged goods, which are sold for remnants, at a sacrifice, and caused by scrimps made by poor seams, can be entirely avoided by using this Machine—a matter which should interest every Manufacturer. The goods being stretched and sewed while in that condition, leaving the goods as smooth at the seam as elsewhere, and stretched enough to allow for all shrinkage in the Bleach and Dyeworks.

We refer with pleasure to Cocheco Printworks, Dover, New Hampshire; Pacific Mills, Lawrence, Massachusetts; Dunnell Manufacturing Company, Pawtucket, Rhode Island; W. H. Locke, Passaic, New Jersey, who are using this Machine for joining the rolls at the Printing Machine, doing away entirely with Hand Seams.

No. 3.—SEAMER AND STRETCHER. (Power.)

The above represents our POWER SEAMER, with a capacity for sewing 1,000 seams per day for Wet or Dry Goods, now in use at Pacific Mills, Lawrence, Massachusetts, and Lawrence Manufacturing Company, Lowell, Massachusetts.

Price £30 10 0

PATENT MACHINE-MADE SPLIT LINCH AND COTTER PINS
For Railway Use, Machinery, &c., &c.

BESSANAUNDIGHTLIDREYENREYCOSN — BAILEY & COY (letters on pins spelling BAILEY & CO)

Inch long	1	2	3	4	5	6	7	8	9	10	11	12	Wire Gauge per Gross
1	3/4	3/0	2/8	2/4	2/0	1/9	1/6	1/5	1/4	1/3	1/2	1/1	,,
1¼	3/8	3/4	3/0	2/7	2/3	1/11	1/8	1/6	1/5	1/4	1/3	1/2	,,
1½	4/0	3/8	3/4	2/11	2/6	2/1	1/10	1/8	1/7	1/6	1/5	1/4	,,
1¾	4/6	4/0	3/8	3/3	2/9	2/3	2/0	1/10	1/9	1/8	1/7	1/6	,,
2	5/0	4/6	4/0	3/6	3/0	2/5	2/2	2/0	1/11	1/10	1/9	1/8	,,
2¼	5/6	5/0	4/4	3/9	3/3	2/8	2/4	2/2	2/1	2/0	1/11	1/10	,,
2½	6/0	5/6	4/8	4/0	3/6	2/11	2/6	2/4	2/3	2/2	2/1	2/0	,,
2¾	6/6	6/0	5/0	4/4	3/9	3/2	2/9	2/6	2/5	2/4	2/3	2/2	,,
3	7/0	6/6	5/6	4/8	4/0	3/5	3/0	2/9	2/7	2/6	2/5	2/4	,,
3¼	7/6	7/0	6/0	5/0	4/4	3/8	3/3	2/9	2/9	2/8	2/7	2/6	,,
3½	8/0	7/6	6/6	5/6	4/8	3/11	3/6	3/3	3/0	2/10	2/9	2/8	,,
3¾	8/8	8/0	7/0	5/10	5/0	4/2	3/9	3/6	3/3	3/0	2/11	2/10	,,
4	9/4	8/6	7/6	6/3	5/4	4/6	4/0	3/9	3/6	3/3	3/2	3/0	,,

Orders under £2 charged Ten per cent. extra.

BAILEY'S SPIRAL SPRINGS.

Having some experience in the manufacture of Springs, we are prepared to quote prices for any description, either black or bright, and plated with nickel silver. Under our patent for Safety Valve Springs, we keep stock of those sorts we use for our various Safety Valve and Spring Balance arrangements.

CRICKMER'S PATENT ELASTIC METALLIC PACKING

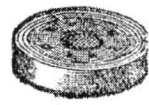 2/3 per lb.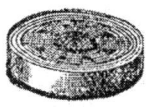

For Pistons, Piston Rod, Stuffing Boxes, Pumps, Joints, &c. Requires very little tallow to lubricate it. The steam enters the mesh of the wire gauze, and thereby lubricates the rods, &c., without leaving a solid sediment behind, which is the case with other packings.

Directions for use, and all particulars, on application.

Manchester Sponge Cloths, 30/- per gross,

For Cleaning Machinery, &c., cheaper than Cotton Waste, and more economical in every way. Twopence worth of caustic soda will clean one gross if placed along with them in boiling water.

COTTON WASTE.

COMMON COLOURED	BEST COLOURED	GREY	COMMON WHITE	BEST WHITE
per cwt.	per cwt.	per cwt.	per cwt.	per cwt.

Orders for tons bought in the open market, at competition rates for large purchasers, on commission, at market rates—5 per cent. charged for buying. In all cases cash must accompany orders of this sort. Our knowledge of the Manchester Cotton Market is here placed at the disposal of our friends.

Prices of Pistons and Packing Rings.
RAMSBOTTOM'S PATENT.

Piston Rings under 3½ inches diameter, 1/2 per set of three Rings; in Brass, 1/9 per set.

Section No.		Description	Per inch in diameter	Complete Pistons at per inch in diameter	Brass Rings at per inch in diameter
1		Three rings 3½ inches and under 9 inches in diameter	5d	7/6	9d
2		Three rings 9 inches and under 16 inches in diameter	7d	10/6	10d
3		Three rings 16 inches and under 20 inches in diameter	9d	12/6	1/-
4		Three rings 20 inches and under 28 inches in diameter	1/0	16/0	1/7
5		Three rings 28 inches and under 38 inches in diameter	1/10	18/6	2/9
6		Three rings 38 inches and under 48 inches in diameter	2/6	20/6	3/9
7		Three rings 48 inches in diameter and upwards	3/6	22/6	5/9

RINGS ARE MADE TO ANY SPECIAL SECTION WHEN REQUIRED.

N.B.—More than 13,450 Pistons on this principle are now at work. All Rings bear the above Trade Mark.

MACK'S PATENT TUBE SCRAPER,
FOR
Locomotive, Marine,
And Portable Boiler Tubes.

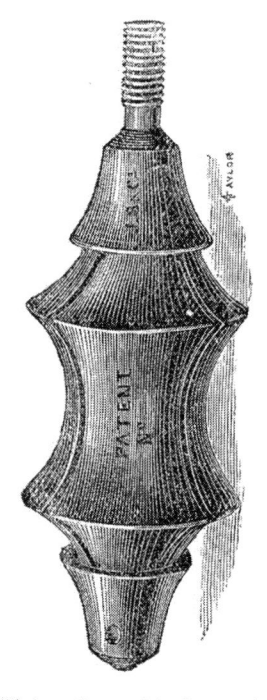

This invention consists of segments of chilled iron, kept in position by the caps, and made elastic by springs.

Diameter				Each
2	...	...	...	10/-
2¼	...	...	...	12/6
2½	...	...	...	14/-
3	...	...	...	15/-
3¼	...	...	...	16/-
3½	...	...	...	18/6

1 Coupling and Rod to piece up with each.

BAILEY'S HAMMER SHAFTS, specially selected of North Country English Timber.

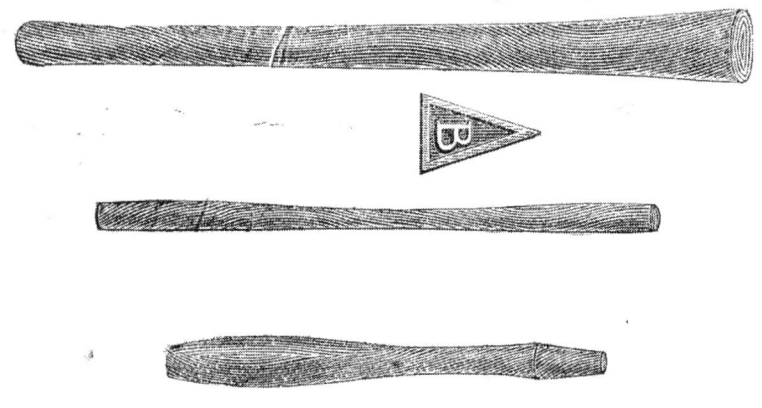

	Per doz.
	s. d.
12 inches long	3 0
14 " "	3 4
16 " "	3 6
18 " "	4 0
20 & 21 "	4 6
25 " "	6 0
30 " "	7 0
33 " "	7 6
36 " "	8 6
39 " "	9 0
42 " "	10 0

	s. d.		s. d.		s. d.
Sets or Tool Shafts, 39 inches long, per dozen	6 0	Mallet Shafts, 4 ft. long, per doz.	12 6	Boiler Makers Mallets, 10 in. by 6 in., with rounded ends, per dozen	35 0
Assorted lengths "	5 0	Mallet Shafts, 4 ft. 6 in. long "	14 0		

BROWN AND BAILEY'S PATENT LOCKED BOLT.

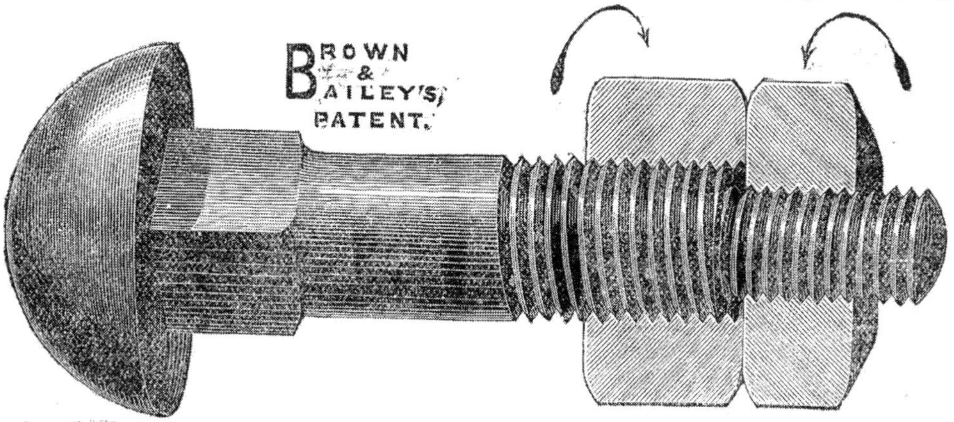

The novelty of the above Invention consists in the arrangement of the Threads acting in contrary directions right and left-handed, by this means securing a perfect lock

Particularly applicable to Railways and a variety of Engineering Purposes.

Best Hand-Made Rivets—$\frac{1}{4}$in., 29s.; 5-16in., 26s.; $\frac{3}{8}$in., 23s.; 7-16in. 22s.; $\frac{1}{2}$in., 20s.; 9-16in., 19s. 6d.; $\frac{5}{8}$in., 18s. 6d.; $\frac{3}{4}$in., 18s. 0d.; $\frac{7}{8}$in., 17s. 6d.; 1in., 17s. 6d. per Cwt.

BEST BEST DITTO, 1s. PER CWT. EXTRA.

Our Manchester Finish Bolts are of the highest class quality, our chief demand being for use by the Chief Engineers and Tool Makers in the Manchester District.

One of our Specialities is COACH SCREWS.

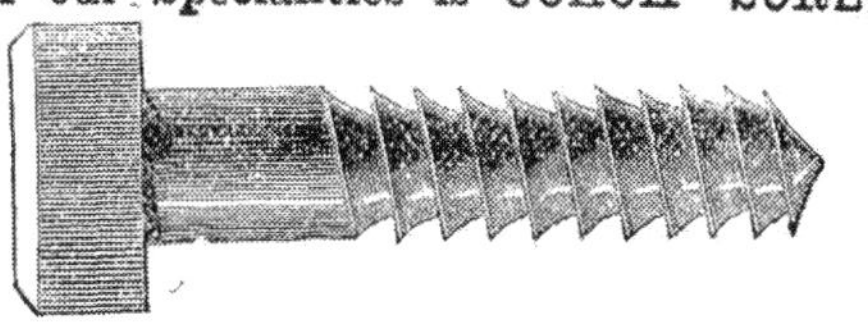

Forged and cut by a Patent Process.

List of Prices for Patent Pointed Coach Screws—Square Head.

WEIGHT SIZES PER HUNDREDWEIGHT.

Length from under Head to Point.	$\frac{3}{8}$in.		7-16in.		$\frac{1}{2}$in.		$\frac{5}{8}$in.		$\frac{3}{4}$in.		$\frac{7}{8}$ in.		1in.	
	s.	d.	s.	d.	s.	d.	s.	d.	s.	d.	s.	d.	s.	d.
$6\frac{1}{4}$in. & upwards, cwt	31	0	29	0	27	0	25	0	24	0	24	0	24	0
$4\frac{3}{4}$in. to 6in. long ,,	34	0	31	0	28	0	26	0	25	0	25	0	25	0
$3\frac{1}{4}$in. to $4\frac{1}{2}$in. long ,,	37	0	34	0	29	0	27	0	26	0	26	0	26	0
$2\frac{3}{4}$in. to 3in. long ,,	—		—		32	0	29	0	28	0	28	0	28	0
2in. to $2\frac{1}{2}$in. long ,,	—		—		34	0	30	0	29	0	29	0	29	0
Under 2in. long ,,	—		—		36	0	31	0	—		—		—	

If with hexagon Heads, 1s. per cwt. extra.

COUNT SIZES, PER GROSS.

			Per Gross. s.	d.
$\frac{1}{4}$in. diam.,		under 2in. long	3	3
$\frac{1}{4}$,,	,,	2in. up to and including $2\frac{1}{2}$in.	3	9
$\frac{1}{4}$,,	,,	above $2\frac{1}{2}$in. up to and including 3in...	4	3
$\frac{5}{16}$,,	,,	under 2in. long	4	0
$\frac{5}{16}$,,	,,	2in. up to and including $2\frac{1}{2}$in.	4	6
$\frac{5}{16}$,,	,,	above $2\frac{1}{2}$in. up to and including 3in.	5	0
$\frac{3}{8}$,,	,,	under 2in. long...	5	0
$\frac{3}{8}$,,	,,	2in. up to and including $2\frac{1}{2}$in.	5	6
$\frac{3}{8}$,,	,,	above $2\frac{1}{2}$in. up to and including 3in.	6	0
$\frac{7}{16}$,,	,,	under 2in. long	5	9
$\frac{7}{16}$,,	,,	2in. up to and including $2\frac{1}{2}$in.	6	9
$\frac{7}{16}$,,	,,	above $2\frac{1}{2}$in. up to and including 3in.	7	6

If with Hexagon Heads, 1s. per cwt. extra.

Best Hand-Made Rivets.—$\frac{1}{4}$in., 29s.; 5-16in., 26s.; $\frac{3}{8}$in. 23s.; 7-16in., 22s.; $\frac{1}{2}$in. 20s.; 9-16in., 19s. 6d.; $\frac{5}{8}$in., 18s. 6d.; $\frac{3}{4}$in., 18s.; $\frac{7}{8}$in., 17s. 6d.; 1in. 17s. 6d. per cwt.

BEST BEST DITTO, 1s. PER CWT. EXTRA.

Our Manchester finish Bolts are of the highest class quality, our chief demand being for use by the Chief Engineers and Tool Makers in the Manchester District.

Bailey's Best Manchester Finish Bolts, for Machinery and Engine use.

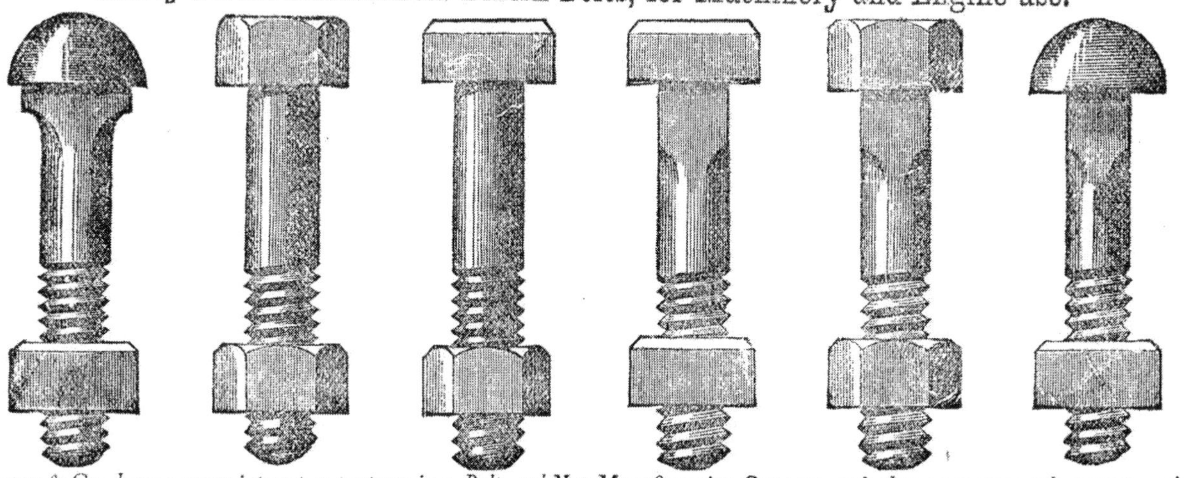

J. Bailey & Co. *have a large interest as partners in a Bolt and Nut Manufacturing Company, and they can consequently execute orders for such goods under the best condition for their friends.* In asking for Prices, please say if Manchester finish or commoner quality will do.

BAILEY'S BEST MANCHESTER-FINISH BOLTS,

For Machinery and Engine Use.

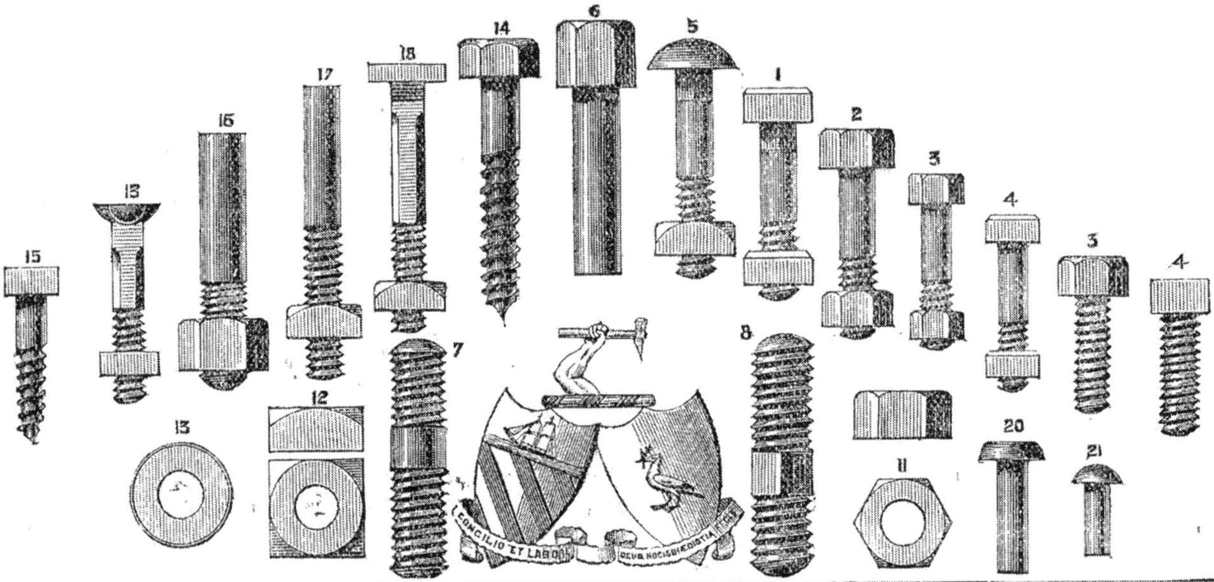

BOLTS, Per Gross.

In	$\frac{1}{4}$	$\frac{5}{16}$	$\frac{3}{8}$	$\frac{7}{16}$	$\frac{1}{2}$
$1\frac{1}{4}$	4/3	4/11	5/10	7/5	9/6
$1\frac{1}{2}$	4/7	5/4	6/4	7/11	10/2
$1\frac{3}{4}$	4/11	5/8	6/10	8/6	10/10
2	5/4	6/0	7/5	9/0	11/7
$2\frac{1}{4}$	5/8	6/4	7/11	9/6	12/3
$2\frac{1}{2}$	6/0	6/8	8/6	10/0	13/0
$2\frac{3}{4}$	6/4	7/1	9/0	10/6	13/8
3	6/8	7/5	9/6	11/1	14/5
Hex. Heads extra	1/-	1/1	1/2	1/4	1/6
Hex. Heads extra	1/3	1/3	1/6	1/6	1/6

SET SCREWS, Per Gross.

In	$\frac{1}{4}$	$\frac{5}{16}$	$\frac{3}{8}$	$\frac{7}{16}$	$\frac{1}{2}$	$\frac{9}{16}$
$\frac{3}{4}$	3/6	4/0	4/6	5/0	6/9	—
1	3/10	4/4	4/11	5/7	7/6	—
$1\frac{1}{4}$	4/2	4/8	5/5	6/1	8/2	9/8
$1\frac{1}{2}$	4/6	5/0	5/10	6/7	8/11	10/9
$1\frac{3}{4}$	4/10	5/5	6/3	7/2	9/8	12/-
2	5/4	5/10	6/8	7/7	10/4	13/-
Hex. hds. ex	1/-	1/1	1/2	1/4	1/6	1/9

Hexagon Nuts, ℔ Gross.

Blank.		Tapped.	
$\frac{1}{4}$	3/9	—	4/3
$\frac{5}{16}$	4/0	—	4/6
$\frac{3}{8}$	4/3	—	4/9
$\frac{7}{16}$	4/9	—	5/4
$\frac{1}{2}$	5/7	—	6/4
$\frac{9}{16}$	6/1	—	7/2
$\frac{5}{8}$	7/11	—	9/6

Square Nuts, Per Gross.

Blank.		Tapped.	
$\frac{1}{4}$	2/0	—	2/6
$\frac{5}{16}$	2/3	—	2/9
$\frac{3}{8}$	2/6	—	3/0
$\frac{7}{16}$	3/3	—	3/9
$\frac{1}{2}$	4/0	—	4/9
$\frac{9}{16}$	4/9	—	5/10
$\frac{5}{8}$	6/7	—	8/2

BOLTS, Per Cwt.

Square Nuts. Blank.		Hexagon Nuts. Screwed.	
$\frac{9}{16}$	36/3	—	40/0
$\frac{5}{8}$	34/4	—	36/9
$\frac{3}{4}$ to 1	33/0	—	35/8

Hexagon Nuts, Per Cwt.

Blank.		Tapped.	
$\frac{5}{8}$	41/-	—	45/-
$\frac{3}{4}$	37/10	—	41/0
$\frac{7}{8}$	36/9	—	40/0
1	36/9	—	40/0
$1\frac{1}{8}$ to $1\frac{1}{2}$	36/9	—	40/0

Square Nuts, Per Cwt.

Blank.		Tapped.	
$\frac{5}{8}$	31/6	—	34/8
$\frac{3}{4}$ to 1	30/6	—	33/7

COACH SCREWS.

Per Gross.

In.	$\frac{1}{4}$	$\frac{5}{16}$
$1\frac{1}{2}$	—	—
2	5/6	6/-
$2\frac{1}{2}$	6/-	6/6
3	6/6	7/-
$3\frac{1}{2}$	7/-	6/6

Per Cwt.

$\frac{3}{8}$	42/0
$\frac{7}{16}$	40/0
$\frac{1}{2}$	38/10
$\frac{9}{16}$	37/9
$\frac{5}{8}$	36/9
$\frac{3}{4}$ to 1	35/8

Bolt Ends, for Piecing, ℔ Cwt

Inches	Nuts Sq.	Nuts Hex.	Inches	Nuts Sq.	Nuts Hex.
$4 \times \frac{1}{2}$	26/-	30/-	$9 \times 1\frac{1}{8}$	20/3	24/3
5 ,, $\frac{5}{8}$	22/6	26/-	10 ,, $1\frac{1}{4}$	—	24/3
6 ,, $\frac{3}{4}$	21/3	25/-	11 ,, $1\frac{3}{8}$	—	24/3
7 ,, $\frac{7}{8}$	20/3	24/3	12 ,, $1\frac{1}{2}$	—	25/-
8 ,, 1	20/3	24/3	14 ,, $1\frac{3}{4}$	—	25/-

Count Bolts with heads above double diameter of Bolt will be charged extra.

$\frac{5}{8}$ Bolts and all above (Hexagon Heads), 2/2 per cwt. extra.

Strong Washers, $\frac{1}{2}$ in and above, 30/- per cwt.

ALL WHITWORTH'S PITCH AND FIRST-CLASS MANUFACTURE.

Special Quotations for Brass Screws, Studs, Nuts, &c. **These prices are subject to alteration with or without notice.**

BAILEY'S
PATENT PORTABLE AND OTHER FORGES AND BELLOWS.

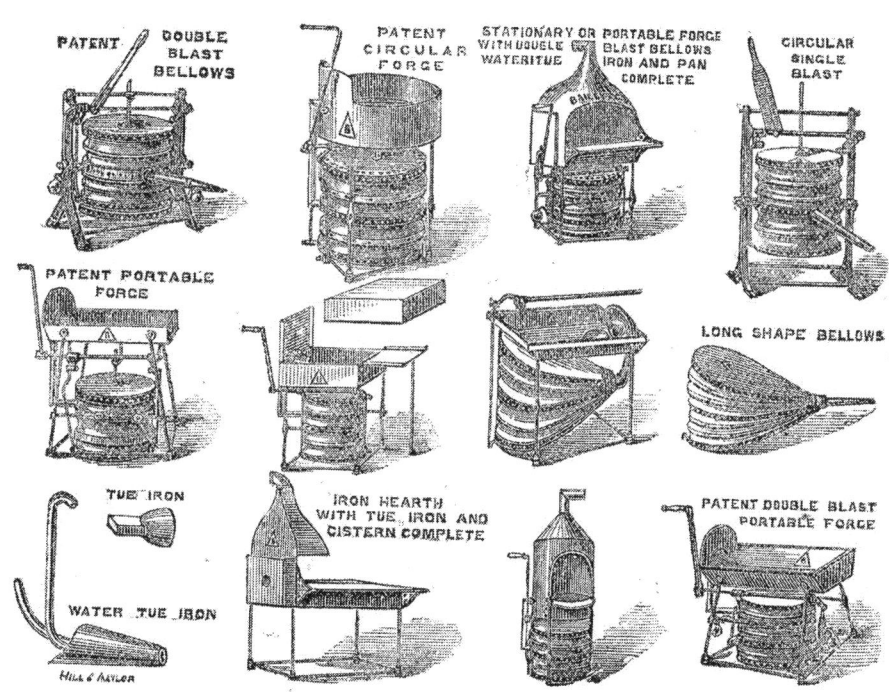

O 1.
Patent Double Blast Bellows.

18 inches	... ...	£5 15 0
20 ,,	... ...	6 12 0
22 ,,	... ...	7 14 0
24 ,,	... ...	8 16 6
26 ,,	... ...	9 18 0
28 ,,	... ...	11 10 0
30 ,,	... ...	13 8 0
32 ,,	... ...	15 0 0
34 ,,	... ...	17 10 0
36 ,,	... ...	20 0 0

On account of the expense of carriage, the weights are not included in price, and are not supplied with the Bellows.

O 9.

No. 1 18 inches	...	£6 5 0
,, 2 20 ,,	...	6 18 0
,, 3 22 ,,	...	7 14 0
,, 4 24 ,,	...	8 16 0

O 21.
Cast-iron Tue Irons,
18/- per cwt.

O 23.

12 inches	... ...	£0 18 0
13 ,,	... ...	1 0 0
14 ,,	... ...	1 2 0
15 ,,	... ...	1 4 0
16 ,,	... ...	1 6 0
17 ,,	... ...	1 8 0
18 ,,	... ...	1 10 0

O 6.
Patent Circular Forge.

x 0	16-inch Bellows		£4 12 0
x 1	18 ,,	,,	5 0 0
x 2	20 ,,	,,	5 16 0
x 3	22 ,,	,,	6 15 0
x 4	24 ,,	,,	7 18 0

O 18.
Emigrant's Portable Forge.

18 inches	... ...	£6 5 0
20 ,,	... ...	6 18 0
22 ,,	... ...	7 14 0
24 ,,	... ...	8 16 0

O 13.
Iron Hearth, with Tue Iron and Cistern, complete.

26 x 22 inches	...	£4 0 0
28 x 24 ,,	...	4 10 0
30 x 26 ,,	...	5 2 0
32 x 28 ,,	...	5 16 0
34 x 30 ,,	...	6 12 0
36 x 32 ,,	...	7 10 0
38 x 34 ,,	...	8 10 0
40 x 36 ,,	...	9 12 0

O 3.

16 inches	... ...	£8 15 0
18 ,,	... ...	9 13 0
20 ,,	... ...	10 12 0
22 ,,	... ...	11 12 0
24 ,,	... ...	12 14 0
26 ,,	... ...	13 14 0

O 17.
Long Shape Portable Forge.

A	18-inch Bellows		£4 10 0
B	20 ,,	,,	5 0 0
C	22 ,,	,,	6 5 0
D	24 ,,	,,	7 10 0

O 5.
Patent Circular Forge, with Chimney and Hearth Plate.

Stands in less room than any other Forge made. Adapted for Light Trades and Jobbing Work.

16 inches	... ...	£6 2 0
18 ,,	... ...	6 12 0
20 ,,	... ...	7 8 0
22 ,,	... ...	8 8 0
24 ,,	... ...	9 10 0

O 2.
Circular Single Blast.

16 inches	... ...	£3 14 0
18 ,,	... ...	4 0 0
20 ,,	... ...	4 10 0
22 ,,	... ...	5 5 0
24 ,,	... ...	6 0 0
26 ,,	... ...	7 0 0
28 ,,	... ...	8 8 0
30 ,,	... ...	10 0 0

O 2.
Circular Single Blast—Con.

32 inches	... ...	£11 16 0
34 ,,	... ...	13 16 0
36 ,,	... ...	15 16 0

36 inches and upwards worked by power.

O 14.
Long Shaped Bellows.

16 inches	...	£1 8 0
18 ,,	...	1 12 0
20 ,,	...	1 18 0
22 ,,	...	2 6 0
24 ,,	...	2 14 0
26 ,,	...	3 5 0
28 ,,	...	3 16 0
30 ,,	...	4 12 0
32 ,,	...	5 10 0
34 ,,	...	6 17 0
36 ,,	...	8 16 0
38 ,,	...	11 0 0
40 ,,	...	13 16 0
42 ,,	...	16 10 0

O 10.
Patent Double Blast Portable Forge.

18-inch Bellows	...	£8 0 0
20 ,, ,,	...	9 0 0
22 ,, ,,	...	10 6 0
24 ,, ,,	...	11 12 0
26 ,, ,,	...	13 0 0

BOWDEN'S PATENT PORTABLE CONTINUOUS BLAST FORGES AND FORGE BELLOWS.

Much more durable, less liable to wear and tear, and better in every respect than the old system of Bellows.

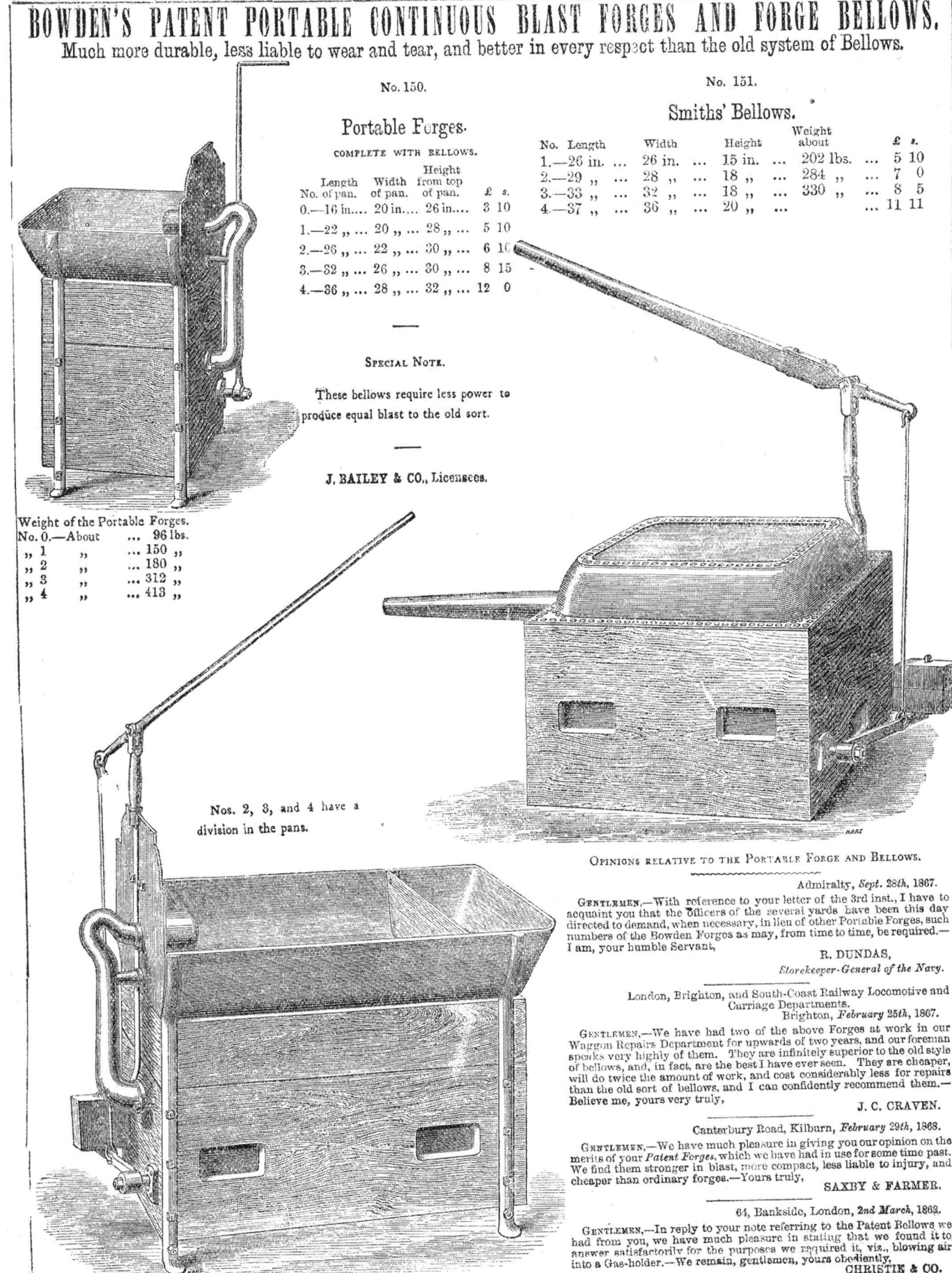

No. 150.
Portable Forges.
COMPLETE WITH BELLOWS.

No.	Length of pan.	Width of pan.	Height from top of pan.	£ s.
0.	16 in.	20 in.	26 in.	3 10
1.	22 ,,	20 ,,	28 ,,	5 10
2.	26 ,,	22 ,,	30 ,,	6 10
3.	32 ,,	26 ,,	30 ,,	8 15
4.	36 ,,	28 ,,	32 ,,	12 0

SPECIAL NOTE.

These bellows require less power to produce equal blast to the old sort.

J. BAILEY & CO., Licensees.

Weight of the Portable Forges.

No. 0.	About	96 lbs.
,, 1	,,	150 ,,
,, 2	,,	180 ,,
,, 3	,,	312 ,,
,, 4	,,	413 ,,

Nos. 2, 3, and 4 have a division in the pans.

No. 151.
Smiths' Bellows.

No.	Length	Width	Height	Weight about	£ s.
1.	26 in.	26 in.	15 in.	202 lbs.	5 10
2.	29 ,,	28 ,,	18 ,,	284 ,,	7 0
3.	33 ,,	32 ,,	18 ,,	330 ,,	8 5
4.	37 ,,	36 ,,	20 ,,		11 11

OPINIONS RELATIVE TO THE PORTABLE FORGE AND BELLOWS.

Admiralty, *Sept. 28th*, 1867.

GENTLEMEN,—With reference to your letter of the 3rd inst., I have to acquaint you that the officers of the several yards have been this day directed to demand, when necessary, in lieu of other Portable Forges, such numbers of the Bowden Forges as may, from time to time, be required.— I am, your humble Servant,

R. DUNDAS,
Storekeeper-General of the Navy.

London, Brighton, and South-Coast Railway Locomotive and Carriage Departments.
Brighton, *February 25th*, 1867.

GENTLEMEN,—We have had two of the above Forges at work in our Waggon Repairs Department for upwards of two years, and our foreman speaks very highly of them. They are infinitely superior to the old style of bellows, and, in fact, are the best I have ever seen. They are cheaper, will do twice the amount of work, and cost considerably less for repairs than the old sort of bellows, and I can confidently recommend them.— Believe me, yours very truly,

J. C. CRAVEN.

Canterbury Road, Kilburn, *February 29th*, 1868.

GENTLEMEN,—We have much pleasure in giving you our opinion on the merits of your *Patent Forges*, which we have had in use for some time past. We find them stronger in blast, more compact, less liable to injury, and cheaper than ordinary forges.—Yours truly,

SAXBY & FARMER.

64, Bankside, London, *2nd March*, 1869.

GENTLEMEN,—In reply to your note referring to the Patent Bellows we had from you, we have much pleasure in stating that we found it to answer satisfactorily for the purposes we required it, viz., blowing air into a Gas-holder.—We remain, gentlemen, yours obediently,

CHRISTIE & CO.

ELLIS'S PATENT AMERICAN BLOWING MACHINE,

For Foundry Cupolas, Smiths' and other Fires, Pneumatic Apparatus, Gas Exhaustion, Mine Ventilation, &c., &c.

USED AT THE UNITED STATES GOVERNMENT DOCKYARDS AND AMERICAN FOUNDRIES.

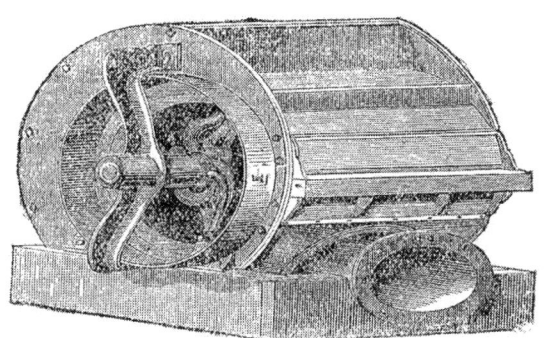 

The Railway Steel and Plant Company, Limited, Newton Heath, near Manchester — Two No. 4, One No. 4½

The Bessemer Steel and Ordnance Company, Limited, East Greenwich — One No. 4

The Glasgow Bessemer Steel Company, Limited — One No. 4½

Messrs. S. Fox & Co., Limited, Deepcar, near Sheffield — Two No. 4½, One No. 4

Messrs. Brown, Bayley, and Dixon, Limited, Sheffield — Two No. 6

CONSTRUCTION AND MODE OF ACTION.

This Blower and Exhauster is made almost entirely of iron. It consists of a cylindrical casing which is open for about one-fourth of its circumference, for the admission of air, and is provided with an outlet for its exit; these openings are seen on the right hand side of the section, the small square wood packing shown being between them. Inside the casing there is another cylinder of smaller diameter, which fits, on one side, close up against the wood packing, and remains in contact with it at all times, not being an eccentric, as it might be mistaken for. This cylinder acts as a driver for the three fan blades or pistons, and makes an air-tight joint against the wood packing. There is a shaft through the machine, on the ends of which the inner cylinder revolves, but which is cranked between the ends, so that the middle part is concentric with the casing, and on this part of the shaft the fan blades or pistons revolve, their outer extremities following the inside face of the casing as closely as can be done without rubbing. The length of crank given to the shaft is half the difference between the diameter of the inner cylinder and that of the casing, and the crank is placed opposite to the point where the inner cylinder touches the wood packing; when passing this point the blades or pistons are wholly withdrawn inside the cylinder, but when passing the place diametrically opposite they are thrust out to the fullest extent, and are always working into or out of the inside cylinder as it revolves. The air is thus continually being drawn in at the upper opening, compressed and delivered through the lower one. The action of the machine bears a resemblance to some of the rotary steam engines which have been designed, and the motion of the pistons in relation to the inner cylinder is similar to that of the rods which work the floats in feathering paddle wheels as related to the wheel. The machine is, in fact, a rotary (but not a centrifugal) pump, and may be said to be a piston and cylinder machine, with a great number of cylinders connected to one shaft.

ADVANTAGES OF THE BLOWER.

This Blower is constructed either to be worked by pulleys and straps, or it is made self-contained, with its own independent engine on the same bed; in any case NO GEARING, and in the latter plan *no belts*, are required.

Compared with a fan, it will melt the same quantity of iron with less than *one-fourth of the power*.

A Blowing Machine, with its engine, is cheaper in first-cost also than a fan and engine.

The Machine is a rotary pump, and effects a direct compression of the blast, the pressure not being dependent on the velocity of rotation.

It will give a much higher pressure of blast than any other rotary apparatus.

As a cupola Blower, it allows a great economy in moulders' time, in coke for melting, and fuel for steam; it effects a saving in oil, strapping, and wear of countershafts; it is simple, durable, and requires no attention beyond moderate lubrication. Smaller cupolas may be used, with less coke for filling up.

The machine itself is noiseless when working, the only sound being a slight one, caused by the rush of the air.

It is the best apparatus made for blowing cupolas, exhausting gases, or ventilating mines; and is suitable for smiths' fires, charcoal or peat blast furnaces, pneumatic apparatus, and other purposes in which a forced blast or a suction is required.

This Blower has been supplied to many Bessemer Steel Works and Large Foundries.

SIZES, PRICES, AND RESULTS.

No. of Blower.	Inside diameter of Cupola in inches.	Indicated Horse Power required.	Volume of Blast delivered per minute, cubic feet.	Quantity of Coke consumed in Cupola cwt. per hour.	Tons of Iron melted per hour.	Number of Smith's Fires blown.	Approximate weight of Machine worked by belts.	Approximate weight of Machine including Steam Engine.	Prices.	Prices. Including Steam Engine on same bed, coupled direct no belt gearing or countershaft used.
3	30	2 to 3	1,620	10½ cwt.	5	20	20 cwt.	40 cwt.	£70	£140
4	30 to 36	3 to 4	2,320	15 ,,	7	30	25 ,,	50 ,,	85	160
4½	36 to 48	4 to 5	3,990	26 ,,	12	50	37 ,,	70 ,,	110	200
5	40 to 50	5 to 6	4,340	28 ,,	13	60	45 ,,	90 ,,	125	230
6	48 to 70	6 to 7	5,870	38 ,,	18	80	52 ,,	102 ,,	150	260

The volumes of blast delivered and quantities of coke consumed given above are such results as would be attained by a velocity of 130 revolutions per minute. The quantity of coke consumed is the only fair test of the capability of a blower, as being, on the one hand, a check on the absurd statements sometimes made of the quantity of air delivered by other apparatus, and on the other, it enables a comparison to be made of the efficiency of the cupola, and may assist in fixing the size of blower required.

Improved Conical Grinding Mill,

FITTED WITH BEST FRENCH-BURR STONES,

Recommended for purposes for which BAILEY's Carr's Mill is not sufficient capacity and power (see page 132).

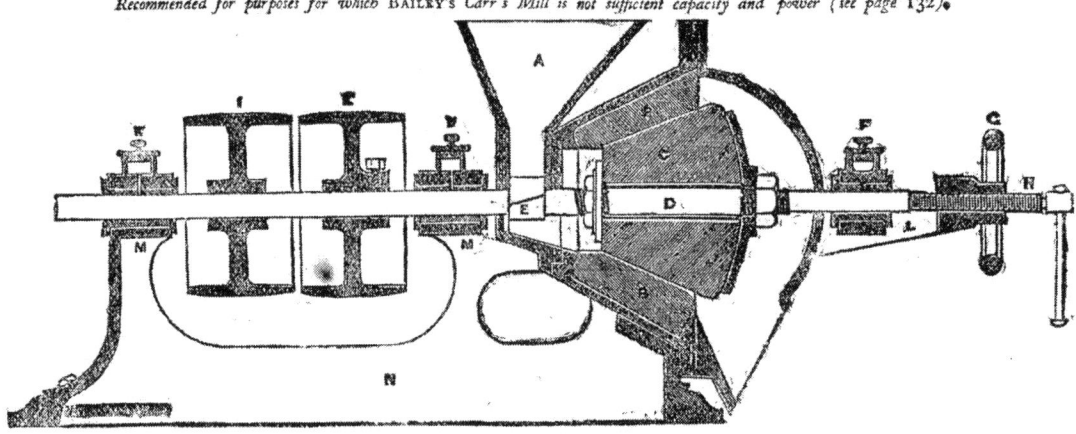

(Scale—1in. to the Foot.)

- A The Hopper.
- BB The Concave Stone.
- C The Conical Running Stone.
- D The Shaft which revolves Stone C.
- E The Feed Roller.
- FFF The Caps for lubricating the Bearings.
- G The Jam Wheel.
- H The Regulating Screw.
- I The Loose Pulley.
- K The Fixed Pulley.
- L The Leather Washer between Regulating Screw and Shaft.
- MM The Bearings carrying the Shaft.
- N The Mill Frame.

The great advantages of these Mills are their portable size and cheapness compared with Flat Stones. They require no setting up, but simply bolting firmly upon a bed-stone. They are then ready for use, and can be driven by any available power.

As Flour Mills they are unsurpassed, and being fitted with the best French-burr Stones, are capable of grinding all hard substances. For paint grinders they are far superior to any other sort of mill, grinding with ease and rapidity all kinds of paint, wet or dry; and they produce colours of far greater brilliancy than those ground by any other method.

Those Mills have been used extensively for grinding Flour, Paint, Coprolites, Lime, Clay, Barytes, Fuller's Earth, Flints, Charcoal, Coffee, Spices, Drugs, Chemicals, &c., &c., and have given universal satisfaction.

For exportation to the Colonies and Foreign Countries these Mills offer every advantage, as they can be fitted up with steam engine, boiler, and every necessary requirement, so that they may be set to work immediately upon arrival.

The price of No. 5, the most useful size for general application, is £45 exclusive of packing; No. 4, £38; No. 3, £32/10/-; No. 2, £24; and No. 1, £19, subject to liberal Discounts for large cash orders, particulars of which, and prices for smaller sizes, can be had on application.

When used as Corn Mills, and especially for Colonial use, these Mills may be had fitted up with revolving Flour-dressing machinery, constituting at once the most portable and effective Flour Mill ever offered to the public.

SCHIELE'S EXCELSIOR NOISELESS FANS.

The advantages of these Fans are:—Simplicity of construction; the cheapest made, consistent with strength and safety; require very small power to drive them; give a much greater volume of blast for their size than any other; are perfectly noiseless in working; are not liable to get out of repair; can be driven at any speed, and placed in any position.

A few of the uses to which these Blast Fans are put are:—Blowing Smiths' Fires, Foundry Cupolas, Furnaces; Increasing Draught under Boilers; Melting Iron; Drying Yarns; Blowing Hot Air; Cooling Worts; Drying Grain; Forcing Air into Shafts, Mines, and Wells; Supplying Fresh Air to Heated Rooms or Manufactories; and a very great variety of purposes where Blast or Draught (hot or cold) is required.

These Fans are now in use by nearly two thousand firms in this country, including many Railway Companies and Public Works; and as the means of producing them is now largely increased, orders can usually be executed on the day of receipt.

PRICE LIST OF THE BLAST FANS.

Diameter of Revolving Fan.	Price.	Smiths' Fires.	Tons melted per hour	Pulleys.	Diameter of Discharge Pipe.	Diameter of Revolving Fan.	Price.	Smiths' Fires.	Tons melted per hour	Pulleys.	Diameter of Discharge Pipe.
6 in.	£3 5s.	—	—	1½ in.	3 in.	20 in.	£13 10s.	14	2½	4 in.	10 in.
9 ,,	£4 15s.	3	—	2½ ,,	4½ ,,	30 ,,	£23 0	30	5	6 ,,	14 ,,
12 ,,	£6 10s.	7	1¼	3 ,,	6 ,,	40 ,,	£39 0	70	10	9 ,,	18 ,,
16 ,,	£10 10s	10	1¾	3 ,,	8 ,,	50 ,,	£64 0	160	20	12 ,,	24 ,,

THE EXCELSIOR COMPOUND VENTILATING AND EXHAUSTING FANS.

(C. SCHIELE & Co.'s Patent of 1863. *Latest Patent.*)

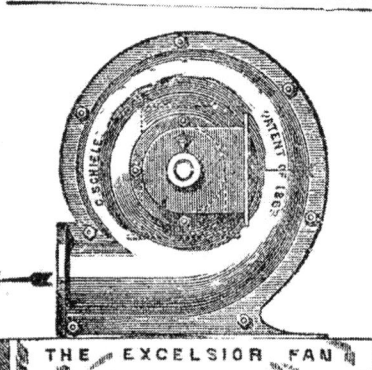

These Fans are the same in principle as the Blast Fan, but different in construction. On each side of the centre or "intake" of the Fan are provided cast-iron elbows, with flanges at their ends; to these flanges can be attached the tin or wooden piping which is conducted to the places from which it is sought to draw foul air, dust, gas, &c. The want of efficient means of mechanical ventilation of mills, manufactories, &c., has been long felt, but no really serviceable machine hitherto introduced. All the difficulties in the way have been overcome by these exhausting Fans. The air-chamber round the tips of the vanes provides a free and quick exit for the particles of dust, fibre, chaff, &c., which are drawn into the Fan, and there is consequently no fouling, which has always been an hindrance to the use of Fans for such purposes. The Fans can be placed in any position in relation to their work, and the elbows can be placed at any angle to suit positions. This Fan is quite as efficient in Blast as in Exhaust, and as the two principles are combined, it may (if required) be used as both at the same time. Owing to the stringent regulations with reference to the ventilation of factories and works where the atmosphere is noxious, these Fans supply a great necessity, and are highly recommended by Government Inspectors.

Size.	Price.	Cubic Feet of Air per Minute.	Diameter of Discharge Pipe.	Size.	Price.	Cubic Feet of Air per Minute.	Diameter of Discharge Pipe.
No. 0	£6 10	600	4½ inch.	No. 3	£29	8,000	11 inch.
,, 1	8 10	1,000	6 ,,	,, 4	£52	20,000	18 ,,
,, 1A	13 10	2,500	8 ,,	,, 5	£85	40,000	24 ,,
,, 2	18 10	4,000	10 ,,				

Special Estimates given for larger sizes.

IMPROVED PATENT UNIVERSAL DISINTEGRATOR.

TO MANUFACTURERS.—In general, for grinding or disintegrating almost any article used in manufacturing businesses, is now in constant use at various works, grinding a great variety of materials too numerous to mention here.

TO FARMERS.—It is of great value for grinding every material required to be ground or reduced for Farm or any other purposes; it grinds all kinds of Seed or Grain, Locust Beans, Bones or Manures, &c., into a meal or flour as required. Straw, Gorse, Hedge Cuttings, Brambles, &c., are ground up into a soft mash, which makes an excellent food for Cattle; or any material that is fed into the mill can be ground to any state required, at the rate of many tons per day, according to the nature of the same.

TO TANNERS.—It is in great demand for grinding every description of Tanning material, English and Foreign Bark being beautifully ground into a fine and raggy state, impossible to be equalled by any other means; a small mill will grind in a day of 10 hours, with 5 horse-power, from 3 to 4 tons of Mimosa, either long rinds or hatched; it will ragg best if damp.

To do such a variety of work with one Machine, it is necessary to grind by percussion. To effect this I enclose within a circular casing a rapidly rotating steel disc, with numerous steel beaters secured on each side; the disc divides the Casing into two compartments serrated on their internal peripheries.

The Material to be ground is fed into the centre of the Mill, and, coming into collision with the beaters, is dashed into atoms against projections on the side of the Casing or serrated periphery.

The grinding is regulated by the hand Wheel, which alters the position of the disc, and also by means of several valves in the discharge, whereby the material may be ground to any degree required.

It will be seen that, besides its simplicity and strength, and the great variety of work this Machine will do, it has many great advantages over other modes of grinding. There are no sharp or cutting edges; but the material is dashed into atoms by the blows from blunt beaters revolving at high velocity, whereby the great friction, wear and tear, and consequently loss of power in the ordinary mode of grinding between two working surfaces, are now brought down to the lowest minimum; therefore it does its work much faster and with a far better result.

They are made of the very best materials, the whole of the working parts are of steel, and they are constructed in the best manner to facilitate their working and manipulation.

CASH PRICES DELIVERED IN LONDON.

No.	Description	Price	No.	Description	Price
1	For Ginger, Spices, &c.	£20 0 0	6	For all kinds of hard substances	£49 0 0
2	For Farmers, Tanners, &c.	22 0 0	7	For Millers	50 0 0
3	For Millers	25 0 0	8	For Dye Woods, and same as No. 5	66 0 0
4	For all kinds of hard substances	26 0 0	9	Hard Materials, Ores, Coprolites, &c.	70 0 0
5	For Tanners, Drysalters, &c.	45 0 0			

Rules for Working sent with each Mill. Spare Discs, Beaters, and Duplicates of all parts kept in stock.

INSTRUCTIONS FOR FIXING AND WORKING.

DRIVING GEAR.—Some consideration is required before deciding upon the plan to be adopted, as much depends upon the driving gear in obtaining a satisfactory result. The belts should be horizontal, if possible, and of a good length, sufficiently long to prevent them slipping without being too tight, say 15ft. between the centres for No. 2 Mills, and 20ft. for No. 15. The speed should not be got up too suddenly.

IN FEEDING do not put the material in too fast, but feed regularly, and keep the Mill going a steady hum, if this is stopped by too heavy feeding it will grind coarse and not so fast.

TO REGULATE the Mill for fine grinding remove the cover on top of the discharge chamber, put in the screen and fix it by the small set screw in front, at the same time set the disc up by means of the hand wheel as close to the front compartment as possible. For coarse grinding remove the screen and set the disc to or from the front compartment, according to the degree of fineness required. It is sometimes found necessary to regulate the Mill in a different manner to the above, which entirely depends upon the nature of the material. Should this be the case, please apply for further instructions.

THE BEATERS are required to be forged out of the very best steel, and hardened on the face as hard as it is possible to make them. They should be exactly alike, both for shape and weight, but it will be found by far the cheapest plan to get them from the maker, as they are required to be made in special tools to make them properly, without which they will be found very expensive to make. They should be put on with cold rivets made of the best iron; Lowmoor is best if it can be obtained. *It will be found necessary to keep a few Beaters in stock in case of accident.*

A SPARE DISC.—It is a great advantage to have a spare disc with spindle and pulley complete, in case of an accident, to the one in the Mill, which could be replaced by the spare one, and the Mill going again in a few minutes, while the damage, (which is never more than knocking off a few beaters) can be replaced at leisure.

SHAKING OR VIBRATION is caused by the disc being out of balance, *which should never be allowed to continue.* To correct this take out the spindle with the disc and pulley keyed upon it, and place the journals on two thin straight edges of steel or iron, each fixed perfectly level. The heaviest side of the disc will then be sure to come down to the bottom, then drill a $\tfrac{3}{8}$ inch hole through the top or lightest side, about 1 in. from the periphery, in which is to be riveted a small flat piece of iron sufficiently heavy to exactly balance the disc, so that any part of the periphery when brought up to the top will there remain. It is necessary to try the piece before riveting it, in case any may require to be filed off.

In closing the Mill be careful not to let any material get between the joints. Duplicates of any part can be supplied if required.

Should any further information be necessary, please apply to J. BAILEY & CO., Albion Works, Salford.

Patent Horse Mortar Mill for One or Two Horses.

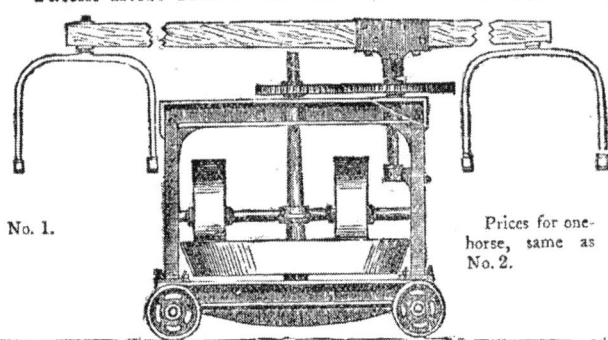

No. 1.

Prices for one-horse, same as No. 2.

Improved Hand Mortar Tempering Machine.

By the use of this Machine a man and a boy can supply a large number of masons, and the mortar is made much better and finer than in the ordinary way, and with less than half the quantity of water—thus the mortar sets quicker than usual. The Machine cannot choke or get out of order, and is well adapted for making cement or plaster.

Price... £9 10s.

EXTRA STRONG
Patent Steam Mortar Mill.

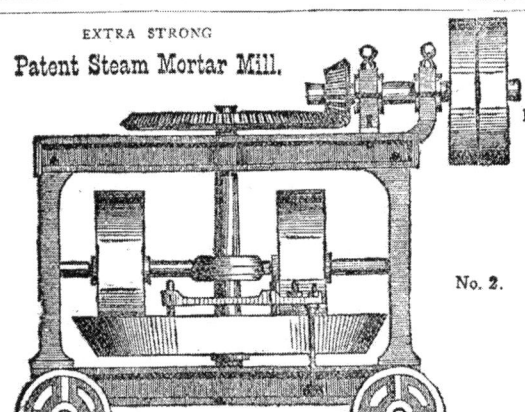

No. 2.

On wheels, or fixed; fast and loose Pullies, strong gear, &c.

3 ft. 9 in. diam.
4 ,, ,, ,,
4 ,, 6 in. ,,
5 ,, 5 ,, ,,
6 ,, ,, ,,
7 ,, 9 in. ,,

Prices on application.

Bailey's Paint Mills.

These Mills will grind any description of Paint or Colours, either in Oil or Water, and effect a considerable saving of time and trouble. They grind the colour finer than can be done by hand in half the time, and quite do away with the use of strainers, or the necessity of reducing the colour on a grinding stone.

PRICES:
No. 1, 16in. high 8in. diam. ... ... £2 10s.
,, 2, 21in. ,, 12in. ,, ... £4 0s.
,, 3, 22in. ,, 15in. ,, ... £5 10s.
If to work by power, Pulleys extra.

Improved Mortar Mill.

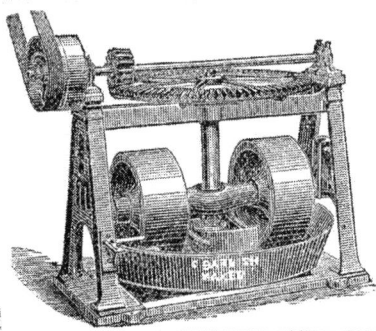

PRICES.

4 ft. diam. of pan, ... £45 10s.
4 ,, 6 in. diam. of pan 55 0s.
5 ,, diam. of pan ... 74 10s.
6 ,, ,, ... 93 0s.
7 ,, ,, ... 115 0s.
8 ,, ,, ... 190 0s.

Mather's Patent Paint and Colour Mill.

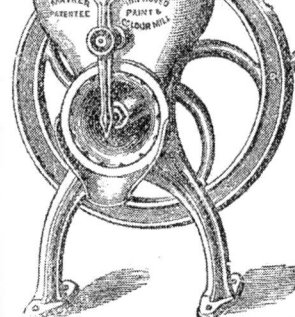

The best and cheapest Mill ever invented.

Price ... £2 5s.

No Engineer, Millwright, Chemist, Painter, or Ironmonger, should be without it.

Carr's Patent Paint and Drug Mill.

Approved by some of the most eminent Chemists, and awarded the Silver Prize Medals of the Manchester and Liverpool, and the Middleton Agricultural shows.

EXTRACTS FROM TESTIMONIALS.

From Messrs. SIMPSON, MAULE & NICHOLSON, 9, *Fenchurch Street, London.*—We are much pleased with the small Mill; it works in a very satisfactory manner.

From Messrs. SWAISLAND & STABLE, *Croyford, London.*—We are much pleased with it; it is very effective for the purpose, and very superior to anything we have in use.

From Mr. CHARLES HOLLIDAY, *Water Bond Colour Works, Huddersfield.*—I have much pleasure in saying that the small Mill I bought gives me entire satisfaction, and works perfectly both by hand and steam power.

From Mr. J. DUTTON, *Rock Ferry, Birkenhead.*—The Mill you sent me answers admirably for powdering all kinds of Salts, and for many other things, such as Opium, Scammony, Soap, Almonds, Mace, &c. It also effects a great saving of time and labour in mixing various Powders, such as Tooth Powder, Lemon and Kali, &c., and proves a very useful apparatus in the shop.

From Messrs. E. H. SMYTH & Co., 21, *Duke Street, Edinburgh, and 69, Coleman Street, City, London.*—The small Levigator Mill we recently got from you works most efficiently, and is a great economiser of time.

The chief feature in this Machine is, that although it can be turned with ease by a boy, it has immense frictional power for levigating purposes. This is caused by the runner being driven at a much greater speed, but in the same direction, than the bowl. The surfaces being Minton ware, they are clean, smooth, and durable.

(*Read the Testimonials.*)

The price has hitherto (Feb. 1862) been £14 nett, but feeling satisfied that the great body of Chemists and Druggists have been restrained from purchasing at that price, it is now reduced to £11 nett cash, delivered in Manchester; £12 10s. if packed for export.

The diameter of the bowl is 18in., and it and the runners are made of Minton ware. It is useful for Painters, Chemists, Grocers and Cooks, for titurating and mixing Medicines, Vegetable Powders, Ointments, Paints, Sugar, Salts, Spices, Herbs, Meat for Potting, and will grind the COARSEST EMERY INTO A NEARLY IMPALPABLE POWDER in a few seconds. The Pan can be tilted for emptying, as shown in the dotted lines; it can be worked by hand or power.

Butterworth's Patent Machines for Cutting Leaf, Cavendish, and Roll Tobacco.

These are the only Machines that do not require a Wood Block for the knife to cut upon, by which improvement the cutting edge of the Knife remains sharp, and therefore seldom requires sharpening. They are Self-Feeding, and can be regulated in one moment to cut different sizes of cuts from **very** fine to coarse. They are especially adapted for Cigarette Manufacturers.

			£	s.	d.
Size No. 1 Machine, to Cut Cavendish	...	Net Price,	4	4	0
„ No. 2 „ to Cut Cavendish and Roll	...	„	6	10	0
„ No. 3 „ intended for Small Manufacturers, for Cutting Leaf, Cavendish, and Roll	...	„	20	0	0
„ No. 4 „ Do. do. do.		„	45	0	0

No. 3 and 4 for Steam Power, extra.
Improved Hand Cutters, each ... ... per Doz.
Do. do. extra finished and ornamented, each „
Improved American Hand Cutters, each ... „
Do. do. extra finished and ornamented, each „

Nos. 1 and 2 Machines stand upon Polished Wood Frames. Packing Cases charged 5 per cent. extra.

Butterworth's Tobacco Spinning Machine, "The Premier."

The **intermittent** rolling and compressing action of the hand-board—a desideratum hitherto unaccomplished by mechanical means—is accomplished in a superior manner in this Machine by rollers acting intermittently.

No drag or injury to the Twist is caused in winding it on the bobbin; uniform winding is effected by peculiar mechanism, which acts in a positive manner.

One Machine can be made to spin all sizes, if required, from Pigtail to thick Irish Roll.

They are easily worked by hand or engine power. Where manufacturers have not available steam power in the spinning room, small Steam Engines, specially adapted for the purpose of driving one or more Machines, are made, which can be fixed in the spinning room or where most convenient. Prices, from £90 to £120 each.

FOR Crushing or Flattening the Stalks of Tobacco.

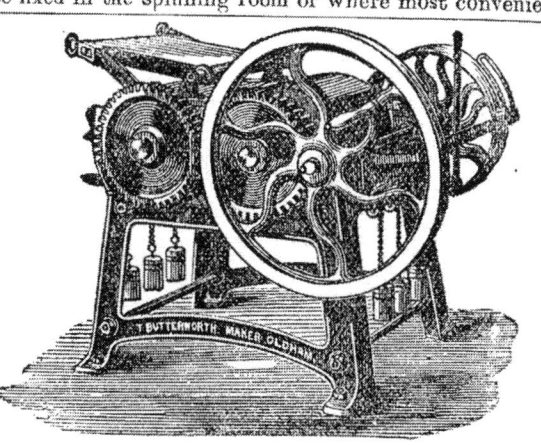

These Machines are expressly made to crush or Flatten the Stalks, that they may be Spun into Roll, or Cut with Leaf. With them the Stalk is Crushed or Flattened almost to the thickness of Leaf.

No. 2 MACHINE,	No. 3 MACHINE,
To Work by Steam Power.	To Work by Steam Power,
£35 0 0	£50 0 0

Important to Managers of Gas Works, &c.

LYONS' PATENT MACHINES,
FOR
WEIGHING, MEASURING AND RECORDING.

Specially adapted for Gas Works for the retail business in Coke and Coal.

As used at the Manchester and other Gas Works. Special Machines for Corn Potatoes, and other purposes, to Order.

No. 1. END VIEW.

Bushel Measuring Machine, with Index.

No. 2.

Measuring and Weighing Machine.

1st. ACCURACY.—The measure is supported at a convenient elevation from the ground for filling into bags, and so prevents over-filling. When the measure has been filled, the man will, in emptying it, cause it to turn half over, and before he can again fill the measure the shaft must make one complete revolution, which will be indicated by the pointer in the register.

2nd. ECONOMY OF LABOUR.—This soon explains itself; the measure being fixed at filling height forms the ground line, and capable of revolving, shows that the weight has only to be *once* lifted, and requires only *one* attendant, instead of *two*, as required in the old style of filling; thus saving *one-half* in labour and wages.

3rd. A CHECK AGAINST FRAUD.—Each measure is supplied with a Check Box, and the filler will be held responsible for the correct tallying of the checks in the box with the indicator attached to his measure. The Indicator is concealed and locked up by the manager or other appointed official holding the key.

4th. The work performed by a man, in any given time, is shown by referring to the index from time to time.

All the above-named advantages are secured by using No. 1 Measuring Machine. No. 2 Weighing Machine has all the advantages of, and may be used for the same purpose, as No. 1 Machine, and, in *addition*, accurately *weighs* quantities of $\frac{1}{2}$ cwt. at a time.

PRICES.
No. 1 Measuring Machine, ... £12/0/0
No. 2 Weighing ,, ... £15/0/0

IMPROVED
ROAD SCRAPERS
For Hand Power.
A valuable Machine for collecting Mud from roads
Price £3 15s.

Improved Revolving Screen
For Sand, Gravel, or Concrete.

A most valuable machine for screening Sand, Gravel, or Cinders, also for Agricultural and Contractors' work. It is easily worked by Hand, or can be fitted for Power.

The Machine can be made either single or double length, for either one or two sizes, made with pierced iron, with any size hole required.

Price for double length, 6ft., for 2 sizes,
10 Guineas.
Price for single length, 4ft., for 1 size,
6 Guineas.
If with pulley for power, **1 Guinea** extra.

STONE OR BONE CRUSHER,
TO WORK BY HAND OR POWER.

An invaluable Machine for Inspectors of Highways and others who have the making and repairing of roads, especially for ASPHALTE for footpaths.

No. 1 MACHINE.

PRICE 17 GUINEAS.

This Machine is well adapted for Crushing Stones to about the size of walnuts and fine gravel mixed. It is provided with a Screen to separate the gravel from the stone, if required, or the Screen can be removed, and the gravel and stone remain mixed, which makes an invaluable material for patching roads, where the ordinary stone is too large. Can be worked by two men.

If with Driving Pulleys, 2 Guineas extra.   Screen, 1 Guinea extra.
Revolving Screen, 2 Guineas. extra.

Town Surveyor's Office, 5, Buckwell Street, Plymouth,
November 15th, 1871.

SIR,—The "Patent Stone Crusher" supplied by you to the Local Board of Health, Plymouth, in April last, has been used under my direction since that period in preparing gravel for footpaths, and I beg to certify that it is well adapted for that purpose, particularly where tar paving is adopted. To make good tar paving the stone must be regular in size, as well as the layers in thickness, both of which are materially assisted by your machine.

I am, Sir, your obedient Servant,
ROBERT HODGE, C.E.,
Chief Surveyor to the Corporation of Plymouth, and Board of Health.

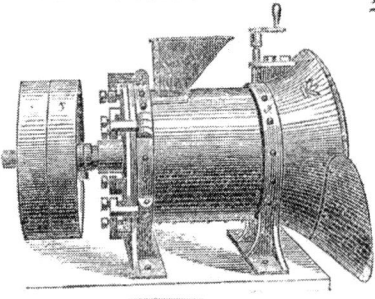

No. 5

TESTIMONIAL.
From the SILICATE PAINT. CO.
24, Fenwick Street,
Liverpool.

The No. 5 Paint Mill we purchased of you gives us every satisfaction; we are much pleased with the way it does its work, and we hope to send you further orders. We like the principle of the Mill, and can get through more work with it than anything of the kind we have used.

No. 5 Mill, Price ... ... £25.
If with Pugging Apparatus, £33.

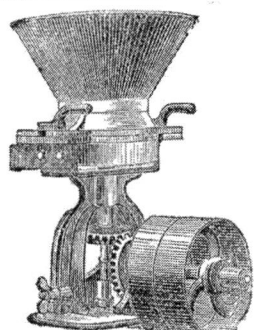
No. 3

These Paint and Colour Mills have been especially constructed for the use of Wholesale Manufacturers, and are capable of turning out a large amount of work. The No. 5 Mill is very compact, easily worked, and is readily taken apart for cleaning, and is capable of turning out more paint in a given time than any other Mill at the price in the market.

Small Power or Hand Paint Mill
No. 3. ... ... £5 10 0
,, 5. ... ... 25 0 0

Bailey's Copying Presses.

No.		£	s.	d.
0. Quarto, Black Japanned and Marbled, Brass Balls		1	4	0
2. " "		1	13	0
5. " 10 x 12 "		2	9	6
3. Foolscap, Mottled and Marbled, 10 x 15		3	6	0
1A. Folio, Mottled and Marbled		3	14	6
Demy Royal, 15 x 21		7	1	0
Royal, 18 x 24		9	11	0

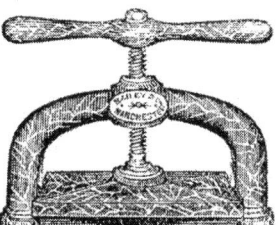

No.		£	s.	d.
0. Quarto, Black Japanned and Marbled		1	0	0
2. " "		1	4	0
5. " Mottled and Marbled, 10 x 12		2	0	0
1A. Foolscap, Mottled and Marbled		2	1	0
3. " " 10 x 15		2	18	0
2. Folio, "		3	10	0

No.		£	s.	d.
0. Quarto, Plain Black Japanned		1	0	0
1. " "		1	2	0
1. Foolscap, Black Japanned and Marbled		1	15	6
1. Folio, "		2	18	0

Bailey's Extra Strong Shippers' Export Copying Press,

12 × 20 inch, Weight about 3 cwt., Price £6 10s.

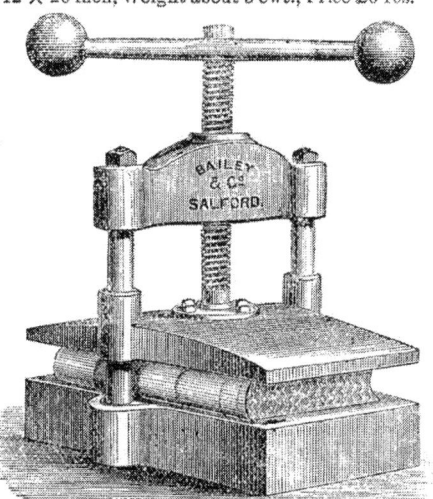

Highly recommended for Railway Companies, large Firms, Corporations, etc.

Bailey's Embossing Presses.

SCREW EMBOSSING PRESSES
(Without Dies.)

For Plain, Cameo, and Relief Printing, and for Companies' Dies. With Steel or Rubber Springs,

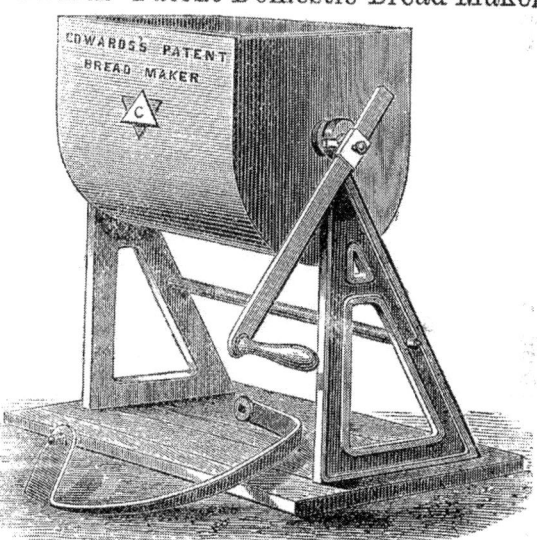

		£	s.	d.
1A. Black Japanned and Marbled, suitable for dies up to 1½ inch		3	0	
2A. " " 2 in.		4	0	
3A. " " 2½ in.		5	0	
1A. Mottled and Marbled, suitable for dies up to 1½ in.		3	3	
2A. " " 2 "		4	4	
3A. " " 2½ "		5	5	
1B. Black Japanned and Marbled, or Fileted, with Steel Springs and Solid Brass Ram Box, suitable for dies up to 1½ inch		3	10	
2B. " " 2 in.		5	0	
3B. " " 2½ in.		6	10	

Edwards' Patent Domestic Bread Maker.

By this invention every family is enabled to make its own Bread, superior to the very best which is supplied by Bakers. In the absence of all Adulteration there can be no comparison, whilst in cheapness the Home-Made Bread produced by this Machine shows to very great advantage.

ENAMELLED WROUGHT-IRON TROUGH.

1st Size (No. 2271), to make 2lbs. to 4lbs. of Bread ... 0 15 0 each
2nd Size (No. 2174), " 4lbs. to 14lbs. of Bread ... 1 10 0 "
The first size has the legs cast on the body.

Lever Embossing Presses.
No. 2

Extra strong, with Die complete, engraved with name and address, either round or oval, for envelopes or letter paper,
£1 10s.

Lever Embossing Presses.
(Without Dies).
No. 1

With Die complete, engraved name and address,
£1 1s.

No.				per doz
1B. For dies up to 1 inch				84/-
2B. " " 1½ "				132/-
3B. " " 2 "				192/-
1C. " " 1 "				138/-
2C. " " 1½ "				180/-
3C. " " 2 "				210/-

Orders not accepted for less than a dozen at these prices.

BAILEY'S WHEEL HOOPING SLACKING PAN.

Important to Wheelwrights, Carriage Builders, &c. Price complete, £45; Size, 6 feet in diameter; 24 in. deep.

The extravagant use of water in cooling hoops, and the indifferent manner in which it is done, has caused this machine to be designed. The moment the hoop is fixed the wheel may be lowered into the water, preventing the wood being burnt, and also preventing unequal and destructive contraction. There are many other obvious advantages apparent to those engaged in this business.

The Patent Bread-Kneading Machine.

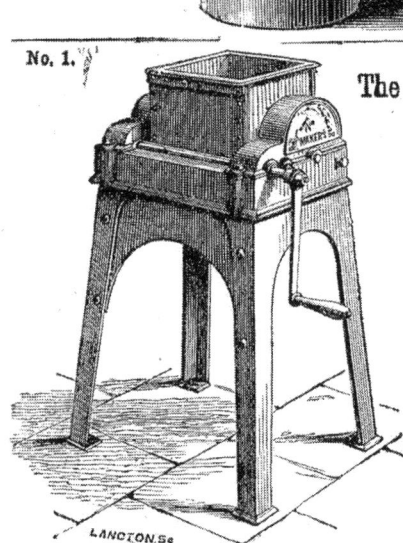

No. 1.

J. BAILEY & CO. beg to invite the attention of Bakers, Managers of Public Institutions, & Private Families to this valuable Invention.

ADVANTAGES.—The advantages of Machine-made Bread:—First, *Cleanliness*—the use of the Machine preventing all contact that the Dough must otherwise have with the hands and arms. Secondly, *Saving of Time.* Thirdly, *Economy.* A greater quantity of Bread produced from the same amount of flour.

The No. 1 small size KNEADER, suitable for families. It is capable of kneading from 6 to 14 lbs. of flour; requires very little power to work it.

Instructions.—Place in the Machine 14 lbs. of dry flour, in the centre of which pour half-a-pint of water, in which there has been previously dissolved 2 ozs. of German, or its equivalent in Brewers' or other barm; slightly mix a little of the flour with the aforesaid barm and water, so as to form a light dough or sponge on the top of the flour, and leave to ferment. If German Barm is used, the process will require one hour, or thereabouts; but, as in ordinary baking, the time required will be in proportion to the quantity of barm used. When the sponge has been left to ferment for the specified time, take three quarts of tepid water, in which 2 ozs. of salt have been dissolved, commence to turn the handle and add the water, when the operation will be completed in two minutes; then place a small trough or other receptacle under the Machine, and draw the spring at the side of the frame. This will allow the box to turn completely over, and a few turns of the handle will entirely empty the Machine of its contents. PRICE £5.

No 2 KNEADER is similar in construction to No 1, but larger and stronger—adapted for the requirements of large Schools, Institutions; and small Baking Establishments. Two men can knead with this Machine at the rate of 60 lbs. of Flour in two minutes. PRICE £14.

No. 3—Larger and Stronger, capable of thoroughly mixing one Sack of Flour in eight minutes by two men; if worked by Power, in a much shorter time. PRICE £25. If fitted for Power (in which case a stronger Frame is requisite), PRICE £30. Larger sizes made to order.

Hancock's Patent Mixing Machine.

No 1 Machine will mix about Six Pounds of Powder Cement Colour, Drugs, &c., at one time. £1 5s.

No. 2 Hand Machine will mix about Twenty Pounds of Powder at one time. £2 2s.

This is a very useful Machine for many purposes.

Steam Power Mixers. £15.

These Machines will mix from 20 to 50 Tons of Powder a-day.

LARGE PAINT MILL JIGGING AND MIXING APPARATUS,
FOR COLOUR AND CEMENT MANUFACTURERS,
PRICE £120. (Subject to fluctuations of Metal Market.)

BAILEY'S Improved Hop Press.

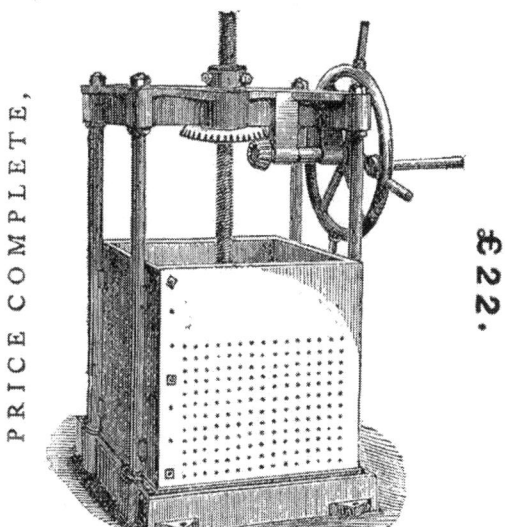

PRICE COMPLETE, £22.

This improved Hand Power DOUBLE-ACTION HOP PRESS, has been specially designed to meet the requirements of BREWERS, &c. The Box is strongly made of Cast Iron—is 28 inches square, perforated on all sides, and stands on a CAST IRON TANK, into which the liquor drains, and is drawn off by a tap or other arrangement at the bottom. The Press-Plate, Screw and Gearing, are VERY SIMPLE AND POWERFUL, so that a pressure of some tons can be applied BY ONE MAN. When the Hops have been pressed, by a simple arrangement THE BOX IS RAISED BY THE SCREW, and from the bottom plate THE HOPS ARE EASILY REMOVED. The Machine is complete in itself, NO FOUNDATION BEING REQUIRED, it is very compact, and by its use A CONSIDERABLE SAVING IS EFFECTED, as numerous testimonials conclusively prove.

BAILEY'S IMPROVED TIRE BENDING MACHINE.

This Machine is composed of

Three Rollers in One Frame,

set in position by

One Double-acting Screw,

so that a bar of Iron can be bent to any desired sweep with far greater truth than is obtainable by any other method

After being welded,

A Tire can be replaced between the Rollers

without removing any part of the machine.

With this very important Improvement

this Tire Bender is confidently recommended as one of the best in the market No Coach Builder or Wheelwright should be without one.

PRICE £5.

BAILEY'S HYDRAULIC MACHINE,

To put and take Wheels for Locomotives, Wagons, and Railway Carriages on and off their Axles.

The Cylinder is 8 in. bore, with stroke 1 ft. 9 in., and cast with strong projecting arms fixed on a strong and deep bed, which also forms cistern for a Brass Pump, with plunger, lever, and weight, fitted with link and guides, let-off safety valve. Provision is made in bow and lever to alter stroke of Pump for quick and slow speeds. Crossheads similar to those on cylinder and attached to chain worked over pulleys for tension bars to pass through Wheel Carriage, with revolving table, elevating screw and inclined plane, mounted on wheels. The Ram-head has a drum bar fixed to it, and a chain attached to the end, which is connected to chain wheel to draw ram back. The Hoop or Cylinder is bored to fit Ram-head, and used when forcing wheels on.

PRICE

BAILEY'S GAS FIXTURES FOR IRON AND BRASS TUBES.

(Prices opposite side.)

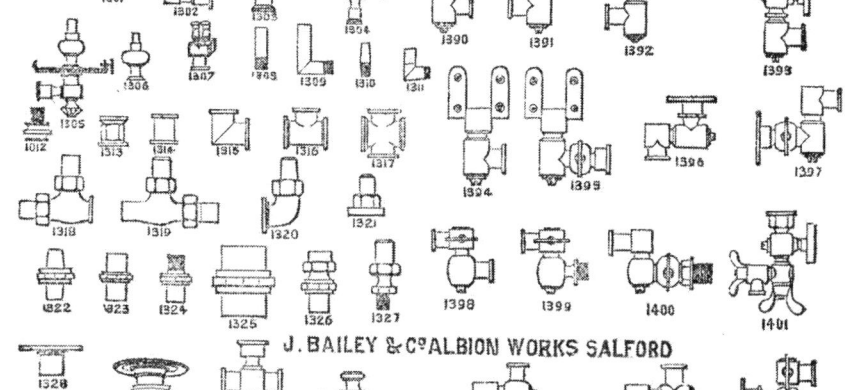

Iron Tubes supplied at 60 o/o discount off list. When iron is low, we are enabled to do a little better. Purchasers of large quantities should ask for special quotations.

Brass Tubes and other metal tubes at market rates.

Cast Iron Pipes with Flanges or Sockets.

Special quotations on application with specification of quantities and size.

This list is nett, except for large quantities.

For Foundry or Works' Gas Fittings, when required extra strong special quotation to drawing.

Gas Meters, by all the principal makers, supplied at their prices.

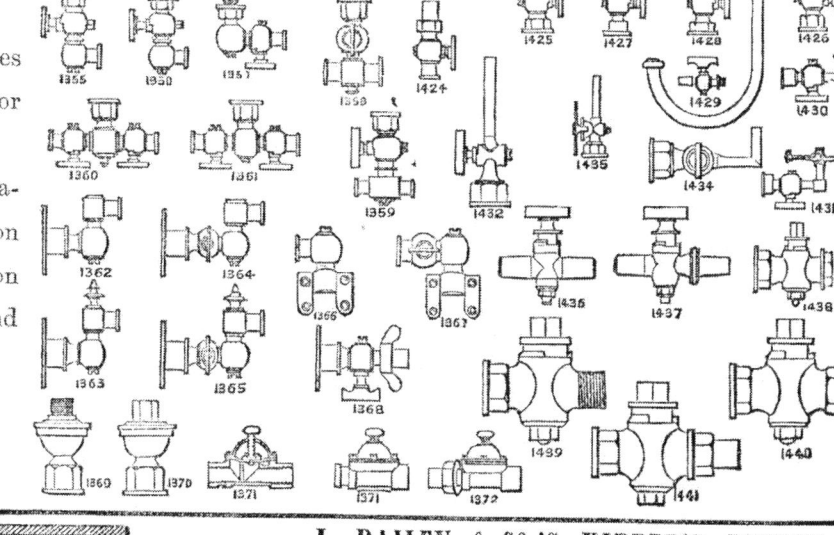

J. BAILEY & Co. ALBION WORKS SALFORD

J. BAILEY & CO.'S KIDDER'S PATENT GAS REGULATOR.

Directions for fitting up Kidder's Patent Gas Regulators.

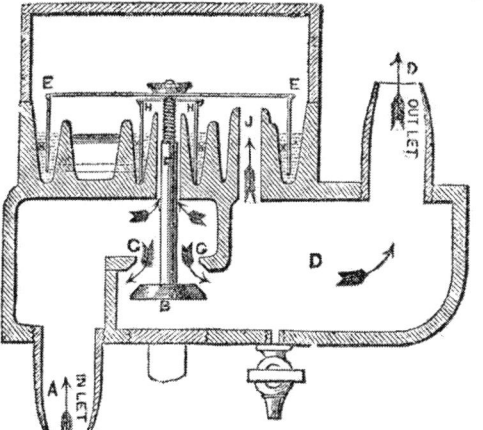

THE REGULATORS MUST, IN ALL INSTANCES (IF POSSIBLE), BE PLACED UPON THE OUTLET COUPLING OF THE METER, where it will be less subjected to being altered (as some persons have done), and the *greatest care must be used that it sets perfectly level*, in order that the Mercury shall be level, and not run to one side, as they will prevent the Gasometer from acting freely, and thereby partly stopping its action, and working to the injury of the consumer. *Re-set until it stands level*; and, with perfect burners and nice adjustment with the weights, EVERY REGULATOR is warranted perfect, and must, in every instance, save from 20 to 40 per cent. in consumption. After the connections are made, remove the cover (and not till then) and pour in the mercury between the small cap, or gasometer.

Scale of Prices, inclusive of Mercury.

½ inch bore, for 3 Light Meter ... 20/-
¾   „   5 Light Meter ... 25/-
1   „   10 Light Meter ... 36/-
1¼   „   20 Light Meter ... 45/-
1½ in. bore, for 30 & 45 Light Meter 50/-
2   „   60 Light Meter ... 70/-
3   „   Cast Iron Meter ... 90/-

When not furnished by the Agent, care must be taken to clean the mercury used, by straining it through buckskin or chamois **leather.**

After the regulator is set, and mercury put in, apply a pressure gauge to a burner, light four burners, and *take off all the weight from the gasometer*. If the pressure is under four-tenths of an inch, and light too small, add on weights, commencing with the smaller, and so increase as required until they are the right size; but do not go over seven-tenths of an inch by the pressure gauge. If the lights burn too free with all the weight off, *add mercury until it is right*, thereby reducing the consumption to **a very low point.** *The less weight there is upon the gasometer the less consumption.* Use cement in every instance in setting regulators, *and not white lead.*

BAILEY'S LIST OF PATENT WELDED WROUGHT IRON TUBES,
FOR GAS, STEAM, AND WATER.

Ask for Discount before ordering.

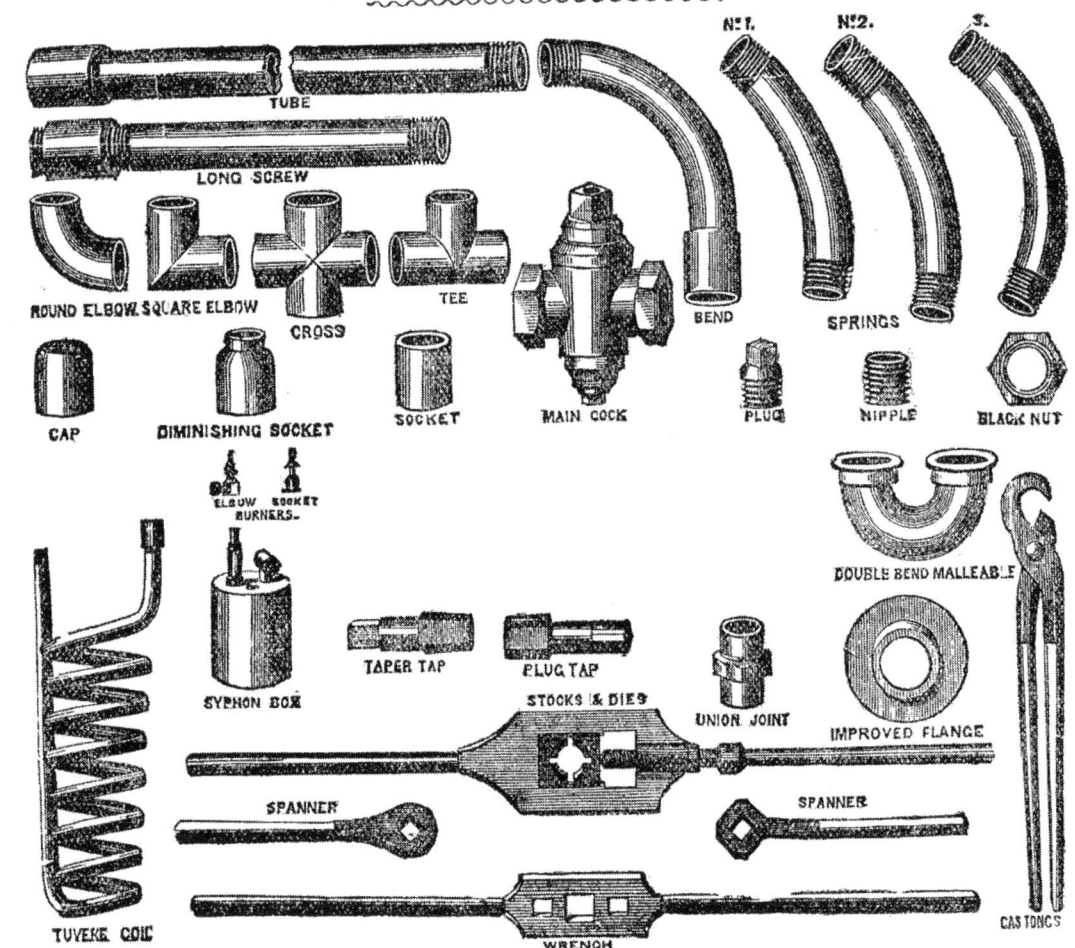

BUTT WELDED TUBES.

		INSIDE DIAMETER in Inches		1/8	1/4	3/8	1/2	3/4	1	1¼	1½	1¾	2	2¼	2½	2¾	3	3½	4
				s. d.	s. d.	s. d.	s. d.	s. d.	s. d.	s. d.	s. d.	s. d.	s. d.	s. d.	s. d.	s. d.	s. d.	s. d.	s. d.
TUBES	1	Tubes from 2 to 14 feet	per foot	0 2	0 2½	0 3	0 4½	0 6	0 8	0 11	1 2	1 6	1 9	2 6	3 3	4 0	4 6	5 6	7 0
	2	Do. do. 12 to 23½ inches	each	0 4	0 5	0 7	0 9	1 0	1 4	1 8	2 0	2 6	3 0	4 0	4 9	6 0	7 0	8 0	9 0
	3	Do. do. 3 to 11½ "	"	0 2	0 3	0 4	0 6	0 8	0 11	1 1	1 4	2 0	2 3	4 0	4 9	6 0	6 0	12 6	15 6
	4	Connecting Tube, 12 to 23½ inches	"	0 5	0 7	0 9	0 11	1 2	1 6	2 0	2 6	3 3	4 0	4 5	6 7	6 6	7 6	8 6	10 0
	5	Do. do. 3 to 11½ "	"	0 4	0 5	0 6	0 8	0 10	1 1	1 3	2 0	2 6	3 0	4 5	6 5	6 6	6 6	16 0	32 6
	6	Tubular Bends and Lamp Bends	"	0 5½	0 6½	0 7	0 8	0 11	1 3	1 9	2 3	3 3	4 3	6 6	10 0	12 0	19 0	26 0	
	7 8 9	Springs, Various Elevations	"	0 4	0 5	0 6	0 7	0 9	0 11	1 4	1 8	2 6	3 3						
FITTINGS	10 11	Socket or Pipe Unions, Wt. Iron	"	...	2 0	2 6	3 0	4 0	5 6	6 9	8 0	9 0	10 0	12 0	14 0	16 0	18 0	22 0	28 0
	12	Elbows, Equal or Diminished	"	0 6	0 6½	0 7	0 8	0 10	1 1	1 2	1 9	2 3	3 0	3 6	5 8	8 6	11 0	14 0	20 0
	13	Tees do. do.	"	0 6	0 6½	0 7	0 9	1 0	1 3	1 9	2 6	3 0	3 9	6 0	9 0	12 6	16 6	24 0	30 0
	14	Crosses do. do.	"	0 10	1 0	1 0	1 5	1 9	2 3	3 0	3 6	4 6	5 3	10 6	16 0	21 0	30 0	42 0	50 0
	15	Sockets, Plain	"	0 1½	0 1½	0 2	0 3	0 3½	0 4	0 6	0 7	0 9	1 0	1 6	2 6	3 0	3 6	5 0	7 0
	16	Do. Diminished	"	...	0 3	0 4	0 5	0 6	0 7	0 9	0 11	1 1	1 3	2 0	3 0	4 0	5 0	7 0	9 0
	17	Flanges	"	0 8	0 9	0 10	1 0	1 2	1 4	1 6	1 9	2 0	2 6	3 9	5 0	6 9	8 6	10 0	11 6
	18 19	Caps and Plugs	"	0 2	0 3	0 3	0 4	0 5	0 6	0 8	0 10	1 0	1 3	2 6	3 6	4 9	7 0	10 0	
	20 21	Backnuts and Nipples	"	0 1	0 2	0 2	0 3	0 3½	0 4	0 6	0 8	0 10	1 0	1 9	2 3	3 0	3 6	4 6	5 6
	22	Union Bends, or Elbows	"	...	2 6	3 0	3 9	5 0	6 3	8 6	11 0	13 6	16 0	19 0	22 0	25 0	30 0	36 0	
	23	Elbows, Round Backed, Wt. Iron	"	0 7	0 7	0 8	0 9	1 0	1 4	1 11	2 6	3 0	3 10	6 6	10 0	13 0	16 0	25 0	32 0
	24	Iron Main Cocks	"	2 3	2 3	2 9	3 6	4 6	6 6	8 6	11 0	14 0	18 0	27 0	36 0	44 0	50 0	75 0	90 0
	25	Do. do. do. Brass Plugs	"	...	...	4 6	5 6	7 6	10 6	15 0	19 6	25 0	32 0	47 0	60 0	90 0	110 0	140 0	190 0
	26	Do. do. do. Roundway	"	...	...	3 6	4 0	5 6	7 6	10 0	13 0	17 0	22 0	38 0	54 0	62 0	70 0	100 0	160 0
	27	Do. do. do. Do. Brass Plugs	"	...	...	5 0	6 6	9 0	13 0	19 0	28 0	36 0	42 0	60 0	85 0	105 0	120 0	180 0	280 0
	28	Spanners, for Cocks, Wt. Iron	"	...	...	1 0	1 4	1 8	2 0	2 4	3 0	3 6	4 0	6 9	6 0	7 6	9 0	12 0	14 0
	29	Do. do. Malleable Ct. Iron	"	...	...	0 7	0 8	0 10	1 2	1 8	2 2	2 9	3 3	4 9	6 0	7 6	9 0	12 0	14 0
	30	Syphon Boxes, 1 Quart	"	...	...	...	11 0	12 0	13 0	14 0	15 0	15 6	16 0	18 0	...	...	...	...	...
	31	Do. do. 2 do.	"	...	...	...	...	16 0	17 0	18 0	19 0	21 0	23 0	25 0	30 0	35 0	40 0	...	...
	32	Do. do. 3 do.	"	...	...	...	...	20 0	22 0	24 0	25 0	26 6	28 0	32 0	35 0	40 0	45 0	50 0	56 0
	33	Do. do. 4 do.	"	...	...	...	...	21 0	23 0	25 0	27 0	29 0	31 0	34 0	38 0	42 0	47 0	54 0	60 0
	34	Malleable Cast Round Elbow	"	0 6	0 6½	0 7	0 8	0 10	1 2	1 9	2 3	3 0	3 6	5 6	9 0	12 0	15 0	30 0	40 0

BAILEY'S PRICE LIST OF GAS FITTINGS FOR IRON & BRASS TUBES.

GAS FITTINGS.

No. — ¼ ⅜ ½ ¾ inch.
1300 Elbow Burner for Brass Tube 2/6 3/6 per doz.
" " " Iron " 3/6 5/3 6/6 8/6 "
1301 Socket " Brass " 2/ 3/ "
" " " Iron " 3/ 4/ "
1302 Elbow, with Glassholder, lacquered, for Brass Tube, ⅜in. 4/3 "
" " " " " Stronger 5/6 "
" " " " " " ½in. 5/6 "
1303 Socket " " " " ⅜in. 3/9 "
" " " " " " ½in. 4/6 "
1304 Burner Socket, with ornamental Glassholder " " " ⅜in. 9/6 "
1305 Elbow " " " " " 13/0 "
1306 Burner Socket " " " " 3/0 "
1308 Straight Connecting Piece, Tube ... ... " 1/0 "
1309 Elbow " " " ... ... " 1/6 "
1310 Straight " " Cast ... ... " 1/6 "
1311 Elbow " " " Long ... " 3/3 "
" " " " " Short ... " 2/6 "

⅜ — ½ x ⅜ — ⅝ x ⅜ inch
1312 Nose Piece, for Brass Tube 1/9 2/ 3/ per doz.

¾ x ⅜ — ⅜ x ⅜ — ½ x ⅜ inch
" " " Iron " 2/ 3/ 4/ per doz.

⅜ — ½ x ⅜ — ½ — ⅝ x ½ — ⅝ inch
1313 Socket " Brass " 1/9 2/3 2/6 3/3 4/6 per doz.

½ — ⅜ inch
" " " Iron " 2/3 4/6 per doz.

⅛ — ¼ — ⅜ — ½ x ⅜ — ½ inch
1314 " rough " Iron " 1/9 2/ 3/6 5/6 6/6 per doz.

⅜ — ½ x ⅜ — ½ — ⅝ inch
1315 Elbow " for Brass Tube 2/3 2/9 3/6 4/9 per doz.
1316 Tee " " " " 2/6 3/3 3/6 5/ "
1317 Cross " " " " 4/ 4/9 5/ "
1318 Union Tee " " " " 6/ 7/6 8/9 11/ "
1319 " " Tinned Ends 6/ 7/6 8/9 11/ "
1320 Elbow for Brass Tube, with Union 4/ 5/ "
1321 Cap and Lining for Iron Tube,
¼ ⅜ ½ ⅝ ¾ 1 1¼ 1½ 1¾ 2 inch
1/9 2/1 3/ 3/6 4/6 6/6 12/6 15/ 21/ 24/ per doz.

¼ ⅜ ½ ⅝ ¾ 1 inch
1322 Tighted Union, Tinned Ends 3/ 3/6 4/3 5/6 8/9 15/ per doz.

⅜ — ½ x ⅜ — ½ — ⅝ — ¾ inch
1323 Union Joint, for Brass Tube 2/9 3/6 3/9 4/6 8/ per doz.
1324 Ditto male and female ditto 2/9 4/3 6/ "

¼ ⅜ ½ ¾ 1 1¼ 1½ 1¾ 2 inch
1325 Union Joint for Iron Tube 4/6 6/ 9/6 14/6 21/ 34/ 57/ 66/ 84/ per doz.
1326 Ditto, tighted ditto 6/6 9/6 12/ 18/ 30/ 45/ 76/ 88/ 109/ "

⅜ ¼ ⅜ ½ inch.
1327 Male Union Screw, for Iron Tube, with tinned outlet 3/ 4/ 6/ 9/9 per doz.

⅛ ¼ ⅜ ½ ⅝ ¾ 1 inch
1328 Ceiling Plate, for Brass Tube 3/6 5/ 6/ 7/6 13/ per doz.
" " " " Iron " 3/6 5/ 6/ 7/6 13/ 19/ "
" " " male " " " 4/ 5/6 6/6 10/ 15/ 21/ "
1329 Winged Union for Brass Tube 4/ 5/6 6/6 "

⅜ — ½ x ⅜ — ½ — ⅝ x ½ — ⅝ — ¾ x ½ inch
1330 Pendant Body " Brass " 7/ 8/ 10/ 12/ 13/ 14/ per doz.

½ x ⅜ — ⅝ x ½ — ¾ x ⅝ — 1 x ¾ inch
1331 " " " " " 9/ 12/6 17/6 30/ per doz.

¼ x ⅛ — ⅜ x ¼ — ½ x ⅜ — ¾ x ½ inch
" " " " Iron " 9/ 12/6 17/6 30/ per doz.
1332 Ball Body " " " Prices special according to size.
1333 Horse Singer with Union Joint, 3-in and 5-in Comb Burners, each, 7/
" " " " " if with Ball Joint " 8/

3 — 4 — 5 — 6 inch
1334 Comb Burners for Horse Singers, ... 2/6 2/9 3/ 3/6 each.
1335 Ceiling Hook and Rose, with 2½-in Screw, ... per doz., 4/
1336 Elbow and Union " 5/

¼ x ⅛ — ¼ — ⅜ x ¼ — ⅜ — ½ x ⅜ — ½ inch
1350 Single Swivel, for Brass Tube 5/9 7/ 8/ per doz.
" " " Iron " 7/ 8/ 9/6 11/ 13/6 16/ "
1351 " " male & female " " " 9/ 9/9 11/ 12/6 "
1352 Double Swivel. " Brass " 7/9 8/9 9/9 "
" " " " Iron " 8/9 9/9 11/9 13/6 16/6 18/6 "
1353 " " male & female " " " 9/ 10/ 11/6 13/6 18/ 20/ "
1354 Universal Swivel " " " 12/9 13/9 17/6 19/3 24/ 30/ "
" " " " Brass " 11/9 12/9 13/6 "
1355 Cock and Swivel " " " 11/6 13/3 14/ "
" " " " Iron " 13/3 14/ 17/6 19/6 21/ 24/ "
1356 " " male & female " " " 14/9 15/6 18/6 20/ 23/ 28/ "
1357 Ditto " " " 14/9 15/6 18/6 20/ 23/ 28/ "

⅜ — ½ x ⅜ — ½ inch
1358 Tee Cock, for Brass Tube 11/ 12/ 14/ per doz.
1359 Ditto to Swivel " " " 14/ 15/ 16/ "
1360 Double Tee Cock " " " 16/ 17/ 19/6 "
1361 Ditto to Swivel " " " 19/ 20/ 24/ "

¼ — ⅜ — ½ — ⅝ — ¾ inch
1362 Pendant Top " " " 11/ 13/ 16/9 23/ per doz.
" " " " " " 13/ 16/9 23/ "
1363 " " with knob, lacquered for Brass Tube 14/ 16/ 20/ 27/ "
1364 Bracket Back " " " 14/ 17/6 24/ 32/ "
" " " " Iron " 17/6 24/ 32/ "
1365 " " with knob, lacquered " Brass " 17/ 21/ 28/ 36/ "

⅜ — ½ x ⅜ — ½ inch
1366 Wing Back " " " 8/ 10/ 11/6 per doz.

¾ x ⅜ — ¾ — ⅝ x ¾ inch
" " " " Iron " 10/0 11/6 14/6 per doz.

¾ x ⅜ — ¾ — ⅝ x ¾ inch
1367 Wing Back and Cock, for Iron Tube 16/ 17/6 23/6 per doz.

GAS FITTINGS—*Continued.*

No. — ⅜ — ½ x ⅜ — ½ inch
1367 Wing Back and Cock, for Brass Tube 12/6 16/0 17/6 per doz.
1368 Back, with Winged Union for Brass 18/6 20/6 "

¼ — ⅜ inch
" " " " " " Iron 20/6 24/6 per doz.

¼ ⅜ ½ ¾ 1 inch
1369 Ball Joint, male and female, for Iron Tube 13/9 17/6 21/9 29/9 50/ per doz.
1370 " " female " " " 13/9 17/6 21/9 29/9 50/ "
Ball Joints, without tail pipes, screwed at top, male or female to Iron tube
⅛ ¼ ⅜ ½ ¾ 1 inch
10/ 12/ 16/ 18/ 24/ 35/ per doz.
The balls of the ⅛ and ¼ sizes are screwed out to ⅜ iron, larger sizes, 2-8 iron

⅜ ½ ⅝ ¾ ⅞ 1 inch
Tail pipes for the above, for Brass Tube, 2/ 2/3 3/3 4/6 5/9 7/ per doz.

¼ ⅜ ½ ¾ 1 inch
" Iron " 2/3 3/3 4/3 7/ 15/ per doz.

½ ¾ 1 1¼ 1½ 2 inch
1371 Carter's Gas Valves, for Iron Tube 2/3 2/7 3/4 6/ 8/ 15/ each
1372 Do. with union joint " " " 2/9 3/4 4/1 7/9 10/ 18/6 "

EXTRA STRONG

ROUGH MILL FITTINGS.

SCREWED FOR IRON PIPE.

No.		¼ x ⅛	¼	⅜ x ¼	⅜	½ x ⅜	½ inch	
1390	Single Swivel	11/	12/	14/	15/	17/	20/	per doz
1391	Double "	14/	15/	16/	18/	20/	24/	"
1392	Universal Swivel	23/	25/	27/	30/	33/	37/	"
1393	Cock and Swivel	18/	20/	22/	23/6	26/	29/	"
1394	Wing Back	16/	17/	18/	21/	25/	28/	"
1395	Wing Back and Cock	22/	24/	26/	33/	35/	39/	"
1396	Pendant Top		24/		27/6		34/	"
1397	Bracket Back		31/9		35/		42/	"
1398	Double Swivel, with Cock in square	13/	14/	16/	20/			"
1399	Do. male and female do.	13/	14/	16/	20/			"
1400	Cock and Swivel, male and female	15/	16/	24/	26/	30/		"
1401	Universal Cock and Swivel	24/	34/	36/	39/			"
1402	" Pendant Top		20/		26/			"
1403	" " "		32/		38/			"
1404	Bracket Back, with Cock in square		19/		23/		34/	"
1405	Double Swivels	10/	12/6	14/6				"
1406	Cock and Swivel	19/6	22/					"

No.			⅜	¾	⅜ inch
1407	Full-way Gas Cock	... ...	9/6	14/6	18/6 per doz.
1408	Do. and Union	... ...	12/6	18/	22/6 "
1409	Universal Wing Back	... ...		28/	"

GAS COCKS.

⅜ — ½ inch
1410 Connector Cock, Lacquered, for Brass Tube 18/ 24/ per doz.
1411 " " " " " " 18/ 24/ "

⅜ — ½ — ⅝ inch
1419 Cock, with winged Union, for Brass 10/ 12/ 14/ per doz.

¼ — ⅜ — ½ inch
" " " " " " Iron 12/ 14/ 18/ per doz.

¼ x ⅛ — ¼ — ⅜ x ¼ — ⅜ — ½ x ⅜ — ½ inch
1420 Gas Cock, female, for Brass Tube 6/ 7/3 8/ per doz.
" " " " Iron " 7/3 8/ 10/3 11/ 14/ 16/ "
1421 Nose Cock, the male end in all sizes screwed ⅜in. brass,

⅜ — ½ — ⅝ inch
For Brass Tube 6/ 7/9 8/6 per doz.

¼ — ⅜ — ½ inch
" Iron " 7/ 8/6 12/ per doz.

⅜ — ½ — ⅝ inch
1422 Gas Cocks, male, for Brass Tube 6/6 7/6 per doz.
1423 " tinned ends 7/ 7/6 9/6 "

¼ — ⅜ — ½ x ⅜ — ½ inch
1424 " with union " " " 9/6 10/9 11/9 per doz.
1425 " " " Iron " 12/ 15/ "

⅛ — ¼ — ⅜ x ¼ — ⅜ — ½ inch
1426 " strong " " " 8/ 10/ 12/ 14/ 18/ per doz.
1427 Pillar Cock, the male end in all sizes screwed ⅜ in. brass

⅜ ½ ⅝ ¾ ⅞ 1 inch
For Brass Tube 7/ 8/ 11/ 12/6 15/6 18/6 per doz.
1428 Pillar Cock, the male end in all sizes screwed ⅜in. brass

¼ — ⅜ — ½ inch
For Iron Tube 9/ 10/6 14/ per doz.
1429 Cigar Cock ... ... 5/6 per doz.

¼ — ⅜ — ½ inch
1430 Elbow Cock for Brass Tube 7/6 9/ per doz.
" " " Iron " 9/ 11/6 16/ "
1431 " with glassholder " Brass " 11/ 12/6 "
" " lacquered 14/6 16/ "

⅛ — ¼ — ⅜ — ½ — ¾ inch
1432 Straight Lamp Cock " Iron " 10/ 10/6 11/6 12/6 13/6 ℔ doz.
1433 Cock-up " " " " 13/ 14/6 "
1434 Elbow Lamp Cock " " " 10/6 11/ 12/ 13/3 14/6 "
1435 Lamp Cock, with quadrant lever " " " 13/ 14/ 15/ 17/ "

⅜ — ½ — ⅝ — ¾ inch
1436 Way Cock, tinned ends 9/6 12/ 16/ 23/ per doz.
1437 " with union ditto 13/ 15/ 20/ 30/ "
1439 Main Cock, usual pattern, male and female

¼ ⅜ ½ ¾ 1 inch — 1¼ 1½ 1¾ 2 inch
10/ 12/6 16/6 26/6 40/ per doz. 7/9 10/ 16/ 20/ each
1440 female 10/ 12/6 16/6 26/6 40/ " 7/9 10/ 16/ 20/ "
1441 with union 12/ 15/ 19/6 31/ 47/ " 9/ 11/6 18/ 22/6 "

THE EXCELSIOR GAS MACHINE,

(FOGARTY'S PATENT).

J. BAILEY & CO., Manufacturers.

Purpose — The Machine is designed for lighting residences, hotels, Mills, factories, churches, shops, railway stations, railway carriages, and villages, supplying a superior quality of gas at a moderate cost.

Production — The gas is AUTOMATICALLY PRODUCED as fast as required—there is never a large stock on hand—dispensing altogether with the unsightly gasholder; and as the material is already purified, the gas itself requires no subsequent purification, but is fit for use as soon as made, the disagreeable smell arising from the purification of coal gas is entirely avoided.

Attendance — It is perfectly automatic, and requires but little attention—TEN MINUTES IN THE DAY BEING ALL THE TIME REQUIRED TO MANUFACTURE a continuous supply of gas, and it is so very simple that, with a few hours' instruction, any man of ordinary intelligence can manage it. On account of the small care and attention the Machine requires there is no necessity to employ skilled, or even ordinary labour specially to make the gas, as any person about the premises can look after the machine without interfering with his other work.

Quality of Gas — From the peculiar construction of the Machine, it is capable of maintaining a perfectly uniform quality of gas at all times and at all temperatures, on which account it is especially adapted for furnishing a supply of gas for gas engines, the use of which is now limited to the vicinity of coal gas works. In all cases it is warranted to be perfectly safe and reliable to supply gas in sufficient quantity, and of uniform quality, to the full number of burners at which it is rated, equally well in winter as in summer.

Material — The material used is Gasoline, one of the lighter products derived from the distillation of petroleum, having a specific gravity of .665, a boiling point of 86° Fahrenheit (30° centigrade), and being of a density of 85° of Beaumé's Hydrometer. It is extremely volatile, to which property it owes its gas-producing value.

Capacity — The Machine itself is very simple in its construction, is warranted to be PERFECTLY SAFE, to supply the full number of FIVE FOOT BURNERS it is rated at, and to furnish through either argand or open burners, at ALL TIMES, a clear, soft, and brilliant light, entirely free from smoke or smell. It is durable, not liable to get out of order.

Cost of Production — The cost of the gas produced will, of course, vary in different localities, but in most cases it will be found that, on a SMALL SCALE, gas can be made from gasoline more cheaply than from coal; 3.69 imperial gallons of gasoline will produce 1,000 cubic feet of superior gas.

Insurance — Gasoline is not more dangerous than any other equally volatile combustible, and with proper care can be used and handled with perfect safety. In THE EXCELSIOR GAS MACHINE there has been adopted, with a view to safety, every device which the accumulated experience of many years could suggest, and with such success that, where the Machine is known, insurance companies take risks upon buildings lighted by it upon the same terms as if they were lighted by coal gas, and invariably reduce their rates wherever the EXCELSIOR GAS is substituted for lamps.

Safety — Gasoline, as a LIQUID, is not dangerous at all, it is only when it has been reduced to the form of vapour that it becomes so. Every chemist is aware that while in the liquid form it cannot explode, or even burn, and that even in the form of vapour it will neither explode nor burn until it has been mixed with air, in the proportion of ten cubic feet of air to one of vapour. The gasoline used in THE EXCELSIOR GAS MACHINE is enclosed in an extremely strong and perfectly air-tight tank, buried in the earth outside of any building, so that it is impossible for fire to reach it, its only communication with the Machine being through a small pipe, through which flame cannot pass, and the Machine itself, when in operation, does not contain more liquid than would suffice to fill a small lamp. Gasoline gas is no more explosive than coal gas. If a room is filled with coal gas and a light taken into it, it will cause an explosion; under the same circumstances an explosion will be caused with gasoline gas, and not otherwise.

Advantages Claimed

1st. The Machine makes at all times, and in all temperatures, a cheap, brilliant gas, of uniform quality.

2nd. It makes a gas which is practically free from condensation.

3rd. The proportions of the mixture of vapour and air are under absolute control.

4th. On account of the gas produced being always of uniform quality, it can be burned through open burners, whereas the air gas usually made requires to be burned through argand burners.

5th. Its simplicity of construction—a few hours' instruction being sufficient to enable any man of ordinary intelligence to manage it.

6th. The little attention it requires—ten minutes in the day being all the time required to insure a continuous supply of gas.

7th. Its safety—the hydro-carbon liquid being placed in strong iron tanks, absolutely air-tight, and buried in the ground outside of any building, so that fire cannot possibly reach it, while the quantity of liquid contained in the Machine when in operation does not exceed that required to fill a small lamp.

8th. It does not require a large unsightly gasholder full of gas, but makes it continuously as it is required for use.

9th. Its reliability—it contains but a few moving parts, and these are so simple that there is but little liability of their getting out of order.

10th. No smoke or smell is produced in making the gas, which requires no after-purification, but is ready for use as soon as made, thereby avoiding the disagreeable smell produced by the purification of coal gas.

11th. The small space the Machine occupies, a building seven to ten feet square being all that is required up to 500 lights.

PRICES:
A Machine usually at work on the Manufacturer's Premises.

Machine for 20 lights, with Tank and Pump complete	£75	
,, 40 ,, ,, ,,	85	
,, 60 ,, ,, ,,	100	Gasoline supplied
,, 100 ,, ,, ,,	125	
,, 150 ,, ,, ,,	150	at
,, 200 ,, ,, ,,	200	
,, 300 ,, ,, ,,	250	per Gallon.
,, 400 ,, ,, ,,	300	
,, 500 ,, ,, ,,	350	

Delivered at the Railway Station, Manchester. Packing cases extra. Half price allowed for empty cases if returned, carriage paid, within one month.

Experienced workmen sent to erect the machine at the lowest possible cost.

Special estimates given for any number of lights up to 10,000.

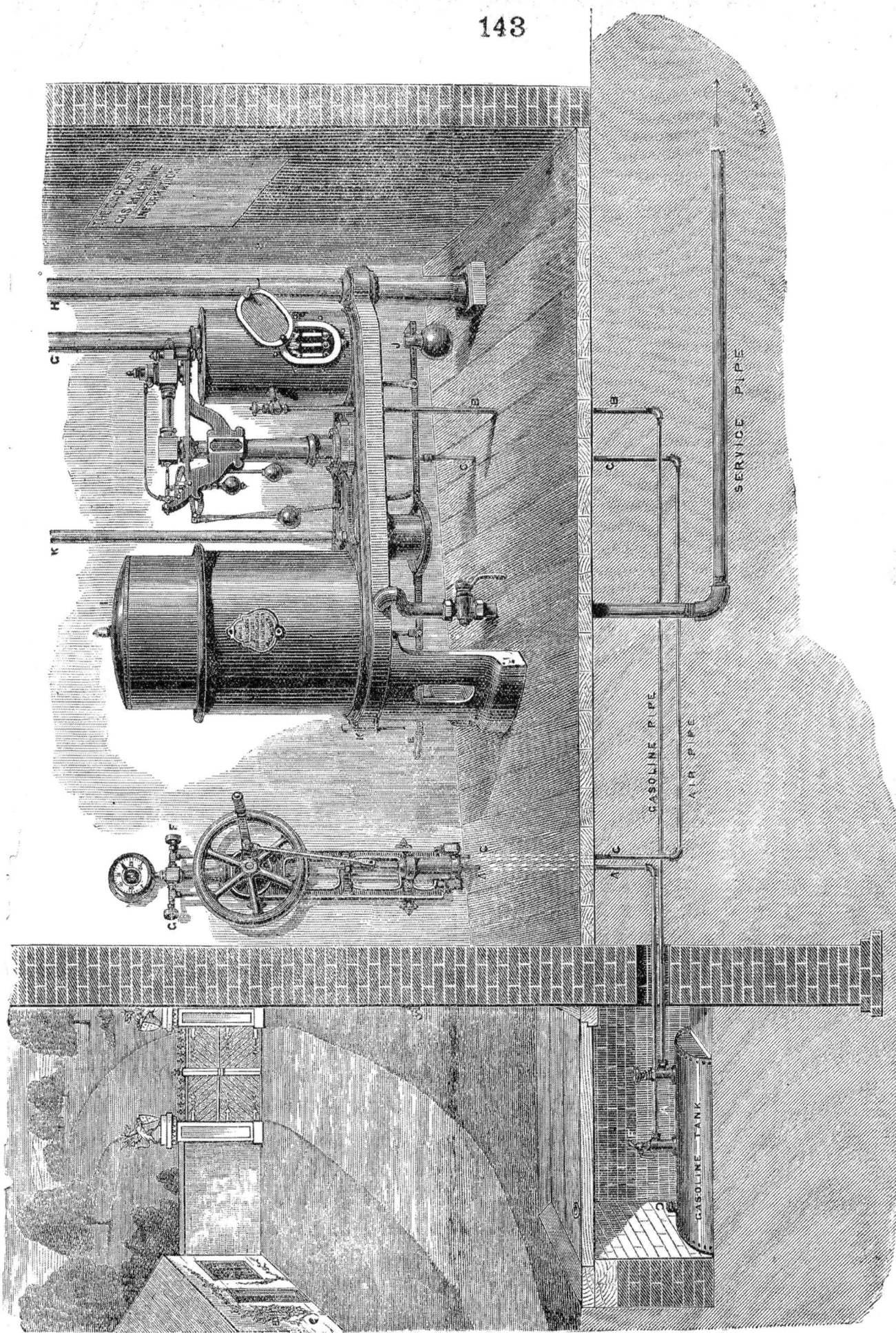

THE EXCELSIOR GAS MACHINE, awarded Prize Medals, Vienna, 1874, &c., &c.

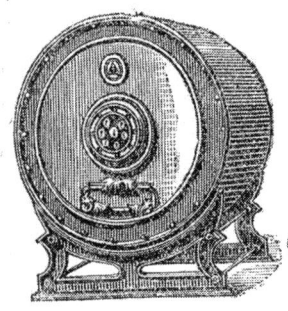
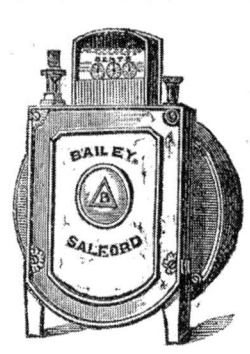

GAS AND WATER METERS.

J. BAILEY & CO. supply Wet or Dry Gas Meters, of most approved Makes, at Current Prices.

THE NEW PATENT HOT WATER METER
FOR STEAM BOILERS (FROST'S PATENT),

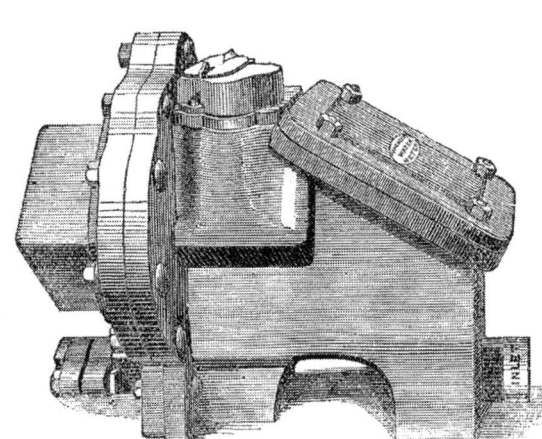

Designed specially for measuring the water evaporated in Steam Boilers, where ordinary Cold Water Meters are not suitable.

The above Meter is in extensive use, and has the approval of many eminent Engineers, to whom it has been submitted. It is, we believe, the only efficient and reliable Hot Water Meter made.

SIZES AND PRICES.

Internal Diameter of Inlet and Outlet Pipe	Quantity of Water each Meter is capable of Passing	Horse Power of Boiler supplied	Price
¾ inch	250 gals. per hour	20 to 40	£13/4/0
1 ,,	500 ,, ,,	40 to 80	18/15/0
1½ ,,	1000 ,, ,,	One or more	26/5/0
0 ,,	2000 ,, ,,	Boilers.	37/16/0

Prices of Cold Water Meters for Towns' Water on application.

WILKINSON'S
Patent Improved Self-Acting Hydraulic Double-Dip Cup Arrangement,
FOR RELIEVING THE PRESSURE IN GAS RETORTS.

QUICKLY AND EASILY APPLIED, IS SELF-ACTING, SELF-SEALING, SELF-CLEANSING, A GREAT SAVING.

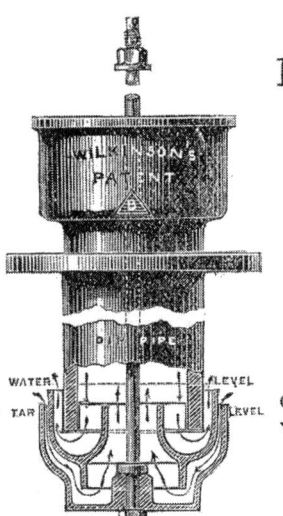

Single Cups.			Double Cups.		
No. 1	3 in.	10/0	No. 4	3 in.	15/0
,, 2	4 ,,	12/6	,, 5	4 ,,	20/0
,, 3	5 ,,	15/0	,, 6	5 ,,	25/0

These cups are easily and quickly applied to the ordinary dip pipe in the ordinary main, and can be put in without disturbing existing arrangements in the least; they offer no obstruction whatever to the gasway in the main, being almost entirely submerged in the water.

They work equally well with or without the exhauster, as far as regards their own action.

The first cost of cups, rod, and fixing is only small, and little trouble fixing.

Once in position, they require no further care or attention in work; remaining constantly self-acting and self-sealing.

By their use, the exhauster is enabled entirely to relieve the pressure from the retorts, and thus prevent excessive deposit of carbon, and effecting a great saving in fuel.

Their use also prevents the gas from passing through the tar in the main, on its way from the retorts.

When the retort is charged, and the gas begins to flow into the main through the dip pipe and cup (*see illustration*), the water is instantly flashed out of the annular basin, and a clear way is opened between the retort and the main. The basin will remain empty during the full flow of gas from the retort, but as the gas ceases to flow, gradually the basin fills, until, when the mouth of the retort is again opened, the dip pipe end is instantly sealed up.

By the use of the under cup, the water to seal is taken from the surface level of the water in the main, free from tar.

The illustration represents the double dip cup, as attached to an ordinary dip pipe within the hydraulic main, and the direction of the arrows shows the flow of the gas from the retort into the main through the basin of the upper cup, and also shows the direction of the flow of water through the lower into the upper cup in the centre.

Cups made to suit dip pipes of any diameter.

The single or double cup supplied to order, with or without rods and nuts.

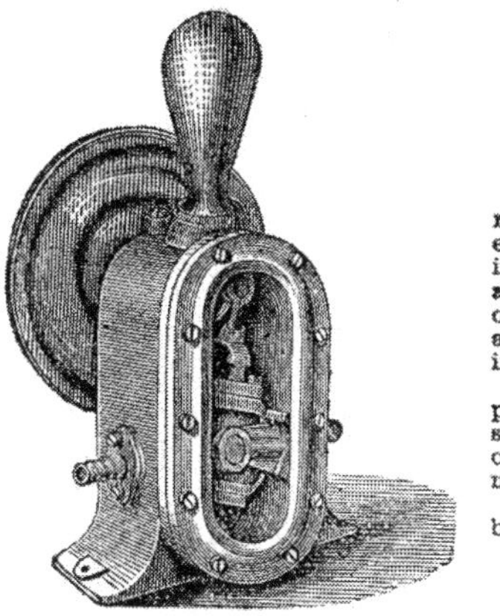

Improved Hydraulic Motor.

The hydraulic motor represented in our illustration is intended to run one or more sewing machines, or other light machinery, and may be used in any house provided with a regular water supply. The apparatus consists of an oscillating engine placed within a perfectly watertight outer casing, into which the water enters at one side and leaves at the other, as indicated by arrows. The oscillating engine cylinder, driven by the water, swings in bearings, as shown, suitable entrance and exit ports of the bearing permitting alternately the entrance and discharge of water from the cylinder. The piston rod of the cylinder is pivoted to a crank disc of the driving shaft. The power is transmitted to the machinery by a friction cone and belting, and can be arranged to run the same at different speeds. A brake device could be applied to produce the instant stoppage of the motor.

The regulating air chamber, shown at the top of the inclosing casing, secures uniformity of motion under varying pressures. A glass front shows the working of the interior parts of the apparatus. The casing is to be attached by fastening screws to any suitable point at or near the sewing machine, and the water can be conveyed thereto by rubber pipes. No oiling is necessary, as the apparatus works entirely in water, which forms a sufficient lubricant. The motor is capable of making from 120 to 500 revolutions per minute, with an average water consumption of forty gallons.

It will be obvious that in tall buildings where the pressure is great, the water used to drive this machine may be utilized by flowing into a cistern, and then used for other purposes.

£5 0s. 0d.

OPEN PRESSURE WATER METER,

For measuring water and other fluids not under pressure.

By this the water of a boiler may be measured at suction-pipe of pump.

To pass	100	gallons per hour,	½ in. joint,	... ...	£3	15	0
,, ,,	200	,, ,,	¾ in. ,,	... ...	5	0	0
,, ,,	400	,, ,,	1 in. ,,	... ...	6	10	0
,, ,,	600	,, ,,	1⅛ in. ,,	... ...	8	0	0
,, ,,	800	,, ,,	1¼ in. ,,	... ...	9	0	0
,, ,,	1000	,, ,,	1½ in. ,,	... ...	10	0	0
,, ,,	2000	,, ,,	2 in. ,,	... ...	16	10	0
,, ,,	3000	,, ,,	2¼ in. ,,	... ...	23	0	0
,, ,,	4000	,, ,,	2½ in. ,,	... ...	28	0	0
,, ,,	6000	,, ,,	3 in. ,,	... ...	35	0	0

These meters should be fixed over a supply cistern of small dimensions; if 100 gallons an hour be used let the cistern hold 5 gallons of water, so for ordinary calculation divide the number of gallons per hour by 20 for the size of cistern required.

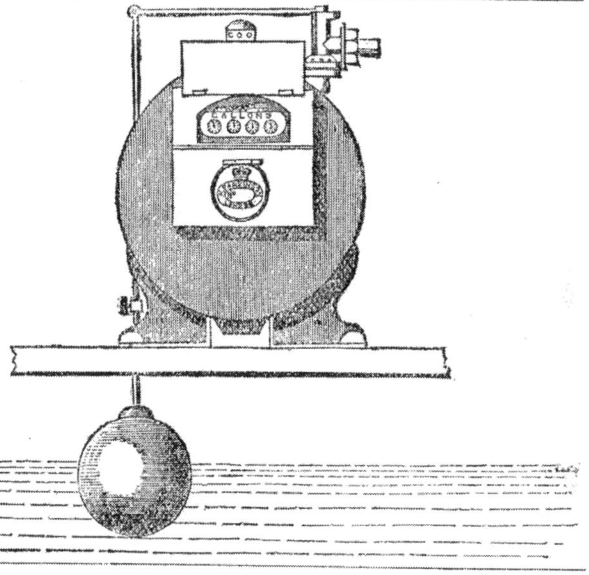

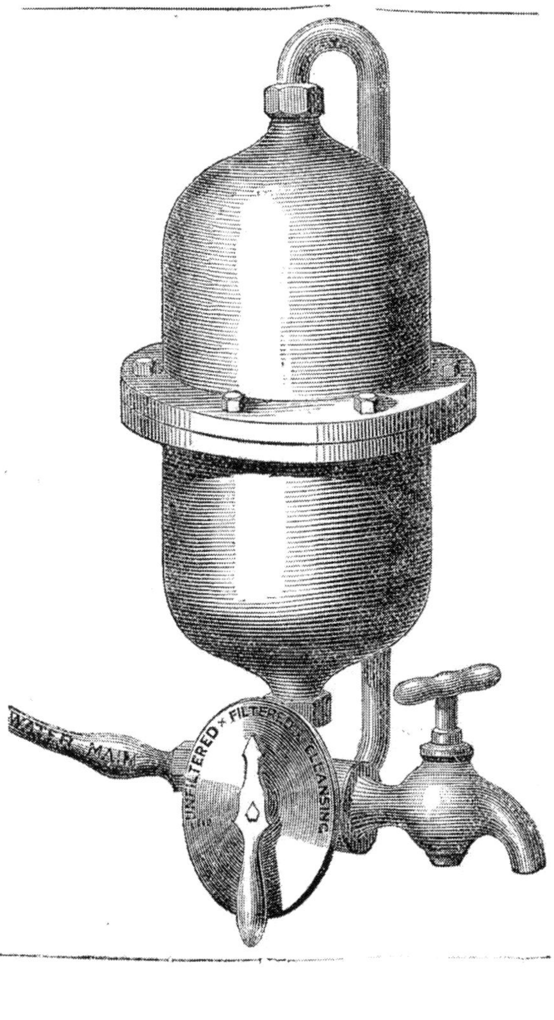

CLEMESHA'S

Patent Self-cleansing High-pressure Water Filters.

The efficiency of these Filters is acknowledged by all who have seen them to be most remarkable.

The following are some of the advantages possessed by these Filters:

1st.—They give a *continuous* supply of thoroughly filtered water.

2nd.—Being attached to the Water Main, they require no filling, as do ordinary Filters.

3rd.—They remove from water all organic impurities, and other matters held in suspension and some of the mineral bases held in solution.

4th.—They render water *bright, free from odour, and colourless*, and better adapted for manufacturing and all domestic purposes.

5th.—They can be *instantly cleansed without cost or loss of time*, by turning the hand on the dial plate from a point thereon marked Filtered to a a point marked Cleansing.

6th.—Under a steady pressure their purifying powers will continue unimpaired for years.

7th.—Their use will to a great extent prevent the scaling of Steam Boilers.

8th.—For large Houses and Public Institutions, they can be fitted on the water main in a cellar, and will supply filtered water through all the ordinary taps in the building.

9th.—They cost much less than Filtering Cisterns, Filter more efficiently, and give a much greater supply.

10th.—They are the *only* Filters that will filter water as rapidly as supplied by the water mains.

These Patent High-pressure Self-cleansing Filters are made in the following sizes, viz.:—

No. 1	will filter	300	gallons per day	... ...	£3	10	0	¼	inch Pipe.
No. 2	,,	600	,,	... ...	5	5	0	⅜	,,
No. 3	,,	1000	,,	... ...	7	7	0	½	,,
No. 4	,,	1500	,,	... ...	10	0	0	¾	,,
No. 5	,,	3000	,,	... ...	15	15	0	1	,,
No. 6	,,	6000	,,	... ...	20	0	0	1¼	,,
No. 7	,,	12000	,,	... ...	30	0	0	2	,,

For Manufacturing or other purposes these Filters are made to supply up to 250,000 gallons per day.

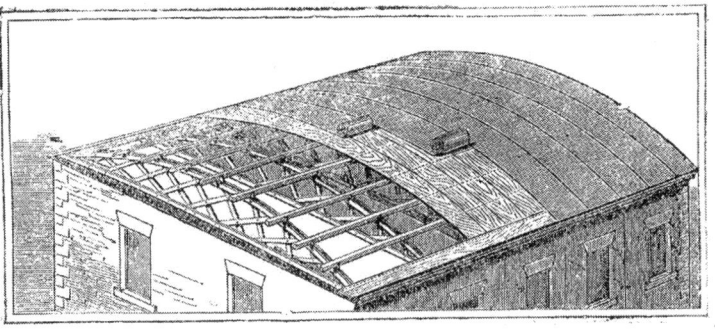

HAIR FELT FOR **Covering Boilers** AND **Steam-Pipes.**

SHIP SHEATHING Felt.

WATERPROOF INODOROUS FELT.

ASPHALTE ROOFING FELT.

This Felt is the cheapest Roof that can be made, costing one-fourth the price of Slates, and much less than Tiles and Thatch, while it makes a most durable light Roof, and requires very little support.

It is much used of late years for lining under Slated or Tiled Roofs, Zinc or Lead Flats, and under Floorings, to protect the Ceiling beneath from wet or damp, and at the same time deadening sound.

It is a valuable Lining for Granaries, Stores, &c., as rats, mice, insects, or other vermin will not touch it.

This Felt suits any climate, as it does not crack from change of temperature, and, being non-conducting, resists the heat of the sun and the cold of the frost. It is made 32 inches wide, and packed in rolls of any required length.

PRICE ONE PENNY PER SQUARE FOOT.

VENTILATOR & SMOKE CONDUCTOR,

Suitable for Ventilation of all kind of Buildings.

PRICES:

			£	s.	d.
9 in. Internal Diameter, with Square Base	...	1	3	0
10 in. Ditto ditto ditto	...	1	7	0
12 in. Ditto ditto ditto	...	1	15	0
18 in. Ditto ditto Round Base	...	4	10	0
24 in. Ditto ditto ditto	...	6	10	0

In submitting this Ventilator and Smoke Conductor to the public, while claiming nothing more than the novel adaptation of the well-known and thoroughly reliable system of directing currents of air, the principle being sound and well tried, can, with every confidence, be recommended, the construction being such that no matter from what direction the wind may blow a rapid upward current is produced, and down draft prevented.

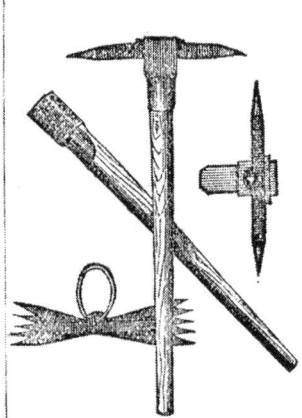

MINERS' PICKS

Of every description supplied at the lowest Market Prices.

Improved Powerful Strongly-Geared Plate Straightening and Bending Rolls.

The upper roll is raised and lowered by screws, and the upper part of cheeks made loose, to take off if required. The Cheek B at the non-geared end of machine swings on a pivot opposite to Bolt A on other side of Cheek B. By detaching the Bolt A, the Cheek B can be swung off, leaving the end of upper roll clear, so that in case of a complete RING being bent it can be taken off without deranging the machine, which is fitted with pulleys, strap guides, and reversing motion. By means of the Swing Cheek B a complete Circle or Ring can be taken off with more despatch and ease than by any other arrangement. The Rolls are cast on end in dry sand, and keyed on wrought iron centres, which pass through their entire length.

Prices.

To take plates 6ft. wide, Rolls 8in. diameter,	£155 0 0
,, 7ft. ,, 8in.	170 0 0
,, 7ft. ,, 12in.	195 0 0
,, 8ft. ,, 12in.	205 0 0
,, 9ft. ,, 12in.	225 0 0

NOTE.—The 9ft. Machine-top Roll is 14in. diameter.

J. BAILEY & CO.,

METAL MANUFACTURERS AND MERCHANTS.

COPPER.

Ingot Copper, tough Ingot, per cwt.; best selected ... ... per cwt.
Seamless Copper Tubes, 1½in. outside, and not exceeding 1 in. diam. to No. 14wg, (if thinner than 14wg, 1d. per lb per gauge extra) ... per lb.
Do. above 1 in ,, ,, 1¾in. ... to No. ,, ,, ,, ,, ,, ,, ,,
Do. ,, 1¾in. ,, ,, 3½in. ... to No. ,, ,, ,, ,, ,, ,, ,,
Do. ,, 3½in. ,, ,, 4½in. ... to No. 12wg, (if thinner than 12wg, 1d. per lb. per gauge extra) ,, ,,
Do. ,, 4½in. ,, ,, 5in. ... to No. 12wg, ,, ,, ,, ,, ,, ,,
Do. ,, 5in. ,, ,, 5½in. ... to No. 12wg, ,, ,, ,, ,, ,, ,,
Do. ,, 5½in. ,, ,, 6in. ... to No. 10wg, ,, ,, ,, ,, ,, ,,
Do. ,, 6in., price according to size.
Brazed Copper Gas and Steam Tubes, above ⅝in. diameter, and not exceeding 4½in. diameter ... ... ,,
Do. do. do. do. ⅜in. to ⅝in., ½d. per lb. extra.
Reeded or Fluted Copper Tubes, for Lightning Conductors and Twisted Wire and Strand ... ... ,,
Tinned Copper Pipes, 2d. per lb. extra.
Wrought Copper Rivets, ⅜in. No. 7wg and larger, and Washers to suit ... ... ,,
Tinned Copper Rivets and Washers, 2d. per lb. extra.
Copper Sheets, 24 × 48in., 8lbs. and upwards ... ...
Rolled Copper, in Strips ... ... ,,
Engineers' Piston and Pump Rods Covered with hard drawn Brass or Copper ... ... ,,
Copper Wire per lb. per cwt. ,,
Copper Wire Covered with Cotton or Silk. (See Electric Dpt. list) ... ... ,,

BRASS.

Brass Locomotive and Marine Boiler Tubes, Seamless, 1¾ to 4in., not thinner than 12wg (½d. per lb. extra for each gauge thinner) per lb.
Do. do. do. do. under 1¾ to 1¼in. outside diameter do. do. do. ,,
Do. Condenser Tubes, Seamless, above 1in. to 1¼in. ,, to 18wg, ... ,,
Do. do. do. do. above ⅝in. to 1in. outside to 19wg, ... ,,
Do. do. do. do. ⅝in. outside to 19wg, not exceeding 10 feet long ... ... ,,
Do. Machine Tubes ... ... ,,
Do. Gas Tubes, ⅜in. and larger ... ... ,,
Extras: ¼ and 5-16in., per lb.; Rope and Twisted, ; Receded, ; Mandril-drawn, 1d., or if cut to lengths, if thinner than 20wg, per gauge extra.
Brass Beading or Edging, ... ,,
Do. Angle Edging ... ... ,,
Do. Bell Tubes, Open Joints ... ... ,,
Do. Sheets, 24 × by 48in., 8lbs. and upwards, best quality ... ... ,,
Extras: 6 and 7lb. Sheets, ½d. per lb.; 4 and 5lb. Sheets, 1d. per lb; Brass Shapes cut to patterns, 1d. per lb.
Extras above 24 in. wide, ½d. per lb.; above 30in. wide, 1d. per lb.; above 36in. wide, 1½d. per lb.
Rolled Brass, 2 @ 6in. to No. 32wg, or above 6 @ 12in., to No. 30wg, ... ,,
Extras: Widths under 2in. ½d. per lb.; 2 to 6in., 33 to 35wg, ½d. per lb.; thinner, 1½d. per lb.; above 6 to 12in., Nos. 31 and 32wg, ½d. per lb.; Nos. 33 and 34wg, 1d. per lb; Nos. 35 and 36wg, 1½d. per lb.
Rolled Brass, above 12 to 18in., to [illegible]wg, ... ,,
Ext[illegible]s. 29 and 30wg, ½d. per lb.; Nos. 31 and 32wg, 1d. per lb.; No. 33wg, 2d. per lb.
Rolled Tagging Brass ... ... ,,
Do. Opticians' Brass, best quality ... ... ,,
Do. Dipping Metal, do. ... ... ,,
Do. Gilding Metal, do. ... ... ,,
Do. Engraving Metal, do. ... ... ,,
Do. Doctor Metal, do. ... ... ,,
Do. German or Nickel Silver ... ... ,,
Yellow Solder, No. 0 per lb.; Nos. 1 and 2 per lb.; No. 3 and upwards ... ... ,,
Ingot Brass, No. 1 per cwt.; No. 2 per cwt.; No. 3 ,,

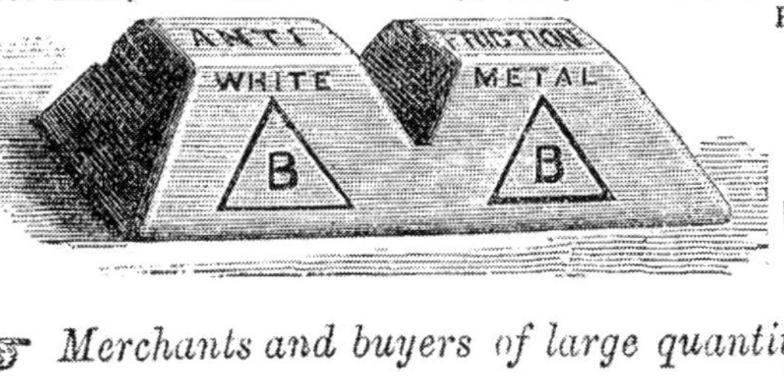

Bailey's White Anti-Friction Metal, for Waggon Brasses, Steps, Bearings, cheaper than Brass and far more durable, in Ingots, of lbs. each. ... ,,

Special Quotations for Light and Heavy Castings of Brass and Copper.

BELLS—SIGNAL, CHURCH, FACTORY, ELECTRIC, AND OTHER BELLS, SPECIAL.

☞ *Merchants and buyers of large quantities of Metal for Shipment are requested to specify quantity, in asking for fine quotations.*

The full Market rate allowed on Old Metal, in exchange for Goods.

Bailey's Price List of Best Sheffield Files and Rasps.

Flat, Half-round, Square, Round, Entering, Taper Cotter, Horse Shoe, Flat and Half-round Rasps.

Mill Saws, one or two Square Edges Single and Double Cut.

Topping Files, Single and Double, left at point, and Safe Edges.

In. 1 to	Rough and Bastard (Per dozen. £ s. d.)	2nd Cut Flat and ½ Round Gun-stockers' and Round Rasps (Per dozen. £ s. d.)	Smooth & Cabinet Files and Rasps (Per dozen. £ s. d.)	Dead Smooth and extra Smooth Cabinets (Per dozen. £ s. d.)
4	0 4 9	0 5 6	0 6 9	0 10 3
4½	0 5 3	0 6 0	0 7 6	0 11 3
5	0 5 9	0 6 9	0 8 3	0 12 6
5½	0 6 3	0 7 6	0 9 0	0 13 6
6	0 7 0	0 8 3	0 9 6	0 14 6
6½	0 7 6	0 8 9	0 10 6	0 15 9
7	0 8 6	0 9 9	0 11 6	0 17 6
7½	0 9 6	0 10 9	0 12 3	0 18 6
8	0 10 6	0 12 0	0 13 6	1 0 0
8½	0 11 0	0 12 9	0 14 6	1 2 0
9	0 12 0	0 13 6	0 15 6	1 3 6
9½	0 13 6	0 15 3	0 17 0	1 5 6
10	0 15 0	0 17 0	0 19 0	1 8 6
10½	0 16 6	0 18 6	1 0 6	1 11 0
11	0 18 0	1 0 0	1 3 0	1 15 0
11½	1 0 0	1 2 0	1 5 0	1 18 0
12	1 1 6	1 4 0	1 6 6	2 0 0
12½	1 3 0	1 5 6	1 8 0	2 2 0
13	1 5 0	1 7 0	1 10 0	2 5 0
14	1 10 0	1 13 0	1 16 0	2 14 0
15	1 16 0	1 19 0	2 2 0	3 3 0
16	2 3 0	2 7 0	2 12 0	3 18 0
17	2 10 0	2 15 0	3 3 0	4 14 0
18	3 0 0	3 5 0	3 14 0	5 11 0
19	3 8 0	3 15 0	4 4 0	6 6 0
20	4 1 0	4 9 0	4 19 0	7 9 0
21	4 13 0	5 1 0	5 13 0	8 10 0
22	5 6 0	5 15 0	6 8 0	9 12 0
23	6 1 0	6 12 0	7 6 0	11 0 0
24	7 0 0	7 11 0	8 6 0	12 10 0

EXTRAS.

All above 24 inches, 20/- per inch extra.

Flat Files, double cut on the edge, to advance ½-inch.

Topping, Square Cut Edges, advance half-inch.

Mill Saw, Two Round Edges, advance half-inch.

Feather Edge and Knife Files, to advance 3 inches.

Three-square, Hand, Equalling one safe Edge. Parallel Cotter, Pillar, Needle, Round off, Bone, Pottance, Round Edged Flat. Extra thin Flat, and Flat and High-back Half-round.

In. 1 to	Rough and Bastard (Per dozen. £ s. d.)	2nd Cut (Per dozen. £ s. d.)	Smooth (Per dozen. £ s. d.)	Dead Smooth (Per dozen. £ s. d.)
4	0 5 3	0 6 0	0 7 6	0 11 3
4½	0 5 9	0 6 9	0 8 3	0 12 6
5	0 6 3	0 7 6	0 9 0	0 13 6
5½	0 7 0	0 8 3	0 9 6	0 14 6
6	0 8 6	0 9 9	0 11 6	0 17 6
6½	0 9 6	0 10 9	0 12 3	0 18 6
7	0 10 6	0 12 0	0 13 6	1 0 0
7½	0 11 0	0 12 9	0 14 6	1 2 0
8	0 12 0	0 13 6	0 15 6	1 3 6
8½	0 13 6	0 15 3	0 17 0	1 5 6
9	0 15 0	0 17 0	0 19 0	1 8 6
9½	0 16 6	0 18 6	1 0 6	1 11 0
10	0 18 0	1 0 0	1 3 0	1 15 0
10½	1 0 0	1 2 0	1 5 0	1 18 0
11	1 1 6	1 4 0	1 6 6	2 0 0
11½	1 3 0	1 5 6	1 8 0	2 2 0
12	1 5 0	1 7 0	1 10 0	2 5 0
12½	1 8 0	1 10 0	1 13 0	2 10 0
13	1 10 0	1 13 0	1 16 0	2 14 0
14	1 16 0	1 19 0	2 2 0	3 3 0
15	2 3 0	2 7 0	2 12 0	3 18 0
16	2 10 0	2 15 0	3 3 0	4 14 0
17	3 0 0	3 5 0	3 14 0	5 11 0
18	3 8 0	3 15 0	4 4 0	6 6 0
19	4 1 0	4 9 0	4 19 0	7 9 0
20	4 13 0	5 1 0	5 13 0	8 10 0
21	5 6 0	5 15 0	6 8 0	9 12 0
22	6 1 0	6 12 0	7 6 0	11 0 0
23	7 0 0	7 11 0	8 6 0	12 10 0
24	7 19 0	8 12 0	9 8 0	14 2 0

EXTRAS.

All above 24 inches, 20/- per inch extra.

Pin Files and Tanged Horse Rasps, to advance 1 inch.

Round off with points, to advance 1 inch.

Needle exceeding breadth of Hand Files as Equalling cut on both Edges.

Equalling and Cotter Files, extra thin, to advance 1 inch.

Hand and Equalling Cut both Edges, or with one double cut Edge.

Lock, Arch, Riffler, Tumbler, Oval Saw Files, Cant, Taper, Cross, Bellied Three Square.

Double Tanged Mill Saw, Topping two round Edges.

In. 1 to	Rough and Bastard (Per dozen. £ s. d.)	2nd Cut (Per dozen. £ s. d.)	Smooth (Per dozen. £ s. d.)	Dead Smooth (Per dozen. £ s. d.)
4	0 6 3	0 7 6	0 9 0	0 13 6
4½	0 7 0	0 8 3	0 9 6	0 14 6
5	0 7 6	0 8 9	0 10 6	0 15 9
5½	0 8 6	0 9 9	0 11 6	0 17 6
6	0 9 6	0 10 9	0 12 3	0 18 6
6½	0 10 6	0 12 0	0 13 6	1 0 0
7	0 11 0	0 12 9	0 14 6	1 2 0
7½	0 12 0	0 13 6	0 15 6	1 3 6
8	0 13 6	0 15 3	0 17 0	1 5 6
8½	0 15 0	0 17 0	0 19 0	1 8 6
9	0 16 6	0 18 6	1 0 6	1 11 0
9½	0 18 0	1 0 0	1 3 0	1 15 0
10	1 0 0	1 2 0	1 5 0	1 18 0
10½	1 1 6	1 4 0	1 6 6	2 0 0
11	1 3 0	1 5 6	1 8 0	2 2 0
11½	1 5 0	1 7 0	1 10 0	2 5 0
12	1 7 0	1 10 0	1 13 0	2 10 0
12½	1 10 0	1 13 0	1 16 0	2 14 0
13	1 13 0	1 16 0	1 19 0	2 19 0
14	1 19 0	2 3 0	2 8 0	3 10 0
15	2 6 0	2 11 0	2 18 0	4 6 0
16	2 15 0	3 0 0	3 7 0	5 2 0
17	3 4 0	3 10 0	3 19 0	5 18 0
18	3 14 0	4 2 0	4 11 0	6 18 0
19	4 7 0	4 15 0	5 6 0	8 0 0
20	5 0 0	5 8 0	6 0 0	9 0 0
21	5 14 0	6 3 0	6 16 0	10 6 0
22	6 11 0	7 1 0	7 16 0	11 16 0
23	7 10 0	8 1 0	9 2 0	13 14 0
24	8 8 0	9 2 0	10 8 0	15 12 0

EXTRAS.

All above 24 inches, 20/- per inch extra.

Hand and Equalling with round Edges, advance One inch; if double cut, Two inches.

Two-tanged Mill Saw, Two round Edges, advance half-inch.

BEST REFINED CAST STEEL SAW FILES.

In. 1 to	Taper Saw Files: 2nd Cut Single (Per dozen. £ s. d.)	Taper Saw Files: 2nd Cut Double (Per dozen. £ s. d.)	Taper Saw Files: Smooth Single (Per dozen. £ s. d.)	Frame Saw Files and Gulleting: 2nd Cut Single (Per dozen. £ s. d.)	Frame Saw Files and Gulleting: 2nd Cut Double (Per dozen. £ s. d.)	Blunt Segment Saw Files, and Taper Cut to Point: 2nd Cut Single (Per dozen. £ s. d.)	Blunt 2nd Cut Double, and Band Saw, 2nd Cut Single (Per dozen. £ s. d.)
3½	0 4 0	0 4 9	0 5 6	0 4 9	0 5 9	0 5 0	0 6 6
4	0 4 6	0 5 3	0 6 0	0 5 3	0 6 3	0 5 6	0 7 6
4½	0 5 0	0 6 0	0 6 3	0 5 9	0 6 9	0 6 6	0 8 6
5	0 5 6	0 6 6	0 7 0	0 6 6	0 7 6	0 7 6	0 9 6
5½	0 6 6	0 7 6	0 8 0	0 7 6	0 8 6	0 8 6	0 10 6
6	0 7 6	0 8 6	0 9 0	0 8 6	0 9 6	0 9 6	0 12 0
6½	0 8 6	0 9 6	0 10 0	0 9 6	0 10 6	0 10 6	0 13 6
7	0 9 6	0 11 0	0 11 0	0 10 6	0 12 0	0 12 0	0 15 6
7½	0 10 6	0 12 0	0 12 6	0 12 0	0 13 0	0 13 6	0 17 6
8	0 12 0	0 13 6	0 14 0	0 13 6	0 14 6	0 15 6	0 19 6
8½	0 13 6	0 15 0	0 15 6	0 14 6	0 16 0	0 17 6	1 1 6
9	0 15 6	0 17 0	0 16 0	0 16 0	0 17 6	0 19 6	1 4 0
9½	0 17 6	0 19 6	0 19 6	0 18 0	0 19 6	1 1 6	1 6 6
10	0 19 6	1 1 0	1 1 0	1 0 0	1 2 0	1 4 0	1 9 0
11	1 4 0	1 6 0	1 6 0	1 5 0	1 7 0	1 9 0	1 14 0
12	1 9 0	1 11 0	1 11 0	1 10 0	1 12 0	1 14 0	2 0 0
13	1 14 0	1 17 0	1 17 0	1 16 0	1 19 0	2 0 0	
14	2 0 0	2 3 0	2 3 0	2 3 0	2 6 0		

REAPER KNIFE FILES.

In.	Plain and Swaged. Single (Per dozen. £ s. d.)	Plain and Swaged. Double (Per dozen. £ s. d.)	Knife Shape. Single (Per dozen. £ s. d.)	Knife Shape. Double (Per dozen. £ s. d.)	Cant Shape. Single (Per dozen. £ s. d.)	Cant Shape. Double (Per dozen. £ s. d.)
7	0 8 6	0 9 0	0 8 6	0 9 6	0 12 6	0 13 6
8	0 9 3	0 10 0	0 9 6	0 10 6	0 13 6	0 14 9
9	0 11 6	0 12 9	0 11 9	0 13 3	0 16 3	0 17 6
10	0 13 6	0 15 6	0 13 9	0 16 0	0 19 0	1 1 3

EXTRAS.

Taper Saw Files, Double Cut Smooth, to advance half inch on Single Smooth.

Frame Equalling Saw Files, 3 inches on Frame Saw price.

EXTRAS.

Rubbers, Rough and Bastard ... ... 1/3 per lb.
Ditto. Second Cut ... ... 1/5 „
Ditto. Smooth ... ... 1/7 „

	Rough and Bastard.	2nd Cut.	Smooth.
1 lb. Rubber	1/8 per lb.	1/9 per lb.	1/10 per lb.
2 „ „	1/5 „	1/6 „	1/7 „
3 „ „	1/4 „	1/5 „	1/6 „

Strong Flat Files & Half-thicks, Rough & Bastard 1/5 „
Do. do. do. Second Cut 1/7 „
Do. do. do. Smooth 1/9 „
Three-Square, 1d. per lb. extra to Flat Files.

Horse Mouth Rasps, 5/- each.

Bread Rasps, handled, 30/- per doz.

Single improved Shoe Rasps, ½ inch on Flat prices.

Double do. do. 1 do.

Last Makers' Rasps, to advance 2 inches.

Saddle Tree Rasps, to advance 3 inches.

All Parallel Files to advance 1 inch on their respective descriptions.

All quarter inches the price of the next size above.

Round, Half-round and Cross Files, Double Cut Second Cut, to advance half an inch.

Do. Double Cut Smooth, to advance 1 inch.

Flat, Three-Square and Hand Files, Rough and Middle Cut, above 14 inches, 6d. per dozen extra to Bastard Cut.

New Cut Files to advance 1 inch.

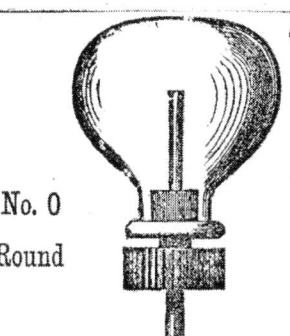

No. 0 Round

OVER THREE MILLION FIVE HUNDRED THOUSAND SOLD.

PROTECTED UNTIL THE YEAR 1880.
By Her Majesty's Royal Letters Patent.

REGISTERED TRADE MARK.

THE "NEEDLE" LUBRICATOR,

On a Patent Pneumatic and Self-Acting Principle, in Glass.

DESCRIPTION.

A—Globe in glass.
B—Stopper in wood.
C—Metal Tube.
D—Moderator Tube.
E—Metal Needle Rod.

The Stopper is made of wood, in preference to metal, because it allows the neck of the Globe to expand or contract, by heat or cold, without breaking the glass.

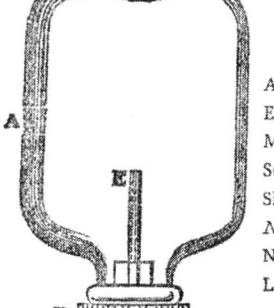

ADVANTAGES.

A saving of 75 per cent. in oil.
Economy of labour. Durability.
More effectual lubrication.
Supply of oil always seen.
Simplicity of construction.
No expense in fitting.
Not likely to get out of order.
Lubrication ensured without heating the bearings first, as in most others.
Incomparably the *best* and cheapest.

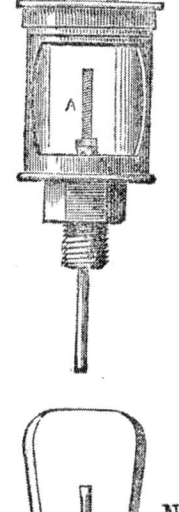

No. 4 Flat

No. 1 Round

(LIEUVAIN'S PATENT).
ALREADY EXTENSIVELY ADOPTED IN THIS COUNTRY AND ON THE CONTINENT,
And in Her Majesty's Dockyards and Railway Works, &c.
Nos. 1, 2, 3, 4, 5, 6, 7 and 8—Price 1s. each.
A SAMPLE LUBRICATOR SENT ON RECEIPT OF POSTAGE STAMPS FOR THE AMOUNT.

This simple, efficient, and inexpensive Self-acting Lubricator is composed of a strong globe of glass (A) (see sketch) having a neck or outlet fitted with a stopper of wood (B) through which is a conical metal tube (C) forming the only exit for the oil. In order to regulate the supply of oil, a metal rod or needle (E) passes through the tube.

The apparatus is filled with oil and turned neck downwards, and the lower end of the stopper is fitted, or, if necessary, pared down to fit the oil hole over the bearing of the shaft; the needle (E) alone descends, and comes into contact with the parts required to be lubricated, the least movement of which produces an oscillation or vibration of the needle, which disengages a small portion of oil and causes it to descend from the globe, the quantity being in proportion to the speed. When the machinery stops, or is not in motion, no oscillation of the needle takes place, and the pressure of air at the base of the tube, also the partial vacuum formed in the globe, prevents the oil from descending until the machinery is again set in motion.

Its economy in saving of oil is incredible; an ordinary globe, containing but a small quantity will lubricate a small shaft, turning 150 to 200 revolutions per minute, for upwards of a month.

Approximate capacity of the respective numbers in Liquid Measure—No. 1, 2 oz.; No. 2, 1½ oz.; No. 3, 1½ oz.; No. 4, 1 oz.; No. 5, 1¼ oz.; No. 6, ½ oz.

NOTE.—Should the oil descend too freely, in consequence of the Lubricator being fixed in a high temperature, or other cause, the needle rod should be replaced by a thicker one; or, on the contrary, if insufficiently, the rod should be slightly filed on one side, or a thinner one substituted. These alterations, however, are rarely necessary. The needles should be clean and free from rust before putting the Lubricator to work.

The largest size, No. 0—Price 2s. each.

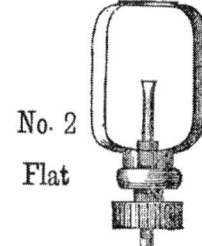

No. 2 Flat

No. 5 Round

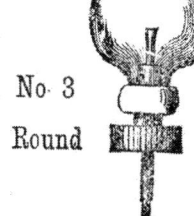

No. 3 Round

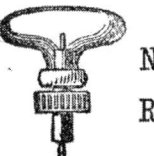

No. 6 Round

CAUTION.—*All Lubricators sold under this patent are marked "Lieuvain's Patent," without which they will be considered infringements. It is intended to protect this patent to the utmost, and all parties are respectfully cautioned against infringing same by* USE, SALE, *or* MANUFACTURE *of colorable imitations. The unparalleled success of this patent has induced parties to sell other Lubricators, fraudulently describing them as "The Needle Lubricators;" such persons are warned that the Solicitors to this patent will institute criminal proceedings against them under the "Merchandise Marks Act, 1862."*

ENTERED AT STATIONERS' HALL.

THE "HAVRE" LUBRICATOR.

REGISTERED TRADE MARK—"LIEUVAIN'S PATENT."

On a Patent Pneumatic Self-acting principle, in glass, mounted in gun metal.

Is specially recommended when an Oiler is required to be securely fixed for Engines, Connecting Rods, Cranks, etc., etc., etc.; it can be replenished with oil without removal from bearing; it possesses the *efficiency, economy,* and *simplicity* of the "Needle" Lubricator, Lieuvain's Patent (the public appreciation of which latter invention is attested by their being over 3,000,000 in operation), and of which it is a modification. The "HAVRE" LUBRICATOR was first exhibited by Mons. LIEUVAIN at the International Exhibition at Havre, 1868, and gives the most unqualified satisfaction. *Observe*—No cement is used; joints are made by leather only, and new globes can be refitted, if required, without difficulty or expense.

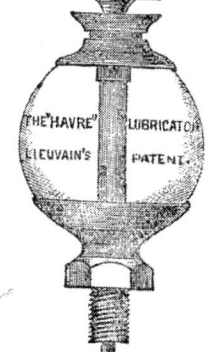

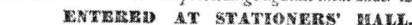

No. 7 Flat

No. 8 Round

Diameter of Globe in inches			1 in.	1½ in.	2 in.	2½ in.	3 in.	3½ in.
Sizes			No. 0	1	2	3	4	5
Prices each			2/6	3/-	3/6	4/-	4/6	5/-

OIL CANS

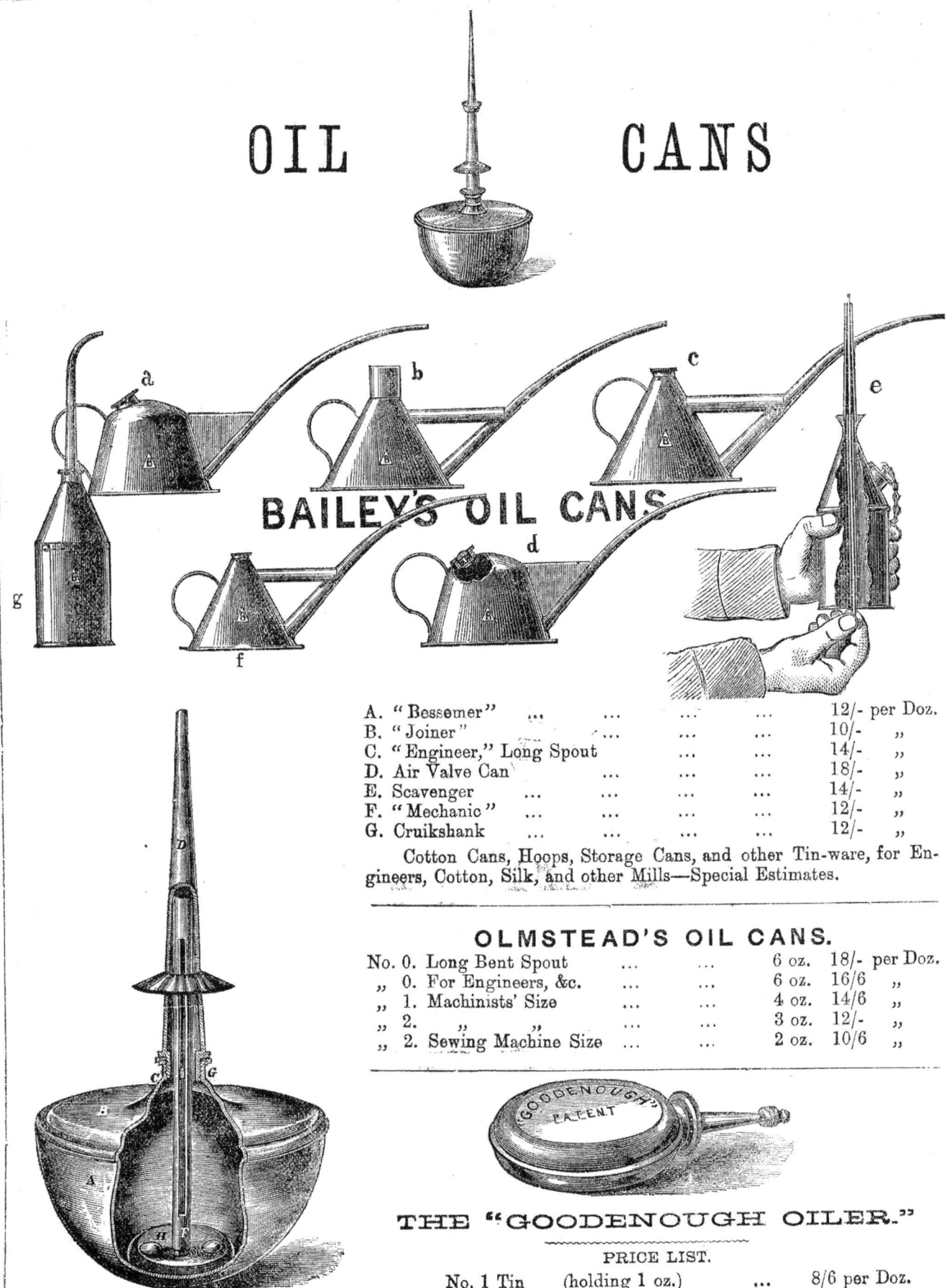

BAILEY'S OIL CANS.

A. "Bessemer"	...	12/-	per Doz.
B. "Joiner"	...	10/-	,,
C. "Engineer," Long Spout	...	14/-	,,
D. Air Valve Can	...	18/-	,,
E. Scavenger	...	14/-	,,
F. "Mechanic"	...	12/-	,,
G. Cruikshank	...	12/-	,,

Cotton Cans, Hoops, Storage Cans, and other Tin-ware, for Engineers, Cotton, Silk, and other Mills—Special Estimates.

OLMSTEAD'S OIL CANS.

No. 0. Long Bent Spout	...	6 oz.	18/- per Doz.
,, 0. For Engineers, &c.	...	6 oz.	16/6 ,,
,, 1. Machinists' Size	...	4 oz.	14/6 ,,
,, 2.	...	3 oz.	12/- ,,
,, 2. Sewing Machine Size	...	2 oz.	10/6 ,,

THE "GOODENOUGH OILER."

PRICE LIST.

No. 1 Tin   (holding 1 oz.)   ...   8/6 per Doz.

White's Patent Oil Feeders.

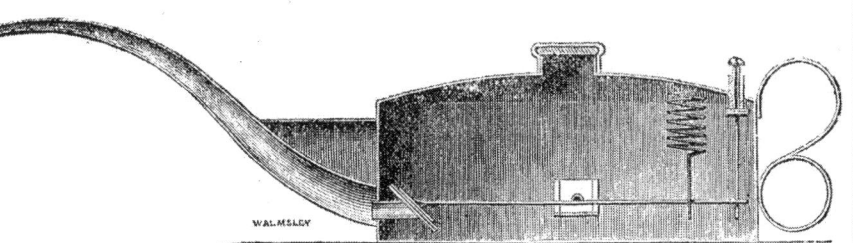

As supplied to Her Majesty's Dockyards, the Royal Arsenals, Mint, &c.

PRICES (with Screw Top and Strong Chain),

Nos.	0	1	¼-pint 2	3	½-pint 4	5	1 pint 6	7	Quart 8
	15/-	17/6	20/-	22/6	25/-	28/-	32/-	36/-	42/- per dozen, wholesale.

BUCKINGHAM'S PATENT OILER.

PRICES:
No. 1, 12/- per doz.
No. 2, 15/- "
No. 3,

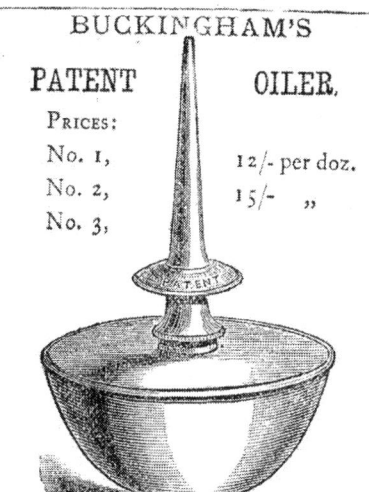

RADCLIFFE'S PATENT OIL CANS

SAFETY & ECONOMY

Are the best, most economical, and by far the strongest and most durable of any in the market; specially made to stand the rough usage of those possessing an excess of physical over the mental qualification. There are none cheaper in the market, taking strength into consideration.

Fig. 5 is a section showing the Patent Valves.

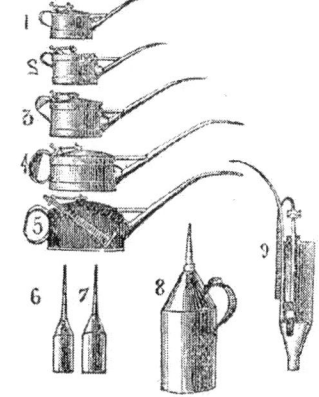

		Per Doz.
¼-pint	No. 1	18/-
½-pint	" 2	21/-
¾-pint	" 3	25/-
1 pint	" 4	31/-
1½ pint	" 5	38/-
Quart	" 5 A	42/-

RADCLIFFE'S PATENT Piston Shafting OIL CAN,

For Oiling Shafting in motion. Economy and safety. Several hundreds in use.

Complete, 15/- each.

J. BAILEY & CO., LICENSEES.

RADCLIFFE'S Patent Locomotive OIL CAN,

Very good and strong,

72/- per Dozen.

Brass Oil Cups, with Lids, made any size.

THE "SKYLIGHT" LUBRICATOR.

Adapted also (3d. extra each size) for loose pulleys and the wheels of vehicles of every description, causing the same free working of the wheels on the axles as it effects when applied to the journals or bearing parts of Engines and other machines,

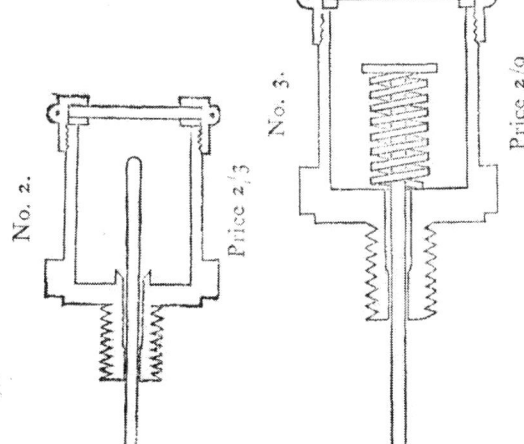

No. 1. Price 2/-
No. 2. Price 2/3
No. 3. Price 2/9

PATENT METALLIC KEGS—Continued.

No. 6—Tanks.

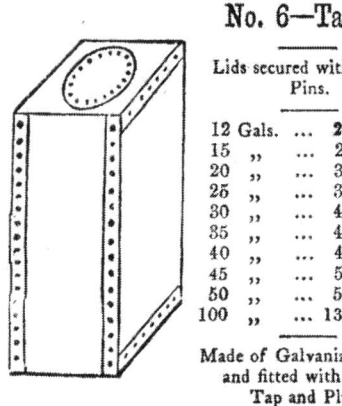

Lids secured with Screw Pins.

12 Gals.	...	25/3 each.
15 ,,	...	28/9 ,,
20 ,,	...	32/6 ,,
25 ,,	...	35/6 ,,
30 ,,	...	42/6 ,,
35 ,,	...	46/- ,,
40 ,,	...	48/3 ,,
45 ,,	...	51/9 ,,
50 ,,	...	56/6 ,,
100 ,,	...	135/- ,,

Made of Galvanized Iron, and fitted with Brass Tap and Plug.

No. 7—Patent Iron Casks,

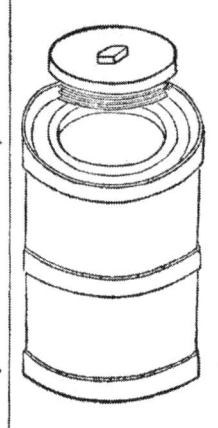

With Screw Lid.

9½ Gals.	...	25/3 each.
13½ ,,	...	28/9 ,,
26½ ,,	...	39/9 ,,
36 ,,	...	56/- ,,
45 ,,	...	63/9 ,,
50 ,,	...	69/6 ,,
75 ,,	...	96/9 ,,
100 ,,	...	120/- ,,

No. 8—Patent Iron Casks.

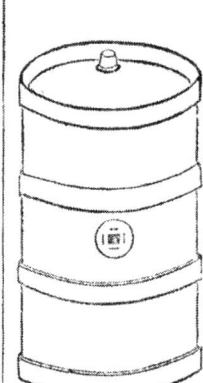

With Four Iron Hoops and Metal Screw.

9½ Gals.	...	20/- each.
13½ ,,	...	23/- ,,
26½ ,,	...	34/6 ,,
36 ,,	...	50/9 ,,
45 ,,	...	58/6 ,,
50 ,,	...	64/3 ,,
75 ,,	...	92/- ,,
100 ,,	...	115/- ,,

Made any size.

This Metallic Cask is tinned inside and outside, and painted outside, and is strongly hooped. It has a Screw Bung, and is perfectly air-tight.

STRONG GALVANIZED WROUGHT IRON CISTERNS

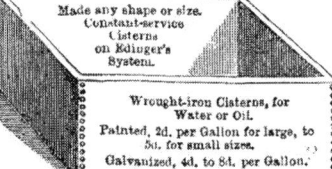

Made any shape or size. Constant-service Cisterns on Edinger's System.

Wrought-iron Cisterns, for Water or Oil. Painted, 2d. per Gallon for large, to 5d. for small sizes. Galvanized, 4d. to 8d. per Gallon.

CAST IRON CISTERNS,

of any capacity, to special quotation, delivered fitted up, or for export, in pieces, ready for building up.

SIZES	CONTENTS	OPEN Per Gallon.	CLOSED Per Gallon.
2 ft. 1 in. × 1 ft. 6 in. × 1 ft. 8	30 Gallons	0s. 10d.	1s. 5d.
2 ft. 4 in. × 1 ft. 6 in. × 1 ft. 10	40 ,,	0 9½	1 3
2 ft. 8 in. × 1 ft. 8 in. × 1 ft. 10	50 ,,	0 9	1 1
2 ft. 8 in. × 2 ft. × 1 ft. 10	60 ,,	0 8½	
3 ft. 1 in. × 1 ft. 10 in. × 2 ft.	70 ,,	0 8	
3 ft. 1 in. × 2 ft. 3 in. × 2 ft.	80 ,,		
3 ft. 1 in. × 2 ft. 3 in. × 2 ft. 6	100 ,,		
3 ft. 4 in. × 2 ft. 6 × 2 ft. 6	125 ,,		
3 ft. 4 in. × 2 ft. 6 × 3 ft.	150 ,,		

Others to Special Quotations.

Painted, 1d. per Gallon less. Other Sizes and Shapes can be supplied to order in a few days.
Constant Service Cisterns, or very narrow Shapes extra; also, Divisions, Bolts, and Fittings, when required.
Terms and other particulars on application.
Edinger's system is to have water supplied to houses on constant service, with a small Cistern for drinking purposes, another for Closet, &c. As the water is drawn off for use, it runs in again directly without waste; enough water for present use is kept in hand and efficient flushing is secured.

BAILEY'S EXTRA STRONG RIVETED GALVANIZED IRON FIRE BUCKETS.

PRICE:

12 in. diam.	24/- per doz.
14 in. ,, ...	36/- ,,

Every Purchaser of a Fire Pump should have at least Six Buckets, always full of water, and in the immediate vicinity of the Pump.

BAILEY'S BREWING PANS,

WROUGHT IRON,

Suitable for Brewers, Bleachers, Dyers, and others.

Made in all sizes from 30 Gallons and upwards, and supplied at 40/- per cwt.

Prices for Cast Iron Enamelled or all Copper on application.

PATENT METALLIC KEGS,
For White Lead, Paint, Colours, Oils, Printers' Ink, &c.

These Kegs are lower in price than wooden ones; they do not absorb the Oil contained in White Lead and Paint, but preserve them for any length of time; they do not require any coopering, and are easily headed and unheaded; all the contents can be entirely taken out, whereby a considerable saving is effected; they can be used any number of times; are easily repaired, and are painted inside and out. *N.B.—All sizes given are outside measurements.*

PRICES.

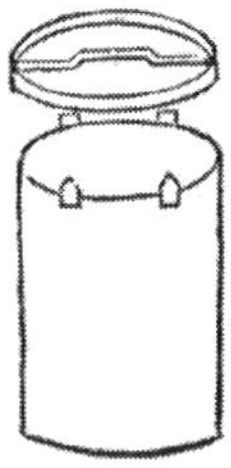

No. 1.

Diam.	Depth.	Per Doz.	Diam.	Depth.	Per Doz.
5 in.	× 4 in. to 9 in.	11/-	9 in.	× 14 in.	27/-
6 ,,	× 10 ,,	12/-	9 ,,	× 16 ,,	30/-
6½ ,,	× 11 ,,	13/-	10 ,,	× 12 ,,	33/-
7 ,,	× 13 ,,	15/-	10 ,,	× 15 ,,	34/-
7½ ,,	× 11 ,,	17/-	10 ,,	× 18 ,,	36/-
7½ ,,	× 14 ,,	18/-	11 ,,	× 14 ,,	42/-
8 ,,	× 13 ,,	20/-	11 ,,	× 18 ,,	48/-
8 ,,	× 15 ,,	21/-	12 ,,	× 18 ,,	54/-
			12 ,,	× 22 ,,	60/-

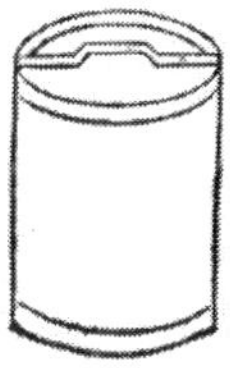

No. 2—Hooped Top and Bottom.

Diam.	Depth	Per Doz.	Diam.	Depth	Per Doz.
10 in.	× 16 in.	43/-	14 in.	× 20 in.	84/-
11 ,,	× 18 ,,	51/-	14 ,,	× 22 ,,	86/-
12 ,,	× 15 ,,	59/-	14 ,,	× 24 ,,	90/-
12 ,,	× 17 ,,	60/-	15 ,,	× 21 ,,	96/-
12 ,,	× 19 ,,	63/-	15 ,,	× 24 ,,	102/-
12 ,,	× 21 ,,	65/-	16 ,,	× 23 ,,	108/-
14 ,,	× 16 ,,	81/-	16 ,,	× 26 ,,	114/-
14 ,,	× 18 ,,	83/-	17 ,,	× 25 ,,	120/-

No. O 1—Paint Cans.

1¼ Pints	4½ in.	× 3 in. deep	4/6	per Doz.
1¾ ,,	4¾ ,,	× 4½ ,,	5/3	,,
2 ,,	4¾ ,,	× 4¾ ,,	6/3	,,
3 ,,	5¾ ,,	× 4½ ,,	7/6	,,
5 ,,	6½ ,,	× 5¼ ,,	8/6	,,
8 ,,	6½ ,,	× 6 ,,	9/6	,,

No. O 2—Paint Buckets.

2 Pints	6 in.	× 6 in. deep	11/-	per Doz.
3 ,,	7½ ,,	× 6¾ ,,	12/6	,,
4 ,,	7¾ ,,	× 7½ ,,	13/6	,,
5 ,,	9 ,,	× 8½ ,,	14/6	,,
6 ,,	9 ,,	× 10 ,,	15/-	,,

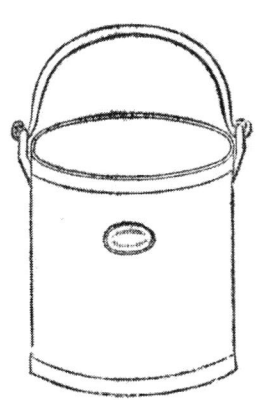

No. O 3—Mill Painters' Buckets.

GALVANIZED.

10	11	12	13 in. diameter.
34/9	37/6	40/9	47/- per doz.

No. O 4—Impoved House Buckets.

GALVANIZED.

	10	11	12	13 in. diam.
Light	18/-	20/6	23/-	26/- per doz.
Strong	21/-	24/-	27/-	29/6 ,,

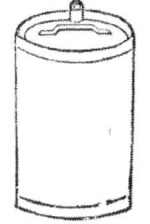

No. 3—Patent Metallic Casks.
With Tight Top and Bottom.

Gals.	Diam.	Height.	Strong.	With Brass Screw Taps.	
1	6½ in.	× 10 in.	22/-	½ in.	92/6 doz.
2	8 ,,	× 13½ ,,	33/-	,,	104/9 ,,
3	9 ,,	× 16 ,,	46/3	,,	119/- ,,
5	11 ,,	× 17 ,,	63/-	,,	135/6 ,,
7	12 ,,	× 19 ,,	90/6	,,	176/- ,,
9	12 ,,	× 23 ,,	115/6	,,	185/- ,,
12	14 ,,	× 24 ,,	146/-	⅝ in.	221/- ,,

Drum Shape

No. 3a.

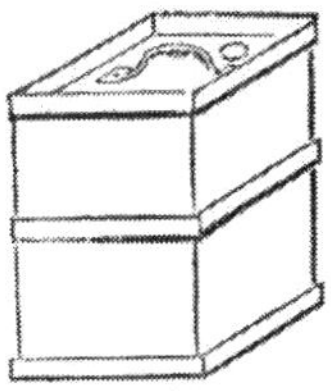

Gals.	Per Doz.		With Brass Screw Taps
1	24/9	½ in.	95/3
2	36/3	,,	109/-
3	49/6	,,	121/-
4	60/6	,,	130/-
5	73/-	,,	140/-
6	79/3	,,	169/-
8	108/-	,,	177/-
10	132/-	,,	205/-
12	151/9	⅝ in.	231/-

Square Shape.

If with Brass Screw Bungs, 1/- and upwards extra.

No. 4—Patent Metallic Casks.
For Oil, Naptha, Turpentine, &c.

Gals.	Strong.		With Brass Screw Taps.	
1	29/-	½ in.	99/-	per doz.
2	40/-	,,	112/-	,,
3	53/-	,,	126/6	,,
5	69/6	,,	143/-	,,
6	82/6	,,	152/-	,,
8	115/6	,,	185/-	,,
10	141/-	,,	211/-	,,
12	172/6	⅝ in.	235/-	,,

Taper Neck Shape

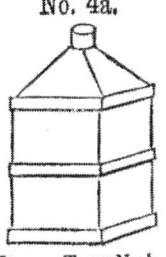

No. 4a.

Gals.			With Brass Screw Tap	
1	31/6	½ in.	101/9	per doz.
2	43/-	,,	115/6	,,
3	56/-	,,	129/-	,,
5	74/-	,,	146/6	,,
6	86/-	,,	155/-	,,
8	121/-	,,	190/-	,,
10	145/-	,,	218/-	,,
12	165/-	⅝ in.	242/-	,,

Square Taper Neck Shape

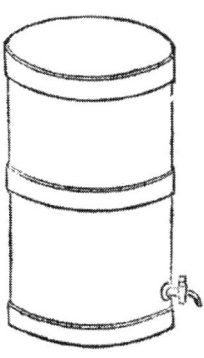

No. 5—Patent Metallic Cisterns,
With loose Covers and Brass Screw Taps.

Gals.			Strong.
10	...	...	21/- each.
20	...	...	30/- ,,
25	...	...	35/- ,,
30	...	...	48/3 ,,
40	...	...	63/3 ,,
50	...	...	74/9 ,,
75	...	...	103/6 ,,
100	...	...	120/9 ,,
150	...	...	138/6 ,,
200	...	...	166/9 ,,

These Cisterns are also made with Tight Covers, and Brass Screw Bungs, at 3/6 each and upwards, extra.
Any Sizes can be made.
Made of best Tinned or Galvanized Iron, and painted outside.

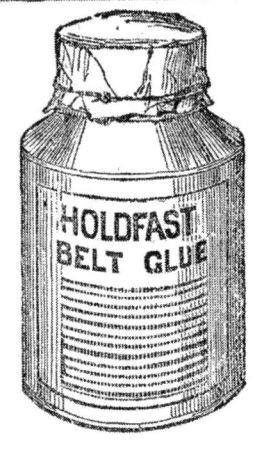  

Baker & Co's Improved Holdfast Belt Glue
FOR FASTENING BELTS,
USED TO ALL KINDS OF MACHINERY.

ADVANTAGES TO BE OBTAINED.

No Rivets or Lacing Holes are required, as they frequently wear away in going over the Pulleys.

There is very little Delay in the Stoppage of Machinery, as the Glue will set in a few Minutes' time.

The Belts will sooner give way in any other part than where they have been fastened by this process.

The Joints being the same thickness as any other part, obviates all Jarring when passing over the Pulleys which occurs by the present system.

The Glue is not effected by Dampness, and no ordinary Heat will have any effect upon it.

It will answer for any kind of Belts, either New or Old, Greasy, or otherwise.

SOLD IN BOTTLES, 5/- AND 10/- EACH.
Full Directions for Use on each Bottle.

Large Consumers will be Liberally Treated with.   Numerous Testimonials may be seen on application.

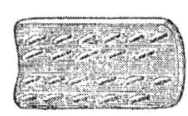  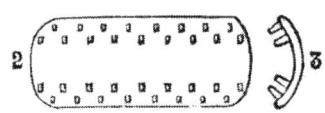

Harris's Patent Strap Fastener.

This Patent mode of connecting Straps or Belts is an improvement on lacing or stitching. It is easily applied, and the joint is as strong as any other part of the strap.

INSTRUCTIONS FOR USE.

Lay the casting teeth uppermost on something solid, and put one end of the strap on one of the sets of teeth, and force or hammer it firmly on to them; then place the other end of the strap on the opposite set of teeth, and force it down firmly in the same manner: this done, the strap is ready for use.

In applying this Fastener, the strap not being weakened by making holes or bevelling, the joint is necessarily stronger than when laces are used.

Care must be taken not to strike over both sets of teeth at the same time, otherwise the *curve* would be destroyed; and the *curve* is that which gives the requisite angle to the teeth to prevent them from working loose.

In case of broad straps, say 6-inch, use two 3-inch Fasteners.

Width of Strap,	$\frac{1}{2}$in.	1in.	1$\frac{1}{4}$in.	1$\frac{1}{2}$in.	1$\frac{3}{4}$in.	2in.	2$\frac{1}{4}$in.	2$\frac{1}{2}$in.	2$\frac{3}{4}$in.	3in.	3$\frac{1}{2}$in.
Prices,	12/-	18/-	18/-	24/-	24/-	30/-	33/-	36/-	39/-	42/-	48/- per Gross.

N.B.—To separate the Strap from the Fastener, run a knife between the teeth from end to end.

List of Prices of Improved Tanned Leather DRIVING STRAPS,

ALL STRETCHED BY MACHINERY BEFORE DELIVERY.

"Very varied materials are employed for straps, the most serviceable of all being leather."—*Vide "Mills and Millwork,"* W. FAIRBAIRN, C.E., &c., &c.

BAILEY & CO. have made arrangements with a Company who are the proprietors of a number of valuable Patents, relating to the treatment of Hides for the production of Leather, and the method of making it into Driving Straps for Machinery, with a view to ascertain the very best processes applicable to such purposes, and who have recently carried out a series of careful experiments and tests, and are possessed of extensive, well-arranged premises, appointed with the best Machinery and appliances, and who perfected a system of manufacture, the products of which have been submitted to, and have received the unqualified approval of some of the most experienced judges in the trade. J. B. & CO. can therefore offer IMPROVED TANNED LEATHER DRIVING STRAPS at extremely moderate prices, and with the fullest confidence in their thorough reliability in every respect.

These Prices are subject to Alteration without notice.

BEST STRAPPING.

2 in. and under	...	2/9 per lb.
2 in. to 3¼ in.	...	3/- „
3¼ in. to 6 in.	...	3/4 „

Broader Strapping to special quotations.

BEST SINGLE STRAPS.

Width	Per Foot s.	Per Foot d.	Width	Per Foot s.	Per Foot d.
1 inch	0	4½	5 inch	2	5
1¼ „	0	6	5½ „	2	8
1½ „	0	7	6 „	2	11
1¾ „	0	8	6½ „	3	3
2 „	0	9	7 „	3	6
2¼ „	0	10½	7½ „	3	9
2½ „	1	0	8 „	4	1
2¾ „	1	2	8½ „	4	5
3 „	1	3½	9 „	4	9
3¼ „	1	5	9½ „	5	1
3½ „	1	7	10 „	5	6
3¾ „	1	8½	10½ „	5	11
4 „	1	10	11 „	6	4
4¼ „	1	11½	11½ „	7	0
4½ „	2	1	12 „	7	8
4¾ „	2	3			

DOUBLE STRAPS.

Width	Per Foot s.	Per Foot d.	Width	Per Foot s.	Per Foot d.
3 inch	2	9	9 inch	9	2
3¼ „	3	0	9½ „	9	9
3½ „	3	3	10 „	10	3
3¾ „	3	5	10½ „	10	9
4 „	3	8	11 „	11	4
4¼ „	3	11	11½ „	11	11
4½ „	4	2	12 „	12	6
4¾ „	4	4	..	..	
5 „	4	7	..	..	
5½ „	5	1	..	..	
6 „	5	6	..	..	
6½ „	6	1	..	..	
7 „	6	8	..	..	
7½ „	7	4	..	..	
8 „	8	0	..	..	
8½ „	8	7	..	..	

BEST SINGLE STRAPS are made exclusively from the best parts of the backs of the primest Hides, and are recommended for heavy work, and where small pulleys are driven at high velocities. DOUBLE STRAPS are employed where extra strength is required. *Straps for Portable Engines made up endless and Waterproof.* EXTRA STRONG LACES, 1s. 3d., 2s. 6d., and 4s. per dozen.

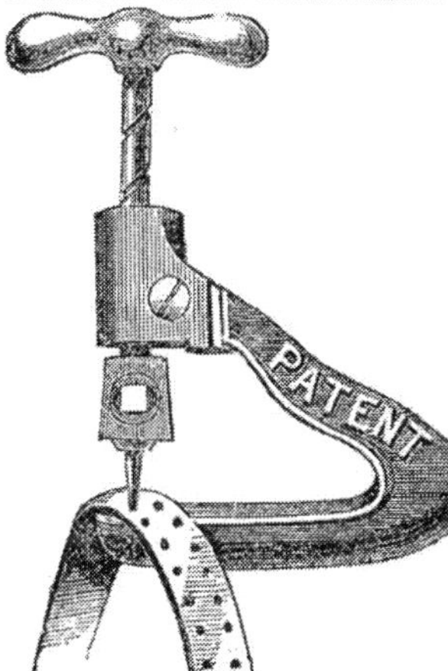

BAILEY'S SCREW STRAP PUNCHES FOR DRIVING BELTS.

SHOULD BE IN EVERY WORKS WHERE MACHINERY IS USED.

No. 1. For BELT 4 in. wide and under, with 2 Punches. Depth of Jaw to punch 2¾ inches. } **12s. 6d.**

No. 2. Large size for heavy Straps and for Saddlers, &c., with 3 Punches, largest ⅜ in. diameter. Depth of Jaw 7 inches, will do Straps 14 in wide. } **20s. 0d.**

BAILEY'S

CHEAP SMALL

HORIZONTAL ONE & TWO-HORSE ENGINES

For Brewers, Grocers, Tobacconists, &c.

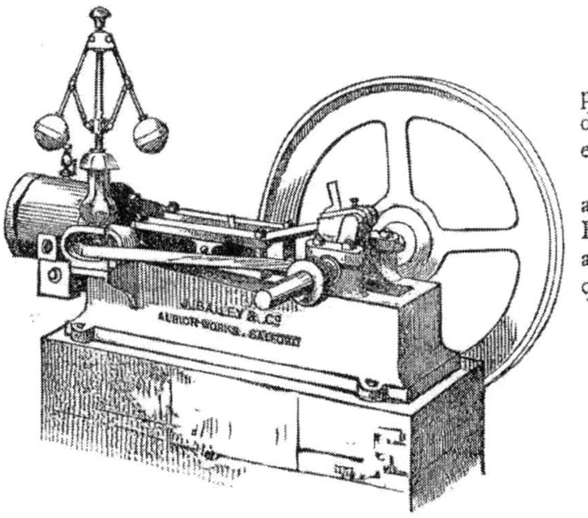

These Engines will do for Carr's Mill (see page 132), Oil Tester (see page 87), Bottle Washing Machines (see page 192), &c., and they can be driven for high speed from the fly wheel, and from a pulley on the other end for low speeds.

These are well-made horizontal engines, complete, with fly wheel, and extra length of shaft on opposite side to which a pulley can be fixed. Engineers who wish them made with their name plate on can be supplied at a price which they will find it impossible to make them at, in consequence of the quantities we make at once.

NETT CASH PRICE.

Nominal Horse power	CYLINDER		Price at Works, with Pump and Governors
	Diameter	Stroke	
2	4½	7	£20 0 0

10 o/o extra, if packed for export.

PRICE LIST OF VULCANIZED INDIA-RUBBER MECHANICAL GOODS.

All Goods Manufactured by this Company are made according to the American process, which is acknowledged to be the most perfect, as by it, Strength, Elasticity, and Durability are most permanently retained.

	PRICES PER POUND.					
	FA	A	1B	B	D	C
Vulcanized Sheet Rubber						
36in. wide, ⅛in. and upwards thick. Under ⅛in., 6d. per lb.; and 1-16th, 1s. per lb. extra.	3/9	3/6	3/0	2/5	1/10	1/4
Insertion Rubber						
1-16 in. thick, and under ⅛in. thick	4/9	4/6	4/0	3/0	2/5	2/0
Do. ⅛in. thick and upwards - -	3/9	3/6	3/0	2/5	1/10	1/4
Corrugated Rubber						
1-16 in. thick and upwards - -	3/9	3/6	3/0	2/5	1/10	
Washers						
For Flange Joints of Steam & Water Pipes, 1in. diameter and upwards	3/9	3/6	3/0	2/5	1/10	1/4
Do. Flat for Steam Gauges, under 1 in diameter - - -	6/0	5/6				
Do. Round do. do. do.	8/0					
Socket Rings						
For Pocket Joints of Water and Gas Pipes - - - - - -	3/9	3/6				
Valves						
For Marine and Land Engines, Pumps, &c., of any size up to 6ft. in diameter, the A quality is most strongly recommended as superior to all others for valves. Valves ordered in great haste, requiring to be cut out of the sheet, will be charged 9d. per lb. extra to cover the waste	3/9	3/6	3/0	2/5	1/10	
Bucket Rings						
For Hot and Cold Water Pumps -	3/9	3/6	3/0	2/5	1/10	
Buffer Rings						
For Buffer, Draw Bar, and Bearing Springs - - - - - -	3/9	3/6	3/0	2/5	1/10	
Wheel Tires (NOISELESS)						
For Carriage Trucks, &c. - -	3/9	3/6	3/0	2/5	1/10	1/4
Deckle Straps						
For Paper Manufacturers - -	5/6					
Packing Sheet						
Under 1 in. thick (Canvas & Rubber)		1/6				
Rope Packing (ROUND OR SQUARE)						
For Glands, Stuffing-Boxes, &c. ⅜in. diameter and upwards - -		1/4½				
¼in. and under - - - -		1/9				
Bevel, 3d. per lb. extra.						
Core Packing (ROUND OR SQUARE)						
⅜in. and upwards - - - - -		1/9				
¼in. and upwards - - - - -		2/0				

Canvas and Rubber Washers, cut from Sheet, - 2/6
Canvas and Rubber Washers, cut from Cylinder, - 1/6
Gas Bags, for repairing Mains, - - - - - 8/3

Vulcanized Solid India-Rubber Tubing,

For Acids, Gas, and Chemical Purposes, where little pressure is used. Sizes, internal diameter, and Prices per foot run.

INCHES -	⅛ or 3/16	¼	5/16	⅜	7/16	½	⅝	¾	⅞	1	1¼	1½	1¾	2
No. 1 quality,	0/3	0/3¾	0/5	0/5½	0/7	0/8	0/11	1/3	1/6	1/10	2/6	2/11	3/3	3/8
No. 2 "	0/2½	0/2¾	0/3¼	0/3¾	0/5	0/5½	0/7	0/11	1/1	1/6	1/9	2/0	2/6	2/10

These Prices are *for Tubing of ordinary substance*. Any thicker will be charged at 6/9 per lb. for No. 1 quality under 1 inch, and 5/9 per lb. one inch and upwards; and for No. 2 quality, 5/5 per lb. under one inch, and 4/5 per lb. one inch and over.

No extra charge for Tubing or Spiral Wire up to two inches. All orders will be executed *on Wire*, unless specified without.

TRADE PRICE LIST OF VULCANISED RUBBER HOSE PIPES,

For Railway and Steam-Packet Companies, Brewers, Distillers, Chemical Works, Fire Engines, Plumbers, Gas-Fitters, Gardening, Agricultural, and other purposes.

DELIVERY HOSE.

SIZE Internal Diam	PRICE PER FOOT						SUCTION HOSE, on Spiral Wire, extra to Prices of Delivery.
Inch	1-ply	2-ply	3-ply	4-ply	5-ply	6-ply	
¼	0/5	0/6	0/8	0/11	1/1	1/6	0/1
⅜	0/5	0/7	0/9	1/0	1/2	1/8	0/2
½	0/6	0/8	0/10	1/1	1/4	1/10	0/2
⅝	0/7	0/9	0/11	1/3	1/6	2/0	0/2
¾	0/8	0/10	1/1	1/5	1/9	2/4	0/3
⅞	0/9	0/11	1/3	1/8	1/11	2/8	0/3
1	0/11	1/1	1/5	1/10	2/2	2/11	0/3
1¼	1/1	1/3	1/7	2/1	2/6	3/4	0/4
1½	1/3	1/5½	1/10	2/4	2/10	3/8	0/4
1¾	1/5	1/8	2/0	2/7	3/1	4/0	0/5
2	1/7	1/10½	2/3	2/10	3/6	4/4	0/6
2¼	1/9	2/1	2/6	3/2	4/0	4/8	0/7
2½	1/11	2/3	2/9	3/6	4/3	5/0	0/8
2¾	2/1	2/5½	3/0	3/10	4/7	5/6	0/9
3	2/3	2/8	3/3	4/2	5/0	6/0	0/10
3¼	2/6	2/10½	3/6	4/6	5/5	6/6	0/11
3½	2/8	3/0½	3/9	4/10	5/10	7/0	1/0
3¾	2/11	3/4	4/3	5/3	6/3	7/6	1/1
4	3/2	3/8	4/7	5/7	6/8	8/0	1/2
4¼	3/6	3/11	4/11	6/0	7/1	8/6	1/3
4½	3/9	4/3	5/3	6/5	7/6	9/0	1/4
4¾	4/0	4/7	5/7	6/10	8/0	9/6	1/5
5	4/3	4/11	6/0	7/4	8/6	10/0	1/6
5¼	4/6	5/3	6/5	7/10	9/0	10/6	
5½	4/10	5/7	6/10	8/4	9/6	11/0	
5¾	5/2	6/0	7/3	8/10	10/0	11/6	
6	5/6	6/5	7/9	9/4	10/6	12/0	

Embedded Suction Hose, Per Foot.		
Inch	3-ply	4-ply
¾	2/2	2/7
⅞	2/4	2/9
1	2/6	2/11
1¼	2/10	3/2
1½	3/1	3/6
1¾	3/6	4/0
2	4/0	4/7
2¼	4/8	5/3
2½	5/2	5/10
2¾	5/9	6/6
3	6/3	7/3
3¼	6/9	7/11
3½	7/6	8/9
3¾	8/3	9/5
4	9/0	10/3

Specially Prepared Delivery and Suction Hose, for STEAM and BREWERS, 10 per cent. extra on these prices.

ANY LARGER SIZES MADE—PRICES ACCORDINGLY.

N.B.—1-inch 1-ply, 2-inch 2-ply, and 3-inch 3-ply, are nearly equal in strength, 1-inch 2-ply, 2-inch 3-ply, and 3-inch 4-ply Delivery Hose will stand a working pressure of 75 lbs.

EMBEDDED SUCTION HOSE SPECIAL PRICES.

STOCK LENGTH OF ALL HOSE, 60 FEET.

VULCANIZED SOLID INDIA-RUBBER CORD,

For Springs, Packing, &c., very Elastic.

INCHES DIAMETER, ...	⅛	3/16	¼	⅜	½	⅝	¾	⅞	1
Best Quality—Price per lb. ...	8/0	8/0	7/6	7/3	7/0	6/9	6/6	6/3	6/0

Other Sizes in proportion.

NON-CONDUCTING FELT,
(RICHARDSON'S PATENT)
FOR COVERING STEAM BOILERS, PIPES, &C.

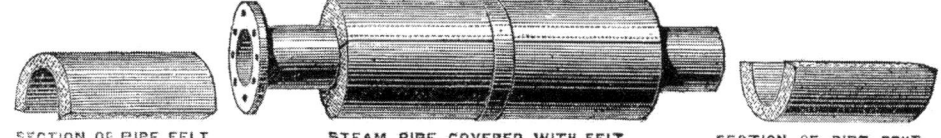

SECTION OF PIPE FELT — STEAM PIPE COVERED WITH FELT — SECTION OF PIPE FELT

SOLD BY JOHN BAILEY & CO., ALBION WORKS,
SALFORD, LANCASHIRE,
SOLE AGENTS FOR LANCASHIRE AND YORKSHIRE.

This FELT is unequalled in efficiency as a non-conductor, and in compactness, durability, and cheapness. As a covering for Steam Boilers, Pipes, Cylinders, or other heated surfaces, it is most effectual in preventing the radiation of heat therefrom. It is simply affixed to the surface by flour paste, or any other ordinary adhesive composition.

After six years' trial, we can recommend it to our friends with confidence, and subjoin a price list for your consideration. We shall also be happy to forward samples, or give any further information you may require, and hope to be favored with your orders.

TESTIMONIAL.

GENTLEMEN,
We have pleasure in stating that during the last two years we have used your Paper Felt for covering our Steam Pipes. It has given us great satisfaction, and we consider it to be the best material at present made for this purpose.

Yours obediently,

WIDNES SOAP COMPANY, WARRINGTON,
June 15, 1872.

WILLIAM GOSSAGE & SONS.

PRICES.

For Pipes not exceeding 1 inch external diameter, $1\frac{1}{2}$d per lineal foot ... $\frac{1}{2}$ inch.

1 inch	,,	$1\frac{1}{2}$,,	,,	2d	,,	... $\frac{1}{2}$,,
$1\frac{3}{4}$,,	,,	$2\frac{1}{4}$,,	,,	3d	,,	... $\frac{5}{8}$,,
$2\frac{1}{2}$,,	,,	3 ,,	,,	4d	,,	... $\frac{5}{8}$,,
$3\frac{1}{4}$,,	,,	$3\frac{3}{4}$,,	,,	5d	,,	... $\frac{5}{8}$,,
4 ,,	,,	$4\frac{1}{2}$,,	,,	6d	,,	... $\frac{3}{4}$,,
$4\frac{3}{4}$,,	,,	$5\frac{1}{2}$,,	,,	8d	,,	... $\frac{7}{8}$,,
$5\frac{3}{4}$,,	,,	$6\frac{1}{2}$,,	,,	10d	,,	... 1 ,,
$6\frac{3}{4}$,,	,,	$7\frac{1}{2}$,,	,,	1/-	,,	... 1 ,,

Boiler Felt, $\frac{1}{4}$ inch thick, $1\frac{1}{4}$d per square foot
,, $\frac{1}{2}$,, $2\frac{1}{4}$d ,,
,, $\frac{3}{4}$,, $3\frac{1}{4}$d ,,

} In Sheets 24-in. × 18-in.

For Boilers that are to be lagged, the $\frac{1}{4}$ sheets laid up to the rivet heads, and the whole covered with $\frac{3}{4}$-in. Felt, would, in most cases, be sufficient.

For High Pressure Boilers that are not to be lagged we should recommend the $\frac{1}{2}$-in. and one thickness of $\frac{3}{4}$-in. Felt.

This Cement is much cheaper and makes a better cement than red lead. The joints are also less liable to break in consequence of a toughness and elasticity which it possesses.

An order for a single cask is solicited. Those who once try it will use no other.

BAILEY'S "HOLDFAST" STEAM JOINT CEMENT

In 1 cwt. Metal Cases, 35/- complete.
In 2 cwt. do. 70/- do.
Sample in 28 lb. Case, complete, 10/6 each.

As used by some of the Chief Manufacturing, Mining, and Engineering Firms in this Country and Abroad.

This cement is supplied in powder, which only requires the addition of boiled oil to form it into a thick paste, which prepares it for use.

It is constantly used by us for our various joints in the manufacture of Valves, &c., and years of experience have enabled us to prepare it of such a quality as will form a good sound joint where many others have failed.

To prevent deterioration when kept in stock, it is prepared in air-tight cases. A trial is solicited.

NOTICE.—In consequence of the great success of this cement, many of our friends have been imposed upon by fraudulent imitations. We hereby give notice, that a reward of £20 will be given to any one giving us information that will lead to the conviction of any one infringing our trade mark.

JOHN BAILEY & CO.,
Sole Proprietors of the "Holdfast" Cement.

Unsolicited Testimonial, selected from many others:—
(From Messrs. E. P. MAPLES & CO.)

SPALDING, *Oct. 5th*, 1867.

It is the best cement of the kind we have ever used.

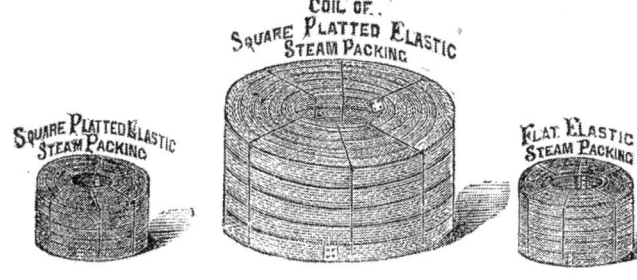

SQUARE-PLATTED
ELASTIC STEAM PACKING
FOR
Pistons, Piston Rods, D Valves, Pumps, &c.
Price 2s. 3d. per lb.

This Square-Platted Elastic Steam Packing is manufactured with a machine more than twice the dimensions of any other machine of the same kind, weighing nearly three tons—thus being able to weave a square plat any diameter from $\frac{3}{8}$ths of an inch to 3 inches at one platting, rendering the same exceedingly flexible and easier to bend round the piston rod or pump than if the sizes were obtained by platting round and through a number of cores of hemp to obtain the desired diameter, which is compulsory by any other machine.

Instructions for applying the Square-Platted Elastic Steam Packing.

All stuffing boxes that do not require the Steam Packing larger in diameter than one inch, can be lapped round the piston rod or pump in a spiral form, then pressed down into the stuffing box; but for stuffing boxes that require a larger diameter of packing it will be found necessary to cut off as much of the packing as will go once round the piston rod, and press the same to the bottom of the gland by means of a piece of wood, if too deep for the fingers; then cut as many more lengths as the stuffing box will require to fill it, placing each joint in an opposite direction. Be very careful not to screw down the cap too tight, or you take away its great flexibility and injure its lubricating properties. In many cases the fingers will be found sufficient. Should the Steam Packing in any case be a little too large for the stuffing box, flatten the same a little with a hammer or piece of wood, but by no means force the Packing into the box.

ELASTIC CORE
Red Lead Rope Packing,
FOR
STEAM JOINTS, MANHOLES, CYLINDER COVERS, &c.

By Royal  Letters Patent.

The Patentee desires to call particular attention to his Improved Lead Rope Packing, which has acquired and maintained a great celebrity amongst all the Iron Works and Manufacturers throughout the United Kingdom, and acknowledged to be the best material ever used for making steam joints, manholes, cylinder covers, and for all hydraulic purposes.

It is manufactured by a peculiar process, by means of which its properties are so concentrated that it is capable of resisting the greatest pressure of steam, hydraulic, hot or cold water. The joints made of it can be repeatedly broken, and the same ring used again, provided one side is chalked to prevent the ring being torn off. If this be done, the joint will remain good for use many times. It also enables the operator (having a wire in the centre) to bend it to any shape, and it will remain there. A manhole, 16 in diameter, made out of No. 0 Joint Packing, will not exceed 3½d., or a 5in. Ring, 1d.

Arranged in sizes—¼ in. diameter, known as No. 0
⅜ " " No. 1
½ " " No. 2
⅝ " " No. 3
¾ " " No. 4

No. 0 or No. 1 are sizes suitable for steam joints or manholes, &c., that have been faced, and No. 2 and upwards for unfaced joints or manholes, &c. Nos. 1 and 2 are the most useful sizes.

1s. 10d. per lb.
In Coils of ¼ cwt., ½ cwt., and 1 cwt each.

DIRECTIONS.—To be kept in water or a damp place.

A stock of this should be kept at all Works where Steam Power is used.

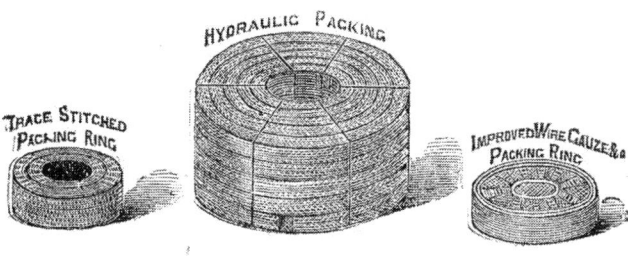

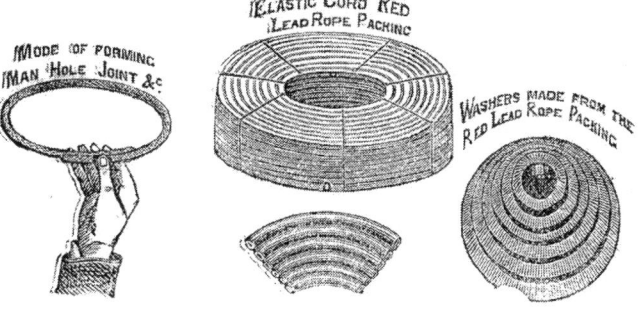

IMPROVED TRACE-STITCHED STEAM PACKING RING, FOR PISTON RODS, PUMPS, &c.

JOHN BAILEY & Co. have great pleasure in recommending this Improved Steam Packing Ring as being far superior to the Wire Gauze Packing Ring. The improvement consists in the stitching together by sewing machine four or five of the inside layers or thicknesses of webbing "similar to the stitching of a trace," by which a complete inner circle is formed, so that when applied to the piston rod it will retain its form without separating, which is the fault of the Wire Gauze Packing Rings. Price 2s. 3d. per lb.

In giving an order, the diameter of the piston rod and the outside measurement of the stuffing box are required.

WIRE GAUZE STEAM PACKING RING, FOR PISTON RODS, PUMPS, &c

Notwithstanding the great competition there is in these Rings, J. B. & Co. beg to inform their customers that they continue to manufacture these Rings from the very best material, combined with good workmanship, and repudiate the cheap article made from jute, which is sold by many makers as the best article at a reduced price. Price 2s. 3d. per lb.

HOWARTH'S PATENT VENTILATORS.

PRICES OF No. 1 VENTILATOR.

No. 1

Painted Stone Colour, made with square bottom, so as to fit outside square wooden base.

Diameter	£	s.	d.	Wood Base £	s.	d.
6-inch Diameter	1	8	0			
8 ,, ,,	1	10	0	0	10	0
9 ,, ,,	1	12	0	0	12	0
10 ,, ,,	1	17	0	0	14	0
11 ,, ,,	2	3	0	0	14	0
12 ,, ,,	2	10	0	0	14	0
14 ,, ,,	3	0	0	0	16	0
16 ,, ,,	4	0	0	0	17	0
18 ,, ,,	4	15	0	1	3	0
21 ,, ,,	5	15	0	1	5	0
24 ,, ,,	7	0	0	1	8	0
27 ,, ,,	8	5	0	1	10	0
30 ,, ,,	9	10	0	1	12	0
33 ,, ,,	10	15	0	1	14	0
36 ,, ,,	12	10	0	1	16	0
39 ,, ,,	14	5	0	2	0	0
44 ,, ,,	15	10	0	2	5	0
48 ,, ,,	18	0	0	2	10	0

Prices of No. 1 Ventilator, made ornamental, painted stone colour, and square bottom, so as to fit outside square wooden base.

Diameter	£	s.	d.	£	s.	d.
6-inch Diameter	1	10	0			
8 ,, ,,	1	15	0	0	10	0
9 ,, ,,	2	0	0	0	12	0
10 ,, ,,	2	5	0	0	14	0
11 ,, ,,	2	10	0	0	14	0
12 ,, ,,	3	0	0	0	14	0
14 ,, ,,	3	10	0	0	16	0
16 ,, ,,	4	10	0	0	17	0
18 ,, ,,	5	5	0	1	3	0
21 ,, ,,	6	5	0	1	5	0
24 ,, ,,	7	15	0	1	8	0
27 ,, ,,	9	0	0	1	10	0
30 ,, ,,	10	5	0	1	12	0
33 ,, ,,	11	15	0	1	14	0
36 ,, ,,	13	10	0	1	16	0
39 ,, ,,	15	15	0	2	0	0
44 ,, ,,	17	0	0	2	5	0
48 ,, ,,	19	10	0	2	10	0

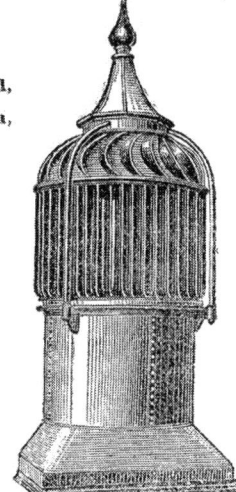

No. 1 Ventilator, Ornamental.

Prices of No. 1 Ventilator, painted stone colour, made with plain round bottom, so as to fit on round tubes.

Diameter	£	s.	d.
6-inch Diameter	1	5	0
8 ,, ,,	1	7	6
9 ,, ,,	1	10	0
10 ,, ,,	1	15	0
11 ,, ,,	2	0	0
12 ,, ,,	2	5	0
14 ,, ,,	2	15	0
16 ,, ,,	3	15	0
18 ,, ,,	4	8	0
21 ,, ,,	5	8	0

Prices of No. 1 Ventilator, made Ornamental, painted stone colour, with plain round bottom, so as to fit on round tubes.

Diameter	£	s.	d.
6-inch Diameter	1	8	0
8 ,, ,,	1	12	0
9 ,, ,,	1	15	0
10 ,, ,,	2	0	0
11 ,, ,,	2	5	0
12 ,, ,,	2	15	0
14 ,, ,,	3	5	0
16 ,, ,,	4	5	0
18 ,, ,,	5	0	0
21 ,, ,,	6	0	0

No. 1 Ventilator, to fit on Plain Round Tube.

PRICES OF No. 4 VENTILATOR
FOR CURING SMOKY CHIMNEYS.

For small Fireplaces.

	£	s.	d.
10-in. diameter—3ft. 0in. high	2	0	0
10-in. diameter—3ft. 6in. high	2	5	0
10-in. diameter—4ft. 0in. high	2	10	0

For Bedroom and Diningroom Fireplaces.
Made extra strong and durable.

	£	s.	d.
11-in.—3ft. 0in. in height	2	10	0
11-in.—3ft. 6in. in height	2	15	0
11-in.—4ft. 0in. in height	2	17	0

If made Fireproof, 7s. 6d. each extra.

For Dining-room and Small Kitchen Fireplaces.

	£	s.	d.
12-in.—3ft. 0in. in height	2	15	0
12-in.—3ft. 6in. in height	3	0	0
12-in.—4ft. 0in. in height	3	5	0

For Kitchen Fireplaces.

	£	s.	d.
14-in.—3ft. 0in. in height	2	17	0
14-in.—3ft. 6in. in height	3	0	0
14-in.—4ft. 0in. in height	3	5	0

If made Fireproof, 7s. 6d. each extra.

All the above Prices are subject to alteration according to the Price of Material, &c. Extra charge for Fixing.

No. 2 EJECTOR VENTILATOR.

No. 4 Ventilator for Chimneys.

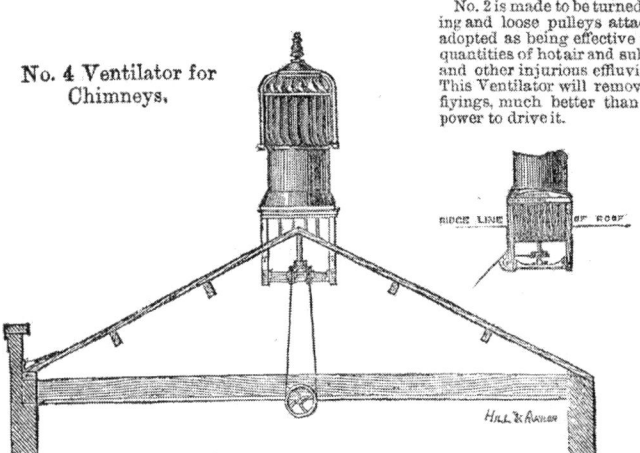

No. 2 is made to be turned by steam or other power, having driving and loose pulleys attached. This kind is most extensively adopted as being effective in expelling accumulations of large quantities of hot air and sulphurous gases, dirt and waste flyings, and other injurious effluvia from gasing and other workrooms. This Ventilator will remove hot air, dust or steam, and waste flyings, much better than a fan, and only requires 1-16th the power to drive it.

Stockport Ropery, and Croft Flax Mills.

I have very great pleasure in bearing testimony to the efficiency of your Ventilators. I have now twenty-six at work in various parts of my works, more particularly in the Card room in my Flax Mill. Before putting in your Ventilators my people suffered very much from the thick heavy dust that is present in all hemp and flax fibres; and before trying your Ventilators I tried various other methods of clearing my rooms with very little success. I am now glad to say my rooms are almost free from dust, and have great pleasure in bearing testimony to their efficiency and recommending them to others.
HENRY HANSON.

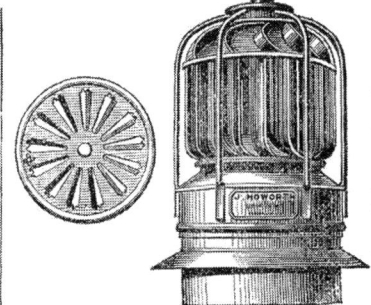

No. 5.
Railway Carriage Ventilator.

These are on the same principle as the No. 1 Ventilator, and are used for Ventilating and taking away Smoke from Railway Carriages, and are in use on several Railways in England and Ireland.

Price on application to the Works.

A shows the Ventilator as fixed outside the Carriage. **B** shows the Valve inside the Carriage, *which opens and closes* as required.

NETT PRICES OF No. 2 VENTILATORS.—(Made to turn by Steam Power, with Wood Base, Cast Iron Crossbearer, Footstep, Driving Pulley, and Guide Pulleys, complete:—
24-in. diameter, £16 10s.; 30-in. diameter, £20; 36 in. diameter, £24 10; 48 in. diameter, £35.

W. H. Bailey's Patent Adjustable Cavendish

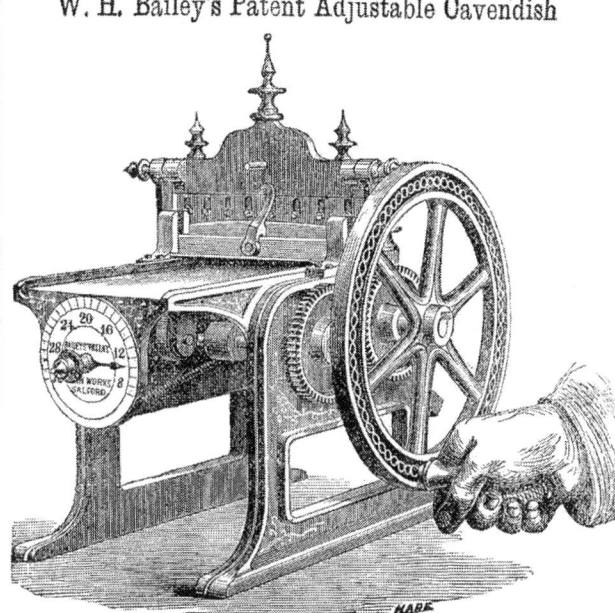

TOBACCO CUTTER with Bottom Feed,
PRICES:—
No. 1—To Cut 2 Cakes at once, 5 inches wide,... £4/10/0
" 2— " 1 " " ...£2/15/0

BAILEY'S FOUNDRY BRUSHES.

PRICES:—
Per Doz.
No. 1   39/-
" 2   32/-
" 3   35/-
" 4   48/-

No. 1.　　No. 2.　　Nos. 3 & 4.
Steel Wire Brushes for Cleaning Iron or Brass Castings when Hot.

Bailey's PATENT STOVE,
For Plumbers, Gasfitters, etc., etc.

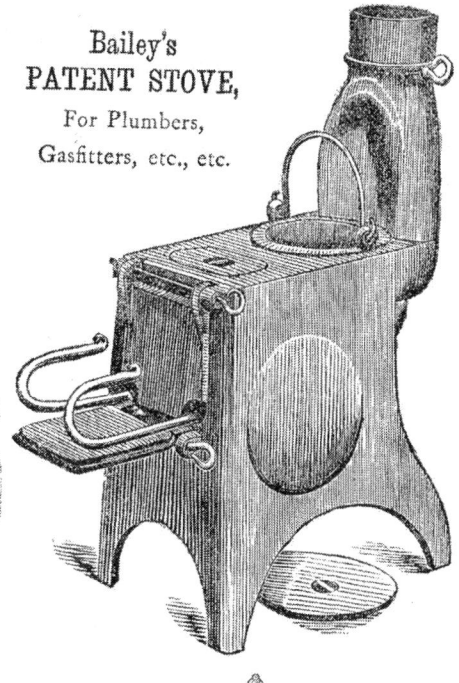

Price, 37/6

Weight of Stove—about One Hundred weight, Sixteen Pounds.

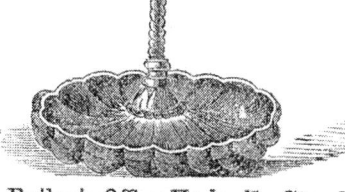

Bailey's Office Umbrella Stand,
All Brass, with Iron Cup, 25/-

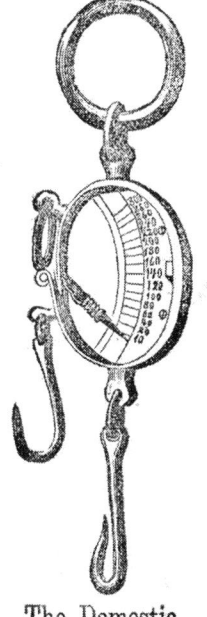

The Domestic Steelyards.
PRICES:—
200lbs., ... 5/- each.
240lbs., ... 7/- "
300lbs., ... 7/6 "
400lbs., ... 10/- "
500lbs., ... 15/- "

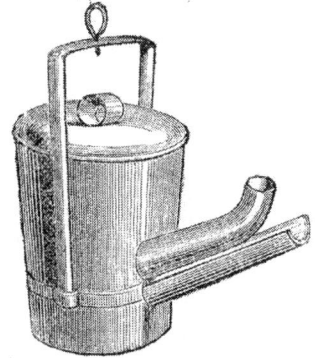

Strong Iron Miner's Oil Lamp.
Price 30/- per dozen.

Bailey's Tinman's Stove for Gas.
Will heat Two Soldering Irons in ten minutes after being lighted, and always keeps the Irons clean and hot.
Price 12/6 each.

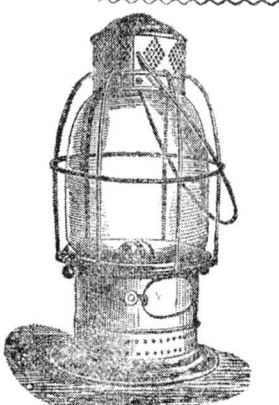

Patent Milwaukee Lantern.
For Engine Rooms, Warehouses, Railways, Stables, &c. Gives a clear and brilliant light. Price 6/6 each.

BAILEY'S Strong-Hand Power Flock Dressing Machines.
For Saddlers, Upholsterers, etc.
Price £5 each, complete.
Very useful in the Colonies.

BAILEY'S FIRE BRIGADE FITTINGS.

View from a Photograph taken in the Salford Corporation Fire Brigade Yard.

LANDING HOSE PIPE REEL,
All Wrought Iron, with Handle,
25/- each.

No. 1 Hose Reel and Tool Box on wheels, to hold 500 yards of **Woven** Linen Hose Pipe, as illustrated	...	£15 0 0
No. 2 Do. with Springs, more suitable for long distances and rough roads, for Local Fire Brigades	...	20 0 0
Fire Ladders, well painted, with Staples all to Template, interchangeable, in lengths 6 feet 6 inches long, Brigade pattern	each	0 17 6
Firemen's Helmets	...per dozen	
Firemen's Belts and Hatchet	,,	
Hatchet, with Long Handle	,,	1 1 0
Do. Short Handle	,,	0 10 6
Canvas Water Buckets	per doz.	
* Bailey's Improved Hose Cart, complete, with Two Ladders, one Lantern, well painted	...	16 10 0

This Cart is used by the Chief Town Brigades in Manchester District, and it is also recommended for Warehouses, Works, and large establishments

* This will hold the following assorted Fire Brigade articles:—200 Yards of 2½ in. Canvas Hose Pipe, 2 Stand Pipes, 1 Hand Pump, 2 Branch Pipes, 6 Canvas Buckets, 1 Large Axe, 1 Ceiling Hook and 2 Ladders outside.   Price, complete, with these Fittings, £57 10 0

PATENT FIRE ENGINE.

No. 1,—WITH 4 WHEELS AND SHAFTS.

The attention of Manufacturers, Proprietors of Extensive Works, Railway Companies, and others, is called to the above Newly-patented Fire Engine.

No. 1 represents PORTABLE FIRE ENGINE, in which is combined compactness, great power, and effective execution. It is constructed entirely of wrought-iron, brass and copper, the wheels either wood or wrought-iron, all the Hose and Apparatus being carried in the tank. It can be worked either from the tank filled by buckets, or from suctions placed in a river or reservoir, &c. It will throw about one hundred gallons of water per minute to a distance of 110 to 115 feet. The valves and works are easy of access, and it is not liable to get out of order. It can be worked by ten men, and is the cheapest and best Engine extant.

No. 1. (Fittings supplied with each Engine included in the annexed Prices.	7-inch Pumps
	£ s. d.
12 feet of Patent Vulcanized India Rubber Suction Hose, lined with wire … …	
Two pairs of gun metal Unions, and do. lapp'd on to Hose, complete … …	
One Copper Suction Rose, or Strainer	
40 yards of Patent Woven Hose (to stand 150 lbs pressure) … … …	75 0 0
Two pairs of gun metal Unions, and ditto lapp'd on to Hose, complete … …	
One Copper Delivery Pipe	
Three bell metal Jets, various sizes to suit the Engine … … …	
Two Hose and Suction Wrenches … …	
One Screw driver and Handle … … …	

IMPROVED
FIRE ESCAPE,

As used by the Royal Society for the Protection of LIFE from FIRE in LONDON, and various Provincial and Continental Towns.

This engraving represents the FIRE ESCAPE in full working order; it consists of one main ladder (3 storey) on wheels, behind which a strong copper-wire netting is fixed, lined with strong canvas (which undergoes a preparation to render it fireproof,) and down which women or children may be sent with perfect ease and safety. No. 2 ladder is fixed by levers, &c., which upon being hoisted reaches to the fourth storey. No. 3 is a loose ladder suitable for the second storey; in case of emergency another small ladder attached to the guiding lever may be attached to No. 2, and thus reach the fifth storey, the whole machine being very light and portable, four men only being required to work it. It can also be easily lowered when a railway arch or any other obstruction is in the way.

PRICE £100 0 0

BARBOUR'S AMERICAN SPREADING NOZZLE.

All are screwed to fit the ordinary hand pipes as used by London and Manchester Fire Brigades.

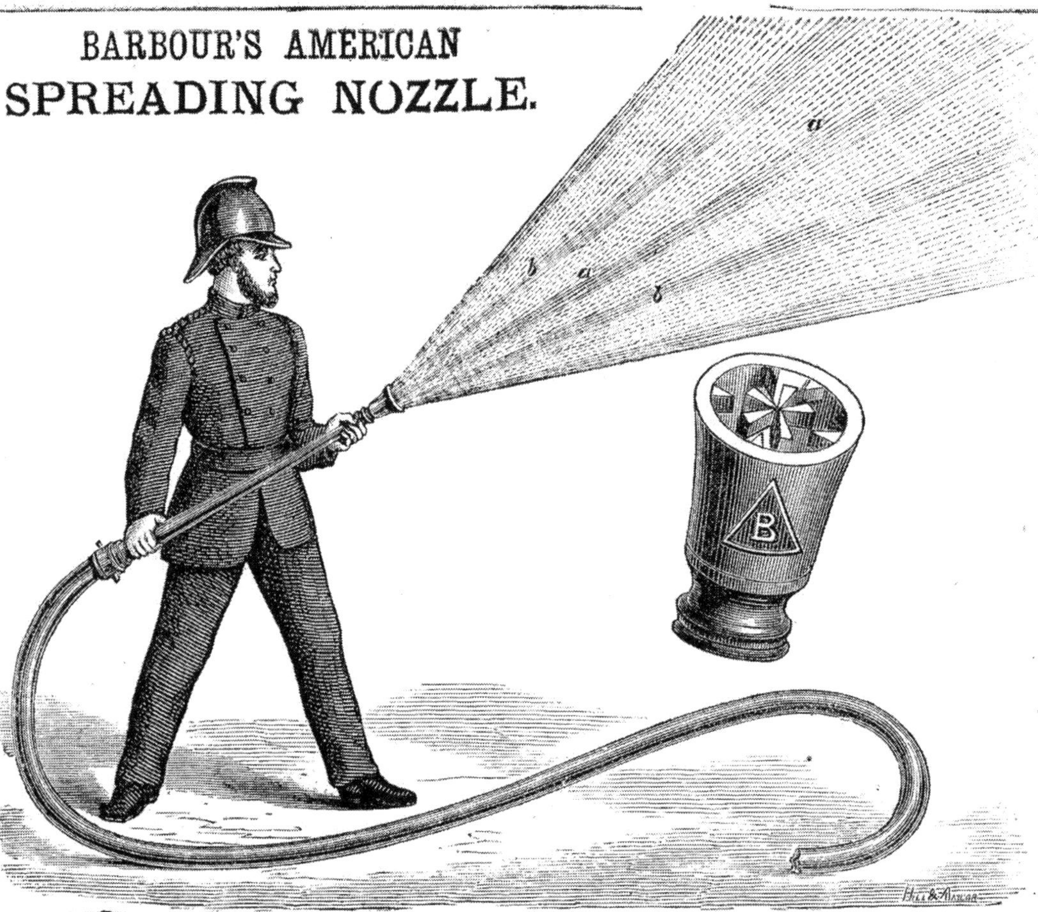

PRICE, EACH,	
Jet, ½in. bore,	£1 5 0
⅝in. bore,	£1 10 0
¾in. bore,	£1 12 0
⅞in. bore,	£2 0 0
1in. bore,	£2 5 0

The efficacy of a jet of water used either for the extinction of fires, watering flowers, or for washing the walls or windows of buildings, as frequently depends upon the character of the jet as upon the quantity of water delivered; and the arrangement of the spreading nozzle shown in the above illustration, and which is adjustable, so as to deliver either a solid stream or one more or less diffused, is doubtless one of great utility. By a turn of the wrist, a number of metal fingers (the whole or half of them) are made to enter the stream, and so change its character from a solid jet, as shown at *a a*, to a spreading one, indicated by the lines *b b*; the entire movement causing the water to be fully diffused, so as to cover from two to four hundred square yards of ground with a fine shower. Economy of water, dispersion of the smoke, and the capability of nearly approaching a fire, are among the advantages of the use of these nozzles, which are largely employed both in America and in this country, and are said to render a jet from four to eight times as effective as an ordinary one.

PERMANENT WATER PILLAR
VERSUS
PORTABLE STAND PIPES.

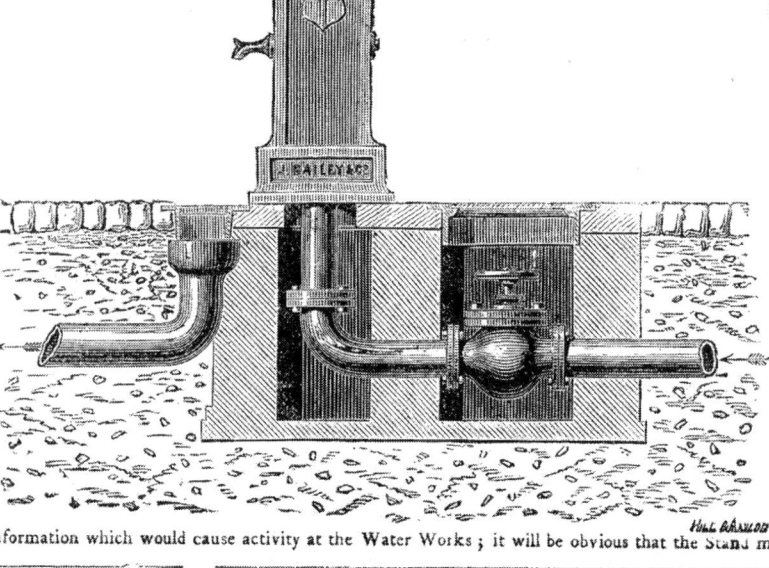

In calling attention to this Stand Pipe, J. B. & Co. wish to refer to the old and absurd Portable Copper Stand Pipes which are carried about by Firemen, and often are the causes of serious delay; cases have been known, on dark cold nights, where from 10 to 15 minutes have been lost, firstly, in finding the grid or hole, and then in coupling up. Why such a system yet exists in many large towns is unknown, as not one word of defence can be said in favor of the antique instrument so common as an appliance for extinguishing fire.

Lamp Posts, Pillar Letter Boxes and Telegraph Terminals are not found inconvenient on the curbstones of the footpath, or against walls in the streets, and why not Water Pillars? which can be instantly used either for Town Purposes or for Works, Private Residences, Railway Stations, &c.

The Water Pressure Gauge on the top is a very important addition, for the moment a fire is discovered, and the police and other telegraph is used to summon the Fire Brigade, the message states fire at:..., and the pressure at this place is only 40 feet, thus giving information which would cause activity at the Water Works; it will be obvious that the Stand may be used for Water Cart purposes, &c.

PATENT POWERFUL FIRE PUMPS.

Invented by the Chief of the Manchester Fire Brigade, and manufactured by J. BAILEY & CO., Albion Works, Salford, Lancashire.

TRIAL BETWEEN "L'EXTINCTEUR" AND THE "MANCHESTER" FIRE PUMP, AT LUCKENWALDE, near BERLIN, PRUSSIA, March 23rd, 1870.

To-day, in the presence of the undersigned, Tozer's "Manchester" Powerful Hand Pump was tried by Mr. Edward Hennings, from Berlin, and we hereby declare that the results of the same were not only completely satisfactory to us, but far surpassed our expectations of this little apparatus. The transport of the same to the scene of the fire, wherever it may be, is easy and ready, so that by means of this Engine the fire is immediately to be got at, and as the filling of the engine needs no other manipulation than pouring water in, comparatively greater results are obtainable from the same.

It is specially to be observed that the working of this Engine by one person throws the water nearly sixty feet.

We consider this Engine the most useful which householders, and especially proprietors of manufacturing establishments, can procure.

At the same time, an "Extincteur" was practically tried by a gentleman present. This rival trial showed that the "Manchester" Engine operated far more effectually, and its precision came out strongly superior.

C. W. FAHNDRICH, F. G. EMISCH, H. GEBHARDT, L. F. TIETZ, FERD. KREUTER, H. BOLTZE, J. KNOCHENHAUER, F. W. BOCK, LUDWIG OTTO, Town Councillors, present at the above trial.

I certify, moreover, that the "Extincteur" after its first complying, was refilled with tartaric acid from the laboratory. Only after exactly twenty minutes—not less—was the necessary pressure produced, notwithstanding repeated shakings of the apparatus to produce the same.

E. HENNINGS.

Testimonial from Mr. SCABELL, Fire Brigade Director & Privy Councillor, Berlin, March, 26th, 1870.

At the trial the "Manchester" Hand Fire Pump threw in one minute, with sixty strokes of the handle, one cubic foot of water, and sent the same fifty feet horizontally, and forty feet perpendicularly.

This trial amply testifies that the before-mentioned Hand Fire Pump recommends itself as a portable, easily-worked, fire extinguishing apparatus, in every respect answering the end for which it is intended: for the preservation of property in places which are at a distance from public fire brigades, and for the owners of manufactories, etc., etc.

L. S. SCABELL, Fire Brigade Director.

PROPERTY SAVED ESTIMATED AT £50,000 VALUE.

Duke Street, Broughton, April 18th, 1867.

Messrs. J. BAILEY & Co.

GENTLEMEN,—In answer to yours of this date, I have great pleasure in expressing my unqualified satisfaction with Tozer's Patent Hand Pumps. They have on many occasions more than equalled my most sanguine expectations; and although I might give you numerous instances of the great service they have been in preventing the spread of fire, I think that one good example will suffice. *At the great fire in the London and North Western Railway Co.'s Warehouses, in May last, they were principally the means of saving No. 3 Warehouse.* A number of the Pumps were taken into places where it was utterly impossible to carry the jets, and by this aid the fire was extinguished inside the building, and comparatively little damage done by water. In many cases of smaller fires, the Hand Pumps have been used solely in extinction.

I remain, Gentlemen,
Your obedient Servant,

ROBT. A. DREW.
Captain Broughton Volunteer Fire Brigade.

Hathersage Works, near Sheffield,
April 15th, 1867.

DEAR SIRS,—The Hand Pumps we have had now some time in use we consider as extremely serviceable for fire, and other appliances for which we have used it. Being so easy of carriage, *it has been of service in extinguishing two fires* which have been very serious.

Yours truly,
ROBT. COOKS & Co.

THREE FIRES EXTINGUISHED IN A COTTON MILL

Hollingworth, near Rakewood Mills, Littleborough.
April 27th, 1867.

Messrs. J. BAILEY & Co.

GENTLEMEN,—In reply to yours of the 26th inst., we have great pleasure in giving our testimony in favour of TOZER'S Hand Pump. *It has been the means of extinguishing three fires that would in all probability have destroyed the Mills but for having one.*—Yours respectfully,

THOS. & WM. HALLIWELL.

THE NEW PORTABLE FIRE ENGINE — J. BAILEY & Co., ALBION WORKS, SALFORD — PATENT POWERFUL UMP FIRE 5.5.0 COMPLETE READY FOR USE

MANCHESTER HAND PUMP, with 20ft. of best woven hose, union joints, rose, jet, and strong galvanised iron cistern painted, to hold 7 gallons. ... £5 5s. complete.

PADDINGTON FIRE PUMP, on wheels, strong galvanised iron cistern painted, 2ft. 6in. long, 1ft. 6in. wide, 1ft. 6in. deep, to hold 28 gallons (see p. 67). £7 10s. "

One Month's Trial allowed before Purchase.

The "Manchester,"
PRICE, £5 5 0

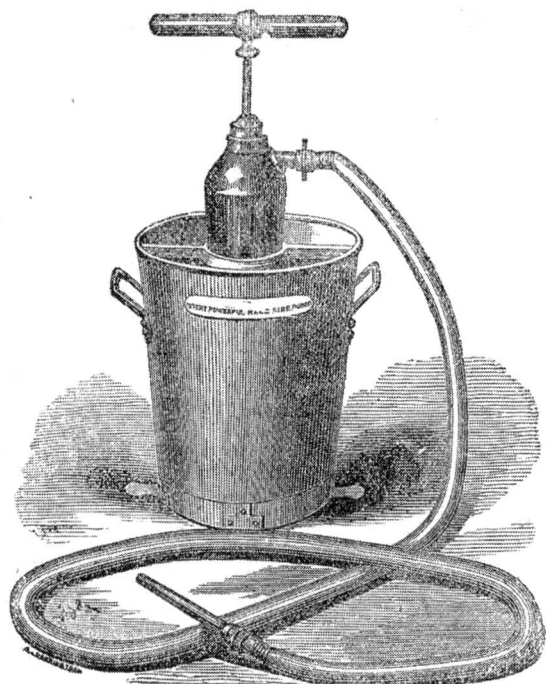

Since J. BAILEY and Co., introduced these cheap and strong popular little Engines, the trade mark has often been infringed. Please note that J. Bailey and Co. are the Sole Makers.

The "Paddington,"
PRICE, £7 10 0

PATENT POWERFUL PUMPS,
(For Prices, etc., see page   )

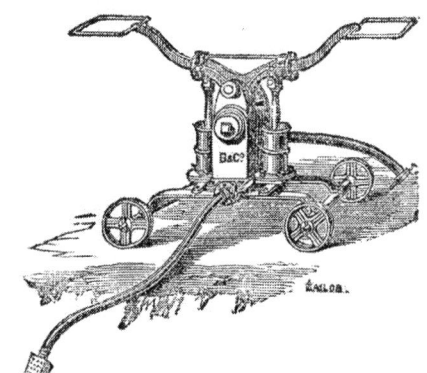

BAILEY'S FACTORY, FARM, SHIP OR WAREHOUSE FIRE ENGINES.

Bailey's Double-Barrel Fire Engines.

The chief features of this Pump are—simplicity of construction, immense strength, and the ease by which the valves are cleaned. It will deliver 70 feet.

PRICES, WITH GUN METAL BARRELS.

A	3½-in. diameter	£17 10 0
B	4-in. "	£25 0 0
C	5-in. "	£30 0 0

Extra for A and B :—10 feet of 2-inch Suction Hose, with Rose (best wired rubber), and 20 feet best Delivery Hose (flax), with Connexions, Jet, and Branch Pipe, £6 10s.

Extra for C :—10 feet 2½-inch Suction Hose, and 20 feet of Best Woven Linen Fire Brigade Delivery, with Tozer's Patent Unions and Jet, £8 10s.

30-feet lengths of 2½-inch Best Woven Hose Pipe for delivery, with Unions to fit Unions of Pump C, screwed London pitch, and Manchester Fire Brigade Pattern, £3 3s.

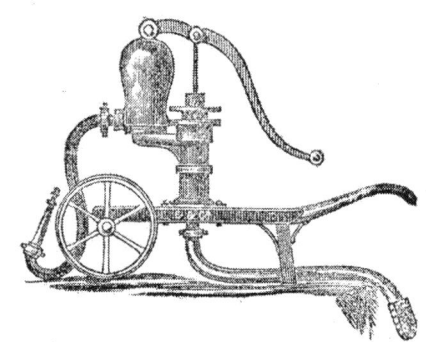

BAILEY'S SINGLE-BARREL HAND FIRE ENGINE.

Diameter of Ram, 3 inches,

Price £10 0 0.

Suction and Delivery Hose extra.

THE MANCHESTER "EXPRESS" HAND FIRE ENGINE.

TRADE MARK "EXPRESS."

J. BAILEY & Co. Sole Proprietors & Makers.

TOTAL WEIGHT, 56 Lbs.

This modification of our Patent Powerful Hand Fire Pump has been designed specially for Manufactories, Railway Stations, and for Colonial use, to meet a want felt for one to draw its own water; and also to be very light and strong, as well to enable it to be quickly transported.

The Discharge Pipe is the best Fire Brigade linen hose, and all the fittings are made after the same pattern.

C Price, with 10 feet of Hose and Discharge Pipe, and 5 feet of Suction and Grid,... £6 6 0

D If with 20 feet of Discharge, and 2 pair Unions, ... 6 12 0

E 40 feet and 4 pair Unions, 7 2 0

P.S.—If it will be wanted for garden purposes at any time, we will include a small rose, without extra charge.

SPECIAL NOTICE.—The air chamber is copper, and everything can be taken in pieces, examined, and cleaned. This is important for exporters.

THE MANCHESTER PORTABLE DOUBLE-BARREL HAND FIRE PUMPS,

With 29 feet of best wove hose, complete,

F Price £8 10s.

This is designed to be carried empty to remote places in large buildings, where is is difficult to wheel large Pumps; water is poured in from buckets, and either one or two men can work it, as each Pump is light, portable, powerful, and durable, entirely independent of the other, although, of course, two men working it will send a greater body of water.

IMPROVED HOSE REEL

Is made principally of Wrought Iron, and is nicely Japanned.

It is useful for keeping and moving flexible Hose or Water Pipe, from place to place, either in Gardens, Roads or Lawns.

PRICE.

No. 1.............22/6
 ,, 2.............31/6
 ,, 3.............42/-

IMPROVED SWING WATER BARROWS,

With Galvanized Iron Cistern, and Malleable Iron Frames.

The framing of this Barrow is so arranged that it requires no axletree; this brings the cistern several inches nearer the ground, which considerably lessens the labour in using. The cistern being oval, renders the Barrow more complete; it will pass through narrower doorways than those of the usual form.

To hold 18 Gallons, 40s.   To hold 30 Gallons, 50s.

Extra Cistern, for 18 Gallons, 15/6 extra. Do. for 30 Gallons, 21/- extra.

Bailey's Fire Brigade Fittings,

FOR THE

STAIRCASE OF A WAREHOUSE, COTTON MILL, PUBLIC BUILDING, &c.

As supplied to the Winter Gardens and Aquarium, Southport, and several other Public Companies.

"A PLACE FOR EVERYTHING, AND EVERYTHING IN ITS PLACE."

The great fire at Over, in Cheshire, caused a loss of many thousands of pounds, and ten lives; and the old saying was never more forcibly understood when the evidence was given before the Coroner, October 30th, 1874:—

William Bullock, Spinner, said—I immediately ran to the bell and rang an alarm. *They used to have buckets at each mule, but they could not find them when the fire was discovered.*

By Mr. Haigh, jun.—There were two dozen buckets bought some time ago, and each spinner had one at the end of his mule; but they were borrowed by other people, and became "anybody's buckets," and on Tuesday none could be found. Whether this was owing to the smoke or not he could not say.

Mr. Haigh said there were six or eight dozen buckets in the place altogether

It will be seen, that although the firm had taken every human precaution to prevent fire spreading, that one of perhaps the finest Cotton Mills ever erected was destroyed in consequence of the buckets not being at hand when required.

ESTIMATE FOR ONE LANDING, not including Woodwork.

	£	s.	d.
One 2½ inch Valve, with Brass Cap and Chain	1	18	0
One Copper Hand Pipe, 2 feet long, complete, with Jet	1	7	6
One Key	0	1	6
One 40 feet length of 2½ inch Fire Brigade Hose of Woven Linen, fitted with a pair of Tozer's Fire Brigade Pattern Swivel Unions	3	0	0
Eight Galvanized, Strong Riveted, Iron Fire Buckets, with the word "Fire" painted on the front @ 2/6	1	0	0
One Tozer's Patent Manchester Pattern Fire Pump, with 20 feet of India Rubber Hose	5	5	0
	£12	12	0

HAVING often been requested to state the best set of Fittings for this purpose, our experience of what has been found of actual value has caused us to introduce the Fittings as illustrated, and which may be supplied, as per estimate, complete or singly. The value of the articles in case of fire will be apparent to the most superficial.

    1st. The Manchester Fire Pump, with its small hose pipe, if brought to bear upon a small fire, has in vast numbers of cases been known to extinguish them long before the large hose could be got to work.

    2. The buckets can be filled immediately, or kept filled, and, being always ready, also be the means of extinction before the large fittings could be got to work. Anyone removing a bucket from its place should be instantly discharged.

    3. In valuing the above observations, it is of importance to consider that all fires are small at the commencement.

    4. The 40 feet length of 2½ inch hose pipe can be attached to the valve, and the unions being Fire Brigade pitch and pattern, can be coupled to any which may be brought to assist.

    5. The small cock under the valve can be used for filling buckets at the same time as it supplies water to the large pipe.

    6. The instructions, which should be plain, will, of course, vary with the circumstances.

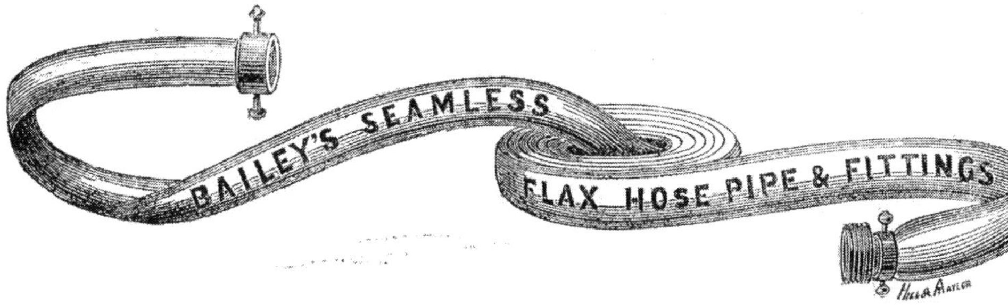

TOZER'S PATENT SWIVEL UNION.

Invented by Mr. Tozer, Chief Superintendent of the Manchester Fire Brigade, and used by the chief Fire Brigades in the United Kingdom.

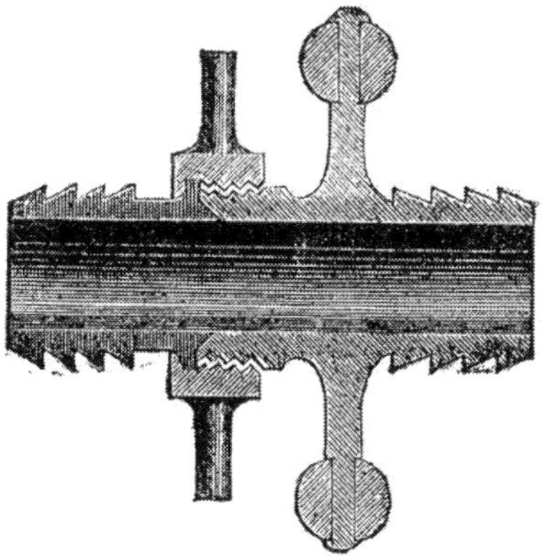

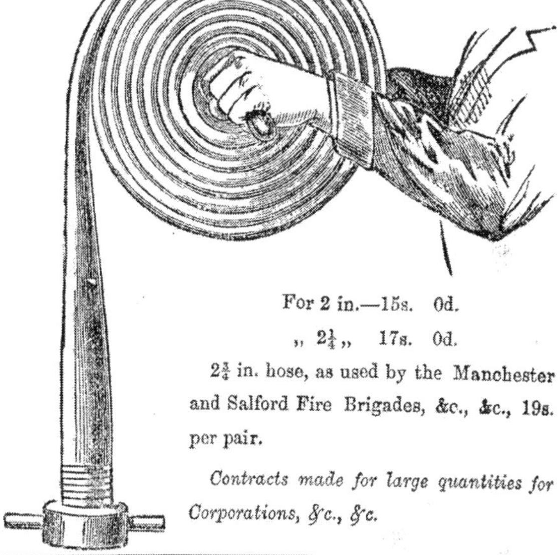

The simple improvement here illustrated, consists of the swivels which enables the coil of hose pipe to be brought into use with greater speed, in the most effectual manner. All that is required to be done when the hose is wanted, is to hold the coil by means of the union in the centre, the weight of the other end causes the hose to rotate rapidly.

For 2 in.—15s. 0d.
„ 2¼ „ 17s. 0d.
2¾ in. hose, as used by the Manchester and Salford Fire Brigades, &c., &c., 19s. per pair.

Contracts made for large quantities for Corporations, &c., &c.

PATENT SEAMLESS FLAX HOSE PIPE.

No. 1—Super quality, hand wove, very strong, for Fire Brigades, or any other purpose requiring great strength and resistance to the escape of water, warranted equal to VOUCHER'S, and on delivery, not to burst under a pressure of 300lbs. to the square inch.

Size	1 in.	1¼	1½	1¾	2	2¼	2½	2¾	3	Made up to 10 inches
Price per yard	s. d. 1 6	s. d. 1 9	s. d. 2 0	s. d. 2 3	s. d. 2 6	s. d. 2 9	s. d. 3 0	s. d. 3 3	s. d. 3 6	

No. 2—Fine quality, machine wove, from very fine Line Flax Yarn, warranted a good substantial Hose, and on delivery, not to burst with a pressure of 250 lbs. to the square inch; extensively consumed both at home and abroad.

Size	½ in.	¾	1	1¼	1½	1¾	2	2¼	2½	2¾	3
Price per yard	s. d. 0 10	s. d. 0 11	s. d. 1 0	s. d. 1 3	s. d. 1 6	s. d. 1 9	s. d. 2 0	s. d. 2 3	s. d. 2 6	s. d. 2 9	s. d. 3 0

The various qualities of Hose may be had Lined with India-rubber and cloth, at the following prices:—Up to 2½ in., 6d.; 2¾ to 4 in. 9d; 4¼ in., 9d.; 4½ in. 1s.; 6¼ in. to 7 in., 1s. 6d.; 7¾ in. to 10 in., 2s. per yard nett extra. Shrinking in the process not allowed for.

Best Copper-riveted Leather Hose

{ Made from 25 to 40 feet, in one length, riveted only on one side. As portable as canvas, and will bear unusual pressure.

1 1¼ 1½ 1¾ 2 2¼ 2½ 2¾ 3 3½ 4 inch inside diameter.

Prices on application.

No. 54D.—Leather Fire Buckets.

Leather Fire Bucket, large, best quality, painted outside and inside, each
„ „ smaller, best quality
} Prices on application.

BAILEY'S Best Irish Flax Hose Pipe.

1	1¼	1½	1¾	2	2¼	2½	2¾	3	inches.
1/9	2/-	2/3	2/6	2/9	3/-	3/3	3/6	3/9	per yard.

J. BAILEY & CO. having devoted a great amount of attention to the manufacture of a special high class quality of Fire Engine Hose Pipe, have made arrangements which enables them to supply carefully-selected Flax Piping of the very best manufacture, in fact if a higher price were paid, a superior manufacture could not be obtained.

As is usually the case when a reputation has been earned, endeavours are made by improper people to supply an inferior article at higher prices, and pirate an ancient name. To prevent doubt or fraud, J. B. & Co. have found it necessary to stamp every 20-foot length with a Shamrock as engraved.

Foreign buyers who order through merchants and agents should insist on this BRAND when ordering, if they desire a high quality.

STAND PIPES.

B. 1. Single ends, 53/- each.
Double do. 65/- do.

B. 2. Single ends, 46/- each.
Double do. 55/- do.

Square Street Case for Hydrants, 9/- each
Round Street Case for Sluice Valve
Spindle, 8/- each.

A. Hydrant with Brass Valve, 18/- each.
With Face of Brass for Stand Pipe, 20/- each.

B. Ball Hydrants, 84/- per dozen.
With Brass Facings, for Stand Pipe, 108/- per dozen.

No. 1003.
SLUICE Landey Valve.
£ s. d.
Bore, 2 in., 2 10 0
" 2½ " 3 7 6
" 3 " 4 0 0

No. 1004
GUN METAL LANDEY VALVE,
With Cap for wrought iron Pipe.
£ s. d.
Bore, 1 in., 1 0 0
" 1½ " 1 7 6
" 2 " 2 5 0
" 2½ " 3 3 0
" 3 " 4 5 0

No. 1005.
Screwed for Iron Pipe.
£ s. d.
Bore, 1 in. 0 16 0
" 1½ " 1 3 0
" 2 " 1 17 6
" 2½ " 2 18 0
" 3 " 3 17 0

⁎ It is important to note that the London Manchester, and other chief towns all use 2½-in. Hose Pipes in their Fire Brigades.

No. 2001.
BAILEY'S LANDEY VALVE,
With Bucket-Cock in iron, with gun metal Fittings and Cap and Chain, and Cock for Bucket.

Bore, 2 in. . . 38s.
" 2½ " . . 45s.
" 3 " . . 55s.

No. 1002.
GUN METAL LANDEY COCK
£ s. d.
Bore, 1½ in. . . 1 2 6
" 2 " . . 2 2 0
" 2½ " . . 3 0 0
" 3 " . . 3 15 0

BAILEY'S
Steam Fire Extinguishing Apparatus.

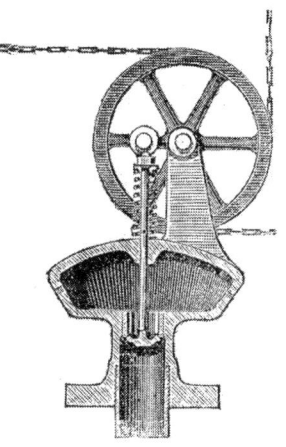

With Flange, and Screwed for Pipes of two inches bore. May be fixed in any position. Price each, with Pulley ready for fixing, 50/-, and in dozens, £24 per doz.

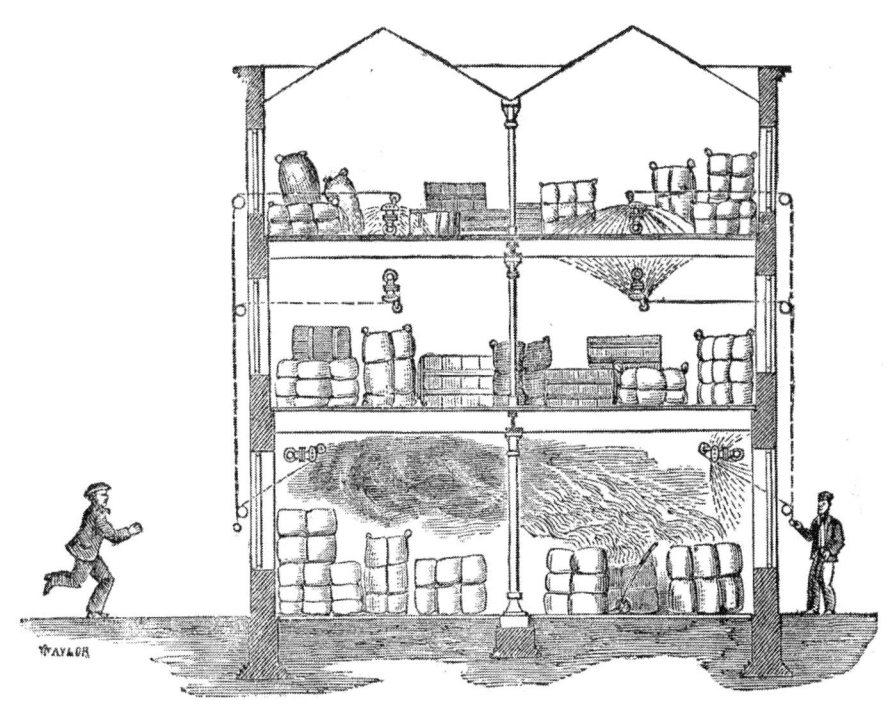

The use of Steam for extinguishing Fire has been well known for some time to be very effective. It is often used on board Steam Ships, and in Cotton and other Mills with success. It will be obvious that the Steam does not put the Fire out because of the water in it; but because the space it occupies in a room excludes the oxygen of the atmosphere, which is requisite to support combustion, the result being the Fire goes out, because it cannot burn, there not being sufficient air for the purpose. The Valves are so arranged that, with ordinary ingenuity, any mill mechanic could fix them, and if need be, where Steam is required for warming, they may be fixed on the same Pipes. The Ropes or Chains may be fixed at the outside of the mill, or in the house of the watchman, at any convenient distance. There is no occasion for the Steam to be always on, as one Stop Valve near the Boiler can be used to fill the Pipes, and afterwards the Special "Pull" used to extinguish the Fire.

There is no mystery about this invention. It is simple, cheap, and effective, and can at once be put to work by the most ignorant watchman.

HALL'S
Fire Escape for Works.

Proprietors of Mills and places employing a great number of people will do well to provide easy means of Escape for the workpeople, by means of

Hall's Wrought-Iron Ladders,

Which have been fixed to some of the most important Cotton Mills in Lancashire. Mr. HALL is the Captain of the Salford Corporation Fire Brigade, and his experience in that capacity has caused him to direct special attention to this subject.

Prices sent on description of Building.

BAILEY'S STEAM JET PUMPS FOR WELLS, BILGE WATER, &c.

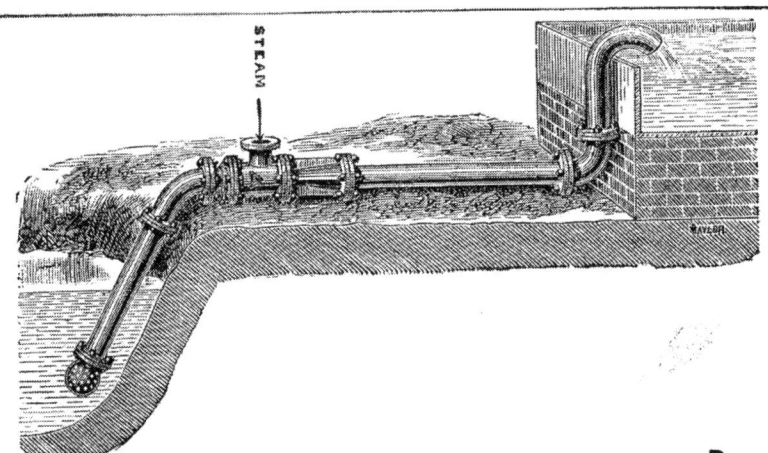

FOR FILLING TANKS, CISTERNS, &c.

In this case, a Portable Engine may be brought and coupled up when only for occasional use.

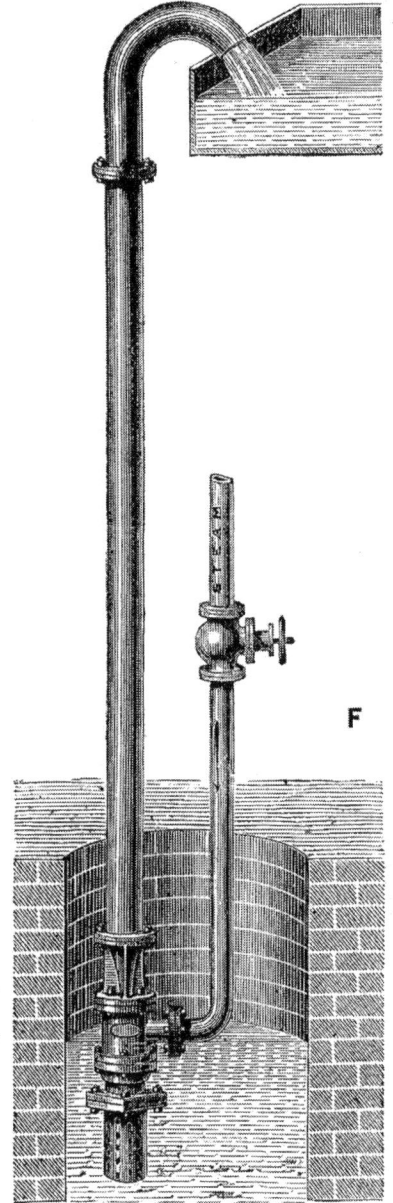

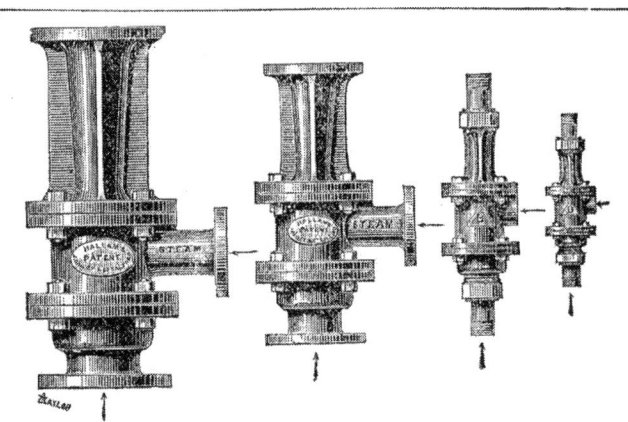

See Special Circulars.

HALLAM'S PATENT STEAM JET PUMPS, or EJECTORS,

FOR LIFTING WATER FROM WELLS, STEAM SHIPS, YACHTS, TANKS, RIVERS, RESERVOIRS, &c.
REDUCED PRICE LIST.—In Cast Iron, with Gun-metal Fittings.

Which please quote in ordering.

No.	5.	4.	3.	2.	1.	0.	0A.
Bore of Water Delivery Pipe	Inches. 3	Inches 2	Inch. 1½	Inch. 1	Inch. ¾	Inch. ½	Inch. ½
Bore of Steam Pipe	1½	1¼	1	¾	½	⅜	¼
Delivery in Gallons per Hour, at 50lbs. pres.	5,000	2,500	1,500	800	500	200	100
Price	£12 10 0	£10 0 0	£7 10 0	£4 10 0	£3 3 0	£2 2 0	£1 10 0

For further details see BAILEY's Supplementary List of Boiler-Fittings, Injectors, Jet Pumps, Pyrometers, Water-heaters, and other useful goods for Engineers. Post free.

These Ejectors will lift Water equal to any ordinary lift pumps, and will discharge it to any height according to the pressure of the steam used. Dirty water does not injure them. They are much in use, and are found valuable for Brewers and others who may lift and warm the water at the same time; also for bilge water in Yachts and larger Steamboats; for Dry Docks, Tanks, Gas Works, Agricultural operations, Drainage and Sewage Works, Dyers, Mining operations, Railway Tanks (to enable the locomotive to raise water to the tank for feeding the boilers), and many other purposes which will be apparent to those engaged in Engineering operations.

For further particulars, ask for Special Circulars of Injectors and Ejectors.

(*Instructions for fixing and working on application.*)

BAILEY'S BRASS LIFT & FORCE PUMPS, ENGINE FRAMES, &c.

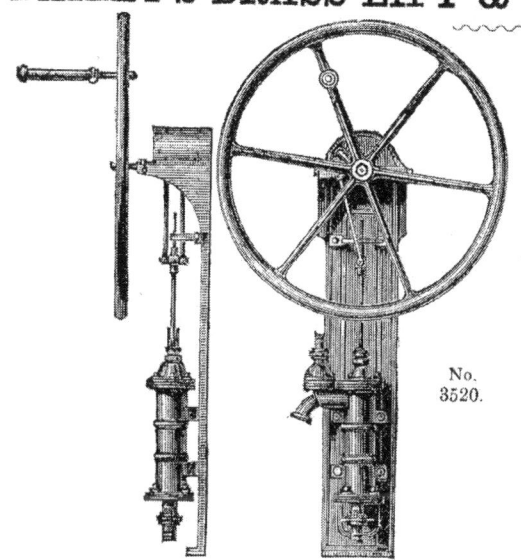

BAILEY'S STRONG BRASS LIFT AND FORCE PUMPS.

On Iron Standard, Wrought-Iron Crank, with Fly Wheel, without Unions, Cock as shown, extra where required.
Bore, 3 in., £9 18s.   3½ in., £11.   4 in., £12 5s.

No. 351.—Strong Lift and Force Pump, with wrought-iron Handle, each:—

1½ in. Brass,	£3 10 0	3 in. Brass,	£6 0 0	4 in. Brass,	£8 0 0
2 ,, ,,	3 15 0	3½ ,, ,,	7 0 0	5 ,, ,,	16 0 0
2½ ,, ,,	5 0 0	If with Iron Pumps, one-third less in price above 2in.				

No. 352.—Strong Brass Lift and Force Pumps, on Iron Standard, Wrought Iron Crank, with Fly Wheel, without Unions,

3	3½	4in.
£8 15 0	£9 12 6	£11 10 0

This improvement upon the ordinary Force Pump on Plank has the advantage of the Rotary motion and Fly Wheel, *which greatly decreases the labor*.

No. 353.—Strong Iron Frame, with Wrought Crank, Connecting Rods, and Fly Wheels for two Barrels ... ... each £23 5 0
  ,,   ,,   ,,   three ,, ... ,, 30 10 0
If Cast Iron instead of Wrought Crank, for two Barrels less ,, 2 0 0
No. 354.—Iron Frame, to work one Barrel with Fly Wheel, each £10 0 0
  ,,   ,,   ,, two   ,,   ,, ,, 12 12 6
,, 355. ,,   ,, one, lighter pattern ,, 9 0 0
,, 356. ,, Single Barrel Brass Pump 3   3½   4in.
  £15 0 0   £16 0 0   £17 7 6

,, 357.—Iron Frame, with Multiplying Power, Single Crank, 14 15 0
  ,,   ,,   ,,   ,, Double Wrought Crank, 16 16 0
,, 358.—Engine Frame for Double Pumps, for Steam Power.
,, 359.—Treble Gun Metal 3in. Pumps, with or without Valve Doors, on Iron Frames, for Steam Power, with Fast and Loose Pullies, for raising hot liquor or water.

Tinned Copper Pipe, or Iron Flange Pipe, Air Vessels and other Brewers' Fittings made to order.

EDWARDS'S PATENT FRICTIONLESS LIFT AND FORCE PUMPS.

No. 1   No. 2   No. 3   No. 1 F on Plank.   No. 1 F   No. 351

These PUMPS, the cheapest and most durable in the market, raise water, or other fluid, either hot or cold, from the usual depth; the handles can be set to any required angle to the spout, and no skill whatever is required, either in fixing or taking them to pieces, to replace any of the parts. They are admirably adapted for domestic purposes, and for liquid manure, bilge water, and for solutions in tan pits, breweries, clay mines, &c.; they may be had galvanized and in malleable cast iron—more durable than brass—at less than half the cost, and their principle of construction is such, that however much they may be battered, or put out of shape, they will continue to work freely, making them invaluable on shipboard, &c.

Force Pumps (No. 1 F) are made upon the same principle, to raise and force water to a height of Thirty or Forty feet from the level of supply.

In hot climates these Pumps are far more durable than those fitted with leather.

All the Pumps are prepared for receiving either Hose, Lead, or Gas Pipe Suction, and Rising Main, as may be ordered.

PRICES IN CAST-IRON, WITH MALLEABLE CAST-IRON HANDLES.

PUMP No. 1, equal to a 2½ inch Barrel Pump,	...	...	...	17/6	PUMP No. 1 F	...	...	...	...	...	25/-
,, ,, 2 ,, 3 ,, ,,	...	...	...	25/-	,, ,, 1 F, with plank	...	...	...	...	35/-
,, ,, 3 ,, 4 ,, ,,	...	...	...	35/-						

BAILEY'S IMPROVED LIFT AND FORCE PUMPS, FOR SHALLOW OR DEEP WATER.

Fitted with Patent Metallic Buckets and Conical Oscillating Valves. Will Pump either Hot or Cold Liquid.

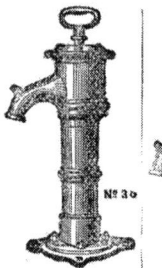

No. 30.—2½ in. Pump, 16 in. high, fitted with Rod and bow handle, bored and tapped to suit 1¼ in. wrought-iron tube, price 15s. 0d.

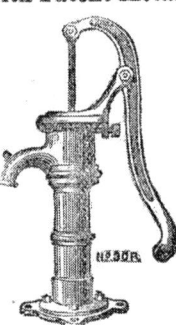

No. 30 R.—2½ in. Pump, 16 in. high, for 1¼ in. iron tube, price 18s.

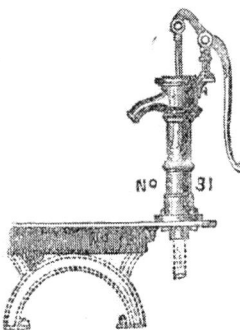

No. 31.—2½ in. Universal Pump, 21in. high, 13in. under spout, fitted with reversible cap and handle, bored and and tapped for 1¼in. iron tube, price £1 4s.

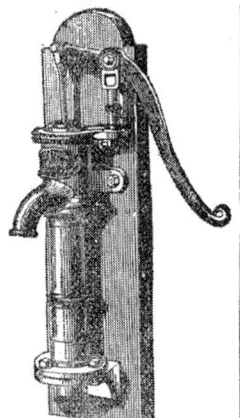

No. 31BP.—2½ in. Pump, same as No. 31, with brackets and lugs, bolted to strong wood plank, price £1 13s.

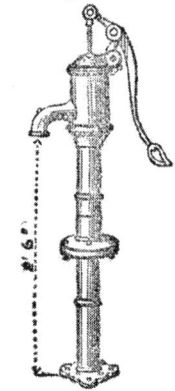

No. 33XX.—2½in. Pump, 40in. high, 30 in. under spout, fitted with reversible handle, and standard pipe for either 1½ in. flanged pipe or iron tube, price £1 13s.

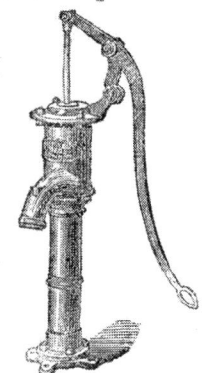

No. 33R.—2½in. Pump, 24 in. high, 13in. under spout, with reversible cap and handle, bracket and lugs for bolting to a wall, plank, or cart, to suit 1½ in. iron tube, price £1 13s.

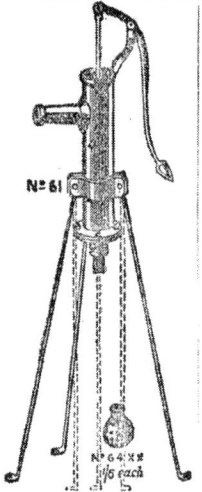

No. 61.—4½in. strong galvanized iron Pump, for Liquid Manure, fitted with wrought-iron tripod, portable legs and connecting piece, to suit 2in. suction hose or iron tube, price £3 3s.

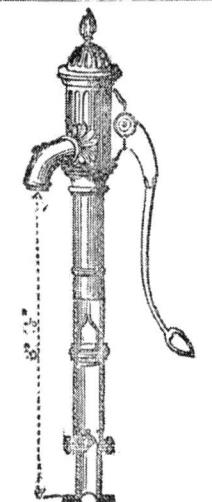

No. 41.—Improved Pump, with fluted pattern head and cap, 3 ft. high under spout, fitted with tail-piece, &c., to suit flanged pipe, price:

Bore	£ s. d.	Bore	£ s. d.
2½in.	2 3 0	3½in.	2 14 0
3in.	2 10 6	4in.	3 0 0

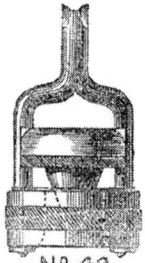

No. 42.

Patent Brass Buckets, with oscillating conical valve enlarged view, extra charge for above on Pump or Barrel.

2½in.	5/- each
3 "	7/- "
3½ "	9/- "
4 "	10/6 "
4½ "	12/- "

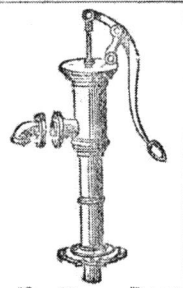

No. 33 F.—Patent Lift and Force Pump, 2½ in., fitted with flanged base-plate, to suit 1½ in. iron tube for suction and rising main, 24in. high, 14in. under branch, price £2 10s.6d.

No. 33VV.—2½ in., fitted with Patent elbow air-vessel, and retaining valve, to suit 1½in. iron tube for suction and rising main, 24in. high, 14 in. under elbow (as 58VV), price £3 12s.

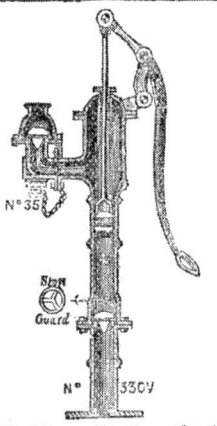

No. 33ov.—3in. Pump fitted with Patent elbow, retaining valve and dome cap, to suit either 1½ in. flanged pipe or iron tube for suction and rising main: 42in. high, 30in. under elbow, price £3 6s. Can be bored and tapped for 2in. suction and rising main, if expressly ordered, which will cause it to be worked with greater ease.

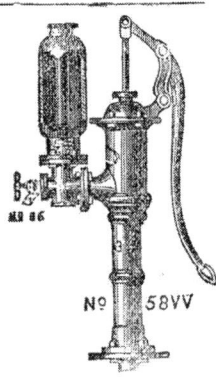

No. 58VV.—3½in. Pump, fitted with Patent elbow, air-vessel, and retaining valve, flanged base-plate; to suit 2in. iron tube, for suction and rising main 30in. high, 22in. under elbow, price £4 4s.

IMPROVED WATER OR LIQUID MANURE CART.

The wheels are wrought-iron, with wide tyres, and jolting is avoided by india-rubber springs. For conveying and distributing Liquid Manure it is invaluable. This Cart is confidently recommended to Agriculturists and others, as the strongest and most convenient implement yet introduced. No farm should be without one. One horse is sufficient to work the 200-gallon Cart.

To hold 140 gals., painted, £13; 200 do., £15; 250 do., £17. Galvanized, 140 gals., £15; do., 200, £17; do., 250, £19. Width of 140-gal., 4 ft.; do. 200-gal., 4ft. 6in.; do. 250-gal., 4ft. 8in.

This woodcut represents the Improved Water or Liquid Manure Cart, fitted with Pump and Spreader, the Shafts turned back, and the Lids open.

Extra charge for Portable Pump ... £2 5 0
India-rubber Suction Pipe, 10 ft. long, with Clip and Strainer ... 1 15 0
Spreader for any size Cart ... 0 15 0

The Pump and Strainer can be detached from the Cart in one minute.

Longer lengths of Suction Pipe can be had if required.

INDEPENDENT PILLAR PUMPS, FOR HAND OR STEAM POWER.

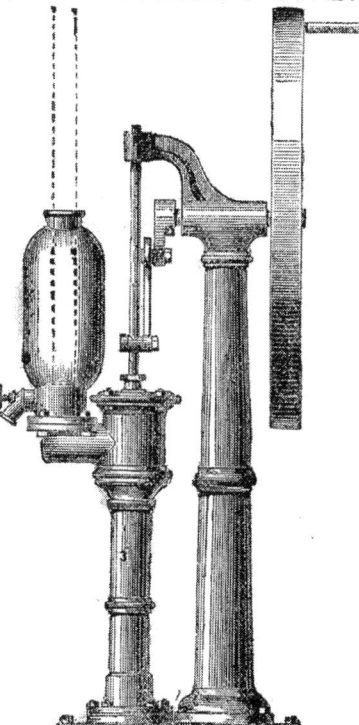

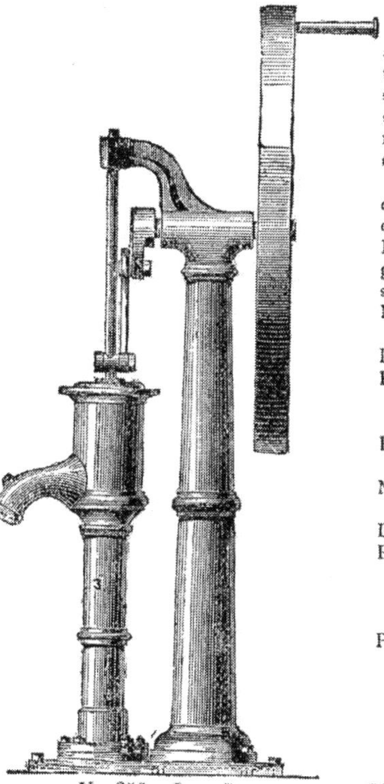

These Pumps will fulfil all the conditions required, whether for ordinary pumps, for shallow wells, or for lifting from any depth up to 50 feet, and forcing to a moderate height; and the PRICES ARE MUCH LOWER than those necessarily required for pumps with ENGINE FRAME, fly-wheel and crank of the *usual* construction.

The fly-wheels are made flat on the outer edge, to take a strap for steam power, if required, and each Pump is fitted with Patent Bucket and Conical Valve. The height from ground to spout varies from 12 inches in the small size to 18 or 20 in. in the larger sizes.

No. 350.—LIFT PUMP, for Wells not exceeding 25 feet deep :—

Diameter of Barrel	2½in.	3in.	3½in.	4in.
Prepared for wrought iron suction	1¼	1½	2	2
Price of Pump AS SHOWN	£6 3s.	£6 12s.	£7 4s. each	Special quotations.

No. 360.—LIFT AND FORCE PUMP, for Wells not exceeding 26 feet deep :—

Diameter of Barrel	2½in.	3in.	3½in.	4in.
Prepared for wrought iron suction and rising main	1¼	1½	2	2
Price of Pump with retaining Valve, air-vessel, and draw-off cock, AS SHOWN	£8 2s.	£8 8s.	£9 each.	

If without the draw-off cock and fitting, 7/6 less

No. 350.—LIFT PUMP.

No. 360.—LIFT AND FORCE PUMP.

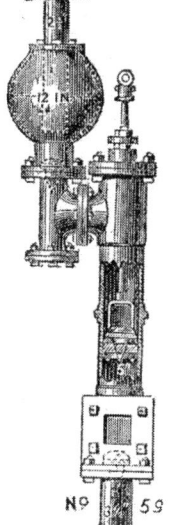

5in. fitted for power, with gland and stuffing-box, extra strong turned rod and cotter joint to disconnect bucket, T pipe with retaining valve, globular air-vessel, 12in. inside, to suit 3 or 3½in flanged suction, and 2½in rising main pipes, for motive power, 39in. high, 31in. underbranch, price £8 8.

Another use for the Manchester Fire Pump, (*see page* 166), showing how it may be used as a Force Pump for Baths, Cisterns, and other purposes.

Quotations sent on application, for Lead Pipe, with Cock and Union Joint attached, when required.

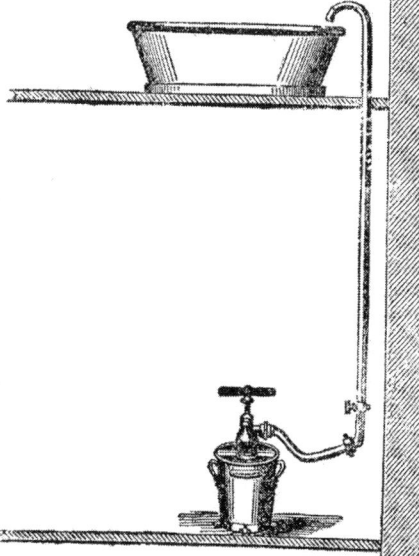

DOUBLE-ACTION LIFT AND FORCE PUMP, No. 14.

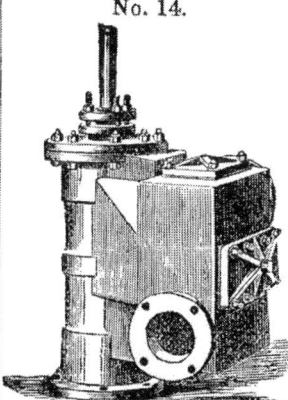

These Pumps are exceedingly compact, strong, simple in action, and all the working parts are easily accessible. Being on the double action principle, viz., to raise water at both the up stroke and down stroke, one of these pumps is equal in capacity to two single-action pumps of the same diameter, whilst only one set of gear is required to work it. They are adapted to work by hand, or they are fitted to portable and ships' engines and cranes, and being proportioned throughout for lifting and forcing, they are available for all ordinary purposes, whilst in an emergency they may be used as FIRE ENGINES or for SHIPS' PUMPS of the most powerful description.

Bore of Barrel.	Stroke.	Price with Brass lined internal barrel bored	If with Standards, Guides, and Slings, extra.	Gallons per hour at 40 strokes per minute
4in.	12in.	£19 10/-	£3 0/0	2,500
6 „	14 „	32 8/-	4 4/4	6,000
8 „	14 „	40 16/-	4 16/0	11,500

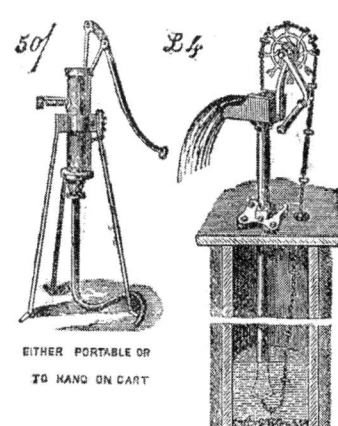

EITHER PORTABLE OR TO HANG ON CART

The use of the CHAIN PUMP is found to be very advantageous in many ways. They have no valves, will pump thick liquids of any kind, and are never affected by frost. Also a larger amount of water can be raised by them than by any other Pump of the same power. For the Colonies, and all countries where repairs are difficult they are particularly adapted. They are especially useful for Liquid Manure Tanks, Brick Yards, Irrigation, &c.

PRICES.

No. 1.—An Improved Chain Pump, with working barrel two inches diameter, cast iron flange, wheel, handle, with chain and disc complete, 10 feet, £4. If more than 10 feet, 5s. per foot for extra wrought iron piping, discs, and chain. This Pump will raise about 500 gals. per hour.

No. 2.—This Pump is the same as No. 1, but made larger and stronger, and is capable of raising 1,000 to 1,800 gals. per hour, according to the depth of the well. Price £6 6s. If more than 10 feet, 8s. 6d. per foot for extra wrought iron piping, discs, and chains.

No. 3.—Larger than the above, to raise 3,000 gals. per hour. Worked by two men. Price £8 8s. for 10 feet. Extra length, 11s. 6d. per foot.

LIQUID MANURE PUMPS.

Improved Liquid Manure Pumps, with Patent Bucket and Sucker, not liable to choke, with 4½ inch Barrel and Legs, £3 15s. Ditto for attaching to Cart, which can be instantly taken off when not in use, £3 10s. Flexible Rubber Suction Pipe for ditto, best quality, 3s. per ft.

BAILEY'S DEEP-WELL PUMPS FOR HORSE OR BULLOCK POWER.

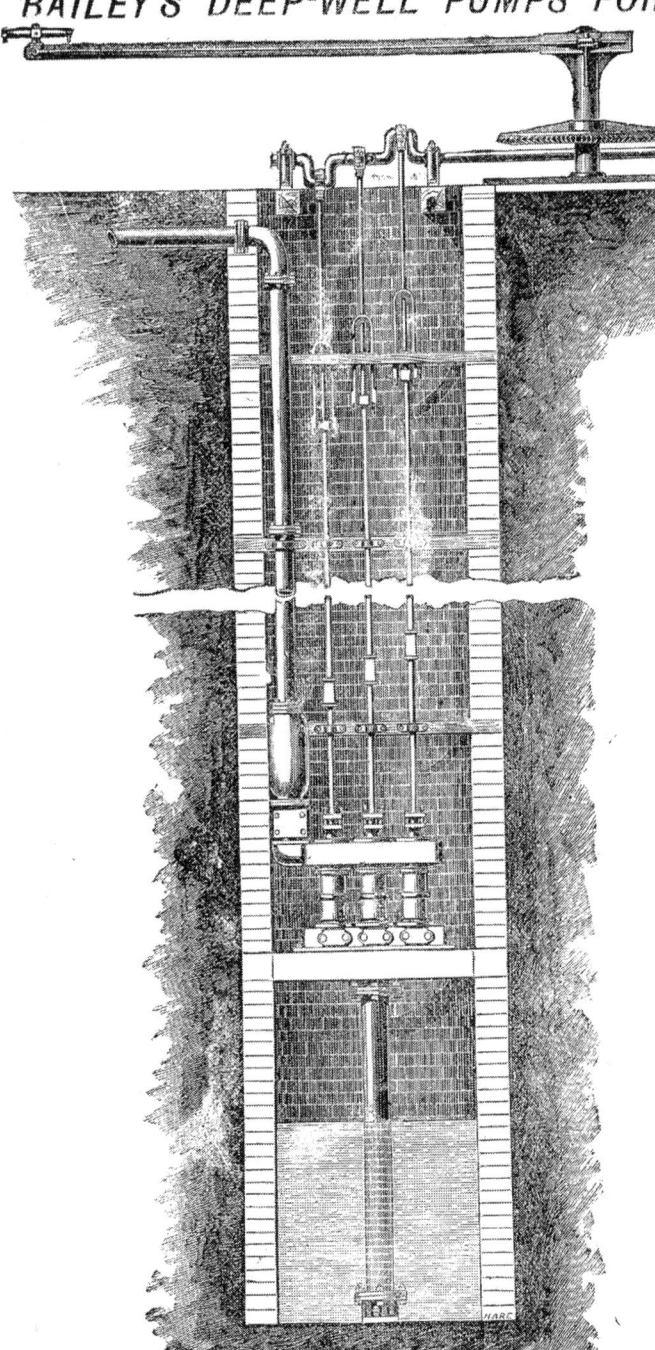

Deep Well Pumps for Horse or Bullock Power with strong Single-speed Pillar Horse Gear on Iron Base Plate, fitted with swivel yoke for one horse, bevel wheel and pinion, wrought-iron crank and suitable bearings, slings and guides, pump-rods, rising main pipe up to ground line, with all bolts, nuts, and packings; the pumps are made extra strong with full water-ways, doors to give access to the buckets and valves, brass valves (or patent oscillating conical valves if preferred), gun-metal stuffing-boxes, suction pipe and strainer for bottom of well, all complete for 30 ft. deep, as shown in the engraving; exclusive of well-stages or guides, which are usually formed of timber.

Double Pumps

Bore of Working Barrel	Price complete for Well 30 ft. deep. Double Brass Pumps	Extra per foot if exceeding 30 ft. deep	Approximate Gals. ⅌ hour	
			At 20 strokes per minute	At 30 strokes per minute
	£ s. d.	s. d.		
3 inches	75 12 0	5 0	500	700
3½ ,,	79 5 0	5 3	650	900
4 ,,	82 16 0	6 0	900	1200
5 ,,	104 8 0	8 6	1500	2000

For Gearing to increase the speed of working, £6 extra.

Treble Pumps

Bore of Working Barrel	Price complete for Well 30 ft. deep. Treble Brass Pumps	Extra per foot if exceeding 30 ft. deep	Approximate Gals. ⅌ hour	
			At 20 strokes per minute	At 30 strokes per minute
	£ s. d.	s. d.		
3 inches	91 4 0	6 0	760	980
3½ ,,	96 0 0	6 3	980	1350
4 ,,	112 0 0	7 6	1350	1900
5 ,,	134 8 0	9 0	2100	2900

For Gearing to increase the speed of working, £6 10s. extra.

The internal diameter of the suction and rising main pipes for low lifts should not be less than two-thirds of the diameter of the Pump; and in all *Deep Wells* it is recommended that the pipes should be the *same diameter* as the barrel: this will ensure much greater ease in working.

STRONG SINGLE-SPEED PILLAR HORSE OR BULLOCK GEAR, mounted on Iron Base Plate, with one pole and swivel yoke, bevel wheel and pinion, and suitable bearings, strap head connecting rods, slings and guides, ready for welding to the pump rods, but EXCLUSIVE OF PUMPS.

	Strong Gear	Lighter Gear
Suitable for Single-Barrel Pump, with a single crank or arm	£41 0	£34 16
For Double do., with wrought-iron double crank	48 0	42 0
,, Treble do., do. treble do.	57 15	51 12

For Second motion Shaft and pair of Spur wheels to increase the speed, £5 to £6 extra.

Each Pole with Swivel Yoke, £1 15s. extra.

Prices of Pumps only.

IMPROVED SINGLE, DOUBLE, AND TREBLE-BARREL LIFT AND FORCE PUMPS FOR DEEP WELLS, with full water-ways and valves; door to each valve to give easy access for repairs, &c. The barrels all bored and flanges faced, all necessary valves, buckets, and rods, gun-metal stuffing-boxes, and iron bows or cotters, *ready for attaching to the well-rods.*

Diameter of Barrels	Single Barrels		Double Barrels		Treble Barrels	
	Iron	Brass	Iron	Brass	Iron	Brass
	£ s. d.	£ s. d.	£ s. d.	£ s. d.	£ s. d.	£ s. d.
2½ inches	8 2 0	9 6 6	13 4 0	15 12 0	18 0 0	21 12 0
3 ,,	9 0 0	10 10 0	15 0 0	17 8 0	21 0 0	24 12 0
3½ ,,	10 16 0	12 6 0	17 8 0	20 8 0	24 0 0	28 16 0
4 ,,	13 4 0	14 14 0	19 16 0	22 16 0	32 8 0	38 8 0
5 ,,	21 0 0	24 0 0	30 0 0	33 12 0	48 0 0	54 0 0
6 ,,	31 4 0	34 16 0	45 2 0	50 8 0	69 12 0	78 0 0

If with Cast-Iron Air Vessel, extra. If with Copper Air Vessel, extra.
For Hot Liquor, add 11/- per barrel.

BRASS CASTINGS,
HEAVY OR LIGHT,

At from ... 10½d. per lb.

More or less, according to the Metal Market.

BAILEY'S STRONG LIFT & FORCE PUMPS.

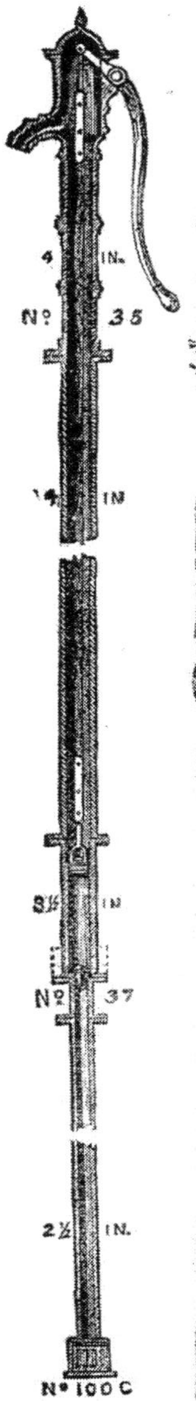

Deep Well Pump, No. 100 C.

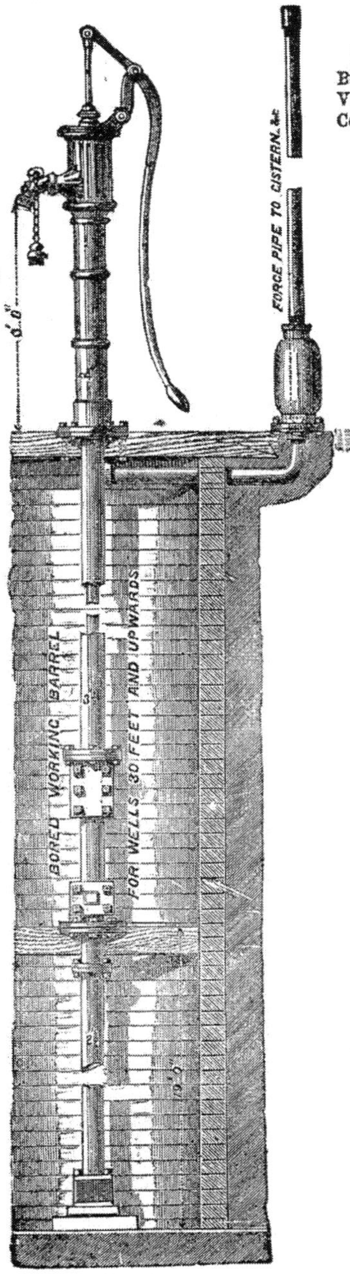

No. 101.

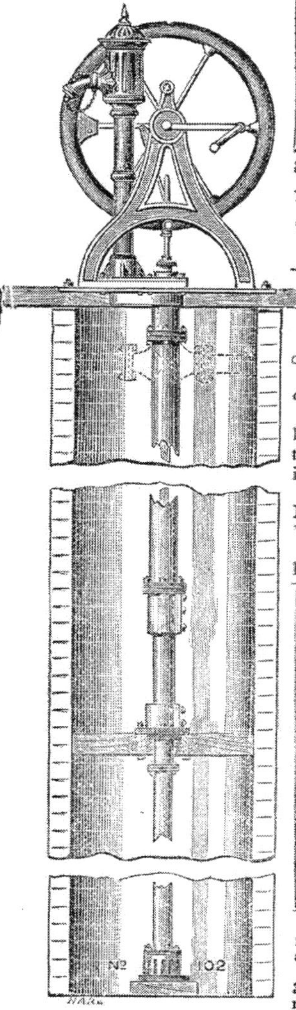

No. 102.

Fitted with Patent Metallic Buckets, and Conical Oscillating Valves. Will Pump either Hot or Cold Liquors, or Pulpy Matter.

LIFT PUMPS, FOR WELLS, FROM 27 TO 100 FEET DEEP.

N.B.—For example, refer to 100C, which illustrates both principle and specification.

No.	**Fluted Pattern Pump Head**; fitted with strong wrought Iron-handle, 9 ft. of flanged main pipe and wood rod (rendered impervious) with iron forked strap at each end, bored working barrel, 2ft. 6in. long, fitted with all the latest improvements, 18ft. 6in. of flanged suction pipe with patent strainer, including bolts, nuts, and patent washers for all the pipe joints, ready for fixing, in all 30 ft. :—	Bored Working Barrel. (No. 37.)	Suction Pipe. (No. 45.)	Price complete for 30 ft. Deep.	Extra per foot, if exceeding 30 feet deep. For Main Pipe & wood rods	Extra with Bucket, Door, &c. to Working Barrel, No. 38.	Extra for Copper Lining fitted into Bored Metal Barrel
100A	Complete for Wells 30 ft. deep (and exceeding)	2½ in.	1½ in.	£5 8 0	2s 6d	11s 0d	8s 0d
100B	Ditto do. do.	3 „	2 „	6 0 0	3 0	12 0	9 0
100C	Ditto do. do.	3½ „	2¼ „	6 18 0	3 6	14 6	10 6
100D	Ditto do. do.	4 „	2½ „	7 16 0	3 9	18 0	13 0
100E	Ditto do. do.	4½ „	3 „	9 0 0	4 0	24 0	15 0

SPECIAL NOTE.—Nos. 100B and 100C Pumps are recommended for Wells varying from 50 to 80 ft. deep; unless a larger supply of water is required, and more power is applied to work larger barrels.

N.B.—The extra price per foot is for main pipe [with wood rod], which is fixed above the barrel, and uniformly ½ inch larger in diameter than the bore of barrel; bolts, nuts, and patent elastic washers for all the pipe joints are included.

The suction pipes with patent strainer are 18 ft. 6 in. long, which are fixed below the barrels, and about one-third less in diameter than the bore of barrels for these Pumps. These proportions will ensure proper action, provided all the parts are fixed perfectly plumb, and firmly bolted together.

LIFT AND FORCE PUMPS FOR SHALLOW OR DEEP WELLS.

Many Thousands of these Pumps are now in efficient working order, after several years' incessant use, under every variety of condition, and **experience has proved that the Valves** are applicable for pumping hot or cold water or other liquors, and that their efficacy, durability, and economy, is unaffected by heat or cold, or by climatic influences.

The Pumps now illustrated and described (Nos. 101 to 102) have been specially designed to give a maximum of effective result, with a minimum of labour, every facility being afforded for examination and repair in case of need.

To obtain this result, the Forcing Pipe is taken from below the ground line, and the rising main is made of large proportions to admit a wood rod, which is coated and rendered permanently buoyant, and impervious to the destructive action of the water; also, the necessity of Guides, with the attendant friction, is avoided, and an important saving is effected in cost of erection, and subsequent wear and tear.

The Gland and Stuffing Box are placed outside the Cap, and are perfectly accessible. When required as a Force Pump, the Standard Head being of large capacity, acts as an Air Vessel, assists in reducing the shock on the Valves, as well as the labour in working, and without additional cost.

N.B.—**The Retaining Valve** assists materially in economising the power exerted when forcing to any considerable height, and should never be omitted.

No. 101.—PATENT LIFT AND FORCE PUMP for Well 30 feet deep: consisting **of the Standard Head**, which has an extra large and strong flange at the bottom, for bolting to the foundation. The Head is fitted with strong wrought iron Handle and vibrating Links, the Nozzle is screwed to take a Brass Plug, which is used when the Pump is required for forcing, and is attached by a strong tinned Chain, as shown; the rod is turned, and works in a Metallic Gland and Stuffing-Box. A 9 ft. length of Flanged Rising Main Pipe, ½ in. larger in diameter than the Bore of the Pump Barrel, the wood Pump Rod which is rendered impervious, passing through this pipe and communicating with the Working Barrel, bored throughout, and fitted with Bucket with Sword Joint, and Brass Coupling; Clack Valve and Doors for access to both Bucket and Valve. [Length of Barrel with Tailpiece, 3 feet]. The Suction Pipes 18 ft. and Strainer at the bottom of the lower pipe, 6 in. long.

Total depth from ground line, 30 ft. 6 in.

No.		Bored Working Barrel, No. 38, K.	Main Pipe.	Standard Head.	Suction Pipe and Strainer.	Price complete, for 30 ft. 6 in. deep.	Extra per foot if exceeding 30 ft. 6 in. for Main Pipe with Wood Rod.	Extra for Copper Linings fitted into Bored Metal Barrels.
								each
101A	Complete for Wells 30 ft. 6 in. deep	2½ in.	3 in.	3 in.	1½ in	£9 18 0	2s 6d	8s 0d
101B	Ditto do. do.	3 „	3½ „	3½ „	2 „	10 10 0	3 0	9 0
101C	Ditto do. do.	3½ „	4 „	4 „	2¼ „	11 14 0	3 6	10 6
101D	Ditto do. do.	4 „	4½ „	4½ „	3 „	12 18 0	3 9	13 0

The whole of the pipes can be easily and securely bolted together, and are supplied with patent washers and bolts and nuts for each joint. Side branch pipe for forcing, retaining valve, pipe for forcing vertically, supplied to suit special purposes, and *charged extra* in each case, as are also the other accessories.

No. 102.—Strong Crank Frame, or Well Engine Pump; accurately fitted, and bolted to a cast-iron foundation plate, 36 in. by 18 in.; the Standard Head and the general arrangement is similar to No. 101, but the pump is worked with a crank motion and fly-wheel, as shown:—

Bore of Barrel	Main Pipe	Standard Head	Suction Pipe	Price complete for Well 30 ft. 6 in. deep	Extra if exceeding 30 ft. 6 in. deep per Foot	Extra for Copper Lined Working Brl.	Extra for Brass Buckets and Valves per set
2½ in.	3 in.	3 in.	1½ in.	£23 15 0	£0 2 6	£0 8 6	£0 5 0
3 „	3 „	3 „	2 „	24 6 0	0 2 6	0 9 0	0 7 0
3½ „	3½ „	3 „	2½ „	25 0 0	0 3 0	0 10 6	0 9 0
4 „	4 „	3 „	2½ „	25 16 0	0 3 6	0 13 0	0 10 6

No. 280.

BAILEY'S
FRAME PUMP,
WITH FLY-WHEEL.

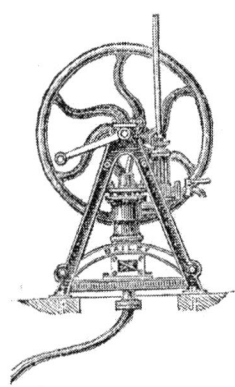

IMPROVED DOUBLE ACTION STATION FORCE PUMP, mounted on cast-iron frame, with fly-wheel, for hand or power. This is an exceedingly simple and durable form of Pump, having but *one working barrel*; it is fitted with gun-metal plunger and bucket, and delivers at BOTH the UP and DOWN STROKE, discharging the same quantity as ordinary *Double Barrel* Pumps. It is suited for filling Tanks at Railway Stations, or in Private Establishments, &c. The Pump, as shown will draw from a depth of about 25 feet from ground-line to water-level in well, and will force to any reasonable height or horizontal distance. It is equally applicable for *Deep Wells*, fixing the working barrel down the well about 15 or 20 feet above the water-level. Prices as below, with Brass Plunger, Gland, and Buckets finishing with flanged inlet and outlet for suction and delivery pipes:—

Gals. per Hour at 30 to 35 Strokes per Minute.	Price for Manual Power.
500 to 700	£26 10 0
700 to 900	28 12 0
900 to 1200	37 0 0

BRASS DEEP WELL PUMPS, &c.

No. 362.—Strong Double Brass Barrel Deep Well Pumps, with Cast Iron Top and Bottom Chambers,

	3	3½	4in.
	£11 7 6	£13 2 6	£15 15 0
,, 363. ,, with Doors to repair Valves	15 0 0	19 0 0	21 10 6
,, 364. Treble ,, ,,	22 2 6	26 5 0	31 10 0

,, 365. Brass Pumps, on Square Tail,

	2½	3	3½	4in.
	£3 15 0	£4 15 0	£5 15 0	£7 2 6
Extra Strong	4 5 0	5 12 6	6 12 6	7 15 0
,, 366. ,, ,, Double	11 5 0	13 7 6	16 7 6	
,, 367. ,, ,, Treble	16 16 0	20 5 0	24 5 0	

,, 368. Deep Well Weighted Pump Handles, with Wrought Iron Slings, Guide, and Conducting Rod, mounted on Strong Oak Plank 2 2 0

,, 369. Wrought Iron Work for Lift and Force Pumps mounted on Oak Plank,

	3	3½	4in.
	£1 18 3	£2 0 0	£2 2 0
If Weighted Handle,	2 0 0	2 2 0	2 2 0

,, 370.—Brass Lift and Force Pumps, on Oak Plank, Wrought Iron Work,

	2½	3	3½	4in.
	£4 17 6	£5 12 6	£6 8 6	£7 5 0
,, 371.—Very Strong	£5 10 0	6 10 0	7 15 0	8 7 6

No. 372.—Brass Lift and Force Pumps, fitted on Oak Plank, with Brackets, Wrought Iron Work,

	2½	3	3½	4in.
	£4 17 6	£5 12 6	£6 8 6	£7 5 0
,, 373. ,, with Taper Tail Piece, very strong,	£5 10 0	6 10 0	7 15 0	8 7 6

,, 374.—Brass Pump on Oak Plank, Vibrating Standard, £5 5 0   6 1 0

Brass Lift and Force Pumps, screwed top and bottom for Iron Pipe, extra,

2½	3	3½	4in.
£0 5 3	£0 6 9	£0 9 0	£0 10 6

Force Pump on Oak Plank, best quality, fitted with Copper Air Vessel, and 1 inch Draw-off Cock,

2½	3	3½	4in.
£6 11 6	£7 12 6	£8 18 6	£10 0 0

*** Pumps of any size, and to suit any requirements, made to order.

,, 375.—Copper Air Vessel for 2½ or 3in. Pumps,
  15in. × 8in. £1 5 0
 ,,   ,,   3½ ,,   4in. ,, 16in. × 9in. 1 10 0
,, 375a.   ,, *Extra Strong* for Deep Wells, from 1 12 6
,, 376.—Bolts with Washers and Nuts 3, 4, 5, 6, 7, 8in.
  2/6 2/8 3/ 3/5 3/9 4/1 per doz.
,, 377.—Brass Bushes for Pump Rod Joints, each, 0 2 6
,, 378.—Well Rod Joint, with Brass Bush, ⅝in. 3/6, ¾in. 0 4 6
,, 379.—Cast Iron Pump Stage for Wells, from 1 4 6
Well Rods, including Joints and Bush, in 12ft. lengths
 ⅝in., per foot 0 0 7½
 ,,   ,,   ¾in. ... 0 0 9

TABLE SHOWING THE QUANTITY OF WATER RAISED PER HOUR BY SINGLE-BARREL PUMP, WITH 9IN. STROKE.

	20 Strokes.	25 Strokes.	30 Strokes per minute.		20 Strokes.	25 Strokes.	30 Strokes per minute.
2 inch	124 Gallons.	155 Gallons.	185 Gallons.	3½ inch	376 Gallons.	470 Gallons.	564 Gallons.
2½ inch	192 ,,	240 ,,	288 ,,	4 inch	491 ,,	614 ,,	737 ,,
3 inch	277 ,,	346 ,,	415 ,,				

BAILEY'S IMPROVED HYDRAULIC RAMS

For the Automatic Raising of Water for Mansions, &c.,

FITTED WITH PATENTED SPRING ADJUSTMENT.

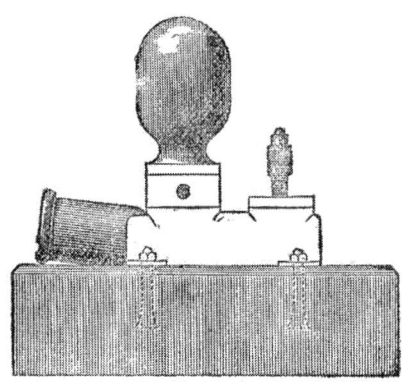

The above illustration shows my Improved Hydraulic Ram for supplying country Mansions, Farmsteads, &c., with water.

This Machine can be fixed in any place where a stream can be held up so as to give a fall of two feet or upwards. It will force water to a vertical height equal to from twenty to thirty times the height of the fall, drive the water any horizontal distance which may be required, and work day and night without any attention whatever. Great attention has been given to the details and proportions of the Machine, and it is offered to the public with confidence that wherever tried it will give satisfaction. The Improved Ram can be taken in pieces for examination and adjustment without breaking any of the joints in the pipes. If the supply of water is limited, the Ram may at a small cost be made to work intermittently, so as to accommodate itself to the varying feed. The cost of repairs is not nearly as much as in the case of an ordinary pump. In preference to using a larger size than $3\frac{1}{2}$ inches two Rams discharging into one pipe are recommended, the wear and tear in very large sizes being greater in proportion than in smaller ones.

The following table will prove useful in choosing the size of Ram required:—

Size of Pipes.		Price.	Quantity of water required per minute.	Water delivered in 24 hours.
Injection.	Delivery.			
$1\frac{1}{2}$ inches	$\frac{3}{4}$ inch	£7 0 0	4 to 10 gallons.	400 to 900 gallons.
2 ,,	1 ,,	10 0 0	7 to 15 ,,	800 to 1300 ,,
$2\frac{1}{4}$,,	1 ,,	10 0 0	8 to 20 ,,	1200 to 2500 ,,
$2\frac{1}{2}$,,	1 ,,	15 0 0	12 to 26 ,,	1600 to 3000 ,,
3 ,,	$1\frac{1}{4}$,,	20 0 0	20 to 40 ,,	3500 to 4000 ,,
$3\frac{1}{2}$,,	$1\frac{1}{4}$,,	25 0 0	25 to 60 ,,	3500 to 4500 ,,

Estimates given for Rams, Injection Pipes, Grate Box, and Valve, on receipt of the following particulars:—

1st. Quantity of water at command, in gallons, per minute.

2nd. The greatest fall which can be obtained by holding up the stream or spring.

3rd. Perpendicular height to which the water must be forced.

4th. Distance measured along the surface from fall to place of delivery.

BAILEY'S POWER PUMP, FOR STRAP OR GEARING.

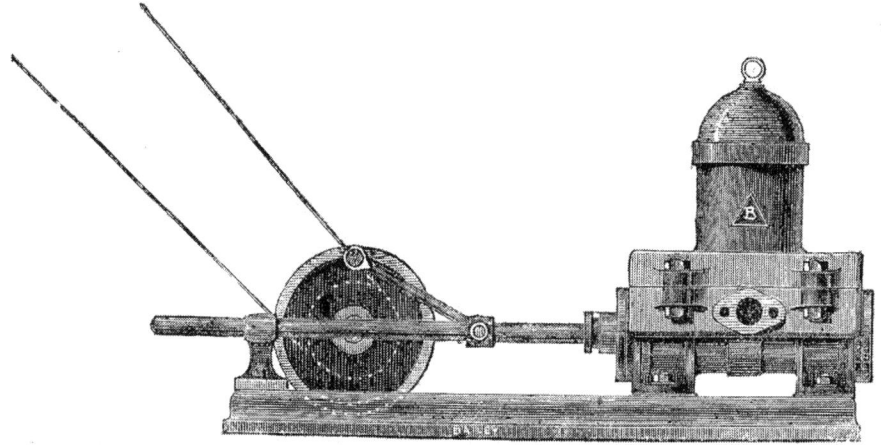

These Pumps are double acting, and are fitted on cast iron base plate, with pedestal driving pulley, of sufficient diameter, ready for use.

They are used for feeding boilers, and many other useful purposes.

Diameter of Pump	Length of Stroke	Gallons per Hour	Price £ s. d.
2 inches	9 inches	850	10 10 0
3 inches	10 inches	1,940	15 10 0
4 inches	12 inches	2,000	20 0 0
6 inches	12 inches	7,200	30 0 0

Other Sizes Special Quotations.

The following are a few of the firms now using BAILEY'S Steam Pumps, working with steam and compressed air. (*For Prices and Illustration, see next page*):—

Messrs. Leech, Cotton Spinners, Stalybridge.
Messrs. Wells, Birch, Ryde & Co., Hoyland Collieries, Hoyland.
Messrs. Whyatt & Sons' Dye Works, Openshaw.
Messrs. Piggott & Farrar, Barnsley.
Messrs. R. Walker & Co., Openshaw.
Messrs. Leitch, Sugar Refinery, Liverpool.
Messrs. Ashton, Bleach Works, Hyde.
The Silkstone & Dodworth Coal Company, Dodworth.
Messrs. A. & A. Crompton, Shaw, near Oldham.
Messrs. Watkinson & Sons, Buckley, near Mold.
The Wharncliffe and Woodmoor Colliery Company, Carlton.
Messrs. Dodgson & Grundy, Ashton-under-Lyne.
Mr. Adshead, Cotton Spinner, Stalybridge.
Mr. Airey, Victoria Brewery, Wigan.
Hyde & Haughton, Colliery Company, Denton.
C. & A. Hampson, Steam Beetling Works, Droyleden.
Mostyn Coal and Iron Co.

Mr. Holford, Colliery Owner, Chesterfield.
Mr. Forrest, Oaks Pit, Mold.
Mr. John Lancaster, Ashby-de-la-Zouch.
Mr. T. Williamson, Stalybridge.
The Denton Colliery Co., near Manchester.
The Dunkirk Colliery Co., Dukinfield.
The Vancouver Coal Mining & Land Co., Vancouver's Island.
Messrs. Jasper & Co., Sugar Refiners, Liverpool.
Messrs. Whitehead & Booth, Ridge Hill Collieries, Stalybridge.
The Astley and Tyldesley Coal and Salt Company.
Messrs. Kershaw, Cotton Spinners, Guide Bridge.
Mr. Aydon, Longton, Staffordshire.
Messrs. Lees' Colliery, Oldham.
The Manchester, Sheffield & Lincolnshire Railway.
Earnest Reuss, Manchester.
Buckton Vale Print Works, near Stalybridge.
Mr. Timmis, Stourbridge.

BAILEY'S STEAM PUMP,
Williamson and Walker's Patent.
BAILEY & CO., Makers.

All double acting. Delivers a constant stream. Will force to any height.

All pumps tested with steam and water to a high pressure before leaving the Manufactory.

PARTICULARS AND PRICES OF STEAM PUMP.

No.	Diameter of Steam Cylinder	Diameter of Pump	Length of Stroke	Gallons Per Hour approximate	Total Length	Total Width	Weight Approximate			Price
	Inches	Inches	Inches		Inches	Inches	Cwts.	Qrs.	Lbs.	£
1	4	2	9	850	40	11	2	0	10	18
2	6	3	10	1,940	44	12	3	1	0	26
3	6	4	10	2,000	48	12	4	2	9	30
4	8	4	12	3,150	56	14	6	2	18	40
5	6	6	12	7,200	56	14	8	1	0	40
6	8	6	12	7,200	56	16	9	3	0	50
7	10	6	12	7,200	58	18	10	0	20	60
8	8	8	12	12,000	58	18	10	2	14	65
9	10	8	12	12,000	58	20	15	1	0	75
10	12	8	15	12,600	66	22	20	0	0	85

Providing the length of stroke is the same, any combination can be arranged between the steam and water cylinders. The prices stated in this list do not include stop or other valves.

CAN BE WORKED WITH STEAM OR COMPRESSED AIR.

These Pumps are daily at work in Collieries, Sugar Refineries, Bleach Works, Cotton Mills, Copper Works, &c., giving the most unqualified satisfaction.

When required, Purchasers may see their own Pumps working at our Manufactory here before delivery.

Estimates rendered on application for sizes up to 40-inch Cylinders.

This Steam Pump is altogether exceedingly simple, having but two moving parts, with the exception of Pump Valves; and from the entire absence of metallic percussion, a silent action is maintained.—*See Engineer, February 7th, 1873.*

The Pumping Engine has created a great amount of attraction, and we feel certain it has extended your reputation and increased your orders.—*Extract from Letter sent by the Wigan Exhibition Committee, consisting of eminent Mining Engineers.*

See "Treatise on Boilers," by N. P. Burgh, M.J.M.E.

Silver Medal awarded Manchester and Liverpool Agricultural Show.

WILLIAMSON and WALKER's Steam Pumps have had awarded them the following Prize Medals:—Manchester and Liverpool Society, North Lancashire Society, and the Silver Medal of the Pomona Exhibition of Machinery, Manchester, 1875.

(For References where at work, see previous page.)

BAILEY'S WORKS STEAM FIRE ENGINE,

When used as Boiler and Engine Feeder.

WILLIAMSON AND WALKER'S PATENT.

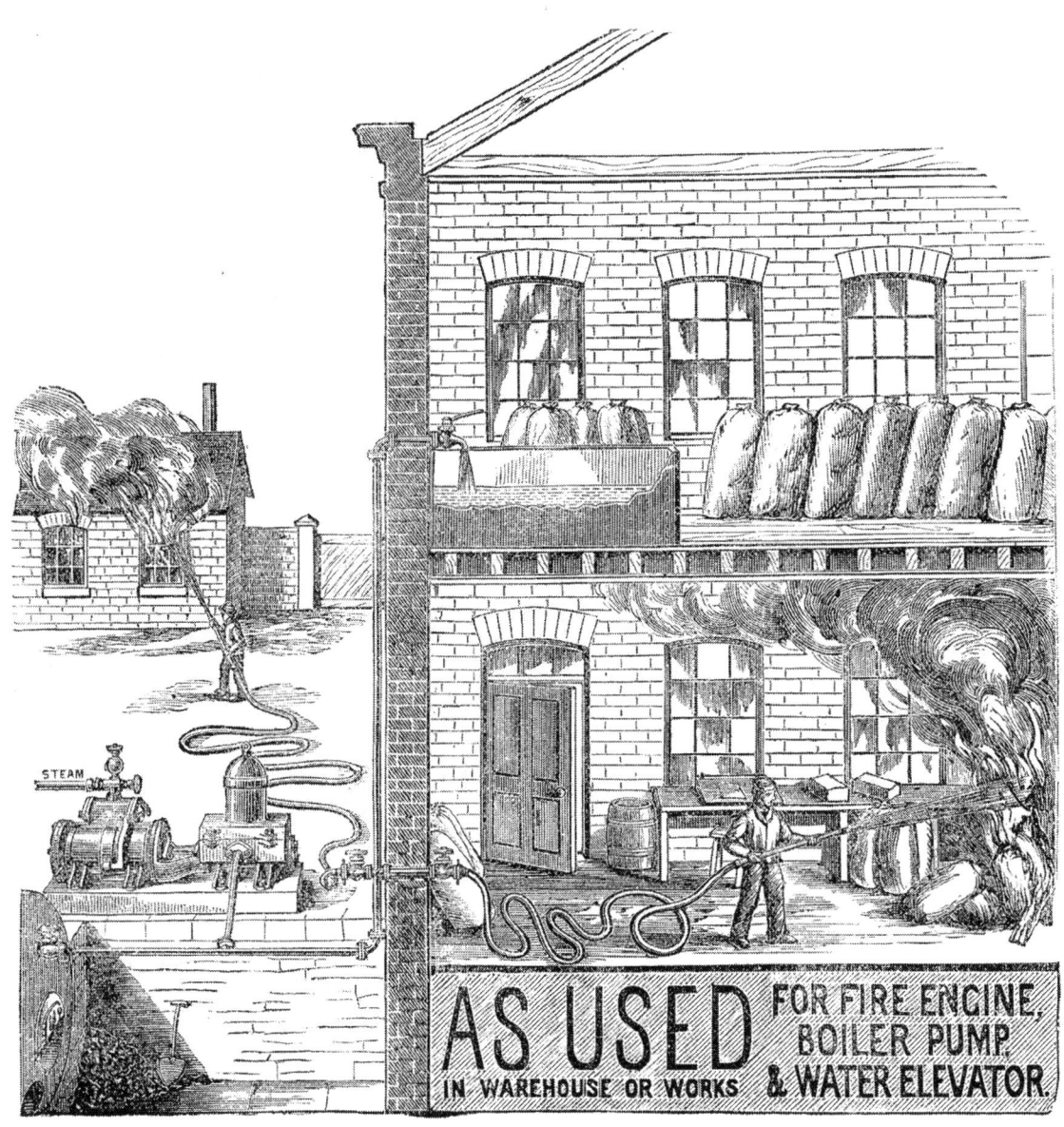

The size we recommend for this purpose is the No. 4, which has a capacity equal to 3,150 gallons per hour; it will feed two or three boilers, and, so long as steam is up, it can be used as fire engine day or night as required.

PRICE £50.

Special quotations for Hose Pipe, Landing Valves, Hand Pipes, and other Fittings, on receipt of specification. All Pumps are well tested previous to delivery.

CAMERON'S PATENT STEAM 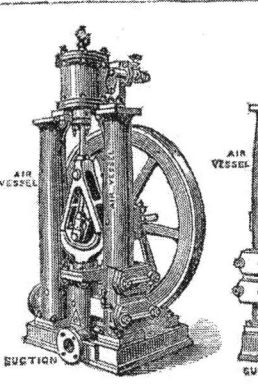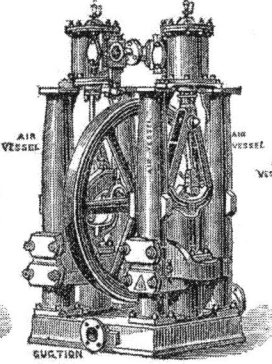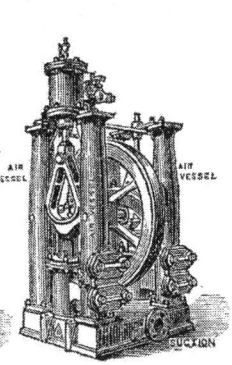 DONKEY AND OTHER PUMPS

DESCRIPTION.

These Pumps, from their compact form and satisfactory working, are now well known and extensively used for a variety of purposes, viz., in Factories and Works, &c., to feed Boilers, force water and chemical liquids. The larger sizes are excellent Steam Fire Engines. Many fires have been promptly extinguished by their assistance. They are also much used in clearing Mines of water, and can be specially made to force any height. The exhaust steam can be utilized in heating water or condensed.

The columns support the Steam Cylinder, and are Air Vessels for the Pump; the Piston and Valve-rods are steel, working through brass glands and bushes; the Stroke is limited by a crank; the Connecting-rods have brass steps and cottars; the Pump valves lift vertically, and are made of brass—each has a separate door. All the working parts and packings are easy of access, and capable of adjustment.

To ENSURE SATISFACTION the thickness of all hollow castings is carefully gauged, and then tested to 300 lbs. water pressure; finally, the Pumps are tested at actual work, drawing water 25 feet vertically, and forcing against a high pressure.

N.B.—*The suction pipes should be well tested by water pressure, and the joints made perfectly tight. Air-leaks in the suction pipe are generally blamed on the Pump, and are very difficult to discover when the pipes are laid. If the Pump has to draw above a few feet vertically, a roomy stop valve should be fitted in the suction pipe near the water.*

When ordering, please state Steam Pressure and duty the Pump is required for.

REDUCED PRICE LIST, JULY 1874.

	Ram Diameter	Strokes		Content of Pumps per hour		To Feed Boiler. Horse Power 2½ cubic feet allowance per H.P.	PRICES Delivered Here		
		Length	Number	Gallon	Cubic Feet		With one Ordinary Cylinder	With two Cylinders, one above each Pump	Extra with Governors & equilibrium regulating Valve
Single-acting, with Ram	2	3	120	240	38	15	£18		
,, ,,	2½	4	90	375	60	25	22		
,, ,,	3	5	72	540	86	35	26		£6
,, ,,	3½	,,	,,	735	117	45	28		6
,, ,,	4	6	60	960	153	55	35		7
,, ,,	4½	,,	,,	1215	194	80	37½		7
,, ,,	5	,,	,,	1500	240	100	40		7
,, ,,	6	8	45	2160	345	140	52		8
Double-acting with two Rams	2	3	120	480	77	30	28	£36	
,, ,,	2½	4	90	750	120	50	34	42	
,, ,,	3	5	72	1080	172	70	40	50	6
,, ,,	3½	,,	,,	1470	234	90	43	53	6
,, ,,	4	6	60	1920	307	110	50	60	7
,, ,,	4½	,,	,,	2430	388	160	55	65	7
,, ,,	5	,,	,,	3000	480	200	60	70	7
,, ,,	6	8	45	4320	691	280	80	90	8
,, ,,	7	9	40	5800	928	370	100	115	9
,, ,,	8	10	36	7680	1228	500	130	150	10
,, ,,	10	12½	30	12000	1920	750	180	210	12
,, ,,	12	15	25	17280	2765	1000	240	280	14
,, ,,	15	,,	,,	27000	4320	1700	310	360	16
,, ,,	20			48000	7680				

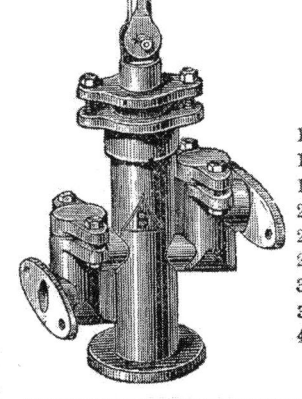

BAILEY'S FORCE PUMPS FOR ENGINES, &c.

All Iron, Brass Valves.				With Brass Plungers, Glands and Valves.			
1¼ in.	...	...	£1 4 6	1¼ in.	...	...	£2 0 0
1½ ,,	...	...	1 17 6	1½ ,,	...	...	2 15 0
1¾ ,,	...	...	2 5 0	1¾ ,,	...	...	3 10 0
2 ,,	...	...	2 10 0	2 ,,	...	...	4 10 0
2¼ ,,	...	...	2 15 0	2¼ ,,	...	...	5 10 0
2½ ,,	...	...	3 2 6	2½ ,,	...	...	7 10 0
3 ,,	...	...	3 17 6	3 ,,	...	...	10 0 0
3½ ,,	...	...	4 10 0	3½ ,,	...	...	12 10 0
4 ,,	...	...	6 7 6	4 ,,	...	...	15 0 0

Pumps with Lever for Feeding Small Boilers, &c.

PRICES:

25 per cent. extra on Pumps with Brass Valves.

THE EXCELSIOR STEAM PUMPS.

Fly-wheel and all rotary motion dispensed with.

Delivers a constant Stream, and will force to any height.

Is sure in action, the first Motion to the Steam Valves being given direct from the Pump or Piston Rod.

Can be worked either by Compressed Steam or Air.

It is now working at all speeds from 2 strokes to 100 per minute, and against all pressures from 4 lbs. to 400 lbs. per inch.

Is so simple in construction that it can be taken to pieces in a few minutes.

ALL DOUBLE ACTING.

We wish to call the attention of Owners of Mills and Works to the great *power* and *efficiency* of these Pumps for Fire purposes; for a small extra outlay any Millowner secures not only one of the simplest and most economical Boiler-feeders, but also a **Steam Fire Engine**, equalling in efficiency the most powerful Steam fire Engine yet introduced to the Corporations of the principal cities and towns in the country.

Being always at work on the premises, in case of fire, it can be applied instantaneously.

PARTICULARS AND LIST OF PRICES.

No. of Pump.	Diameter of Pump.	Diameter of Cylinder.	Diameter of Suction Pump.	Diameter of Steam Pipe.	Length of Stroke.	No. of Strokes.	Gallons per Hour.	Dimensions of Foundation Plate.	Price
1	1½-in.	3 in.	1 in.	½ in.	6 in.	100	450	3 . 11 by 1 . 2	£24 4 0
2	2 ,,	4 ,,	1¼ ,,	½ ,,	6 ,,	100	800	3 . 11 ,, 1 . 2	£26 15 0
3	2½ ,,	4 ,,	1½ ,,	¾ ,,	9 ,,	80	1,500	5 . 0 ,, 1 . 4	£31 12 6
4	3 ,,	5 ,,	2 ,,	1 ,,	12 ,,	60	2,100	6 . 2 ,, 1 . 6	£42 7 6
5	4 ,,	6 ,,	3 ,,	1 ,,	15 ,,	40	3,000	7 . 3 ,, 1 . 8	£58 0 0
6	5 ,,	7 ,,	4 ,,	1¼ ,,	15 ,,	40	5,000	7 . 9 ,, 1 . 11	£73 15 0
7	6 ,,	9 ,,	5 ,,	1½ ,,	18 ,,	40	7,300	9 . 3 ,, 2 . 2	£90 15 0
8	6 ,,	12 ,,	5 ,,	2 ,,	18 ,,	40	7,300	9 . 3 ,, 2 . 2	£110 0 0
9	7 ,,	10 ,,	6 ,,	2 ,,	24 ,,	30	12,000	11 . 3 ,, 2 . 6	£133 0 0
10	8 ,,	10 ,,	7 ,,	2 ,,	24 ,,	30	16,000	11 . 3 ,, 2 . 6	£145 0 0
11	8 ,,	12 ,,	7 ,,	2 ,,	24 ,,	30	16,000	11 . 3 ,, 2 . 6	£170 0 0
									Double Rams.
12	8 ,,	8 ,,	2 ,,	2 ,,	12 ,,	60		10 . 0 ,, 1 . 11	£101 15 0

Brass Lined or Solid Brass Water Cylinders, extra.   Estimates for larger Pumps on application.

ALL THE ABOVE CAN BE RUN AT DOUBLE THE STROKES GIVEN WITHOUT ENDANGERING THEIR SAFETY.

This Pump is eminently adapted for the undermentioned purposes:

FOR FEEDING BOILERS WITH HOT OR COLD WATER.
  ,, STEAM FIRE ENGINES FOR MILLS OR MANSIONS.
  ,, PUMPING LIQUIDS OR SEMI-LIQUIDS IN PAPER MILLS.
  ,, CHEMICAL WORKS, BLEACH WORKS, DYE WORKS.
  ,, BREWERIES, TANNERIES, COLLIERIES, GAS AND WATER WORKS.

The Stilwell Water Heater, Injectors, Steam Traps, and other useful goods for Steam Engine Proprietors, described in Bailey's Supplementary List of Engine and Boiler Fittings, post free.   All Engineers at home or abroad are requested to ask for it.

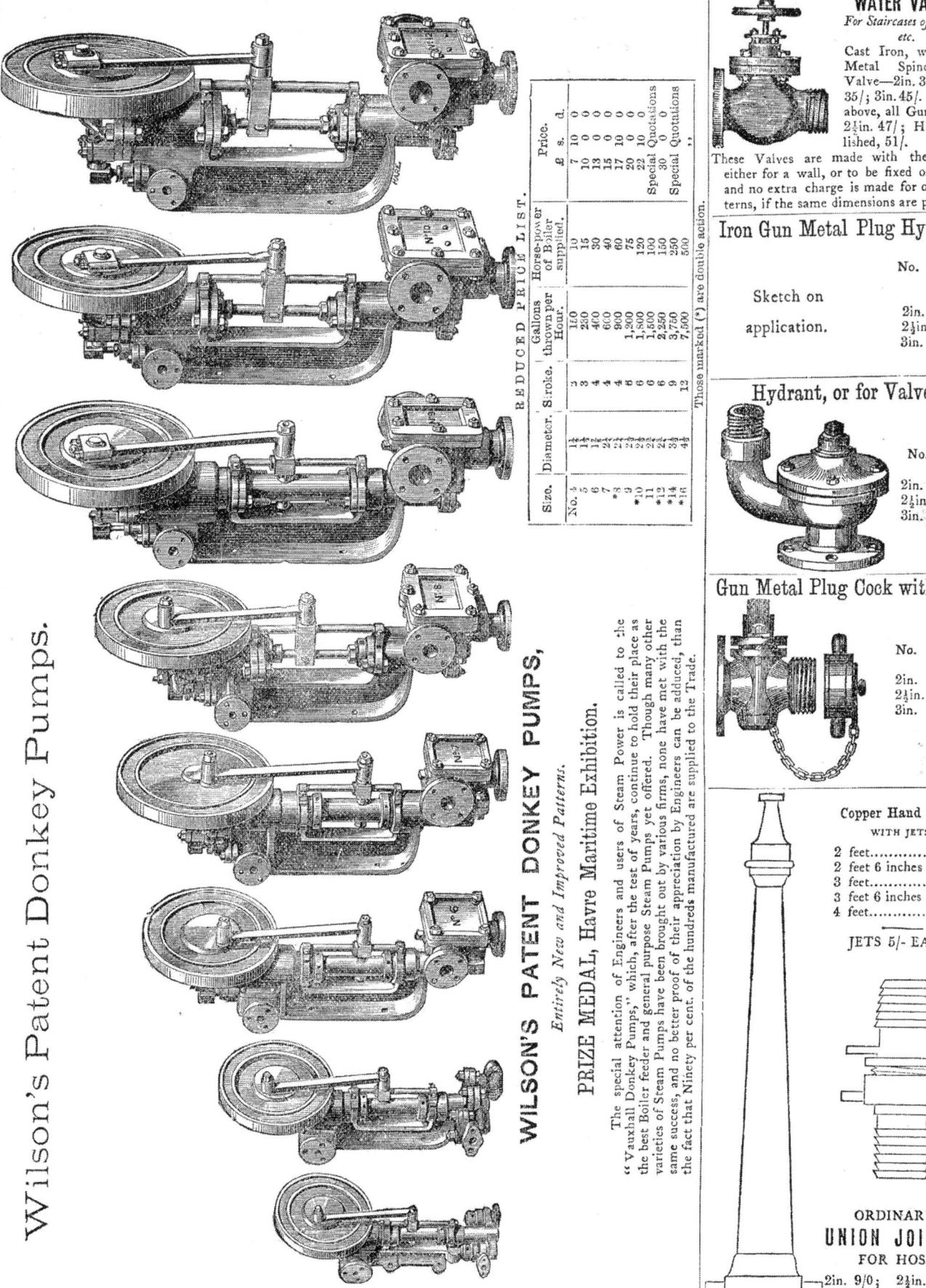

Wilson's Patent Donkey Pumps.

WILSON'S PATENT DONKEY PUMPS,
Entirely New and Improved Patterns.

PRIZE MEDAL, Havre Maritime Exhibition.

The special attention of Engineers and users of Steam Power is called to the "Vauxhall Donkey Pumps," which, after the test of years, continue to hold their place as the best Boiler feeder and general purpose Steam Pumps yet offered. Though many other varieties of Steam Pumps have been brought out by various firms, none have met with the same success, and no better proof of their appreciation by Engineers can be adduced, than the fact that Ninety per cent. of the hundreds manufactured are supplied to the Trade.

REDUCED PRICE LIST.

Size.	Diameter.	Stroke.	Gallons thrown per Hour.	Horse-power of Boiler supplied.	Price. £ s. d.
No. 5	1¾	3	150	10	7 10 0
6	2	3	230	15	10 0 0
7	2½	4	400	30	13 0 0
*8	2¾	4	600	40	15 0 0
*9	3	4	900	60	17 10 0
*10	3½	6	1,200	75	20 0 0
12	4	6	1,500	100	22 10 0
*13	4½	6	1,800	120	Special Quotations
*14	5	9	2,250	150	Special Quotations
*15	6	9	3,750	250	30 0 0
*16	8	12	7,500	500	Special Quotations

Those marked (*) are double action.

WATER VALVE,
For Staircases of Works, etc.

Cast Iron, with Gun Metal Spindle and Valve—2in. 30/; 2½in. 35/; 3in. 45/. Valve as above, all Gun Metal, 2½in. 47/; Highly Polished, 51/.

These Valves are made with the flanges either for a wall, or to be fixed on a floor, and no extra charge is made for other patterns, if the same dimensions are preserved.

Iron Gun Metal Plug Hydrant

Sketch on application.

No.
2in. 30/-
2½in. 35/-
3in. 40/-

Hydrant, or for Valve

No.
2in. 30/-
2½in. 35/-
3in. 40/-

Gun Metal Plug Cock with Cap

No.
2in. 30/-
2½in. 35/-
3in. 40/-

Copper Hand Pipes,
WITH JETS.

2 feet	22/6
2 feet 6 inches	25/6
3 feet	27/6
3 feet 6 inches	35/0
4 feet	39/0

JETS 5/- EACH

ORDINARY UNION JOINTS,
FOR HOSE

2in. 9/0; 2½in. 12/0; 3in. 17/0.

BARREL PUMPS.

HAND ROTARY FORCE PUMP.
Without Hose or Discharge Pipe.

Will lift water 25 feet, and force it to any distance; can be worked by hand or power. No 1, Price 76/; No 2, 88/; No 3, 105/; No 4, 150/; and No 5, 180/
Delivering in Gallons per Minute, at sixty Revolutions:
No. 1, 10 gals; No 2, 13 gals; No 4, 25 gals; No 5, 30 gals.

PRICES, &c.—No 1, 1-in suction, 1-in discharge, for ¾ hose, Iron, £3 15   Bronze, £8 75
" 2, " " " " " " 4 10 " 10 0
" 3, 1¼ " " 1 " " 5 10 " 11 0
Above prices include suction pipe, hose coupling, hook and holder. Brass suction pipe furnished at extra prices.

IMPROVED REVOLVING-TOP CISTERN PUMPS.

With Bolt Fastenings and Brass Valve Seats.

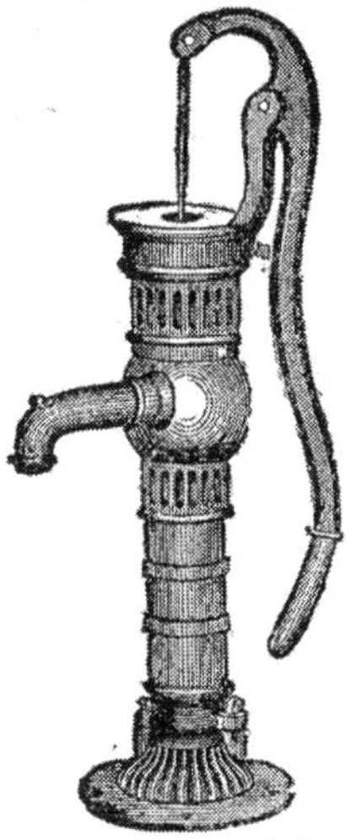

	Price
No 1, 2 inch bore,	16/-
2, 2¼ "	18/-
3, 2½ "	20/-
4, 2¾ "	23/-
5, 3 "	25/-
6, 3¼ "	32/-

GOULD'S ROTARY POWER PUMPS.

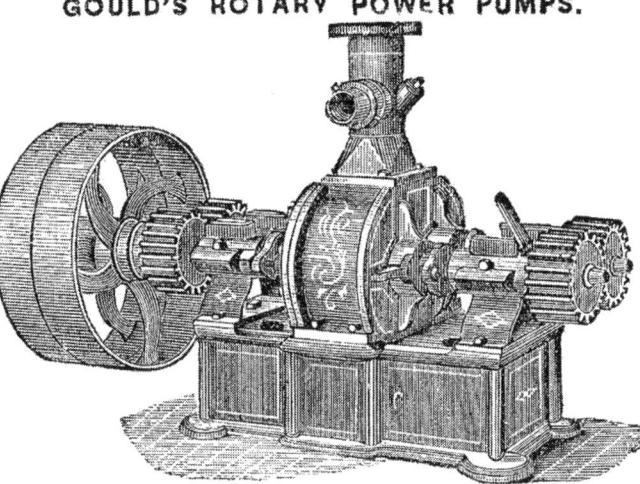

PRICE LIST.

	Suction.	Discharge.	
No 1,	2 inch	1½ inch	£21
2,	2¼ "	2 "	- 26
3,	3 "	2½ "	- 36
4,	5 "	4 "	- 50
5,	6 "	5 "	- 62
8,	10 "	8 "	- 158
10,	12 "	10 "	- 225

No. 4, and upwards, are supplied with couplings instead of pulleys.

CAPACITY.

		Speed per min.
¼ gal. ea. rev.		225 to 250
½ "	"	175 to 200
1 "	"	150 to 175
1½ "	"	125 to 150
2½ "	"	100 to 125
9¼ "	"	60 to 75
17 "	"	40 to 60

IMPROVED HYDRAULIC RAMS

For the supply of Dwellings, Factories, Villages, Railroad Stations, Gardens, &c., with Running Water.

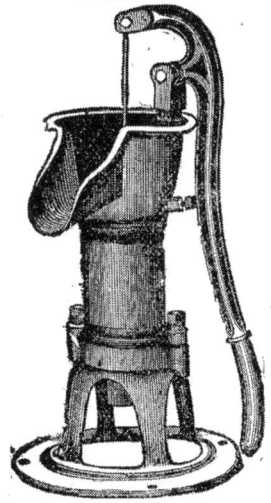

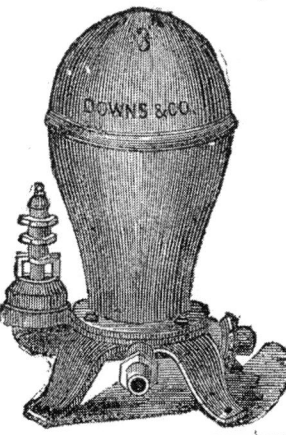

Ten feet fall is sufficient for forcing water to an elevation of one hundred and fifty feet. More than ten feet fall is not desirable, the wear of the Ram being too great.

No 2,	¾ in. Drive Pipe	36/
" 3,	1 "	"	44/
" 4,	1¼ "	"	56/
" 5,	2 "	"	88/
" 6,	2½ "	"	160/
" 7,	4 "	"	300/

ROTARY PUMP ON FRAME.

	Revolutions	Gals. per Minute	All Iron Price	Brass Price
No. 1	120	20	110/	200/
" 2	120	25	130/	225/
" 3	120	30	155/	255/
" 4	120	50	200/	320/
" 5	120	60	225/	370/

Pitcher-Spout Cistern Pump

No.	in. bore	Price	No.	in. bore	Price
1,	2½	17/-	3	3½	21/-
2,	3	19/-	4	4	23/-

BENNISON'S PATENT CENTRIFUGAL PUMPS.

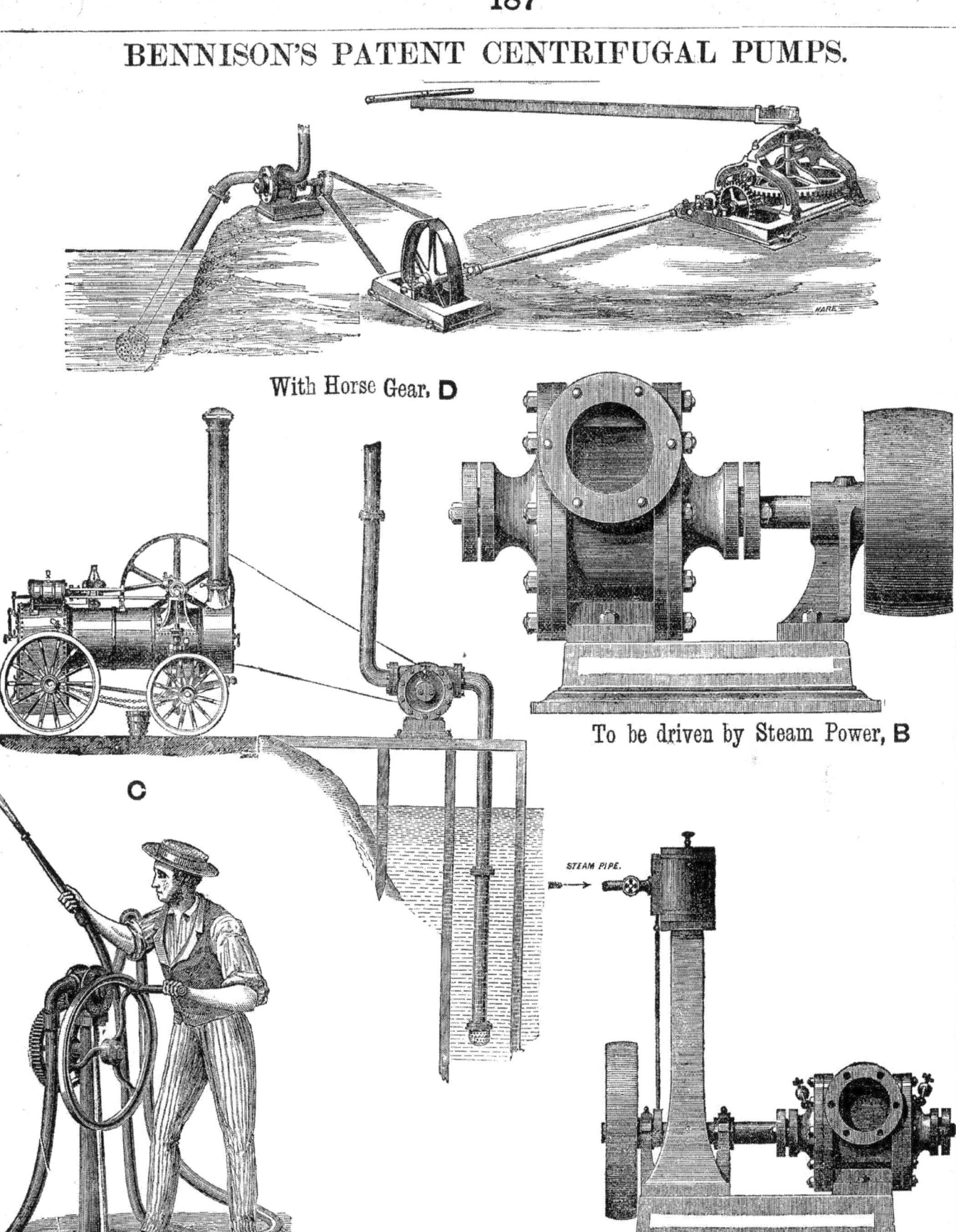

With Horse Gear, D

To be driven by Steam Power, B

C

Hand Pump, A

E

BENNISSON'S PATENT
HAND & STEAM-POWER CENTRIFUGAL PUMPS.

Letter A.

Small Hand Pump, with 1 inch pipes, mounted on pillar, with gearing and fly wheel complete, to deliver 9 to 15 gallons per minute. Easily worked by one man ...	£6 10 0
Hand Pump, to deliver from 20 to 30 gallons per minute ...	10 10 0
Hand Pump, to deliver from 40 to 60 gallons per minute ...	16 10 0

If we have not sent you the Price List of BAILEY's Injectors for feeding Boilers, please ask for it.

Letter B—to be driven by steam power.

No. of Pump	000	00	0	1	2	3	4	5	6
Gallons of Water per minute	25	45	80	150	260	4	6	750	1200
Diameter of Suction and Discharge Pipes	1 in.	1½ in.	2 in.	3 in.	4 in.	5 in.	6 in.	7 in.	8 in.
Revolutions per minute				200 to 400			100 to 250		
Diameter of Driving Pulley	4 in.	5 in.	6 in.	9 in.	12 in.	15 in.	18 in.	21 in.	24 in.
Price	£5 5	£10	£15	£22 10	£35	£50	£70	£95	£125

For localities where frequent removals are necessary these Pumps are mounted on a two-wheeled carriage.

Applicable for purposes of Irrigation, Drainage, Works of Construction by Contractors, Engineers, Builders, &c., for Emptying Docks, Mining Operations, and for numerous manufacturing and other purposes.

Engines and Boilers complete, to drive the above, as illustration C.

This engraving shows our New Improved Gear, fitted with frame and pulley, suitable for working the above Pump, or Saw Benches, Cotton Gins, &c., where great speed is required (D cut).

Price of Gear, exclusive of Frame and Pulley ...	£13 0 0
„ „ Two-horse do. ...	14 10 0
A strong Cast Iron or Oak Frame, fitted with pulley 3 ft. in diameter, and connected with spindle, by a spring clutch ...	4 10 0
If fitted with 4 ft. Pulley ...	5 10 0

E quality, with Engine combined, on application.

Those who will investigate the merits of the STILWELL PATENT WATER HEATER, will find that this is not an over-drawn or over-colored statement. Particulars will be sent on application.

It is only applicable to High-pressure Engines, and a guaranteed saving is given to purchasers.

BAYLEY AND BAILEY'S PATENT WATER VALVES.

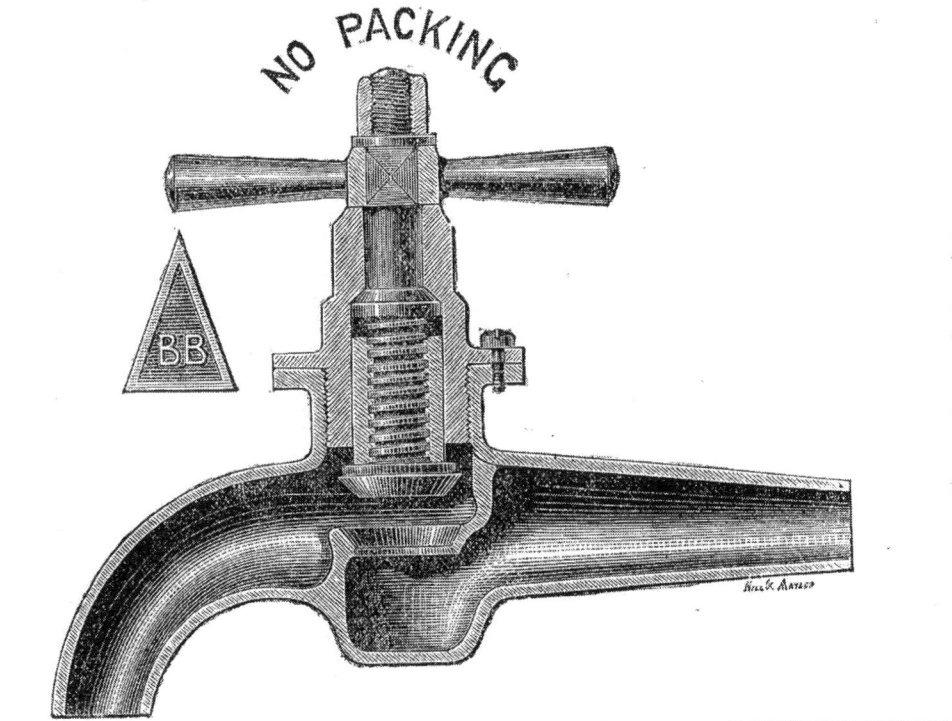

DESCRIPTION.

These Valves have no stuffing-boxes. The illustration shows their superiority to practical men without any further comment being required. All have leather facings. Brass only if ordered specially.

PRICES.

Bore—⅜, ½, ⅝, ¾, 1 in.
Per Doz.—30/- 36/- 45/- 60/- 90/-

IMPORTANT TO WATER WORKS ENGINEERS.

WATER-PRESSURE REDUCING VALVE (Greenhalgh's Patent.)

This valve is fitted with piston-leathered plunger, which, when weighted to the desired pressure, will permit 20, 30, 40, or other lbs. pressure to be delivered in low parts of a town, even if there be 80, 100, or any higher pressure on the inlet side. In preventing bursts, and in economising water and pumping power its merits are obvious. Working parts all gun metal.

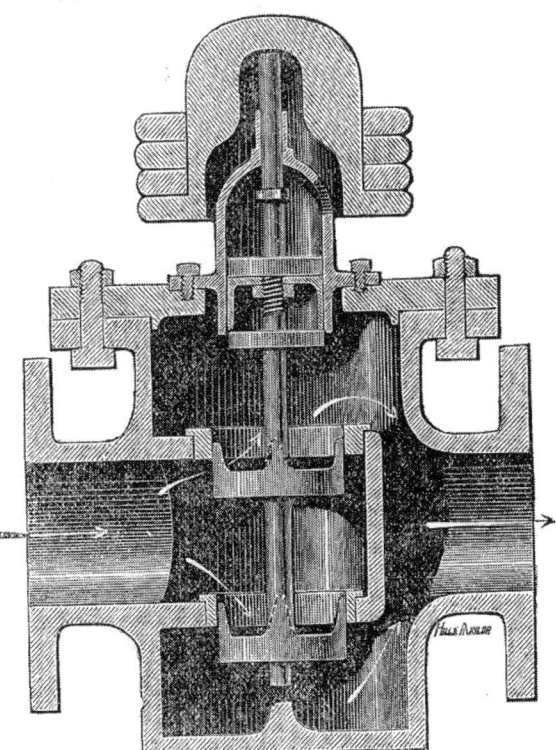

PRICES,

including weights, or lever with weight complete, for

2 in. bore	... ...	£6 0 0
3 ,,	... ...	9 0 0
4 ,,	... ...	12 0 0
5 ,,	... ...	15 0 0
6 ,,	... ...	18 0 0
8 ,,	... ...	24 0 0
10 ,,	... ...	30 0 0
12 ,,	... ...	36 0 0

These are made all brass, if less than 2 inches, for dwelling-houses. In ordering, please state for water pressure, to prevent confusion, as many are made by us for steam, of a modified form, for which see BAILEY's "SUPPLEMENTARY LISTS" of Boiler Fittings, *post free*.

Bailey's Air Compressors.

Large Pumping Engines often require the Air Chamber, refilling with air during the time the engine is working, the air having become absorbed by the water. These Air Compressors are designed for permanent fixtures against the engine house wall, being connected to the air vessel of the Pumping Engine by means of pipe and union. The pumps are supplied with or without pressure gauge. These may be used as test pumps for cylinders.

		With Gauge.	Without Gauge.
No. 1. With Brass Barrel 3 inch bore × 8 inch long	...	£10 0 0	8 0 0
No. 2. ,, ,, 2½ ,, × 6½ ,,	...	8 10 0	7 0 0

If more than 30 lbs pressure is required, No. 1 should be ordered with smaller barrel and extra strong ; same price charged.

These pumps are used for many other purposes, for which compressed air is required ; and if required to be made into exhausters, by reversing the valves, they are sold at the same prices with a vacuum gauge on the top, and made to order accordingly.

This class of pump was originally designed for use as Air Compressors for the Fogarty Air Gas Machines, made by J. BAILEY & Co. We find that 20 to 30 lbs. pressure may be obtained with ease.

Bailey's Patent Gas-Fitter's Test Pump and Gauge.

Price, with Gauge complete, £3 10s.

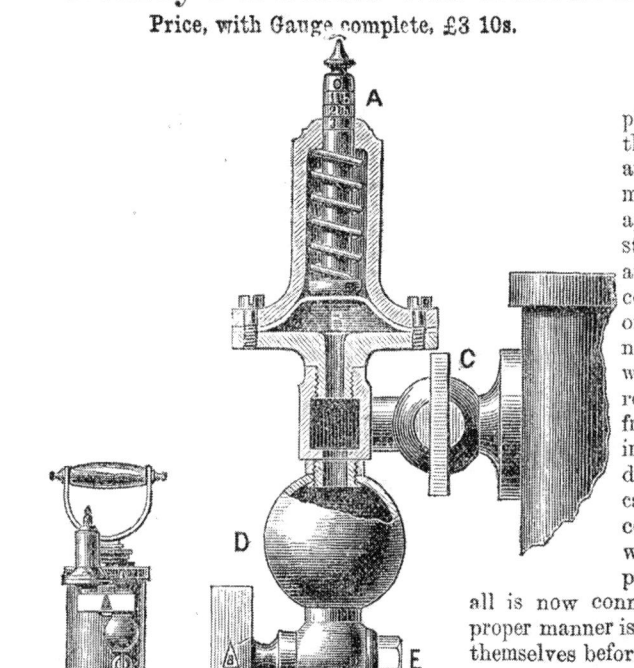

GAS EXPLOSIONS IN PRIVATE FAMILIES.

We refer to those explosions which occur from leaks in the pipes that have for the most part been laid inside the houses themselves, that are inward of the meter, and independent of any valves which the gas companies may have affixed to their mains. A long bill of indictments might be got up even against these house-service pipes, and against the mischief stored up in the upper parts of rooms which are unventilated at the cornice or chimney-breast or stored up between the ceiling of the room and the floors above. If, as a late writer on sanitary matters explains, we employ a gas-fitter who is not a gas-fitter, but a jack-of-all-trades, a "blacksmith, whitesmith, glazier, brazier, plumber, and bell-hanger," all rolled into one, we may safely look out for nuisances arising from our gas pipes in the positive degree, waste of money ; in the comparative degree, bad smells ; and in the superlative degree, suffering and death. The same writer explains how careless we in England seem to be about our gas supplies, the companies caring not one farthing what desperately bad work may be done inside the house, and the householder apparently caring as little, content if his fitter informs him that all is now connected to the meter, and that he may light up. The proper manner is to test house pipes—we do not speak of testing the pipes themselves before they are laid, for that the pipe-makers mainly do ; but to test them after every ramification of iron barrel and composition tube has been duly fitted up. We will suppose a mansion to be fitted up by a gas-fitter for the proprietor, every pipe in its place, and all ready for screwing up the brackets or pendants. This being so, the gas-fitter stops up all the outlets with screwed caps or other contrivances, all but one, and to this he affixes a forcepump, with a few drops of sulphuric ether dropped into its interior. The pump is now connected with a gauge, and set to work up to some moderately high pressure, sufficient, at all events, to find out any weaknesses, such as small holes or opening seams owing to imperfect welding. When the gauge registers a certain figure the pumping is stopped, and if the pressure lessens, it is evident that the pipes are somewhere unsound, and those imperfections are sought for. If they cannot be found by the smell of the escaping ether, the pipes are lathered over with soap and the leaks detected by the bubbles. This experiment is repeated until the gauge ceases to show a loss of pressure, and then only need the fitter trouble the gas company about an attachment to their mains. The official of the company, for he is an official in every sense of the word, looks at the dial, which now indicates no loss of pressure, and hands over his authorisation to connect. This is an amount of precaution that in our country we very rarely attempt ; indeed, we question if twenty journeymen gas-fitters out of a hundred ever heard of it.—*The Sanitary Record*, April, 1875.

The gas-fittings in all large establishments should be tested periodically, thus preventing heavy gas bills as well as danger from explosion.

By Her Majesty's  Royal Letters Patent.

THE PATENT HIGH-PRESSURE
SELF-CLEANSING FILTERS.

The efficiency of these Filters is acknowledged by all who have seen them to be most remarkable.

THE FOLLOWING ARE SOME OF THE ADVANTAGES POSSESSED BY THESE FILTERS:—

1st. They give a *continuous* supply of thoroughly filtered water.

2nd. Being attached to the Water Main, or Double-Acting Pump they require no filling, or Cistern, as do ordinary Filters.

3rd. They remove from water all organic impurities, and other matters held in suspension, and some of the mineral bases held in solution.

4th. Being made of pure animal Charcoal, they render water *bright, free from odour, and colourless*, and better adapted for manufacturing and all domestic purposes.

5th. They can be *instantly cleansed without cost or loss of time*, by turning the hand on the dial plate from a point thereon marked Filtered to a point marked Cleansing.

6th. Under a steady pressure their purifying powers will continue unimpaired for a good length of time.

7th. For Manufacturing purposes these Filters are invaluable. Being fixed on the main water pipe on entering the premises, the whole of the supply is filtered water through all the ordinary taps in the building.

8th. Their use will, to a great extent, prevent the scaling of Steam Boilers. Water can be taken from the hot well of a condensing engine, and filtered before entering the boiler.

9th. They cost much less than Filtering Cisterns, filter more efficiently, and give a much greater supply.

10th. They are the *only* filters that will filter water as rapidly as supplied by the water mains.

11th. They occupy little space; and may be attached to pipes in any part of the building.

12th. The supply of water is regulated by the hand on the dial plate, on which three points are indicated:—Unfiltered, Filtered, and Cleansing.

Diameter of Pipe	Single Cylinder	Double Cylinder
2 inch	£33 0 0	£44 0 0
3 „	60 0 0	77 0 0
4 „	105 0 0	132 0 0
5 „	150 0 0	180 0 0
6 „	200 0 0	240 0 0

These Filters are in use at Print Works, Bleach Works, Paper Works, Dye Works, Breweries, Public Baths, Hospitals, Asylums, Reformatories, Hotels, Restaurants, Spirit Merchants, Soda Water Manufacturers, Lancashire and Yorkshire Railway Co., Manchester Royal Exchange, Manchester Royal Infirmary, Private Houses, &c.

Steam Pumps can be attached to these Filters, to use Rain, Top, or River Water.

These Patent High-pressure Self-cleansing Filters for Manufacturing purposes are made in the following sizes, viz.:—2in. pipe, 3in. pipe, 4in. pipe, 5in. pipe, 6in. pipe. They can be made to filter up to 250,000 gallons per day.

Useful Inventions for Innkeepers, etc.

Bailey's Self-acting Bottling Machine
For 4 Bottles ... £4 0 0
With Copper Pan, for 6 Bottles ... 5 19 0

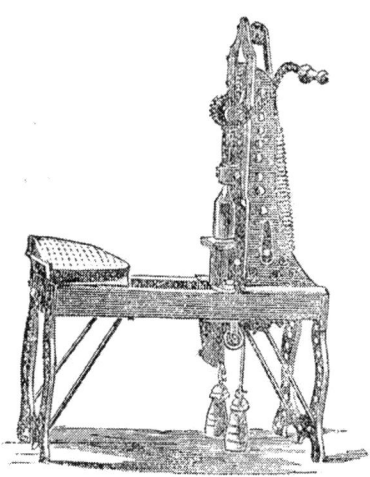

Bailey's Self-acting Corking Machine
Price, with Single Thimble, £5 10 0

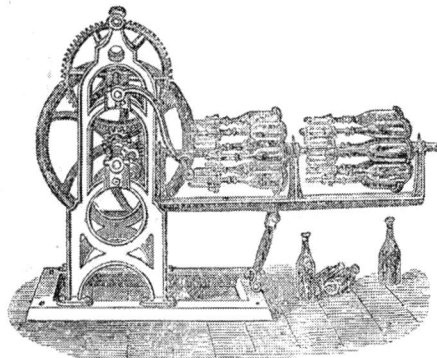

Hickling's Patent Bottle Washing Machine.
REVISED PRICE LIST.
No. 1—Machine to clean 16 Bottles at once, or 40 to 50 Gross per day £12 0 0
" 2 " 8 " ... 10 0 0
" 3 " 6 " ... 7 10 0
With fast and loose Pulleys for Steam Power extra ... 0 17 6
Shot measuring Apparatus for putting shot into bottles ... 0 7 6
Apparatus for transferring shot from one set of bottles to next size, suitable for
No. 1 Machine ... 0 12 6
" " 2 " ... 0 10 6
" " 3 " ... 0 7 6
All suitable for Bottles any size.
Iron Points, which are far superior to Shot for washing Bottles, 3d. per lb. or 27/- per cwt.

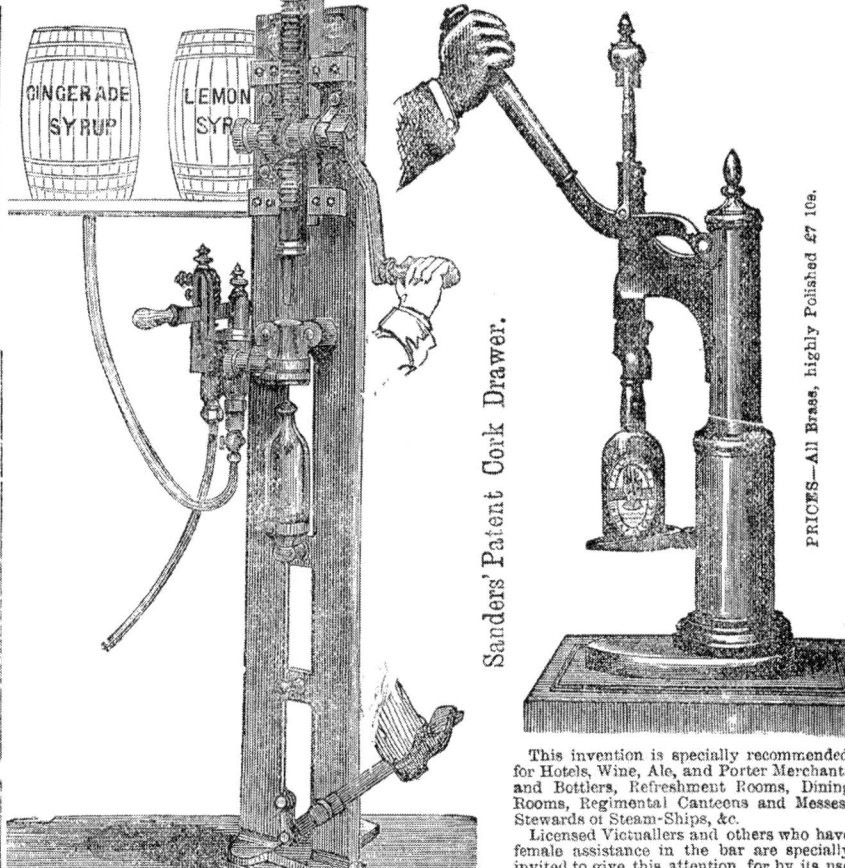

LEE'S NEW SYRUPING & FLAVOURING MACHINE,
(HOPE'S PATENT),
Which contains many *advantages* over the *best* methods hitherto practised for supplying the Bottle with Syrup or other ingredients, either in a liquid or gaseous form.
Among the numerous advantages may be noticed the following:—
1—It avoids the necessity of a separate operation in Syruping. 2—It prevents a waste of Syrup. 3—It supplies an equal quantity to each bottle. 4—It can be regulated to supply more or less as may be required. 5—It can be made to supply an unlimited number of different Syrups, &c. 6—It can be fixed to any Bottling Apparatus. 7—It is easily understood. 8—It works as easily as the ordinary Tap on Bottling Apparatus. 9—It reduces the removal, and consequently the Breakage of Bottles. 10—It prevents wasps and other insects from entering the Bottle while Syruping. 11—Syruping and Bottling are reduced to one operation. 12—No detriment to the Bottling process whatever.
PRICE—Complete, £6 each, ready for fixing to Bottling Machine; complete, with Bottling Machine, £12 10s.; Bottling Machine separate, £8.

Aerated Water Manufacturers, Waterloo Works,
Waterloo Bridge, Greengate, Salford.
Messrs. BAILEY & Co., Albion Works, Salford.
Gentlemen.—Your Syruping Machine gives complete satisfaction. It is the most efficient and complete thing we have seen, both in expense, room, and labour, and supplies a necessity long felt.   We are, faithfully yours,
S. LINGARD & CO.,
Per James Lingard.

Aerated and Mineral Water Stores, Jersey.
Mr. LEE,
Sir,—I have much pleasure in stating that your Syruping and Flavoring Apparatus answers all that can be desired, to my entire satisfaction. It only requires to be seen at work to be appreciated.   Yours truly,
THOMAS KINE.

Sanders' Patent Cork Drawer.

PRICES.—All Brass, highly Polished £7 10s.

This invention is specially recommended for Hotels, Wine, Ale, and Porter Merchants and Bottlers, Refreshment Rooms, Dining Rooms, Regimental Canteens and Messes, Stewards of Steam-Ships, &c.
Licensed Victuallers and others who have female assistance in the bar are specially invited to give this attention, for by its use the tightest cork may be drawn by a child.
It is also highly ornamental for a Table or Counter.
Numerous Testimonials from well-known respectable Licensed Victuallers and others on application.

Sanders' Patent Liquor Blender and Ale Regulator.
(Patented in England, France, America, Belgium, &c.)

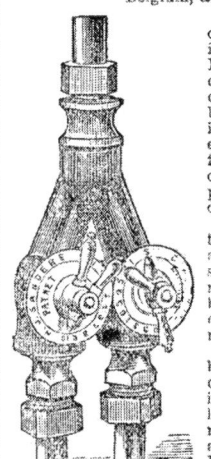

This useful Machine has been invented by the Patentees at the oft-repeated request of several large Innkeepers; its object being to enable to draw from two or more casks in any given proportion with one Pump.
It is unnecessary to enumerate the advantages of such an arrangement, as they must be obvious to all dealers in fermented liquors.
The Machine, being made on correct principles, is durable, and not liable to derangement, whilst its action is certain. It may be fixed close under the Pump, or in a convenient place in the cellar.
The Dial is divided into tenths. In using, put the fingers pointing to the figures representing the proportion required thus :—3 and 7; 4 and 6; 5 and 5; 1 and 9, &c.
N.B.—Very fresh and flat Beer may be drawn together with certainty, and no liability of either being disturbed.
PRICE—£2 5s.; if Six or more are ordered at one time, £1 5s. each. Each warranted perfect and to work well.
As we have had enquiries as to the possibility of Beer running out from one barrel into the other, we wish to say that it is impossible.

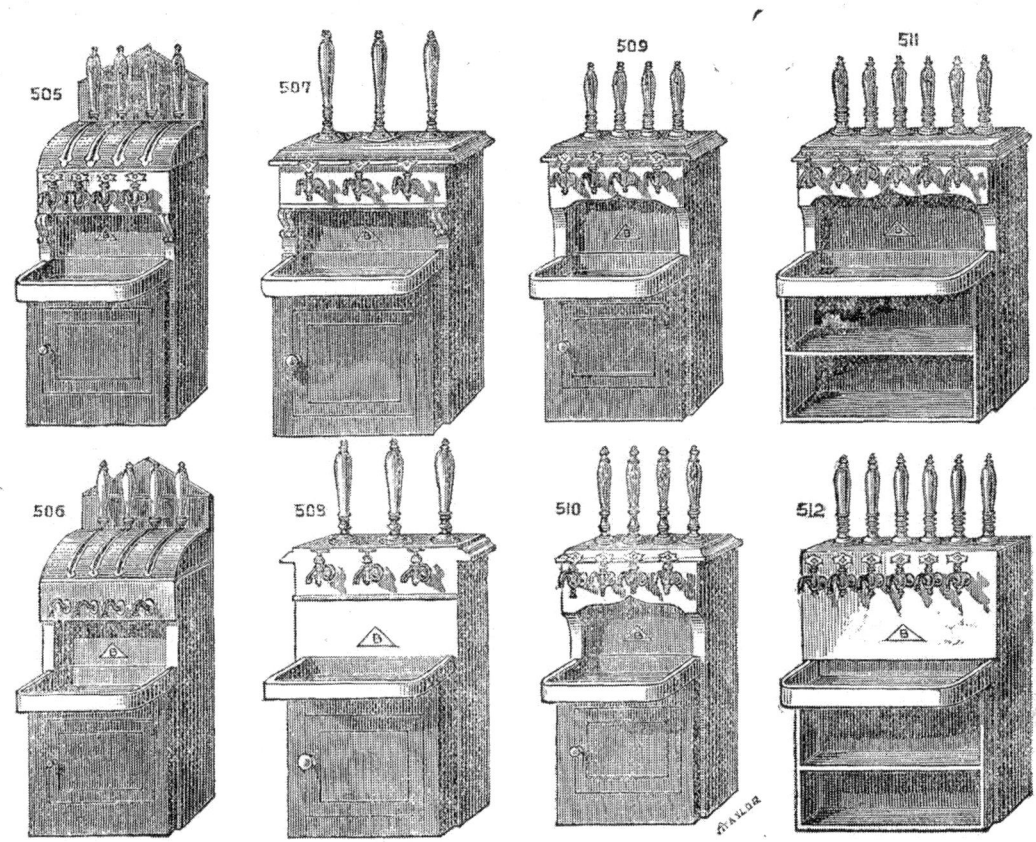

BEER MACHINES.

No. 505—Best quality Beer Machines, in Mahogany or Rosewood Cases, with a Tapping Cock to each Motion and Wrench.

2 Motions with Spouts,	£5 5 0	...	With Front Stop Cocks,	£5 9 0
3 ,, ,,	7 2 0	...	,, ,,	7 8 0
4 ,, ,,	8 15 0	...	,, ,,	9 6 0
5 ,, ,,	10 15 0	...	,, ,,	11 5 0
6 ,, ,,	12 12 0	...	,, ,,	13 3 0
8 ,, ,,	16 10 0	...	,, ,,	17 0 0

No. 507—Quadrant Action Beer Engine, in Mahogany Case, with a Tapping Cock to each Motion.

2 Motions with Spouts,	£6 18 0	...	With Front Stop Cocks,	£7 2 0
3 ,, ,,	9 8 0	...	,, ,,	9 14 0
4 ,, ,,	11 17 0	...	,, ,,	12 5 0
5 ,, ,,	14 6 0	...	,, ,,	14 16 0
6 ,, ,,	16 15 0	...	,, ,,	17 7 0
8 ,, ,,	22 0 0	...	,, ,,	22 16 0

No. 509—Quadrant Action Beer Engine, in Mahogany Case, with Tapping Cock to each Motion.

2 Motions with Front Stop Cock,	...	...	...	...	£6 15 0
3 do. do.	...	...	...	...	9 5 0
4 do. do.	...	...	...	...	11 10 0
5 do. do.	...	...	...	...	14 0 0
6 do. do.	...	...	...	...	16 7 0

No. 511—Improved Strong Quadrant Action Beer Engine, in Mahogany Case, and Tapping Cock to each Motion.

2 Motions with Best Front Stop Cock,	...	...	...	...	£7 6 0
3 do. do.	...	...	...	...	10 0 0
4 do. do.	...	...	...	...	12 12 0
5 do. do.	...	...	...	...	15 6 0
6 do. do.	...	...	...	...	18 0 0

No. 506—Good Quality, in Mahogany Cases, with Tapping Cock to each Motion.

2 Motions with Spouts,	£4 5 0	...	With Front Stop Cocks,	£4 9 0
3 ,, ,,	5 15 0	...	,, ,,	6 0 0
4 ,, ,,	7 3 0	...	,, ,,	7 12 0
5 ,, ,,	8 13 0	...	,, ,,	9 4 0
6 ,, ,,	10 3 0	...	,, ,,	10 16 0

No. 508—Quadrant Action Beer Engine, Front and Top of Case covered with Pewter, Tapping Cock to each Motion.

2 Motions with Best Front Stop Cocks,	...	...	...	£8 18 0
3 do. do.	...	...	...	11 19 0
4 do. do.	...	...	...	14 18 0
5 do. do.	...	...	...	18 8 0
6 do. do.	...	...	...	21 10 0

No. 510—Ball Motion Beer Engine in Mahogany Case, Tapping Cock to each Motion.

2 Motions with Front Stop Cocks,	...	...	...	£6 6 0
3 do. do.	...	...	...	8 12 0
4 do. do.	...	...	...	11 0 0
5 do. do.	...	...	...	13 6 0
6 do. do.	...	...	...	15 12 0

No. 512—Improved Stove Quadrant Action Beer Engine, Front and Top of Case covered with Pewter, Tapping Cock to each Motion.

2 Motions with Front Stop Cocks,	...	...	...	£8 10 0
3 do. do.	...	...	...	11 8 0
4 do. do.	...	...	...	14 5 0
5 do. do.	...	...	...	17 2 0
6 do. do.	...	...	...	20 0 0

If with Ornamental Handles, from 2/- each extra.

SPIRIT FOUNTAINS, COUNTER BEER PUMPS, &c.

480—Improved Spirit Fountain with Six Cocks, Tin Tube for Connecting, ...	£6 6 0
,, Do. do. do. Plated in best manner,	9 15 0
481—Best Liquor Cocks, on Brass Polished Plate, fixed on Mahogany, with Union to each Cock at back, no Pipe, ... per Cock from 6/3 to	0 8 0
482—Liquor Barrel Tapping Cock, with Union, ... each	0 2 6
483—Liquor Fountain Cock, Octagon, Revolving Head,	0 4 9
484— Do. do. best quality, Bent Union,	0 3 9
485— Do. do. do. with Boss,	0 4 0
486— Do. do. do.	0 4 3
488—Best Strong Beer Machine Tapping Cock, ...	0 4 9
489—Turn-down do. do. ...	0 6 0
490—Stocker's Patent, Strong do. ...	

491—Driving Cap for Tapping Cocks, ...	£0 0 10
492—Hop Strainer for do. ,, per doz. ...	0 6 0
493—Front Spout for Beer Machines ... each ...	0 2 3
494—Best Front Cock with Boss ... ,, ...	0 5 3
496— Do. Octagon London Pattern, ... ,, ...	0 7 0
497—Improved Counter Pillar Engine, ...	2 4 0
500—Ball Lever Strong Counter Beer Pump, with Guide Rods, ...	2 0 0
501—Quadrant do. do. do. ...	2 4 0
502—Improved do. do. do. ...	2 10 0
503— Do. Best Quality and Extra Strong do. ...	2 3 0
Ornamental Handles, extra from 2/- each	
Plated Furniture, ... each	0 9 6

Bailey's Beer or Spirit Racking and Bottling Cocks, &c.

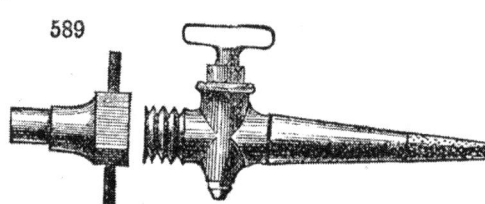

588 Beer Machine Tapping Cock, VERY STRONG & GOOD 60/- per doz.

589 BAILEY'S EXTRA STRONG & DURABLE LONG BARREL TAPPING COCK, 72/- per dozen.
All who purchase these send us further orders. It is the best in the market at the price.

587 Bailey's Extra Strong Beer Cocks
¾ in. — 49/0
⅞ in. — 64/0
1 in. — 76/0

		Per doz.
No. 981, Rough London Porter Cocks, screw bottom		31 6
No. 982, Rough London Porter Cocks, screw Lock		37 0
No 983, Beer Cocks, Nut Bottoms		29 0
" " " Strong		32 6
" 984, " " Small		18 9
" 985, " " Lock		21 0
" 986, Racking Cocks, Strong Nut Bottom		

⅝ ¾ ⅞ 1 inch
41/- 49/- 64/- 76/- per doz.

" 987, Racking Cocks, Lock
¾ ⅞ 1 inch.
47/- 58/- 76/- 88/- per doz.

" 990, Wine Bottling Cocks, Screw Bottom		23 0
" 991, Wine Bottling Turned Barrel, Nut Bottom		33 6
" " Wine Bottling Turned Barrel, Nut Lock		37 0
" 993, Spirit Cocks, Globe Barrel, Screwed Shank		16 0
" " Spirit Cocks, Globe Barrel, Screwed Lock		18 0

No. 599
GOODRING'S PATENT CRYSTAL MEASURING TAP.
Price each, **12/6**

This simple invention is for Measuring Spirits, Wines, Medicines, &c., direct from the cask or vessel in which it is screwed. The Tap, by being turned one quarter of a revolution, allows the liquid to enter the measure; when it is full to the required mark, a quarter turn empties the liquid into the jug.

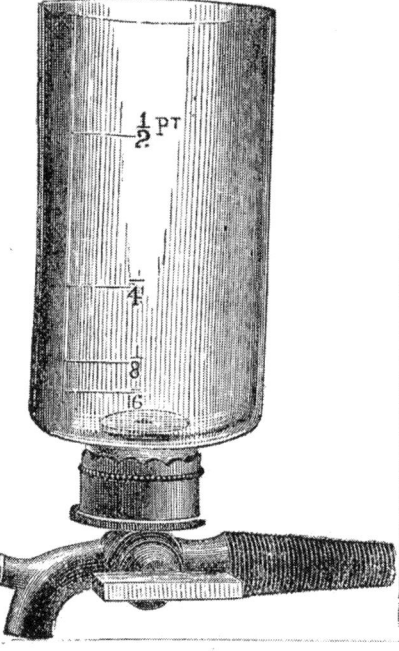

No. 600.
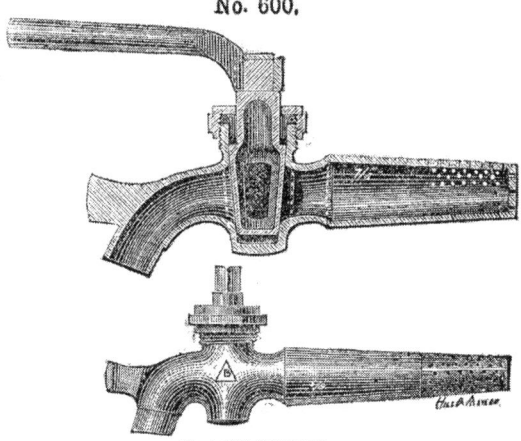

BAILEY'S LEAKLESS BEER COCKS
For Lever Keys with Glands.
⅞ in. ... 5s. 6d. each. | ⅝ in. ... 4s. 6d. each.
Keys 6d. and 9d. each.

VIEW FROM A PHOTOGRAPH.

The chief Publicans of Manchester and Liverpool, and many other towns, have these in daily use, and their reputation has greatly increased our trade in this Department.

No. 586

BAILEY'S CORK VALVE SPIRIT WINE AND LIQUOR COCKS,
PRICE **6/-** each;

With Union and Lock Nut, 7/- each.   With Taper Screw for Bungs in Casks, 6/6 each.
Mounted on highly-polished brass plate for the counter, 8/- each, ready for screwing on Mahogany Back.

This Spirit Cock is the most durable in the market, and only requires to have a cork inserted when it leaks; it is then as good as new.

TURRET CLOCK DEPARTMENT.

JOHN BAILEY & CO.,
MANUFACTURERS OF TURRET CLOCKS,
FOR

CHURCHES,	STABLES,	EXCHANGES,	INFIRMARIES,
CHAPELS,	BREWERIES,	GAS WORKS,	MARKET HALLS,
SCHOOLS,	TOWN HALLS,	COLLEGES,	CUSTOM HOUSES,
MILLS,	RAILWAY STATIONS,	HOTELS,	&c., &c., &c.

EXTRACTS FROM TESTIMONIALS.

Selected from a few hundred which J. B. & Co. have received.

TESTIMONIAL FROM THE LATE RIGHT HON. THE EARL OF ROSSE, F.R.S., F.R.A.S., &c.

The Castle, Parsonstown, Ireland, March 22, 1859.

Gentlemen—In answer to your letter, I beg to say that the Church Clock here PERFORMS VERY WELL; I believe MUCH BETTER THAN LARGE CLOCKS USUALLY DO.

ROSSE.

Bank Field, Halifax, October 27, 1857.

I have much pleasure in stating that the Clock constructed by Mr. BAILEY has met with my entire approval.

E. AKROYD.

From the late RICHD. ROBERTS the eminent inventor,

Globe Works, Faulkner Street, Feb. 27, 1857.

I have great pleasure in stating that I have seen Clocks made by Mr. BAILEY, which, for WORKMANSHIP AND FINISH, I THINK SUPERIOR TO ANY I HAVE SEEN BY OTHER MAKERS. I consider Mr. BAILEY's charges very moderate.

RICHD. ROBERTS.

☞ *In consequence of employing Steam Power and Improved Machinery,* **PRICES ARE VERY MUCH REDUCED.**

THE PRIZE MEDAL

TURRET CLOCKS
MANUFACTURED BY
Messrs. JOHN BAILEY & CO

Have the merit of being exceedingly simple, very strong, well-made, and replete with all the most modern improvements, and in consequence of being made in quantities by improved machinery, a Church Clock can be produced for less than £75, complete, which formerly could not, and cannot even now from some makers, be had for more than double the price.

The Testimonials received from the Right Hon. the Earl of Rosse, F.R.S.; Chancellor of Dublin University, the Right Rev. the Lord Bishop of Manchester, and other distinguished learned personages, sufficiently demonstrate the superiority of the Public Clocks erected by Messrs. J. B. & Co. They perform equally well in Northern Russia or Finland, in Jamaica or South America, as in this country.

View of the GREAT TURRET CLOCK exhibited by J. BAILEY & CO. in the Central Avenue of the Royal Agricultural Show, when held at Manchester, in July, 1869. Total height, 100 feet.

Patronized by most of the principal Church Dignitaries, Governments, Corporations, Railway Companies, &c., in the world, amongst which may be mentioned—

The Right Rev. the Lord Bishop of Manchester. The Right Hon. the Earl of Rosse, F.R.S. G. C. Leigh, Esq., M.P. Sir F. Crossley, E. Akroyd, Esq., Halifax. English, Chilian, and Peruvian Governments, Manchester, Salford, Halifax, and Warrington Corporations, Ulverston, Knaresborough, Elland and Stainland Local Boards. South Portuguese, Great Western, Belfast, Jamaica, and numerous other Railway Companies.

Estimates for any description of Turret Clock upon particulars being given.

TURRET CLOCK DEPARTMENT.

The Illustration next Page represents a Clock engraved from a Photograph, complete with the most modern improvements, Maintaining Power, Compensated Pendulum, internal set Dial, Patent Wire Ropes, best Gun Metal Wheels, Steel Pinions, and finished with great care.

Nos. 18, 19, and 20 in Price List are similar in design to this.

Prices of Church Clocks.

No. 21.—Turret Clock, with 2 Dials 6ft. diameter, blue and gold, strong enough for a bell of from 10 to 15 cwt., ... £100 0 0

22.—Do., with 4 Dials, ... 125 0 0
(This is a very usual size for a Town Clock.)

23.—Do., with Dials 5ft. diameter, ... 110 0 0

If "Ting Tang" quarters, add to these Prices 25 per cent.

When ordered for export careful attention is paid to the packing, and full instructions sent for fixing.

J. BAILEY & CO.,

Turret Clock Makers to the British & Foreign Governments,

The Chief Railway Companies, Corporations, &c., at home and abroad,

ALBION WORKS,

SALFORD, MANCHESTER.

Turret Clock Department established A.D. 1832.]

MODERN CHURCH CLOCK.

For Description of this Clock, see next page; for Prices of them, see preceding page.

Bailey's Turret Clocks.

On the following two pages will be found engravings of one of the large turret clocks manufactured by the well-known firm of Bailey & Co., of the Albion Works, Salford, Manchester. It is what is known in workshop parlance as the "lathe-bed" pattern, in contradistinction to those which are called the "cage" pattern, made by our forefathers out of strips of wrought-iron bolted together to form a cage, and bushed with brass where requisite. There are points of superiority about this clock to which we think profitable attention may be directed by those engaged in mechanical pursuits. The adjusting of the external dials by means of the internal minute dial is very simple. The old-fashioned way to do this was to have a long bearing on the pallet shaft to enable the pallet wheel to be disengaged, and thus to "run down" the clock until the right time was indicated outside. If this was done in a clumsy manner, very often the teeth were damaged, and sometimes entirely stripped by allowing the pallet to slip into gear when the wheel was revolving at a great speed. Messrs. Bailey effect the operation in a totally different way. Fig 1 is plan of hour shaft with a friction clutch lock-nut and set dial, Fig. 2 is the friction clutch, and Fig. 3 is elevation of dial and bevel, and on reference to the large engraving it will be seen with what ease the upright shaft which leads to the dials may be adjusted by this simple arrangement. The pendulum has appeared in many shapes in the hands of horologists; many of the means of compensating for the effects of temperature on their length seem to be ingeniously contrived to create a great evil in order that a little one may be cured. The most approved system of compensation is the mercurial. A steel rod carrying a glass jar containing mercury, the expansion of the mercury upwards will compensate for the lengthening of the steel rod downwards, and thus keep the centre of oscillation at one fixed distance from the point of suspension. The compensation is only applicable to small clocks. If a wood pendulum rod be used, well dried and varnished, its expansion is very trifling, and very little compensation is required. Figs. 4 and 5 show the front and side elevation of the wood pendulums used in the large clocks made by Messrs. Bailey & Co. At the bottom of the rod, at Fig 4, is a cotter pin, upon which rests a brass rod standing up the centre, about 12 inches long; the bob rests on this rod, a cotter pin driven through its centre causing all the weight to rest on the upright brass rod; the expansion of the rod of wood and the suspension springs is compensated by the expansion of the small brass rod. The way in which these large pendulums are adjusted will be seen and understood by reference to the upper ends of Figs. 4 and 5. A brass nut is let into the rod through which works a bolt having a milled head resting on the crutch. This crutch is so arranged that the pendulum slides between its two jaws. This simple manner of adjustment at the top of the pendulum is an obvious improvement on the plan of adjustment used at the bottom, as it enables a slight adjustment to be made without stopping the clock. The horizontal adjustment for the springs at the top of the pendulum has been copied from the small French clocks. This enables the clock to be put in beat if a slight variation takes place after it has been fixed.

When winding the heavy weights of the striking parts of large clocks the winch handle cannot be used direct on the drum shaft; a pinion wheel being added to the wheel similar to the arrangement of a hoisting crab; Fig. 7 shows a plan adopted by Messrs. Bailey for using the first pinion of the train for this purpose. It will be observed that the pinion works loose from the second wheel when required for winch purposes, the ratchet wheel and clicks enabling this to be done, but when required for the clock purposes it is equal to a fast pinion wheel, and thus does duty for both. This improvement is so obvious that no comment is required. Although the clock here illustrated has been designed by Mr. W. H. Bailey, it is only doing justice to the late Richard Roberts, of Manchester, to say that the specific improvements mentioned have been very slightly altered from his designs, with the exception of the framework. The wheels in this clock are of hard gun metal, engine cut, and the pinions are of hardened steel. The drums have a worm cut on them to enable the wire rope to coil freely. A number of these clocks are being fixed at home and abroad by Messrs. Bailey & Co., one of a larger size, and to strike the quarters, having during the past few days been fixed at Walkden Church, near Manchester, having been presented by Mr. William Crompton, ex-mayor of Wigan, an extensive iron and coal proprietor.—*Engineer, June, 1875.*

BAILEY'S
TURRET CLOCKS FOR CHURCHES AND PUBLIC BUILDINGS.

Turret Clocks to Strike the Hours.

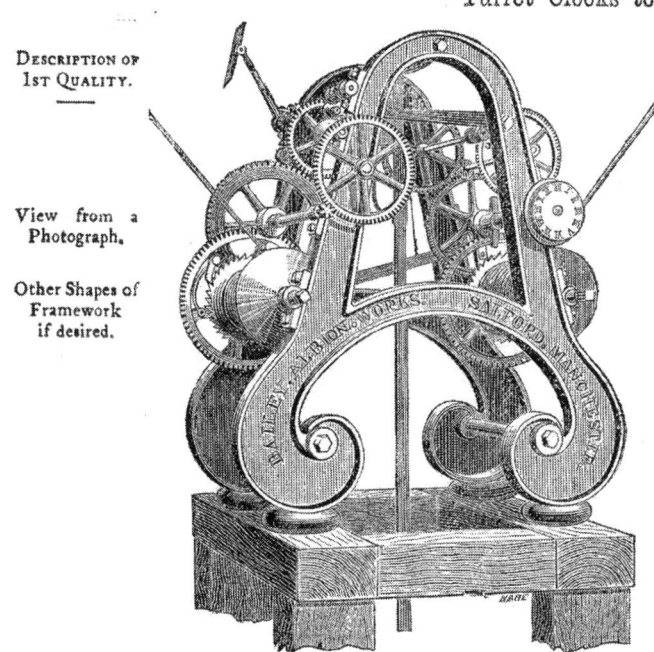

DESCRIPTION OF 1ST QUALITY.

View from a Photograph.

Other Shapes of Framework if desired.

Turret Clock, to go eight days, dead-beat escapement, maintaining power, internal dial to set hands, patent wire ropes, weights, compensating *pendulum*, hammer, levers, and all complete and ready for fixing, the larger wheels of iron, and the smaller of best gun-metal, engine cut, and the pinions of steel, with one cast-iron dial and hands complete.

If required of extraordinary "*Best Best*" finish, and of more expensive material and quality, with Dennison's Gravity escapement.

Of sufficient power for Bell of 28 lbs.	No. 7.—Dial 18 inch,	£15 10	7A	£20 0
	" 8.—Do. 2 ft.	17 10	8A	22 0
Ditto for Bell of 100 lbs.	" 9.—Do. 2 " 6 in.	25 0	9A	32 0
	" 10.—Do. 3 "	35 0	10A	40 0
	" 11.—Do. 4 "	40 0	11A	50 0
Powerful enough for Bell of 250 lbs	" 12.—Do. 3 "	40 0	12A	50 0
	" 13.—Do. 4 "	50 0	13A	60 0
	" 14.—Do. 5 "	55 0	14A	60 0
	" 15.—Do. 5 "	60 0	15A	70 0
For 5 cwt. Bell	" 16.—Do. 6 "	65 0	16A	76 10
	" 17.—Do. 7 "	80 0	17A	90 0
10 cwt. Bell to 15 cwt.	" 18.—Do. 5 "	60 0	18A	70 0
	" 19.—Do. 6 "	75 0	19A	86 10
	" 20.—Do 7 "	85 0	20A	100 0

The above do not include bells or fixing.

For prices of extra Dials, see following page. If a purchaser is unable to select a Clock from this list, on receipt of particulars as follows, the price will be sent :—

Numbers of Dials ... ?
Diameter of present Bell, if any ... ?
Must we include price of Bell ... ?

Chiming Clocks, to strike the hour and chime quarters, "ting tang," or Westminster chiming, from £80 to £500, according to size of bells and dial

Export, add 7½ o/o on the above prices for packing ; the greatest care taken in executing Foreign Orders ; if purchasers abroad wish for any information we shall be glad to send it.

For the Trade—Clock or Watchmakers who will represent us, or who wish for prices, will find their interests consulted.

Our Facilities—We make more Public Clocks than all the firms put together in the North of England, and every improvement is immediately introduced, and old designs discarded ; we cast our own Gun Metal, cut our own Wheels, Paint, Engrave, and Gild our own Dials, and perform every operation on our premises by means of first-class Machinery and the *best paid Workmen* in the Kingdom, under our own management, assisted in each department by Foremen and Managers of ability and experience. The consequence is an ever-increasing trade in this department, caused by the satisfaction our workmanship produces among purchasers.

BAILEY'S DOUBLE & SINGLE DIAL TIMEPIECES,
For Shops, Railway Stations, and Show Rooms, &c., to wind behind.

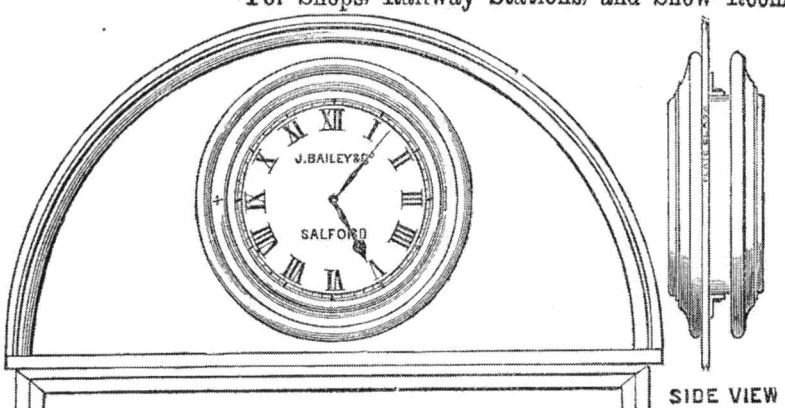

SIDE VIEW

Double Dial Timepiece, in one case, with eight-day movement, strong spring, brass plates and wheels, steel pinions hardened, hands to be set by the hands of the internal dial, glass on front of both dials, complete and ready for fixing :—

		£ s. d.
No. 1—Dials, 14 in.	...	10 10 0
" 2.—Do. 16 "	...	14 10 0
" 3—Do. 18 "	...	20 0 0

If the internal dials and case are for weight like No. 248, p. 92, the price extra, to go with weight and long pendulum will be £3 each.

Railway and other Public Companies who wish for Estimates for Clocks for the Tropics, or for long or short lines of Railway, will find our prices moderate and workmanship excellent.

TURRET CLOCK DEPARTMENT.

Small Turret Timepieces and Clocks for Railway Stations, Works, &c.

A, View of Works, and **C**, View of the No. 2 £15 Works or School Timepiece, with Cast Iron Dial, Raised Figures; can be fixed by any Joiner.

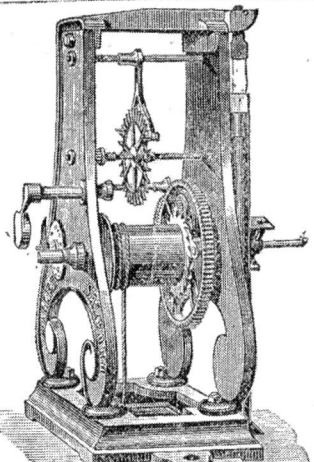

TURRET TIMEPIECES, i.e. (not to strike).	With Gun Metal Wheels, Steel Pinion and dead beat escapement one dial. B quality.	If with gravity escapement, and most superior finish, one dial. A quality.	PRICE EACH. For extra Dials, gilded, Dial motion and Hands, Bevel Wheels.
	£ s. d.	£ s. d.	£ s. d.
No. 1, with dial, 18in diameter, to fix against dead wall, and movement eight-day, dead-beat escapement, complete with all, ready for fixing	10 10 0		2 15 0
No. 2 Timepiece, with 2ft. dial, blue and gold, with cast-iron Rim, as Photograph, with roller pallet escapement, dead-beat, all complete	15 0 0	20 0 0	3 0 0
No. 3, if 3ft. dial	16 10 0	21 10 0	6 10 0
No. 4, 4ft. dial and stronger works	20 0 0	26 0 0	10 0 0
No. 5, 6ft. dial	30 0 0	36 0 0	12 10 0
No. 6, 8ft. dial	50 0 0	60 0 0	16 10 0

All warranted Two Years. A third quality at lower prices.

The above are all well tested before delivery, and in the larger ones the main wheels are Iron, and all the rest of the very best Gun Metal, Engine cut and finished, the Pinions of Steel, and all very superior manufacture.

No. 1A Timepiece with two internal Dials, 14in. and one dail external 24in. complete, price £20.
For illustration see opposite page

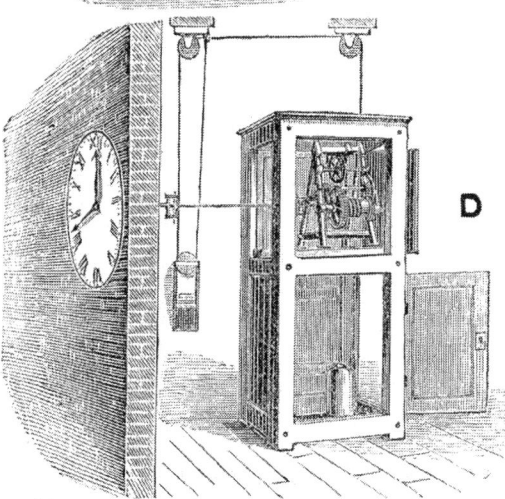

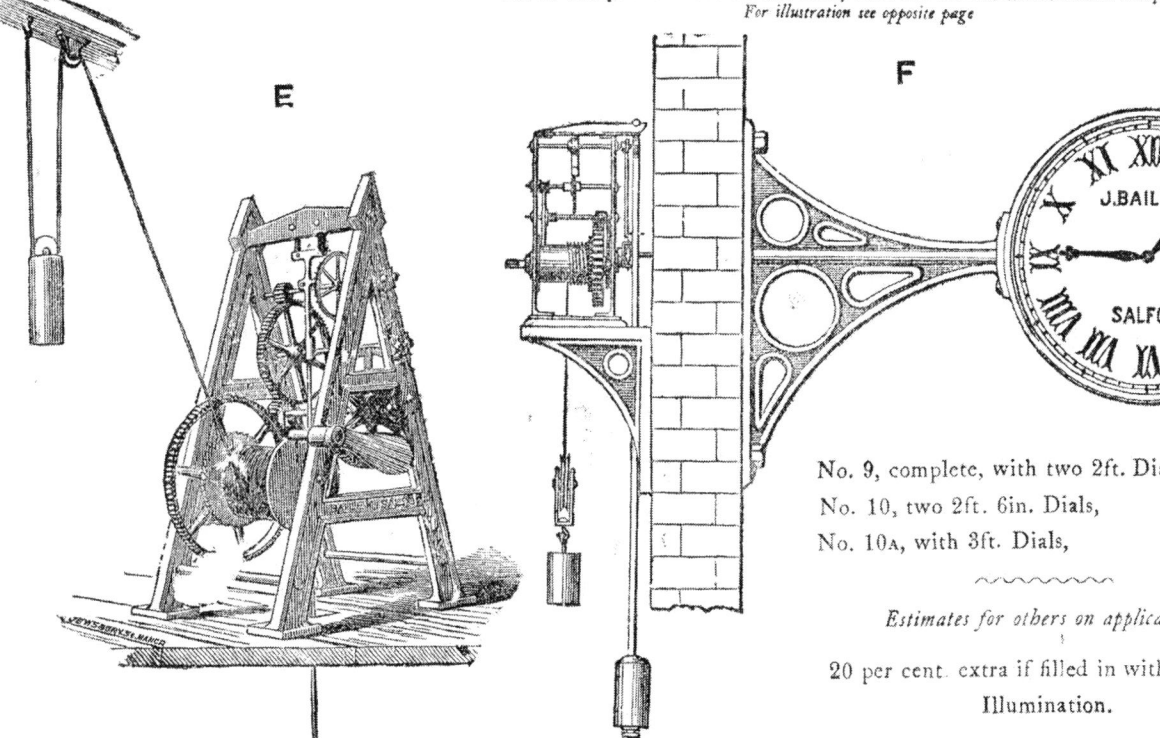

No. 9, complete, with two 2ft. Dials, £21 10

No. 10, two 2ft. 6in. Dials, ... 26 0

No. 10A, with 3ft. Dials, ... 40 0

Estimates for others on application.

20 per cent. extra if filled in with glass for Illumination.

Explanation of Illustrations on this Page.

A, View from a Photograph of the Timepieces Nos. 1, 2, 3, 4. C, View from Photograph of No. 2 Timepiece Dial. D, View of Timepiece made for the Chief Station of the Railway of Boca and Eusenadá, South America, with Case, complete. E, View of larger Timepieces, suitable for 4 to 8 feet Dials. F, Railway Station Timepiece.

IMPROVED TIME REGULATOR, for Works' Yard, the Office, and the Stores.
THREE DIALS DRIVEN BY ONE MOVEMENT,
BY MESSRS. BAILEY AND CO.

In workshops where a large number of workmen are employed, and distributed over the building in various rooms, stores, or offices, it is essential that the time of day should be shown alike on all the dials, but that has hitherto been an impossibility, from the circumstance that, as each dial has the works in its own case, they cannot be kept so exact as to ensure the pendulum springing at the same speed to move the handles at the same rate. Thus in (say) half-a-dozen clocks in one house, there is always a discrepancy of time between them. This may appear a small matter to those who have plenty of time to spare, and who have no compulsory feeling to keep time; but in factories it is necessary that time should be kept to the second, and that excuses as to the difference of time shown by one clock over another should be abolished, and that all the clocks in the building, even to the entrance towers, should be governed by one set of going mechanism, placed within some part of the works, and kept under lock and key, to be seen only for the purpose of winding. Such an arrangement of mechanism has been introduced by Messrs. J. BAILEY & Co., of the Albion Works, Salford. It will be seen by the above engraving, of which fig. 1 is a general view of an office and of a store-room above, with a clock in each, and a dial outside in the yard, all showing the same time exactly. There is a spindle in connexion with the wheels of each clock, which are turned by the going mechanism indicated in the store by bevel gearing. The moving power is composed of a powerful train of wheels from a barrel and weight, as clearly seen in the detached view, fig. 2. It will be observed that the pendulum is at the back of the works, near the wall, and is clear of the barrel arbor in its vibrations. The maintaining power levers close over the winding square, so that it is impossible to wind it without lifting it, and of course setting it in motion. The set dial is an important feature in the mechanism, as it sets all the hands simultaneously by a peculiar motion sleeve pinion, which can be tightened up by a thumbscrew to bring it in gear with the clock-work. The escapement is the "dead-beat," and, instead of using the anchor pallot, Messrs. BAILEY & Co. fit steel studs, with hardened rollers upon the ends, to engage with teeth of the wheel; these rollers are renewable at any time by ordinary mechanics not versed in horology. The introduction of the rollers is important, as they will work with less friction than ordinary pallets, and necessarily last a much longer time. Altogether, the idea is very good and simple, the arrangement being carried out in a very satisfactory manner.—(*From the "*MECHANICS' MAGAZINE.*"*)

Copy of a Letter received by the founder of our Firm, from the late Earl of ROSSE, the eminent Astronomer.

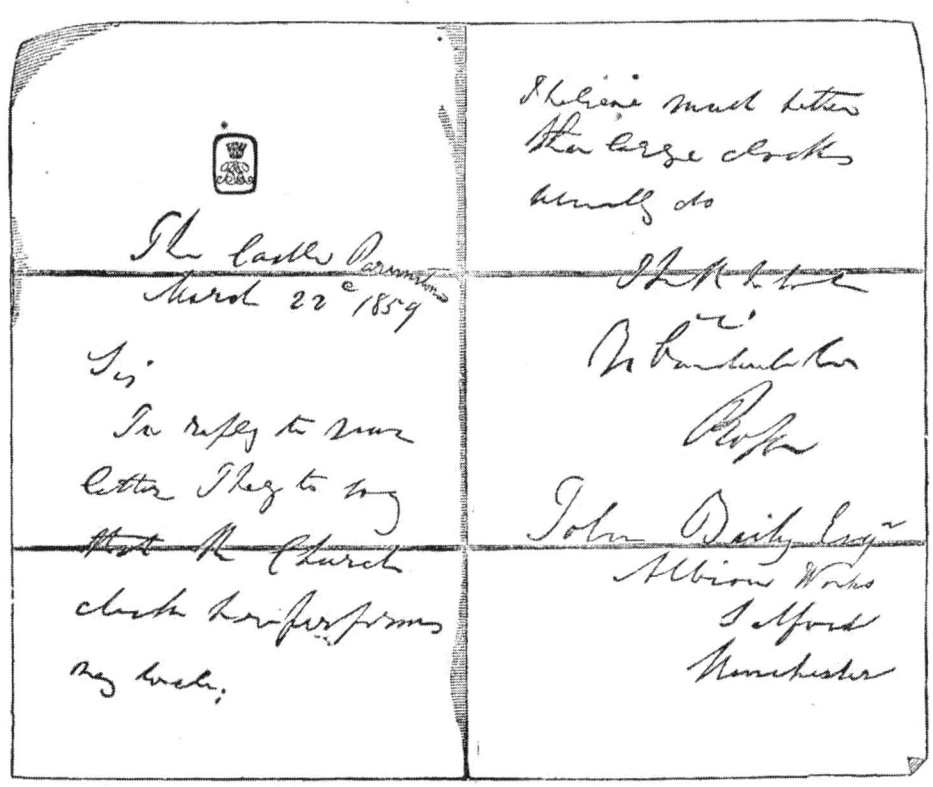

BAILEY'S REGISTERED DESIGN
HALL, VESTRY, OR DINING-ROOM BRACKET TIMEPIECES.
The dial blue dead ground, and gold hands and figures, remarkably handsome.

Price with dial 14 in. diameter, to go eight days, steel pinions, and brass wheels, not to strike,

£5 10 0

Six shillings extra, if packed in case.

To strike the hours, on Gong, with Cathedral tone, 14 in. dial,

£8 8 0

If packed in case six shillings extra.

ART TREATMENT.
If Architects or others require special designs with our most improved style of Art embellishment for Entrance Halls, &c., we shall be glad to quote, or to make to architects' own designs.

BAILEY'S BELLS AND BELL-TOLLING AND CHIMING MACHINES.

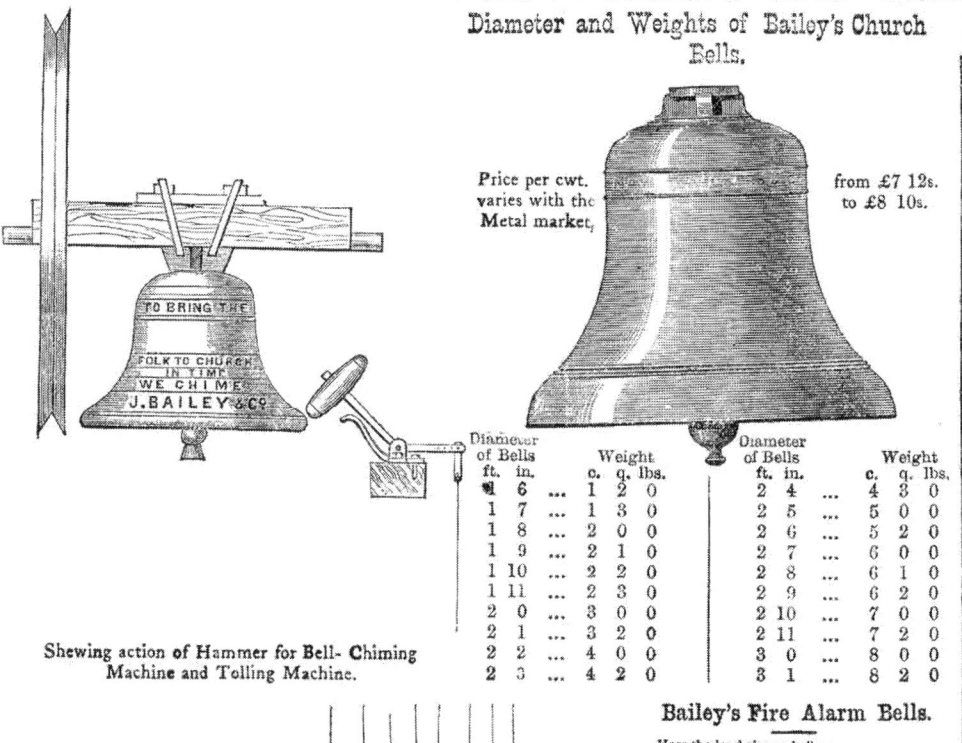

Diameter and Weights of Bailey's Church Bells.

Price per cwt. varies with the Metal market, from £7 12s. to £8 10s.

Diameter of Bells ft. in.	Weight c. q. lbs.	Diameter of Bells ft. in.	Weight c. q. lbs.
1 6	1 2 0	2 4	4 3 0
1 7	1 3 0	2 5	5 0 0
1 8	2 0 0	2 6	5 2 0
1 9	2 1 0	2 7	6 0 0
1 10	2 2 0	2 8	6 1 0
1 11	2 3 0	2 9	6 2 0
2 0	3 0 0	2 10	7 0 0
2 1	3 2 0	2 11	7 2 0
2 2	4 0 0	3 0	8 0 0
2 3	4 2 0	3 1	8 2 0

Shewing action of Hammer for Bell-Chiming Machine and Tolling Machine.

Bailey's Fire Alarm Bells.

Hear the loud alarum bells—
    Brazen bells!
What a tale of terror now their turbulency tells!
  In the startled ear of night
  How they scream out their affright!
    Too much horrified to speak
    They can only shriek, shriek,
      Out of tune,
In a clamorous appealing to the mercy of the fire,
In a mad expostulation with the deaf and frantic fire
  Leaping higher, higher, higher,
  With a desperate desire,
  And a resolute endeavour
  Now, now to sit or never
By the side of the pale-faced moon,
  Oh, the bells, bells, bells,
What a tale their terror tells.—E. A. POE.

Bailey's Bell-Tolling Machine.

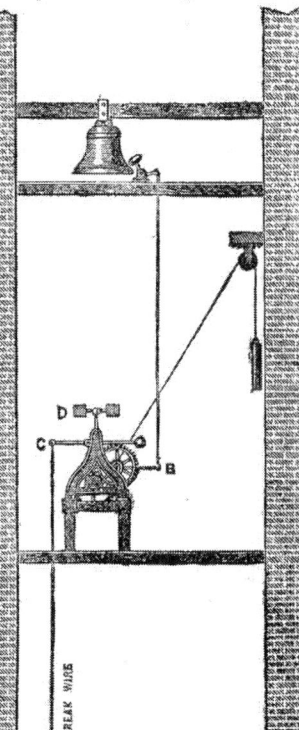

This does away with the cost of a man for tolling, morning and evening, in Churches; it only requires to be wound, and at any time the wire A may be pulled, and it will then go for half an hour with great regularity; it can be stopped by the same means. This is a very useful Machine in a Church tower, and saves a small sum per annum.

PRICES.

Including two speeds, one for tolling for Service, and one very slow, for Funerals, both of which can be regulated at will.

No.		Diameter ft. in.	£ s. d.
1.	For Bells	2 0	10 0 0
2.	Ditto	2 6	15 0 0
3.	Ditto	3 0	20 0 0
	Over 3 ft. in diameter		25 0 0

And upwards.

All ready for fixing, not including Bell. Any joiner can fix in a few hours.

Bailey's Bell-Chiming Machine.

Each Machine has three changes by the adjustment of the drum.

For 3 bells, price	...	...	...	...	£20	Bells	
„ 4 „	...	...	...	...	25	6 8 10	
„ Bells, if largest bell 5 cwt.	...	...	...	...£30 £40 £50			
„ „ „ 10 „	...	...	...	...	40 60 70		
„ „ „ 20 „	...	...	...	...	60 80 100		

The Machines are very strong and made in accordance with the size of the Bells, the changes for change-Chiming are done so well, that to the ear the effect is similar to change-Ringing.

One important feature in these Machines is the handles to the levers which will enable the Bells to be played upon, *a la pianoforte*, by hand by any man of ordinary musical attainments.

BAILEY'S BEST **BRONZE BELL.** NETT PRICES.

Diam.		Extra with Yoke and Lever	Diam.		Extra with Yoke and Lever
9 in.	24/-	10/-	14 in.	102/-	14/-
10 in.	33/-	11/6	16 in.	168/-	16/-
12 in.	68/6	12/-	18 in.	202/-	19/-

Bailey's Electric Bells,

FOR WAREHOUSE, FACTORY, or Domestic Use.

In Metal Cases, very strong and good.

PRICES ON APPLICATION.

Bell Alarm Machine for Fire Brigade Stations.

To go ten minutes, with two hammers, complete, ready for fixing, without bell,

No. 4, ...£10 0 0
„ 5, For very large bell 15 0 0

Special quotation for electric arrangement to enable the alarm to be released from a distant Police Station.

BAILEY'S SPRING AND WEIGHT TIME-PIECES AND CLOCKS.

BÜRK'S PATENT WATCHMAN'S CLOCK.

No. 246.

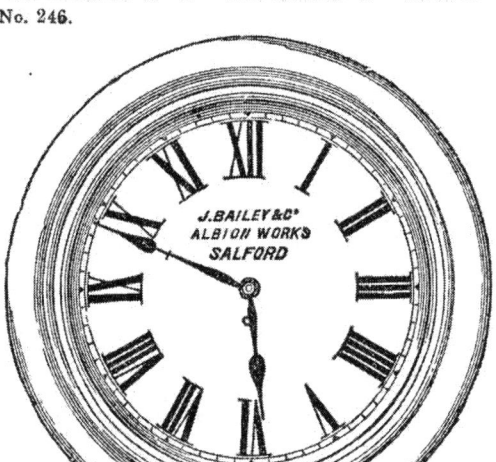

Bailey's First-class Timepieces,

For Railway Station Rooms, Platforms, Offices, &c., of the very best manufacture, and as supplied to the chief companies, with spring movements, French polished cases, works best brass and steel, same shape as the Watchman's Peg Clock :—

No. 1.—12 in. dials	...	...	...	£2 10 0
,, 2.—14 ,, ,,	...	...	...	3 15 0
,, 3.—16 ,, ,,	...	...	...	6 0 0
,, 4.—18 ,, ,,	...	...	...	6 15 0
,, 5.—24 ,, ,,	...	...	...	10 10 0

Special estimates on application.

No. 247.

Bailey's Timepieces,

Same as No. 246, but with trunk case and long pendulum :—

12 in.	...	£3 0 0	To strike the hours,	£5 10 0
14 ,,	...	4 4 0	,, ,,	8 10 0
16 ,,	...	6 9 0	,, ,,	16 0 0

Chime Clocks, in long case, £20 each.

BAILEY'S WEIGHT CLOCK,

With seconds pendulum, in French-polished mahogany case, dead-beat escapement, thirty-nine inch pendulum.

No. 248.

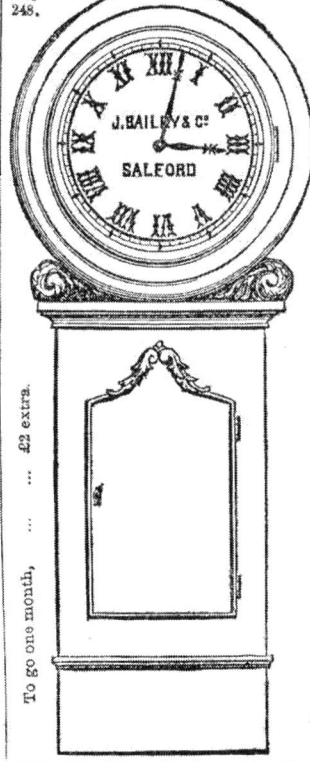

To go one month ... £2 extra.

With 14 in. dial. ... £6 10; 16 in. ... £8 10
To strike hours, 14 in. £8 10; 16 in. £12 0

At each of the stations where the watchman passes, a key for impressing a sign is fixed in a manner suitable in a likewise fixed box. The watchman carries with him the clock locked up, and on arrival at each station inserts the key into a hole in front of the clock, and turning it round each key impresses a sign on a paper dial which is fixed inside upon a ring, which is carried round by the pointer, thereby indicating the proper time. Each paper dial is divided into 12 hours, and every hour into 6 subdivisions, indicating 10 minutes each. Every key impressing a different sign, it clearly shows the time the watchman has passed each station.

When the clock is delivered for inspection, it is opened and the paper dial taken out, and after having been wound up another paper dial is applied for use by fixing the black end of the paper dial on the small pin attached to the ring through the centre of the figure 6. In fixing the paper dial round the ring, the pin meets again the centre of the figure 6 on the opposite end of the paper dial. The clock is handed over to the watchman after having been locked, and the key is kept by the principal.

The key for winding up the clock is likewise used for setting it. The arrangement of the clock does not allow of a minute finger, but the key turns round the minute tube, and the wire projection fixed to the key indicates instead, and affords the means to set the clock to the minutes.

About 400 paper dials are provided with each clock, and a book into which they are placed for permanent record, arranged to hold the paper dials for 52 weeks of 7 days. The back of the paper dials is prepared with red gum, and when wetted to place them in the book, the red matter makes the marks more visible.

See also Recorder Department.

Price complete, with 6 Keys, £6 10s.

Bailey's MEAN TIME

Best REGULATOR

For Entrance Halls of Public Buildings, to Regulate the Time of Towns or Cities.

And for the Entrance Halls of the Residences of Gentlemen.

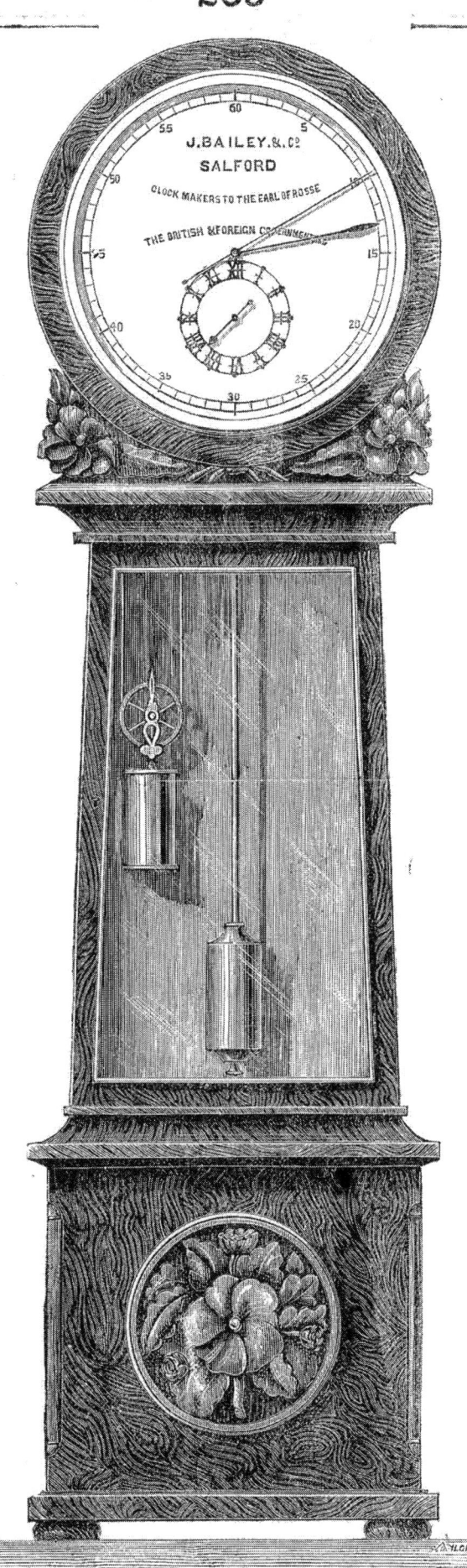

No. 1—Dead Beat Escapement, Cylindrical Pendulum, Iron and Zinc Compensating, Enamel Dial, —in Oak or Mahogany Case—to go 14 days, £21

„ **2**—Dead Beat or Roller Escapement, Jewelled, Compensating Pendulum, of Steel and Brass Rods, Enamel Dial—in Oak or Mahogany Case—to go 8 days, £25

„ **3**—Gravity Escapement, Compensating Pendulum, Plate Glass Front, Centre Seconds — in Oak or Mahogany Case —to go 14 days, £35

„ **4**—Dead Beat Escapement, Jewelled Pallets, Mercurial Compensating Pendulum, Enamel Dial Plate Glass Front —to go 14 days, £40

No. 5—Dead Beat or Gravity Escapement, Jewelled, Mercurial Compensating Pendulum, Plate Glass Front, Enamel Dial, with Arms or Crest carved in bottom panel of Case—to go 28 days £55
Silvered Dial, £3 extra.

„ **6**—Dead Beat or Gravity Escapement, Mercurial Compensating Pendulum Escapement, Jewelled throughout, Movements cased in metal, damp and dust proof, suitable for the Colonies, most splendid workmanship—in Oak or Mahogany — to go 28 days, … … £60

These First-Class Timekeepers are all warranted of the best description; all the works being of the best possible finish, and thoroughly adjusted, and Compensations tested before delivery.

BAILEY'S MEAN TIME

GOTHIC

No. 1—Dead Beat Escapement, Cylindrical Pendulum (Iron and Zinc Compensating) Blue and Gold Dials—in Oak or Mahogany case—to go 14 days, ... £24

„ **2**—Dead Beat or Roller Escapement, Jewelled, Compensating Pendulum, of Steel and Brass Rods, Blue and Gold Enamel Dial—in Oak or Mahogany Case—to go 8 days, ... £28

„ **3**—Gravity Escapement, Compensating Pendulum, Plate Glass Front, Centre Seconds, Blue and Gold Enamel Dial—in Oak or Mahogany Case—to go 14 days £38

„ **4**—Dead Beat Escapement, Jewelled Pallets, Mercurial Compensating Pendulum, Blue and Gold Enamel Dial, Plate Glass Front—to go 14 days, £44

BEST REGULATOR.

DESIGN.

No. 5—Dead Beat or Gravity Escapement, Jewelled, Mercurial Compensating Pendulum, Plate Glass Front, Blue and Gold Enamel Dial, with Arms or Crest carved in bottom panel of Case—to go 28 days, £60

„ **6**—Dead Beat or Gravity Escapement, Mercurial Compensating Pendulum, Escapement Jewelled throughout, Movements cased in Metal, Damp and Dustproof, suitable for the Colonies, most splendid workmanship—in Oak or Mahogany Case—to go 28 days, ... £70

This style of Standard Clock is one of the most complete and beautiful specimens of Horological Art ever offered. The painters' and enamellers' skill, combined with the mechanical exactness and finish, enables us to say that it is unsurpassed for quality and beauty of workmanship.

THE FIRST LIGHTNING CONDUCTOR.

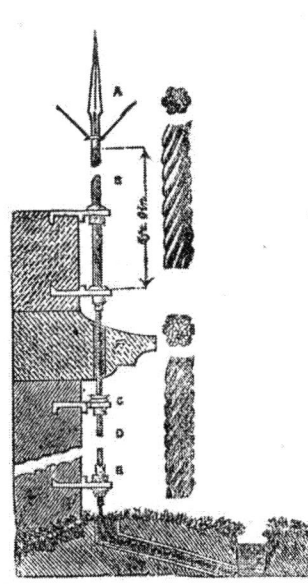

Benjamin Franklin, with his son, in the fields near Philadelphia experimenting with the first Lightning Conductor, A.D. June, 1752.
[*Extracted from an old American book on Electricity.*]

Lightning Conductors supplied for Private Residences.

BAILEY'S VILLA CONDUCTOR,
60 feet long, Copper Strand, ⅜-in. all ready for fixing, £3.
(Special Estimates for other Buildings.)

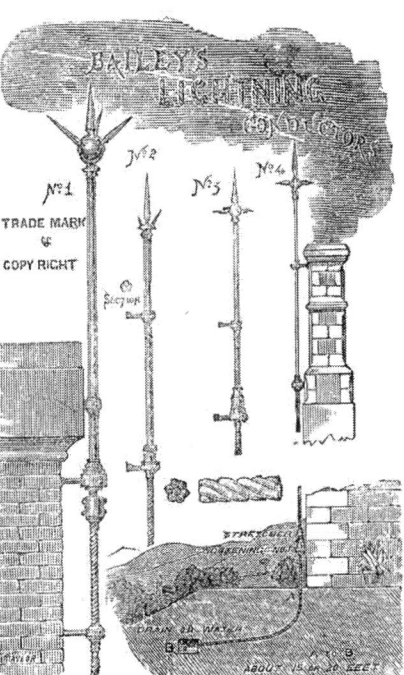

HAVE BEEN SUPPLIED BY
J. BAILEY & CO,
TO

The British Government, for the Mint of Hong Kong.
Sir William Armstrong, Elswick Forge.
Sir Francis Crossley, Somerleyton.
North of England Carriage and Iron Company, Limited.
Norwich Cathedral.
The Barrow Hæmatite Iron and Steel Company.
Church of English Martyrs, Preston.
Bowling Iron Company, near Bradford.
Loftus Iron Company, Saltburn-by-the-Sea.
Landore Siemens Steel Company, Swansea.
Consett Iron Company, near Durham.
Rochdale Corn Mill Company, Rochdale.
North of England Industrial Coal and Iron Company, Limited, Middlesbro'.
Kirkleatham Ironstone Company, Middlesbro'.
Alexander Annandale & Sons, Dunbar.
Wharton Hall Colliery Company, Little Hulton, near Bolton.
Parton Hæmatite Iron Company, Parton, near Whitehaven.
Cumberland Iron Mining and Smelting Company, Millom, Cumberland.
Whitley and Monkseaton Coal Company, Newcastle-upon-Tyne.
Cannock and Wimblebury Colliery Company, Hednesford.
Stockton Malleable Iron Company, Stockton-on-Tees.
Crompton & Potter, Little Lever, Bolton.
Mellards Trent Foundry Company, Rugeley.
Woodhouse, Son, & Andrews, Barrow-in-Furness.
Henderson & Sons, Aberdeen.
Whittle & Son, Whitehaven.
Bell Brothers, Brandon Works, near Durham.
Baker & Co., Fenton, Potteries.
Hutchinson & Co., Widnes.

And many hundreds of names of Firms, Church Dignitaries, Private Gentlemen, and Noblemen, can be furnished for the satisfaction of intending purchasers, in all parts of the United Kingdom, or abroad.

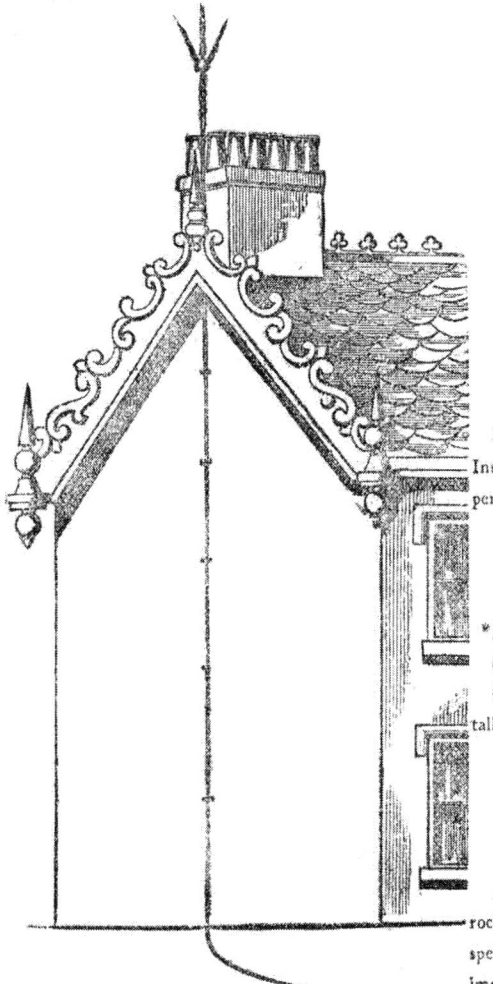

LIGHTNING RODS.

No. 1. For Chimneys over 200 feet high.
No. 2. For Ordinary Mill Chimneys.
No. 3. Villa or Mansion Rods.
No. 4. Fancy do., gilded.

PRICES.

Length of 60 feet or more unfixed, complete, with Insulators, Holdfast Elevating Tube, &c., ⅜-in. 1/0 per foot; ½-in. 1/6 per foot; ⅝-in. 2/0 per foot.*

* ⅜-in. is used for Domestic Erections, Dwellings, &c.
½-in. for Factory Chimneys, Church Steeples, &c.
⅝-in. is used for large Iron Works Chimneys, very tall Spires, Cathedrals, &c.

Materials supplied to Builders, &c.

☞ In fixing Conductors never terminate in sand, rock, or clay. If a drain and water cannot be got, special advice will be given, as a Lightning Conductor improperly fixed is far more dangerous than none at all.

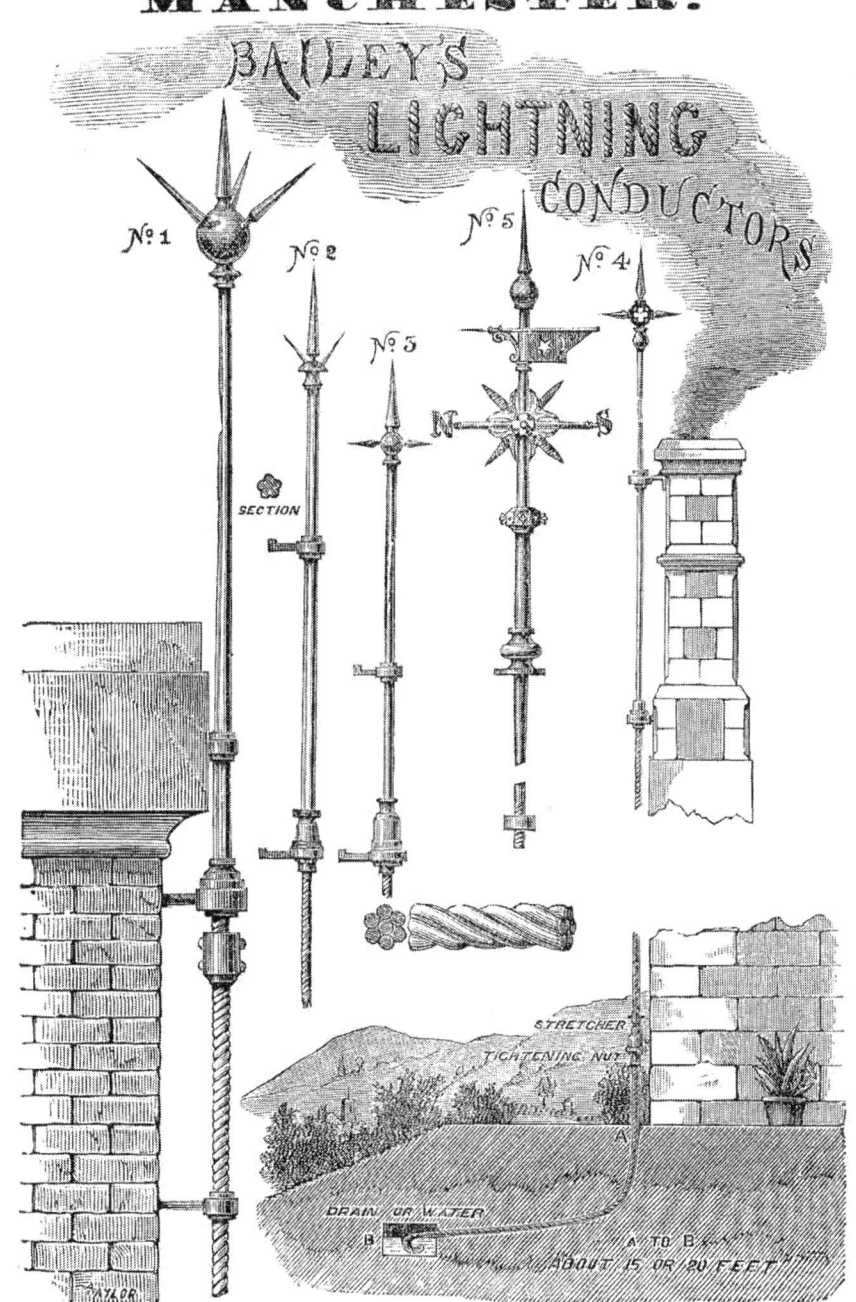

J. BAILEY & CO.
Electricians, Turret Clock Makers, Bell Founders, and Lightning Conductor Manufacturers,
MANCHESTER.

BAILEY'S LIGHTNING CONDUCTORS

N.B.—When fixing Conductors never let the end terminate in clay, sand, or rock; damp earth will do, but it is much better for it to terminate in a well, drain, gutter, or cesspool, or it may be attached to the water pipes, if in the earth.

J. BAILEY & CO. have directed particular attention to this branch of their business, and the accumulated experience of years and practical application of Conductors to all classes of buildings, enables them to supply Conductors which, as far as human knowledge can guide, will render a building absolutely safe.

Any ordinary builder may fix to Villa Residences, if our instructions are observed.

References can be given from the chief Church of England, Dissenting and Roman Catholic Clergymen in the United Kingdom. ESTIMATES ON APPLICATION.

J. BAILEY & CO. hold more Prize Medals than any other firm in the same branches of business in Europe.

One of the Chimneys of the Barrow Hæmatite Steel and Iron Company Limited, Barrow-in-Furness, 260 feet high.

The Lightning Conductor of this Chimney, and those of the Chimneys belonging to the Barrow Shipbuilding Company, and, nearly without exception, all the Works' Chimneys in the neighbourhood, were fixed by J. BAILEY & CO., Manchester.

Galileo, sitting in the Cathedral at Pisa, observed the swinging of a lamp, and therefrom his mind first conceived the advantages to be derived from laws of oscillation. In his honour this marking board is called by his name, its principle being that of a simple pendulum.

Although the pendulum has been used in many ways—for time, for music, for governing steam engines, for dictating the length of the yard measure or the contents of an ale cask, the novel application of this unerring principle is quite as new as its first discovery

THE GALILEO BILLIARD MARKING BOARD,

(Orme & Son's Patent),

AN ENTIRELY NEW MOTIVE POWER APPLIED TO BILLIARD MARKING.

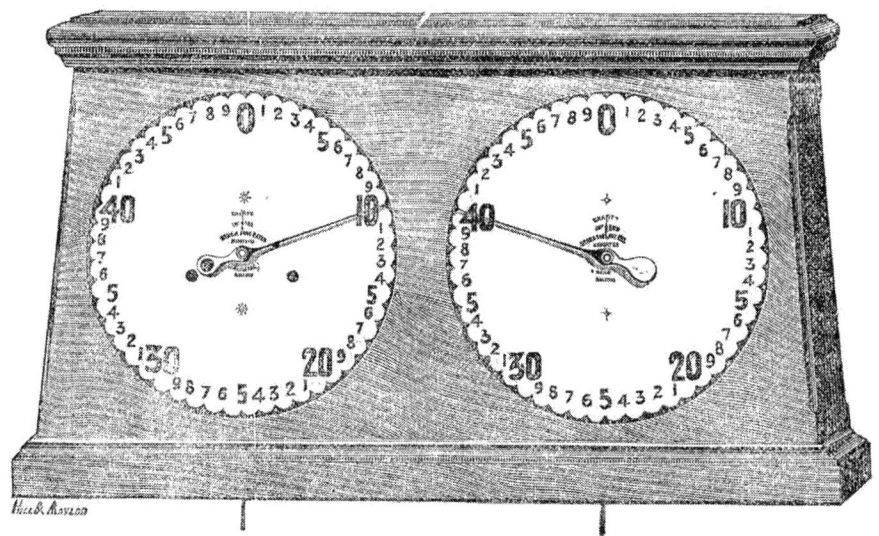

Whereby the points of the Game can be accurately Registered without leaving the Table.

In marking from the table, either one point or fifty, or any intermediate number can be scored upon the board with one pull of any one of the small knobs fastened at convenient positions at the sides and ends of the table.

The motion is perfectly simple and unerring, requiring no clockwork, springs, electricity, winding-up, or any care whatever.

Its power will last as long as brass and iron will wear.

The effect is obtained by a simple pull, which relieves a pendulum, otherwise kept out of perpendicular, and this, acting upon an escapement, moves the pointers or fingers round the dials; the pull being released, stops the finger at exactly the desired number.

In addition to being actuated from the table, the fingers can be set in motion by a simple arrangement of bell ropes fixed in any part of the room, convenient to the seats, or they can at the board be moved backwards or forwards, as desired.

The advantages of the apparatus are :—

1.—That it can be used from any part of the billiard table or room.
2.—That if a mistake in scoring is made it can be instantly rectified.
3.—That it is so simple of construction there is nothing to get out of order.
4.—That from its peculiar construction, it neither requires winding-up or any other attention whatever.
5.—That it is of very handsome exterior, and may be placed in any part of the billiard room; and further, that any bellhanger can fix the apparatus.

The movements and dials of the Marking Board are made by Messrs. J. BAILEY & Co., Albion Works, Salford, the extensive horological engineers.

The Marking Board attached to a Billiard Table, can be seen at

ORME & SON'S,

(Billiard Table Makers to H.R.H. The Prince of Wales,)

St. Ann's Street, Manchester.

S. H. SMITH'S NEW PATENT DUPLICATE-MARKING "WHIST" TABLE.

DESCRIPTION OF TABLE.

This very useful novelty claims to furnish all the aids to a really enjoyable game of Whist. Used as an ordinary table it is a handsome piece of furniture—as a whist table it is remarkably convenient. The Inventor has not only made the comfort of the player paramount, but he has endeavoured to construct a table at once useful and unique. The four legs of the table form a square; but the top and sides are concave, in order to place the player as near his work as possible. A circle of green cloth covers the centre, and prevents that sliding of cards so annoying to players. At each side of the table a novel contrivance is secured to the legs, to hold (quite protected) the glass or coffee cup of the player (two on each side); and immediately in front a small drawer is fixed, with loose perforated zinc bottom. This drawer is designed for the pipe or cigar of the player, the ashes of which fall through into the bottom of the drawer, and out of sight; there is also a place for matches. By using a small spring the drawer will pull out half length for use by players, or full length if required. Behind each drawer there is also a compartment capable of holding two packs of cards, or a number of cigars.

The marking arrangement is quite a novelty; its simplicity and *certainty* are unapproachable. Four dials are sunk at the four corners of the table, and are worked by a screw from two opposite corners, turned by a seven-eighth inch knob. Upon a player scoring, he turns this knob until the finger on the dial points to the number made; his partner's right-hand dial will be found to indicate the same number. This arrangement affords a veritable game at whist, as the players need never ask the state of the game—the dial on the right showing the figures in his or her favour, and those on the left the score of the opponents. There is also a neat addition for short whist.

A trial of the table at once gives rise to a feeling of tidiness which is absent at an ordinary card table. No glasses to impede rapid and correct play; no cigar or tobacco dust on either table or carpet; in short, no disorderly appearances so offensive to good taste, and so common to an ordinary table. The Patent Duplicate-Marking Whist Table certainly lends an air of comfort to the pastime which no other table can offer.

THE ADVANTAGES CLAIMED BY S. H. SMITH'S PATENT DUPLICATE-MARKING WHIST TABLE ARE AS FOLLOW:—

1—A table from which cards cannot slide.
2—Markers sure and immovable, by which own and opponents' score can be seen at a glance.
3—No glasses on table; therefore no liability to accident therefrom.
4—A small drawer for reception of pipe or cigar when not in use; and perforated zinc bottom for ashes. The drawer may be in use a whole evening and give no indication of dust, the grid covering the ashes.
5—A handy corner for a glass or coffee cup (two to each player,) by which same can be used and replaced, without the least motion from the table.
6—A piece of furniture suitable, from its elegance, to stand in any Club or private room; and if loose top is added, the table is suitable to an abundance of purposes in a sitting room.
7—Its greatest recommendation is, that all these advantages can be secured at a little more cost than the price of an ordinary Whist Table.

PRICE COMPLETE, £9 9 0

Important to Harbour Boards, Lighthouse Authorities, etc.

BAILEY'S
AUTOMATIC FOG BELL,

To sound 1, 2, 3, every three or five minutes in a fog, for Piers, Lighthouses, Landing Stages, Harbour Mouths, &c., with Bell of 10 cwt., in Cast-Iron Case, as illustrated, to go five hours with once winding; all Gun-Metal, highly lacquered wheels, all steel, work painted. £300 complete each.

Special contracts when more than one wanted.

If any different Signal required, it can be altered to any Code.

J. BAILEY & CO.,
Importers and Manufacturers.

12 MONTHS' REGULATOR CLOCK,

This Clock requires Winding only Once a Year.

In real Gilt Bronze Square Case (size, 15 inches, 9½ by 6½), with fancy bevelled top and pillars, fine bevelled crystal glass sides, enamelled dials, ruby pallets, visible escapements, and with either mercurial or compensated pendulum. The movement of the highest finish, and goes correctly for twelve months, requiring to be wound only once during that time; under a square glass shade, on a richly gilt stand, resting on four gilt legs, with an elevation covered with rich blue or crimson silk velvet, giving the Clock a magnificent appearance. Size, complete, 22 by 12 by 9½. Price £24 each.

The same article, with addition of showing in front the position of the moon on each day of the year, the date of the month, and the day of the week, richly engraved ormolu face, £30.

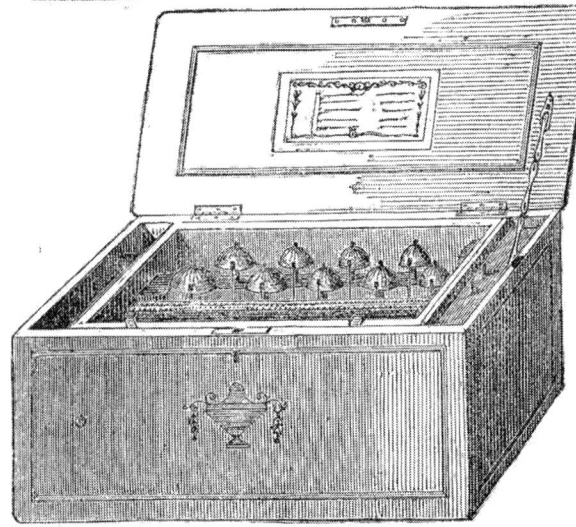

MUSICAL BOXES
OF SUPERIOR MANUFACTURE.

An elegant and entertaining piece of Furniture for first-class Drawing Rooms, a *sine-quâ-non* for Children's Parties, and a graceful Wedding Present. The prices are low for this class of Instrument.

No. of Tunes	Length of Barrel in inches.	Large Table Boxes, Glass Covers and Patent Winders, each	No. of Tunes	Length of Barrel in inches.	Large Table Boxes, Glass Covers and Patent Winders, each
4	4½	Inlaid Rosewood Case £2 15	8	10	6 bells in sight £11 1
6	8¼	,, ,, 3 18	8	12	9 ,, ,, 11 17
8	10¼	,, ,, 4 18	10	13	9 ,, ,, 13 13
6	10¼	,, ,, 6 4	12	14	6 ,, ,, 14 10
8	14	,, ,, 8 16	6	10½	Voix Celeste 12 6
6	10	,, ,, 8 16	6	,,	,, ,, 13 13
6	10½	6 bells in sight 9 15	8	,,	,, ,, 16 18
6	12	6 ,, ,, 10 0	8	,,	,, ,, 18 17
6	12	9 ,, ,, 10 16	10	,,	,, ,, 25 10
			12	,,	,, ,, 28 10

Prices quoted for larger quantities and sizes, on legs and large Cases, with Flute, Drum, Bell, Castagnettes, etc., with changeable Drums, suitable for Hotels, Exhibitions, etc., from £25 to £100.

BAILEY'S ROYAL POLYTECHNIC BAROMETER,

With ADMIRAL FITZROY'S "Prize Medal" BAROMETER combined.

This newly-invented Instrument meets a want that has been universally felt, viz.: a correct indicator of approaching weather, and that the indications should be simple, intelligible, and reliable.

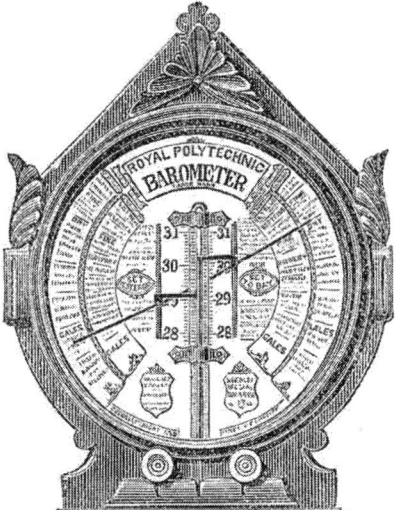

- IT IS ELEGANT IN FORM.
- IT IS SIMPLE IN ITS MECHANISM.
- IT IS ACCURATE IN ITS INDICATIONS.
- IT IS NOT LIABLE TO GET OUT OF ORDER.
- IT IS SELF-EXPLANATORY.
- IT IS COMPENSATED FOR TEMPERATURE.
- IT IS EASILY FIXED.
- IT IS GUARANTEED FOR ACCURACY.
- IT IS SUITABLE FOR USE IN ANY SITUATION.

- IT IS THE CHEAPEST BAROMETER MADE.
- IT IS RELIABLE AS A WEATHER GUIDE.
- IT IS THE ONLY BAROMETER THAT WILL GIVE SEPARATE INDICATIONS IN SUMMER AND WINTER.
- IT IS THE ONLY BAROMETER THAT WILL INDICATE APPROACHING FROST AND FOG, WIND OR CALM, WITH OTHER UNCERTAIN CHANGES IN THE WEATHER.

PRICE LIST.

All Frames are Carved and made from Solid Wood.

	£	s.	d.
No. 1, in English Oak, with One Thermometer	3	3	0
No. 2, in Antique Dark Oak with One Thermometer	3	5	0
No. 3, in Antique Dark Oak, with Two Thermometers, and larger column of Mercury	3	10	0
No. 4, in Antique Dark Oak, with Two Mercurial Thermometers, and extra large column of Mercury	4	0	0
No. 5, in White Oak, with One Thermometer	3	7	6
No. 6, in White Oak, with Two Thermometers, and larger column of Mercury	3	12	6

DESIGN, TITLE, AND COPYRIGHT REGISTERED.

PRICE LIST.

All Frames are Carved and made from Solid Wood.

	£	s.	d.
No. 7, in White Oak, with Two Mercurial Thermometers, and *extra* large column of Mercury	4	0	0
No. 8, in Black and Gold Frame, richly gilt, with Two Thermometers	4	4	0
No. 9, in Black and Gold, richly carved, engraved and gilt with Wedgewood Medallion; Two Thermometers and large column of Mercury	6	6	0
No. 10, richly carved and ornamented Gothic design, very elaborate, same fittings as No. 9	8	8	0

Securely Packed in Case for the Country, 3s. extra.

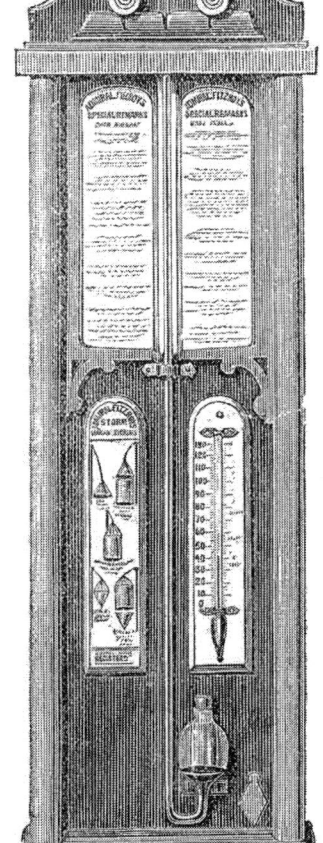

HEIGHT, 3 feet 6 inches.   WIDTH, 1 foot.

J. BAILEY AND CO.,

Sole Licensed Manufacturers for the Northern Counties, Scotland, and Ireland.

This Instrument is suitable for all Countries North of the Equator.

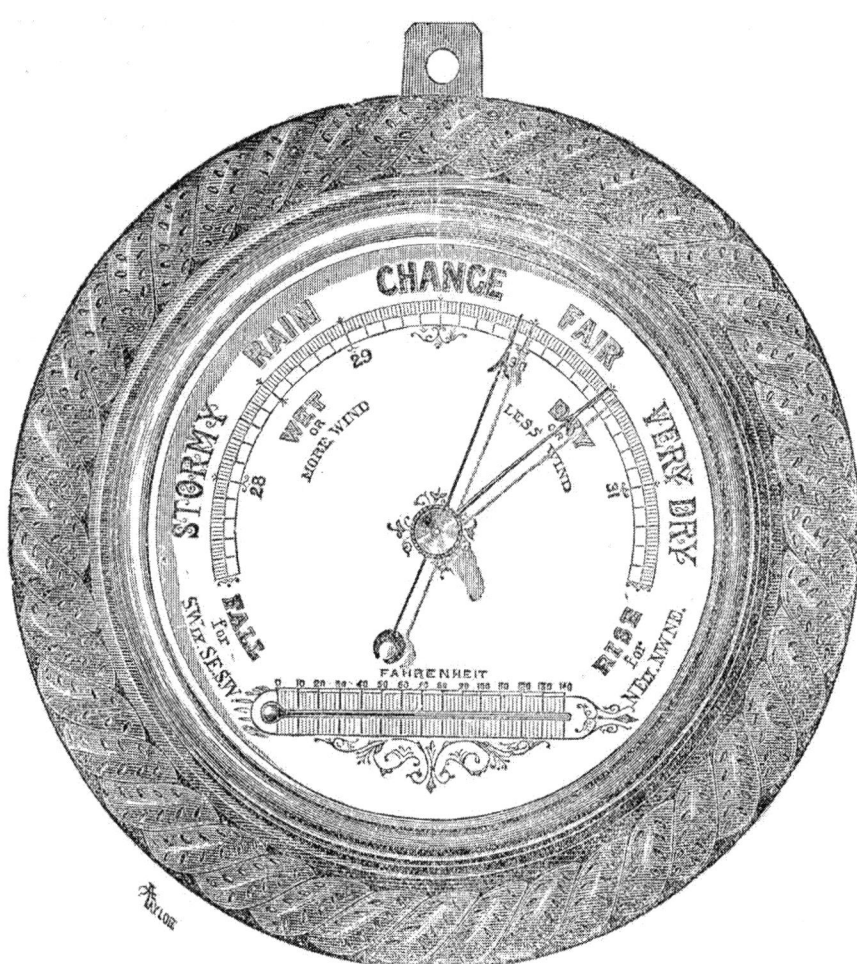

BAILEY'S CABLE-PATTERN BAROMETER,

35/- each.

In Carved Oak frame. A useful Library, Office, or Drawing-room Ornament. Diam. of Dial, five inches.

COAL PIT AND SURFACE BAROMETERS.

No. 1.—Best Pit Barometer, oak case, enamelled face, Vernier to read to $\frac{1}{100}$, and Thermometer attached £2 10 0
No. 2.—Best Pit Barometer, ivory face, (second quality) ... 1 15 0
No. 2A.—Improved Pit Barometer, strong oak case, glass-covered face, and Thermometer, (see Plate No. 2A) 2 5 0
No. 3 & 4.—Best Surface Barometers, glass-covered face, two Vernier (see Plate No. 4) 2 15 0
No. 5.—Second Quality Surface do. 1 5 0
Colliery Standard Barometers, with Kew Certificate ... 5 15 0

In all Collieries there should be a Standard to check the ordinary Barometers by.

The above Barometers have Portable Tubes, with Safety Travelling Screws to secure them against injury in transit, and have engraved Ivory Scales.

The No. 2 A Pit Barometer is especially adapted for underground work.

The above instruments are very handsome and well-finished goods, and although they are especially introduced for Pit purposes, are equally useful for Meteorological purposes, for the Study, the Laboratory, or the Entrance Hall of private gentlemen.

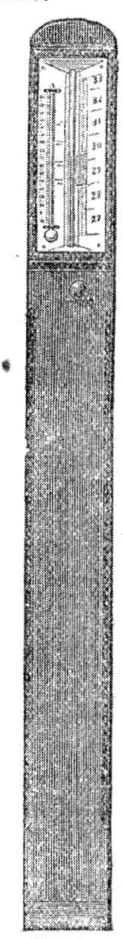

No. 2A.

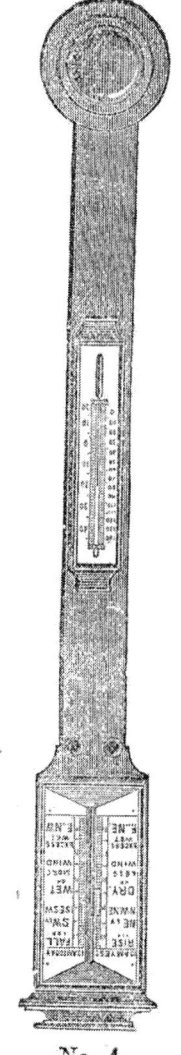

No. 4.

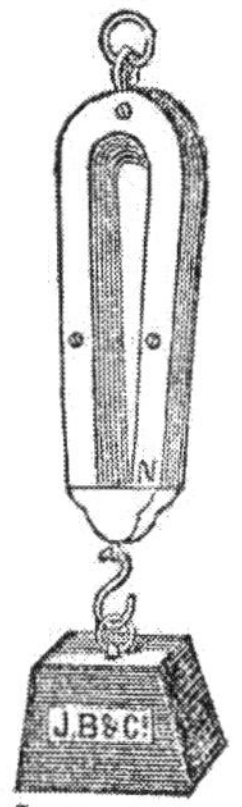

TELEGRAPH DEPARTMENT.

List of Prices

OF

BAILEY'S COMPOUND MAGNETS.

Long.			Each. £	s.	d.
3 in.	2	bars	£0	1	6
4 ,,	2	,,	0	3	9
,,	3	,,	0	4	0
5 ,,	2	,,	0	4	6
,,	3	,,	0	6	9
6 ,,	2	,,	0	5	0
,,	3	,,	0	7	6
,,	4	,,	0	10	0
,,	5	,,	0	12	6
,,	6	,,	0	15	0
7 ,,	2	,,	0	6	3
,,	3	,,	0	9	6
,,	4	,,	0	12	6
,,	5	,,	0	15	9
,,	6	,,	0	18	9
,,	7	,,	1	2	0
8 ,,	2	,,	0	7	6
,,	3	,,	0	11	3
,,	4	,,	0	15	0
,,	5	,,	0	18	9
,,	6	,,	1	2	6
,,	7	,,	1	5	3
,,	8	,,	1	10	0
9 ,,	2	,,	0	9	0
,,	3	,,	0	13	3
,,	4	,,	0	18	0
,,	5	,,	1	2	0
,,	6	,,	1	5	3
,,	7	,,	1	11	0
,,	8	,,	1	16	0
,,	9	,,	2	0	0
,,	10	,,	2	5	0
,,	11	,,	2	8	6
,,	12	,,	2	12	6
10 ,,	2	,,	0	10	0
,,	3	,,	0	15	0
,,	4	,,	1	0	0
,,	5	,,	1	5	0
,,	6	,,	1	10	0
,,	7	,,	1	16	0
,,	8	,,	2	0	0
,,	9	,,	2	5	0

Long.			Each. £	s.	d.
10 in.	10	bars	£2	8	6
,,	11	,,	2	15	0
,,	12	,,	3	0	0
11 ,,	2	,,	0	11	3
,,	3	,,	0	17	3
,,	4	,,	1	2	6
,,	5	,,	1	8	2
,,	6	,,	1	13	9
,,	7	,,	2	0	0
,,	8	,,	2	5	0
,,	9	,,	2	10	0
,,	10	,,	2	16	3
,,	11	,,	3	2	6
,,	12	,,	3	7	6
12 ,,	2	,,	0	12	6
,,	3	,,	0	18	9
,,	4	,,	1	5	0
,,	5	,,	1	11	3
,,	6	,,	1	17	6
,,	7	,,	2	5	0
,,	8	,,	2	10	0
,,	9	,,	2	16	3
,,	10	,,	3	2	6
,,	11	,,	3	8	9
,,	12	,,	3	15	0
14 ,,	2	,,	0	17	6
,,	3	,,	1	6	3
,,	4	,,	1	10	0
,,	5	,,	2	3	9
,,	6	,,	2	12	6
,,	7	,,	3	1	3
,,	8	,,	3	10	0
,,	9	,,	3	18	9
,,	10	,,	4	9	6
,,	11	,,	4	16	3
,,	12	,,	5	5	0
16 ,,	2	,,	1	2	6
,,	3	,,	1	13	9
,,	4	,,	2	5	0
,,	5	,,	2	16	3
,,	6	,,	3	7	6
,,	7	,,	3	18	9

Long.			Each. £	s.	d.
16 in.	8	bars	£4	10	0
,,	9	,,	5	1	3
,,	10	,,	5	12	6
,,	11	,,	6	3	9
,,	12	,,	6	15	0
18 ,,	2	,,	1	7	6
,,	3	,,	2	1	3
,,	4	,,	2	15	0
,,	5	,,	3	8	9
,,	6	,,	4	2	6
,,	7	,,	4	16	3
,,	8	,,	5	10	0
,,	9	,,	6	3	9
,,	10	,,	6	17	6
,,	11	,,	7	11	3
,,	12	,,	8	5	0
20 ,,	2	,,	1	12	6
,,	3	,,	2	8	9
,,	4	,,	3	5	0
,,	5	,,	4	1	3
,,	6	,,	4	17	6
,,	7	,,	5	13	9
,,	8	,,	6	10	0
,,	9	,,	7	5	3
,,	10	,,	8	2	6
,,	11	,,	9	0	0
,,	12	,,	9	15	0
22 ,,	2	,,	1	17	6
,,	3	,,	2	16	3
,,	4	,,	3	15	0
,,	5	,,	4	13	9
,,	6	,,	5	12	6
,,	7	,,	6	11	6
,,	8	,,	7	10	0
,,	9	,,	8	8	9
,,	10	,,	9	7	6
,,	11	,,	10	6	3
,,	12	,,	11	5	0
24 ,,	2	,,	2	2	6
,,	3	,,	3	3	9
,,	4	,,	4	5	0

Long.			Each. £	s.	d.
24 in.	5	bars	£5	6	3
,,	6	,,	6	7	6
,,	7	,,	7	10	0
,,	8	,,	8	10	0
,,	9	,,	9	11	3
,,	10	,,	10	12	6
,,	11	,,	11	13	9
,,	12	,,	12	15	0
26 ,,	2	,,	2	7	6
,,	3	,,	3	11	3
,,	4	,,	4	15	0
,,	5	,,	6	0	0
,,	6	,,	7	2	6
,,	7	,,	8	6	3
,,	8	,,	9	10	0
,,	9	,,	10	13	9
,,	10	,,	11	17	6
,,	11	,,	13	1	3
,,	12	,,	14	5	0
28 ,,	2	,,	2	12	6
,,	3	,,	3	18	9
,,	4	,,	4	15	0
,,	5	,,	6	11	3
,,	6	,,	7	17	6
,,	7	,,	9	3	9
,,	8	,,	10	10	0
,,	9	,,	11	16	3
,,	10	,,	13	2	6
,,	11	,,	14	8	9
,,	13	,,	15	15	0
30 ,,	2	,,	2	17	6
,,	3	,,	4	6	3
,,	4	,,	5	15	0
,,	5	,,	7	3	9
,,	6	,,	8	12	6
,,	7	,,	10	1	3
,,	8	,,	11	10	0
,,	9	,,	13	1	9
,,	10	,,	14	7	6
,,	11	,,	15	16	3
,,	12	,,	17	5	0

LIST OF PRICES FOR Bailey's Single or Foundry Magnets, HORSE SHOE SHAPE.

No.	Long.	per Doz. £	s.	d.
000	2½ in.	0	2	3
00	2¾ ,,	0	2	6
0	3 ,,	0	3	0
½	3¼ ,,	0	3	9
1	3½ ,,	0	4	6
2	4 ,,	0	6	0
2½	4½ ,,	0	7	6
3	5 ,,	0	9	0
4	6 ,,	0	16	6
5	7 ,,	1	2	6
6	8 ,,	1	10	0
7	9 ,,	1	12	6
8	10 ,,	2	5	0
9	11 ,,	2	12	6
10	12 ,,	3	0	0
11	13 ,,	3	2	6
12	14 ,,	3	15	0
13	15 ,,	4	2	6
14	16 ,,	4	10	0
15	17 ,,	5	5	0
16	18 ,,	6	0	0
17	19 ,,	6	15	0
18	20 ,,	7	10	0
19	21 ,,	8	5	0
20	22 ,,	9	0	0
21	23 ,,	9	15	0
22	24 ,,	10	10	0
23	25 ,,	10	15	0
24	26 ,,	12	0	0
25	27 ,,	12	15	0
26	28 ,,	13	10	0
27	29 ,,	14	0	0
28	30 ,,	15	0	0

Breadth and thickness in proportion. *Three inch Magnets, with grooved ends, for thermometers, 7/6 per dozen.*

STRAIGHT MAGNETS FOR TOYS.

3 inch, 12s. per Gross.
3½ ,, 16s. 6d. do.

3½ inch, 3-16th inch square, 12s.
4 ,, 3s. per Dozen.

5 inch, 3s 9d. per Dozen.
6 ,, 4s 6d do.

Any kind of Magnet made to Sketch on the shortest notice.

CUT CARBONS FOR BUNSEN'S BATTERIES.

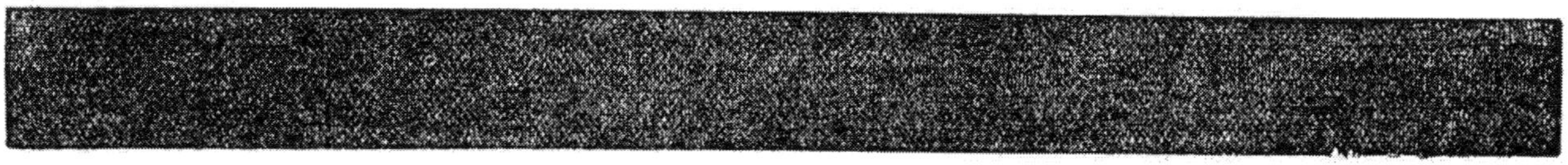

			s.	d.
3¼ inch long, by ¾ in.	... ...	each	0	6
4 ,, ,, 1 ,,	... ...	,,	0	8
5 ,, ,, 1¼ ,,	... ...	,,	1	0
6½ ,, ,, 1¼ ,,	... .	,,	1	3
8 inches long, by 2 in.	... ...	each	1	9
10 ,, ,, 2¼ ,,	... ...	,,	2	0
12 ,, ,, 2½ ,,	... ...	,,	3	0

Great reduction in prices for large quantities.

TELEGRAPH DEPARTMENT.

Telegraph Apparatus.

See full Illustration.—Special Circular on application.

No. of Article.		£	s.	d.
1.—*Bailey's "Albion" A B C Telegraph, in handsome metal case; particularly suitable for export and for Mills, or Private and Railway use,		6	0	0
2.—Ditto, with Bell,		8	0	0
3.—*Ditto, with Bell and 8 cells Leclanché Battery, in box complete, to work for two years without attention, any distance up to ten miles,		10	0	0

* For every mile above ten miles, add 4/- for increased Battery power. This is the only Alphabetical Telegraph suitable for hot climates. Colonists having extensive cattle runs, or other large estates, will find this Apparatus strong, serviceable, and perfectly reliable, and as simple in construction as an American clock; any child who knows its alphabet can work it immediately. (See BAILEY's Complete Outfit for a Colonial Telegraph.)

4.—Breguet's A B C Telegraph,	7	0	0
Ditto, with Bell,	10	0	0
5.—Breguet's Magnetic A B C Telegraph, requires no Battery,	20	0	0
6.—Ditto, with Clockwork Bell,	26	0	0
7.—Siemen's Magnetic A B C Telegraph for 5 miles,	18	0	0
8.—Ditto, larger size, 20 miles,	20	0	0
9.—Ditto, with Polarised Alarum on Iron stand, with Terminals, &c., complete,	30	0	0
10.—Wheatstone's Magnetic A B C Telegraph, as used by Her Majesty's Postal Telegraph Department,	30	0	0
Ditto, with Bell,	36	0	0
11.—Wilder's Magnetic A B C Telegraph,	18	0	0
12.—Ditto, with Bell, Tell-tale and Switch, complete,	24	0	0
13.—Crossley's A B C Telegraph, combining Communicator, Indicator and Bell, in box complete. When the box is closed the Bell is in circuit, but upon opening the lid, the distant current actuates the Indicator. A most complete and very beautiful arrangement, price	10	0	0
With 8 cell Battery in box	12	0	0

Henley's, Wilde's, Tyer's, and every other description of A B C Telegraph.

14.—Single Needle Telegraphs, to work with a handle or by Highton's Keys,—undemagnetisable coils, Lightning Protectors and Standard Resistance, ... £4 10s. to	7	15	0
15.—Bright's Bell Telegraph,—two Bells and Keys,	6	0	0
16.—Ditto, ditto, with Relay,	12	0	0
17.—Bailey's Morse Printing Telegraph,	15	0	0
18.—Ditto, Ink Writer (Patent),	20	0	0

The Morse Instruments are constructed to work in connection with those in use throughout Great Britain, the Continent of Europe, Egypt, America, the Colonies, &c.

19.—Bailey's Morse Printing Key, for working in two directions on one Line wire,	1	0	0
20.—Tyer and Norman's Train Signalling Telegraphs, as recommended by the Board of Trade, per set,	20	0	0
21.—Galvanometer, No. 1, in square Mahogany or Oak case,	2	0	0
22.—Ditto, No. 2, with Keys for sending messages, if required	2	17	6
23.—Ditto, No. 3, in round Brass case,	3	0	0
24.—Ditto, No. 4, in Watch case for the pocket,	4	0	0
25.—Crossley's Electro-Magnetic Speed Indicator,—suitable for every description of Engine or Nautical or Meteorological Apparatus in motion. Placed in a Private room or Counting-house, it indicates the exact speed of either one, two, or any number of Engines, distance being no object. Price, with Switches for six Engines or Machines, with Battery complete,	10	10	0
25A.—Ditto, for one or two Engines,	9	10	0

(Connecting wire according to distance).

26.—Chatwood's Patent Electric Log, an accurate and reliable Indicator for nautical use. (J. B. & Co., Sole Makers).

27.—Magnetic Exploders for Mines, &c., single shot,	7	0	0
28.—Ditto, to fire 8 fuses at once, giving immense lifting power,	12	0	0
29.—Ditto, with six directing keys, for Time Guns, &c.,	25	0	0
30.—Fuses for Experimental Use, No. 1, ... per doz.		2	0
31.—Ditto, for Blasting, No. 2, ,,		4	0
32.—Ditto, for Cannon or Submarine work, No. 3 ,,		5	0

33.—(Gutta Percha covered wire for above, 3d. per yard or £20 per mile).

34.—Electro-Magnetic Counters for Turnstiles in Theatres, &c., &c., for indicating each time a door is opened, when a pump works, for tallies in Docks, the passing of a train, weighing of coal, the punctuality of a watchman, distance in each case being no object. Made to drawing, or for Inventors. Prices forwarded upon application.

Bailey's Electric Bells, Indicators, &c.

35.—Bailey's Electric Bell, No. 1, Single Stroke, gravity arrangement,		7	6
36.—Bailey's do., No. 2, Trembler movement,		10	0
37.—Bailey's do., No. 3, do., for household use,		15	0
38.—Bailey's do., No. 4, do., larger size,		18	0
39.—Bailey's do., No. 5, do., for Halls, Lodge-gates, &c.,	1	4	0
40.—Bailey's do., No. 6, do., with 7 inch Gong,	2	0	0
41.—Bailey's do., No. 7, do., with two Bells and oscillating hammer, for Factories, Stables, Fire Alarms, and large Buildings,	3	0	0
42.—Bailey's Registered Dust-proof and Damp-proof *Single stroke* or Trembler Bell for Collieries, Mines, &c., *in strong* METAL CASE, and for Code of Signals, 7 in. diameter,	3	10	0

The Best Colliery or Railway Signal ever produced.

43.—Magnetic Bell Apparatus complete, from	2	2	0

INDICATORS FOR HOUSEHOLD USE, in Box complete.

No. of Article.		£	s.	d.
44.—From 1 to 10 Indicators, at per Indicator			15	0
45.—Above 10 to 500, per Indicator			12	6
46.—Bailey's "Reliable" Indicators, at per Indicator		1	0	0

The "Reliable" Indicator continues to ring the Bell till attention is given to it, if required to do so; is perfect in action, cannot get disarranged. All the points of contact are platinised; a *sine quâ non* for Electrical work in the neighbourhood of sea air.

47.—Bell Buttons, Pushes, or Pear-shaped Drops in Oak, Satinwood, Rosewood, Mahogany, Birch, &c., &c., with springs and connecting screws, complete, 1/6 each; 15/- per doz.; per gross, assorted		7	0	0
48.—Ditto, in Ebony, 2/6 each; 26/- per doz.; per gross, assorted		14	0	0
49.—White or Cream Porcelain Bell Pushes, with springs, &c., complete, 2/- each; 20/- per doz.; per gross, assorted		10	10	0
50.—Black and Gold do., 3/6 each; 36/- per doz.; per gross, assorted		16	10	0
51.—Bell Actions, for ordinary Bellropes, 3/- each; 30/- per doz.; per gross, assorted		12	0	0
52.—Ivory Pushes, Presselles, &c., from ... 5s. to			12	6
53.—Outdoor Pulls, in Marble, Brass, &c., according to order.				
54.—Flexible Cord, containing conducting wire in crimson and various-coloured silk, an indispensable comfort to the invalid, per yard,			2	0
55.—Bailey's Dust-proof and Damp-proof Key for Colliery and Railway Signals, in strong Iron Case, with Code of Signals,		1	0	0
56.—Door and Window Contact Makers for Alarms,			3	0
57.—Electric Thermometers or Fire Alarms,			10	0
58.—Bailey's Portable Bell and Battery combined, in elegant Mahogany case, for special or temporary use; peculiarly adapted for Invalids, as the Bell can be rung without any effort; with 20 yards of flexible conducting cord and Presselle,		3	0	0

(This is also very suitable for Cabin use on board Ship).

59.—J. Bailey & Co's Estimate for Fitting Hotels, Mansions, Clubs, &c., with Electric Bells, including their "Reliable" Indicators, Batteries, Wires, and fixing complete, is **40/- per Pull** or Push, and as they are, when **"once done, well done,"** they are cheaper than any system known. As compared with the old system of Crank Bells in large buildings, the first cost is no greater, while there is immense saving in the perfect security against reopening walls, cutting up floors, carpets, &c. The comfort of Electric Bells is all that can be desired. The Indicators can be fitted in cases to any design, and form a very handsome piece of furniture for the Servants' Hall or Entrance Lobby.

Railway Fares charged extra. Foreign Orders sent out complete, with drawings and full instructions for erecting and fitting the wires, which can be carried out by any carpenter without further explanation. An invaluable boon to those up the country

SPEAKING TUBES FOR OFFICES, WORKS, &c.

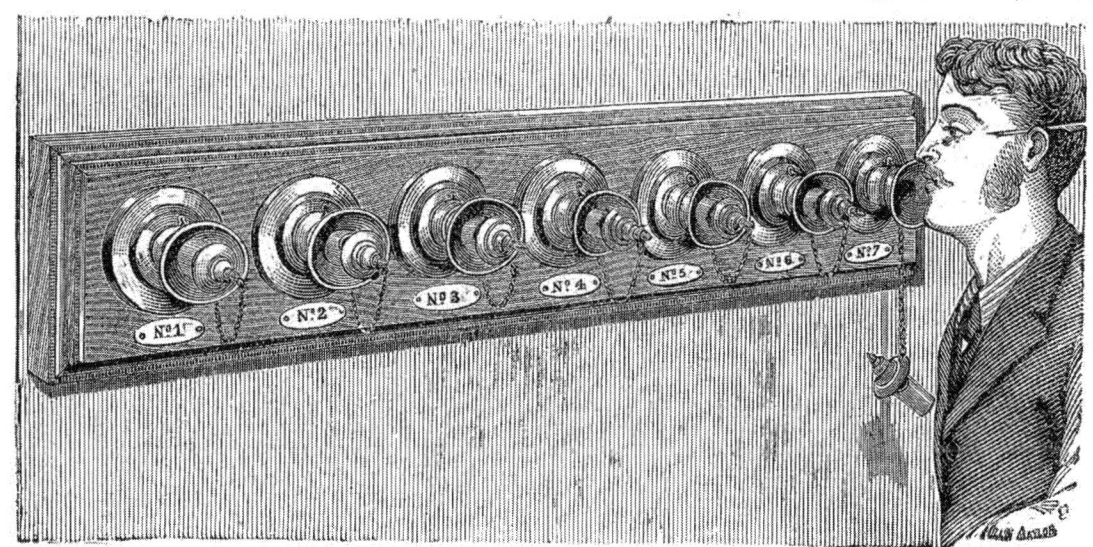

View, from a Photograph, of Mouthpieces and Whistles made for an extensive Works in Germany.

Ivory Mouthpieces fitted as illustrated, complete, 15/0 each, for Four or more, mounted on Mahogany board.
Estimates for bends, elbows, &c., all complete, fixed or unfixed.   Send rough sketch giving distance.

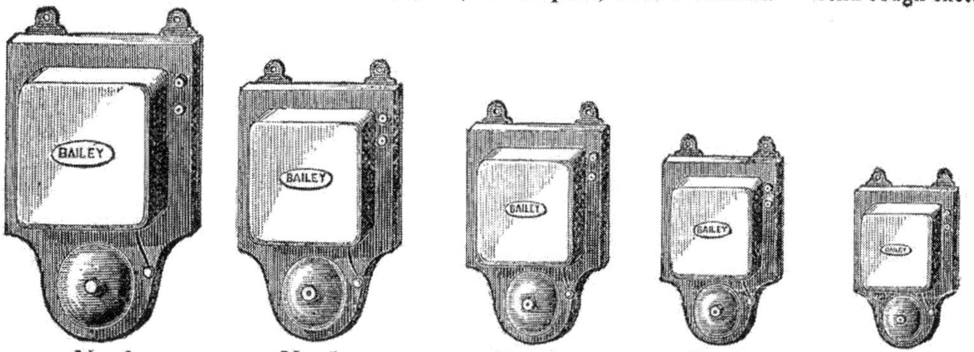

	PRICES OF ELECTRIC BELLS.
No. 2,	10/0
,, 3,	15/0
,, 4,	18/0
,, 5,	24/0
,, 6,	40/0

No. 6.   No. 5.   No. 4.   No. 3.   No. 2.

EVERY DESCRIPTION OF TERMINAL   ELECTRIC TELEGRAPH   MADE TO ORDER.

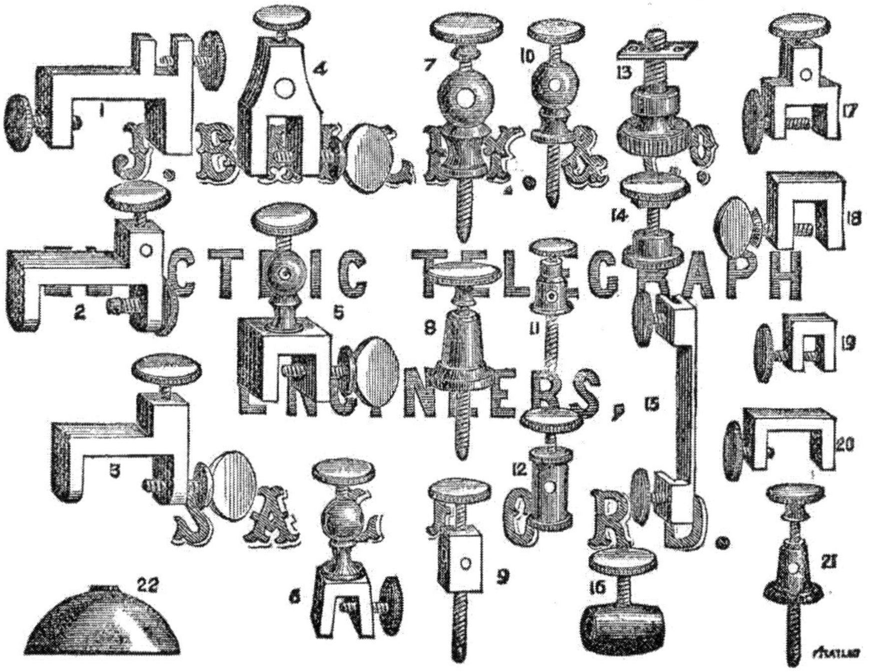

BAILEY'S ELECTRIC BELL FITTINGS.
BELL AND INDICATOR COMPLETE FOR RESIDENCES.

From a Photograph. The Front Door is Ringing, and shows the Black Spot.

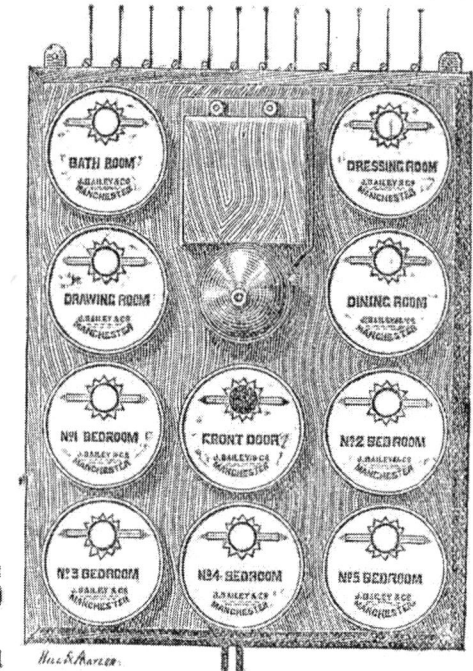

BAILEY'S
4 in. diameter
ELECTRICAL SEMAPHORE INDICATORS

These are kept in stock, and can be arranged as above in any numbers, and the Bell fixed, either separately or on the same board.

Complete estimates of all the materials required on receipt of a description of the number of the rooms, and roughly giving their dimensions.

Hotels, Public Buildings, Clubs, &c., fitted up on the most scientific and approved principle.

ESTIMATE.

Nine Rooms and front Door, fitted and working complete, with all materials, within five miles of Manchester.

£20.

Manufacturers of Materials for Telegraph Lines, for Railway Companies, Governments, etc.

See LIST OF PRICES.

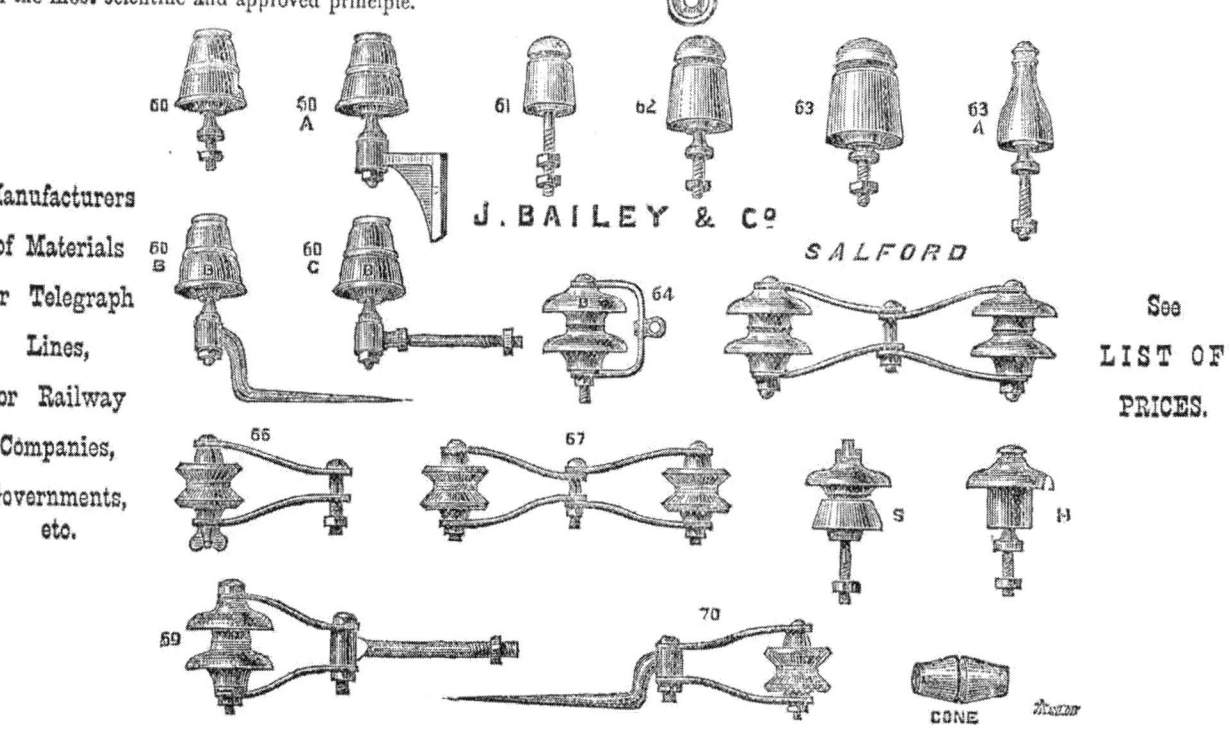

J. BAILEY & Cº SALFORD

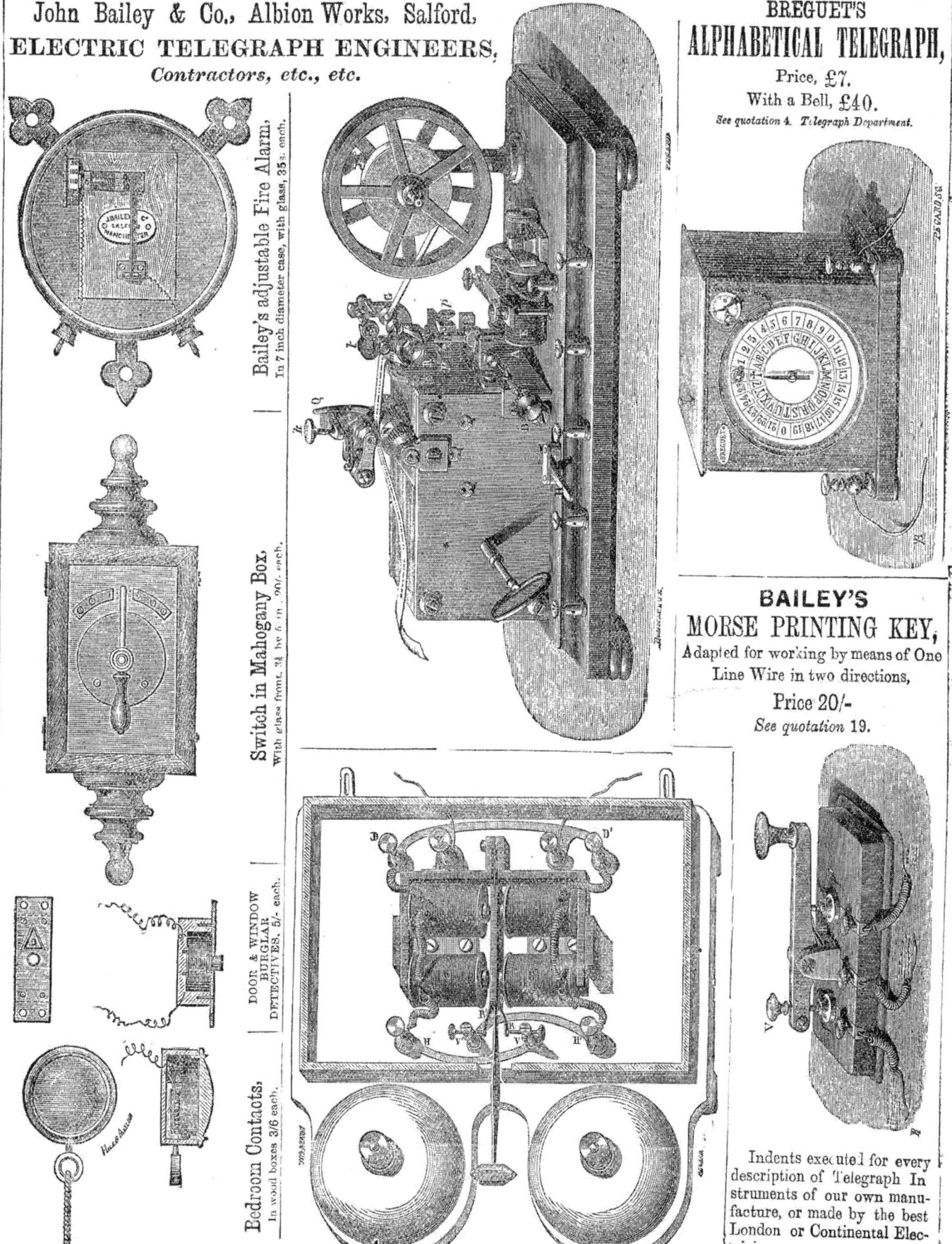

ELECTRIC BELL FITTINGS,

FOR

Offices, Dwelling-houses, Works, &c.

ILLUSTRATED AS FIXED AT AN EXTENSIVE IRON WORKS IN DERBYSHIRE.

Illustration represents Manager's Office, fitted up to communicate with the Errand Boy's Room, in which are the Semaphore Indicators, on which are the Foremens' names.

The cost per room for work of this description depends very much on circumstances. To enable our friends to arrive at an idea of the cost of a system of ten signals, we append the following estimate of an actual job of this description.

	£	s.	d.
10 Cream-coloured Pushes, mounted with brass backs, on mahogany board, for Manager's office, with the name of the foreman of each department in gilt letters under each push, at 8/-	4	0	0
10 Indicators, mounted, with circular white dials and black discs, the dials indicating the name of the foreman of each department, written on, at 20/-	10	0	0
1 No. 4 Bell to signal, and 1 to acknowledge, at 18/-	1	16	0
2 Ledwiché Batteries, in boxes and cells, at 40/-	4	0	0
500 yards of Gutta Percha Covered Wire, at 2d.	4	3	4
Total, ready for fixing	£23	19	4

The above details will enable purchasers to form an idea of the cost of Electrical Apparatus for larger or smaller jobs. Of course, the amount of wire will vary with the distance. Two wires from each Indicator will be about the quantity required. The Pushes and Indicators are of good durable quality, and not of the fragile toy-like description often sold for such purposes.

Alphabetical Telegraph Instruments,

EITHER ELECTRICAL OR MAGNETIC,

As used by the "British Government Telegraph Department," and others

SPECIAL QUOTATIONS ON APPLICATION.

L. J. CROSSLEY'S
ELECTRICAL ENGINE, PUMP, HOIST & SPEED INDICATOR.

J. B. & Co. have the pleasure to announce that Mr. L. J. CROSSLEY, the Meteorological and Electrical authority, has appointed them the Manufacturers of his Electrical Speed Indicator, an instrument which, placed in the private room or office of the proprietor or manager of the works, indicates the exact speed of either one, two, or any number of Engines, or the motion of a Hoist, Crane, Pump, Weighing Machine, &c., distance being immaterial.

Reduced Price of Indicator for one Engine or Machine, £6 6s.

Leclanche Battery and Connecting Wire according to distance.

The engraving shows the arrangement for two Engines for attachment to the shaft or lever by which motion is communicated.

The dial is 7 in. diameter. It may be fixed by any Electrical bell-hanger, or we will quote for Wire and Battery, if supplied with rough particulars of distance, &c.

This Indicator is not intended for continuous action. It is generally used to test one or two minutes by a watch at any time the manager chooses to put the peg in to make communication.

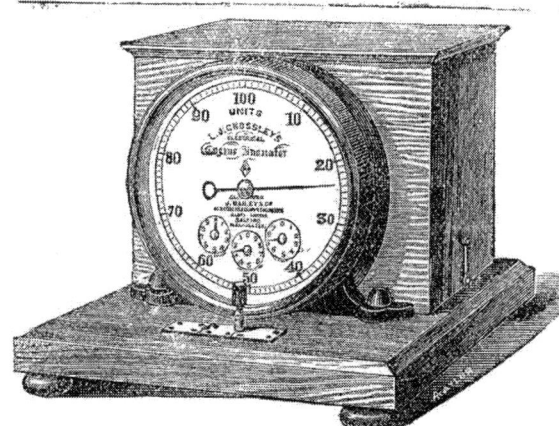

JOHN BAILEY & CO.,
ALBION WORKS, SALFORD,
ELECTRIC TELEGRAPH ENGINEERS AND CONTRACTORS.

THE LECLANCHÉ BATTERY.

Highly recommended by R. S. CULLEY, Esq., Chief Engineer to the Postal Telegraphs in Great Britain, C. V. WALKER, Esq.; W. H. PREECE, Esq.

Requires no attention for TWO YEARS.

LIST OF PRICES, &c.,

Size	Diam.	Height	Each	Per Dozen	In quantities of 100 or more
No. 1	5 inch	9 inch	6/6	5/6 each	5/0 each.
,, 2	4⅝ ,,	8 ,,	5/0	4/6 ,,	4/3 ,,
,, 3	3¾ ,,	7 ,,	4/0	3/6 ,,	3/3 ,,
,, 4	3¾ ,,	5 ,,	3/6	3/0 ,,	2/9 ,,

No. 1 is chiefly used for Electric Bells in Mansions, &c.
,, 2 ditto ditto but smaller size.
,, 3 For Telegraph Instruments and long Circuits. This size supplied to the Postal Telegraph Departments, and the chief Railway Companies.
,, 4 For Experiments and Scientific amusements.

BAILEY'S PREPARED SAL AMMONIAC,
Ready for recharging the Leclanché Battery, in boxes, 6d. per Element; 5/- per dozen. Each box contains sufficient for twelve months' supply for one Element. Water is the only liquid used—No Acids.

JOHN BAILEY & CO., have the most favorable opportunities for introducing new Apparatus to Electrical Telegraph Engineers, Railway Companies, &c.

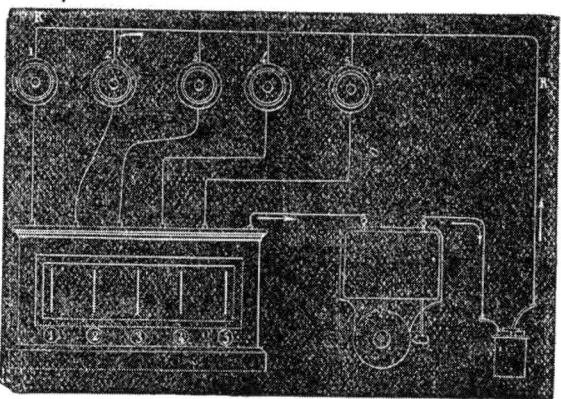

BAILEY'S SYSTEM OF ELECTRIC BELLS.
Mansions, Warehouses, &c., fitted-up complete.
For Prices—See Telegraph Department, quotation 59.

ELECTRIC BELL BUTTONS,
In Wood, Ivory, China, Brass, &c., &c.,
From 1/- to £2
See quotations 47 to 50 Telegraph Department.

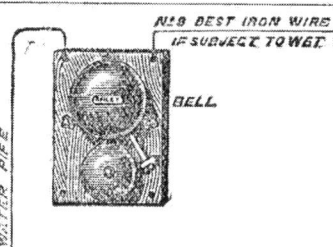 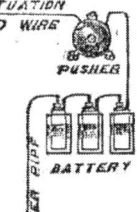

Bailey's Dust and Damp-Proof Electrical Signal Bell, ... Price £3. 10s. Pushers, £1.

The Bell is 7in. diameter, is designed and much used for Code Signals for Collieries; also used by the Chartered Gas Company, Woolwich, for Telegraphing the Vacuum required. In dry places, Iron Wire, Galvanized, is about 12/- per 100 yards. Prices for all materials on application, if rough sketch be sent of distance.
SPECIAL NOTE.—Any number of these Pushers may be fixed to one Wire when required, the Current being sent through those at rest.

BAILEY'S DOUBLE-WIRE SYSTEM FOR TRAMWAYS OR INCLINES.
This is well adapted where a great number of "Pushes" cannot be fixed with convenience, and where it is desirable to Signal from any part of a Tramway.

This is done by fixing Parallel Wires, so———————————————A———————————————
————————————————————B————————————————

The Bell being in the Engine-House when a Signal is sent, it is done by simply pressing the two Wires together with the thumb and finger. For Estimates, send rough Sketch and give distances. This cannot be fixed in very wet Pits, as only bare uncovered Iron or Copper Wire can be used. The materials for a long distance are very inexpensive, and the fixing is very simple.

BRASS CLEANING MACHINE.

PARKINSON'S PATENT
MAGNETTING MACHINE,

For separating small Particles of Iron or Steel from Brass or other Metals or Materials, for Brass Founders, Engineers, &c.

ABOUT 250 IN USE.

The principal object of the above Machine is to remove the small particles of Iron or Steel which are generally found mixed with Brass Filings, Borings, and Turnings, but it may also be used to separate the small particles of Iron mixed with the earth used in the Manufacture of porcelain, and for other purposes.

The mixed filings, or other materials, are fed into the Hopper **A**, from whence they drop into the trough in which the Magnet Roller revolves. The Magnets are fixed in a spiral or screw form on this Roller, which revolves slowly, and traverses the filings or other materials to the opposite end of the trough, from whence they drop through the spout **C**, into a receptacle below; the small particles of Iron and Steel adhering to the Magnets are removed by the revolving Brush **E**, into the Box below. The Machine is perfectly self-acting, and the attendant has only to keep the Hopper **A** supplied with the Brass Filings, or other material to be cleaned.

Directions to be observed in using the Machine.

First.—Before Putting the Turnings into the Hopper A, pass them through a ¼in. Riddle, so that all large lumps of Metal and Waste may be removed.

Second.—The speed of the Brush Roller should run 70 revolutions per minute, and revolve in the direction of the Magnet Roller.

PRICE, READY FOR USE, £18.

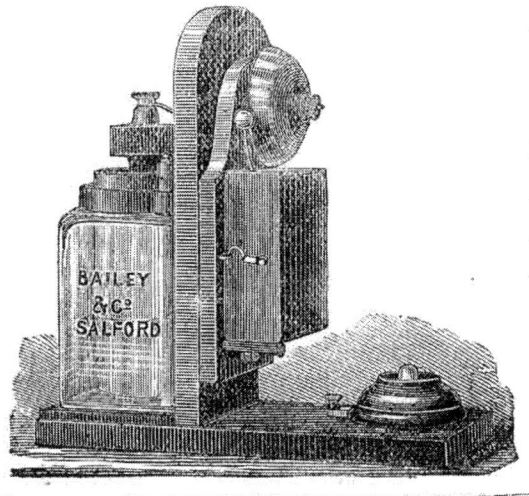

BAILEY'S EDUCATIONAL BELL.
(COPYRIGHT.)

In consequence of many of our friends at a distance requiring Instructions for fixing our Electric Bells and Telegraphs, we arranged for one of them a small Model, complete with "PUSH," with "TREMLER BELL," and with "LECLANCHE BATTERY," all mounted on a board of Mahogany, French Polished, and connected ready for ringing. A small amount of Salamoniac and water will keep the Apparatus right for twelve months. This enables purchasers of Bells, by studying the connections, &c., to fix them themselves, and, in addition to this, it is a cheap instructive Model. It is brought out at a price barely remunerative, in order to render BAILEY's Electric Instruments more popular.

PRICE 25/-
The same Bell separate, 10/6 each.

BAILEY's A B C TELEGRAPH INSTRUMENTS, as used by the chief Colliery Proprietors, Gas Works, and Manufacturers, to connect two or more offices of works. *(See page 107.)*

BAILEY's SYMPATHETIC DIALS from 7 inches to 6 feet in diameter. Prices on application.

THE BRITISH WORKMAN'S CLOCK,

All Metal.   No Wood about it.

1502

Not to Strike.

Much used for Works at home and abroad. We recommend this for Cotton Mills, Work Rooms, Offices, &c. For Dining, Breakfast, and Sitting Rooms, Stables, Saddle Rooms, Servants' Halls, &c. Dials, 14 inches, going 12 days. In Ornamental Iron Cases. The regulation is extremely simple, and they are easier to repair than any Clock now in the market. No glass being used in the construction of these Clocks, they are not liable to be damaged in transit. Also, the case being of Iron, they are not injured by heat or damp, and are well adapted for Colonial and Foreign use; and the key-holes being bushed, no dust can possibly enter.

Price £0 16s. 0d.

Packed in Three Dozen Cases for Export.

THE CITIZEN CLOCK.

All Metal.   No Wood about it.

TRADE MARK,  "CITIZEN."

This elegant Eight-Day Clock we have sold in immense numbers. It will do either for Bed Room or Office, Kitchen or Smoke Room, in fact,

"For up stairs or down stairs,
Or in my Lady's Chamber."

PRICE £0 12s. 6d.

Packed in Three Dozen Cases for Export to the Trade.

MYSTERIOUS CLOCK,

(MECHANICAL, NOT ELECTRIC,)

WITH AUTOMATICAL HANDS.

This new and wonderful clock consists of a transparent bevelled glass dial, 16 inches in diameter, to which is attached the whole mechanism, so constructed as to be entirely invisible. Simply suspended by a wire or cord in any place or position, it indicates the time with perfect exactitude. Being transparent it may be looked at from either side; placed before a light, it serves as a night clock.

The hands, which are of metal, richly engraved, move automatically by means of the displacement of the centre of gravity. They possess this striking peculiarity, that though they may be made to revolve with great rapidity *in either direction*, they return and *set themselves*, at the right time. The mechanism is simple, not easily disarranged, and in case of need, can be repaired by any watchmaker.

Any name and address desired can be put on the dial.

Price £7 10s. 0d.

THE NEW CLOCK BAROMETER,

Indispensable in every Country House.

Price £3 3s. 0d.

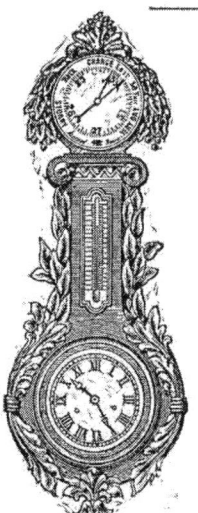

Height, 27 Inches.
Breadth, 10 Inches.

The case is of iron, bronzed, and forms a handsome ornament for the Dining Room, Library, Hall, &c.

The Clock goes 12 days, strikes hours and half-hours, and is a sound movement, well finished, and keeping accurate time.

The Barometer is Aneroid, the kind which, for its convenient size and other advantages has come into such universal requirement.

The Thermometer is carefully graduated, and may be relied on as exact.

The Dials of the Clock and of the Barometer are protected by strong plate glass, which cannot be broken except by extreme violence.

POCKET ANEROID.

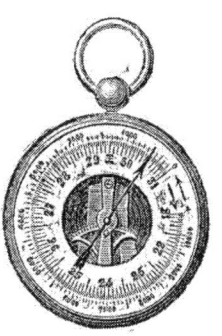

No. 2463.—Diameter, 2¼ in., weight, 2½ oz.; visible movement, extra-strong crystal glass. Altitude Scale to 3,000 yards; Compensated for Temperature. In Travelling Case. This is specially suitable for Sportsmen and Tourists, and cannot be damaged by any ordinary accident.

Price £2 10s. 0d.

ANEROID BAROMETER,

FOR MEASURING MOUNTAIN HEIGHTS.

No. 2430.—Best Silvered Dial, 4½ inches diameter, divisions on raised ring, Revolving Index, and Altitude Scale to 14,000 ft.; Compensated for Temperature.

Price £4 10s. 0d.

ROYLE'S PATENT
SELF-CLEANSING STEAM TRAP,

For Liberating Air and Water from Steam Pipes, Steam Engines, Steam Hammers, Drying Cylinders, Dressing Machines, Steam Worms, Sugar Pans, Combing Machines, Wool Driers, Tentering Machines, and Steam Apparatus generally.

Price £2 15s. 0d.

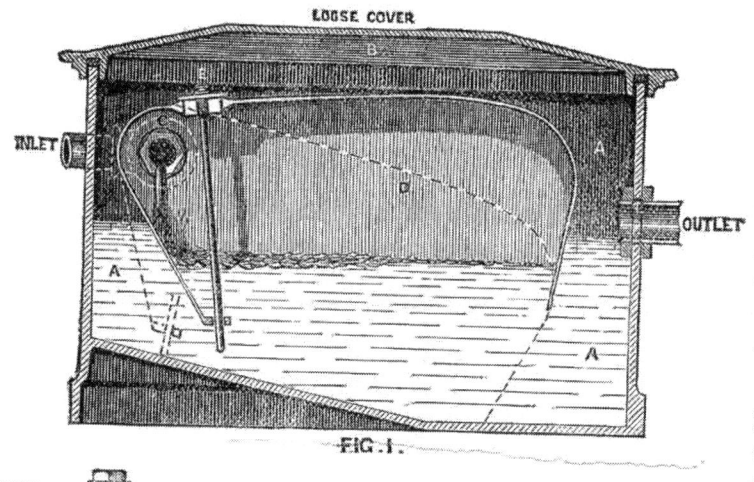

FIG. 1.

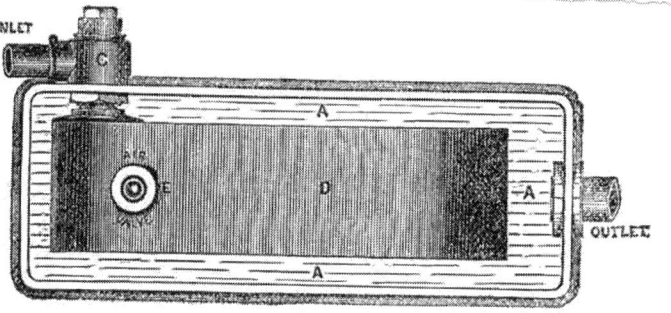

FIG. 2.

Description and Action.

A, Reservoir; **B**, Cover to same; **C**, Plug Cock; **D**, Bottomless Vessel forming a self-acting lever-handle for opening the Cock **C** when the condensed water accumulates in the steam pipes, and for closing the same immediately the water has escaped; **E**, air Valve.

ACTION.—The Bottomless Vessel **D** is kept in equilibrium in its highest position in the reservoir **A**, by the steam trapped beneath it, so long as the Steam Pipes are dry, and sinks by condensation, and so opens the Plug Cock **C** immediately any condensed water requires to escape. This condensed water simply falls directly into and amongst the water contained in the Reservoir **A**, (the overplus flowing away by the outlet pipe) whilst a free escape for air is provided through the Air Valve **E**.

SUMMARY OF ADVANTAGES.

1.—It is entirely open to the atmosphere, and therefore accessible for examination, even whilst under working pressure.

2.—It is practically self-cleansing; as the water of condensation falls direct into the reservoir A,—any scum or sediment settling to the bottom, and being swept away by the first rush of water upon starting.

3.—It will work equally well at high or low pressure.

4.—Its extreme simplicity and durability,—enclosed ball-floats, flange-joints, holding-down bolts, levers, stuffing-boxes, &c., being all dispensed with.

5.—Its action and working condition can be always seen and tested by simply lifting the loose cover B.

6.—A freer discharge for the Air and water condensation than is possible with any valve trap.

7.—It is thoroughly reliable, there being ample power to open or close the plug-cock C, which is surrounded with a steam-jacket, to ensure equal expansion throughout, and therefore easy working.

BAILEY'S
PATENT
VERTICAL STEAM TRAP

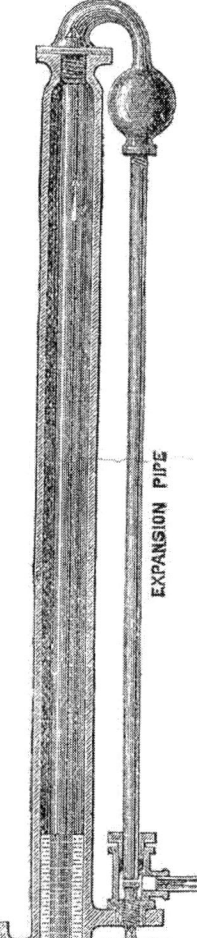

The "Vertical" is an adaption of the old expansion trap in a most complete form. This may be fixed either upright or horizontal, and water may be delivered in the most automatic manner from steam-pipes without loss of steam; there is no mystery about it, it being so plain and simple that those who run may read. It will not only permit the water to come out of the trap, but it will force the water into any receptacle many feet above it.

THE ACTION IS AS FOLLOWS:—

Where water accumulates in the pipes it runs in at the inlet of the iron case, and its pressure causes it to ascend the internal tube: it then descends into the expansion pipe, causing it to contract and to lift itself out of the stop at the bottom end; the water rushes out, and the moment hot steam begins to blow through, the pipe increases in length and closes the stop: it again opens when colder water accumulates. Thus, it will be seen, by taking advantage of the laws of expansion and contraction, one of the most perfect and reliable instruments ever invented is produced. No floats, springs, levers, joints, ethoé genus rerum are here found.

The space it occupies is about Three Feet Six Inches high.

No. 1—Inlet for ½ inch Gas Thread,	...	...	...	£2	10	0
No. 2 ,, ¾ inch ,, ,,	...	...	...	2	15	0
No. 3 ,, 1 inch ,, ,,	...	...	...	3	5	0
No. 4 ,, 1¼ inch ,, ,,	...	...	...	4	0	0
No. 5 ,, 1½ inch ,, ,,	...	...	...	5	0	0
No. 6 ,, 2 inch ,, ,,	...	...	...	6	10	0

Average height about 3 feet 6 inches.

GRINDROD'S PATENT GAS PIPE SCREWING MACHINE,

To Screw 1, 1¼, 1½, and 2 inches, Without Taps, } £6 6s.

This is a very useful Tool, and for large Pipes enables one man to do the work of two without the physical exertion necessary in the use of Screw Stocks and Dies. Its Portability and Lightness are additional advantages which a practical man will at once appreciate.

FOR EXPORT PURPOSES THIS TOOL IS FOUND HIGHLY ADVANTAGEOUS.

POST FREE, AN ACCOUNT OF
BAILEY'S PATENT PYROMETERS,
With Illustrations of their Application for Making Bread, the Indication of Waste Heat in Flues, and other useful purposes;

Also Illustrations, Description, and Prices of Bayley's Patent Recorders, Hallam's Patent Injectors, Jet Pumps, Governors, Water Heaters, and other useful Inventions interesting to Engineers, Mechanics, and other Tradesmen, as well as Amateurs.

J. BAILEY & CO.,
Inventors, Patentees, Manufacturers, Brass Founders, Electric Telegraph Engineers, Turret Clock Makers, &c.,

ALBION WORKS, SALFORD, MANCHESTER.

HALLIDAY'S PATENT
WAGON OILING MACHINE,

For Oiling Colliery Tub Wagons, Mining, and Quarrying Wagons, &c.

This apparatus mechanically OILS THE AXLES AND BEARINGS OF COLLIERY TUB WAGONS, and other small Wagons used in Mines and Quarries. It saves at least fifty per cent. of Oil, besides reducing the labour to a very considerable extent.

It will be seen from the illustration above, that the Invention consists of a cistern containing Oil, in which is a small brass pump, with pipes so attached as to come into juxtaposition with the axle bearings and pedestals of the wagon. Every time the pump lever is depressed small jets of Oil are forced upon these bearings, &c., and the Wagon is effectively oiled.

At every Colliery some hundreds of these Wagons are in use, each of which has to be turned upside down, and oiled with a can or brush. This necessarily involves great trouble and loss of time, and also causes an immense waste of Oil. By means of HALLIDAY'S Patent, this labour and attendant waste is avoided, as the surplus Oil is not lost, but runs through a small filter into the cistern again. The invention has no detail, and is not liable to get out of order, neither is it cumbrous, but can be easily fixed where considered most convenient.

The Machine has stood the test of experience, and has been working with great satisfaction at a number of Collieries, to which reference as to results can be made.

PRICES:

Machine for Oiling ordinary-sized Wagons, with fast wheels	£10 10s. 0d.
" " " loose wheels	12 0s. 0d.

Made by J. BAILEY & Co., Albion Works, SALFORD, MANCHESTER.

IMPROVED 40-INCH HYDRO EXTRACTOR,

For Bleachers, Dyers, Sugar Refiners, &c. For Drying Purposes in Hospitals and Wash-houses, and Extracting Moisture from all kinds of Pulps.

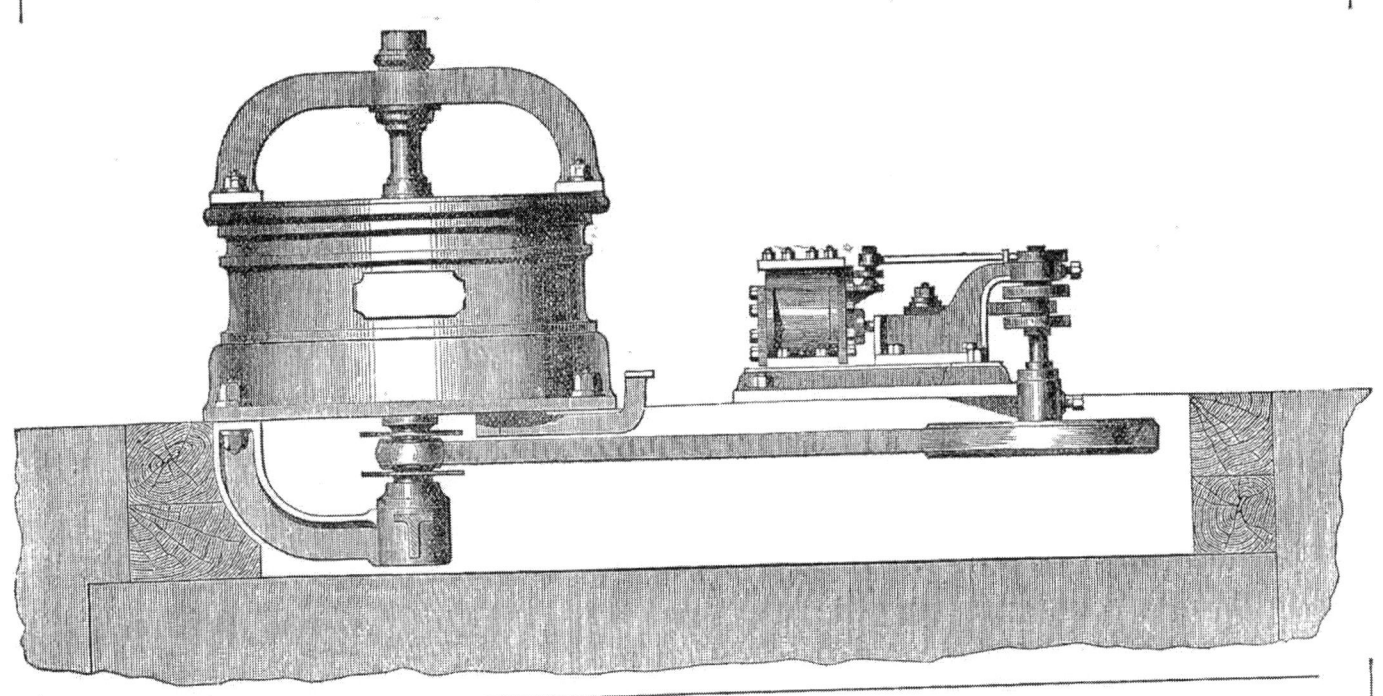

PATENT HAY AND COTTON PRESS.

This can be rolled about from place to place, or it may be made into small pieces for transport over difficult country.

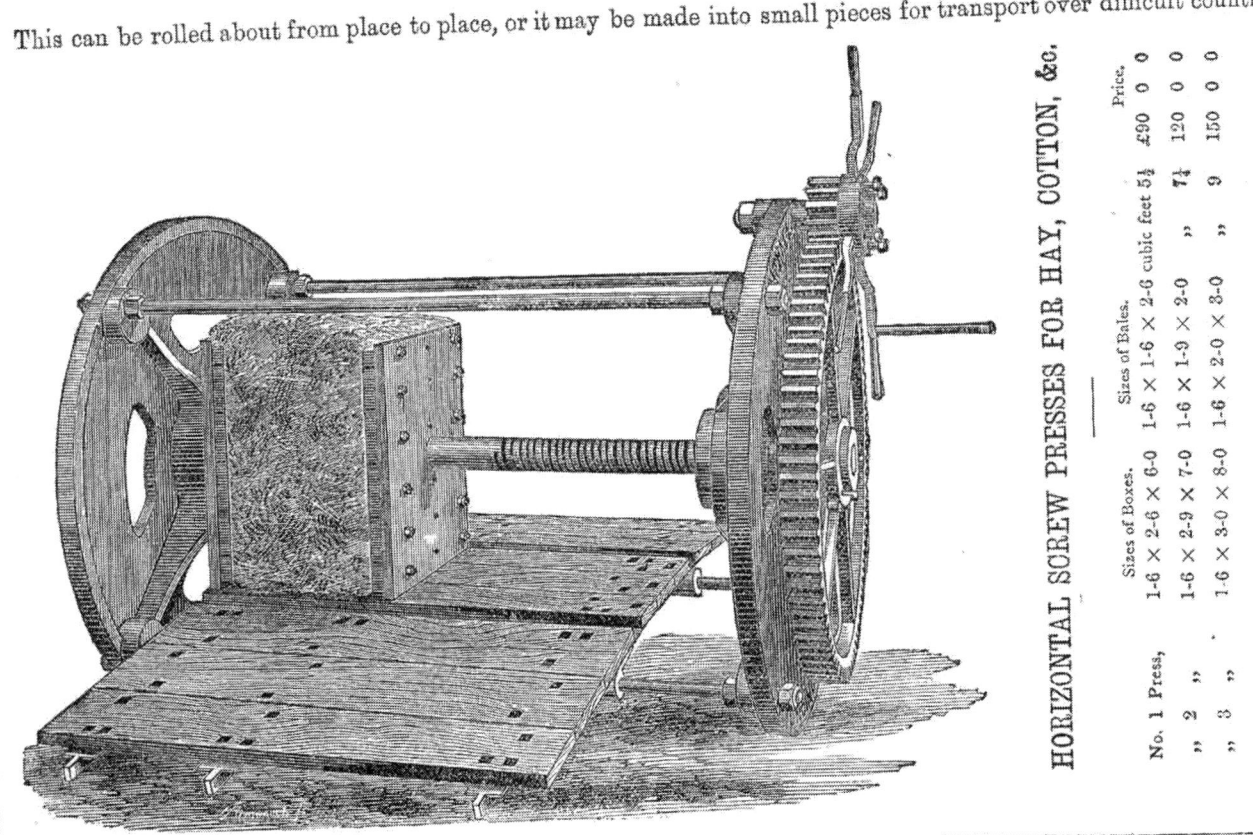

		Sizes of Boxes.	Sizes of Bales.		Price.
No. 1 Press,		1-6 × 2-6 × 6-0	1-6 × 1-6 × 2-6 cubic feet	5½	£90 0 0
,, 2 ,,		1-6 × 2-9 × 7-0	1-6 × 1-9 × 2-0 ,,	7¼	120 0 0
,, 3 ,,		1-6 × 3-0 × 8-0	1-6 × 2-0 × 3-0 ,,	9	150 0 0

HORIZONTAL SCREW PRESSES FOR HAY, COTTON, &c.

OXIDE PAINT,

FOR IRON WORK OR TIMBER STRUCTURES, BOILERS, BRIDGES, GIRDERS, ETC.

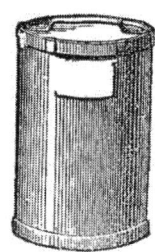

Ground in Oil,
Packed in 1 cwt. Cases,
35s. each.

Dry, or Native State,
ready for Mixing,
£25 per Ton.

"Warton Native Oxide of Iron" is the speciality of this firm. This remarkable mineral production was discovered by Mr. H. J. Walduck, in searching for the ordinary Hœmatite ores peculiar to the Limestone formation of the North of Lancashire. The "Warton" Oxide, however, far surpasses any other kind of iron ore in purity, and is remarkable for the fine state of division of its particles, which renders it admirably adapted for use as a pigment, either mixed with water or oil. Specimens of it, and of a water colour sketch drawn with oxide as it leaves the mines without preparation of any kind, may be seen at the Geological Museum, Jermyn Street, London. Professor Church, of the Royal Agricultural College, Cirencester, writes:—

"This native red Oxide of Iron is of remarkable colour and unusual purity. Ten parts of it contain 9½ parts of chemically pure ferric oxide. It contains minute traces of oxide of copper, an ingredient which has not, I believe, been before detected in similar native ores of iron. The amount of this oxide is, however, very small, only about 1 in 10,000 of the ore. I cannot attribute the peculiar brilliancy of this ferruginous pigment to the occurrence of this minute quantity of copper in it. Titanic Acid was carefully sought for in this sample, but not found."

Mr. Riley, the metallurgist, of Leeds, says:—"This Oxide of Iron is in the state of an impalpable powder free from grit and dirt, and uniform in quality throughout the mass. It is nearly a chemically pure per oxide."

For any description of paint work this beautiful mineral is of great value, and it should be noticed that its use is attended with no deleterious effects to those employed in applying it. It is, moreover, an excellent material for making steam joints, and is rapidly superseding red lead for this purpose, and also as a pigment.

We would advise consumers to obtain this oxide direct from the mine, as, its staining properties being so extraordinary, it is very liable to be adulterated by paint manufacturers.

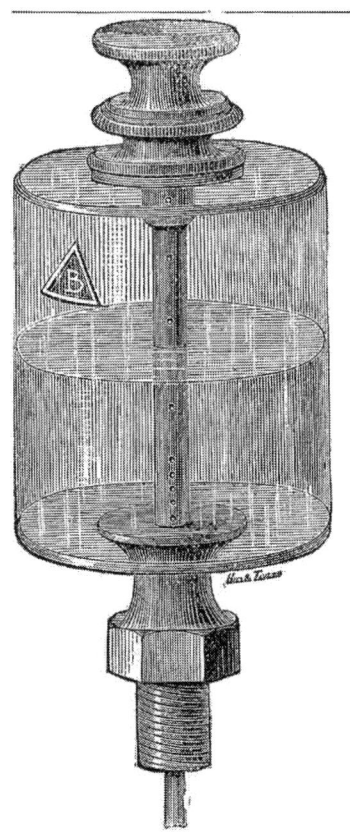

LARGE GLASS LUBRICATORS.

"THE ATMOSPHERIC,"

FOR

BEARINGS OF ENGINES OR SHAFTING.

Diameter in Inches						
5	.	.	.	.	at 12/6	} Extra Large
4	.	.	.	.	„ 8/6	
3	.	.	.	.	„ 4/6 ;	Per Doz. 48/7
2½	.	.	.	.	„ 4/0	„ 43/2
2	.	.	.	.	„ 3/6	„ 37/10
1¾	.	.	.	.	„ 2/6	„ 29/0

LEE & ROGERS'
PATENT
WROUGHT-IRON RIBAND SPIRAL PILLARS.

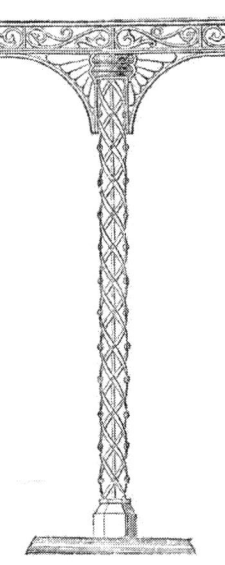

Among the most recent Novelties in the application of Bar Iron in cases in which Wood, Stone, or Cast Iron were formerly used, is the Patented Manufactures of Open-Work for Pillars, Posts, Poles, &c., &c.

The Strength of these Riband Pillars, their power of supporting vertical weight, and of resisting lateral strain, is abundantly evident both from their structural form and from the efficiency with which they have been found to answer all the practical purposes to which they have been applied.

A Post from 10 to 12 feet high, 8 inches diameter, and made from Iron 1 inch by $\frac{1}{4}$ thick, will support a weight of from 3 to 4 tons vertically, and will weigh about 2 cwt., including cap and base—that is to say, these Pillars support a vertical pressure of thirty-five times their own weight.

Iron Riband Poles may be used with the greatest advantage in all cases in which weight has to be supported or strain resisted, as well as in all cases in which a tall upright standard is employed. But their great strength and lightness render them specially suitable as *Railway Signal Posts*, *Telegraph Poles*, *Gas and Lamp Pillars*, and *Pillars* for Verandahs, Arbours, Rosaries, Kioskos, Conservatories, Porches, &c.—*Standards* for Training Plants, *Roofing Columns*, for Railway Stations, Arcades, Markets, Sheds, Covered Approaches, and also for Temporary Structures of all kinds; *Gate Pillars and Posts*, *Pillars for Park Fencing*, *Finger or Sign Posts*, and, in short, almost all classes of purposes for which Cast Iron or Wooden Pillars have hitherto been used.

The special advantages of the Patent Riband Pillars are their DURABILITY, STRENGTH and LIGHTNESS, their elegant appearance, their superiority over wooden Pillars in being exempt from dry rot, the ravages of insects, and the effects of damp. In strength they are much superior to wood, while they have the advantage over cast iron of being the least expensive of all metal supports. Their pleasing appearance is susceptible, where required, of the highest adornment, either by using them as trellises for climbing plants and flowers, or by enriching the design of the Pillars themselves.

ROOFING COMPLETE.

The Messrs. Bailey & Co. are prepared to Contract not ony for the Pillars of covered Structures, but for the Frame Work and Roofing as well. The following Prices are calculated for Pillars 15 feet high under the eaves, and the covering of Galvanized Corrugated Iron of 22 guage, as well as the necessary Ridging, Down Spouts, Eaves, Bolts, Rivets, &c.

SPAN From Outside to Outside the Pillars	LENGTH OF ROOF						
	25 feet	30 feet	40 feet	50 feet	75 feet	100 feet	140 feet
15 feet	£35	£40	£48	£60	£70	£90	£100
18 feet	48	55	65	75	90	110	170
20 feet	55	65	78	87	95	115	200
25 feet	55	70	85	95	115	140	225
30 feet	65	78	92	112	130	170	265
35 feet	75	90	100	120	150	195	310
40 feet	82	100	110	130	190	250	385

ALPHA PATENT
Portable Gas-Making Apparatus.
Now Made with SELF-FEEDING ARRANGEMENT.
Specially Constructed for Country use.

By Means of this Apparatus any person can INSTANTANEOUSLY make his own Gas, without requiring ANY HEAT. The Gas produced is of a superior illuminating and heating power to coal gas, and is also purer. There is no danger with the Apparatus whatever, and the gas produced is NON-EXPLOSIVE. It may be fitted to any existing gas-piping.

THE PROCESS IS VERY SIMPLE:—The reservoir being filled with Gasoline, the weight wound up, and the main-tap turned on, the Gas is ready for lighting. The Apparatus, being now supplied with a SELF-FEEDING ARRANGEMENT, gives a perfectly steady and uniform light, and all the attention required is winding up the weight, and refilling with Gasoline when empty. The Gas is PRODUCED IN THE SAME QUANTITY AS IT IS BEING CONSUMED, so that NO WASTE OR EVAPORATION is possible.

The Apparatus is sent out READY FOR WORKING, requiring simply filling; and, being self-contained, it is particularly ADAPTED FOR EXPORTATION, and there is no fear of it getting out of orde.

SUITABLE GASOLINE can be supplied direct from the Works, or by local Agents.

FULL INSTRUCTIONS SENT WITH EVERY APPARATUS.
No. 2 Will supply 25 lights, £30 (about 24 in. square). No. 3 will supply 60 lights, £55 (about 30 inch square).
SMALLER AND LARGER SIZES IN COURSE OF CONSTRUCTION.

N.B.—The Guages and Feed Tap are now dispensed with, being superseded by the adoption of a Self-Feeding arrangement.

THE "UNIVERSAL" SCREW-STOCK,

For Engineers' Use.

No. 5698.   REGISTERED JULY 17th, 1875.

WITH 1 PAIR OF ADJUSTABLE TAPER DIES, SCREWING 4 SIZES, AND TAPER AND PLUG TAPS.
WHITWORTH STANDARD THREADS.

The advantages of the REGISTERED "UNIVERSAL" SCREW-STOCK consists in its improved arrangement and construction, whereby Two adjustable reversible Dies are admitted, by which FOUR Sizes may be screwed.

The Dies, made from the best Cast Steel, are tapered to half their thickness, which causes them to work much easier.

The processes of manufacture being simplified, it is produced at much less cost than the ordinary Screw-stock, and its simplicity, compactness, and general handiness for mechanical use, should insure for it a wide market.

No. 5698. To Screw.	With Taper and Plug Taps to each size.	No. 5698. To Screw.	With Taper and Plug Taps to each size.	No. 5698. To Screw	With Taper and Plug Taps to each size.
$\tfrac{1}{4}, \tfrac{5}{16}, \tfrac{3}{8}, \tfrac{1}{2}$	2 0 0	$\tfrac{5}{16}, \tfrac{3}{8}, \tfrac{1}{2}, \tfrac{5}{8}$	2 6 0	$\tfrac{1}{2}, \tfrac{5}{8}, \tfrac{3}{4}, \tfrac{7}{8}$	2 18 0
$\tfrac{5}{16}, \tfrac{3}{8}, \tfrac{7}{16}, \tfrac{1}{2}$	2 2 0	$\tfrac{3}{8}, \tfrac{7}{16}, \tfrac{1}{2}, \tfrac{5}{8}$	2 7 0	$\tfrac{1}{2}, \tfrac{5}{8}, \tfrac{3}{4}, 1$	3 5 0
$\tfrac{1}{4}, \tfrac{3}{8}, \tfrac{7}{16}, \tfrac{1}{2}$	2 1 0	$\tfrac{1}{4}, \tfrac{3}{8}, \tfrac{1}{2}, \tfrac{3}{4}$	2 9 0	$\tfrac{5}{8}, \tfrac{3}{4}, \tfrac{7}{8}, 1$	3 6 0
$\tfrac{1}{4}, \tfrac{3}{8}, \tfrac{1}{2}, \tfrac{5}{8}$	2 5 0	$\tfrac{3}{8}, \tfrac{1}{2}, \tfrac{5}{8}, \tfrac{3}{4}$	2 10 0	$\tfrac{7}{8}, 1, 1\tfrac{1}{8}, 1\tfrac{1}{4}$	4 5 0

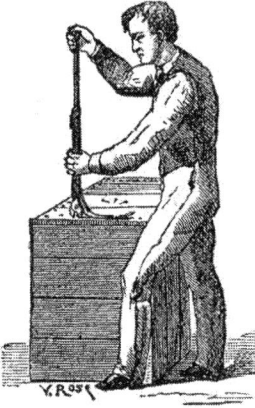

WILLIAMS' PATENT NAIL PULLER.

By its use the nails are drawn out straight and good, the cases are not broken or injured, and the time saved is sufficient to induce all who have cases to open to obtain one.

To use it, place the jaws over the head of the nail, with the short lever in a line with the grain of the wood, strike the rammer down two or three times, lift it up and pull it towards you.

No. C. 1402   Price 8/6 each.   **A smaller size for light work, 7/- each.**

HAND-LEVER
Punching and Shearing Machines

Suitable for Coppersmith, Whitesmiths, Blacksmiths, and all Workers in Iron, &c.

	Centre of Punch to back of Gap.	Weight lbs.	Price. £ s. d.
No. 1.—To punch $\tfrac{1}{4}$-in. through $\tfrac{1}{4}$-in. plate	$2\tfrac{1}{4}$-in.	56	4 0 0
No. 2.—To ,, $\tfrac{3}{8}$-in. ,, $\tfrac{3}{8}$-in. ,,	3-in.	140	5 10 0
No. 3.—To ,, $\tfrac{1}{2}$-in. ,, $\tfrac{3}{8}$-in. ,,	$3\tfrac{1}{2}$-in.	224	7 0 0

The Price includes 1 Punch, 1 Die, and 1 pair Cutters.

CAST IRON PIPES,

FOR COLD AND HOT WATER AND SANITARY GOODS.

RAIN WATER GOODS.

Sizes		2	2½	3	3½	4	4½	5	6
		s. d.	s. d.	s. d.	s. d.	s. d.	s. d.	s. d.	s. d.
Pipes, (6 ft. lengths) ℔ yd.		0 11	1 1	1 4	1 6	1 9	2 3	2 10	3 3
Heads, ...	ea.	1 1	1 3	1 6	1 10	2 0			
Ditto, large pattern ...	,,	1 6	1 8	1 10	2 2	2 6			
Shoes	,,	0 8	0 10	1 0	1 2	1 7			
Boots	,,	1 1	1 4	1 6	1 9	2 2			
Elbows (square)	,,	1 0	1 2	1 4	1 9	2 2			
Ditto (obtuse)	,,	1 2	1 4	1 6	2 0	2 6			
Plinth Pipes, 2½ in. proj. ...	,,	1 4	1 9	2 0	2 9	3 9			
Swan Necks, 3 in. ,, ...	,,	0 10	1 0	1 3	2 2	2 3			
Ditto 6 in. ,, ...	,,	1 0	1 3	1 6	2 1	2 6			
Ditto 9 in. ,, ...	,,	1 3	1 6	1 10	2 4	3 0			
Ditto 12 in. ,, ...	,,	1 8	2 0	2 6	3 0	3 9			
Half Round Gutters, ℔ yd.	...			0 7¼	0 7½	0 8	0 9½	11½	1 6
Ditto Angles and Nozzles, ...	ea.			0 8½	0 9	0 11	1 0	1 3	1 8
Ditto Stop Ends (loose), ℔ doz. ...	...			2 0	2 0	2 4	2 4	2 9	3 0

Sizes		3	3½	4	4½	5	6
		s. d.	s. d.	s. d.	s. d.	s. d.	s. d.
O. G. Gutters, (plain clips) ℔ yd. ...	...	......	0 11	1 1	1 3	1 5	2 3
Ditto Angles and Nozzles, ...	ea.	......	1 0	1 2	1 4	1 6	2 6
O. G. Gutters, (Lion clips) ℔ yd. ...	...	......	1 0½	1 2½	1 5	1 8	2 6
Ditto Angles and Nozzles, ...	ea.	......	1 1	1 3	1 6	1 9	2 9
Ditto Stop Ends, (loose), ℔ doz. ...	...	......	2 3	2 9	2 9	3 0	3 0
Nozzles, cast on Gutters ...	...	......	0 4	0 4	0 4	0 6	0 9
Stop Ends, ditto	...	......	0 2	0 2	0 2	0 3	0 3

Sizes		4	4½	5	6	7	8
Smoke Pipes (6ft. lengths) ...	℔ yd.	1 9	2 3	2 10	3 3	5 0	6 0
Ditto Elbows	ea.	2 2	3 0	3 6	4 6	6 6	7 6
Ditto ditto with soot door ...	,,	3 9	4 6	5 6	6 6	8 6	10 0

Pipes, Boots, Shoes, &c., if with angle ears, 2d. each extra. Short Lengths of Pipe charged 1d. per yard extra. Pipe Nails, 8d. per doz. Bolts and Nuts, 4/6 per gross.

HOT WATER GOODS.

No. on Sheet	Sizes	2	3	4
		s. d.	s. d.	s. d.
	Socket Pipes, in 6 and 9 ft. lengths, ℔ yd. ...	1 3	2 2	2 9
	Ditto under 6 ft. ,, ,, ...	1 5	2 4	2 11
	Coil ditto 6 and 9 ft. ,, ,, ...	1 4	2 3	2 10
	Ditto under 6 ft. ,, ,, ...	1 5	2 4	2 11
	Ditto under 3 ft. ,, ,, ...	1 6	...	...
	Trough ditto 6 and 9 ft. ,, ,, ...	3 6	4 6	6 0
5	Blank Spigots	0 4	0 6	0 10
9	Ditto Sockets	0 8	1 1	1 8
12	Common Elbow	1 6	2 6	3 0
,,	Ditto shorter and lighter	1 3	1 11	2 6
12A	Long Elbow	2 0	3 4	4 0
13	Double Socket ditto	1 5	2 8	3 2
13A	Long ditto ditto	1 11	3 6	4 6
14	⅛th ditto ditto	1 5	2 8	3 2
14A	Long ditto ditto	1 9	3 3	4 0
15	Double Elbow, 4½ rise	1 6	2 9	3 10
,,	Ditto ditto 7 ,, ...	1 8	3 0	4 2
,,	Ditto ditto 9 ,, ...	1 10	3 3	4 6
18	**S** Pipe, with 2 sockets	2 7	3 10	5 0
19	Elbow Boiler Top	3 0	3 9	4 2
20	Flange and Socket Elbow (short)	1 7	2 7	3 3
21	Ditto ditto (long)	2 2	2 11	3 10
22	Boiler Top, straight	2 6	3 0	3 6
23	Close Syphon	1 8	3 3	4 2
24	Open ditto	1 10	3 6	4 10
25	Three-way ditto	3 0	5 0	7 2
26	Spigot Outlet Syphon	2 5	3 10	5 0
27	Socket ditto	2 7	4 5	5 6
28	Three-way Syphon Spigot Outlet	3 6	5 0	7 2
29	Ditto ditto Socket ditto	3 10	5 9	8 3
30	Elbow Syphon	2 9	4 0	5 6
31	Three-way ditto	3 7	5 6	8 3
32	**T** Pipe, Double Socket and Socket Branch ...	2 9	4 8	5 6
33	Ditto Socket Branch	2 2	4 0	4 9
34	Ditto double Socket and Spigot Branch ...	2 2	4 6	4 9
35	Ditto Spigot Branch	2 0	3 4	3 10
		3 x 2	4 x 2	4 x 3
36	Ditto dbl. Socket and dimng. Sckt. Branch ...	3 7	4 0	5 0
37	Ditto ditto ditto Spigot ditto ...	3 4	3 9	4 6
		2	3	4
38	**H** Pipe	3 4	4 10	6 6

No. on Sheet	Sizes	2	3	4
		s. d.	s. d.	s. d.
39	Branch Pipe	3 4	4 10	6 6
40	Ditto ditto	3 3	4 9	6 4
41	**Y** Pipe	3 6	5 3	6 9
42	Cross ditto	3 4	4 9	6 6
43	Flange Socket, long	1 8	2 8	3 4
44	Ditto Spigot, long	1 3	2 3	2 6
45	Double Socket	1 6	2 3	3 3
46	Sliding Collar	1 1	1 3	1 9
		3 x 2	4 x 2	4 x 3
47	Diminishing Sockets	2 1	2 3	3 6
48	Ditto Pipe	1 4	1 6	2 0
49	Ditto Nipples	1 1	1 2	1 6
	Ditto Elbows	2 4	3 2	3 6
		2	3	4
50	Four-way Elbow Syphon	4 9	8 6	11 0
51	Ditto Syphon	4 3	7 9	9 6
52-53	Coil Syphons ... ... ℔ cwt.	18 8	16 4	15 0
54-55	Throttle Valves, improved	10 6	12 6	13 9
	Stop ditto with brass screw	12 0	15 0	17 6
60	Flange Socket, short	1 3	2 2	2 10
		3 x 2	4 x 2	4 x 3
61	Diminishing Spigot Pipe	1 11	2 5	3 0
			3	4
	Loose Trough, 3 ft. long		3 0	4 0

Soot Hole and Plug	6 × 3½ 2/-	9 × 6 3/-		
Cistern and Cover	12×10×6 4/-	18×12×8 7/-	20×15×8 9/-	24×15×12 15/6
Double Furnace Doors and Frames, flush			23×13 13/-	29×17 16/6
Ditto ditto recessed			25×16 16/6	31×20 18/6
Ditto Sliding ditto		18×14 11/-	24×21 19/-	30×27 30/-

Expansion Box and Cover, 12 × 12 × 24, with 4 sockets, 27/6
Ditto ditto 2 ditto 25/-
Coil Blocks, with inverted sockets for 2 in. pipe ... ... ℔ cwt., 13/6
Furnace Bars, Bearers, and Dead Plates ,, 11/-
Ornamental Gratings, various ,, 14/- to 18/8

ESTIMATES GIVEN FOR COIL CASES.

This List is liable to alteration, according to Metal Market.

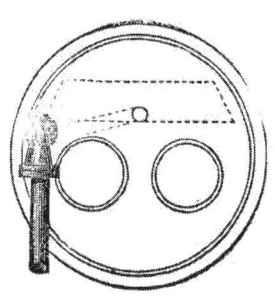 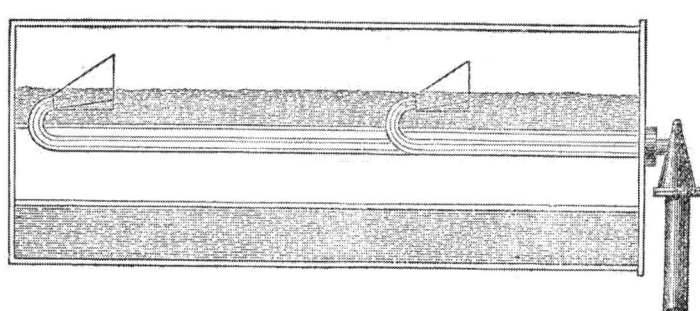 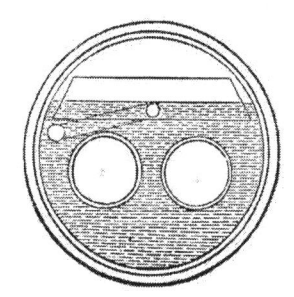

PRICE LIST
OF
NEEDHAM'S PATENT SURFACE SCUMMING APPARATUS,
FOR STEAM BOILERS,
CONSISTING OF

Surface Scummers, Steam-Piping, Flanges, New Brass Blow-off, and 9ft. length of 2 inch Drain-Pipe.

Several Thousands of them are in use giving satisfaction.

Length of Boiler	Prices.	Length of Boiler.	Prices.
7 to 16 feet	£12 0 0	25, 26, to 27 feet	£15 0 0
17 „ 18 „	12 10 0	28, 29, „ 30 „	15 10 0
19 „ 20 „	13 0 0	31, 32, „ 33 „	16 0 0
21 „ 22 „	14 0 0	34, 35, „ 36 „	16 10 0
23 „ 24 „	14 10 0	37, 38, „ 39 „	17 0 0

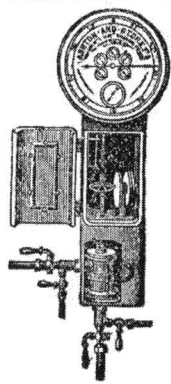

ASHTON & STOREY'S
STEAM POWER CONTINUOUS INDICATOR.

A, Power Meter for any size Cylinder, showing ft. lbs. per circular inch, £25 0 0

PRICES—exclusive of delivery.

For Power Meter, suited to any size of Cylinder, showing ft. lbs. per circular inch	25 0 0
If with dial to show horse power per minute adapted to the size of cylinder, extra	1 10 0
If with large dial arranged to show horse power, instead of ft. lbs., to suit special size of cylinder, extra	1 10 0
If with portable barrel mounted to take paper diagrams, extra	3 3 0
B, For Portable Engines small size Instrument in Box,	15 0 0

HILL'S PATENT FIRE ESCAPE and LOWERING TACKLE.

Sole Makers, J. BAILEY & CO.

As used for Lowering Weights.

This simple invention is fully explained by the Engravings as a neat means of lowering weights or saving life when escaping from buildings on fire.

It will be observed that the instrument consists of a short piece of hard wood, round which a rope is coiled, thus causing an adjustable, powerful, and easily controlled friction, which enables a man to descend at a slow or quick velocity from any height that the rope is suitable for.

Another great advantage, in addition, is, that anyone who wishes to assist the person descending may hold the end of the slack rope, and thus control his descent if he has become weak, insensible, or incapable of lowering himself. The assistant may be either above or below. Ladies can thus be lowered with safety.

All sorts of Fire Brigade Fittings in Manufactories should have a small quantity of this tackle for the use of work people.

Superintendents of Fire Brigades are respectfully requested to investigate its merits for use by Firemen when engaged in their dangerous avocation.

No. 1—For Dwelling Houses, with   feet of rope
,, 2—For Works and Warehouses, Mills, &c., with   feet of rope

Trials with this invention have, in all cases, been pre-eminently successful.

Sample Orders invited.

With this invention one man can lower 1 ton weight with ease. Special Instruments made for special purposes.

The Ashcroft Patent Compound Safety Valve and Low Water Detector.

(Continued from Page 47.)

For ensuring Safety against danger from Low Water, High Steam, and High Water.

Prices of Smaller Sizes will shortly be published, for Agricultural, Portable, and Marine, or Locomotive Boilers, with Spring Balance instead of Weights.

When once fixed, it cannot possibly be tampered with.

PRICES:

With 3 inch Valve, ... £7 10 0
 „ 4 „ do. ... 10 0 0

Complete, ready for fixing, allowance being made for a Cast Iron Neck to go between it and the Boiler of 6 inches in depth.

One dozen Fusible Caps sent with each.

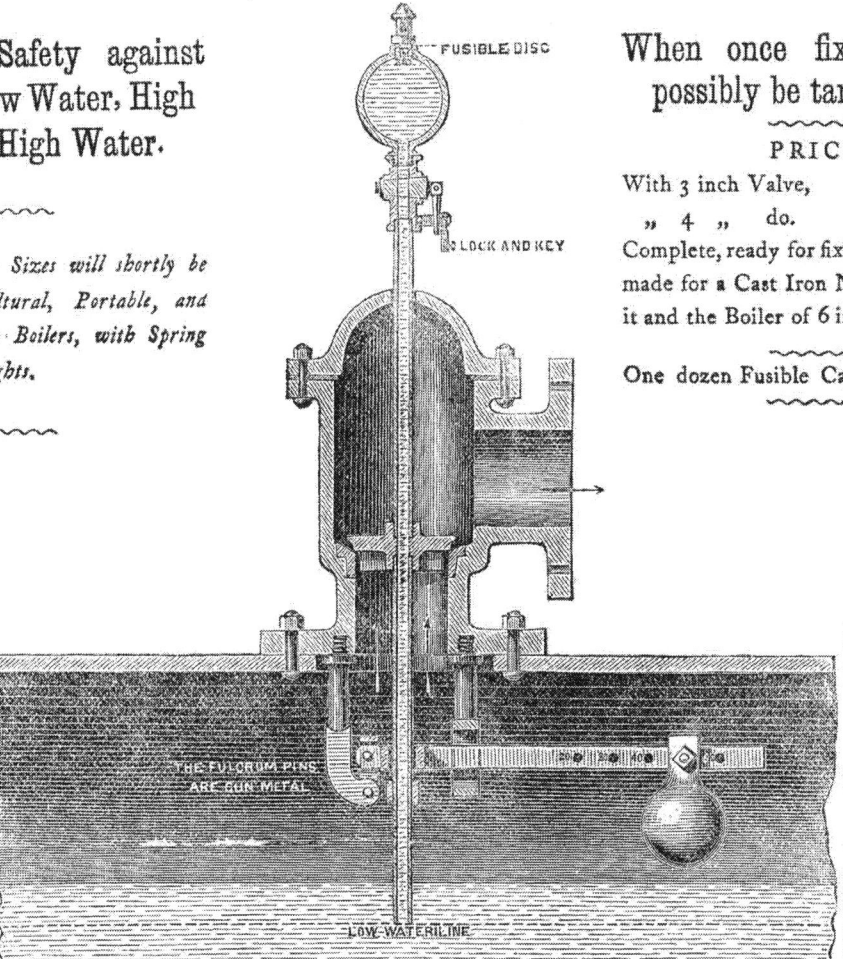

The whole is so constructed as to be bolted to an ordinary cast-iron Necking riveted to Boiler shell, and thus admits of being easily and readily applied, without entailing any deviation from the ordinary fittings usually supplied to every Boiler.

It may not be unimportant to state that, when the water is too high, it surrounds the Valve Weight, and causes steam to blow off at one-third less pressure than it would otherwise do, thus rendering the Invention *perfect in every sense.*

1. A Low Water Alarm that cannot be tampered with, and which does not stop the Boiler when the water is low.

2. A Safety Valve which is beyond the reach of any one who might be inclined to overweight it.

3. A High Water Valve, which will cause the Steam to escape at one-third less than working pressure, preventing priming and those accidents and loss in attendance on it.

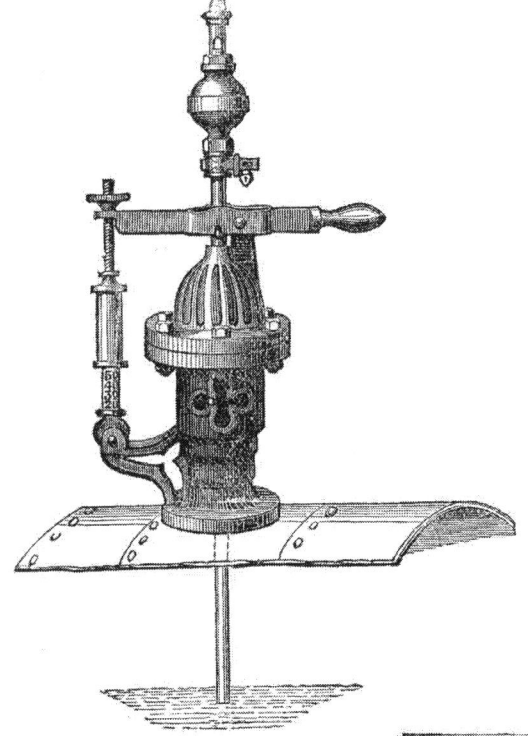

ASHCROFT PATENT SPRING BALANCE
SAFETY VALVE,
AND
LOW-WATER ALARM,
FOR
SMALL PORTABLE & STATIONARY BOILERS,
ALSO USED AS AN AUXILIARY VALVE.

This Valve is 2 inch bore, and is fitted on the Large Boiler in the centre, with an Ashcroft Low-Water Alarm, making it a most complete guardian of the Boiler against accident from High Steam or Low Water.

Price, with 1 dozen Discs ... £6 10s. 0d.

THE MEASURING INSTRUMENT,

(BY ROYAL LETTERS PATENT.)

For general Measuring Purposes, instead of the Measuring Tape. To use it, it is simply necessary to advance it along the surface or object, when the hands will indicate the length in feet, inches, and fractions of inches. It registers to 100 feet, weighs under 3 oz., and requires only one person to use it. Is most simple and accurate, and is recommended by the Press for the use of Engineers, Architects, Surveyors, Timber Merchants, Upholsterers, &c., and for the general public, for Picture Hanging, taking dimensions of rooms, &c., and for general use,

Price 10s. 6d. each.

Illustrated Prospectus Post Free from the Works.

THE CHARTOMETER.

(BY ROYAL LETTERS PATENT.)

The only Instrument that Registers Distances on Maps, Scaled Drawings, &c. By advancing it along any route on a Map the actual distance is indicated on the dial in miles, yards, &c., according to the Scale.

Changeable Dials are provided for various Scales of Maps, and a set is contained in the Leather Case that holds the Instrument.

The most accurate Distance Indicator—Recommended by the Press for the use of Engineers, Architects, Surveyors, Navigators, Tourists, Canoeists, Bicyclists, Hunting and Sporting People, &c., &c., and for the general public. Invaluable for ascertaining Cab Fares.

Illustrated Prospectus Post Free from the Works   Silver Medal awarded at the Manchester Exhibition (Pomona) 1875.

J. BAILEY & CO., Albion Works, Essex Street, Salford, Manchester.

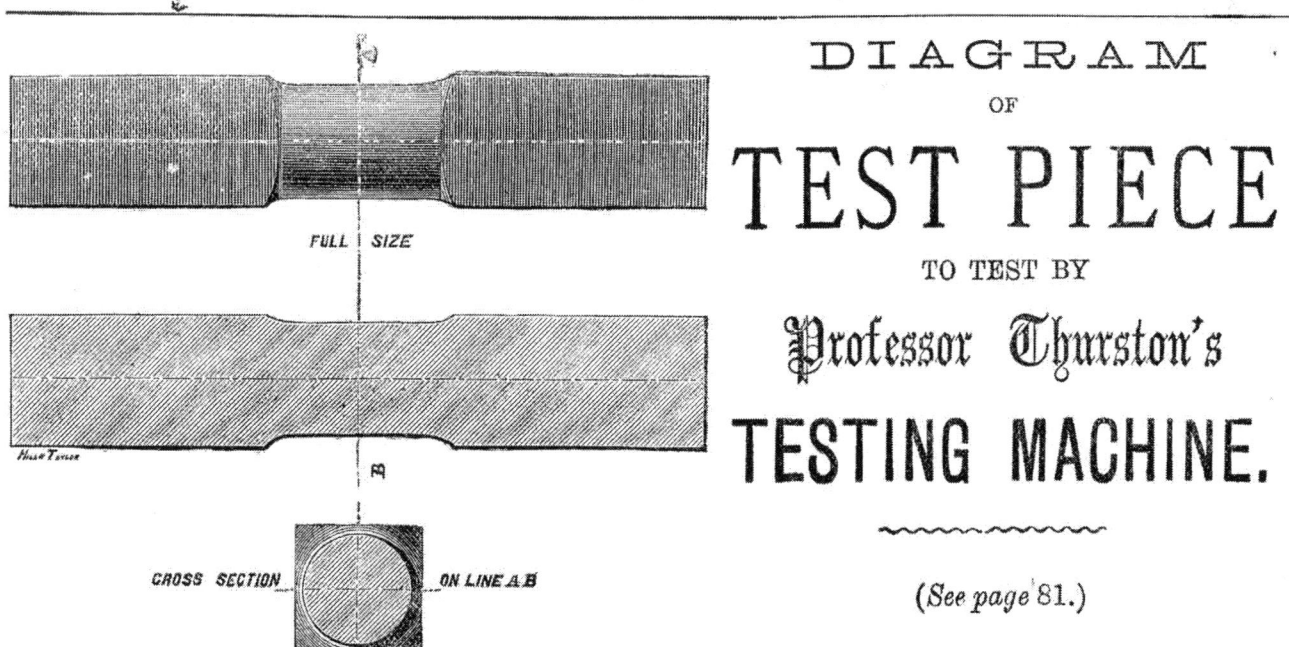

DIAGRAM OF TEST PIECE TO TEST BY Professor Thurston's TESTING MACHINE.

(See page 81.)

The above Illustration gives the exact size of a piece of Iron, Steel, Copper or other metal to be prepared for testing by the Thurston Machine.

☞ We are prepared to test Specimens at a charge of £1 for each Test and Diagram.

NEW PATENT HOT-WATER BOILERS

For Heating Conservatories, Dwelling Houses, Mansions, Public Buildings, etc.

EASILY, EFFECTUALLY, AND SAFELY.

PATENT INDEPENDENT BOILERS WITHOUT BRICKWORK.

PATENT HORIZONTAL TUBULAR BOILER,

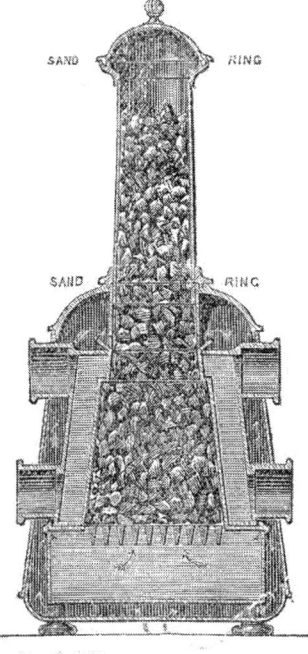

The most powerful Boiler known, for heating greenhouses, public buildings, &c., and requires less depth of stoke-hole than any other boiler. The fire is placed under and in it.

No.	Dimensions.	Heating power of 4in. pipe	Price.	Fittings per set*
1	1ft. 8in. sqr.	350 ft.	5 10 0	2 16 6
2	2ft. 0in. ,,	750 ft.	8 10 0	3 13 0
3	2ft. 4in. ,,	1000 ft.	12 0 0	5 0 0
4	2ft. 9in. ,,	1500 ft.	16 0 0	6 19 0
5	3ft. 5in. ,,	2000 ft.	20 0 0	10 5 0
6	4ft. 0in. ,,	3500 ft.	30 0 0	12 11 0
7	5ft. 0in. ,,	5000 ft.	45 0 0	17 17 0

* Fittings comprise—top plate, furnace doors, bars and bearers, dead plate, damper, soot door, fire irons

A 2 C WITH PATENT CASING.   **A 2 C** WITH PATENT CASING.

We have just introduced an important feature into the system of HEATING BY HOT WATER by Inventing and Patenting a HOT AIR CASING for Boilers, of which the following are some of the prominent advantages:—

Economy of Fuel! Prevention of Radiation! Utmost Utilization of Heat! Perfect Combustion Ensured! No Brickwork Required! Perfect Portability! Effectually Heats Buildings! No Danger from Fire!

As will be seen by the sectional Drawing, this NEW PATENT CASING consists of an arrangement of Chambers, whereby a continuous current of *heated* atmospheric air is introduced both *under and above* the burning fuel, thus bringing the heated gases into a state of perfect combustion before they pass away to the Smoke flue. The heat is thus enormously increased, and a corresponding economy of Fuel insured. As necessary results of this perfect combustion very little smoke is given off, and the smoke flue, instead of being very hot, is always comparatively cool. The new atmospheric inlet is self-acting, and when in use sustains a uniform heat for a greater length of time than is obtainable by other means. The feeder shown is for continuing the combustion for a longer time.

No. A 2	Heating Power in 2in. Pipe.	Fire will last.	WITHOUT Patent Casing.	No. A 2 C	Heating Power in 2 in. Pipe.	Fire will last.	WITH Patent Casing.
Size 1 ...	200 feet	6 hours.	£4 4 0	Size 1 ...	200 feet	8 hours	£5 15 0
,, 2 ...	350 ,,	8 ,,	£5 5 0	,, 2 ...	350 ,,	10 ,,	£7 0 0

THE APPLICATION OF THIS INVENTION TO OTHER BOILERS, FURNACES, &c., IS IN COURSE OF PREPARATION.

IMPROVED THROTTLE VALVES.

No. 9,
Bored and accurately fitted with Brass Disc and Spindle.

	Mark	2-inch	3-inch	4-inch
No. 9, Cast Iron Throttle Valve, with double Sockets	D S	10/6	12/6	16/-
Do. with one Socket and one Spigot End	S S	10/6	12/6	16/-

NEW PATENT
HIGH PRESSURE VALVES
FOR STEAM, WATER, OR GAS.
Patented in America, Canada and all European Countries.

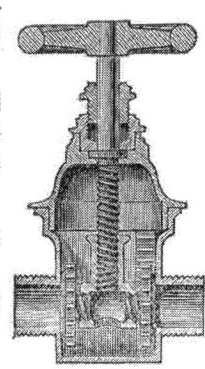

- IT IS THE ONLY VALVE WHICH CLEANSES FACES AND SEATS BEFORE CLOSING!
- IT IS THE ONLY VALVE THAT CAN BE OPENED AND ALL THE WORKING PARTS EXAMINED AND CLEANED WHILST UNDER PRESSURE!
- IT HAS A STRAIGHT UNOBSTRUCTED PASSAGE!
- THE AREA OF THE APERTURE IS EQUAL TO THAT OF THE PIPE!
- DOUBLE WEARING CAPACITY!
- CAN BE FIXED IN ANY POSITION!
- ADJUSTABLE & INTERCHANGEABLE DISCS!
- FRICTION REDUCED TO A MINIMUM!
- POSSIBILITY OF LEAKAGE REDUCED TO A MINIMUM!
- CAN BE PACKED UNDER PRESSURE!
- NOTHING BUT METAL USED IN THE CONSTRUCTION!
- SPECIALLY DESIGNED TO RESIST GREAT PRESSURE!

No. 12. GUN METAL Valve.

This New Patent Valve is supplied in the following sizes and patterns, fitted with wheel handles.—Screwed sockets, male ends, and screwed unions are tapped for wrought iron pipe.—Flanges sent round unless ordered otherwise.

DESCRIPTION.	Mark.	½-inch. s. d.	¾-inch. s. d.	1-inch. s. d.	1¼-inch. s. d.	1½-inch. s. d.	2 inch. s. d.
With double screwed sockets, female ends	D S	5 0	7 0	10 0	13 0	16 6	26 0 each
„ double screwed male ends	D M	5 0	7 0	10 0	13 0	16 6	26 0 „

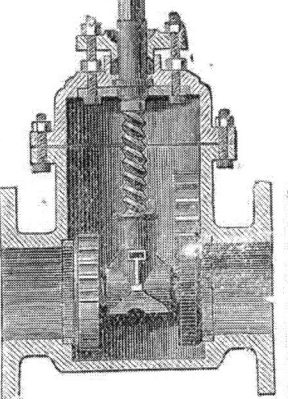

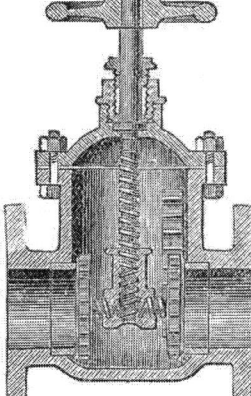

No. 12. CAST IRON VALVE, For Steam, Water, or Gas.

No. 12a. CAST IRON, WITH GUN METAL WEARING PARTS

DESCRIPTION.	Mark.	2 inch. s. d.	3-inch. s. d.	4-inch. s. d.
With double Flanges	D F	35 0	50 0	70 0 each
„ double Sockets	D S	35 0	50 0	70 0 „
„ one Socket and one Spigot end	S S	35 0	50 0	70 0 „

The above are supplied with either wheel or square-headed spindle at choice, without deviation from the price.
Cast Iron Valves, with Gun Metal wearing parts, No. 12 H, for underground purposes, same prices as No. 12.

For other Valves, see pages 50 to 60, in body of book.

Bailey's Patent Tidal River, Water Works, and Tank Recorders and Indicators.

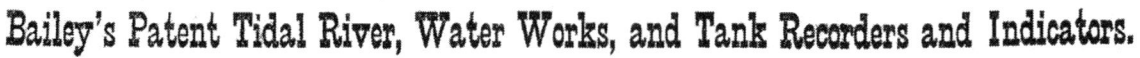

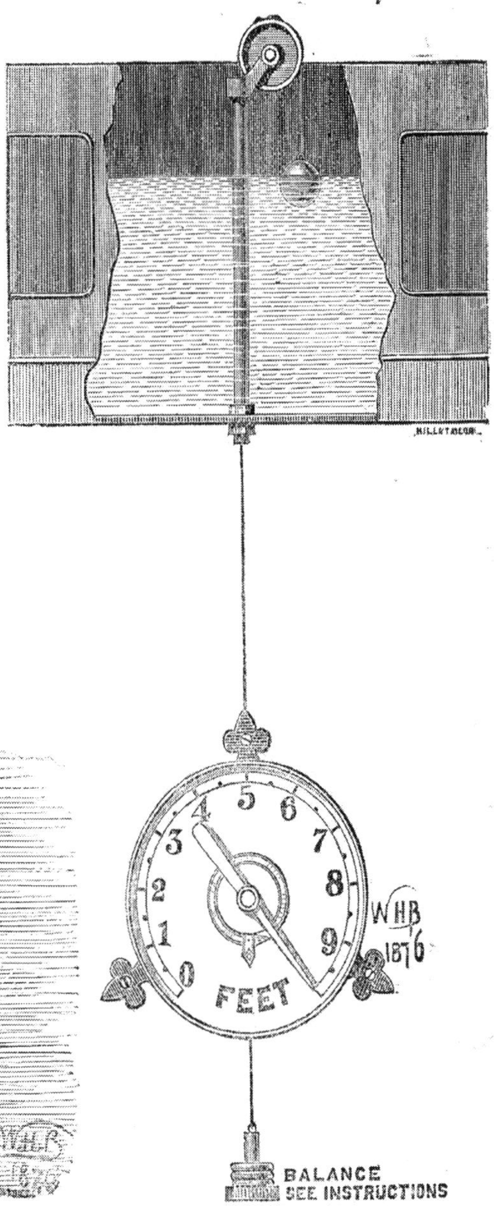

These Recorders have been designed, at the suggestion of Mr. Charles Hawksley, C.E., of Westminster, for the various extensive works in which he has been engaged upon. The Birmingham Sewerage Works and others have them at work. The price very much depends on the duty to be performed. The one illustrated has a dial 7 inches in diameter; the case is cast iron; the drum revolves once in 24 hours; the clock goes 8 days, and the scale on diagram is 1 inch to the foot, there being 4 feet fluctuation of water. Price, £35 for instrument with float; great depths special prices.

The Tank Indicators, as shown, are very useful for Water Works, Railway Tanks, &c., either above or below; for small fluctuations the dial is marked to the exact inches, but if the fluctuation be much, an inch to a foot is advisable; the balance weight is adjustable and falls through less space than the float, by an ingenious arrangement. If the float has 15 feet, the weight has only say 15 inches to travel.

MAXIMUM VARIATION

	For 3ft. or less	For 10ft. or less	For 20ft. or less
	£ s. d.	£ s. d.	£ s. d.
Diameter of Dial, 7 inches ...	2 2 0	3 3 0	5 5 0
" 8 " ...	3 10 0	4 4 0	6 10 0
" 10 " ...	4 4 0	5 10 0	8 8 0

Not including Pipe, Float, or Chain.

FOR DEEP WELLS, SEE NEXT PAGE.

BAILEY'S DEEP WELL TIDAL Indicators,

SOUTHPORT PATTERN.

Specially designed for the Pumping Stations of Southport Waterworks, and used elsewhere also.

Large size, 2 feet dial, blue and gold letters, white mounts, with float, cord and balance weight for Well 120 feet deep, very strong, 7 feet high.

Complete, as illustrated,
£40 0 0

Second size, do. do. as above, with dial 15 inches in diameter, and frame in proportion,

£25 0 0

Third-sized Wells of 50 feet deep, dial 12 inches,

£15 0 0

For Wells of less or greater depth, or any modification, please ask for prices.

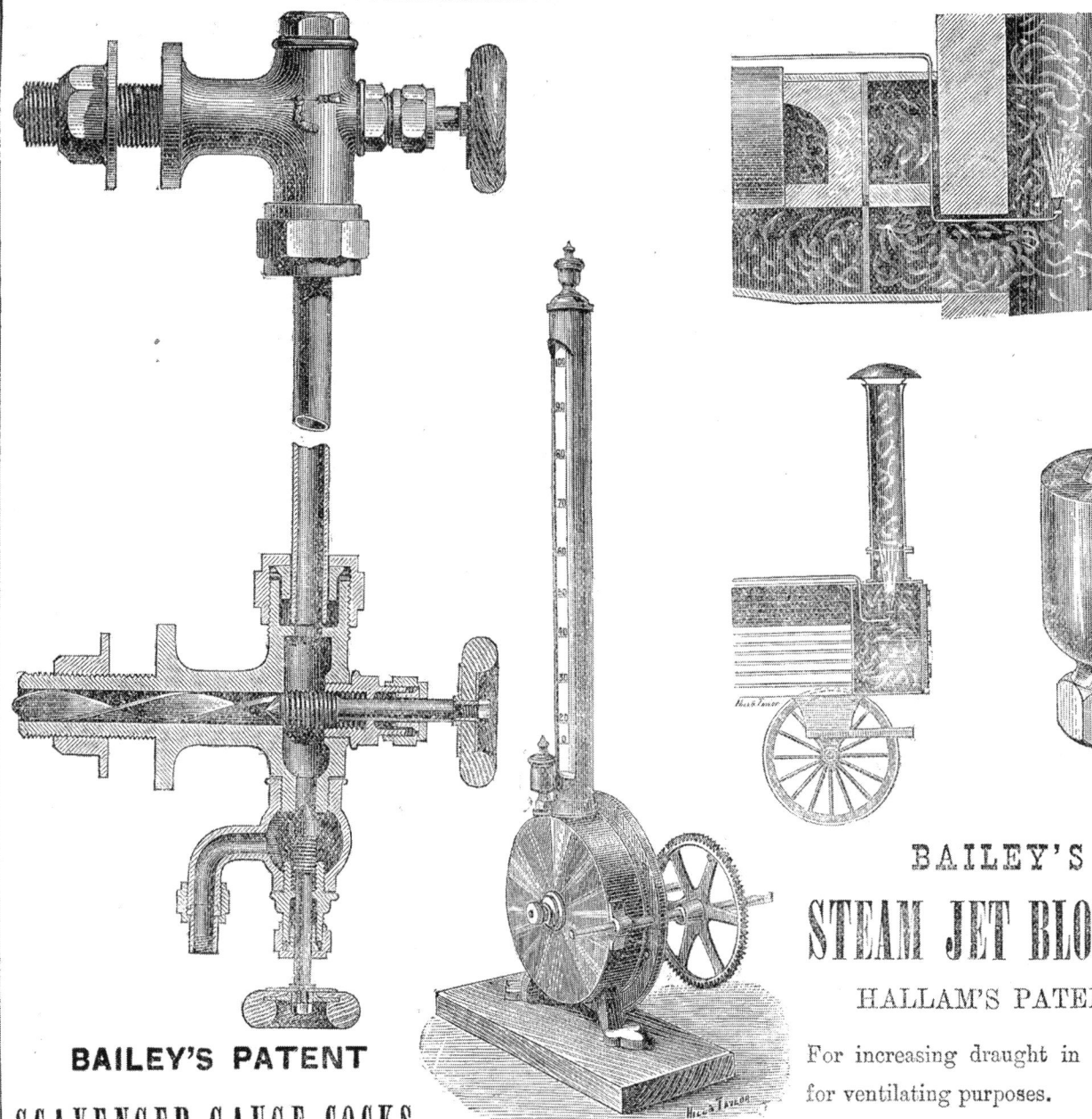

BAILEY'S PATENT
SCAVENGER GAUGE COCKS,

"MARINE PATTERN,"

Very strong, specially made, in the first instance, for Messrs. J. F. FOSTERS' extensive Works at Denholme, in Yorkshire.

For ¾ in. Glass, very heavy   £3   3   0
     ⅞ in.   ,, ...   3 10   0
Per Set.

For ordinary Gauges, see pages 33, 34, 35, of this book.

BAILEY'S
GYROMETER,
OR
SPEED INDEX,

For indicating the revolutions per minute by means of the columner height of a fluid in Glass Tube,

£5 5s. 0d. each.

BAILEY'S
STEAM JET BLOWER,
HALLAM'S PATENT,

For increasing draught in flues and for ventilating purposes.

~~~~~~

			£	s.	d.
No. 1, for 6 H. P. Boilers and under			2	2	0
,, 2 ,, 10 H. P. Boilers			3	3	0
,, 4 ,, 20 ,,	,,		4	10	0
,, 5 ,, 60 ,,	,,		6	10	0
,, 6 ,, 120 ,,	,,		8	0	0

When required for Ventilating purposes, they are placed inside a pipe of proper dimensions.

For Steam Jet Pumps and Injectors, see Special List.

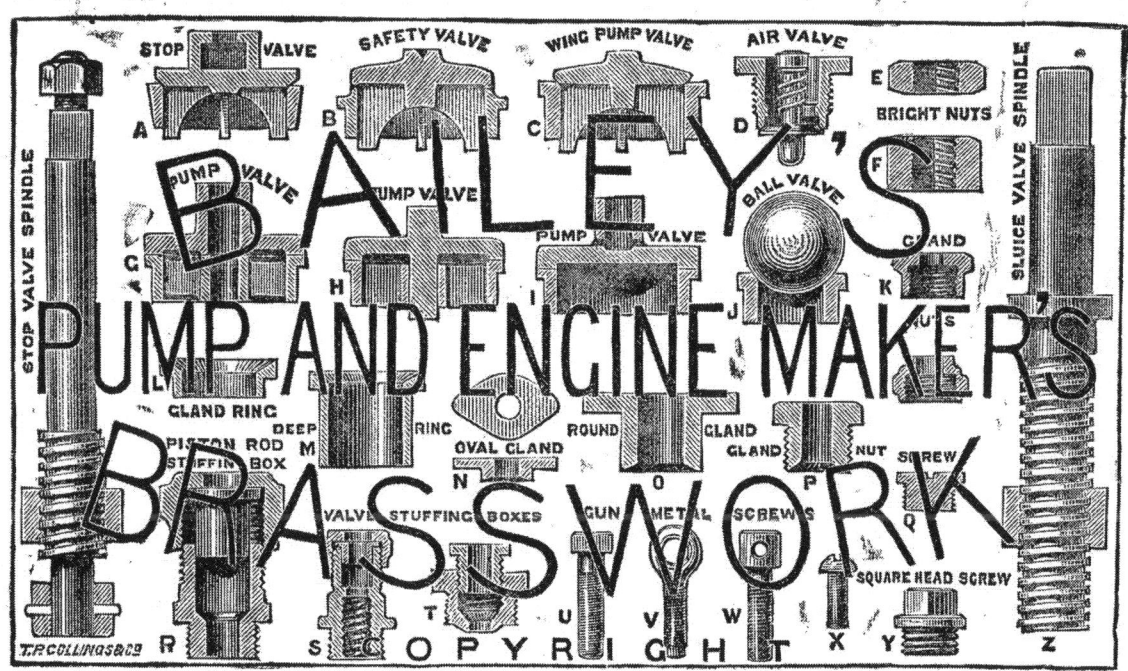

Engineers and Machinists supplied to drawing with every description of Glands, Valves, Spindles, Brass Nuts, finished bright, either of our own patterns, or to special drawings.

Our special tools and division of labour enable us to do this class of work generally much cheaper than Engineers can do it themselves.

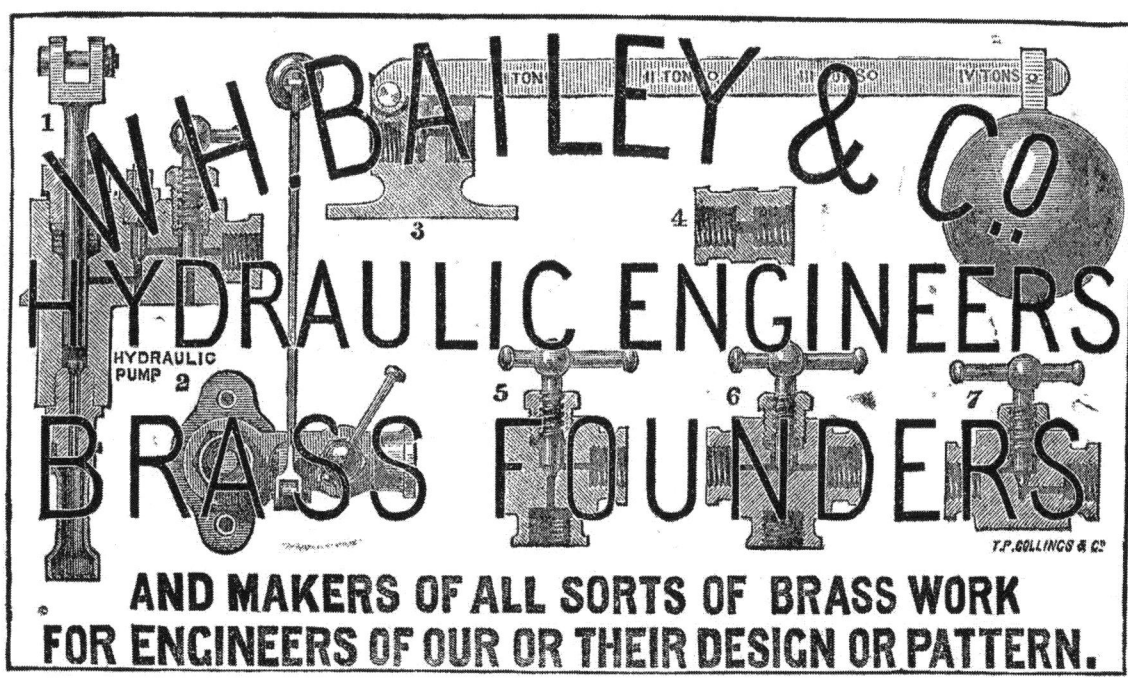

HYDRAULIC PUMP WORK,
READY FOR FITTING UP,
TO ORDER, OR FROM OUR OWN PATTERNS.

RACK SAW BENCH.

Rack Saw Bench will take a 6ft. Saw (Saws not included). Tail is 16 feet long, of Red Deal, 9 × 3. The Middle is made of Well-seasoned English Oak, and fitted with Cast Iron Girders, to carry Rollers, Spindle and Fence Bearings. A Pulley is supplied on end of Spindle. The Head is 20 feet long, and is made of Red Deal or Pitch Pine, 11 × 3. The Rollers, which are turned true, out of Elm, 4½ inches diameter, have Spindles running through them. The Table Planks are Pitch Pine, with a Rack let in each the whole length, one is 15 inches and the other 12 inches wide by 2¼ thick. The Fence Gauge is planed up true, and is made very strong; the Spindle is Screw Cut into a Brass Nut, moving the gauge 1 inch at a revolution. Price, £75. £1 per Foot Extra for Additional Lengths. This Bench can be made Self-Feeding at an extra charge of £10. *Prices, with Iron Tops, and for Fixtures, on Application.*

PATENT HAND POWER COMBINED CIRCULAR AND BAND SAWING MACHINE,

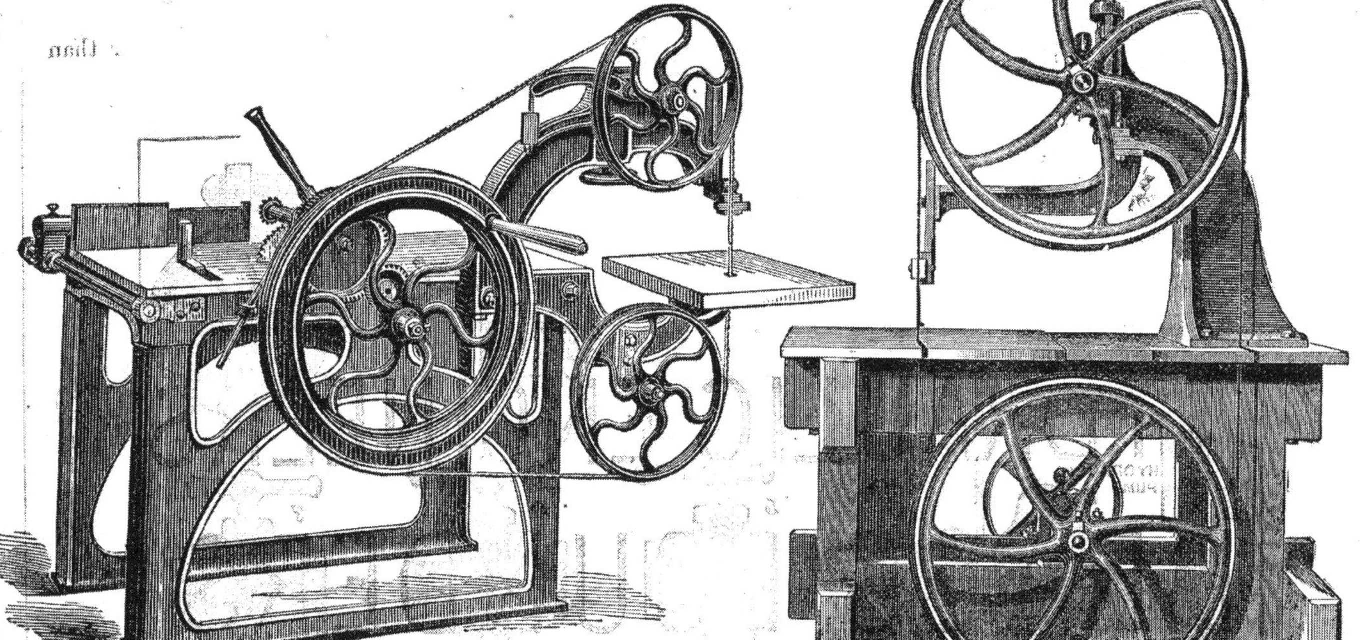

Will cut with 14 in. Circular Saw, 4½ in. deep; with Band Saw, 6 in. deep.

Table 4 feet by 2 feet, made of Iron and planed true on the top. Fitted with Rising and Falling Spindle, Self-acting Feed Motion; Parallel Fence made to cant, so as to cut bevels, and also to turn over end of bench, to be out of the way of cross-cutting. Fitted with Weight and Roller, for keeping timber to Fence.

With this Bench one man can cut 3 inches deep, at the rate of 10 feet in four minutes, thus effecting a saving of 150 per cent. over the Hand Saw.

Band Saw Apparatus is fitted with square table, made so as to cant over for cutting to any bevel; with this may be cut any irregular, curved, or ornamental design, with an date not attained before by any Hand power Machine. The Band Saw is fitted with a new arrangement for securing equal tension to saw at all times.

Price of above Machine, with one 14 in. Saw, and one Band Saw ... £22 0 0
„   „   if fitted with Boring Apparatus, and one patent Auger ... 24 0 0

BAILEY'S WASHER CUTTER, FOR INDIA RUBBER MERCHANTS, &c.

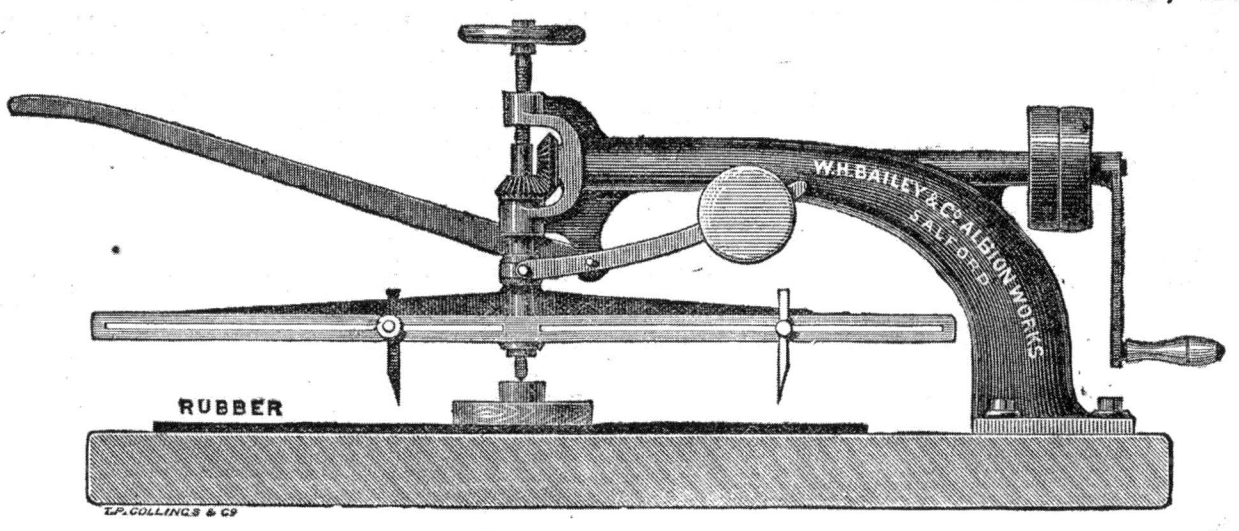

This useful Machine needs no description.
It cuts inside and outside of a Washer at once it is adjustable.

For Rings, No. 1, 36 inches in diameter	£25 0 0
No. 2, 20 inches in diameter	20 0 0
No. 3, 12 inches in diameter	10 0 0

It will Cut Felt and Thin Wood, Cardboard, Cloth and other Materials.

SMITH & COVENTRY'S PATENT STEEL TOOLHOLDERS,

For use in the Lathe, Shaping Machine, Slotting Machine and Planing Machine.

TRADE MARK

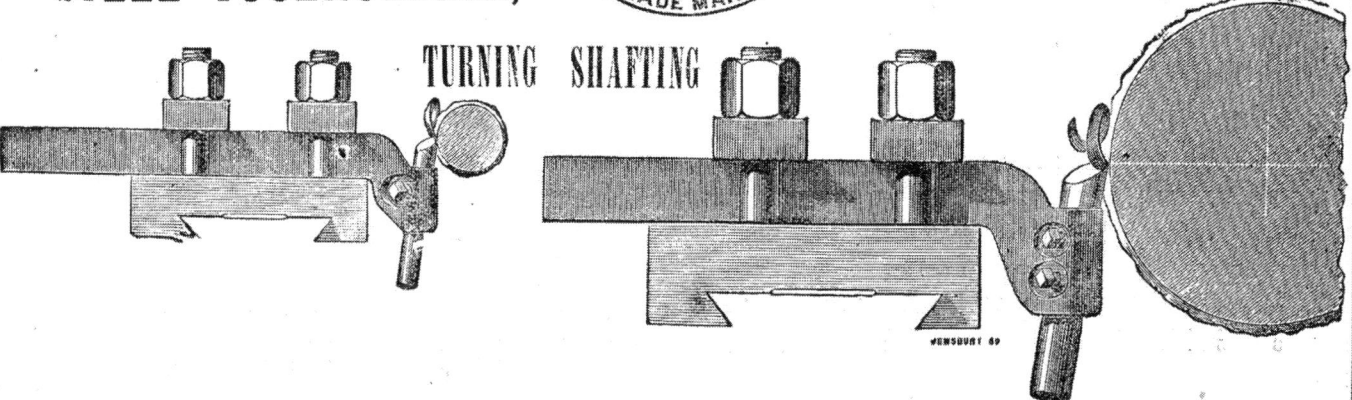
TURNING — SHAFTING

THESE TOOLHOLDERS, WHEN MADE WITH ROUND SHANKS, ARE ADMIRABLY ADAPTED FOR SCREW CUTTING.

When ordering, state whether the Toolholders are for Turning or Planing.

They are supplied of the following Sizes:—

Depth of Cutter.	Size of Shank.	Price of Toolholder.	Price of Tools per Dozen.	Suitable for use in
In.	In.	£ s. d.	£ s. d.	
⅝	¾	1 0 0	0 6 0	Lathes to 6in. centres, Shaping Machines to 5in. Stroke.
⅞	1	1 10 0	0 8 6	Ditto 8in. ,, ditto ditto 7in. ,,
1¼	1¼	2 0 0	0 17 0	Ditto 10in. ,, ditto ditto 10in. ,,
1⅝	1⅜	2 10 0	1 8 0	Ditto 15in. ,, ditto ditto 16in. ,, Planing Machines to 3ft. wide.
2¼	1¾	3 5 0	2 14 0	Ditto 18in. ,, ditto ditto 20in. ,, ditto ditto 5ft. ,,
3	2¼	5 10 0	5 12 0	Ditto 24in. ,, ditto ditto 24in. ,, ditto ditto 8ft. ,,

ANGLE GAUGES 6s. EACH.

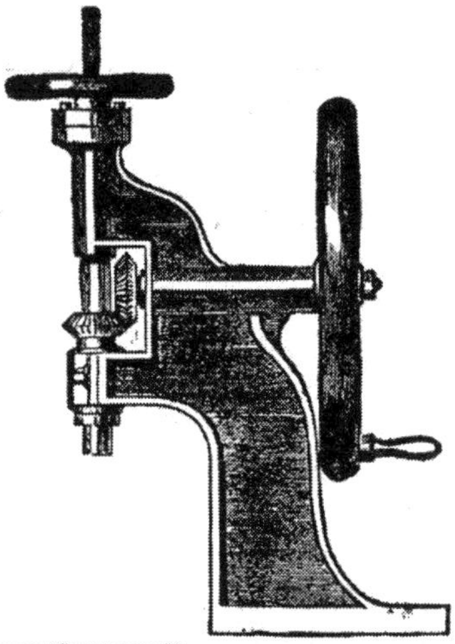

BAILEY'S
BRITISH BLACKSMITHS' DRILLING MACHINES.

These really strong and useful Machines are in great demand on account of their cheapness, combined with their power and the small space they occupy. They have been greatly improved upon lately, and are now sent out with three pulleys, to be worked by a strap when the handle is not required. The price remains the same as in the old pattern.

Fly Wheel, 16 inches diameter; Height, 22 inches, 6¼ centres;
Bed Plates, 9 inches × 7½; Pulleys, 9, 7, and 5 inches.

Price £6 6s. 0d.

BAILEY'S
FRICTION
RATCHET BRACE.

Price 1s. 6d. per inch.

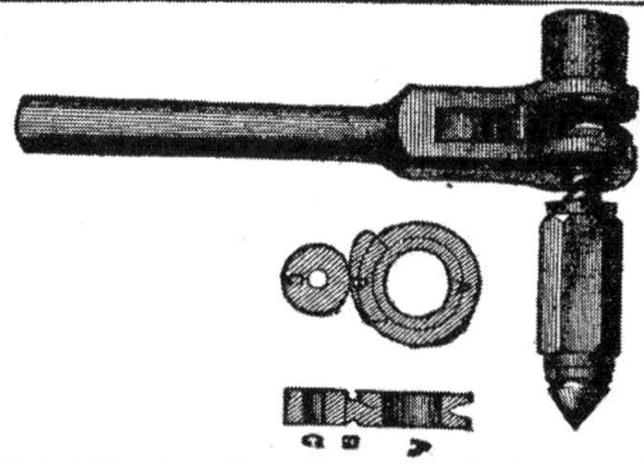

A. Friction Wheel. **B.** Bevelled Wedge. **C.** Roller.

This Brace is simple in construction; when the handle is moved forward the wedge tightens instantly, but it is perfectly free when moved backwards. It is noiseless and, having no backlash, makes a full stroke; therefore it drills a hole in much less time, and works in a smaller space than any other.

THE "WOOTON" PATENT CABINET SECRETAIRE.

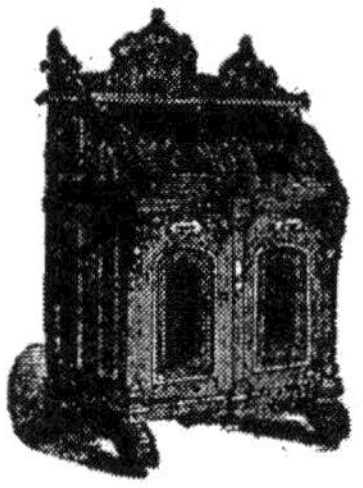

OUTSIDE MEASUREMENTS.

No.	Height.	Width.	Depth.	Height of Guard.
1	4 ft. 7½ in.	3 ft. 3½ in.	2 ft. 1½ in.	13½ in.
2	4 ft. 10½ in.	3 ft. 6½ in.	2 ft. 3 in.	14 in.
3	5 ft. 1½ in.	3 ft. 9½ in.	2 ft. 4 in.	14½ in.

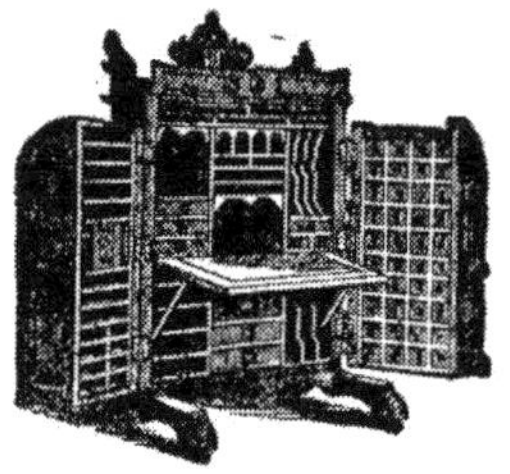

INSIDE MEASUREMENTS.

No.	Depth of Body.	Depth of Pigeon Holes.	Size of Writing Table.	Size of Upper Book Space	Height of Lower Book Space.	Size of Lower Drawers.	Size of Upper Drawers.
	IN.	IN.	IN.	IN.	IN.	IN.	IN.
1	11½	9½	30 × 19	13	19¼	14 × 4¼	2½ × 9⅜
2	12½	10	36 × 24	15¼	19¼	15 × 4½	2¼ × 10⅜
3	13½	10½	40 × 26	17¾	19¼	16 × 4¼	2¾ × 11⅜

DESCRIPTION AND PRICES.

The "ORDINARY" grade is the cheapest and plainest desk we manufacture of this design. It is made, however, of good material, and possesses most of the advantages of the other grades as to convenience, capacity and solidity. Double Spring Four-Tumbler Lock.

No. 1, £22; No. 2, £24; No. 3, £26.

The "STANDARD" has several extra drawers in the interior, and is composed of light and dark woods, nicely shaded in fine contrast with the exterior—which has raised moulded panels laid in veneers, finished in French polish. Uniform Berlin Bronze Hardware, including letter box; spring letter plate. New Patent Bank Lock.

No. 1, £27; No. 2, £30; No. 3, £33!

The "EXTRA" is an elegant desk. The external is beautifully panelled and finished in French veneers in best style. The interior is of Maple, Spanish cedar, or similar woods, in full harmony with the exterior. It is furnished with silver or nickel plated hardware or full bronze. New Patent Bank Lock.

No. 1, £42; No. 2, £46; No. 3, £50.

The "SUPERIOR" is an elaborately finished cabinet, constructed in the best style. It is elegantly decorated externally with appropriate designs and carvings, and ornamented with Marquetry in splendid style. The interior finish is of Holly or Satin woods, trimmed or stripped in ebony; writing table and drawer fronts to match. Real Bronze Hardware entire, and altogether a most superbly got up article. New Patent Bank Lock.

No. 1, £90; No. 2, £105; No. 3, £120.

IMPROVED FILING BOXES FOR PIGEON HOLES, 1s. each.

GRINDROD'S
Patent Screwing Machine.

PORTABLE MACHINE.

A Grindrod's Patent, with Dies to screw, from 1 inch to 2 inch pipe. Price, £7 10s. 0d.

B Bench Machine on "Swivel" Fixture, where Vice is not used, same size as **A**. Price, £8 8s. 0d.

Wood Cut on application.

105, EAST PARADE, LOW STREET,
KEIGHLEY,
December 20th, 1876.

GENTLEMEN,

In reply to your favour, I am highly satisfied with the Patent Screwing Machine. On the 6th December I left my place, at 7 o'clock, with the Patent Screwing Machine, and went to work. I cut six 2-in. Tubes and screwed twelve Tube ends, put the Tubes altogether complete, and was back again at my place at 1-30. This work, with the old stocks, would have taken me (with a man to assist) three times as long.

Yours truly,
JAMES BALDWIN.

ALSO SEE PAGE 228.

Further testimony in favour of New Screwing Machines, if requisite.

PATENT MITRE CUTTER.

No. 1 Mitre Cutter, 4 in. wide by 2 in. deep, with one set of irons ... Price £4 0 0
„ 2 „ 7 in. „ 4 in. ... „ £6 0 0

The Improvement in this Mitre Cutter consists in having a second pair of irons, to take one or more finishing cuts after the first pair. Both pair of irons work on the same principle as the old wood Mitre Block and Plane.

Moulds for Cornice Work, &c., can be cut with the Machine which it is impossible to cut by the old Mitre Block and Hand Plane.

All Gilt and other Moulds that can be Mitred by the old Mitre and Hand Plane can be done on this Machine much more rapidly and correctly.

FRONT VIEW.

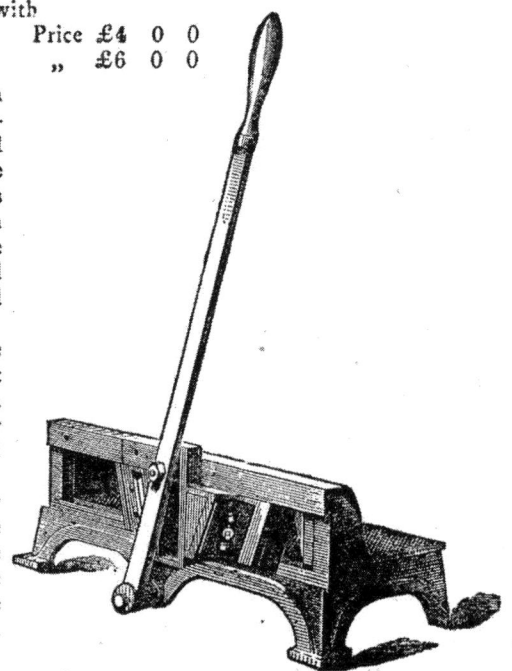

BACK VIEW.

LARD AND TALLOW PRESSES.

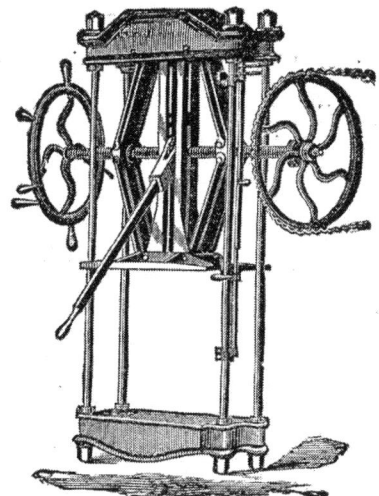

Cloth Press.

In offering our LARD AND TALLOW PRESS to the trade, we can safely guarantee to purchasers an increase of from 5 to 15 per cent. more product from an equal quantity of scrap, than can be obtained with the ordinary Screw-press, and a saving of labour of at least 50 per cent.

An ordinary Hoop or Cylinder may be used with this press; but as the power exerted is so much superior to the Screw-press, that few of such Hoops in use can withstand it, we construct one peculiarly adapted to its use which must recommend itself for its simplicity, convenience and strength. When the pressing is completed, the doors are unfastened and swung open, the cake is removed, the doors are swung together and fastened.

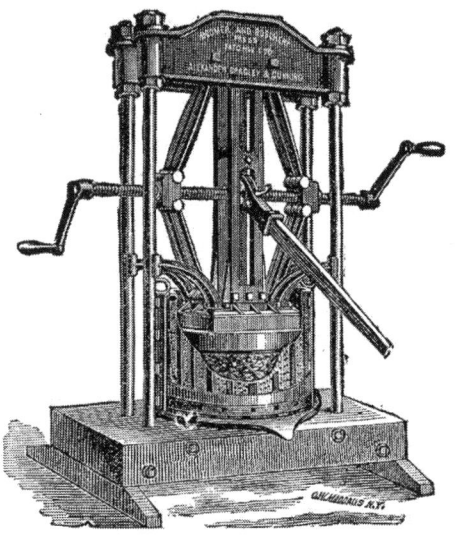

Lard and Tallow Press.

PAPER PRESSES.

Size		Size of Platen or Table	Distance between Rods	Ordinary distance between Follower and Base when down.	Rise of Follower	Size of Rods	Length of Lever Arms	Power in Tons	Ordinary Height of Press	Price
				INCHES.						
No. 0	Standing.	21 x 25	21	1	8	1	6	10	2 ft. 6 in.	£28
,, 00	,,	21 x 25	21	24	14	1	10	15	4 ft. 2 in.	32
,, 1	,,	24 x 36	30	28	17	1¼	12	50	6 ft. 4 in.	65
,, 2	,,	26 x 34	34	32	22	2	16	100	7 ft. 9 in.	80
,, 3	,,	30 x 44	30	40	34	2¾	22	175	9 ft. 6 in.	120
,, 4	,,	36 x 48	36	46	38	3½	28	300	11 ft. 5 in.	200

LARD AND TALLOW PRESSES.   Hoop.

No.	Width between Rods	Size of Screw	Length of Arm	Size of Rods	Ordinary Height between Follower and Bed	Rise of Follower	Power in Tons	Price	Diameter	Height	Price
1	2 ft. 6 in.	2 in.	12 in.	1¼ in.	20 in.	17 in.	50	£43	24 in.	24 in.	£17
2	2 ft. 10 in.	2¼ in.	16 in.	2 in.	24 in.	22 in.	80	50	27 in.	27 in.	24
3	3 ft. 3 in.	2½ in.	20 in.	2¾ in.	28 in.	28 in.	200	90	32 in.	32 in.	35
4	3 ft. 10 in.	3 in.	24 in.	3¼ in.	32 in.	34 in.	400	200	36 in.	36 in.	50

CLOTH AND BALING PRESSES.

No.	Size of Table	Rise of Follower	Full space for Goods	Dimensions of Bale	Power in Tons	Height of Press	Price
1	40 in. x 23 in.	2 ft. 6 in.	4 ft. 4 in.	40 x 23 x 18	80	9 ft.	£75
2	40 in. x 36 in.	4 ft.	5 ft. 6 in.	40 x 36 x 18	175	10 ft. 6 in.	100
3	68 in. x 44 in.	3 ft.	6 ft.	68 x 44 x 36	250	10 ft. 6 in.	150
4	36 in. x 48 in.	3 ft. 2 in.	7 ft.	37 x 48 x 46	400	11 ft. 5 in.	200

Nos. 1 and 2 can be worked by Hand or Power, but we recommend Power for Nos. 2, 3 and 4.

AUTOMATIC POWER ATTACHMENT,

Including Chain, Belt and Wheel, ... £16 0 0

HENDERSON'S PATENT IMPROVED WESTON'S PULLEY BLOCKS.

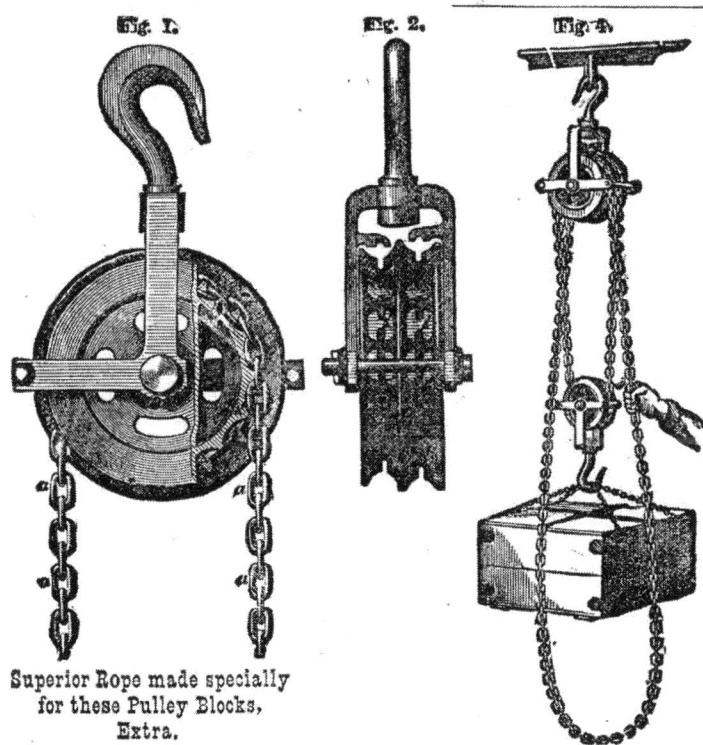

Fig. 1.   Fig. 2.   Fig. 4.

Superior Rope made specially for these Pulley Blocks, Extra.

These are the same in principle as the ordinary Weston's Pulley Blocks, without their chief failing, viz :—The quick wearing away of Pulleys and Chains. Henderson's Patent provides an additional bearing, viz., a recess for the intermediate upright links, thus giving more than twice the bearing surface to Chains and Pulleys. See side elevation, A A.

The Pulley Blocks with this important improvement are offered at the same price as ordinary Weston's Pulley Blocks.

First-Class Materials and Workmanship. Every Block is tested to the full power before leaving the Works. For Prices of other Pulley Blocks, see pages 90 to 94.

PULLEY AS FIGURE 4

Tested to	Price of Blocks	Bright B B Chain per ft.
¼ Ton	£0 12 6	0s. 6d.
½ ,,	1 0 0	0 6
1 ,,	1 10 0	0 9
1½ ,,	2 0 0	0 10
2 ,,	2 10 0	0 11
3 ,,	5 0 0	1 1
4 ,,	6 0 0	1 3

Worked from below, and should have a Chain fully four times the length of the lift.

WITH SPOCKET WHEEL

Tested to	Price of Blocks	Chain per ft.
2 Tons	£3 15 0	0s. 11d.
3 ,,	5 10 0	1 1
4 ,,	6 15 0	1 3

By using a rope over Spocket Wheel one man can lift from one to two tons. This kind worked from below.

These require Chains three times the length of Lift.

PULLEY WITH RATCHET

Tested to	Price of Blocks	Bright B B Chain per ft.
1 Ton	£2 10 0	0s. 9d.
1½ ,,	3 0 0	0 10
2 ,,	3 10 0	0 11
3 ,,	5 0 0	1 1

When worked from above only, the Chain should be fully double the length of lift.

WITH SPOCKET WHEEL AND SPUR GEAR

Tested to	Price of Blocks	Chain per ft.
4 Tons	£6 15 0	1s. 3d.
5 ,,	10 0 0	2 3
6 ,,	12 0 0	2 4
8 ,,	16 0 0	3 0
10 ,,	20 0 0	3 6

By using a rope over Spocket Wheel, one man can lift from 2 to 3 tons, two men 4 to 5 tons, three men 6 to 8 tons. This kind worked from below.

These require Chains three times the length of Lift.

WATER WASTE PREVENTER VALVE
AND
REGULATOR.
(HOWARD'S PATENT.)

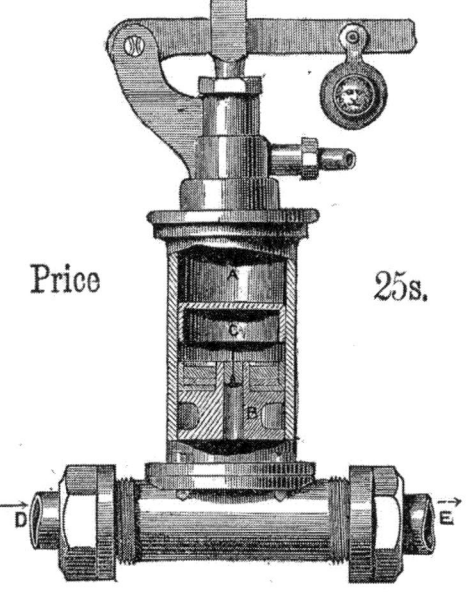

Price 25s.

The Valve consists principally of a Chamber A, in which work the Stoppers B and C.

Water enters either from a cistern, or direct off the main by the Aperture D, and leaves by E, as shown by the respective arrows.

The action of lifting the Closet Handle relieves the Stopper C, which, rising, allows the Stopper B to leave its seating when a flow of water takes place.

By a small perforation through the Stopper B, water is admitted betwixt the Stoppers B and C, and gradually, but regularly, restores the Stopper B to its seating, and stops the flow.

No further complete flush can be obtained until the Stopper C has fallen upon B, a distinct interval being thus secured; and, during the flow, it is immaterial whether the handle is held up or not.

FOR USE ESPECIALLY IN WATER CLOSETS.

This Water Waste Preventer Valve combines simplicity of action with efficiency in the attainment of what it professes to effect, viz :—A sufficiency of flush without waste of water, leaving the pan luted, and obviating the necessity of holding up the handle while the water is running.

It is recommended to Water Companies as really a reliable Valve, which will supply consumers with sufficient for their wants, while waste is rendered impossible; and it is recommended to consumers as a cheap and effective means of meeting the requirements of the Companies, rendering an expensive Water Waste Preventer Cistern unnecessary, and at the same time saving the outlay of a Bellows Regulator in First Class Closets.

For Second Class Closets it is a most satisfactory substitute for the noisy cast-iron W.W. Cisterns commonly used.

It has been submitted to the inspection of several distinguished Water Engineers, who have all expressed opinions favourable to its use, and leave has been at once granted, on application, by the Metropolitan Water Companies, that it should be applied within their several districts.

Price, with Closet complete, £2 15s.

SECTIONS OF USUAL IRON MERCHANT SHAPES

BAILEY'S MILD STEEL BARS

FOR PISTON RODS, WHEEL TYRES, CONNECTING RODS, CHAINS, &c. &c.

This mild Steel is exclusively used for Piston Rods, where great strength is required with little weight. We use it for our Steam Pumps. It is made from ¾ inch to 2 inches. It is used also for Wheel Tires and for Forgings by the Manchester Carriage Company, and by Wheelwrights in Manchester and neighbourhoods. The sections are the same as ordinary merchant bar iron.

Price—17s. 6d. per cwt. in quantities of not less than two or three cwt.

If in Tons, Special Quotation, according to Metal Market. Sample orders for a few bars will have attention.

Size, 27 × 35 and ⅛ to ¾ in. thick,

BAILEY'S SPECIALLY PREPARED MILL BOARDS
FOR STEAM PIPE JOINTS, VALVE LIDS &c.

Price, 25s. per Cwt.

For many purposes we recommend these Boards in preference to India-rubber Rings. They make a perfectly Steam-tight Joint, and last much longer than India-rubber. If ordered in less quantities than one Cwt. at a time, 4d. per lb.

Patent Safety Belt Shipper.

It prevents accidents by being used at a safe distance. It effects great saving by putting on the Belts without stopping the Engine.

No. 1 Size Belts up to 2¼ in.	...	...	25s.
,, 2 ,, from 2¼ to 4 in.	...	...	30s.
,, 3 ,, ,, 4 to 8 in.	...	...	36s.

IMPROVED FRICTION CRANE,

For General Contractors and Builders' purposes, for Hand or Steam power.

These Cranes have all their actions combined under one lever of Breaking, Winding and Lowering.

Price—No. 1, ... £15 10 0
No. 2, ... £18 10 0

BAILEY'S FIRST-CLASS TAPS,

Machine Working Taps, for Tapping Nuts.

Hand Working Taps.

For Nuts, and Machine Uses.

Master Taps, for Cutting Dies.

For Prices, see other Portions of this Book.

Master Taps, for Cutting Dies for Iron Piping.

Working Taps, Taper and Plug, for Iron Piping.

DAVIS & BAILEY'S ADJUSTABLE SPIRIT LEVEL, PLUMB, AND INCLINOMETER,

Unequalled in Accuracy, Durability, and Simplicity. Each Level fully Warranted.

No. 1, 6 inch, 	Price, 11/6 each.	No. 2, 12 inch, 	18/0 each.
No. 3, 18 inch,			22/6 each.
No. 4, 24 inch,			25/0 each.
No. 5, 30 inch, Wood.			27/6 each.

BAILEY'S SPIRIT LEVELS. Each Level Warranted.

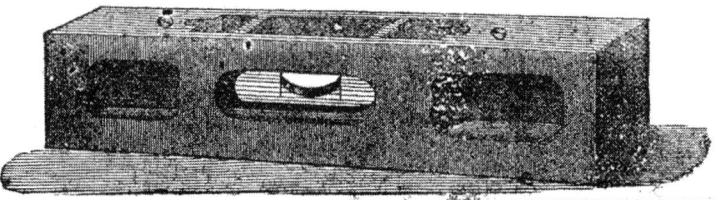

No. 1, 3½ inch, 8/6.   No. 2, 7 inch, 12/6.

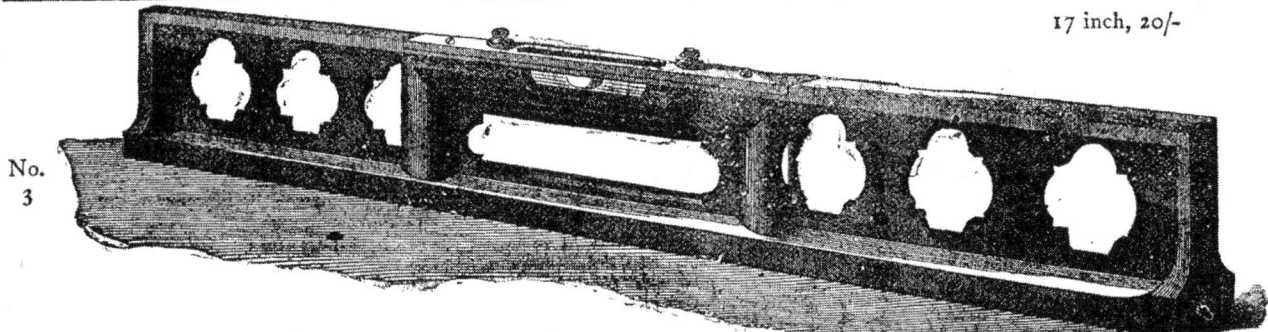

No. 3   17 inch, 20/-

The above are constructed with Iron Stocks; are strongly mounted, and of the best materials and workmanship in all parts, and are thoroughly adjusted and tested in every case. They are pronounced the most accurate and convenient for all classes of Mechanics.

LEFEBORE'S PATENT CLITOGRAPH

For Levelling or Measuring Angles.

This instrument denotes inclinations or slopes, by sub-divisions of an inch, for the length in feet, both for Vertical and Horizontal direction. It therefore enables the operator to give immediately, at one single trial to a line or surface any desired direction, either horizontal, vertical, or inclined, simply because the instrument indicates exactly the amount of rectification required for each foot in length.

This instrument combines the advantages of the common level and plumb-line, with greater precision, and is useful to Miners, Manufacturers, Civil and Mechanical Engineers, Architects, &c.; also, for adjusting Gas and Water Main Pipes, &c.

Levelling operations, at small distances, are made on the ground with the same instrument. It is particularly adapted for drainage, irrigation, water and gas courses, &c., and for all other kinds of surveying purposes.

PRICES:—

No. 1, with Brass Frame £1 15 0
No. 2, with Brass Frame, and Socket Pillar for mounting on a stick, ... £3 15 0

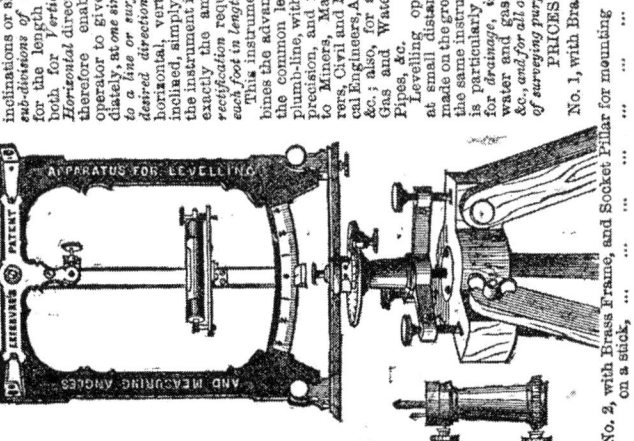

BAILEY'S HYDROSTATIC LEVEL,

For Civil & Mechanical Engineers, Surveyors, Builders, &c.,

For Measuring Large Distances.

This new and exceedingly useful instrument is constructed as follows:—Two Glass Tubes fitted in heavy Gun Metal Pedestals, with Cocks connected with a pipe as long as the distance to be levelled. One of the Tubes is filled with water till it will be seen in the other tube—the difference in the tubes gives the result of the level or plane. This instrument will be found valuable by Railway Engineers, Manufacturers, &c.

Price, complete, with 6 feet of Tube, 35/-

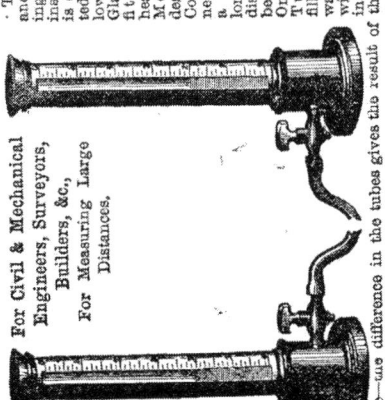

BAILEY & BROWN'S PATENT COMPOUND

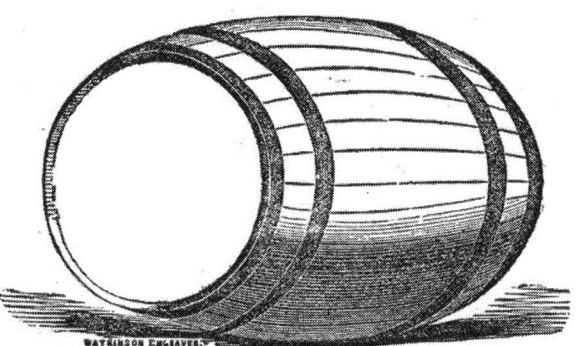

For Preventing Corrosion and Incrustation in Steam Boilers.

In introducing their Patent Compound for the Prevention of Corrosion and Incrustation in Steam Boilers, B. and B. are aware that many altogether worthless preparations are sold for such purposes. They have therefore taken every possible means of having the Patent Compound which they manufacture tested by the experience of parties practically acquainted with Steam Boilers, and from the result of that experience they have the greatest confidence in recommending it as an important economiser to all employers of Steam Power.

On being put into the Boiler, the Compound acts directly on the Mineral matter contained in the Water, neutralising the Acids and precipitating the residue to the bottom, thereby preventing Incrustation, and preserving the inside surface of the Boiler from Corrosion.

In applying the Compound, 1 lb. to 2 lb. should be used per horse power per month, except in cases where the state of the Boilers and the quality of the water may require a departure from this rule, either for the purpose of increasing or decreasing the quantity to be applied.

The best method of applying the Compound is not to put it into the Boiler once a month, but daily, or weekly, by means of a half or a $\frac{3}{8}$-inch gas-pipe bent in the form of a Siphon, with a tap in any part of it, one end attached to the Suction-pipe of the Pump or Injector, the other inserted into the solution of the Compound. This mode enables the consumer to blow off the Mineral Sediment that is constantly falling to the bottom, and thereby keeps the Boiler clean.

B. and B. have been at much trouble and expense in analysing the waters from canals, rivers, reserves, &c., in various parts of the country, of which they have kept a careful record, and are prepared to make a Compound which will preserve Boilers and remove all Calcareous or Stony Deposits of every kind.

Sold in Casks from 3 cwt. each, at 21s. per cwt.

TESTIMONIALS.

Owen's College, Manchester,
Nov. 30th, 1866.

GENTLEMEN,—I have made a careful analysis of the BOILER COMPOUND sent by you. I found that it does not contain the LEAST TRACE of ammonia, nor any other substance which would injure boiler plates.

I am, gentlemen, yours truly,
C. SCHORLEMMER.

Victoria Finishing Works, Radcliffe,
August 1st, 1873.

SIRS,—The scale I now send you is out of my steam boiler, and has been removed by means of your valuable Composition, supplied to me for that purpose.

I shall be glad if you will at your earliest convenience send me another cask; and further, I shall be glad to be used as a reference.

Yours truly,
J. B. LOMAX.

London Road Mill, Manchester,
September 13th, 1865.

We have used Mr. BROWN'S Boiler Compound for about four months, and find it gives every satisfaction.

LEWIS & EDWARD WILLIAMS.

Disley, near Stockport, April 26th, 1865.

DEAR SIR,—I have sent per rail a small parcel containing incrustations taken out of our boilers since using your Patent Compound for the prevention of it. I could fill you a bucket or two similar to the sample I have sent. We never had anything that answered our purpose so well. Can confidently recommend it.

Yours truly,
PRO JAMES MARSHALL & SONS,
D. WALMSLEY.

Tame Street Mill, Ancoats, Manchester,
September 13th, 1865.

We have used Mr. BROWN'S Boiler Composition for about four months, and find it gives every satisfaction.

LEWIS WILLIAMS & SON.

And other References, if requisite.

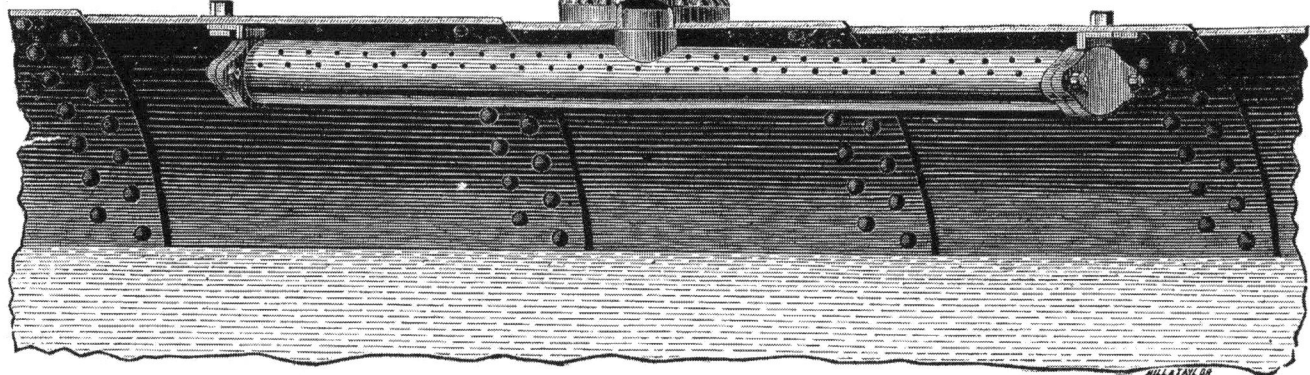

BAILEY'S STARTING VALVE AND ANTI-PRIMING PIPE

This is recommended by First-Class Engineers whose difficulty is experienced in obtaining dry steam.

Prices, complete with 1 Junction Valve, 1 block to Curve of Boiler, fitted and faced with bolts to Valve; 1 Pipe with holes and bracket ends complete, ready for fixing:—

2-inch £4 4 0		3½-inch £7 0 0		5-inch £9 10 0
2½-inch 4 17 6		4-inch 7 10 0		6-inch 13 0 0
3-inch 5 10 0				

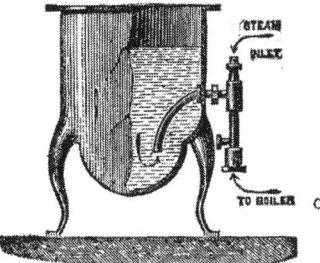

BAILEY'S PATENT BOILER COMPOSITION INJECTOR AND CISTERN

For Mixing and Feeding Boilers with Liquids for preventing Incrustation.

This is a cast-iron Cistern on 3 legs, to which is attached our Injector; it must be placed on the top, or above the Boiler, and can be used as required.

No. 1 will empty 10 Gallons in about 5 minutes, Price, £5 0s. 0d.

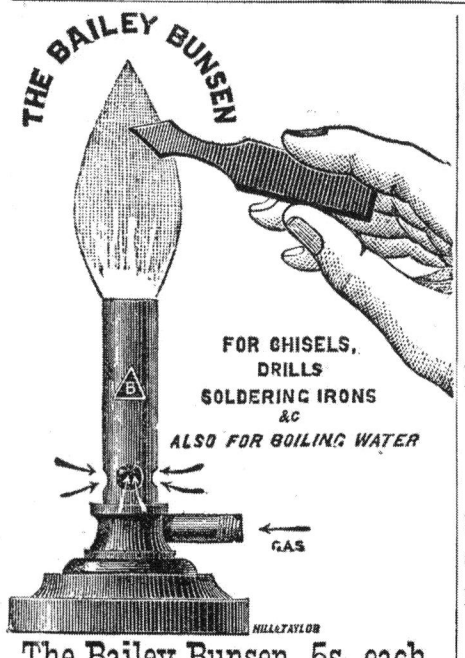

THE BAILEY BUNSEN

FOR CHISELS, DRILLS SOLDERING IRONS &C ALSO FOR BOILING WATER

The Bailey Bunsen, 5s. each.

Complete with short Tube and Mouth-piece.

10s. 6d.

THE BAILEY BUNSEN BLOW PIPE, with short Tube and Mouth-piece.

This will do for brazing small articles, and is useful for other purposes.

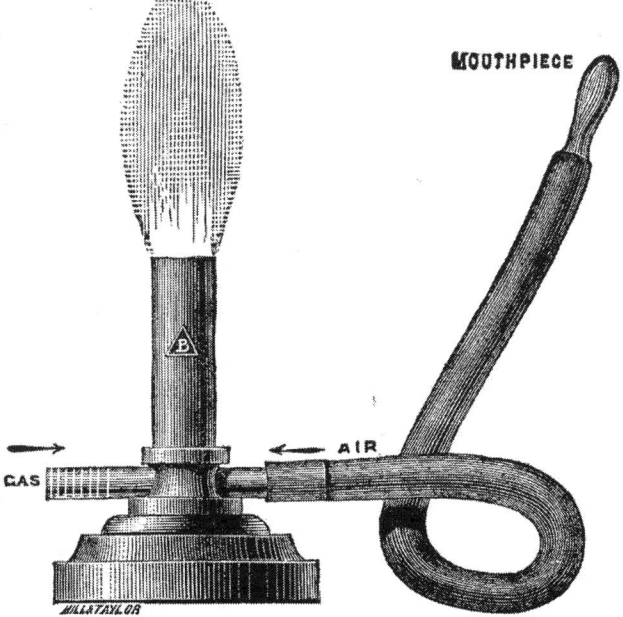

BRIDGETT'S PATENT

GUN-METAL PACKING,

For Piston Rods.

SHEWING SPACE REQUIRED

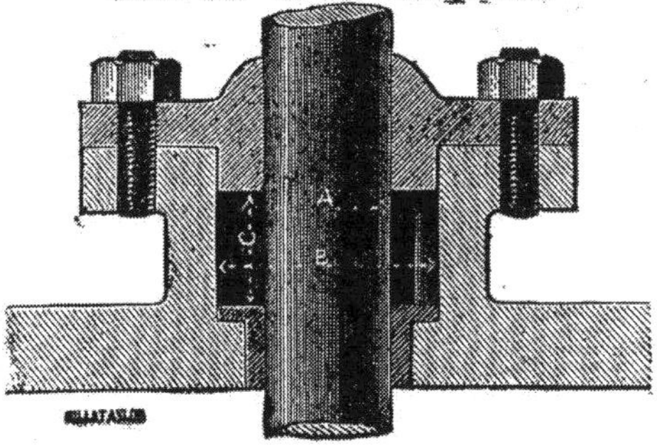

SHEWING PACKING OUT OF PACKING-BOX

ELEVATION

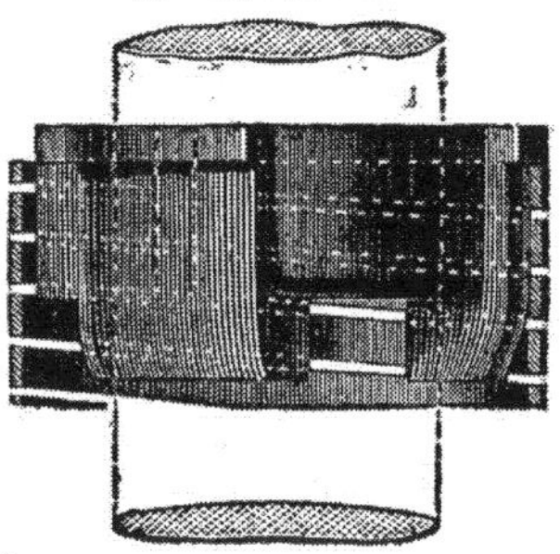

PLAN

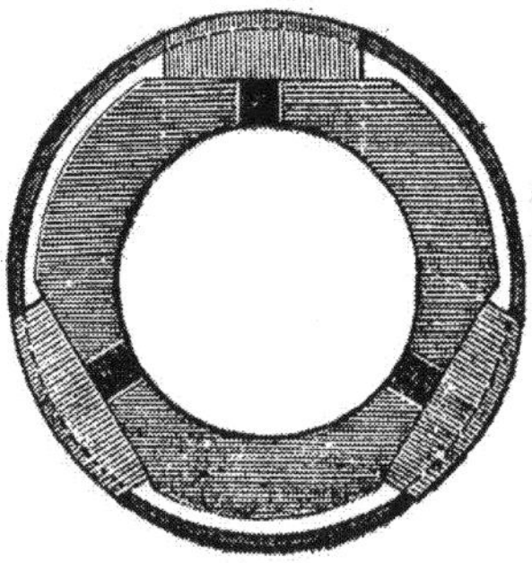

The important advantages secured by using this Packing are:—

From its peculiar construction it remains steam-tight until worn nearly through, and, being made of hard gun-metal, lasts for years.

It requires no attention, gives no trouble, and causes much less friction than ordinary packings.

The Piston Rod becomes splendidly polished, instead of fluted and grooved, as is usually the case.

All new Engines should be fitted with it, or it can be applied to those already at work.

It is eminently suitable to place between End-to-End Cylinders of Compound Engines.

Being made by special machinery, secures great accuracy.

The sizes in the list are kept in stock, but Packing to suit any odd size of Piston Rod or Packing Box will be supplied to order.

N.B.—When the Piston Rod and Crosshead are in one forging, a form of spring is supplied which does not require passing over the end of the Piston Rod.

LIST OF PRICES.

TRIAL ORDERS will be followed by Orders to adopt it generally.

A	B	C	Price each	A	B	C	Price each	A	B	C	Price each
2	$3\frac{7}{8}$	$1\frac{5}{8}$	40/-	$2\frac{3}{4}$	$4\frac{3}{4}$	$2\frac{1}{4}$	55/-	$3\frac{1}{2}$	$5\frac{1}{2}$	$2\frac{7}{8}$	70/-
$2\frac{1}{8}$	...	...	42/6	$2\frac{7}{8}$	...	...	57/6	$3\frac{5}{8}$	...	...	72/6
$2\frac{1}{4}$	$4\frac{3}{8}$	$1\frac{7}{8}$	45/-	3	5	$2\frac{1}{2}$	60/-	$3\frac{3}{4}$	6	3	75/-
$2\frac{3}{8}$	...	...	47/6	$3\frac{1}{8}$	...	...	62/6	$3\frac{7}{8}$	...	...	77/6
$2\frac{1}{2}$	$4\frac{1}{4}$	2	50/-	$3\frac{1}{4}$	$5\frac{1}{4}$	$2\frac{5}{8}$	65/-	4	$6\frac{1}{2}$	$3\frac{1}{4}$	80/-
$2\frac{5}{8}$	...	...	52/6	$3\frac{3}{8}$	...	...	67/6	$4\frac{1}{8}$	...	...	82/6

W. H. BAILEY & CO.,
Albion Works,
SALFORD,
MANCHESTER.

These sizes are nominal, as we make to special dimensions in most cases.

BAILEY'S STEAM PUMPS,

For Stationary Purposes, for Works or Warehouses.

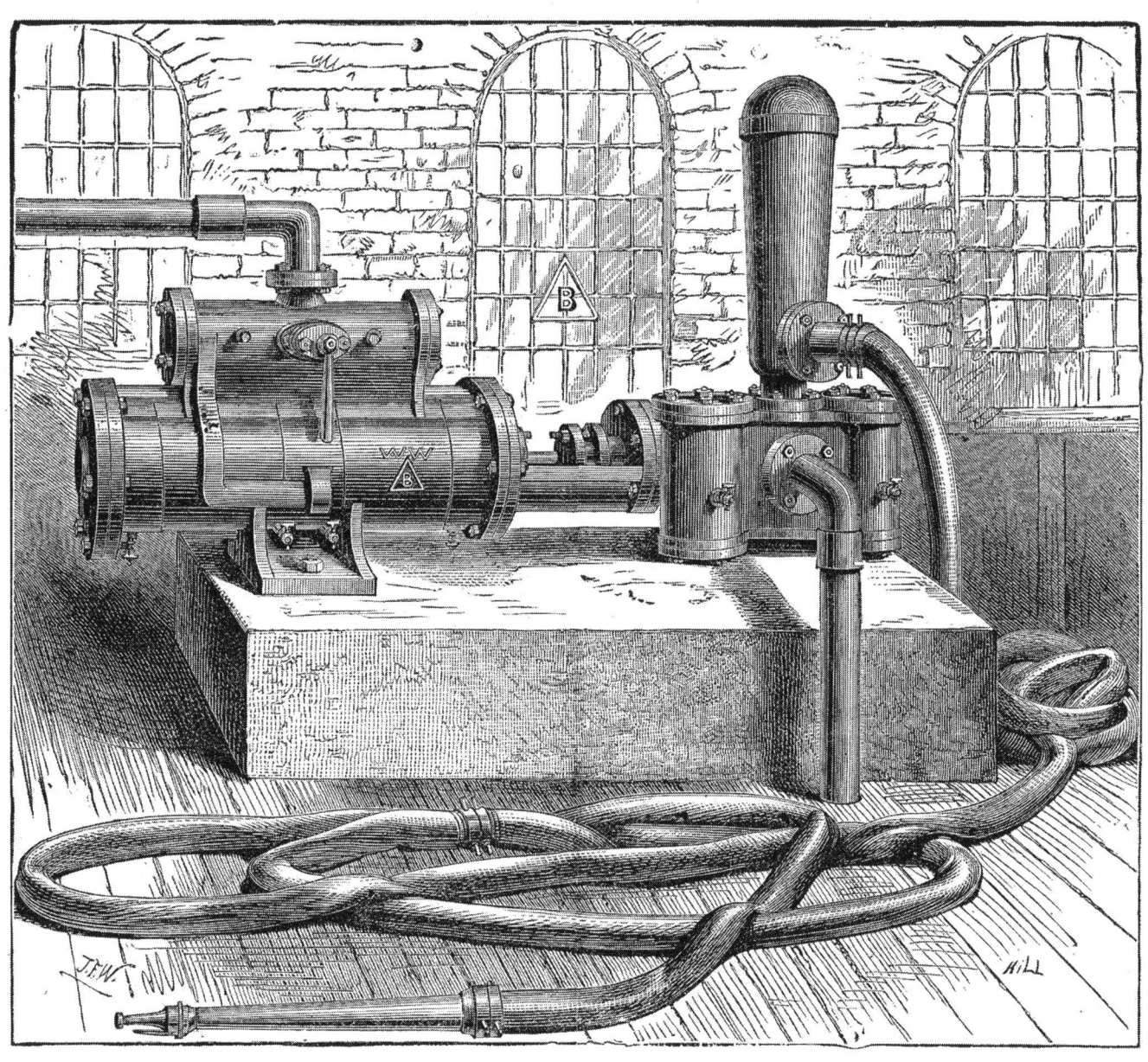

These Pumps have been awarded Prize Medals by the Chief Societies.

They are fully described in our Supplementary Catalogue of Pumps, Injectors, Pyrometers, &c., which please ask for.

IMPROVED VERTICAL WELDED AND RIVETED COMBINED STEAM BOILER.

BAILEY'S PATENT

B.R.

BOILER MOUNTINGS

HERE ILLUSTRATED

On the Boiler,

Fully illustrated and described on pages 36 to 39,

Including BAILEY'S B.R. FITTINGS—viz., Safety Valve, Steam Gauge, and One Pair Water Gauge Cocks combined; also Fusible Plug and Blow-off Cock, as shown, exclusive of Injector.

Approximate Horse-power	Size of Boiler	Price, including Two Tubes and Fittings	Injector and Fittings.
½	36 × 21	£16 10 0	£4 0 0
¾	42 × 21	17 10 0	4 0 0
1	42 × 24	23 0 0	4 0 0
1¼	48 × 24	28 10 0	4 0 0
1½	48 × 27	32 10 0	4 0 0
1¾	54 × 24	30 0 0	4 0 0
2	54 × 27	32 10 0	4 0 0
2¼	54 × 30	37 10 0	4 0 0
2¾	60 × 30	40 0 0	4 0 0
3¼	60 × 33	44 0 0	4 0 0
4	66 × 36	51 10 0	4 0 0
5	66 × 42	59 10 0	4 0 0
5½	72 × 42	62 10 0	4 0 0

All Boilers tested with Steam before delivery, and also tested by Hydraulic pressure to 120 lbs. per square inch.

CHIMNEYS EXTRA, ACCORDING TO LENGTH.

BAILEY'S Double-Water CYLINDER PUMPS FOR Two Sorts of Liquids.

VIEW FROM A PHOTOGRAPH.

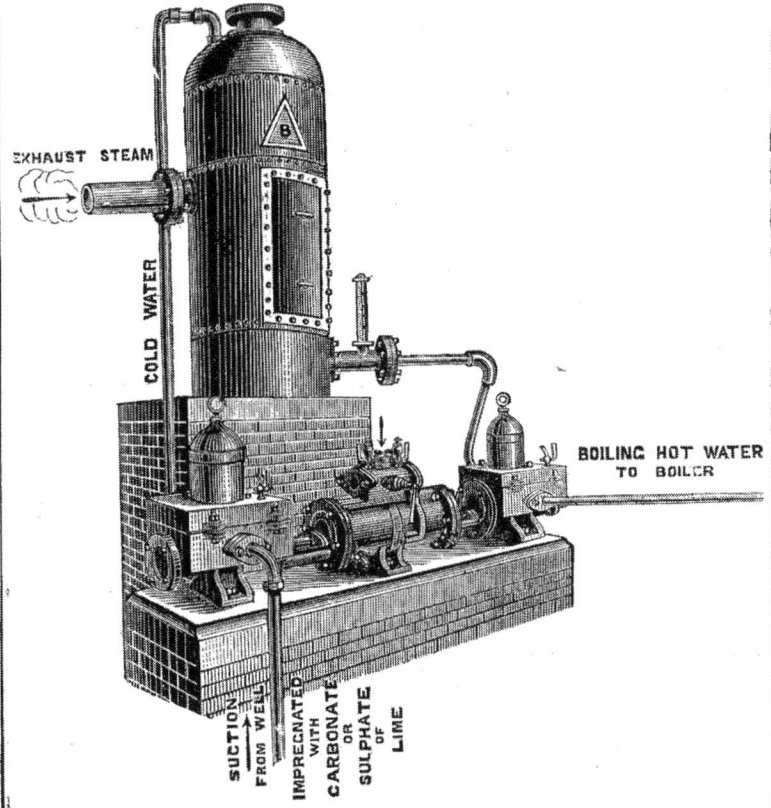

The Double Cylinder Pump here illustrated pumps water from a well to the STILLWELL PATENT WATER HEATER, (*see page* 64). After it has been made boiling hot, and the sediment removed by the Heater and Filter, the Hot Water Cylinder pumps it into Boiler.

As used at Gas Works.

They are fully described in our Supplementary Catalogue of Pumps, Injectors, &c., which please ask for.

The B. R. Boiler Fitting (Bailey's Patent) having been adopted by Messrs. Deakin, Parker & Co. on their very superior Boilers and Engines, W. H. Bailey & Co. have great pleasure in calling attention to its compactness.

COMBINED VERTICAL ENGINE AND BOILER,

OF IMPROVED TYPE.

See pages 36 and 37 for the B. R. Fitting.

FEATURES:

Simplicity, Compactness, Fewness of Parts.

Engines are unaffected by the expansion of the Boilers, there being a sliding connection at Cylinder end.

The Governors are of the high-speed spring type.

The equilibrium valves are horizontal, and close upon the steam chests, and Bailey's Boiler Fittings are used.

The Slide Bars are adjustable.

The Fly Wheels are turned and balanced.

The Ash-pits have Cast-Iron bases and sliding draft doors.

Double Safety-Valves are supplied with each Boiler.

PRICES.
3 H.P. Boiler,	6 ft. 0 in. × 2 ft. 6 in.,	Cylinder	5 in. diameter,	10 in. stroke	...	£80	nett.	
4 "	6 " 6 " × 2 " 9 "	"	6 " "	10 " "	...	£90	"	If with Bailey's Patent Injectors, extra.
5 "	7 " 0 " × 3 " 0 "	"	7 " "	14 " "	...	£105	"	
6 "	7 " 6 " × 3 " 3 "	"	8 " "	14 " "	...	£120	"	

Firing tools £1 1s. 0d. extra.

All the above are steam jointed, run and tested before sent out. All Boilers are of the cross tube type. These Boilers and Engines are supplied by Messrs. W. H. BAILEY & Co., at the same prices as the makers.

NOTICE OF REDUCTION IN PRICE.

BAILEY'S WORKS AND VILLAGE, OR INSTITUTION
IMPROVED PORTABLE FIRE-ENGINE,
For Two Men, or more.

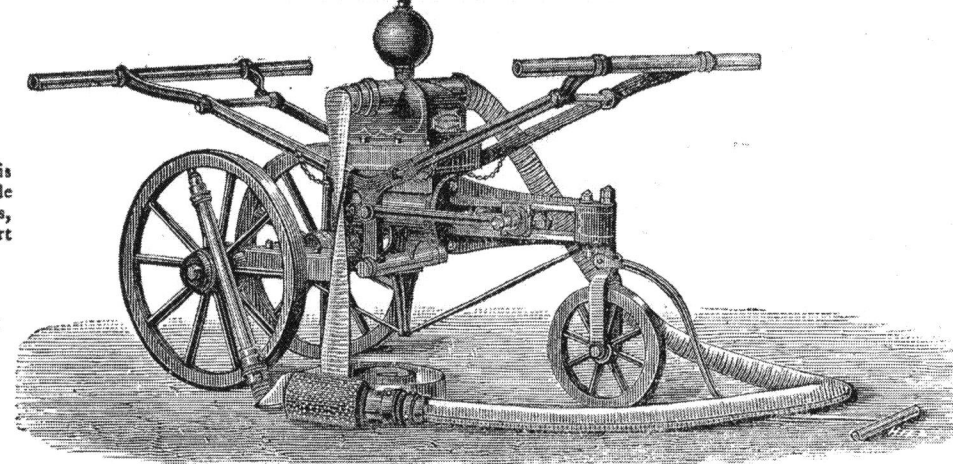

Since we have taken this Photograph, they are now made with Wrought-Iron Wheels, which are superior for export and rough use.

These Engines are strong, and, having few parts, are not liable to get out of order. The pumps are double-acting; the suction and delivery valves are on the top of the pump barrel; and, by a simple arrangement, *all the valves are covered by one valve chest.* They are particularly adapted for Private Establishments, and for Irrigation.

FITTINGS:
- Forty yards 2-inch Patent Linen Hose, in two lengths
- Two Pairs of Gun-Metal Unions
- Copper Branch Pipe
- Two Brass Nozzles
- One Pair of Hose Wrenches, and Screw Wrench

Reduced Price, £30.

Complete and Ready for Work, carefully Tested.

Also makers of Steam Pumps, Horizontal Pumping Engines, Single and Double-acting, for feeding Boilers, Irrigating, or Pumping out of Mines; Safety Valves, Steam Reducing Valves, Steam and Water Valves, Brass and Iron Valves, and Cocks of all descriptions. Press Pumps on the most improved constructions. Shafting, Gearing, &c.

For further particulars of Pumps, see this Book, Pump Department, and our Special Supplementary List of Pumps, Injectors, Pyrometers, Water Heaters, &c., Post Free.

BAILEY'S STEAM PUMPS & BOILERS COMBINED.

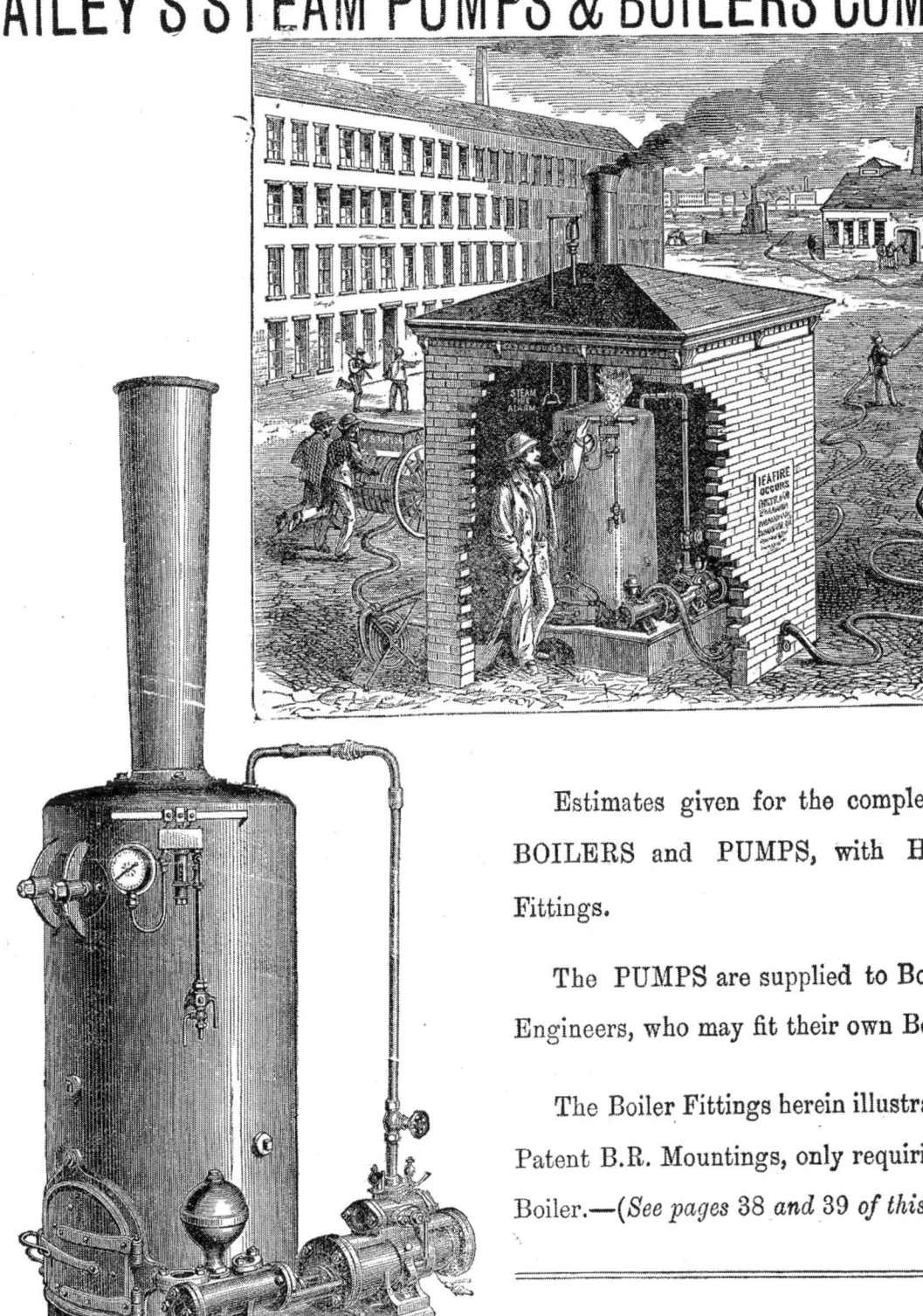

Estimates given for the complete Fitting up of BOILERS and PUMPS, with Hose Pipes and Fittings.

The PUMPS are supplied to Boiler Makers and Engineers, who may fit their own Boilers.

The Boiler Fittings herein illustrated are Bailey's Patent B.R. Mountings, only requiring two holes in Boiler.—(*See pages* 38 *and* 39 *of this Book.*)

For further particulars, see Supplementary Catalogue of Pumps, Injectors, &c., which please ask for.

Every Fire is a small one when it starts.

BAILEY'S "DOWSER," (TRADE MARK) Is much used in Mills in Lancashire and Yorkshire.

With Bucket, 10/6 "DOWSERS" Without Buckets, Per Dozen.

PRICE COMPLETE 10/6

REDUCING VALVE, with Spring instead of Weights.

These are used where Weights are inconvenient, Prices 10% higher than those with Weights.

(*See Reducing Valves*).

These are used either for Steam or Water.

BAILEY'S STEAM, HOT AIR, AND HOT LIQUOR THERMOMETER,

With Circulating Pipe, for Front of Vats, Hot Air Chambers, Retorts, &c., to 400 degrees, Price 42s.

This Thermometer is described page 11, without the bend, Price 30s.

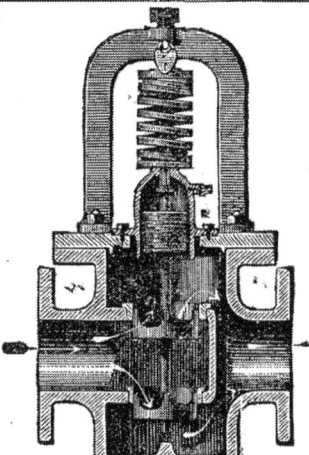

Bailey's Boiler Insurance Companies' Pattern Blow-off Cock,

For front of first-class Boilers, with Brass plate of instructions, Double Gland Companion to the Feed Regulator Valve (*see page* 42), which is placed on the opposite side of Boiler.

For ordinary sort, straightway, see page 52, No. 806.

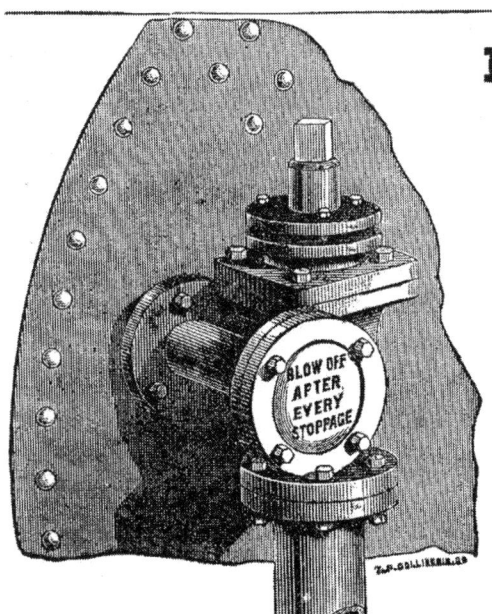

Bore.	£	s.	d.	Bore.	£	s.	d.	Bore.	Iron Bodies Gun-Metal Plug £ s. d.
1	1	15	0	2½	5	15	0	2	2 16 0
1½	2	5	0	3	8	0	0	2½	3 10 0
2	4	10	0	4	13	10	0	3	4 6 0
								4	10 16 0

A COMPARISON between the Lip Area of an Ordinary Safety Valve and HALLAM'S DOUBLE-LIP VALVES,

WHICH WE SHALL BE GLAD IF ALL ENGINEERS WILL READ.

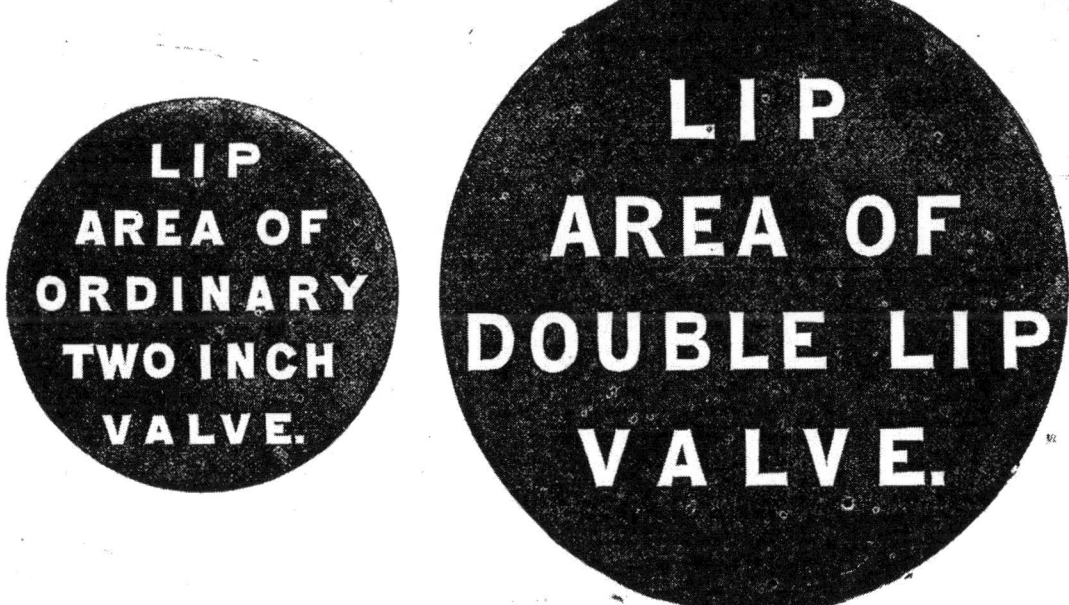

These Valves are much lower in Price than the ordinary Valves, especially so if the area is taken into consideration.

Whilst the area of the ordinary Safety Valve varies as the square of its diameter, the circumferential or lip-opening varies simply in proportion to the diameter; therefore enlarged lip-opening requires a rapidly augmenting load, since to increase the lip-opening one-half necessitates a more than double load,—this with Safety Valves directly loaded with dead weight becomes serious at high pressure.

To provide increased circumferential or lip-opening a number of Valves arranged together are sometimes used, but this merely mitigates one evil at the expense of the ultimate discharging power. Thus two Safety Valves, each having an area of one square inch, will, if raised from their seat a distance of one quarter-inch, or the fourth of their diameter, afford a discharge area of two square inches, which is their utmost capacity,—whereas, if a two-inch ordinary Valve be raised a distance of half-an-inch, equal to one-fourth its diameter, the maximum discharge area equals three square inches, or one-half more.

HALLAM'S PATENT SAFETY VALVE for a given diameter provides nearly double the amount of circumferential or lip-opening afforded by ordinary Valves. Repeated observations and experiments show that ordinary Safety Valves scarcely under any circumstances rise from their seat to a greater extent than one-sixteenth of an inch, and that with Safety Valves even of large size the pressure in a boiler may and does increase considerably beyond that to which they are loaded, especially if the whole steam the boiler is capable of generating be discharged through them. Hallam's Patent Safety Valve, on the contrary, lifts from its seat in proportion as the weight of steam to be discharged increases,—indeed, will give at once a discharge area equal to that of outlet from boiler immediately the working pressure is exceeded; it also requires less weight to load it, which decreases cost of carriage, and, being less bulky, occupies less space when fixed.

Ordinary Valves. 60 lbs. pressure.			Ordinary Valves. 60 lbs. pressure.		
Diameter	Lip-Opening	Dead Load	Diameter	Lip-Opening	Dead Load
2 inch	6¼ inch	180 lbs	2 inch	10½ inch	120 lbs.
3 ,,	9½ ,,	420 ,,	3 ,,	16½ ,,	247 ,,
4 ,,	12½ ,,	750 ,,	4 ,,	22¼ ,,	420 ,,

TESTIMONIALS.

LINEN AND COTTON DYE WORKS, HORROCK'S LANE, RED BANK,
MANCHESTER, *December 5th*, 1874.

I have great pleasure in testifying to the efficiency of the "Hallam's Patent Safety Valve." I have one attached to one of my boilers, and find it will rise and discharge the whole steam generated by the boiler, and again close with a range of pressure under one pound per square inch.

When just rising, the variations in opening and closing the throttle valve are indicated by the steam discharged from the valve.

Yours respectfully,
JOHN JOHNSON.

61, POLYGON AVENUE, ARDWICK, *January 20th*, 1874.

I have much pleasure in certifying having used one of your Patent Safety Valves during the recent evaporative tests of my new Sectional Boiler, at pressures varying from 80 to 100 lbs. pressure on the square inch, and that its behaviour and certainty of action was all that could be desired.

Yours faithfully,
JAS. SHEPHERD.

HALLAM'S PATENT
DOUBLE-LIP SAFETY VALVE.

No. 595.

VIEW

OF THE

DEAD-WEIGHT

PATTERN.

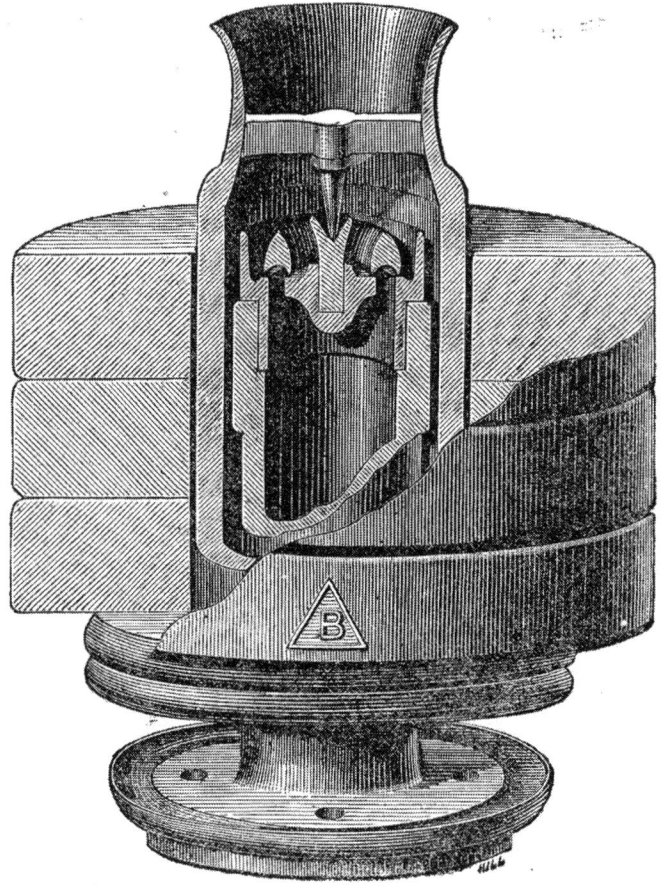

REDUCED PRICES.

2in.	3in.	4in.
£4 4s.	£6 5s.	£8 0 0

These are for Valves to 30 lbs. pressure. For higher pressures, extra weights, 12s. per cwt.

In criticising the cost, it will be borne in mind that there are here TWO VALVES IN ONE, *at the price of one.*

SPECIAL VALVES FOR SMALL BOILERS.

¾in.	1in.	1½in.
£2 0s.	£2 10s.	£3 10.

A Safety Valve should be so constructed as to permit, under no circumstances or conditions, the pressure of steam to exceed that at which the Boiler is worked; that so soon as this pressure is attained it should at once discharge the surplus steam generated, and close immediately. This is effected without lowering the steam below the working pressure.

The following are some of the qualities possessed by this Valve :—

1st—*It cannot stick or adhere to its seat.*
2nd—*It rises and discharges the surplus steam directly the maximum working pressure is exceeded, and closes immediately the pressure falls, with a range under no circumstances exceeding one pound per square inch.*
3rd—*It is so arranged that it cannot be wedged or fastened down.*
4th—*When the valve rises, the discharge area being very large, the steam is rapidly voided, and the noise made by blowing off cannot fail to arouse the attention of the Engineman, and warn him to close the damper.*
5th—*It provides double the area, with a given lift for discharge, compared with ordinary Valves.*

These Valves are highly commended by all who have used them.

FURTHER TESTIMONIALS.

CROWN IRON WORKS, WEST GORTON, *May 19th*, 1874.

We have had one of your Patent Safety Valves fixed alongside one of the ordinary Mushroom Valves on our Boiler for some time past, and are exceedingly well pleased with it. Its action is instantaneous, both with rising and with falling steam; it opens or shuts off completely at the exact pressure to which it is set, and allows the free and vertical escape of about three or four times the volume of any other valve we have seen of equal area. It leaves the other valve nothing to do, and alone is far safer and more effective than the pair we had in use before. We shall be glad to show it to any of your friends at any time.

For GEO. L. SCOTT, Limited.
WM. E. HEYS, Secretary.

41, LOWER MOSLEY STREET, MANCHESTER, *July 3rd*, 1874.

DEAR SIR,—We have much pleasure in stating that the Boiler, &c., you fitted up for us gives entire satisfaction. Your Safety Valve works most accurately, and with the greatest certainty it allows an escape at the given pressure, and closes on the diminution of within 1 lb. of steam. We shall be pleased to show it to any of your friends.—Yours respectfully,

Pro ARNOLD CONSTABLE & CO.
H. LAMB.

MANCHESTER SECTIONAL BOILER COMPANY,
Works—Brewery Street, Downing Street, Ardwick; Offices—8, St. Ann's Place, St. Ann's Square,
Manchester, October 9th, 1874.

DEAR SIR,—Shortly after you left our Works this morning, the pressure in the Boiler rose rapidly and instantaneously The "Safety Valve" burst forth with a terrific discharge of steam.

No. 596.
TWIN DOUBLE-LIP SAFETY VALVE,
With Ashcroft Low Water Alarm Combined.

See page 45 for the Ashcroft Detector.

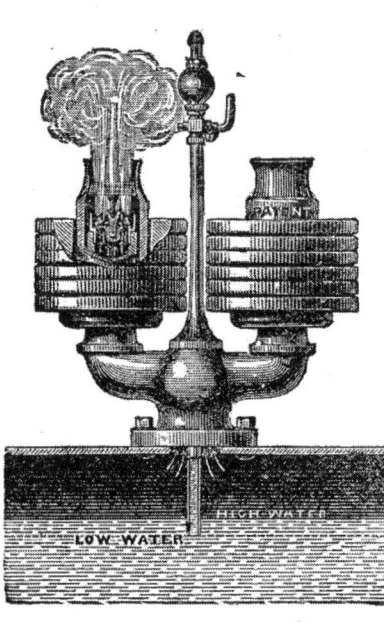

PRICES.
Weighted to 30 lbs.
2in.	...	£10 18 0
3in.	...	15 0 0
4in.	...	18 10 0

This is a superior fitting for High-class Boilers.

No. 597.
TWIN DOUBLE-LIP SAFETY VALVE.

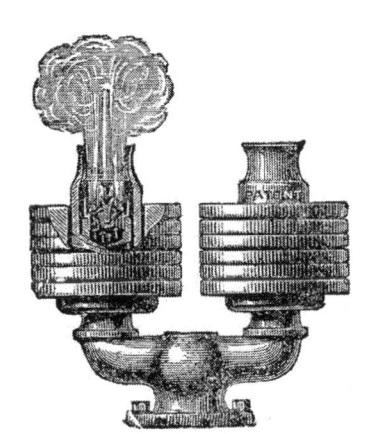

2in.	...	...	£8 8 0
3in.	...	...	12 10 0
4in.	...	...	16 0 0

No. 598.
DOUBLE-LIP VALVE,
With Ashcroft Alarm, &c., for Low Water.

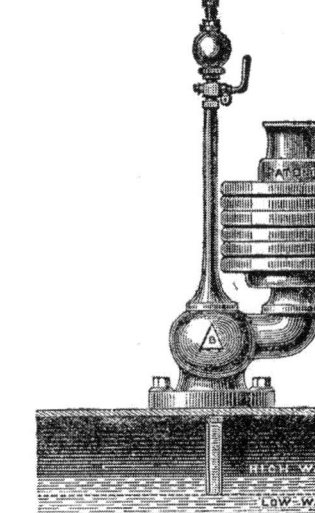

2in.	...	...	£6 10 0
3in.	...	...	8 15 0
4in.	...	...	10 0 0

DOUBLE-LIP VALVE,
With Lever and Weight.

1½in.	...	...	£2 10 0
2in.	...	...	3 10 0
3in.	...	...	4 15 0
4in.	...	...	6 6 0

In ordering, be careful to give the blow-off pressures. Weights for higher pressures 12/6 per cwt. extra.

The following are a few of the firms who have the Hallam's Double-Lip Valves at work, and speak highly of them:—

Messrs. Rylands & Sons, Limited, Gorton Mills, Manchester.
    „   „   „   Swinton Lane, „
    „   „   „   Crawshaw Brook „
    „   „   „   Chester Street Mill „
    „ Gratrix, Bros., Queen's Brewery, Moss Side „
Manchester Gas Works, „
Tinker, Sheuton & Co., Hyde.
Willonby, Brothers, Plymouth.
G. Plant & Co., „
Sectional Boiler Co., Manchester.
Coghlon & Dury, Albert Forge, Leeds.

M. R. Woolstenholme, Boiler Maker, Hunslet, Leeds.
J. L. Kennedy & Co., Harkhead, near Stalybridge.
The Mersey Wood Co., Bootle, near Liverpool.
Manchester Machine Tool Co., Cornwall Street, Openshaw.
Hardman, Brothers, Rawtenstall.
Old Garrat Dyeing Co., at their Gaythorn Works, Manchester.
Lewis Williams & Co., London Road Mills, „
Williams & Pemberton, Boiler Makers, „
Tetlow & Sons, Hallins Road, Hollinwood, „
J. Tomlinson & Son, Builders, Chester Road, „
&c., &c., &c.

BAILEY'S EXTRA LARGE ENGINE COUNTER

The large Engine Counter has been designed for large Engines, Screw Ships, &c. The dials are four inches in diameter. When ordering, please say if for reciprocating or rotary motion. The besels are polished brass, and the whole appearance good and substantial, in contradistinction to the toys that are often sold for this purpose, to 100,000.

Price, £8 10s. 0d.

LYNDE'S PATENT EQUILIBRIUM RESERVOIR REGULATOR,

Invented by J. G. LYNDE, Esq., C.E., City Engineer of Manchester.

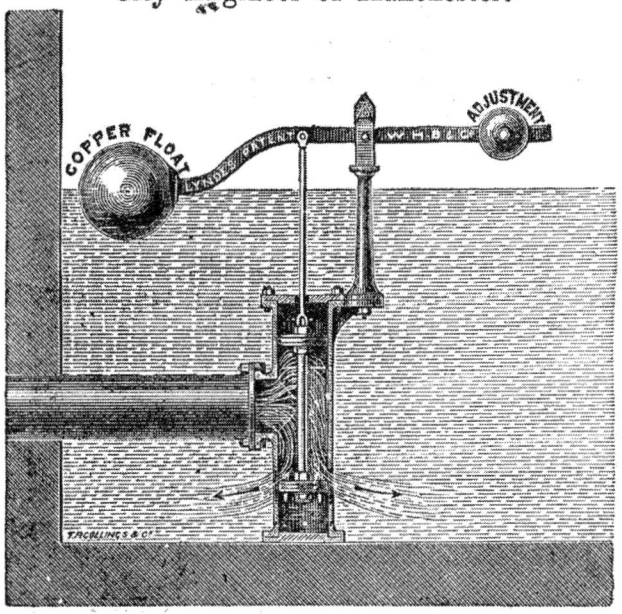

This simple Regulator is a perfect Equilibrium Valve, and will regulate for any pressure or head of water coming from a higher level, or from a pump. The chief parts are of brass —the Piston and Piston-rod. The Pins are Gun-Metal, the Float of Copper.

PRICE,		£	s.	d.
Complete, 3-in. Bore	…	15	0	0
,, 4 ,,	…	20	0	0
,, 5 ,,	…	25	0	0
,, 6 ,,	…	30	0	0
,, 7 ,,	…	35	0	0
,, 8 ,,	…	40	0	0
,, 10 ,,	…	50	0	0
,, 12 ,,	…	60	0	0

BAILEY'S EXTRA SIZE EQUILIBRIUM BALL VALVE.

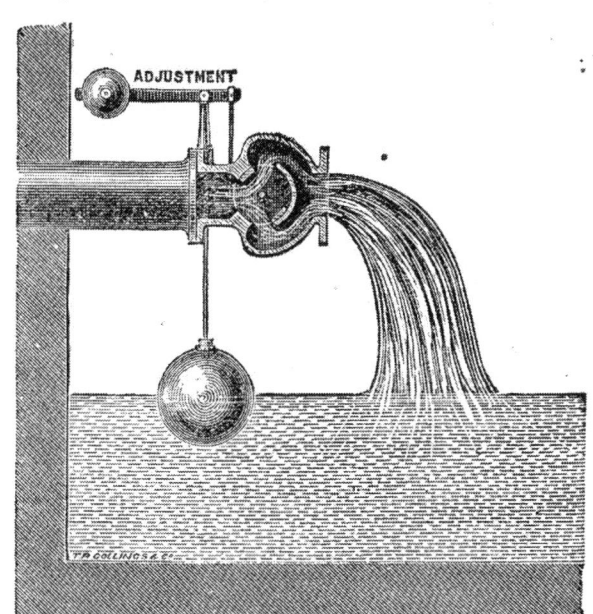

PRICE,		£	s.	d.
Complete, 2-in. Bore	…	6	0	0
,, 2½ ,,	…	7	10	0
,, 3 ,,	…	9	0	0
,, 3½ ,,	…	10	10	0
,, 4 ,,	…	12	0	0
,, 5 ,,	…	15	0	0
,, 6 ,,	…	18	0	0
,, 7 ,,	…	21	0	0
,, 8 ,,	…	24	0	0
,, 10 ,,	…	30	0	0
,, 12 ,,	…	36	0	0

Bailey's Patent Vertical Steam Traps

Have a special feature in addition to their well-known perfect action—namely, they will force water out of the pipes to a higher level. This is a great advantage, and practical men appreciate it.

These Traps are applied to Drying Cylinders, Stoves, Steam Hammers, Engine Cylinders, and pipes generally on which condensed steam accumulates. They are warranted perfect in action. All are tested before delivery.

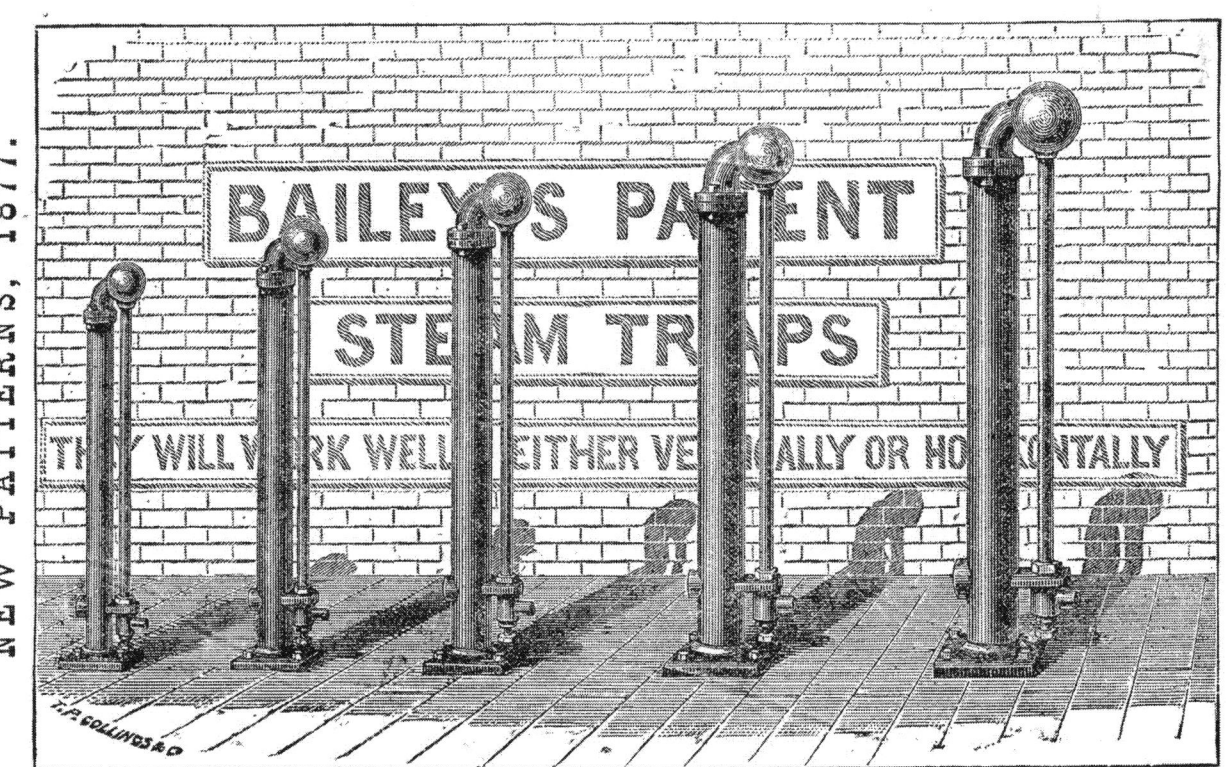

NEW PATTERNS, 1877.

BAILEY'S PATENT STEAM TRAPS

THEY WILL WORK WELL EITHER VERTICALLY OR HORIZONTALLY

The old Patterns are discarded for these.

For prices and description, see page 227 of this Book.

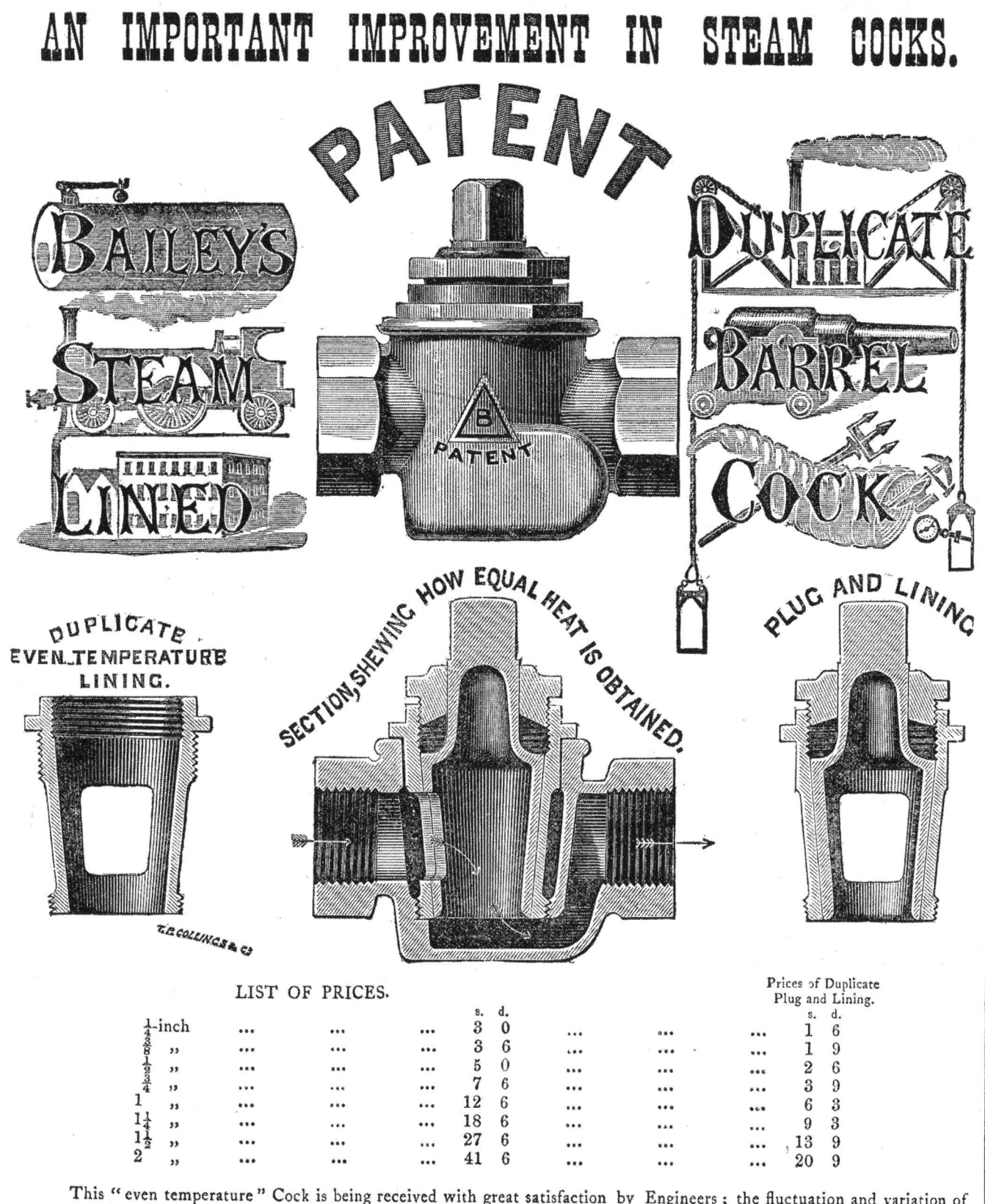

BAILEY'S SUET LUBRICATOR

PRICES.	External Diam.	1	1¼	1½	2	2½	3	3½	4	5	6 inch.
	For Engines up to	1	2	4	6	10	20	30	40	70	100 h.p.
	Screwed Whitworth Thread	¼	⅜	½	½	¾	¾	¾	¾	1	1 inch.
	Price	9/-	10/6	12/6	15/-	19/-	30/-	37/6	45/-	55/-	70/- each.

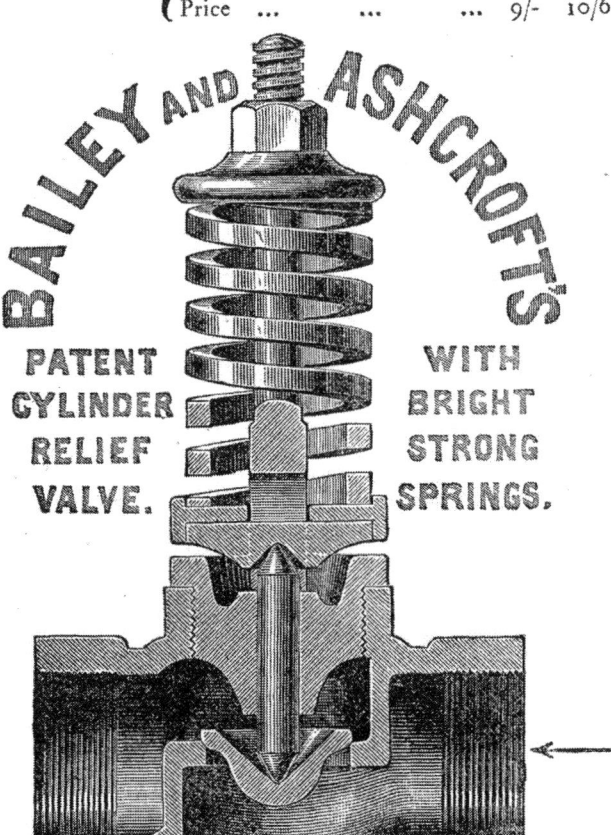

BAILEY AND ASHCROFT'S PATENT CYLINDER RELIEF VALVE.
WITH BRIGHT STRONG SPRINGS.

PRICES
- 1-in ... £1 0 0 ... 2-in ... £2 10 0
- 1¼-in ... 1 6 0 ... 2½-in ... 3 10 0
- 1½-in ... 2 0 0 ... 3-in ... 4 10 0

These Valves are much used for Engine Cylinders and other purposes. The sudden starting of Engines when water has accumulated has been the cause of many serious accidents.

These Valves are strong, well made, and of a design which Engineers appreciate.

BAILEY'S
BALL & EXTRA STRONG SWIVEL BALL JOINT AND UNION,
FOR STEAM, WATER, OR GAS.

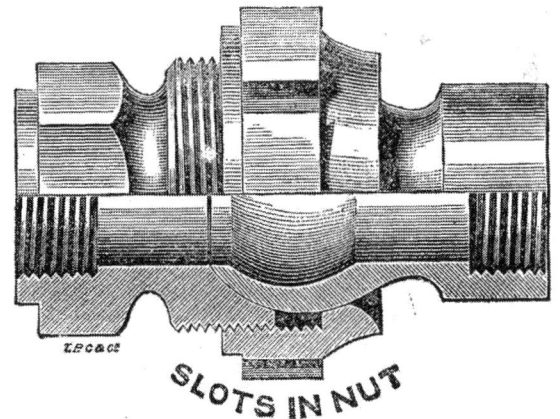

SLOTS IN NUT

1-inch	...	...	...	...	7/6
1¼ ,,	...	...	...	...	10/6
1½ ,,	...	...	...	...	12/6
2 ,,	...	...	...	...	20/-
2½ ,,	...	...	...	...	27/6
3 ,,	...	...	...	...	35/-

We have Patterns of nearly every conceivable description of Union Joints, Special Valves, Couplings and other Fittings for Locomotive, Stationary, Marine and Portable Engines.

Special quotations sent for either rough or finished BRASS WORK.

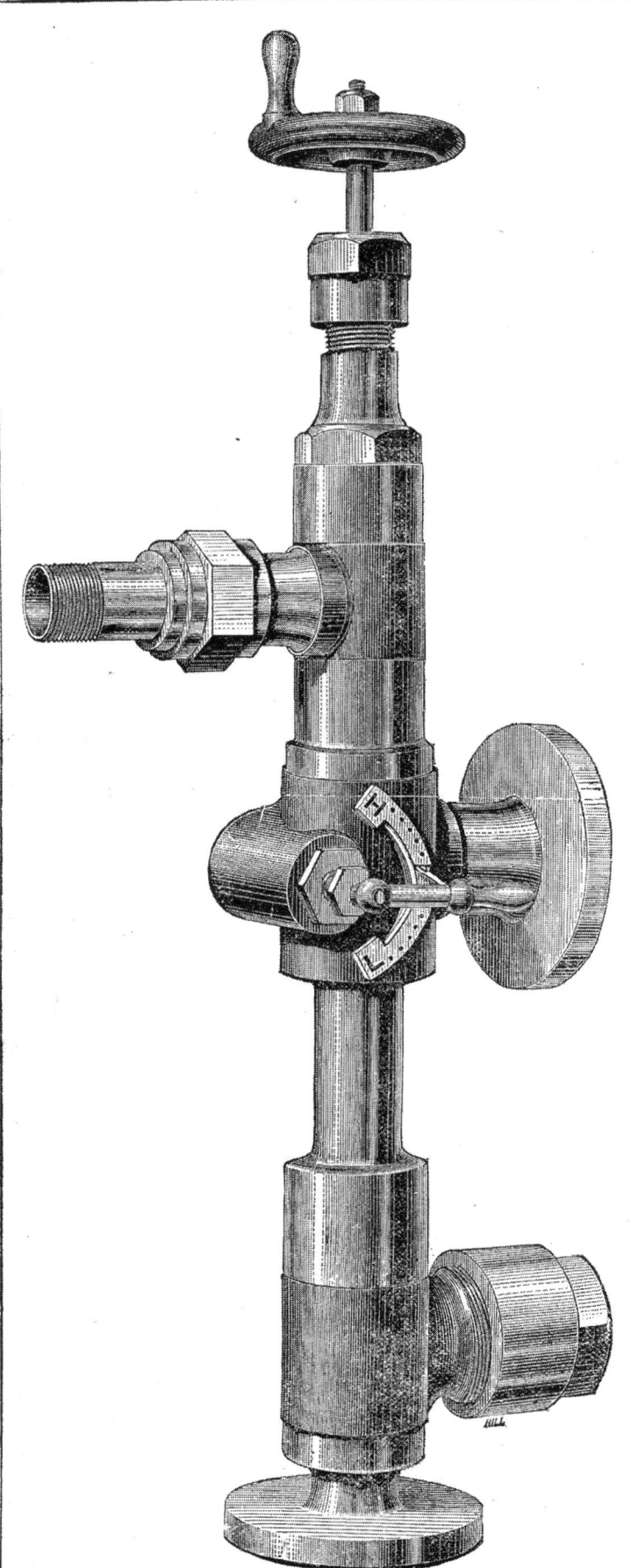

Many Thousands in Use.

BAILEY'S

PATENT

INJECTORS

Have recently been much improved, and are now the most superior to any for lifting and forcing water into Steam Boilers.

For prices, see page 41;

ALSO SEE

SUPPLEMENTARY LISTS

OF

Pumps, Injectors, Pyrometers, Hydraulic Motors, &c.,

POST FREE.

RECENT TESTIMONY.

16th December, 1876.

Memo.

From JAMES TAYLOR, Millwright and Engineer, Romsey.

Re HALLAM'S INJECTOR.

GENTLEMEN,—Some time since, I purchased from you one of these for a customer of mine, which has answered its purpose admirably.

Yours respectfully,

J. JOHNSON.

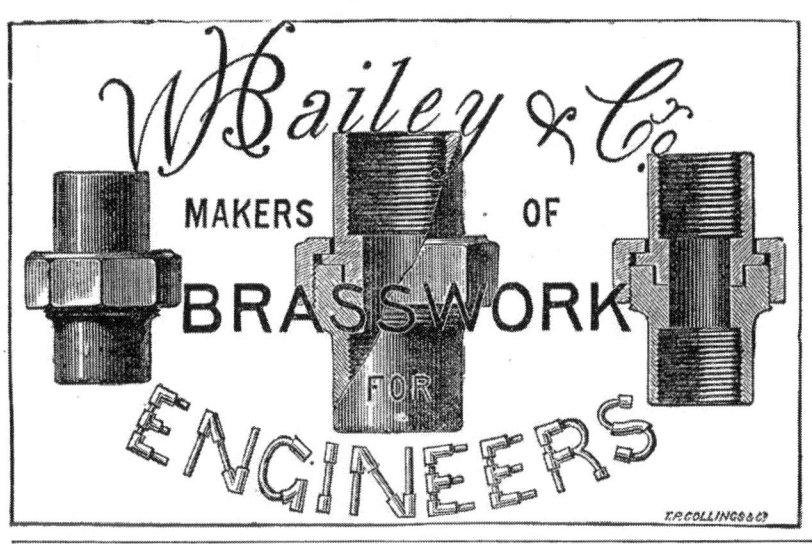

BAILEY'S EXTRA-STRONG UNION JOINTS,

For Gas, Water and Steam.

See page 50

Bore, Gas Pipe Size,	¼-in.,	⅜-in.,	½-in.,	⅝-in.,	¾-in.,
PRICE,					
,,	1-in.,	1¼-in.,	1½-in.,	1¾-in.,	
PRICE,					
,,	2-in.,	2½-in.,	3-in.		
PRICE,					

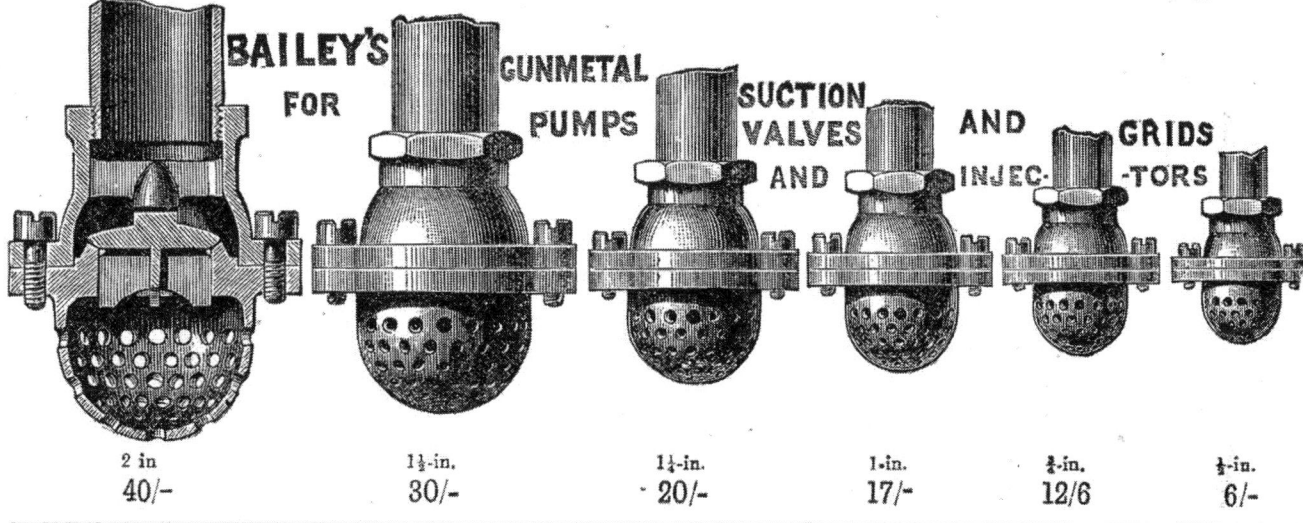

2 in	1½-in.	1¼-in.	1-in.	¾-in.	½-in.
40/-	30/-	20/-	17/-	12/6	6/-

STILLWELL'S PATENT MUD FILTER AND DIRT EXTRACTOR.

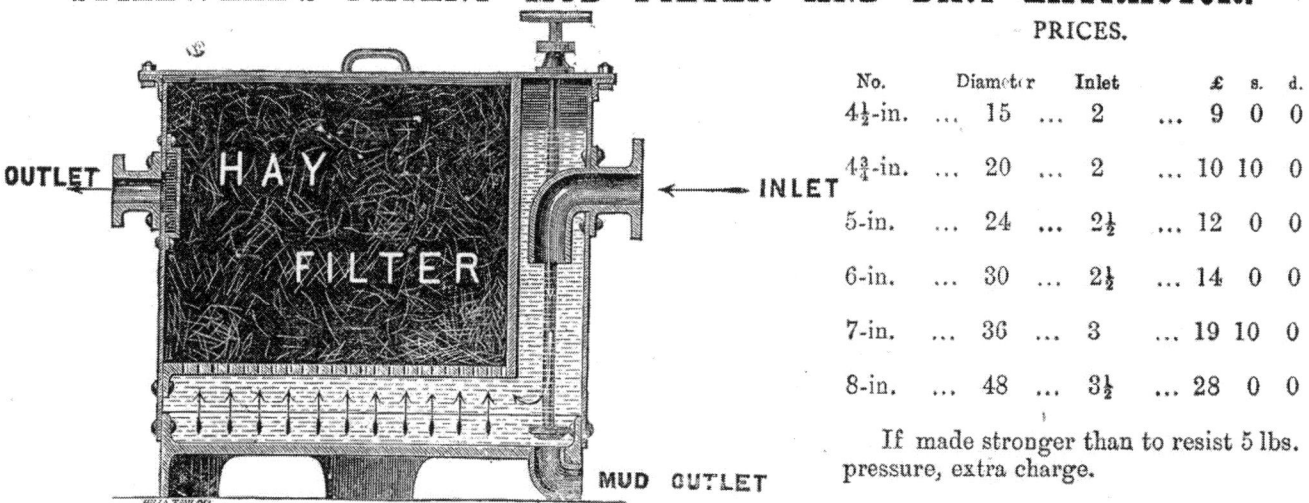

PRICES.

No.	Diameter	Inlet	£	s.	d.
4½-in.	15	2	9	0	0
4¾-in.	20	2	10	10	0
5-in.	24	2½	12	0	0
6-in.	30	2½	14	0	0
7-in.	36	3	19	10	0
8-in.	48	3½	28	0	0

If made stronger than to resist 5 lbs. pressure, extra charge.

This is useful for Canal, Ditch, or Stream Water, for extracting the mechanical impurities quickly. The Filter is of hay, which may be removed weekly, or at any other interval; the Mud Valve enables the bottom to be cleared out. The pressure these will stand is about 5 lbs. on the square inch, say equal to a head of water about 12 feet high.

BALDWIN & BAILEY'S PATENT ABSOLUTE "VACUUM" GAUGE,

COMPLETE IN FRENCH-POLISHED CASE.

WITH FIRST-CLASS BAROMETER,

ACCURATELY TESTED,

£6 6s.

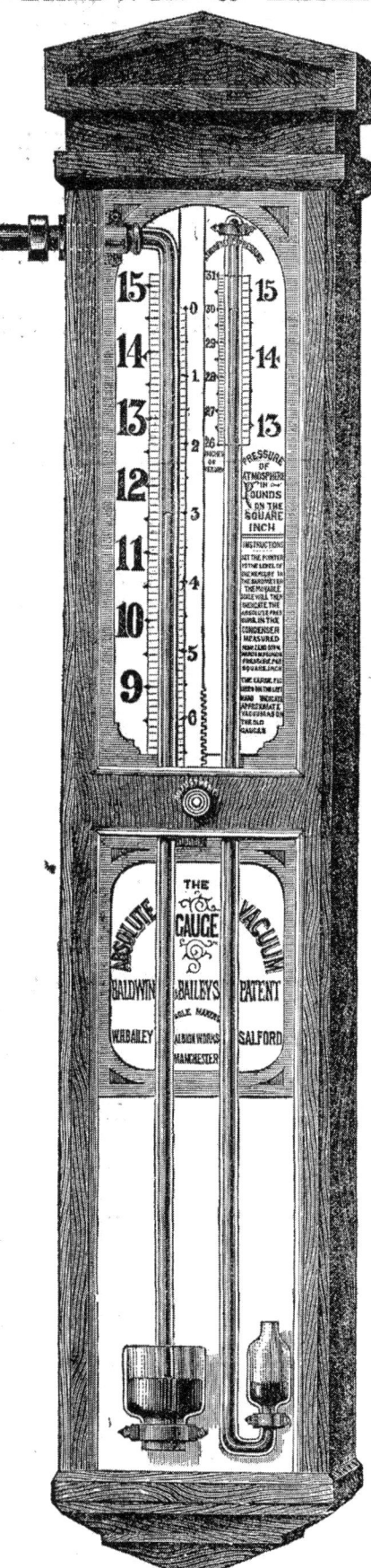

INSTRUCTIONS.

All Indicator Diagrams should have the absolute pressure in the Condenser and the absolute pressure of the atmosphere written upon them, as shown by the ABSOLUTE "VACUUM" GAUGE at the time they are taken.

If the mercury in the tube attached to the Condenser fluctuates, as it will in some engines, the highest and lowest points should be noted, and Marked L for least, and G for the greatest, *absolute pressure* in the Condenser, as shown on the sliding scale.

The position of the mercury in the glass tubes in the engraving shows an absolute pressure in the Condenser of 3 lbs., and the pressure of the atmosphere to be 14¾ lbs., or 14.75 lbs.

The ABSOLUTE "VACUUM" GAUGE may be placed in the Office, and coupled by a pipe to the Condenser a hundred yards distant, if required.

The present form of steam engine is open to great improvement, since it only utilises about twelve per cent. of the heat given to the steam by the boiler.

Extensive experiments on Steam Engines varying from 500 to 750 horse power have been conducted by Mr. Thomas Baldwin, Consulting Engineer, of Manchester, for the purpose of ascertaining *the weight of steam used per indicated horse power per hour*, after it has left the boiler; he has also directed his attention to the value of the loss of steam during its action in the cylinder of the engine, caused firstly by loss of heat, and secondly by a portion having become liquified, and passed in that condition into the condenser

These experiments have caused some startling facts to be revealed, for in some of what appeared to be the best engines working expansively, it has been shown that they were consuming nearly double the amount of steam they should do, when tested by the indicator; this has been ascertained by both measuring and weighing the condensed steam in the form of water passing from a surface condenser, and also by measuring the water pumped from the ordinary condenser by the air pump, and taking its temperature and the temperature of the injection water, and also by carefully indicating the engines and ascertaining the absolute pressure by fixing the *Zero Line*, or line of *no pressure*, on the Indicator diagrams, which can be done with great accuracy when the ABSOLUTE "VACUUM" GAUGE is used.

The Patent ABSOLUTE "VACUUM" GAUGE being one of the results of these experiments, its use must be at once apparent to owners of engines, for fixing the *Zero Line*, or line of *no pressure*, on Indicator diagrams, and showing at once if the condenser is doing its proper duty.

All Engineers know the importance of keeping down the pressure in the condenser, and they also know that when that pressure is greater than it ought to be a *serious expenditure of coal* is the consequence.

The ABSOLUTE "VACUUM" GAUGE enables a considerable amount of fuel to be saved, as it at once shows when the engine is drawing air, or leakage is taking place in the piston, or steam, or exhaust valves, in which case the *absolute pressure* in the condenser is generally increased.

It is important to remember that a *good condenser* should never show, when the ABSOLUTE "VACUUM" GAUGE is used, A GREATER ABSOLUTE PRESSURE THAN ONE POUND ON THE SQUARE INCH. Any condenser showing more than this is open for improvement.

Fifty or Sixty Horse power is often lost owing to the pressure in the condenser being greater than it ought to be, which may be at once detected with the ABSOLUTE "VACUUM" GAUGE.

With a good condenser the mercury in the gauge will remain nearly stationary, if the exhaust valve is properly set.

If the valves are not properly set, the mercury will often fluctuate in the tube, and it will sometimes do so when the air pump is out of order.

A pipe fitted into the exhaust passage, near the slide valve, and attached to the ABSOLUTE "VACUUM" GAUGE, will show very clearly if the steam is obstructed in its passage from that point to the condenser. *If it is obstructed*, the distance between the surfaces of the mercury in the two tubes will be considerably increased, and the consequence will be increased back pressure on the piston of the engine, and *serious loss of power and fuel*.

The height of the column of mercury in the right-hand tube will vary with the pressure of the atmosphere, it being simply a first-class barometer, but the absolute pressure measured by the sliding scale of the ABSOLUTE "VACUUM" GAUGE will remain constant, if all the parts of the engine are in good working order.

☞ In some large engines ONE-QUARTER OF A POUND of increase in the ABSOLUTE PRESSURE in the condenser indicates a loss of TEN HORSE POWER, that is to say, if the cylinder be 55 inches in diameter, the loss will be FORTY HORSE POWER, if the absolute pressure in the condenser is increased ONE POUND per square inch, as read on the sliding scale of the ABSOLUTE "VACUUM" GAUGE, and this loss increases with the increased size of the cylinder.

Do not allow the temperature of the water in the hot well to exceed about 100° Fahrenheit, because the temperature of steam having an absolute pressure of *one pound* on the square inch has a temperature of 102° Fahrenheit, and any increase above this temperature will increase the *absolute pressure* in the condenser, and consequently the *back pressure* on the piston.

Shortly will be published, a Pamphlet on the economical working of Condensing Engines, with special relation to the use of the ABSOLUTE "VACUUM" GAUGE.

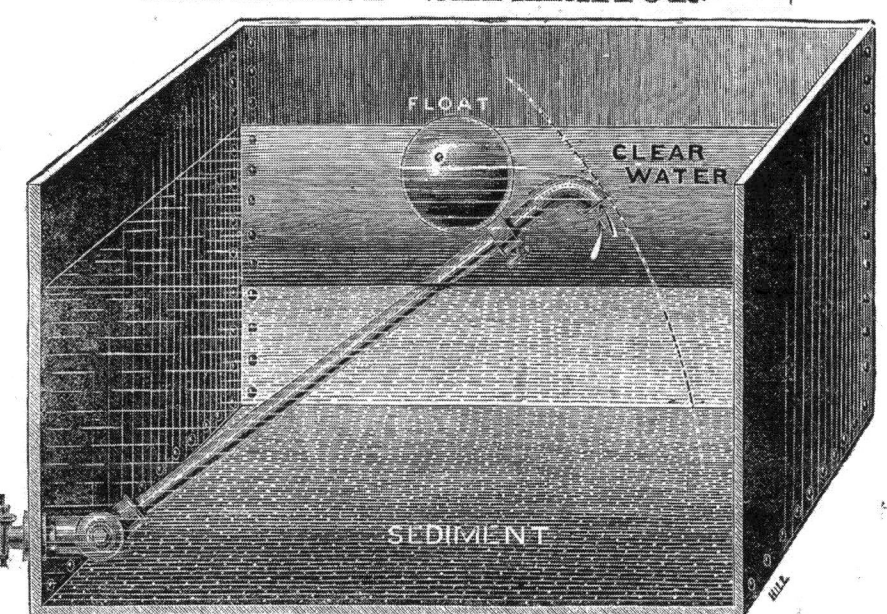

SEDIMENT SEPARATOR.

BAILEY'S PATENT "Tell-Tale" Oil Cistern.

To be able to "see at a glance" how much Oil is in stock, to check waste, to have an idea of consumption, or to guide the delivery—the dial indicating the number of gallons—is useful.

The Dial has an arrangement under it to enable the cock to be locked up.

PRICES, COMPLETE.
READY FOR WORK, AS ILLUSTRATED.

40 Gallons	...	...	...	...	£4 0 0
50 Gallons	...	...	...	...	5 0 0
60 Gallons	...	...	...	...	6 0 0
80 Gallons	...	...	...	...	8 0 0
100 Gallons	...	...	...	...	10 0 0
150 Gallons	...	...	...	...	12 10 0
200 Gallons	...	...	...	...	14 0 0

These "Tell-Tale" are made for a variety of purposes, and may be had separately, either for House Cisterns, Water works, Wells, &c., &c.

PLUM'S PATENT Clear Water Separator, AND DRAW-OFF COCK,

For drawing off the light and clean portion of Water, or any other liquid, and leaving the sediment untouched.

Complete, as illustrated, ready for fixing to a cistern, the arm from one to three feet long; if longer than three feet, extra will be charged.

With Brass Flange Cock, Lock Nut, Iron Pipe and Copper Ball.

Bore, ½-in. ⅝-in. ¾-in. 1-in. 1¼-in. 1½-in. 2-in.

20s., 25s., 28s. 6d., 45s., 65s., 80s., 110s.

Special for larger sizes.

Bailey's Oil Pump,
ON CAST-IRON FRAME,

With Fly Wheel Unions on Outlet and Inlet, with Brass Barrel.

2½-in. Bore, 6-in. Stroke	...	...	...	£7 0 0
3-in. Bore, 8-in. Stroke	...	...	...	£8 0 0

BAILEY'S FITTERS' FRIEND SHAPER

For either Hand or Power.

Traverse, 13 inches; Stroke, 2¼.

Price, with Top Driving,
£25 0s. 0d.

This Tool, which is daily at work, was designed for our Turret Clock Department Fitters, for small work. It will do for either flat, semi-circular, or round purposes. Long articles that want ending can be put in the Side Vice.

TREGONEY AND WALKER'S PATENT HYDRAULIC MOTOR.

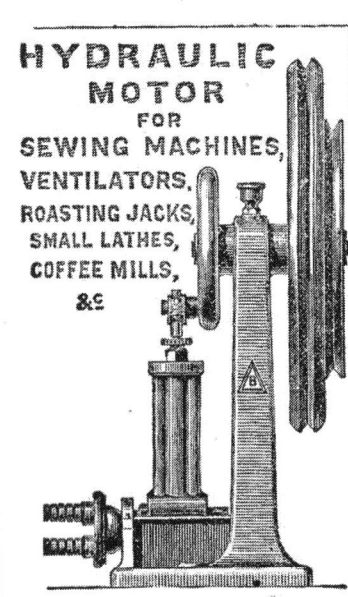

HYDRAULIC MOTOR FOR SEWING MACHINES, VENTILATORS, ROASTING JACKS, SMALL LATHES, COFFEE MILLS, &c.

These are only made one size, in order to be produced in quantities cheap.

Price for Sewing Machines, &c., Total height, 16 inches, } £4 4 0

To be had of all Sewing Machine Dealers and Merchants of Domestic Machinery at home and abroad, or direct from the Manufacturers, W. H. BAILEY & Co.

HYDRAULIC MOTORS
(HAAG'S PATENT.)
Sole Makers, W. H. BAILEY & Co., Salford.

HAAG'S PATENT WATER MOTORS GIVE 86 Per Cent OF USEFUL EFFECT.

MADE FROM ¼ HORSE POWER.

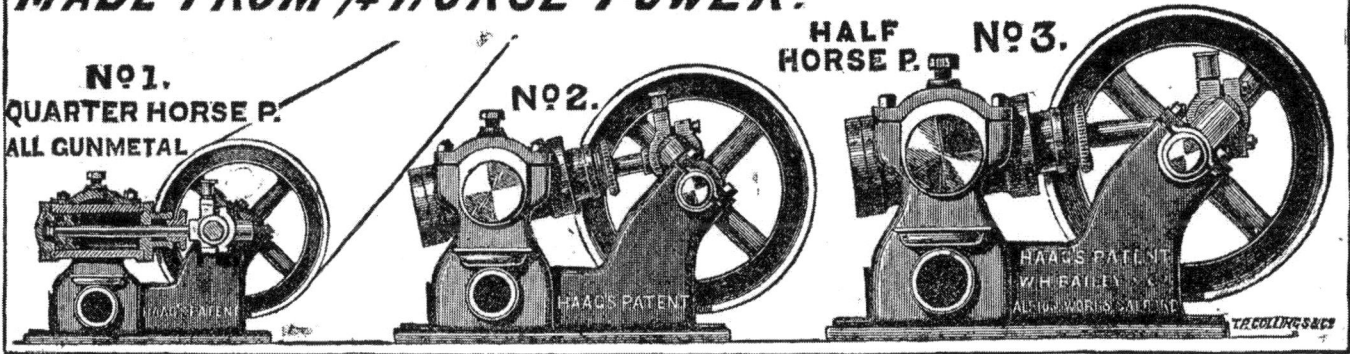

¼ Horse Power.	½ Horse Power.	1 Horse Power.	These Powers are at 45 lbs. of water pressure.
£6 0 0	£10 0 0	£15 0 0	

(Other Sizes, see Pump, Injector and Motor List.)

These are well finished, and are fitted with gun metal parts where required. The small sizes all brass. These will do for steam, if specially stated when ordering.

BAILEY'S HYDRAULIC ORGAN BLOWER.

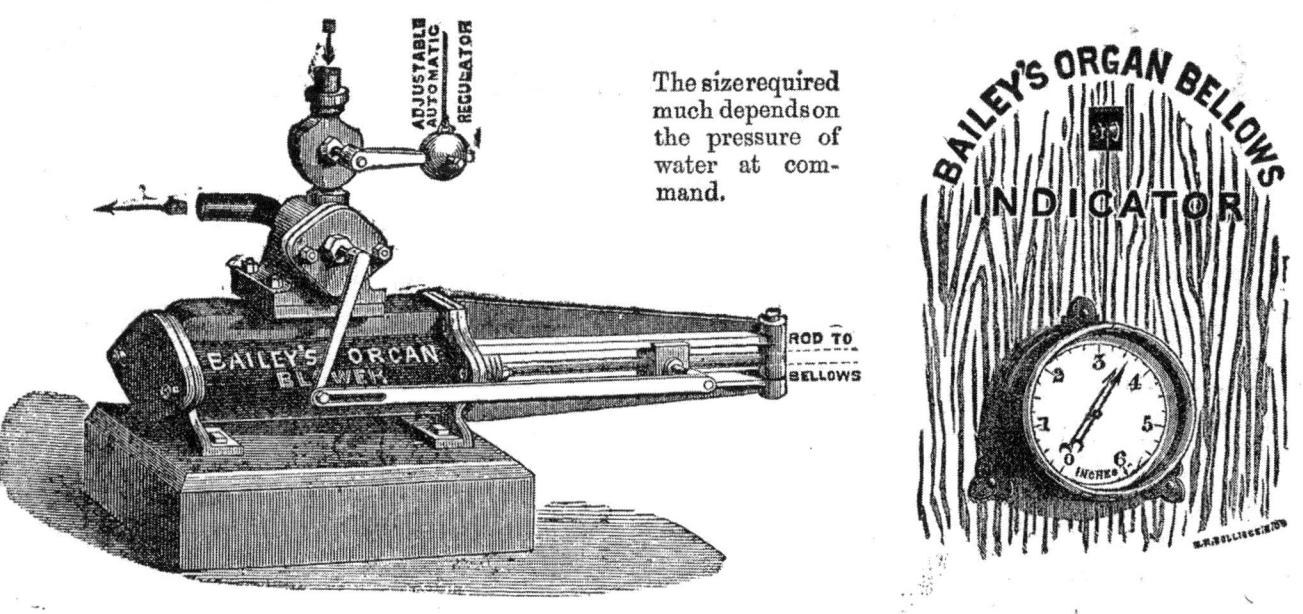

The size required much depends on the pressure of water at command.

2-inch Diameter,	9-inch Stroke	...	£10 0 0
2¼ "	9 "	...	12 10 0
3 "	10 "	...	20 0 0
3½ "	12 "	...	30 0 0

4-inch Diameter for 6-inch Stroke, Chapel Pattern, 21s. each.

Any length of Stroke to Order.

Extra Size, 7-inch Diameter and 10-inch Stroke, for Large Organs, 50s.

These Dials are to regulate the man who blows the Organ, instead of the uncouth lead weight.

STEAM ENGINES.
W. H. BAILEY & Co., Sole Makers.

HAAG'S PATENT.

These simple Steam Engines are not liable to derangement. They are very strong, and will resist a great amount of wear and tear.

No.	13	14	15	16	17	18	19	20
Horse Power ...	½	1	2	2½	3	4½	6	8
Bore, Inches ...	2⅜	3⅛	4	4¾	5½	6½	7	8
Stroke ...	3⅞	4¾	6	7	8	9	10¼	12
	£6	10	14	20	30	40	60	75

The "finish" of these Engines is good and sound, but if any are wanted with much polish and first-class bright job for window purposes, for shopkeepers and others, add 10 per cent. to the prices.

These Engines are useful for driving Chaff-Cutters, Pumps, Screwing Machines, Printing Presses, Sausage Chopping Machines, Mangles, &c.

YOUNG'S DIAMOND GRINDSTONE TURNER.

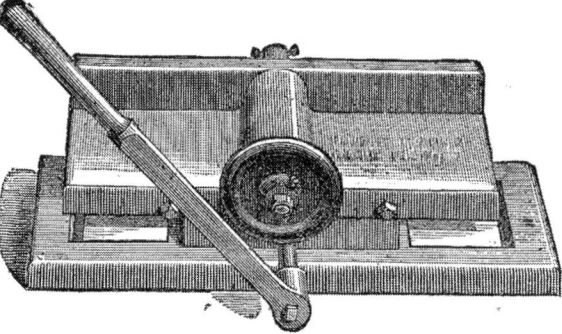

This Apparatus is simple, effective and durable, and gives the most unqualified satisfaction generally.

Adopted extensively by Engineers, Millwrights, etc., and in numerous Factories throughout the kingdom.

The above illustration represents the Machine in perspective.

The Machine is fixed to frame of Grindstone by bolts coming up through the openings shown in sole.

The Diamond is fixed by a peculiar arrangement in the nozzle, which is shown at top part of illustration.

The Diamond is set to its work or withdrawn at pleasure by turning the small hand wheel at back of Machine, and is adjusted backward and forward across face of stone by the moving of the lever handle shown above.

This Machine will keep the stone in perfect true face, and will do in five minutes more work than can be done by a steel bar in an hour.

Price, without Diamond, £4.

Discounts to Shippers and the Trade.

BAILEY'S
Smoke-Preventing Bridge Furnace Bars,

[ERSKINE'S PATENT.]

For Stationary, Portable, Locomotive, Marine, Agricultural, Brewers' and other Boilers, Stoves, Ovens, Kilns, etc., etc.

We have patterns of all sizes for Cotton Spinners, Bleachers, Bakers, Sugar Refiners, Brewers, Japanners, Calico Printers, Dyers, etc., etc.

SIDE VIEW.

This has been truly described as The Bunsen Burner Fire Bar, the theory of the two being identical.

THIS arrangement is a *simple and self-acting means* of reducing Smoke. This is accomplished by a peculiar construction of Furnace Bars, which act by practically admitting *hot air* to the furnace. Most of the Smoke is consumed as produced in the body of the furnace, and any portion which may have escaped combustion is met at the bridge end of the fireplace by a distinct ingress of *hot air*, which at once consumes it, so that scarcely a trace of Smoke is perceived at the outlet of the chimney. This stream of hot air is admitted through the vertical position of the Bars, as shown in the plate, the smoke being consumed in passing over the brick bridge. These Bars give a greater space and better distribution of air than any others, thus securing a better consumption of fuel, for, as the Carbon of the smoke is actually burned by means of *hot air*, its value is gained as fuel, whilst no diminution of the steam in the boiler *can* take place, as no cold air is admitted.

All engineers acknowledge that air, or, say oxygen, admitted in proper proportions, will entirely prevent Smoke. This is often accomplished by admitting cold air, which is but a clumsy way to economise at one end and lose what is gained at the other.

ADVANTAGES OVER THE BAR IN COMMON USE.

1. They are far more durable, having a better distribution of air space, which prevents their destruction.
2. They generate steam more quickly, and with less labour.
3. They prevent soldering and clinkering to a great extent.
4. Being light Bars, a less weight per boiler is required.
5. They are most effectual smoke burners.
6. They improve the draught, by admitting an abundance of warm oxygen.
7. No special preparation required.

☞ They will last fully double the length of time of the old fire bars, as well as to *effectually prevent Smoke*.

SAMPLE ORDER FORM.

Please send us one set of Fire Bars, length over all,　　　　　inches. *Width of Furnace,*　　　　　inches.

☞ ENGINEERS ARE REQUESTED TO READ THIS.

An Account of a Public Trial of the Bunsen Burner Fire Bars *versus* the Common Bars.

THE SMOKE NUISANCE.—We are glad to be able to announce that the smoke nuisance, which is one of the banes of all large manufacturing towns, may now be all but entirely obviated at a trifling cost. On Thursday last, some highly interesting experiments were made with two boilers belonging to Messrs. Tysoe and Hope, Hope Street, Salford, in the presence of upwards of twenty practical gentlemen, specially invited. Amongst the firms there represented may be mentioned the following:—Messrs. Tysoe and Hope's, Tysoe and Son's, Harvey and Son's, Hall, Poole and Co.'s, Lancashire and Yorkshire Railway Co., the Bridgewater Trustees, Rowbotham and Ezard, George Grant and Sons, of Glasgow, T. B. Crompton's, Ancoats Vale Rubber Company ; and the following gentlemen :—Messrs. W. Routledge, C.E., Councillor John Bailey (Salford), Sam Mason, Major Bowers, Councillor Ashton, Deputy-Chairman of the Health Committee (Manchester), Councillor Muirhead, Manchester, Alderman Priestley, Huddersfield, Frank Preston, etc. The experiments commenced at eleven o'clock a.m., and were brought to an end about half-past twelve ; and, as already stated, were made with two double-flue boilers, side by side, the flues of both running into one shaft ; they were built by Clayton, of Preston—one in 1868, the other in 1869. The latter was fitted with Erskine's Patent Bars, the former with the ordinary fire bars, and first one was fired up, and then the other ; and when only one of both the flues of each boiler was fired up at a time, the superiority of the patent bars over the ordinary ones was most manifest. INDEED, SO MARKED WAS THE DIFFERENCE IN FAVOUR OF ERSKINE'S PATENT, THAT IT WOULD BE WELL IF ALL LOCAL AUTHORITIES HAD THE POWER TO COMPEL ALL THE FIRMS TO ADOPT IT, FOR WE ARE CONVINCED THAT THEN WE SHOULD HEAR NO MORE OF THE SMOKE NUISANCE, WITH WHICH WE ARE NOW DAILY INFESTED. This is not the place for a description of the bars, but we may say that the consumption of smoke is accomplished by their peculiar construction admitting hot air to the furnace. Most of the smoke is consumed as produced by the hot air admitted into the body of the furnace. Any portion which may have escaped combustion during its passage is met at the farthest end of the fireplace by an additional and distinct ingress of hot air, which at once consumes it, so that scarcely a trace of visible smoke is perceived at the outlet of the chimney. It is also alleged that a certain economy attends the use of this apparatus ; for, as the carbon of the smoke is actually burned by means of hot air, the value of this is gained as fuel, whilst no diminution of the tension of the steam in the boiler can take place, since no cold air is admitted. As to this latter statement we cannot speak of our own knowledge, but that, by means of the patent bars, smoke is either consumed, or in some other way destroyed, is certain. After the experiments were over, many of the gentlemen present congratulated the patentee on the unmistakeable success of the experiments.—Mr. Moore called attention to the fact that these patent bars had many advantages over the old kind of bars ; for not only did they never get red-hot, but the smallest possible coal might be burnt upon them, while they would last three times as long as the ordinary bars.—Mr. W. Routledge, C.E., said he considered that the result of the day's experiments was highly satisfactory, and thoroughly successful.—Mr. Johnson, Locomotive Superintendent of the Lancashire and Yorkshire Railway Company, said they had tried the patent bars in the furnaces of two locomotives, AND THEY HAD NEVER, EVEN AFTER A 90 MILES' RUN, BEEN ABLE TO MAKE THEM RED-HOT, although every attempt had been made to do so ; while the ordinary bars would become red-hot before starting. He considered that they well answered their purpose, and, with careful firing, would reduce smoke to its smallest possible quantity.—Mr. John Tysoe said that after his experience of the patent bars he was quite satisfied, and felt confident that, if the boiler flues were only kept clean, as they all ought to be, IT WAS ALMOST IMPOSSIBLE FOR A MAN TO MAKE ANY SMOKE WHERE THE FURNACES WERE FITTED WITH THESE BARS. A gentleman representing the Ancoats Vale Rubber Works said they had had the bars in their boiler furnaces fourteen months, and he had never seen one of them red-hot ; and he was thoroughly convinced of THEIR EFFICACY IN CAUSING THE CONSUMPTION OF SMOKE.—Mr. Sam Mason also spoke in commendation of the patent.—Mr. Councillor Bailey said the experiments he had that day seen had convinced him that the smoke nuisance ought now no longer to exist, and he would warn those who were summoned before the Salford Council Nuisance Committee for the offence "to look out" after this. (Hear, hear, and laughter.)—Mr. Jessie Timmins, Mechanical Engineer to the Bridgewater Collieries, said he had been requested by Mr. Fereday Smith to attend the experiments which they had just witnessed, and he was glad to say he should have no difficulty whatever in reporting to that gentleman in favour of these patent bars to do away with the smoke nuisance, and he (Mr. Timmins) was glad to find that this could now be in great part, if not entirely, accomplished. By using these patent bars, and paying proper attention to firing, nobody need fear being summoned for having smoky chimneys.—Mr. Councillor Ashton, Manchester, as Deputy-Chairman of the Smoke Nuisance Committee of that Corporation, had witnessed the experiment with great pleasure, and was thoroughly convinced that the patent bars, when used, would accomplish that which was claimed for them. In all cases which henceforth came before him he should tell the offending parties they might prevent the nuisance for which they were summoned if they felt so minded, by using Erskine's patent fire bars. (Hear, hear.)—Mr. Alderman Priestley, Huddersfield, also bore testimony to the efficacy of the patent. The smoke question has often been before the Huddersfield Town Council, where it was argued by some of the members of that Corporation that if they enforced the law against those who offended against it by sending forth too much smoke from the chimneys of their works, they would drive, in time, the trade out of the town. Now, he did not believe in that argument ; nor did he see why anything should be permitted that was of advantage to a few as against the many. At any rate, from what he had that day seen this need no longer be so ; for, by using Erskine's fire bars, smoke need not be, and would not be, a nuisance at all ; and he therefore hoped they would at once adopt the plan.—The company soon after dispersed.—From the *Salford Weekly News*, June 25, 1874.

PREVENTION OF THE SMOKE NUISANCE.

Most of the smoke is consumed as it is produced by the hot air admitted into the body of the furnace. Any smoke which may have escaped combustion during its passage is met at the furthest end of the fireplace by an additional and distinct ingress of hot air, which at once consumes it. Two boilers were experimented upon, one fitted up with the patent apparatus, and the other with the ordinary fire bars. The result was, that while a very dense volume of smoke was given off by the latter, the smoke emitted when the former was tried was scarcely visible. The difference was very marked, and most of the gentlemen present declared then, and at a meeting which took place subsequently, that the experiment was conclusive as to the efficiency of Erskine's apparatus. It is also claimed for the new invention that it effects a large saving of fuel.—From the *Manchester Examiner and Times*, June 24, 1870. See also *Manchester Guardian, Manchester Courier* and other local papers.

SPECIAL NOTE.—These Bars, lasting, as they do, much longer, besides possessing this well-known and admitted superiority, are in reality no higher in price than the old sort of Bars.

The small cost of a trial Order we beg to call attention to.

BAILEY'S BUNSEN BURNER BARS

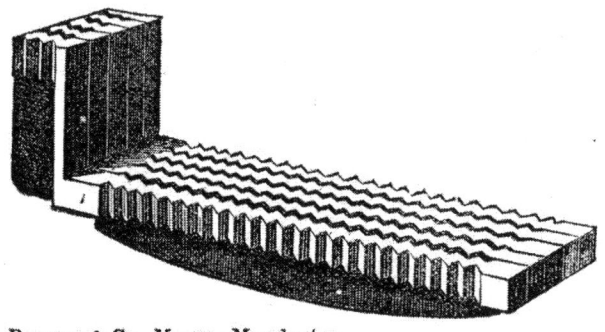

HAVE BEEN SUPPLIED TO THE UNDERMENTIONED.

In many cases repeated Orders have been received.

Brennan & Co., Messrs., Manchester
Chadwick, Mr. J., Manchester
Storey & Co., Messrs., Manchester
Lewis, Williams & Co., Messrs., Manchester
Taylor, Mr. J., Manchester
Hardy, G. H. & Son, Messrs., Manchester
Gregson, Mr. James, Manchester
Dodd, Mr. Nathaniel, Manchester
Holt, Mr. J., Manchester
Johnson, T. & Co., Messrs., Manchester
Heywood, Mr. J., Manchester
Bazley & Co., Messrs., Manchester
Dodgshon, Mr. Edmund, Manchester
Griffiths, Mr. T., Manchester
Boddington & Hart, Messrs., Manchester
Newton & Co., Messrs., Manchester
Crook, Mr. H., Manchester
O'Neil, W. & J., Messrs., Manchester
Greatorex Bros., Messrs., Manchester
Blair, Mr. J. H., Manchester
Chadwick, Robert, Finisher, &c., Hulme Street, Oxford Road, Manchester
Politaihi, H., Finisher, Oxford Road, Manchester
Fryer, Benson & Foster, Sugar Refiners, Oxford Road, Manchester
McCreadie, Jno., York Street Saw Mills, Charles Street, Oxford Road, Manchester
Tysoe & Hope, Messrs., Salford
Worral, J. & J. M., Messrs., Salford
Harvey & Sons, Messrs., Salford
Hall, Poole & Co., Messrs., Salford
Briggs, Mr. F., Salford
Clayton, Mr. G. R., Salford
Foster, Mr. J., Salford
Silitoe & Seares, Messrs., Salford
Dewhirst, Samuel & Co., Messrs., Salford
Goodier, Mr. J., Salford
Holdsworth & Gibb, Messrs., Eccles
Evans & Syddal, Messrs., Eccles
Ermen & Engels, Messrs., Eccles
Moore and Waddington, Messrs., Patricroft
Bagley and Co., Messrs., Patricroft
Hyde, R. and Co., Messrs., Stalybridge
Platt, Mr. Robert, Stalybridge
Erman, Mr. G., Pendlebury
Knowles and Son, Messrs., Pendlebury
Bower, Mr. Major, Pendlebury
Vickers, Mr. T., Newton Heath

Baxter, J. and Sons, Messrs., Hollinwood
Buckley, W. and Sons, Messrs., Hollinwood
Windsor Mill Co., Hollinwood
Grimshaw, Mr. J. H., Gorton
Buckley and Sons, Messrs., Gorton
Ashton Bros., Messrs., Hyde
Andrew and Sons, Messrs., Harpurhey
Rixson, J., Waste Manufacturer, Tottington Road, Bury
Dickenson and Co., Messrs., Middleton
Waterside Mill Co., Ashton
Wilkinson and Constantine, Droylsden
Walker, Mr. Robert, Droylsden
Hardy, Nathan and Son, Messrs., Failsworth
Kershaw, Leese and Co., Messrs., Stockport
Ashton, Bros., Messrs., Stockport
Ashworth, Bros., Messrs., Todmorden
Clemenson and Co., Messrs., Dukinfield
Radcliffe, Samuel and Sons, Rochdale
Radcliffe, Samuel and Sons, Oldham
Lees, Mr. G. H., Oldham
Lees, H. and J. W., Messrs., Oldham
Leese and Wrigley, Messrs., Oldham
Broadbent and Sons, Messrs., Oldham
Greaves, Mr. Hilton, Oldham
Sun Mill Company, Oldham
Jones and Sons, Messrs., Bolton
Wainwright and Hardcastle, Bolton
Briercliffe, Mr. R., Farnworth
Topp and Hindley, Messrs., Farnworth
Briggs, Mr. R., Burnley
Cooke, Williams and Co., Messrs., Warrington
Walker and Sons, Messrs., Warrington
Lees, Mr. J. H., Warrington
Bulcock, Mr. A., Clitheroe
Holden, Mr. F., Clitheroe
Seville, S. and E., Messrs., Lees and Mossley
Hall, Rowland, Huddersfield
Rhodes, Mr. James, Hey, near Lees
Almond Iron Works, Linlithgow
Ross, Alex. and Co., Messrs., Glasgow
Boddington and Co., Messrs., Burton-on-Trent
Vipond, J. and Co., Messrs., Pontypool
Stott, J. and A., Flixton
Stott, J. and A., Manufacturers, Urmston
Ainsworth, Thomas, Cleator Mill, Whitehaven
Cleator Iron Ore Co., Cleator, near Carnforth, etc., etc.

In ordering, please send length of Bars required, and diameter of Flue.

RECENT TESTIMONIAL.

From H. R. WILLIAMS & CO.,
The Lime Street Warehouses, Lime Street, London, *January 10th*, 1877.

Memo.

Gentlemen,

We are glad to report that the Fire Bars you sent us are very satisfactory, and beg to enclose our cheque for the account, which please return in course of post duly receipted. We shall be glad to receive two more sets of the same dimensions at your early convenience.

THE BUNSEN BURNER FIRE BARS

PRICES.

For Small Furnace Boilers, such as Bakers' Ovens, Hot Hearth Purposes, etc.

Length	Width	Price	Length	Width	Price
12 inches	18 inches	£0 16 0	15 inches	24 inches	£1 2 0
12 ,,	21 ,,	0 18 0	18 ,,	21 ,,	1 4 0
12 ,,	24 ,,	1 0 0	18 ,,	24 ,,	1 10 0
15 ,,	18 ,,	0 18 0	24 ,,	24 ,,	2 0 0
15 ,,	21 ,,	1 0 0			

For Furnaces, the following Widths and Lengths:—

Length	Width	Price	Length	Width	Price
36 inches	24 inches	£2 11 6	60 inches	32 inches	£6 6 0
36 ,,	27 ,,	2 18 0	60 ,,	36 ,,	6 10 0
36 ,,	30 ,,	3 5 0	66 ,,	24 ,,	4 15 0
36 ,,	33 ,,	3 11 0	66 ,,	27 ,,	5 5 0
42 ,,	24 ,,	2 15 0	66 ,,	30 ,,	5 10 0
42 ,,	27 ,,	3 2 6	66 ,,	36 ,,	6 10 0
42 ,,	30 ,,	3 7 0	72 ,,	24 ,,	5 3 0
42 ,,	33 ,,	3 11 6	72 ,,	27 ,,	5 16 0
42 ,,	36 ,,	3 18 0	72 ,,	30 ,,	6 10 0
48 ,,	24 ,,	3 0 0	72 ,,	33 ,,	7 2 0
48 ,,	27 ,,	3 9 0	72 ,,	36 ,,	7 14 6
48 ,,	30 ,,	3 18 9	72 ,,	39 ,,	8 7 0
48 ,,	33 ,,	4 7 6	72 ,,	42 ,,	8 17 0
48 ,,	36 ,,	4 17 0	84 ,,	24 ,,	6 15 0
54 ,,	24 ,,	3 5 0	84 ,,	27 ,,	7 10 0
54 ,,	27 ,,	3 15 0	84 ,,	30 ,,	8 5 0
54 ,,	30 ,,	4 5 0	84 ,,	33 ,,	9 2 6
54 ,,	32 ,,	4 13 0	84 ,,	36 ,,	9 17 6
54 ,,	36 ,,	5 5 0	84 ,,	39 ,,	10 2 6
60 ,,	27 ,,	4 1 6	84 ,,	42 ,,	10 17 6
60 ,,	30 ,,	4 14 0			

OTHER PRICES IN PROPORTION.

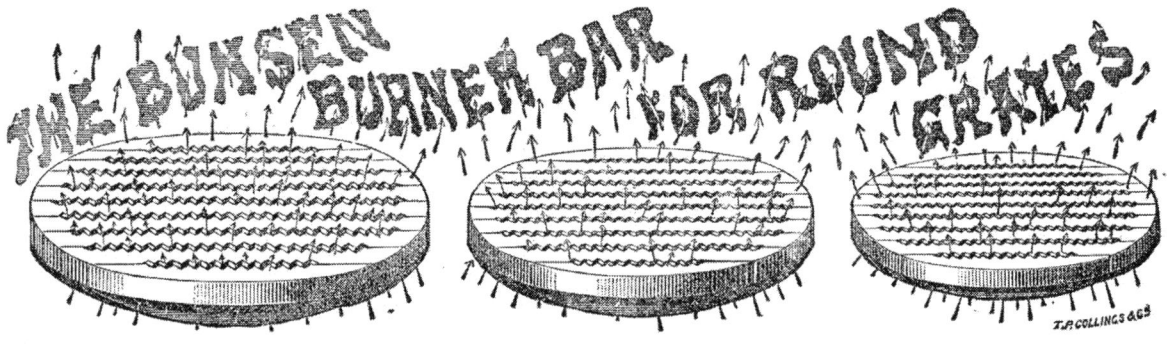

CIRCULAR BARS.

2 ft. 0 in. in diam., per set, £1 12 6	3 ft. 3 in. in diam., per set, £3 2 0	4 ft. 0 in. in diam., per set, £5 12 0
2 ,, 3 ,, ,, ,, 2 0 0	3 ,, 6 ,, ,, ,, 3 17 6	4 ,, 3 ,, ,, ,, 6 15 0
2 ,, 6 ,, ,, ,, 2 8 0	3 ,, 9 ,, ,, ,, 4 13 0	4 ,, 6 ,, ,, ,, 8 5 0
2 ,, 9 ,, ,, ,, 2 15 6		

BAILEY'S GALVANIZED MACHINE-MADE WIRE NETTING,

GALVANIZED AFTER MADE;

Rolled and Drawn Wire, Wire Nails, Wire Netting and Wire Rope,
OF EVERY VARIETY.

1½-inch Mesh Wire Game Netting,
Made any width up to 4 feet.

1⅝-inch Mesh Wire Netting,
Made any width up to 6 feet.

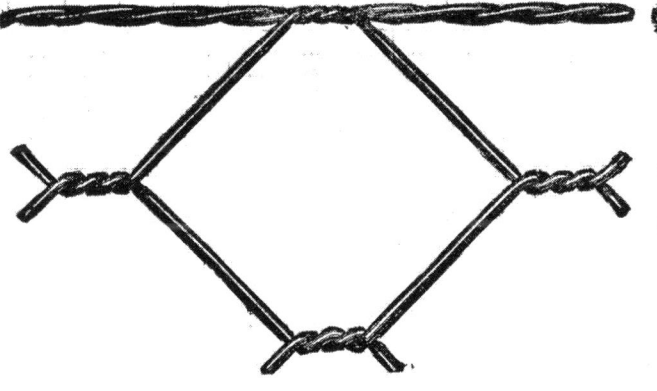

This Mesh is suitable for small Rabbits, Poultry and Game generally.

This Mesh is most in use as a Game Netting for Rabbits, Hares, etc.

2-inch Mesh Wire Netting.
Made any width up to 6 feet.

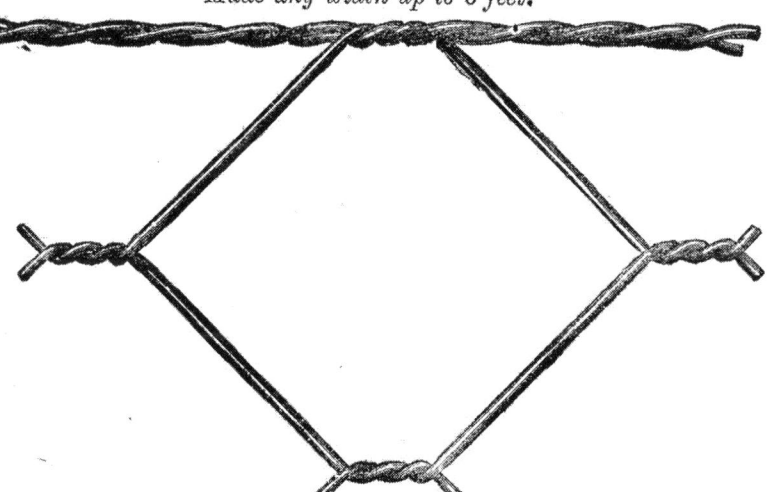

Suitable for larger Game.

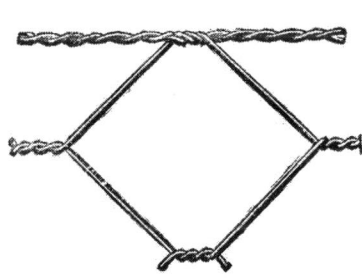

PRICES.

Gauge	Galvanized 1½ 24 inches wide	Galvanized 1⅝ 24 inches wide	Galvanized 2 24 inches wide
	d.	d.	d.
No. 16	9	7	7 per yard.
,, 17	7	5¼	5½ ,,
,, 18	5½	5	4¼ ,,
,, 19	5	4	3½ ,,

Other widths at proportionate prices.

Low Quotations given to large Buyers of Galvanized Iron Wire for Fencing Bolts, etc. Special Quotations to specifications from Managers of Estates, etc.

Length under Head

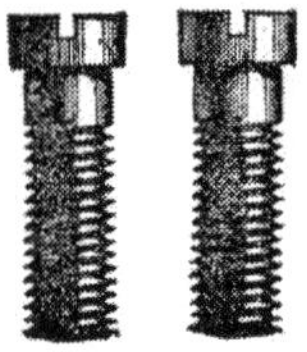

CHEESE-HEADED SET SCREWS. Price per Doz.

Diameter	Size of Head	3/4 in.	7/8 in.	1 in.	1 1/8 in.	1 1/4 in.	1 1/2 in.	1 3/4 in.	2 in.	2 1/4 in.	2 1/2 in.	2 3/4 in.	3 in.
5/16 in.	7/16 in. diameter, 1/4 in. deep	1/10	2/0	2/2	2/4	2/8	3/0	...	...	...	...	...	...
3/8 in.	1/2 in. ,, 5/16 in. ,,	2/2	2/4	2/6	2/8	2/10	3/2	3/6	...	...	...	...	...
1/2 in.	5/8 in. ,, 5/16 in. ,,	2/6	2/8	3/0	3/3	3/6	4/0	4/6	5/0	5/6	...	...	...
5/8 in.	7/8 in. ,, 7/16 in. ,,	...	...	4/4	4/6	4/8	5/0	5/4	5/9	6/3	6/9	7/3	...
3/4 in.	1 in. ,, 1/2 in. ,,	...	...	...	...	5/0	5/4	5/8	6/0	6/6	7/0	7/6	8/0

COUNTERSUNK OR CONE-HEADED SET SCREWS. Price per Doz.

Length over all

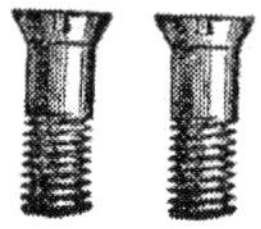

Diameter	Size of Head	3/4 in.	7/8 in.	1 in.	1 1/8 in.	1 1/4 in.	1 1/2 in.	1 3/4 in.	2 in.	2 1/4 in.	2 1/2 in.	2 3/4 in.	3 in.
1/4 in.	1/2 in. diameter, 3/16 in. deep	2/2	2/4	2/6	...	...	...	...	...	...	...	...	...
5/16 in.	9/16 in. ,, 3/16 in. ,,	2/2	2/4	2/6	...	...	...	...	...	...	...	...	...
3/8 in.	5/8 in. ,, 3/16 in. ,,	2/6	2/8	2/10	3/0	3/3	3/6	...	...	...	...	...	...
1/2 in.	13/16 in. ,, 1/4 in. ,,	2/8	2/10	3/2	3/6	4/0	4/6	5/0	...	...	...	...	...
5/8 in.	1 1/16 in. ,, 3/8 in. ,,	...	...	4/10	5/2	5/6	5/10	6/2	6/6	7/0	7/6	8/0	...
3/4 in.	1 1/8 in. ,, 3/8 in. ,,	...	...	...	...	6/0	6/4	6/9	7/2	7/8	8/2	8/8	9/2

BRIGHT TURNED STUDS. Price per Doz.

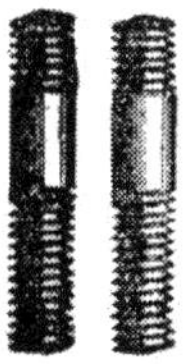

Length	2 in.	2 1/4 in.	2 1/2 in.	2 3/4 in.	3 in.	3 1/4 in.	3 1/2 in.	3 3/4 in.	4 in.	4 1/4 in.	4 1/2 in.	4 3/4 in.	5 in.	5 1/4 in.	5 1/2 in.	5 3/4 in.	6 in.
1/2 in. diameter	4/3	4/6	4/9	5/0	5/3	5/6	6/0	6/6	7/0	7/6	8/0	8/6	9/0	9/6	10/0	10/6	11/0
5/8 in. ,,	4/6	4/9	5/0	5/3	5/6	6/0	6/6	7/0	7/6	8/0	8/6	9/0	9/6	10/0	10/6	11/0	11/6
3/4 in. ,,	4/9	5/0	5/3	5/6	6/0	6/6	7/0	7/6	8/0	8/6	9/0	9/6	10/0	10/6	11/0	11/6	12/0
7/8 in. ,,	5/0	5/3	5/6	6/0	6/6	7/0	7/6	8/0	8/6	9/0	9/6	10/0	10/6	11/0	11/6	12/0	12/6
1 in. ,,	5/3	5/6	6/0	6/6	7/0	7/6	8/0	8/6	9/0	9/6	10/0	10/6	11/3	12/0	12/9	13/0	13/9

Length under Head

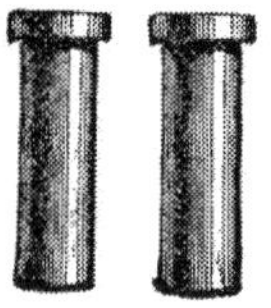

	1 in.
1/4 in. Diameter, 3/4 in. long ...	2/0
3/8 in. ,, 1 1/2 in. ,, ...	2/6
1/2 in. ,, 1 1/2 in. ,,	3/9

Oil Pins finished bright all over.

JOINT PINS MADE TO ORDER. Price per Doz.

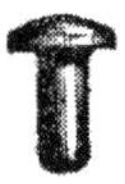

Shank	Collar	1 1/2 in.	1 3/4 in.	2 in	2 1/4 in.	2 1/2 in.	2 3/4 in.	3 in.	3 1/4 in.	3 1/2 in.	3 3/4 in.	4 in.
1/2 dia.	1 1/16	2/3	2/6	2/9	3/0	3/3	3/6	...	...	...	...	...
5/8 ,,	13/16	2/6	2/9	3/0	3/3	3/6	3/9	4/0	...	...	...	...
3/4 ,,	15/16	...	...	3/6	3/9	4/0	4/3	4/6	4/9	5/0	5/3	5/6
7/8 ,,	1 1/16	...	...	4/6	4/9	5/0	5/3	5/6	5/9	6/0	6/3	6/6
1 ,,	1 3/16	...	...	...	...	5/4	5/8	6/0	6/4	6/8	7/0	7/4

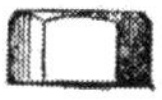

BRIGHT FINISHED HEXAGON NUTS. Price per Gross.

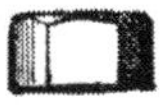

Made to Whitworth's standard gauges, both in the threads and across the flats; the outer surfaces are very true with the threads, the boring, tapping and facing being done at one setting.

	1/4 in.		3/8 in.		7/16 in.		1/2 in.		9/16 in.		5/8 in.		3/4 in.		7/8 in.		1 in.		1 1/8 in.		1 1/4 in.	
	Thick	Price	Thick	Price	Thick	Price	Thick	Price	Thick	Price	Thick	Price	Thick	Price	Thick	Price	Thick	Price	Thick	Price	Thick	Price
Ordinary Nut ...	...	...	3/8	17/0	7/16	18/6	1/2	20/6	9/16	23/6	5/8	25/6	3/4	35/6	7/8	47/0	1	61/0	1 1/8	82/6	1 1/4	100/0
Lock Nut ...	...	...	...	...	...	...	3/8	20/6	...	...	7/16	25/6	1/2	33/6	9/16	42/0	11/16	55/6	13/16	74/6	7/8	92/0
Deep Nut ...	...	...	...	...	...	...	5/8	24/0	11/16	28/0	13/32	31/0	15/16	43/0	1 1/16	55/0	1 1/4	74/0	1 3/8	96/0	1 1/2	118/0
Bright Washer ...	1/16	3/6	1/16	5/0	...	...	3/32	7/6	...	...	1/8	12/0	1/8	17/6	5/32	25/0	3/16	28/0	7/32	40/0	1/4	50/0

Length under Head

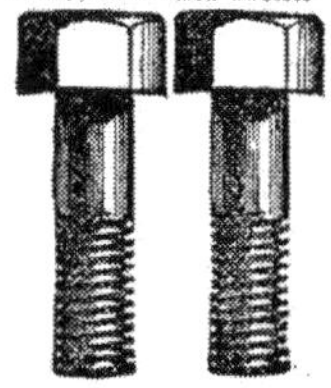

HEXAGON-HEADED SET SCREWS. Price per Doz.

	1 1/2 in.	1 3/4 in.	2 in.	2 1/4 in.	2 1/2 in.	2 3/4 in.	3 in.	3 1/4 in.	3 1/2 in.	3 3/4 in.	4 in.	4 1/4 in.	4 1/2 in.	4 3/4 in.	5 in.	5 1/4 in.	5 1/2 in.	5 3/4 in.	6 in.
1/2 in. dia.	5/6	5/7	5/8	5/9	5/10	5/11	6/0	6/2	6/4	6/6	...	...	...	...	...	...	...	...	...
5/8 in. ,,	...	...	7/6	7/8	7/10	8/0	8/2	8/4	8/6	8/8	8/10	...	...	...	...	...	...	...	...
3/4 in. ,,	...	...	11/4	11/6	11/8	11/10	12/0	12/2	12/4	12/6	12/8	12/10	13/0	13/3	13/6	...	...	...	...
7/8 in. ,,	...	...	15/0	15/2	15/4	15/6	15/8	15/10	16/0	16/2	16/4	16/6	16/8	16/10	17/0	17/3	17/6	17/9	18/0
1 in. ,,	...	...	20/0	20/3	20/6	20/9	21/0	21/3	21/6	21/9	22/0	22/3	22/6	22/9	23/0	23/4	23/8	24/0	24/4
1 1/8 in. ,,	...	...	25/0	25/4	25/8	26/0	26/4	26/8	27/0	27/4	27/8	28/0	28/4	28/8	29/0	29/4	29/8	30/0	30/4

Length under Head

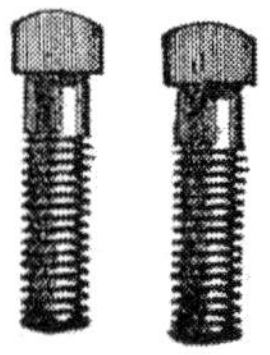

SQUARE-HEADED SET SCREWS. Price per Doz.

	5/8 in.	3/4 in.	7/8 in.	1 in.	1 1/8 in.	1 1/4 in.	1 3/8 in.	1 1/2 in.	1 5/8 in.	1 3/4 in.	1 7/8 in.	2 in.	2 1/4 in.	2 1/2 in.
5/16 in. diameter	1/8	1/9	1/11	2/1	2/3	2/5	2/7	2/9	2/11	3/1	...	...	...	...
3/8 in. ,, ...	...	2/0	2/2	2/4	2/6	2/8	2/10	3/0	3/2	3/4	3/6	...	...	...
1/2 in. ,, ...	...	2/4	2/6	2/8	2/10	3/0	3/2	3/4	3/6	3/8	4/0	4/6	5/0	5/6

The above, if with heads shaped to standard sizes,.........5/16 in. diameter, 9d ; 3/8 and 1/2-in. diameter, 1/- per dozen extra.

INGRAM & STAPFER'S

Dimensions of Base,
30 × 18,
Diameter of Friction Bowl,
6 in.
Diameter of Bearings,
6 in.

OIL-TESTING APPARATUS.

RAILWAY AND STEAM BOAT COMPANIES' PATTERN.
Price £20.
Ordinary Size,
£8 8s.

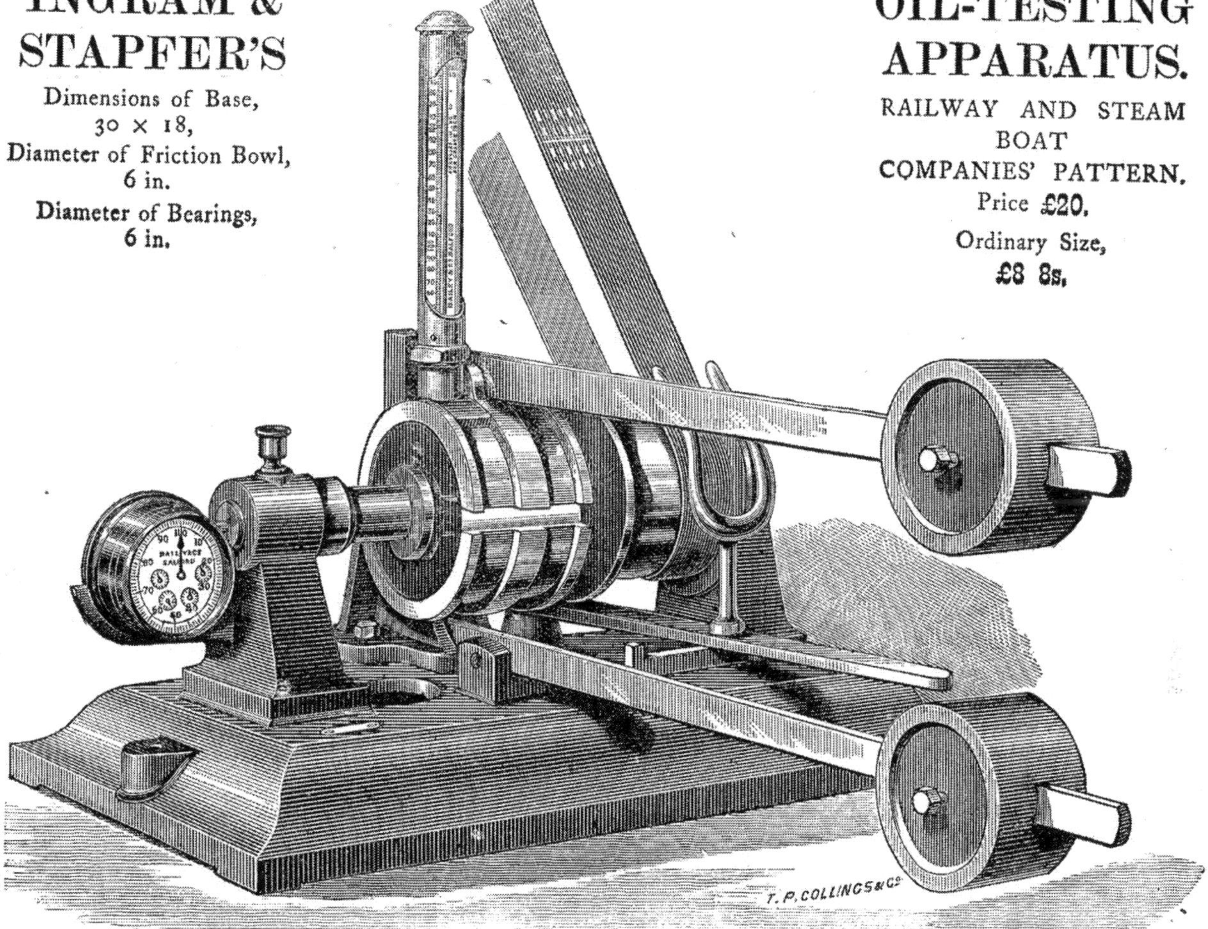

The illustration shows the arrangement of Ingram and Stapfer's Oil-Testing Apparatus, as manufactured by Messrs. W. H. Bailey and Co., of Salford. It consists simply of a shaft running in two brass bearings, which may be compressed to any desired extent by means of the weighted levers, as shown. The top bearing is fitted with a thermometer, and the shaft drives a counter, as shown, to indicate the number of revolutions made by the apparatus, the quality of the oil being tested by the number of revolutions made before a certain temperature is recorded by the thermometer. Testing different classes of lubricants with a view to ascertain how they are affected by atmospheric influences is effected by leaving the oil upon the apparatus for a certain time after the first run, and noting the results of a second experiment.

A further test is effected by removing the lower bearing, as shown in the annexed sketch, and allowing the shaft to run in a small reservoir containing a known quantity of oil, which after a given time is weighed, the deficiency indicating the loss of oil. Messrs. Bailey and Co. have, we believe, manufactured a large number of these Oil Testers of a smaller size. Of those of the type illustrated, which are adapted for testing grease as well as oils, the first was made for the railways of New South Wales, and the second for the Manchester, Sheffield and Lincolnshire Railway. The same firm are also, we are informed, employed in the manufacture of Professor Thurston's Apparatus for testing the strength of materials, one of which was exhibited in the Loan Collection of Scientific Apparatus at South Kensington. The first of these instruments was made by Messrs. Bailey for the College of Engineering in Yokohama, Japan.—*Extract from Examiner, January, 1877.*] For further particulars and descriptive matter, see pages 87 and 88 of this Book.

PATENT AMERICAN

The dough having been reduced to condition by the Breaking-down Rollers, it is brought to this Machine and placed on the feeding table. The rollers, which act as the thicknessing rollers, are first adjusted to the size required for the biscuits; the dough then passes through them to the endless Canvas Belt on which it travels, and is brought by the simple action of the Machine under the Cutters

BISCUIT MACHINE

and Dockers. At every rise of the latter, a fresh part of the sheet of dough is brought forward, and at the down stroke is cut into the required form. The biscuits thus formed, docked and impressed, are carried forward, transferred to the baking tins, and pass to the oven. These Machines can be fitted with any form of cutter, but, at the prices quoted, are fitted with a set of 3-inch Lunch Cutters.

Patent American Biscuit Machine—Hand Power, £55; Steam Power, £88.
CUTTERS ADAPTED TO THESE MACHINES EXTRA.

	Steam.	Hand.			Steam.	Hand.
5-inch Circular Cutters and Dockers (Ship)	£11 10	£9 8	Pic-Nic	...	£18 14	£14 6
4-inch " " (Large Lunch)	13 4	10 9	Fancy	...	26 8	20 14
3-inch " " (Lunch)	14 6	12 6	Cracknel	...		

THURSTON'S PATENT OIL TESTER

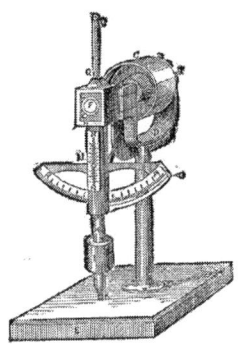

Price £8 10s. Each.

The following is the method adopted in conducting tests upon the Machine for Testing Lubricants:—

A certain quantity of the unguent is dropped upon the journal of the Machine, and spread evenly over its surface. The two cams being turned so as to throw the brasses apart, the pendulum is carefully lipped over the journal, care being taken not to rub off any of the oil. The cams are then thrown out of bearing, and the spiral spring is compressed to the desired tension, as indicated upon the scale. The nut and washer on the end of the spindle being put in place, the Machine is ready for use. Care must be taken that the washer mentioned above does not bear against the brasses of the pendulum, so as to cause friction, since this would affect the readings. The temperature indicated by the thermometer should be noted before starting; at the end of one minute after starting, the temperature and the reading of the scale upon the half-circle are taken. These readings of the thermometer scale are then taken at the end of every two minutes. The spindle is allowed to run until the bearing becomes dry or gummed, or heated to 300°. If the pendulum is oscillating when a reading is to be taken, it may be steadied by a touch of the hand.

In order to get the same weight of oil at each test, twenty drops of the oil are weighed out by being dropped upon the scale-pan from a brass pipette having a hole of about $\frac{1}{32}$ inch in diameter—thus the weight of one drop being known, drops enough to make the standard weight are put in the journal at each trial.

The weight generally used is 332 milligrammes, or about 5 grains avordupois. This quantity has been found to give the right amount of lubrication for most cases with the Institute Machine. After the close of a trial, the journal and brasses are wiped clean and cooled to the temperature of the air. Care must be taken, if water is used, to cool the heated parts, to wipe out any which may have worked in around the thermometer, or may have entered between the thermometer and the spindle; for if this is left, the formation of steam will prevent a correct indication of the rise in temperature. The scale upon the half-circle is the scale of values in inch-pounds of the total friction for different angles at which the pendulum may hang. The moment of the weight of the pendulum, measured by a balance attached to the centre of the bob, multiplied by the distance from the centre of the bob to the centre of the spindle, when the pendulum is in a horizontal position, is evidently equal to the product of the force of the friction into the radius of the journal when the friction is sufficient to maintain the pendulum in the given position. The Machine is so adjusted that this product is equal to forty inch-pounds. To make this adjustment, fix upon the distance of the centre of the bob from the centre of the spindle, and increase or diminish the weight of the bob to make the moment correct. Thus, in the Institute Machine, the distance of the centre of the bob from that of the spindle was set at (*ten* inches, then $40 \times \frac{1}{8}$ inches, the radius of the journal) was equal to X, or the weight $\times 10$; hence X, the weight must equal $2\frac{1}{2}$ pounds, and the bob was turned down until the pendulum, in a horizontal position, weighed $2\frac{1}{2}$ pounds hung from the centre of the bob.

The Index Plate has two scales, the right hand one being the pressure per square inch upon the pound. The left hand one is the total pressure upon the journal, due to both the weight of the pendulum and the pressure of the spring. The reading of the scale on the half-circle, or "arc," divided by the reading on the left hand side of the Index Plate, gives the co-efficient of the length of time the test continues.

The capacity for reducing heating of the journal is shown by a comparison of the readings of the thermometer and the time records.

JUDGE'S REPORT OF THE AMERICAN INSTITUTE.

We find that the machine does all that is claimed for it, and is a great improvement over similar machines previously used for testing lubricants, in that it records, at the same time, the power of any lubricant to resist pressure, the co-efficient of friction, the pressure per square inch of journal, and the temperature of the same at any instant.

We therefore recommend the highest award allowable by the Rules of the Institute,

"THE SILVER MEDAL."

We are, however, of the opinion that the machine merits a higher award.

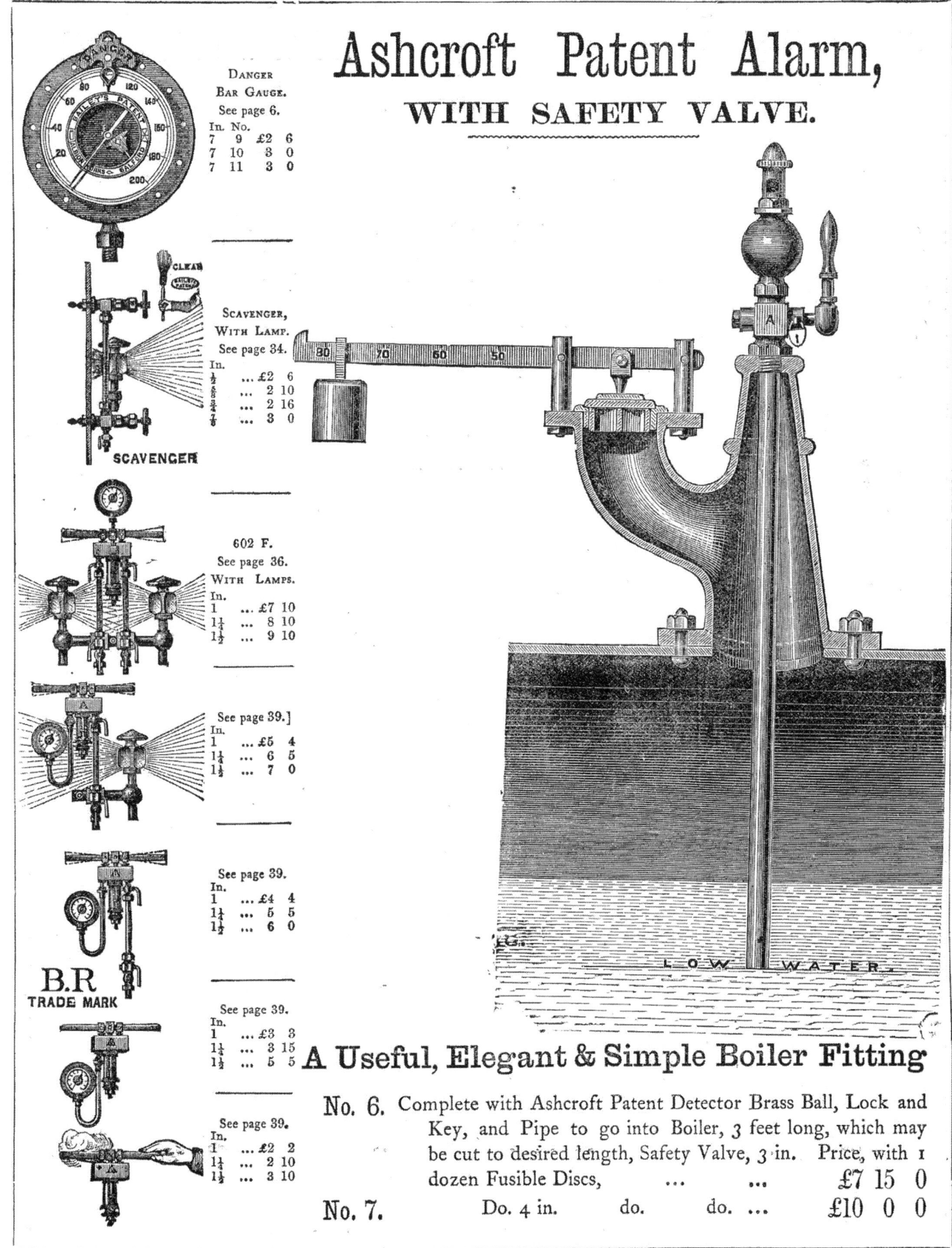

Ashcroft Patent Alarm,
WITH SAFETY VALVE.

DANGER BAR GAUGE.
See page 6.

In.	No.		
7	9	£2	6
7	10	3	0
7	11	3	0

SCAVENGER, WITH LAMP.
See page 34.

In.		
½	...£2	6
⅝	... 2	10
¾	... 2	16
⅞	... 3	0

602 F.
See page 36.
WITH LAMPS.

In.		
1	...£7	10
1¼	... 8	10
1½	... 9	10

See page 39.]

In.		
1	...£5	4
1¼	... 6	5
1½	... 7	0

See page 39.

In.		
1	...£4	4
1¼	... 5	5
1½	... 6	0

See page 39.

In.		
1	...£3	3
1¼	... 3	15
1½	... 5	5

See page 39.

In.		
1	...£2	2
1¼	... 2	10
1½	... 3	10

A Useful, Elegant & Simple Boiler Fitting

No. 6. Complete with Ashcroft Patent Detector Brass Ball, Lock and Key, and Pipe to go into Boiler, 3 feet long, which may be cut to desired length, Safety Valve, 3 in. Price, with 1 dozen Fusible Discs, ... £7 15 0

No. 7. Do. 4 in. do. do. ... £10 0 0

BAILEY'S PATENT TALLY OR COUNTER,

FOR

Corn, Coal, Wool, and other Factors,

With 4in. Dial, Price 25s.

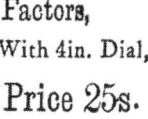

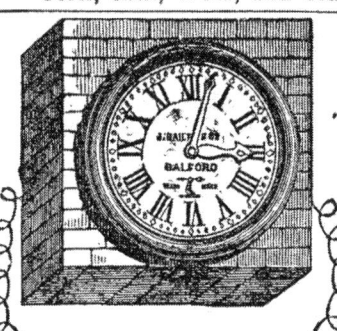

BAILEY'S PATENT WELL INDICATORS

FOR

WATER IN Tanks, Reservoirs, Wells, Rivers, &c.,

£5 5s.

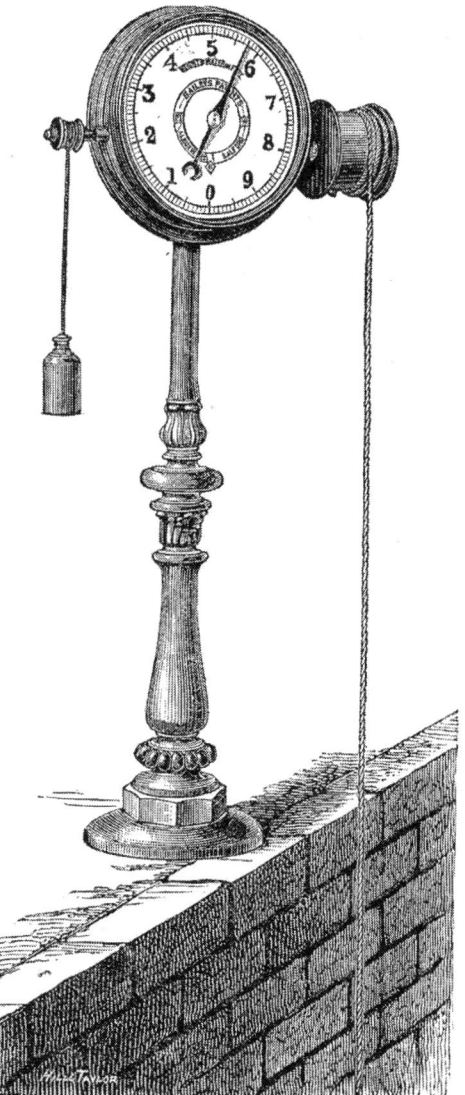

BAILEY'S SYMPATHETIC DIALS.

It will be seen that by simply winding one Clock all the others are kept in unison with it, rendering the system of great value in large Mansions, Town Halls, Railway Stations, &c.

Price of Prime Movers or Regulators, with self-acting maintaining power:—

A quality, in Mahogany case £10

B do. similar movement, not quite so highly finished £8

Prices for large Dials will be sent on application.

Where the distance is great we use galvanized Iron Wire, at 10s. or 12s. per 100 yds.

The Leclanché Battery is used, the number of cells varying with the number and situation of the Dials.

Sympathetic Dials for Internal Use.

No. 1 ... 7 in. in diam. for office use, bracket pattern ... £2 10 0
„ 2 ... 12 in. in diam. round heads 3 3 0
„ 3 ... 14 „ „ „ 4 10 0

Sympathetic Dials for External Use.

Gold Figures and Blue Ground of Iron, ready for bolting to Wall or Tower.

No. 4 ... 18 in. £6 10 0
„ 5 ... 24 „ 8 10 0
„ 6 ... 36 „ 10 0 0

☞ Batteries according to distance and number of Dials. Insulated Wire, 2d. per yard. Estimates for materials on receipt of details and rough plan of the building.

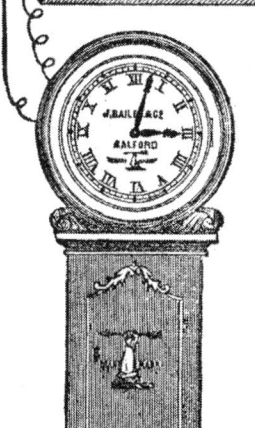

PARKINS' PATENT SIGNAL BELL AND INDICATOR,

OR

Combined Audible & Visible Signal

With 6in. Bell ... 20s. ⎫ Indicator 15s.
„ 8 „ „ ... 27s. 6d. ⎪ „ 15s.
„ 10 „ „ ... 40s. ⎬ „ 18s.
„ 12 „ „ ... 50s. ⎪ „ 18s.
„ 18 „ „ ...100s. ⎭ „ 20s.

SPRINGS.

14lb. Springs ... 1s. 9d. each.
28lb. „ ... 3s. 6d. „
36lb. „ ... 4s. 0d. „

Small Springs, to work Bell only, 6d. each.

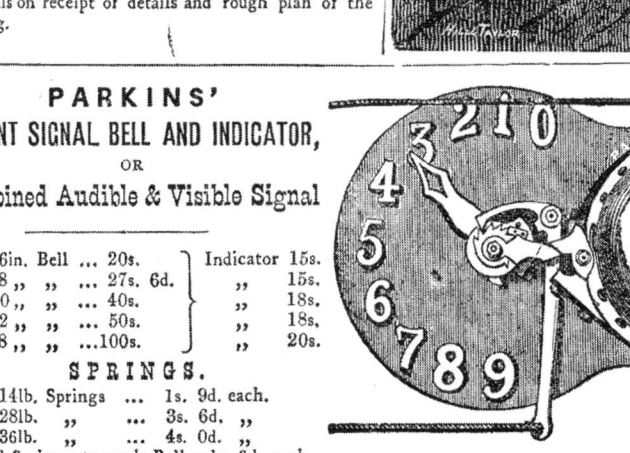

Telegraph Department.

Insulators, Shackles, &c.

Trade Mark, "PERFECT TEST."

W. H. BAILEY & Co. have upwards of 70 different forms of Insulators and Shackles, and Fittings belonging to them, and adopt as far as possible one uniform Gauge for Arms, Bolts, Pins, Brackets, Straps, &c., having been guided by the requirements of the Chief Engineers to the Postal Telegraph Department, and the Railway Companies. Any pattern forwarded to them will meet with careful attention, and they will quote a price for the same in their special White Porcelain, or in Brown Ware, in which their own Insulators, &c., are made.

The Prices quoted below are for leading qualities only.

Every Insulator is tested and labelled with W. H. B. & Co.'s Trade Mark, "Perfect Test."

No. of Article		£	s.	d.
60	Bailey's Special Double Insulator, in compressed White Porcelain or Brown Ware, with ½ in. galvanized iron pin, 1/- each; 10/- per doz.; per 1,000 ...	37	0	0
61	Small X, with ½ in. galvanized iron pin, 7d. each; 6/6 per doz.; per 1,000	25	0	0
62	Varley's No. 8, with ⅝ in. galvanized iron pin, 1/6 each; 15/- per doz.; per 1,000 ...	42	0	0
63	Varley's No. 11, with ½ in. galvanized iron pin, 1/- each; 10/- per doz.; per 1,000 ...	37	0	0
63A	Ebonite, with ½ in. galvanized iron pin, 1/9 each; 18/- per doz.; per 1,000	62	10	0
64	Double Bell Shackle, with galvanized iron straps and bolts, single fitting, 1/6 each; 15/- per doz.; per 1,000 ...	50	0	0
65	Ditto, ditto, double fitting, 2/6 each; 1/7/0 per doz.; per 1,000	95	0	0
66	Real Shackle ditto, single fitting, 1/3 each; 12/- per doz.; per 1,000	42	0	0
67	Ditto, ditto, double fitting, 2/- each; 1/2/0 per doz.; per 1,000	80	0	0
68	Galvanized Iron Roofs, 12 × 8, punched, 4d. each; 3/6 per doz.; per 1,000	12	0	0
69	Single Shackles for terminal work, with large galvanized iron spike or bolt, Bell, 2/6 each; 1/7/0 per doz.; per 1,000 ...	95	0	0
70	Ditto, ditto, Reel; 2/- each; 1/2/0 per doz.; per 1,000	80	0	0

Insulators and Shackles, designed or manufactured to the order of Inventors or Proprietors, can be inserted in this list under a special number. Terms upon application.

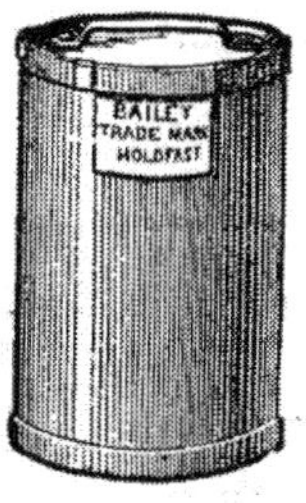

71—BAILEY'S "Holdfast" Insulator Bolt Cement. *Entirely free from sulphurous compounds;* is tough and elastic, and dries hard, and only requires a moderate heat to prepare it for use. An order for a single Cask is solicited. Those who once try it, will use no other. The cases being airtight, it will not spoil by being kept in stock.

	£	s.	d.
Sample, in 28 lb. case, ...	0	9	0
In 1 cwt. metal case, ...	1	10	0
In 2 cwt. metal case, ...	3	0	0

Telegraph Tools, &c.

No. of Article.		£	s.	d.
72	Iron Telegraph Vice and Stretcher 5 inches, ... each,	1	2	0
73	Ditto, ditto, 5½ in. ,,	1	4	0
74	Steel ditto, ,,	1	8	0
75	Wrought Keys to suit above, each		2	8
76	Drawing Tongs, 7 in. ,,		6	0
77	Ditto, Steel (Dutch pattern) ,,		9	9
78	Cutting Pliers, 5 in. per doz.	1	4	0
79	Ditto, Extra strong, 8 in. ,,	2	14	0
80	BAILEY'S TELEGRAPH TOOL CHEST, containing 2 Hammers, 2 Files, Spade, Pick, 2 Saws, Tar Pot and Brush, 2 Chisels, Mallet, Fire Pot, 2 Soldering Irons, Spirit Lamp, Gimblets (2), Auger, Hand - Vice, 2 Screw-Drivers, Drawing Knife, Spokeshave, Square, Battery Can, Syringe, &c.	5	5	0

Galvanized Iron Wire and Insulated Wire.

Galvanized Iron Telegraph Wire, charcoal annealed.

	B.W.G. No. 8.	B.W.G. No. 9.	B.W.G. No. 10.	B.W.G. No. 12.	B.W.G. No. 16.
81—Per 100 yards.	0 10 0	0 8 0	0 6 6	0 5 0	0 3 0
82—Per cwt.	1 10 0	1 15 0	1 18 0	2 0 0	2 5 0

		£	s.	d.
83	Gutta Percha Covered Connecting Wire, 2d. per yard; per mile	12	10	0
84	India Rubber covered and taped, for Electric Bells, 2d. per yard; per mile	12	10	0
85	Patent Caoutchouc Covered Wire, for leading in and out-door work, 6d. per yard; per mile	40	0	0
86	Ditto do. for Colliery and Pit Signals, and subterranean work, 9d. per yard; per mile	58	0	0

87—Special quotations will be sent for BAILEY'S SELECTED TELEGRAPH LINE WIRE, killed, tested and prepared according to the Postmaster-General's specification.

Upwards of thirty different descriptions of Insulated Wire can be inspected in our Telegraph Department.

Silk and Cotton Covered Wire

Per lb.

88—Silk Covered,

No.	12	14	16	18	20	22		
	6/-	6/6	7/-	7/6	8/-	8/6		
	24	26	28	30	32	34	35	36
	9/-	9/6	10/-	10/6	12/-	13/-	15/-	16/-
	37	38	39	40	41	42/-	43	
	17/6	20/-	22/-	24/-	30/-	36/-	42/-	

89—Cotton Covered,

No.	12	14	16	18	20	22			
	3/-	3/6	3/9	4/-	4/6	5/-			
	24	26	28	30	32	34	35	36	37
	5/6	6/-	6/6	7/-	7/6	8/-	8/6	9/-	9/6
	38	39	40	41	42	43			
	10/-	10/6	12/-	14/-	16/-	18/-			

Special Prices quoted for quantities above £10 in value.

W. H. B. & Co. guarantee that the Copper from which the wire is drawn is of 95 o/o minimum conductivity, and that the Insulation is well maintained. As it is to the interest of all scientific men that the copper wire used in electrical instruments shall be of the best quality, there should be general co-operation to discourarge, as much as possible, the use of inferior copper.

ADDRESS—

W. H. BAILEY & CO.,

ELECTRIC TELEGRAPH ENGINEERS,

ALBION WORKS,

ESSEX STREET, SALFORD,

LANCASHIRE.

90—W. H. BAILEY & Co.'s *Estimate for Materials* FOR A PRIVATE TELEGRAPH FOR THE COLONIES, &c., FOR ONE MILE COMPLETE, Poles not included, but *including requisite tools:—*

	£	s.	d.
1 Mile Best Selected Galvanized Iron Wire, No. 8	6	0	0
2 Single Terminal Shackles ...	0	5	0
30 Bailey's White Porcelain Insulators, with Galvanized Iron Bracket and Screws ...	3	0	0
30 Galvanized Iron Pole Caps and Nails		12	0
50 yards Insulated Copper Wire ...	1	5	0
Solder		2	0
No. 16 Binding Wire		2	0
	11	6	0
Telegraph Tool Chest, containing the articles enumerated in quotation 80, and also 1 pair Pliers, Vice, Stretcher and Key	6	14	0
Case containing Two Sets BAILEY'S A B C Telegraph, with Bells and Batteries complete. (See quotation No. 3)	20	0	0
	38	0	0
91—Ditto, for 2 miles, Tools and Apparatus...	50	0	0
92—Ditto, for 5 miles, ...	84	0	0
93—Ditto, ,, 10 ,, ...	140	0	0

TO OUR FOREIGN AND COLONIAL FRIENDS we shall be glad to make our services available for the engagement of Telegraph men and clerks, thoroughly competent to fix or work both line and apparatus.

W. H. BAILEY & Co. will send full Instructions to all purchasers to enable them to fix.

Batteries.

		£	s.	d.
94	Smee's Battery, pints 7/6; quarts		10	0
95	Set of Six in Vulcanite Cells and Mahogany Trough ...	5	0	0
96	Grove's Platinum Battery ...		12	0
97	Set of Ten in a Tray ...	6	0	0
98	Bunsen Batteries, 4in., 5/-; 6in., 7/-; 9in., 10/6; 12in. ...		12	6
99	Improved Sulphate of Lead Battery, to last twelve months, per cell	4	0	0

[This must not be confounded with the ordinary Sulphate of Lead Battery, which soon clogs up and is practically useless.]

100—Bailey's Leclanché Manganese Battery. [For prices, see Illustration.]

101—Bailey's Prepared Battery Charge for Leclanché Batteries, in boxes, per doz. 5 0

102—Daniel and Muirhead Batteries made specially to order.

Miscellaneous.

		£	s.	d.
103	Binding Screws and Terminals, see Illustrated Price List.			
104	Sulphate of Lead, ... per lb.		0	9
105	Bichromate of Potash ,,		1	6
106	Sulphate of Mercury, per oz.		0	9
107	Sea Salt, per lb.		0	3
108	Porous cells, per inch.			
109	Zinc Rods, Plates, &c., pure ... ... per lb		2	0
110	Platinized Silver, per oz. Troy		10	0
111	Platinum Foil or Wire ,,	1	12	0
112	Gutta Percha Tissue, 24in. wide, ... per yard		2	6

113—Porous Slabs, Stoneware Cells and Troughs, Nitric and Sulphuric Acid, Mercury, Sulphate of Copper, etc., at Market Prices. Special quotations for large quantities.

Clock Department—Additional Matter, see pages 195 to 206.
Patronized by the British and Foreign Government Departments.

BAILEY'S DOUBLE DIAL
Railway Station, Barracks, Workshop, Mechanic's Institute, or School Timepiece.

The Dial outside is complete with dial motion and coupling ready for any thickness of wall.

The figures are cast on Dial, and are gilded. The rim is o.g., the background blue or chocolate.

In ordering please state thickness of wall, and sufficient ¼-inch rod will be sent to couple up.

The inside Dial is 14 inches The weights and pendulum and works are all complete in case.

With 2 feet outside Dial, £20.
18-inch outside Dial, £17.
14-inch outside Dial, £14.

The 14-inch Dial, being small, has a glass over it to protect the hands.

BAILEY'S ENGLISH-MAKE HIGH-CLASS
8-DAYS' MANTEL-SHELF STRIKING CLOCK,

With 8-inch White Enamel Dial, and French Polished Case.

THE HOURS ARE STRUCK ON A GONG.

This Clock is suitable for a first-class Office, good Dining-room, or Board-room of a Company.

EXTRACTS FROM TESTIMONY.

Price, £8 8s. 0d.

Testimonial from J. B. Morrison, Esq.

MURIE HOUSE, PERTHSHIRE,
Memo. December 20, 1876.

The Turret Clock is a very great success, and I shall have much pleasure in recommending your firm to a friend who wishes to put one up.

BAILEY'S
"BARONIAL PATTERN"
(TRADE MARK)
ENTRANCE HALL AND DINING ROOM CLOCK.

BLACK AND GOLD AND ORMOLU MOUNTINGS;

18 Inches High,
16 Inches Wide,
9½ Inches Deep.

The Circles are Engraved and Silvered.

STRIKES HOURS ON CATHEDRAL TONE GONG;

CHIMES THE QUARTERS on BELLS In imitation of the Bells of the Houses of Parliament, Westminster.

The Ornaments on Dial are Chased and Gilt.

The whole Workmanship of the best class Old English Workmanship,

£35 0s. 0d.

We beg to call special attention to our Stable Clocks, not to Strike, with Blue and Gold Dials, Two feet Diameter, ready for fixing, which can be done by any joiner.

Value £15 Each.
SEE TURRET CLOCKS.

Automatic Horse Feeder, Damper, Closer, or Gas Turn Cock, &c.

COTTRELL'S PATENT CLOCK,

FOREIGN MANUFACTURE.

W. H. BAILEY & CO., Sole Agents.

TIME DROP ATTACHMENT FOR ALARM CLOCKS.

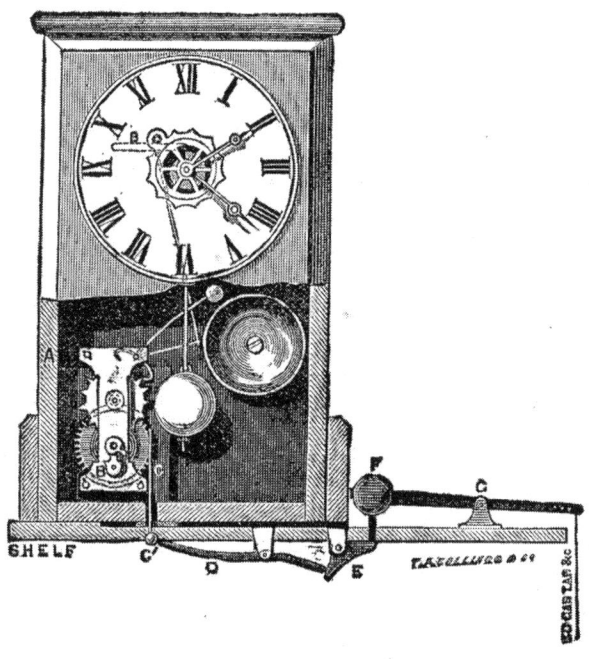

This is an ingenious device connected with ordinary clock mechanism, which may be attached to the door of a furnace to turn on the draft; with the faucet of a water pipe, to turn off or on the water; or with the valve of a gas pipe, to turn off the gas at any time; say, in Dwelling-houses at twelve o'clock, or any given time every night, and thus save the leakage in Mills: it can turn off the gas every night at six o'clock, and thus save a great amount, and do it in a more regular manner than a careless attendant. Horses should be fed early by means of a swivel trap door, a "feed" may be placed in position, and upset, say at five o'clock, thus giving the horse time to digest before the work begins. A rod, C, passes through the bottom of the case of the clock, and has a loop formed upon its upper end, to enable it to be hung upon the teeth of the wheel of the alarm mechanism, B. To the lower end of the loop rod, C, is pivoted the end of a lever, D, which is pivoted to the bottom of the clock, A, when said lever, E, rises into a horizontal position, so that it may receive and hold any object hung upon it. With this construction, as soon as the alarm mechanism starts, the loop rod, C, will drop, which withdraws the end of the lever, D, from the arm of the angle lever, E, so that the object hung upon or from its other arm may drop. In case it is not wished to sound an alarm when the alarm mechanism, B, starts, the bell, or hammer, or both, may be detached. The lower end of the loop rod is provided with a handle, for convenience in hanging it upon a wheel of the alarm mechanism. The object, in falling, may release a weight which performs the required operation.

Prices for more superior Clocks, to go Eight Days, on application.

THIRTY HOUR CLOCKS, PRICE 35s. EACH.

Without the Levers, F. & G., which can be supplied by us to Order, or made by any Bellhanger.

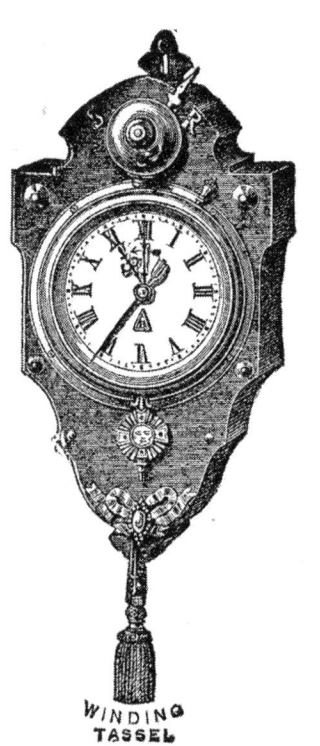

WINDING TASSEL

PATENT
TASSELL WINDING CLOCK,

WITH ADJUSTABLE ALARM,

NO KEY REQUIRED.

THE CASE IS OF METAL, NICKEL PLATED;

IT IS

A HANDSOME, CHEAP CLOCK,

FIT FOR A GOOD BED-ROOM,

30/- EACH.

See also Page 65.

BAILEY'S PATENT
STEAM KETTLES

FOR

PRODUCING HOT WATER FOR WORK-PEOPLE'S BREAKFAST

AND ALSO FOR

Dyers, Bleachers, Brewers, Public Baths, Workhouses, Hotels, Hospitals, &c.

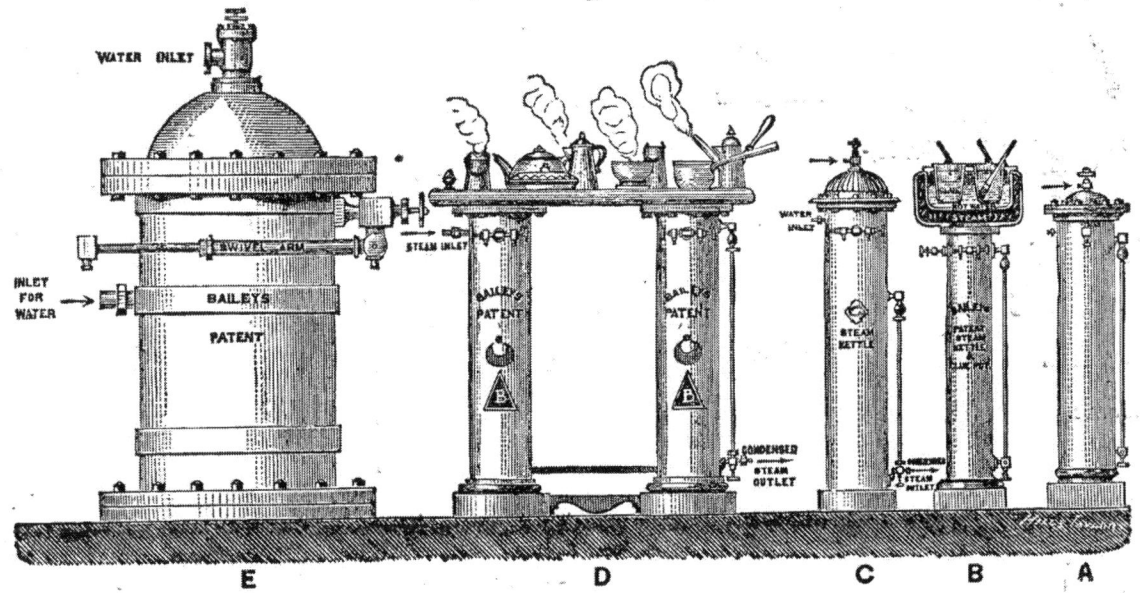

A	This quality is a small size, suitable for works of about 40 or 50 men. It is also suitable for Restaurants, Hotels, &c., for Coffee.	£6 6 0
B	For Joiners, Cabinet Makers, Printers, Bookbinders, &c., for Glue as well as Metals.—This quality is a size larger than A, the cut not giving a proper proportion. It is suitable for 100 men, and being fitted with three glue pots, it is useful for both purposes. When fixed in the centre of a joiner's shop it warms it as well.	£9 9 0
C	This size is the one most in demand; it is suitable for 100 men—will deliver the requisite amount in 15 or 20 minutes. It is in use in Machine Works, Bleach Works, Locomotive Fitting Shops, Cotton Spinning Factories, Hotels, &c., giving the highest satisfaction.	£8 10 0
Double C NOT ILLUSTRATED	The C is found not large enough for more than 100 men, unless more than half-an-hour be taken to fill the cans, which is too long where stated meal times exist. In this case two Kettles coupled together are recommended for 150 to 200 or 300 men: the advantage of having two is, that only one stop valve to both steam and water and one fixing is required. One steam trap is only requisite. The price is therefore less than two singly. Complete,	£15 0 0
D	Hot Hearth and Double Kettle Combined.—This will not require much description. The Hot Hearth is of great advantage. It is useful for works having from 100 to 300 men, and is admirable to place in a works Dining-room, as it acts as a stove as well as fulfilling its other uses. Complete,	£20 0 0

In very large establishments, where more than 200 hands are employed, it is sometimes more advisable to have three or four of the C quality placed in different parts of the building, than to have one very large Kettle.

E	HOT WATER KETTLE FOR DYERS, BATHS, BREWERS, &c. This contains 7 copper coils, and will supply hot water 212° through a full-bore 1 in. pipe, or slightly lower temperature full-bore 1¼ in. pipe. The swivel arm, with telescopic arrangement, enables tubs and buckets to be filled with facility.	£55 0 0

BAILEY'S PATENT GLUE, SIZE, AND PASTE POTS.

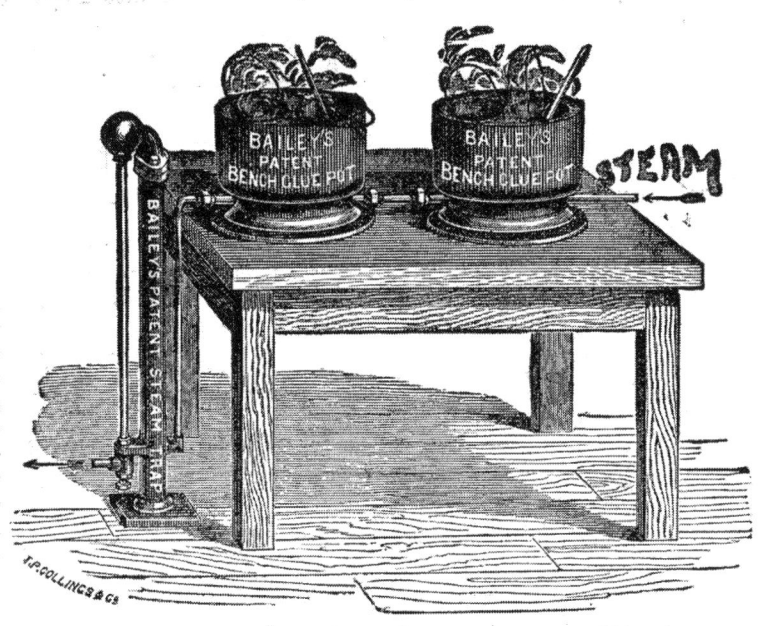

These Patent Glue Pots give the greatest satisfaction where used.

They are simple, cheap and durable.

Pattern Makers, Joiners, Carpenters, Bookbinders, Printers, Paper Bag Makers, Pill Box and Card Case Makers, Pattern Card Makers, Lithographers, Stereotypers and those requiring hot paste or glue, will find their merits worth investigation.

With 3 Pots, on Legs, K quality, 63/- with Steam Trap.

For Bench Purposes, with 2 Pots only, without Steam Trap, 38/- each.

BAILEY'S PATENT Steam Kettle
For filling FOOT WARMERS *for* RAILWAYS.

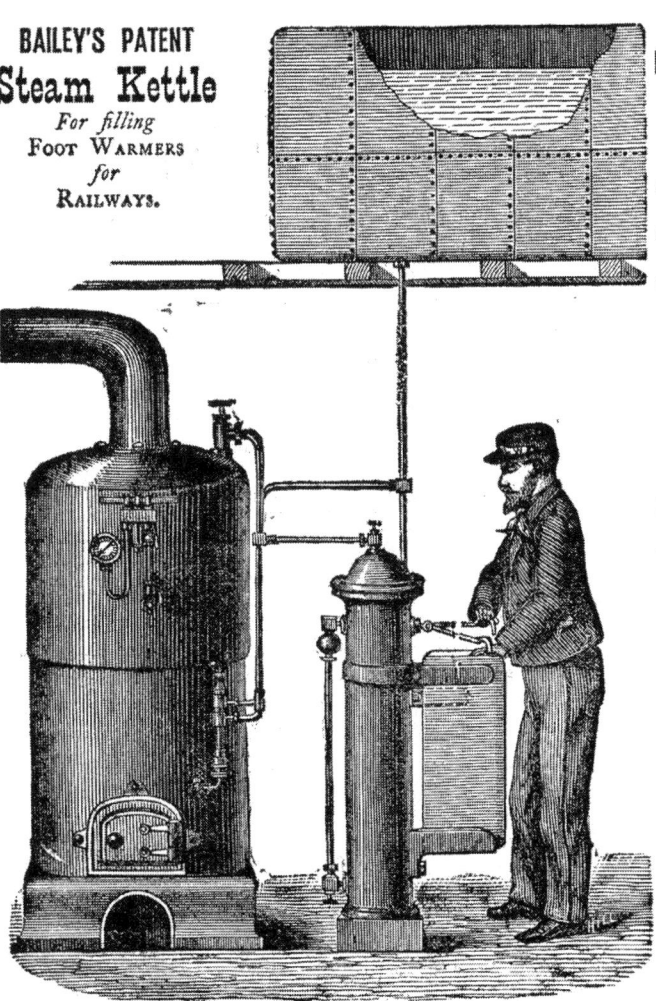

IMPORTANT TO RAILWAY COMPANIES.

This modification is for filling Foot Warmers; two can be filled at once, with great rapidity.

Price, £10 each,

M Quality.

If with Boiler and Injector Gauge, Stop Valve and all fittings, except Tank Boiler, 60 by 30 inches,

£55 10s. 0d.

BAILEY'S PATENT Steam Stoves
COMPLETE

With Steam Traps for Offices, Ships, Stores, &c., &c., all complete with Steam Trap.

These have been altered since this Cut was made, and they now have Flat Tops.

Quality N, 3 ft. 6 in., 10 in. diameter,
£4 10s. 0d.

Quality O, 3 ft. by 8 inches,
£4 0s. 0d.

Where steam exists, this is the cheapest way to warm a room or ships' cabins.

BAILEY'S PATENT STEAM PAN,

For Hotels, Institutions, Hospitals, Asylums, &c.

Also used for Cattle Food, and for Manufacturing Purposes.

This is similar to the Steam Glue Kettle, with a four-gallon Tin Steam Pan placed on the top. The Hot Water Bath is boiled by the Steam Double-cased Pan. The raw steam may be turned on under the Pan to commence with.

Price, with Four-gallon Tin Pan, H quality, £5 5s.

OTHER SIZES MADE TO ORDER.

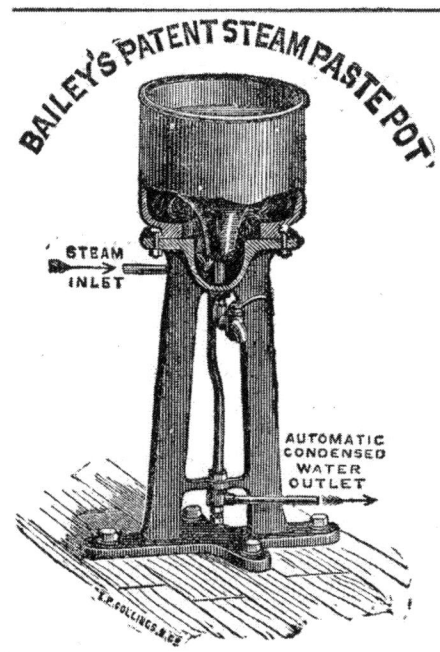

Important to Printers, Bookbinders, Newspaper Proprietors, &c., &c.

BAILEY'S PATENT STEAM PASTE POT

FOR

Stereotypers' Mixtures,

Pill Box Makers' Paste, &c.

Complete with Top, as illustrated, to hold about 3 gallons, £5 5s. G quality.

Supplementary Matter to page 65 in Book, where see details of the invention.

BAILEY'S
PATENT STEAM KETTLE

Hot Water for Breakfast or Tea

FOR

WORKS, HOTELS, STEAM-SHIPS, HOSPITALS, PRISONS, ASYLUMS, &c.; also for DYERS, BLEACHERS, &c.

Direct from the Waterworks Main, or from an overhead Cistern,

WITH HOT HEARTH.

This is also an excellent Steam Stove for Warming a Room.

Extra Large Size, D quality, Price £20.

TESTIMONIAL FROM MANCHESTER, SHEFFIELD & LINCOLNSHIRE RAILWAY,
Locomotive Dept., Gorton, Manchester,
December 7th, 1876.

With reference to your letter *re* Patent Steam Kettle, I like it very much, as it is very suitable, and takes up very little room. It is better and cleaner in every respect to our old mode of boiling the water, and is fixed close to the shop, and consequently must save the men's time.

Yours truly, S. PERKINS, Chief Engineer.

MIDLAND RAILWAY COMPANY,
Superintendent's Office, Locomotive Dept., Derby,
2nd January, 1877.

PATENT STEAM KETTLE.

GENTLEMEN,—In reply to yours, 28th ultimo, which has been handed to me by Mr. Allport, I beg to say, we are well suited with the Hot Water Apparatus we have got in our mess rooms.

Yours truly, SAMUEL JOHNSON, Chief Engineer.

MEMO. FROM THE STAR CORN MILLERS' SOCIETY, LIMITED.
STAR CORN MILL,
Oldham, January 10th, 1877.

GENTLEMEN,—Herewith we forward cheque for payment of your No. 1 Steam Kettle. We are glad to testify to the simplicity and efficiency of your Kettle, which gives every satisfaction, and will be a great boon to all who use it.

This Apparatus is also used for mixing "BRAN MASH" for Horses, &c., where STEAM BOILERS ARE USED ONLY.

A quality, ... Price £6 6s.

Livery and Gentlemen's Stables should not be without one, as a supply of Hot Water can be had at any moment.

The Horse Keeper at a Works can, of course, use the Steam Kettle at all hours where steam power is used.

BAILEY'S FLOAT INDICATOR,
FOR TANKS.

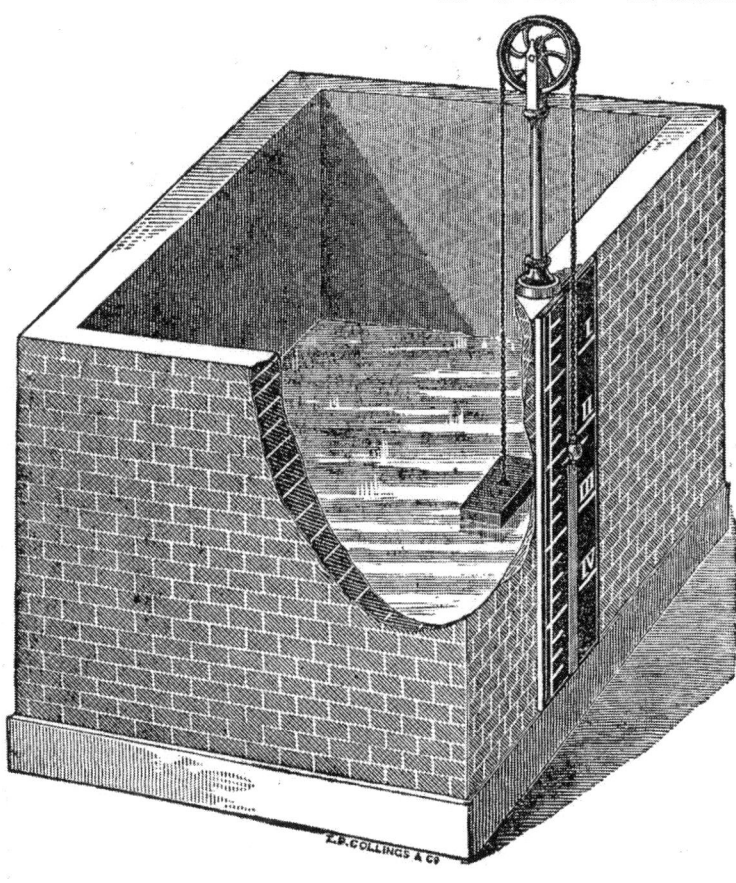

With Panelled Board, Wooden Float and Balance Pointer, to ...

5 feet	60/-
6 "	65/-
7 "	70/-
8 "	75/-
9 "	85/-

We make all sorts of Recorders, Deep Well Indicators, Reservoir Gauges, Tidal Clocks and other instruments for investigating the fluctuations of water for Waterworks Engineers, and Experimental purposes.

BAILEY'S PATENT HOT HEARTH.

This is 24 inches long and 40 inches wide; the steam is admitted above, and the condensed water discharged on an automatic matter, by means of the steam trap which is supplied with it. The water may be conveyed away by small pipe.

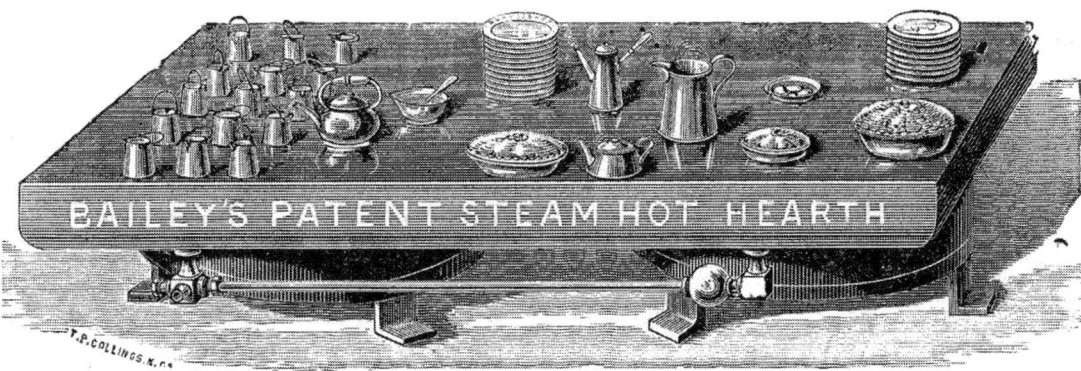

PRICE, COMPLETE, **£7 7s. 0d.**

If bright on the Top, for First-class Kitchens, **£8 15s. 0d.**

Sheet Iron Doors and Case over this can be fitted by any tinsmith.

USEFUL NOTE.—Steam at 50 lbs. pressure has a temperature of 300 degrees Fahrenheit.

MACKENZIE'S PATENT BLOWERS, FOR BLAST PURPOSES,
FOR SMITHS' FIRES, IRON FOUNDERS, VENTILATING PURPOSES, &c.

BAILEY'S STEAM PUMPS.

BAILEY'S HYDRAULIC PRESS PUMPS, FOR HEAVY PRESSURES.

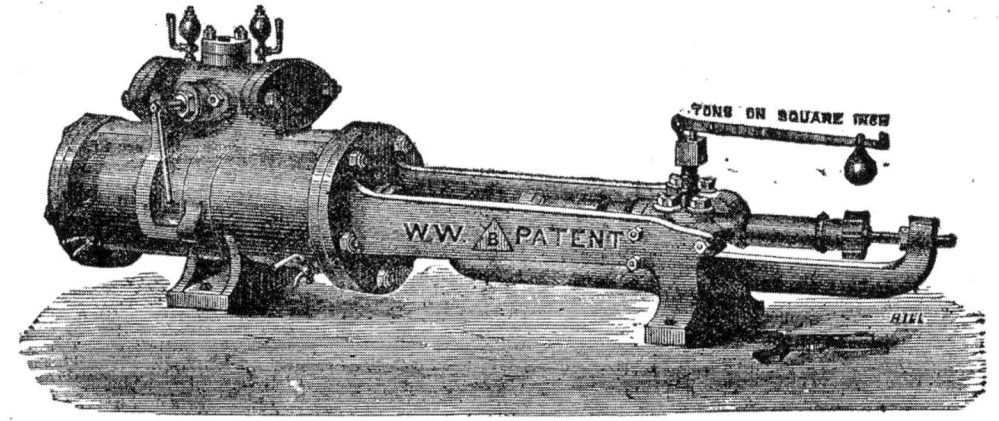

For Prices and Descriptions, see Supplementary Catalogue of Pumps, Injectors, Pyrometers, &c., which please ask for.

BAILEY'S STEAM PUMPS,

WILLIAMSON AND WALKER'S PATENT,

For Feeding Boilers, Fire Engines, Colliery Plantations, Quarries, Ships and other purposes.

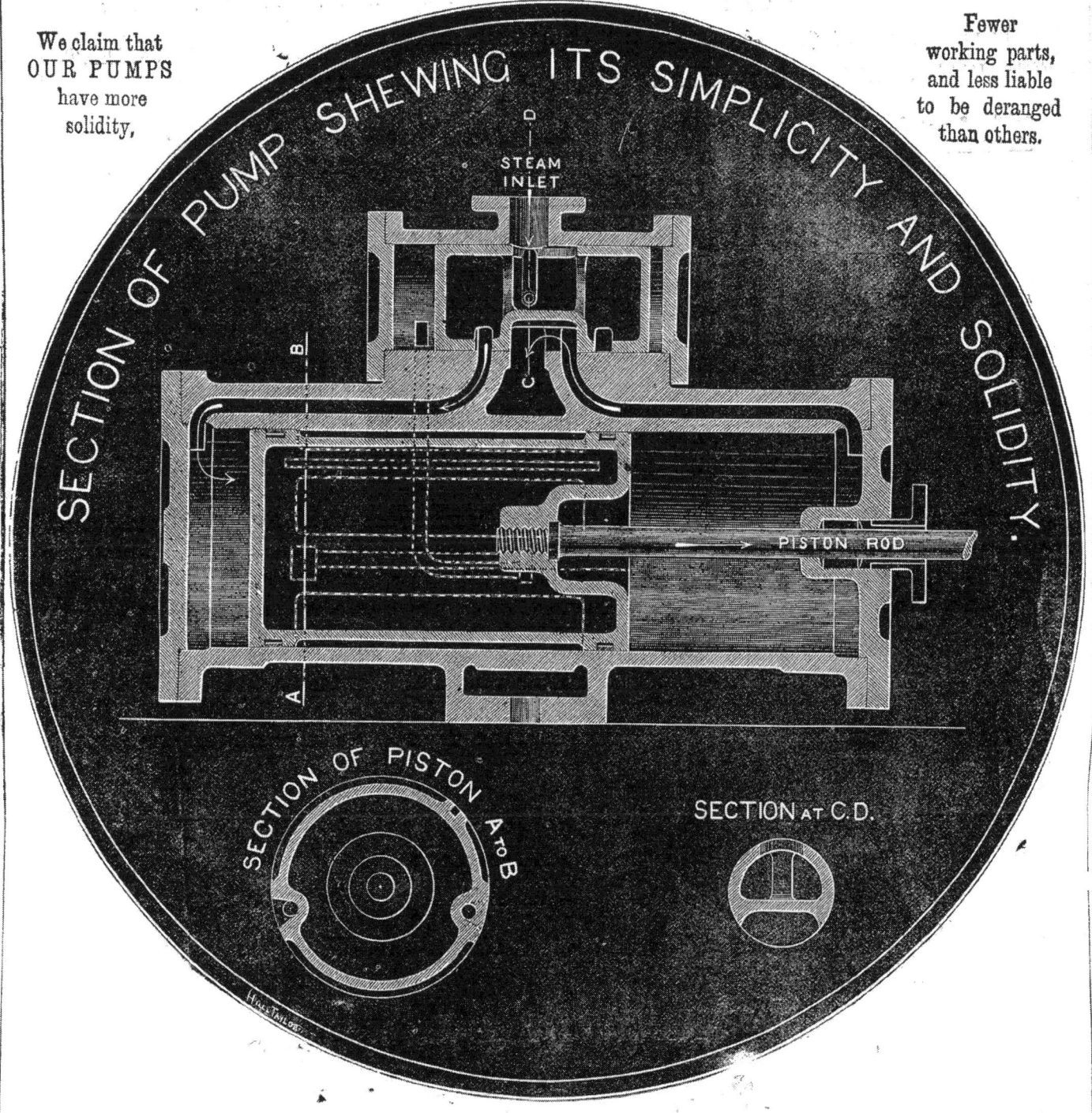

We claim that OUR PUMPS have more solidity,

Fewer working parts, and less liable to be deranged than others.

For further particulars of our Pumps, Pyrometers, &c., see our Illustrated Supplement and Catalogue, which please ask for.

BAILEY'S TESTING MACHINES.

The various Machines we make for testing are *not* described in this Book. We have recently made a set of TESTING APPARATUS FOR THE JAPANESE GOVERNMENT TECHNICAL COLLEGE, AT YOKAHAMA, consisting of

Friction Brakes, Dynamometers, &c.

PARTICULARS ON APPLICATION.

The following is a List of some of our Testers, Indicators and Recorders:—

	£ s. d.		£ s. d.		£ s. d.
Rubber Tube Tester	5 10 0	3-Horse Power Tester (Bailey's Friction Brake)	15 0 0	Domestic Pyrometer	1 15 0
Wine and Soda Water Bottle Tester	10 0 0	1-Horse Power Do. Brake	6 10 0	Steam Thermometer	1 10 0
Paper Tester	2 10 0	Watchman's Clock	5 5 0	Water Pressure Recorder	12 0 0
Cement Tester	20 0 0	Paper Machine Indicator	2 10 0	Cotton Mill Clock	4 4 0
Iron, Steel and Brass Tester (Thurston's)	45 0 0	Gas Meter Index	0 8 6	Deep Well Recorder	20 0 0
3-Horse Power Tester (Bailey's Dynamometer)	25 0 0	Baker's Pyrometer	2 15 0	Tank Indicators	4 4 0
		Still Pyrometer	4 4 0	Tide Gauge	50 0 0
				Wind Recorder	12 10 0

Yarn Tester, £6 10s.

BAILEY'S POCKET STEAM TEST GAUGE,
In Mahogany Box.

Designed for the use of Engineers, for Testing Gauges in large Works, and for Locomotive and Portable Engines, etc. Supplied with Three Nipples, ¼, ⅜ and ½ in. Price, complete, £2/2/0.

SPECIAL LISTS
OF
STEAM PUMPS,
INJECTORS,
WATER MOTORS,
BOILER FEEDERS,
SLUICE VALVES,
POST FREE,
ON APPLICATION.

Ask for BAILEY'S Supplementary Lists of Engine and Boiler Fittings.

NOTICE TO ADVERTISERS, INVENTORS, PATENTEES, AND MANUFACTURERS OF MECHANICAL GOODS.

BAILEY'S
ILLUSTRATED INVENTIONS,

The most Complete Book of Engineers' Sundries and Useful Inventions ever Published.

W. H. BAILEY & CO. send this Book by post to their various customers throughout the World. These include the chief Engineers, Machinists, and Machine Factors and Dealers in London, Manchester, Birmingham, Sheffield, Glasgow, Dublin, Hamburg, St. Petersburg, Berlin, Paris, Turin, Pesth, and others in Europe, North and South America, the British Colonies, and everywhere where the Steam Engine has penetrated.

W. H. BAILEY & CO. have over Fifteen Thousand regular customers in various parts of the world.

In addition, we have on our books the names of several thousands of Engineers, Iron and Brass Founders, Ironmongers, Boiler Makers, Railway and Steamship Companies (at home and abroad), Ship Chandlers, Gas and Water Works Managers, Brewers, Distillers, Publicans, Corn Millers, Bread and Biscuit Makers, Sugar Refiners, Oil Refiners, Soap Makers, Manufacturing Chemists, Gas Fitters, Plumbers, Painters, the British and Foreign Governments, &c., &c., to whom it is sent regularly by post.

Doing a regular business with all the above classes, and having travellers, agents, or representatives in nearly every manufacturing district in the world, W. H. B. & Co. are compelled of necessity, *in selling their own goods,* to bring this Catalogue under the notice of all their customers; advertisers, therefore, will see that no better medium can be had for bringing their manufactures before the above varied classes of people.

The book is also advertised in the chief mechanical papers here and abroad, at the price of three shillings and sixpence, and given away to wholesale dealers gratis.

As a book of reference, therefore, among these varied classes of people,

IT OFFERS ADVANTAGES AS AN ADVERTISING MEDIUM

possessed by no other, and, in addition, the representatives of the firm have instructions to further the interests of advertisers in any possible manner.

The following are the terms for advertisements inserted in all issued during twelve months, and for six months one half, from date of publication:—

	£ s. d.
One whole page (about 7 inches by 9½ inches of matter, size of this sheet)	£20 0 0
Half page	12 0 0
Quarter page	7 0 0

A fresh edition every June and December.

Advertising accounts due four months after the date of publication.

The attention of Manufacturers and Dealers is particularly directed to the advantages thus offered for bringing their goods under the notice of the various classes of consumers referred to.

Advertisements received now will be inserted in our next edition. Full particulars on application to the Manager, Publishing Department.
W. H. B. & CO.

☞ **No Advertisements received which in any way compete with W. H. BAILEY & CO.'S own manufacture.**

BAILEY'S ILLUSTRATED INVENTIONS.

INDEX TO ADVERTISEMENTS.

	PAGE
Title Page	1
Index to Advertisements	2
Amateurs' Lathe, Manchester Pattern	24
Appleby Brothers, Engineers	9
Ashworth Brothers, Pumping Engines	3
Bailey and Co., Weighing Machinery, &c.	27
Bailey and Son, Manufacturers of Chemicals for Telegraphic, &c., purposes	20
Baker's Rotary Blower and Gas Exhauster	10
Barningham & Co. Limited, Rails, &c.	31
Barraclough, Thomas, Flax, Hemp, and Jute Machinery	18
Bradley and Bumstead, Horizontal Engines	14
Brazier and Son, Chemical Plumbers	22
Broadbent, Henry, Lathes	32
Brown's Patent Pipe Tongs	30
Burnett, Sir William, Preservation of Timber and Canvas	22
Cameron & Son, Steam Pumps	30
Clarke, H., Bicycle Manufacturer	22
"Climax" Boiler Composition Company, Birkenhead	8
Crane, P. Moir and Co., Oil Merchants	29
Cunliffe and Croom, Tool Makers	11
Dean and Son, Wholesale Stationers	12
Domestic Washer, &c.	25
Donald, John, and Son, Bars, Angle Tees, &c.	21
Egg Boiler for Bailey's Steam Kettle	26
Gravity Tallow Cup	28
Green, W. H., Venetian Blinds	22
Grindstones for Tools	23
Halliday's Mechanical Stoker and Fuel Economiser	23
Handasyde, C. H., and Co., Boiler Composition	21
Haynes and Jefferis, Ariel Wheels and Bicycle Manufacturers	20
Haywood, Joseph, and Co., Table Cutlery, &c.	22
Hill and Taylor, Engravers on Wood, &c.	22
Hollow Plug Tallow Cup	23
Hudswell, Clarke, and Rodgers, Patent Wrought Iron Drums	17
Ironfounders' Gauge	24
James, I. and Son, Liquid Manure Carts, Bone or Stone Crushers	20
Lloyd, R., and Co., Change Wheels for Lathes	21
Lowe's Patent Stench Traps	24
Lowther and Bailey, Oil and Tallow Cups	24
Mapplebeck, W. B., Malleable Iron Castings	16
Massey, B. and S., Steam Hammers	32
Mathews, J., and Co., Paint, Colour, and Drysaltery Merchants, Liverpool	6
Matthews, J., and Co., Vertical Boiler Makers, &c., Somerset	4
Patent Screw Wrench	24
Patent Water Gauge Glass	30
Phillips' Gas Baths	21
Radcliffe, Frank, Colliery Tubs, &c.	16
Railway Spring Company, Sheffield	22
Rownson, Drew, and Co., Cyclops Patent Blowers	7
Sutcliffe, Leonard W., Engineer	16
"Syren" Low Water Alarm	26
Thomas, Evan, Davy Lamps, &c.	22
Topham, Charles, Mincing and Sausage Machines, &c.	26
Twibill, Joseph, Fuel Economiser	19
Twibill, Joseph, Smoke Extincteur	18
Warren & Co., Knife Cleaning Machines, &c.	26
Westray, Copeland and Co., Engineers	5
Westray, Copeland, and Co., Rock Drills	4
Wightman's Printing Presses	12
Wilkinson, W. B., and Co., Stable Flooring	22
Wilson, John G., Patent Agent	13
Wooton Patent Cabinet Secretaire	15

ASHWORTH BROTHERS'
PATENT "SIMPLEX" RAM PUMPS,

Double-Acting, with One Ram,
Quadruple-Acting, with Two Rams,
Also Single-Acting Ram Pumps.

Useful to Millowners as forming an excellent Steam Fire Engine, Feeder for Boilers, &c.

Useful for Dyeworks, Gas & Water Works, &c.

CAN BE USED AS AN ENGINE FOR DRIVING PURPOSES, BEING SELF-CONTAINED.

CONSTRUCTION OF THESE PUMPS.

The bed-plate being *hollow* is an air vessel and a reservoir for water, and the columns which support the steam cylinder are air vessels for the pump.

The cylinder is fitted with metallic piston; and the piston and valve-rods are of steel, working through brass glands and bushes. The connecting rods have brass steps and cottars. The stroke is limited by a crank on the fly-wheel shaft. The valves are of brass, and lift vertically, each having a separate door. All the working parts and packings are easy of access, and capable of ready adjustment and repair.

The pumps are tested to a high pressure before being sent out, and warranted to work well.

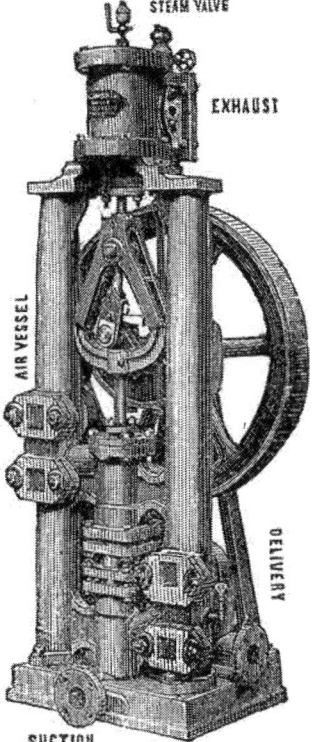

Double-Acting, with Two Rams.

The "SIMPLEX," Double-Acting, with One Ram.

AWARDED FOUR FIRST PRIZE MEDALS.

"SIMPLICITY" and "DURABILITY," two features most important and essential in any piece of Machinery—and particularly in Pumping Engines—are allowed by all experience, and competent judges, to pertain especially to the Ram Pump.

The only hindrance to their being preferred over all others, and taking the entire field hitherto, has been the comparative small quantity of water the Single-acting Ram Pump will draw; or that the Double-acting Ram Pumps so far introduced are so complicated or defective in construction as to cause more trouble in keeping in order than the advantage in extra draw of water will cover.

In the construction of our Patent Ram Pump, however, we have managed to remedy these defects; and can offer DOUBLE-ACTING WITH ONE RAM, AND QUADRUPLE-ACTING WITH TWO RAMS, which possess all the advantages pertaining to any kind of Double-acting or Quadruple-acting Pumps hitherto used, and have at the same time that simplicity and durability which has made the Single-acting Ram Pump so general a favourite with colliery owners and others.

A reference to the Pump, as given above, will give an idea of its construction. It will be seen that there are two ram chambers, one over the other, and that the chambers are CAST TO THE COLUMNS.

When the columns are set to the boring table, both of the ram chambers are bored out, and the top of the columns recessed to receive the end of the steam cylinder before the columns are moved, thus ensuring PERFECT CONCENTRICITY between the circle lines of the steam cylinder and the two ram chambers.

All practical men and engineers will at once see the importance of this. It enables us to make perfect fits of the most important working parts, and reduces the friction to a minimum.

It will be seen from the woodcut of the Pump that there are two glands and stuffing boxes, one opposite to the other—that they are the same kind of glands and stuffing boxes as those used in the Single-acting Ram Pump—and are packed in exactly the same manner.

MADE SPECIALLY STRONG FOR DEEP LIFTS FOR MINING PURPOSES.

We beg to draw the attention of Engineers, Steam Users, &c., to our

High Pressure Multitubular Boilers

These Boilers are lagged with wood, and which is covered with sheet iron, well painted, giving the Boiler a neat appearance, and preventing radiation of heat. They are very economical in working, and as no foundation or brickwork is required, are most convenient for fixing and moving when desired. They can also be easily entered by a man, to be cleaned.

FULL PARTICULARS & PRICE LISTS ON APPLICATION.

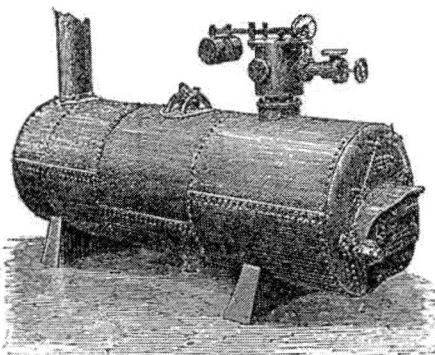

Single-Acting, One Ram.

ASHWORTH BROTHERS,
Moss Brook Foundry, Machine & Boiler Works,
Rock Street, Collyhurst Road, & Ashley Lane, Manchester.

WARING'S IMPROVED SELF-FEEDING ROCK DRILL

BY FAR THE MOST SIMPLE AND EFFECTIVE MACHINE FOR ALL DESCRIPTIONS OF

MINING WORK.

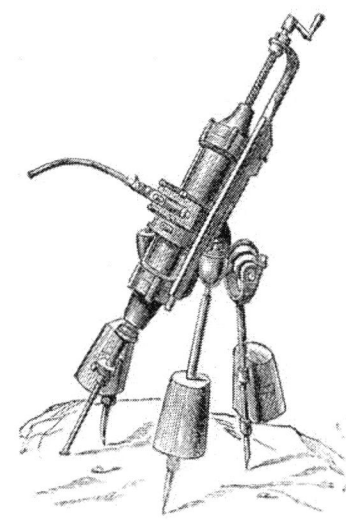

MAKERS OF

AIR COMPRESSORS

AND GENERAL

MINING MACHINERY.

PRICES

AND

TESTIMONIALS

ON APPLICATION.

SOLE MANUFACTURERS FOR GREAT BRITAIN,

WESTRAY COPELAND & CO.,
BARROW-IN-FURNESS.

MATTHEWS' PATENT
VERTICAL HIGH PRESSURE BOILER,
FOR LAND AND MARINE ENGINES.

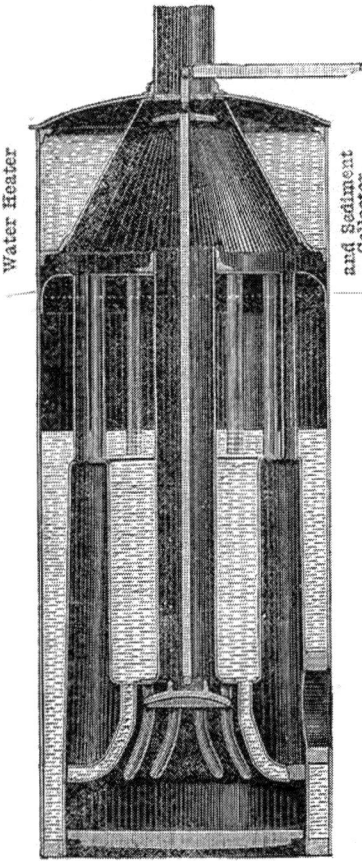

Water Heater and Sediment Collector.

The great feature in these Patent Boilers is the extraordinary extent and beautiful arrangement of FIRE BOX HEATING SURFACE, by which the hot gases from the fire are thoroughly utilised, and the largest ECONOMY of FUEL and SPACE is attained, combined with GREAT POWER.

The MATTHEWS' PATENT BOILER is excellently adapted for Road Locomotives, Steam Hammers, Pumps, and Rock-boring Machinery.

They can be lowered into Mines, Tunnels, Shafts, and Workings with great facility, as they are entirely self-contained. No fixing is required.

They are suited for Marine Engines in Tug Boats, Steam Launches and Yachts, and for use on Ships' Decks. They occupy comparatively little room.

For Stationary and Semi-portable Engines, the MATTHEWS' PATENT WATER HEATER, fixed on top of Boiler is recommended, the waste gases from Boiler *heating the feed water* and *depositing the sediment*, in itself effecting a *large saving* in *fuel* and *wear and tear* of the *Boiler*.

The circulation of water in these Boilers is perfect, and every part is *accessible* for *inspection* and *cleaning*, thus ensuring *safety* and *durability*.

These Patent Boilers are built to carry pressures of from 60lbs. to 120lbs. per square inch. Sizes, from 2 to 40 horse power; above that, two or more Boilers. They stand on their own foundation, and require no brick work or chimney stack.

All Boilers fitted with BAILEY'S PATENT SAFETY PLUG.

For Particulars and Prices apply to

J. Matthews & Co.
2, LION CHAMBERS, BROAD STREET, BRISTOL, ENGLAND.

Patented in Great Britain and Foreign Countries.

BEESLEY'S PATENT
Punching, Shearing, & Angle-Cropping MACHINE.

SECTIONAL ELEVATION.

END ELEVATION.

THE ABOVE ILLUSTRATIONS REPRESENT A MACHINE OF THE FOLLOWING DIMENSIONS:—

PUNCH TEST.	ANGLE TEST.	DEPTH OF GAP.
$1\frac{1}{4}$in. through $1\frac{1}{4}$in.	4in. by 4in. by $\frac{5}{8}$in.	30in.

SOLE MAKERS,

WESTRAY COPELAND & CO.,
BARROW-IN-FURNESS.

PRICE LISTS AND PARTICULARS ON APPLICATION.

JOHN MATHEWS & CO.,
OIL MERCHANTS AND DRYSALTERS,
MANUFACTURERS OF PAINTS, COLOURS, VARNISHES, AND GREASE,
HATTON GARDEN WORKS, LIVERPOOL.

PAINTS.
- White Lead Paints
- " Zinc Paints
- Green Paints, all shades
- Blue Paints, all shades
- Red Paints, Venetian
- " Indian
- " Turkey
- Black Paints
- Stone-colour Paint
- Yellow Paints
- Ochre Paints
- Brown Paints, Spanish
- " Umber, English
- " " Turkey, raw
- " " " burnt
- " Purple
- Chocolate
- Lead-colour Paint
- Oxide iron Paints, all shades
- Patent Drier
- Putty, Best Linseed Oil and Whiting

DRY COLOURS.
Anti-corrosion Paints in powder, all colours

BLUES.
- Ball Blues
- Brunswick Blues
- Celestial
- Chinese
- Lime
- Prussian
- Ultramarine Blues
- Blue Black

BLACKS.
- Drop Black
- Charcoal Blacking
- Ivory Black, genuine
- Lamp Black, loose
- " 2, 4, 8, & 16 oz. pkgs.
- Mineral Black
- Vegetable Black

BROWNS.
- Crocus
- Colcothar
- Purple Brown, all shades
- Spanish Brown, lump
- " powdered
- Terra-sienna, raw and burnt
- Umber Turkey, raw and burnt
- " English
- Vandyke Brown

DRIERS.
- Litharge, Flake
- " powdered
- Lead, Sugar of

GREENS.
- Arsenate-copper
- Bronze Green
- Brunswick Green, all shades
- Chrome Green
- Emerald Green
- Mineral Green
- Paris Green
- Verdigris

LEADS.
- Lead, Black, picked lump
- " powdered, loose
- " " in packages
- " Dry, White
- " " Orange
- " " Red

REDS.
- Lakes, all kinds
- Chinese Red
- Derby Red
- Persian Red
- Red, Indian
- " Venetian
- Raddle
- Vermillion, Chinese
- " English
- " Imitation
- Chalk, Carpenters' Red

WHITES.
- Barytes, Sulph.
- " Carb.
- Chalk, French
- " English
- Flake White
- Mineral White
- Paris White
- Terra-alba
- Whiting

YELLOWS.
- Chromes
- Imperial Yellows
- Ochres

VARNISHES, &c.
- Body Copal
- Fine Pale Polishing Copal
- Pale Cabinet
- Carriage
- Furniture Varnish
- Oak
- Gold Size
- Paper Varnish, fine transparent
- Black Japan, superfine

- Black Lacquer, best
- Brunswick Black
- Turpentine
- Oil Gold Size
- Pale Maple
- Black Varnish
- Bright Varnish
- Pattern Varnish

GREASE.
- Coom
- Yellow, Locomotive or Railway
- Anti-friction, or Wagon, Pine or Rosin
- Anti-friction, New Brown
- Engine, White
- Mill, Black, No. 1
- " Brown, No. 2
- Water-wheel
- Wire-rope
- Cart

DRYSALTERIES, &c.
- Alum
- Ammoniac-sal
- Asphalt
- Arsenic
- Bath-bricks
- Borax
- Blue Stone, or Sulph. Copper
- Brimstone
- Brushes, Painters'
- Cement, Portland and Roman
- Charcoal, Blacking
- Chloride Lime
- Clay, China, in ½ ton casks
- Copper, Sulph.
- Cudbear

- Coal Dust
- Copperas
- Emery
- Glue
- Iron Liquor
- Indigo
- Methylated Finish
- Naptha
- Pitch
- Prussiate Potash
- Rosin
- Rotten Stone
- Sal-ammoniac
- Saltpetre
- Sheepwash
- Shellac Gum Benzoin
- Soda
- Soap, Soft
- Tar, Stockholm
- " Coal
- " Oil
- Tallow, Refined Engine
- Waste, Engine

OILS.
- Machinery Oils
- Refined Olive
- " Lard
- Galipolli
- Refined Rape
- Sperm Oil
- Refined Colza Oil
- " Petroleum
- Raw Linseed
- Boiled "
- Spirits, Turpentine
- Castor Oil
- Tar Oil
- Cylinder & Valve Oils
- Fish Oils

THE "PIONEER LUBRICATING OIL."
(REGISTERED TITLE.)

This is a dark, opaque, natural Oil, *possessing remarkable properties as a Lubricant*, for either heavy or light bearings. It is about *Rape Oil consistency*, flows freely from the Oil-can, and is used in *Needle Lubricators* of even the smallest size. It has a large sale for all kinds of *Machinery* and *Engines*, as well as for *Railway Wagons* and *Carriages*, the boxes of which merely require stuffing with Waste which is afterwards saturated with the Oil.

It is **free from Glutinous Matter** so generally present in Machinery Oils, and **does not clog or set**, in which respect, as well as in its **durability**, it will compare most favourably with the more expensive Oils, whilst its *Cost* (2s. 6d. per Gallon) is in striking contrast with that of the *cheapest Lubricant hitherto adopted*. It contains **no acid, and does not stain** "bright work."

The adoption of this Oil on Machinery, which, from the use of other Oils, has become *foul*, exhibits its **detergent properties**; the gummy deposit is speedily removed, and the Machinery assumes a clean appearance; and, as long as the Oil is in use, there is an **absence of anything like setting or drying**.

In introducing the "**PIONEER LUBRICATING OIL,**" the Proprietors were not unaware of *two great disadvantages* which Oils of this class generally labour under. The **dark colour** is apt at first sight to create a *prejudice* which the **smell** usually confirms, and whilst the *Colour* cannot be so improved as to compare with that of Olive or Rape Oil, the *offensive smell* in this instance *does not exist*, and in comparing it with *Oils of similar appearance*, the purchaser is invited to take into consideration the *annoyance* arising from the use of other Oils abounding in *offensive Volatile Constituents*, which evaporate rapidly when the Oils come into use, and, pervading the Workshop or Engine-room, *are a continual nuisance*.

No fear need be entertained as to the **safety** of the "Pioneer Oil," to prove which, pour a little into an open vessel, and *plunge into it a lighted match*, which it will at once *extinguish*.

Sold in Casks (containing about 40 gallons each), at 2s. 6d. per Gallon of 9 lbs., delivered free to Rail or Wharf **in Liverpool**. The quotation reads *Casks free*, which is of itself a *consideration of One Penny per Gallon* as compared with other Oils.

JOHN MATHEWS & CO., HATTON GARDEN, LIVERPOOL.

CYCLOPS PATENT BLOWERS.

FOR ORDINARY SMITHS' HEARTHS.

Are much more powerful and worked more easily than the ordinary Smiths' Bellows; take up very little room, and require but little fixing; can be worked by hand, treadle, or overhead pulley; are fitted with either belts or chain gear, and with patent lubricators.

PRICE COMPLETE, WITH PATENT TUYERE, £7.

DELIVERED FREE TO ANY RAILWAY STATION IN ENGLAND.

KEYSTONE PATENT PORTABLE FORGES

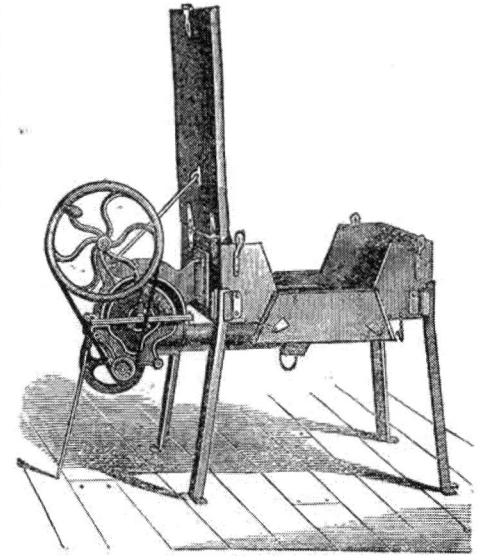

These are the lightest, strongest, most powerful, and most portable yet introduced; have no leather or wood to decay, and are virtually indestructible; are made in Forty-six different varieties, and with both Lever and Rotary Motions.

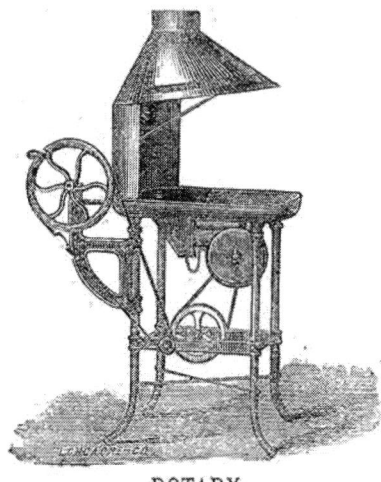

MINER'S FORGE (OPEN.)

MINER'S FORGE (CLOSED.)   ROTARY.   LEVER.

ROWNSON, DREW, & CO.,
225, Upper Thames-st., 113, Queen Victoria-st., & Paul's Wharf, London, E.C.

IMPORTANT TO STEAM USERS AND OTHERS.

THE CLIMAX
BOILER ANTI-INCRUSTATION AND CORROSION COMPOSITION,

Adapted for all kinds of Boilers and Economisers—free from acids or oils—harmless and efficient—recommended by the highest chemical and practical authorities, after the severest tests. Supplied to H.M. India and other Departments, &c.

Terms:—20s. per Cwt., or £18 per Ton. Contracts entered into.

McIVOR'S IMPROVED
FIBROUS NON-CONDUCTING COMPOSITION,

For covering Steam Boilers, Cylinders, Pipes, and other heated surfaces—prevents radiation of heat and condensation—rapidly generates steam—keeps stoke-hole and engine-house cool, and saves 15 to 25 per cent of fuel—easy of application—most durable and cheap.

STEAM AND PUMP PACKINGS—SELF-LUBRICATING AND OTHERS,

Suitable for all kinds of Engines and Pumps—capable of resisting the highest pressure—cheapest and best.

"LION" MACHINE BANDS AND LACES,

Tested to be 30 per cent. stronger than ordinary oak-tanned or other Belting—suitable for the lightest or heaviest machinery—good substitute for gearing—stands more fatigue and lasts much longer than any other kind—is light and pliable—lugs the pulley and does not slip.

ALL KINDS OF MACHINERY LEATHER SUPPLIED.

MARINE FIRE PREVENTER AND ANNIHILATOR,
"WEARE'S PATENT,"

The most combustible cargo carried with safety—any fire in the largest ship extinguished in a few minutes, without injury or removal of the cargo, by a Gas—adapted for vaults or fire-proof buildings, &c.

THE MOST SIMPLE AND EFFICIENT FIRE ENGINE KNOWN.

ACID BOXES, "Weare's Patent,"

Constructed to carry Muriatic, Sulphuric, and other Acids to all parts safely and cheap.

THOROUGHLY CLEAN ANYTHING WITH LITTLE LABOUR BY USING THE
CLIMAX DETERGENT.

Wholesale, 1s. 3d. per Gallon; Single Casks, 1s. 6d.

"ERSKINE'S" IMPROVED PATENT SMOKE CONSUMER AND FUEL ECONOMISER,

By far the Cheapest and most Efficient Smoke Consumer and Fuel Economiser known. References to some of the largest steam users. A guarantee given indemnifying users from any loss or fines arising from information laid by Smoke Nuisance Inspectors.

REFERENCES AND FULL PARTICULARS ON APPLICATION TO

THE CLIMAX BOILER COMPOSITION CO.,
109, VITTORIA STREET, BIRKENHEAD.

INFLUENTIAL COMMISSION OR PURCHASING AGENTS WANTED.

APPLEBY BROTHERS,

EMERSON-ST., SOUTHWARK, LONDON, S.E.,

Engineers, Millwrights, Ironfounders, &c.

SPECIALITIES.

(No. 43.) Locomotive Steam Crane, to lift, turn, travel, and alter radius, all by Steam.

(No. 16.) Semi-portable Winding and Pumping Engine for Small Shafts, or for Wire Tramways, Open Cuttings, &c.

Behrens' Rotary Steam Pump and Engine combined.

(No. 1 B.) Hand Wharf Crane.

STEAM CRANES, Locomotive and Fixed.
Gantry Steam Cranes.
HYDRAULIC CRANES and Machinery of every kind.
OVERHEAD TRAVELLERS, for Hand and Steam Power.
Fixed Station or Wharf Cranes.
Portable Station and Accident Cranes.
PLATFORM & WAREHOUSE CRANES.
Fixed and Semi-fixed WINDING and PUMPING ENGINES, PUMPING ENGINES for WATER WORKS.
SHIPS' DECK ENGINES, Winches, and Distilling Apparatus.
Screw Propeller Engines.
Steam and Hand TRAVERSERS, for Railways and Coal Depots.
Bank, Hotel, and Warehouse LIFTS: Hydraulic, or Hand.
Contractors' Locomotives.
Steam PILE DRIVERS.
ROCK DRILLS & AIR COMPRESSORS.
Concrete Mixers, Contractors' SKIPS.
Dredging Apparatus for sinking Cylinders, &c.
Builders' HOISTS, various, and all kinds of Contractors' Machinery and Plant.
Steam PUMPS, Centrifugal Pumps, House Pumps, Pumps for Contractors, for Hand, Horse, or other power, for manufacturing or other purposes.
HIGH CLASS ENGINES of all kinds.
Boilers, Shafting, Mill Gearing, &c., &c.

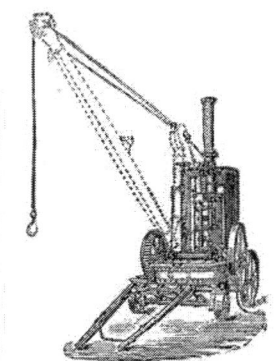

(No. 13.) Contractors' Steam Crane, Builders' Hoist or Portable Engine.

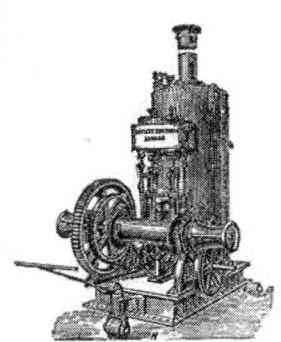

(No. 13 B.) Deck Hoisting Engine, with two Cylinders.

(No. 1 A.) Portable Hand Crane.

BAKER'S PATENT
ROTARY BLOWER & GAS EXHAUSTER,
FORCED BLAST.

Highest Premium (Silver Medal and Diploma) Awarded by Franklin Institute, 1874; also Scott Legacy Medal and Premium, 1875.

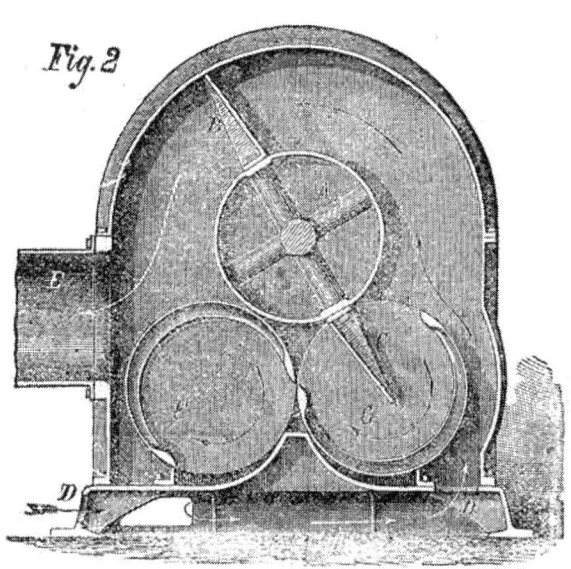

Fig. 2

BAKER'S BLOWER POSSESSES THE FOLLOWING SPECIAL ADVANTAGES:—

1st. Strength!
2nd. Durability!
3rd. Fewness of parts!
4th. Ease of motion!
5th. Less pulsation than any of its class!
6th. Can be run direct from an engine!
7th. Will not be affected internally by wearing of gears!
8th. Requires no lubrication whatever internally!
9th. It requires no dubbing to make it temporarily tight!
10th. Will exhaust, as well as blow!
11th. Dust will not injure it!
12th. Dampness will not change its form!
13th. It runs steadily without jerking the belts!
14th. Will blow hot or cold air equally well!
15th. It requires less power for the amount of air discharged!
16th. Its entire absence of friction internally!

Size	Displacement of Air at each revolution in cubic feet.	Suitable for Cupola.	£	No. of Smoke Fires.
No. 1½.— 1½		...	...	...
,, 3.— 3		16 to 18 in.	30	8
,, 6.— 6		18 to 28 ,,	48	16
,, 9.— 9		28 to 33 ,,	60	24
,, 13.—13		33 to 38 ,,	80	32
,, 17.—17		38 to 42 ,,	95	40
,, 25.—25		42 to 50 ,,	120	55
,, 30.—30		50 to 60 ,,	135	67
,, 60.—60		...	...	...

LARGE SIZES FOR COLLIERY VENTILATION IN PROGRESS.

W. H. BAILEY & CO., WHOLESALE AGENTS, ALBION WORKS, SALFORD, MANCHESTER.

CUNLIFFE & CROOM, MACHINE TOOL MAKERS.

Brass Finishing Machine.

MAKERS OF
CAPSTAN-HEAD LATHES,
HAND AND SCREW
CUTTING LATHES,
FOOT LATHES;
ALSO
SLIDE RESTS,
JAWED CHUCKS,
AND OTHER
ENGINEERS' TOOLS

Planing Machine.

MAKERS OF
Planing Machines,
Shaping Machines,
Drilling Machines,
Slotting Machines,
Milling Machines,
AND
Brass Finishing Machines.

Milling Machine.

STRONG SELF-ACTING, SLIDING, SCREW CUTTING, AND SURFACING LATHES.

Centres.	Length of bed.	Prices in Manchester.	Extra if with gap.	Additional length per ft. of bed.
in.	ft.	£ s.	£ s.	£ s.
5	5	40 0	1 10	1 3
6	6	51 0	1 15	1 8
7	8	64 0	2 0	1 14
8	10	75 0	2 5	2 0
9	12	86 0	2 8	2 4
10	16	110 0	2 12	2 8
12	16	140 0	3 0	2 15
14	20	180 0	4 0	4 0

LIGHT SELF-ACTING, SLIDING, AND SCREW CUTTING FOOT LATHES.

5 centres, 5ft. bed, £45, extra if with gap, £1 10s.
6 ,, 6ft. ,, £56, ,, ,, £1 15s.

HAND TURNING LATHES.

Centres.	Length of bed.	Prices in Manchester. Single speed.	Double gear.	Extra if with slide rest.	Extra if with gap.
in.	ft.	£ s.	£ s.	£ s.	£ s.
5	5	12 10	17 0	5 10	1 8
6	6	15 10	20 0	6 10	1 12
7	8	18 0	24 10	7 10	1 16
8	10	22 0	32 0	8 10	2 0
9	12	26 0	38 0	9 16	2 3
10	16	38 0	53 0	10 10	2 7

FOOT TURNING LATHES.

Centres.	Length of bed.	Prices in Manchester. Single speed.	Double gear.	Extra if with slide rest.	Additional per ft. of bed.
in.	ft.	£ s.	£ s.	£ s.	£ s.
4	4	15 0	18 10	4 10	0 15
5	5	16 10	20 0	5 10	1 0
6	6	18 10	23 0	6 10	1 5

POWERFUL PLANING MACHINES.

Made self-acting in all cuts, with adjustable traverse and quick return motion.

Length planed.	Width planed.	Height planed.	Prices in Manchester.	Additional per ft. of table.
ft. in.	ft. in.	ft. in.	£ s.	£ s.
3 0	1 6	1 6	50 0	3 10
4 0	2 0	2 0	70 0	4 5
6 0	2 6	2 6	120 0	5 10
8 0	3 0	3 0	140 0	6 10
10 0	3 6	3 6	180 0	8 10

LIGHT HAND AND POWER PLANING MACHINES.

Length planed.	Width planed.	Height planed.	Price for hand only.	Price for power.
ft. in.	ft. in.	ft. in.	£ s.	£ s.
2 0	1 0	0 9	24 0	30 0
3 3	1 4	1 0	29 0	35 0

SHAPING MACHINES.

7in. stroke, 3ft. 0in. bed, fixed head ...... price £40
9in. ,, 3ft. 6in. ,, traversing head ,, 58
12in. ,, 6ft. 0in. ,, ,, ,, 110

BRASS FINISHING MACHINES.

Prices in Manchester.
With dividing apparatus and top cone £28 0
Extra with top driving apparatus 2 0
Brass Finishers two Jawed Chucks 4 10

MILLING AND GROOVING MACHINES,

With self-acting transverse slide.

Prices in Manchester. Single speed.	Double geared.	Extra for parallel vice.	Extra for dividing apparatus.	Extra top driving apparatus.
£ s.	£ s.	£ s.	£ s.	£ s.
35 0	39 0	3 0	4 10	2 0
42 0	48 0	4 0	4 10	3 10

JAWED CHUCKS.

Diam. of plate	10in.	12in.	14in.	16in.	18in.	20in.	24in.
Price, 3 Jaws	£5 10	£6 10	£7 10	£8 10	£9 10	£10 10	£12 10
,, 4 ,,	£6 10	£7 10	£8 10	£9 10	£10 10	£12 10	£13 10

SLIDE RESTS.

Ht. of Hdstck.	4in.	5in.	6in.	7in.	8in.	9in.	10in.	12in.
Prices in Manchester	£4 10	£5 10	£6 10	£7 10	£8 10	£9 10	£11 10	£14 10

PILLAR DRILLING MACHINE.

Prices in Manchester.
Single speed £36
Double geared £55
Bench Drill £15

Packing and Packing Case, add 5 per Cent.   If delivered F.O.B. in Liverpool, Hull, or London, 2½ per Cent. extra.

BROUGHTON IRON WORKS, EDWARD STREET, BROUGHTON LANE, MANCHESTER.

DEAN & SON,
WHOLESALE AND EXPORT FANCY STATIONERS,
PUBLISHERS AND MANUFACTURERS OF

VALENTINES, BIRTHDAY, EASTER, AND CHRISTMAS CARDS,
PERFUMED AND FANCY CHROMO-PRINTED ALMANACKS.

SHIPPERS AND THE TRADE SUPPLIED WITH

Albums	Cards for Printing on	Lead Pencils	Purses
Account Books	Cards for Drawing on	Ledgers, Journals, and Day	Rubber Bands
Artists' Materials	Copying Papers	Books, cheap style	Sketch Books
All Requisites for a Printing Office	Drawing Boards	Memorandum Books	Stove Ornaments
	Drawing Books	Mechanical Toys or Steam Engines	Tissue Papers
Black Bordered and other Note Papers	Dye and Embossing Presses		Wallets
	Envelopes	Papers of all kinds	Writing Inks, &c., &c.
Blotting Books	Fancy Papers	Pencils	Dean's Celebrated Oil Colour Toy Books, 1d. 2d. 3d. 6d. 1s. & 1s. 6d.
Bookbinders' Requisites	Games and Toys	Pens, Steel	
Bouquet and other Papers	Leather Goods	Playing Cards	Dean's Untearable Cloth Toy Books.

Send for Trade-priced and Illustrated Catalogue.

LONDON: 160A, FLEET STREET.

WIGHTMAN'S AMATEUR PRINTING PRESSES.

THE LITTLE STRANGER PRESS.

(All Iron.) Planed Iron Surface, with all recent improvements. Constructed in four different sizes.

This Press is also supplied with a set of Registered Movable Hinges, which can be altered either for a light or strong impression, and is quite simple to work.

This Press is preferred by our best class of customers for the following reasons:—being iron, will last a lifetime, and is not liable to get out of order.

TESTIMONIAL.

High Wycombe,
July 1st, 1875.

Sir,
The Machine still answers admirably. I have made it to pay for itself a long time ago by printing amongst my friends.

Yours truly,
H. KIRBY.

TESTIMONIAL.

Aveton Gifford, Devonshire.

My Dear Sir,
I have received the Press all right, it answers very well indeed. I have enclosed a card of the first trial, it works beautifully. Will you please send a list of ornaments.

I am, dear Sir, yours truly,
C. H. STEAR.

No. 1, with chase, to print 7in. by 5in., **30s.**
 „ 2,   „   „   8in. „ 6in., **40s.**
 „ 3,   „   „   9in. „ 7in., **50s.**
 „ 4,   „   „   10in. „ 8in., **60s.**

With 2lbs. of type, type case, ink, ink roller, slab, quoins, furniture, reglet, and leads, 10s. extra.

Packing Cases are charged 2s. each, which are returnable.

WORKS:—JACK LANE, MEADOW ROAD, LEEDS.

TO INVENTORS AND PATENTEES.

BRITISH AND FOREIGN
PATENT OFFICE,
AND DESIGNS' REGISTRY,
71, MARKET STREET, MANCHESTER.

JOHN G. WILSON,

Associate in Arts of the Oxford University, Articled Mechanical Engineer & Draughtsman,

Offers his services to Inventors and Patentees in working out and securing Inventions by Letters Patent or Registration. Having been favoured with business for several years past by some of the principal firms in this country and abroad, J. G. W. has received many unsolicited Testimonials, one of which is subjoined, from Messrs. W. H. BAILEY & Co., the Publishers of this Catalogue.

[COPY]. *Albion Works, Salford, February 28th, 1869.*

MR. WILSON,—Dear Sir,—Having employed you to take out Patents for us for some years past, we have always been pleased with the able, conscientious, and punctual manner in which you have performed such duty. It always gives us pleasure to recommend you to our friends who wish to protect Inventions in this country and abroad. Yours, W. H. BAILEY & Co.

PROVISIONAL PROTECTION

for simple Inventions, obtained for Six Months, at a cost of £8 8s., enabling an Inventor to work or sell his Invention in the meantime, and thereby prove whether it is worth while to procure a complete Patent before incurring much expense. The full cost of

ENGLISH PATENTS,

through this Agency (including Provisional Protection), averages from £35 to £45.

Every description of Patent business transacted. The novelty of Inventions ascertained. Application for Patents taken up from any stage.

FOREIGN PATENTS.

J. G. W. has made this branch a special study, and believes that, consistent with giving proper attention to preparing the necessary documents and drawings, his prices will be found to bear favourable comparison with those of other responsible Agents.

The following prices include the cost of preparing the specification and Drawings, Government Duties, Stamps, and all other expenses, except Consular and Notarial Fees, which are not often required:—

United States of America … £18	*Austria* …	£14
France … 12	*Italy* …	15
Belgium … 8	*India* …	35
Prussia … 15	*Russia* …	45

Patents obtained in other Countries at equally moderate prices.

A Circular of information and costs, and list of references upon application.

JOHN G. WILSON, PATENT AGENT, 71, Market Street, Manchester.

BRADLEY AND BUMSTED,
ENGINEERS & MILLWRIGHTS,
BRASS AND IRON FOUNDERS,
MAKERS OF HORIZONTAL ENGINES OF THE HIGHEST CLASS.

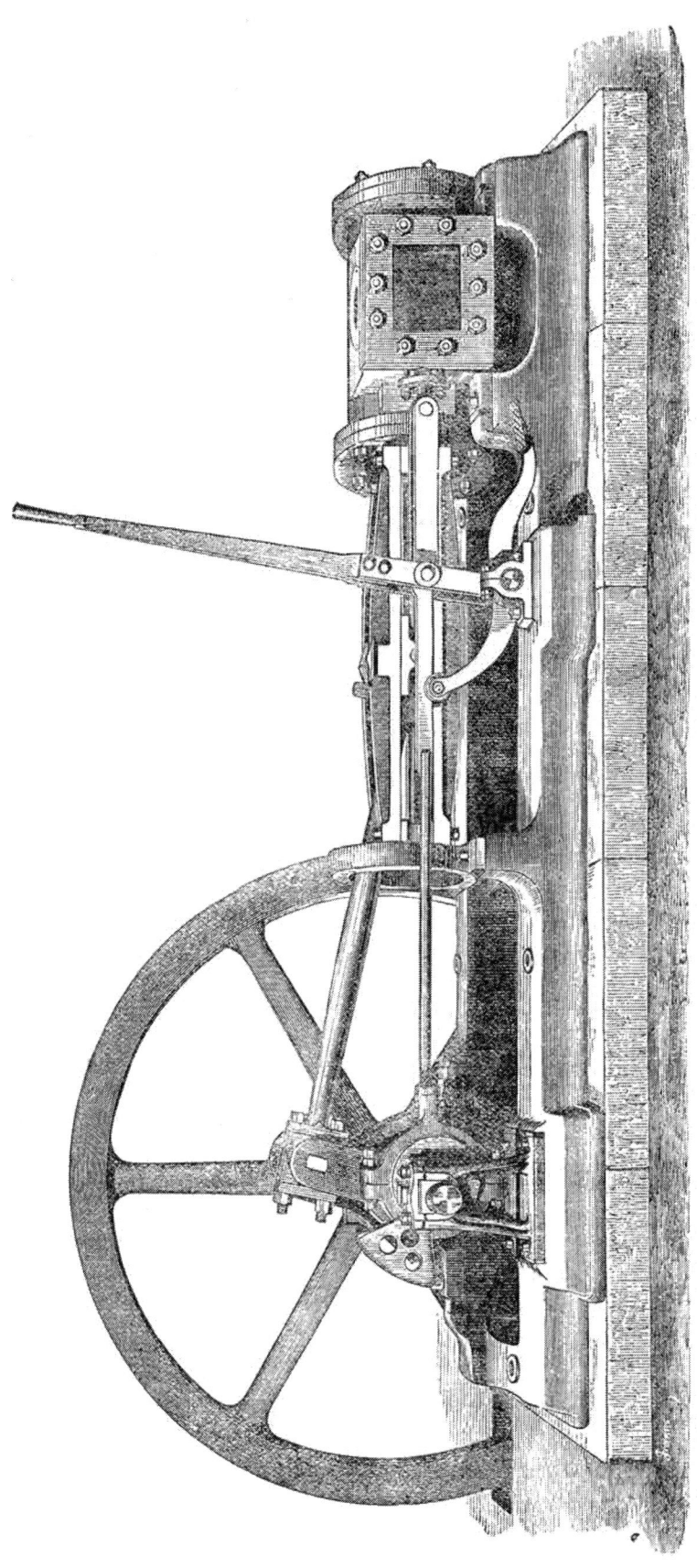

Working Parts made to Gauges, of the Best Materials, and Patent Yellow Metal used in all Bearings.

CANNOCK CHASE WORKS,
HEDNESFORD, NEAR STAFFORD.

THE "WOOTON" PATENT CABINET SECRETAIRE

CONTAINS more available interior space than any other Office Desk made, there being nearly one hundred different apartments, consisting of Drawers, Shelves and Pigeon Holes of various dimensions; all accessible to the operator when seated, and secured by a single lock.

Every article needed in business has a place in this Desk, so that the Writing Table is wholly unincumbered, which admits the closing of the entire Desk at any stage of business, in the shortest possible space of time, *with everything in its proper place.* It needs to be seen to be appreciated.

Every Business Man should have One!
Every Professional Man should have One!
Every Private Gentleman should have One!
Nothing more suitable for Presentation purposes.
Rapidly taking the place of all other Styles of Desk.

PRICES FROM £20 TO £120.

"As time to the man of business means money, it would be difficult to attach too much importance to the advantages derivable from method and order in the arrangement of his letters and documents. Under the best system papers have a habit of accumulating with wonderful rapidity, and how often, from want of simple contrivances for their preservation, are they lost or mislaid so as not to be forthcoming at the proper time. There has been a long-felt want of a good desk suitable for office or library, which should afford not only the means of writing with facility, but also give space for a methodical and easy arrangement of documents, such as is not the case with the narrow drawers found in the ordinary pedestal tables. Little or no improvement has taken place of late years in desk manufacture on this side the Atlantic, and it has been reserved for our ingenious American friends across the water to show us what can be done in this respect.

The Wooton Cabinet Office Secretaire is an invention new to this country, although in the United States it has gained great popularity, and we have read numerous testimonials from purchasers speaking of it in the highest terms of praise.—*Furniture Gazette, November 6th.*"

THE BEST DESK IN THE WORLD.

Catalogues Sent Free on Application to the WOOTON DESK CO.

Agencies in all the Principal Cities in the Kingdom.

45, GORDON STREET, GLASGOW.

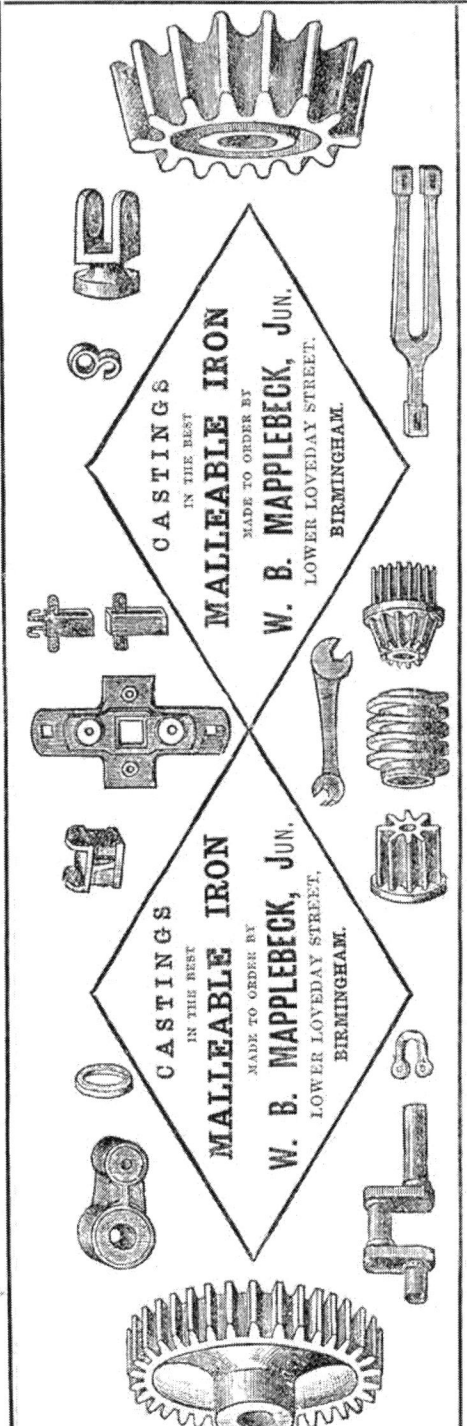

CASTINGS IN THE BEST MALLEABLE IRON MADE TO ORDER BY W. B. MAPPLEBECK, JUN. LOWER LOVEDAY STREET, BIRMINGHAM.

LEONARD W. SUTCLIFFE,
ENGINEER,
Tool, Machinery Merchant and Shipper.

PLANT BOUGHT AND SOLD

FOR CASH OR ON COMMISSION.

NEW AND SECOND-HAND MACHINERY
ALWAYS ON HAND.

ALL ORDERS PROMPTLY ATTENDED TO.

GOODS PACKED FOR SHIPMENT.

OFFICES:
IRENE CHAMBERS, 25, MARKET STREET, MANCHESTER.

ATTENDANCE—MANCHESTER ROYAL EXCHANGE, TUESDAYS & FRIDAYS.

NOTE.

SPECIFICATIONS and ESTIMATES given and CONTRACTS entered into for supplying Engines, Boilers, Tools, and Machinery of every description to Railway Companies, Shipbuilders, Colliery Owners, Engineers, Machinists, Boiler Makers, and Contractors, also for Factories, Foundries, Iron and Steel Works, and Rolling Mills, Breweries, Dyeing, Bleaching, Chemical, and Printing Works, Corn, Rice, Sugar, and Paper Mills, &c., &c., at the lowest possible prices, consistent with good workmanship, material, and design, combined with prompt delivery.

PENDLEBURY FOUNDRY, NEAR MANCHESTER.

Colliery Tubs or Trams, made of Iron, Steel, or Hard Wood, for export or home use; Cages: Single, Double, or Treble Decks; Self-acting Tipplers, for Tipping Coal every way; Wagon and Tub Forgings, Wheels and Axles, and every Colliery requisite. Prices on application.

GREAT ECONOMY FOR MILLOWNERS!

DRIVE YOUR SHAFTING WITH
Rodgers' Patent Wrought-Iron Drums,

INSTEAD OF GEARING.   MANY THOUSANDS IN USE!

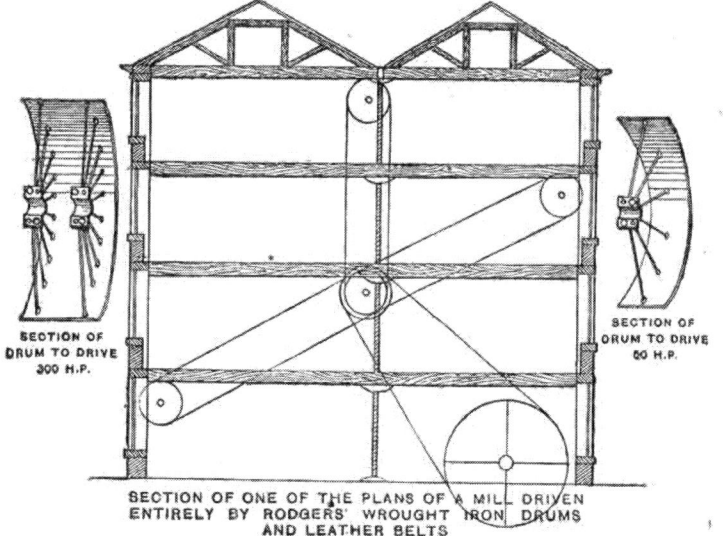

SECTION OF ONE OF THE PLANS OF A MILL DRIVEN ENTIRELY BY RODGERS' WROUGHT IRON DRUMS AND LEATHER BELTS

ADVANTAGES.

1. Leather belts on these drums will drive fully 25 per cent. more than on cast-iron ones, viz: a belt 6in. wide will drive as much as one 8in. wide on a cast-iron drum, and will last **longer**.

2. These drums are not only considerably **lighter** but also infinitely **stronger** than cast-iron ones.

3. In case of **Fire** they can be easily repaired: we have repaired hundreds at a small cost.

4. For **Main Driving** purposes they are invaluable, especially in case of a new mill, no expensive ashlar work being required to withstand the jars of costly gearing.

ADVANTAGES.

5. The wrought-iron drums and belts are more easily and quickly fixed than gearing, and cost **less**.

6. Greater **Economy** in steam power, as it requires less power to transmit the same effective force with belts than it does with gearing.

7. Very much greater **Economy** in subsequent repairs as compared with gearing.

8. The power is transmitted evenly, faithfully, **noiselessly** and without the jar arising from defective or worn gearing.

9. They require no cases for transport or shipment.

They can be supplied up to **24 feet** diameter.

For Prices and Particulars apply to the SOLE MAKERS,

HUDSWELL, CLARKE, AND RODGERS,
RAILWAY FOUNDRY, HUNSLET, NEAR LEEDS.

MR. JOSEPH TWIBILL,

THE INVENTOR OF THE UNIVERSALLY-USED FUEL ECONOMISER,

Has succeeded also in solving the problem of SMOKE BURNING.

TWIBILL'S PATENT
SMOKE EXTINCTEUR

PREVENTS SMOKE AND SAVES COALS!

No Steam Boiler User should be without this valuable Patent!

TO BE SEEN IN OPERATION AT

TWIBILL'S ECONOMISER AND ENGINEERING WORKS,
HULME, MANCHESTER.

FLAX, HEMP, JUTE, COIR, MANILLA, AND ALOE FIBRE MACHINERY.

Seed Rolls, Breaking, Softening, Scutching, Brushing, and Preparing Machinery for FLAX and HEMP. COIR MACHINERY, Husk Rolling, Extracting, Willowing, and Spinning Machines.

COMPLETE ROPERIES, for every size and kind of Ropes and Cables up to 20ins. circumference; Spinning and Bobbining Machines, Reels, Tarring Apparatus, Foreboard, and Travelling Rope-laying Machines; Jacks, Register Plates, Tubes, Rails, Hackles, Accessories, &c.

COMPLETE TWINE FACTORIES, for Twines, Cords, Fish-lines, Sash-cords, Spun-yarn, &c.; Spinning, Twisting, and Topping Frames; Dressing, Sizing, Drying, Polishing, and Balling Machines.

Looms and Preparation Machinery for Weaving MATTING, SACKING, BAGGING, SAIL-CLOTH, CANVAS, &c.

Machinery for the Manufacture of OAKUM, FISHING NETS, FLAT ROPES, WIRE ROPES, SQUARE and ROUND GASKETTING.

HYDRAULIC and SCREW PRESSES, for packing Flax, Hemp, Jute, Coir, &c.

Machines for utilizing Cotton, Flax, Hemp, Woollen and Silk Waste. Shoddy and Mungo Machinery.

JUTE Teasing and Softening Machines.
MANILLA Brushing and Heckling Machines.
SPECIAL MACHINERY FOR PREPARING AND SPINNING NEW FIBRES.

TOW Willowing, Cleaning, and Teasing Machines.
Fibre SINGEING and PLAITING Machines.
WOOL Washing, Drying, Burring, and Packing Machinery.

Ronald's Patent Fibre Brushing, Heckling, and Spinning Machines.
Ronald's Patent Self-contained Rope-laying Machines.

CATTLE GEAR, WATER-WHEELS, TURBINES, BOILERS, STEAM ENGINES, FUEL ECONOMISERS, MILL-GEARING, &c. MILL STORES OF EVERY DESCRIPTION.

THOMAS BARRACLOUGH, 97, BRIDGE STREET, MANCHESTER.

TWIBILL'S FUEL ECONOMISER

AND BOILER FILTER,

In operation to thousands of Boilers,

For using up Waste Heat escaping from Steam Boilers,

HEATING,

CIRCULATING, & FILTERING

WATER,

AND

SAVING 25 PER CENT. IN FUEL.

TWIBILL'S ECONOMISERS

Are used throughout this country, and during many years have been exported to manufacturing towns on the Continent of Europe, America, India, Australia, Russia, Turkey, Norway, and Sweden, and have become an indispensable adjunct to Steam Boilers.

J. T. & Co. invite special attention to their Patent Quadruple Scrapers, Seamless Copper Tubes, and greater facilities for cleaning or repairs, the result of **25** years' experience and working.

J. TWIBILL & CO.,

ECONOMISER & ENGINEERING WORKS,

MANCHESTER.

All sizes and duplicates kept in stock.

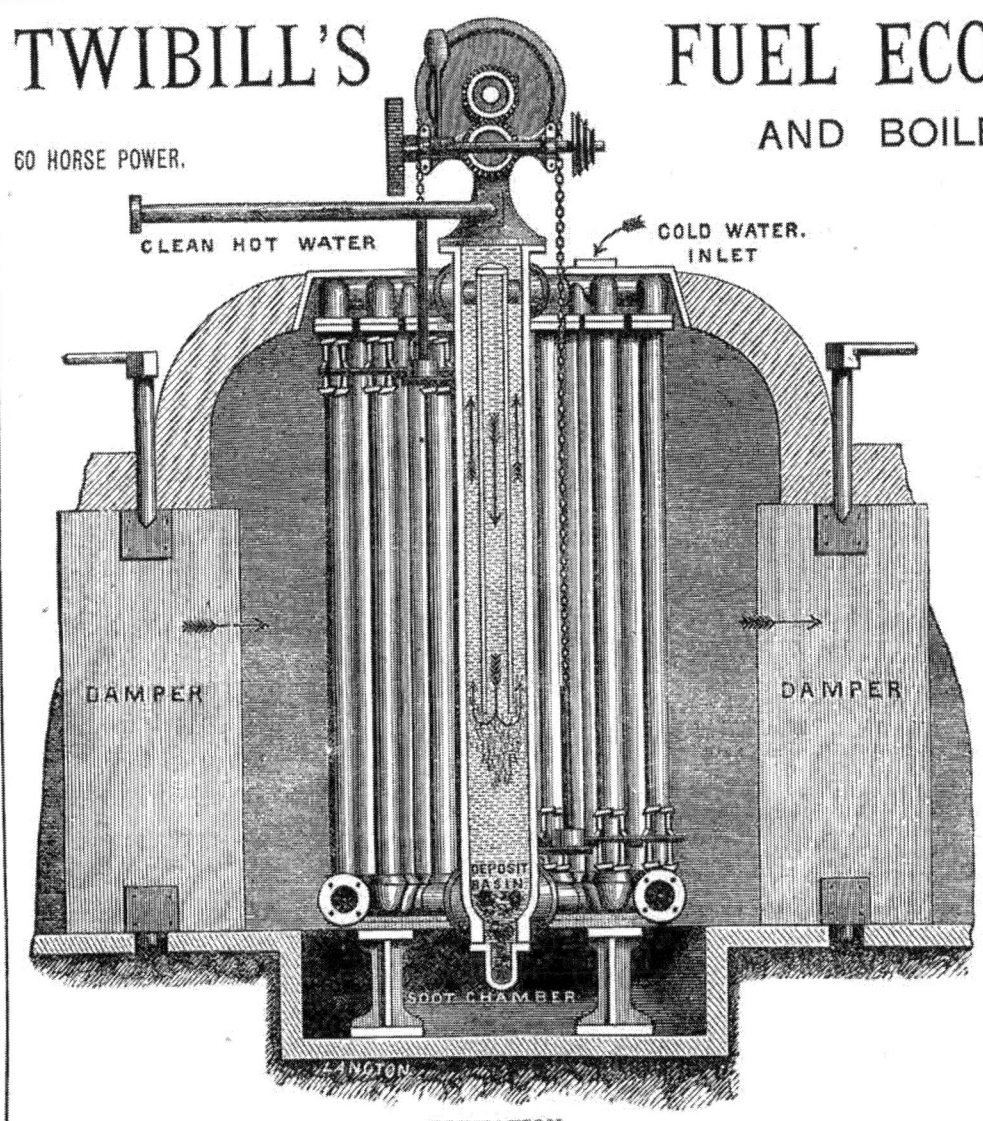

ELEVATION.

Price £125, Cast Iron; £200, Seamless Copper Tubes.

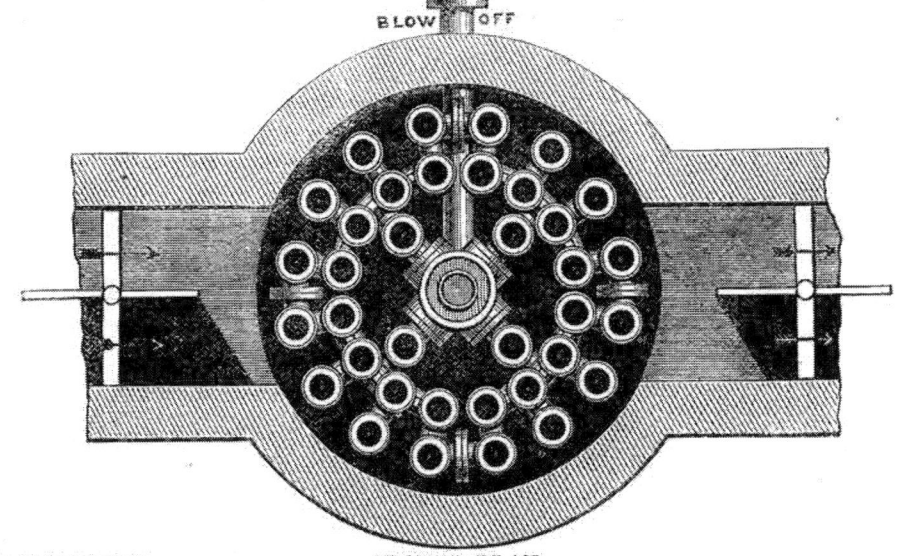

60 HORSE POWER.   GROUND PLAN.

ADVERTISEMENTS.

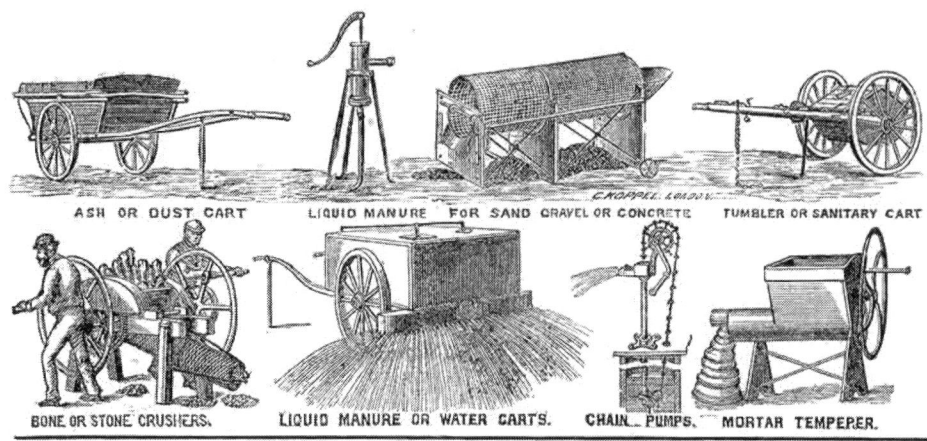

31 FIRST ROYAL
AND OTHER PRIZES
HAVE BEEN AWARDED FOR
LIQUID MANURE AND STREET WATER CARTS,
BONE, STONE, SAND, CONCRETE, OR LIME CRUSHERS,
FOR HAND OR STEAM POWER,
Tumbler and Sanitary Carts, Clod Crushers, Liquid Manure and Chain Pumps, and Mortar Temperers.

The Bone Crushers are now made to work well with 2 men, or 1 horse, or 2 horses, according to size.

I. JAMES & SON,
TIVOLI, CHELTENHAM.

WILLIAM BAILEY & SON,
BY APPOINTMENT,

Manufacturers of Chemicals for Telegraphic, Photographic, Pyrotechnic, and other purposes.
Contractors to Her Majesty's War Office, Admiralty, Post Office, India Office, and other Government Departments. Also to the principal Railway and Telegraph Companies in Great Britain.

Great attention is given to the Manufacture of Chemicals and other preparations for Commercial and Scientific use.

Works—HORSLEY FIELDS, WOLVERHAMPTON.
London Offices—2 and 3, ABCHURCH YARD, CANNON STREET, E.C.

The following Specialities are particularly recommended—

BAILEY'S TANNATE OF SODA, for preventing incrustations in Steam Boilers, and removing the scale already formed therein, a considerable saving of fuel being also effected. PRICE 36s. PER CWT.

BAILEY'S CLEANSING POWDER possesses very remarkable detergent properties, and when mixed with either fresh or sea water, cleanses every variety of Wood or Metal to which it may be applied. PRICE 28s. PER CWT.

BAILEY'S SANITARY FLUID is specially adapted for Purifying the Atmosphere in Factories, Workshops, Hospitals, and Public Institutions, and for disinfecting purposes generally. PRICE 1s. 6D. PER GALLON.

BY ROYAL LETTERS PATENT.

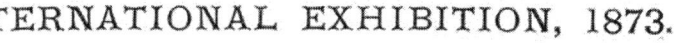

HIGHEST PRIZE MEDAL
LONDON INTERNATIONAL EXHIBITION, 1873.

THE "ARIEL" BICYCLE
FOR
LADIES OR GENTLEMEN.

MAKERS OF THE CELEBRATED 7 FEET "ARIEL," THE LARGEST BICYCLE EVER MADE.

Machines made as light as required for Road or Racing.

Testimonials from all parts of the World.

THE "ARIEL" CARRIAGE, BATH CHAIR, AND PERAMBULATOR WHEELS AND AXLES, WITH INDIA-RUBBER TYRES.

In consequence of the easy running, a vehicle on these wheels requires less than the usual horse power for draught. They are suitable for all kinds of light vehicles, from the elegant Park Phaeton in Rotten Row, to the humble Delivery Cart of the town or suburban tradesman where expedition is required.—*Carriage Builders' Gazette, July 1st,* 1875.

Full particulars free on application to London Retail Depôt, 11, *Prince's Street, Leicester Square, W. Representative for Wholesale Trade,* A. C. Hickling, 32, *Kentish Town Road, N.W.*

HAYNES & JEFFERIS,
MANUFACTURERS AND PATENTEES,
ARIEL WORKS, COVENTRY.

JOHN DONALD & SON,
IRON AND HARDWARE MERCHANTS,
42, CADOGAN STREET, GLASGOW.

IN STOCK:—Bars, Angles, Tees, Plates Sheets, Hoops, Nails, Chains, Iron Tubes, Anvils, Vices, Bellows, Steel, Files, Hammers.

Patent Injector Fans & Exhausters.   Portable Punching Bears.   Machine-made Horse Shoes.   **PATENT ANHYDROUS LEATHER BELTING & HOSE.**

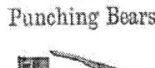 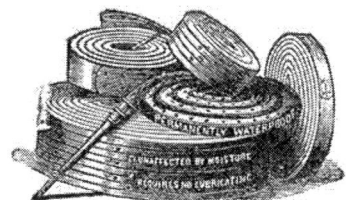

The best in the Market.   The Trade supplied.   Unaffected by Moisture.   Permanently Waterproof.

Prices and List of Stock Sizes on application.   A STOCK ON HAND.

GAS BATHS.
GAS BOILERS, FOR HEATING CONSERVATORIES.
GAS STOVES, FOR WARMING AND FOR COOKING.
GAS MULLERS, FOR WINE, BEER, AND FOR WARMING THE BAR, &c.

THE BEST MANUFACTURED AT

PHILLIPS',
10A, FEATHERSTONE BUILDINGS, HOLBORN, LONDON.

CHANGE WHEELS FOR LATHES,

From the most complete sets of Machine-cut Metal Patterns in the kingdom, and unrivalled for the beauty and accuracy of the castings.

GRADUATED STEEL STRAIGHT EDGES, TRY SQUARES, with hardened edges, and **VERNIER CALLIPERS**, &c., mechanically perfect.

ENGINEERS AND MACHINISTS' TOOLS OF EVERY DESCRIPTION.

PRICE LISTS ON APPLICATION.

RICHARD LLOYD AND CO.,
MILL AND MACHINE IRONMONGERS AND MECHANICAL TOOL MANUFACTURERS,
135, STEELHOUSE LANE, BIRMINGHAM.

HANDASYDE'S COMPOSITION,

FOR THE REMOVAL & PREVENTION OF INCRUSTATIONS IN STEAM BOILERS.

FREE FROM ACIDS.   IN EXTENSIVE USE BOTH AT HOME AND ABROAD.

Special Terms for Export Orders.   Agents Wanted (Commission or Purchasing): only those who can command a sale need apply.

C. H. HANDASYDE & CO., DALKEITH, N.B.

ADVERTISEMENTS.

EVAN THOMAS,
MANUFACTURER OF ALL KINDS OF
MINERS' SAFETY LAMPS,
AND SOLE MAKER OF HIS
PATENT IMPROVED CLANNY LAMP,
WITH ELASTIC GLASS RING,
Which admits of the expansion of the glass without the risk of breakage.

PRICES AND DESIGNS ON APPLICATION.

CAMBRIAN LAMP WORKS,
7, CARDIFF STREET, ABERDARE.

Evan Thomas's Improved Patent Clanny Lamp.
REFERENCES.
A India-rubber band. B Brass Washer. C Screw.

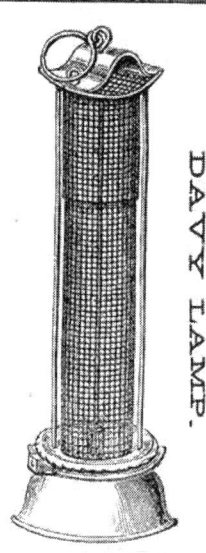

DAVY LAMP.

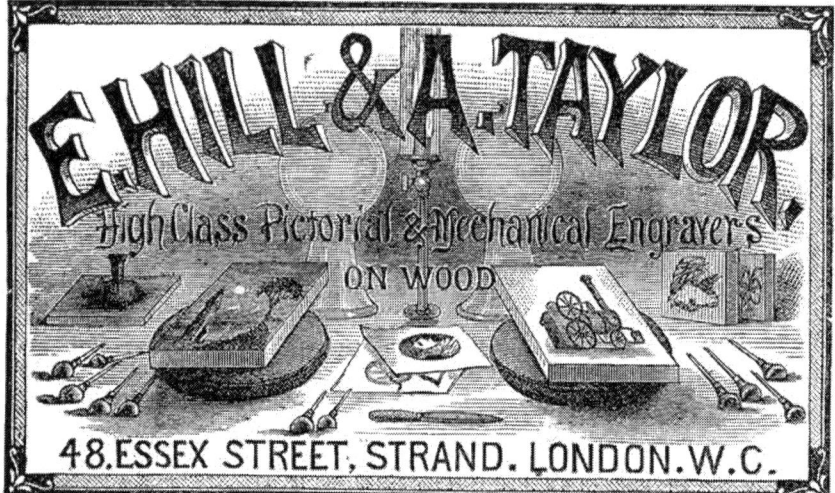

E. HILL & A. TAYLOR,
High Class Pictorial & Mechanical Engravers ON WOOD
48, ESSEX STREET, STRAND, LONDON, W.C.

VENETIAN BLINDS.
By the adoption of new and patented machinery for making and painting Venetian Blinds, the Trade can now be supplied with a far superior article, beautifully varnished, at 7d. per foot. Old Blinds re-made equal to new for 4d. per foot. Send for samples and full particulars to

HENRY W. GREEN,
KILBURN BLIND WORKS, LONDON, N.W.

EXHIBITION MEDAL, 1874.
WILKINSON'S STABLE FLOORING
Has, after considerable inquiry, been adopted by the War Department for Stables at Shorncliffe Camp, Canterbury, Weedon, Birmingham, Newcastle, &c. It has also been largely used for stables and stable-yards of the nobility and gentry in various parts of the kingdom, and is specified by many leading London and provincial architects. 400 (stable floor) references on application.

W. B. WILKINSON & CO., Newcastle-on-Tyne.
Established 1841.

CHEMICAL PLUMBERS, SANATORY BUILDERS AND DECORATORS.—BRAZIER & SON, 100, Blackfriars-road, S.E. Every description of work executed with efficiency and despatch on the latest improved principles, combined with economy. Manufacturers of the improved full-sized lead D traps, jointed with the oxy-hydrogen blow-pipe. Estimates prepared. Established 70 years.

SIR WM. BURNETT & CO.'S
PROCESSES for the PRESERVATION of TIMBER and CANVAS from DRY ROT, MILDEW, WHITE ANTS, and PREMATURE DECAY; also for rendering WOOD UNINFLAMMABLE.

SIR W. BURNETT & CO. respectfully invite the attention of Architects, Civil Engineers, and all interested in the Preservation of Timber or Canvas, to the merits of this process, the efficacy of which has been fully established by its successful operation in all parts of the world for upwards of thirty years.

Testimonials can be seen, and all further information obtained, on application by letter or personally at the

OFFICE, 99, CANNON STREET, LONDON, E.C.

BICYCLES & BICYCLE WHEELS.
Spider or Wood-wheeled Machines, U-Iron Rims, Bent Wood Rims, Sadles, Rubber Tyres, Cement, &c. List, one stamp, for postage.
H. CLARKE, Bicycle Manufacturer, Baker-st., Wolverhampton.

JOSEPH HAYWOOD & CO.,
GLAMORGAN WORKS, SHEFFIELD,
GENERAL MERCHANTS, &c.,
MANUFACTURERS OF
Table Cutlery, Pocket, Pen, and Sportsmen's Knives, and Pruning Knives,
RAZORS,
PLATED DESSERTS.

PROTECTED BY THE CUTLERS' COMPANY. CORPORATE MARK.

THE RAILWAY SPRING COMPANY,
MANUFACTURERS OF EVERY DESCRIPTION OF
RAILWAY SPRINGS,
MILLSANDS, SHEFFIELD.

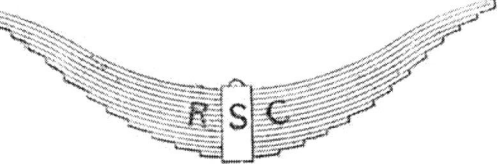

GRINDSTONES
FOR TOOLS, &c.

Stones in Stock from 6 inches to 8 feet Diameter.

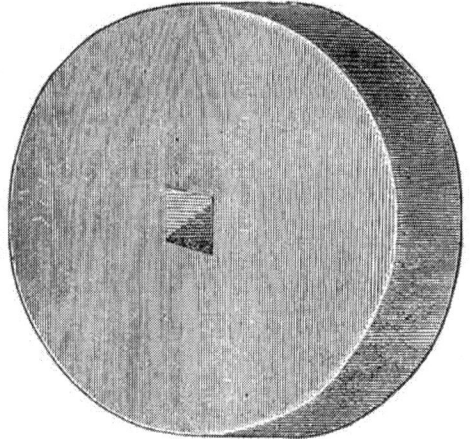

Diameter. Ft. In.	Thickness. Inches.	Price. £ s. d.
2 0		0 13 0
2 2	3 to 4	0 15 0
2 4		0 17 0
2 6		1 0 0
2 8	3 to 6	1 4 0
2 10		1 6 0
3 0		1 8 0
3 2	,,	1 10 0
3 4	,,	1 12 0
3 6	,,	1 14 0
3 8	,,	1 17 0
3 10	,,	2 0 0
4 0	6 to 8	2 6 0
4 2	,,	2 10 0
4 4	,,	2 15 0
4 6	,,	3 0 0
4 8	,,	3 6 0
4 10	,,	3 12 0
5 0	,,	4 0 0

HALLIDAY'S MECHANICAL STOKER
AND FUEL ECONOMISER,
Adapted for Single or Double Flued Land or Marine Boilers.

PRICES:

No. 1 - - £15 0 0
No. 2 - - £20 0 0

Fire Doors and Frames £2 extra.

HALLIDAY'S STOKER increases the generation of Steam from a given boiler space to the extent of twenty per cent. as compared with hand firing. It saves not less than ten per cent. in the consumption of fuel when the same quality is used as in the ordinary method of firing.

Its cost will be fifty per cent. less than any other Stoker at present offering, and from its simplicity and efficiency cannot fail to meet the great want of the day—

"A CHEAP AND PERFECT MECHANICAL STOKER."

BAILEY'S HOLLOW PLUG TALLOW CUPS.

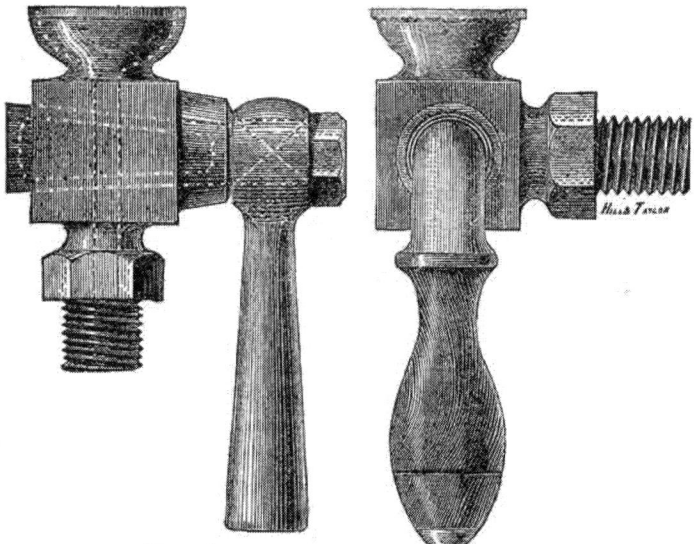

In ordering, say if angle or straight.

No. 1, screwed to ¾in. gas thread, 10s. 6d. each.
,, 2,   ,,   ½in.   ,,   8s. 6d. ,,

BAILEY'S
Ironfounders' Gauge,
FOR INDICATING LOW BLAST PRESSURES,
WITH USEFUL TABLE ON DIAL.

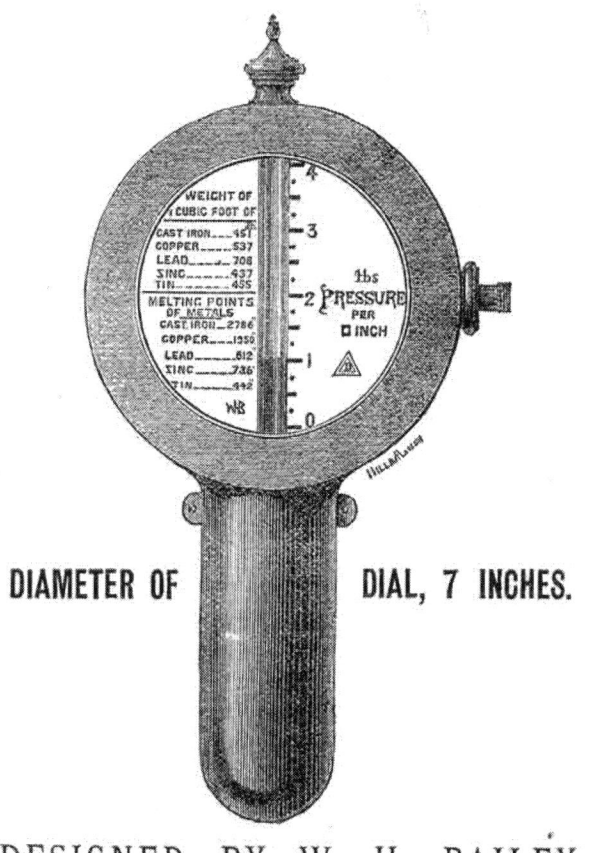

DIAMETER OF DIAL, 7 INCHES.

DESIGNED BY W. H. BAILEY.

TO 4 LBS. PRESSURE.

Price 35s. Each.

W. H. BAILEY & CO., ALBION WORKS, SALFORD, MANCHESTER.

LOWE'S PATENT STENCH TRAPS,
Suitable for all Sewers, Drains in Gardens, Cellars, Yards, &c.

THE BEST MEANS OF PREVENTING THE ATMOSPHERE BEING POISONED BY SEWAGE GAS.

PRICES AND DIMENSIONS.

	LONG.	WIDE.	DEEP.	£	s.	d.			LONG.	WIDE.	DEEP.	£	s.	d.	
A	36 in. ×	16 in. ×	18 in.	4	0	0	each.	E	12 in. ×	5¼ in. ×	6 in.	0	9	0	each.
B	30 in. ×	13½ in. ×	15 in.	3	0	0	,,	F	9 in. ×	4 in. ×	4½ in.	0	5	6	,,
C	24 in. ×	10¾ in. ×	12 in.	1	14	0	,,	G	6 in. ×	2⅞ in. ×	3 in.	0	4	0	,,
D	18 in. ×	8 in. ×	9 in.	1	0	0	,,	H	4 in. ×	1¾ in. ×	2 in.	0	3	6	,,

LARGE QUANTITIES, SPECIAL CONTRACT.

From the above perspective view and section the advantage of the improved Stench Trap will be at once perceived, the principal feature being the form of the bottom and end, as shown in the section, which, when the grate is removed and a rake or other instrument introduced, will enable the operator to draw the dirt up the incline with great facility. Where filth has to be removed, it should be easy to accomplish, or it is very liable to be badly done, or neglected altogether.

The letters A B, &c., refer to the different sizes: the dimensions are taken from the outside measure. The arrow points the direction to set the trap, in case of the channel being on an incline. The grid is fastened with a chain, and is not liable to stick fast, or get broken by being allowed to fall.

PATENT IRON HANDLE SLIDING SCREW WRENCH,
WARRANTED.

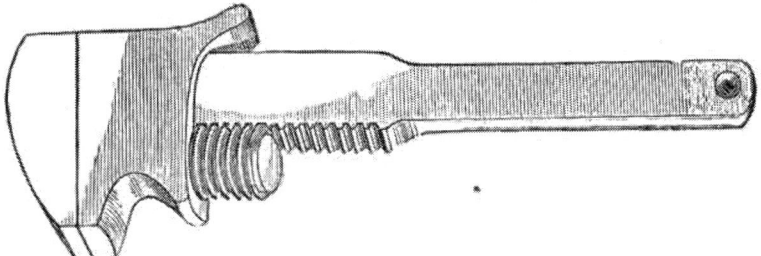

	26/-	30/-	38/-	52/-	70/-	100/-	120/-
C1161.	6	8	10	12	14	16	18-in.

This Wrench is made of a form to give the greatest strength with the least weight of Iron, it being much lighter than any other of the same size. It is easily adjusted, for on lifting the screw out of gear, the jaw will slide freely up or down, or it can be shifted to any nicety by means of the Screw.

AMATEURS' LATHE.
MANCHESTER PATTERN.

Complete, with Planed Bed (V and flat), Treadle and Hook, Crank and Driving Wheel, Hand Rest, Driving Chuck, Drill Chuck, and Two Centres:—

No. 4, 4in. Centres (3 Speeds), 3ft. 6in. Bed £10 0 0
,, 5, 5in.   ,,   (4 Speeds), 3ft. 6in. Bed 11 5 0
,, 6, 5in.   ,,   (4 Speeds), 4ft. Bed 11 16 0

Compound Slide Rests extra, 4in., £4 10s.; 5in., £5.—NETT.

Brass Time Checks for Checking Workmen, including Die and Stamping, 20/- per Dozen.

W. H. BAILEY & CO., ALBION WORKS, SALFORD, MANCHESTER.

THE "DOMESTIC" WASHER.

The "Domestic" Washer,

WITH WRINGER AND MANGLE COMBINED.

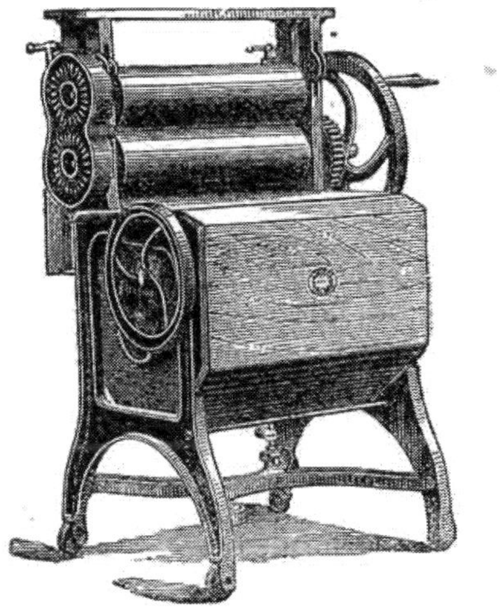

No. 1.—Our Family Machine.. £6 6 0

No. 2.—Twice as large 8 8 0

The "Domestic" Washer,

WITHOUT WRINGER & MANGLE.

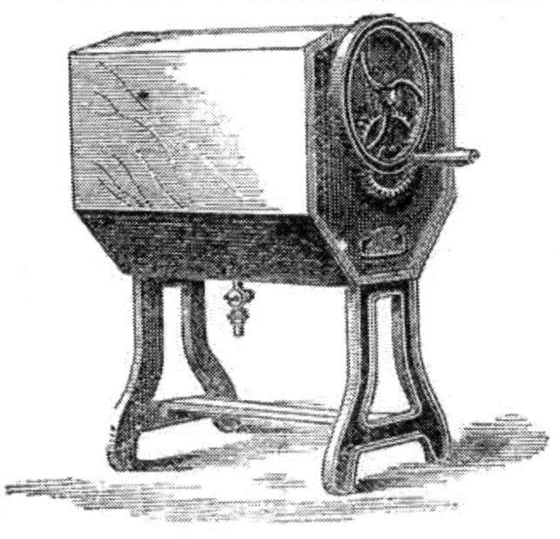

No. 3...£3 15 0 No. 4...£5 0 0

The "Domestic" Washer has the following special advantages :—

1.—A child ten years old washes easily with it.
2.—No wear or tear of material.
3.—Will wash more clothes at once than any other Machine of the same value.
4.—Requires only six gallons of water.
5.—Requires only same space as an ordinary Wringer.

Nos. 3 & 4 can have Bar to suit India Rubber Wringer for 5s. extra.

The "Domestic" Washer,

WITH INDIARUBBER WRINGER.

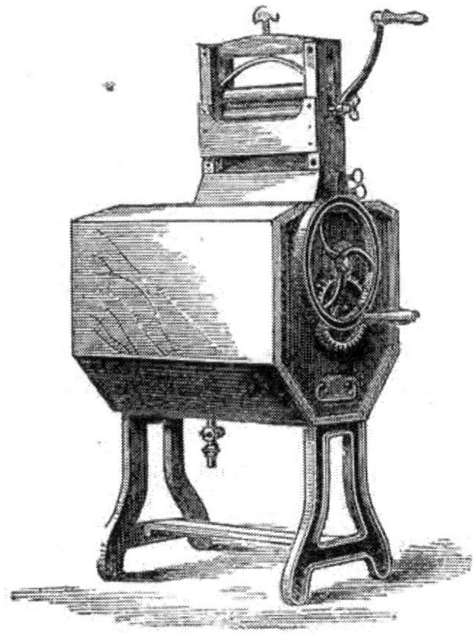

No. 5...£5 5 0 No. 6...£7 7 0

WRINGING AND MANGLING MACHINES.

No. 8.

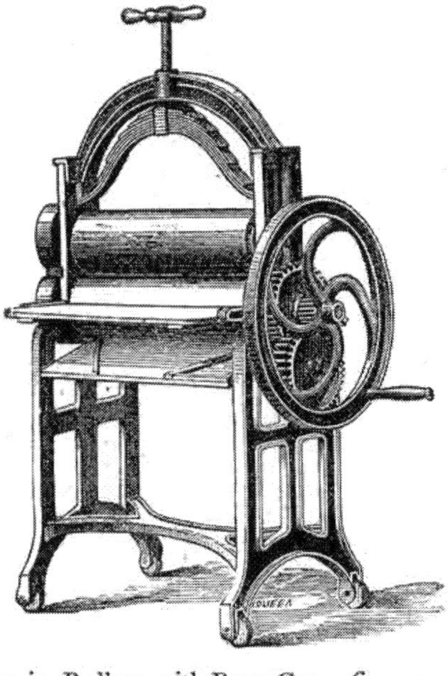

20in. Rollers, with Brass Caps £2 10 0
24in. do. do. ... 3 5 0

No. 7.

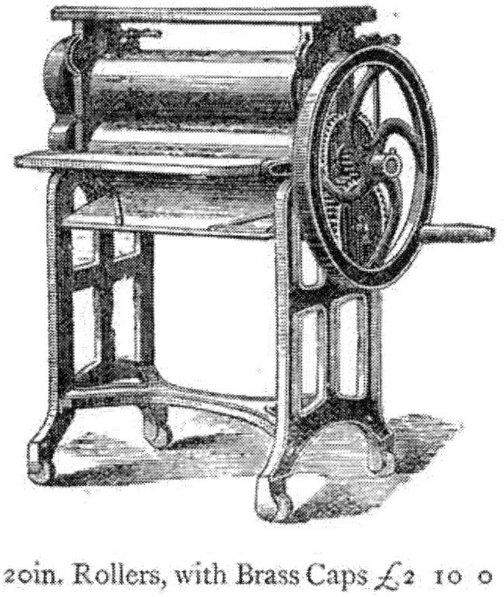

20in. Rollers, with Brass Caps £2 10 0
24in. do. do. ... 3 5 0
26in. do. do. ... 3 10 0
28in. do. do. ... 3 15 0
30in. do. do. ... 4 0 0

No. 10.

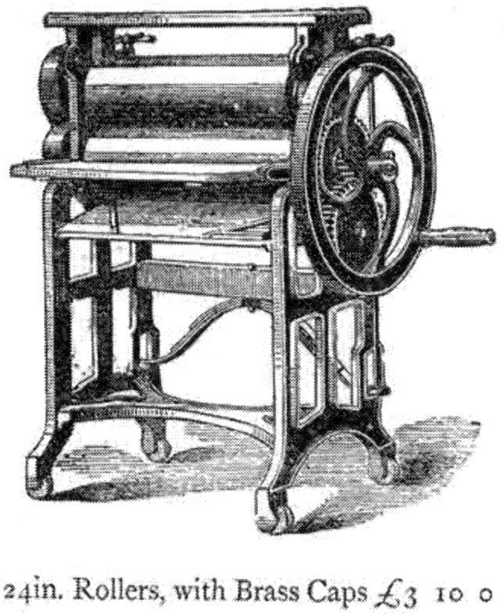

24in. Rollers, with Brass Caps £3 10 0
26in. do. do. ... 3 15 0
28in. do. do. ... 4 0 0
30in. do. do. ... 4 5 0

N.B.—We desire specially to point out that in all Wringing and Mangling, or Combined Washing, Wringing, and Mangling Machines supplied by us, ALL ROLLERS are of the best QUARTERED SYCAMORE, well seasoned, no self Rollers being used.

All Machines are delivered to the nearest Railway Station CARRIAGE PAID.

W. H. BAILEY & CO., ALBION WORKS, SALFORD, MANCHESTER.

BAILEY'S "Syren" Low Water Alarm,
FOR STEAM BOILERS.

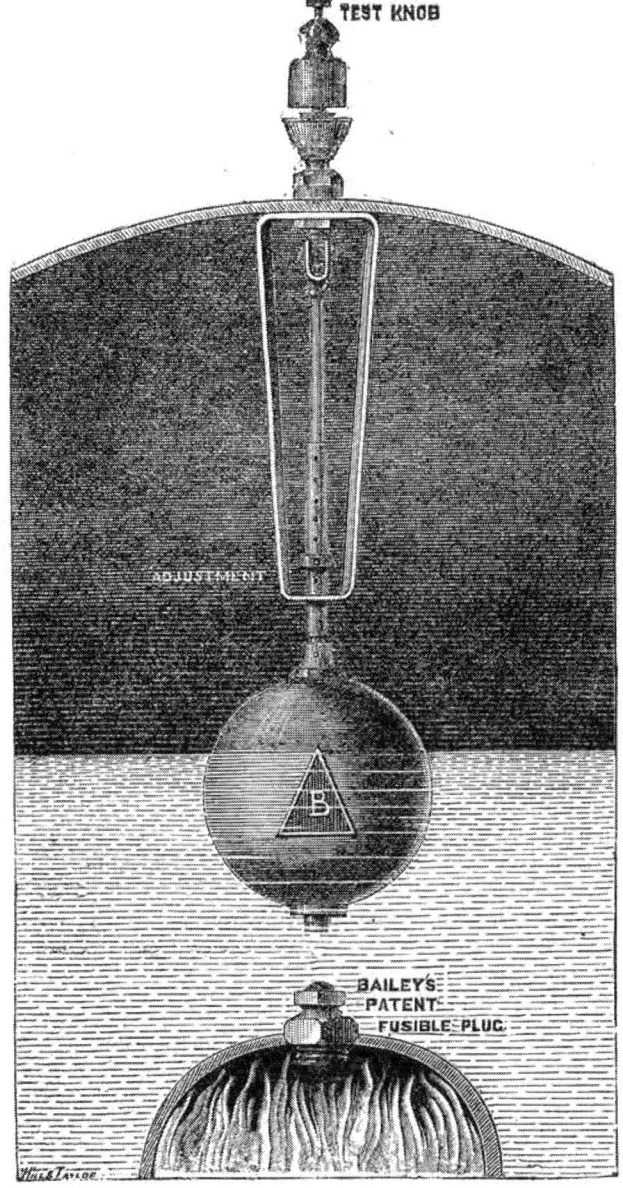

COMPLETE, £2 10s. 0d.

This is much in use, and gives great satisfaction. By pressing down the knob, the Whistle can be made to sound at any time.

For other Whistles see Steam Fitting Department in another portion of the Book.

MANUFACTURERS:
W. H. BAILEY & CO., Brassfounders, &c.,
ALBION WORKS, SALFORD.

WARREN AND CO.,
Manufacturers of the PREMIER ROTARY
KNIFE CLEANING MACHINES,
PREMIER PREPARED EMERY,
TOWEL RAILS, STEEL POLISHERS, &c

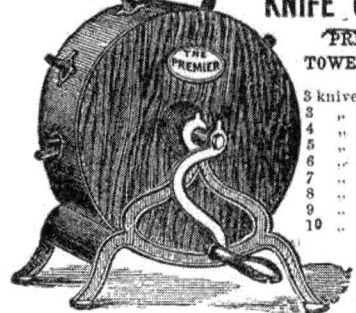

		Low Stand.	High Stand.
3 knives	(iron mounts)	£1 1 0	
3 "	(brass mounts)	1 10 0	
4 "	"	2 2 0	£3 0 0
5 "	"	3 3 0	4 4 0
6 "	"	4 15 0	5 5 0
7 "	"	5 15 0	6 6 0
8 "	"	6 15 0	7 7 0
9 "	"	7 15 0	8 8 0
10 "	"	8 15 0	9 9 0

The above machines are fitted with best materials and workmanship.

To be had through Merchants, Shippers, and Factors.

78 & 79, OXFORD STREET, BIRMINGHAM.

CHARLES TOPHAM,
COLEMAN STREET, BUNHILL ROW, LONDON,
MANUFACTURER AND PATENTEE OF
MINCING AND SAUSAGE MACHINES,
SAUSAGE FILLERS, COFFEE MILLS, AND GENERAL DOMESTIC MACHINERY.

ILLUSTRATED PRICE LISTS, POST FREE.

HOW TO BOIL EGGS
FOR WORKMEN'S BREAKFASTS BY
BAILEY'S PATENT STEAM KETTLE.

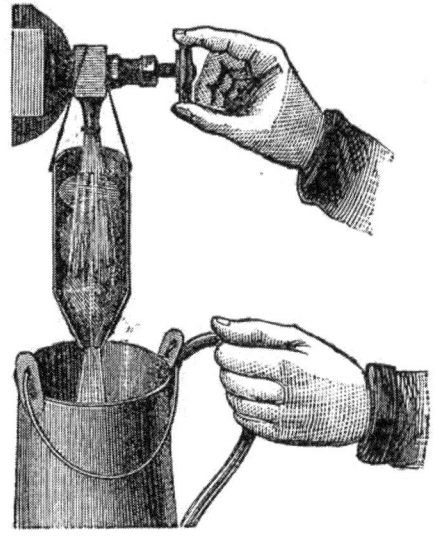

The Steam Kettle for supplying hot water for work people, illustrated and described at page 65 of this book, may be used for boiling eggs by using a small funnel as illustrated; hung by means of a wire handle to the valve. The stoker who minds the boiler generally does this work at large establishments, and will soon by a little practice become a perfect egg boiler. Owners of good eggs may mark their property with a black lead before handing them to him, this prevents confusion. The extra egg apparatus may be made by any tinsmith, or may be had from us at 3/6 each, made of sheet copper.

W. H. BAILEY & CO.,
PATENTEES & MANUFACTURERS.

WEIGHING MACHINERY

COUNTER WEIGHING MACHINE.

Q Z

Suitable for Brass Founders, Piece Goods, and where very fine and accurate weighings are indispensable.

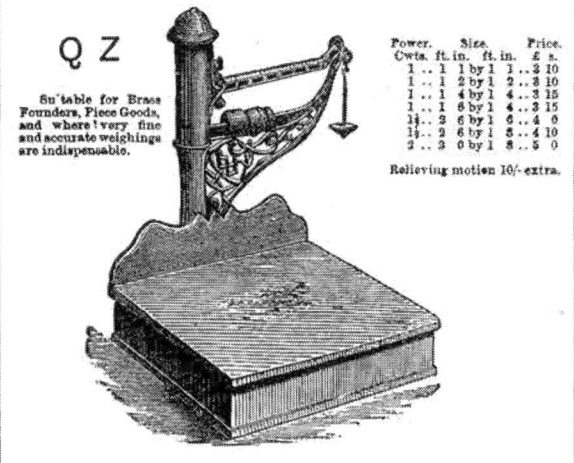

Power.	Size.		Price.
Cwts.	ft. in.	ft. in.	£ s.
1	1 by 1	1	3 10
1	1 2 by 1	2	3 10
1	1 4 by 1	4	3 15
1	1 6 by 1	4	3 15
1½	2 by 1	6	4 0
1½	2 6 by 1	8	4 10
2	3 by 1	8	5 0

Relieving motion 10/- extra.

PORTABLE PLATFORM WEIGHING MACHINE

T

Suitable for Gas, Chemical, and other Works.

With Pockets for Planks.

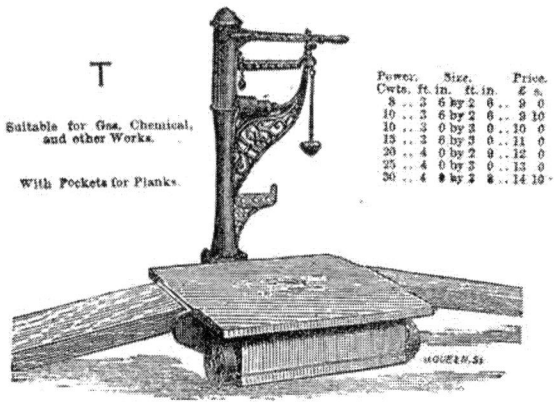

Power.	Size.		Price.
Cwts.	ft. in.	ft. in.	£ s.
8	3 6 by 2	6	9 0
10	3 6 by 2	6	9 10
10	3 0 by 3	0	10 0
15	3 6 by 3	0	11 0
20	4 0 by 2	9	12 0
25	4 0 by 3	0	13 0
30	4 8 by 3	8	14 10

PORTABLE PLATFORM WEIGHING MACHINE

H

For Wool Bales, Cotton Waste, and Leather Dealers, &c., &c., and all kinds of bulky goods.

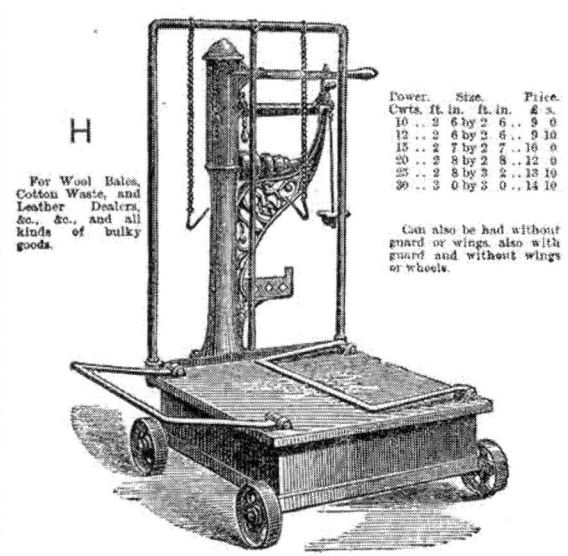

Power.	Size.		Price.
Cwts.	ft. in.	ft. in.	£ s.
10	2 6 by 2	6	9 0
12	2 6 by 2	6	9 10
15	2 7 by 2	7	16 0
20	2 8 by 2	8	12 0
25	2 8 by 3	2	13 10
30	3 0 by 3	0	14 10

Can also be had without guard or wings, also with guard and without wings or wheels.

For Railways, Roads, Collieries, Iron Forges, Rolling Mills, Mines, Markets, Warehouses, Paper Makers, and all Commercial Uses.

—

**W. H. BAILEY & Co.
Albion Works,
ESSEX STREET,
SALFORD,
MANCHESTER.**

PORTABLE PLATFORM WEIGHING MACHINE.

Y

For Stores, Railway Parcel Offices, Shops, &c. This Machine is also fitted, when desired, with back guard, at from 5/ to 15/ extra; also with four wheels and axles, at from 5/ to 15/ extra.

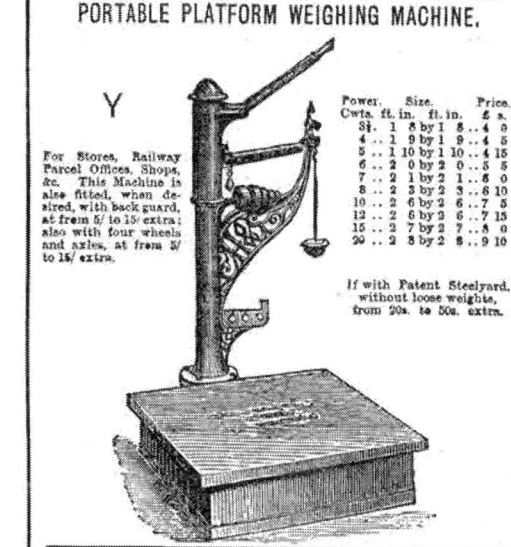

Power.	Size.		Price.
Cwts.	ft. in.	ft. in.	£ s.
3½	1 8 by 1	8	4 0
4	1 9 by 1	9	4 5
5	1 10 by 1	10	4 15
6	2 0 by 2	0	5 5
7	2 1 by 2	1	5 0
8	2 3 by 2	3	6 10
10	2 6 by 2	6	7 5
12	2 6 by 2	6	7 15
15	2 7 by 2	7	8 0
20	2 8 by 2	8	9 10

If with Patent Steelyard, without loose weights, from 20s. to 50s. extra.

PORTABLE PLATFORM WEIGHING MACHINE.

X S

For ordinary purposes. This Machine can be fitted with wheels and axles, at from 10/ to 30/ extra, and cradle for bar iron at from 25/ to 80/ extra.

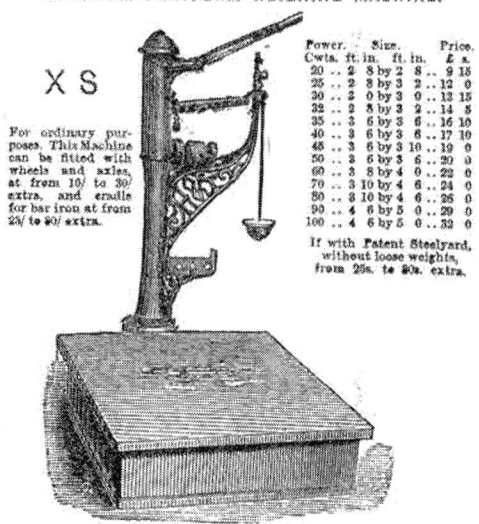

Power.	Size.		Price.
Cwts.	ft. in.	ft. in.	£ s.
20	2 8 by 2	8	9 15
25	2 8 by 3	2	12 0
30	3 0 by 3	0	13 15
32	3 8 by 3	8	14 5
35	3 6 by 3	6	16 10
40	3 6 by 3	6	17 10
45	3 6 by 3 10		19 0
50	3 6 by 3	6	20 0
60	3 8 by 4	0	22 0
70	3 10 by 4	6	24 0
80	3 10 by 4	6	26 0
90	4 6 by 5	0	29 0
100	4 6 by 5	0	32 0

If with Patent Steelyard, without loose weights, from 25s. to 80s. extra.

PLATFORM DORMANT WEIGHING MACHINE.

W V

Sunk flush with floor, for Warehouses, Railway Platforms, &c., &c. Manufactured with Patent Steelyard, without loose weights, when desired; also with chequered platforms, at prices proportionately higher.

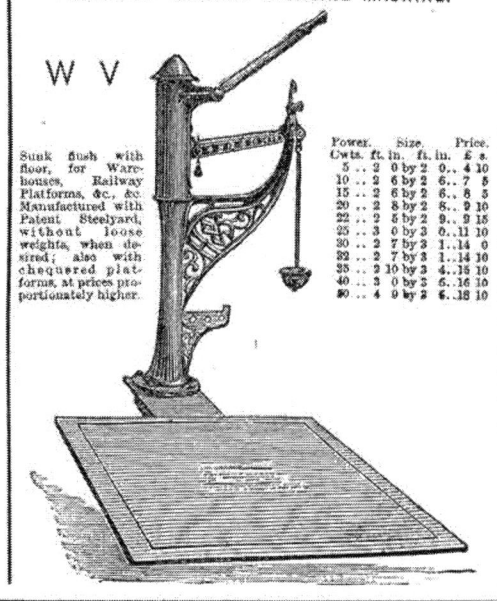

Power.	Size.		Price.
Cwts.	ft. in.	ft. in.	£ s.
5	2 0 by 2	0	4 10
10	2 6 by 2	6	7 5
15	2 6 by 2	6	7 15
20	2 8 by 2	8	9 10
22	2 5 by 2	9	9 15
25	3 0 by 3	0	11 10
30	2 7 by 3	1	14 0
32	2 7 by 3	1	14 10
33	2 10 by 3	4	15 10
40	3 0 by 3	5	16 10
50	4 0 by 2	6	18 10

The Gravity Tallow Cup

Is especially adapted for use when

Messrs. Crane's Patent Oil

Is used for

Steam Engine Cylinders.

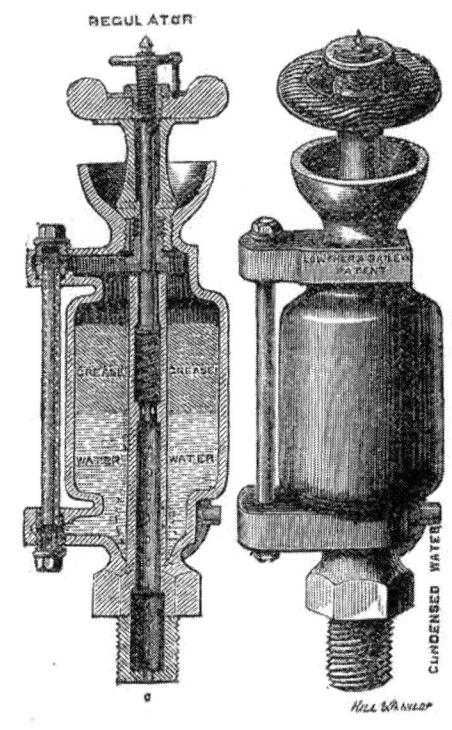

FOR PRICES AND PARTICULARS SEE PAGE 77 OF THIS BOOK.

There will be read an account of important facts in connection with the incrustation of Steam Boilers which must be of interest to all who study BOILER ECONOMY.

W. H. BAILEY & CO., ALBION WORKS, SALFORD, MANCHESTER.

CRANE'S PATENT OIL,

FOR CYLINDERS AND VALVES OF COMPOUND SURFACE-CONDENSING ENGINES,

AS SUPPLIED TO H.M. DOCKYARDS AND FLEET.

MANUFACTURED BY

DUCIE BUILDINGS, BANK STREET, MANCHESTER,

TRADE MARK

P. MOIR CRANE & CO.,

AND 25, WATER STREET, LIVERPOOL.

WORKS: CLAYTON.

THE superiority of this Oil over all others as a lubricant for the internal parts of Compound Surface-Condensing Engines has been fully proved by its use for some years past by most of the principal Steamship Companies. It is now regularly supplied to H.M. Dockyards and Fleet, to the German, Danish, and Italian Navies, and to the leading Steamship Companies of London, Liverpool, Glasgow, Southampton, &c. By its use the cylinders, valve casings, and condensers are kept perfectly free from the deposit, which was so serious an objection to the lubricants formerly employed; and as the Oil does not turn acid, the internal parts of the machinery, as well as the boilers, are not corroded by it.

The following are some of the advantages possessed by this Oil:—

1. It stands a higher heat without grinding.
2. It *remains in its original form of an Oil* in cylinders, condensers, and boilers, and from its so remaining does not form a scum or soapy substance on the surface of the water, but allows the steam to escape regularly through it, whereby *priming*, arising from local causes, is prevented.
3. A better vacuum is maintained.
4. It does not become sticky or gummy upon any of the working portions of the Machinery.
5. It is absolutely free from acid, and *no acid can be generated from it:* the great cause of the rapid destruction of the boilers of H. P. Compound Surface-Condensing Engines is thus removed. The high temperature to which the lubricants are exposed in the high pressure cylinder decomposes fatty Oils, such as Olive or Tallow, forming Oleic and Stearic acids, which rapidly eat into the boilers. CRANE'S Patent Oil is not thus decomposed by heat, and consequently *preserves* instead of injuring the boilers.

These results will be obtained if CRANE'S Oil is used *alone* for valves, cylinders, and piston-rods.

P. MOIR CRANE & Co.'s patent rights cover the application of all Oils of the class possessing these advantages, and any infringement will be promptly dealt with.

India Rubber Valves, specially prepared to withstand the action of this Oil, are now supplied by all the well known makers.

P. MOIR CRANE & Co. guarantee the Oil genuine only when supplied direct, or through their authorised Agents. All casks branded with the trade mark of the firm.

CRANE'S SPINDLE AND MACHINERY OILS.

THE high character of the above Oils has been fully established by the results of actual working, during many years past, in some of the largest Cotton and Flax Spinning Mills, Machine Works, &c., throughout the country. They are at present in extensive use by numbers of the principal firms in the above trades, to whom reference can be made.

P. MOIR CRANE & Co.'s works at Clayton, covering nearly three acres of ground, have been erected specially for the manufacture of Lubricating Oils, and are now amongst the largest of the kind in the kingdom. They are thus enabled to supply their Oils direct to the consumers upon the most advantageous terms, and also to ensure a uniformly good quality.

P. MOIR CRANE & Co. take this opportunity of drawing the attention of consumers to the following advantages which their Oils possess:—

1. They are entirely free from any tendency to gum or clog upon Machinery, being in this respect superior even to Sperm.
2. They are perfectly safe to use, possessing a high point of ignition.
3. They are prepared of different degrees of body, so as to be suitable both for light and heavy Machinery.
4. Being bagged at a low temperature, these Oils will stand a considerable degree of cold without congealing, and the lubricating power is improved thereby.
5. The moderate price of these Oils, combined with their quality, renders their use as lubricants extremely economical.

LONDON: W. ALLAN & CO., 38, Leadenhall Street.
NEWCASTLE-ON-TYNE: G. A. BUSHELL, 38, Quay Side.
GLASGOW: ARTHUR, GOODWIN & CO., 163, St. Vincent Street.
HULL: R. BARTON, 4, Castle Street Chambers.

DUNDEE: MATHERS BROS., 9, Bain Sqr.
CORK: W. & H. M. GOULDING.
CALCUTTA: J. NICOL FLEMING & CO.
HAMBURG: E. HAGAN & CO.
ROTTERDAM: WIJNMALEN & HAUSMAN.
AMSTERDAM: CORNS. KONING, JUN.
ANTWERP: F. MONU, 15, Quai St. Pierre.

CHRISTIANIA: JENSEN & JARMANN.
SINGAPORE: THE BORNEO CO., Limited.
HONG KONG: T. G. LINSTEAD.
SHANGHAE: J. M. CANNY & CO.
BOMBAY: WM. NICOL & CO.
STETTIN: A. WEYLANDT.
PORT SAID: R. BROADBENT.
COPENHAGEN: ARNOLD SALMONSEN.

JOHN CAMERON'S SPECIALITIES

(ESTABLISHED 1852.)

ARE ALL SIZES OF

STEAM PUMPS,
Shipbuilders' Tools,
BAR SHEARS.

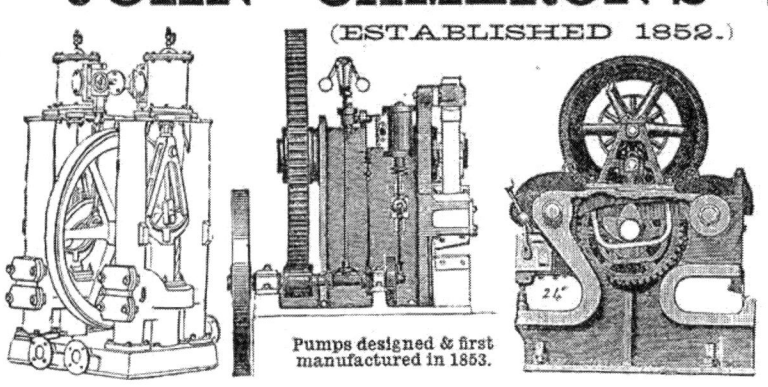

Pumps designed & first manufactured in 1853.

WORKS:
OLDFIELD ROAD IRONWORKS,
SALFORD, MANCHESTER.

BROWN'S PATENT PIPE TONGS.

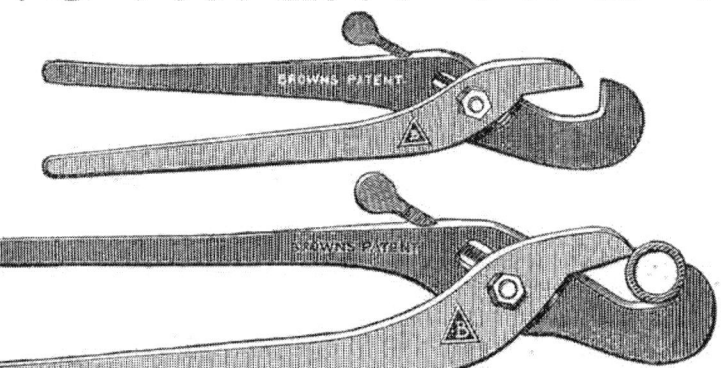

Adjustable,
Compact,
Durable,
Quick,
Powerful,
Light,
Satisfactory.

For Pipe. Inches.

No. 2 ¼ to 1¼ 15s.
" 3 1 " 2½ 20s.

The two complete in case, with handle to carry,

£2 2s.

☞ PLEASE NOTICE THE FACILITY FOR ADJUSTMENT.

PATENT ENAMELLED
𝔚ater 𝔊auge 𝔊lasses,
FOR STEAM BOILERS.

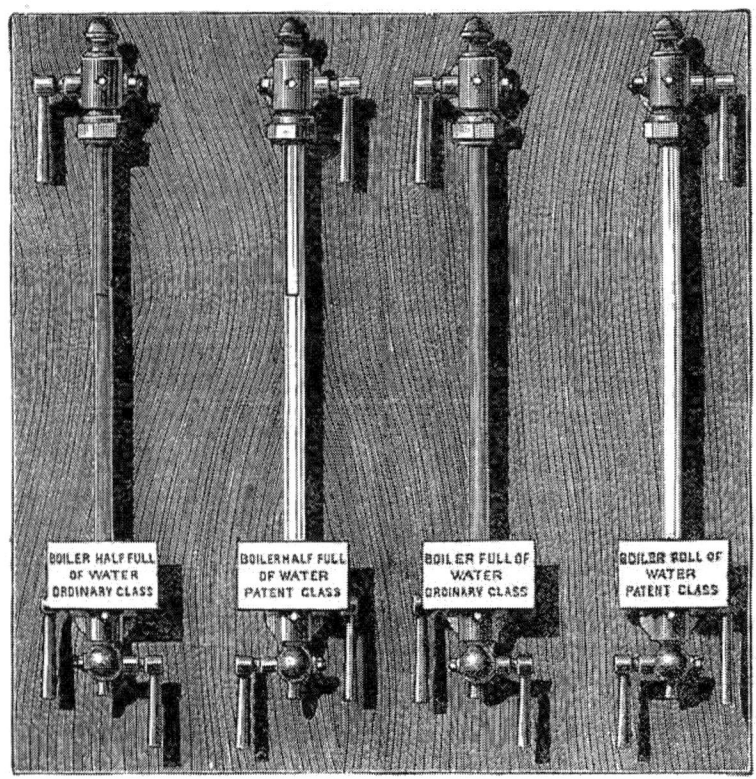

PRICE LIST.

Length Inches	⅜in. Per Doz.	½in. Per Doz.	¾in. Per Doz.	⅞in. Per Doz.	1in. Per Doz.
12	8/9	10/6	12/0	13/0	14/8
13	9/3	11/0	12/6	14/0	16/0
14	9/9	11/6	13/0	15/2	17/3
15	10/3	12/0	13/6	16/2	18/6
16	10/9	12/6	14/0	17/2	19/3
17	11/3	13/0	14/8	18/3	21/0
18	11/9	14/0	15/2	19/3	22/3
19	12/3	15/0	16/2	20/3	23/6
20	12/9	15/8	17/2	21/3	25/0
21	13/3	16/2	18/3	22/3	26/0
22	13/9	16/8	19/3	23/3	27/6
23	14/3	17/2	20/3	24/3	28/6
24	14/9	17/8	21/3	25/6	29/6

W. H. BAILEY & CO., ALBION WORKS, SALFORD, MANCHESTER.

W. BARNINGHAM & CO. LIMITED,

Manufacturers of

RAILS, CHAIRS, SWITCHES
AND CROSSINGS,
Fish Plates, Bolts, Spikes,
BAR IRON, ANGLES, AND ROLLED GIRDERS.

CONTRACTORS' RAILS, WHEELS, AXLES, &c.

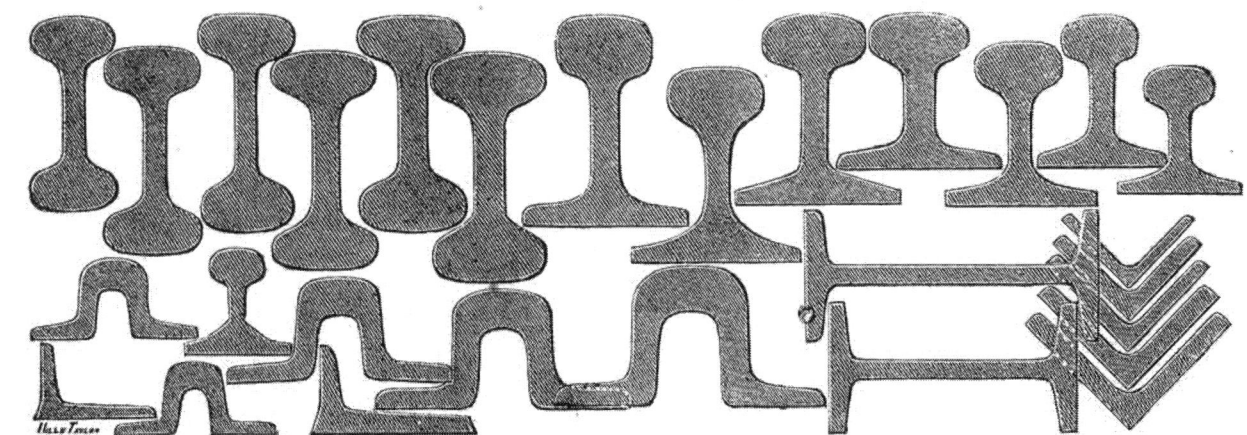

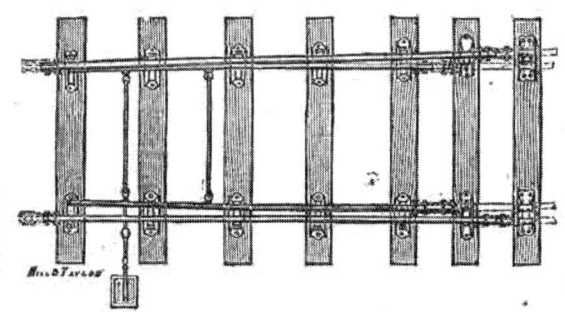
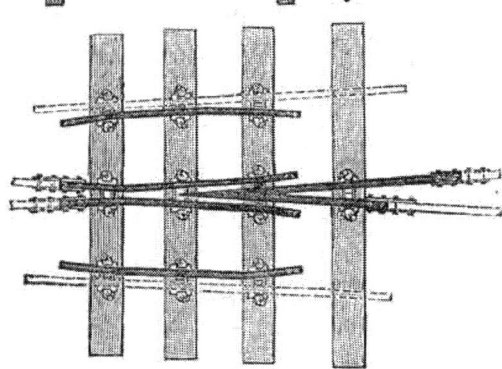

TURNTABLES, MORTAR MILLS.
BARNINGHAM'S PATENT RAIL-STRAIGHTENING MACHINES.
WROUGHT-IRON BRICK WAGONS,
AND GENERAL PLANT FOR BRICKMAKERS' DRYING STOVES.
Ironwork for Constructive Purposes, &c.

PENDLETON IRON WORKS, MANCHESTER.

HENRY BROADBENT,
THE HOLLINGS TOOL WORKS,
Sowerby Bridge, Yorkshire.

12 inch Lathe.

9 inch Lathe.

PARTICULARS ON APPLICATION

Maker of superior Sliding & Screw Cutting Lathes; Planeing, Slotting, Drilling, Punch & Shearing Machines; Iron Founder, &c.

B. & S. MASSEY, OPENSHAW, MANCHESTER, ENGLAND.

PRIZE MEDALS AWARDED :—Paris, 1867; Havre, 1868; Highland Society, 1870; Liverpool, 1871; Moscow, 1872; Vienna, 1873; Scientific Industry Society, 1875; Leeds, 1875.

PATENTEES AND MAKERS
OF DOUBLE AND SINGLE-ACTING
STEAM HAMMERS

Of all sizes, from ¾ Cwt. to 20 Tons, with Self-acting or Hand Motions, in either case giving a perfectly DEAD BLOW, while the former may be worked by Hand when desired. Large Hammers, with Improved Framing, in Cast or Wrought Iron. Small Hammers, working up to 500 blows per minute, in some cases being worked by the Foot of the Smith, and not requiring any separate Driver.

SPECIAL STEAM STAMPS
For Forging, Stamping, Punching, Bolt-Making, &c.
STEAM HAMMERS

For Engineers, Machinists, Shipbuilders, Steel Tilters, Millwrights, Coppersmiths, Railway Carriage and Wagon Builders, Colliery Proprietors, Ship Smiths, Bolt Makers, Cutlers, File Makers, Spindle and Flyer Makers, Spade Makers, Locomotive and other Wheel Makers, &c.; also for use in Repairing Smithies of Mills and Works of all kinds; for straightening Bars, bending Cranks, breaking Pig Iron, &c.

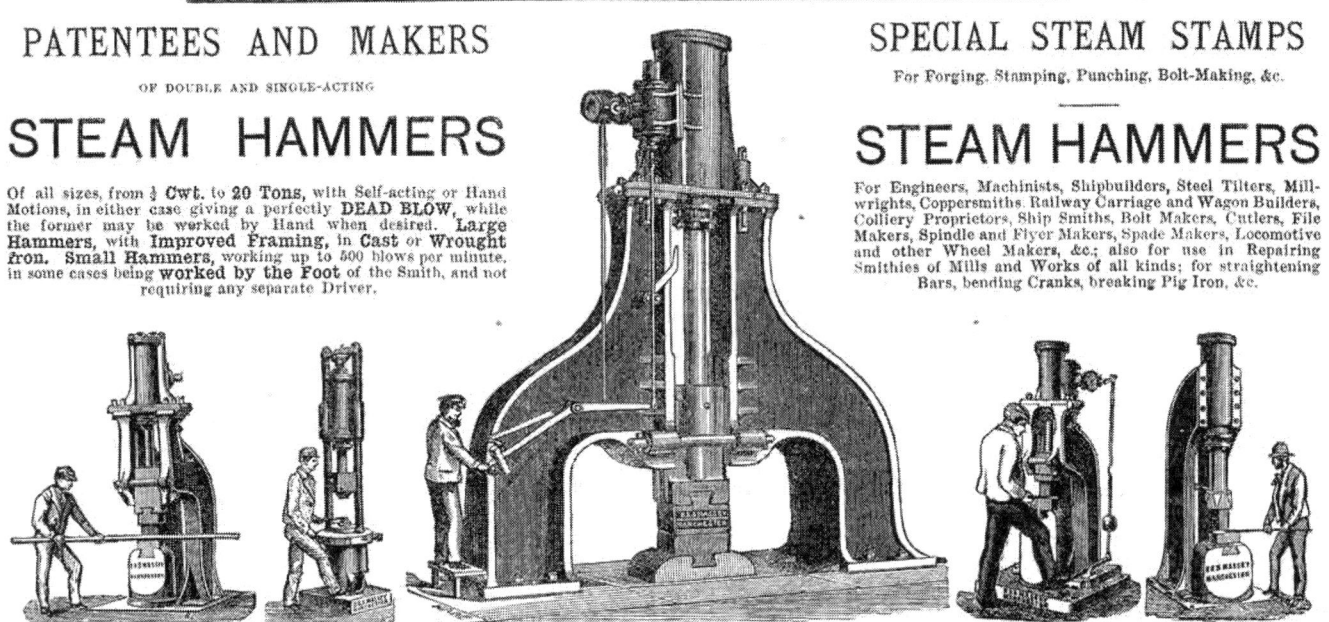

General Smithy Hammer.   Special Steam Stamp.   Steam Hammer for Heavy Forging.   Small Hammer, with Foot Motion.   General Smithy Hammer.

From 60 to 100 Steam Hammers and Steam Stamps may usually be seen in construction at the Works.

J. W. STEAD'S IMPROVED AND PATENT WEIGHING MACHINERY,

J. W. STEAD'S Patent PIT-BANK MACHINES are made to any dimensions and power, and with or without turntable or rails.—NO SPRINGS.—NO LOOSE WEIGHTS.—NET WEIGHT shown at a glance.

J. W. STEAD'S SELF-CONTAINED WEIGHBRIDGES entirely supersede masonry and brickwork foundations. They are *strong, well-finished, accurate and durable.* Send for particulars.

FOR

RAILWAYS, IRON WORKS, WOOLLEN MILLS,
CORPORATIONS, COLLIERIES, PAPER MILLS,
MARKETS, CHEMICAL WORKS, GLASS WORKS,
GAS WORKS, COTTON MILLS, WAREHOUSES,

AND ALL COMMERCIAL PURPOSES.

J. W. STEAD, GLOBE FOUNDRY, PENDLETON, MANCHESTER.

HARTLEY & SUGDEN,

Atlas & Premier Works, HALIFAX, England,

PATENTEES AND MANUFACTURERS OF

WROUGHT-WELDED BOILERS,

FOR HOT WATER HEATING APPARATUS, KITCHEN RANGES, &c., &c.

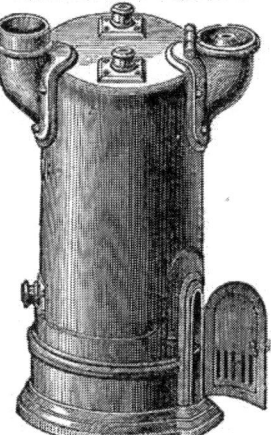

Independent Dome-Top Boilers.

Prize Medal & Grand Diploma	Gold Medal—1872.	Prize Medal & Grand Diploma
BRUSSELS INTERNATIONAL EXHIBITION, 1876,	NATIONAL CONTEST PRIZE MEDALS, FOR	BRUSSELS INTERNATIONAL EXHIBITION, 1876,
FOR BOILERS.	BOILERS & LAWN MOWERS.	FOR LAWN MOWERS.

Patent Climax Boiler.

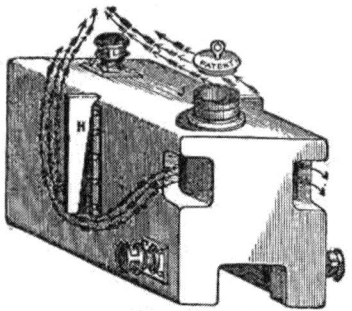

FRONT ELEVATION

Gold-Medal Boiler.

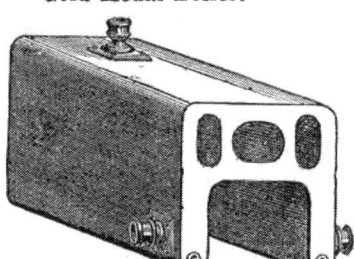

Patent Saddle Boiler, with Top Feeder.

ELEVATION SHOWING METHOD OF SETTING CHARGING

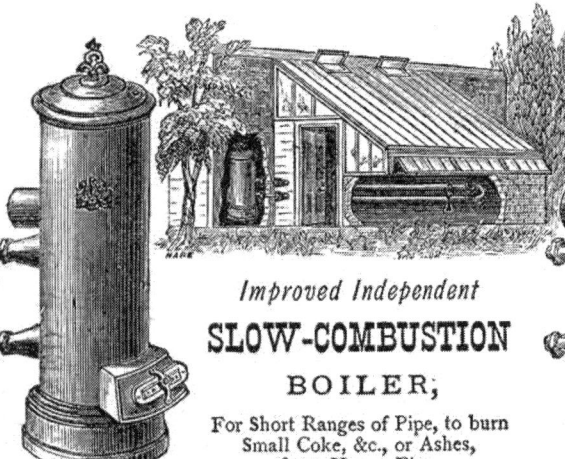

Improved Independent
SLOW-COMBUSTION BOILER;
For Short Ranges of Pipe, to burn Small Coke, &c., or Ashes, from House Fires.

Welded Independent Vertical Steam Boiler.

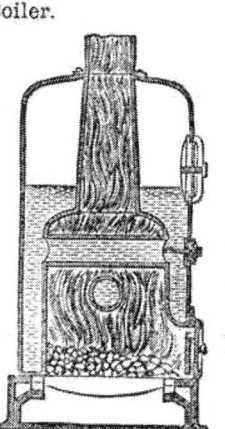

NATIONAL CONTEST PRIZE-MEDAL LAWN MOWERS.

THE OSBORNE.
(REGISTERED TITLE.)

THE WINDSOR.
(REGISTERED TITLE.)

All our Lawn Mowers will be found complete, with all the Latest Improvements; will cut long or short Grass, Bents, &c. Every Machine is warranted to give satisfaction.

Goods supplied through the Trade only. Merchant Shippers supplied on Liberal Terms.

J. & J. BRADDOCK,
GLOBE METER WORKS, OLDHAM,
Gas Engineers and Manufacturers of Wet and Dry Gas-Meters,
Of the best material and workmanship only, carefully adjusted to the requirements of the British Sales of Gas Act and Foreign Standards of Measure.

Gas-Station Meter.

WET METERS.

Size of Meter. Lights	Price. £ s. d.
2	1 8 0
3	1 13 6
5	2 10 0
10	3 17 6
15	4 16 6
20	5 16 6
30	8 18 0
50	13 6 6
60	15 11 0
80	18 18 0
100	22 5 0
150	30 0 0
200	37 16 0
250	44 10 0
300	50 0 0
400	55 10 0
500	61 0 0
600	66 10 0

DISCOUNT.

DRY METERS.

Size of Meter. Lights	Price £ s. d.
2	1 4 6
3	1 10 0
5	1 16 6
10	2 7 0
20	3 5 0
30	4 10 0
50	6 5 0
60	8 8 0
80	10 12 0
100	13 15 0
150	18 17 0
200	25 4 0

DISCOUNT.

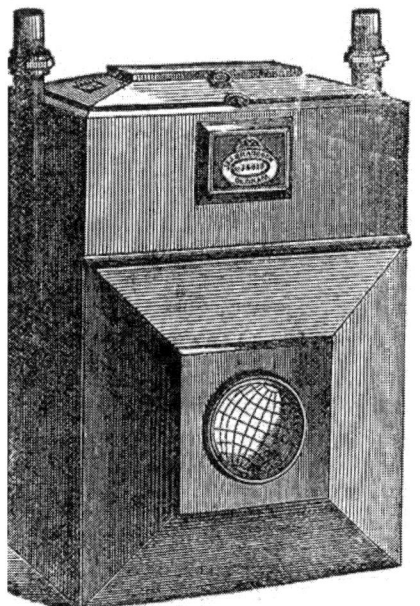
Dry Gas-Meter.

Round Meter.   Wet Gas-Meter.

PATENT GOVERNORS, GAUGES, INDICATORS, EXHAUST-GOVERNORS, DISTRICT-GOVERNORS, TEST-HOLDERS, MAIN COCKS, GAS-COOKERS, &c.

All Sizes of Consumers' Meters kept in Stock, and Orders almost invariably despatched on the day of Receipt.

DEAKIN, PARKER & CO.
ENGINEERS,
SANDON STREET WORKS, SALFORD, MANCHESTER.

CLASS C.

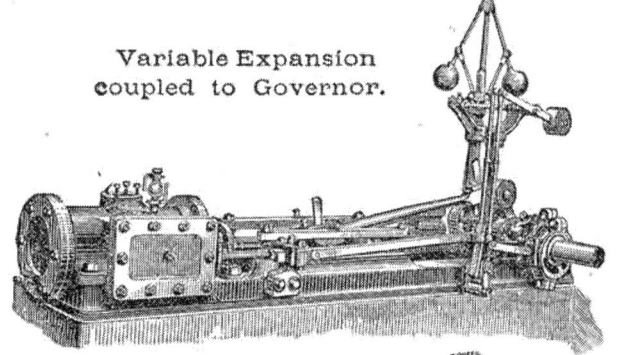

Variable Expansion coupled to Governor.

CLASS A.

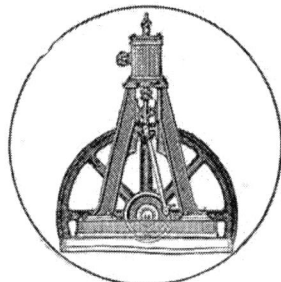

CLASS K.

Condenser. CLASS D.

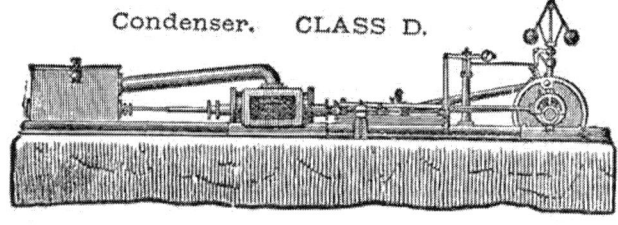

CLASS J.

High Class Compound Condensing Engines, of most compact, durable and simple design.

All Engines, of whatever class, guaranteed to work well.

Compound as made for Turkish Government.   Compound as made for Manchester Corporation.

CLASS I.
PRICES AND PARTICULARS.

Diameter of Cylinders			4 in.	5 in.	6 in.	7 in.	8 in.	9 in.	10in.	12in.	14in.	16in.	18in.	20in.	22in.	24in.	26in.	28in.	30in.	32in.
Nominal Horse Power			2	3	4	5	7	8	10	14	16	22	25	32	40	48	55	65	75	90
Indicated ,,			2½	4½	8	11	14½	19	23½	33	53	68	82½	120	145	164	193	250	320	372
Length of Stroke			8 in.	10in.	12in.	14in.	16in.	18in.	20in.	24in.	28in.	32in.	36in.	42in.	42in.	48in.	48in.	54in.	60in.	60in.
Revolutions per Minute																				
Diameter of Fly Wheel		Ft.	2½	3	3½	4.0	4.6	5.0	6.0	7.6	8.0	8.6	9.0	9.6	10.0	10.6	11.0	11.6	12.0	14.0
Weight ,,		Cwt.	2	2½	3½	5	7½	10	15	25	35	45	60	70	80	90	100	120	140	160
Width ,,																				
Diameter of Crank Shaft		In.	2¼	2½	2¾	3	3¼	3¾	4	4½	5¼	6¼	7	7½	8	8¼	8¾	9	9¼	9½
Length			2.6	3.0	3.6	4.0	4.6	5.0	5.6	5.6	5.6	5.6	5.6	6.0	6.0	6.6	7.0	7.6	8.0	8.0
Approx. Weight Complete		Cwt.	10	15	20	25	30	40	50	80	100	130	160	200	240	280	360	420	480	500
			£	£	£	£	£	£	£	£	£	£	£	£	£	£	£	£	£	£
PRICES—Class A			30	40	51	64	75	84	96	120	152	190	238	320	420	510	648	744	864	1080
,, ,, C			36	46	63	78	91	102	116	144	184	222	274	360	464	558	700	800	924	1144
,, ,, D			58	71	93	113	130	147	166	204	254	302	364	460	574	678	830	940	1074	1301
,, ,, E			30	40	45	50	55													
,, ,, F			30	40	45	50	55													
,, ,, H			30	40	51	64	75	84	96	138	152	218	272	368	483	586				
,, ,, J				75	90	105	120	&c.												
,, ,, K				75	90	105	120	&c.												

ADVERTISEMENT.

IMPORTANT TO STEAM POWER USERS.
HULME & LUND'S
PATENT NOISELESS DONKEY PUMPS,

AWARDED SPECIAL   PRIZE MEDAL

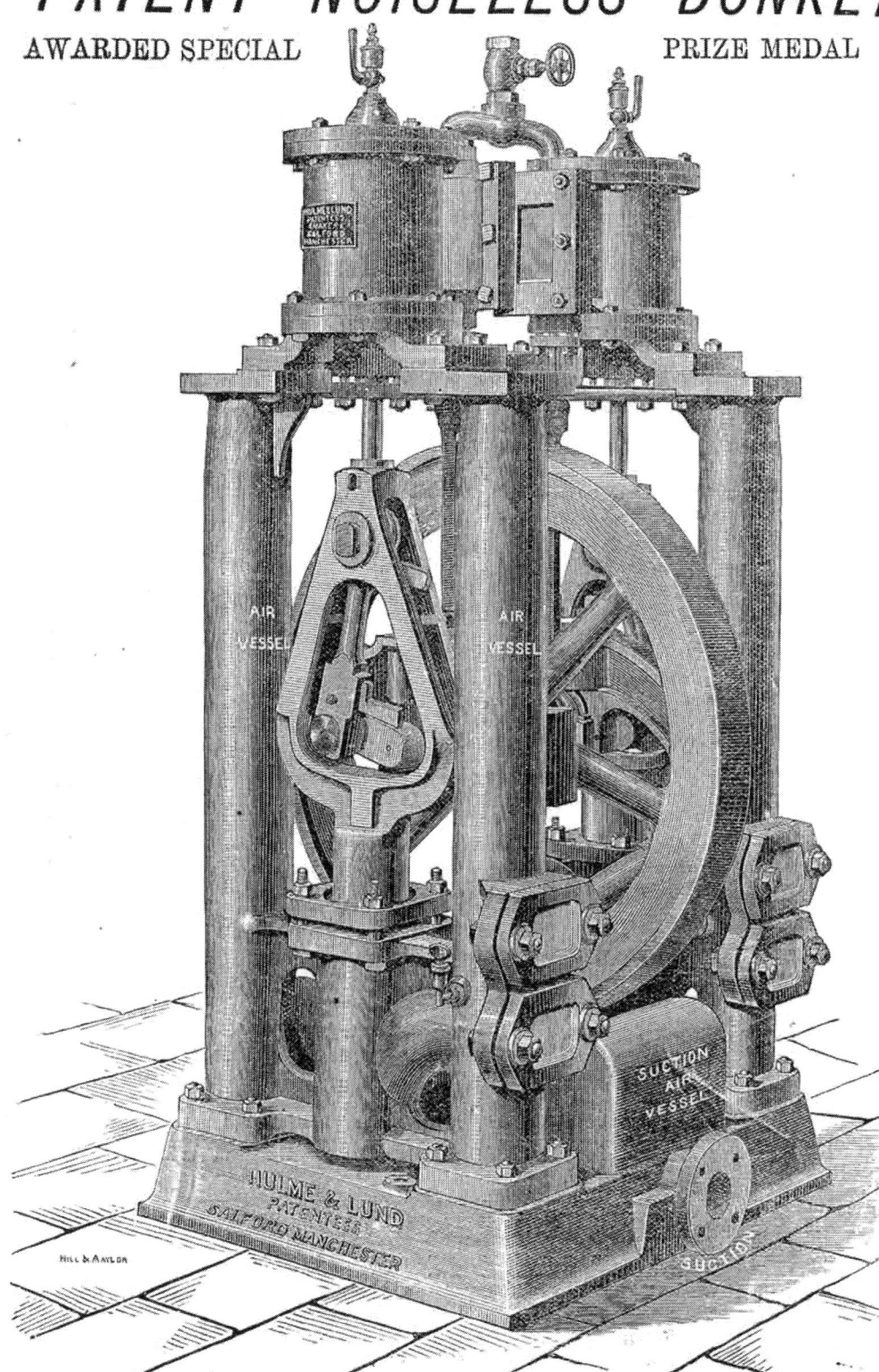

AT THE
Pomona Exhibition,
MANCHESTER,

For Feeding Boilers with Hot or Cold Water, and as Steam Fire Engines at Mills and other Works,

For this they are invaluable, being the simplest and most durable Pump made; all working parts are easy of access and adjustment; they can be understood, and managed by any Fireman, Watchman or Labourer; made in all sizes, from 2-in. upwards, single and double-acting.

These Pumps are much used in Deep Mines, and can be specially made to force water from any depth, some now forcing 1,140 feet high in one direct lift. They are also well adapted for driving self-stoking Apparatus, the Scrapers of Economisers, Machine shop or any small Machinery.

OUR
Horizontal Pumping Engines,

Double-acting, with One Ram,

Quadruple-acting, with Two Rams,

Have long Strokes, Crank and Fly-Wheel, specially designed for Fire Engines, and for raising very large quantities.

Our Pumps are strong and well made, and are tested at actual work, forcing against a high pressure before delivery. Warranted to work well.

References to, and Testimonials from, Collieries, Mills, Iron, Brick, Bleach, Dye, Chemical and other Works, on application to

WILBURN IRON WORKS, Wilburn Street, Regent Road, SALFORD, MANCHESTER.
Also Makers of Steam Engines.   All Sizes of Pumps in Stock or Progress.

ADVERTISEMENT.

August, 1875.]   8-IN. STROKE, SINGLE-GEARED, AND THREE-SPEEDED   [No. 43.

SHAPING & PLANING MACHINE,

Of New Design, and with IMPROVED ARRANGEMENTS, by Andrew Muir.

(From a Photo.)

Internal Curve Motion on Tool-box to shape hollow objects, ¼-in. to 11-in. radius, extra... £2 10 0
Improved External Curve Motion Chuck to fix on front of table, with Steel Conical Mandrel, to shape round objects, ¼-in. to 19½-in. radius ... 3 15 0

Similar Machine, 10-in. Strokes, extra. do. £2 10 0
Ditto, do. 12-in. do. do. 5 0 0

This Universal Self-acting Shaping Machine is specially designed to Shape, Plane, or Groove the small parts of Machines expeditiously, cheaply, and accurately, which were heretofore considered too small to be shaped by a Machine-tool, and were therefore finished by skilled workmen; whereas this Tool only requires the attendance of a boy, who can mind one or more Machines at the same time.

It can be fixed and worked on a Lathe-bed or Work-bench, or on legs, with shelves, as shewn.

It has a three-speeded Cone-pulley, 6, 8, and 10-in. diameter, and 2½-in. wide, with a pinion working into a wheel which is cast in one piece with the Slot-disc, with a variable stroke from ¼-in. to 8-in. long, and will plane an object 3-ft. long, self-acting. The Tool-box has a full swivel, and is graduated into degrees.

	£ s d
All complete (without Legs), with top Cone-pulley and Screw-keys delivered on Rails in Manchester	£38 10 0
EXTRAS, IF REQUIRED.	
If fitted on Legs, with Shelves, as shewn	2 10 0
Patent universal overhead Driving Apparatus, for fixing and working on ceiling, wall, or any other required position, consisting of fast and loose Pulleys, 12-in. diameter and 3¼-in. wide, two Hangers, Counter-shaft, Sliding-bar, Strap-forks, and definite-safety starting and knock-off strap motion	3 10 0
8-in. Jaw Parallel Vice-chuck, with key, to fix on top and side of table	3 10 0
8-in. Jaw Parallel Vice-chuck, with a self-adjusting Swivel-jaw, to hold all kinds of taper or irregular-shaped objects, such as taper-keys, work in the rough, &c.	4 10 0
Improved Dividing Apparatus, with a set of 6 Nut-mandrels, to hold any number of nuts up to 8-in. long, for 2, 4, 6, or 8 sides, for shaping wrought-iron nuts, &c.	10 10 0
If fitted with heavier Fly-wheel and handle, so as to work by hand, where power is not available	1 10 0
Packed in Strong Case for Shipment and delivered on Rails in Manchester	2 0 0
Packed in Strong Case for Shipment, and delivered f.o.b. London, Liverpool, or Hull	2 15 0
Gross Weight, about 16 cwt.	

Constructed by ANDREW MUIR & CO., Albion Works, Strangeways, MANCHESTER.

ADVERTISEMENT.

ANDREW MUIR AND COMPANY
ALBION WORKS, STRANGEWAYS, MANCHESTER,

Designers and Constructors of LABOUR-SAVING MACHINE TOOLS, for General and Special Purposes.

PUNCHING & SHEARING MACHINES, PLATE EDGE PLANING MACHINES, RAILWAY WHEEL TURNING LATHES

ANDREW MUIR'S PATENT AND OTHER POWER LATHES,

For Screw-Cutting, Sliding, Surfacing and Hand, with Expanding Gap and other Beds, from 5-in. to 36-in. Centres.

ANDREW MUIR'S PATENT FOOT LATHES FOR AMATEURS,

And when Engine-Power is not available. From 5-in. to 12-in. Centres.

☞ SPECIAL MACHINERY for Sewing Machine Makers, Small Fire-Arms, Rifled Ordnance, Armour Plates, &c.

ANDREW MUIR'S IMPROVED AMERICAN HOLLOW-MANDREL LATHES,
WITH CAPSTAN OR TURRET RESTS,

For Sliding, Screwing, Heading, Ending, Finishing and Cutting Off Screws, Pins, Studs, Washers, &c., from $\frac{1}{8}$-in. to 1-in. diameter, at the rate of from 20 to 60 per hour, according to the size and complexity of the objects turned.

PLANING, SHAPING, SLOTTING, DRILLING, BORING AND MILLING MACHINES,
SINGLE AND DOUBLE GRINDSTONES.

Prices and Plans for Special or General Machine Tools for any Purpose on Application.

ADVERTISEMENT.

ELECTRO-TYPING AND WOOD ENGRAVING.

Views of Buildings, Machinery Works, produced of a Photograph, on paper the size required,

IF SENT TO

W. H. BIRD, 18, Albert Street, MANCHESTER.

TO PRINTERS, BOOKBINDERS & STATIONERS.

Letterpress Machines and Presses, Litho. Machines, Cutting Machines, Rolling Machines, Arming, Hydraulic & Standing Presses, and all kinds of Printing & Bookbinding Materials.

Send for Second-hand Lists, to W. H. BIRD, 18, ALBERT STREET, MANCHESTER.

NORTON'S PATENT "ABYSSINIAN" TUBE WELLS.

NORTON'S IMPROVED PATENT REGISTERING TURNSTILES.

LE GRAND AND SUTCLIFF,

PROPRIETORS OF LETTERS PATENT,

ARTESIAN WELL ENGINEERS, &c.,

MAGDALA WORKS, 100, BUNHILL ROW, LONDON.

CLARKE & MARRIOTT,

VULCAN FOUNDRY AND ENGINEERING WORKS.

MANUFACTURERS OF ALL KINDS OF CUT TACK MACHINES, &c.

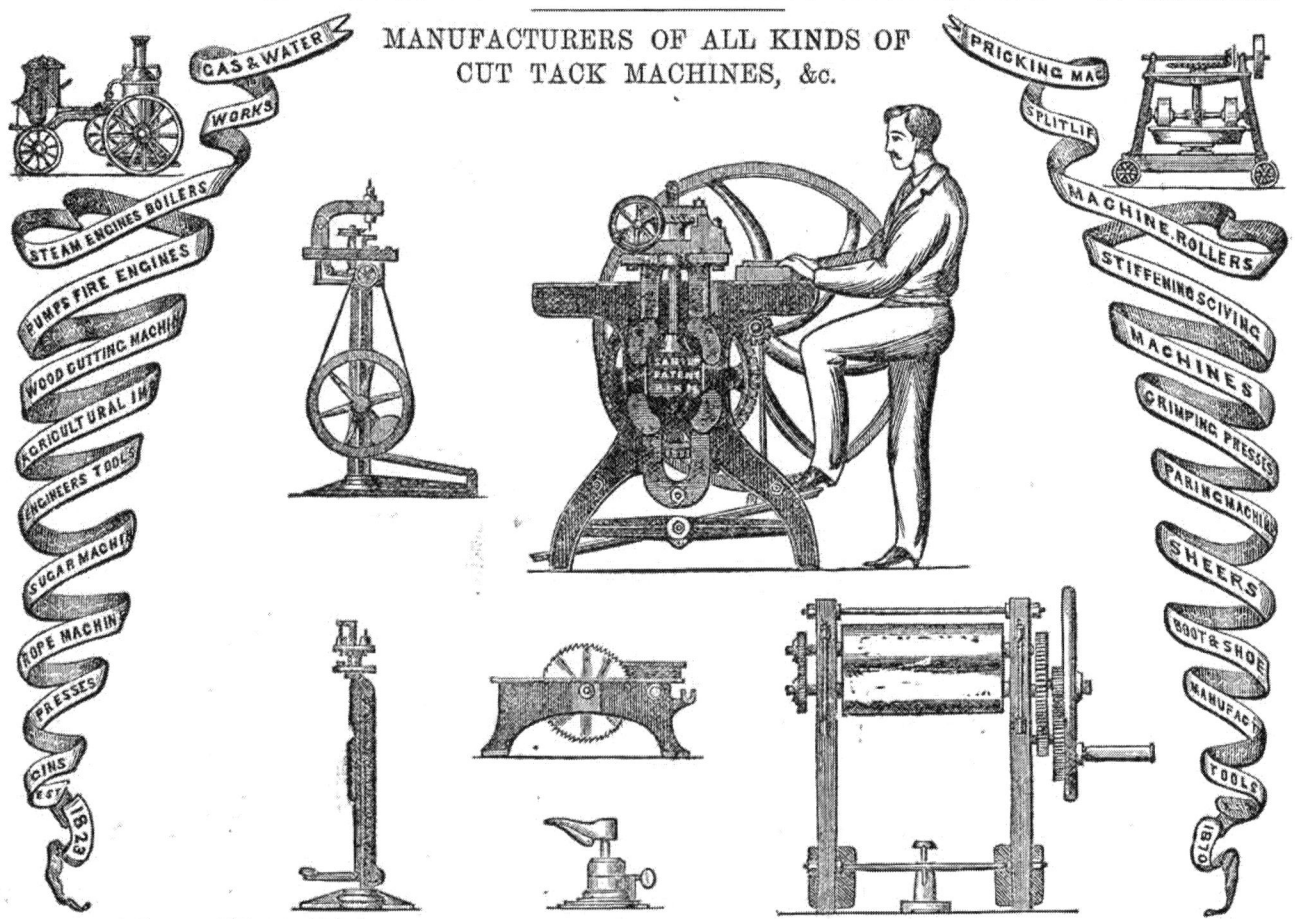

44, SHADWELL STREET, BIRMINGHAM, ENGLAND.

CUNLIFFE AND CROOM,
ENGINEERS AND MACHINE TOOL MAKERS.

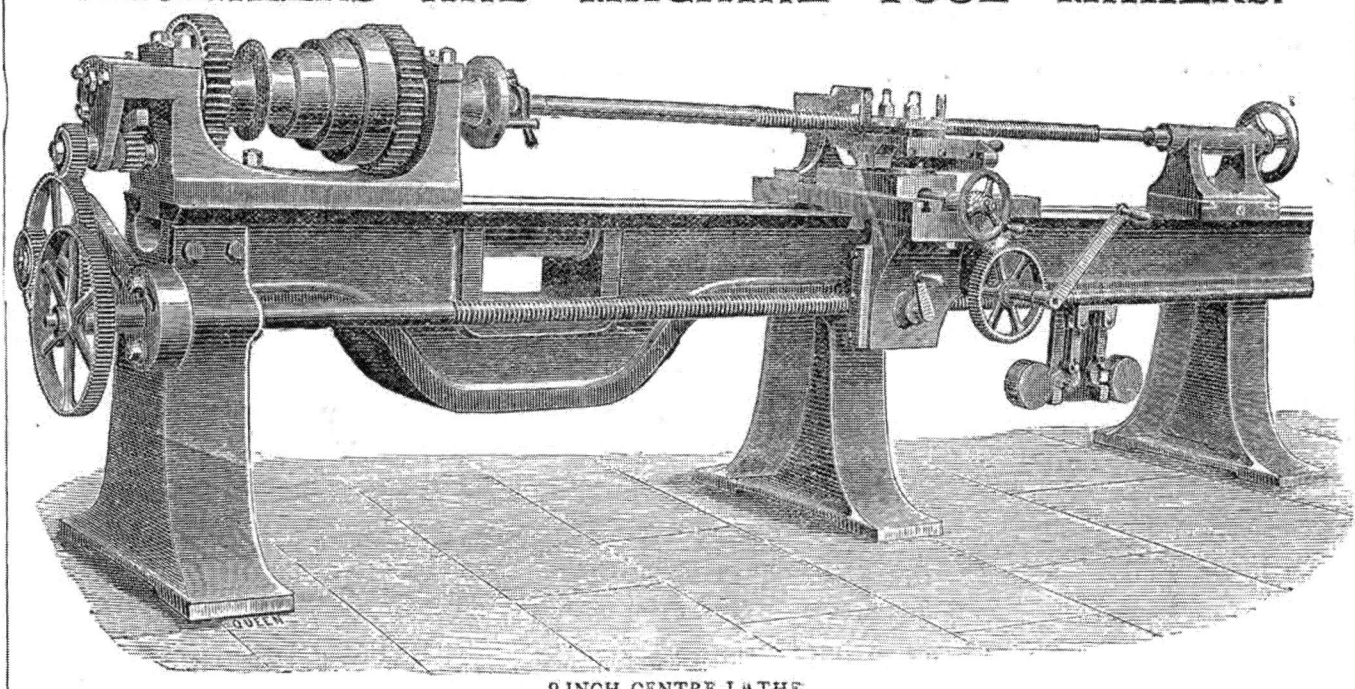

9-INCH CENTRE LATHE.

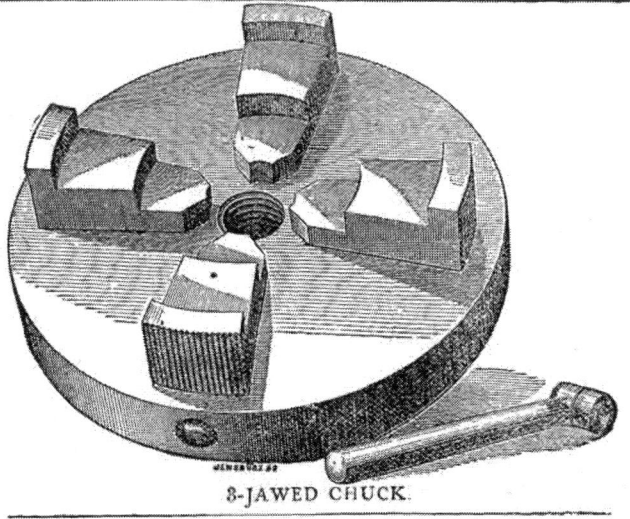

3-JAWED CHUCK.

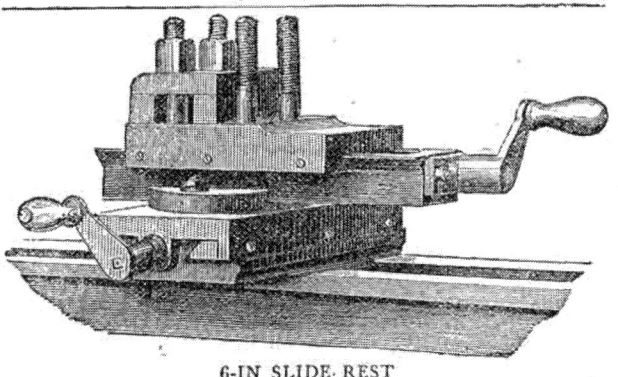

6-IN SLIDE-REST.

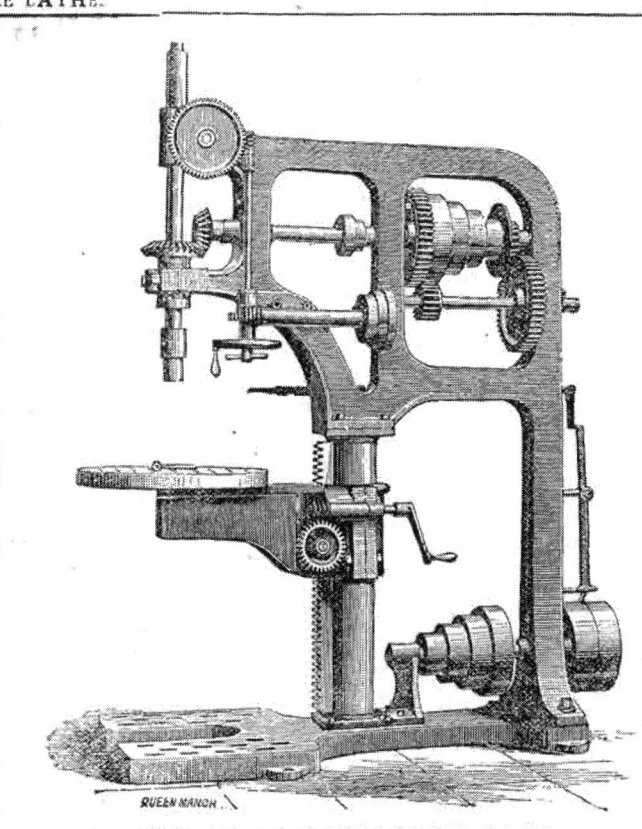

SINGLE-SPEED AND DOUBLE-GEARED VERTICAL DRILLING MACHINES.

For Prices, &c., see our other Advertisement, page 11.

Broughton Iron Works, Edward Street, Broughton Lane, Manchester, England.

EDWARD MERCER,
MACHINE TOOL MAKER, &c.,

(SOLE LICENSEE AND MANUFACTURER),

SPAW STREET, next to New Bailey Street, CHAPEL STREET, SALFORD,

MANCHESTER,

(Five Minutes' walk from Exchange. 'Busses pass every Five Minutes.)

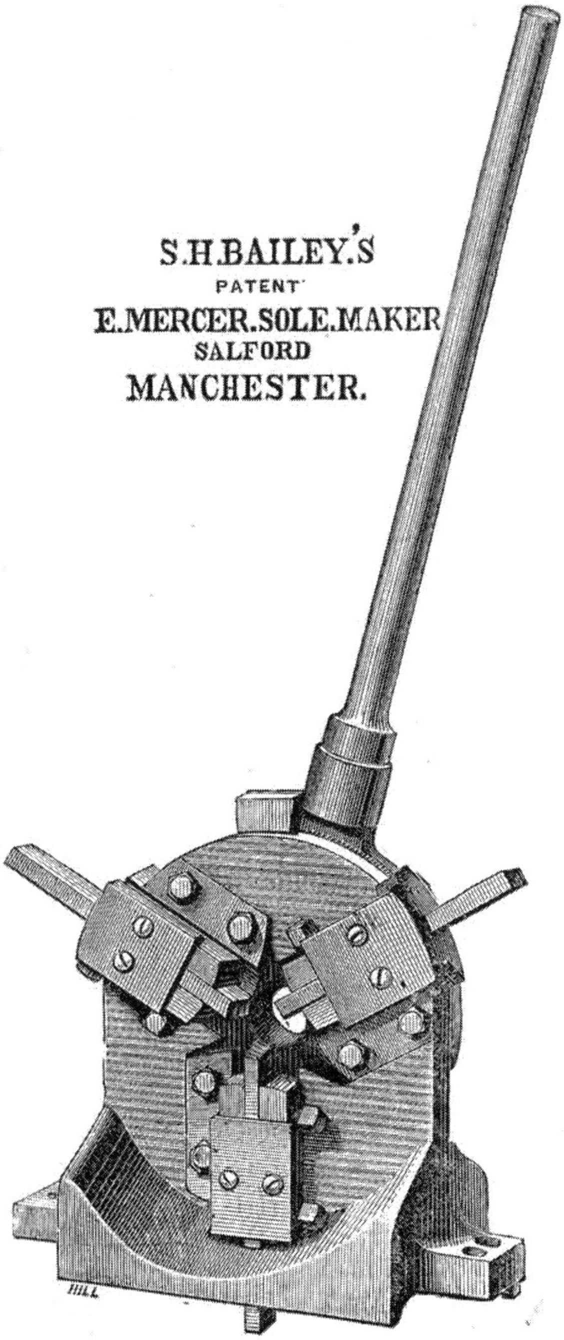

S. H. BAILEY'S
PATENT
E. MERCER. SOLE. MAKER
SALFORD
MANCHESTER.

In bringing this PATENT SCREWING APPARATUS under your notice, I beg to inform you that the principal Screw Bolt Manufacturers of Lancashire are now using them.

The great advantage over all other Machines is that the dies do not require to be filed or fitted in. You can cut the dies off the black steel, and you get more wear out of one set of these dies than you would do out of 10 or 12 sets of the other one-cut Machines; the head is not so complicated, and less liable to get out of order, and, if by any accident or wear, it is soon put right again at a very small cost.

N.B.—This Patent Chasing Head can be fitted on any other Screwing Machine or Lathe.

No. 1. Screwing Apparatus, to screw from $\frac{1}{4}$ to $\frac{1}{2}$ in., £13   5   0
No. 2. Screwing Apparatus to screw from $\frac{1}{2}$ to 1 in., £17   10   0
No. 3. Screwing Apparatus, to screw from $\frac{3}{4}$ to $1\frac{1}{2}$ in., £22   0   0
No 4. Screwing Apparatus to screw from $1\frac{1}{4}$ to 2 in., £33   0   0

Larger sizes made to order.

Further Particulars on application.

For Export, these Machines may be ordered through

Messrs. W. H. BAILEY & CO.,

Or their various Agents.

ADVERTISEMENT.

PATENT SCREWING MACHINES.

EDWARD MERCER

MACHINE

Tool Maker,

ETC., ETC.,

SPAW STREET, next to New Bailey St.,
CHAPEL STREET, SALFORD,

MANCHESTER.

*(Five minutes' walk from Exchange.
'Busses pass every five minutes.)*

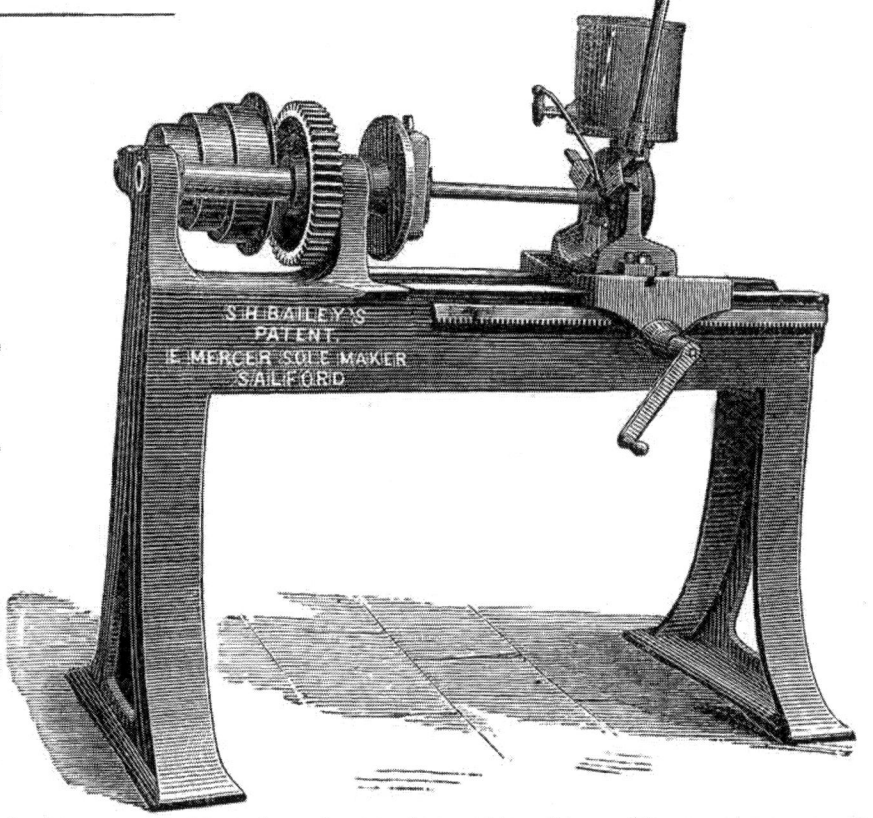

ALBION WORKS, SALFORD,
January 20th, 1877.

I have great pleasure in strongly recommending this Machine.

It is far superior to all Machines we have in use, or any I have ever seen.

(Signed,)   W. H. BAILEY,
Chairman of Directors,
Manchester and Liverpool Screw Bolt Co

THE Inventor of these Machines having had a large practical experience in screwing, and screwing machinery, as manager of the Screwing Department of the Manchester and Liverpool Bolt and Nut Company, has the greatest confidence in bringing them into the market, and they will do more work than any other, and he has no hesitation in saying, that they will do it in a far better manner.

These Machines will produce work at a considerable less cost than others, owing to the dies having about TEN TIMES THE AMOUNT OF WEARING OR CUTTING SURFACE THAN any other patent one-cut Machine has.

One of the very great advantages to the workman they possess is the cutting-edges of the dies being exposed to view without having to take them out; and it is impossible for them to get filled up with cuttings in the space where the dies work.

The dies being in separate boxes, and not a portion of the cams, as in other machines, they can be taken out for sharpening without disturbing each other.

In cases of accident to any portion of the chasing apparatus, it can be easily replaced at a comparatively small cost.

The dies being held rigid by means of screws, the boxes cannot wear bell-mouthed, as in other Machines, which causes great uncertainty in the working of them; but in this case they are as firm and cut as true as if held in a slide rest.

The chasing or screwing apparatus is so simple and easy of management that any ordinary boy or girl can work it with ease, and without requiring so much of a man's time being devoted to them.

An active boy or girl can screw from 25 to 30 gross of $\frac{1}{2}$-inch bolts per day of ten hours—24 $\frac{5}{8}$", 20 $\frac{3}{4}$", 18 $\frac{7}{8}$" and 14 1".

Common oil, or a mixture of oil, soap and water, may be used for running on the dies whilst in process of cutting.

No. 1.—A single-speed Machine, for screwing from $\frac{1}{4}$-inch to $\frac{1}{2}$ inch, with dies, $\frac{1}{4}$", $\frac{5}{16}$", $\frac{3}{8}$", $\frac{7}{16}$", $\frac{1}{2}$" £37 10 0

No. 2.—A single-geared Machine, for screwing from $\frac{1}{2}$-inch to 1-inch, with dies $\frac{1}{2}$", $\frac{5}{8}$", $\frac{3}{4}$", $\frac{7}{8}$", and 1"; also, extra dies down to $\frac{3}{8}$" may be supplied with this Machine, at per set 55 0 0

No. 3.—A double-geared Machine, for screwing from $\frac{3}{4}$" to 1 $\frac{1}{2}$", with dies $\frac{3}{4}$", $\frac{7}{8}$", 1", 1 $\frac{1}{8}$", 1 $\frac{1}{4}$", 1 $\frac{3}{8}$", and 1 $\frac{1}{2}$". (Smaller sizes of dies may be supplied.) 77 0 0

No. 4.—A double-geared Machine, for screwing from 1 $\frac{1}{4}$" to 2", with dies from 1 $\frac{1}{4}$", 1 $\frac{3}{8}$", 1 $\frac{1}{2}$", 1 $\frac{3}{4}$", and 2" 94 0 0

No. 5.—A Tapping Apparatus, suitable for No. 1 Machine, including sockets for holding the nuts; also, tap sockets, and $\frac{1}{4}$", $\frac{5}{16}$", $\frac{3}{8}$", $\frac{7}{16}$", and $\frac{1}{2}$" taps. 6 0 0

No. 6.—A Tapping Apparatus, suitable for No. 2 Machine, including sockets for nuts and taps; also, $\frac{1}{2}$", $\frac{5}{8}$", $\frac{3}{4}$", and 1" taps, 9 0 0

No. 7.—A Tapping Apparatus, suitable for No. 3 Machine, including sockets for nuts and taps; also $\frac{3}{4}$", $\frac{7}{8}$", 1", 1 $\frac{1}{8}$", 1 $\frac{1}{4}$", 1 $\frac{3}{8}$", and 1 $\frac{1}{2}$" taps 13 0 0

No. 8.—Tapping Apparatus, suitable for No. 4 Machine, including sockets for nuts and taps; also taps 1 $\frac{1}{4}$", 1 $\frac{3}{8}$", 1 $\frac{1}{2}$", 1 $\frac{3}{4}$", and 2" 14 0 0

Each Machine is fitted with saddle, carrying the screwing apparatus; also with a head-stock, having a hollow spindle, carrying a right and left-hand screw chuck, for holding the drivers for bolt-heads and taps, and for gripping long bolts; bed formed into a trough for holding oil, and provided with improved drawing-off tap; oil-can with tap and stand; complete top-driving apparatus; set of master-taps; set of rose-bits and rimer; together with a set of screw-keys.

Larger sizes of Machines made to order.   Further particulars on application.   Inspection earnestly invited.
The Machine can be seen working at the Works.

KENDALL & GENT,
MACHINE TOOL MAKERS,

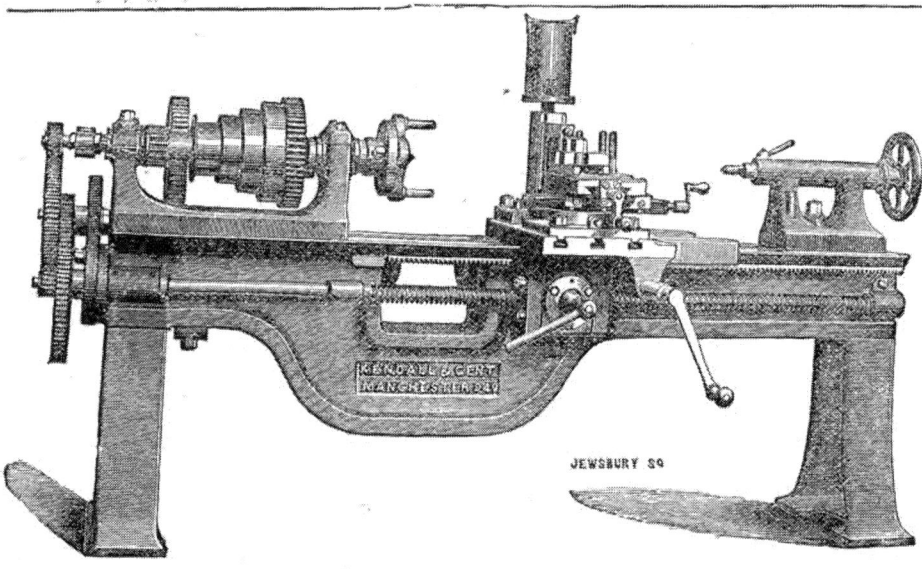

HAND-SLIDE,
SCREW-CUTTING,
Sliding, Break-Cap & Boring
LATHES.

DOUBLE-TURNING, BORING,
AND CAPSTAN LATHES.

Planing, Drilling, Slotting
AND
Shaping Machines.

Sole Makers of

BROWN'S PATENT
"ONE-CUT"
SCREWING MACHINES,
Patent Self-Acting
TUBE CUTTERS,
Patent Slot
DRILLING MACHINES.

Special Machinery for BRASS WORK,
SEWING MACHINISTS, &c.

General Engineering Contractors,
VICTORIA WORKS.
SPRINGFIELD, SALFORD, MANCHESTER, ENGLAND.

ADVERTISEMENT.

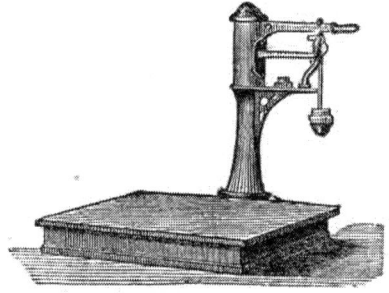

Counter Weighing Machines

For OFFICES, STORE-ROOMS, BRASS FOUNDERS, &c., where quick and accurate weighing is required.

Power. No.	Cwt.	ft. in.	ft. in.	£ s. d.	
1	1	1 0	× 1 0	3 10 0	Non-Relieving.
2	1	1 2	× 1 2	3 10 0	
3	1	1 4	× 1 4	3 15 0	
4	1½	2 6	× 1 6	4 5 0	Relieving.
5	2	2 6	× 1 6	4 15 0	

Portable Platform Weighing Machines,

For GROCERS, PROVISION DEALERS, MACHINISTS, IRON FOUNDERS, RAILWAYS, CANAL CARRIERS, CHEMICAL WORKS, MERCHANTS, MANUFACTURERS, WAREHOUSES, &c.

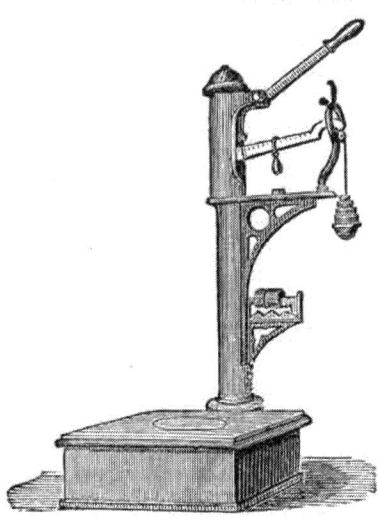

Power. No.	Cwt.	ft. in.	ft. in.	£ s. d.
1	3½	1 8	× 1 8	3 15 0
2	4	1 9	× 1 9	4 0 0
3	5	1 10	× 1 10	4 5 0
4	6	2 0	× 2 0	4 15 0
5	7	2 0	× 2 0	5 10 0
6	8	2 3	× 2 3	5 15 0
7	10	2 6	× 2 6	6 10 0
8	15	2 6	× 2 6	7 10 0
9	20	2 8	× 2 8	8 10 0
10	25	2 8	× 3 2	10 10 0
11	30	3 0	× 3 0	11 10 0
12	32	2 10	× 3 4	12 10 0
13	40	3 4	× 3 9	14 10 0
14	45	3 4	× 3 10	15 10 0
15	50	3 5	× 3 10	16 10 0
16	60	3 6	× 3 10	18 10 0
17	70	3 10	× 4 4	20 10 0
18	80	3 10	× 4 6	22 10 0

EXTRAS.

Back Frame, or Guard to	Nos. 1 to 7	10/ each.	If Mounted on 4 Wheels and Axles	1 to 7	10/ each.	
,, ,, ,,	,, 8 to 11	15/ ,,	,, ,, ,, ,,	8 to 11	15/ ,,	
Fitted with Folding Wings	9 to 12	17/ ,,	,, ,, ,, ,,	12 to 16	20/ ,,	
,, ,, ,,	13 to 18	20/ ,,	,, ,, ,, ,,	17 to 18	30/ ,,	

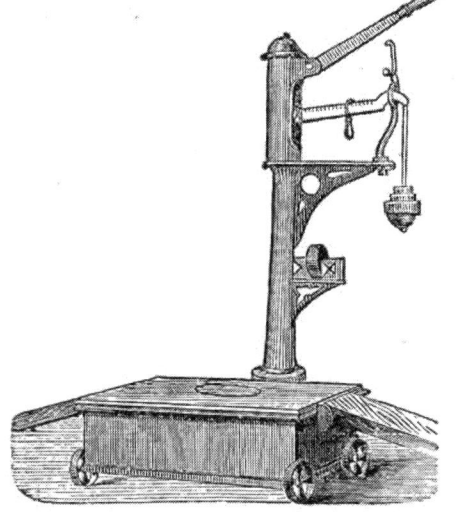

PORTABLE PLATFORM, fitted with Pockets or Plank Rests,

For CHEMICAL AND OTHER WORKS, &c., requiring to weigh materials in barrows.

Cwt.	ft. in.	ft. in.	£ s. d.
10	3 0	× 2 6	8 0 0
10	3 6	× 2 6	8 10 0
15	3 6	× 2 6	9 15 0
20	4 0	× 3 0	11 0 0
25	4 0	× 3 0	13 0 0

SPENCER & CO., Machinists, &c.,

HOLLINWOOD, MANCHESTER,

ENGLAND.

PLATFORM MACHINES, Dormant, sunk flush with Floor,

For Railways, Canal Carriers, Merchants and Manufacturers, Warehouses, Chemical Works, Collieries, &c., &c.

These Machines can be fitted with our Patent Steelyard, which requires no loose weights; also with Chequered Platform, if desired, at prices proportionately higher.

No.	Cwt.	ft. in.	ft. in.	£ s. d.
1	6	2 0 ×	2 0	6 5 0
2	8	2 0 ×	2 0	6 15 0
3	10	2 6 ×	2 6	7 0 0
4	15	2 6 ×	2 6	7 15 0
5	20	2 8 ×	2 8	9 0 0
6	20	3 0 ×	3 0	10 0 0
7	20	3 0 ×	4 0	11 10 0
8	20	4 0 ×	4 0	15 0 0
9	22	4 0 ×	2 6	10 0 0
10	25	2 7 ×	3 1	11 0 0
11	25	3 0 ×	3 0	12 0 0
12	32	2 8 ×	3 2	13 0 0
13	32	3 0 ×	3 6	15 0 0
14	32	4 0 ×	4 0	16 10 0
15	40	3 0 ×	3 0	15 0 0
16	40	3 6 ×	3 0	16 0 0
17	40	4 0 ×	3 10	18 10 0
18	40	4 0 ×	4 0	19 10 0
19	50	4 0 ×	4 0	20 0 0
20	50	4 0 ×	3 6	19 10 0
21	60	4 0 ×	4 0	21 0 0
22	60	4 0 ×	6 0	22 0 0

Self-Contained Weighbridges,

For Two-Wheeled Carts.

Tons.	With Relieving Apparatus.		Without Relieving Apparatus.	
	ft. in. × ft. in.	£ s. d.	£ s. d.	
3	4 0 × 6 0	26 0 0	24 0 0	
4	4 6 × 5 6	30 0 0	28 0 0	
5	5 0 × 6 0	34 0 0	32 0 0	
6	5 0 × 6 0	38 0 0	35 0 0	

Made in sizes **A**   **B** and **C**
110/-   140/-   180/-
Will take in 12 in.   12 in.   15 in.
Will drill holes ½ in.   ½ in.   ¾ in.

BENCH DRILLING MACHINE.

Also Makers of Self-Acting, Sliding, Surfacing & Screw-Cutting Lathes, Hand Lathes, Planing, Shaping and Slotting Machines.

Crab Winches, Cranes, Patent Pipe Screwing Machines, &c., &c., &c.

JAMES SPENCER & CO.,
HOLLINWOOD, MANCHESTER.

JAMES SPENCER & CO.,
HOLLINWOOD, MANCHESTER,
IMPROVED SELF-CONTAINED WEIGHBRIDGE.

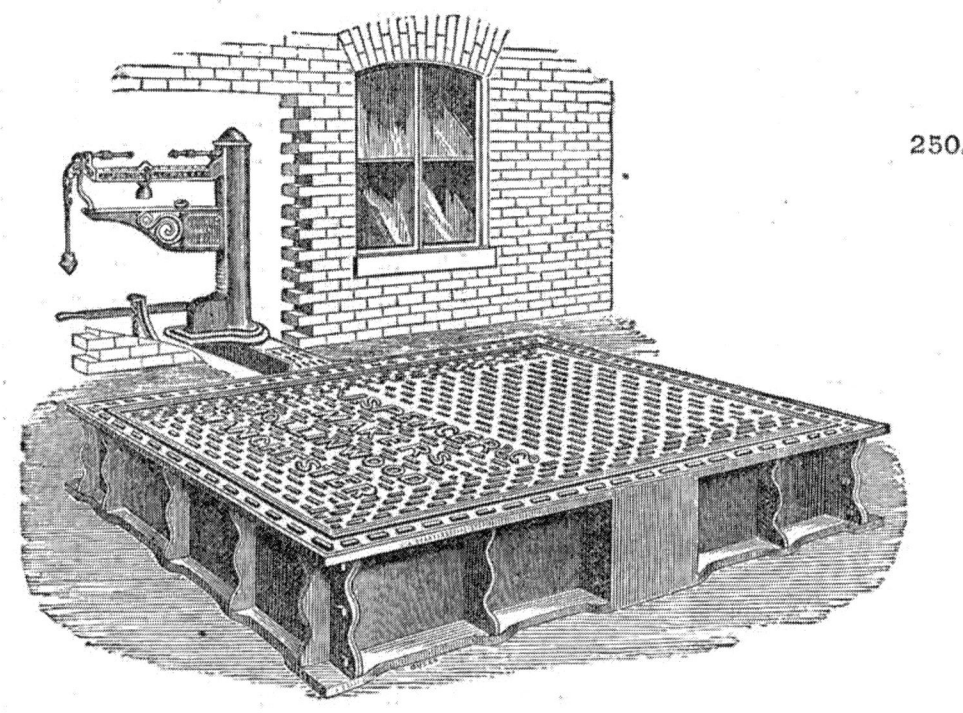

250.

The above Illustration represents our Improved Self-contained Weighbridge, for Carts, Road and Railway Wagons. Made in sizes from four pounds to sixty tons power, and graduated to any National standard. These Machines require no masonry in fixing, and can be removed and re-fixed at a small cost.

FOR CARTS AND ROAD WAGONS, &C.

No.	Lbs. Tons.	Dimensions of Platform. Ft. In. × Ft. In.	Without Relieving Apparatus £ s. d.	With Patent Relieving Apparatus £ s. d.
1	4 to 6	12 0 × 6 3	52 0 0	56 0 0
2	4 to 7	12 0 × 6 3	54 0 0	58 0 0
3	4 to 8	12 0 × 6 3	56 0 0	60 0 0
4	4 to 10	12 0 × 6 6	63 0 0	68 0 0
5	4 to 10	12 0 × 7 0	65 0 0	70 0 0
6	4 to 12	12 0 × 6 6	66 0 0	71 0 0
7	4 to 12	12 0 × 7 0	68 0 0	73 0 0
8	4 to 15	12 0 × 6 6	70 0 0	76 0 0
9	4 to 15	12 0 × 7 0	72 0 0	78 0 0
10	4 to 15	15 0 × 6 6	87 0 0	93 0 0
11	4 to 20	12 0 × 6 6	76 0 0	84 0 0
12	4 to 20	12 0 × 7 0	78 0 0	86 0 0
13	4 to 20	14 0 × 7 0	88 0 0	96 0 0
14	4 to 20	14 0 × 8 0	98 0 0	106 0 0
15	4 to 20	15 0 × 6 6	91 0 0	99 0 0
16	4 to 20	16 0 × 8 0	112 0 0	120 0 0
17	4 to 20	14 0 × 9 0	—	—
18	4 to 20	14 0 × 8 0	—	—
19	4 to 25	16 0 × 8 0	122 0 0	130 0 0
20	4 to 25	14 0 × 8 0	108 0 0	116 0 0
21	4 to 30	16 0 × 8 0	130 0 0	140 0 0
22	4 to 30	16 0 × 8 0	—	—
23	4 to 40	16 0 × 8 0	—	—
24	4 to 50	16 0 × 8 0	—	—

JAMES SPENCER & CO.,
ENGINEERS AND MACHINISTS,
ETC., ETC., ETC.

Will Drill Holes 2 in. diam., 8½ in. deep.
Will admit an article 24 in. diam.
£30 0s. 0d.

Will Drill Holes diam., 8½ in. deep.
Will admit an article 30 in. diameter.
£40 0s. 0d.

Will Drill a Hole 12 in. deep, 10 in. diam.
Will admit an article 4 ft. 0 in. diameter.
£70 0s. 0d.

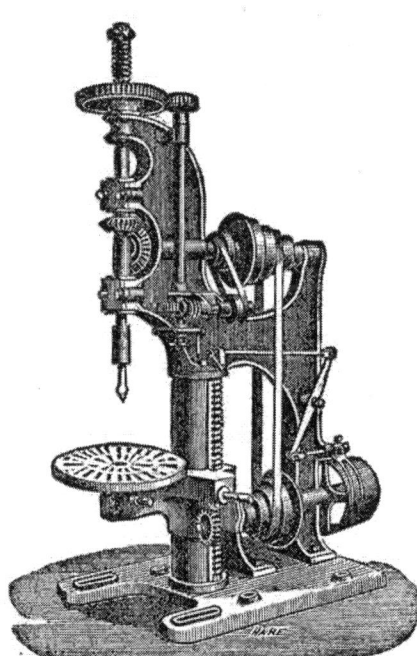
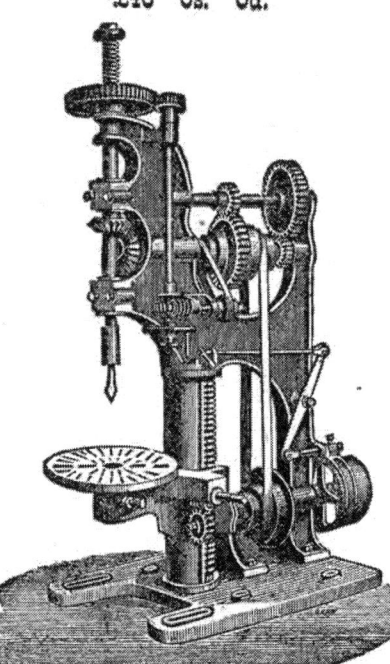
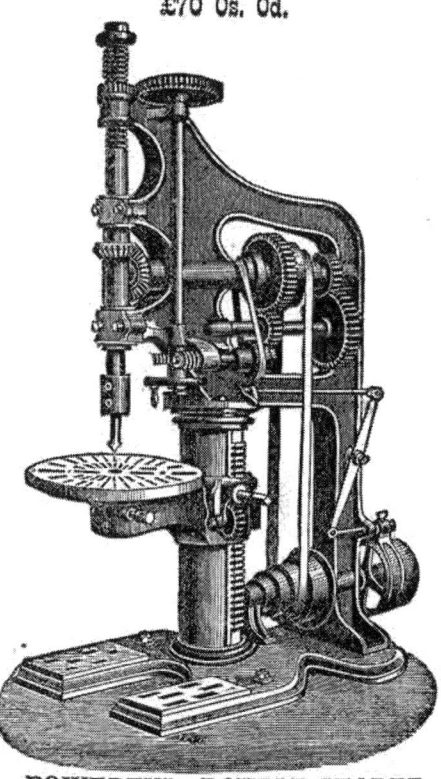

SINGLE-GEARED DRILLING MACHINE, £30 0s. 0d.

DOUBLE-GEARED DRILLING MACHINE, £40 0s. 0d.

POWERFUL DOUBLE-GEARED DRILLING MACHINE, £70 0s. 0d.

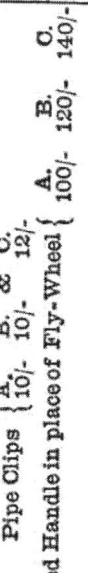

Pipe Clips { A, 10/-. B, 12/-. C, }
A, 100/-. B, 120/-. C, 140/-.
If with Cranked Handle in place of Fly-Wheel

Self-feeding Drilling Machine.

A.—Machine, to drill up to 1 in. diam. £5 4s.
B.   do   do   1½   do   6 5s.
C.   do   do   2   do   7 6s.

This Machine entirely supersedes the Ratchet or Swing Brace in point of time and efficiency, as well as being adapted to Drill at almost any angle.

For huge and ponderous work, not easily removed to the Drilling Machine, it will be found a desideratum long wanted.

Screw the Drill-stock or Bracket firmly to the work-bench or the article to be drilled. This being done, lock the upper tooth wheel, by turning the eccentric gearing against it to the left hand. Then run down the spindle, by turning the handle until it reaches the article being drilled. Put on the feed motion, by turning the eccentric to the right hand. After the hole is drilled, the spindle is immediately drawn back, by locking the upper wheel, as before, and reversing the handle.

The above Drills are capable of drilling holes at almost any angle, or in almost any position, and will be found a most invaluable tool in Mills and Workshops of any kind.

JOHN FLETCHER & SONS,

Engineers, Ironfounders, &c.,

EAGLE FOUNDRY, BOOTH ST.

SALFORD, MANCHESTER,

(Three minutes' walk from the Manchester Royal Exchange),

PATENTEES AND SOLE MAKERS OF

SELF-ACTING GRINDING & MIXING MILLS,

Especially suitable to Ironfounders, Contractors, Manufacturing Chemists, Cement, Emery and Flint Grinders, Firebrick and Tile Makers, Copper, Lead and Iron Ore Miners, Manure Manufacturers, Builders, etc.

CAN BE SEEN IN OPERATION AT THE PATENTEES' WORKS.

EXTRACT FROM TESTIMONIAL:—"I consider that the improvements that you have introduced are of great value."—WILLIAM FAIRBAIRN (Fairbairn Engineering Company, Manchester).

JOHN FLETCHER & SONS'

MACHINE-MOULDED TOOTH-WHEEL, FLY-WHEEL,

AND

PULLEY CASTINGS, & MILL GEARING,

Which can be supplied Bored and Turned, if required.

Thousands of their Wheels and Pulleys are now in use.

PRICE LISTS ON APPLICATION.

ADVERTISEMENT. 51

BROADBENT'S PATENT IMPROVED BLAKE STONE BREAKER.

Fitted with Positive Drawback Motion; saves power, and prevents choking.

No spring required; takes less power than any other Stone Breaker.

AWARDED TO Robert Broadbent & Sons FOR STONE BREAKING MACHINE EXHIBITED AT SOUTHPORT SEP. 1876.

ROBERT BROADBENT & SON,
Patentees and Sole Makers,
PHŒNIX WORKS, STALYBRIDGE.

ESTABLISHED 1836.

Formerly Manufacturers to the late Mr. H. R. MARSDEN, having made for him, in less than four years, 336 STONE BREAKERS.

FITTED WITH REVERSIBLE CUBING JAWS.

GUARANTEED TO BE NO INFRINGEMENT OF BLAKE'S OR ANY OTHER PATENT.

Copy of TESTIMONIAL *from the* MANCHESTER CORPORATION.

Highways Department,
City Hall, Manchester,
Oct. 18th, 1876.

Mem./
We have had one of Messrs. Broadbent and Son's Patent-Improved 15 × 9 Stone Breakers [Blake's Machine] working at our yard for the past three months, and its work is giving us every satisfaction.

S. MASSEY, Chief Clerk.

We beg to endorse the above testimony from our own knowledge.
W. H. BAILEY & Co.,
Albion Works, Salford.

Size of Machine at mouth.	Price of fixed Machine.	Extra when mounted on wheels.	Extra for Screen.	Production of Road metal per day of 10 hours.
Inches.	£ s. d.	£ s. d.	£ s. d.	Tons.
10 × 7	140 0 0	10 0 0	7 10 0	40
15 × 7	180 0 0	10 0 0	10 0 0	55
15 × 9	200 0 0	10 0 0	10 0 0	65
20 × 9	240 0 0	...	15 0 0	80
24 × 12	350 0 0	...	15 0 0	120
24 × 16	375 0 0	...	15 0 0	130

All sizes of Machines may always be seen in stock at the Works.

These machines may be had through Messrs. W. H. BAILEY & CO., or their Agents.

W. F. COLEMAN,
Midland Boiler Works, LOUGHBOROUGH.

MANUFACTURER OF

Every description of Cornish, Vertical Cross Tube, Multitubular, and Launch Boilers, Tanks, Girders, Bridges, &c., Vertical Cross Tube Boilers from 1 to 10 h.-p. generally in Stock or progress.

PRICES ON APPLICATION.

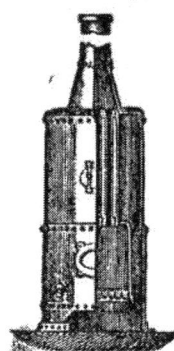

"We are enjoined not to hide the discovery of blessings found by the way. No. 2 HINDOO PEN.

"They come as a boon and a blessing to men, The Pickwick, the Nile, and the Waverley Pen."
1,200 Newspapers Recommend them. See *Graphic*, 10th February, 1875.
1s. per Box. 1s. 1d. by Post. Sold Everywhere.
PATENTEES—MACNIVEN & CAMERON,
23 to 33, BLAIR STREET, EDINBURGH.

Shippers supplied on Liberal Terms.

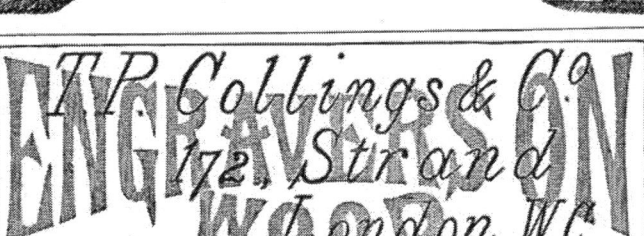

T. P. Collings & Co., 172, Strand, London. W.C. ENGRAVERS ON WOOD

B. & S. MASSEY,
OPENSHAW, MANCHESTER, ENGLAND.

PRIZE MEDALS AWARDED:—Paris, 1867; Havre, 1868; Highland Society, 1870; Liverpool, 1871; Moscow, 1872; Vienna, 1873; Scientific Industry Society, 1875; Leeds, 1875; Paris, 1875; Manchester and Liverpool Society, 1876; U. S. Centennial, Philadelphia, 1876.

PATENTEES AND MAKERS
OF DOUBLE AND SINGLE-ACTING
STEAM HAMMERS

Of all sizes, from ½ Cwt. to 20 Tons, with Self-acting or Hand Motions, in either case giving a perfectly DEAD BLOW, while the former may be worked by Hand when desired. Large Hammers, with Improved Framing, in Cast or Wrought Iron. Small Hammers, working up to 500 blows per minute, in some cases being worked by the Foot of the Smith, and not requiring any separate Driver.

SPECIAL STEAM STAMPS
For Forging, Stamping, Punching, Bolt-Making, &c.

CIRCULAR SAWS FOR HOT IRON.
STEAM HAMMERS

For Engineers, Machinists, Shipbuilders, Steel Tilters, Millwrights, Coppersmiths, Railway Carriage and Wagon Builders, Colliery Proprietors, Ship Smiths, Bolt Makers, Cutlers, File Makers, Spindle and Flyer Makers, Spade Makers, Locomotive and other Wheel Makers, &c.; also for use in Repairing Smithies of Mills and Works of all kinds; for straightening Bars, bending Cranks, breaking Pig-Iron, &c.

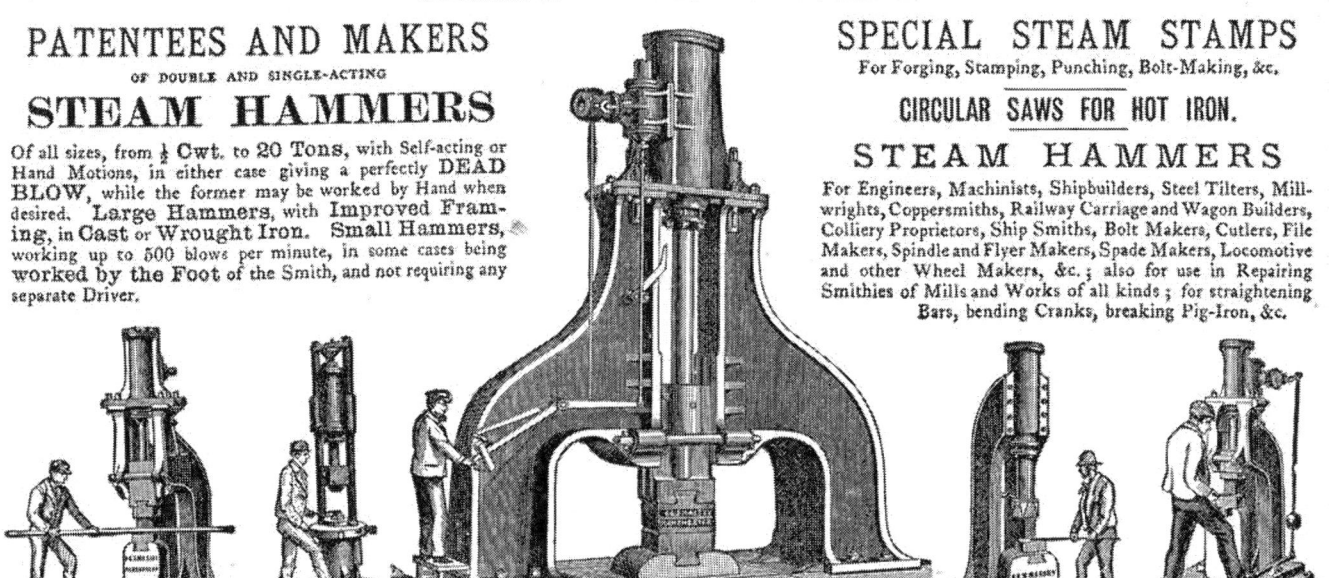

General Smithy Hammer.   Special Steam Stamp.   Steam Hammer for Heavy Forging.   General Smithy Hammer.   Foot Motion Hammer.

From 60 to 100 Steam Hammers and Steam Stamps may usually be seen in construction at the Works.

ADVERTISEMENT.

OUR PATENT SELF-INDICATING MACHINE FOR COLLIERIES IS UNEQUALLED.

ESTABLISHED 1852.

HODGSON & STEAD,

CERTIFICATE FOR GENERAL EXCELLENCE, MANCHESTER, 1875.

Prize Medals: Manchester, Stalybridge, Southport.

Prize Medals: Manchester, Stalybridge, Southport.

MASSIVE DEEP CAST-IRON FRAMING.

MASSIVE DEEP CAST-IRON FRAMING.

WEIGHBRIDGE, WEIGHING MACHINE,

CRANE, AND TURNTABLE MANUFACTURERS,

IRON FOUNDERS, &c.,

EGERTON IRON WORKS, WINDSOR ST., REGENT ROAD,

SALFORD, MANCHESTER.

ALL KINDS OF WEIGHING APPARATUS FOR

RAILWAYS,	BLAST FURNACES,	MARKETS,	PAPER MAKERS,
ROADS,	IRON FORGES,	WAREHOUSES,	COTTON MILLS,
COLLIERIES,	ROLLING MILLS,	MINES,	WOOL MERCHANTS,

AND ALL COMMERCIAL USES, OF THE MOST APPROVED CONSTRUCTION, ADAPTABLE TO EVERY NATIONAL STANDARD.

☞ There are Thousands of our Weighbridges and Weighing Machines in use in the United Kingdom, and abundant reference can be given as to their accuracy and durability. Prices and Special Tenders on application to the offices, **SALFORD**, or any of the undermentioned.

DEPÔTS FOR

LONDON:	YORKSHIRE:	DERBY:	SOUTH WALES & FOREST OF DEAN:
11, Queen Victoria Street.	Victoria Road, Dewsbury.	61, Uttoxeter New Road.	
H. B. MILLS, MANAGER.	D. NIELD, MANAGER.	S. HUMBLE.	Dock Street, Newport, Mon.

ADVERTISEMENT.

ESTABLISHED 1868.

HARDMAN STREET OIL WORKS, MANCHESTER.

ENGINE, SHAFTING, SPINDLE AND LOOM OILS.

Our Oils having been used for years by some of the largest Engineers, Cotton and Woollen Spinners and Manufacturers, proves that they are worthy of the character given them when first introduced.

The superiority of our Oils consists in their being specially refined and prepared for Spinning and Weaving Machinery. Having many years' experience in the manipulation and refining of various Oils, we can uphold their superiority. Although they possess great body and gravity, they keep limpid, and are rendered free from gum and acid. Having a very high firing point, they are among THE VERY SAFEST AND BEST OILS which can be used.

Notwithstanding the many other Oils in the market, THE DEMAND FOR OUR OILS KEEPS INCREASING; this pleasing fact gives us great confidence in recommending them to those who have not favoured us with a trial, both as regards their superiority and moderate price.

SPECIAL QUOTATIONS FOR CONTRACTS AND LARGE QUANTITIES FOR SHIPMENT.

CYLINDER AND PISTON OILS.

It is a well-established fact that where tallow or any fatty matter is used for lubricating the cylinders, pistons, valves, etc., of Steam Engines, that, owing to the action of the steam upon the oleine of the tallow or fatty Oils, oleic and other acids are produced; these acids attack the inside of the cylinder or whatever parts are exposed to their action, forming oxide of iron, thereby causing a gradual eating away of the metal.

Where the steam is condensed and re-used, these acids attack the boiler, more particularly where the water is impregnated with lime, forming salts of lime, which is very injurious to boilers.

This gradual decomposition in most cases is slow, and may not be noticed for some time, yet it is a matter which should be carefully considered. Where the acids referred to are allowed to act undisturbed, it is found that the inside of the cylinder becomes uneven, preventing the piston head from working satisfactorily, causing the Engine to work with an irregular motion, allowing a waste of steam and power.

In order to prevent these injurious effects, we beg to direct attention to our Hydro-Carbon Oil, specially adapted for lubricating the cylinders, pistons, and valves of Steam Engines. As this Oil does not generate acid or decompose with the action of steam, it prevents the formation of acids and protects the parts exposed, keeping the cylinder and the other parts in a clean, easy-working condition, and preventing the formation of scale in the boilers.

M. WELLS & CO.,
OIL IMPORTERS & REFINERS,
Inventors and Sole Manufacturers of the Crystal Sperm Oil,
A Superior Oil for Steam Engines and heavy bearings.

WATSON'S CYLINDER OIL.

NO GUMMING. NO CORROSION.
CHEAPER THAN TALLOW. PERFECT LUBRICATION.

TRADE MARK ON EACH CASK.

A SUBSTITUTE FOR TALLOW IN THE LUBRICATION OF STEAM CYLINDERS.

Marine Engineers have long felt the want of a lubricant for Cylinders which will **leave no deposit, either in the Cylinders, Condensers, or Steam Pipes**, and which will at the same time keep the metal surfaces **clean** and **uncorroded**. This Oil, containing a large proportion of the richest carbon (hence its dark colour), answers all these objects, and only needs one trial to prove its efficiency.

WATSON'S SUPER SPERM OIL.

NO CLOGGING. NO CORRODING.
NO SMELL. NO SMELL.

TRADE MARK ON EACH CASK.

A SUBSTITUTE FOR WHALE SPERM, AT HALF THE COST.

This Oil has a higher body than the best Whale Sperm, and will lubricate **gallon for gallon with that oil**. It is entirely free of gumming or clogging tendency, and will remain moist and soft **after every other oil has dried up**. In the hottest factory no **odour of oil** will be felt, and spindle or loom will require no cleaning where this oil is used.

DAVID WATSON,
BATHVILLE WORKS,
BATHGATE, SCOTLAND.

SURFACE PLATES.

RALPH TAYLOR, SURFACE PLATE MAKER.

Having had over Twenty Years' Experience with some of the principal Tool Makers in Manchester, as a Fitter and Foreman, I have had much practice in getting up Surfaces of various kinds (Surface Plates included). I have made this my *special* business, and by making them in quantities, I have been able to fix upon the following Prices :—

SIZE	PRICE	SIZE	PRICE
4 × 3	£0 6 0	15 × 10	£2 3 0
6 × 4	0 12 0	18 × 12	2 18 6
9 × 6	1 2 6	24 × 18	5 8 0
12 × 8	1 14 0	30 × 20	7 10 0

Other Sizes and Shapes Made to Order.

8, GORDON STREET, BROUGHTON, MANCHESTER.

EXCELSIOR GAS BATH,
WITH LINEN WARMER, £5 10s. 0d.
GAS BATHS IN GREAT VARIETY.
REFLECTOR COOKING STOVES,
15s. 6d., 30s., 45s., 50s., 52s. 6d., £3 10s. to £10
GAS CONSERVATORY BOILERS,
FROM £2 5s. 0d.

G. SHREWSBURY, 59, OLD BAILEY.
Factory,—98, BARRINGTON ROAD, EAST BRIXTON, LONDON, S.W.

W. H. PLATT AND COMPANY,
ASHTON-UNDER-LYNE,
Manufacturers of every description of

ENGINE AND PUMP PACKINGS,
Specially made for and adapted to
Marine, Locomotive, and Stationary Engines, Steam Hammers, Pumps, &c.

"TALC GLYCERINE," for very High-Pressure Steam, Steam Hammers, &c., suitable for any description of Engines. Self-Lubricating and very durable.
"THE GRAPHITE," a very useful Packing. Self-Lubricating, adapted for either Steam, Hydraulics, or Pumps.
"SQUARE HEMP PACKING," (India Rubber Core), useful for any purpose, Chemical, Dye or Print Works, Paper Mills, &c.
"RED LEAD PACKING," for Manhole Lids, Cylinder Covers, Valve Covers, Steam Pipes, &c.
"GAUZE RINGS," "JUNCTION RINGS," &c., &c.
ASBESTOS, SOAPSTONE, &c.

All sizes in Stock from ¼-in. to 5-in. Orders completed same day as received. Samples and Prices on Application. Shippers and the Trade supplied. Carriage Paid to any part of the United Kingdom.

56   ADVERTISEMENT.

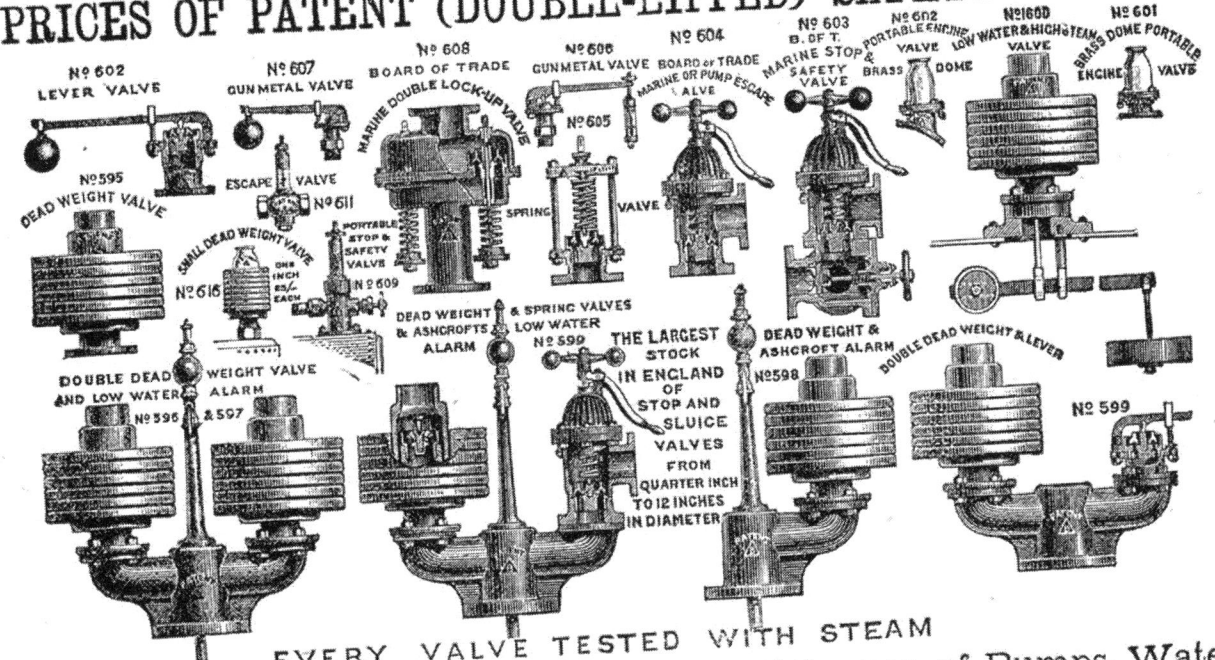

ANCIENT PLOUGH (*vide* STRUTT.)

ROBERT LANGTON,
ENGRAVER ON WOOD,
ALBERT CHAMBERS,
CORPORATION STREET, MANCHESTER.

LATE OF CROSS STREET.

PRICES OF PATENT (DOUBLE-LIPPED) SAFETY VALVES.

EVERY VALVE TESTED WITH STEAM

For Prices, see Bailey's Supplementary Catalogues of Pumps, Water Motors, Injectors, Pyrometers, etc. *Post Free on application.*

W. H. BAILEY & CO., ALBION WORKS, SALFORD, MANCHESTER.

ADVERTISEMENT.

EDWIN COTTERILL & Co.'s SAFES.

The following Challenge was given at the ROYAL AGRICULTURAL SHOW, at ASTON, BIRMINGHAM:—

PUBLIC CHALLENGE.

To prove whose Safes are really reliable, EDWIN COTTERILL & Co. are prepared to test their Safes by placing £100 in one of them against ANY SAFE EXHIBITED IN THE SHOW. Safes that WILL NOT STAND A TEST are worthless.

July 20, 1876.

N.B.—The highest price of our Safes was £95, and the Sicker Safe Co. exhibited one at £225, and another at £255. (See Show Catalogue.) Our Challenge was NOT accepted.

Safe No. 12, Without Fittings.

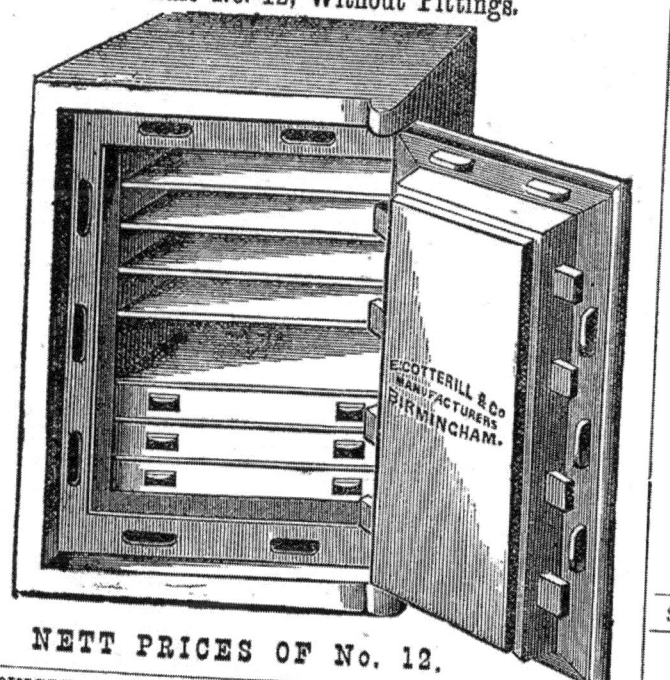

Safe No. 13, Without Fittings.

NETT PRICES OF No. 12.

SINGLE DOOR SAFES.				DOUBLE DOOR SAFES.				
	Outside Dimensions in Inches.		Price without Fittings.		Outside Dimensions in Inches.		Price with Fittings.	
No.	Hgt.	Wth.	Dth.	£ s. d.	No.	Hgt. Wth. Dth.	£ s. d.	
1	22	16	16	9 0 0	13	30 30 24	22 10 0	With two Drawers at bottom
2	24	18	18	10 10 0	14	33 33 24	27 0 0	Do. do.
3	26	20	20	12 0 0	15	36 36 26	30 10 0	Do. do.
4	28	22	22	13 10 0	16	40 36 26	34 0 0	Do. do.
5	30	24	24	15 10 0	17	48 38 28	40 0 0	Do. and Shelf above.
6	33	26	24	18 0 0	18	54 40 28	46 10 0	Do. do. do.
7	36	26	24	22 0 0	19	60 48 30	58 0 0	Do. do. do.
8	42	26	24	24 10 0	20	66 54 30	70 0 0	With 3 drawers, 2 feet from the bottom, cupboard 2½ inches above drawers, partition above and below drawers.
9	48	28	26	26 15 0				
10	54	30	26	30 0 0				
11	60	30	26	33 0 0				
12	60	32	28	36 10 0	21	72 60 30	82 10 0	With 4 drawers, 2 feet from the bottom, cupboard 18 inches above drawers, partition above and below drawers.

For price of Fittings, see Note at Foot.

NOTE.—Extra for Fittings in this quality: Single Door Safes, One Drawer top or bottom, 16s.; two Drawers top or bottom, 30s.; for each additional Drawer, 16s. Cupboard charged as two Drawers; Shelves, 7s. 6d. per foot in width; Partitions, 7s. 6d. per foot in height.

Specifications, Drawings, and Estimates supplied free.

NETT PRICES OF No. 13.

SINGLE DOOR SAFES.				DOUBLE DOOR SAFES.				
	Outside Dimensions in Inches.		Price without Fittings.		Outside Dimensions in Inches.		Price with Fittings.	
No.	Hgt.	Wth.	Dth.	£ s. d.	No.	Hgt. Wth. Dth.	£ s. d.	
1	24	18	18	13 0 0	12	30 30 24	33 10 0	With two Drawers at bottom
2	26	20	20	15 10 0	13	33 33 24	36 0 0	Do. do.
3	28	22	22	18 10 0	14	36 36 26	42 10 0	Do. do.
4	30	24	24	22 0 0	15	40 36 26	47 10 0	Do. do.
5	33	26	24	25 10 0	16	48 38 28	56 10 0	Do. and shelf above.
6	36	26	24	27 10 0	17	54 40 28	65 0 0	Do. do.
7	42	26	24	30 0 0	18	60 48 30	80 0 0	Do. do.
8	48	28	26	35 10 0				
9	54	30	26	41 0 0				
10	60	30	26	46 10 0	19	66 54 30	95 0 0	With 3 drawers, 2 feet from the bottom, cupboard 21 inches above drawers, partition above and below drawers.
11	60	32	28	50 0 0				
					20	72 60 30	115 0 0	With 4 drawers, 2 feet from the bottom, cupboard 18 inches above drawers, partition above and below drawers.

For price of Fittings, see Note at Foot.

NOTE.—Extra for fittings in this quality: Single Door Safes, one Drawer at top or bottom of Safe, 16s.; two Drawers at top or bottom, 30s.; for each additional Drawer, 16s. Cupboard charged as two Drawers; Shelves, 7s. 6d. per foot in width; Partitions, 7s. 6d. per foot in height.

No. 13 or 14 Safes, *without the Steam Chambers*, for Gold Dust, Bullion, or Jewellery, &c., with or without Fittings.

Specifications, Drawings, and Estimates supplied free.

Export Agents—CLOSE & LEGG, 28, Jewry Street, E.C.

ADVERTISEMENT.

TURNER'S PATENT ELASTIC TUBULAR COTTON PACKING RINGS,

With or without wire gauze. These are an improved form of Crickmer's Packing, to meet the requirements of high pressures, but are equally adapted for low pressures.

Crickmer's Metallic Packing. Self-Lubricating Packing.
Patent White Canvas Core Packing.
Patent Platted Cotton and Flax Core Packings made round or square. Red Lead Rope Packing, for Cylinder Covers, Manholes, &c., &c.

Boiler Composition, for the removal and prevention of incrustation. Many times the strength of soda, and is manufactured in iron boilers, which is the best guarantee against injury to the plates.

TURNER'S PATENT ELASTIC METALLIC WASHERS,

For securing the Joints of Steam and Water Pipes.

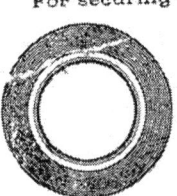

A great advantage is here gained by strengthening the ordinary india-rubber Washers with thin metal-flanged hoops, so as to take the pressure from the india-rubber, and prevent it from squeezing inside the pipes. They may be safely applied under any pressure without the addition of cement.

A good opportunity for Rubber Depots and the Trade generally.

Prices, &c., on application.

TURNER BROTHERS,
CLOD MILLS, ROCHDALE.
Shippers and the Trade supplied.

W. GAMBLE,
AGENT, BROKER, MERCHANT, AND AUCTIONEER,
WREXHAM,

Solicits business, under either of the above heads, in

COAL, COKE, IRON,

AND EVERY DESCRIPTION OF MANUFACTURED GOODS.
New or Second-hand

PLANT AND MACHINERY

Of every kind, and Stores in general. Particulars and favourable prices on application.

Ironworks, Collieries, Lead Mines, Slate & Stone Quarries for Sale & Wanted

Sales of same conducted by Public Auction.

Cannock Chase Coal by Canal and Railway.

THE Company send Coal by Railway, in trucks, to all Stations, and load Canal Boats at their extensive Wharves on the Anglesey Branch of the Birmingham Canal, adjoining the Colliery; and also at Hednesford Basin, Cannock. For prices, apply to

JOHN N. BROWN,
Anglesey Chambers, New Street, Birmingham.
LONDON OFFICE, 455, NEW OXFORD STREET.

CELEBRATED "WATER OF AYR STONE" HONE,
UNRIVALLED FOR EDGED TOOLS AND POLISHING PURPOSES.
Supplied and Shipped as under to all parts of the World:—

Marble and Lithographers' Polishers.   Small Hones and Joiners' Blocks.
Curriers' Octagon Clearing Stones.   Engravers' Polishing Blocks.
Segments for Circles.   Wheelstones and Lapstones.   Turned Handle Hones.
Pencils and Slips of every description.

Apply to JOHN C. MONTGOMERIE,
"WATER OF AYR STONE" HONE WORKS,
DALMORE, STAIR, AYRSHIRE, N.B.

HORSE CLIPPERS,
EQUAL TO ANY IN THE MARKET

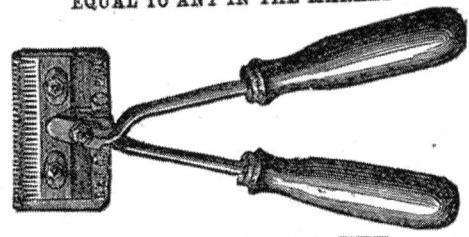
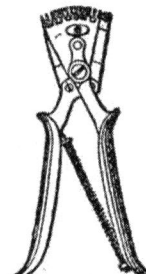

FROM 7/6 EACH.
Special Terms to Merchants and Shippers.
Samples supplied on approval.

5/-
THE TOILET.

The Sphinx Key Ring and Puzzle.

The only useful, safe Ring, easy to open or close by the owner; a Puzzle to others.

Plated, with Initials, 6d.;
Full Name, . . 1/-

ALSO,

The Nepaulese Puzzle Finger Ring;
A GEM.

Money returned if secret is found out in one hour's time.
13 STAMPS.
Same as Napkin Ring, 3/6.

AIME-HUGON, Sole Agent, 24 George St. Tower Hill, E.C.

EMERY WHEELS.

The Mitchell's Emery Composition Wheel Company (Limited),

20, DAVID STREET, MANCHESTER,
MAKER OF
Emery Wheels, Machines, Emery and Glass Cloths.
LIBERAL TERMS TO SHIPPERS.
Price lists free, on application.   Please address in full.

MACNAUGHT, ROBERTSON AND CO.,
IRON, STEEL, AND GIRDER MERCHANTS,
BANKEND, SOUTHWARK, LONDON, S.E.

Bar, Red, Hoop, Angle, Tee, Channel, Sheet, Plate and Sash Iron of every quality and description; Chequered Floor Plates, Bulb and Deck Beam Iron, Bolts and Nuts, Bolt Ends, Rivets, Chain Forgings, Steel, Files, Zinc, Anvils, Vices, Swage Blocks, &c.; Gas, Steam, Galvanized and Boiler Tubes and Fittings; Scotch, Welsh, and Middlesbrough Pig Iron; ENGLISH and BELGIAN Rolled and Riveted Girders and Joists, Flitch Plates, Builders' Bond Hooping and Bridge and Contractors' Rails.

Prompt deliveries from Stock or Works.

New Section Sheets, Tables of Strengths, and Price Lists, forwarded on receipt of Card.

ADVERTISEMENT.

WM. HEYWOOD & CO.,
MACHINISTS,
HULME, MANCHESTER.

Paper Coloring or Staining Machines,
Suspending or Drying Machines,
Paper Polishing Machines,
Color Grinding and Mixing Machines,
Book Paging Machines,
Elastic Braid Machines.

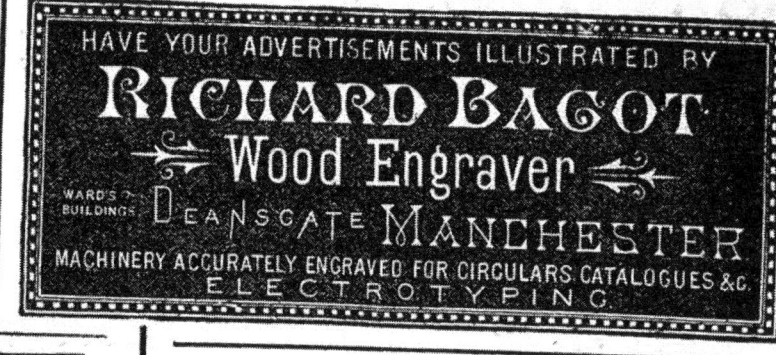

HAVE YOUR ADVERTISEMENTS ILLUSTRATED BY
RICHARD BAGOT
Wood Engraver
WARD'S BUILDINGS, DEANSGATE, MANCHESTER
MACHINERY ACCURATELY ENGRAVED FOR CIRCULARS, CATALOGUES &c.
ELECTROTYPING.

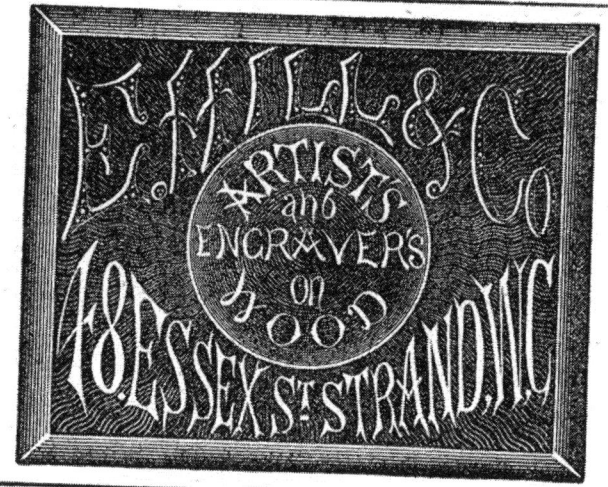

E. M. ILL & CO.
ARTISTS and ENGRAVERS on WOOD
48, ESSEX ST, STRAND, W.C.

LOCKWOOD & LEITH,
CAUSTIC SODA MANUFACTURERS,
ST. HELENS,
LANCASHIRE.

BLACKMORE & CO.'S
PATENT BOLTING CLOTHS,
WITHOUT SEAMS,

Are the best and most perfect articles for precision and despatch in

DRESSING FLOUR & CLEARING OFF.
ESTABLISHED 1783.

SOLD AT THE MANUFACTORY,
WANDSWORTH, LONDON, S.W.,
Where all particulars may be obtained.

Plans of the Bolting Machine, Price Lists, etc., post free, on application.

BAILEY'S WATER REGULATOR ORGAN BLOWER
SEND FOR A CIRCULAR
PATENT
ONE MAN'S POWER £10
W. H. BAILEY & CO. ALBION WORKS SALFORD MANCHESTER
CHURCH CLOCK MAKERS

THIS BLOWER IS PERFECTLY NOISELESS. *Send for* CIRCULARS.

A POSITIVE CURE FOR SMOKY CHIMNEYS.
"THE CLIMAX"
(DE SA'S PATENT),
BY HER MAJESTY'S ROYAL LETTERS PATENT.

This ingenious design is based on simple scientific principles, and is entirely new in construction, being the result of twelve years' study and experience, and well deserves special attention.

THE GREAT MERITS OF THIS INVENTION:

- It prevents down draughts.
- It is noiseless, being a fixture.
- It requires no cowl or cap.
- It provides for every action of the wind.
- It is handsome in appearance.
- It accelerates up currents.
- It cannot get out of order.
- It is easily swept.
- It provides free escape of smoke.
- It can be fitted by any bricklayer.

The "Climax" can be adapted as a universal Ventilator.

5 ft. 6 ins. high, and made in Zinc, Galvanized Iron, and Copper.
Prices and Discounts to be had from the
SOLE PROPRIETOR AND MANUFACTURER,
J. D. WRIGHT,
4, LUPUS STREET, LONDON, S.W.

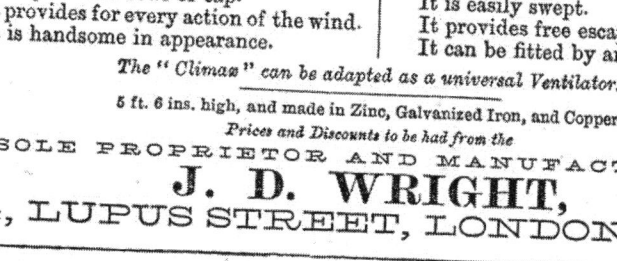
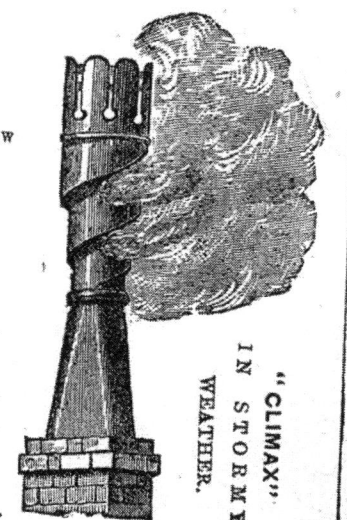

ADVERTISEMENT.

BAYLISS, JONES AND BAYLISS,
PATENTEES AND MANUFACTURERS
OF

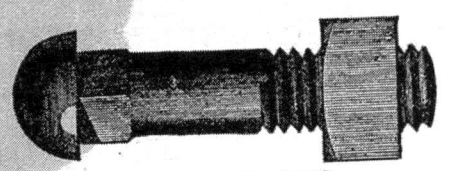

FISH BOLTS,
FANG BOLTS,
RAIL SCREWS,
CHAIR SPIKES,
DOG SPIKES,
TWISTED SPIKES,
BROBS,

RAILWAY AND TRAMWAY FASTENINGS OF EVERY DESCRIPTION.

Patent Strained Wire Fencing,
Continuous Bar Fencing,
Wrought-Iron Hurdles,
Field and Entrance Gates,
Wire Standards,

Galvanized Wire Netting, Galvanized Sheep Netting, Fencing Wire, (Iron and Steel) Wire Strand, Fencing Staples, Straining Brackets, Best Crane Chains, &c., &c.

Manufactory: **VICTORIA WORKS, WOLVERHAMPTON.**
LONDON OFFICES: 3, CROOKED LANE, KING WILLIAM STREET, E.C.
Illustrated Catalogue, containing 270 Illustrations, free on application.

B. & S. MASSEY,
OPENSHAW, MANCHESTER, ENGLAND.

PRIZE MEDALS AWARDED:—Paris, 1867; Havre, 1868; Highland Society, 1870; Liverpool, 1871; Moscow, 1872; Vienna, 1873; Scientific Industry Society, 1875; Leeds, 1875; Paris, 1875; Manchester and Liverpool Society, 1876; U.S. Centennial, Philadelphia, 1876.

PATENTEES AND MAKERS
OF DOUBLE AND SINGLE-ACTING
STEAM HAMMERS

Of all sizes, from ½ Cwt. to 20 Tons, with Self-acting or Hand Motions, in either case giving a perfectly DEAD BLOW, while the former may be worked by Hand when desired. Large Hammers, with Improved Framing, in Cast or Wrought Iron. Small Hammers, working up to 500 blows per minute, in some cases being worked by the Foot of the Smith, and not requiring any separate Driver.

SPECIAL STEAM STAMPS
For Forging, Stamping, Punching, Bolt-Making, &c.
CIRCULAR SAWS FOR HOT IRON.
STEAM HAMMERS

For Engineers, Machinists, Shipbuilders, Steel Tilters, Millwrights, Coppersmiths, Railway Carriage and Wagon Builders, Colliery Proprietors, Ship Smiths, Bolt Makers, Cutlers, File Makers, Spindle and Flyer Makers, Spade Makers, Locomotive and other Wheel Makers, &c.; also for use in Repairing Smithies of Mills and Works of all kinds; for straightening Bars, bending Cranks, breaking Pig-Iron, &c.

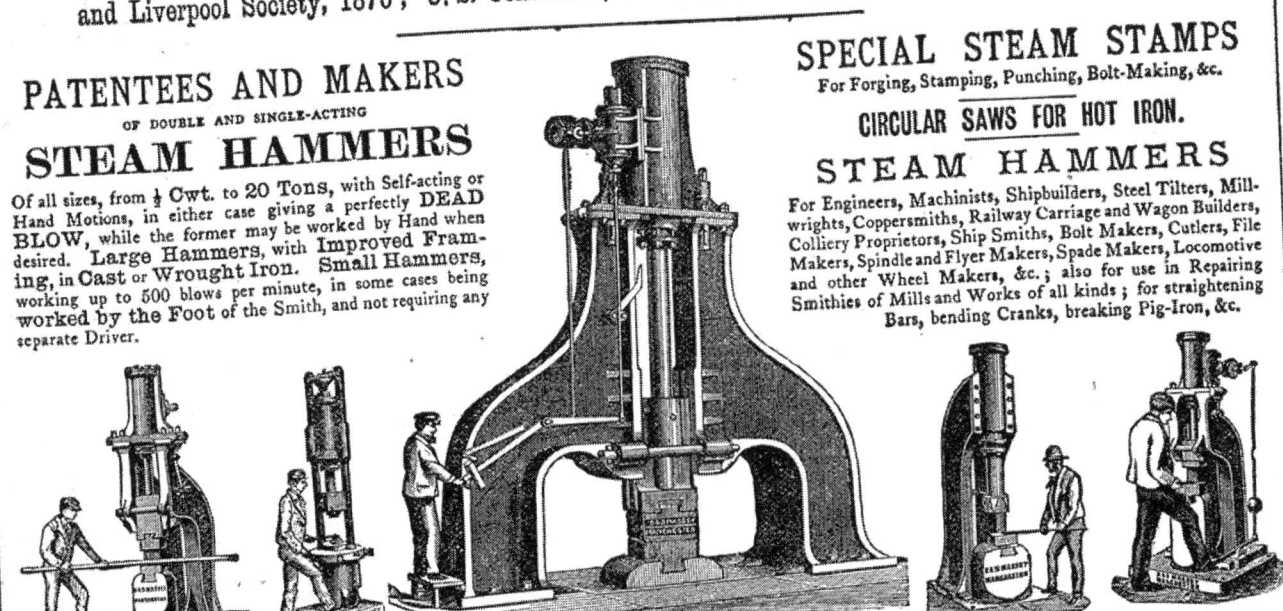

General Smithy Hammer. Special Steam Stamp. Steam Hammer for Heavy Forging. General Smithy Hammer. Foot Motion Hammer.

From 60 to 100 Steam Hammers and Steam Stamps may usually be seen in construction at the Works.

DEFERRED PAYMENTS.

HUDSWELL, CLARKE & RODGERS,
ALSO MAKE
Greatly Improved LOCOMOTIVE TANK ENGINES, on 4 or 6 Wheels.

NEW LOCOMOTIVES, with Cylinders 8 in., 10 in., and 13 in. diameter, always in stock, or in progress. SECOND-HAND LOCOMOTIVES, of various sizes, for Sale or Hire.

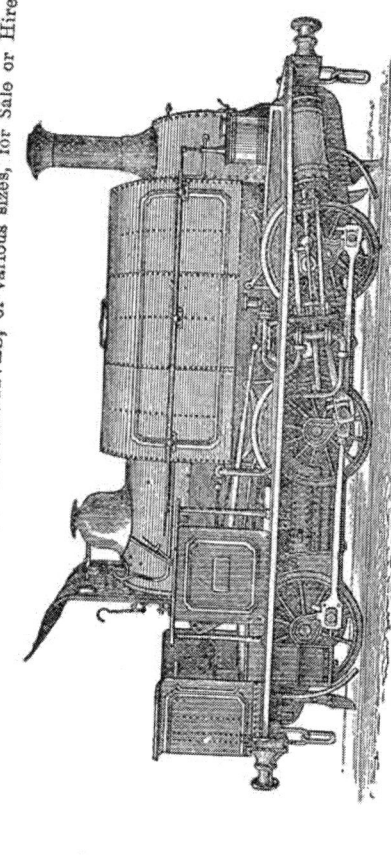

FIRE BOXES—Copper. TUBES—Brass. TYRES—Steel. AXLES—Steel. BOILER PLATES & MACHINERY of the best Yorkshire Iron.

Sole Makers of RODGERS' PATENT WROUGHT-IRON SPLIT DRUMS, &c.

TERMS:—CASH, OR

SUPPLEMENTARY LIST OF ADVERTISEMENTS,
Received immediately before going to Press.

		Pages			Pages
Appleby, Bros.	London	9	Hill, E.	London	22
Bird, W. H.	Manchester	40	Hulme and Lund	Salford	37
Braddock, J. & J.	Oldham	35	Kendall and Gent	Salford	44
Broadbent, Robert, and Son	Staley Bridge	51	Le Grand and Sutcliff	London	40
Clarke and Marriott	Birmingham	40	Macniven and Cameron	Edinburgh	52
Coleman, W. F.	Loughborough	52	Mapplebeck, W. B., Junr.	Birmingham	16
Collings, T. P., and Co.	London	52	Massey, B. & S.	Openshaw, Manchester	52
Cunliffe and Croom	Manchester	41	Mathews, J. W., and Co.	Liverpool	6
Deakin, Parker and Co.	Salford	36	Mercer, Edward	Salford	42, 43
Eagle Edge Tool Co., Limited	Wolverhampton	45	Muir, Andrew, and Co.	Manchester	38, 39
Fletcher, John, and Son	Salford	50	Spencer, James, and Co.	Hollinwood	46, 47, 48, 49
Hartley and Sugden	Halifax	34	Stead, J. W.	Pendleton	33

Terms for Advertisements in next Edition on application.

More Books by Chris McKay

Big Ben: The Great Clock and the Bells at The Palace of Westminster
A definitive history of the clock and bells. Covers the clock tower, clock and bells along with the men involved, E.J. Dent, F. Dent, E.B. Denison, G.B. Airy, C. Barry and others. The technical side of the clock is covered in detail.

Publisher	Oxford University Press
Size	288 Pages, 260 B&W Halftones, Plus 8pp of colour plates. Hardback.
ISBN	978-0-19-958569-4
Publication Date:	2010

The Maintenance, Repair, Restoration, Conservation and Preservation of Turret Clocks
The book is aimed at the professional clock restorer who is sometimes asked to work on a turret clock. A 100% practical how-to-do-it guide plus a lot on conservation.

Publisher	Self published by the author
Size	Quarto.
ISBN-13	978-1517127206
ISBN-10	1517127203
Publication Date:	2016

The Turret Clock Keeper's Handbook (New Revised Edition)
This book is for anyone who looks after a turret clock. Instruction is given on basic activities like setting to time, regulation, correcting striking. There are chapters on health & safety issues plus a guide on conservation and how to select a suitable restorer.

Publisher	Self published by the author
ISBN-13	978-1492317708
Size	A4, 84 pages, 60 plus B&W line illustrations.
Publication Date	2013

Longitude's Legacy James Harrison of Hull 1792–1875: Turret Clockmaker. The Last of the Harrison Clockmakers
A history of the other side of John Harrison's family comprising his brother James and his successors. The main thrust is the work of James 4 who was an ingenious turret clock maker who worked in Hull. This James was obviously well aware of the work of John Longitude.

Publisher	Self published by the author
ISBN-13	978-1511810333
ISBN-10	1511810335
Size	Quarto. 288 pages, over 240 black & white illustrations
Publication Date	2015

A List of Church, Turret and Musical Clocks, Manufactured by John Moore & Sons. 38 & 39 Clerkenwell Close, London
A facsimile of an old catalogue circa 1877. Moore was a major manufacturer of turret and domestic clocks. This list was intended as a piece of give-away advertising material.

Publisher	Self published by the author
ISBN-13:	978-1514858967
ISBN-10:	1514858967
Size	8" x 5.25", 50 pages
Publication Date:	2015.

Printed in Great Britain
by Amazon